THEY MADE HISTORY

A BIOGRAPHICAL
DICTIONARY

THEY MADE HISTORY
A BIOGRAPHICAL DICTIONARY

Geoffrey Wigoder

SIMON & SCHUSTER
A Paramount Communications Company

New York   London   Toronto   Sydney   Tokyo   Singapore

Academic Reference Division
Simon & Schuster
15 Columbus Circle
New York, New York 10023

A Paramount Communications Company

Printed in Israel

printing number
1 2 3 4 5 6 7 8 9 10

Library of Congress Cataloging-in-Publication Data

Wigoder, Geoffrey, 1922–

They made history: a biographical dictionary / Geoffrey Wigoder.

p.   cm.
Includes bibliographical references.
ISBN 0-13-915257-1

1. Biography—Dictionaries. 2. History—Miscellanea.   I. Title.

CT103.W54 1993

920.02—dc20
                                                93-25031
                                                CIP

CONTRIBUTORS

Michael Ajzenstadt
Caren Benjamin
Ian Brown
Chrystal Corcos
Tania Davidson
Matti Diamond
Roza El-Eini
Steven Frais
Paul Frosh
Lisa R. Frydman
Elizabeth Goldfine
Ari Gorlin
Rashie Grahame
David Hamburger
Pamela Hogle
Margo Lee Kossof
Ruth Lang
Ayala Levine
Debra Levitt
Gary Michael

Yael Oberman
Terrye Pico
Mandy Rabin
Susan Hersch-Sachs
Raphael Ruderman
Rohan Saxena
Fern Seckbach
Shalva Segal
Susanna Shabetai
Joseph Shutkin
Inez Singer
Gabriel Sivan
Debra Slonim
Julie Stahl
Stewart Telman
Michael Weinstock
Vera Weisz
Danny Wool
Emmy Zitter
Julie Zuckerman

Managing Editor: Rachel Gilon
Assistant Editors: Georgette Corcos, Danny Wool
Copyeditors: Rohan Saxena, Susanna Shabetai
Illustration Research: Ari Gorlin
Typesetting, and Pagination: Michael Abramson —
                                    The Jerusalem Publishing House
Printing and Binding: Keter Enterprises Ltd., Jerusalem

FOREWORD

The title of this book, *They Made History*, seems to presuppose a judgment in the historiographical debate as to whether individuals can influence the course of history. Tolstoy addresses this issue in *War and Peace* by questioning whether the novel's outstanding protagonists, Napoleon and Kutuzov, indeed "made history" or were merely the puppets of historical currents. He concluded that human actions are determined by natural laws and that there is no free choice. Without presuming to enter into this discussion, it is surely not exaggerated to hold that in every sphere of human endeavor, outstanding personalities have taken what Neil Armstrong on landing on the moon called "one giant step for mankind." And it is not farfetched to believe that those who took these giant steps did in fact make history.

In this gallery of the great, we have viewed the broadest historical panorama, and not just the march of politics, diplomacy, and wars. For us, history covers the entire spectrum of human endeavor, incorporating all aspects of the natural and social sciences, culture, religion, and discovery and exploration that have advanced the march of civilization and broadened the human experience.

Not everyone in this book has contributed positively. Hitler too made history. Many appear because of their role in the sweep of political and military developments that led to the founding of nations and countries. Others can definitely be said to have advanced the well-being, knowledge, and perceptions of humankind, often breaking through to new horizons. Jesus and Aristotle, Galileo and Copernicus, Newton and Freud made history no less than Alexander the Great, Julius Caesar, and Franklin D. Roosevelt. We have also included the trailblazers in the arts — Shakespeare and Goethe, Rembrandt and Picasso, Beethoven and Gershwin — although we have excluded the performing arts as essentially interpretative. Another restriction we have imposed on ourselves is to exclude people still alive on the assumption that, in the context of a project such as ours, only after an individual's death can one achieve the necessary perspective on his or her significance and life's work.

It is evident that any choice must be subjective. No two people would come up with identical lists of the "greats" of history. The editor has consulted with many, but accepts that the final selection is his. He can assert that all those included have indeed made history, while accepting that there is a multitude of others with a similar claim who cannot be included due to reasons of space.

In these biographies and in the "boxes" accompanying many entries, we have often given informal details, stories, and sayings that throw light on the subject. We hope that these will give a more human and personal picture than that usually conveyed in encyclopedias, which are often limited to the main biographical details.

Finally, I would like to thank the publishers, Charles E. Smith of Simon and Schuster and Shlomo S. Gafni of the Jerusalem Publishing House, for their enthusiasm and guidance; Georgette Corcos and Danny Wool, who brought the project to fruition; and all those who have advised on, written for, and participated in the production of *They Made History*.

Geoffrey Wigoder

"History is the essence of innumerable biographies."

Thomas Carlyle

A

ABBAS I (the Great; 1571–1629), shah of Persia 1588–1629. Abbas was the most important emperor of the modern Persian state. He was a successful military strategist and competent administrator who brought his realm increased renown, extensive territory, and unprecedented wealth. He was the son of Shah Muhammad Khubadanda of the Safavid dynasty. In 1581 the ten-year-old Abbas was appointed nominal governor of the province of Khorasan. When Shah Muhammad died in 1586 the country was plunged into anarchy; for two years civil war raged in Persia. Abbas came to the throne in 1588; his first act as shah was to restore order to the kingdom.

At the time of Abbas's accession to the throne Persia was an ailing kingdom. Its powerful neighbors, the Ottoman Turks on the west and the Uzbeks on the east, threatened the country; the Turks had even annexed much of Persia's western territory. Abbas set out on a well-calculated venture to restore his kingdom to its former glory. In 1590 he signed a treaty with the Turks recognizing their conquests in the west. This allowed Abbas to focus his attention on the Uzbeks to the east. Abbas's great victory over the Uzbeks in 1598 was achieved in a surprise attack near the Afghan city of Herat. The Uzbeks were defeated, allowing Abbas to conquer Mazanderan and most of Afghanistan.

In 1602, his power consolidated, Abbas was finally ready to take on the Turks. In 1605 his 60,000 men defeated more than 100,000 Turkish troops at the Persian Gulf port of Basra. Abbas extended his conquests past the Euphrates, well into Turkish territory. The Ottoman Emperor Ahmed I ceded Shirvan and Kurdistan to Abbas in 1611. In 1618 Abbas defeated a coalition of Turks and Tartars at Sultanieh; the terms of the peace treaty included the restoration of all Persian territory formerly ceded to the Ottoman Empire. Abbas then turned his attention southward to the Persian Gulf. In 1622, following a year-long siege Abbas, aided by the British, captured the strategic port city of Hormuz. To assure Persian ascendancy at the entrance to the gulf, trade was diverted from Hormuz to the town of Bandar Abbas, named in Abbas's honor. The fol-

lowing year Abbas revoked his treaty with Turkey and took Baghdad and Diyarbakir. Abbas had extended his realm from the Tigris River to the Indus.

Abbas was an able monarch who developed the infrastructure of his country and enacted new laws to benefit the commercial status of Persia. A system of roads, the Sang Farsh (stone carpet), was constructed to ease trade. This highway system, com-

Helmet of Abbas the Great

plete with bridges and caravansaries, can still be seen in Iran. Abbas also moved his capital to Isfahan, which he rebuilt into one of the most remarkable cities in the world at that time.

Abbas stressed the common belief in Islam as a unifying factor among the many diverse tribes and peoples of his realm. He himself was a devout Muslim who once walked 800 miles on a pilgrimage to Meshed. He was tolerant of other religions but despite his open-minded character, Abbas was often extremely superstitious.

Abbas was also extremely jealous of his own children and was frightened that they would seize his throne. He had his eldest son, Safi Mirza, assassinated; his second son, Tahmap Mirza, was blinded, and his fourth son was beheaded. His third son, Khudabanda, escaped Abbas's wrath by committing suicide. When Abbas died in Mazanderan in 1629, his young grandson, Safi, succeeded him as shah.

I. B. Munshi, *History of Shah Abbas,* 2 vols, 1978.
P. Sykes, *History of Persia*, Vol. II, 1969.

ABD AR-RAHMAN I (731–788), founder of the Umayyad dynasty in Spain. Abd ar-Rahman was born in Damascus, the grandson of the tenth Umayyad caliph, Hisham, through the liaison of one of his sons with a slave girl. Abd ar-Rahman was forced to flee Damascus in 750 after the fall of the Umayyad dynasty to the first Abbasid ruler, Abu al-Abbas. He roamed through Egypt and North Africa for five years, developing bonds of friendship with the local Arab and Berber populations.

Throughout his travels in North Africa, rumors reached Abd ar-Rahman of the troubled state of affairs in Muslim Spain. The Muslim empire was beginning to suffer the consequences of its vast size, and inadequate communications prevented effective rule of the periphery from Damascus and Baghdad. As a result Spain was divided into small cantons with rival governors, each struggling for ascendancy. As the sole remaining heir of the Umayyads, Abd ar-Rahman saw this as an ideal opportunity to assert himself. Leading an army of Berbers and slaves, He crossed to Spain in 755, ostensibly to settle the disputes between the warring local rulers but, in fact, to establish his own authority.

Abd ar-Rahman easily made himself ruler of the Iberian Peninsula. Only the Saracens in the north did not succumb to him and he declared himself emir of Andalusia in 756. The term "emir" had previously meant "military lord"; under Abd ar-Rahman the meaning was more similar to king. With his capital at Córdoba, Abd ar-Rahman had established the first Muslim state independent of the caliphate.

Abd ar-Rahman ruled Andalusia for thirty-three years. The first twenty years were spent consolidating his kingdom and suppressing revolts against his authority. In 758 an Abbasid emir, Yusuf al-Fihri, laid siege to Córdoba for a year. The siege was only lifted after the death of Yusuf near Toledo in 759. The next fifteen years were marked by re-

gional rebellions which were crushed and attempts to subdue the Saracens which failed. The Saracens, however, aware that their position was steadily worsening, sent messengers to *Charlemagne in 777, begging him to help them against the Umayyads. Charlemagne readily consented; he saw this an ideal opportunity to restore Christianity to Spain. He abandoned his war with the Saxons and led his forces past the Pyrenees. His armies then split in two, with one flank attacking Gerona in the east, the other invading the Basque regions of the western seaboard. After a successful campaign the two forces met at Saragossa but they failed to subdue the city. Charlemagne was then recalled to Germany by a fresh outbreak of hostilities by the Saxons; his retreat and the ensuing disaster his men faced are the subject of the French epic, *The Song of Roland.* That account, although composed some two hundred years after the battles, gives a fair account of the assistance the Basques offered Abd ar-Rahman by attacking the rear of Charlemagne's retreating army. The defeat of Charlemagne assured Umayyad Spain a lengthy respite from the threat of foreign invasion.

Abd ar-Rahman spent the remainder of his reign peacefully consolidating his conquests. The diverse population of Syrians, Yemenites, Berbers, local converts, and North Africans was united under the banner of Islam. The capital, Córdoba, was fortified by a series of walls and an aqueduct was built to insure an adequate supply of water to the city. His enormous building campaign included such architectural treasures as his palace, known as the Munyat ar-Rusfah, and a large central mosque, which he did not live to see completed. The mosque, as well as other buildings completed by Abd ar-Rahman, can still be seen in Córdoba, where it currently serves as a Roman Catholic church. His efforts to beautify the city and turn it into a center of learning made Córdoba, during his lifetime, a city to rival Baghdad, Damascus, Constantinople, and the great cities of Europe.

A. Mackay, *Spain in the Middle Ages*, 1977.
M. Watt, *A History of Islamic Spain*, 1965.

ABD EL-KADER (1808–1883), Algerian nationalist and military leader, son of Mahi ad-Din, a prominent religious leader of the Qadiriyah Muslim brotherhood. Abd el-Kader distinguished himself by his looks, intellect, and horsemanship. He joined his father in opposing Turkish rule over Algeria and when the authorities threatened to clamp down on Mahi ad-Din, Abd el-Kader and his father planned a pilgrimage to Mecca but they were imprisoned for two years before being allowed to set out.

For Abd el-Kader this journey presented an opportunity to study in the Islamic universities of Egypt, Syria, and Baghdad. Upon their return to Algeria many legends were spread by Mahi ad-Din about his son. It was reported that in Baghdad a holy man saluted him by crying, "Hail to the sultan." Mahi and his son were surprised by the changes that had taken place in Algeria. The Turkish government had been replaced by the French and while at first this was seen as a positive development, the French were considered pagans and soon came to be less popular than the Muslim Turks. Mahi's call for holy war against the French was put into effect by Abd el-Kader, who succeeded his aging father in 1832. He moved to Mascara and obtained the allegiance of rival tribes. Realizing that he stood no chance against the superior French forces, he chose to lay siege to Oran and moved his base into the interior of the country.

The French general Louis-Alexis Desmichels could not combat Abd el-Kader's guerrilla tactics and concluded that the Algerians could best be controlled by a treaty. In 1833 Abd el-Kader occupied Tlemcen; the French occupied Arzew and Mostaganem. The deadlock was broken by the treaty of Desmichels, signed in February of the following year. According to the official version of the treaty, Abd el-Kader recognized French hegemony over Algeria. In fact, a secret document signed a month later recognized Abd el-Kader as the leader of the Muslim tribes ("Commander of the Believers"), and offered French support to him in that capacity. The treaty led to French intervention after radical Muslims attempted to overthrow him because they accused him of acting as a European — he was rumored to have begun wearing a hat and planned to marry a Christian. However, Desmichels's support of Abd el-Kader was unpopular in Paris and he was replaced by General Camille Trézel.

Trézel led several successful campaigns against Abd el-Kader, yet each time his own mistakes, such as failing to leave adequate troops to protect his military acquisitions, led to a renewal of Abd el-Kader's fortunes. His popularity was erratic throughout this period; his successes brought him renewed support but his failures left him with only a handful of followers. After a year of indecisive skirmishes he was left with only 150 troops. However, he rallied support and in 1837 the Tafna Treaty led to effective mutual recognition by the French and the Algerians.

The peace lasted two years, during which time he considerably expanded the area under his control. He also enlisted the support of Léon Roches, a French deserter who had converted to Islam. Roches advised him to create a regular army in the European fashion, including martial music, training, and uniforms; a munitions factory was also established.

French settlement activity led to a breach of the peace in 1839 but Abd el-Kader's troops were no match for the French armies. He was forced several times to move his capital until he finally established a roving tent city, *Smalah*, from which he administered his contracting realm. Finally, after a promise of safe-conduct Abd el-Kader surrendered in 1847. The promise was not kept and he was arrested and imprisoned in France, to be released only in 1852. After a brief stay in Turkey he settled in Damascus, where he received a considerable pension from the French government and was awarded the French Legion of Honor for saving 12,000 Christians from a Muslim mob.

Abd el-Kader's tactics were adopted by Algerian nationalists in the 1950s and he was accorded the status of national hero. His banner was adopted as the national flag of Algeria upon independence in 1962. In 1968, Abd el-Kader's remains received an official burial in Algeria.

M. Bennoune, *The Making of Contemporary Algeria, 1830–1987*, 1988.

R. Danziger, *Abd al-Qadir and the Algerians*, 1977.

ABDULHAMID II (1842–1918), Ottoman emperor. Abdulhamid was the son of Sultan Abdulmecid I; his mother was an Armenian member of the harem. His accession to the throne in 1876 followed the ouster of his mentally ill brother Murad V. Abdulhamid was endorsed by the liberal Society of New Ottomans. In his bid for power he had made significant overtures to the growing liberal faction by proposing a constitution, granted the year he ascended the throne, providing for the establishment of a bicameral parliament. Midhat Pasha, involved in the ouster and supposed murder of former despot Abdulaziz, was appointed prime minister.

Abdulhamid's apparent liberalism, however, was merely a ploy to assure his accession. The empire was crumbling and he believed that only the sternest measures would ensure its survival. Using the pretense of a war with Russia sparked by the harsh Turkish suppression of Balkan separatists, a state of emergency was declared and the constitution was suspended. Midhat was tried for his role in the assassination of Abdulaziz and exiled to Arabia, where he was mysteriously strangled.

The Russo-Turkish war (1877) was a disaster for the Ottomans. The terms for peace dictated by the Treaty of San Stefano demanded that Turkey relinquish its Balkan possessions. Later territorial losses included Tunisia (1881) and Egypt (1882). To consolidate what remained of his realm Abdulhamid emphasized pan-Islamic nationalism, which was rejected by both the Christian Armenians of Anatolia (whose revolt in 1894 was cruelly suppressed) and by the inhabitants of Yemen and Mesopotamia, who favored pan-Arabism devoid of Turkish interference.

Abdulhamid's tyrannical regime sparked several conspiracies. Token reforms in education (the University of Istanbul was established as a trade school in 1900) and transportation (new railways linked Constantinople with Europe and Mecca) failed to assuage the volatile situation and Abdulhamid feared for his life. His understandable paranoia, however, rapidly took on insane proportions and he retreated to the Yildiz palace, never to emerge. The palace was an enormous labyrinth but Abdulhamid increased the confusion by continu-

ABOUT ABDULHAMID

I can still see him before me, this Sultan of the declining robber empire. Small, shabby, with his badly dyed beard which is probably freshly painted only once a week. The hooked nose of a Punchinello, the long yellow teeth with a big gap on the upper right. The fez pulled low over his probably bald head; the prominent ears serving as a "pants' protector," i.e., they keep the fez from slipping down onto his pants. The feeble hands in white, oversize gloves, and the ill-fitting coarse loud-colored cuffs. The bleating voice, the constraint in every word, the timidity in every glance. And this rules! Only on the surface, of course, and nominally.

From the *Diary of Theodor Herzl*, 1901.

ally adding and removing walls, windows, and doors to disorient even his most faithful retainers. Every chamber contained a bed — the emperor would never sleep in the same room twice — and countless ashtrays to contain an endless flow of cigarette butts; bright lights always burned to allay his terror of darkness. He even extracted his own teeth and prepared his own medicines to avoid supposedly hostile doctors.

Yildiz also contained extensive torture chambers, but there is no evidence that Abdulhamid personally took part in the abuse of prisoners. Contemporaries described screams of agony coming from behind the palace walls that could be heard throughout Constantinople. "Abdul the Damned," or "Bloody Abdul," was responsible for the deaths of at least half a million people.

The European powers were only too willing to abandon the demented emperor whose policies were determined by his astrologer, in favor of the liberal-leaning Committee for Union and Progress, the forerunner of the Young Turks. The Young Turks revolted in 1908. Abdulhamid responded by restoring the constitution but his complicity in a 1909 reactionary coup attempt led to his final ouster. His brother was declared Emperor Muhammad V. Abdulhamid spent the remainder of his life under house arrest in Thessalonica.

F. Ahmed, *The Young Turks*, 1969.
J. Haslip, *The Sultan: The Life of Abdul Hamid II*, 1973.
Lord Kinross, *The Ottoman Centuries: The Rise and Fall of the Turkish Empire*, 1978.

ABDULLAH, MUHAMMAD (1905–1982), Kashmiri nationalist politician. Muhammad Abdullah was born in Sorrah on the outskirts of Srinagar, the Kashmiri capital. The tall, imposing Abdullah studied at the Islamic College in Lahore and at Aligarh University, where he was well known for participating in Indian nationalist activities. At the time, the Indian nationalist movement was torn along ethnic lines. The majority Hindus, led by Mahatma *Gandhi and Jawaharlal *Nehru, advocated a secular state encompassing all of India's minorities. The sizeable Muslim minority, led by Muhammad Ali *Jinnah, favored the partition of the country and the formation of a Muslim state of Pakistan. The ethnic dilemma was particularly acute in Abdullah's home state of Kashmir; although the majority of the population was Muslim there were sizeable Hindu and Sikh minorities. Furthermore the population was governed by a Hindu maharajah.

The early years of Abdullah's nationalist agitation were directed against the British. In 1931 Abdullah, then unemployed, began attending anti-British gatherings. He quickly rose to the head of the local movement and was instigator of a revolt in 1931. Although he was arrested and jailed, Abdullah's reputation spread throughout the country. He was now referred to as Sher-E-Kashmir, the "Lion of Kashmir."

While in prison Abdullah came to the conclusion that the Muslims of Kashmir should organize themselves as a political force to overthrow the despotic maharajah and take part in the impending deliberations about their own future. In 1932 he organized the All Jammu and Kashmir Muslim Conference, a political party advocating democratic reforms in Kashmir as a first step toward participation in Indian independence. The British recognized the growing dissatisfaction with the rule of the maharajah and urged him to implement reforms; the maharajah responded by imposing martial law. A failed revolt that year was followed by a campaign of civil disobedience in 1934. The British, seeing their own authority dwindling, forced an election on the reluctant monarch. The new state assembly, the Praja Sabha, was to consist of seventy-five members, thirty-five of whom were appointed, the remainder to be divided along ethnic lines. Despite only 8 percent of the population being eligible to vote, Abdullah's Muslim Conference won fourteen out of the twenty-one seats reserved for Muslims. The conference walked out of the assembly in 1936, but two years later, in a second election, they won nineteen seats.

Despite the party's initial successes, Abdullah soon found himself at odds with other party leaders. Although a devout Muslim, he had been influenced by the democratic, secular ideals advocated by Nehru and supported the notion of a unified India. Others in the party supported Jinnah's bid to create a separate Muslim state. The Muslim Conference split in 1939 over whether non-Muslims should be allowed to join the party. Abdullah, who supported the participation of all Kashmiris in the nationalist process, formed a second party, the All Jammu and Kashmir National Conference.

Abdullah was often more popular outside Kashmir than in that state. His rejection of a separate Muslim state lost him the support of the Muslims; his rejection of the continued rule of the maharajah lost him the support of the Hindus and Sikhs. Despite his waning popularity at home he joined Indian negotiators in talks with the British in 1946. That same year Abdullah once again found himself in jail for nationalist and antimaharajah agitation. In 1947 elections were held but Abdullah's call from prison to boycott the election resulted in a particularly low turnout. Although the rival Muslim conference claimed sixteen seats, the election results were questionable. Abdullah, again the power broker of Kashmir, was released from prison. He seized power in a coup in 1947, banishing the maharajah and declaring Kashmir an integral part of India. Despite the ensuing India-Pakistan War over Kashmir, Abdullah was remarkable in his ability to achieve for Kashmir greater autonomy than any other Indian state.

Despite his achievements, Abdullah was disillusioned with the Indian government. Since neither India nor Pakistan seemed to provide a suitable solution for the question of Kashmir, he demanded independence in 1953. The Indian government intervened and Abdullah was again arrested. He spent the next twenty years in preventive detention and exile, constantly corresponding with his followers about Kashmir. Over the years Abdullah's opinions moderated. Soon after his release in 1973 he was elected chief minister, a position he held from 1975 until his death in 1982. "The Kashmiri government....will be a joint government of the Hindu and the Muslim. That is what I am fighting for!" he declared.

M. Abdullah, *The Testament of Sheikh Mohammed Abdullah*, 1974.

S. Gupta, *Kashmir: A Study in India-Pakistan Relations*, 1966.

J. Korbel, *Danger in Kashmir*, 1966.

ABDULLAH IBN AL-HUSAYN (1882–1951),

first king of Jordan. Abdullah was the son of *Husayn ibn Ali, sharif of Mecca, a descendant of the prophet *Muhammad, and hereditary guardian of the Muslim shrines in Mecca and Medina. Under suspicion by the Ottoman authorities for plotting to liberate Arab lands from Turkish rule, Husayn was forced to settle in Constantinople, where he could be placed under surveillance; Abdullah and his brothers, Ali and Faisal, joined their father there. In Constantinople Abdullah received a broad education and became his father's spokesman. Following the Young Turks' revolution he returned with his father, now emir, to Mecca but was again in Constantinople from 1912 to 1914 to represent Mecca in the Ottoman parliament.

Abdullah supported his father in the Arab revolt against the Turks in 1916 and served in his father's government as foreign minister. After the war he was offered the Iraqi throne but the British refused to consider Abdullah's appointment, claiming that as a Sunni Muslim he would be opposed by the majority Shiite population. When the brief reign of his brother King Faisal I of Syria was terminated by the French, Abdullah led 2,000 men toward Damascus in defense of Faisal's honor. They arrived in Amman in 1921 but British colonial secretary Winston *Churchill, fearful of provoking the French, offered Abdullah the crown of the new emirate of Transjordan as compensation. Abdullah was to serve for a six-month trial period, under the supervision of the British high commissioner for Palestine.

Transjordan was in a state of anarchy, with warlike Bedouin tribes exerting influence on different regions of the country. Only with considerable British financial assistance could Abdullah begin to assert his authority. Abdul Aziz *Ibn Saud, king of Nejd, was an additional threat; after conquering Hejaz he advanced toward Amman. To protect their interests in Transjordan the British founded the Arab Legion, an Arab military force. Under British command, the legion repulsed Ibn Saud and secured the port of Aqaba for Abdullah. Several Beduin revolts were also suppressed but the Beduins only accepted Abdullah after the legion commander incorporated them into the military.

A constitution and legislature were created in 1928 as negotiations for total independence began. The lengthy negotiations, in which Abdullah was accused of gross mismanagement of British grants, ended in the formation of the Kingdom of Transjordan in 1946. Independence was a reward for Abdullah's support against pro-Axis Iraq and French Vichy Syria during World War II.

Extensive British involvement in local affairs hindered American recognition of the nation's in-

King Abdullah ibn al-Husayn of Jordan

dependence and, thereby, the country's admission to the United Nations. Abdullah was also censured by Arab nationalists for his recognition of the right of Jews to settle in western Palestine and his acceptance of the 1947 UN partition resolution to resolve the Arab-Jewish conflict. The king conducted a series of meetings with Jewish representative Golda *Meir, who expressed willingness to recognize Abdullah's annexation of territories slated for an Arab state in return for peace. A new treaty with Britain also recognized Abdullah's rights to the territory and limited British influence in internal affairs.

Arab pressure forced Abdullah to participate in the Arab invasion of Israel in 1948. He was officially commander of the joint Arab forces but in fact his role during the war was minimal. Arab governments rejected Transjordan's occupation of the West Bank in favor of the mufti of Jerusalem, Haj Amin al-Husayni's All-Palestine government in Gaza. Nonetheless, Abdullah incorporated the West Bank into his kingdom in 1950 and the country's name was changed to the Hashemite Kingdom of Jordan.

Although many Palestinians played important roles in Abdullah's administration, the king was unpopular with Arab nationalists for supposed collaboration with the British and the Zionists. He was assassinated by a follower of al-Husayni while entering the Jerusalem al-Aqsa Mosque. His son Talal succeeded him, but was deposed because of his unstable mental health in favor of his grandson Husayn (Hussein).

M. Abu Nowar, *The History of the Hashemite Kingdom of Jordan*, 1989.

K. T. Nimri, *Abdullah Ibn Hussain: A Study in Arab Political Leadership*, 1977.

M. C. Wilson, *King Abdullah, Britain and the Making of Jordan*, 1987.

ABELARD, PETER (Pierre Abélard or Abailard; 1079–1142), French scholar. A poet, logician, moral philosopher, and theologian, he was one of the most famous and controversial teachers of his age. He is seen by some as a champion of free thought and rationalism in the face of obscurantism and intolerance. Among others he is known for the elopement, castration, condemnation, and confinement which were responsible for the popular literature about him. However, he was undoubtedly one of the most influential names in medieval history; he greatly improved the schools of his day and laid the foundations for the establishment of universities. His attempts at rational and humanist interpretations of the Catholic faith were far ahead of his times. Although condemned and criticized for skepticism and freethinking during his lifetime, he is now recognized as an outstanding theologian and logician.

Abelard was born at Le Pallet in Brittany and studied with Roscelin Compiègne in Loches and William of Champeaux in Paris. He later criticized both teachers severely for their handling of the

Peter Abelard leading Héloïse to the convent of Argenteuil

question of universals. After leaving William of Champeaux he set up his own schools, first at Melun, then at Corbeil, and finally in Paris. In 1113 a decision to study theology took him to the school of Anselm of Laon but, disillusioned and impatient, he opened his own school. He began his teaching career there with a difficult exposition on the text of the prophet Ezekiel, which drew students away from his former master. Anselm's unfavorable reaction convinced him to return to Paris, where he received a position as master of the cathedral school.

Much has been made of Abelard's subsequent love affair and elopement with Héloïse, niece of Canon Fulbert, who had engaged Abelard as her private tutor. As master of the Parisian cathedral school, Abelard had attracted students from all over Europe but when Héloïse became pregnant he married her secretly and left his illustrious teaching career in order to flee with her to his family home in Brittany. After the birth of their son, Astralabe, the couple returned to Paris where Abelard was castrated by Héloïse's angry and vengeful uncle. Héloïse became a nun at Argenteuil and Abelard returned to his teaching and to the problem of explaining Catholicism in rational terms. He later wrote an autobiography, to which Héloïse replied with her famous love letters.

At the instigation of his opponents Abelard was accused of heresy and summoned to defend his activities before the Council of Soissons. The verdict was condemnation and confinement to the abbey of Saint Denis, where his intellectual pursuits soon created an atmosphere of hostility. He then retired to the deserted hermitage of the Paraclete in Champagne with some of his students and, as he had done before, established what was to become an important school. Although he was elected abbot of the Breton abbey of Saint Gildas in 1155, he chose to remain at the Paraclete and when the nuns of Argenteuil were expelled from their convent in 1129, he gave the community to Héloïse.

After two more years as spiritual director of the Paraclete, Abelard returned to Paris and picked up the threads of his teaching career there, founding a school on the left bank of the Seine which was to eventually become the University of Paris. He was still, however, plagued by opponents and in 1140 the Council of Sens condemned his works and forbade him to teach. En route to appeal this decision with the pope in Rome he stopped at Cluny, where he was persuaded to remain. He died there in the middle of writing *Dialogue between a Jew, a Christian and a Philosopher*, on the subject of monotheism.

Abelard's motto was "Understand that thou mayest believe" and his method was the application of logic to the science of theology. In his emphasis on dialectical discussion he is seen as a precursor of *Thomas Aquinas. His own thesis was that truth is to be attained by weighing opposing positions.

In his theory of universals he asserted that a universal is a word which expresses an image by virtue of abstraction from many things with a certain common likeness. In ethics his contribution was the belief that action is to be considered in the light of the doer's subjective intentions. His works include *The Story of My Calamities*, *Thus and Otherwise*, and a number of philosophical and theological treatises including *Know Thyself* and *Christian Theology*.

D. E. Luscombe, *The School of Peter Abelard*, 1969.

K. M. Starner, *Peter Abelard: His Place in History*, 1981.

M. Worthington, *The Immortal Lovers*, 1960.

ABRAHAM (Abram; c. nineteenth century B.C.E.), first of the patriarchs of the children of Israel, traditional founder and disseminator of monotheism. Information on Abraham's life is found in the Bible (Gen.11:26–25:10). He is first referred to as Abram ("exalted father"; Gen.11:26–17:4), with God later changing his name to Abraham (Gen.17:5), explained as "father of a multitude of nations," a folk etymology.

After establishing Abraham as the tenth generation from Noah, the biblical story starts with his moving from his birthplace, Ur of the Chaldees (in modern Iraq), with his father Terah, his wife Sarah (Sarai), and his brother Haran's son, Lot. They tarried at Haran in northern Mesopotamia where Terah died, and it was there that God commanded Abraham to leave all things familiar to him — his land, his birthplace, and his kindred — and go wherever God would send him, with the divine promise that his descendants would become a great nation. Abraham set forth with Sarah and Lot for Canaan where, at Shechem, God promised for the first time to give the land to Abraham's descendants; Abraham then journeyed southward to the Negeb.

Famine caused Abraham to seek relief in Egypt (Gen.12:10–20), where Pharaoh's eye fell upon the beautiful Sarah. Under the impression that Sarah was Abraham's sister, Pharaoh took her to his palace and gave rich gifts to Abraham. Divine plagues alerted Pharaoh to the fact that Sarah was Abraham's wife and he returned her to Abraham, telling him to leave Egypt.

Back in Canaan Abraham prospered and was "very rich in cattle, in silver, and in gold." The herdsmen of Lot, who had also fared well, quarreled with those of Abraham, and to keep peace the two separated, with Lot moving east to the Dead Sea region and Abraham remaining in the Negeb.

When a group of invading kings from the east made war against the kings of Sodom, Gomorrah, and other cities, capturing Lot in the process, Abraham led a force of 318 of his own men in routing the invaders, rescuing Lot and returning the plunder and captives. Abraham himself refused any share in the spoils, even when they were offered to him by Melchizedek king of Salem (possibly Jerusalem). God then concluded a solemn covenant with Abraham, promising him that the land from the Nile (the great river of Egypt) to the Euphrates would be set aside for Abraham's descendants.

The next episode describes how Sarah gave Hagar, her maidservant, to Abraham as a concubine, as she herself remained childless. *Ishmael, the child of this union, born when Abraham was eighty-six, was also destined by God to become the ancestor of a great nation. Thirteen years later God reiterated his promises to Abraham and instituted circumcision as the everlasting token of his pledges. Abraham and all males in his household, including Ishmael, then thirteen, were circumcised on the same day.

Abraham's legendary hospitality was displayed upon the visit of three men who appeared at the door of his tent in the terebinths of Mamre. They proved to be divine messengers (the Hebrew word is synonymous with angels) who informed him that Sarah would bear him a son within the coming year. To the doubts expressed by Abraham on the grounds of both his and Sarah's advanced age (their late nineties), the messengers responded that they should have faith in God's power.

God then revealed to Abraham through the messengers that he intended to destroy the hopelessly wicked cities of Sodom and Gomorrah. Abraham, fearful that the innocent would perish with the guilty, endeavored to avert this disaster by asking that all be spared if only fifty, only forty, even only ten righteous people could be found in these cities. God agreed, but the minimum number of ten unblemished individuals could not be discovered and Sodom and Gomorrah were destroyed. Although Lot and his daughters were spared, his wife was turned into a pillar of salt for turning back to view the destruction of the city.

God fulfilled his promise of a son when Sarah conceived and gave birth to Isaac. At her insistence Abraham reluctantly expelled Hagar and Ishmael.

The supreme test of Abraham's trust took place some time later when God commanded him to offer his son Isaac as a sacrifice. (It is not clear how old Isaac was at the time, but he is called a "lad.") Abraham's unhesitating acceptance of the call was seen as a sign of supreme devotion, but at the crucial moment an angel stayed his hand and provided a ram to be sacrificed instead of Isaac. This vivid episode gained for Abraham the reputation of the man of perfect faith.

After Sarah's death in Kiriath Arba (Hebron), Abraham purchased the nearby Cave of Machpelah for a burial site. The cave was to be the burial sepulcher of the patriarchal couples Abraham and Sarah, Isaac and Rebecca, and Jacob and Leah, and its traditional location is revered by Jews and Muslims to this day.

Abraham married again after Sarah's death and had more children. He died at 175 and Isaac and Ishmael conducted the funeral.

Scholars disagree as to the historicity of Abraham, but the plausibility of the details of his life have been confirmed by archeology and comparative studies. In any case, both Jews and Muslims revere Abraham as the originator of their faiths and peoples and he is widely accredited with the birth of the belief in monotheism.

J. van Seters, *Abraham in History and Tradition*, 1975.

ABU BAKR (c.573 – 634), father-in-law of *Muhammad; the first caliph. Born Uthman ibn Abdullah in Mecca, he was a successful merchant who also gained a reputation as a judge, interpreter of dreams, and local historian. Uthman met Muhammad the prophet in 610 and became the first male convert to Islam the following year. He was originally called Abd al-Kaaba, Arabic for "servant of the temple," but received the name Abu Bakr, meaning, "father of the virgin," when Muhammad married his daughter Aishah. Abu Bakr was also called Abd Allah (servant of God) and al-Siddik (the righteous one) because of his devotion to Muhammad.

Abu Bakr was a close friend and adviser to Muhammad and was the only person to accompany him on the *hegira*, Muhammad's migration from Mecca to Medina in 622 to escape persecution by the local authorities. During the next ten years, as the new religion spread, Abu Bakr remained in the background, often counseling Muhammad on Arab intrigues. He was already an elderly man with a stooping gait and a white beard dyed red. Although he was a far from imposing figure, Abu Bakr was well loved for his charity and for his nearness to the prophet.

Before his death Muhammad expressed his desire that Abu Bakr should succeed him by having him offer prayers for the people. When Muhammad died in 632, Abu Bakr went to the balcony of Muhammad's palace, which overlooked the anxious crowds waiting for news of the prophet, and declared, "Oh you believers! Know that the Prophet Muhammad is dead. But you who have faith in God, know that God is alive and can never die." Despite the protestations of Muhammad's son-in-law *Ali, Abu Bakr was appointed caliph, an Arabic term for deputy. He himself defined the title by saying, "Call me not the Caliph of the Lord. I am but the Caliph of the Prophet of the Lord."

Although Abu Bakr reigned for only two years and three months, the period was important in Islamic history. Muhammad's death shook the new religion and many adherents sought to shake off the strict yoke of Muhammad's authority. The people of Nejd revolted against the tribute they were forced to pay; the people of the Hejaz sought to discard the new religion entirely. Even the city of Medina, capital of the caliphate, was threatened by religious upheaval. Abu Bakr suppressed these revolts in just two years and encouraged the campaign of Khalid, in which Iraq and Syria were attacked and overcome. The spread of Islam to Byzantium and Persia began during his reign.

He was instrumental in organizing Islam as a religion. At the urging of *Omar, Abu Bakr wrote down the sayings of Muhammad and deposited them with the Prophet's widow, Hafsa. These writings later became the basis for the Koran, the Islamic scripture. Abu Bakr died in 634; it was rumored that he had been poisoned. Although he had had access to the wealth of his country, he died possessing only the clothes he was wearing, a servant, and a camel.

F. Gabrieli, *Mohammed and the Conquests of Islam*, 1968.

W. Muir, *The Caliphate*, 1924.

M. Syrier, *The Religious Duties of Islam as Taught by Abu Bakr*, 1971.

Oh people! Now I am ruler over you, albeit not the best among you. If I do well, support me; if ill then set me right. Follow the true, wherein is faithfulness; eschew the false, wherein is treachery. The weaker among you shall be as the stronger among me, and the stronger shall be as the weaker, until, if the Lord wills it, I shall have taken from him that which he has wrested. Leave not off to fight in the ways of the Lord; whosoever leaves off, him verily, shall the Lord abase. Obey me as I obey the Lord and his prophet. Wherein I disobey, obey me not. Now rise to your prayers, and may God have mercy on you.

**Abu Bakr's speech
on inauguration as caliph**

ADAMS, JOHN (1735–1826), statesman, diplomat, and lawyer who became the second president of the United States 1797–1801. Born in Braintree (now Quincy), Massachusetts, Adams could say even in those very early days that he was a fourth-generation American. After attending Harvard College and receiving his bachelor's degree in 1755, he became a schoolmaster in Worcester, Massachusetts, where he lived in the home of a prominent Worcester lawyer, James Putnam, who inspired him to study law. After three years, he was admitted to the Boston bar in 1758.

His law practice led him to be active on behalf of the Revolution. As a lawyer he argued against the Stamp Act before the royal governor, pointing out that it was truly taxation without representation since the colonists were not represented in the British parliament that passed this law. Although he was strongly opposed to the Stamp Act, he disapproved of the so-called Stamp Act riots. First and foremost he was an advocate, to the point of defending British soldiers who fired on civilians in the Boston Massacre. He grew closer to the revolutionary cause by appearing in important cases connected to it, such as the smuggling charges against John Hancock, a prominent colonist.

In 1774 he was one of the Massachusetts delegates to the first Continental Congress and in the second Continental Congress, became one of the leaders of the Revolution. He was appointed to a committee charged with drafting the Declaration of Independence. Adams's greatest contribution to the Declaration of Independence, of which he was a signatory, was to serve as the driving force that supported and defended it through Congress.

Between 1778 and 1788 Adams primarily served his country as a diplomat. In 1778 he was a congressional commissioner to France and in 1780–1782 served in the Netherlands, securing its recognition of the United States as an independent country. He negotiated a treaty of amity and commerce with the Netherlands as well as, most important in those days, a loan. In 1783 he was one of the negotiators who drafted the Treaty of Paris, which officially brought the American Revolution to an end. From 1785 to 1788 he served as the first U.S. ambassador to England.

In 1788 Adams returned home and the following year was elected the first vice president of the United States, an office to which he was reelected in 1792. This was followed by his election as president in 1796.

During his presidency John Adams's notable achievements included the establishment of the Department of the Navy in 1798, the signing of the Alien and Sedition Acts and, in 1800, the signing of a treaty with France that averted war. In 1800 he was defeated by Thomas *Jefferson for the presidency. Both he and Jefferson died on the same day — the fiftieth anniversary of the signing of the Declaration of Independence — the year after Adams's

BY JOHN ADAMS

Yesterday the greatest question was decided which ever was debated in America; and a greater perhaps never was, nor will be, decided among men. A resolution was passed without one dissenting colony, that these United Colonies are, and of right ought to be, free and independent States.

**In a letter to his wife,
Abigail, July 3, 1776**

I have come to the conclusion that one useless man is called a disgrace, that two are called a law firm, and that three or more become a congress! For ten years King George and his Parliament have called, cullied, and diddled these colonies with their illegal taxes — Stamp Acts, Townshend Acts, Sugar Acts, Tea Acts — and when we dared stand up like men they stopped our trade, seized our ships, blockaded our ports, burned our towns, and spilled our blood — and still this congress won't grant any of my proposals on Independence....

At the Second Continental Congress

Wherever a general knowledge and sensibility have prevailed among the people, arbitrary government and every kind of oppression have lessened and disappeared in proportion.... Liberty cannot be preserved without a general knowledge among the people who have a right, from the frame of their nature, to knowledge.... And the preservation of the means of knowledge among the lowest ranks is of more importance to the public than all the property of the rich men in the country.... Let us dare to read, think, speak, and write. Let every order and degree among the people rouse their attention and animate their resolution.... In a word, let every sluice of knowledge be opened and set a-flowing.

From an article in the *Boston Gazette*, 1765

- An ounce of mother wit is worth a pound of clergy.
- Education makes a greater difference between man and man than nature has made between man and brute.

Letters to his wife, 1775–1776

son, John Quincy Adams, was elected president of the United States.

C.D. Bowen, *John Adams and the American Revolution*, 1950.

R. A. Brown, *The Presidency of John Adams*, 1975.

M. D. Peterson, *Adams and Jefferson*, 1976.

P. Smith, *John Adams*, 2 vols., 1962.

ADENAUER, KONRAD (1876–1967), first chancellor of the Federal Republic of Germany. He was born to a devout Catholic family in Cologne and studied at the universities of Freiburg, Munich, and Bonn, graduating with a law degree in 1899. In 1906 he served on the Cologne city council, where he remained until 1917, when he was elected mayor. He proved his competence by preventing riots by retreating German soldiers in the aftermath of World War I. As early as the time of British occupation he advocated the creation of a federal state in Germany to resolve that country's problems. He opposed the French proposal to establish an independent Rhineland and the British for their attempted mistreatment of the civilian population. On one occasion the British insisted that all males be required to tip their hats to British officers on the street. Adenauer simply remarked that he "could not imagine that the British would want to humiliate a vanquished people in this way," and the order was rescinded.

From 1917 to 1933 Adenauer took little interest in the national politics of the Weimar Republic, despite serving as a delegate in the Prussian Diet as mayor of Cologne. His life revolved around his city and his family. In 1926 the Catholic Center party proposed him as chancellor but after failing to form an acceptable coalition, he returned to Cologne. As lord mayor he was already the highest paid politician in the country.

Being a Centrist Democrat, Adenauer was opposed to Adolf *Hitler and did everything he could to distance himself from him. When Hitler first visited Cologne as chancellor, prior to the election in which he gained absolute power, Adenauer refused to greet him at the airport, claiming that Hitler was visiting the city as part of his political campaign and not as chancellor. Nazi flags were removed from a bridge Hitler was to cross, since it was considered municipal property. Hitler never forgave Adenauer; upon assuming control he had him removed from power. Adenauer was banned from Cologne and even arrested briefly following the so-called Night of the Long Knives purge in 1934. He eventually retired to his new estate at Rhondorf, where he lived peacefully until the attempt on Hitler's life in 1944. Although he refused to take part in the plot he was arrested and nearly sent to Buchenwald concentration camp, but escaped. Only after his wife was arrested and beaten was he captured but this time his son, an army lieutenant, approached the Gestapo and secured his father's release. Adenauer returned to his estate until the end of the war when, in keeping with occupation policies, he was reappointed mayor of Cologne.

The occupation forces and Adenauer soon disagreed over British demands that surrounding forests be cut down for firewood. This time his refusal to comply with British orders led to his dismissal and a second prohibition against entering Cologne. Instead of retiring again, Adenauer chose to enter national politics. He joined the rightist Christian Democratic Union (CDU), serving as its leader by merit of his age. When tensions between the Soviets and the West came to a head in 1949, he represented the CDU in the committee drafting a constitution for the proposed Federal Republic of Germany to be formed out of the American, British, and French zones. In the elections his party won a slim majority. The Bundestag elected Adenauer chancellor by a margin of one vote, his own.

BY ADENAUER

- God made a great mistake to limit the intelligence of man but not his stupidity.
- In politics, patience is of major importance, and I have a great deal of patience.

Once in power Adenauer refused to form a coalition with the opposition Social Democrats. *Der Alte* (the "Old Man"), as he was affectionately known, served as chancellor (1949–1963), foreign minister (1951–1955), and as president of the CDU (1950–1966). He opposed neutrality and sought to forge closer ties with the West, and particularly with France. Deeply upset by the Holocaust, he signed an agreement with Israel to pay that country reparations. His first opportunity to assert independence came when he convinced the Allies to curb the dismantling of factories for reparation payments. The next year Germany and France signed the Schuman Plan, creating an international authority in western Europe to direct steel and coal production in what became the predecessor of the European Economic Community. With the Cold War threatening Europe, Germany also joined the North Atlantic Treaty Organization (NATO), thereby allowing it to restore its army. Much of his time in office was spent healing the economic wounds of Germany and creating what came to be known as the "economic miracle." In 1955 Germany gained full independence. It was now a member of the EEC, NATO, and the UN.

Perhaps the most significant event of Adenauer's career was the signing of the Franco-German treaty of friendship and cooperation on January 22, 1963, putting an end to the centuries-long hostility between the two countries. That year, at age eighty-eight, he resigned as chancellor in favor of Ludwig Erhard. Until his death Adenauer kept an office in the Bundestag and often commented — sometimes with wry remarks — on affairs of state.

D. Cook, *Ten Men and History*, 1981.

R. Hiscocks, *The Adenauer Era*, 1966.

ADLER, ALFRED (1870–1937), psychiatrist; founder of the school of individual psychiatry. Although often neglected and occasionally maligned in the history and theory of psychology, he was a creative pioneer in examining interpersonal relationships, in social psychology and group psychotherapy, and in psychosomatic medicine.

Adler was born in a Vienna suburb, the sickly second son of a struggling grain merchant. He barely passed medical school in Vienna, and after a stint in a clinic and the army, opened his own practice there. At this time, he already showed a definite interest in social medicine, publishing a booklet in which he demonstrated that poor work conditions and economic straits, and not just biological factors, may precipitate disease.

In 1902, he met Sigmund *Freud and became an early member of the inner circle with which Freud surrounded himself. During the next nine years, Adler contributed a great deal to the development of psychoanalytic thought. It was he who coined the term "inferiority complex." He spoke of organ inferiority, whereby a deficient part of a person's body may lead to feelings of inferiority and attempts to compensate by striving for superiority. This he believed could have far-reaching ramifications for personality and neurosis.

Disagreement on theoretical grounds, in which Adler diminished the role of sexual factors in neurosis, as well as personal competitiveness, led in 1911 to a rupture between Freud and Adler. Adler went on to establish "individual psychology." He emphasized the uniqueness and indivisibility of each human being. He stressed that the personality may be reflected in every action and in every memory. Indeed, one of his well-known innovations was to inquire after earliest memories, which, he believed, regularly revealed much about a personality.

Eventually he developed a psychology that encompassed all human behavior and psychopathology. He stressed the role of environment and society in neurosis. He believed that human behavior is derived form the individual's sense of community and from his own strivings for superiority. He maintained that each person is not simply a victim of unconscious conflicts, but a being who, with sufficient courage, can discover the hidden goals which determine his behavior and the fictions which may mar his perspective of the world, and in this way change his lifestyle. Thus he believed psychotherapy can lead a patient from secluded self-preoccupation to productive functioning within the community.

His other important contributions include his attention to sibling position in forming character (creating for example, the responsibility-laden eldest, or the pampered youngest), and the concept of masculine protest, a reaction to the unjustified male domination of society. He also became an advocate of therapeutic education, counseling teachers and parents and setting up experimental schools. He was, however, always denied the university post he coveted.

An unassuming man who conducted his meetings in the coffee houses of Vienna, Adler was alienated from his Judaism. He did not want to be a member of a religion limited to one ethnic group. At the age of thirty four, he had himself and his children baptized and became a Protestant. Late in life, in dialogues with a Lutheran minister, he attempted to reconcile psychology with religion and psychotherapy with salvation.

Foreseeing the Nazi menace, he relocated, in his last years to the United States. He died of a heart attack during a lecture tour in Scotland.

F. Ellenberger, *The Discovery of the Unconscious*, 1970.

W. A. Kaufmann, *Freud Versus Adler and Jung*, 1980.

P. Roazen, *Freud and His Followers*, 1975.

AESCHYLUS (525–456/5 B.C.E.), first of the great ancient Greek dramatists. Through his innovations Aeschylus established the tragedy in its final form while dramatizing issues that have remained timeless to this day. He retained the chorus of the earlier Greek dramatists, the Thespians, but added a second actor, enabling dialogue and the presentation of action rather than narration of events. These changes were integral to his presentation of new themes: the rise of democracy in Athens and the struggle for greater human dignity even when opposed by superior powers, whether of the state or the gods.

The first half of the sixth century B.C.E., which preceded the birth of Aeschylus, had witnessed the elevation of Athens into a major city-state; it changed from an agricultural society to a more powerful, urban one. As Athens changed politically and economically, its culture was transformed as well. The old chthonic or earth gods, who ruled crops and agriculture, were integrated with the heavenly Zeus and his pantheon. Then, as Athens moved toward democracy under *Pericles, the dynamic relationship of the gods of heaven and earth was made to incorporate yet another partner — human beings struggling toward civilization. Decisions of justice were no longer to be determined by the chthonic gods' need for vengeance, nor seen as the retribution of the more considered yet still unmerciful law of Zeus. As Greece became democratic, the old laws gave way to a new standard of mercy that at the same time incorporated the traditions of the old gods. It was these social and cultural transformations that Aeschylus dramatized in his plays.

Aeschylus was born into the Eupatrid family of old Attic aristocracy in the town of Eleusis, not far from Athens. The town, the site of the temple of Demeter, the ancient earth goddess, was the scene of secret mystery rites and initiations carried out by torchlight during the nights of winter. Aeschylus witnessed these rites as well as the sacred processions, accompanied by song and the retelling of the myth of Demeter, from Athens to the sanctuary of Demeter in Eleusis. These rites and myths formed the background for Aeschylus's drama, which was

---

Now listen to the sufferings of mankind,
In whom, once speechless, senseless, like an infant,
I have implanted the faculty of reason...
At first, with eyes to see, they saw in vain,
With ears to hear, heard nothing, groping through
Their lives in a dreamlike stupor, with no skill
In carpentry or brickmaking, like ants
Burrowing in holes, unpracticed in the signs
Of blossom, fruit and frost, from hand to mouth
Struggling improvidently, until I
Charted the intricate orbits of the stars;
Invented number, that most exquisite
Instrument, and the alphabet, the tool
Of history and chronicle of their progress;
Tamed the wild beasts to toil in pack and harness
And yoked the prancing mounts of opulence,
Obedient to the rein, in chariots;
Constructed wheelless vehicles with linen
Wings to carry them over the trackless ocean...
This is my record. You have it in a word:
Prometheus founded all the arts of man.

From *Prometheus Bound*

---

composed in the mythic language of his youth yet which liked that past with the new world view of his contemporaries — the pre-Socratic (see *Socrates) philosophers and the founder of Athens's democratic government. The subjects of his drama reflect these wider changes occurring within Greek culture and society during his lifetime.

Aeschylus first competed in the Dionysia Festival in the year 500 B.C.E. at the age of tweny-five. He failed at that time to win a prize, although he must have written with great conviction — legend has it that as a teenager he had a vision of the god Dionysus commanding him to write, and from that moment on he was inspired in his efforts. In 490 B.C.E.,

when Aeschylus was thirty-five, the Persian Empire under the rule of *Darius invaded the Peloponnesus in its first bid to conquer the Greek city-states. Aeschylus and his brother Cynegirus joined the battle at Marathon. His brother was killed trying to capture a Persian boat but Aeschylus survived. It was not until 484 B.C.E., after Aeschylus had matured in the crucible of war, that he was victorious at the Dionysia — but his winning drama was lost to posterity, along with many others of his more than ninety plays. In 480 B.C.E., when Greece was again invaded by the Persians under Darius's son *Xerxes, Aeschylus joined the battle once more. No doubt this served as the background for one of his extant plays, *The Persians*, which won him first prize at the festival in 472 B.C.E.. The play contrasts the failure in war of autocratic Persia with the triumph of democratically-ruled Athens.

Aeschylus would win thirteen victories at the Dionysia but in 468 B.C.E. lost the competition to another of Greece's great tragedians, the younger *Sophocles. The following year Aeschylus again won the competition with his Oedipus trilogy, known to posterity as *Seven against Thebes*, the surviving one-third of the work.

Aeschylus's latest plays are his most famous. The *Oresteia* trilogy tells the tragic history of a blood feud within the royal house of Atreus. Its production paralleled a tumultous period in Athens's fledgling democracy as radical elements ascended to power through bloodshed, exiling their more conservative contenders. The *Oresteia* is composed of three parts: *Agamemnon*, *Libation Bearers*, and *Eumenides*. Beginning with the story of the Greeks stalled on their way to engage the battle for Helen of Troy, the play tells the story of the Greek leader Agamemnon, who sacrifices his daughter Iphigeneia in order to propitiate the gods. Agamememnon's deed is avenged by his bitter wife Clytemnestra; Orestes, Agamemnon's son, is then ordered by the god Apollo to avenge his father's murder and he does so, committing matricide, a crime for which he is pursued by the Furies, the goddesses of earth. Caught in an endless cycle of blood revenge, Orestes takes refuge at the altar at Delphi and asks for mercy based on the circumstances of his action. While the old gods call for Orestes's death, Athena comes to his aid, arguing for new notions of justice that will also placate the old gods. Aeschylus's conclusion of the play makes a plea for Athens to end its recent cycle of violence and return peacefully to its new democratic experiment.

Aeschylus's last play, *Prometheus Bound*, was also possibly written as a trilogy, although only one part survives intact. Again the subject of the play revolves around the relationship between godly powers and human beings — the latter struggling for their independence.

Aeschylus died at Gela, in the south of Sicily. His grave was marked by an epitaph perhaps composed by Aeschylus himself:

This tomb the dust of Aeschylus doth hide,
Euphorion's son, and fruitful Gela's pride.
How tried his valor Marathon may tell,
And long-haired Medes [Persians] who knew it
all too well.

A. E. Haigh, *The Tragic Drama of the Greeks*,
1968.
J. Herington, *Aeschylus*, 1986.
G. Thomson, *Aeschylus and Athens*, 1973.

AKBAR (1542–1605), third and greatest Mogul
emperor. Akbar, named Jalal-ud-Din Muhammad
Akbar, was the grandson of *Babur, founder of the
Mogul empire and son of the second Mogul emperor, *Humayun; he was also a descendant of
*Genghis Khan and *Tamerlane. At the time of
Akbar's birth Humayun had been defeated by an
Afghan usurper, Sher Shah, and was forced to flee
his capital, Delhi. Akbar was born in exile in the
city of Umarkot in Sind. By the time he ascended
the throne at age fourteen his father had managed to
restore a section of his empire under a Persian protectorate. Within only two decades, Akbar had expanded his inheritance to its original boundaries and
beyond. The name Akbar, Arabic for "great," was
adopted to describe this man noted for his military,
administrative, and religious achievements and his
warm, humane personality.

Akbar's first task on taking over the kingdom
was to defeat all rival claimants to the throne.
Chief among these was the Hindu minister Hemu,
whom he defeated at Panipat. Akbar went on to
conquer the territories of his father's original kingdom and the surrounding areas. By 1562 he had
conquered the Punjab, Hultan, Ganges, and Juman
basins from Panipat to Allahabad, Gwalior, Ajmer,
Kabul, and Rajputana. He consolidated his authority over the influential Hindu region of Rajputana
by making a series of marriage alliances with the
local royal family. By 1576, he had conquered
Malwa, Clitor, Ranthambhor, Kalinjar, Gujarat, and
Bengal. In his last wave of conquests
(1586–1592), he overran Kashmir, Sind, Baluchistan, Kandahar, part of Orissa, the Deccan, Khan-
desh, Berar, and Ahmadnagar.

Akbar was not only a remarkable military leader
but was also a notable administrator. He had sur-
veyors measure the land area of the empire so that
land revenues could be accurately calculated, then
divided the territory in fifteen *subas*, or provinces,
to ease administration. Many of his administrative
reforms were adopted by the British in later years.
Despite the Mogul Empire's devout Islamic culture,
he allowed for complete freedom of religion for all
his subjects. Many Hindus were appointed to
prominent positions and he did away with the hated
jizya, a poll tax levied on all Hindus making religious pilgrimages.

Akbar himself came to doubt many of the important precepts basic to Islam. He preferred reason to
the written word of the Koran and saw validity in

other religious beliefs, particularly those of Hinduism (he believed in the transmigration of souls
upon death rather than the traditional Muslim belief
in a heavenly paradise). His split with Islam was
nearly total when he rewrote the fundamental prayer
of that religion to read, "There is no God but Allah,
and Akbar is his vice-regent." On three occasions
he summoned Jesuit missionaries to teach him the
principles of Christianity but each time rejected fundamental Christian beliefs such as heaven, the Trinity, and the incarnation of Christ. His interest in religious beliefs led him to convene a council of sages
of all the major religions of India. Akbar then chose

Akbar – a contemporary drawing

from each religion those beliefs which appeared
most reasonable to him and incorporated them into a
new religion, the *Din-i-Ilahi* ("Divine Faith"), which
was to unify his empire but came to nothing. He
erected houses of worship, *ibadat khana*, in which
members of all religious persuasions could worship.

Although Akbar was illiterate, each evening he
had his servants read to him. He established an extensive library of twenty-four thousand books containing works translated from many languages and
staffed his court with noted intellectuals.

Akbar was unwilling to forego the pleasures allowed him by his position. He had a stable of five
thousand elephants and it was said that his harem
numbered five thousand but this figure probably included eunuchs and slaves in addition to wives,
concubines (said to number three hundred), and
many young children. Akbar had seven children by
his consort: his sons Salim, Murad, and Danyal,
and four daughters. Toward the end of Akbar's
reign, Salim rebelled against his father but the two

were reconciled shortly before Akbar's death in Agra in 1605.

F. Augustus, *The Emperor Akbar*, 1973.
L. Binyan, *Akbar*, 1932.
P. Du Jarric, *Akbar and the Jesuits*, 1979.

AKHENATON (Amenhotep IV; reigned c.1379– 1362 B.C.E.), pharaoh of Egypt and religious reformer. Akhenaton, the son of Amenhotep III and his commoner wife, Tiy, was one of the greatest religious reformers of the ancient world; he is often credited with being the first monotheist. Physically very weak and thin, with a bulging pot belly, Akhenaton was very different from his father, a remarkable builder and hunter. Rather than spend his time at the hunt or at other physical activities common to Egyptian princes, Akhenaton was an intellectual who spent much of his youth poring over Egyptian religious texts.

At the time of his ascent to the throne, Egypt's Eighteenth Dynasty was undergoing radical social changes. The country was an economic and military power which ruled Nubia, Palestine, and Phoenicia, as well as Upper and Lower Egypt. Extensive foreign trade allowed for other cultures to make their mark on Egyptian society and many Egyptians had adopted modes of dress and habit unfamiliar to the otherwise isolated Egyptian culture. Even the pharaoh had become little more than a figurehead monarch, removed from mundane matters of state. The pharaohs had relinquished their authority in favor of priests and bureaucrats who administered religious and secular rites and laws, for which they received great wealth and prestige.

Egyptians worshiped an immense pantheon of gods and goddesses, each requiring its own rituals. The gods of Egypt were generally depicted in human or animal form, often combining elements of the two. Two important gods were Re, worshiped in Heliopolis, and Amon, worshiped in Thebes; there was animosity between the adherents of these two gods. A few years before Akhenaton's birth a new deity, Aton, appeared in the Egyptian pantheon. Aton was originally depicted similarly to Re, as a human figure with the head of a falcon and a sun disk over his head; the whole figure was surrounded by a coiled serpent. Gradually the human and animal elements of Aton disappeared, leaving only the sun disk to represent the god.

Akhenaton assumed the throne sometime during the latter years of his father's reign. Immediately upon coming to power he began to promote the worship of Aton. The temple of Re-Harakhte, in the royal capital of Thebes, was abandoned for new temples erected to Aton at Karnak. Unlike the older temples, which were dark, imposing edifices containing majestic statues of the gods and their subjects, the new temples were less imposing and well lit by windows. Aton, the sun disk, had to be worshiped where his rays could reach. Much of the ritual was performed in the open air. The ritual was less devel-

oped than that of other gods; rather than consisting of a series of commandments and ceremonies, it demanded of its adherents merely to be grateful to Aton for the life that they were given. There was no tradition of divine rewards and punishments.

Akhenaton became a zealous champion of Aton. In the sixth year of his reign, he changed his name from Amenhotep ("Amon is satisfied") to Akhenaton ("he who serves Aton"). His capital was moved from Thebes, the city sacred to Amon, to Amarna, renamed Akhetaton, meaning, "place of Aton's power." A crusade was waged against the old gods: their statues were destroyed, and their names were erased from temples and documents. Their images were replaced with those of Akhenaton and his consort, Nefertiti. The traditional funeral hymn was rewritten; references to Osiris, god of the dead, were replaced with the name of Akhenaton; Akhenaton composed new hymns to Aton.

The new city of Akhetaton was a remarkable architectural feat, containing wide boulevards, villas, gardens, and pools. At the center of the city stood an open temple to Aton. The city was decorated with a new style of art in which the subjects were depicted as they appeared rather than being idealized by the artist. Akhenaton was depicted with all his physical defects and Nefertiti was shown as a hag, in a style that was closer to caricature than art.

Akhenaton was not a radical reformer. He had returned the monarchy to its former potency, causing him to be regarded by many as a reactionary. New nobles were created to replace the old aristocrats, leading to dissent among Egypt's leading families. In his zeal for religious reform, Akhenaton had neglected commerce and the military and his administration was infiltrated by corrupt officials. Many of his former subjects and allies in Africa and Asia were abandoned. During the twelfth year of his reign, the queen mother visited Akhetaton to warn him of the slow disintegration of his kingdom. He apparently accepted her advice; he was separated from Nefertiti and promoted Smenkhare, his son-in-law and possibly his younger brother, to a leading

Akhenaton and Nefertiti

How manifold are your works! They are hidden from the sight of men, O Sole God, like unto who there is no other. You did fashion the earth according to your desire when you were alone, all men, all cattle, great and small, all that are upon the earth, that run upon their feet or rise up on high, flying with their wings. And the lands of Syria and Kush and Egypt — you appoint every man to his place and satisfy his needs. Everyone receives his sustenance and his days are numbered. Their tongues are diverse in speech, and their qualities likewise, and their color is differentiated, for you have distinguished the nations.

Thou made the waters under the earth, and bring you them forth (as the Nile) at your pleasure to sustain the people of Egypt even as you have made them live for you, O Divine Lord of them all, tiring yourself with them, the Lord of Every Land, shining forth for them, the Aton Disk of the Daytime, great in majesty.

From Akhenaton's prayer to Aton inscribed on the tomb of Ay

role in the administration of Egypt. Akhenaton, who was sickly, died soon after. He was succeeded briefly by Smenkhare and then by Tutankhaton. Tutankhaton rejected the reforms of his predecessor, restoring the old gods to their former eminence. He himself changed his name to Tutankhamen, in honor of Amon, the god Akhenaton had tried to destroy.

C. Aldred, *Akhenaton, Pharaoh of Egypt*, 1968.
W. H. McNeill and J. W. Sedlar, eds., *The Ancient Near East*, 1968.

ALARIC (370–410), king of the Visigoths from 395. A descendant of the Balthi, one of the leading Goth families, Alaric was born on an island in the delta of the Danube River. In his youth the Visigoths were forced to migrate westward because of attacks from the Huns at their rear. The Eastern Roman emperor, *Theodosius the Great, took on the Visigoths as mercenary forces and Alaric became a commander in Theodosius's army. Upon the death of Theodosius in 395 Alaric hoped to receive a more important position in the government of the new Eastern emperor, Arcadius, but was disappointed. In 397, however, he attained a much greater position when the Visigoths elected him as their king. Turning toward Greece he sacked Corinth, Argos, and Sparta, sparing Athens only in return for a heavy ransom.

After Alaric was defeated by the Western Roman general, Flavius Stilicho, Arcadius commissioned him to move north toward Italy; Alaric accordingly proceeded to establish a Visigoth kingdom in Illyricum. His attempted invasion of Italy in 402 was again rebuffed by Stilicho. Honorius, the Western Roman emperor, subsequently convinced Alaric to join forces with him in what he believed would be an inevitable war with the Eastern Empire. The death of Arcadius in 408 preempted the projected attack on the East, and Alaric demanded four thousand pounds of gold as indemnity. He was paid at Stilicho's insistence but Honorius subsequently had Stilicho executed. Alaric invaded Italy, besieged Rome, and demanded a large ransom. In 409 a second siege resulted in Rome's capitulation and the deposing of Honorius. When the emperor regained power within a year, Alaric invaded Rome for the third time and captured the city in 410. Traitors opened one of the gates and when Alaric gave his forces six days to take what they wanted, they proceeded to sack the city. This event sent shock waves throughout the Roman world and was seen as the end of Roman civilization. Alaric had intended to go on to invade north Africa, but died before he could act on his intentions.

A. Pignanoli, *Le Sac de Rome*, 1964.

ALBA, DUKE OF (Fernando Alvarez de Toledo; 1507–1582), Spanish statesman and military figure and a controversial figure in European history: To the Spanish, he was one of the greatest military minds their country produced; to the inhabitants of the Low Countries, he was a brutal conqueror who nevertheless failed to quell their demand for religious and political liberty.

Orphaned at an early age, Alba was raised by his grandfather, himself a prominent military figure, who insisted that his young grandson accompany him to the battlefield. He was only six years old when he witnessed the invasion of Navarre; by seventeen, he had defeated the French at Fuenterrabia and was appointed governor of that region. As Duke of Alba, a title he inherited in 1531, his military acumen proved invaluable to the Holy Roman Emperor *Charles V. He commanded the imperial troops that captured Tunis, and was assigned, after the disastrous Algerian campaign of 1541, to reorganize the army, stressing his own unusual combination of severity and loyalty toward his men. On one occasion, when his men threatened to mutiny over delayed salaries, Alba offered himself as a hostage until the money arrived.

Although his uneasy marriage lasted fifty-three years, his only known love affair occurred while he was still single. While visiting a remote village during one of his campaigns he fell in love with a peasant girl, who, unknown to him, became pregnant. Many years later he visited the town and was impressed by a young matador. When asked who his father was, the boy replied, "Why, sir, none other than you." Alba accepted the boy's claim and adopted him.

For his impressive victory over the Protestant troops of Elector John Frederick of Saxony in 1547, Alba was promoted to several important positions in Italy. By 1556, however, Charles had abdicated the imperial throne, to be succeeded by his brother *Ferdinand I. The Spanish throne was inherited by Charles's son *Philip II, who promoted Alba to his council of ministers. Charles once warned Philip that Alba was "ambitious, sanctimonious, and hypocritical, and perhaps he may even try to tempt you with women." Alba was a competent statesman surpassed by none in his understanding of foreign affairs. Moreover, he was a paradox — well-educated but anti-intellectual cosmopolitan but xenophobic — and an able champion of the Counter-Reformation. His arrogant behavior was unpopular with the king and while Philip regularly called his ministers "cousin," the derogatory epithet "uncle" was reserved for Alba.

As a self-proclaimed champion of the Catholic church, Philip undertook to subvert the rapid spread of Protestantism in the Spanish-controlled Low Countries. Concluding that a strong arm was needed to check any potential uprising, he commissioned Alba to restore order in the provinces. The appointment had a secondary motive: whereas Alba was acknowledged as Spain's most competent military commander, his feuds with other ministers, led by Ruy Gómez, had escalated to violence. On one occasion, Philip's son Don Carlos tried to stab Alba.

Philip originally intended to accompany Alba to the Low Countries, but was convinced by Gómez that the expedition was hardly worthy of his attention. Alba also expected to have total support from the crown in mustering troops, only to complain that his best division consisted of "eight ranks of boys with no beards and no shoes." Despite these setbacks, Alba arrived in the Netherlands in 1567.

Alba's hasty analysis of the situation blamed the lenient measures taken by Philip's sister, Margaret of Austria, the duchess of Parma, for the deteriorating situation. While he tended to be wary of the local leadership and brought his own bureaucrats from Spain to administer the provinces, the duchess sought compromise by favoring the local nobility. Alba immediately instituted the Council of Troubles, a judiciary committee of inquiry with himself as the final authority. Soon known as the Tribunal of Blood, the council supposedly executed over eighteen thousand people (the real number is significantly lower — 8,957 were condemned, of whom 1,083 were executed) often after no more than a slanderous report by a malicious neighbor or a rival businessman. Two of the Council's earliest victims were Counts Egmont and van Hoorne, local favorites of the duchess and staunch royalists who, even as they died, were unsure of what crimes they were guilty.

By 1568 the unstable situation exploded. Backed by the Protestants of northern Germany, *William the Silent of Orange and his brother Louis of Nassau revolted against Alba. Rather than attack, Alba stationed his men behind the dikes and waited for Louis to leave his camp. When he did, the rout was total, and William retreated to Germany.

Because of Alba's extravagance, the cost of maintaining a Spanish presence in the Low Countries became increasingly cumbersome and the subject of much criticism. As his reserves became depleted he contemplated imposing a "tenth-penny tax" sales tax on the provinces. The proposed tax nearly sparked a second revolt, with many quipping that Dutch traders might willfully abandon their campaign for religious freedom but would never allow their purse strings to be threatened.

Meanwhile, the Sea Beggars and other small groups of Dutch patriots waged a relentless campaign against Alba. Aided by the French, William captured Brielle while Louis took Mons and Valenciennes. Only by restoring the notorious "tenth-penny tax" could Alba drive William to the north. Finally, tired of the incessant warfare, Alba petitioned Philip to be relieved of his command. His petition was granted in 1573.

Alba returned to court life and the bitter rivalry that preceded his appointment to the Low Countries. Unlike other ministers, he pursued a militant stance against the Dutch that he advanced at every possible opportunity. To Philip, Alba was an excerable bore: stripped of his honors, he was exiled to his estate under house arrest. However, Philip soon realized that Alba remained his most able military commander and in 1580 recalled him to lead his armies against Portugal. In a stunning victory at the Bridge of Alcántara (1581), he defeated the Portuguese king and enthroned Philip in his stead. Alba died in Lisbon the following year.

W. S. Maltby, *Alba*, 1983.

ALBERTUS MAGNUS, SAINT (Count of Bolstädt; c.1200–1280), German scholastic theologian and scholar. He was born in Lauingen in Swabia to a noble family. In 1223, after spending several months studying in Bologna and Padua, he entered the Dominican order in Padua, then under the influence of Jordan of Saxony. In 1228 he was sent to Cologne to teach theology and in 1245 went to Paris, where he became a master of theology and one of the foremost theologians at the university; one of his students was *Thomas Aquinas. In 1248 he was sent to reorganize the *studium* (school) at Cologne; in 1254 was appointed provincial (head of the order) in Germany; and in 1260 was elected bishop of Ratisbon, holding this position for only two years before resigning in order to devote himself to teaching and writing.

A scholar of immense erudition and a veritable encyclopedia of knowledge who seemed to write with authority about everything, he was called Albert the Great and given the title of Doctor Universalis. Aside from his immense capacity for knowledge he was notable for his forays into philosophy in an era when the statutes of his order dictated that the brethren "shall not study in the books of the

Gentiles and the philosophers although they may inspect them briefly." He therefore encountered understandable hostility and criticism when he attempted to reconcile theology with philosophy. He believed, however, that within certain limits philosophy was valid and necessary for the pursuit of truth and that it should be studied in its own right. He was unique in his determination to counter the medieval certainty that true philosophy was to be found exclusively in the divine message of the Bible, and its interpretation through meditation and contemplation; in this sense his ideas are considered transitional to the thinking of Thomas Aquinas. His guide to and authority on philosophy was primarily *Aristotle and he sought to present the whole of Aristotle to the West and to establish the union of theology and philosophy which would become the foundation of scholasticism.

Albertus was also interested in the sciences and medicine and engaged in biological research, at the same time becoming the subject of legends which depicted him as a magician. He wrote a treatise called *The Secrets of Women* which became a popular textbook on pregnancy and childbirth in the Middle Ages. He was altogether a prolific writer, albeit difficult to read. The Paris edition of his works (1890–1899) filled thirty-eight volumes. The principal works include *Summa de Creaturis*, a treatise on man and his immortal soul, and *Summa Theologiae*, an account of God as the cause and goal of all creatures. Pope Pius XI declared him a saint and doctor of the church in 1932.

M. Haren, *Medieval Thought*, 1985.

D. Knowles, *The Evolution of Medieval Thought*, 1962.

J. A. Weisheipl, ed., *Albertus Magnus and the Sciences, Commemorative Essays*, 1980.

ALCIBIADES (c.450–404 B.C.E.), Greek politician and general. He was the nephew of the Greek statesman *Pericles, who raised Alcibiades after his father's death in 447 B.C.E. Although he was a pupil and friend of *Socrates, Alcibiades developed some of the worst aspects of Sophistic training.

Alcibiades married into a wealthy family and his expensive public displays helped to win him support among the common people. He became the leader of radical democrats in 420 B.C.E. and was opposed only by the Athenian statesman Nicias, who had secured a peace treaty between the Athenians and the Lacedaemonians. At the initiative of Alcibiades, who wished to expand the Athenian empire, and despite the opposition of Nicias, an expedition was undertaken against Syracuse with Alcibiades as one of its commanders. After his departure he was blamed for the mutilation of all the statues of Hermes and in his absence was charged with impiety and sentenced to death.

Alcibiades escaped to Sparta where he revealed to the Spartans the Athenian plans against them and helped them defeat the Athenians. With his assistance, the Spartans became more involved in the Aegean Sea region, and at his urging many Ionian states revolted against Athens. Difficulties with the Spartan leaders and intimations of an assasination plot against him, however, convinced him that a further change was called for and he fled to the Persian satrap Tissaphernes, attempting to convince him to assist the Athenians against Sparta. Tisaphernes remained unconvinced that assisting Athens was in the Persian interest and Alcibiades turned next to the Athenians at Samos. They accepted his offer and with his assistance secured several important victories. The sentences against him were revoked and after returning to Athens he was elected extraordinary commander in 407 B.C.E.

The failure of his expedition to Notium in 406 B.C.E. led to renewed accusations by his enemies and he was removed from his duties. Once again he turned to the Persians, taking refuge in Phrygia with Pharnabazus, a satrap of King Artaxerxes II of Persia. This time, however, his maneuvering failed him. At the request of the Athenians, Pharnabazus arranged for the murder of Alcibiades; his residence was set on fire during the night and as he fled his burning home he was felled by a volley of arrows.

F. F. Benson, *The Life of Alcibiades*, 1928.

S. Forde, *The Ambition to Rule*, 1989.

G. Hatzfeld, *Alcibiades*, 1951.

ALCOCK, SIR JOHN WILLIAM (1892–1919), pioneer aviator. Born in Manchester, England, the eldest son of a horse dealer, Alcock's interests centered on the new century's means of transportation. He began work as an apprentice at the Empress Motor Works but his interest in motor cars soon gave way to an enthusiasm for flying. He began learning in Brooklands in 1910 and, as mechanic to French pilot Maurice Ducrocq, acquired skills which were to make him into one of the country's foremost pilots. He gained his flyer's license in 1912 and worked as a racing pilot before World War I.

In 1914 Alcock was commissioned into the Royal Naval Air Service. For several years he served as a flying instructor in Kent and then was sent on active service on the Turkish war front. He gained a reputation as a highly competent and brave pilot with a warm and generous nature that easily won admirers. He received a gallantry award after emerging triumphant from a dogfight with three enemy seaplanes. Returning from a bombing raid on Constantinople, he was forced by Turkish anti-aircraft fire to ditch his plane in the sea. Alcock and the other two members of the crew were not spotted by British ships. When their Handley Page bomber started to sink they swam ashore but were captured, and Alcock spent more than a year as a prisoner.

In 1919 Captain Alcock became a test pilot for Vickers Aircraft Company, eager to win the £10,000 prize offered by the *Daily Mail* newspaper for the first nonstop flight across the Atlantic. On June 14 Alcock took off from Saint John's in Newfoundland in a Vickers Vimy bomber, with Lieutenant Arthur Brown as navigator. It was a flight dogged by disaster and as severe a test for Alcock's skills as could be imagined. In succession the radio failed and then the exhaust pipe fell off causing poisonous fumes to invade the cockpit. Alcock and Brown wore specially heated suits against the cold and these also failed them. Then, as if this had not been disastrous enough, they encountered a snowstorm and the engines kept clogging with ice. Showing great daring, Brown climbed out onto the wings in a strong wind, and bent down and chipped away the ice. He had to repeat this feat five times. It was a moment of great relief as well as achievement when they touched down in Clifden in the west of Ireland, sixteen hours and twenty minutes and almost two thousand miles after takeoff.

The secretary of state for war, Winston *Churchill, presented the *Daily Mail* prize and spoke in flowery terms of "that terrible waste of desolate water... in almost ceaseless storms and shrouded with an unbroken canopy of mist. Across this waste, through this obscurity, went two human beings, hurtling through the air, piercing cloud and darkness." Churchill went on to depict the implications for uniting the English-speaking world and crowned his speech by announcing the award of Knight Commander of the British Empire to both Alcock and Brown. Alcock did not live to enjoy his fame long. A few months later, flying an amphibian airplane to Paris, he ran into a severe storm and died after a crashlanding.

J. Blake, *Flight: The Five Ages of Aviation*, 1987.
H. Evans, *Front Page News*, 1984.
H. Penrose, *Wings Across the World*, 1980.

ALEXANDER THE GREAT (Alexander III of Macedon; 356–323 B.C.E.), king of Macedonia, and conqueror of the eastern world. His great reputation is based on his military genius, his remarkable conquests of the East, and his zeal to promote Hellenism in the lands that he conquered. He was the son of *Philip II of Macedonia and Olympias of Epirus. When he was thirteen his father engaged *Aristotle to tutor him in poetry, drama, and politics; the scholar gave Alexander a thorough education, also stimulating his interest in science, medicine, and philosophy. There was some friction between Alexander and his father as the latter's various marriages left the question of Alexander's succession to the throne uncertain. When Philip was murdered in 336 B.C.E., Alexander, not yet twenty, wasted no time ascending the throne and executing his rivals.

From his father Alexander inherited an excellent army and a war against Persia. He went immediately to Thessaly, where partisans of independence had gained ascendancy, and reestablished Macedonian control of Greece. Then, having had himself elected general of all the Greeks in the campaign against Persia, he moved quickly to counter the defecting Thracians and en route back to Greece crushed the threatening Illyrians. Finally he hastened back to Thebes, which had revolted in his absence. There he set an example which brought the other Greek states into abject submission by destroying the city and selling its citizens into slavery.

In the spring of 334 B.C.E. Alexander resumed the battle against Persia. He set out with an army of forty thousand Greek and Macedonian troops and crossed the Hellespont. At the Granicus river, near Troy, he achieved a brilliant victory against a large army of Persians and Greek mercenaries and turned to a now-submissive Asia Minor while Darius II of Persia advanced into Syria. Alexander won a historic victory against him at Issus in November 333 B.C.E. and, rejecting the Persian king's peace offers, turned toward Phoenicia. He defeated and destroyed Tyre, then went on to Palestine and besieged Gaza. Next came his conquest of Egypt and the foundation of the new city of Alexandria, which was to become the literary, scientific, and commercial center of the Greek world. In Egypt he went to the Oasis of Siwa to consult the oracle of Ammon, god of the sun, and was hailed there by the high priests as the son of Ammon — a title usually accorded to pharoahs — which confirmed his belief in his divine origin.

**BY AND ABOUT
ALEXANDER THE GREAT**

- If I were not Alexander, I would be Diogenes.

  Alexander the Great

- Were I not Napoleon, I would be Alexander.

  Napolean

- My son, seek out a kingdom equal to yourself. Macedonia has no room for you.

  Philip of Macedonia

- In the course of many campaigns, he captured fortified towns, slaughtered kings, traversed the earth to its remotest bounds, and plundered innumerable nations.

  I Maccabees 1:2

- When in the world I lived I was the world's commander
  By east, west, north and south I spread my conquering might
  My scutcheon plain declares that I am Alexander.

  Shakespeare, *Love's Labour Lost*

Alexander the Great in battle; a mosaic from Pompeii

Darius had meanwhile reorganized his forces but Alexander won another victory against him at the battle of Guagamela in October 331 B.C.E. After securing the Iranian city of Susa with its store of treasures, he completed his destruction of the Persian empire after a mere three years of warfare by making his way to Persepolis, the Persian capital; there he plundered the royal treasury and burned the city.

As the Persian empire had once included part of western India, Alexander crossed the Indus River in 326 B.C.E. and marched through the Punjab, but his army refused to continue advancing indefinitely. Alexander told them, "Go home and tell them that you left Alexander the Great to conquer the world alone." However, only a quarter of his original army returned with him to Persia. The return to Greece, by sea to the Persian Gulf and overland across the desert, was fraught with difficulties.

His reign after his return was increasingly autocratic, and execution for misconduct was not uncommon. He also incurred Macedonian disfavor by attempting to enforce a policy of cooperation with the Iranians, adopting Persian ceremonial at court, himself marrying the daughter of Darius, and encouraging his soldiers to take Iranian wives. The Macedonians finally rebelled when he tried to incorporate Iranians into the army, but a reconciliation was reached at Opis in the summer of 324 B.C.E.

After a year spent organizing and surveying his empire, Alexander spent his final months planning further conquests and expeditions. He died in Babylon of a severe attack of fever and was buried in Alexandria, leaving his empire "to the strongest." Having failed to appoint a capable successor, however, he contributed to the breakup of the empire he had so brilliantly consolidated.

An excellent soldier and military strategist, Alexander was flexible and resilient and won his soldiers' devotion by leading them into battle and often incurring injuries in the process. His conquests inaugurated a new period in history by extending the influence of Greek civilization and opening the doors to Greek traders and settlers who followed in the wake of his army, often settling in one of a number of "Alexandrias" he had founded along his march. Not surprisingly, legends about him abounded and a romance of which he was hero appeared in Egypt c.200 C.E. and became widely popular in the Middle Ages in western European languages.

P. Green, *Alexander the Great*, 1970.
J. R. Hamilton, *Alexander the Great*, 1973.
J . M. O'Brien, *Alexander the Great, Invisible Enemy*, 1992.

ALEXANDER I (1777–1825), czar of Russia.The son of Czar Paul I and grandson of Catherine the Great, Alexander was born in Saint Petersburg. He was raised in the liberal atmosphere of his grandmother's court, where he received a Western education under the tutelage of Frédéric César La Harpe, a Swiss revolutionary. This education was not in keeping with the military training usually provided to a future heir to the throne, nor were La Harpe's republican sentiments compatible with the aristocratic upbringing Alexander received from his reactionary father. Even as a youth Alexander felt torn by the conflict between his grandmother's liberalism and his father's extreme conservatism.

Czar Paul was wary of his son's flirtations with liberalism and planned to disinherit him. His unpopular opposition to Catherine's reforms, however, soon led to his downfall and Paul was deposed and murdered in a coup of which he had prior knowledge; on March 12, 1801, Alexander became czar.

Upon assuming the throne Alexander began a major campaign to modernize Russia along the model of post-revolutionary France. He gathered several of his friends along with his tutor, La Harpe, in a so-called Secret Committee which set lofty goals for itself, including emancipation of the serfs, the promotion of industry, and the creation of a constitutional monarchy. A constitution was written which was partially implemented but for the most part the committee was a failure and was soon abandoned. Despite his liberal leanings Alexander was an autocrat who envisioned himself fulfilling the role of an enlightened despot. He interfered in all proposed reform legislation and often imposed his reforms on a reluctant populace. La Harpe, who soon realized that he had failed to mold Alexander according to his own philosophies, left Russia and returned to Switzerland.

Upon assuming the throne Alexander proclaimed Russian neutrality in the European wars, but this, too, was short-lived. *Napoleon, who had previously cited Alexander as an example of the enlightened despot he wished to emulate, threatened European stability. In 1804 Russia joined Britain, Sweden, and Austria in a coalition against France. Alexander found himself at war; his armies were unprepared and easily defeated at Austerlitz, Eylau, and Friedland. But rather than humiliate Russia, Napoleon concluded with Alexander the Treaty of Tilsit on July 7, 1807. The treaty created an alliance between France and Russia against Britain. Alexander was now free to fulfill his own territorial ambitions. He wrested Finland from Sweden in 1809 and added the Ottoman province of Bessarabia in 1812. The next year he successfully concluded a nine-year war with Persia by annexing most of Georgia. Yet despite the military advantages offered Alexander by the treaty, the Tilsit agreement was unpopular among the people. France's isolation in Europe had been extended to Russia; trade suffered and the economy faltered. In 1812 Russia finally abrogated the treaty. The French response was immediate; on June 24 of that year Napoleon invaded Russia. The war between France and Russia was disastrous for both sides. The French made rapid advances across Russian territory and soon reached Moscow. The city was set afire and this act of barbarism so infuriated Alexander that he refused to reach any accord with Napoleon. The French were left no option but to begin a disastrous retreat; they were ill-provided for the bitter cold of a Russian winter and countless French troops died in what is considered the turning-point of Napoleon's career. Although Russia had been thoroughly despoiled by the French invasion, its unwillingness to succumb to the French was considered the first great victory against Napoleon. Russia emerged from the war as the major European power at the Congress of Vienna (1814–1815).

During Napoleon's Hundred Days bid to regain his empire, Russia joined the Quadruple Alliance with Austria, Britain, and Prussia. At Alexander's behest this alliance served as the nucleus of the short-lived Holy Alliance, formed on September 26, 1815, to unite all of Christian Europe.

It has been said that the flames of burning Moscow served as a spiritual inspiration for Alexander. He underwent a religious transformation in which he tried to govern Russia according to divine will. Religious figures suddenly became prominent in his administration, often to the detriment of the country.

Alexander did not fulfill any of the ambitious projects he had set for himself upon assuming the throne and his final years were spent in morose religious speculations. Nor could he find consolation in his family life. He had married the German princess Louise of Baden-Durlach when he was only sixteen years old. The Empress Yelizaveta Alekseyevna, as she came to be known, had only one child, a girl, who died in infancy. For many years Alexander carried on an affair with Maria Naryshkina; only toward the end of his life did his grief over the child's death reconcile the czar with his empress.

The final years of Alexander's reign were no less stormy than the early years. In 1820 he was faced with a mutiny in the Semenovsky regiment, the same regiment he had commanded as prince and which had carried out the coup that brought him to the throne. In 1825 Alexander received news that the Greeks had rebelled against the Ottomans. Despite the previous agreements not to interfere in the internal affairs of Europe, Alexander set out to help. On the way he died suddenly at Taganrog. His close friend and adviser, Klemens *Metternich, remarked, "The novel is over; history begins." Alexander was succeeded by his brother, *Nicholas I.

M. Paleologue, *The Enigmatic Czar: The Life of Alexander I of Russia*, 1969.

A. Palmer, *Alexander I*, 1974.

H. Troyat, *Alexander of Russia*, 1982.

ALEXANDER II (1818–1881), czar of Russia; son of Czar Nicholas I. As a boy he received the standard education accorded to a member of the royal family, studying humanities, history, statecraft, and military science. In 1841 he married the German princess Marie of Hesse-Darmstadt, who adopted the Russian name Maria Alexandrovna and bore him six sons and two daughters.

Alexander II succeeded his father to the throne of Russia in 1855 during the disastrous Crimean War (1854–1856). Seeing the effects of the war on Russia, Alexander sued for peace after the fall of Sebastopol. Although he was a kindly and sentimental

The assassination of Alexander II

monarch Alexander had no original ideas on how to run his country, which was already showing signs of defeat on the battlefield, and often vacillated between the opinions of his various advisers. Although Alexander was a conservative he recognized the need for economic reforms in Russia so as to fully exploit the country's rich natural resources. He believed that the Crimean fiasco was symptomatic of a widespread deterioration of the economy and of the morale of the people.

On February 19, 1861, Alexander took great strides to end the morass into which Russia was sinking. He issued a proclamation ushering in the "Era of Great Reforms." His manifesto called for changes in all aspects of the Russian administration. Practices of government finance were called into question and amended and the judicial system was reorganized along the pattern of the French system. He ordered universal military training in which all members of society – nobles and peasants – underwent similar regimentation and instruction. Towns and rural districts received a degree of local autonomy allowing them to collect taxes for their own use. Progress was made in the areas of civil liberties and academic freedoms.

The most important element of Alexander's proclamation, however, was the emancipation of the serfs. Until that time approximately three-quarters of the Russian population lived as serfs, indebted to aristocratic landlords. Alexander believed that maintaining the people as serfs was actually counterproductive because all their labors benefitted others, thereby discouraging them from producing more and improving their lot. At the same time, the liberation of the serfs was a dangerous move in that it would enrage those aristocrats whose livelihood depended on retaining this system. Alexander therefore moved slowly and cautiously in his plan, first introducing committees "for improving the position of peasants" in the outlying provinces of Poland and Lithuania. As the new idea slowly took root it was expanded to include other Russian provinces and additional freedoms, eventually leading to total emancipation. Historians debate whether Alexander intended that the liberated serfs would remain dependent on the upper classes, or whether he envisioned the eventual formation of communal councils to oversee the land. Whatever his true intentions, Alexander's reforms were popular and earned him the title of Czar Liberator.

Alexander's popularity was not long-lived; both sides of the political spectrum attacked him. The reactionaries complained that he was discarding the sacred traditions of Russia and overturning the traditional structure of a well-functioning society; the radicals and liberals protested that the long-needed reforms were too slow and insufficient. Even Alexander's entourage began criticizing him with impunity. Continued agitation by peasants and intellectuals led to further unrest. One growing movement, the Nihilists, with their total rejection of the traditional standards of Russian society, threatened to undermine the regime. Alexander became disillusioned with his earlier reforms and rejected many of them. He centered his efforts on restoring Russia's pride, which he did by a successful series of conquests in the Balkans, the Caucasus, and Asia. In the Russo-Turkish War of 1877–1878 he managed to regain South Bessarabia, Kars, and Ardahan, territories lost to Turkey in the Crimean War. Yet Alexander's victories were overshadowed by his disillusionment over the failure of his reforms; his disappointment developed into severe depression by 1880 and the government of the country passed into the hands of Count Mikhail T. Loris-Melikov. Alexander spent most of his time at leisure, preoccupied with a love affair with Princess Yekaterina Dolgorukaya. Following the death of the Czarina Maria Alexandrovna, Alexander married the princess in a secret ceremony.

Alexander never relinquished his dream of reforms. On March 1, 1881, he drove through the streets of Saint Petersburg on his way to grant further political concessions. A bomb was thrown at his carriage and Alexander was killed. Following the assassination, his program of reforms was rejected by *Alexander III, his son and heir. As a French diplomat said at his funeral, "A liberator's is a dangerous job!"

W. E. Mosse, *Alexander II and the Modernization of Russia*, 1958.

H. Seton-Watson, *Decline of Imperial Russia, 1855–1914*, 1961.

ALEXANDER III (1845–1894), czar of Russia.

Because he was the second son of Czar Alexander II he was trained for a military rather than an imperial career. The sudden death of his older brother, Nikolay, when Alexander was twenty put Alexander into the position of heir, a role for which he was ill-prepared. He was a stocky, surly individual, not adept at statecraft or diplomacy. His disposition was further coarsened by his tutor, K. P. Pobedonostev, a fanatic Russian nationalist and reactionary. In 1866 Alexander married his brother's fiancee, Princess Dagmar of Denmark, who assumed the Russian name of Maria Fyodorovna. He became czar in 1881 following the assassination of his father.

Unlike his liberal father, who earned the title Czar Liberator for the concessions he made to the people, Alexander III followed the advice of Pobedonostev and rejected his father's reforms. The autonomy granted to the rural districts, cities, and peasant communes or *zemstvos*, was revoked. All decisions, even those affecting the appointment of provincial midwives, were placed under the direct authority of the czar. The attitude of Alexander's regime can be summed up in the words of one of his advisors, who referred to parliamentarianism as "the great lie of our times."

Alexander III was a chauvinistic Russian nationalist who sought to unify his far-flung empire through a policy of Russification. Russian was enforced as the sole language of instruction in the schools, including those in the Baltic provinces, Poland, and Finland. The Russian Orthodox Church, whose power Alexander II had reduced in the provinces, was reinstated as the sole legitimate religion. Jews in particular were singled out for harsh treatment, often despite the protests of foreign governments. Others who suffered were aristocrats in the Baltic provinces and Poland, who had earlier received a charter from Alexander II permitting them to practice their own religions. One such noble, Mikhail B. Barclay de Tolly, of Scottish descent, had his child baptized according to the Lutheran rite. When asked by Alexander how he dared baptize his children according to that rite, Barclay quoted the law of Alexander II. On the spot, Alexander rescinded the law. Despite Alexander's warnings, Barclay baptized his second child according to the Lutheran rite; he was promptly dismissed from the royal guard and army.

> As the rule of Alexander II was the mildest and most liberal, so that of his son and successor is by far the most despotic experienced by the Russian people since the days of Ivan the Terrible.
>
> **M. Lanin (a contemporary Russian journalist)**

Alexander prided himself on being like his subjects. His behavior was often childish and boorish, showing utter disregard for the opinions of his advisers and the sentiments of his subjects. He was the object of assassination plots; for instigating one of these plots Vladimir Ilyich *Lenin's elder brother, Vladimir, was hanged in 1887. At the same time, Alexander was capable of magnanimous gestures to benefit his countrymen. In one instance he provided eighteen million rubles of his own money to relieve impoverished villages. He was often surrounded by competent advisors, notably his interior minister Count Mikhail T. Loris-Melikov, who supported the establishment of a cabinet and basic laws as a forerunner to a constitution. These ideas were quickly rejected by the czar; Loris-Melikov was replaced by Count Nikolay R. Ignatiev, a reactionary pan-Slavist.

Alexander continued the policy of Russian expansionism in Asia and the Far East but avoided major military conflicts. One of his important decisions was the abrogation of the traditional Russo-German Alliance in favor of a new Franco-Russian Alliance, concluded on December 31, 1893. This alliance paved the way for Russian participation in World War I on the side of the Allies. Alexander died suddenly on October 20, 1894, shortly after the conclusion of the new alliance. He was succeeded by his ill-fated son, *Nicholas II.

C. Lowe, *Alexander III of Russia*, 1895.

H. Rogger, *Russia in the Age of Modernization and Revolution: 1881–1917*, 1983.

H. W. Whelan, *Alexander III and the State Council*, 1982.

ALEXANDER NEVSKY (c.1220–1263), Russian prince and military hero. He was the son of Yaroslav II, grand prince of Vladimir, and in 1236, when only sixteen years old, was elected prince and military leader of the republic of Novgorod. The many minor Russian states were then subject to constant incursion by their neighbors to the west. While Swedes and Germans attempted to assert their control of the Baltic by barring Russian access to the sea, smaller tribes such as the nomadic Finns and Lithuanians were staking their own territorial claims in the region.

When the Swedish army invaded Novgorod in 1240, Alexander met it at the juncture of the Neva and Izhora rivers. In his first major encounter, he succeeded in repelling the invaders, himself wounding the Swedish commander. He commemorated his victory by adopting the title Nevsky ("of the Neva") and came to consider himself the rightful heir to Novgorod by merit of his success. When he began to meddle in municipal matters, the citizens voted to have him expelled. Soon, though, they were soon forced to ask him to return.

The Baltic region was then inhabited by a mixture of Russian followers of the Orthodox church and nomadic pagans. The Teutonic Knights, a zealous order of German Catholics, eagerly responded to the call for a crusade issued by Pope Gregory IX and invaded Novgorod. Nevsky, at the head of a small army, marched forward to meet them. The battlefield had been carefully chosen: the channel connecting Lakes Chud (Peipus) and Pskov. It was mid-April in the year 1242, and the ice-covered lakes were beginning to thaw. Nevsky hoped that if the Germans were kept on the thin ice their heavy armor would be their downfall. As the Germans marched across the frozen lake, Nevsky feigned retreat. German troops concentrated on the center of the Russian lines while Nevsky was moving his troops around the lake to the German flanks. Finally, he attacked. The Germans could not maneuver on the slippery surface and many fell through the ice to the freezing water below. The battle became known as the "Massacre on the Ice" and saved the Russian people from Teuton domination.

With his western boundary safe, Nevsky concentrated on securing himself from the Mongol Golden Horde in the east. Unlike many of his contemporaries, he realized that no military action could defeat the Mongols, and chose to follow his father's lead and to come to an accommodation with them. His father was poisoned in 1246 by a Russian nationalist. Nevsky and his younger brother Andrew journeyed to meet Khan Batu, prince of the western Mongols. Batu favored Nevsky to succeed his father as prince of Vladimir, but was unwilling to make the appointment without the consent of the Great Khan in Karakorum. The two brothers trekked to Mongolia, only to find that the Great Khan disapproved of Batu and rejected his advice. Vladimir was given to Andrew; Nevsky received Novgorod and Kiev in compensation. Andrew, however, attempted to organize a revolt against the Mongols. He was denounced to Batu's son by Nevsky and deposed. Nevsky now ruled Vladimir, Novgorod, and Kiev, uniting three of the leading Russian principalities.

As prince, Nevsky had considerable autonomy. He reorganized the legal system, fortified the western frontier, and fostered the growth of the Orthodox church. He was criticized, however, for his commitment to the Mongols and faced several revolts, one led by his own son.

The Russian nobles revolted against the khan in 1262. Nevsky had opposed the revolt, but fearing reprisals, he again made the long journey to Karakorum to appeal for mercy. The journey was a success. Not only was the tax burden reduced, but the khan agreed to forego his plan to enlist Russian troops for an excursion against Iran. Nevsky turned for home, but died at Gorodets along the way. At his funeral his friend, the Metropolitan Cyril, prophecied, "The sun of Russia has set. Now we shall perish." Nevsky's united Russia disintegrated shortly after.

Russians have long esteemed Nevsky for preserving his country and church from foreign intrusion. More than an historical figure, he has become a symbol of Russia's determination to assert its independence. The same year that Nevsky's great-great-grandson finally expelled the Tatar descendants of the Golden Horde, Nevsky's tomb was suddenly rediscovered. He was canonized in 1547 and reinterred in Saint Petersburg by *Peter the Great in 1725.

E. A. Presniakov, *The Formation of the Great Russian State*, 1970.

S. Vernadsky and M. Kayovitch, *The Mongols and Russia*, 1953.

ALFRED (Aelfred the Great; 849–899), king of the West Saxons (Wessex). The youngest of the five sons of Aethelwulf, Alfred was crowned in 871 on the death of his brother Aethelred. He came to the throne in the midst of a Danish invasion. Although he defeated the Danes at Ashdown in 871 and prevented their invasion of Wessex, they attacked again in 875 and 878 and this time encountered no effective resistance. His country overrun, Alfred retreated to Atheleny in the marches of Somerset and reassembled his army. In 878 he defeated the Danes at Edington, in Wiltshire. The country was now split into two: a Danish part, northwest of the London-Chester road, and the Anglo-Saxon part dominated by Wessex. In 886 he conquered London and with the submission of Northumbria, he ruled all England. In the years of peace that followed Alfred devoted himself to his kingdom. He strengthened his fortifications and his navy and enforced compulsory military service — measures which proved invaluable when the Danes returned in 893 and were forced to withdraw after four years of battle.

Alfred's successful resistance to the Danes marked him as the first Anglo-Saxon leader to repel Scandinavian invasions in England and although he did not succeed in freeing all the territories from Danish rule, he laid the foundations for the unification of England. During periods of peace, brief though they were, he was also notable for codifying the law, establishing unity, and reforming the administration of the kingdom by extending and consolidating the shire system of local government.

Alfred also contributed greatly to the education of his people by encouraging the monasteries as centers of learning and establishing a school for nobles in his own court. Himself a talented writer, he translated several works and encouraged the translation of all philosophical and theological works from Latin into Anglo-Saxon, thus promoting the development of Anglo-Saxon into a literary language.

A. Cook, *Asser's Life of King Alfred*, 1902.
A. J. Frantzen, *King Alfred*, 1986.
J. Pelling, *King Alfred*, 1977.

ALI (c.600–661), son-in-law of *Muhammad; the fourth caliph of the first Muslim state. Ali was the son of Abu Talib, an indigent relation of Muhammad. Because his father could not afford to support him, Ali was sent to be raised by Muhammad. Ali supported Muhammad's new religion, becoming one of the first converts to Islam when he was only ten

years old. In return Muhammad raised Ali as if he were his own child and later gave him his daughter, Fatimah, as a wife. When Muhammad, to escape persecution in Mecca, was forced to flee the city in 622 Ali lay in Muhammad's bed, impersonating the prophet so that he could escape undetected. Prior to his escape Muhammad took Ali to the sacred shrine of the Kaaba; Ali climbed on Muhammad's shoulders and smashed the idols placed in the shrine.

Ali exhibited remarkable military prowess, assisting Muhammad in his conquests. He also served as the prophet's scribe, writing down the prophecies and visions which later formed the basis of the Koran. Many Muslim leaders expected Ali to succeed Muhammad after the prophet's death in 632; however, to Ali's consternation, *Abu Bakr was chosen in his stead. Ali was reluctant to accept Abu Bakr as caliph and gradually became a peripheral figure in the Islamic hierarchy, occasionally voicing his opinions against the caliphs. Most of Ali's time during these years was spent transcribing the Koran. He was openly critical of the policies of Uthman, Muhammad's son-in-law who became caliph, but did not participate in his assassination in 656.

Following the murder of Uthman, the Muslims of Medina chose Ali as his successor. His election was opposed by the aristocracy of Mecca, who feared that Ali's austere lifestyle would threaten the wealth they had accumulated from Islamic conquests. One prominent leader of the opposition to Ali was Aishah, Muhammad's widow. Dissension also came from the Umayyads, the family of Uthman, who suspected that Ali was somehow implicated in Uthman's murder; they cited Ali's refusal to bring the perpetrators to justice as proof of their claim.

The dissension rapidly increased and Ali's supporters were soon at war with the opposing factions. The decisive battle between the two parties took place near Basra, in Iraq, in December 656. Ali had previously moved his capital to Kufa, in Iraq, to distance himself from the opposition. The Battle of the Camel, so named because Aishah led her forces from a screened chamber on the hump of a camel, was won by Ali, but the victory was far from decisive. The next year, Muawiya, Umayyad governor of Syria, challenged Ali's authority. Ali was winning the ensuing battle of Siffin, in northern Iraq, when the opposing troops approached with copies of the Koran tied to the points of their spears. They asked for a truce so that the question of succession to the caliphate could be brought to arbitration. The result of the arbitration remained uncertain, although Ali was probably defeated. Though Ali had been reluctant to accept arbitration, preferring military victory to support his claim, many of the supporters who had encouraged him to reach a peaceful agreement with Muawiya abandoned his cause.

Although Ali and Muawiya eventually worked out a truce in 660, splitting the Islamic world between them, there was no true peace. Muawiya built up a power base in Syria, Egypt, and Hejaz; Ali concentrated his forces in Iraq and Persia. Further problems ensued when a group of Muslim secessionists, the Kharijites, threatened Ali's authority in the area left to him. Ali was assassinated in 661, struck from behind with a poisoned sword. The Muslim world was temporarily reunited under Umayyad rule from Damascus. But Ali's two sons, Husayn and Hassan, refused to accept Umayyad rule, and established their own dynasty, the Fatimids, named after their mother. Their followers, who called themselves the Shiat Ali (Party of Ali) never accepted the central authority of Muawiya and the succeeding caliphs. They continued the struggle to restore Islamic hegemony to the family of Muhammad while developing their own interpretation of the Koran and its creed. This sect, the Shiites, is still a powerful force in Islam, particularly in Iran. Ali is revered and his teachings, collated several hundred years later in a book, *the Road of Eloquence*, are venerated.

M. J. Chirri, *The Brother of the Prophet Mohammed: The Imam Ali*, 1982.

F. Gabrieli, *Mohammed and the Conquests of Islam*, 1968.

AMBROSE, SAINT (339–397), an early church father, one of the four traditional doctors of the Western church. Ambrose was born in Trier, then in the Roman province of Gaul. After the death of his father, the local praetorian prefect, while Ambrose was still a child, his mother brought the family to Rome. The aristocratic young Ambrose was destined for a civic career and studied Greek and law to that effect. His first appointment was as advocate to the court of Probus, praetorian prefect of Italy. In 370 he moved to Milan to serve as governor of the provinces of Emilia and Liguria.

In 373 both the Arian and Orthodox bishops of Milan died. Since no candidate acceptable to both parties could be found to fill the bishopric, riots threatened the city. Ambrose rushed to the cathedral to appeal for reconciliation when, according to legend, a child cried out, "Ambrose for bishop." Ambrose had not even been baptized, but his unforeseen nomination was unanimously acclaimed. Within eight days he was baptized and ordained bishop. He abandoned his wealth and became an ascetic.

Ambrose was responsible for several important liturgical and ritual innovations. A sworn enemy of pagans and heretics, he adapted some pagan rituals, such as the funeral rite, to church services. He was an articulate preacher whose addresses were known for their pithy maxims; his sermons drew heavily both on biblical texts, interpreted literally, morally, and allegorically, and on the Greek writings of Philo of Byblus, Origen, and Saint Basil. He championed the cult of the Virgin *Mary and of the martyrs after discovering sacred relics supposedly belonging to the Christian martyrs Gervasius and Protasius. Today he is best known as the father of liturgical hymnology, although only four of the ninety-one

---

ABOUT SAINT AMBROSE

To Saint Ambrose is attributed the origin of the saying, "When in Rome, do as the Romans do," because it is said that when Saint Augustine arrived in Milan in 387 he noted that the church there, unlike in Rome, did not fast on Saturdays. He consulted Saint Ambrose, bishop of Milan, whose original reply was: "When I am in Rome I fast on a Saturday; when I am in Milan, I do not. Follow the custom of the church where you are."

---

hymns attributed to him have been authenticated, with the celebrated *Te Deum* not among them. None of the original music he composed for his hymns survived; the florid Ambrosian chants known today date from the Middle Ages.

Ambrose was no less renowned for challenging the un-Christian behavior of the government. When the Arians (who held that *Jesus is not of the same substance as God), supported by Empress Justina, demanded use of a local church, Ambrose appealed to the emperor and the matter was dropped. More threatening than the Arians was the pagan revival, espoused by his own relative, Quintus Symmachus, and the senate. An attempt was made to restore the Altar of Victory in Rome, but Ambrose again successfully appealed to the emperor. However, even Emperor *Theodosius I was not immune to Ambrose's zealous defense of the church. On one occasion, after a bishop incited a mob to destroy a synagogue, the Jewish community appealed to the emperor and the bishop was ordered to pay for its restoration. Ambrose wrote to Theodosius, castigating him for recognizing the rights of Jews over Christians. In response, Theodosius outlawed both the private and public observance of paganism.

Ambrose's most famous encounter with Theodosius followed the revolt of Thessalonica in 390. Theodosius's reprisal, in which 7,000 were slaughtered, caused the infuriated Ambrose to declare, "The emperor is within the church, not above the church." Threatened with excommunication, Theodosius performed a public penance for the massacre. Yet despite the occasional tensions between the two men, Ambrose was trusted by the imperial household and occasionally performed diplomatic missions. The emperor was eager to heed Ambrose and often, at his behest, pardoned Christian criminals sentenced to death.

Many pagans were attracted by the chaste, unassuming character of the bishop who had stood up to kings. In his *Confessions*, Saint *Augustine pays lavish tribute to Ambrose as the single individual who inspired him to join the church. Saint Ambrose's tomb can still be seen in the basilica of Saint Ambrogio in Milan. Among his surviving writings are a commentary on the Gospel of Luke, descriptions of the duties of bishops and nuns, and a refutation of Arianism. His feast is celebrated by the Roman Catholic Church on December 7.

F. H. Dudden, *The Life and Times of Saint Ambrose*, 2 vols., 1935.

A. Paredi, *Saint Ambrose: His Life and Times*, 1964.

AMENHOTEP III (reigned 1417–1379 B.C.E.), pharaoh of Egypt. Amenhotep, son of Thutmose IV, was one of the great builders and reformers of the Egyptian 18th dynasty. His full regnal name was Amun-Hotpehek-Wase. There is some speculation that Amenhotep's mother was not an Egyptian but a Mittani princess. This would have been extraordinary for the time, given the insular attitudes of the Egyptian ruling classes. It is known that his wife, Tiy, was a commoner, another break from tradition for a dynasty whose kings regularly married their sisters so as not to contaminate the royal stock.

While still a youth, Amenhotep was placed under the tutelage of Yuya, master of the horse. Not only did Yuya teach the prince the art of war, he inflamed his passion for the hunt. One legend reports that while still a young child, Amenhotep succeeded in capturing a large herd of wild cattle.

After acceding to the throne Amenhotep turned his attention to advancing Egyptian prestige among neighboring states. The Amarna tablets tell of embassies established and trade being carried on with the other powers of the time, notably Assyria, Babylonia, the Hittites, and the Mittani. Much of the wealth garnered by Amenhotep went to embellish his capital, Thebes.

His royal complex of palaces and harems encompassed eighty acres. In addition, he had constructed for Tiy a huge artificial lake measuring thirty-seven hundred by seven hundred cubits. The vast temples of Karnak and Luxor are also credited to Amenhotep.

His tranquil reign and the extensive trade carried out in his name transformed Thebes into a thriving cosmopolitan city. This spurred dissatisfaction among many of the nobles and priests, who regarded an isolated Egypt as indispensable to their own interests.

Amenhotep ruled Egypt for thirty-eight years. Contemporary portraits from the final years of his reign show him to be ailing. Some scholars have suggested that his son and heir, *Akhenaton, ruled jointly with his father in the last years of his reign. Upon his death Amenhotep was buried in the funerary temple he had already prepared for himself. Although the temple was the largest of its kind, all that remains of it today are enormous statues, the Colossi of Memnon.

C. Aldred, *Akhenaton, Pharaoh of Egypt*, 1968.

AMENHOTEP IV SEE AKHENATON

AMUNDSEN, ROALD (1872–1928), Norwegian explorer; first person to reach the South Pole. Although Amundsen originally studied medicine, he dreamed of exploring the unknown Arctic regions and abandoned university life to join the navy. His first experience in the polar regions was in 1897 as first officer on a Belgian Antarctic expedition. He later conducted oceanographic research off Greenland and fixed the location of the North Magnetic Pole, becoming the first person to sail through the northwest passage north of Canada.

His original goal was to become the first person to reach the North Pole. An expedition was carefully planned, financed by a grant from the Norwegian parliament and by mortgaging his house. For a ship, he borrowed the *Fram* from another Norwegian Arctic explorer, Fridtjof *Nansen. Amundsen took personal charge of every aspect of the planned journey, even supervising the manufacture of his team's underwear. He was shattered when, on April 6, 1909, Robert *Peary beat him to the Pole.

After some consideration, however, Amundsen simply decided to change his plans and become the first person to reach the South Pole. Not even his men were told of his new objective, and preparations continued unchanged. Even when Robert *Scott announced his own planned assault of the South Pole, Amundsen, driven by personal rivalry, rushed ahead. He was determined to beat Scott in the race to the Pole.

On September 6, 1910, the eve of the *Fram*'s departure from Madeira, Amundsen finally described his true plans to his crew and offered them the choice to disembark. Cables to the Norwegian parliament and to Nansen apologized for the undisclosed new route. Another was sent to Scott, notifying him that Amundsen intended to reach the Pole first. As they reached the Antarctic coast, the two teams had a tense meeting. Each took care to keep its itinerary a well-guarded secret. Amundsen moored his boat in the Bay of Whales on January 3, 1911; he was already sixty miles south of Scott.

It took three weeks to set up a base camp. The Pole was only 480 miles away, but the harsh Antarctic winter was approaching, delaying any attempt for at least eight months. During the long winter, the explorers reviewed their supplies and discovered several ingenious ways to lighten their loads. While Scott used Siberian ponies to carry his loads, Amundsen preferred dog-driven sledges, which he cut to save weight. A strict regimen of work and leisure was introduced, and the plentiful supplies were rationed. Free time was spent reading, listening to their few records, doing needlework, and even using a steam bath carved out of the ice.

As summer neared, the men were anxious to begin their journey. They had forgotten to bring the 1912 edition of the *Nautical Almanac* containing vital astronomical observations necessary to determine their course, so they were forced to reach the Pole by December 1911 at the latest. For eight weeks they took bets over when conditions would improve sufficiently so that they could begin. The first day agreed upon had to be canceled because of a blizzard. The next day, eight men and eighty-six dogs set out with six sledges. Conditions worsened after three days and they were forced to turn back.

Amundsen set out again with four companions on October 20, 1911. Four sledges pulled by fifty-two dogs carried provisions for four months. Keeping to a strict routine, they traveled for five hours each day, covering about twenty miles. Two hours were spent digging a snow cavern, and the remainder of the time resting. The team advanced rapidly, but Amundsen was constantly plagued by the fear that Scott had already reached the Pole. Nearer the Pole, steep slopes, 10,750 feet high, blocked their passage. Since no route was found around the towering mountain range they named Queen Maud's Range in honor of the Norwegian queen, Amundsen decided to climb it. Upon reaching the top, most of the dogs were so exhausted that they had to be shot — the men called the site the Butcher's Shop. Closer to the Pole, stormy weather and icy winds tormented them in a place they named the Devil's Ballroom.

At 3:00 p.m. on Friday, December 14, 1911, Amundsen reached the South Pole. Scott had not yet arrived. The five men planted the Norwegian flag and Amundsen composed a letter to King Haakon. He also wrote a note to Scott asking him to deliver the letter if he did not survive. After three days, Amundsen turned back to camp. Exactly one month later, on January 17, Scott reached the Pole but perished on his way back from hunger and cold. Amundsen reached his base safely on January 25. He was anxious to leave Antarctica and bring news of his triumph to the world.

During World War I Amundsen made a fortune in neutral shipping but his pioneering expedition through the northeast passage over the Siberian coast led to his financial ruin. In 1926 he was the first to fly over the North Pole. Two years later, in search of a lost Italian airship in the Arctic, Amundsen's plane disappeared and was never found.

W. Herbert, *A World of Men: Exploration in Antarctica*, 1968.

R. Silverberg, *Antarctica Conquered: The Great Explorers in Their Own Words*, 1965.

ANDERSEN, HANS CHRISTIAN (1805–1875),

Danish author. On New Year's Day, 1835, Hans Christian Andersen wrote to a friend, "I am now beginning some fairy-tales for children, I shall try to win the future generation, you know!" and with this prophetic statement launched the project that was to insure his fame. This novelist, travel writer, lover of theater and above all "childrens' poet," grew up in poverty in the town of Odense. Andersen received little formal instruction; his narrative talents were inspired by Jean de La Fontaine's fables and the tales of the *Arabian Nights*. His shoemaker father, imaginative and romantic like his

---

SOME OF ANDERSEN'S BEST-LOVED TALES

The Tin Soldier
The Emperor's New Clothes
The Tinder Box
The Princess and the Pea
The Snow Queen
The Nightingale
The Ugly Duckling
The Fir Tree
The Red Shoes
The Little Match Girl
The Little Mermaid

---

son, made Hans a marionette theater and the small boy entertained himself by making costumes for the puppets and writing plays inspired by theater posters advertising plays which he could himself rarely afford to attend.

Andersen was a lonely child who did not mix well with his peers and therefore spent long hours daydreaming or amusing himself by exchanging stories with elderly women at the hospital he visited with his grandmother. He first worked in a factory but his singing abilities won him admirers and patrons. At the age of fourteen, determined to seek his fortune in the theater he had always loved, he set off for Copenhagen. Although he soon proved to be a poor actor, he won the attention of a director of the Royal Theater, Jonas Collin, who saw to it that Andersen was educated. After struggling through the courses, Andersen graduated and began to write.

During the following years he wrote travel books and novels which brought him substantial success. In 1829 he published his first important works, *A Journey on Foot from Holm Canal to the East Point of Amager*, *Fantasies and Sketches*, and a book of poems. In 1835 he began *Fairy Tales*, finishing the last of four series of tales in 1871–1872. His novel *Improvisatore* (1835) was translated into English in 1845. During a visit to England and Scotland in 1847 he received an overwhelming reception and met Charles *Dickens, who had come to London expressly to meet Andersen. "Whatever you do," Dickens wrote to him that year, "don't leave off writing, for we cannot afford to lose any of your thoughts. They are too purely and simply beautiful to be kept in your own head."

Initially Andersen himself thought little of the fairy tales which he was steadily producing, and which eventually were to represent the pinnacle of his work. The first of these stories were based on existing folk tales and Andersen contented himself with developing and recreating them, but in 1843 he began creating his own. The tales are rich in their descriptions of nature and studded with humor, yet at first they were not very popular with the public. Eventually they too found favor, both in his homeland and abroad, and today all over the world they are regarded as his most valuable work.

Andersen also wrote *O.T.* (1836), *Only a Fiddler* (1837), *Picture Book Without Pictures* (1840), *The Two Baronesses* (1849), and *To Be or Not to Be* (1857), as well as three travel books: *A Poet's Bazaar* (1842), *In Sweden* (1849), and *In Spain* (1863).

C. Green, *Hans Christian Andersen, Teller of Tales*, 1986.

F. J. Marker, *Hans Christian Andersen and the Romantic Theater*, 1971.

R. Spink, *Hans Christian Andersen: The Man and His Work*, 1981.

ANTHONY, SAINT (Antony of Egypt; c.251–356), Egyptian anchorite credited with founding monasticism. The son of a wealthy Christian family, he hated school, never learned Greek, and was reliant on Coptic translations of religious texts throughout his career. Orphaned at twenty, he began frequenting religious services and soon felt that the texts read were directed at him personally. He was particularly struck by the verse: "If you want to be perfect, go, sell what you have and give to the poor" (Matthew 19:21). After sending his younger sister to a convent, he joined a group of ascetics living in a cemetery.

Anthony lived in a tomb for fifteen years, learning the life of a hermit before setting out across the desert to an abandoned fortress at Pispir, overlooking the Nile. For twenty years he lived there, seeing no one. Food was thrown to him over the fortress walls; visitors seeking his advice were turned away. As his reputation spread, an entire community of anchorites developed around the fortress. Although they had no contact with the saint, the anchorites were inspired by his holy solitude. Legends grew according to which Anthony was constantly besieged by demons, often disguised as wild beasts, enticing and provoking him to forgo his seclusion.

When Anthony finally joined his followers, they expected to see an emaciated individual crawl from behind the walls, but were astounded to see that he was as youthful and vigorous as on the day he began his seclusion. Anthony remained with his followers for five years, teaching the principles of a monastic life under rule (an innovation) before abandoning them for a second retreat into the desert (c.310). For the next forty-five years he lived at a remote spot between the Nile and the Red Sea. The rule he now imposed upon himself allowed him to see visitors and he occasionally visited the anchorite community at Pispir. He is known to have visited Alexandria on two ocasions: in 311, to lend support to Christian martyrs, and about 350 to preach against the Arian heresy (see *Arius). Among his visitors at the monastery was *Athanasius, who sought shelter there from rival bishops.

Athanasius's gripping biography of the saint as a simple yet heroic Christian submitting to his destiny persuaded many Christians throughout history to emulate Anthony by joining monastic orders.

Anthony died at the age of 105; the site of his grave was kept secret to avoid its becoming a place of veneration. At the site of his final retreat, a monastery, Mar Antonius, was founded.

Anthony was not the first Christian ascetic. His importance lies in his emphasis on seclusion and in his initiating retreat into remote regions. Because of his fondness for desert expanses, Saint Anthony is the patron saint of herdsmen. His feast is celebrated on January 17. The temptation of Saint Antony became a popular theme of art and literature.

R. C. Gregg, ed., *Athanasius: The Life of Anthony and the Letter to Marcellinus*, 1980.

ANTHONY, SUSAN BROWNELL (1820–1906), reformer, teacher, and leader of the early women's suffrage movement. Born in Adams, Massachusetts, Anthony was raised in a progressive household in which her father respected his daughters' intelligence and gave them a good education. As one of eight children, Anthony saw her quiet, worn-out mother as a symbol of married life and it made her eager to improve the condition of married women in the United States.

Growing up in a Quaker household, Anthony heard women speaking freely and participating equally in church affairs. She was sent to a boarding school in Philadelphia, and received an education superior to that usual for girls at that time.

In 1838 Anthony experienced discrimination firsthand after a brush with what she considered unfair property laws in Rochester, New York. Rochester was considered a center of reform and many abolitionist and temperance workers became friends of the family; Anthony became known for her honesty, sense of humor, and sympathetic view of people. While working as a schoolteacher in nearby Canajoharie Academy she joined the local chapter of the Daughters of Temperance, soon becoming an officer of the organization.

Anthony became bored with teaching and returned home to Rochester, where she directed her father's farm for two years and became increasingly involved in reform circles. In 1852 she organized the first women's state temperance society in the United States, and soon became active in the antislavery movement.

After attending several reformers' conventions at which women were not allowed to participate fully, Anthony heeded the advice of her friend Elizabeth Cady Stanton and began to work full-time for the women's rights movement, becoming secretary of the National Woman's Rights Convention. As she toured the country with Stanton, she was the main organizing force behind the tours, though Stanton gave the speeches. In March 1860, she and Stanton were successful in lobbying to change a New York

State property law to give women the right to keep their own earnings, enter into contracts, or use their earnings as they saw fit. Widows now had the same property rights as widowers.

Anthony soon turned her attention to suffrage for women, helping to found the National Woman Suffrage Association in 1869, which she served as the vice-president-at-large until 1892, when she became the president. From 1868 to 1870, she was the proprietor of a weekly newspaper, *The Revolution*, whose motto was "The true republic — men, their rights and nothing more; women, their rights and nothing less." With Stanton, Anthony helped to bring previously taboo subjects, such as divorce, into public debate.

In 1872 Anthony cast a ballot in the presidential election, as she felt she was entitled to do according to the 14th amendment of the Constitution. She was arrested and fined $100 but never paid the fine. As the debate over women's suffrage heated up, Anthony continued fighting for her cause. "Abraham Lincoln said, 'No man is good enough to govern another man without his consent.' Now I say to you, 'No man is good enough to govern any woman without her consent,'" she said in 1895. Her pioneering led to women's suffrage in the United States in 1920.

She organized the International Council of Women, and, along with Stanton, Matilda Joslyn Gage, and Ida Husted Harper, published a four-volume history of their cause, called *The History of Women's Suffrage* (1902). In the last years of her life, though she suffered from a serious heart condition, she continued to work for women's rights, attending her last convention two months before her death at the age of eighty-six. Anthony's last public words were said at her eighty-sixth birthday celebration: "Failure is impossible."

E. DuBois, ed., *Elizabeth Cady Stanton and Susan B. Anthony: Correspondence, Writings, Speeches*, 1981.

While I do not pray for anybody...to commit outrages, still, I do pray...for some terrific shock to startle the women of this nation into a self-respect which will compel them to see the abject degradation of their present position; which will force them to break their yoke of bondage, and give them faith in themselves....The fact is, women are in chains, and their servitude is all the more debasing because they do not realize it. O, to compel them to see and feel, and to give them the courage and conscience to speak and act for their own freedom, though they face the scorn and contempt of all the world for doing it.

Susan B. Anthony, 1870

M. Gurko, *The Ladies of Seneca Falls: The Birth of the Woman's Rights Movement*, 1974.

AQUINAS, THOMAS   SEE THOMAS AQUINAS

ARCHIMEDES (c.287–212 B.C.E.), one of the greatest mathematicians of all times, both for his contributions to theoretical mathematics, which anticipated many modern discoveries, and for his mechanical inventions, among them the lever. Son of the astronomer Pheidias, he was born in Syracuse, Sicily and educated in Alexandria. Although he spent time in Egypt he lived most of his life in the vicinity of Syracuse and was a friend of the Syracusan king Hieron II.

A popular story is related about Archimedes's discovery of the law of hydrostatics (the principle of Archimedes), which states that a body immersed in a fluid is buoyed up with a force equal to the weight of the fluid displaced. Hieron had asked Archimedes to verify whether his crown was indeed made of pure gold. While taking a bath Archimedes noticed the bath water overflowing and suddenly perceived that the volume of water displaced was equal to the volume of his body submerged inside the bath. He then realized that if he put the crown into a vessel filled with water and weighed the water that overflowed and then did the same with a piece of pure gold the weight of the crown, the weight of the water that overflowed would be equal only if the crown also were of pure gold. Without stopping to dress he ran through the streets of the city shouting, *Eureka!* ("I have found it.")

He invented the spiral pump, which raised water from a lower to a higher level by winding a tube around an inclined axis. His discovery of the principle of compounded pulleys was responsible for his famous remark, "Give me a firm spot on which to stand, and I will move the earth." He showed Hieron how little force was needed to move a ship with pulleys. Although he devoted most of his energy to his studies and was little involved in public life, when the Romans besieged Syracuse he put his skills to work for the defense of his native city. He invented such mechanical devices as catapults and a system of concave mirrors which used the rays of the sun to ignite the sails of the Roman ships. Nevertheless, the city fell in 212 B.C.E. and Archimedes was killed by a Roman soldier who came upon him while he was working on a problem of geometry in the sand. According to the story he was so involved in his work that all he said to the soldier was, "Do not disturb my diagrams."

Archimedes was responsible for creating the fields of hydrostatics and statics in mechanics. Although he wrote works on geometry, mathematics, optics, astronomy, and mechanics, he did not write about his inventions. His extant works include: *On Quadrature of the Parabola*; *On the Sphere and Cylinder*; *On Spirals*; *On Conoids and Spheroids, Measurement of the Circle*; *Book of Lemmas, On the Heptagon*; *On Equilibrium of Planes*; and *On Floating Bodies*. He requested that his best-known

works — on the sphere and the cylinder — be inscribed on his tombstone.
D. C. Ipsen, *Archimedes*, 1981.

ARIOSTO, LUDOVICO (1474–1533), Italian Renaissance poet. He was born in Reggio Emilia to an official of the court of Ferrara. His lifetime, coinciding with some of the greatest moments of the Renaissance, was influenced by the period's historical events and its literary and artistic achievements.

Although he initially studied law to please his father ("my father kept me to that rubbish for five years"), Ariosto also acquired an education in the humanities. From an early age he began to write, and after several years of law eventually gained his father's consent to pursue a literary career. The economic necessity posed by his father's death, however, forced him to take employment as a courtier when he was twenty-six. His comedies, which were enjoyed by Cardinal Ippolito d'Este, secured him a position and from 1503 to 1517 he served in Ippolito's court. He subsequently entered the service of the cardinal's brother, Alfonso, duke of Ferrara. In Ferrara he fell in love with a beautiful married woman, Alessandra Benucci. Her husband died soon after and they continued their romance clandestinely because Ariosto was officialy a priest. Eventually they wed in secret.

In 1521 Ariosto became governor of the province of Garganana in the Apennines. His service in that turbulent region was far from pleasant and after three years he requested leave to return to Ferrara. His earnings had finally given him the means to buy the house and garden of which he had always dreamed and from 1528 he spent the rest of his life in Ferrara in retirement with his crippled brother Gabriele and his son Virginio.

His greatest poem was *Orlando Furioso*, one of the classics of Italian literature. The first version, in forty cantos, appeared in 1516; the final version, with forty-six cantos, in 1532. A romantic epic dealing with the wars of *Charlemagne against the Saracens and the love of Orlando for Angelica, a Cathay princess, it was ostensibly a continuation of the unfinished epic poem *Orlando Innamorato* by Matteo Maria Boiardo. In fact it was also a glorification of the Este family and a representation of Charlemagne's battle to protect Europe from Islam. Its chief aim was to entertain. Remarkable for its diversity and sheer length (almost 39,000 lines), it was a brilliant success. During the many years it took to complete, the poem was constantly evolving in response to Ariosto's own revisions as well as comments and suggestions by friends, for the manuscript accompanied him on his many journeys in service of the Este family and was read aloud wherever he could find a listener.

His other works include *La Cassaria* (1508), *Gli Suppositi* (1509), *Il Negromante* (1520), and *La Lena* (1529), as well as plays which pioneered European comedy.

N. Borsellino, *Ludovico Ariosto*, 1973.
A. V. Cameron, *The Influence of Ariosto's Epic and Lyric Poetry on Ronsard and his Group*, 1973.
R. Griffin, *Ludovico Ariosto*, 1974.

ARISTOPHANES (c.450–c.385 B.C.E.), Greek comic. There are few known biographical details of his life; he had three sons but nothing is known of them. It is known that he lived through the Peloponnesian war (431–404 B.C.E.) but the extent of his involvement and the nature of his political views are unclear. What remains of Aristophanes are his plays: eleven comedies that are extant and references to some thirty others.

Aristophanes was a master of Old Comedy, a style which combined a basically serious intent with a goal of exuberant entertainment — and above all Aristophanes entertained. His plays, though based on real life, were set in an imaginary timeless universe of his own creation. He had a genius for the fantastic and a supreme mastery of language whether his subject was comic, serious, absurd, weighty, or trivial. With a particular talent for parody and satire, he excelled at portraying and ridiculing his fellow man. No figure, whether prominent or ordinary, poet, or politician, was spared his scathing tongue. The chief objects of his satire were politics and morality, but he also found opportunity to mock anything from the latest fashions to the latest economic theories. His extant plays are *Acharnians, Knights, Clouds, Wasps, Peace, Birds, Frogs, Ploutos, Lysistrata, Thesmophoriazousai*, and *Ecclesiazousai*.

THE EXTANT PLAYS OF ARISTOPHANES

Acharnians, produced in 425, won first prize in the Lenaea. It concerns the private peace treaty that the hero concludes with Sparta in opposition to public opinion.

Knights, produced in 424, won first prize at the Lenaea. It is a savage attack on Cleon, who loses his popularity in the Demos to a man who defeats him in his own vices.

Clouds, produced in 423, placed third in the Dionysia. It deals with the differences between a father and his son who adopts new ideas. These ideas are represented by Socrates, who is ridiculed and to whom all the absurdities of the Sophists are ascribed.

Wasps, produced in 422, won second prize in the Lenaea. It takes its theme from — and ridicules — the ability of the Athenians to serve in the jury-courts.

Peace, produced in 421, won second prize in the Dionysia. The hero flies to Olympus where he rescues the girl, Peace, from War and marries her.

Birds, produced in 414, won second prize in the Dionysia. Two Athenians, disgusted with their city, convince the birds to build a new city in the air, and one of them becomes its king

Lysistrata, produced in 411. The Athenian and Spartan women decide to compel their husbands to restore peace by refusing to have sexual relations with them.

Thesmophoriazousai, produced in 411. The Athenian women, while celebrating the *Thesmophoria*, are preparing to attack Euripides, who manages to escape with his friend.

Frogs, produced in 405, won first prize in the Lenaea. Inasmuch as Athens is short of poets, Dionysius descends to Hades to bring Euripides back, but finds Aeschylus to be a better poet and fetches him instead.

Ecclesiazousai, produced probably in 391. The women take over the government of the city and replace private property by communal ownership.

Ploutos, produced in 388. The blind, and hence erring, Ploutos ("Wealth") is cured and as a result, just and unjust people get what they deserve.

E. David, *Aristophanes and Athenian Society of the Early Fourth Century*, 1984.
G. Murray, *Aristophanes*, 1933.
A. Solomons, *The Living Aristophanes*, 1974.

ARISTOTLE (384–322 B.C.E.), Greek philosopher; student of *Plato. Aristotle's works cover almost every conceivable topic including logic, philosophy of science, physics, astronomy, meteorology, biology, psychology, metaphysics, ethics, politics, rhetoric, and theory of poetry. He had an encyclopedic mind and though he admired and was influenced by *Socrates and Plato, in many ways he went beyond the two in his inquiries. In some of his writings Aristotle expresses an affinity for Platonic thought and in others refutes it. One of their differences was on the subject of ideal forms. While Plato held that there existed ideal forms that could not be perceived by the senses, Aristotle maintained that every object has both Form and Matter which are inseparable and can be studied only in that object. Aristotle believed that nature was purposeful and did nothing by accident and that a philosopher's responsibility was to observe the objects in nature to discover their purposes.

Though scholars have worked out different theories in an attempt to explain the development of Aristotle's philosophy, it is almost impossible to know with certainty when Aristotle developed any one idea as there exists no accurate chronology of his writings. What is certain is his influence on eastern and western civilizations, and on Christianity, Islam, and Judaism.

Aristotle was born in the Greek colony of Stagiros in Macedonia. His father, Nicomachus, was a court physician to King Amyntas III of Macedonia (father of *Philip II and grandfather of *Alexander the Great). It is likely that as a youth Aristotle studied medicine and biology in the family tradition, and although he did not become a physician, his early studies probably had some influence on his later interest in biology and the natural sciences.

Aristotle's parents died when he was young; at age seventeen he went to Athens and entered Plato's Academy (367 B.C.E.), where he remained for some twenty years lecturing, writing, and researching. His studiousness and intelligence reportedly earned him the nicknames the Mind, (from Plato) and the Reader, (from his fellow students). At the Academy he wrote dialogues (which now only exist in fragments) and began his work in the natural sciences.

Aristotle left Athens around the time of Plato's death (348/47 B.C.E.). Some suggest that he left because the Academy did not choose him to succeed Plato but others say that it had more to do with the political climate in Athens. After Philip II conquered the Greek city-state of Olynthus, anti-Macedonian feeling spread to Athens and Aristotle might have been subjected to abuse had he stayed. He and a group of followers, including Theophrastus of Eresus (his eventual successor), settled in Assos in Asia Minor, where Aristotle became an adviser to the ruler Hermias. He married Hermias's niece Pythias, with whom he had one daughter, also named Pythias. When Aristotle married he was in his late thirties, which he regarded as the ideal age for men to marry (with eighteen as the ideal age for women). Pythias did not live long and after her death Aristotle took a companion, Hermeias (it is not clear if they were married), with whom he had a son, Nicomachus.

In about 345/44 B.C.E. Aristotle moved to the island of Lesbos, where he and Theophastus established a philosophical circle in the fashion of the Academy. Judging from the many place names from this area in his writings, he conducted much of his biological research during his stay on Lesbos.

A few years later (343/42 B.C.E.), Aristotle went to Pella in response to an invitation from Philip II to tutor his thirteen-year-old son, the future Alexander the Great. It is not certain how much influence the tutor had on his pupil in the three years they spent together, for many of their ideas are divergent. For one thing, Aristotle told Alexander to completely dominate the barbarians (non-Greeks) and not to intermix with them, to treat them "as beasts or plants," as *Plutarch later reported. But Alexander did no such thing and, in fact, actively promoted intermarriage between his soldiers and the people they conquered.

Aristotle returned to Stagiros, where he remained until 335/34 B.C.E., when he traveled to Athens. There, he founded his own academy, later called the

Lyceum, for it was located in a gymnasium attached to the temple of Apollo Lyceus on the outskirts of Athens. The school, which boasted the first large library, differed from Plato's Academy in that it stressed the systematic collection of material and became a leading research center. At the Academy mathematics was the focus of inquiry, but at the Lyceum biology and history were central. In addition, the predominant writing style at the Lyceum became that of expository analysis as opposed to the dialectic style of the Academy. Here Aristotle wrote and organized what later became the largest parts of his corpus of works. Each morning he would walk with his students during their philosophical discussions and eventually the Greek term *peripatetic*, meaning "walking about," became synonymous with Aristotelian philosophy.

The death of Alexander the Great in 323 B.C.E. signaled the revolt of many of the Greek city-states, including Athens. Anti-Macedonian feelings ran high and Aristotle was charged with impiety, as Socrates had been. "Proof" of his crime was a poem he had written twenty years before as a eulogy to King Hermias which compared him to the gods. He left the city for Chalcis (now Khalkis) on the Strait of Evripos. In a letter to Antipater, a deputy of Alexander, he wrote that he would not allow Athens to sin twice against philosophy, a reference to the sentence imposed on Socrates. He died the following year, reportedly from a stomach illness.

Aristotle

BY ARISTOTLE

- Anybody can become angry – that is easy. But to be angry with the right person and to the right degree and at the right time and for the right purpose and in the right way – that is not within everyone's power and is not easy.
- Our characters are the result of our conduct.
- We should aim at leveling down our desires rather than leveling up our means.
- A friend is a single soul dwelling in two bodies.
- There was never a great genius without a touch of madness.
- Every act of necessity is disagreeable.
- I have gained this by philosophy: I do without being ordered what others do out of fear of the law.
- Man is a political animal.
- One may go wrong in many different ways but right only in one.
- One swallow does not make spring.
- The good is that at which all things aim.

Copies of busts of Aristotle exist and give the impression of a handsome man with noble features. Written descriptions report that he was thin-legged, had small eyes, spoke with a lisp, and dressed well. He was said to have had a quick and sharp wit and once, when told someone had insulted him, reportedly said, "He may even scourge me, as long as it is in my absence." Aristotle's kindness has been noted in anecdotes and especially in reference to the kind treatment of slaves and servants he expressed in his will.

There are a number of surviving works (in part or whole) that have been attributed to Aristotle. Scholars believe more than one hundred of his works have not been found.

Aristotle's main works include *Metaphysics*, consisting of fourteen volumes covering a range of philosophical concepts such as the nature of being or substance, causality, God, and nature; *Organon*, a compilation of logical works; *Physics*; *On the Heavens*; *Nicomachean Ethics*; *Politics*, a comparison of over 150 governments; *Rhetoric*; and *Poetics*.

The extant works of Aristotle were not written for publication but as teaching aids. His contribution to thought was immense and it was Aristotle who founded the scientific method. In his works on logic he introduced the study of logical propositions and developed the system of syllogisms. In his *Ethics* he expounded the concept of the Golden Mean: human happiness consists in virtue, defined as the mean between two extremes.

It was said of him that "he set in order all parts of philosophy," and at that time all knowledge was seen as a whole. He laid the foundation for research work and its exposition within the framework of defined branches of science. He established the model for the correct definition of scientific subjects: by definitions and assumptions, by classification and orderly arrangement of the material, and by careful progression from one stage to the next. He laid the foundations for the sciences of zoology, anatomy, and physiology, transforming mere information into science. His works on rhetoric and politics are classics and in his *Poetics* he taught that tragedy is based on imitation and associated with a catharsis of fear and pity. One of his chief contributions to philosophy was his division of all things into Matter and Form. God, the Prime Mover, is pure Form or thought. In man, the highest Form is represented by reason.

Aristotle's thought has been studied and expounded since his time. For three centuries after his death his school remained a center of research. The influence of Aristotelianism was paramount in the Middle Ages and was basic in Islamic and Jewish philosophy and Christian scholasticism. Many of our major concepts – energy, substance and essence, subject and predicate, potential and actual, quantity and quality – can be traced back to the immense contribution and originality of Aristotelian thought.

J. L. Ackrill, *Aristotle The Philosopher*, 1981.

F. Brentam, *Aristotle and His World View*, 1978.

A. Edel, *Aristotle and His Philosophy*, 1982.

J. H. Randall, *Aristotle*, 1960.

W. D. Ross, *Aristotle*, 1955.

ARIUS (c.250–c.336), Christian theologian and heretic who denied the godhead of Christ. Arius, probably born in Alexandria, studied under Lucian of Antioch before assuming the position of deacon under Peter of Alexandria. His role as deacon was, however, short-lived. Peter excommunicated Arius in 311 for associating with the heretical Meletians, who denied the divinity of Christ. Although Peter's successor, Achillas, restored Arius to communion two years later, Arius, then presbyter the church of Baucalis, soon found himself in conflict with Achillas's heir, Bishop Alexander. During a sermon Arius proposed that God the Father created the Word (Logos) prior to the creation of the world. Unlike the Meletians, who then claimed that *Jesus Christ was the adopted son of the Word, Arius claimed that Christ was Logos incarnate. Christ was therefore a creation of a higher status than humanity but, nonetheless, a creation of God the Father. He argued that if God begat the Son, the Son would then have a beginning and not be eternal. No other being could share God's being; Christ was subordinate to God.

Arius's ideas infuriated Bishop Alexander. Although Arius had attempted to synthesize the classical teachings of the church with the Meletian heresy, church fathers took his opinions as a threat to orthodoxy and their own standing. At the time, the church was undergoing a vigorous evolutionary process; many Christians who had reverted to paganism because of Roman oppression began to re-

Christ is the Logos [Word] incarnate.
Christ is capable of change and subject to change.
Therefore the Logos is capable of change and subject to change,
And not equal to God.

From the *Thalia*

turn to the fold. Some elders wished to reject these returning Christians because of their past sins; some favored forgiving them their lapses from faith. Other hardliners had rejected the highly urban church lifestyle, preferring to dwell as ascetics in the desert. Arius's teachings, based on common sense rather than pure faith, were seen as a further blow to the authority of the church and Arius was again excommunicated.

Despite his excommunication Arius did not abandon his beliefs. He published the *Thalia*, a book of lyric hymns in which he expounded his philosophy for the masses. Although only fragments of the book survive in quotations, it was apparently a popular work that attracted both laymen and some church elders. But despite its populist appeal the reception of the *Thalia* by the upper echelons of the church hierarchy threatened to tear the infant church apart. The Emperor *Constantine himself intervened in the debate by convening the Council of Nicaea in 325. Constantine's intentions were purely political; he believed that the rift in Christendom would affect his throne. Many of the bishops gathered at Nicaea did so to promote their own interests. Arius's position was supported by only a minority of the council's participants; upon refusing to retract his views, he was exiled to Illyria. Although he continued to promote Arianism, others, notably Valens and Eusebius, became its foremost champions. In 333 Constantine summoned Arius and after sitting with him for several hours, was convinced that Arius's views were far from heretical and ordered *Athanasius, the bishop of Alexandria, to restore him to communion. Athanasius's refusal led to his own banishment. However, Arius was not to benefit from the repeal of his excommunication. On the morning on which he was to be readmitted, he was walking with Eusebius in Constantinople when he suddenly fell ill. Seeking refuge in a public toilet, he began vomiting heavily and losing body fluids. Legend relates that his body became so shriveled that he fell between the grids in the floor into the sewer below and died. Arius's supporters claimed that he was poisoned by disciples of Athanasius but his opponents claimed that divine retribution prevented the heretic from partaking of the sacrament.

H. O. J. Brown, *Heresies*, 1989.

R. C. Gregg and D. E. Groh, *Early Arianism*, 1981.

C. Kannengeisser, *Arius and Athanasius*, 1991.

ARKWRIGHT, SIR RICHARD (1732–1792), British inventor whose innovations in spinning machinery fostered the Industrial Revolution. Richard Arkwright was born to a humble family in the town of Preston, Lancashire, the youngest of thirteen children. As a child he was expected to learn a trade and therefore received little formal education. He was apprenticed at eighteen to Edward Pollit, a wigmaker in Bolton. While working there he developed a new method for dyeing hair, enabling him to have his own business.

Upon his father's death Arkwright inherited a small shop. He continued in the wigmaking profession but took an interest in cotton spinning. By 1767 Arkwright had made considerable improvements on a spinning machine invented several years earlier by Louis Paul. His own model – the famous spinning frame – was exhibited at the Preston fair of 1768, where it attracted much attention. In June of that year Arkwright opened a horse powered spinning mill in Nottingham incorporating his own improvements. Despite the cost involved, he had found partners who foresaw great promise in his innovations. Arkwright obtained a patent on his first spinning machine in 1769.

Although the new machinery had mechanized some of the spinning process, much of the work continued to be done by hand. Arkwright spent the next years developing machinery for carding, drawing, and roving. In 1771 he bought property in Cromford, Derbyshire on which he constructed a water-driven mill, and by the following year was producing a superior quality of yarn. Earlier machinery had produced threads that were suitable only for use as woof in weaving; Arkwright's threads were strong enough to be used as warp.

Despite the protests of competing spinners, who expected his improvements to cost them business, in 1775 Arkwright received additional patents on his machinery. At the same time, these competitors began to imitate Arkwright's machinery; he sued them for patent infringements in 1781, but lost his case because his patents were said to be lacking in specifications. A second suit in 1785 was also lost. Despite his legal failures Arkwright was earning a fortune from his own mills and from the sale of his machinery. By 1789 he owned five mills in Derbyshire and three in other counties. Several other mills had adopted his machinery. However, because he had initiated the large-scale production of yarn he was also the object of agitation on the grounds that his inventions cut the demand for labor; in 1779 his mill in Chorley was destroyed by a mob.

Although he was not an original inventor, preferring to improve on previous inventions, his innovations won him the esteem of his community. Arkwright was knighted in 1786 after delivering his county's congratulatory address to King *George III following an assassination attempt. The next year he was appointed high sheriff for his county. Arkwright earned over £200,000 in his career and spent the last years of his life completing the formal education he had missed as a child and in the construction of Willersly Castle, dying before its completion.

R. S. Fitton and A. P. Wadsworth, *The Strutts and the Arkwrights*, 1958.

R. Guest, *A Compendious History of the Cotton Manufacture*, 1968.

ARRHENIUS, SVANTE AUGUST (1859–1927), Swedish chemist; founder of physical chemistry. Arrhenius was born in Vik, Sweden. From an early age, he showed remarkable intellectual prowess, teaching himself to read at the age of three, but his true aptitude was for mathematics, the love of which came to him from watching his father, an estate manager, tally figures. Attending the University of Uppsala, he studied mathematics, chemistry, and physics, fields he would later combine in his scientific work. He completed a doctorate in chemistry at the University of Stockholm in 1884.

Arrhenius's doctorate was unlike any other presented at the university. He combined his previous training to develop an entirely new theory of electrolysis, according to which chemicals dissolved in a liquid to generate conductivity separated into electrically charged particles (ions) even if no current is passed through the solution. The doctorate was unpopular with his examiners; it combined principles of what were, until then, two distinct disciplines, chemistry and physics, and was argued by theoretical hypotheses acquired from mathematics rather than by proven experimentation, a conventional technique Arrhenius was loath to employ. No one could deny that his thesis showed brilliance and was therefore qualified to pass, but because of his unorthodox methodology, Arrhenius was awarded the lowest possible grade.

Rejection did not deter him. Convinced of his theory's validity, he sent copies of his thesis to several leading chemists, with whom it gradually gained recognition. For two years Arrhenius lectured at the University of Uppsala while his theory was more and more widely discussed in prominent scientific circles. Finally, in 1886, he received a fellowship at the Swedish Academy of Sciences, allowing him time to work on his original thesis. Between 1886 and 1890 Arrhenius developed his theory along with several other important findings related to it, among them, an equation determining the rate of chemical reactions and the discovery that the rate of dissociation of a substance in liquid increases with dilution. With the publication of his findings, Arrhenius became one of the leading chemists in the world.

For the remainder of his life he was sought after by leading institutions in Europe and America, but his love for his native country precluded the option of teaching abroad. In 1896 he was appointed rector of the Royal Institute of Technology in Stockholm and was made a member of the Swedish Academy of Sciences in 1901.

Arrhenius also received countless awards and prizes in recognition of his life's work, the most notable being the Nobel prize for chemistry in 1903. When the votes of the Nobel committees for both physics and chemistry were counted, he was found to be the leading contender in each field. A bitter debate ensued over which prize to grant Arrhenius. One suggestion was that he receive half of each prize, but this was rejected by the physics committee. Another proposal recommended that he receive one prize in 1903 and the second in 1904, but it was argued that by then his importance might wane. Eventually he was awarded the Nobel prize for chemistry, becoming the first Swede to win a Nobel prize.

Later in life Arrhenius served as the director of the Nobel Institute for Physical Chemistry. He also expanded his scientific research to include such diverse fields as immunology, geology, and even cosmology. His theories in these fields have never been accepted by mainstream scientists.

E. Farber, *Nobel Prize Winners in Chemistry*, 1952.

B. Harrow, *Eminent Chemists of Our Time*, 1927.

J. Kendall, *Great Discoveries by Young Chemists*, 1954.

ASOKA (reigned c.273–232 B.C.E.), third Mauryan emperor of India; religious reformer and advocate of Buddhism. Asoka was one of the hundred sons of Bindusura and the grandson of *Chandragupta, the first Mauryan emperor of northern India. Asoka was serving as viceroy of Ujjain in Malwa at his father's death. Bindusura's death prompted a bloody war of succession; Asoka was the only son to survive. Some historians choose to point to contemporary records in which Asoka shows his concern for his brothers and sisters as discrediting the legend. There was, however, an unexplained four-year gap between his father's death and his own coronation.

Little information is available on the early years of Asoka's forty-year reign. Some thirteen years after his accession Asoka attacked Kalinga near the Bay of Bengal in an attempt to expand his realm. Despite his military victory Asoka was appalled by the carnage of war. There were 100,000 casualties and 150,000 prisoners were taken; millions more may have died from famine and disease. The sight prompted a radical transformation in Asoka. Whereas he had previously enjoyed the life of a royal prince, the memory of Kalinga inspired him to adopt the philosophy of *ahimsa*, or noninjury of living things. Asoka abandoned the hunt and became a vegetarian. He provided for his subjects by planting trees, digging wells, and building hospitals and began exporting medicinal herbs to many of the neighboring states.

Asoka adopted the *dharma*, Buddhist laws encouraging respect for one's parents and teachers, charity, honesty, moderation, and tolerance of all people. He exhorted his officials to treat his subjects as if they were his own children. Although Asoka's empire was the largest that the dynasty would know, he abandoned military conquests, preferring to send missionaries abroad in a program he referred to as "conquest through faith." (He did not, however, disband the army, nor did he abolish capital punishment.) Asoka's missionaries reached as far as Greece in Europe, Egypt in Africa, and Burma and Ceylon in Asia.

In his own realm Asoka established a group of educators, the *dharma-mahamatras*, who roamed the country preaching the teachings of the *Buddha. He is said to have built 8,400 temples, some of which can still be seen. Perhaps his greatest achievement was carving the teachings of the *dharma* on countless cave walls and pillars throughout the kingdom. These records provide historians with a thorough understanding of Asoka's reign. They are highly ornate monuments, polished by a technique that has yet to be reproduced, written in both Pali and local languages. The writings designate Asoka as *Devanampiya* ("Beloved of God") and *Piyadashi* ("One concerned about the welfare of his subjects").

Little is known about Asoka's personal life. He was apparently polygamous but only one wife, Kalivaki, is known. Two of his children, a son, Mahendra and a daughter, Sanghamitra, may have been missionaries in Ceylon. Asoka was not succeeded by his oldest son, Tivara; however, two grandsons, Dasaratha and Samprati, divided the empire after Asoka's death. They were unable to consolidate their power and within fifty years the Mauryan empire had crumbled.

Some scholars are skeptical as to whether Asoka actually embraced Buddhism. Although he adhered to the *dharma*, there is no record of other important Buddhist principles, such as the Four Noble Truths and the Eightfold Way, being promoted during his reign, while the principles of *dharma* and *ahimsa* are common to Buddhists, Jains, and Hindus. These scholars claim that Asoka was actually the founder of a new universal faith combining the pacifist principles common to all Indian religions. Some legends contradict this claim, telling that Asoka spent his final years attempting to prevent schisms developing in Buddhism.

M. A. Nikam and R. P. McKeon, *Asoka, King of Magadha*, 1958.

J. S. Strong, *The Legend of King Asoka*, 1984.

- Even to one who should wrong him, what can be forgiven is to be forgiven.
- The subdued brothers should not be afraid of me; they should trust me and receive from me happiness, not sorrow.

From Asoka's rock inscriptions

ATATURK, MUSTAFA KEMAL (1881–1938),

founder and first president of the Turkish Republic. He was born in Salonika to poverty-stricken Turkish parents who lived in a deteriorated hut in a cobbled alleyway. Mustafa was a loner, willful and opinionated, unusually self-sufficient, and resented any restriction or disagreement, traits which made him unpopular with his schoolmates. His father died when he was nine, leaving the family destitute. They moved to an uncle's farm, where Mustafa took well to the outdoor work. Against his mother's wishes, he sat for and passed the examination for the Salonika military cadet school. He was successful in his military subjects and excelled at mathematics but did not get on well with the other cadets. A teacher gave him the nickname of Kemal, meaning "perfection," a name by which he was known from then on. His sexual interests developed early and at age fourteen he started an affair with a neighbor girl. At seventeen he graduated from the cadet school and went on to the Senior Military School in Monastir, from which he graduated in 1899 and entered the War College in Istanbul. While in Istanbul, he began a wild life of drinking, gambling, and consorting with prostitutes. Women for him were never more than sex objects and he felt no affection for any of his conquests.

During his years at the War College, Mustafa Kemal joined the Vatan, a secret revolutionary society. He graduated in 1905 with the rank of captain. While waiting to be posted to an assignment he headed the Vatan and was arrested for his activities, spending several months in prison before being sent to a cavalry regiment in Damascus. There he organized a branch of the Vatan, gaining widespread support among the discontented officers. Realizing that Damascus was a backwater and that Salonika was the center of revolutionary activity, he applied for a transfer. In Salonika he joined the secret revolutionary movement, the Committee of Union and Progress (CUP), popularly known as the Young Turks. As an outsider and newcomer, Mustafa Kemal was not in a leadership position but he constantly questioned and criticized the leaders. The CUP seized power in 1908 and proclaimed a constitution, staying in power until 1918. In the 1912 Balkan War, Mustafa Kemal was in charge of the defense of the Gallipoli peninsula and in 1913 was sent to Sofia as military attaché. In World War I he twice defeated the British in Gallipoli and stopped the Russian advance on Turkey. After the war the victorious Allies swooped in to carve up the empire among themselves. The British occupied Istanbul and the CUP government was firmly taken under their control. Mustafa Kemal aroused the Turks' nationalist feelings and opposed both the sultan, who favored placing the country under English protection, and the CUP government. In 1919 he declared a rival nationalist government in Ankara. Together with his supporters, he convened the Grand National Assembly, of which he was elected president.

The sultan allowed elections in Istanbul, where "Kemalists" won considerable support, but the British occupiers dissolved the new parliament. When the CUP-backed sultan's government was about to sign a crippling treaty that Britain and her allies had forced on them, Mustafa Kemal was incensed. Rousing his supporters to action, he directed campaigns against the Armenians, Georgians, and French. Aware that he could not rally enough strength to hold on to the entire Ottoman empire, he declared to a French official, "You may have Syria and Arabia, but keep your hands off Turkey. We claim the right of every nation, to be a free community within our national boundaries, not one inch more but not an inch less." He successfully beat back a Greek invasion in 1922, pushing the Greeks to the sea at Izmir. Mustafa Kemal was convinced that only he could lead the Turks to modernization. "I am Turkey," he said. "To destroy me is to destroy Turkey." After seizing power, the Grand National Assembly government negotiated a new treaty with the Allies at Lausanne in 1923, achieving nearly all of the objectives they had outlined at their first congress. Mustafa Kemal immediately forced through the assembly a bill separating the sultanate from the caliphate, the position of religious

Ataturk with his wife Latife

leadership of the entire Muslim world. He then abolished the sultanate, the first step in his sweeping reform plan, and in 1924 abolished the caliphate as well, sending the caliph into exile. He also pushed through a bill declaring Turkey a republic, with himself as president.

Mustafa Kemal blamed Islam for keeping Turkey in a backward state and in his determination to modernize and westernize, he ruthlessly attacked the religious institutions. One of his first campaigns was to abolish the traditional fez and replace it with western-style brimmed hats. He crushed opposition to the wearing of these hats, which interfered with the religious Muslims' bowing during prayer and were forbidden by the Koran, by making fezzes illegal. He discouraged women from wearing the traditional veil and encouraged western-style clothing. He also brought western-style music to Turkey in order to adapt traditional dances, requiring all government officials to learn western dances.

Mustafa Kemal abolished the religious code of law and adopted instead the Swiss civil code, Italian penal code, and German commercial code. He outlawed polygamy, instituted civil marriage, confiscated the Wakf (the religious endowment) property and fund and closed down the religious schools, instituting a nationwide system of secular schools. Further changes included introducing the metric system, Gregorian calendar, and the system of telling time by numbering hours from midnight instead of from dawn, as had been traditional. Blaming the complicated Arabic script of Ottoman Turkish for the mass illiteracy and linguistic isolation of Turks from the western world, he adopted a Latin alphabet for the Turkish language and started a mass literacy campaign, even refusing to release prisoners at the end of their term if they could not demonstrate mastery of the new alphabet. Turkish became the only legal language for the conduct of business and for education. Mustafa Kemal endorsed reforms granting equality to women, giving them the right to vote and to hold public office. He required all Turks to adopt surnames, taking for himself Ataturk or "father of the Turks."

Many of these reforms engendered resistance from the public, but he ruthlessly crushed all opposition, surviving at least two assassination attempts. Mustafa Kemal was fanatical in his drive to re-create Turkey as a modern republic. An extreme egocentric, he was given to periods of deep depression and would spend days brooding alone at home or engaging in bouts of drinking and gambling, and then be galvanized into action by some crisis or sign that his reforms were failing. He felt he had to be a dictator but only long enough to prepare the Turks for democracy. As he said in 1932, "Let the people leave politics alone for the moment, let them interest themselves in agriculture and commerce. For ten or fifteen years more I must rule. After that, perhaps I may be able to let them speak openly." He died, still in office, in 1938.

W. P. Hansen and J. Haney, eds., *Kemal Ataturk*, 1987.

J. P. D. Kinross, *Ataturk: The Rebirth of a Nation*, 1964.

G. Lewis, *Ataturk and His Republic*, 1982.

V. D. Volkan, *The Immortal Ataturk*, 1989.

ATHANASIUS (c.293–373), bishop of Alexandria noted for his struggle against the Arian (see *Arius) heresy. While the subject of controversy in his own time, Athanasius's role was crucial in establishing the generally accepted Christian doctrine that Christ is of the same nature as the Father. Even as a young boy Athanasius was drawn to the church. He was once seen by Bishop Alexander of Alexandria playing in a church, pretending to be bishop. Alexander was impressed by Athanasius, who had meticulously baptized one of his playmates in play. The baptism was recognized, and Athanasius was chosen as Alexander's ward.

Athanasius accompanied Alexander to the Council of Nicaea in 325. The council condemned the Arian heresy, which denied Christ's divinity; the Arian doctrine was advocated by Bishop Eusebius of Nicomedia. It also proposed a solution to the problem of the Melitians, Christians whose faith had lapsed during times of persecution. Melitian laymen were reaccepted into communion but the clergy was not. Alexander left the task of implementing the decisions made at Nicaea to his choice as his successor. An election in 328 confirmed Alexander's choice of Athanasius, over considerable opposition from the Arian party and their allies, the Melitian clergy.

Consecrated that same year, Athanasius began strengthening his see. His episcopal authority was extended into Libya in the west and Sudan in the south. However, the Arians and the Melitians were also consolidating their power. The Roman emperor, *Constantine, acceded to Eusebius's plea to allow the aging Arius to receive communion before his death and wrote to Athanasius that Arius had signed the creed adopted by the council of Nicaea. Athanasius still refused to accept Arius, but his reasoning so impressed Constantine that the matter was dropped. Eusebius, however, demanded revenge. The Melitians' complaints of ill treatment by Athanasius were exaggerated by the rumor that Athanasius had murdered a Melitian bishop and used his bones for sorcery. The bishop suddenly reappeared, but Athanasius's harsh treatment of the Melitians was well known and he was excommunicated. Athanasius's appeal to Constantine was rejected when Eusebius produced evidence of a dock strike in Alexandria planned by the bishop to halt the supply of Egyptian grain to the capital. Church and state had conspired against Athanasius; in 335, he was removed from his see and exiled to Gaul.

Following Constantine's death in 337, the empire was divided among his three warring sons: Constantine II (Gaul), Constantius (Egypt and the East), and Constans (Italy and North Africa). Athanasius's friendship with Constantine II led to his restoration to Alexandria in 337, but Eusebius appealed to Constantius, and Athanasius was again exiled in 339. Athanasius fled to Rome, where he was warmly received by Pope Julius I. Constans also welcomed Athanasius and urged Constantius to restore him to Alexandria. The death of Eusebius in 342 reduced the controversy surrounding Athanasius and he was allowed to return to Alexandria in 346.

For the next ten years Athanasius officiated largely undisturbed. He was still opposed by Constantius who, from 350, was the sole Roman emperor, but civil war prevented Constantius from interfering in church affairs. The Arian bishop Valens, Constantius's lackey, incited him anew against Athanasius. In 356, 5,000 troops marched on Alexandria to install an Arian bishop, George, in Athanasius' stead. Athanasius escaped to the monastic communities of the desert, where he remained a fugitive for five years. Relentlessly pursued by Constantius's secret police, his own vast espionage service assured his safety. When Constantius died in 361, Athanasius received a hero's welcome in Alexandria.

The new emperor, Julian the Apostate, originally admired Athanasius for his unflinching convictions. Athanasius was reinstated before Julian realized that it was foolish to expect his support against the Christians because Athanasius, despite the persecution he had suffered, was also a Christian. Athanasius was a potential foe who had actually increased the church's influence, and therefore had to be expelled. The order of expulsion was extended by Julian's successor, the Arian emperor Valens.

The threat of a Gothic invasion in 366 convinced Valens of his need for extensive support from all quarters. Athanasius was restored to Alexandria, where he died. His firm conviction in his creed and his prolific writings and correspondence made him, more than any of his contemporaries, responsible for the acceptance of the creed of Nicaea by the church. The feast of Saint Athanasius is celebrated on May 2. The profession of faith known as the Athanasian Creed is now recognized as dating from a later period and does not represent the thought of Athanasius.

While in his twenties, Athanasius wrote two short treatises. One of them, *De Incarnatione* (On the Incarnation), became a classic of Christian theology. Later he wrote works in defense of the decision of the Council of Nicaea, proclaiming the divinity of the Son of God, directed against the Arians.

F. L. Cross, *The Study of Saint Anthanasius*, 1945.

C. Kannengeisser, *Arius and Athenasius*, 1991.

E. P. Meijering, *Orthodoxy and Platonism in Athanasius*, 1968.

ATTILA THE HUN (c.406–453), ruler of the Huns, called by his Christian enemies "The Scourge of God." In 433 Attila succeeded his uncle Rua as king of the Huns, a Mongol tribe from Asia that had slowly migrated westward, driven to leave by exhausted soil and their own, enemies. Living off cattle and war, they had subjugated some of the German tribes while other tribes, fleeing them, had been driven to seek sanctuary within the Roman Empire which they later subdued. Rua left his kingdom, which at the time of his death extended from the Don River to the Rhine, to his two nephews, Bleda and Attila.

History does not provide accurate information about Attila. The Roman historians of the day were so twisted by hatred of what he had already done and fear of what he might do that they seem to be describing a demon rather than a human being. Attila's use of psychological warfare — such as using exaggerated reports of his cruelty to immobilize his enemies with terror or encourage them to surrender — may have contributed to this hatred.

Attila was illiterate but extremely intelligent, his conquests depending more on cunning than force, and he ruled his people by playing on their superstitions. He was not the savage that his Roman opponents termed him, often showing more honor, justice, and mercy than they did. He lived simply, ate and drank moderately, and had many wives, but did not indulge in Roman-style debauchery.

The first eight years of Bleda and Attila's reign were mostly spent warring with other barbarian tribes, which gave the Huns control in Central Europe. Bleda's ambitions and role in these conquests are unknown. Attila wanted to rule all of Europe and the Near East. Both the Eastern and Western Empires paid him a yearly tribute, protection money against his depredations, saving face by claiming it was payment for services rendered. In 441 his troops defeated Constantinople's army, threatening Constantinople itself until the Eastern emperor promised to triple his yearly tribute.

The decaying, decadent Rome of Attila's day was a tempting target. The shrinking native population left rich farmland uncultivated while the wealth accumulated from centuries of conquest and exploitation created a high standard of living attractive to barbarians seeking new land to accommodate their expanding population. The empire's contracting borders meant that it no longer had access to the raw materials particularly grain, on which it was dependent, and it no longer had dependable markets for its goods. Barbarians who had been settling along the frontiers for centuries, immigrating individually or by official invitation of the emperor, had become Romanized. The German tribes outside the empire were primarily Christian and, after five centuries of contact with Rome, also aspired to the acquisition of Roman culture. Rome's army and administration were mostly in German hands. Assassination had become the most common way for emperors to gain power.

Attila became the most powerful man in Europe when Bleda was murdered in 444, (rumor had it that Attila was responsible for Bleda's death). His conquests continued and in 447 the Huns invaded the Balkans, sacking towns and enslaving thousands.

> He was a man born into the world to shake the nations, the scourge of all lands, who in some way terrified all mankind by the rumors noised abroad concerning him. He was haughty in walk....a lover of war yet restrained in action, mighty in counsel, gracious to suppliants, and lenient to those once received under his protection. He was short of stature, with a broad chest and a large head; his eyes were small, his beard was thin and sprinkled with gray. He had a flat nose and swarthy complexion...
>
> **Jordanes (Gothic historian)**

They wreaked such devastation that the Balkans were ruined for centuries and the Danube ceased to be the main route for East-West trade, to the detriment of the cities along its banks.

The two Roman emperors, Theodosius II and Valentinian III refused to continue to pay Attila tribute and Attila seized the pretext offered to him by Honoria, Valentinian's sister, to attack. Banished to Constantinople after her seduction by a chamberlain, Honoria sent a ring to Attila with an appeal for help. Attila promptly declared that the ring was a proposal of marriage entitling him to both Honoria and a dowry of half of Europe. When this demand was refused, he declared war. In 451 he joined forces with the Franks and the Vandals and marched into Gaul, sacking, burning, massacring, and striking terror into the hearts of its inhabitants. It took the combined might of the Visigoths and Rome in the Battle of the Catalaunian Plains, one of the bloodiest battles of history to secure an indecisive victory for Rome. The Roman forces were too exhausted and divided to go after Attila when he retreated.

In 452 Attila invaded Italy itself, destroying and looting. Attila could have reached Rome virtually without opposition — the road was open before him — but his army was suffering from plague and food shortages. He had a conference with an imperial delegation consisting of Pope Leo I and two senators. Exactly what happened at that conference is unknown, but Pope Leo took credit for Attila's immediate retreat. Attila left, threatening to return in the spring if his demands for Honoria were not met. While waiting for the bride who would bring him half an empire, Attila celebrated his marriage with another young women, Ildico. He put aside his usual restraint and drank and feasted. He then died during the night of a burst blood vessel, choking on his own blood. Chaucer recalled the event in *The Canterbury Tales*, "Looke, Attila, the gret conquerer... / Deyde in his sleep, with shame and dishonor, / Bledynge ay at his nose in dronkenese."

His kingdom was divided among his sons but they were unable to maintain control of their subject peoples because of jealousies and conflicts among themselves. They eventually succeeded where the two Roman Empires had failed: they destroyed Attila's empire.

C. D. Gordon, *The Age of Attila*, 1960.
O. Manchen-Helfen, *The World of the Huns*, 1973.
E. A. Thomsohn, *A History of Attila and the Huns*, 1948.

ATTLEE, CLEMENT RICHARD (1883–1967), leader of British Labor Party and prime minister. Attlee was born into a prosperous middle-class family and educated at Haileybury, an exclusive private school, before going to Oxford to study law. He practiced as a lawyer for a brief spell after leaving the university, but soon devoted himself to political activity. In 1907 his concern for social reform led to his taking up residence in a settlement house in London's poverty-stricken East End. His political career began in the same year when he joined the socialist Fabian Society, and from 1908 he was active in the more radical Independent Labor Party. He became mayor of the London East End borough of Stepney in 1919 and was returned to Parliament to represent the London constituency of Limehouse in 1922.

Attlee's organizational skills were quickly noticed in the Parliamentary Labor Party, and he served in the first Labor government (1924) as undersecretary for war. From 1929 to 1931 he was chancellor of the duchy of Lancaster and postmaster general, but when the Labor prime minister, Ramsay *Macdonald, formed a national coalition government in 1931, Attlee resigned and joined other Labor politicians on the opposition benches while Macdonald was expelled from the party he had led.

In 1931 Attlee became deputy leader of the Labor Party, first under Arthur Henderson and later under the pacifist George Lansbury. The country was in severe economic depression and the Labor Party's parliamentary position was weak. Many extreme proposals were made at the time, and it seems that Attlee, though he never publicly admitted it, privately subscribed to Sir Stafford Cripps's view that the party should set up a temporary dictatorship should it win an election. By the mid-1930s the foreign aggression of Adolf *Hitler and Benito *Mussolini had become the main political issue and the pacifism of Lansbury was considered both practically untenable and an electoral liability. Attlee, described as "a natural adjutant, but not a general," replaced him as party leader in 1935. This was the first time the position was held by a man not of working-class origin.

With the declaration of war against Germany in 1939 Attlee refused to bring the Labor Party into the national government under Neville Chamberlain. He supported the war but was doubtful of Chamberlain's ability to lead the country. In May 1940, after the fall of Norway and Denmark, he joined the new government under Winston *Churchill and for the rest of the war served in the war cabinet as deputy prime minister. The coalition government worked smoothly and Attlee and his Labor colleagues had a fairly free hand in the administration of domestic affairs, while Churchill conducted the war. Churchill was reported to have derided him as "a sheep in sheep's clothing" and "a typical British understatesman" but the two worked well together and by the end of the war in Europe, Attlee had become an extremely accomplished government leader. In July 1945, following a landslide Labor election victory, he became prime minister.

The new Labor government introduced a massive program of nationalization of major industries and laid the foundations of the welfare state, instituting welfare and educational reform and creating the National Health Service. The domestic economy was controlled by strict "austerity," which included the continuation of wartime rationing. In foreign affairs, all pretense of a socialist foreign policy independent of the superpowers vanished when Britain accepted the United States's Marshall Plan for European recovery and joined the North Atlantic Treaty Organization for western defense. The government also directed the dissolution of the British Empire, granting independence to many dominions and colonies, including India, Burma, and Ceylon, and giving up control of Egypt and Palestine.

Attlee, though considered somewhat uninspiring and inscrutable, secured his position throughout by establishing a close relationship with his most likely challenger within the party, Ernest Bevin, and his administrative skills were always beyond question. He remained prime minister until 1951, when Labor lost the general election, and stayed on as party leader until 1955. Upon relinquishing the leadership he was made Earl Attlee of Walthamstow, Viscount Prestwood. He published two volumes of memoirs: *As It Happened* (1954) and *A Prime Minister Remembers* (1961).

K. Harris, *Attlee*, 1982.

P. Hennesy, *Never Again*, 1992.

AUGUSTINE, SAINT (Augustine of Hippo; 354–430), bishop of Hippo (now in Algeria) and an early Christian church father. The volume of his writing exceeded that of any other ancient author and he exerted a profound influence on his contemporaries and succeeding generations. His adoption of Platonic philosophy as a basis for his own religious and political thought made it the dominant philosophical system in western Europe. His view of the Christian religion as an organic system of faith influenced ecclesiastical organization in the Middle Ages as well as relations between church and lay society. His political ideas, as represented in *The City of God*, were at the foundation of the medieval Christian state, which sought to realize the ideal theocratic regime, with the church leading the way to salvation.

He was born in Roman North Africa to Patricius, a pagan who later converted to Christianity, and Monica, a devout Christian who was later canonized by the church. His early life is described in his autobiographical *Confessions*. Written from the viewpoint of his conversion to Christianity, they are severely critical of his past life — he called it "his misspent youth" — including the years during which he lived with a mistress, by whom he had a son named Adeodatus.

He read extensively and *Plato exerted a strong influence on him. After studying at Carthage he began teaching rhetoric. *Cicero's *Hortensius* led him to become interested in philosophy and he experimented with several philosophical systems. Augustine spent nine years as a Manichaean because its fundamental principles of conflict between good and evil seemed at the time the most plausible basis for a philosophical and ethical system. It was also relatively lenient with novices which, judging from his petition, "Lord make me pure and chaste — but not just yet," must have suited him at the time. Eventually disillusioned, he turned to skepticism, then to Neoplatonism, and finally to Christianity. One day, according to his own account, he heard a voice saying, "Take and read." He opened the Scriptures and read the first passage he saw, which was, "Not in rioting and drunkenness, not in chambering and impurities, not in contention and envy, but put ye on the Lord Jesus Christ, and make not provision for the flesh in its concupicences" (Romans 13:13–14). He immediately embraced Christianity and was baptized in 387 along with his son, much to the joy of his mother. The following year he returned to Africa where he was to become bishop of Hippo in 355. Finding in himself a bent and a desire for Christian exegesis, he began a lifelong career in justifying and interpreting the Christian faith.

Augustine was primarily a religious thinker who desired to know and represent God and the human soul. "I desire to have knowledge of God and the soul. Of nothing else? No of nothing else whatsoever," and, "O God always one and the same, if I know myself, I shall know Thee." Philosophy was but a means to that end, a body of knowledge from which he could draw illustrations and explanations. He saw Christianity as an organic system of faith that could create conditions for salvation through the knowledge of God and the correct behavior of the faithful within the church. He taught that the only true church was characterized by unity, holiness, catholicity, and apostolicity, and became so convinced of this truth that he eventually believed it was justifiable to coerce the intractable to join the church.

His political program, which suggested the identification of the state with Christian society, implied the exclusion of non-Christians from the political body. Although pagans were treated severely, Jews were tolerated and barred only from public office and land tenancy. In order to prevent propagation of heresy, the church had to investigate and punish heretics — this goal was at the root of the Inquisition at the end of the twelfth century.

BY SAINT AUGUSTINE

- Whosoever reads these words, let him go with me, when he is equally certain; let him seek with me, when he is equally in doubt; let him return to me, when he knows his own error; let him call me back when he knows mine.
- This is the sum of religion: to imitate whom thou dost worship.
- The human will receives the Holy Spirit through which there arises in his heart a delight in and a love of that supreme and unchangeable Good which is God.
- Thou hast made us for thyself and our heart is restless until it rest in Thee.
- What else is our end, but to come to that realm of which there is no end.
- He is a vain preacher of the word of God without who is not a heaven within. There is no salvation outside the Church.

Augustine was a persuasive writer, excellent stylist, and prolific author. Aside from his famous *Confessions* (397), he wrote *The City of God* (413–426), in which he is represented as a divided man, one part embodying ancient culture, the other the new Gospel; but as the book clearly illustrates, Christianity is ascendant. Ten of its twenty-two books are concerned with refuting the pagan notion that worshiping the gods brings prosperity in this life or the life to come, while the other twelve discuss the history, progress, and destiny of the city of God and its eventual triumph over the city of this world. Other works include *Retractations* (428), *Epistles* (386–429), and numerous treatises.
P. Brown, *Augustine of Hippo*, 1967.
H. Chadwick, *Augustine*, 1986.
E. Gilson, *The Philosophy of Saint Augustine*, 1960.

AUGUSTUS (63 B.C.E.–14 C.E.), first Roman emperor. His mother was the daughter of Julia, Julius *Caesar's sister. Upon his father's death in 59 B.C.E. he was adopted by Julius Caesar; though originally named Gaius Octavius, he received the name Gaius Julius Caesar Octavianus after Caesar's death.

The news of Caesar's death and of being designated the main heir in Caesar's will reached Augustus while he was studying in Apollonia. He was only nineteen when Caesar was murdered but determined to avenge the death and secure his own political position. His rival *Mark Antony was defeated in a campaign at Mutina and Augustus won popular support by paying the legacy promised the people in Caesar's will out of his own pocket when Mark Antony refused to surrender Caesar's property or pay the legacy.

In 43 B.C.E. Augustus made peace with Antony and a triumvirate was formed between them and the Roman general Lepidus. They signed an agreement whereby each swore to give up in death any friend who was demanded as a victim by the others; this pact led to the deaths of 300 senators and 2000 knights. *Cicero, for whom Antony had a personal hatred, was not spared.

The following year Caesar was officially deified and Augustus was regarded as a god's son. That year, too, the triumvirate defeated the forces of Marcus Junius, Brutus, and Gaius Cassius at Philippi. Their victory consolidated their control of the Roman world, which they proceeded to divide up among themselves, according the west to Augustus, the east to Antony, and Africa to Lepidus. Lepidus was soon deposed and the empire redivided among the two others (Antony by now had married Augustus's sister). While Antony alienated the Romans by his fondness for things Egyptian, among them *Cleopatra, Augustus made himself popular among the people and aristocracy of Italy by his temperance, adherence to Roman ideals, generosity in the realm of public building, and the opportunities he offered for advancement. Under the pretext of attacking Cleopatra he instigated a propaganda war against Antony; one ploy was the publication of Antony's will, which left inheritances to Cleopatra's children and requested burial in Alexandria. In 31 B.C.E. he defeated the combined forces of Antony and Cleopatra at Actium; with Antony's suicide, he became the sole master of the Roman world and was accorded by the senate the divine title of "Augustus" (exalted).

Although the peace he had achieved was preserved within the empire, Augustus did successfully wage war against Africa, Asia, Gaul, Spain, and Dalmatia. Within the empire he sought to resolve various problems of society and state. He hoped to achieve a revival of Roman morals through the encouragement of marriage, an increasing birthrate, and a reduction in luxury. Laws were passed to diminish slavery and improve the position of freed slaves. For administrative purposes, the country was organized into *regiones*; military reforms were also implemented. Thus he achieved the so-called *pax Augusta* for his empire, fostering the internal peace,

BY AUGUSTUS

- I found Rome brick and left it marble.
- Make haste slowly.
- The noisesomeness of far-fetched words.
- (On his deathbed):
  Since well I've played my part, all clap your hands and from the stage dismiss me with applause.

Augustus

law, and security which brought prosperity to his citizens.

Augustus was a patron of the arts and a friend of *Ovid, *Horace, *Virgil, and Livy; the Augustan age was known as one of literary and artistic triumphs.

Although married three times he had no heir and thus reluctantly left the throne to his stepson *Tiberius. After his death he was deified. By a decree of the senate the sixth month was named Augustus (today August) in his honor.

M. Griebel, *Augustus*, 1990.

A. H. M. Jones, *Augustus*, 1970.

AURANGZEB (Alamgir I; Muhi-ud-Din Muhammad; 1618–1707), sixth Mogul emperor. Aurangzeb expanded the Mogul empire to its broadest geographical extent but was the last truly important emperor prior to the Mogul decline. The third son of Shah Jahan, he had a stormy childhood. The emperor Jahangir, wary of Shah Jahan, kept Aurangzeb and his brother Dara Shukoh hostage for several years to insure their father's loyalty. The brothers only received their freedom upon Shah Jahan's ascension to the throne.

Even as a youth Aurangzeb distinguished himself by his courage. Once, when he was only fourteen years old, the royal family went to inspect two combating elephants. When one elephant charged the crowd only Aurangzeb remained seated, unperturbed, on his horse. The elephant charged the boy, who responded by hurling his spear at its head. Infuriated, the elephant felled Aurangzeb's horse; Aurangzeb quickly got up and, unsheathing his sword, faced the elephant in defiance. Only then did the army manage to kill the beast. Shah Jahan was so impressed by Aurangzeb's display of courage that he called him *Bahadur* ("hero"). As he grew older Aurangzeb, like his brothers, took an active role in the imperial administration, serving as viceroy of Dacca and Afghanistan.

Shah Jahan became ill in the final years of his reign and although he had earlier designated his eldest and favorite son Dara to inherit the kingdom, his second son, Shujoh, viceroy of Bengal, saw in his father's illness an ideal opportunity to make his own bid for the throne and had himself declared emperor. The youngest son, Murad, viceroy of Gujarat, soon followed with a bid of his own and Aurangzeb, sensing an impending civil war over the succession, followed suit. Aurangzeb made a pact with Murad by which they would divide the empire between them. Dara was defeated in the battles of Dharmat and Samugarh (1658), forcing him to flee to his father in Agra. Aurangzeb and Murad conquered Agra and held Dara Shukoh and Shah Jahan captive. Upon arresting his father, Aurangzeb made the callous remark, "It is your own doing." He then turned on Murad, having him tried and executed by an Islamic court for killing an adviser in Gujarat. After defeating Shujoh in the battle of Khajwa he chased him from Bengal to Dacca and finally to Arakan, where Shujoh and his family were executed. Dara managed to escape his imprisonment in Agra but was defeated in the battle of Deorai. Rather than simply murder his brother, Aurangzeb had him tried as an apostate.

Aurangzeb was crowned following the arrest of his father in 1658 but only after the defeat of Dara in 1659 was he officially enthroned as emperor. He styled himself *Alamgir* ("The Conqueror of the World"). The title was appropriate: Aurangzeb expanded his empire in every direction. In 1661 he conquered Assam and Garhgaon; in 1666 he occupied Chittagong in the Bay of Bengal. In 1691 Aurangzeb captured Tanjore and Trichinopoly, the farthest south the Mogul empire was to extend. For the next twenty years the Mogul empire played a prominent role in world politics. Aurangzeb received emissaries from Central Asia and Mecca, and even from Ethiopia.

Aurangzeb proved to be an unpopular monarch, inspired by a fanatical urge to create a *dar-al-Islam* (Islamic realm). The most conspicuous victims of his policies were the Hindus who were banned from holding high office. In 1679 Aurangzeb reinstituted the *jizya*, or poll tax, on non-Muslim subjects. It was forbidden to erect new Hindu temples and many ancient temples were pulled down, their idols sometimes buried under the stairs leading to mosques. Every attempt was made to make converts and new Muslims were rewarded handsomely.

Unlike the first half of his reign, Aurangzeb's final twenty years were turbulent. Although he crushed the Afghan rebellion (1667–1675), the war was costly. In 1679 he quelled the Rajputs, bringing to an end the friendship between them and the Moguls that had existed since the reign of *Babur. Aurangzeb lost Sikh support in the Punjab after executing the Sikh leader, Tegh Bahadur, for failing to convert to Islam. But perhaps the greatest threat to Mogul hegemony was the revolt of Maratha. Shivaji, king of Maratha, revolted in defiance of Aurangzeb's anti-Hindu measures. Upon his defeat, he was succeeded by his son Shambuji. Shambuji's defeat and ensuing execution only aggravated the tensions. Shambuji's brother, Raja Ran, continued to confront Aurangzeb; he was succeeded by his wife, Tara Bai, who acted as regent for their infant son. Aurangzeb, a devout Muslim, was faced with the humiliating prospect of being challenged by a woman. He was also faced with family unrest. His eldest son, Muhammad, was executed for treason in 1676; his fourth son, Akbar, also revolted against his father, for which he was exiled to Persia.

Aurangzeb was in the midst of the disastrous Deccan War (1681–1707) when he died. His unpopular policies had led to revolts throughout the empire, seriously damaging the centralization of authority. He had failed to notice the European encroachments in India that would lead to British domination within a century. Finally, his own death was followed by a bloody war of succession among his three remaining heirs, Muazzam, Ajam, and Kam Baksh, not unlike the one Aurangzeb had fought with his brothers almost fifty years earlier.

F. Bernier, *Aurangzeb in Kashmir*, 1989.
R. Joshi, *Aurangzeb*, 1978.

AUSTEN, JANE (1775–1817), British novelist. She began writing stories as a child and had completed *First Impressions*, which was to become *Pride and Prejudice*, by the time she was twenty-one. She led a quiet life, as uneventful as those she described in her novels, and kept much to herself, avoiding conspicuousness and saving her observant eye, brilliant tongue, and shrewd judgments for her books. The seventh of eight children and one of two daughters, she had a very close relationship with her elder sister Cassandra, to whom she wrote many of the letters that are extant. These letters give the minute details of her life but reveal little of great dramatic interest. She lived in a cottage with her mother and sister and no room of her own and concealed her manuscripts under the blotting paper on the drawing room desk. As is evidenced in her books, she had a very high opinion of the value of marriage and of the love that should unite husband and wife. Nonetheless she never married despite four suitors, one of whom she agreed to marry only to withdraw her acceptance the following morning.

In 1801 Jane's father, a rural rector well connected with the gentry, retired and moved the family

---

Emma Woodhouse, handsome, clever, and rich, with a comfortable home and happy disposition, seemed to unite some of the best blessings of existence; and had lived nearly twenty-one years in the world with very little to distress or vex her...The real evils indeed of Emma's situation were the power of having rather too much her own way, and a disposition to think a little too well of herself.

From Jane Austen's *Emma*

---

to Bath, which distressed Jane greatly. The years in Bath were difficult, clouded by the decline and death of her father and the illness of her mother. She had written early versions of *Sense and Sensibility*, *Pride and Prejudice*, and *Northanger Abbey* but the rejection of her writing by two publishers was a great disappointment.

After her father's death in 1805 the family moved first to Southampton, then in 1809 to Chawton, where they lived in one of the homes of Jane's brother Edward. It was there that she finally met with success as a writer. Between 1811 and 1816 two of her three early novels were published in revised form and other successes followed. Her health began failing in 1815 but she did not accept that she was an invalid until 1817, when she moved to Winchester for better medical treatment, which failed to help. She died at the age of forty-one, leaving behind a legacy which included *Sense and Sensibility* (1811), *Pride and Prejudice* (1813), *Mansfield Park* (1814), *Emma* (1816) and *Persuasion* (1816).

Austen is regarded as one of the greatest English novelists. All her works deal with relationships between young men and women. In the course of the novels, various defects are corrected through hard lessons learned from difficult experiences. Her characters are the English country gentry and although her novels never moved beyond the confines of that world, her mastery of it was complete and her delicacy, naturalness, detail of character, and ironical sense of humor have insured her continued popularity.

Lord D. Cecil, *A Portrait of Jane Austen*, 1978.
J. Halperin, *The Life of Jane Austen*, 1984.
P. Honan, *Jane Austen, Her Life*, 1988.

AVERROËS (Abu al-Walid Muhammad ibn Ahmad ibn Muhammad ibn Rushd; 1126–1198), Moorish philosopher, doctor, and jurist. The greatest of the medieval Islamic Aristotelians, he integrated the Islamic and Greek traditions into his own system and significantly influenced Scholasticism, the brand of theological philosophy which, from the time of *Thomas Aquinas until the Reformation, dominated European thought.

Born to a distinguished family of jurists in Córdoba, Spain, Averroës was educated in the traditional Muslim sciences, medicine and philosophy. He became chief judge of the city of Seville as well as holding the position of personal physician to its Almohad caliphs, Abu Ya'qub Yusuf and Abu Yusuf Ya'qub. His initial meeting with the former, in 1169, constituted a crucial watershed in his life and career. Impressed by his erudition, Abu Ya'qub requested Averroës to produce a definitive Arabic commentary upon *Aristotle. As a result, Averroës wrote a series of works over the next twenty-five years, ranging over the whole Aristotelian corpus, *Plato's *Republic*, and Porphyry's *Isagoge*. Fifteen of his thirty-eight clear and penetrating commentaries were later translated and included in the Latin version of Aristotle's complete works produced in thirteenth-century Europe; they added considerably to the understanding of that philosopher and made Averroës famous throughout the West, while having a great impact on both Jewish and Christian thought. He was careful to remove those Neoplatonic elements which had crept into previous Aristotelian exegeses, clearly demonstrating where his predecessors al-*Farabi and *Avicenna had departed from Aristotle's thought.

As early as 1162 he produced original writings; however, few of his works on law and medicine survive. His most important original works were composed in the years 1179 and 1180. The *Decisive Treatise on the Agreement between Religious Law and Philosophy*, the *Examination of the Methods of Proof Concerning the Doctrines of Religion*, and *The Incoherence of the Incoherence* postulated the establishing of the true, inner meaning of religious beliefs as the correct aim of philosophy. They also propounded his view that metaphysicians using syllogistic proof were competent (indeed, obliged) to interpret the doctrines in prophetically revealed law, whereas traditional Muslim theologians relying on dialectical arguments were not. The third of these works constituted a masterly defense of philosophy from al-*Ghazali's attack upon it in *The Incoherence of the Philosophers*; among other things, he accused the latter of wholly misunderstanding the central question of the attributes of God and in what way He could be said to possess such faculties as speech and sight.

Averroës's views did not depart wholly from Islamic orthodoxy: he accepted that religious law constituted the only truth for both philosopher and layman, while asserting that "philosophy is the companion and foster-sister of the Shari'a" (Islamic religious law). Moreover, he considered Islam to have superseded Judaism and Christianity, and that its law was superior to Greek law because it had been prophetically revealed. However, his refusal to accept what was contradicted by demonstration, his rejection (based on Aristotelian principles) of creation out of nothing, and his antipathy to the orthodox clerics of his time (whom he likened to the sophists of Plato's day), all earned him the enmity of the religious establishment, which also controlled the legal system.

In his political philosophy he adopted the views of Plato, which he considered valid for an Islamic state, too. Taking happiness as the highest good, he was moved to criticize certain conventions, such as the low position assigned to women in Islam. Such unhindered critical speculation about matters popularly considered immutable and unquestionable served to further arouse hostility against him.

An alliance of traditional jurists and theologians, backed by the reflexively fanatical mob, succeeded in getting Averroës stripped of high office and banished to Lucena in 1195; the Almohads remained sympathetic to him but were obliged to appease public opinion at a time when the state required the undivided loyalty of its people to help face external threats. His writings were burned and a prohibition was placed on all studies not directly connected with religious law. He was later recalled, however, to the caliph's presence, and after his death in Marrakesh his body was transferred back to Córdoba.

C. Genequand, *Ibn Rushd's Metaphysics*, 1986.
S. Harvey, *Averroës on the Principle of Nature*, 1977.

AVICENNA (Abu Ali al-Husayn ibn Abd Allah ibn Sina; 980–1037), Persian philosopher, physician, and scientist. Born in Bukhara, Avicenna demonstrated his energy, prodigious memory, and exceptional intelligence at an early age; By the time he was ten he had memorized the Koran and soon outgrew the tutors his father employed to teach him; he then pursued his own course of studies into Islamic law, medicine, and metaphysics until the age of eighteen. He mastered these subjects with ease, claiming difficulty only with metaphysics: he read *Aristotle's *Metaphysics* forty times without understanding it, but eventually chanced on a commentary by al-*Farabi which illuminated the work for him.

His philosophical output notwithstanding, it was as a man of medicine that he was to be most renowned in Europe, where translations of his works into Latin led to his being called "Prince of the Physicians." Within Persia he had already made his name in this field by the age of twenty-one, when he cured the Samanid Prince Nuh ibn Mansur and was rewarded with access to the extensive royal library. When the Samanids were overthrown by Mahmud of Ghazna in one of the Turko-Persian conflicts that characterized that turbulent age, he fled to the court of Shams ad-Dawlah in Hamadan; there he began his encyclopedic *Book of Healing*, a massive treatise covering logic, the natural sciences, geometry, astronomy, arithmetic, music, and metaphysics.

This magnum opus was later abridged into the *Book of Salvation* by its author. Also dating from this period is Avicenna's best known work, the *Canon of Medicine*, a masterful scholarly synthesis presenting the theories and diagnostic techniques contained both in the works of the Greek doctors of the Roman imperial age and in the writings of other Arab physicians (Avicenna had lost his own clini-

Avicenna at work

cal notes while traveling); it is perhaps the single most famous book in the history of medical literature and was considered authoritative for several centuries.

Avicenna survived numerous intrigues against him at the court of Hamadan (which even led to his imprisonment at one time) and was appointed vizier in addition to his role as personal physician to the prince. While his days were filled with court duties, he devoted his nights to the composition of his writings and to general philosophical and scientific discussions with his disciples; these nights were generally accompanied by musical performances and carousing. Only his incredible constitution allowed him to live a life that would have exhausted any ordinary individual.

His philosophical debt to Muhammad al-Farabi was always evident in his philosophical works which, fusing Aristotelian and Neoplatonic elements, achieved a clarity that earlier philosophers had not. Those works included the first one on Aristotle in Persian, which was written while Avicenna was accompanying Prince Ala ad-Dawlah of Isfahan (in whose service he found refuge after Shams ad-Dawlah's death in 1022) on a military campaign. It was during campaigning that Avicenna contracted a stomach disorder, exacerbated from exhaustion, from which he died.

In attempting to found a discernibly oriental philosophy, Avicenna was the progenitor of the mystical theosophy which imbued subsequent Islamic philosophy. His *Book of Directives and Remarks* described the mystical path culminating in the direct and uninterrupted vision of God; his Supreme Being was characterized by both necessity and complete unity, from whom emanated all other being. His views were roundly attacked as misleading, dangerous, and heretical by al-*Ghazali, but translations of part of his philosophical endeavor into Latin in the twelfth century blended with Saint *Augustine's writings to significantly inform European scholasticism.

D. B. Burrell, *Knowing the Unknowable God: Ibn Sina, Maimonides, Aquinas*, 1986.

D. Gutas, *Avicenna and the Aristotelian Tradition*, 1988.

S. Kemal, *The Poetics of al-Farabi and Avicenna*, 1991.

B

BAB, THE (Mirza Ali Muhammad; 1819 or 1820–1850), religious reformer and leader; founder of Babism, the precursor of the Baha'i religion. Ali Muhammad, a descendant of the prophet *Muhammad, was born into the traditional Shiite Muslim community. Shiites had religious leaders, *imams*, who ruled over them in the distant past. The last imam was said to have died in 819; he was followed by a series of "Hidden Imams," whose identity was unknown. As the millennium of the last imam's death approached, Muslim mystics foretold the birth of a new imam who would revolutionize the faith. Ali Muhammad, whose birth coincided with the 1000th anniversary of the death of the last imam, was considered a fulfillment of the prophecy.

Ali Muhammad was born in Shiraz, Persia; his father, a cloth merchant, died when he was three so Ali Muhammad was raised by an uncle. He was an intelligent child, given to religious speculation and meditation. At seventeen he entered the family business, but spent a year in Iraq visiting Shiite shrines. At Karbala, Haj Sayyid Kazin, head of the Shaykhi movement, introduced him to the mystic rituals and beliefs of that sect. The meeting of the two men had a marked influence on Ali Muhammad. Although he returned to Shiraz and married in 1842, he frequently visited the neighboring forests to meditate and pray. In 1844 he declared himself the Bab, or Gate.

This declaration has been given two interpretations: he believed himself to be the precursor of the Hidden Imam whose arrival was imminent; he regarded himself as that Hidden Imam, a belief which developed throughout his career until, in prison, he declared himself a manifestation of God.

The first person to whom the Bab declared himself was Mullah Hussayn, who was convinced of the Bab's transcendental knowledge and was staggered by the intensity of a book, the *Kittab-al-Awwal* (The First Book), that the Bab had written. Whereas many ridiculed the Bab, Mullah Hussayn remained an impassioned disciple and had the title, Babu'l-Bab (Gate to the Gate) conferred on him. The two gathered a significant following led by eighteen foremost disciples. Adherents of the growing sect became known as Babis. That same year the Bab made a pilgrimage to Mecca. Before going, he wrote to the Sharif of Mecca, declaring himself to be the *Mahdi*, or Muslim messiah.

Both the government and the clergy regarded the Bab as a threat to civil order. Many Babis claimed that since his appearance, the laws of the Koran were no longer valid. Women abandoned the veil and other symbols of male dominance, claiming that they were now equal with male adherents. The Bab was arrested and brought to Shiraz, where he denied his claim to being the precursor of the Hidden Imam. He later explained his repudiation in a letter, saying that he was not the Gate to the Hidden Imam but to God Himself.

The Bab escaped to Isfahan, where the Christian governor, a known opponent of the regime, offered him sanctuary and even an army to defend himself; while he accepted asylum, he refused military assistance. At the same time, he did not dissuade his followers from bearing arms in self-defense. In Isfahan, the Bab established his religious ascendancy

The Baha'i Temple on Mount Carmel, Israel, standing over the tomb of the Bab

> I am that divine fire which God kindles on the Day of Resurrection, by which all will be resurrected and revived. Then, either they shun away from it or enter Paradise through it.
>
> **From a sermon of the Bab**

by claiming that he could, in just three hours, write one thousand sentences on any topic and produced a brilliant commentary on a particularly obscure portion of the Koran as proof.

Following the death of the governor in 1847, the Bab was imprisoned. According to Shiite tradition he finally recanted his claim to be the Mahdi in a letter, which is still preserved in the Iranian Parliament. This letter has not, however, been authenticated and its contents, even if genuine, might still reflect the Bab's earlier uses of double-talk to save his life.

The Babis were not shaken by the imprisonment of their leader; many violent clashes with the government ensued in which thousands of Babis met their death. The Persian government finally concluded that only the Bab's death would end the uprisings which threatened the regime's stability. In Tabriz the Bab was sentenced to death for apostasy. That night, his followers congregated around him in his cell. One follower, Mirza Muhammad Ali, begged the Bab to be allowed to share in his martyrdom; his request was granted.

The next day the two men were dragged through the streets of Tabriz. First, Mirza Muhammad Ali was suspended from a parapet with ropes and shot by a firing squad. The Bab was then suspended but when the smoke cleared, the ropes had been cut and the Bab was nowhere to be seen. After a careful search, he was found in a nearby barracks, unscathed. Again he was taken for execution, and his bullet-ridden body was cast outside the city walls. His followers bribed local officials to have the body removed for secret burial. Some years later the Bab was reinterred on Mount Carmel in Palestine. In Haifa, a magnificent shrine today stands over the tomb. A disciple of the Bab, the Baha'ullah, later combined the teachings of the Bab with his own beliefs to form the Baha'i faith. This claims to incorporate the best of all religions, teaching the unity of all mankind, without regard to race, color, or creed. W. M. Miller, *The Bahai Faith: Its History and Teachings*, 1974.

BABUR (Zahir-ud-Din Muhammad; 1483–1530), first Mogul emperor of India. Babur ("lion"), a Barlas Turk, was the son of the ruler of Fergana in present-day Afghanistan. He had an impressive lineage: on his father's side he was descended from *Tamerlane; on his mother's side, he was distantly related to *Genghis Khan. Upon succeeding his father as

ruler of Fergana in 1494, Babur set off to capture Tamerlane's old realm of Transoxiana, an important trade route between India, China, and Babylonia. Although only a child, Babur's congeniality and his skill in resolving disputes among his supporters earned him a respectable reputation, allowing him to attract a considerable army of local mercenaries. Between 1494 and 1504 he fought the Moguls and Uzbeks to defend Fergana and conquer Samarkand, Tamerlane's capital. He managed to occupy Samarkand for one hundred days in 1501, until his defeat by the Uzbek leader Shaibani Khan at Sar-i-pul forced Babur to retreat to Kabul. Still a teenager, he later wrote how he sobbed at the loss of Tamerlane's city. All attempts to recapture the city (1511–1512), as well as his native Fergana, failed.

Despite his inability to regain his realm, Babur did not abandon his dream of establishing an empire. Finding Tamerlane's old lands inaccessible, Babur focused his attention on India in the south and occupied Kandahar in 1522. Noting Babur's success, Alam Khan, uncle of Ibrahim Lodi, the sultan of Delhi, invited Babur to join Lodi of Lahore, Daulat Khan, and himself in a coalition against his nephew. Babur agreed and began his conquest of northern India with war against Ibrahim and the Rajputs (landowners). Ibrahim was killed at Paniput in 1526 and Babur proceeded to occupy Delhi and Agra. The following year he vanquished the Rajput ruler, Rana Sanga, at Khanua, and in 1529 routed the Afghans in the Battle of the Gogra, adding Bihar and Bengal to his empire. Babur now had complete control of northern India. He styled himself Padishah, "ruler of kings."

Babur's early failures can be attributed to his young age when he assumed his father's throne. Although he was often commended for his intelligence, his most important decisions were made at the behest of his grandmother, Isan. Throughout much of his childhood he was dictated to and forced to assume positions and roles he did not want. Babur was married to the princess Ayishah when he was only five years old. The marriage was an unhappy one as Babur was infatuated with Baburi, a young boy serving in his retinue. Babur later married Maham, mother of his heir *Humayun, but this marriage also proved unhappy because of his affair with Bibi Marika, the daughter of Shah Mansur.

Despite the immense power he wielded toward the end of his life, Babur maintained simple tastes, preferring to ponder Islamic mystical texts than to amass great wealth. Upon conquering Agra, he received untold priceless jewels as gifts, among them the Koh-i-noor diamond (now part of the crown jewels of Great Britain). Babur kept only the smallest portion for himself, distributing the remainder among his soldiers and retinue.

Babur died suddenly at Agra in 1530. His empire, though immense, had yet to be consolidated. Humayun was unable to preserve the realm from foreign incursions, leaving the task of creating the

Mogul state to his son, *Akbar. The events of Babur's reign are recorded in his diaries, which have been preserved in translation until the present day.

W. Erskine, *India under Babur and Humayun*, 1972.
H. Lamb, *Babur the Tiger, First of the Great Moguls*, 1961.

BACH, JOHANN SEBASTIAN (1685–1750), German composer. Bach's testimony to the world is the music he wrote and not the story of his life, a story of travels from court to court, of securing musical positions for longer or shorter terms, and of writing sublime music. Born in Eisenach in central Germany, he received a sound humanistic and theological education at the Lateinschule. He came from a musical family, both his father and grandfather having been musicians. His parents had died by the time he was ten and Johann Sebastian and his brother Jacob moved in with their elder brother Johann Christoph, the organist at Ohrdruf, near Eisenach, where Bach studied keyboard and enjoyed a wide curriculum at the local Lyceum, comprising religion, reading, writing, mathematics, singing, natural sciences, and history.

In 1700 Bach moved north to Lüneburg, thirty miles from Hamburg, where he continued his education. His next stop was Arnstadt, where he was appointed organist at the Neukirche (which in 1935 was renamed after Bach). His duties at the time were very light and he was left with considerable time for composing and organ-playing. Bach did not yet write elaborate music because the musicians at the church were far from professional. Bach, however, tended to alienate his semicompetent musicians with his rude remarks. There were also complaints that he was not a good disciplinarian, took little interest in the choir (even allowing his girl cousin to sing in it at a time when women were barred), had improvised at the organ during hymn-singing, and had even slipped out during sermons. Nevertheless, Bach's name was becoming well-known and several positions were offered to him; his next one was in Mühlhausen, where he also began to teach music.

Bach then went to Weimar to be organist at the duke of Weimar's court and, later, *konzertmeister* as well, which required him to compose a monthly cantata. He wrote most of his organ work at Weimar. From the court in Weimar Bach moved in 1717 to the court in Köthen, where the prince was a young man who loved and understood music. Bach's final move, to Leipzig in 1723, was not a happy one for him in certain respects. He considered it a step downward on the social scale and had little respect for his employers, who treated him as a mediocrity and were angered by his refusal to teach Latin as part of his duties. In addition seven of the thirteen children born to him in Leipzig died and, toward the end, he began to lose his eyesight. There were also the positive aspects, which attracted him. Bach went to Leipzig as the cantor at

the famous Thomaskirche and as the local civic director of music, one of the most prestigious positions in German musical life at the time. Bach's duties in Leipzig were much more varied and demanding than his activities in the previous courts in which he was employed. Moreover there was more financial security in Leipzig and the city itself, a flourishing commercial town, was more interesting to live in than any of his previous homes. As cantor Bach was responsible for the music of the four main churches in Leipzig, as well as for other musical activities in the city. He was also supposed to provide, for an extra fee, music for weddings and funerals. During Bach's first weeks in Leipzig there was a funeral for the postmaster's widow and it was probably for this occasion that Bach wrote the now famous motet *Jesu meine Freunde*. The Leipzig years were filled with musical duties of varied scope but most of Bach's time was devoted to composing works for special occasions ranging from funerals to birthdays to weddings, as well as writing congratulatory cantatas and sacred compositions for church.

In 1729 Bach was appointed director of the *collegium musicum*, a position that brought major changes in the composer's activities in the city. The *collegium*, which had been founded by Telemann in 1702, was an association of professional musicians and university students who gave regular weekly concerts. Together with the sacred music which he continued to compose, he could now embark on writing more instrumental works.

Bach continued to compose and perform until his death, although in the last few years of his life, as his health began to deteriorate, his musical activities decreased. In 1747 he was invited by *Frederick the Great to visit the court at Potsdam and on his arrival the king exclaimed with delight, "Gentlemen! Old Bach has arrived." He had to examine the king's piano and organs, and on his return to Leipzig included a theme written by the king in a trio, which he sent to the king as a "musical offering."

Bach died in Leipzig; his second wife, Anna Magdalena, who had also been his collaborator in writing out his music, survived him by a decade, dying in poverty in 1760. By his two wives he had twenty children, of whom nine survived him; several of them were themselves famous musicians and composers.

Bach's musical output was immense. This most prolific musical genius wrote in almost every musical form except opera. His chamber music contains some of the pinnacles of the genre; the keyboard music is demanding and rewarding for listener and performer alike, but it is above all the vocal music — the cantatas and especially the passions and the masses — that sets Bach apart from any other composer. Listening to the *Saint Matthew Passion* or to the *B minor Mass* is always a riveting emotional experience.

Like many composers who did not enjoy great success in their lifetime, Bach's music emerged in all its profundity only many decades after his death; only then did composers begin to acknowledge Bach's greatness. Charles Gounod said that "Bach is a colossus of Rhodes, beneath whom all musicians pass and will continue to pass. Mozart is the most beautiful, Rossini the most brilliant, but Bach is the most comprehensive: he said all there is to say." Claude *Debussy added that Bach is "a benevolent God, to whom musicians should offer a prayer before setting to work so that they may be preserved from mediocrity." Bach himself once said that he has "always kept one end in view, namely, with all good will to conduct a well-regulated church music to the honor of God."

Bach's music was rediscovered in the early nineteenth century and has never left the world's concert stages and recording studios since. In the last few decades, with the emergence of the so-called early music movement in which musicians began to perform baroque music on instruments which sound as close as possible to the instruments of the time, the music of Bach has come to be appreciated in a new light: no longer big symphonic sounds for the suites or the *Brandenburg Concerti*, no longer the grand piano for the *Goldberg Variations*, but the more elegant sound of the harpsichord instead.

M. Boyd, *Bach*, 1983.

W. Felix, *Johann Sebastian Bach*, 1985.

A. Schweitzer, *J. S. Bach* , 2 vols., 1935.

BACON, FRANCIS (1561–1626), English philosopher, statesman, and essayist. He was born in London, the son of Sir Nicholas Bacon, lord keeper of the Great Seal and lord chancellor. Educated at Trinity College, Cambridge, in 1576 Bacon was admitted to Gray's Inn to study law, becoming a barrister in 1582. From 1584 he was a member of Parliament; seeking to advance himself at court, he offended Queen *Elizabeth by his opposition in the Commons to the government's tax policies of 1593.

His new acquaintance, Robert Devereux, earl of Essex, pressed for Bacon's appointment as attorney general in 1594; however, the position was granted to Sir Edward Coke, who became Bacon's long-standing rival. Essex, as Bacon's patron and one of the queen's favorites, recommended him for various posts at court, but his efforts were unsuccessful. Elizabeth later relented and made Bacon her "Learned Counsel Extraordinary." The appointment brought him little recognition or financial benefit, and necessitated his involvement in the condemnation of his friend and patron, the Earl of Essex. In 1600, when Essex failed to suppress the Earl of Tyrone's rebellion in Ireland and subsequently returned against orders, Bacon participated in the prosecution of Essex at a disciplinary tribunal initiated by the queen. When Essex was arraigned for high treason in 1601 following his attempted insurrection, Bacon was again requested to take part in the prosecution. Essex was proclaimed guilty, sentenced to death, and executed. Three years after the trial Bacon defended

- I have taken all knowledge to be my province.
- If a man will begin with certainties, he shall end in doubts, but if he will be content to begin with doubts, he shall end in certainties.
- There are four classes of Idols which beset men's minds. To these, for distinction's sake, I have assigned names — calling the first class, Idols of the Tribe; the second, Idols of the Cave; the third, Idols of the Marketplace; the fourth, Idols of the Theater.
- Nature to be commanded, must be obeyed.
- Nuptial love maketh mankind; friendly love perfecteth it; but wanton love corrupteth and embaseth it.
- Some books are to be tasted, others to be swallowed, and some few to be chewed and digested.
- He that will not apply new remedies must expect new evils: for time is the greatest innovator.

Francis Bacon

his behavior in his *Apologie in certaine imputations concerning the late Earl of Essex*.

Bacon's critics have held that he was a faithless friend who deserted Essex in his hour of need; However, others have expressed the view that he had no choice but to obey the commands of the queen and privy council; to refuse to participate in the trial would have resulted in Bacon's own condemnation and could have been of no benefit to Essex.

Bacon was knighted in 1603, when *James I came to the throne. He wrote numerous letters offering his services to the new king and demonstrating his desire to prove himself a loyal subject with no ulterior motive. He was appointed one of the commissioners for the union of Scotland and England; king's counsel (1604); solicitor general (1607); and attorney general (1613). Following Bacon's proposal to that effect, his rival, Coke, was removed from his post as chief justice of the common pleas and appointed to the King's Bench. The two men became embroiled in the controversy over the relationship between king and state; Bacon championed the royal prerogative, while Coke spoke out for the common law and an independent judiciary.

Bacon forged relationships with the king's favorites, Robert Carr, earl of Somerset, and George Villiers, earl of Buckingham. These associations, together with persistent efforts to serve the king and his letters of self-recommendation, ensured the progress of his career. After Coke's dismissal Bacon became lord keeper of the Great Seal in 1617. He was subsequently appointed lord chancellor (1618),

Francis Bacon

raised to the peerage as Baron Verulam (1618), and created Viscount Saint Albans (1621).

Bacon enjoyed a prominent position in court and society. He was a lavish host and industrious in his management of the royal finances. But in 1621 the House of Lords, on allegations initiated by Coke, charged him with bribery. He confessed to general guilt, was deprived of the Great Seal, and condemned to confinement in the Tower of London. He remained there for only a few days, but after his release was banished from parliament and prevented from holding any state office. Despite his attempts to regain favor with the king, Bacon never received a full pardon.

Finding himself excluded from public service, he concentrated his energies on producing and expanding his philosophical, literary, and professional writings. It was his ambition to create a new philosophy to replace that of *Aristotle, based on a correct interpretation of nature. Rejecting Aristotle's system of deductive logic, he relied on inductive methods based on all possible knowledge and looked for causes not only in science but also in morality and politics. He has been called the creator of scientific induction.

His principal philosophical works are the *Advancement of Learning* (1605); the *Novum Organum* (1620); and *De Augmentis* (1623), an enlarged Latin edition of the *Advancement of Learning*. The most important of Bacon's literary works is the *Essays*, first published in 1597 and issued, in final

form, as fifty-eight essays in 1625. In these "dispersed meditations," as they were subtitled, Bacon attempted to interpret human experience and invited the reader to examine rather than accept ideas. Other significant literary publications include *De Sapientia Veterum* (1609), the *History of Henry the Seventh* (1622), and *Apothegms New and Old* (1625). His longest and most important professional treatises are *Elements of the Common Law* (1630) and *Reading on the Statute of Uses* (1642).

Bacon's death followed a cold caught while stuffing a fowl in order to observe the effect of cold on the preservation of flesh.

F. H. Anderson, *Bacon: His Life and Thought*, 1962.
A. Dodd, *Bacon's Personal Life Story*, 1986.
A. Quinton, *Francis Bacon*, 1990.

BADEN-POWELL, ROBERT STEPHENSON SMYTH (Baron Baden-Powell of Gilwell; B-P: 1857–1941), soldier and founder of the world scout movement. He was born in London, educated at Charterhouse, and earned a commission in the Thirteenth Hussars cavalry regiment, serving in India, Afghanistan, and South Africa. In 1884–1885 he pioneered the use of observation balloons in wars in the Sudan and Bechuanaland. He was assistant military secretary in South Africa and Malta, and served in a number of campaigns in Africa. At one time, he did some spying, disguised as a mad butterfly enthusiast. With net in hand, he surveyed military fortifications in Germany, Tunisia, and Algeria. At the end of each day, he drew the butterflies he had captured but inside the sketches were layouts of the fortifications and the size and location of their guns. He later described these days in a book, *My Adventures as a Spy* (1915).

In the Boer War he was a general in the British army. Even then he accomplished a reconnaissance trip into the Drakenburg Mountains, dressed in ragged clothing and wearing a beard. He spoke to the local farmers and gathered much invaluable information as well as drawing maps that were of great importance to the British campaign. His epic defense of Mafeking with a small garrison, which the Boers were unable to capture during a siege which lasted from October 1899 to May 1900, made him a national hero. The relief of Mafeking was the signal for wild rejoicing in Britain and the name passed into the language to mean extravagant behavior by crowds.

From 1900 to 1903, holding the rank of inspector general, Baden-Powell organized the South African constabulary. He recruited and trained men, helping them to develop self-reliance, resourcefulness, and courage. The success of this program served as the model for his later work with the Boy Scouts. Returning to England, he was inspector general of cavalry and retired from the army in 1910.

Baden-Powell is chiefly remembered as the founder of the scout movement. His early experience in reconnaissance had been the basis of his

BY AND ABOUT
ROBERT BADEN-POWELL

- All well, four hours' bombardment. One dog killed. (Dispatch at outset of siege of Mafeking)
- Beneath the British flag, all men are free.
- Country first, self second.
- Make yourselves good scouts and good rifle shots in order to protect the women and children of your country if it should ever become necessary.
- We have all got to die some day; a few years more or less of our lives don't matter much if by dying a year or two sooner than we should otherwise do from disease we can help to save the flag of our country from going under.

Robert Baden-Powell

- Baden-Powell would have made an ideal headmaster in a Victorian adventure story. A ripper when the going was good but an alarming man to have as your enemy.

Thomas Pakenham

book *Aids to Scouting* (1899) but this term gained new meaning with his proposal for a Boy Scout movement. Scout troops began to spring up all over England and to aid the organizers, he wrote *Scouting for Boys* (1908).

In 1909 Baden-Powell was knighted. In the same year, with the assistance of his sister, Agnes, he founded the Girl Guides, later known in the United States as Girl Scouts.

At the insistence of King Edward VII, Baden-Powell retired from the army to devote his time to the scouting movement. His wife, Olave, (1889–1977) also did a great deal to promote the Girl Guides).

Baden-Powell initiated the concept of young people, boys and girls, joining a voluntary brotherhood or sisterhood under the guidance and leadership of adults. In 1916 he broadened the movement by organizing the Wolf Cubs in Great Britain (Cub Scouts in the United States), for boys under the age of eleven. In 1920, the first International Boy Scout jamboree was held in London, and he was acclaimed Chief Scout of the World. He encouraged Juliette Gordon Dow of Savannah, Georgia, to bring the principles of girl scouts and girl guides to the United States in 1912. Lady Baden-Powell was instrumental in internationalizing the movement by arranging for the first International Conference of Girl Scouts and Girl Guides in 1920. In 1929 Baden-Powell was created a baron for his service to scouting.

His dedication to the Scout movement — which ultimately became international — was expressed

through his books. These works serve as a reference even today. They include *The Wolf Cubs Handbook* (1916); *Girl Guiding* (1917); *Aids to Scoutmastership* (1920); *What Scouts Can Do* (1921); *Rovering to Success* (1922); *Scouting and Youth Movements* (1929); *Paddle Your Own Canoe* (1933); *Adventures and Accidents* (1934); *African Adventure* (1936); and *Birds and Beasts in Africa*. The last two books, as well as his autobiography, *Lessons of a Lifetime* (1933) were written in Kenya, where he had moved due to ill-health and where he died.

E. Edwin, *Baden-Powell*, 1959.
E. E. Reynolds, *Baden-Powell*, 1957.

BAIRD, JOHN LOGIE (1888–1946), father of television. He was born in Helensburgh, Scotland, and educated as an engineer at the Royal Technical College and at Glasgow University. After a short, unsuccessful engineering career Baird developed the basic theory that would ultimately result in workable television. Strapped for cash, he advertised for assistance in the London *Times* in June 1923. A motion picture entrepreneur, Wilfred E. L. Day, realized the merit of Baird's idea and provided financial backing and equipment. Baird filed the first of his many patents in 1923. His Flying Spot, patented in 1926, allowed transmission of real television images with halftones, which had not previously been available. He patented color television in 1928, and in 1941 applied for a patent to cover his invention of three-dimensional color television, which viewers found difficult to watch, particularly if they were not directly in front of the image. Although he patented many inventions, Baird deliberately kept his Super Sensitive Photocell a secret from his competitors.

Baird wrote numerous scientific articles. It appears, however, that he had a preference for disseminating his ideas and technical inventions through public demonstration. In 1925 he set up a simple television apparatus for three weeks in Selfridge's, a London store. It was reported that the images were "recognizable, if rather blurred." By 1927 he was able to transmit a television picture that was recognizable and had steady images; they traveled by telephone line from his London laboratory to Glasgow, Scotland, a distance of 438 miles. He received the first license to broadcast television from the British Broadcasting Corporation in 1926. The subject of his first transmission was Bill, his ventriloquist's dummy, and a young office boy. In 1928 he gave the first public demonstration of color television and one observer said that "the illusion is very striking." By 1930 he was telecasting two and a half hours a week with sound.

In October 1931 Baird toured the United States and visited the laboratories of General Electric and Bell Telephone to observe their research techniques and progress in the field of television. Not only was Baird not impressed with the Americans' work, but he was quoted as saying that he saw "no hope for television by means of cathode ray bulbs." Returning to England, he continued his research. A disastrous fire completely destroyed his laboratory in 1936. After it was rebuilt he continued the development of television based on his original ideas and incorporated developments made by his American rivals. By 1939 Baird was forced to recant his views of 1931 when he demonstrated his color television on a cathode ray tube; that transmission covered a distance of two miles.

In a related development in 1926 Baird invented Noctovision, which utilized infrared rays to make objects visible in the dark.

A. Abramson, *The History of Television, 1880– 1941*, 1987.

BAJAZET (BAYEZID) I (c.1354–1403), sultan of the emerging Ottoman Empire; elder son of Sultan *Murad I. During his father's reign he served as the governor of Anatolia, where his remarkable military exploits earned him the epithet Thunderbolt. Bajazet ascended the throne following the assassination of Murad by Serbian insurgents in 1389. His first act as monarch was to have his younger brother Yakub strangled by a bow string to prevent any attempt to usurp the throne. This fratricide was only the first in a long line of royal murders of their siblings by Ottoman emperors, a tradition that, at one point, would be enacted as law.

Bajazet avenged his father's death by conducting a massacre of the Serbian population of Kosovo. But rather than encourage further Serbian hostility he concluded an alliance with the Serbian leader Stephen Bulcovic by which Serbia received autonomy within the empire. Bajazet's amicable relationship with Bulcovic endured throughout his reign; Bulcovic, in turn, remained a constant ally.

Bajazet was an impulsive monarch who would rather cavort with the women and boys of his harem than conduct affairs of state. He was fascinated with Islamic mystical philosophy and had a private chamber built in the Bursa mosque where he could meditate and confer with Muslim philosophers, often at the expense of his subjects' well-being.

At the same time, Bajazet was a proficient militarist who proved his ability by frustrating several threats to his realm. Revolts in the Balkans and Anatolia were crushed and local rulers were exiled. In 1391 Byzantine emperor, John V Paleologue was subdued; his heir, Manuel, was made a vassal of Bajazet and given the title Groom of the Chamber. Constantinople itself capitulated after a seven-month siege; the terms of the city's surrender included the establishment of an Islamic court in the city. In 1395 Bajazet declared himself Heir to the Caesars. To solidify his claim Bajazet planned the murder of the entire Paleologue family but was discouraged by his advisers, who convinced him, rather, to blind and maim surviving Byzantine dignitaries.

Christian Europe, led by King Sigismund of Hungary, felt threatened by Islamic expansion under the Ottomans. An army of crusaders, led by Hungary

and Venice, crossed the Danube to attack the Turks, only to find no opposition awaiting them. The crusaders easily advanced through the Balkans, reaching Nicopolis in Bulgaria. There, Bajazet was waiting; he easily defeated the crusader forces and returned to Turkey to complete the absorption of Constantinople into his empire.

The tide, however, was about to turn against Bajazet. The Mongol conqueror, *Tamerlane, claimed Anatolia as his own in 1399. His championship of local rulers expelled by Bajazet won him the support of the populace; Bajazet was no match for Tamerlane. On July 20, 1402, his armies were destroyed and Bajazet was taken prisoner. He died in captivity the following year. Many touching stories are told about Bajazet's captivity and belittlement by Tamerlane. He was kept chained in an iron cage, sometimes serving as Tamerlane's footstool. Although many historians attribute Bajazet's death to an apoplectic seizure, there is ample reason to accept the traditional story that Bajazet put an end to his own life.

Were it not for the escape of Bajazet's sons Suleiman and Mehmed, Bajazet's tragic death would have signaled the end of the Ottoman Empire, but the two brothers waged a bloody war of succession and in 1413 Mehmed was able to assume the title of sultan.

J. P. D. Kinross, *The Ottoman Centuries: The Rise and Fall of the Turkish Empire*, 1978.

BAJAZET (BAYEZID) II (c.1447–1512), Ottoman emperor. The elder son of Emperor *Mehmed II, he was noted for his consolidation of Ottoman power and his infamous law whereby, upon assuming the throne, the new emperor was to dispose of his brothers and their children so as to insure an unsullied reign. Although Mehmed did not appoint a successor, it was assumed he favored his younger son, Jem, over Bajazet. Both filled administrative positions as provincial governors but Bajazet was an intellectual who avoided combat in favor of academic pursuits; Jem was more inclined to war. Mehmed's grand vizier endorsed Jem's claim to the throne, but Bajazet, who had forged matrimonial ties with leading janissaries, received their support and assumed the throne.

In the ensuing civil war Jem declared himself emperor at Bursa, but his reign lasted only eighteen days. Bajazet proved himself a capable military commander and Jem was forced to flee. He did not want to kill his brother, but Bajazet rejected Jem's proposal that the empire be partitioned between them. Bajazet suggested that Jem live in retirement in Jerusalem. Jem waived Bajazet's offer and sought sanctuary with the Knights Hospitalers stationed on the island of Rhodes.

Until his sudden death in 1495, Jem remained a threat to Bajazet. Both the pope and France saw in Jem an ally to lead them in a successful crusade to regain Jerusalem. Although nothing came of these plans, Bajazet remained alert to the impending threat and did little to consolidate his father's conquests, refusing to lead his armies to a distance where his authority could be challenged (in fact, Bajazet was the first Ottoman emperor not to lead his armies into battle). Nonetheless, he succeeded in subduing Bosnia (1483) and extended his authority to the banks of the Dniester (1484) and from there to Crimea. A truce was signed with King *Matthias Corvinus of Hungary, securing his northern European boundary.

Much of Bajazet's reign was spent improving the economic situation of the empire, ailing as a result of his father's policies. He put an end to the devaluation of the currency and restored private lands that had been confiscated. When King *Ferdinand and Queen *Isabella of Spain expelled their Jewish community in 1492, Bajazet welcomed the refugees to Turkey, recognizing them as the nucleus of a much-needed middle class.

Bajazet's reign witnessed the rise in Safavid Persia of the mystical Muslims, the Sufis; many of the Turcoman tribesmen in Anatolia were influenced by this movement. Known as the Kizil Besh ("red hats"), they threatened both the Ottoman and Mameluke empires, leading Bajazet to make border concessions to the Mamelukes in Syria to rid himself of these tribesmen.

Only after Jem's death was Bajazet able to focus his attention on the empire's principal rival, Venice. The Turkish navy was expanded, and Bajazet gained control of the eastern Adriatic coast, conquering Lepanto, Modon, Coron, and Navarino. Peace was signed with Venice in 1503, but Venice was never able to regain its former glory because the vast Ottoman navy now controlled the Mediterranean basin.

In his final years, Bajazet sought to defeat the Safavids. At the time he favored his son Ahmed, who shared his temperament, as his successor, but when Ahmed adopted the practices of the Kizil Besh, Bajazet was forced to recognize his headstrong son *Selim as heir. Before the war with the Safavids was concluded, Selim deposed his father and exiled him to Demotika. Bajazet died en route; it is supposed that Selim had him poisoned. His legacy to Selim was a mobile army and a dominant navy.

J. P. D. Kinross, *The Ottoman Centuries: The Rise and Fall of the Turkish Empire*, 1978.

BAKUNIN, MIKHAIL ALEXANDROVICH

(1814–1876), Russian anarchist and writer. He was born near Tver to an aristocratic family. After completing his studies at the Saint Petersburg Military Academy in 1832 he enlisted in the army, but resigned his commission three years later, frustrated by failing to get a promotion. He planned to study in Germany, but soon after his arrival there in 1841, discovered that the revolutionary idealism debated in coffee houses and street corners was far more engrossing than the classroom. His own philosophy can be traced to the fashionable philosophers of the

Mikhail Bakunin

period such as Pierre Proudhon, who postulated that an ideal society must entail total personal freedom, and Karl *Marx, who advocated revolution to overthrow the existing social order. Taking Marx's hypothesis to its extreme, Bakunin claimed that a new society can only be formed after the existing society has been annihilated. "The urge for destruction is also a creative urge," an essential dogma in Bakunin's later writings, was already posited in his first published article in 1842.

Seeking to advance his revolutionary studies, Bakunin moved to Paris where, with his magnetic personality and aristocratic background, he became a prominent figure in the radical community. His doctrines, although still unclear, caused considerable concern to the Russian ambassador, who arranged that his holdings be confiscated and his title revoked unless he return to Russia to face charges of sedition. The French government, not wishing to upset its Russian allies, yielded to the ambassador's petitions and expelled Bakunin from Paris.

Returning to Germany, Bakunin became a prominent spokesman for the establishment of a federation uniting the Slavic peoples of the Russian, Austrian, and Ottoman empires. Only after the failure of the revolutionary fervor of 1848 did he advance the need for an international revolution uniting the proletariat of all nations. Competition and contention, he now believed, were the inherent result of even the most enlightened nationalism. He had witnessed how the old establishment — the ruling dynasties and the church — had exploited the xenophobic attitudes of the peasants to crush the short-lived liberal regimes.

For his role in the revolution in Dresden Bakunin was condemned to death. At the intervention of the liberal-minded King of Saxony, this sentence was commuted to life imprisonment and later to deportation to Russia. There, faced with intolerable prison conditions, he consented to sign a well-publicized confession describing his revolutionary activities and attributing them to his intense hatred of Germany. His ploy succeeded, and Bakunin's sentence was again commuted, this time to exile in Siberia. He was placed under the supervision of the regional governor, General Nicholas Muravayev-Amursky, himself a liberal who secretly shared many of Bakunin's beliefs. Furthermore, it seemed that Bakunin had actually moderated some of his radical opinions. Once again, he espoused his pan-Slavic ideology, and approached both the general and possibly even the czar proposing that they act as temporary dictator of his envisioned Slavic federation. After his marriage to a young Polish peasant in 1858, it seemed that Bakunin was ready to settle down. In fact, all the while, Bakunin carefully plotted his escape. With Muravayev's help, Bakunin was able to reach Japan. From there he sailed to the United States, eventually reaching London in 1861.

Over ten years of exile and imprisonment had not dampened any of Bakunin's personal charm, which had attracted so many followers. Furthermore, he had crystallized his political philosophy, a challenge to traditional socialist dogma. His writings are often rambling and incoherent, and many important elements of his ideas are the subject of much debate, but common to all interpretations is his belief that the means of production should become common property rather than state property as proposed by socialism. Workers would then form productive organizations rather than unions to promote efficiency. An anarchist state, according to Bakunin, is a federation of self-governing communities based on economic rather than national considerations. Although he considered the position of the worker to be central to this new order, others, including intellectuals, religious dissenters, socialists, communists and even criminals were also important. Bakunin loathed religion and often said that "even if God existed, it would be necessary to abolish him." He considered Satan to be the first revolutionary.

Although he differed in many important respects from communism and socialism, Bakunin continued to participate in their conferences and congresses, such as the International Alliance of Social Democrats in 1868 and the First International in 1872. Marx, however, was so perturbed by Bakunin's radical ideology that he had him expelled from the International for purportedly supporting a clandestine revolutionary circle. For the remainder of his life, Bakunin continued expounding his ideology of violent social upheaval to a small but fanatical group of followers.

Shortly after his death in 1876 the movement emerged as a potent force in Europe and America, primarily due to a wave of political assassinations. Among the victims were Czar *Alexander II, King Umberto of Italy, presidents Carnot of France and McKinley of the United States, and Empress Elizabeth of Austria. Although the Bolshevik victory in Russia led to a decline in Bakunin's popular appeal, many of his predictions regarding state socialism proved true. He forewarned of the dangers of a swollen bureaucracy and predicted that the atrocities committed by an eventual communist regime in Russia would even outdo those of the czar.

A. Kelly, *Bakunin*, 1982.
A. Masters, *Bakunin*, 1974.

BALBOA, VASCO NÚÑEZ DE   SEE NÚÑEZ DE BALBOA, VASCO.

BALZAC, HONORÉ DE (1799–1850), French author; a developer of the realistic novel. From his father Balzac absorbed his devotion to the Napoleonic era, writing as a young man that "what *Napoleon could not achieve with his sword, I shall accomplish with my pen"; A fascination with the occult, earned from his mother, suffuses many of his important works. His grandmother taught him cards (she would often let him win to provide him with pocket money) and told him Parisian gossip. He was born in Tours and when he was ten his parents enrolled him in the Collège de Vendôme, a prestigious institution run by radical priests who encouraged their students to read even those books censored by the government and church. There, Balzac was an unpopular and below-average student, but he once confided to a friendly priest how he relished being sent to the garret as punishment because it enabled him to read. In Vendôme he developed his ambivalent attitude toward the church, much influenced by the writings of *Voltaire and his own philosophy of the Christian occult. During the six years he spent there he was visited just once; he eventually returned home on the verge of mental collapse.

Soon after, his family moved to Paris and Balzac entered law school. Working in a law firm, he earned a reputation for humor rather than diligence, illustrated by a note sent to him: "Mr Balzac is requested not to come today as there is much work to be done." In law school, Balzac had several affairs with prostitutes and courtesans; although short, overweight, poorly groomed, naturally rude, and a sloppy dresser, he had piercing eyes and a romantic nature that overcame all his physical shortcomings. His most important liaison was with Mme. de Berny, a friend of his mother's with whom he maintained an amorous relationship throughout his life.

Despite his parents' protests, Balzac decided to abandon law for writing. His father provided a stipend for two years in return for 50 percent of the son's income and Balzac moved to a poorly furnished attic, where he began a compulsive regimen, writing twenty hours each day, subsisting on stale bread and as many as fifty cups of coffee. In winter, he wrote in bed because of the bitter cold. To relax he took lengthy walks, studying the common people he encountered. After a year, he produced a drama about Oliver *Cromwell so pitiable that he nearly returned to law; two novels produced in his second year were just as poor.

Honoré de Balzac - a contemporary photograph

Balzac was on the verge of abandoning writing when a friend offered to share 800 francs with him if he would write a trashy popular novel. Using the pseudonym Lord R'hoone, he wrote fifty pages per day; the resulting book, although of no literary merit, was immensely popular. He continued writing similar stories and also began accumulating debts by developing expensive tastes in food and clothes. In 1829 he founded a publishing firm with money his mother lent him on condition that he renounce his latest mistress, the duchess d'Abartes. The venture failed, however, because of Balzac's poor business sense.

Thirty years old and deeply in debt, he began his first serious novel, *Les Chouans* (1829), about a peasant uprising in Brittany. The novel was ignored by most of the critics, so Balzac turned to writing codes of behavior for the popular market. One such code, *La Physiologie du mariage*, published to cover a debt, became an instant success, with the result that *Les Chouans* gained widespread attention. Balzac finally won the acclaim he coveted and was befriended by other leading French authors such as Alexandre *Dumas, George Sand (with whom he is suspected of having had an affair) and Victor *Hugo. He continued to write at a remarkable rate; in 1831 alone he produced seventy-six novels, articles, and reviews, excluding the trashy novels he continued to write under various pseudonyms. His strict regimen demanded that he write at least fifteen printed pages per day, apart from the constant revisions he made on finished work. His revisions became the horror of printers, who went through at least ten revisions and often a lawsuit until Balzac was prepared to allow anything to be published.

In the following twenty years, Balzac produced many important works, among them *Le Père Goriot* in 1834, *La Fille aux yeux d'or* (a controversial study of lesbianism) in 1835 and the trilogy *Illusions perdues* between 1837 and 1843. Characters frequently reappear throughout his works, which fill over 100 volumes and which he called the Human Comedy, intended to portray "every situation in human life" in an "*Arabian Nights* of the Occident." His characters include exaggerated specimens from all sectors of French society; the upper class is lethargic, the middle class is pretentious, and the lower class lives in inescapable squalor.

Balzac cultivated many peculiarities for which he became famous: he spent enormous sums on his clothes, only to ruin them by wiping his mouth with his sleeve; he bought elaborate walking sticks with ornate gold knobs, one of which he claimed contained the nude portrait of a mistress. When writing, not even clothing was allowed to disturb him; he either wrote naked or in a monk's robe when cold. He also spent freely on expensive gifts for friends and mistresses, and in supporting his aged mother, who continued to nag him throughout his life. Even when ill, Balzac refused to forsake his writing.

To cover his continuing debts Balzac sought to marry a wealthy heiress, and had numerous affairs with members of the aristocracy. The most prominent was Eveline Hanska, a Russian noblewoman who wrote Balzac an anonymous letter out of boredom. Balzac's reply and the ensuing correspondence culminated in a meeting in Switzerland and an amorous liaison. When Hanska's husband finally died, Balzac resolved to marry her, but she refused until she received the czar's consent. In 1850 she became pregnant, and Balzac himself successfully petitioned the czar for permission to marry her. Shortly thereafter he died, leaving Eveline to cover his debts of half a million francs. "A tomb such as this is proof of immortality," eulogized Hugo.

N. B. Gerson, *The Prodigal Genius: The Life and Times of Honoré de Balzac*, 1972.

H. J. Hunt, *Honoré de Balzac: A Biography*, 1969.

C. Prendegast, *Balzac, Fiction and Melodrama*, 1978.

Fire broke out in this quarter at 9 Rue des Lesdiguieres in the head of a young man on the fifth floor. The fire brigades have been working on it for months but cannot put it out. The young man is consumed with passion for a beautiful woman he has not met. She is called Fame.

Balzac, in a letter to his sister Laure

BANDARANAIKE, SOLOMON WEST RIDGEWAY DIAS (1899–1959),

Ceylonese nationalist and statesman; prime minister of Ceylon (Sri Lanka). Bandaranaike was born in the Ceylonese capital of Colombo. His wealthy father sent him to be educated abroad. Bandaranaike studied at Oxford and was called to the British bar at age twenty-five. Rather than pursue a legal career in Britain, Bandaranaike immediately returned to Ceylon, where he became involved in local politics.

Bandaranaike joined the National Congress party, representing it in the Colombo municipal council in 1927. At that time, in response to rising nationalist tensions in Ceylon, the new constitution of 1931 allowed a considerable degree of self-rule.

Bandaranaike allied himself with the nationalist forces, representing the United Nationalist party in the state council in 1931. That same year, despite his Christian upbringing, he declared himself a Buddhist. Following his reelection in 1936, Bandaranaike was made a minister. Upon independence in 1948, he was elected to the newly constituted house of representatives, serving as minister of health and of local government.

Bandaranaike, however, soon found himself at odds with the party leadership. He resigned his post in 1951 to form the Sri Lanka Freedom party and served as leader of the opposition from 1952 until the election of 1956. Rather than confront the United Nationalist party alone in that election, Bandaranaike managed to muster the support of several smaller left-wing parties for his own Freedom party, forming the People's United Front. The Front easily won the election, making Bandaranaike prime minister. The new party had an avowedly nationalist platform, including the removal of British naval bases on the island (achieved in 1957), and the promotion of the majority Sinhalese Buddhist culture. To the dismay of the sizeable Tamil minority, Sinhalese was made the official language of the country, sparking riots in the northern and western regions. Bandaranaike's neutralist foreign policies led to a reduction in Western support and the economy began to falter shortly after. Bandaranaike's popularity fell as a consequence of increasing ethnic and economic tensions; in 1959 the coalition fell apart. Unwilling to relinquish power, Bandaranaike made a series of concessions that often alienated him from his supporters.

Bandaranaike planned to appeal for foreign support for his foundering government. He was preparing to travel to the United States to address the UN General Assembly and to meet with President Dwight *Eisenhower when, on September 25, 1959, he was shot by Talduwe Somarama, a deranged Buddhist monk. Bandaranaike died the next day. Lengthy negotiations to create a new government were only concluded in 1960 when Sirimavo Bandaranaike, the late prime minister's widow, became the first woman prime minister in history.

A. J. Wilson, *Politics in Sri Lanka: 1947–1973*, 1974.

BANTING, SIR FREDERICK GRANT (1891–1941),

Canadian physician and medical researcher, discoverer of insulin; first Canadian recipient of the Nobel Prize. The youngest of five children, Banting was born on a small farm in Alliston, Ontario. He was educated in Ontario and studied medicine at the University of Toronto School of Medicine, receiving his medical degree there in 1916. He served in the Canadian Army Medical Corps during World War I and in 1917 was assigned to Ramsgate Hospital, England. Shortly thereafter he served in France, where he suffered shrapnel wounds in the right forearm. He was awarded the Military Cross for bravery.

After the war, Banting returned to Canada, practicing medicine in London, Ontario, from 1918 to 1920. During this period he also taught anatomy and physiology at Western University in London, Ontario (now the University of Western Ontario). This led to his research work on the pancreas and especially its so-called islets of Langerhans. In 1922 he worked at the University of Toronto with his assistant, Charles H. Best, a medical student. At that time, Banting was the first to succeed in extracting the hormone insulin from the pancreas of dogs and utilizing this in treating diabetes. His work ultimately made it possible to treat diabetes mellitus victims and prolong their lives. Accordingly, in 1923 Banting, together with John J. R. MacLeod, received the Nobel Prize in physiology and medicine for being the first to obtain a pancreatic extract of insulin.

Strange as it may seem, it appeared that Macleod's contribution to the research resulting in Banting's monumental work on insulin was solely in permitting Banting to use his laboratory at the University of Toronto for the research work. Banting, furious that the Nobel Prize had not been given to himself and Best jointly, gave Best half of his share of the Award. Apparently not wanting to be outdone by Best, Macleod, in turn, gave his share of the Nobel Prize award to J. B. Collip, who had worked in purifying and standardizing insulin in Macleod's lab after Banting and Best had extracted it.

At the time of the Nobel Prize award, Banting was appointed Professor of Medical Research at the University of Toronto. Honor followed honor, including an annuity award by the Canadian Parliament in 1923. In 1930 the Banting Institute was established at the University of Toronto. Banting's work did not stop with insulin; he went on to do important research on the adrenal cortex, cancer, and silicosis. From 1930 until his death, Banting served as the director of the Banting-Best Department of Medical Research at the University of Toronto.

In 1934 he was knighted. His public activity was also extensive, and included serving as chairman of the medical research committee of the Canadian National Research Council as well as chairman of the Canadian Associate Committee on Aviation Medical Research. During World War II, an important part of his work was establishing and maintaining liaisons with British researchers through continuous visits to England. Just after taking off on one of these trips in February 1941, he died in an air crash near Musgrave Harbor, Newfoundland.

S. Harris, *Banting's Miracle: The Story of the Discoverer of Insulin*, 1946.

A.Y. Jackson, *Banting as an Artist*, 1943.

L. Stevenson, *Sir Frederick Banting*, 1947.

BARBAROSSA   SEE FREDERICK I.

BARENTS, WILLEM (c.1550–1597), Dutch navigator and first explorer to winter in the Arctic. Barents led three exploratory Arctic Ocean voyages along the northern edge of the European-Asian landmass in search of a northeast passage for trade with India and the Orient. Discovery of such a passage would allow Dutch shipping interests direct routes to the East without risking clashes at sea with the then dominant Portuguese and Spanish.

Barents made significant contributions for explorers who followed him by preparing excellent navigational charts of the areas he explored and by leaving valuable meterological records. In 1594 and 1595 he sailed along the coast of northern Europe and reached the vicinity of Novaya Zemlya. He discovered Spitsbergen, the Barents Sea and Barents Island were later named in his honor. On his third and final voyage, in 1596, he sailed too far north in the cold weather and his ship was caught in the ice pack. He and his crew involuntarily became the first explorers to winter in the Arctic. They built a makeshift hut for shelter on Novaya Zemlya, and burned coal for heat (the hut was discovered intact in 1871). From his records, historians conclude that a tragedy was avoided one night when a concerned sailor opened the hut's door and allowed fresh air to enter the structure. Improper burning of the coal created poisonous carbon monoxide gas, which caused the sailors sleeping in upper bunks to become ill. The fresh air prevented death and allowed the affected men to recover.

In the spring Barents led his men out of the Arctic in open boats, since his ship had been crushed by the ice; he and some of his men died of exposure before reaching warmer waters. The survivors were saved by Russians, who cured their scurvy. They were picked up by a Dutch ship and caused a sensation in Amsterdam when they arrived in Arctic dress.

V. Stefansson, *Unsolved Mysteries of the Arctic*, 1939.

D. Sugden, *Arctic and Antarctic*, 1982.

BARRY, JOHN (1745–1803), American revolutionary war naval officer. Barry was born in Tacumshane, Ireland; he had no formal education and went to sea as a young boy. By 1760 he had settled in Philadelphia, becoming a shipmaster there in 1766 at the age of twenty-one. At thirty-one he became one of the first captains commissioned by the Continental Congress.

Barry's first command was the frigate *Lexington*, with which he captured the British ship *Edward*, on April 7, 1776. This was the first capture of a British vessel by an American warship during the Revolutionary War. Later on, using four small boats he seized a quantity of supplies from a British craft in the Delaware River near Philadelphia.

He later commanded the *Effingham*, but this ship was kept in Philadelphia by the British blockade of the Delaware River. During the period of the blockade, Barry saw duty in the army for a brief time, leading a volunteer company of artillery and fighting at the Battle of Trenton. Soon he was back at sea; from 1780 to 1783 he commanded the frigate *Alliance*, on which he made his first voyage to France, taking Colonel John Laurens there on a diplomatic mission.

Upon Barry's return from France in April 1781, the *Alliance* saw considerable action. Off the coast of Newfoundland it was attacked by two British privateers, the *Mars* and the *Minerva*. This developed into a grueling fourteen-hour battle in which the *Alliance* ultimately forced its attackers to surrender.

In May 1781 the *Alliance* was once again attacked by two British ships, the *Atalanta* and the *Trepassy*. Although reputedly badly wounded in this encounter, Barry managed to hold his rebellious crew to their guns until he was able to drive between his attackers with the assistance of a favorable breeze, thus forcing both ships to surrender. In 1782 Barry made a second voyage to France in order to take the Marquis de *Lafayette home after the Battle of Yorktown.

On March 10, 1783, the *Alliance*, under Barry's command, fought the last naval battle of the Revolutionary War against the British vessel *Sybil*, in the straits off the Florida coast.

The United States Navy was reorganized in 1794, during George *Washington's second term as president. Barry was named senior captain and given command of a new frigate, the *United States*. Between 1798 and 1800 he found himelf involved in yet another war, a short one with France. In the course of this war, Barry served as commander of all U.S. warships in the West Indies. Thereafter, from 1800 to 1801, he commanded the U.S. naval station at Guadeloupe in the West Indies.

In the United States, Barry has often been called "father of the navy" because of the large number of young naval officers that he trained who became outstanding names in U.S. naval history. These included, among others, Stephen Decatur, Richard Somer, Charles Stewart, and Jacob Jones. When Barry died in Philadelphia, he was at the head of the U.S. Navy officers' list.

R. G. Albion, *Makers of Naval Policy, 1798–1947*, 1980.

W. B. Clark, *Gallant John Barry*, 1938.

BAYEZID OR **BAYAZID**   SEE BAJAZET

BEACONSFIELD, EARL OF SEE DISRAELI, BENJAMIN

BECKET, SAINT THOMAS (Thomas à Becket; c.1118–1170), archbishop of Canterbury, Roman Catholic saint. Born in London to a Norman merchant family, Thomas Becket's pious mother — the only woman who ever had a place in Becket's life — strongly influenced her son. He grew up in an England divided among powerful lords and torn apart by civil wars between the weak rival claimants to the throne of Henry I. The clergy ruled England during that period, insofar as it was ruled at all.

Physically attractive, brilliant, and verbally adept, Becket came to the attention of the foremost prelate in England, the archbishop of Canterbury, Theobald, who sent him to Italy to study law. At twenty-five he became one of the eager and ambitious young clerks surrounding Theobald. With the prudent use of tact, charm, and an astute judgment of character, he set out to become indispensable to Theobald and succeeded, rapidly becoming Theobald's favorite as well as being generally respected.

In 1154 Henry II became king of England, ending almost twenty years of civil war. Faced with the enormous task of restoring order to a war-ravaged country, he needed men with loyalty and administrative skills. Theobald, wishing to have the position filled by an ally who could be depended on to protect the church's interests, suggested Becket, then thirty-six, for the position of high chancellor.

A man of action, skilled in administration, organization, diplomacy, debate, and war, Becket was a superb chancellor, becoming almost as wealthy and powerful as the king. Known for his lavish hospitality, he lived in opulent luxury. He was on excellent terms with Henry II throughout his seven years as chancellor. Friends as well as colleagues, they hunted, ate, and drank together.

Henry was determined to unite England under a strong central monarchy. Fighting to break the barons, he appointed Becket the new archbishop of Canterbury in 1162, believing that Becket would support him in his efforts to bring the church under his control. Until this time Becket had merely been a lay person associated with the church; he did not want to become archbishop of Canterbury but eventually yielded to pressure from all sides, including the papal legate, who wanted a strong archbishop to defend the church's prerogatives.

Becket changed his way of life completely on becoming archbishop. He resigned as chancellor (despite Henry's opposition) and abandoned his wealthy, luxurious way of life. Determined to live a physically stern and austere life, he wore coarse clothing, with a haircloth next to his skin, scourged himself frequently, gave much charity, and washed the feet of thirteen beggars every night. As chancellor he had worked tirelessly for the crown. As archbishop his first loyalty was to the church and he became the unyielding defender of all the church's rights and privileges, even against the throne. Becket's relationship with the king changed, too. As archbishop, Becket felt that he was the king's spiritual mentor, but Henry could not relate to his old hunting and drinking companion that way; their bitter quarrels killed Henry's love for Becket.

The core of their dispute was whether the church in England would be independent, with ties to Rome, or subordinate to the king. The surface cause of their conflict was the king's desire to establish a uniform system of justice for all as opposed to the church's wish to maintain the clergy's right to be tried in an ecclesiastical (where their crimes often went unpunished) rather than civil court. The Constitution of Clarendon (1164) was designed to put an end to many clerical immunities. Becket refused to sign the constitution (which was promulgated nonetheless) and Henry tried him for feudal disobedience at the royal court. When his own bishops found him guilty, he fled England for France.

Believing that only excommunication and interdiction could move Henry, Becket turned to the pope, submitting his resignation. Pope Alexander III defended Becket, publicly recognizing him as the church's champion, but as he himself was plagued by rival popes backed by *Frederick I, he was not in a strong enough position to oppose Henry fully and sent Becket to live for a time as a simple monk.

Becket remained in exile for six years. Attempts to effect a reconciliation with Henry were always bogged down by the intransigence of one or the other, Becket having abandoned tactful charm for unyielding, righteous stubbornness. Henry only yielded when the pope finally threatened him with interdiction if he refused to restore Becket to his see.

Becket returned to England in triumph in 1170 and immediately excommunicated the bishops who had opposed him. Henry was furious when he heard of this, exclaiming, "What! Shall a man who has eaten my bread...insult the King and all the kingdom, and not one of the lazy servants whom I nourish at my table does me right for such an affront?" Four knights heard his words and, apparently without Henry's knowledge, went to Canterbury where they murdered Becket at the altar of the cathedral, just four weeks after his return to England.

Becket dead succeeded where Becket living had not. Horrified, Christendom responded to his murder by declaring him a saint and excommunicating Henry for his part in the assassination. Henry declared his innocence to the pope, ordered the apprehension of the assassins, and restored all the rights and properties of the church. Finally, he came to Canterbury as a penitent, barefoot, wearing a hair shirt, begging the monks to whip him for his part in Becket's death. Becket was canonized in 1173 and his tomb became the most popular shrine in England. The drama of the conflict between the king and the "turbulent priest" is the subject of modern plays by T. S. *Eliot (*Murder in the Cathedral*,

1935) and Jean Anouilh (*Becket ou l'honneur de Dieu*, 1959; *Becket or the Honor of God*, 1961).

F. Barlow, *Thomas Becket*, 1986.
T. Jones, ed., *The Becket Controversy*, 1970.
M. D. Knowles, *Archbishop Thomas Becket*, 1950.
R. Winston, *Thomas Becket*, 1967.

BECQUEREL, ANTOINE HENRI (1852–1908),

French physicist whose work at the turn of the century led to the discovery of radioactivity. He came from a family of distinguished scientists. His grandfather, Antoine Becquerel, was professor of physics at the Musée d'Histoire Naturelle in Paris, and initiated his family's research into the nature of phosphorescence. Antoine's son, Edmond, succeeded his father as professor at the Musée and continued studying the chemical action of light. He was renowned as an expert on fluorescence, with particular expertise in the photo-emissions of uranium salts.

Edmond's son Antione Henri studied at the École Polytechnique in Paris, which was almost a prerequisite for any Frenchman contemplating a serious scientific career. He was awarded his doctorate in 1888, and the following year was admitted to the Académie des Sciences. By 1895, Becquerel had assumed the chair of physics at the Musée, as well as having received a professorship at the École Polytechnique. It was apparent from the incisive papers he published that his appointments were not the result of nepotism, but well earned recognition of his talent. He also inherited his family's legacy of knowledge and involvement in fluorescence and phosphorescence.

Also in 1895 Wilhelm *Roentgen, a German scientist, announced his discovery of unexplained emissions with remarkable properties from cathode tubes, which he called X-rays. This sensational news spread quickly to France when Henri Poincaré, an associate of Roentgen, showed examples of the first X-ray photographs to his colleagues at the Académie des Sciences. Becquerel was intrigued, particularly once Poincaré explained that the X-rays appeared to emanate from the region of the cathode tubes where the glass would fluoresce. He quickly returned to his laboratory and the next day began preparing experiments to test the connection between fluorescence and X-rays. To his disappointment, the fluorescent and phosphorescent materials he initially tested did not emit X-rays.

Not to be diverted, in early 1896 Becquerel began investigating afresh with a phosphorescent uranium salt with which his father had been experimenting. By February 24 he reported to the Académie that a covered photographic plate, when placed in the sun with a sample of the salt lying on it, did indeed show evidence of exposure. He believed that he had successfully demonstrated that a phosphorescing material emitted X-rays, and when the weather became overcast a few days later he stored his experimental apparatus indoors, placing his wrapped photographic plates in a dark drawer, leaving quite by chance the uranium salts lying in place above them.

Several days later, the sun shining brightly, he returned to his laboratory to resume his experiments, expecting to find a faint silhouette of the salts fogging the photographic plates from the residual phosphorescence of the salts. Instead, he found a well defined and vivid image on the developed plates. He immediately recognized that whatever had caused the exposure was not the result of a phosphorescent effect as he had previously assumed. He named the mysterious cause of the exposure Becquerel rays, later identified as alpha particles, beta particles, and gamma rays, the emissions of nuclear decay.

Just as Roentgen's discovery had been made quite by chance, so too did Becquerel stumble across the first evidence of what was to become known as radioactivity. Becquerel was quoted as saying that he believed he was predestined to discover the phenomenon of radioactivity due to the remarkable confluence of factors of time and family that centered on him.

He spent the last years of his life investigating the properties of uranium. In 1903 he was awarded the Nobel prize for physics jointly with Marie and Pierre *Curie. His son, Jean, became the physics professor at the Musée d'Histoire Naturelle after his father's death in 1908.

E. Serge, *From X-Rays to Quarks*, 1980.

BEETHOVEN, LUDWIG VAN (1770–1827),

German composer; one of the giants of music. He was born in Bonn to a musical family of Flemish origin. His grandfather, after whom he was named, was a choir director, while Beethoven's father gave his child basic instruction in music. After the age of eleven his only schooling was in music and even on his deathbed he was being instructed in simple multiplication by his nephew. The young boy studied the piano and the violin as well as theory and all other necessary musical disciplines. At twelve he composed "Nine Variations for Piano on a March of Dressler." A clumsy child who knocked his inkpot into his piano, he could never learn to dance rhythmically. At fourteen he was appointed deputy court organist in Bonn. Later he also began playing the viola in several local theater orchestras. When he was seventeen he performed in Vienna for W. A. *Mozart, who said: "Keep your eyes on him. Someday he will give the world something to talk about." When his mother died in 1787 the musician had to start providing for his two younger brothers as his alcoholic father could not be counted on for any help. Beethoven then gave piano lessons and was lucky enough to encounter several wealthy admirers. He also continued to compose for performances at aristocratic gatherings or in homage to royalty.

In 1792 he left Bonn for Vienna where he studied with Franz Joseph Haydn (who nicknamed him the "Great Mogul") and other musicians (one of whom concluded, "He will never do anything properly").

He maintained himself with the financial help of several aristocratic benefactors, among whom his success was immediate despite his temper and arrogance. In return the composer dedicated some of his works to these noblemen.

In 1795 Beethoven made his performing debut in Vienna, playing the solo part in one of his piano concertos, and took the city by storm. A year later he began touring, playing the piano in Prague, Berlin, and other German cities. He was popular as a pianist, a composer, and a social figure who was more than welcome in the city's many aristocratic circles. He had a servant and bought stylish clothes; for a short time he owned a horse. He also had quite a few influential students and before long had become, after Haydn, the most eminent musician in Vienna. When a rich nobleman commissioned a score he owned the autographed copy for only six months, after which it reverted to the composer. Beethoven had many friendships with women and would have liked to marry but never found a wife because of his idealized standards.

His career took a turn for the worse when he began to lose his hearing. He first noted signs of the affliction in 1798 and in 1802 wrote the "Heiligenstadt Testament" in which he laments the loss of his hearing. This testament, written in the village of Heiligenstadt, was discovered only after the composer's death. In it he says, "I was on the point of putting an end to my life. The only thing that held me back was my art. For indeed it seemed to me impossible to leave this world before I had produced all the works that I felt the urge to compose; and thus I have dragged on this miserable existence." In a postscript he added: "Oh, Providence — do but grant me one day of *pure joy*. For so long now the inner echo of real joy has been unknown to me. Oh when, oh when, Almighty God, shall I be able to hear and feel this echo again in the temple of Nature and in contact with humanity? Never? No! Oh, that would be too hard." As he wrote this he was composing his cheerful Second Symphony.

There are many theories about Beethoven's illness but whatever the cause, his growing deafness changed his life completely in spite of the fact that he continued to compose and conduct. He also never ceased to hope that a remedy would eventually be found. After 1818, however, the only way in which Beethoven could communicate with the outside world was through his conversation books, in which someone would write a question for him and the composer would answer in writing as well. These books contributed greatly to the study of Beethoven's own character but not all were preserved.

The deaf Beethoven continued to compose with the same vitality and energy as when he had been younger and healthier, and his illness, tantrums, and moods never influenced the style of his music. Passages of anger and joy can be found in Beethoven's music both before and after his illness. He also continued to present concerts of his own works in which he played the piano parts in chamber music and the solo piano in his own piano concertos.

In 1803 he began to write an opera based on J. N. Bouilly's *Léonore, ou L'Amour conjugal*. The result was his sole opera, *Fidelio*. The premiere took place on November 20, 1805, only a few days after the French army entered Vienna. There were only three performances at the time. *Fidelio* was performed again a year later and returned to the stage in a revised version only in 1814.

In a creative outburst between 1802 and 1808, Beethoven wrote some of his major masterpieces, including the Fourth, Fifth, and Sixth Symphonies, the Razumovsky string quartets, the violin concerto, the triple concerto, the fourth piano concerto, and two of his famous piano sonatas, the *Appassionata* and *Waldstein*.

Despite severe financial difficulties he declined an offer made in 1808 to become *kapellmeister* in Kassel. He wished to remain in Vienna where he continued to compose and perform, although his life outside his music was far from pleasant. His deteriorating health, continuous quarrels with friends and relatives, and bad temper were a constant part of his daily life. He was overly suspicious; he exaggerated his poverty, which was sometimes real but never became destitution; he was untidy (he was once arrested when mistaken for a tramp), naive, and far from pleasant. Although he had many friends and admirers, he spent most of his life alone.

The last fifteen years of Beethoven's life feature what scholars call his third style. During these years Beethoven composed epics such as the Ninth Symphony, the *Missa Solemnis*, and the late string quar-

Ludwig van Beethoven, by Perugino

> O you my fellow-men who take me or de-
> nounce me as morose, crabbed, or misan-
> thropic, how you do me wrong! You know not
> the secret cause of what seems thus to you. My
> heart and my disposition were from childhood
> up inclined to the tender feeling of goodwill. I
> was always minded to perform even greater ac-
> tions; but only consider that for six years past I
> have fallen into an incurable condition, aggra-
> vated by senseless physicians, year after year
> deceived in the hope of recovery and in the end
> compelled to contemplate a lasting and incur-
> able malady. Born with a fiery, lively temper-
> ament inclined even for the amusements of soci-
> ety, I was early forced to isolate myself, to lead
> a solitary life. If now and again I tried for once
> to give the go-by to all this, how rudely was I
> repulsed by the mournful experience of my de-
> fective hearing; but not yet could I bring my-
> self to say to people "Speak louder, shout, for I
> am deaf."
>
> **From Beethoven's Testament
> (written in 1802)**

tets. At the first performance of the Ninth Symphony he stood in the orchestra quite unaware of the
massive applause until his attention was turned to
the audience. At the end of 1826 he was stricken
with a fever that developed into pleurisy and died in
Vienna. Twenty thousand people attended his funeral. His last words, on receiving a present of good
wine from his publishers on his deathbed, were,
"Pity, pity, too late."

M. Broyles, *Beethoven*, 1987.

M. Hamburger, ed., *Beethoven: Letters, Journals,
and Conversations*, 1951.

D. Matthews, *Beethoven*, 1985.

W. S. Newman, *Beethoven on Beethoven: Playing
His Piano Music His Way*, 1988.

BEGIN, MENAHEM (1913–1992), Israeli prime
minister, leader of the Jewish underground movement, the Irgun, during the British mandate over
Palestine, proponent of Revisionist Zionism (a
strongly nationalist approach which opposed the
Zionist mainstream as too moderate), and Nobel
peace prize recipient. Born in Brest Litovsk, Poland,
to an ardent Zionist family, at the age of fifteen he
joined the Zionist youth movement, Betar, which
advocated the immediate establishment of a Jewish
state in Palestine.

Growing up in Poland, Begin felt the dangers of
anti-Semitism. By 1939 he had become the Betar
commissioner in Czechoslovakia and later the Betar
chief in Poland, where he tried to expedite immigration of Jews to Palestine. After Poland was invaded

in 1939, Begin and a few members of his family escaped to Vilna, then under Soviet rule, but his parents and a brother died in the Holocaust. The Soviets sent Begin to a Siberian concentration camp for
his Zionist activities, and for the next two years he
was either in Soviet prisons or in a work brigade
near the Arctic Circle. His eight-year sentence was
commuted when Adolph *Hitler invaded Russia, and
he was allowed to join the Polish force formed by
General Wladyslaw Anders and sent by the Allies to
the Middle East. In 1942 he made his way to Palestine, where he became the Betar chief in Jerusalem.
From 1943 he commanded the Irgun Zvai Leumi (literally the "National Fighting Army"), the paramilitary underground aligned with revisionist Zionist
factions. In 1944 the Irgun declared war on the
British forces in Palestine, and Begin planned and
executed a guerilla campaign against them. At one
point, he ordered the execution of two British soldiers in retaliation for the execution of two of his
men. Not only was Begin hunted by the British, but
he and his organization were usually at odds with the
Hagana, the Jewish underground self-defense organization under the leadership of David *Ben-Gurion.
Begin was forced to move around in disguise to hide
his identity, at times dressing as a meek doctor or a
bearded talmudic scholar.

Evading capture, in 1946 Begin ordered the bombing of the King David hotel, in which ninety-one
persons (Britons, Jews, and Arabs) were killed. His
goal was to bring worldwide attention to the plight
of the Jews in Palestine struggling for statehood and
to perform a symbolic act of resistance against the
British. His most controversial act, however, came in
early 1948 when the Irgun, together with the even
more militant Stern group, carried out a massacre in
the Arab village of Deir Yassin, in which 254 villagers were killed. For the Palestinians, the massacre
became a symbol of Jewish ruthlessness.

When the mandate of the British government in
Palestine ended and Ben-Gurion proclaimed the independence of the State of Israel in May 1948, Begin
and his group emerged from the underground but almost provoked a civil war when they tried to bring in
a ship loaded with weapons in violation of an Arab-
Israel cease-fire. Ben-Gurion ordered his men to fire
on the ship; sixteen Irgun men were killed and Begin
was dragged away from the ship as it was sinking.
With the establishment of the state, Begin founded
his parliamentary party, Herut ("Freedom"), which
advocated a Jewish state on both sides of the Jordan
River. He emerged as a formidable orator and led
frenzied opposition to the reparations agreement
with West Germany in 1952. He remained in the opposition on other issues also, initially representing
only a small minority of voters.

As the 1950s and 1960s wore on, Begin began to
acquire respectability and from 1967 to 1970 he was
minister without portfolio in a government of national unity. In the wake of the Six Day War in
1967, right-wing nationalist attitudes became more

fashionable. Begin's advocacy of intensive Israeli settlement in the formerly Jordanian-controlled areas of the West Bank, together with the impact of the 1973 Yom Kippur War, in which Israel was caught by surprise, led to rising popularity for Begin's party, now called the Likud. His impassioned populist oratory was especially appealing to the growing proportion of Jews in Israel who came from countries that had been under Muslim rule and Begin and the Likud rode to power for the first time in the 1977 national election.

A few months after the election, at the initiative of Anwar Sadat, Begin hosted the Egyptian president in Jerusalem, in what became the first official step in the process that led to the signing of a peace treaty between the two countries in March 1979. During the negotiations, in which American president Jimmy Carter was actively involved, Begin proved a tough negotiator. Although he agreed to relinquish Sinai, he refused to freeze settlement activity on the West Bank. For his efforts in the peace process, he won the 1978 Nobel peace prize jointly with Sadat. Throughout his term of office, Begin increased in number and size the Jewish settlements in the West Bank.

Shortly before the 1981 Israeli national elections, in which Begin was reelected, he ordered the bombing of an Iraqi nuclear reactor, an act that drew widespread international condemnation. In 1982 Begin ordered the invasion of Lebanon, ostensibly to drive Palestine Liberation Organization members perpetrating terrorist attacks on northern Israel out of the area. The war turned out to be a terrible failure for Israel, the first war for which there was no consensus among the Israeli public. It dragged on and Begin was deeply affected by the growing roster of Israeli casualties. At this point his wife died and Begin went into a depression that brought him to resign from public life in September 1983. He lived thereafter as a recluse in his own home, leaving only to visit his wife's grave each year on the anniversary of her death. He wrote two books, *White Nights*, on his experiences in Soviet prison camps, and *The Revolt* on his fight against the British.

> The defenselessness of the Jews was the real scourge of life, for centuries, but mainly in our generation. That must never happen again. Therefore, we decided to take up arms and fight for liberation. In order to have a State, an army, a means of national defense. That was the prime mover. And to make sure that the Jewish State is secure, that the borders are unbreakable, that the land is unconquerable. That is the second prime mover of all our actions, when we were in opposition and now in the government.
>
> **Begin's interview with *Rolling Stone*,
> November 3, 1977.**

A. Perlmutter, *The Life and Times of Menachem Begin*, 1987.
E. Silver, *Begin: The Haunted Prophet*, 1984.

BELISARIUS (c.505 – 565), Byzantine military leader. Belisarius, like the emperor *Justinian for whom he fought, was probably of Illyrian origins. He came to the emperor's attention while serving in the imperial bodyguard and was appointed commander of the eastern armies at the age of twenty-five. Belisarius was among the most illustrious military commanders of all times. In his entire career, despite extraordinary odds and adverse conditions, he lost only one battle. However, he also was the victim of imperial machinations fueled by the emperor's weak character and the intrigues of his own wife, Antonina.

Belisarius's first major battle, in 530, was against the enormous Persian army stationed at Dara in Mesopotamia. His victory was so overwhelming that despite his defeat the following year at Sura he returned to the capital with no blemish to his reputation. In 532 the Nika insurrection threatened to overthrow Justinian, but Belisarius proved his loyalty to the emperor by quashing the rebellion in a bloody massacre at the hippodrome. So impressed was Justinian by the young officer's resourcefulness and bravery that he appointed Belisarius to fulfill his greatest ambition, the recovery of the lost western provinces, including Rome, from the Goths and Vandals.

With only 15,000 men, Belisarius defeated and captured Gelimer, the Vandal king of Africa. The booty he brought to Constantinople included the golden candelabrum from the temple in Jerusalem, brought to Carthage from Rome eighty years earlier. Justinian celebrated Belisarius's victory as a traditional Roman triumph, the first held in 500 years.

The following year Belisarius undertook an expedition to recover Italy. Entering through Sicily, he was besieged in Rome for a year but managed to defeat his Ostrogoth adversaries and continued to Ravenna, where he captured the Goth king Vittigis. The Goths acknowledged Belisarius's ability by offering him the kingship in Vittigis's stead. Belisarius's rejection in favor of Justinian was without precedent, but the emperor feared Belisarius's status and ordered him to return to Constantinople. Belisarius was reassigned to the eastern frontier, although this time Justinian denied him funds to wage a successful campaign against the Persians or even to pay his troops. After three years. Belisarius was stripped of his command under suspicion of disloyalty. He returned briefly to Italy in 544 but his lengthy absence had caused irreparable damage to his earlier victories. Lacking funds and troops, he was able to recover Rome only briefly before retiring to Constantinople.

Much of the resentment against Belisarius was instigated by his wife Antonina, a favorite of the empress Theodora. Trained as a sorceress, ancient historians claim that she beguiled Belisarius by a love potion which caused him to overlook her shortcomings. She bore Belisarius a daughter, Joannina, but failed to produce a son. Instead, Belisarius adopted a young boy, Theodosius, with whom Antonina carried on a passionate affair. Belisarius knew of this but somehow Antonina was able to persuade her husband that there was nothing going on between her and Theodosius; on the contrary, anyone who criticized her behavior was cruelly hunted and killed by Belisarius at his wife's instigation. One friend, Constantine, was murdered for merely expressing sympathy. Antonina's wrath knew no bounds; she even harassed Photius, her son from a previous marriage, for siding with Belisarius. With the assistance of Theodora, Photius was imprisoned and tortured until he eventually escaped to Jerusalem to become a monk.

Justinian recalled Belisarius in 559 to defend the empire against the encroaching Huns. Belisarius fought bravely but was falsely implicated in a plot against the emperor and he was imprisoned for a year before being restored in 563. Two years later he died. Ancient legends describe a broken Belisarius, impoverished and blind, wandering the streets of Byzantium before his death.

Belisarius's tragic life was described by his contemporary, Procopius, in his *Anecdota*. He was also the subject of an historical novel, *Count Belisarius*, by Robert Graves.

J. J. Norwich, *Byzantium*, 1989.

Procopius, *The Secret History*, 1966.

BELL, ALEXANDER GRAHAM (1847–1922), American scientist and educator of the deaf who invented the telephone. Bell was born in Edinburgh, Scotland, where he was educated at Edinburgh University and the University of Scotland. In 1865 he moved to London with his father, Alexander Melville Bell, becoming his professional assistant. The elder Bell was a highly regarded scientist in the field of vocal physiology. In the course of his work the senior Bell invented a system of symbols indicating the position of the human vocal cords in speech, known as visible speech. The invention of the telephone by Alexander Graham Bell was a natural outgrowth of his work for the deaf.

As early as 1865 Bell developed the idea that it was possible to transmit speech by electrical waves. While working with his father in London, Bell sought to improve his knowledge in the field by taking courses in anatomy and physiology at University College, London. In 1868 he adapted his father's visible speech system at a school for deaf children in Kensington. By 1869 his father had made him a full partner in his professional work. The elder Bell became familiar with North America in the course of a lecture tour there in 1868 and the family moved to Canada in 1870. While on a lecture tour in the United States, the elder Bell had stimulated interest in his visible speech system. This led to the employment of Alexander Graham Bell at the Boston Day School for the Deaf, where he trained teachers in the use of visible speech in 1871. By October 1872 he was conducting his own private school in Boston to train teachers in this method, for which he developed a system of notations. In 1873 he was appointed a professor of vocal physiology and the mechanics of speech at Boston University.

Bell had been conducting studies of the human ear while he tried to invent a so-called phonautograph. This was to be an instrument that would explain how to make tone vibrations correctly to deaf pupils. The idea was that this could be done by comparing visual representations of the sounds that deaf pupils made with standard records of the same. From this work, he developed the concept of the membrane element in the telephone. By March 10, 1876, the first telephone apparatus had been invented and perfected by Bell. He was able to transmit the first intelligible and audible sentence to his assistant, "Mr. Watson, come here, I want you." Basically, the apparatus made it possible to reproduce the tones and overtones of a steel spring that in turn could yield the tones and overtones of the human voice.

Bell obtained patents for his invention of the telephone. Immediately, other claimants contested Bell's right to his invention. This resulted in what was at the time the most important and prolonged patent litigation in U.S. history. Some sixty-six legal cases developed about this invention, culminating in a decision by the U.S. Supreme Court that found Bell to be the inventor of the telephone.

Financing the further development of this invention was not easy. Eventually, Gardiner G. Hubbard, a well-known citizen active in the education of the deaf, gave Bell the assistance he needed for the commercial development of the telephone and other inventions. In 1877 the telephone company trusteeship known as the Bell Telephone Company was established with Hubbard as its first trustee. His daughter, Mabel, who had been deaf from early childhood, married Bell.

In 1880 France awarded Bell the Volta prize of 50,000 francs in recognition of his invention of the telephone. This led to extensive research and invention, especially for the benefit of the deaf, through the establishment of the Volta Laboratory by Bell. There he invented the photophone to transmit speech over a ray of light by means of the variable resistance of silenium to light and shade, as well as the induction balance to locate metallic objects in the human body. Both of these inventions were not patented but were given to the world by Bell. In the Volta Laboratory, Bell invented the audiometer and brought his scientific inventions ever closer to service for the deaf.

Never to be limited to a single direction, Bell became interested in the field of aviation and was one of the first to consider aerial locomotion practicable. He founded the Aerial Experiment Association, under whose auspices the first public flight of a heavier-than-air machine took place in 1908. By 1915 the first transcontinental telephone line was established from New York to San Francisco. In 1920 Bell was recognized by his birthplace and childhood

ABOUT ALEXANDER GRAHAM BELL

One afternoon Mark Twain, who lost more than one hard-earned fortune by investing it in harebrained schemes described to him in glittering terms, observed a tall, spare man, with an eager face and kindly blue eyes coming up the path with a strange contraption under his arm. Yes, it was an invention, and the man explained it to the humorist, who listened politely but said he had been burned too often.

"But I'm not asking you to invest a fortune," explained the man. "You can have as large a share as you want for $500." Mark Twain shook his head; the invention didn't make sense. The tall, stooped figure started away.

"What did you say your name was?" The author called after him.

"Bell," replied the inventor a little sadly, "Alexander Graham Bell."

Vansant Coryell in
"On the Trail for Financing,"
The Christian Science Monitor

home, Edinburgh, Scotland, which elected him a burger and brother of the city as well as conferring upon him the freedom of the city.

R. V. Bruce, *Alexander Graham Bell and the Conquest of Solitude*, 1973.

C. D. Mackenzie, *Alexander Graham Bell, the Man Who Contracted Space*, 1928.

E. Montgomery, *Alexander Graham Bell*, 1963.

BENEDICT OF NURSIA, SAINT (c.480 – 547), early Christian anchorite, father of Western monasticism. Little is known about his life; the hagiography in the *Dialogues* of *Gregory the Great allows for some sifting of fact from legend, while his character can be construed from the Rule of Saint Benedict. Born in Nursia, Italy, Benedict apparently received a classical education in Rome. He was surrounded by wanton companions but at the age of around twenty rejected the debauchery of Rome in favor of a simple, religious life. Benedict did not originally plan to become a hermit. At first he was accompanied by his nurse, who attended to his physical needs while he studied and prayed.

One day the nurse was sifting flour when the sieve broke. Benedict miraculously restored the sifter in what was his first miracle. After this event he retreated to a cave to pursue a hermit's life. Initially only Romanus, a local monk who provided him with food and a coarse monk's habit, was allowed in his company, but as Benedict's reputation grew he attracted a considerable following. Monks from Vicovaro invited Benedict to be their abbot, little an-

ticipating that he would not only try to revitalize their religious life but would even interfere in their temporal existence by becoming a self-proclaimed law-giver. In the growing tension, an attempt was made to poison Benedict's food; he fled the monastery accompanied by a small group of followers willing to accept his authority. Benedict organized his disciples into twelve monasteries of twelve monks and an abbot; he was abbot of a thirteenth monastery. The monasteries flourished until a jealous local priest forced him to flee. Benedict reestablished himself at Monte Cassino and lived there until the end of his life.

To run his monastery, Benedict composed the Rule. Its seventy-three chapters became the basis of later European monastic tradition. Beginning with an exhortation to identify with Christ, Benedict stressed the role of the abbot, not only as a teacher but as an authoritative father figure. The rule calls on monks to practice obedience, silence, and humility, and explains how these traits can best be acquired. Benedict was not a radical anchorite (a person living alone for religious reasons): he encouraged his monks to perform community services as cenobites (people living together in a religious community) before isolating themselves from the world. Nor did he deny the pleasures of the material world; unlike other orders, which insisted on austere regimentation, Benedict contended that monks should receive adequate physical comforts. His recommended menu included one pound of bread per day, meat once a day, and at least two cooked dishes at each meal. Wine, though not encouraged, was not proscribed. Benedict also insisted that his monks sleep six to eight hours each night and allowed for an additional siesta in the summer months. Monks were to be provided with adequate blankets and pillows and with warm clothing in the winter. The popular Benedictine Rule spread throughout the region and was adopted by Benedict's twin sister, Scholastica, for her own convent located nearby.

Benedict achieved renown for his miracles (he is usually depicted with a serpent and a raven, commemorating two of his miracles) and his prophetic powers. Even the Gothic king Totila, then at war with the Byzantine Empire, sought his advice. To test Benedict, Totila first sent an officer dressed in royal attire pretending to be the king, but Benedict detected the impersonation and asked to see the real king. Benedict told Totila that he would conquer Rome, cross the seas, and rule for nine years; the prophecy was fulfilled exactly as Benedict had said. Benedict also foretold the exact hour of his own death. When the time came, the ailing abbot was brought to the chapel. He received communion and died, and was buried in Monte Cassino in the same grave as his sister, Saint Scholastica.

It appears that the Benedictine Rule fell into disuse for some time before being restored throughout Europe by *Charlemagne. Today Saint Benedict is credited with founding and encouraging the liberal

Saint Benedict, by Perugino

Western monasticism that eventually prevailed in Europe. In 1964 Pope Paul VI declared Benedict patron saint of all Europe. His feast is celebrated in the West on July 11.

T. Kardong, *Together unto Life Everlasting: An Introduction to the Rule of Benedict*, 1987.
I. Schuster, *The Story of Saint Benedict and His Times*, 1951.

BEN-GURION, DAVID (1886–1973), Zionist leader and first prime minister of the State of Israel. He was born in Plonsk, a small town in Poland. The sixth child of eleven, tragedy struck him early in life, as six of the children died young, and his mother died when he was eleven. Ben-Gurion (who changed his last name from Green when he moved to Palestine), was raised in a Zionist home; his father founded a Hebrew school, at which Ben-Gurion studied. At age sixteen he left home for Warsaw, where he taught Hebrew and became involved in politics. He became caught up in the political fervor sweeping the town and joined the Socialist Zionist movement.

In 1906 he settled in Palestine, worked in agricultural settlements, and soon became active in politics. In the Galilee he first encountered the problems of Jewish defense against Arab attacks and decided that villages must be guarded by Jewish watchmen instead of by hired Arab or Circassian guards.

To prepare himself to represent Palestine's Jewish community in the Turkish parliament he enrolled at Istanbul University to study law, but the outbreak of World War I cut short his studies. He returned to Palestine but was arrested in 1915 and accused of forming a society to rebel against the ruling Ottomans. Expelled, he moved to the United States, where he concentrated on organizing a group to convince people to settle in Palestine. "A homeland is not given or got as a gift; it is not acquired by privilege or political contracts; it is not bought with gold or held by force. No, it is made with the sweat of the brow. It is the historic creation and the collective enterprise of a people, the fruits of its labor, boldly spiritual, and moral, over a span of generations," he wrote. He joined the British Jewish Legion to fight on the side of the Allies and returned to Palestine in British army uniform.

His next task was to unite the labor movement, as well as to work for the realization of the Balfour Declaration, in which the British had promised to create a Jewish national home in Palestine. In 1920 a general union of workers, the Histadrut, was created, and Ben-Gurion served as its secretary-general from 1921 to 1935. He was now the leading figure in the Jewish community and in 1930 he founded Mapai, the Palestine Labor party. During the 1920s and 1930s, Ben-Gurion was involved in international Zionist movements, including the Jewish Agency, of which he was chairman from 1934 to 1948.

As Arab resistance to Jewish settlement increased and manifested itself in the form of violence against Jews, Ben-Gurion argued that the two peoples could live together and made several attempts to negotiate with Arab representatives. When widespread Arab riots broke out in 1936 Ben-Gurion organized Jewish self-defense, both through legal methods with the British authorities, as well as through the Hagana, the Jewish underground.

Increasing Arab pressure led the British to limit Jewish immigration just at the time when Jews needed more than ever to escape from Nazi Europe. Ben-Gurion fought the British immigration restrictions but suspended the struggle against British policy in order to concentrate on the fight against the Nazi threat. During the war, however, he led the Zionist movement to declare that its aim was the establishment of a Jewish state; after the war, Ben-Gurion continued working to achieve that goal, which had become urgent in view of the refusal of the countries of the world to admit the tragic survivors of the Holocaust. He also led the underground struggle of the Haganah against the British in Palestine.

Finally, in November 1947 the United Nations General Assembly passed a resolution recommending that Palestine be partitioned into Jewish and Arab states. The decision was rejected by the Arabs, who attacked Jewish towns and communication throughout Palestine, and Ben-Gurion redoubled his efforts to organize and mobilize the Jewish defense.

On May 14, 1948, when the British ended their mandate and left Palestine, Ben-Gurion, who had been chosen a month earlier by the Zionist General Council to be the de facto prime minister and minister of defense, read the Proclamation of Independence, which announced that the state of Israel had come into being. Immediately following his announcement the armies of Egypt, Syria, Jordan, Lebanon, and Iraq invaded the country from all sides. Ben-Gurion presided over the new state's defense and over each strategic decision. He faced challenges not only from the Arab countries but also from within the Jewish community; he was constantly in conflict with the underground radical group, the Irgun, led by Menahem *Begin, and even ordered one of the ships of the Irgun to be sunk. The tide of battle eventually turned against the Arabs and by July 1949 armistice agreements were signed between Israel and all the countries (except Iraq) that had attacked the infant Jewish state.

Except for a two-year retirement, Ben-Gurion (popularly known as 'B.G.') was Israel's prime minister and its dominant personality for fourteen years. During this period the country absorbed over two million immigrants from many parts of the world, developed its economy (partly with the help of a controversial reparations agreement with Germany) and its agriculture, and built up a strong army. The neighboring Arab states continued to threaten Israel's existence and in October 1956, Ben-Gurion — in collaboration with Britain and France — led the brief Sinai Campaign, which defeated the Egyptian army and gave the country a period of tranquility. One of Ben-Gurion's great dreams was the "conquest of the desert" and he set a personal example by settling in Sdeh Boker in the arid Negeb desert. In 1963 he retired there in order to write a history of the Jewish people's return to its homeland.

Dissatisfaction with the policies of his successors brought him out of retirement and he founded the Rafi party, which broke away from his own Mapai party; its adherents found only limited support and eventually returned to the Labor party. Ben-Gurion finally retired from political life in 1970. He wrote extensively and many volumes of his writings — books, articles, diaries, and letters — have been published by the institute established in his name in Sdeh Boker.

A. Avi-Hai, *Ben-Gurion: A State Builder*, 1974.
M. Bar-Zohar, *Ben-Gurion, A Biography*, 1978.
S. Teveth, *Ben-Gurion: The Burning Ground 1886–1948*, 1987.

BENTHAM, JEREMY (1748–1832), British philosopher, economist, and theoretical jurist. Immensely influential on the process of reform in the nineteenth century, Bentham is now best remembered for his espousal of the philosophical doctrine of Utilitarianism. More generally, he is notable as one of the first to attempt to discover scientific solutions to social problems, and — as a radical — for paving the way to socialism.

The son of a London attorney, Bentham was a precocious child; by the age of four he had learned to read and was already commencing his studies in Latin. He entered Queen's College, Oxford, in 1760 and graduated with a degree in law in 1763 at the age of fifteen. However, he was more interested in indulging his scientific curiosity through chemical experiments, and in engaging in abstruse speculations on legal theoriesBegin than in studying lawbooks. To his father's disappointment it became clear that he was not disposed to rise to the lord chancellorship (the apex of the English judicial system), the post to which the elder Bentham felt Jeremy's talents should lead him. Called to the bar, Bentham did his best to disentangle himself from the career that had been prepared for him; his extreme shyness only increased his aversion to such a histrionic profession.

The publication in 1776 of his first book, *A Fragment on Government*, brought Bentham to the attention of Lord Shelburne, who remained his friend and supporter. The work may be seen as marking the beginning of British philosophical radicalism. Bentham's trip to Russia to visit his brother, who was working there, resulted in his *Defense of Usury*, outlining his laissez-faire economic philosophy, which owed much to the theories of Adam *Smith.

His next work, the *Introduction to the Principles of Morals and Legislation*, made Bentham famous; in it he introduced his view that the aim of legislation should be to fulfill "the greatest happiness of the greatest number," on the assumption that happiness is good while pain is bad. Defining utility as "that property in any object whereby it tends to produce pleasure, good or happiness, or to prevent the happening of mischief, pain, evil or unhappiness to the party whose interest is considered," he went so far as to elaborate a "hedonistic calculus" to enable the computation of the effect of actions on the general good. Acknowledging the divergence between private and public interests, he argued that the role

> - I know not one country in which the Jew is truly free to follow his heart's desire — even if the law does not formally discriminate against him. The freedom of action of Jews is limited in every single place, either by the law and the police or by the political and social reality. The Jews in the diaspora do not control the forces which surround them and they are unable to do as they wish as Jews.
> - The State of Israel will not be tested by its strength or economy but by its spirit. We have inherited a great heritage and it is binding. It will be tested by the moral image it will give its citizens, by the human values which will determine its internal and external relations, by its faithfulness in deed and word to the supreme command of Judaism: "Thou shalt love thy neighbor as thyself."
>
> **Ben-Gurion**

The preserved remains of Jeremy Bentham in the University of London; his skull lies beneath his feet

of the legislator is to harmonize these interests through judicious use of the legal apparatus.

As his influence increased, Bentham, a pleasant and benevolent individual, gathered around him a number of good friends who supported and elaborated his ideas; it was also they who arranged for the publication of many of his writings, to which he was curiously indifferent. Especially significant was James Mill, who was instrumental in encouraging Bentham's nascent radicalism; his son, John Stuart *Mill, was to continue to disseminate influential theories deeply rooted in Benthamite doctrine. Bentham was also intimately connected with the economist David *Ricardo, while Robert Owen — the father of socialism — was also a good friend.

Bentham was by nature more interested in security than liberty: "wars and storms are best to read of, but peace and calms are better to endure" argued the man who was made a citizen of France by its revolutionary government. However, the logic of his ideas led Bentham to espouse the radical cause; in his *Catechism of Parliamentary Reform* he advocated a widening of the franchise, the introduction of the secret ballot, and equal electoral districts (recommendations that were the basis of resolutions to Parliament in 1818); He was a vigorous campaigner for prison reform, came to propound the emancipation of women; and argued for the better treatment of animals on the grounds that "the question is not 'can they think?' but 'can they suffer?'"

While vulnerable to rigorous logical scrutiny and deficient in many of its psychological assumptions, Bentham's philosophy was of great value as the foundation for his perceptive critique of existing institutions; people were receptive to his views and he lived to see many of his recommendations enacted.

His followers founded University College, London, and Bentham's mummy, kept there in a cupboard, is brought out to preside over college feasts.

J. Bentham, *An Odyssey of Ideas*, 1962.
J. R. Dinwiddy, *Bentham*, 1989.
R. Harrison, *Bentham*, 1983.

BERGSON, HENRI LOUIS (1859–1941), French philosopher. He was extremely popular because of an ability to couch his original philosophical ideas in clear language comprehensible even to the layman. He was born in Paris. His father, a Polish Jew, had been a pupil of *Chopin; his mother was English. As a student at the Lycée Condorcet he gravitated toward both mathematics and letters, but eventually settled on the latter, to the disappointment of his mathematics professor. He taught high school in Angers and Clermont-Ferrand before returning to Paris in 1889 to publish his doctoral thesis, *Time and Free Will* (1889). He taught at the Collège de France from 1900 to 1921, was elected to the French Academy in 1914, and in 1928 was awarded the Nobel prize for literature.

After World War I he was active in the promotion of international understanding and served briefly as the chairman of the League of Nations' Committee for Intellectual Cooperation before poor health forced his retirement. Toward the end of his life he became close to the Roman Catholic church, and would have converted were it not for his wish to be with his fellow Jews when they were being persecuted by the Nazis. Accordingly, after the Vichy government offered to exempt him from certain anti-Semitic laws, he publicly renounced all his previous posts and honors rather than accept privileged treatment.

Rebelling against previous philosophical assertions of a fixed and rigid reality, Bergson saw time, movement, and change as the essence of reality. He contended that there are two kinds of time: the mathematical conception of time, measured by clocks, which is in effect an illusion, and the real time of direct experience, a continuous flow in which one period merges imperceptibly and irreversibly into the next. His rejection of the mathematical conception of time evolves, in his doctoral thesis, *Time and Free Will*, into an argument against determinism. There he argues that a moment of choice cannot be represented as oscillation on a point on a line between various branches, in which the direction chosen is predetermined, because deliberation and choice are temporal, rather than spatial, activities.

In *Matter and Memory* (1896), Bergson tackled the mind-body relationship and concluded that memory is independent of the body, converging with it temporally and not spatially. He proposed the existence of two kinds of memory: habit memory consists of mechanisms or habits which are activated in response to certain stimuli and thus permit adaptation to specific situations; and pure memory, an accumulation of events as they occur in time that retains all of our past. He saw the brain as a filter which allowed specific memories to surface as they pertain to a given situation, thus leading to acceptance of part of the mind as being unconscious or subconscious.

In his most famous and popular work, *Creative Evolution* (1907), Bergson proposed the domination of the material universe by a vital force (*élan vital*), which is responsible for its continuous creative evolution, a process which he saw as the basis of reality and which could only be comprehended by intuition as opposed to reason. The book expresses his dissatisfaction with the materialist account of evolution proposed by thinkers such as Charles *Darwin and Herbert Spencer. He found fault with Darwin's thesis that random variations lead to the adaptations which better equip a certain species for survival. He argued that there must be some force which is responsible for the species' continuity of functioning throughout successive alterations in form, and for their evolutionary progress toward ever-increasing complexity, concluding that it was the *élan vital* which pervaded the evolutionary process and provided this force.

Creative Evolution was widely acclaimed, but the appearance of *Two Sources of Morality and Religion* in 1935 was greeted wih less excitement. Although *Creative Evolution* had seemed to be moving toward equation of the life force with a religious principle akin to God, the later book came much closer to a Christian position, asserting that God is love and the object of love. Intuition of the purpose and reality of the vital force, which could not be understood intellectually, was, according to Bergson, accessible only to certain exceptional persons whom he called mystics. This book also dealt with his notion of closed and open societies. The former, which were conservative and mired in mechanical routine, were an obstacle to evolution and tended to go to war with other closed societies, whereas the establishment of open societies could allow man to progress and grow toward further expression of the life force.

Bergson's ideas were extremely popular and influential among philosophers, novelists, literary critics, psychologists, and sociologists. His book *On Laughter* suggests that laughter serves to foster social discipline because we naturally laugh at whatever in behavior is stiff, clumsy, or machinelike. The comic inherently criticizes society by pointing to its inability to adapt. His idea of memory had, for example, a profound effect on the writings of his wife's cousin, Marcel *Proust, while George Bernard *Shaw propounded the concept of creative evolution in his writings and plays. He was, however, criticized for vague and unfounded argument and insufficient logical analysis. During World War II, despite ill health, he insisted on going out in bad weather and standing in line to be registered as a Jew, and died as a result of the chill he caught on that occasion.

L. Kolakowski, *Bergson*, 1985.
A. R. Lacey, *Bergson*, 1989.

BERNARD OF CLAIRVAUX, SAINT (1090–1153), French monastic reformer, ecclesiastical writer. Born to a noble family at the Château of Fontaines near Dijon in Burgundy, he was destined for an ecclesiastical career and as a child was sent to be educated for this purpose. Shy and reserved, showing no special vocation for the religious life, he nevertheless displayed a talent for writing, particularly ribald verses.

It was following his mother's death when he was seventeen that he became conscious that his "weak character needed a strong medicine," as he himself declared. He entered the monastery of Cîteaux in 1112 despite the protestations of family and friends at his choice of such an austere way of life. Bernard undertook to persuade them to change their way of life instead; the timid young man succeeded in imparting his enthusiasm and inducing thirty members of his family to follow his example.

In 1115 he was given the task by his abbot, Stephen Harding, of founding an abbey of the Cistercian order. Bernard founded the abbey in a deserted valley in Champagne, naming the area *Clara vallis* (the Clear Valley). He soon became one of the most active formulators of church policy, establishing his reputation as the leader of monastic reform of his age. He was at loggerheads with the king, Louis VI, whom he accused of opposing the reform, and with Peter the Venerable, abbot of Cluny, who was both his friend and rival. Already enjoying great prestige, in 1128 Bernard was asked by the Knights Templar at the Council of Troyes to write their code of discipline, which was approved by the council. In one of his most important treatises, *In Praise of the New Knighthood*, he attacked secular chivalry while praising the idealism of religious knights, who sacrifice their private interests to fight against the infidels.

Saint Bernard of Clairvaux, by Fra Filippo Lippi

A champion of orthodoxy, he was to become the virtual dictator of Christendom in western Europe. He criticized the rationalism of Peter *Abelard and had him condemned at the Council of Sens in 1140. He also attacked the Parisian scholars on the grounds that they constituted a new "Babylon." From 1141 to 1143 Bernard opposed Louis VII's government but after a reconciliation between the two, Bernard was able to influence Louis's decision to lead the Second Crusade. When one of his pupils was elected pope in 1143, Bernard of Clairvaux's influence increased subtantially.

He wrote a treatise, *Five Books on Consideration*, for the new pope, Eugenius III, in which he argued for a theocracy, claiming that the rule of the Christian world is the prerogative of the pope alone, while it was the king's and nobles' duty to fight the infidels. He was the spiritual leader of the Second Crusade, preaching for the fulfillment of the duty to protect the Holy Land and the Holy Sepulcher in Jerusalem. While the pope advocated the crusade on both religious and political grounds, Bernard saw it solely as a religious expedition whose intent was the salvation of souls. Moreover, his spiritual concepts were at variance with the lay manners of the Crusaders. Bernard opposed the crusade's anti-Jewish manifestations and his intervention saved the Jews of the Rhineland from persecution.

Under Bernard's administration the Abbey of Clairvaux experienced a period of prosperity and was considered one of the most prestigious monasteries of western Europe, so much so that Alphonso I, king of Portugal, declared his kingdom as vassal of the abbey and undertook to pay an annual tribute.

Toward the end of his life Bernard of Clairvaux was already regarded as a saint, his pupils attribut-ing his activities to the Divine Spirit and considering them as miracles. He was canonized twenty years after his death.

G. R. Evans, *The Mind of Saint Bernard of Clairvaux*, 1985.

E. Gilson, *Mystical Theology of Saint Bernard*, 1940.

B. S. James, *Saint Bernard of Clairvaux*, 1958.

BISMARCK, PRINCE OTTO EDUARD LEOPOLD VON (1815–1898), Prussian statesman; united the German states into the Second German Reich, and served as its first imperial chancellor, imbuing the Reich with Prussian nationalism. Bismarck was born at Schönhausen in the old Mark of Brandenburg to a Protestant and nationalist gentry family steeped in Junker class traditions. Although he inherited his mother's astuteness, he tended to imitate his bullish country father, whom he admired for his values and heritage. As a child Bismarck was enrolled in Berlin's best schools, where he mixed freely with the nobility and made contacts that were to serve him later in his political career.

In 1832 Bismarck attended university, first in Göttingen and later in Berlin, ostensibly to study law. However, he spent a great deal of his time drinking and duelling; in between he read avidly, mostly history, and became quite fluent in six languages. After graduating in May 1835, he took up a position with the Prussian civil service as judicial administrator in Aachen. As a distraction from the monotony of bureaucratic toil, he gambled heavily and chased women from the wealthier classes. In one such pursuit he was absent from his post for over three months, and so ended his brief civil service career.

He then enlisted in the Prussian army, for his mandatory year of military service, which up until then he had tried to evade. On his release in 1839 he returned to the family estate, which had collapsed through neglect following his mother's death. Within seven years he restored the family's prosperity. In 1844, bored and lonely, he ventured again to reenter public service but left two weeks later, unable to withstand life as a subordinate. Aggrieved and cynical, Bismarck saw his life as amounting to little. This changed when he met an evangelical Lutheran, Johanna von Puttkamer, who sought to convert him. By 1847 he was both a devout Lutheran and her husband. Around this time Bismarck became a substitute member of the Pomeranian provincial diet, a small and ineffectual local parliament. In 1847 he was elected to the Prussian Diet, where he championed absolutist Prussian order. He fought for the rights of the monarchy and decried the emancipation of the Jews. His reactionary path seemed certain once he saw that his stance was well received by the king.

In 1848 the revolutionary spirit sweeping across Europe came to Prussia, and following a popular uprising, the king curtailed his own powers and established a German National Assembly and Prussian Parliament, both elected by universal suffrage. Bismarck, a man out of step with the mood of the people, was elected to neither house.

When the king's measures proved ineffective in stopping the political turmoil he ordered the closure of the parliament. A fresh constitution established a new house with limited powers, to be elected by a restricted, more conservative, constituency. Bismarck seized his chance and won a seat in the new legislature. By now he resented the king's compromises and the attempts to subordinate Prussia to greater Germany. Bismarck decried every liberalization or dilution of Prussian identity, until the prerevolutionary confederation of German states was reestablished in 1850.

Bismarck's singular praise of the new-old order made him the obvious choice as Prussia's delegate to the federal diet in Frankfurt. However, he was soon at odds with the Austrian delegate, who constantly reminded the Prussian of Austria's supremacy. He realigned his political views once again and soon came to the notion — which he had previously opposed — of withdrawing the united northern German states from under Austrian domination. Henceforth, he spoke in the diet according to his own political agenda based on Prussian aggrandizement, easily succeeding in keeping Austria out of the free trade zone established in the rest of Germany. Hence, as the Ruhr district developed and northern Germany became the center for an industrialized Europe, Austria became a relative backwater, both economically and politically.

In 1859 the newly crowned King William I chose to moderate Prussian policies and Bismarck was dispatched as ambassador to Saint Petersburg; in 1862 he was appointed ambassador to Paris. In late 1862 Bismarck was recalled to Berlin in the king's desperate attempt to keep parliament from controlling the army. He was appointed prime minister and foreign minister, his only qualification for the job being vociferous opposition to reform.

Bismarck at once proved an autocratic ruler, with no confidants or colleagues. He countenanced no opposition and discussions tended to bring on a nervous crisis, during which he would rant. In his first address to parliament he stated, "the great issues of the day will not be decided by speeches and majority resolution...but by blood and iron."

Bismarck concentrated on foreign policy. In 1863 he deliberately ingratiated himself with Russia by not supporting the uprising in Russian Poland, thus securing Prussia's eastern border. Later that year, following the king of Denmark's death, Bismarck orchestrated a war by Prussia and Austria against Denmark and gained control of the states of Schleswig-Holstein. However, Austro-Prussian cooperation in wartime broke down in peace. The dispute over sovereignty of the lands led in 1866 to a confrontation, and in a few short weeks Austria was defeated at Königgrätz. Prussia thus gained su-

- He who has his thumb on the purse has the power.
- Politics is the art of the possible.
- A conquering army on the border will not be halted by the power of eloquence.
- We Germans fear God, but nothing else in the world.
- Anyone who has ever looked into the glazed eye of a soldier dying on the battlefield will think hard before starting a war.
- This policy can succeed only through blood and iron.

Otto von Bismarck

premacy in northern Germany and Bismarck, by annexing Schleswig-Holstein, ensured its becoming the dominant German state.

French fear of a powerful and united Germany under Prussian leadership gave Bismarck the opportunity to draw the German states together against their common foe. Through masterly statesmanship he effectively isolated France from all other assistance in 1870.

The catalyst for the Franco-Prussian War was the accession of a German prince to the Spanish throne. This horrified the French who, though helplessly overpowered, on July 17, 1870, declared war on Germany. The rout was over in six months, by which time Prussia was demonstrably the new power in Europe. Elated by victory, the people's demand for unity of the states grew and in 1871, by consent of the German princes, the Second Reich was established. William was crowned kaiser and Bismarck was appointed the first imperial chancellor.

Bismarck then set about centralizing power in Berlin, largely in Prussian hands. He had by then shaped a national character in his image — arid, domineering, and ruthless. He adopted the Prussian eagle as the imperial emblem and gave the new nation its motto "Armed might is power, and power is dominion." He was referred to as the "Iron Chancellor."

His next conflict was with the pope. He persecuted Roman Catholics in Germany for twenty years in an attempt to Prussianize them in what became known as the *Kulturkampf* ("war of the cultures"). He sowed the seeds of religious intolerance and grandiose military nationalism that were to grow into Nazism.

The rise of social democracy and growth of German industrialization aggravated his already poor relations with the Reichstag, the federal parliament. The death of William I in 1888 heralded the end for Bismarck. The new emperor, *William II, was a confident and brash young man who had his own ideas on statesmanship that conflicted with those of the chancellor. Eventually, on March 18, 1890, Bismarck was forced to resign.

In retirement he wrote his memoirs which, though they have little historical veracity, are of literary merit, and watched anxiously as the new emperor undid his carefully constructed treaties and plans.

E. Crankshaw, *Bismarck*, 1981.
E. Engleberg, *Bismarck*, 1991.
L. Gall, *Bismarck*, 1986.
A. J. P. Taylor, *Bismarck*, 1965.

BLAKE, WILLIAM (1757–1827), English poet, artist, and mystic. Blake's work was largely unkown to his contemporaries and only achieved full public recognition and acclaim in the early twentieth century. Throughout his life Blake remained something of a lonely individualist with a reputation for eccentricity; indeed, one journalist called him "an unfortunate lunatic whose personal inoffensiveness secures him from confinement."

The struggle for personal and political freedom that infuses Blake's work was something he shared with the wave of revolutionary radicalism sweeping across late seventeenth century Europe. Blake's modest upbringing as the son of a London haberdasher provided him with the opportunity to observe the suffering of the lower classes in England's newly industrialized capital. Throughout his life Blake was violently opposed to injustice and he is the first poet to describe the nightmare urban legacy of the industrial revolution, notably in poems such as "Jerusalem" and "London."

He had no formal education until, at age ten, he went to an art school and was apprenticed to engravers; when he was twenty-two, he went to study at the Royal Academy. Blake was as much a champion of spiritual as he was of intellectual freedom and sharply criticized the Rationalist philosophy of John *Locke and his followers who dominated contemporary English thought. Largely self-taught, Blake was nevertheless widely, if somewhat eclectically, read. His claim to "know nothing except the Bible" was quite untrue, although biblical metaphors and language permeate both his art and his poetry. Blake was also profoundly influenced by the work of Emmanuel *Swedenborg, the Swedish mystic who subscribed to the view that the appearance of ordinary objects was a veil concealing their true essence and that it was necessary to break through this veil to a higher form of reality. This was contrary to the Rationalist opinion that reality is derived from a rational interpretation of our sensory perceptions. Blake's work represents a persistent attempt through verse and art to break through the barriers of ordinary daily life to a higher world of the imagination, a world to which from childhood he believed he had access in visions.

Blake believed that as children, men and women are intuitively closer to the world of the imagination, and this theme of childhood innocence giving way to the perils of adult experience is expressed in the lyrics of his second book of poems, *The Songs of Innocence* (1789) and its sequel, *Songs of Experience*

- Energy is the only life and its form is the body and Reason is the bound or outward circumference of Energy. Energy is Eternal Delight.
- I regard fashion in Poetry as little as I do in Painting.
- Without contraries there is no progression. Attraction and Repulsion, Reason and Energy, Love and Hate, are all necessary to Human Existence.
- I must create a system or be enslaved by another man's.
- As a man is so he sees.
- I will not cease from mental fight,
  Nor shall sword sleep in my hand,
  Till we have built Jerusalem
  In England's green and pleasant land.
- To see a World in a grain of sand
  And a heaven in a wild flower,
  Hold Infinity in the palm of your hand
  And Eternity in an hour.
- One power alone makes a poet; imagination, the divine vision.

William Blake

(1794), in which he shows a strikingly modern perception of childhood. He portrays a world where children are often subject to strong negative and sexual feelings; for the Lockean Rationalist the child's mind was a blank page dependent on external influences to develop its identity. According to Blake, however, man enters the world fully formed mentally as well as physically and only the vicissitudes of adult experience causes him to lose his way. The role of the parent is not to indoctrinate the child with harsh moral codes, for he already has an intuitive morality of his own; instead, all that is required from the adult is security and gentle guidance.

Blake himself had no children. In 1782 he married Catherine Boucher, the illiterate daughter of a market gardener (she signed her name on her marriage document with a cross), whom Blake taught to read and write and even produce engravings in the manner of his own work. Despite severe financial problems in later life and Blake's unpredictable temper, Catherine Blake remained in devoted awe of her husband; a visitor to their home, remarking on the absence of soap, was met with the angry retort from Catherine, "Mr. Blake don't dirty."

It was as an artist, never as a poet, that Blake was able to make a livelihood. Trained as an engraver from the age of ten, he developed a technique which enabled him to print both text and illustration together on one page, which he later colored by hand. It was unfortunately a laborious and time-consuming process which limited the number of copies

William Blake, pencil drawing by John Linnell

Blake could produce, a contributing factor in his failure to reach a wider reading public. This technique, which was used for all except his first book of verse, *Poetical Sketches* (1783), emphasizes the integral nature of Blake's illustrations to any interpretation of his poetry. Initially Blake lived comfortably from the sale of his engravings, but in later life his favorite method of engraving became unfashionable and demand for his work slackened. Blake was forced to rely increasingly on the help of patrons such as the arts enthusiast William Hayley and the sculptor John Flaxman.

The death of Blake's favorite younger brother in 1797 and his trial and acquittal for seditious behavior (alleged criticism of the king, the army, and the country) in 1803 were traumatic events which, coupled with increasing poverty and frustration at home, increased Blake's disillusionment with existing social and religious systems and led him to retreat into a world of private mythology, most clearly expressed in later philosophical works such as *Jerusalem* and *Milton* (1804). In contrast to the approachable lyric poetry of his early books, these last two works are dense with obscure references to ominous and destructive forces, leading the reader into the strange phantasmagoric world of Blake's private symbolism.

Despite the failure of a one-man exhibition of his art in London in 1804, Blake did eventually manage to achieve limited fame as an artist. Toward the end of his life he gave up poetry to concentrate on illustrating the work of other writers such as Geoffrey *Chaucer, John *Milton, *Dante Alighieri, and also

the Book of Job. Illustration for Blake was never merely decorative — it served him as a form of visual comment, even textual criticism. Whether expressed in poetry or illustration, Blake's philosophy, while increasing in complexity, remains consistent. The modern dilemma of psychic disintegration, resulting from alienation with oneself and one's environment, is a repeated motif. The only solution envisaged by Blake is reintegration through art or nature, a theme to be reiterated by all the great Romantic poets. As *Napoleon's rise to power in France signaled the failure of the French revolution and the government in England showed little sign of becoming more liberal, art became Blake's last hope of freedom; he died disappointed in the efficacy of political revolution but convinced of the redemptive power of artistic creation.

J. Bronowski, *William Blake and the Age of Revolution*, 1965.
R. N. Esseck, ed., *Blake in his Time*, 1978.
J. King, *William Blake: His Life*, 1991.
M. Wilson, *The Life of William Blake*, 1948.

BOCCACCIO, GIOVANNI (1313–1375), Italian author and humanist. A literary pioneer, he was one of the first to write prose in vernacular Italian and his masterpiece, the *Decameron*, was crucial to the development of the modern short story. Along with *Dante Alighieri and *Petrarch, Boccaccio is one of Florence's three great literary figures.

Boccaccio was probably born out of wedlock to a Florentine businessman in Paris and taken by his father to Italy as an infant. Little is known of Boccaccio's childhood, though his works imply that the young man who always wanted to be a poet was unhappy at being groomed by his father for a career in business.

Around 1328 his father, who was employed by Florence's largest banking house, sent young Boccaccio to a branch of the business in Naples. Dissatisfied as he might have been pursuing such nonliterary endeavors, Boccaccio's writing career is rooted in these years in Naples. As a member of a banking firm influential with the court of King Robert, Boccaccio came into contact with the aristocrats of the time, exposing him to the courtly values evident in his early works and in some of the tales of the *Decameron* (first published in 1353). At the same time, Boccaccio's involvement in business may well have infused him with the zest for people of all ranks and types that gives the *Decameron* its power — as well, perhaps, as the taste for tales of trickery that gives the work so much of its humor.

Dante had Beatrice to inspire *The Divine Comedy*, and Petrarch had Laura as muse for his poetry. Boccaccio tacitly acknowledged the importance of his years in Naples by creating from his experience there the woman who would serve as his inspiration. Some identify Boccaccio's Fiammetta with Maria d'Aquino, natural daughter of King Robert, while others argue that she did not exist at all. Whatever

Boccaccio, by Andrea del Castagno

the source of Boccaccio's muse, he certainly created the myth of their great love and used her as inspiration and as a persona in his early works.

Even without the *Decameron* Boccaccio would have secured his place as one of the great literary innovators based on his earlier works. While none may be a masterpiece in itself, taken together these early works make up a breathtaking list of literary firsts. *Filocolo* (c.1336) is the first Italian prose romance and *Filostrato* (c.1338) the first Italian romance written in verse by a non minstrel (both Geoffrey *Chaucer and William *Shakespeare used its story of Troilus and Criseida as a source). Dante once complained that no Italian had ever won distinction as a poet of arms, so Boccaccio wrote the *Teseida* (c.1340–1341), the first Tuscan epic and the source for Chaucer's *Knight's Tale*. *Ninfale d'ameto* (c.1342) combines romance with pastoral in Italian for the first time. The *Elegia di Madonna Fiammetta* (c.1344), written from the point of view of Fiammetta herself, is the first Italian psychological romance, and *Ninfale fiesolano* (c.1345) is the first Italian idyll. Displaying a joy in innovation that perhaps surpasses a taste for literature, Boccaccio created in *L'amorosa visione* (c.1343) a long acrostic, using the letters of three sonnets he had written to structure the poem.

As important as these innovations were, Boccaccio's reputation rests largely on his skills as a story-

teller and on one great work. The *Decameron*, composed between 1349 and 1351, is a collection of 100 short tales. Like Chaucer's *Canterbury Tales*, the stories are held together by a frame: seven young women and three young men of Florence's upper class flee the city during an epidemic of the plague to the idyllic countryside where they spend time in gentle pursuits, including taking turns telling stories.

Boccaccio's introduction to the work describes in searing detail the breakdown of order and civilization during the plague. He paints a picture of parents abandoning children, of bodies left unburied, of sick women exposing themselves to the eyes of lowborn men. The order created by the storytellers is maintained beautifully, as each day the one who has been chosen king or queen decides a general theme for the stories. The stories themselves, however, range from the romantic to the ribald, and if one day the courtly tale of a deserving suitor who wins his love are told, on another we hear how a deceitful sinner is granted sainthood. Storytellers can create a beautiful, controlled world as a defense against chaos, but the hint of a world gone mad nonetheless seeps in.

Later in his life Boccaccio turned his talents to the new humanist scholarship, following the lead of his friend and mentor, Petrarch. He compiled two dictionaries, dealing with classical geography and mythology, collected a modest library of manuscripts, and gave a series of lectures on the *Divine Comedy*. Like Petrarch, Boccaccio remained religious but both his writings and his studies foreshadow the transition from a medieval to a more modern, secular world.

Despite illness and poverty Boccaccio spent his last years involved in diplomatic missions for the Florentine government, traveling and meeting with heads of state and church. He died poor but nevertheless heralded as one of the great writers of the time.

T. C. Chubb, *The Life of Giovanni Boccaccio*, 1969.
F. MacManus, *Boccaccio*, 1948.

BOHR, NIELS HENRIK DAVID (1885–1962), Danish theoretical physicist who has been called the founder of modern atomic physics. Bohr was born into a wealthy and cultured family in Copenhagen. His father was a professor of physiology at the university and his mother came from a prominent Danish Jewish family. His maternal grandfather was one of the leading bankers of his generation and a liberal member of the Danish parliament.

In 1911, after receiving his doctorate, Bohr accepted a scholarship to pursue research at Cambridge University, but after some contacts with Ernest *Rutherford, Bohr went to Manchester, where Rutherford had established a prominent center for research into radioactivity. Rutherford's atomic model, consisting of a nucleus and orbiting electrons, had been proposed the previous year, and was wholeheartedly adopted by Bohr when he realized that it formed the basis for an overall theory concerning the properties of atoms. However, Rutherford's model was inherently unstable under the prevailing classical physics theory, which stated that the orbits of the electrons would gradually decay and in the process the atoms would continually emit light. This was contrary to the known facts on atomic stability.

Bohr's atomic theory, expounded in three papers published in 1913, proposed that electrons circle around the nucleus in so-called stationary orbits in which they can continue without losing energy. On the other hand, light is emitted when an excited electron jumps from a stationary orbit of higher energy to one with lower energy. This light is emitted in determinable amounts, or quanta, of energy; hence the theory evolved into the field of quantum mechanics.

In 1916 Bohr returned to Copenhagen, where he was granted a professorship in theoretical physics, and, through his persistence, in 1921 the university's Institute for theoretical physics was inaugurated under his leadership. In 1922 he received the Nobel prize for physics. By the 1930s the Copenhagen Institute, commonly known as the Bohr Institute, became a place of pilgrimage for leading and aspiring scientists. After Bohr's death, it was officially renamed in his honor.

Bohr's work was disrupted by the outbreak of World War II. The institute became a refuge for scientists fleeing the Nazi regime and an escape conduit to England, Sweden, and the United States. When the Germans occupied Denmark in 1943, he himself was forced to seek refuge in Sweden. Once there, he pressured the Swedish government to take action to prevent the planned annihilation of Danish Jews, helping to save almost all of his Jewish countrymen.

In 1944 he was surreptitiously flown to England and then on to the United States, where he was involved in the allied war effort to develop the atomic bomb. With the work already nearing completion, his contribution at Los Alamos was mostly as an inspiration to the younger team members, to whom he was known as "Uncle Nick" (his cover name was Nicholas Baker).

During the years following the detonation of the atomic bombs over Japan, Bohr witnessed the fateful consequences of nuclear warfare, but, with his characteristic optimism, discerned a glimmer of hope in the very horror it embodied. He believed that the prospect of nuclear devastation would make future wars inconceivable. He endeavored to call statesmen's attention to this belief and in 1950 wrote an open letter to the United Nations advocating free exchange of information and scientific knowledge as a first condition to restoring mutual confidence and understanding among the nations of the world. He was active in establishing the first Atoms for Peace conference in Geneva.

Bohr was renowned for his warmth and humility, the nobility of his spirit, and the manner in which he

---

BY AND ABOUT NIELS BOHR

- This matter is so serious that it can only be discussed in a playful way.
- In our description of nature, the purpose is not to disclose the real essence of the phenomena but only to track down, so far as it is possible, relations between the manifold aspects of our experience.

Niels Bohr

- Bohr utters his opinions like one always groping and never like one who believes himself to be in the possession of definite truth.

Albert Einstein

---

encouraged and nurtured his pupils and peers. He died at his home in Carlsberg, active to the end.

P. Dam, *Niels Bohr (1885–1962)*, 1985.

D. Murdoch, *Niels Bohr's Philosophy and Physics*, 1990.

BOLÍVAR, SIMON (1783–1830), Venezuelan soldier and statesman; champion of South American independence. Bolívar was born in Caracas, Venezuela, to one of the most influential families in that city. His father died when Bolívar was only two and his mother when he was nine. His childhood was thereafter marred by a series of unsuccessful attempts to foist him on relatives. At one point he was placed in a boarding school and it was even planned that he would enter the clergy, but it soon became apparent that Bolívar's true calling was the army. An early influence on him was Simon Rodríguez, an eccentric and freethinking tutor who introduced the boy to the teachings of Jean-Jacques *Rousseau, *Voltaire, and similar thinkers.

Bolívar joined the local militia, where he attained the rank of second lieutenant. In 1799 he traveled to Spain to join an uncle; there, he continued his education and received an introduction to life at the royal court. His uncle's arrest and imprisonment in 1802 aroused a contempt for the monarchy that Bolívar bore throughout his life.

He returned to Venezuela in 1807. The country was then aflame with growing nationalist ferment, particularly as a result of the recent abortive attempt of Francisco de *Miranda to achieve independence. Groups of conspirators met clandestinely to promote the cause of independence, and among them was Bolívar. In 1810 Governor Vincente de Emparán was deposed and a ruling junta of local patriots was formed. Despite his lack of formal military experience, Bolívar was appointed lieutenant colonel of the infantry militia. Accompanied by two others, he set out to London to gain backing for the rebels. The mission failed — Britain regarded Spain as a potential ally against *Napoleon and would not risk destroying this alliance — but in London Bolívar met Miranda, whom he convinced to return to South America to lead the independence movement. Their ideas were often radical for their time and included education for women and the construction of a canal cutting through the Isthmus of Panama.

Venezuela was in the midst of renewed revolutionary ardor. A national congress was called in 1811 to draft a constitution for the new state. Although he was not a delegate, Bolívar played an active role in its deliberations. In his first recorded political address he proclaimed, "to hesitate is to perish." Independence was declared on July 5, 1811. Bolívar joined the army commanded by Miranda, but the two soon drifted apart. When Puerto Cabello, commanded by Bolívar, fell to the Spanish as a result of treason, Miranda determined to negotiate an armistice with Spain, abandoning independence. Soon after, Bolívar betrayed him to the Spanish in return for a passport. When asked why he had chosen to betray such a prominent national hero he replied that he did it "to punish a traitor to his country."

Bolívar escaped to the city of Cartagena in neighboring New Granada (now Colombia). That country was facing problems similar to those encountered by the Venezuelans in their bid for independence — disunity and an ineffective federal system of government allowing too much autonomy for local leaders at the expense of the federal government. In his Cartagena Manifesto, Bolívar blamed South American disunity for Venezuela's defeat.

A series of successful campaigns he led against the Spanish resulted in his being awarded the rank of brigadier general. In 1813 he was finally given the opportunity to liberate Venezuela. Bolívar fought six major battles against the Spanish, and became known as El Libertador, (the Liberator) after his conquest of Mérida. The Venezuelan campaign was an outstanding success; Bolívar led his troops into Caracas on August 6, 1813. A nominal local government was established but Bolívar, assuming the role of commander-in-chief, was virtual dictator of the country, molding the regime in line with his belief in a strong centralized government.

Not all Venezuelans were in favor of independence. Many continued to support the royalists and a bloody civil war ensued. Spanish atrocities prompted Bolívar to call for a war to the death; any Spaniard who did not actively support the independence movement was regarded as responsible for earlier defeats and likely to be sentenced to death. At first Bolívar succeeded in conserving his hard-won independence, but royalist forces defeated the patriots in 1814. With Caracas threatened, Bolívar ordered the shooting of the eight hundred Spanish prisoners held in the city, but this only infuriated the Spanish forces. Caracas fell soon after and Bolívar fled to Cartagena to assist in the defense of Bogatá. He then attacked Santa Marta, but as Spanish reinforcements approached the city he fled to Jamaica.

LAST TESTAMENT OF SIMON BOLÍVAR

Colombians!

You have witnessed my efforts to establish liberty where tyranny once reigned. I have labored unselfishly, sacrificing my fortune and my peace of mind. When I became convinced that you distrusted my motives I resigned my command. My enemies have played upon your credulity and destroyed what I hold most sacred; my reputation and my love of liberty. I have been the victim of my persecutors who have brought me to the brink of the grave. I forgive them.

As I depart from your midst, my love for you tells me that I should make known my last wishes. I aspire to no other glory than the consolidation of Colombia. You must all work for the supreme good of the union: my people, by obeying the present government in order to rid themselves of anarchy, the ministers from their sanctuary, by addressing their supplications to heaven, and the military, by using their swords to defend the guarantees of organized society.

Colombians! My last wishes are for the happiness of our native land. If my death will help to end party strife and to consolidate the union, I shall go to my grave in peace.

Bolívar sought American and British aid but this was denied; only Haiti would help the South American patriots. There he established his base of operations for the next three years. In 1816 Bolívar led two hundred fifty men to Venezuela. Despite their lack of weapons and supplies, they fought against royalist troops, winning several decisive victories and massive local support. His army grew considerably; by 1817, he was able to move his headquarters to the provincial capital of Angostura.

One of the outstanding people Bolívar chose to assist him in his wars was General Francisco Santander of New Granada. The two men complemented each other — Bolívar was an ideologue and Santander a pragmatist. Their combined forces men set out on a long, hazardous march to New Granada during the rainy season; the men were ill-equipped and many died of exposure and hunger, yet they defeated the Spanish at the battle of Boyacá and went on to capture Bogotá. In December 1819 Bolívar declared the formation of the Republic of Colombia, comprising Venezuela, New Granada, and Quito (present day Ecuador), as yet uncaptured. He was acclaimed president and Santander vice-president. Bolívar continued his conquests and Venezuela was reconquered after the battle of Carabobo (June, 1821). He now set out to free Quito and success at the battle of Pichincha in 1822 resulted in the liberation of Ecuador.

Only Peru remained in royalist hands; the southern half of the continent had been liberated by José de *San Martín, an Argentinian nationalist whose career paralleled that of Bolívar. The two met at Guayaqil to discuss the liberation of Peru in a meeting that has been the subject of much debate; it is known that they disagreed and that San Martín resigned, leaving the liberation of Peru to Bolívar. Bolívar arrived in Lima in 1823 and the next year, at the battle of Junín, the path was opened for the complete liberation of Peru. The highlands of upper Peru set August 6 as the date of independence; the new country was to be called Bolivia in honor of the Liberator.

That year, Bolívar organized the first conference of the newly independent states of former Spanish America, held in Panama. Colombia, Mexico, Peru, and the Central American states met together in what was the foundation of the Organization of American States. Bolívar was even offered the crown in recognition of his contribution to South American independence, but he rejected the offer in favor of a republican system of government. He was appalled by growing regionalism and nationalist trends among the new countries that portended the end of his dream for a united continent. Bolívar remained president of Colombia, but even in that country there was growing dissatisfaction with his authoritarian rule. Furthermore, Santander, who had effectively governed the country in Bolívar's absence, resented Bolívar's assuming his authority as head of state. The tensions between the two peaked at the national convention at Ocaña (1828), where Santander led the liberals in a successful bid to depose Bolívar.

Bolívar's final years were marked by further disaster. He survived an assassination attempt only to witness the slow breakup of the Colombia Federation and war between Colombia and Peru. In 1829 his home province of Venezuela declared itself independent. Bolívar settled on a ranch in Santa Marta, where he contracted tuberculosis and died.

G. G. Marquez, *The General in his Labyrinth*, 1992.
A. Mijares, *The Liberator*, 1983.
L. B. Prieto, *Simon Bolívar: Educator*, 1986.
J. L. Salcedo-Bastardo, *Simon Bolívar: The Hope of the Universe*, 1983.

BORGIA, Spanish-Italian family, originally from Aragon. The family rose to power in Renaissance Italy. In addition to performing their religious duties as heads of the Roman Catholic church, the popes also ruled the Papal States, which formed a broad band running across the center of Italy. In theory, the Papal States made the papacy the independent, and therefore unbiased, spiritual leader of all Christian lands. In reality, the popes became so involved in ruling and protecting these states that there came to be little difference between them and the secular leaders. Certainly their tactics — deception, intrigue, murder, war — were the same. In Italy (where the Borgia drama was played out) the population's proximity to the all-too-human frailties of high church officials meant that the church, as a religious body, received less respect there than anywhere else in Christendom.

Rodrigo Borja (Borgia; 1431–1503), who later became Pope Alexander VI, was born in Spain. His uncle, Pope Calixtus III, summoned him to Italy and helped him advance rapidly in the church. At twenty-five he became a cardinal, at twenty-six he was appointed vice-chancellor (head of the entire curia), and at thirty-seven he was ordained a priest. A competent, industrious, well-liked administrator, he served as vice-chancellor for thirty-five years under five popes, during which time he became the richest cardinal in Rome. In 1492, at sixty-one, he bought his election to the papacy by promising the other cardinals ample renumeration for their votes. His coronation was splendid and the people of Rome gave him a joyous welcome.

Handsome and sensuous, with graceful manners, a cheerful nature and an eloquent and witty tongue, Rodrigo was always popular with women. In that time popes often had illegitimate children and many used the power and wealth of the church to benefit family members. The easygoing morality of the time made this situation acceptable.

Alexander started his papacy well, embarking on an extensive building program, patronizing the arts, and punishing lawbreakers, but essentially he was a worldly man, who sought to strengthen the papacy through military and economic rather than religious means. Because the church was in poor financial condition, he felt he had to resort to simony (selling of church offices and services) to repair church fi-

Caesar Borgia, by Giorgione

nances. Alexander saw as a major priority the control of the Papal States and the nobles.

In 1494 Charles VIII of France invaded Italy. As he approached Rome many nobles and cardinals sided with him, hoping that he would rid them of Alexander, but Charles feared Spain's reaction to the deposition of a Spanish pope and came to terms with Alexander. To subdue the rebellious nobles and restore church rule over the Papal States — which he now regarded as essential for his personal safety — Alexander needed a good general and army, and so had to raise more money. Church services were put up for sale; dispensations, divorces, positions, and promotions could all be had for a price. He confiscated the estates of dead cardinals and malicious rumors began circulating that cardinals were being poisoned. Alexander rashly ignored public opinion, claiming that Rome was a free city where people were free to say or write whatever they pleased, and that their criticism did not bother him. Rumors of poisoning became inextricably linked to the Borgia name ever since, although historians have not yet discovered any proof.

Alexander found his general in his son **Caesar** (1476–1507). He had tried to use his position as pope to advance Caesar in the church by making him the archbishop of Valencia when he was sixteen and a cardinal at seventeen. However, at twenty-one Caesar decided against an ecclesiastical career and in 1497 his appointment was invalidated through an interpretation of canon law that held that bastards could not become cardinals. Caesar then immersed himself in politics and war. In 1499 Alexander bought Caesar a title and a royal bride (the sister of the king of Navarre) in return for granting the king of France a divorce, a dispensation to remarry, and a large sum of money. Alexander also became the king of France's ally in his plans to invade Italy and annex Milan and Naples; Caesar rode with the invading armies.

Tall, strong, and blond, as well as shrewdly intelligent and unscrupulous, Caeser was a military genius. He reconquered the Papal States and subdued the unruly barons in a remarkably short time. An adept statesman, he outmaneuvered the most seasoned diplomats, holding that, "It is proper to snare those who are proving themselves past masters in the art of snaring others." The Papal States flourished under his rule and by age twenty-eight he was the most powerful man in all Italy. For all his genius, however, his power was based primarily on his father's position.

Alexander died in 1503; the new pope, Julius II, had long been an enemy of the Borgias. Caesar tried to come to some settlement with him, but Julius stripped him of his position and power, and in 1504 had him imprisoned to forestall a civil war. He was in prison for two years before his wife's pleas led her brother to help Caesar escape. He died in 1507 at thirty-one, fighting gallantly against his brother-in-law's enemies.

Lucretia Borgia (1480–1519) was dearly loved by her father, Alexander, and brother, Caesar, but Roman scandalmongers twisted that love into accusations of incest, for which there is no historical proof. Her father alienated Rome by leaving her in charge of his daily business when he was away.

Arranged marriages were the custom then, with rulers making the unions of their children as politically advantageous as possible. Lucretia's first marriage at thirteen aimed at strenghtening papal ties with Milan. The marriage failed and was annulled four years later. At eighteen, she was married to Alfonso, the bastard grandson of Alfonso II, king of Naples, in an attempt to end the traditional enmity between Naples and the Pope. Caesar's marriage and France's war against Naples put a stop to this rapprochement; Lucretia loved Alfonso, but Caesar and Alfonso hated each other passionately. Hired assassins attacked Alfonso, but he escaped and was being nursed back to health by Lucretia when he saw Caesar walking in a neighboring garden. Suspecting Caesar to have caused the assassination attempt, Alfonso tried to kill him. Caesar then had Alfonso murdered, to Lucretia's grief.

Lucretia Borgia, by Bernardino Pintoricchio

Lucretia's third husband was Alfonso, heir to Ercole I, duke of Ferrara, a match by which Alexander hoped to acquire two more Papal States. Lucretia's name had been besmirched by rumors for years. Ferrara had her past investigated, found the rumors to be false, and agreed to the marriage. Lucretia came to be loved and respected for her virtue by the people of Ferrara. She became a linguist and a patron of the arts, devoting herself to Ferrara, her children, and works of charity, and ruling well during her husband's absences. She died at thirty-nine giving birth to her seventh child.

L. Collison-Morley, *The Story of the Borgias*, 1932.
O. Ferrara, *The Borgia Pope: Alexander VI*, 1940.
F. Gregorovius, *Lucrezia Borgia*, 1968.

BOTHA, LOUIS (1862–1919), South African military leader and statesman; first prime minister of the Union of South Africa. The present-day white population of South Africa, both British and Afrikaner, owes its distinctive identity to his vision of a new nation encompassing all the white peoples of the region. Botha was no less British than he was Afrikaner, although he felt more comfortable speaking Zulu than English.

Botha was the seventh of thirteen children. When he was five years old, his family fled British expansionism in Natal by trekking to the Boer-dominated Orange Free State. There, he received little formal education, but excelled at marksmanship and riding. Always astute, he was entrusted with the management of the family farm during the Boer War of Independence (1880). Following his father's death, however, he migrated to the short-lived New Republic in the southeast; although only twenty-one, his heroic expeditions against Zulu marauders earned him an appointment to the state's executive council. The New Republic, however, survived only three years before being annexed by the Transvaal, where Botha was promoted to *veldcornet* (equivalent to general) and elected to the Transvaal parliament.

His years in the Transvaal capital of Pretoria were among the happiest in Botha's life. He and his lively young wife Maatjie contrasted sharply with most of the older and mor staid parliamentarians but developed their own close circle of friends, among them state attorney Jan *Smuts. The two men became inseparable allies, particularly in the parliamentary struggle against Alfred Milner, an advocate of British interests in the Transvaal. At the same time, they recognized the futility of aggression against Britain and resisted any calls for war. War, however, was inevitable and Botha abandoned his parliamentary seat for the front lines.

The tragedy of the Boer War brought Afrikaner culture to the brink of extinction. Despite stunning victories, Botha was unable to force a British retreat from their operational headquarters at Ladysmith, and became convinced that defeat was inevitable. Soon after Botha's appointment as commandant general of the army, British forces captured Pretoria. The Transvaal's stubborn refusal to surrender forced Botha to organize his decimated troops into guerilla bands. The British retaliated with a scorched earth policy — farmsteads were destroyed, and women and children were imprisoned in concentration camps — but the fiercely independent Boer leaders were undeterred.

With no reasonable cause for hope, Botha initiated a meeting with British commander Lord Kitchener; negotiations were conducted over countless games of bridge, until acceptable terms of surrender were reached. The ensuing Treaty of Vereeniging (1902) assured British domination of Boer lands in return for recognition of Afrikaner cultural autonomy. Whereas many Boers, led by General James Hertzog, rejected Vereeniging, Botha and Smuts were pleased by Britain's acquiescence to Boer nationalist aspirations. The majority of Boers agreed with Botha; as head of the Het Volk party, he was elected first prime minister of the Transvaal colony.

Botha and Herzog drifted further apart over negotiations to unite all the crown colonies of southern Africa into the Dominion of South Africa. Botha's willingness to compromise over language and culture in return for maintaining the status quo of the majority black population endeared him to the British, while he maintained his traditional base of support among the Afrikaners. When the Dominion of South Africa was formed in 1910, Botha was recognized as the leader most capable of forging a single national identity out of the two hostile peoples. His compromises were far-reaching; he was willing to forgo the national appellation "Boer" in favor of the generic " Afrikaner." To Hertzog and other Boer leaders, however, Botha was merely hastening the demise of an autonomous Boer national identity. They established the rival National party to champion their own rights against a leader they believed had betrayed them.

Four years later, the National party became a serious threat to Botha's authority among the Afrikaners. Having not yet forgotten their humiliating defeat in the Boer War, they were reluctant to support Britain against Germany in World War I. Many believed that a German victory would enable them to reassert their independence, while the British, recognizing the strategic importance of the southern Cape Province, expected Botha to occupy the neighboring German colony of South-West Africa. Botha went from crushing a civil war to international war as he donned his old uniform to conquer German South-West Africa. The German officers were no match for Botha, an expert in guerilla tactics well acquainted with the harsh terrain. His victory over the German forces entitled South Africa to sign the Treaty of Versailles and become a founding member of the League of Nations.

J. Meintjes, *General Louis Botha: A Biography*, 1970.
B. Williams, *Botha, Smuts, and South Africa*, 1946.

BRADLEY, OMAR NELSON (1893–1981), American general. Born in Clark, Missouri, Omar Bradley overcame the disadvantages of a modest family background to enter the United States military academy at West Point. Upon graduation in 1915 he was commissioned a second lieutenant in the artillery corps but saw no action in World War I. Nonetheless he rose to the rank of major.

Between the world wars Bradley pursued a career as an instructor of mathematics and military science and tactics at several institutions, among them West Point. As commander of the Fort Benning Infantry

School, in Georgia, he impressed General George C. *Marshall with his capabilities and innovative approach. Marshall's patronage enabled Bradley to rise through the ranks.

In 1938, Bradley was appointed to the general staff in Washington, D. C., and therefore did not see active duty in World War II until 1943. As commander of the U.S. Army Second Corps under General Dwight D. *Eisenhower; Bradley led his troops in the final stages of the campaign to drive the Germans out of North Africa. He then served as deputy commander to General George *Patton in the invasion of Sicily.

Bradley's grasp of frontline combat and his well-proven talents as an officer and tactician prompted Eisenhower to give him a key role in planning D-Day. In June 1944 Bradley led the U.S. First Army across the English Channel to storm the Normandy beaches.

Having succeeded in securing a bridgehead on the continent, Bradley was placed in command of all U.S. forces (1,300,000 men) in northwestern Europe. It was the largest contingent of troops ever under the control of one American officer. The relationships he cultivated with soldiers in the field helped him understand the mentality of men such as "the rifleman who trudges into battle knowing that statistics are stacked against his survival." General Patton did not favor Bradley's cautious attitude in advancing his troops.

Breaking out from the Normandy salient, Bradley's army swept across France toward Paris, only to be met by a surprise German counteroffensive. Conflict arose in turn with General Eisenhower who wanted to put some of Bradley's army under the command of British General Bernard *Montgomery. These confrontations climaxed during the Battle of the Bulge, during which, although threatening resignation, Bradley, held his own and led his forces across the Rhine into Germany. There his troops made the first Allied contact with advance units of the Red Army during which, Bradley, although threatening resignation, held his own.

Shortly before the war ended in March 1945 Bradley's contribution to the Allies was recognized with his promotion to full general. After the war he carried out important work as administrator of veterans' affairs. In 1949 he became the first chairman of the Joint Chiefs of Staff — the highest position attainable in the U.S. defence establishment. In 1951 he opposed General Douglas *MacArthur's extension of the Korean War to the Chinese border, saying that this was "the wrong war, at the wrong place, at the wrong time, and with the wrong enemy." That same year Bradley's wartime memoirs, A Soldier's Story, were published; they contained harsh criticism of his colleagues, particularly General Montgomery. After retirement from the army in 1953, Bradley turned to business.

J. Jones, World War Two, 1975.

R. E. Merriam, Dark December: Battle of the Bulge, 1947.

BRAHE, TYCHO (1546–1601), Danish astronomer; second child of an old and noble Danish family, he was raised by a childless paternal uncle. His uncle wanted Brahe to become a statesman and provided him with an excellent Latin education, sending him to the University of Copenhagen when he was thirteen years old.

The solar eclipse of 1560 aroused Brahe's interest in astronomy and he devoted himself to its study until his uncle sent him to the University of Leipzig, employing a tutor to ensure that he studied law, not science. Nevertheless, Brahe continued studying astronomy in secret and came to realize that his books (mostly derived from classical authorities) presented a different picture of the heavens than that revealed by his observations. Deciding that the books were wrong, he concluded that the movement of the planets and stars could only be understood through systematic, continual observation.

Although Brahe's family disapproved of his scientific interests, his careful observations of a new star that appeared in 1572 attracted the attention of Denmark's King Frederick II, who offered him the island of Hveen and generous financial grants so that he could conduct his observations in peace. Brahe accepted Frederick's offer and moved to Hveen with his family (he had formed a relationship with a woman with whom he lived unmarried for twenty-eight years and had eight children). He built an elegant and extensive compound there, which he called Uraniborg, since his work was that of studying the heavens.

The years in Hveen (1576–1597) were happy, active, and productive. Brahe invented instruments with which he made detailed observations of 777 stars. He was aware of Nicholas *Copernicus's theory that the earth revolved around the sun, but did not accept it since his own observations revealed inaccuracies in Copernicus's calculations. Instead, Brahe developed his own theory explaining the movement of the planets claiming that while the planets orbited the sun, the sun and the planets orbited a stationary earth. Word of Brahe's methods and discoveries spread, Uraniborg frequently had visitors, astronomy students were eager to assist him, and Frederick increased his endowments.

The adulation made Brahe haughty, and he offended powerful people. He willingly accepted royal endowments of estates but refused to fulfil his legal obligations and was involved in several law cases over his mistreatment of tenants. His behavior was overlooked during Frederick's lifetime but Frederick's son refused to tolerate it and confiscated the estates. Insulted and angry, Brahe left Denmark in search of a more appreciative patron.

Brahe made only sporadic observations before becoming reestablished with his family and instruments in Bohemia in 1599, where Emperor Rudolph II provided him with a castle and promised him a generous annual grant. However, Brahe's work in Bohemia was limited by lack of

Tycho Brahe in his observatory, a 17th century print

assistants, Rudolph's empty treasury, inferior facilities, and a feud with another astronomer. However, it was in Bavaria that Johannes *Kepler became Brahe's assistant, and Kepler's laws of planetary motion — the basis for modern planetary astronomy — were derived from Brahe's work, which ended with his death just two years after his move to Bohemia.
J. A. Gade, *The Life and Times of Tycho Brahe*, 1947.

BRAHMS, JOHANNES (1833–1897), German composer. He was born in Hamburg, where his father played the double bass in light music ensembles, not always in the most fashionable of places. Brahms's mother was seventeen years older than her husband; young Brahms was brought up as a prodigy by his parents. He began studying the piano at a very young age but performed only in his father's circles, eventually joining his father's ensemble as they played dance music. The young musician almost never used music scores during these performances; instead, he had books to read on the piano rack in front of him.

Brahms began touring as an accompanist, traveling first with a young Hungarian violinist, Eduard Remenyi. The two enjoyed the carefree nature of their adventure much more than the musical aspect of their work. Brahms's reputation as a composer began to grow once he was introduced to Clara and Robert Schumann. The latter wrote that Brahms was the genius Germany has been waiting for ever since the deaths of Ludwig van *Beethoven and Franz *Schubert, and went on to say, "I felt that one day there must suddenly emerge the one who

would be chosen to express the most exalted spirit of the times in an ideal manner, one who would not bring us mastery in gradual developmental stages but who, like Minerva, would spring fully armed from the head of Jove. And he has arrived — a youth at whose cradle the graces and heroes of old stood guard. His name is Johannes Brahms." However, the German composer had his many detractors as well. Richard *Wagner said, referring to Brahms, that "the evil only starts when one attempts to compose better than one can," and Pyotr *Tchaikovsky commented, "I have played over the music of that scoundrel Brahms. What a giftless bastard."

From 1857 to 1859 Brahms was a court pianist, chamber musician, and choir director in Detmold, where he began working on his first piano concerto. He then expected to be named the conductor of the Hamburg Philharmonic Society, but the position was given to another musician. The composer then went to Vienna, which soon became his home.

From 1862 Brahms established himself as a musician in Vienna, where he conducted the choral society and later became the director of the local Society of Friends of Music. He had a worldwide reputation and his many compositions brought him financial success as well. Brahms enjoyed the Viennese lifestyle and was quoted as saying as he left one party, "I beg a thousand pardons if there should be anyone here whom I have not insulted tonight!" All his life he had many friends yet was an independent bachelor. It is hard to explain the gap between his outer benign personality and the inner passion that emerges through his music.

In contrast to many of his forerunners, Brahms created a music culture which remains alive in Vi-

ABOUT BRAHMS

Brahms was a loner who "was occasionally invited to dinner or to a bachelor party where he was relatively at ease; had a faithful housekeeper; and lived contentedly, after receiving his library from Hamburg. He was an enthusiastic collector of musicians' autographs, and characterized himself in numerous letters to friends and other musicians as shy and taciturn. He was sufficiently well-to-do that he could help impecunious fellow musicians or friends, something he did often, generously and tactfully. He never gave up his contacts with relatives in Hamburg and in an anxious and touching manner endeavored to remain on familiar terms with them long after he had really lost all intimate contact with them."

Franz Endler

enna to this day. Today Brahms's four symphonies are cornerstones of the genre, but it took many years until the composer was ready to complete his first symphony. He began working on it in 1855; seven years later he had nearly completed its first movement, yet was still unsure of his ability to write a full-fledged symphony. It took him fourteen more years to complete his first symphony, which was premiered in Karlsruhe in 1876. He then said that this composition was "long and not exactly amiable."

When Brahms died, Vienna staged one of its magnificent funerals for its beloved composer. He left most of his possessions to the Society of Friends of Music, and their archives still hold his manuscripts, autographs, and beloved library.

Brahms's musical output was immense. In addition to his four symphonies and two piano concertos, he composed a violin concerto, a double concerto for cello and violin, a mammoth choral composition, a *German Requiem*, and a vast amount of chamber music, some of which, especially the string sextets, is sublime.

K. Geiringer, *Brahms: His Life and Works*, 1936.
P. Latham, *Brahms*, 1948.
R. Specht, *Brahms*, 1930.

BRAILLE, LOUIS (1809–1852), French pioneer in the development of contemporary reading and writing systems used by the blind. He was the son of a harness maker from Coupvray, France. When he was only three years old, while playing in his father's shop, an awl slipped off the table and struck him in the left eye. Within weeks the ensuing infection left Braille completely blind.

Since few opportunities then existed for the blind, Braille's father insisted that his son pursue a standard education in the village school. With his phenomenal memory, Braille surpassed his sighted classmates and was awarded a scholarship to the prestigious National Institute for Blind Children. There, too, he excelled at his academic studies and took up piano and the organ. At the institute's library, a collection of only three titles, each consisting of twenty volumes with large, embossed letters, Braille taught himself to read by running his fingers over the words. In just a few years, Braille was teaching the younger students the academic and musical skills he had mastered.

Braille's stay at the institute coincided with the visit of Charles Barbier, an artillery captain who had developed a system of night reading for soldiers. The advantages of Barbier's alphabet, a series of raised dots and dashes, was apparent to Braille, and he immediately began to modify it. He abandoned the dashes and placed all the dots in a rectangular grid measuring two by six dots. This new system, first published in 1829 and revised in 1837, included all the letters of the French alphabet (W was added later), punctuation, mathematical symbols, and even musical notation.

Although "Braille" was soon adopted by the institute, its author was better known as a musician and a minor composer. Not long after the death of the institute's director, "Braille" was abandoned in favor of the earlier, more tedious, embossed letters. Braille, now suffering from tuberculosis, was quietly forgotten, only to be rediscovered accidentally. A talented blind musician, a former student of Braille, was asked to play in one of the fashionable salons of Paris. After a moving performance, the girl unassumingly explained that all the credit must go to her teacher, who had developed the system by which she had learned and who was now dying. News of the forgotten system created a stir in the audience, and national recognition was soon forthcoming. The National Institute for Blind Children reintroduced its use in 1854, two years after Braille's death. In 1952 he was reburied in the Pantheon in Paris.

G. Farrel, *The Story of Blindness*, 1956.

BRAMANTE, DONATO (1444–1514), Italian Renaissance architect. Born near Urbino, facts about his youth are obscure, but he is supposed to have studied with Piero Della Francesca in Urbino. In 1477 he was working in Bergamo, where remnants of frescoes attributed to him still exist.

Bramante worked in Milan from about 1481 until 1499, when his patron, Duke Lodovico Sforza, was forced to leave the city. In Milan he worked on many buildings, including the church of Santa Maria Della Grazie, the sacristy of Santa Maria, and the sacristy of San Satiro, which he finished many years later. During this period he also wrote poetry and was involved in staging performances at court. Much of his work in Milan was left unfinished after he fled to Rome when the French occupied the town in 1499; he remained in Rome for the rest of his life. The ancient architectural ruins of the old city fascinated him and he spent days studying their methods of construction, their simplicity, and their functionalism.

In 1502 Bramante built for the Spanish monarchs, *Ferdinand I and *Isabella, a "little temple" on the traditional site of Saint *Peter's martyrdom. This beautiful Tempietto can still be seen in Rome. Built upon circular steps, enclosed by Doric columns with a lovely balustrade over the cornice and a graceful cupola, it is a perfect example of Bramante's use of classical forms to create his own purely Renaissance style.

Not long after Julian II ascended the papal throne in 1503, he decided to replace the old Basilica of Saint Peter and Bramante was commissioned to design a new church to mark the burial place of the saint. He designed a square church, based on the Greek cross, with four strong stone piers joined by arches. Over this was to be a drum to support a soaring dome. The church would be magnificent, whether viewed from the interior or from the outside. Bramante was able to build only the four great stone piers and the basis for the connecting arches as Pope Julius was forced by lack of funds to halt the work.

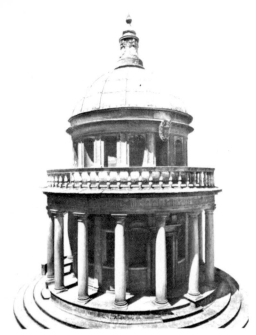

The Tempietto in the cloister of San Pietro in Montorio, Rome, by Bramante

Bramante was put in charge of all other papal constructions. He designed and constructed the Vatican gardens, served as town planner for the major rebuilding of Rome, and designed many monumental buildings. His penchant for simple elegance and functionalism was apparent in his many designs for palazzos. A good example is the house of *Raphael, his pupil. It no longer stands but was a two-story building, with living quarters upstairs. The bottom story was roughly textured – "rusticated" – and designed with a row of stores placed symmetrically on either side of the main entrance.

When Bramante died in 1513 *Michelangelo continued the work on the church, adhering to the plan of the Greek cross. Ten architects worked on Saint Peter's before it was completed in 1629. It is still possible to glimpse the vision of Bramante – and Michelangelo – in the relative simplicity of the western facade.

Generations of architects have been influenced by Bramante's design for Saint Peter's, as well as his further development of the barrel vault with cupolas and domes.

As in the Tempietto, his elegant use of architectural forms and details was all the decoration he needed. He made extensive use of engaged columns, niches, and optical illusions. Bramante was widely admired for his innovative approaches to solving architectural problems and is regarded as the founder of the High Renaissance style in architecture. Michelangelo himself subscribed to the general view that Bramante was the greatest architect of his time. Bramante was buried in Saint Peter's.

J. Burckhardt, *The Architecture of the Italian Renaissance*, 1985.
R. Wittkower, *Gothic and Classic*, 1974.

BRECHT, BERTOLT (1898–1956), leading German dramatist and poet after World War II. He was born in Augsburg, Bavaria, where his father was sales director of a paper mill. He came from a mixed religious background: his father was Roman Catholic and his mother Protestant. Although he himself later became openly anti-Christian, morality per se exerted a strong influence on his life and work and he once said that the Bible was the book that had influenced him most.

He was educated in Munich and Berlin and spent a year at the University of Munich studying medicine and natural science before being called up for military service in 1918. He spent a year in the army as a medical orderly and the experience molded his pacifism and antimilitarism. Although he may have had sympathies for the communist party at that time, it was to be a decade before he became an ardent communist, and for the moment his tendencies were more anarchist.

After leaving the military, he worked as a dramatic adviser and editor, often shocking audiences with his methods of production. He was also a decided antisentimentalist and his first plays, among them *Baal* (1919) and *Drums in the Night* (1920) about a returning soldier hero, were not well liked. In 1928, however, his *Threepenny Opera* (music by Kurt Weill), an adaptation of John Gay's *The Beggar's Opera* (1728), became a popular success. Either missing, or else perversely enjoying, the implied criticism of themselves, the audiences responded enthusiastically to the play's jazzy tunes, slogans, clowning, and irresponsible mood. Brecht and Weill had another success with the opera *Rise and Fall of the City of Mahogany* (1930). By this time Brecht had also become well-known as a poet, publishing *Domestic Breviary* in 1927.

The worldwide depression of 1929 helped to crystallize Brecht's political tendencies and his communist plays date from this period. *The Measures Taken* dealt with communism in China. *He Who Said Yes* advocated the necessity of placing the interest of the community above individual rights. An adaptation in 1932 of Maksim *Gorky's novel *The Mother* depicted the story of a shrewd, witty, strong-willed woman (played by his own wife, Helene Weigel) who takes up the cause of communism, and *Saint Joan of the Stockyards* was set in Chicago. They were didactic and propagandistic and implied the necessity of using violent means to achieve communist ends.

With the Nazi rise to power Brecht's plays were banned and he fled Germany, after a struggle not to leave his two-year-old daughter behind as hostage. After several years in Europe, he moved to the United States in 1942, living in Santa Monica, Cali-

- It's all right to hesitate if you then go ahead.
- What a miserable thing life is; you're living in clover, only the clover isn't good enough.
- From the cradle to the coffin, underwear comes first.
- Who has good luck is good; who has bad luck is bad.
- When praying does no good, insurance helps.
- Do not fear death but rather the inadequate life.
- Those who have no share in the good fortunes of the mighty often have to share in their misfortunes.
- What rapture, oh, it is to know
  A good thing when you see it.
  And having seen a good thing, oh,
  What rapture 'tis to flee it.

Bertolt Brecht

fornia, and working as coeditor of *Das Wort*, a refugee periodical published in Moscow. For the most part, though, his propagandist messages were more anti-Nazi-Fascist than pro-communist. Altogether, his emphasis became much more humanistic and less political than in his younger period. Between 1937 and 1941 he wrote some of his best-known plays, among them the musical critique of war, *Mother Courage; The Life of Galileo; The Good Woman of Szechuan*; and *Herr Puntila and his Man Matti*. *The Caucasian Chalk Circle*, a later play in the same mode, was written in 1944–1945. In 1947 he was subpoenaed to give evidence to the House of Representatives Committee on un-American activities investigating communist sympathizers. The experience was repulsive to Brecht, who left the next day for Europe.

He returned to Germany and settled in East Berlin in 1949. The theater in Schiffbauerdamm was made available to him and he created the Berliner Ensemble to perform his plays and mold it into one of the most acclaimed theatrical companies in the world. Although somewhat more contemplative after his years in exile, he was no more sympathetic a character than he had ever been — thin, gangly, deliberately untidy, and a compulsive womanizer. He saw it as his duty to make people think and his plays generally succeeded in fulfilling his goal of making their audiences uncomfortable. He introduced the "alienation effect," which deliberately blocked the emotional identification of the audience with the action on the stage. Instead Brecht encouraged a detachment necessary to appreciate his deeper message, which was related to real life and not to the theater.

E. Bentley, *The Brecht Memoir*, 1986.
R. Gray, *Brecht*, 1961.
R. Hayman, *Brecht: A Biography*, 1983.

BRONTË, CHARLOTTE (1816–1855), **EMILY JANE** (1818–1848), and **ANNE** (1820–1849), Victorian authors and poets. The Brontë children were born in the small Yorkshire village of Thornton to an Evangelical minister of Irish descent, Patrick Brontë, and Maria Branwell. The Brontës married in 1812 and in the next eight years Maria gave birth to five daughters and one son: Maria, Elizabeth, Charlotte, Patrick Branwell, Emily, and Anne.

Shortly after Anne was born the family relocated to Haworth, near Bradford, Yorkshire, where Patrick Brontë had a parish. The move proved to be too strenuous for his wife, however, and she died soon after, in 1821. Her sister, Elizabeth Branwell, remained with the family to care for the young children. Although the children respected "Aunt Branwell," her extreme religiosity made them uncomfortable. Patrick Brontë made attempts to remarry, but was rejected and lived without a companion for the rest of his life, leaving the children without a mother figure. They grew up on the bleak and misty Yorkshire moors, which sparked their imagination and later influenced their writing.

Tragedy was also a formative influence on the Brontë children. The four eldest girls were sent to boarding school in 1824 but after a few months Maria and Elizabeth fell sick and died. Charlotte and Emily were promptly removed from the school and remained at home, where they were taught by Aunt Branwell. It was in their teens that the children, including Branwell, began to write and define their individual styles. Charlotte and Branwell began writing about the imaginary kingdom of Angria and English voyagers in West Africa, while Emily and Anne wrote of the equally imaginary island of Gondal in the Pacific.

Both Charlotte and Emily began to teach at different boarding schools but neither enjoyed teaching. After spending the late 1830s as governesses, it was decided that the three girls would set up their own school, whereupon Charlotte and Emily were sent to Brussels in 1842 to improve their language skills. Charlotte's experiences in Brussels had a significant impact on her life, for it was here that she fell in love with the schoolmaster, Constantin Heger, who was to be the basis of a character in a later novel. Upon leaving Brussels and returning to England in 1844, it became clear to the sisters that the intended school was not going to succeed. By this time their brother Branwell had taken to drinking and drugs and their father was growing blind. The sisters knew that they could not rely on the men in their family to support them, and it is possible that this knowledge prompted them to begin to write seriously and for publication.

The Brontë sisters first published a book of poems under the pseudonyms of Currer, Ellis Bell and Acton (1845) and although the volume did not sell well, all three sisters continued to write. By the end of June 1846, Charlotte had written *The Professor*, Emily had written *Wuthering Heights*, and Anne had written *Agnes Grey*. All three volumes were rejected by several publishers and it was not until after the completion of Charlotte's next and most famous work, *Jane Eyre*, in 1847 that Anne's and Emily's works appeared. *The Professor* was published posthumously. Anne's *The Tenant of Wildfell Hall* came out in June 1848, but then another series of tragedies befell the Brontës.

Patrick died in the fall of 1848 and Emily died of consumption a few months later, in December 1848. Anne soon developed the same symptoms as her sister and she, too, died the following year at age twenty-nine. Despite her grief, Charlotte continued to press forward with her writing, publishing *Shirley* in October 1849 and *Villette* in 1853, and preparing new editions of her sisters' poetry. *Villette* was somewhat autobiographical, which caused Charlotte a great deal of anxiety as its main character, Paul Emanuel, was modeled after Constantin Heger.

When Arthur Bell Nicholls, Patrick Brontë's curate, asked Charlotte to marry him, she rejected him at first. Nicholls left the village, asked for permission to correspond with her, and soon changed her mind. They were married in July 1854, and their literary career came to an end, although it is unclear if Nicholls caused Charlotte to stop writing. Shortly after the marriage Charlotte became pregnant, but in February 1855 she grew ill and died the next month, leaving two unfinished works, *The Story of Willie Ellin* and *Emma*.

BY AND ABOUT CHARLOTTE BRONTË

- Give him rope enough and he'll hang himself.
- Look twice before you leap.
- Conventionality is not morality. Self-righteousness is not religion. To attack the first is not to assail the last.
- Life, believe, is not a dream,
  So dark as sages say:
  Oft a little morning rain
  Foretells a pleasant day!

Charlotte Brontë

[Charlotte] once told her sisters that they were wrong — even morally wrong — in making their heroines beautiful as a matter of course. They replied that it was impossible to make a heroine interesting on any other terms. Her answer was, "I will prove to you that you are wrong; I will show you a heroine as plain and as small as myself, who shall be as interesting as any of yours."

E. Gaskell, 1857

The Brontë sisters contributed to creating a new kind of heroine, one who was an outsider much as they were. Because their mother died at an early age and their father was a minister, the Brontës did not fit well into a social class and they did not have many friends. Class divisions are apparent in both *Wuthering Heights* and *Jane Eyre*. Jane Eyre is a poor, plain orphan making her own way in the world, yet she is judged for her internal qualities.

The Brontës were considered shocking and coarse, probably because they were unaware of English Victorian standards, having done so much of their own reading among foreign authors or authors of a previous generation. Their contributions to English literature can be found in their honest observations from their own lives and their family's unique and tragic story.

P. Bentley, *The Brontës and Their World*, 1969.

E. Chitham and T. Winnifrith, *Charlotte and Emily Brontë*, 1989.

H. Moglen, *Charlotte Brontë: The Self Conceived*, 1976.

BRUCE, ROBERT (1274–1329), Scottish king and national hero. Robert Bruce bore the same name as his grandfather, a claimant to the Scottish throne after the death of Margaret Maid of Norway in 1290. Edward I of England supported the rival claim of John Baliol in return for recognition of English suzerainty. Baliol, however, had no intention of paying fealty to Edward. In 1295 he signed the Auld Alliance with France in a bid to assert Scottish independence. Edward responded by devastating the country and capturing its royal symbols, among them the Stone of Destiny, believed to have been Jacob's pillow, upon which Scottish kings were crowned. With Baliol exiled to Normandy the revolt was resumed by William Wallace and supported by the native Scottish aristocracy led by Robert Bruce and John Comyn. Edward's military prowess and personal rivalry among the Scottish nobles doomed the revolt. After a crushing defeat at Falkirk in 1298, Wallace fled to France, leaving Bruce and Comyn in command of the disheartened forces. Rivalry among the two resulted in Comyn nearly killing Bruce in a brawl in 1299. At the same time, Bruce shared the Anglo-Norman descent of the English nobility and possessed extensive estates as far south as London. His defection to Edward in 1302, therefore, came as no surprise. In fact, Bruce believed that it was not yet time for Scotland to rise in revolt.

For four years, Bruce feigned fealty to England. By 1306, believing that the disastrous defeats of the past were forgotten, he approached several rebel leaders to probe their readiness to resume hostilities. At a church in Dumfries he described his plans to Comyn, but the animosity between them still lingered. Threatened with betrayal, Bruce killed Comyn. Bruce now faced opposition from both Edward's and Comyn's supporters. Although the country was as yet ill-prepared for war, Bruce fled to

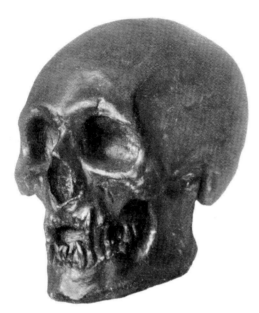

The skull of Robert Bruce

Scone and, with the support of the local clergy, declared himself king (Robert I).

When news of the revolt reached Edward, he swore never to rest until Bruce had been punished. Bruce and his supporters were hounded incessantly; once captured, they were treated callously. A brother was hanged and a sister was suspended in a cage from the walls of Berwick Castle. Only at the last minute was Bruce's twelve year old daughter spared a similar fate. Bruce himself only narrowly eluded capture. The Scottish MacDougal family still possesses a brooch supposedly ripped off Bruce's shoulder in battle. The fugitive king was in despair when, hiding in a cave, he watched a spider spinning its web. Swinging from a slender strand, it narrowly missed the cave's wall several times before finally succeeding in attaching the thread. The spider's perseverance was said to have inspired Bruce to continue the struggle.

His fortune turned upon the death of Edward I in 1307. The new king, Edward II, lacked his father's military acumen, while under Wallace, Bruce had mastered the necessary guerilla tactics for fighting larger forces. Major assaults were often conducted at night. Bruce's men, disguised by dark cloaks, would creep up to the walls of English castles, scale them, and force an entry. Even some of his opponents began supporting Bruce covertly. A secret entrance to Edinburgh Castle was revealed by an aristocrat who used it to visit his mistress in town.

By 1314 only the countryside surrounding Stirling remained in English hands. Bruce's brother Edward, in command of the besieged local castle, agreed to surrender to the English if he was not relieved within a year. British chroniclers claim that One hundred thousand English troops surrounded the castle. Twenty thousand is more likely, and no less a significant adversary to Bruce's six thousand men. Edward, however, disregarded the local topography, vital for Bruce's guerilla tactics. The road to Stirling ran through a forest, below which was a boggy field traversed by several sluggish streams known as burns. By one such stream lay the village of Bannock. In the first day of the Battle of Bannockburn, Bruce repelled Edward twice. Scottish troops attacked the English horses; their enormous corpses prevented English mobility in the bog. On the second day Edward mistakenly placed his archers behind his soldiers, ultimately denying them the protection of a hail of arrows. While the Scottish decimated the imposing English forces, Edward fled so hastily that his contemporaries claim he could not even "make water." Scotland was now completely independent.

Although Bruce had the support of the Scottish clergy, the pope still supported English suzerainty even after Edward himself disclaimed his rights to Scotland in 1323. Bruce pleaded for papal recognition in the Declaration of Arbroath (1320), but it was not received until 1328. Shortly after, Robert Bruce died, possibly of leprosy.
G. W. S. Barrow, *Robert Bruce*, 1965.

BRUNO, GIORDANO (1548–1600), Renaissance philosopher and cosmologist who posited an infinite universe of innumerable worlds; an advocate of tolerance among the quarreling powers of his time. Bruno affirmed the Copernican idea of a universe in motion, dislodging the fixed-Earth notion that preceded it, at the same time deprecating Nicholas *Copernicus's scientism that reduced things to lifeless mathematics in a cosmos Bruno envisioned as animate.

Born at Nola near Naples in 1548, Bruno was baptized Filippo and later called the Nolan after his birthplace. At age fourteen he went to Naples to receive an education in the humanities. Three years later he entered the Dominican order, taking the name Giordano. From the beginning of his association with the Dominicans he was suspected of heresy because of his unconventional ideas, but was nevertheless ordained as a priest, completing his studies in theology in 1572. The following year he was accused of denying the divinity of Christ and a church trial was prepared. Bruno escaped to Rome where he was again accused by the church authorities, this time of murder. He escaped before the trial, deserting his Dominican affiliations and fleeing to the north of Italy; from there he continued to journey throughout Europe.

In 1581 he traveled to Paris and the court of Henry III. The French ruler, fascinated with Bruno's occult doctrine of "memory," appointed him to the post of royal lecturer. In 1582 Bruno published his work *The Candlemaker*, vividly portraying the social corruption of Naples. In 1583 he

> I say that the universe is entirely infinite because it has no edge, limit, or surfaces. But I say that the universe is not all-comprehensive infinity, because each of the parts thereof that we can examine is finite and each of the innumerable worlds contained therein is finite. I declare God to be completely infinite because He can be associated with no boundary and His every attribute is one and infinite. And I say that God is all-comprehensive infinity because the whole of Him pervades the whole world and every part thereof comprehensively and to infinity. That is unlike the infinity of the universe which is comprehensively in the whole but not comprehensively in those parts which we can distinguish within the whole.
>
> You see further that our philosophy is by no means opposed to reason. It reduces everything to a single origin and relates everything to a single end, and makes contraries to coincide so that there is one primal foundation both of origin and of end. From this coincidence of contraries, we deduce that ultimately it is divinely right to say and to hold that contraries are within contraries, wherefore it is not difficult to compass the knowledge that each thing is within every other — which Aristotle and the other Sophists could not comprehend.
>
> **Giordano Bruno**

left for England, taking up residence in the French embassy and publishing his controversial tracts in secret, thereby avoiding the storms that accompanied their publication. At the same time, he visited the court of *Elizabeth I.

In 1584 Bruno published his Italian dialogues; in one of these works, entitled *Ash Wednesday Supper*, he affirmed the proposition that the sun is the center of the solar system, the controversial innovation of Copernicus. Bruno went still further, propounding the then inconceivable notion of an infinite universe with manifold worlds, each its own center. This contradicted the church's doctrine, based on Aristotelian cosmology, of a finite universe with fixed spheres around a single earth. He also differed with *Aristotle's dualism between form and matter, which Bruno held to be united, a neo-Platonic (see *Plato) view of the nature of things. Like *Galileo Galilei, Bruno's attitude toward the Bible was to embrace its moral teachings while dismissing strict adherence to its views of nature and astronomy and, as with Galileo, this attitude led to tragic consequences for Bruno.

In 1591 Bruno incautiously returned to Italy, invited by one of Venice's leading citizens, Giovanni Mocenigo, who was anxious to learn Bruno's techniques of memory and magic. Disappointed by his lessons, Mocenigo betrayed Bruno to the Inquisition.

Bruno eventually recanted his controversial views and was then extradited to Rome, where he spent eight years in prison before facing another trial at the hands of the Roman authorities. This time he refused to recant and in 1600 Pope Clement VIII ordered him executed. Before being burned alive for heresy, Bruno, a believer in knowledge beyond the religious doctrine of his time, confronted his executioners with the words: "Perhaps your fear in passing judgment on me is greater than mine in receiving it." He greatly influenced later philosophers, especially Benedict *Spinoza and Gottfried *Leibniz.

I. L. Horowitz, *The Renaissance Philosophy of Giordano Bruno*, 1952.
J. Kirchhoff, *Giordano Bruno*, 1980.
P. H. Michel, *The Cosmology of Giordano Bruno*, 1973.

BUDDHA, GAUTAMA (c.563–c.483 B.C.E.), Indian philosopher and founder of Buddhism. A man of noble character, intense vision, compassion, and profundity, he established a great new religion which continues to influence millions of lives across the world. As accounts of his life and teachings were written by devoted followers, however, and only many years after his death, it is difficult to extricate fact from legend and myth. Thus a reconstruction of his personal history can only be taken as a general outline.

Although it is not certain exactly when he lived, it is known that he died at about the age of eighty. He was born in Kapilavastu, India, near the border with present-day Nepal, to Queen Maha Maya and King Suddhodana of the Sakya warrior caste, and was originally named Prince Siddhartha. He later acquired many other names, including Sakyamuni ("sage of the Sakya tribe"), Bhagavat ("he who possesses happiness"), Tathagata ("he who has succeeded"), Jina ("the victorious"), and Buddha ("enlightened one").

According to the legends and many paintings of the scene, Buddha entered his mother's womb in the guise of a small elephant and was assisted into the world by a god while his mother supported herself with a fig tree. His mother died shortly after his birth and his father, who feared he would choose the life of an ascetic over that of a warrior and ruler, strove to eradicate any such tendencies by keeping him in the palace and removing any cause of unhappiness or sight of suffering from his life. Educated, intelligent, every material want satisfied, he married when he came of age and seemed to have everything. Yet one day in 533 B.C.E., according to legend, something drew him away from the carefree, self-indulgent life of the palace and into the streets outside, where he encountered an old man, a sick man, and a corpse being carried away for burning. Thus, suddenly introduced to the knowledge that none can escape suffering, he became extremely troubled. As he returned to the palace he met a monk and determined to adopt a similar lifestyle. That night he bade his wife and newborn son a silent farewell and rode into the forest, replacing his royal attire with the simple clothes of an ascetic. This decision is known as the Great Renunciation.

He wandered all over northern India seeking an answer to the problem of suffering and finally elected to study with two Brahman teachers. Unsatisfied, he eventually left them and for the next six years maintained an extremely austere lifestyle, along with five followers, in an attempt to pit mind against body. When he decided to abandon asceticism, his followers left him. Having failed to understand the problem of pain through meditation or self-mortification, he sat quietly one day under a Bodhi tree (tree of enlightenment), reflecting on the human plight, and suddenly experienced the Great Enlightenment, which revealed to him the way of salvation from suffering. A short time later he preached his first sermon in the Deer Park near Benares and established an order of monks. His five former disciples rejoined him there and began to accompany him throughout India to spread his word. He spoke in the vernacular, using language that everyone could understand, and acquired numerous followers, for he accepted everyone regardless of sex or caste. During the rainy seasons when travel was impossible, he would stop for meditation and the sites where he stopped later became permanent retreats. Although, as his fame grew, kings and other

A young and bitter Buddha on the road to enlightenment, a thirteenth century painting by Liang Kai

wealthy patrons began to donate parks and gardens for retreats, Buddha's life remained a simple one of meditation and teaching. He returned briefly to his hometown, where he converted members of his famiy to his beliefs, but for the next forty-five years continued to wander through India teaching. He died in Nepal, apparently of food poisoning. His last words to his disciples, according to legend, exhorted them not to mourn his death: "And now, O *bhikkhus*, I take leave of you. All living elements are transitory. Work out your own salvation with diligence."

Buddha's rejection of metaphysical speculation in favor of logical thinking and his dismissal of Hindu hedonism, asceticism, spiritualism, and the caste system, revolutionized Oriental thinking. His doctrine opposed nonego and impermanence to the basic concepts of Hinduism, i.e., the self and the permanence of Brahman, or Absolute Being. It also opposed a spirit of universal charity and sympathy to the exclusiveness of the caste system, thus attracting millions of followers. His teachings were an attempt to communicate the experience of awakening, a transformation of consciousness in which one is released from the confines of individual personality. He summarized his doctrine in a formula known as the Fourfold Noble Truths concerning suffering, the origin of suffering, the cessation of suffering, and the way to its cessation. The way to cessation is called the Eightfold Way and consists of eight "steps" (right views, right intention, right speech, right action, right livelihood, right effort, right mindfulness, and right concentration). Adoption of the Way leads to a state of peace, *nirvana*, in which all craving for material things ends, although the self is not annihilated.

In the centuries after Buddha's death Buddhism diversified, probably as much as did Christianity, and spread across most of India to Ceylon, Turkestan, China, Korea, Japan, Burma, and Tibet. Although in India it eventually became virtually extinct, it exists throughout Asia in two main forms, the Hinayana in Ceylon (Sri Lanka), Siam (Thailand), Burma, and Indochina, and the Mahayana (the later form) in China, Korea, Tibet, and Mongolia.

The practice of Buddhism has acquired different rituals in different countries but although in popular Buddhism the tendency is to deify him, Buddha is generally recognized as a mortal who realized the ideal of what any man may become.

Carpenter et al., *Founders of Faith*, 1986.
M. Carrothers, *The Buddha*, 1989.
B. Nanamoli, *The Life of the Buddha*, 1972.
M. Pye, *The Buddha*, 1979.

BURKE, EDMUND (1729–1797), British statesman and political philosopher. He was born in Dublin to a prosperous Protestant lawyer and his Roman Catholic wife. The boy was sent to live with maternal relations in southwest Ireland; it was thought a country upbringing would strengthen a

THE WISDOM OF EDMUND BURKE

- I do not know the method of drawing up an indictment against a whole people.
- Kings will be tyrants from policy, when subjects are nobles from principle.
- There is but one law for all, namely, that land which governs all law, the law of our Creator, the law of humanity, justice, equity — the law of nature, and of nations.
- There is a limit at which forebearance ceases to be a virtue.
- When bad men combine, the good must associate.
- Superstition is the religion of feeble minds.
- Toleration is good for all or it is good for none.

weak constitution. Here he received his schooling and absorbed from his surroundings a lifelong concern with the sufferings of the Irish peasantry as well as a keen interest in history and folklore.

In 1744 he began a classical education at Dublin's Trinity College. After graduation in 1748 Burke went to London, ostensibly to follow his father into the legal profession but, in fact, to live the life of a man of letters. In 1757 he married the daughter of a doctor from Bath. In contrast with many of their contemporaries in public life, they enjoyed a devoted marriage, maintaining in Burke's private life the stability he defended in the public sphere.

Burke gained renown with his treatise *A Vindication of Natural Society*, arguing that man could only realize his potential in civilized society. He also began work on *The Annual Register*, a yearly diary of political and cultural events which achieved a considerable following and allowed him entry into the circle of literary men surrounding Samuel *Johnson. Johnson commented: "Burke's talk is the ebullition of his mind; he does not talk from a desire of distinction but because his mind is full."

Burke talked his way into a period of service in Dublin as secretary to Irish chief secretary William G. Hamilton, during which he saw misgovernment and its consequences: "They call for bread and you give them the gallows." Returning to England keen to fight against misuse of power, he turned his talents to public life, aligning himself with the Whigs and, in 1765, entering Parliament.

Burke's opening speeches were a resounding success. In one of these he called for the repeal of the Stamp Act, a major irritant in the American colonies. He wanted to preserve the British North American empire but recognized the impracticality of enforcing royal authority by arms: "it may subdue for a moment, but it does not remove the necessity of subduing again, and a nation is not governed which is perpetually to be conquered." Burke's position on the American conflict placed him in a minority and for almost his entire political career he remained allied to the opposition.

The example he set in party loyalty and his talents for party management played a significant role in the emergence of the modern adversarial political system. He also set a model for disinterested pursuit of public welfare, not seeking to make his fortune from the public purse and believing that a member of Parliament was no mere delegate of the electors but rather their representative, duty bound to exercise his own judgment and not blindly reflect their prejudices. For the rest of his political career, Burke remained true to his principles of defending the liberties enshrined in Britain's unwritten constitution. He expressed his philosophy as "The greater the power, the more dangerous the abuse."

Fear of the moral and social disorder unleashed by the French Revolution spurred him into his greatest campaign, urging British military intervention to save Europe from a terror that would know no restraints. In his *Reflections on the French Revolution* (1790) he produced a work of political literature of enduring value.

His outspoken stand against the revolution isolated him from many in the Whig party. His last years were also embittered by tuberculosis and debts totaling £30,000 until a royal pension ameliorated his circumstances. The greatest tragedy, though, was the death of his son Richard, also of tuberculosis. Richard had aided his father in some of his campaigns and was to have taken his seat in Parliament.

C. B. MacPherson, *Burke*, 1990.
C. C. O'Brien, *The Great Melody: A Thematic Biography and Commented Anthology of Edmund Burke*, 1992.
F. O'Gorman, *E. B., His Political Philosophy*, 1973.

BURNS, ROBERT (1759–1796), Scottish poet. Born in Alloway, Ayrshire, he was the elder son of William Burns, a gardener and, later, tenant farmer. William Burns was well read and of a philosophical turn of mind. His wife, while poorly educated, was well versed in Scottish folklore. From her and from her kinswoman, an old women who worked for the family, the young Burns absorbed the wealth of local legend that inspired his creativity. William Burns and several neighbors hired a private tutor by the name of Murdoch to teach their sons. Robert was a bright pupil and soon acquired a solid grounding in English language and literature.

Young Burns had to help work the farm, but his health was not strong, and hard toil and poor diet aged him prematurely. In his mid-teens he first began writing poems as love songs for local girls and as an escape from periodic bouts of depression. His father died bankrupt in 1784 and Robert Burns became the main breadwinner, struggling to make a meager living from poor land on a farm at Mossgiel.

As a farmer, Burns enjoyed little success but made his name locally in other ways. He had a child by one of his farm servants and, later, twins by Jean Armour, the daughter of a mason in a neighboring town. He wanted to marry Jean, but her family was against the idea, so together they went to church to publicly atone for their sin before parting. Burns continued to live the life of a dissolute farmer, carousing with his cronies and shocking the locals with his outspoken opinions on the church, but he was determined to make another kind of name for himself with the publication of his Scottish poems.

His first poems chiefly in the Scottish Dialect were published in Kilmarnock in 1786. They were a remarkable success, enthused over by the Edinburgh literary elite and also popular with the country people he wrote for. He received a warm reception on his first visit to the capital at the end of that year. His simple country manners and charming conversation won many admirers, from nobles and academics taken by this natural intellectual, to Edinburgh tavern society into which he flung himself with customary abandon. A new, expanded edition of his poems brought him fame beyond the borders of his native land.

Burns hoped to find employment as an excise officer in Edinburgh, but returned to Mossgiel, his future still unclear. He was a welcome guest at aristocratic homes, but the welcome did not extend so far as intimacy with their young ladies and so he returned to Jean Armour, who bore him two more children.

- The best-laid schemes o' mice an' men
  Gang aft a-gley.
- Man's inhumanity to man
  Makes countless thousand mourne!
- But pleasures are like poppies spread
  You seize the flower, the bloom is shed;
  Or like the snowfall in the river,
  A moment white — then melts for ever.
- Inspiring bold John Barleycorn!
  What dangers thou canst make us scorn
  Wi' tippenny, we fear nae evil;
  Wi' usquebae, we'll face the devil!
- Should auld acquaintance be forgot,
  And never brought to min'?
  Should auld acquaintance be forgot
  And auld lang syne?
- My heart's in the Highlands, my heart is not here;
  My heart's in the Highlands, a-chasing the deer.
- Scots, wha hae wi' Wallace bled
  Scots, wham Bruce has aften led.
- O, my Luve's like a red red rose,
  That's newly sprung in June.
- A man's a man for a' that!

Robert Burns

Throughout, Burns still yearned for wider recognition, envisaging himself as Scotland's national poet. He undertook tours of the Border country and the Highlands, visiting sites of historic significance which appealed to his strong patriotic sentiment.

In 1787, the Edinburgh publisher, James Johnson, asked him to find traditional Scottish songs for a work entitled *The Scots Musical Museum*. He traveled widely, rescuing a significant part of a folk tradition on the verge of disappearing. Songs which he discovered, rewrote, and reconstructed reached new heights of popularity; some, like the famous "Auld Lang Syne," which he wrote, except for the first line, remain favorites to this day. He would not accept remuneration, clinging to an ideal of independence which he could not afford to maintain. Shortly before his death he had to write a letter begging for five pounds to pay off a pressing creditor.

In 1788, he legalized his relationship with Jean Armour and they settled on a farm leased at Ellisland near Dumfries, later moving to live in the town. She accepted his infidelities in a cheerful spirit, but his riotous behavior at a country house party resulted in a social boycott by some of his upper-class patrons.

Admitted at last into the excise service, Burns was active in the pursuit of smugglers, a brace of pistols at the ready. His support of radical causes, in particular the French revolution, cast suspicion on him, but he reassured the authorities as to his loyalty. Working to the end on the collation of Scottish songs, he died of a rheumatoid complaint.

A. Bold, *Robert Burns*, 1973.
D. Daiches, *Robert Burns and his World*, 1971.
J. Mackay, *Burns*, 1992.

BYRD, RICHARD EVELYN (1888–1957), American explorer and aviator. He was born in Winchester, Virginia, and at age fourteen he wrote in his diary that he would someday explore the North Pole. A year later he was excited to learn that the *Wright brothers had flown an airplane. From that day forward Byrd kept the themes of exploration and aviation intertwined with his life's goals.

Byrd graduated from the U.S. Naval Academy in 1912 and went on to become an aviator. He spent World War I teaching flying and also invented several aviation instruments. After the war he was assigned to the MacMillan Arctic Expedition in Greenland. On May 26, 1926, Byrd and his aviator friend Floyd Bennett made the first flight over the North Pole. On that day he wrote in his log, before arriving at the North Pole: "To think men toiled for years over this ice, a few hard-won miles a day; and we travel luxuriously a hundred miles an hour. How motors have changed the burdens of man!" Both aviators received the Congressional Medal of Honor for their historic flight. In 1927, accompanied by a third man, they flew nonstop from New York to Paris.

The fame achieved by these two exploits at the time enabled Byrd to raise $800,000 to fund an expedition to the Antarctic. Major funding came from wealthy philanthropists, including John D. *Rocke-feller Jr. and Edsel Ford. Contributions were accepted from the general public as well, including $4.35 from Byrd's eight-year-old son, who had worked all summer to raise the money. The 1928 expedition included forty-two men, four airplanes, powerful radio transmitters, a motor tractor, ninety-five Greenland huskies, and a correspondent from the *New York Times*. Four ships transported the 665 tons of cargo needed for the expedition.

Byrd constructed a base village on the Ross Ice Shelf, known as Little America. From Little America they explored as much surface area as practical and set up an advance base. On November 28, 1929, Byrd and three companions flew the expedition's Ford Tri-motor from the advance base over the 10,500-foot Hump of Liv's Glacier on the way to the South Pole. The next day they became the first to fly over the South Pole. To honor his friend Floyd Bennett, who had died in 1928, Byrd named the airplane in his memory and dropped an American flag weighted with a rock from Floyd Bennett's grave on the South Pole. Byrd flew a circular course around the pole and experienced the rapid crossing of all twenty-four hour time zones as they converged on the pole. He also noted some confusion in that every direction was northward and the positions of east and west had reversed.

Byrd named a newly discovered mountain range Edsel Ford Range and a large plateau, Rockefeller Plateau, in recognition of his chief funders. A large tract of land was named Marie Byrd land in honor of his wife's support for him. For his heroic efforts Byrd was promoted to the rank of rear admiral.

Funding for his second Antarctic expedition was far more difficult, as the stock market crash of 1929 had affected the generosity of his patrons. He raised only $150,000 in cash for the 1934 expedition. Considerable equipment and supplies were donated by industrialists in return for being allowed to advertise that the Byrd expedition was using their products. During this expedition he and two others traveled south of Little America to establish a small base from which to monitor winter weather, but due to the loss en route of a large tractor, only enough supplies to support two men arrived at the station. Byrd believed that three men could spend an Antarctic winter in isolation but that two would only get on each other's nerves. He therefore decided to stay by himself, and wrote the book *Alone* to describe his experiences.

After three months at the station Byrd almost died from carbon monoxide fumes from a faulty burner, as the fresh-air ventilators had become blocked with snow, but he recognized the problem and took corrective measures. Additionally, gas fumes from his radio's generator were making him ill. Although he did not disclose the fact that his health was failing, fellow expedition members at Little America sensed his condition from his radio contacts. A rescue team arrived and stayed two months nursing him back to health before returning to home base.

Byrd took part in two more Antarctic expeditions in 1946–1947 and 1955–1956 and flew over the South Pole during each of these expeditions.

W. Chapman, *The Loneliest Continent*, 1967.
M. Gladych, *Admiral Byrd of Antarctica*, 1966.
E. P. Hoyt, *The Last Explorer*, 1968.

BYRON, GEORGE GORDON, LORD (1788–1824), English poet and one of the best-known figures of the romantic movement. Born in London, he lived with his mother in Scotland until 1798 (his dissolute father having died in Paris in 1791), when he inherited his great-uncle's title and estate at Newstead Abbey, England. From 1801 to 1808 he was educated at Harrow and Trinity College, Cambridge. Although only five foot eight inches tall, he weighed 224 pounds at this time and throughout his life had to battle obesity. He had a foot so crippled that he once begged a doctor to amputate it, but nevertheless was an excellent long-distance swimmer, easily swimming five miles or more. In 1806 *Fugitive Pieces* appeared, a verse collection printed at his own expense. The following year his collection of original poems and translations entitled *Hours of Idleness* was published.

Lord Byron shaking the dust of England from his shoes, by Max Beerbohm

Byron took his seat in the House of Lords in 1809 and spent the next two years traveling with his friend John Cam Hobhouse in Portugal, Spain, Greece, and Turkey. While in Greece, he began work on an autobiographical poem, *Childe Harold's Pilgrimage*. The freedom and spontaneity which he experienced in Greece had a marked influence on him and inspired several of his poems. In 1811 he returned to England and, resuming his seat in the House of Lords, was active over the next two years in the Liberal wing of the Whig party. The first part of *Childe Harold's Pilgrimage* was published in 1812 and brought him fame overnight. The poem was a superb display of his narrative skills, attested to his poetic vitality, and established him as an outstanding romantic poet.

In the years that followed Byron was involved in various amorous exploits. His passionate affair with Lady Caroline Lamb, wife of the future English prime minister, Lord Melbourne, was regarded as scandalous even in fashionable society, where extramarital liaisons were an accepted mode of conduct. Byron then retreated into a more discreet relationship with Lady Oxford. He also maintained a frequent and intimate correspondence with his half-sister, Augusta Leigh. Byron's letters to his confidante, Lady Melbourne (the mother-in-law of Caroline Lamb), hint at intimate relations with Augusta, and he may well have fathered her daughter. He gave vent to the emotions aroused by his affairs in his oriental tales, *The Giaour* (1813), *The Bride of Abydos* (1813), and *The Corsair* (1814). In an attempt to extricate himself from his emotional entanglements, Byron married Annabella Milbanke, Lady Melbourne's niece, in January 1815. The couple settled in London, where Byron soon became exasperated with Annabella's behavior to the point of violent cruelty. She gave birth to a daughter at the end of 1815, but a month later left with the child and returned to her parents. A legal separation followed, and Byron never saw his wife or child again. Wild rumors circulated about him, hinting at incestuous relations with Augusta Leigh, and as a result he felt compelled to leave England.

He arrived in Switzerland in the summer of 1816 and took up residence on the shores of Lake Geneva, becoming friendly with P. B. *Shelley and his wife, Mary Godwin, who together with Mary's half-sister, Claire (Jane) Clairmont, were staying near Geneva. Byron had begun a liaison with Claire before he left England and she gave birth to his child (Clara Allegra) in 1817. He worked on the next portion of *Childe Harold* while continuing to write regularly to Augusta. He was joined in Geneva by his friend Hobhouse and the two made a trip over the Bernese Oberland, which gave Byron the inspiration for *Manfred* (1817). In October he traveled with Hobhouse to Italy. After a stop in Milan he arrived in Venice, where he took an apartment over a draper's shop. His numerous affairs with Italian women caused much scandal in England. During

---

FROM LORD BYRON'S WORKS

He who ascends to mountain tops, shall find
The loftiest peaks most wrapt in clouds and snow;
He who surpasses or subdues mankind,
Must look down on the hate of those below.

Childe Harold's Pilgrimage

The cold in clime are cold in blood,
Their love can scarce deserve the name.

The Giaoure

Let us have Wine and Woman, Mirth and Laughter,
Sermons and soda-water the day after.
Now Hatred is by far the longest pleasure;
Men love in haste, but they detest at leisure.
Society is now one polish'd horde,
Form'd of two mighty tribes, the *Bores* and *Bored*.
Of all the horrid, hideous notes of woe,
Sadder than owl-songs or the midnight blast,
Is that portentous phrase, "I told you so,"
Uttered by friends, those prophets of the past.

Don Juan

---

this "Venetian interlude" Byron wrote the fourth and final canto of *Childe Harold*, the satiric *Beppo*, and began work on *Don Juan*. Cantos I and II of this semiautobiographical masterpiece were published in 1819. Here he revealed his gift for invective and often expressed forceful indignation, despite the lighthearted burlesque of the mock-epic.

Living abroad, Byron accumulated debts, most of which he cleared through the sale of Newstead in 1817, which assured him an annual income. He ignored the appeals of Claire Clairmont concerning their daughter, and Shelley was obliged to act as arbiter. He visited Byron in Venice and arranged for Allegra to be sent to him. Shelley was shocked by Byron's profligacy and the deterioration he found in his friend's appearance, but his continued admiration for Byron's intellect and charm are shown in his poem "Julia and Maddalo."

In 1819 Byron fell in love with Countess Teresa Guiccioli, the nineteen-year-old wife of a wealthy landowner. Soon after their meeting, Teresa had to leave Venice with her husband; Byron, hearing that she had fallen ill, followed her to Ravenna, where his presence apparently effected her recovery. He was then invited by the complaisant Count Guiccioli to live at Ravenna as Teresa's *cavaliere servente* (gentleman-in-waiting). Byron enjoyed great popularity in Ravenna. He was particularly welcomed by the Gamba family (Teresa's father and brother), who initiated him into the *Carbonari*, a secret society whose aim was the liberalization of Italian politics. In 1820 Teresa was granted a legal separation from her husband on the condition that she return to her parents' home. Byron continued to see her intermittently until the spring of 1821, when the whole of the Gamba family was exiled following an abortive revolution. Byron went to Pisa, leaving his daughter Allegra in a convent near Ravenna, where she died the following year.

Despite political and domestic upheavals, Byron continued to write. He completed three more cantos of *Don Juan*; the *Prophecy of Dante* (a translation of the Francesca da Rimini episode from *Dante Alighieri); and four plays *Marino Faliero, Sardanapalus, The Two Foscari*, and *Cain* (all published in 1821). In Pisa Byron spent much time with Shelley and the Gambas, and paid regular visits to Teresa. Shelley invited the essayist Leigh Hunt from England to join Byron and himself in the editing of a new periodical, to be named *The Liberal*. Byron contributed several pieces, including his *Vision of Judgment*, to the first issue of *The Liberal*, which was published in October 1822. He maintained close contact with Mary Shelley, who moved to Genoa, where the Gambas had found asylum and taken a large villa for themselves and Byron. There he continued to write, producing *The Age of Bronze* and *The Island*, and by March 1823 he had completed the fifteenth canto of *Don Juan*.

In April 1823 the Greek Committee in London asked Byron for his active assistance in their war of liberation from Turkey. The opportunity for such noble service appealed to Byron. Leaving for Greece on July 18 after an emotional parting from Teresa, he sailed to the island of Cephalonia, where he awaited instructions from London. He remained on board ship to create an appearance of neutrality, and gave monetary assistance to both rival factions and refugees; but the Greek chieftains had little interest in national unity and sought Byron's money for self-enrichment. With troops and stores from the London Committee, Byron traveled to Missolonghi to join Prince Alexander Mavrocordatos, commander of the forces in western Greece, whose undisciplined troops had not been paid in months. Byron undertook to pay them and proposed to occupy them with a planned attack on the Turkish-held fortress of Lepanto. The attack was delayed when Byron became ill in February 1824. His enthusiasm for the Greek cause was accompanied by fits of depression and agitation over Greek incompetence. Despite the deterioration in his physical condition, he was regarded as the leader and paymaster of the Greek insurrection. On April 9 he contracted a fever and died ten days later. His remains were returned to England where, after being refused burial in Westminster, they were interred in the Byron family vault near Newstead.

M. Foot, *The Politics of Paradise: A Vindication of Byron*, 1988.

L. A. Marchand, *Byron: A Biography*, 1957.

L. A. Marchand, *Byron: A Portrait*, 1970.

P. W. Martin, *Byron: A Poet before His Public*, 1982.

F. Raphael, *Byron*, 1982.

C

CABOT, JOHN (c.1456–c.1499) and **SEBASTIAN** (c.1474–1557), father and son explorers. John Cabot was probably born in Genoa and his name may have been an English adaption of Giovanni Caboto. By the 1470s he had moved to Venice, where he married a local girl and earned his livelihood as a merchant. He had already traveled to Mecca in his youth to develop commercial links in the important Venetian trade in spices from Asia. An educated man and knowledgeable in cartography, he was inspired by Marco *Polo's travel accounts. Hearing that China lay west of Iceland, John believed it possible (independent of Christopher *Columbus) to reach the spice markets from the west by crossing the Atlantic.

By the mid-1480s John Cabot left for the port city of Bristol, England, whose seafarers had sailed further westward than most of their competitors. Cabot sought the support of King *Henry VII for an expedition to China. The commercial interests of Venice would not have countenanced attempts to find an alternative spice route to break their monopoly and in Bristol he had navigators with knowledge and experience of the Atlantic to enlist on this project. In 1496 Cabot and his sons Lewes, Sebastian, and Soncio were granted royal letters patent to sail to all parts of the eastern, western, and northern seas, whatsoever islands, countries, regions or provinces of heathens and infidels in whatsoever part of the world, to any latitude or longitude provided it is land hitherto unknown.... The last provision was meant to ensure that there would be no conflict with Spain: Columbus had been on his first voyage just four years previously and Spain had laid claim to vast tracts of the New World. Another proviso stated that the king was to receive a fifth of the profit and all goods from the newly discovered lands were to be imported through Bristol.

In 1496 Cabot set out from Bristol but was forced to turn back. He set sail again in May 1497 with a crew of eighteen on a small thirty-ton ship named after his wife, Mattea; included on board were Bristol merchants who had experience sailing far out into the Atlantic. They finally sighted land on June 24, although their point of disembarkation is disputed; it was most likely Newfoundland or Maine. Cabot did not venture far into the American hinterland, staying on the shore. He claimed the land for King Henry and noted evidence of habitation, such as the remains of a fire. Convinced he had reached the coast of China, Cabot returned to England, crossing the Atlantic in just thirteen days, although due to a miscalculation he landed in Brittany and not Bristol.

John Cabot was awarded £10 by his royal patron and an annual pension of twenty pounds, but he did not live long to enjoy it. The following year he returned to the North Atlantic with five ships laden with English merchandise and sailed up the coast of Greenland in a futile search for Japan; he died soon after his return to England. His discoveries were the foundation of subsequent British claims in Canada.

His son Sebastian continued his father's tradition of exploration. In 1509 he sailed in a quest for a northwest passage to China, traveling along the coastline of the newly discovered continent of America. He got as far as Hudson's Bay in Canada and claimed discovery of this legendary shortcut to the east. A mutiny forced him to return to England where the new king, *Henry VIII, was not as encouraging as his predecessor had been. At various times in his life he served the king of Spain and the Holy Roman emperor. He returned to England to accept a post as governor of the Merchant Adventurers in 1548.

Sebastian remained active into old age and organized an attempt in 1554 to discover a northeast route to China. The explorers got as far as Russia, where diplomatic contact was initiated with *Ivan the Terrible and trade relations established.

C. R. Beazley, *John and Sebastian Cabot*, 1964.
R. Biddle, *A Memoir of Sebastian Cabot*, 1970.
R. C. Howard, *Bristol and the Cabots*, 1967.

CAESAR, GAIUS JULIUS (100–44 B.C.E.), Roman general and statesman. Caesar, who claimed to be descended from the god Jupiter, came from one of the oldest and noblest families in Rome, many of whose members had served as consuls.

However, by the time of his birth, his family had become impoverished and they lived in one of Rome's poorer districts. He grew up during a period when Rome was being torn apart by civil war between two forces: conservatives, who wanted to preserve the status quo whereby rights and privileges were solely the prerogative of the Roman nobility, and radicals, who wanted to extend those rights to other classes and peoples within the empire.

Caesar excelled in his studies — particularly oratory and writing — and became a military aide in his early teens. At sixteen he married at his father's bidding, but divorced his wife after his father died, marrying Cornelia, the daughter of the head of the radicals. When the conservative dictator, *Sulla, instituted a bloody reign of terror, he ordered Caesar to divorce Cornelia. When Caesar refused, Sulla confiscated his property and ordered his death.

Caesar then fled Italy and only returned after Sulla's death, but soon left for Asia since his enemies were still in power. En route to Asia he was captured by pirates and held for ransom; Once freed, he hired ships and soldiers and attacked, defeated, and crucified the pirates.

Cornelia died when Caesar was thirty-two and he then married Pompeia, Sulla's granddaughter, to effect his reconciliation with the conservatives; this was the first of his political marriages, each of which was contracted to cement political alliances. Marriage did not curtail Caesar's numerous love affairs, however, and some of his most passionate opponents owed their hatred of him to his seduction of their wives, sisters, or daughters. Thus, much of Brutus's hatred for Caesar stemmed from the persistent rumor that he was really Caesar's son, which threatened his claim to membership in the venerable and esteemed Brutus family.

Caesar threw himself into power struggles in Rome; a skilled and unscrupulous politician, he advanced rapidly. He became known for his oratorical eloquence, but his pro-radical, anti-conservative policies caused his fellow senators to mark him as a man to be watched carefully.

Caesar was often short of money. He won fortunes in war only to spend them on politics, buying the support of the masses with games and doles, and of senators with bribes and promises. By 61 b.c.e. he was twenty-five million *sesterces* in debt and his creditors refused to let him leave Rome to become propraetor for Spain until his wealthy ally Crassus guaranteed his debts.

Caesar's Spanish successes paid off his debts and enriched the treasury, but a wary Senate tried to prevent his becoming consul. Caesar outmaneuvered them by making a deal with the triumphant general *Pompey, who was angry about the Senate's refusal to ratify his own agreements. In exchange for Pompey's and Crassus's support, Caesar promised to get Pompey's agreements ratified. Pompey's marriage to Caesar's daughter sealed the pact and the First Triumvirate was formed in 60 B.C.E.

Bust of Julius Caesar

As consul Caesar pushed through financial and agrarian reforms. He also divorced his wife on suspicion of adultery with the popular radical leader Clodius, using the excuse that, "My wife must be above suspicion." He then married Calpurnia, daughter of the radical Piso. He also had himself appointed governor of Gaul (northern Italy and southern France) for five years so that he could deal with the Germanic tribes overrunning that region. Attempting to ensure the continuation of his reforms during his absence, Caesar had his friends elected as consuls and Clodius as tribune for 58 B.C.E.

Clodius, however, decided he did not need Pompey and Caesar anymore; bloody fighting broke out which ended with Rome being ruled by a surprising conservative-Clodius alliance. Their power secure, senators debated the abrogation of Caesar's laws, and whether they should wait and hope Caesar would be killed in war, recall him to stand trial, or arrange for his assassination.

Meanwhile, the Germanic tribes invading Gaul constituted a threat to Rome. Caesar raised, equipped, and paid for extra legions, defeated the invaders, and then organized the administration of Gaul. Announcing the conquest in 56 B.C.E., he sent large amounts of booty to Rome, bribing senators not to repeal his laws and financing Pompey's and Crassus's campaign for the consulate in 55 B.C.E. Caesar's governorship of Gaul was extended for another five years. He secured the Rhine as a frontier and invaded Britain in 52 B.C.E. However, only his brilliant improvisations, acts of daring bravery, and the loyalty of his men saved him from defeat when the Gallic tribes united against him under Vercingentorix in a last bid for independence. Caesar treated the defeated Gauls severely at first, then became such a magnanimous and lenient conqueror that Gaul adopted Roman culture and was to remain a Roman province for three hundred years.

Meanwhile the Roman republic was crumbling. Violence and corruption ruled openly, rival gangs used physical force to determine which laws were passed, crime was rampant; dictatorship seemed a welcome alternative to chaos. Pompey cut his ties with Caesar and the Senate, hoping to depose the latter, granted Pompey special dictatorial powers to fight his erstwhile ally.

Caesar led his troops across the Rubicon River into Italy, beginning his armed rebellion against the Senate; as he advanced he continued his unavailing attempts at negotiation with Rome. Italian cities en route welcomed him as a liberator who supported their claim to full Roman citizenship; business classes were won over by his refusal to confiscate their estates. With Pompey's withdrawal from Italy, Caesar entered Rome unopposed in 49 B.C.E. He restored order there and declared a general amnesty, but his magnanimity did not prevent his enemies plotting against him.

Caesar spent most of the years between his ascension to power and his assassination away from Rome fighting the armies of Pompey or the conservatives. Pompey fled to Egypt and was murdered; following him, Caesar met *Cleopatra, Egypt's beautiful, intelligent, and ruthless queen. He was to restore her to the throne that had been usurped by her vizier; she was to bear him a son. He left her long enough to put down organized rebellions in Asia with a speedy dispatch summarized in his famous report: "I came, I saw, I conquered." Then he returned to Rome with her and their son.

Caesar had grown from a politician to a farsighted statesman. Three times, the Senate granted him dictatorial powers enabling him to institute reforms between military campaigns. His economic reforms restored credit, created a stable currency and eliminated the most extortionate (and profitable) business practices. His social reforms combated urban overcrowding with a colonization program, rural depopulation with extensive land grants to veterans and the poor, unemployment with a massive building program, and the growing number receiving the corn dole with a means test for eligibility, which immediately halved the number of recipients. His political reforms extended Roman citizenship to non-Roman members of the empire, severely punished official corruption, and weakened the Senate by doubling its membership with nonpatrician and nonnative appointees. Other reforms included the adoption of a 365-day yearly calendar (the Julian Calendar), with a leap year, and a month, July, named in his honor.

Caesar decided that only a military campaign to expand the empire and secure its boundaries would provide enough spoils to finance and overcome resistance to any reform. Conservatives feared that a successful campaign would lead to Caesar's establishing a monarchy and plotted to assassinate him; he was stabbed to death in the Senate by a group of nobles including Brutus and Cassius on March 15 (the ides of March), five months after having been declared dictator for life.

M. Gelzer, *Caesar: Politician and Statesman*, 1968.
J. Sabben-Clare, *Caesar and Roman Politics 60–50 B.C.*, 1971.
Z. Yavetz, *Julius Caesar and His Public Image*, 1983.

BY CAESAR

- The die is cast (at the crossing of the Rubicon).
- Why stake your fortunes on the risk of battle? Especially as a victory by strategy is as much a part of good generalship as a victory by the sword.
- All-powerful force, in war above all things, produces momentous changes from very small beginnings.
- The whole of Gaul is divided into three parts.
- In war, trivial causes produce momentous events.
- No one is so brave as not to be disconcerted by unforeseen circumstances.

CALVIN, JOHN (1509–1564), French theologian and ecclesiastical statesman. Born in Noyon, Picardy, the son of middle-class parents, Calvin was educated with the local bishop's sons at the Collège de Montaigu in Paris, where Desiderius *Erasmus had also studied. He pursued advanced law studies and later studied under the outstanding Greek scholar of his era, Guillaume Budé. The next year he published his first book, a study of Seneca's *Concerning Clemency*, which demonstrated his excellent command of Latin, his considerable erudition in matters of ancient history and literature, and his kinship with the humanism of Erasmus and Budé.

The precise reason for Calvin's conversion to Protestantism remains a matter of conjecture. He must have been influenced by the reforming humanist beliefs of his tutors and friends in Paris, while the treatment meted out to his family by the Catholic authorities — his brother Charles's body was publicly hung after his death as a result of his heterodoxy and his father died excommunicate — also contributed to his move. He broke with the church in 1533 after a religious experience in which he believed he had received a charge to restore the church to its pristine purity. In 1534 Calvin moved to Basle, Switzerland, where he devoted himself to theological study.

The fruit of these studies was Calvin's *Institutes of the Christian Religion*. First published in 1536, it has been described as the masterpiece of Protestant theology. Written in Latin and designed as a defense of Protestantism to the king of France, it constituted a manual of spirituality and molded the doctrines of the Protestant movement into a logical system based on the Augustinian premise that man was created for communion with God and remains unfulfilled as long as this need is not satisfied.

Calvin was to expand, revise, and translate this work in many subsequent editions; the definitive French edition appeared in 1560, although as early as 1552 the city council in Geneva was declaring that the book represented a holy doctrine which no man might speak against. It remained the single most influential religious manual produced during the Reformation, immediately enjoying widespread circulation, and assuring Calvin's reputation as a key Reform spokesman.

Calvin visited Geneva in 1536 and was persuaded to remain there by Guillaume Farel, the inflammatory preacher who had incited the city's population to anti-Catholic rebellion. Beginning as a public lecturer, Calvin went on to write *Instruction in Faith* to educate the Genevan citizens in the Reformed faith. However, both he and Farel were forced to leave Geneva by a city council alarmed by the austerity of their proposed regulations.

Calvin took refuge in Lutheran Strasbourg where, in addition to gaining valuable practical experience in the administration of a parish, he was able to become personally acquainted with prominent Lutheran theologians; he never met Martin *Luther himself. The failure of attempts at reconcilliation between Rome and the Reformers left Calvin convinced of the futility of such negotiations; thereafter he was to promote complete conversion to the new Gospel as the only feasible means to end conflict.

In 1541, three years after his expulsion and a year after his marriage to Idelette de Bure, Calvin made a triumphant return to Geneva to save the city from imminent administrative collapse. The ecclesiastical ordinances he established have formed the constitution of the church of Geneva ever since, as well as serving as a model for other Reformed churches and communities. Four ministering orders (doctors, pastors, elders, and deacons) became responsible for the spiritual and social welfare of the community, while the threat of excommunication by the Consistory (a court constituted by the pastors and elders) ensured strict conformity to moral and religious norms.

Although Calvin's only official position in Geneva was that of moderator of the company of pastors, he was the city's guiding light and de facto dictator. His preaching and rigorous Biblical exegesis drew religious refugees from all parts of Europe. Dissent was not tolerated, however, and could be brutally punished. Nevertheless, there was a considerable degree of elective representation in Geneva; thus, as Calvinism spread, its influence on Western democratic institutions was great.

After 1555, the ascendancy of his doctrines within Geneva firmly assured, Calvin concentrated his energies on propagating his creed in other countries, especially France. He displayed his considerable political acumen by enlisting the support of powerful French aristocrats on the side of the Reform Protestants. Similar support was offered to fledgling Reformed movements in other countries. A tireless correspondent, administrator, legislator, and diplomat, Calvin successfully paved the way for the continued growth of the church he had founded, especially through the institutional network he developed, which was copied wherever Calvinism took root. During his lifetime, Geneva could, with some justification, be called a Protestant Rome; after his death, Calvinism played a crucial role in shaping the societies of Western Europe and North America.

W. J. Bouwsma, *John Calvin*, 1988.
A. E. McGrath, *A Life of John Calvin*, 1990.
R. S. Wallace, *Geneva and the Reformation*, 1988.

CAMBYSES II (reigned 529–522 B.C.E.), emperor of Persia. The elder of *Cyrus II's two sons, Cambyses was designated heir with the stipulation that his younger brother Bardiya — Smerdis in Greek — be given the provinces of Khorasmia, Bactria, Parthia, and Carmania. After serving as governor of Babylonia for eight years, Cambyses ascended the throne upon his father's death in 529 B.C.E.

The early years of Cambyses's reign were plagued by dissension among the priesthood and nobility. His first act as emperor was to defy Persian tradition by marrying his two sisters, Atossa and Roxane; he claimed that incestuous marriages were the custom of Babylonia, where he lived. Cambyses shared his father's concern that their claim to the throne would be challenged by rival branches of the Achaemenian family and sought to ensure his line's ascendancy.

The death of Pharaoh Amasis in 525 B.C.E., and the accession of his young son Psamtik to the throne, gave Cambyses the opportunity to invade Egypt. Psamtik's army was routed at Pelesium that same year, and the young pharaoh fled to Memphis where he was captured and executed.

Cambyses remained in Egypt for three years, sending an expedition to conquer Ethiopia and another to destroy the oracle of Amon at Siwa. The latter campaign was a disaster; fifty thousand men were lost in a sandstorm and never returned. *Herodotus claims that Cambyses became insane in Egypt and desecrated its temples, but while it is believed that Cambyses suffered from epilepsy, an exaggerated account of his rule may have seemed necessary to justify his downfall shortly afterward.

During Cambyses's extended absence from Persia, growing civil unrest had evolved into a coup by someone claiming to be his brother Smerdis. It may have been Smerdis who usurped his brother's throne, but most historians believe that Smerdis was assassinated shortly after Cambyses's accession and that the usurper was an impostor. Cambyses died suddenly from a self-inflicted injury during his march back to Persia. Some historians claim that his sword accidentally gashed his thigh and he died from loss of blood; others contend that Cambyses committed suicide in despair at his empire's fate.

C. Irving, *Crossroads of Civilization: 3,000 Years of Persian History,* 1979.

P. Sykes, *A History of Persia,* 1969.

CAMUS, ALBERT (1913–1960), French writer and Nobel prize winner. Camus was born into a poor family in Mondovi, a farming town in Algeria; his father was killed in World War I before Camus's first birthday and he was brought up by his mother, who was deaf and almost mute. Encouraged by his elementary school teachers, he won a scholarship which enabled him to attend high school in Algiers. After graduation he worked his way through the University of Algiers, where he formed and ran a theater group. At seventeen his chosen profession was to be an academic but a severe case of tuberculosis nearly killed him, preventing him from pursuing this goal.

In 1934 he became politically active, joining the communist party in 1935 but leaving it two years later. In 1938 he joined the staff of the left-wing newspaper *Alger Républicain* but after the outbreak of World War II the paper was closed for its pacifist stance. At this time Camus published his first book, *L'Envers et l'endroit (Betwixt and Between),* which included essays and stories of his childhood.

In 1940 he moved to France and, after the fall of France later that year, joined the French underground. The editorials he wrote for the underground newspaper *Combat* were highly influential and when the newspaper was able to come out into the open, Camus was well known. He achieved fame with the novel *L'Etranger* (1942; *The Stranger,* 1946) and the essay *Le Mythe de Sisyphe* (1942; *The Myth of Sisyphus,* 1955 as well as the plays *Le Malentendu* 1944; *(Cross Purpose, 1948)* and *Caligula* (1944, English translation 1948). His portrayal of human isolation and alienation struck a responsive chord. This was the period of the absurd in his writings, born of the confrontation between the yearning for the absolute and the perfect and the impossibility of simplifying the world into a rational, balanced principle. He stressed the need to maintain an awareness of this contradiction — albeit in a state of perpetual tension — thanks to which the hero of the absurd can keep his spiritual freedom in the face of opposing forces.

Camus weighed man's egotism against his need to be socially responsible and his requirement for love and happiness against the knowledge that all his hopes can only end in death. He wrote, "In the darkest depths of our nihilism, I have sought only for the means of transcending it." Despite these oppressive ideas, he attempted to synthesize from them a positive ethical system, basing his belief in a humanistic code

- The absurd is sin without God.
- There is no fate that cannot be surmounted with scorn.
- Men are convinced of your arguments, your sincerity, and the seriousness of your efforts only by your death.
- Absolute freedom mocks justice. Absolute justice denies freedom.
- Don't believe your friends when they ask you to be honest with them. All they really want is to have their good opinion of themselves confirmed.
- The future is the only transcendental value for men without God.
- There's no need to wait around for the Last Judgment — it takes place every day.

Albert Camus

centered on the self but at the same time demanding that man take responsibility for his fellow man. He rejected any idea that there was a god. Disappointed in the religious establishment, he felt that man should take life into his own hands and attempt to solve the suffering of this world rather than sit by idly waiting for a promise of a life in the world to come.

From 1943 he was closely associated with Andre Gide, Louis Aragon, and Jean-Paul *Sartre, and despite his distance from the existentialist movement, he was often identified with it in the postwar years; together with Sartre and Simone de Beauvoir, he was very influential on the postwar generation. His 1945 *Lettres a un ami allemand* (English title: *Resistance, Rebellion, and Death*) condemned racism and militarism. His philosophical work *L'Homme révolté* (*The Rebel* 1951) brought angry reactions from leftist circles over its allusions to a comparison between communist state sponsored terror and fascist terror and led to a painful rift with Sartre.

His powerful novels *La Peste* (*The Plague,* 1947) and *La Chute* (1946; *The Fall,* 1956) marked a change, as his heroes no longer accept surrounding evil but fight it in a spirit of liberal humanism.

In 1957 Camus received the Nobel prize for literature. In his acceptance speech he expressed what he viewed as his obligation to humanity: "Probably every generation sees itself as charged with remaking the world. Mine, however, knows that it will not remake the world. But its task is perhaps even greater, for it consists in keeping the world from destroying itself.... [My generation] has had to reestablish both within and without itself a little of what constitutes the dignity of life and death."

Camus's death in an automobile accident shocked the literary world. After his death his friend Sartre wrote, "He represented in our time the latest example of that long line of *moralistes* whose works constitute perhaps the most original element in French letters.... Whatever he did or decided subsequently, Camus would never have ceased to be one of the chief forces of our cultural activity or to represent in his way the history of France and of this century."

H. R. Lottman, *Albert Camus*, 1978.
R. de Lupper, *Albert Camus*, 1972.
R. J. McCarthy, *Camus*, 1982.
P. Thody, *Albert Camus*, 1989.

CARVER, GEORGE WASHINGTON (c.1864–1943), American botanist, chemurgist, and educator. Carver was not sure of his birth date or exact age but he was born, in Diamond Point, Missouri, the black slave of one Moses Carver. After the Civil War he was informed that he was no longer a slave but chose to remain and work on the Carver plantation until he was about twelve years old. During this time he managed to obtain a grade school education in a one-room schoolhouse in Neosho, Missouri. Upon leaving the plantation he wandered about the countryside supporting himself as best he could working as a farm laborer, cook, and sometimes household worker.

Not content with merely eking out a living, he ultimately managed to obtain a high school education in the vicinity of Minneapolis, Kansas, and by 1890 he had enrolled at Simpson College in Indianola, Iowa, to study art and painting. His art teacher at the college recognized Carver's skill with plants and what seemed to be a natural scientific talent, and encouraged him to enter the land grant college at Ames, Iowa, the Iowa State College of Agriculture and Mechanical Arts, from which Carver received a B.S. degree in 1894.

Upon graduation he joined the staff of Tuskegee Institute (now Tuskegee University) in Tuskegee, Alabama, becoming director of the department of agricultural research, a post he filled with distinction for the rest of his life. He helped to revolutionize the economy of the South by his studies and experiments on plant diseases and soil building. His initial intention was to help poor black sharecroppers in the South by his research, but he succeeded in improving the entire economy of the South by teaching crop rotation and soil improvement methods, as well as by the development of more than 300 by-products from the peanut, soybean, and sweet potato. From the peanut came such products as flour, ink, dyes, soaps, wood stains, insulating board, and that great staple, peanut butter. From the sweet potato, derivative products were produced such as flour, vinegar, molasses, and even a synthetic rubber. Prior to Carver's research, the South had depended upon cotton as its major crop, but cotton used up the soil. Carver showed that nitrogen, which enriched the soil, could be restored to it by planting crops like peanuts and soybeans. In the course of his many years of research, Carver even showed that many products could be devised from cotton waste itself.

Through the years his accomplishments were well recognized. In 1916 he was elected a fellow in the prestigious Society for the Encouragement of the Arts, Manufactures, and Commerce in London, England. In 1923 he was awarded the Spingarn Medal, an award given by the National Association for the Advancement of Colored People annually since 1914 for the highest achievement by a black American, and in 1939 he was awarded the Roosevelt Medal. In 1940 he donated his life savings of $33,000 to establish the Carver Foundation for the continuation of his research.

R. Holt, *George Washington Carver: An American Biography*, 1963.
L. O. McMurry, *George Washington Carver: Scientist and Symbol*, 1981.

CASTLEREAGH, VISCOUNT (Robert Stewart; 1769–1822), British statesman. Scion of an aristocratic Irish family, Robert Stewart, the future Viscount Castlereagh, was born in Dublin, but his mother died during his infancy and his father remarried to Frances, daughter of Lord Camden.

Castlereagh did not complete his studies at Cambridge University, returning instead to Ireland and taking over his father's constituency. Supposedly, his father — newly ennobled as Lord Londonderry — spent £60,000 to get his son elected. Castlereagh was an ineffective speaker but a talented administrator and skilled exploiter of family connections and political influence. His early commitment to reform was set aside when the excesses of the French Revolution reinforced his natural conservative tendencies to defend the status quo that, as Irish chief secretary in the British administration in Dublin Castle, he came to represent.

In 1798 the state of unrest in Ireland broke out into rebellion. Castlereagh had a command in the militia and was involved in the arrest of rebel leaders and in guarding the coast against a French invasion. The rebellion was easily crushed and Castlereagh was convinced the future for Ireland lay in full union with England. In 1800, with judicious use of patronage and bribery, he persuaded the Irish parliament to vote itself out of existence and the United Kingdom was born. The methods used in bringing the union about and his image as an advocate of reform who turned reactionary besmirched his name and provided constant ammunition for political opponents. In Dublin he was burned in effigy and held a threatening mob back from his carriage at pistol point.

The rest of Castlereagh's career was spent in Parliament in London. He first was elected as a supporter of Robert Peel. After serving at the India Office he was appointed secretary for war (1805–1806, 1807–1809), giving this ministry a sense of direction and working to improve the combat worthiness of the British army. He had, however, to bear the blame for a succession of defeats by *Napoleon's forces. In 1809 he was dismissed and when he found out that his political rival, George Canning, had engineered this, he challenged Canning to a duel and wounded him.

Castlereagh remained out of office until 1812, when he was called again to take ministerial office by Lord Liverpool. As foreign secretary he had the delicate task of cementing the alliance of nations against Napoleon. At Vienna and other conferences following Napoleon's defeat at the Battle of Waterloo (1815), he labored to cement a new European order by restoring what he considered legitimate monarchical regimes and insuring that Britain would not be embroiled in further conflict on the continent. His coolness and ability in gaining the confidence of foreign leaders was crucial, and with powerful Prince *Metternich of Austria he established a particular rapport. For the next century Europe enjoyed the absence of major conflict.

Castlereagh's popularity in European capitals was not matched in Britain, where he was one of the most hated political figures. He became identified as an opponent of parliamentary reform and a supporter of repressive measures to curb popular protest. Depressed over the death of his father, he had a mental breakdown in 1822. He had been receiving threatening letters and, according to one account, might have been blackmailed, having been led into a brothel by a man whom he had mistook for a woman. In front of the king and prime minister he accused himself of homosexual crimes and lost his grasp on reality. His wife feared he would harm himself and had all sharp instruments removed from his vicinity, but a small knife was overlooked and with this the deranged Castlereagh killed himself.

C. J. Bartlett, *Castlereagh*, 1966.

W. Hinde, *Castlereagh*, 1981.

H. M. Hyde, *The Rise of Lord Castlereagh*, 1933.

H. M. Hyde, *The Strange Death of Lord Castlereagh*, 1959.

CATHERINE II (the Great; 1729–1796), empress of Russia. She came to power in 1762 after a military coup deposed her eccentric husband, Peter III, who was murdered by the brother of Catherine's lover, Count Orlov. She probably did not authorize Peter's murder, but this event did not contribute to the legitimacy of her rule; nor did the fact that Catherine was a German princess who had converted to Russian Orthodoxy on her arrival at the Russian court of the Empress Elizabeth. From the outset, however, Catherine showed herself determined to rule absolutely — not as regent or consort — and managed to do so successfully for over thirty years.

Arriving at the court of *Peter the Great's daughter Elizabeth in 1744 at the age of sixteen, the German-speaking Calvinist Princess Sophie from the Prussian court of Stettin was required to change her religion, language, and even her name in order to be deemed suitable for the Russian throne. She had come to marry Elizabeth's seventeen-year-old nephew and heir, who was impotent and played with toys in bed. At first she thought of suicide but found consolation in reading and horseback riding. She proved remarkably adaptable and survived the nu-

- Be gentle, humane, accessible, compassionate and open-handed; do not let your grandeur prevent you from mixing kindly with the humble and putting yourself in their shoes.
- My first principle in dealing with men is to make them believe that they want to do what I tell them to do.
- My technique is to praise in a loud voice and to scold in a whisper.

Catherine the Great

merous intrigues and humiliations of Elizabeth's rule until, at the age of thirty-four, her burning ambition to rule Russia was realized in a coup d'etat organized by her lover, Grigori Orlov in which her husband, then reigning as Peter III, was murdered.

Intelligent, lively, and witty, Catherine was an astute manipulator of public opinion and made every effort to consolidate her hold on the Russian throne. She presented herself as a devotee of the Enlightenment, which was then sweeping Europe, and patronized its philosophers. Spokesmen for the Enlightenment such as Denis *Diderot and *Voltaire (with whom she corresponded) believed that people are naturally free and equal and should be encouraged to educate themselves to improve their situation. This optimistic world view did not, however, necessarily encompass democratic government, as social reform was thought to be best undertaken by autocratic rulers. Naturally, many monarchs, among them Catherine, seized upon this philosophy as a pretext for wielding absolute authority. Tension inevitably occurred during her reign between the humane reforms she was genuinely committed to instituting and the repression necessary to maintain a system of government as totalitarian as that in Russia.

Certainly, the backward, unwieldy, and impoverished landmass which constituted the eighteenth-century Russian empire at the beginning of Catherine's reign was not open to any realistic form of democratic government. Russian rulers traditionally ruled by decree, personally authorizing every government decision. Catherine tried early in her reign to institute some kind of limited parliamentary debate by convening a commission to codify the Russian law. She frequently wrote of her sympathy for the oppressed masses and tried to abolish torture and encourage the humane treatment of servants. Despite these and other humanitarian measures, Catherine's reluctance to allow any weakening of her personal control of government led to inevitable repression. Intellectuals such as the writer Alexander Radishchev who dared to criticize her rule were exiled and had their work suppressed. The great Cossack rebellion of 1773–1775 was harshly put

Catherine the Great playing with her grandchildren

down. The near-success of this rebellion also convinced Catherine of the impossibility of freeing the serfs, Russia's peasant class that was legally tied to the land they worked on and considered the property of their noble owners. Indeed, Catherine strengthened the power of the nobility; in 1765 they received exemption from taxation.

Catherine's foreign policy was vigorous and innovative. She pursued many of the same aims as her predecessors, securing Russia's borders and ensuring outlets to the sea. During her reign she engineered the partition of Poland no fewer than three times and positioned an ex-lover, Stanislas Poniatowski, on the Polish throne. By the end of her reign Poland had ceased to exist. On the Asian front Catherine fought two wars with Turkey; the first, in 1768, resulted in the Treaty of Kuchuk Kainardji, whereby Russia gained access to the Black Sea, permitting her to annex the longcoveted Crimea in 1783. From 1787–1792 another successful war with Turkey, ending in the Treaty of Jassy, brought Odessa under Russian control. As a result of these territorial gains the empire's population jumped from nine to twenty-nine million, making Russia a formidable power. The removal of Poland and the Tartar state which had acted as buffers between Russia and western Europe, also increased Russia's interest in European affairs. The empire formed under Catherine the Great was to constitute a continual strategic threat for the next two hundred years. The seeds were also sown for ongoing ethnic problems with the assimilation of millions of non-Russian Ukrainians Poles, and Tartars who bitterly resented Russian rule.

Catherine's economic policy was linked to her territorial expansion; immigration was encouraged, fur, mining, and textile industries set up, and export duties abolished to encourage trade. She tried to encourage the development of towns in the hope that this would lead to the establishment of an educated middle class, as was the case in Europe. Progress was, however, slow in the rural, sparsely populated majority of the empire. Of European origin herself, Catherine tried to instil in the nobility an admiration for European culture. She also exploited Russian traditions when it suited her and cultivated a personality cult, encouraging her subjects to think of her as their little mother.

There is no shortage of vivid stories concerning Catherine's personal life and penchant for young lovers. In fact, for most of her life she was very restrained, taking her first lover, thought to be the father of her eldest son, later Paul I, in desperation after her own marriage remained unconsummated. By the time the Empress Elizabeth died, Catherine was apparently deeply involved with her second lover, Grigori Orlov, who engineered her coup and fathered two of her children. Orlov was succeeded by the cavalry officer and later field-marshal, Grigori Potemkin, to whom she appears to have been most deeply attached and whom she entrusted with many important missions. Only in the last fifteen years of her life, growing increasingly lonely and frightened for the future, did Catherine embark on the promiscuity which so shocked contemporary and later historians.

Opinion remains divided as to whether Catherine the Great was a power-hungry monster or a gifted liberal ruler. She appears to have been genuinely devoted to improving the lot of her adopted country, and by the standards of her time she deserves to be considered one of the most powerful and positive influences in Russian history.

J. T. Alexander, *Catherine the Great*, 1989.
V. Cronin, *Catherine, Emperor of All the Russias*, 1978.
I. de Madiriaga, *Catherine the Great*, 1990.
Z. Oldenbourg, *Catherine the Great*, 1965.

CATHERINE DE MÉDICIS (Caterina de Medici; 1519–1589), queen of France; wife of one French king (Henry II) and mother of three (Francis II, Charles IX, Henry III), a dominant figure in French politics for almost twenty years. A daughter of Lorenzo II de *Medici, she was orphaned at an early age and was educated in a convent. Her marriage at fourteen to the future Henry II of France in 1533 came as a result of a political maneuver between Pope Clement VII and *Francis I. During her husband's reign Catherine did not take part in politics, being eclipsed by his mistress, Diane de Potiers, the woman who dominated his life. After ten years of childlessness, Catherine bore him nine children. She also stayed in the background during the one-year reign of her son Francis II (1559–1560). However, with the accession of her second son, the ten-year-old Charles IX, she became regent of France and retained her hold on the government even after the king attained maturity.

Catherine pursued a moderate policy at the beginning, backing the conciliatory chancellor Michel de L'Hospital. Her attempt to keep a delicate balance in

Catherine de Médicis

French religious life was evident in the edict of January 1562 which, for the first time, gave the Huguenots legal recognition, allowing them to gather for prayer outside walled cities. However, this policy failed with the massacre of sixty Huguenots during a religious service at Vassy by troops of Francis, duke of Guise, which sparked the first of the religious wars of France (1562–1598). Caught between the two warring parties, Catherine adopted an opportunistic position aimed at preserving her own position and that of her children. In 1567, following the attempt of the Huguenots to capture the king at Meaux, she went over to the Catholic side but in 1570, when she suspected the Guises, who were the leaders of the extreme Roman Catholic party, of dealing with the king of Spain, *Philip II, she issued the Edict of Saint-Germain, which again granted the Huguenots freedom of worship. She then clashed with the Huguenot leader, Gaspard de Coligny and, alarmed at the influence he had acquired at the court, tried to solve the problem by concocting a plot for his assassination. Coligny was shot and wounded; two days later servants of the Guises burst into his house and killed him. His murder signaled the beginning of the massacre of Saint Bartholomew's day (1572), to which Catherine consented and in which, it is estimated, 10,000 people lost their lives. This turned out to be a political blunder since it eliminated the advantage that Catherine had as a third party representing royal authority. She continued to be involved in politics during the reign of her third son, Henry III (1574–1589), who made political mistakes of his own. Catherine died a few months before he was assassinated by a fanatical Dominican friar.

J. E. Neale, *The Age of Catherine of Médici*, 1943.
N. M. Sutherland, *Catherine de Médici and the Ancien Regime*, 1966.
P. Van Dyke, *Catherine de Médici*, 2 vols, 1927.
H. R. Williamson, *Catherine de Médici*, 1973.

CATO, MARCUS PORCIUS (Cato the Censor; Cato the Elder; 234–149 B.C.E.), Roman statesman, historian, writer, and orator. He was the son of a farmer in Tusculum and in his youth worked hard on his patrimonial estates, improving his financial circumstances; he became friendly with his neighbor, the noble Lucius Valerius Flaccus, who encouraged and assisted him in entering politics. Cato would go to the forum and offer his services as a lawyer without payment to those who needed them, thus acquiring wide influence. He served in the army in the Second Punic War, taking part in the battle at Metaurus (207 B.C.E.) where Hasdrubal was defeated. He served as quaestor under *Scipio Africanus in Africa in 204 B.C.E. and on his return brought Quintus Ennius, the famous Latin poet, with him to Rome. As governing praetor of Sardinia in 198 B.C.E., his severity caused the usurers to leave the island. In 195 B.C.E. he was consul and conducted a successful war in his Spanish province, for which he was awarded a triumph when back in Rome in 194 B.C.E.. As military tribune in 191 B.C.E. he distinguished himself in the Battle of Thermopylae against Antiochus III. Cato became censor in 184 B.C.E., and, in this capacity, could impose his high moral principles on his fellow senators and on the citizens in general. He levied high taxes on luxurious commodities, expelled offending senators, and severely revised the list of the senate. In leasing public contracts, Cato imposed difficult conditions, thus gaining money for the treasury. He also carried out an extensive building program.

> - The best way to keep good acts in memory is to refresh them with new.
> - Old age has disgraces of its own; do not add to them the shame of vice.
> - It is difficult to argue with a belly, for it has no ears.
> - I would rather see a young man blush than turn pale.
> - I prefer to vie in bravery with the bravest rather than in wealth with the richest or in greed with the greediest.
> - Wise men profit more from fools than fools from the wise; for the wise shun the mistakes of fools but fools do not imitate the successes of the wise.
> - I can pardon everyone's mistakes except my own.
> - I would rather men ask why I have no statue than why I have one.
> - Self-praise and self-depreciation are both alike absurd.
>
> **Cato**

Cato was a conservative who sought to preserve the traditional social order and the old, simple mode of life. He opposed the influx of luxury into Rome and the inroads of Greek culture, forbidding Greek philosophers and rhetoricians to live in Rome. In the course of his life he made a large fortune, but his standard of living remained simple. He preached his ideals of a return to the simplicity of a mainly agricultural state in public speeches and fearlessly prosecuted corrupt magistrates. Cato himself was brought to trial by his enemies forty-four times, but was always acquitted. He regarded the predominance of *Scipio Africanus as dangerous to the constitution; Cato probably instigated the prosecution of Scipio Asiaticus on a charge of speculation, in which his brother Africanus was implicated. As a result Africanus was forced to retire (184 B.C.E.). Cato's concern for Roman subjects is shown in his repeated attacks on misbehaving governors.

Having an aversion to Hellenism, Cato opposed Roman expansion to the east, but sought well-established Roman rule in the west. After visiting Carthage (153 B.C.E.), he strongly advocated its destruction, ending his speeches with "*ceterum censeo Carthaginem delendam esse*," (besides, Carthage ought to be destroyed).

Cato's treatise *De agricultura* (On Agriculture), written about 160 B.C.E., is the oldest Latin prose book extant, though its language was later modernized. It deals with management of estates and is based on personal experience, mainly reflecting conditions in Latium and Campania. No logical arrangement can be discerned in the book, and it includes medical recipes, religious customs, and even magic incantations. Of his other works only fragments have survived. Cato was the first Roman to write history in Latin; his *Origines* described the history of Rome from its founding down to his own time, and included the histories of the various Italian cities. He was also the first Roman to publish his speeches (more than 150). He wrote a didactic encyclopedia for the education of his son, including in it rules on morals, military tactics, farming, and health. He was famous for his witticisms, often crude, and published a collection of sayings. *Plutarch wrote a life of Cato censuring his meanness, especially his practice of selling slaves who were too old to be profitable.

A. A. Edgar, *Cato the Censor*, 1978.

CAVOUR, CAMILLO BENSO, COUNT OF
(1810–1861), Italian statesman who was responsible for the unification of Italy under the house of Savoy. In 1720 the house of Savoy had been awarded Sardinia, Piedmont, and Nice, territories known as the kingdom of Sardinia, into which Cavour was born; his father enjoyed several prestigious government positions.

Cavour entered the military academy in Turin at the age of ten and at fourteen was made a page to Charles Albert, prince of Savoy and Piedmont. When he was sixteen, he was commissioned a second lieutenant in the engineer corps. Political ideas fascinated him but in the wake of the 1830 revolution in France, his liberal political views greatly concerned Cavour's family and the authorities; Cavour was transferred to the remote mountain fort of Bard. Charles Albert, now king of Sardinia, permitted him to resign in 1831.

During the next sixteen years Cavour supervised his family's estate and with his father's help was appointed mayor of a village south of Turin. Throughout this period, he sought to express his liberal views in concrete ways. Concerned with the problems of poverty, he established a society for agricultural improvement and another for the dissemination of education among working-class children. In 1834–1835 he wrote a memoir on poverty in Piedmont and a pamphlet on the history of the Poor Laws in England. Cavour also traveled extensively, taking a firsthand interest in parliamentary life in England and France, attending lectures, visiting schools, prisons, and hospitals. These visits abroad served to convince Cavour of the need to follow the middle path toward sociopolitical and economic reform in Europe. He shunned both the revolutionaries who wished to destroy the existing social order as well as the reactionaries who blindly opposed any change.

When the press laws of the kingdom of Sardinia were liberalized in 1847, Cavour founded the liberal daily, *Il Risorgimento*, utilizing the journal to bring pressure on the king to agree to a constitution and to declare war on Austria, but after the defeat of the Sardinians at Custoza, the signing of an armistice, and the abdication of the king, Cavour opposed renewal of the war in 1849 as advocated by the leftist extremists and chose to support the new king, *Victor Emmanuel II. In 1852, as head of a liberal coalition formed by his own right-of-center moderates with the left-of-center democrats, he became prime minister.

Cavour sought to improve economic conditions and to encourage free trade; in conformity with his policy of social reform, public education was improved and in 1855, privileges previously enjoyed by the Catholic church were abolished (as a result Cavour was excommunicated).

Following a complete reorganization of Sardinia's social, political, and economic structures, Cavour sought to play a greater role in international affairs and Sardinia's participation in the Crimean War (1855) provided such an opportunity. An alliance with Britain and France led to the dispatch of 18,000 men to the Crimea. At the Paris Peace Congress of 1856 Cavour raised Italian problems in the hope of attracting the support of the western European powers against the Austrians. In 1858 he concluded an agreement with Emperor *Napoleon III of France for a war against Austria, in exchange for which France would cede Savoy and possibly Nice. Austria declared war in 1859, but when France concluded a separate armistice agreement, Cavour resigned his office.

He returned to the premiership in 1860; that year Tuscany, Parma, Modena, and the Romagna voted for annexation to Sardinia and Giuseppe *Garibaldi concluded his successful campaign against the Two Sicilies. Cavour sent Sardinian troops to annex the Papal States (with the exception of Latium and Rome). He succeeded in persuading Garibaldi to hand over the south and the annexation (1860) of the kingdom of the Two Sicilies was completed when Francis II abdicated in 1861. Two months before Cavour's death, the kingdom of Italy was proclaimed under Victor Emmanuel II. On his death, Cavour was given absolution by the church and was mourned by a newly united nation.

D. Mack Smith, *Cavour*, 1985.
D. Mack Smith, *Cavour and Garibaldi, 1860*, 1985.
A. J. Whyte, *The Early Life and Letters of Cavour, 1810–1848*, 1976.
A. J. Whyte, *The Political Life and Letters of Cavour, 1848–1861*, 1976.

CERVANTES SAAVEDRA, MIGUEL DE (1547–1616), Spanish novelist. He was born in Alcalá de Henares and educated at the College of the City of Madrid. His father was an indigent doctor with a large family and Cervantes, too, for most of his life was preoccupied with the difficulty of making a living. In 1568 a number of his poems appeared in a volume to commemorate the death of the Spanish queen, Elizabeth of Valois. In 1569 he went to Rome and the following year entered military service.

In 1570 he fought against the Turks in the naval battle of Lepanto. According to a companion's account of the episode, he displayed a form of heroic behavior not unlike that of the knight who was to be the butt of his satire in *Don Quixote*. On the day of the battle he was ill with fever below deck and had every reason to remain there and avoid the fighting. Instead he insisted on taking part. Accordingly he was placed in command of a longboat party in an exposed position to the left of the Spanish fleet, where he received three bullets which maimed his left hand for life, or, as he said, "for the greater glory of the right." He saw further service against the Turks in Tunis, but en route back to Spain, in 1575, he was captured by Barbary pirates, taken to Algeria as a slave, and held there for ransom. During the next five years, until his friends and family finally managed to raise the necessary funds, he made four heroic but vain attempts to escape.

Upon his return Cervantes was unable to find employment and so decided to become a writer. Although he wrote prodigiously between 1582 and 1585, producing some twenty or thirty plays (of which only two are extant), he received little financial reward for his efforts. In 1584 he sold all the rights to his first romance, *Galatea*, which did little to alleviate his financial difficulties. He took government jobs as a Seville commissary, furnishing goods to the fleet of the Armada, and as a tax collector. Probably due to careless bookkeeping, resulting in deficits in the accounts he had received, he was imprisoned more than once. It was around the time of one of these confinements that he first conceived the idea for a story about a madman who imagines himself to be a knight errant and tries to enact the heroic medieval tales of chivalry. The first part of

- All that glitters is not gold.
- Tell me your company and I'll tell you what you are.
- They who lose today may win tomorrow.
- When the head aches, all the members partake of the pains.
- Those who play with cats must expect to be scratched.
- There's no sauce like hunger.

Sayings of Sancho Panza

Cervantes

the novel was published under the title *Don Quijote de la Mancha* (1605), and was so successful that three pirated editions appeared in Madrid almost immediately, while several years later it was translated into English (1612) and French. The pirating and his own lack of financial acumen resulted in Cervantes's failure to reap substantial wealth from this enormously successful book. The second part of *Don Quijote* was published in 1615; a collection of twelve short stories, *Exemplary Novels*, came out in 1613. His last work was *Pérsiles y Sigismunda*. He died within a few days of the death of his great contemporary, William *Shakespeare.

Don Quixote is regarded as the first modern novel and one of the greatest novels ever written. Unlike his predecessors, Cervantes saw his material not from one point of view, but from two contrasting pairs of eyes, those of Sancho Panza and those of Don Quixote. He created that three-dimensional quality which distinguishes the modern novel from what preceded it. Its protagonists, Don Quixote and his servant Sancho Panza, represent two contrasting aspects of human nature. The former is the incurable romantic, dedicated to chivalric ideals of a former age, whereas his servant is the epitome of folk simplicity and worldly common sense. Although initially Don Quixote appears as an insane and extravagant figure of fun, he grows in stature just as Sancho Panza, initially conceived as a simpleminded foil to his master, grows too, so that eventually the master becomes the representative of the ideal while his servant becomes the representative of the real. There are clear differences between the first part of the novel and the second, published

ten years later. Cervantes's fidelity to realistic background becomes more pronounced, whereas the pace of farcical adventures is slowed in favor of a greater emphasis on the characters. The transformation of character which had begun in the first part is also completed. Don Quixote, though his quixotic naivete is undiminished, becomes less a figure of ridicule and increasingly the Platonic philosopher, while Sancho is increasingly his empirical counterpart.

K. P. Allen, *Cervantes and the Pastoral Mode*, 1982.
R. Scheveill, *Cervantes*, 1966.

CÉZANNE, PAUL (1839–1906), French artist; a founder of impressionism. Cézanne was born and grew up in Aix-en-Provence. His parents married when Paul was ten years old. During this time the elder Cézanne had become the owner of a successful bank and the family prospered financially. Still, because of the illegitimacy of Paul and his younger sister Marie, and the couple's humble origins, they were always ostracized by what was considered respectable society in this provincial town.

As a result, the young Cézanne was something of an outsider who found it difficult to form social relationships, a trait that continued throughout his life. Perhaps the most influential person in Cézanne's life was his closest friend from childhood, the writer Émile *Zola. Of their early friendship Zola wrote, "Opposites by nature, we became united forever, attracted to each other by secret affinities, the as yet vague torment of a common ambition, the awakening of a superior intelligence in the midst of the brutal mob."

After school Zola went to live in Paris and Cézanne stayed in Aix to study law in accordance with his father's wishes. He gave up his studies as soon as his father agreed and moved to Paris to be reunited with Zola and begin painting seriously. He produced very little during this period and drifted away from Zola. Always prone to melancholy and fits of temper, he began to have periods of depression and withdrawal that lasted on and off for the rest of his life.

Cézanne returned to Aix determined to please his father; he planned to give up painting and take up the family business. Soon both father and son realized that Paul would never become a banker and he returned to Paris. There he failed to gain acceptance at the École des Beaux Arts. His work, along with that of Camille Pissarro, Pierre Renoir, Claude Monet, and others, was rejected by the art establishment. Cézanne, returned to the countryside, where he remained, except for brief intervals, for the rest of his life.

It was in one of these intervals that he fell in love with a nineteen-year-old model named Hortense Fiquet. He lived with her first in Paris, then in the country, hiding her from his father. His relationship with his father was strained; although the older Cézanne was still supporting his son financially, the allowance was barely enough to live on. Cézanne

- No paintings in a studio are as good as those outside.
- Art is a harmony that runs parallel to nature.
- Color is where the mind and the universe meet.
- Art is what the eye thinks.
- Nature is more depth than surface.

Paul Cézanne

lived off this allowance, and later his inheritance, for his entire working life.

Hortense and Cézanne had a son in 1872 also named Paul, and they married a few years later. Although he was a tender and attentive father, his relationship with his wife was far from ideal. He took sides with his mother, with whom he was very close, and who neither liked nor approved of Hortense. The couple lived apart for most of their married life.

Both official and popular rejection continued to plague Cézanne. He submitted paintings to the salon each year and each year his work was summarily rejected, but eventually his work found a sponsor, a customs official with independent tastes named Victor Chocquet.

Cézanne's technique and style of painting changed gradually throughout his life. His early work was characterized by dark colors. Later, greatly influenced by the impressionist Pissarro, he began using lighter shades and chiseling and softening his style. He finally broke with the impressionists, feeling they too often sacrificed form for color.

Ultimately overwhelmed by criticism, though, Cézanne retired to the countryside, nearly a misanthrope and hermit but still confident of his work. During his last twenty years he concentrated on the landscapes around Aix. He had few visitors as he more or less cut himself off from all his former contacts, including Zola who, after supporting his work for many years, offended Cézanne with his unflattering, thinly veiled portrayal of the artist in his novel *L'Oeuvre*. Locally, he was regarded as an eccentric failure, and the head of the museum in Aix swore that none of Cézanne's paintings would hang on its walls as long as he was director.

His subjects, in the early years, were literary and historical. As his work matured he moved toward more naturalistic subjects: portraits, still lifes, landscapes. His portraits, one of the most famous being *The Portrait of Madame Cézanne*, are a remarkable combination of deadpan, almost inhuman, facial expressions that somehow through color and spacial distortion convey startling humanity.

In his last years the landscape was his only regular companion. Cézanne often chose to paint the same scene from different angles and at different times. These works of Cézanne's differ from similar series by true impressionists because of the presence of a sharp underlying form; however, the roots of his art lie in impressionism. He studied its love of light and shade, but he found impressionism insubstantial, whereas he sought to create something lasting. In his last period he often returned to the theme of people in nature, especially bathers, whom he painted not from life but from other art. To the end, he sought after the universal harmony between nature and mankind.

By the time of his death he had become recognized by his peers but it was not until later that he was acknowledged by the public at large as one of the great painters of the nineteenth century, of whom Pablo *Picasso said, "He was the father of us all." In his last years Cézanne wrote, "The world does not understand me and I do not understand the world. That's why I have chosen to withdraw from it."

M. L. Krumrine, *Paul Cézanne; The Bathers,* 1989.
J. Rewald, *Paul Cézanne: A Biography,* 1968.
R. Shiff, *Cézanne and the End of Impressionism,* 1986.

CHANDRAGUPTA (Chandragupta Maurya; reigned c.324–c.298 B.C.E.), founder of the Mauryan dynasty, the first historical dynasty of India. Little is known about the early life of Chandragupta and even his surname, Maurya, has perplexed scholars. According to one legend, Chandragupta was the illegitimate son of Dhana Nanda, king of Magadha, and his handmaid Mura; it would then be from his mother that Chandragupta inherited the name. He met *Alexander the Great, then campaigning in India, while still a child. The precocious Chandragupta apparently offended Alexander and barely escaped with his life. Other legends state that he was commander in chief of Dhana Nanda's armies; after instigating a failed revolt, he was forced to flee the country.

Sometime during his exile Chandragupta met the Brahman sage Chanakya (Kautilya), author of the *Arthasastra,* a handbook of Indian politics. The two men forged a bond that was to last the remainder of their lives. Chanakya encouraged Chandragupta to conquer Magadha; Chandragupta mustered an enormous army of six hundred thousand infantry, thirty thousand cavalry, nine thousand elephants, and countless chariots. Madagha capitulated sometime between 324 and 321 B.C.E.; Chandragupta continued on to conquer Malwa, Gujarat, and Saurashtra.

Following Alexander's untimely death his Indian territories were governed by Seleucus Nicator. Chandragupta defeated Seleucus in battle in 305, forcing him to concede four Indian satrapies: Kabul, Herat, Kandahar, and Baluchistan. Chandragupta had succeeded in establishing an empire extending over most of northern India and Afghanistan. The extent of Chandragupta's power can best be illustrated by the marital alliance concluded between him and Seleucus; Seleucus agreed to give Chandragupta his daughter for only 500 elephants.

Sometime after the defeat of Seleucus, the Greeks sent an ambassador, Megasthenes, to Chandragupta's court. Megasthenes recorded his impressions in a book, *Indica*. Although the book has since been lost, many other contemporary authors quote it extensively. The book describes Chandragupta's palace at Pataliputra as being even more magnificent than those of the Persian emperors at Susa and Ecbatana. Chandragupta, according to Megasthenes, was a prisoner in his own palace. Despite the glory he had achieved from his conquests, he was apparently regarded as a usurper throughout his life.

Chandragupta was succeeded by his son Bindusura, of whom nothing is known. It was Bindusura's son *Asoka who brought Chandragupta's empire to its zenith.

W. H. Morelan and A. C. Chatterjee, *A Short History of India*, 1945.

H. Morton-Smith, *Dates and Dynasties in Earliest India*, 1973.

CHARLEMAGNE (Charles the Great; 742–814), king of the Franks (768–814); emperor of the West (800–814). Son of Pepin III the Short and grandson of *Charles Martel, he was crowned king, together with his brother Carloman, in 753. At his father's death the realm was divided between him and his brother but soon after, conflict arose between them. At the death of Carloman in 771 Charlemagne became sole king. He eliminated Carloman's family and used the alliance between them and Desiderius, king of the Lombards, as a pretext for invading Italy, ostensibly to extend military help to the Roman church. In 774 he conquered Pavia and was crowned king of the Lombards. Pope Adrian I also granted him the title Patrice of the Romans, which he bore in addition to his two royal titles, authorizing him to intervene in the temporal affairs of Rome under the formal authority of the pope. Returning to his realm Charlemagne embarked on a war against the Saxons (led by his most powerful enemy, Witlekind) which lasted more than thirty years, until 804. Saxony was conquered step by step and its population forcibly Christianized. In his ordinance of 777 draconic measures were prescribed, including the death penalty for opposing conversion. In 787 he responded to a call of Muslim rulers in northern Spain, who were fighting against the Ummayads of Córdoba, and led a raid into Spain. The only results of this expedition were the destruction of Pampelona (Pamplona), capital of the Christian kingdom of Navarre, and the retaliation by the Basques, who wreaked havoc on the rearguard of his army in the Pass of Roncesvalles. But for Charlemagne's military and diplomatic skills, the defeat might have provoked a general revolt by the Saxons. Having crushed his opponents, Charlemagne proceeded to change the structure of his kingdom: in 789 he promulgated a decree aimed at realizing the ideal Christian kingdom, based on the biblical concepts of the Holy People and Sacred Monarchy. The Franks were represented as the heirs of ancient Israel and the Chosen People, while Charlemagne was portrayed as a new King David. His subjects were ordered to swear allegiance to him, every revolt or sign of infidelity being considered an offense against religion. The church was incorporated in the royal system as part of the government subservient to the monarch.

Among Charlemagne's conquests were the duchy of Bavaria (788), the frontier territories of Brittany and the Slavs on the Elbe; but here Charlemagne contented himself with imposing his overlordship. From 797 to 799 he attacked the Avars and conquered their kingdom, enriching his treasury with the booty; once, he had 4,500 captives executed. After many conquests, the idea of a Christian empire was broached at Charlemagne's court. The idea was first given public expression at the council held in 794 at Frankfurt, where many decisions on ecclesiastical and lay reforms of the kingdom were made. The condemnation of Adoptionism, a heresy originating in Spain and that of the decisions of the Council of Nicaea II (787) concerning images left Charlemagne appearing to be the sole leader and defender of Christianity. Then, too, the publication of the *Caroline Books* (a treatise attributed to Charlemagne containing a criticism of the Iconoclasts) was intended to discredit Byzantium and Empress Irene and also to create a new status for Charlemagne. After the death of Adrian I, Charlemagne recognized the new pope, Leo III, and in a letter to him attempted to clarify the division of power, limiting the pope to prayers. A revolt against Leo which compelled him to flee from Rome served Charlemagne's intentions. He received the pope at his camp at Paderborn, where the army was mobilized against the Saxons, and promised to come to Rome to clarify the situation. In 799, after having seen to the completion of his palace at Aix-la-Chapelle (Aachen), which was modeled on the Byzantine imperial palace, he led an expedition to Rome, intending to arbitrate between the pope and his accusers. Leo skillfully prevented this intercession by successfully defending himself against the accusations and positioned himself as Charlemagne's equal. At the Christmas Mass of 800 he crowned Charlemagne Emperor of the Romans, to the great disappointment of the Frankish king, who sought a more powerful title such as Emperor of the Christians. In 802 Charlemagne, who was never to return to Rome, began to organize his empire on religious principles, taking into account the feudal structures of society. He tried to win recognition of his imperial title by the Byzantine Basileus, obtaining it only in 812; his conflict with Byzantium led him to develop relations with the Caliph *Harun ar-Rashid of Baghdad.

The last years of Charlemagne's reign marked the beginning of his empire's disintegration. Because his empire lacked an effective administrative structure, Charlemagne tried to govern by obtaining his vassals' and counts' fealty, but this system was not very efficient and signs of local independence emerged despite the emperor's great prestige. Moreover, the long and continuous wars ruined the free peasants, who began to shirk their military duties. As a result, the first Scandinavian raids were disastrous for the counties along the coast of northern France and the Low Countries.

Charlemagne was a man of contradictions. He adopted the lifestyle and customs of his German ancestors, speaking the Frankish idiom of Austrasia and wearing traditional Frankish clothes — a leather vest or linen tunic. However, Greek was heard at his court and he was a patron of the arts and letters, encouraging the spread of knowledge throughout his empire despite the fact that he did not know Latin. He gathered scholars and intellectuals at his palace of Aix-la-Chapelle and was responsible for the Carolingian Renaissance. Charlemagne took an active part in discussions of the palace academy and was considered after his death to be the patron saint of learning and universities. Yet while demanding a perfect moral life from members of his family and banishing to monasteries those who sinned, he continued to entertain concubines. Nevertheless, Charlemagne became a legendary figure through the centuries, with all the good deeds of his dynasty coming to be associated with his personality.

Subsequent generations were greatly influenced by his depiction in the *Song of Roland*. Charlemagne's romantic image inspired the concept of imperial dignity and also served as a model to *Napoleon.
J. Boussard, *The Civilization of Charlemagne*, 1968.
D. Bullough, *The Age of Charlemagne*, 1966.

CHARLES VII (1403–1461), king of France from 1422. Usually described as a man of weak character, he had a long, eventful reign. He was the eleventh child of Charles VI, and Isabella of Bavaria, and became regent of France in 1418 when his father went mad. His position was precarious: the English army was in possession of a large territory in northern France and the French nobility was divided into two factions, the Burgundians and the Armagnacs. In 1419, at a conference in Montereau, the Armagnacs murdered the duke of Burgundy, John the Fearless, at a meeting where the dauphin (the future Charles VII) was present, thus forcing the Burgundians into the arms of the English. Charles's insane father, who came under the influence of the Burgundians, then accepted the Treaty of Troyes (1420) whereby he declared his son illegitimate and designated Henry V of England regent and future heir to the crown of France. Yet after Charles VI's death in 1422 the dauphin was recognized as king in southern France; however, he was almost powerless and under the influence of his Armagnac councilors. He eventually recovered the occupied parts of his kingdom thanks to the nationalist movement on his behalf inspired by *Joan of Arc. In 1429 she led the French troops against the English, who were besieging the city of Orléans, and liberated it. This opened the way to Rheims

where, in the ancient traditional ceremony, Charles was crowned on July 17, 1429. Joan of Arc had given the king confidence in himself and he became known as Charles the Victorious. However, the king and his advisers decided to do nothing to rescue Joan of Arc when she was captured and handed over to the English in May 1430.

In 1435 Charles concluded the Peace of Arras with Philip the Good of Burgundy. The reconciliation strengthened him vis-à-vis the English and in 1436 he was able to take Paris. This was followed by a period of military standstill in which unruly bands roamed and terrorized the countryside. In the course of these years the king introduced many reforms in the tax system and in the army and, in 1438, issued the Pragmatic Sanction of Bourges, which restricted the authority of the pope over the French church and increased royal control of church revenues.

During this part of his reign Charles was served by a group of loyal advisers, among them the merchant and banker, Jacques Coeur, whom Charles made master of the royal mint and employed as diplomat and administrator of the royal finances. The fact that his advisers were of relatively low social standing caused resentment among the great nobles, who were joined by his own son, the future *Louis XI; their revolt (1440) was suppressed.

Charles's mistress, Agnès Sorel, was influential in court life and also involved herself in political matters. She bore the king four daughters. Her death, soon after the birth of her fourth daughter, was rumored to have been caused by poisoning. The dauphin was suspected but more than a year later, in 1451, Jacques Coeur, whose great wealth had provoked the jealousy of important members of the royal court, was accused. Charles VII ordered his arrest and confiscated his property.

After twenty years of struggle, Charles VII succeeded in driving the English out of the kingdom. At the time of his death only Calais remained in English hands.
M. G. A. Vale, *Charles VII*, 1974.

CHARLES I (Charles Stuart; 1600–1649), king of England from 1625. Born in Dunfermline, Scotland, the second son of James VI of Scotland (later *James I of England). Charles was a sickly child and not expected to live long; he did not speak until he was five and could not walk until he was seven. He grew up in the shadow of his elder brother Henry, the heir-apparent. Henry had the fine physique and prowess that Charles lacked but he fell ill and died in 1612. Charles's favorite sister, Elizabeth, left home to marry a German monarch. Thus deprived of his closest friends, Charles grew up quiet and introverted. He was small in stature and spoke with a Scottish accent and a noticeable stammer. A man of strong religious sentiment, he was a loyal husband to his queen, Henrietta Maria (sister of King Louis XIII of France) and a devoted family man. James VI of Scotland also became king of

England in 1603 and Charles succeeded him as ruler of the two kingdoms in 1625, but his reserved nature and lack of political judgment or diplomatic skill prevented him from cultivating strong bonds with his subjects.

A monarch distant from his people and insensitive to social and political currents, Charles became overly dependent on stronger personalities in his court. He initially came under the influence of the duke of Buckingham, the court favorite of his father. Buckingham's dashing appearance, wit, and talent for flattery captivated the young king but disgusted many of his countrymen. With Buckingham's assassination in 1628, the king turned for support to the queen, catering to her every whim, which ranged from acquiring a pack of pet monkeys to having a dwarf in full armor jump out of a pie and stand at attention at the dinner table. Her extravagances did not meet with the approval of a populace which was also highly suspicious of her Catholicism. The king's love of fine art and his patronage of painters like Anthony Van Dyck and Peter Paul *Rubens gave him an honored place in the development of the arts, but to certain of his subjects money spent on paintings and tapestries seemed a criminal waste.

Charles was a firm believer in the divine right of kings to rule. He placed no trust in his Parliament, which he viewed as little more than a tool for raising taxes, failing to recognize that this institution had assumed an independent power and within its ranks were many men of Puritanical religious views and ideas of political liberty in conflict with his own. For eleven years he sought to rule without their assistance and imposed on the country arbitrary taxes to finance ill-conceived and ultimately futile wars with France and Spain.

In 1639, King Charles's attempts to impose a book of common prayer on his Presbyterian Scottish subjects led to a short war in which his forces were defeated. He was forced to summon Parliament again to raise funds to pursue the campaign in Scotland. The obedience he counted upon was not forthcoming, for Parliament denounced his autocratic approach to government and sought to impeach his leading counselors. One of the king's closest advisers, the earl of Strafford, was impeached, sentenced, and executed and Charles was powerless to save him. Parliament passed, by 159 to 148 votes, a Grand Remonstrance condemning the king's misrule. Plans were set in motion to eliminate the king's control of the army and he feared that the queen would be impeached because the strong feeling against the rise of Catholic influence at court. Desperately trying to assert the authority he believed he still possessed, in 1642 the king went in person with four hundred men to arrest five members of Parliament he accused of treason; the five escaped and the incident served to highlight his weakness.

Efforts to settle the conflict peacefully failed. In London the sentiment of the people was with Parliament and King Charles moved his court north to York. The queen traveled to Holland to pawn the crown jewels; the honor of the monarchy would not stand before the pressing need for funds.

After a series of minor skirmishes, King Charles's armed forces and those of his rebellious Parliament met in a major confrontation at Edgehill in 1643. Before the battle Charles told his soldiers, "Your king is both your cause, your quarrel and your captain. The foe is in sight...." For the first half of what became the English Civil War, the king's forces held the advantage but this was never exploited in a move on London, the capital. From 1645 the tide turned with a major Royalist defeat at Naseby to an army headed by Lord Fairfax and Oliver *Cromwell. By 1646 the king was surrounded in Oxford but managed to escape in disguise to his old enemies, the Scots, encamped at Newark. The following year an agreement was reached between the Scottish commanders and Parliament and the king was handed over. His attempts to forge alliances with the various parties to the conflict were in vain; he was placed on trial at Westminster for treason. In his trial and execution he displayed a strength of character that would have served him well in earlier years. He refused to recognize the court, claiming that no earthly tribunal could judge him; his death warrant was signed by Cromwell. Charles went to his death a proud man; he asked for shirts to wear so that he would not shiver in the frosty January air, saying, "If I tremble with cold, my enemies will say it was from fear; I will not expose myself to such reproaches." Convinced of the justice of his cause, the sight of the sharp ax and block did not frighten the king, as he said with conviction, "I go from a corruptible to an incorruptible crown, where no disturbance can take place."

M. Ashley, *Charles I and Oliver Cromwell*, 1972.
J. Bowle, *Charles I*, 1975.
C. Carlton, *Charles I, the Personal Monarch*, 1983.
K. Sharpe, *The Personal Rule of Charles I*, 1992.

CHARLES II (Charles Stuart; 1630–1685), king of England and Scotland from 1660. The eldest surviving son of King *Charles I was in many ways the opposite in character to his ill-fated father. Tall and handsome with an outgoing personality, devoted to the pursuit of physical pleasures, flexibility to steer a safe course between the conflicting religious and political interest groups threatening to tear the country apart.

In 1645 King Charles I sent his sons Charles and James to France, perhaps fearing that the course of the Civil War would turn against him. Prince Charles returned in 1650 and led an abortive invasion of England from Scotland. Final defeat came in 1651 at the battle of Worcester, where the prince distinguished himself with his courage in the fray. One contemporary described how Prince Charles led out the army and engaged it himself, charging at the head thereof many several times in person, with great courage and success. Despite the talents he displayed in his role as army commander, the battle did not go his way and the parliamentary army entered the city. There is an account of Prince Charles escaping from his lodging by the back door as a parliamentary officer entered by the front.

There followed six weeks of life on the run from the victorious parliamentary forces with a £1,000 price on his head at a time when many families lived on £50 a year or less. Prince Charles utilized his skills as an actor, traveling around disguised as a gentleman's servant. He stayed at a series of safehouses owned by Royalist sympathizers, often Roman Catholics. On one occasion that has since been entered into legend, he hid in an oak tree while soldiers searched the surrounding area. Another time he had to take his horse into a smithy to be shoed. He asked the smith for news of the battle of Worcester and the smith told him the good news of the defeat of the Scots but regretted that that rogue Charles Stuart had not yet been captured. Prince Charles, in his role as a Midlands farmer, commented that he thought Charles Stuart deserved to be hanged more than any other for initiating the invasion and the smith commended him for speaking like an honest man.

Prince Charles escaped to a long and poverty-stricken exile in France. In 1658, the Lord Protector of England, Oliver *Cromwell, died. There followed a period of political uncertainty with growing fears of anarchy. In this climate, one of Cromwell's leading generals, George Monck, invited Prince Charles to return and accept the English crown. He entered London in triumph in 1660 on his thirtieth birthday. The people were anxious to put behind them the conflict of previous years and desired a return to the stability that once characterized the country. The new King Charles II responded by adopting a conciliatory tone toward those who had opposed his father in the Civil War. The men immediately involved in the regicide were brutally executed and Oliver Cromwell's body exhumed and disgraced, but to others clemency was extended and there was a period of widespread satisfaction with the new king's rule; this did not last.

The king's policy of religious tolerance was opposed by a significant segment of the population, who feared that it would open the way for a revival of Roman Catholic power. Charles became involved in a war with the Netherlands over commercial jealousies; although England won two victories, the Dutch admiral, M. A. de Ruyter, sailed up the Thames in 1667, burning several warships, while Charles was occupied with his mistresses. The king's popularity was also adversely affected by the 1670 Treaty of Dover with King *Louis XIV of France. In return for an alliance against the Dutch, Charles promised to become a Roman Catholic and was promised military help if his subjects turned against him. His connection with the king of France and suspicions about the activities of his queen in advancing the Catholic cause eroded the popular support he enjoyed at his restoration. When his queen, Catherine, failed to produce an heir, fear in-

tensified as it became clear that the king's Catholic brother, James, would succeed him. Such fears were amplified by claims in 1679 of the existence of a Popish plot to murder Charles and place James on the throne. Between the years 1679 and 1681 the king almost lost control over the government but through adroit maneuvering he restored his influence and ended his reign in a strong position.

The return of the royal court brought again to London the color that had been lacking during the years of parliamentary rule. The king had little inclination to involve himself with the details of his administration pursuing instead his private interests. He began to rebuild his father's plundered art collection and brought to England a taste for French music and furniture. He had a keen interest in science and encouraged the formation of the Royal Society in 1662, a scientific research foundation still active today. It is recorded that he stayed up one night observing an eclipse of Saturn through a telescope and his interest inspired others. The king was also a lover of parks and gardens, going daily to London's Saint James's Park to feed the ducks and greeting his subjects with the raising of his hat along the way.

Charles had married the Portuguese Princess Catherine of Braganza in 1661. Though he always behaved in a courteous manner toward her, his affections were elsewhere. The queen failed to produce an heir to the throne but the king had scandalized respectable society by having at least fourteen illegitimate children by a succession of mistresses, some noblewomen, but others actresses, like the famous Nell Gwynne (one of his last utterances was, "Don't let poor Nelly starve"). His attitude toward women is indicated in his remark on being told that his mistress Barbara Villiers had converted from Anglicanism to Catholicism. The king is reported to have said "he never concerned himself with the souls of ladies, but with their bodies, insofar as they were gracious enough to allow him." Daniel Defoe summed up Charles's reign as follows:

"The royal refugee our breed restores,
With foreign courtiers and with foreign whores,
And carefully repeopled us again,
Throughout his lazy, long, lascivious reign."

A. Bryant, *King Charles II*, 1955.
A. Fraser, *King Charles II*, 1979.
R. Hutton, *Charles the Second*, 1989.
J. Ogilby, *The Entertainment of his Most Excellent Majestie, Charles II*, 1988.

CHARLES V (1500–1558), Holy Roman emperor, king of Spain (as Charles I), archduke of Austria. Charles's reign was fraught with the difficulties of retaining his many territories and authority in the face of the growth of Protestantism, increasing French and Turkish pressure, and the opposition of a hostile pope. The son of Philip I of Castile and grandson of Emperor *Maximilian I, Charles numbered many other Catholic kings and queens of Europe among his close kin: his maternal grandparents were *Isabella I of Castile and *Ferdinand II of Aragon. He was raised by his aunt, Margaret of Austria, regent of the Netherlands. His regimented upbringing left him little opportunity to form close relationships, a circumstance responsible for his cool and aloof personality which at best inspired respect rather than admiration.

At fifteen Charles assumed rule over the Netherlands, and a year later he became king of Spain when his grandfather Ferdinand died. Insensitive to Spanish traditions, Charles instituted what virtually constituted foreign rule over the country, freely exploiting its resources to further his own ends. When he became king of Germany and was elected emperor-designate in 1519 (finally being crowned emperor by the pope in 1530) he gave his spiritual mentor, Adrian of Utrecht (later Pope Adrian VI, a supporter of the *devotia moderna* religious movement which arose in late fifteenth century Holland) the unenviable task of administering Spain as his regent. A revolt of the Castilian cities soon followed.

A zealous and pious Catholic, Charles struck the first blow in his battle against Protestantism, then gaining force in central Europe, with the 1521 Edict of Worms, which outlawed the writings of Martin *Luther. In 1522, however, he was forced to return to Spain to quell a rebellion and ruled from that country for the next seven years, achieving a rapprochement with the rebellious nobles and adopting the Spanish language, customs, and manners as his own. After his institution of a far stricter degree of administrative centralization there than elsewhere in his empire, Spain became his primary base. Spanish troops served him loyally, while the treasure fleets from the New World helped fund his operations throughout Europe.

Charles's reign was marked by persistent disputes with *Francis I of France, a manifestation of the struggle between the houses of Habsburg (represented by Charles) and Valois to secure hegemony in Europe. In 1525 Francis was captured and forced to marry Charles's sister Eleanor, but he reneged on the terms of the Treaty of Madrid and, with the backing of the anti-Habsburg Pope Clement VII, continued to assert his claim to Burgundy. During a 1527 campaign against the pope, Charles's forces sacked the city of Rome; in 1536 Charles traveled to Rome to challenge Francis to single combat, an offer the latter refused. It was only the more pressing need to unite against the incursions of the Ottoman Turks that prompted the two warring monarchs to engineer an agreement whereby Charles gave up his claims to Burgundy in exchange for Francis's relinquishing his interest in Milan and Naples.

Charles first arrested the Turks' westward expansion into Europe by recapturing Tunis in 1535, a year after its conquest by the enemy. But the cost to him was great, and he became increasingly plagued by the inadequacy of his financial means to preserve

Charles V, by Titian

his holdings, let alone indulge any dynastic ambitions he might entertain. Thus, his 1543–1544 campaign against a resurgent Francis was severely hampered by his shortage of money. Its outcome, though, was successful in that the French king surrendered territory in Canada and agreed to the convocation of a general church council (the Council of Trent) to consider reform, which Charles had been calling for since the mid-1530s.

Charles saw reform as the church's only means to check the spread of Protestantism, which threatened to become especially virulent within his own kingdom; Protestant German princes formed the Schmalkaldic League in 1531. With the backing of the Council of Trent, he went to war against the League, defeating its forces at the Battle of Mühlberg in 1547. However, instead of receiving the credit he regarded as his due for having reasserted the Catholic cause, Charles was criticized by Pope Paul III for tolerating Protestants in Augsburg. Frustrated and angered by perpetual papal opposition, Charles allowed his religious zeal to wane.

Charles's efforts to settle the succession on his son, the future *Philip II, so enraged the German Catholic princes that they allied against him with Henry II of France. Unable to prevent the consequent loss of some of his imperial possessions to France in 1552, Charles barely escaped the humiliation of being captured at Innsbruck that same year. Tired by the constant effort of maintaining his patrimony and dispirited by the election of another hostile pope, Paul IV, Charles made his brother Ferdinand ruler of the German territories in 1554; handed over the Netherlands, Spain and its empire, and his Italian possessions to Philip; and retired to the monastery of Yuste, in Extremadura, Spain, where he died soon afterward.

Given the difficulties of attempting to maintain such extensive possessions, Charles's endeavors were impressive as much for their manner as their scope. An able and forceful statesman, he demonstrated a moral uprightness and sense of personal honor that commanded respect. However, the twenty-eight million ducats in debts he incurred are evidence of the inadequacy of his means. Exploitation of the riches of the Spanish empire in the New World was in its infancy, and Charles was forced to borrow money from the great financial centers of Antwerp, Augsburg, and Genoa at crippling rates of interest. After his death, his former domains were rife with dissent, highlighting the magnitude of his achievement in controlling them.

M. F. Alvarez, *Charles V,* 1977.
E. Armstrong, *The Emperor Charles V,* 2 vols., 1976.
K. Brandi, *The Emperor Charles V: The Growth and Destiny of a Man and of a World Empire,* 1980.

CHARLES XII (1682–1718), king of Sweden.

Charles XII acceded to the throne of Sweden when only fifteen years old after the death of his father Charles XI, assuming power almost immediately. He was a bright, energetic prince with an aptitude for languages and mathematics but his true love was sport, and he excelled in riding and bear hunting. Fascinated with military history, he sought ways to further Sweden's control of the Baltic region.

At age eighteen Charles left Sweden at the head of his armies, never to return to his capital. His first target was Denmark, which had threatened the independence of Sweden's traditional ally, Frederick, duke of Holstein-Gottorp. With Denmark easily crushed, Russian czar *Peter the Great and King Augustus II (the Strong) of Poland feared that Charles would now turn against them. Peter was also seeking an alternative maritime outlet for his growing empire to replace the difficult Arctic route. To establish a Baltic outlet, Russian troops occupied Swedish Livonia and Estonia. Some 40,000 Russian troops were stationed at Narva, in Estonia, to protect the new acquisition. Charles led 10,000 men to Narva where, under the cover of a raging blizzard, he stormed the center of the Russian defenses. This headstrong assault was an extraordinary success; unable to identify their attackers because of the snow, the Russian camp divided into two detached sections. Countless terrified Russians fled the battlefield only to drown in the Narva River. By the battle's end, the number of captured Russians actually outnumbered their Swedish assailants, forcing Charles to release everyone except officers.

The Russian defeat left Charles with three options: the immediate invasion of that country; suing for peace on his own terms; or invading Poland. He chose the last, mistakenly underestimating the popularity of the German-born Augustus. Charles's

decision was made without consulting his officers, who suspected him of loving war for war's sake. Charles felt closer to his troops, preferring the simple uniform and boots of a common soldier to royal garb and fashionable wigs. He admired the rank and file and believed that all competent officers must rise from it. When a young corporal of noble blood applied for promotion, Charles refused to grant the favor and demanded that he first serve in the ranks so as to learn to appreciate his future charges. No one dared question the victorious king, described by one contemporary as "awe-inspiring and almost sinister."

Charles utilized original tactics in his war against Poland. The dreaded Caroline cavalry charge, in tight formation and with sabers drawn, was responsible for the defeat of the combined forces of Saxony and Poland at Klissow in 1702. Charles replaced Augustus with pro-Swedish Stanislas Leszczyński. Augustus escaped to Saxony but was finally defeated in 1706.

Charles, although described by some as an impetuous adventurer, was the most powerful king in northern Europe. He had spent considerable time in Poland trying unsuccessfully to encourage Prussia to participate in an invasion of Russia. Russia would always threaten his Baltic hegemony, he believed, unless he attacked its very heartland by invading Moscow, a strategy shared with *Napoleon and Adolf *Hitler. Peter's reconquest of Livonia and his construction of a new city there, Saint Petersburg, prompted Charles to lead 40,000 men in an assault on the czar, supported by Ukrainian Cossack leader Ivan Mazepa. At first the Russian attempt to ravage the route Charles would take through the Ukraine was foiled by Charles's preparedness; he had brought adequate supplies for just such an exigency. However, the winter of 1708–1709 was the worst

Europe had known in decades. Charles chose an alternative southern route but got lost on the way. Peter defeated Mazepa and the Russians continued their scorched earth policy.

Charles's exhausted troops arrived at the Russian outpost of Poltava in 1709. The ensuing battle was a disaster. Charles was suffering from a fever due to a bullet wound, his reinforcements were waylaid en route, and his generals disagreed on strategy. One third of his infantry had been destroyed in the Russian bombardment before even reaching the battlefield. While fifteen thousand Swedish troops survived the fight, it was only to surrender once Charles had fled.

With only 1,300 men Charles reached the Ottoman Empire. He convinced the Ottomans to attack Russia, and was jubilant when the Turkish army surrounded Peter and his army at Pruth, but peace was declared without concessions to Sweden. The Turks, who hated Charles for inciting hostilities, referred to him as Iron Head. In 1713 his headquarters were burned and Charles imprisoned. Augustus regained Poland, Finland was seized by Russia, and Denmark and Prussia controlled the Baltic.

Accompanied by two companions, Charles made a remarkable journey incognito across Europe, arriving in Pomerania in just fifteen days. On returning to Sweden he made significant economic reforms to allow him to regain his lost empire. His new army consisted of eighty thousand men; but Sweden was never to regain its former glory. Charles was struck down by a bullet during the siege of Fredrikshald (Halden) in Norway. Although the bullet may have been a stray, some historians wonder whether it was fired by an associate of his brother-in-law, Frederick of Hesse, who succeeded Charles to the throne. His military ability and bravery became legendary, his wisdom was admired and cited, and he was regarded as an outstanding hero who was defeated by his ambition.

F. G. Bengtsson, *The Life of Charles XII King of Sweden*, 1960.

R. M. Hatton, *Charles XII of Sweden*, 1968.

M. Roberts, *Sweden's Age of Greatness*, 1973.

CHARLES MARTEL (c.688–741), Frankish ruler who stopped the Moorish invasion of Europe. Martel was the illegitimate son of a Merovingian king's mayor of the palace (official responsible for the palace who effectively ruled the kingdom). Kings of the Frankish Merovingian dynasty had come to prefer debauchery and idleness to the burdens of government; over the generations successive mayors of the palace took advantage of such behavior to assume the royal role in all but name.

In addition to his position as mayor of the palace, Charles's father Pepin II the Younger assumed the title of duke of Austrasia and extended the borders of the Frankish kingdom to include almost all of Gaul. He was survived by three grandsons and his illegitimate son, Charles Martel. Since Pepin's will left everything in his widow's control until his grandsons came of age, Charles was forced to subdue first Pepin's recalcitrant widow and a then rebellious Frankish kingdom before becoming mayor in 719.

With much of Europe still pagan, Charles supported the efforts of Christian missionaries trying to convert the Germanic tribes and repelled Frisian and Saxon attempts to invade Gaul. By 711 the Moors had established themselves in Spain and introduced Islam, and were now crossing the Pyrenees into southern Gaul. They conducted a vicious campaign, burning churches and plundering villages as they crossed Aquitaine (southwest France). Only Charles's 732 victory over them at Tours halted their advance. He met them again in battle on numerous occasions as he conquered his neighbors and added their lands to the Frankish kingdom, but it was the Battle of Tours that broke the momentum of the Muslim push into western Europe and confined them to the Iberian Peninsula.

Charles's relationship with the church was complex. While he made valuable gifts to some abbeys, he confiscated church land and sold church offices to meet his military expenses. He protected missionaries, but once beheaded a monk who protested Charles's quartering of his troops in a monastery. He accepted splendid gifts from the pope (including the keys to Saint *Peter's tomb), but refused to provide military assistance to the pope in his fight against the Lombards, being reluctant to antagonize them after they had supported him against the Moors. Sometimes credited with having saved Europe for Christianity, he was often damned to hell in contemporary sermons.

Content with the reality of power, Charles avoided its trappings. Throughout his reign he preserved the myth that the Merovingian puppet king was the real ruler. Charles's son, Pepin the Short was more ambitious; ten years after Charles's death, Pepin traded support against the Lombards for papal acquiescence to his deposing the Merovingians and starting the Carolingian dynasty in 751. Twenty-seven years after Charles's death, a grandson ascended the throne and became known to history as *Charlemagne, emperor of the West.

J. M. Wallace-Hadrill, *The Long-Haired Kings and Other Studies in Frankish History*, 1964.

CHAUCER, GEOFFREY (c.1342–1400), English poet. Chaucer came from a middle class family of wine importers and merchants who also served as customs collectors. He spent his childhood in London, to which his family had moved before his birth, and was given a strictly religious Latin education in one of its grammar schools becoming a devout Christian. The shortage of books before the invention of the printing press caused great emphasis to be placed on memorization; teachers would dictate from Latin works, which students would write down and then learn by heart. Plots, scenes, and actual lines that Chaucer had memorized would later reappear in his own writings.

FROM THE *CANTERBURY TALES*

- *The original:*
  He was a verray parfit gentil knight.
  But for to tellen yow of his array,
  His hors were gode, but he was nat gay.
  Of fustian he wered a gipoun
  Al bismotered with his habergeoun;
  For he was late y-come from his viage,
  And wente for to doon his pilgrimage.

- *A modern version:*
  He was a true, a perfect gentle-knight.
  Speaking of his appearance, he possessed
  Fine horses, but he was not gaily dressed.
  He wore a fustian tunic stained and dark,
  With smudges where his armor had left mark;
  Just home from service, he had joined our ranks
  To do his pilgrimage and render thanks.

(translation by Neville Coghill)

When Chaucer became a page of the wife of Lionel, Duke of Clarence (third son of Edward III) at the age of twelve, he gained access to Edward's elegant, sophisticated, and French-speaking court. There he became familiar with the ideals of chivalry, in word if not in deed, and they became an important theme in his poetry. The court was also England's administrative center. Permanent administrative careers in the new civil service were becoming available to laymen as well as clerics, and after serving briefly in the Hundred Years' War (during which time he was captured and ransomed by the king), Chaucer started a lifetime of civil service work. By 1367 he was attending to the king and was referred to as our dearly beloved valet.

Governmental use of English rather than French was increasing (Parliament was first summoned in English in 1363). Chaucer translated several of the works of popular French authors and philosophers into English, absorbing much of their style and ideas, which he then imitated in his early works. Written in English, his own works were intended for reading aloud to an audience; they vividly demonstrate the vitality and richness of the English he was instrumental in fashioning.

Chaucer married Philippa de Roet, a lady-in-waiting to the queen and the younger sister of the mistress (later third wife) of John of Gaunt (fourth son of Edward III), in 1366. Both continued to serve the king and queen as courtiers; their married life was marked by the frequent separations necessitated by their positions. As an esquire of the prince's household (1368–1374), Chaucer had a variety of duties ranging from bed-making to diplomatic missions, two of which took him to Italy.

Books were more plentiful in Italy, and Chaucer was able to add to his already extensive collection. His interest in a wide variety of subjects — astronomy, astrology, physics, the psychology of dreams — was reflected in his writing. However, Italy's most important influence on Chaucer's writing was its polished culture and the writings of *Dante Alighieri, Giovamine *Boccaccio, and other Italian authors.

Chaucer was comptroller of customs and subsidies from 1374 to 1386, which was also an extremely productive period for his writing. However, he lost his comptrollership because of a politically-inspired administrative purge, even though he was a cynical observer rather than a supporter of causes. He retired to Kent, where he wrote, served as a justice of the peace, and began to experience the financial problems that would plague him for the rest of his life. In 1389 King Richard II appointed him clerk of royal works, with responsibility for the maintenance of the royal buildings. He later had to relinquish that position for health reasons but still remained in favor at court and was appointed to several minor posts, which he held until his death.

Chaucer's poems included "The Book of the Duchess," "The Hous of Fame," "The Parlement of Foules," "The Legend of Good Women," and "Troilus and Criseyde." But his most popular work was undoubtedly the collection of humorous, warm, lusty short stories collected in the *Canterbury Tales.* Written over a number of years, the *Canterbury Tales* provides a view of life in Chaucer's England that is all the more insightful for its characters having had their inhibitions removed by good company and poor ale. According to the prologue, its thirty travelers were supposed to tell four stories each, but only twenty-three stories were ever finished. Failing health toward the end of his life and anticipation of approaching hellfire accentuated Chaucer's naturally religious tendencies and he added the "Prayer of Chaucer" to the *Canterbury Tales,* asking for both divine and mortal forgiveness for his obscenities and worldliness.

Chaucer's writing and its popularity shaped modern English. He was honored for his services to crown and literature with burial in Poets' Corner in Westminster Abbey.

D. S. Brewer, *Chaucer,* 1973.
G. G. Coulton, *Chaucer and His England,* 1963.
B. A. Hanawalt, ed., *Chaucer's England,* 1992.
D. R. Howard, *Chaucer,* 1987.
G. Kane, *Chaucer,* 1984.
J. D. North, *Chaucer's Universe,* 1988.

CHEKHOV, ANTON PAVLOVICH (or Tchekhov; 1860–1904), Russian playwright and short story writer. He was born at Taganrog in south Russia. His family moved to Moscow in 1869 after his father's business collapsed, leaving the young Chekhov, who was attending the local secondary school, to support himself while completing his education. In 1879 he entered the medical faculty at Moscow university and graduated in 1884. While a student Chekhov took over responsibility as the head of his family and became its main financial supporter through his work as a freelance writer. He turned out many farcical sketches and contributed humorous short stories to journals and magazines, building up a wide popularity among the public. In 1885 Chekhov met A. S. Suvorin, editor of *Novoye Vremya* (New Time), in Saint Petersburg, and in the years that followed his work appeared both in that newspaper and in the *Petersburskaya Gazetta* (Saint Petersburg Gazette). After his graduation, Chekhov worked as a general practitioner in Moscow while continuing his occupation as a writer. On the combination of these activities, he remarked, "Medicine is my legal spouse, while literature is my mistress. When I get tired of one, I go and sleep with the other."

Along with his work as comic author, Chekhov developed his skills as a serious writer and began to examine the condition of human despair and suffering. In 1887 his first full-length play, *Ivanov*, was produced in Moscow and its plot, culminating in the suicide of a young man, demonstrated Chekhov's move toward serious fiction. His first work published in a prominent literary review was a long autobiographical story, *The Steppe*, which appeared in 1888.

Following an expedition to the penal settlement of Sakhalin in Siberia in 1890, Chekhov traveled to Western Europe with Suvorin. He had previously begun work on *The Wood Demon*, a fatuous four-act drama which was produced in Moscow at the end of 1889. Poor reviews by local critics led Chekhov to withdraw the play, which he altered and presented eight years later as *Uncle Vanya*, one of his greatest masterpieces.

By 1892 Chekhov's literary work had proved sufficiently profitable to enable him to acquire a small estate at Melikhovo, near Moscow. It was there that he started writing *The Seagull* in 1895. Melikhovo became Chekhov's main residence for the next four years. During this period he wrote several brilliant short stories in which he portrayed the harsh realities of rural life and contemporary society, including *Ward Number Six* (1892), *The Black Monk* (1894), *My Life* (1896), and *Peasants* (1897). This marked the beginning of Chekhov's break with Russian dramatic tradition, which called for over-emotional sensationalist presentation.

The Seagull was first produced in Saint Petersburg in 1896. The performance was a failure and was booed; Chekhov left the theater after the second act and remarked to Suvorin, "Let people call me a damn fool if I ever write anything else for the stage."

In 1897 Chekhov spent several months at a clinic near Moscow after he suffered a lung hemorrhage, and was diagnosed as having tuberculosis. He spent the winter in the south of France and, returning to Russia in 1898, sold the estate at Melikhovo and built a villa at Yalta, on the Crimean coast, where he spent his convalescence.

Chekhov's reputation as a dramatist was reestablished by the revival of *The Seagull* by the new Moscow Art Theater in December 1898. The novel, intelligent approach of the directors resulted in *The Seagull*'s ultimate success, and in subsequent years, the Art Theater became the chief exponent of Chekhov's dramatic work, including the acclaimed *Uncle Vanya*. Chekhov himself was forbidden to visit Moscow during the theater season on account of his health; however, he had the opportunity to see his plays performed in 1900 when the Art Theater toured the Crimea. He had been elected a member of the Russian Academy in 1897 but resigned when Maksim *Gorky was expelled for political reasons.

Chekhov became attracted to Olga Knipper, one of the actresses of the Art Theater, whom he married in 1901. It was a happy marriage despite the disappointment of not having children and the strain of frequent separations as a result of Chekhov's ill health and Olga's pursuit of her acting career.

Following the Crimea tour, Chekhov was urged to write a play specifically for the Art Theater and produced *Three Sisters*. The first performance took place in 1901 and was well received in Moscow. Although it did not repeat the exceptional triumph of *The Seagull*, with subsequent performances it gradually achieved full recognition.

BY CHEKHOV

• People who are well brought-up usually keep to the following rules of conduct. They have respect for Man, and for that reason are always tolerant, gentle, courteous, and cooperative....They are not garrulous and do not inflict their confidences on people who have not asked for them....They cultivate their aesthetic taste. They strive as far as possible to restrain and ennoble the sexual instinct.

**Excerpt from a letter written by
Chekhov to his brother Nikolai (1886)**

• I must tell you that I am really harsh by disposition, that I am quick-tempered....But I have formed the habit of controlling my impulses, for no decent person should relinquish his hold on himself.

**Excerpt from a letter written by
Chekhov to his wife (1903)**

By 1903 Chekhov's failing health was making his work as dramatist more arduous than ever. He nevertheless completed *The Cherry Orchard* and despite his physical deterioration and his inherent embarrassment on ceremonial occasions, he was persuaded to attend the opening night and received a warm tribute from his audience and colleagues.

Chekhov remained politically unaffiliated in a Russia which was on the brink of revolution, yet his revolutionary rejection of traditional literary devices established his international fame as dramatist and author.

E. Broide, *Chekhov*, 1980.

D. Giles, *Chekhov: Observer without Illusion*, 1968.

V. S. Pritchett, *Chekhov*, 1988.

E. J. Simmons, *Chekhov: A Biography*, 1962.

H. Troyat, *Chekhov*, 1986.

CHENG   SEE SHIH HUANG TI.

CHIANG KAI-SHEK (1887–1975), Chinese military and political leader, head of the Chinese Nationalist government from 1928 to 1949, and then head of the Chinese Nationalist government on Taiwan (Formosa). Chiang Kai-shek, otherwise known as Chiang Chung-cheng, was born in Chikou, about 100 miles from Shanghai, to a prosperous family of salt merchants. At school he already was a rebel, cutting off the pigtail worn by the Chinese as a sign of submission to the Manchu dynasty. He was prepared for a military career and sent to Paoting Military Academy in 1906, spending the next four years training in Japan, studying and serving in the Japanese army. It was during these years in Tokyo that the young Chiang met and formed attachments with compatriots, notably *Sun Yat-sen, who were filled with revolutionary fervor and quickly converted Chiang to their cause.

In 1911 he returned to Shanghai and joined in the revolutionary fighting, which led to the overthrow of the Manchu dynasty. In 1915 he helped fight in the Third Revolution, which saved the fledgling republic from counterrevolutionary forces, and in 1918, he joined Sun Yat-sen's revolutionary group, the Kuomintang (KMT) as a military officer.

At that time China was divided between warring warlords, and Sun — with Chiang Kai-shek as the commander of the southern armies — embarked on a program of unification. However, because Chiang's army comprised rival warlords' gangs, the unification attempt failed. Needing an army of his own, Sun decided to reorganize the KMT according to the Russian system and in 1923 dispatched Chiang to Russia. There for four months he studied Bolshevik military organization, and upon returning to China founded the Whampoa Military Academy. While in Russia, Chiang was introduced to the writings of Karl *Marx and Vladimir Ilyich *Lenin, and was soon basing his thoughts on Leninist doctrine, although he always rejected any attempt to Sovietize China.

After the death of Sun (now his brother-in-law) in 1925, Chiang emerged, backed by his Whampoa officer corps, as the leading successor, and by cleverly maintaining Soviet support while preventing a communist coup, he was strong enough by 1927 to take sole power. He moved his army south and began nurturing the support of foreigners and businessmen in Shanghai. At the same time he worked to suppress the warlords, and by 1928 had gone a long way to unifying the country. In that year he was elected to his first term as president.

While Chiang formulated ideas for broad social reform, he still had to contend with the warlords who continued to dispute his authority. He was especially plagued by communists, who, after having been expelled by Chiang, had withdrawn into the countryside to plan their own army and government, led by *Mao Tse-tung. There was also the impending threat of war with Japan, which invaded Manchuria in 1931.

Chiang decided to crush the communists before taking on the Japanese, a move which proved to be unpopular over the next few years. In response to growing protests over fighting the Japanese, he instituted, in 1934, the New Life movement, based on the cult of *Confucius, in order to boost moral cohesion in the country. At the same time Chiang displayed the ideological confusion that characterized his thinking by promoting western ideals and the Japanese model of Spartan discipline.

War broke out with Japan in 1937 and during the war Chiang took absolute control over the KMT. After four years of fighting alone, China was joined by the Allies, and following Pearl Harbor, Chiang became supreme commander of the Allied air and land forces in the Chinese theater of war. In 1943 he was again reelected to the presidency of China.

The end of World War II brought the resumption of civil war between the communists and Chiang's Nationalists. Negotiations between Chiang and Mao broke down in 1945 and new mediation efforts by U.S. General George *Marshall called for a unified national army and a coalition government. However, by April 1946 all-out civil war was in progress. In 1948 Chiang was elected the first constitutional president of China by the National Assembly and was given virtual dictatorial powers, but time had run out. In 1949 the Nationalist army collapsed in the face of communist attacks and on January 21 Chiang resigned as president. Unable to secure aid from the United States, Chiang flew to Taiwan, where he had organized a base and was soon joined by the remnants of his army and government.

On March 1, 1950, Chiang assumed the presidency of the Nationalist government in Taiwan and in 1954 he secured a mutual defense pact with the United States. In 1960, Chiang was reelected to a third term as president. Holding absolute authority, he built Taiwan into a formidable economic force, while never relinquishing his claim to authority over mainland China. He was succeeded by his son Chiang Ching-kuo as premier in 1972.

P. M. Anthony, *The China of Chiang Kai-shek*, 1973.

B. Crozier, *The Man Who Lost China: The First Full Biography of Chiang Kai-shek*, 1976.

S. A. Hedin, *Chiang Kai-shek, Marshall of China*, 1975.

P. P. Y. Lohl, *The Early Chiang Kai-shek: A Study of His Personality and Politics 1887–1924*, 1971.

CH'IEN-LUNG (Hung-li; 1711–1799), fourth emperor of the Manchu Ch'ing dynasty in China. Ch'ien-lung was the fourth son of Emperor Yung-cheng and a grandson of K'ang-hsi, who established the Manchu dynasty's right to govern. Primogeniture was disregarded by the Chinese, so Ch'ien-lung, considered the most intelligent son of Yung-cheng, was chosen at an early age to succeed his father. Ch'ien-lung was a tall, handsome boy who excelled in horsemanship and archery and was an avid hunter, a hobby he pursued until two years before his death. The focus of his education was orthodox Confucianism but he also showed an interest in the arts, particularly poetry. Some 40,000 verses are attributed to Ch'ien-lung, although he probably composed only a fraction of these.

Ch'ien-lung ascended the throne in 1735. He led a temperate court life, spending the mornings dealing with affairs of state and the afternoons reading, composing verse, or painting. His successful military campaigns brought most neighboring countries under China's influence. He added 600,000 square miles to the empire, its greatest territorial extent, while Sinkiang, Tibet, Burma, and Vietnam offered tribute, as did the Gurkhas of Nepal, against whom Ch'ien-lung led his armies over the imposing plateau of Tibet.

However, Ch'ien-lung's campaigns were a burden on the Chinese economy. Toward the middle of his reign he dismissed his most trustworthy advisers in order to govern the empire on his own. No one dared criticize the emperor. He had seventeen sons and ten daughters, but his chosen heir died at the age of seven. Ch'ien-lung sought solace in his second wife, Ula Nara, but an apparent clash with the emperor caused her to leave the palace for a monastery. Ch'ien-lung then turned to a concubine, Hsiang-fei, a prisoner from Central Asia for whom he built a mosque and even an Oriental bazaar to allay her homesickness. Although Hsiang-fei threatened to kill herself if touched, her considerable influence over the emperor disgraced the court. Only when Ch'ien-lung was away from court did the dowager empress order Hsiang-fei to commit suicide.

Ch'ien-lung turned to literature, amassing an official library, the Ssu-ku Ch'uan-shu, of over 36,000 volumes, divided into classics, history, philosophy, and literature. Each book was copied by hand seven times, to be placed in royal libraries for the emperor and select scholars. At the same time, books not appearing in the library's index were hunted down and destroyed. Often their authors were also liable to the most severe punishments. About 2,500 books were proscribed by Ch'ien-lung's literary inquisition; particularly vulnerable were books critical of the Manchu dynasty for its foreign origins, but other publications included books by people who questioned the corrupt administration. One such author begged Ch'ien-lung to reconsider the appointment of a dissolute official. Angered, Ch'ien-lung asked who taught him to speak in such a manner, to which he replied, *Confucius and *Mencius. The author was banished and his books banned.

In 1780 Ch'ien-lung fell under the influence of Ho-shen, an unscrupulous, power-hungry general who, in effect, governed the country. Ch'ien-lung overlooked Ho-shen's earlier military failures and promoted him and his lackeys to positions of power. The damage to the Ch'ing dynasty was irreparable.

Ch'ien-lung's reign was marked by extremes. He was a mighty soldier and a fervent patron of the arts who abandoned his early policies for dissolute government by incompetent minions. He allowed foreign missionaries to live in China although they were forbidden to preach, but was reluctant to allow other Europeans to advance trade agreements. The British Lord George Macartney visited Ch'ien-lung in Peking, but none of his demands to expand trade links beyond Canton were met. In 1796, Ch'ien-lung abdicated and was succeeded by his son, Chia-ch'ing, but Ch'ien-lung continued to rule in practice until his death. Chia-ch'ing had Ho-shen executed in a futile attempt to correct the damage to the dynasty.

L. C. Goodrich, *The Literary Inquisition of Chien Lung*, 1966.

J. D. Spena, *Emperor of China*, 1975.

CHMIELNICKI   SEE KHMIELNICKI

CHOPIN, FRÉDÉRIC-FRANÇOIS (1810–1849), Polish pianist and composer. He was born near Warsaw to a Polish mother and a French father who had gone to Warsaw to teach French. Young Chopin was brought up in his father's private school among the Polish nobility. He had a happy childhood and always enjoyed a very close relationship with his family, which he expressed in both letters and music. At the age of six Chopin wrote to his father on his name day, "When the world declares the festivity of your name day, my Pappa, it brings joy to me also, with these wishes; that you may live happily, may not know grievous cares, that God may always favor you with the fate you desire, these wishes I express for your sake."

Chopin began playing the piano at a very early age; by the time he was eight he gave his first public performance and was acclaimed as a wonder child. Soon he began composing what would eventually become his renowned short pieces for the piano: polonaises, mazurkas, and waltzes. He was fifteen when his first published work appeared, a rondeau for piano.

Like many musicians of the time, Chopin began touring at a relatively young age; his first concerts, in Vienna, were acclaimed successes. However, once the Polish rebellion against Russian domination ended in defeat, Chopin had to leave his homeland and seek his musical fortunes elsewhere. He traveled to Linz, Salzburg, Dresden, and Stuttgart before arriving in Paris, the center of Polish emigration, in September 1831. In the French capital Chopin continued to perform and began teaching the piano. He mixed with the great composers of his time and moved in high circles. His pupils were almost all aristocratic young ladies.

In Paris in 1837 he met the famous novelist Aurore Dupin Dudevant, who published her works under the name George Sand. Although their characters were different, Chopin and Sand embarked on a lengthy love affair in which, it was said, Sand was the masculine and Chopin the feminine. She dressed like a man, smoked cigars, and held many radical points of view, while he was showing the first signs of tuberculosis. The two parted in 1847; Sand portrayed Chopin in her novel *Lucrezia Floriani* as a weakling. In his letters to Sand it is obvious that he was unable to express with words the emotions and the passion he evoked through his music.

Chopin continued his touring even when he was severely ill with tuberculosis. His last concert in Paris, eighteen months before his death, was an occasion on which, according to *La Revue et Gazette musicale*, "The finest flower of feminine aristocracy in the most elegant attire filled the Salle Pleyel to catch this musical sylph on the wing."

Chopin died in Paris and was buried between Luigi Cherubini and Vincenzo Bellini at the Pere Lachaise cemetery. At his own request, however, his heart was sent to Warsaw for entombment in his homeland.

Chopin will always be remembered for liberating the piano from traditional chorals and orchestral influences. It was Chopin who gave the piano its authoritative assumption as a solo instrument. While his two piano concertos might seem to lack flair and virtuosity, it is, his many smaller pieces for the piano, the ballades, etudes, barcarolles, preludes, and larger sonatas which are still revered by all pianists. In addition to his numerous compositions for solo piano and the few works he wrote for piano and orchestra, Chopin composed chamber music pieces for several figurations, all of which feature the piano.

Chopin was already admired by many other composers during his lifetime. Felix Mendelssohn said that he was glad to be once again with a thorough musician, not one of these half-virtuosos and half-classics who would like to combine in music the honors of virtue and the pleasures of vice. Robert Schumann described his playing the piano: "Let one imagine that an Aeolian harp had all the scales and that an artist's hand had mingled them together in all kinds of fantastic decorations, but in such a way that you could always hear a deeper fundamental tone and a softly singing melody."

W. G. Artwood, *Frédéric Chopin*, 1987.
K. Kobylanska, *Frédéric Chopin*, 1979.
A. Maurois, *Frédéric Chopin*, 1942.

CHOSROES   SEE KHOSROW

CHOU EN-LAI (1898–1976), Chinese communist leader and statesman. Born to a family of provincial gentry in the province of Kiangsu, Chou enjoyed a traditional education. At nineteen he was sent to study at Waseda University in Japan, where he first came into contact with Marxist ideas, although he did not then become a communist. He returned to China in 1919 to study at Nankai University. During the May the Fourth Movement orchestrated by *Sun Yat-sen's Kuomintang nationalists, he joined the protest-and-study activities in Peking, which resulted in his imprisonment for six months. While serving his sentence he met his future wife, Teng Ying-ch'ao.

During his stay in France between 1920 and 1924 Chou became committed to communism and began to develop the organizational skills for which he later became famous. While studying and working there, he began recruiting for the recently-founded Chinese Communist party from among members of the expatriate Chinese community. He also met and exchanged ideas with the Vietnamese revolutionary leader, *Ho Chi Minh.

On his return to China, Chou participated in the Kuomintang-led nationalist revolution of 1924, acting as political commissar in *Chiang Kai-shek's First Army; it was Chou who organized the workers' uprising that delivered Shanghai into Chiang's hands in 1927, although shortly thereafter he was forced to flee south to escape Chiang's suppression of his communist former allies. Elected to the political bureau of the Communist party in 1928, Chou became instrumental in the organization of the party movement in the Nanchang, Swatow, and Canton provinces.

Chou's outstanding personal qualities and political skills were widely acknowledged. He visited the Soviet Union in 1928, and in 1930 was invited to address the sixteenth congress of the Soviet Communist party, an unprecedented honor for a Chinese Communist. For some time it appeared that he might challenge *Mao Tse-tung for the Communist leadership, but in 1931 he accepted Mao's authority, moved to the latter's rural base in southern Kiangsi, and remained closely associated with him thereafter, being elected a vice-chairman of the Party's revolutionary military council.

Chou played the role of political officer during the Communists' 6,000-mile Long March to Yenan in northwest China in 1934–1935. He became the party's chief negotiator in 1935, a role for which his flair amounted to genius. In this capacity he engineered both the capture of Chiang and his release unharmed, in return for concessions from the party's nationalist opponents. With the outbreak of war between China and Japan in 1937, he headed the Communist delegation to the United Front government located in Kuomintang-controlled territory, and he was the chief Communist representative at the abortive American-brokered peace talks aimed at ending the Chinese civil war in 1945.

After the party won power in China, Chou became one of the most important men in the Communist government. As premier of the state council until his death, his was the gargantuan role of chief administrator of the enormous civil bureaucracy: he proved himself a master of policy implementation with an incredible capacity for detail and seemingly inexhaustible reserves of stamina which allowed him to work long hours around the clock. As foreign minister from 1949 to 1958 he masterminded increasing Chinese influence in the developing world: the 1955 Asian-African Bandung Conference was a particular personal triumph for him. In 1956 he was elected one of four vice-presidents to Mao, a position he held until Lin Piao was retained as sole vice-president in 1969.

Chou was a consummate politician: affable, pragmatic, and persuasive. He survived unscathed the various internecine purges that toppled many of the most powerful Communist party members, and was the only leader whose standing was unaffected by the Cultural Revolution (1966–1969), during which he supported Mao while trying to curb the worst brutalities of the Red Guard. He emerged as the third-ranking member of the Chinese Politburo (behind Mao and Lin), while abroad he was the best-known Chinese politician, widely respected as a statesman of international caliber representing the acceptable face of communism.

During the 1960s Chou spearheaded the effort at countering the perceived Soviet threat to China by normalizing relations with Africa and the West, and it was his initiative that led to the historic visits to Peking by U.S. secretary of state Henry Kissinger in 1971 and President Richard Nixon in 1972. After his death from cancer, his ashes were placed in a temple in a sacred corner of the Forbidden City in Peking, and thousands (including many foreigners who for the first time were allowed to enter the Forbidden City) came to pay their respects to one of the principal architects of Communist China.

D. W. Chang, *Zhou Enlai and Deng Xiaoping in the Chinese Leadership*, 1984.
Li Tien-min, *Chou En-lai*, 1970.
J. McCook Roots, *Chou: An Informal Biography of China's Legendary Chou En-lai*, 1978.
D. Wilson, *Zhou Enlai*, 1984.

CHRISTINA (1626–1689), queen of Sweden. Her mother, Maria Eleanora of Brandenburg, never forgave her — the heir to the Swedish throne — for being born female (she was a heavy baby with a caul and the midwives first announced the baby was a boy) and her father, *Gustavus II Adolphus of Sweden, had her educated as a prince. Scorning her femininity, she grew up dressing, swearing, riding, playing, and hunting like a man and always retained a masculine

manner and often wore a man's wig. She despised other women (supposedly because of their ignorance), preferring masculine conversation and was one of the wittiest, most learned women of her age. She was nominally queen from age six after Gustavus was killed fighting for Protestantism in the Thirty Years' War (1632) and in her youth Sweden was well governed by a regency led by Count Axel Oxenstierna. After she took the throne in 1644, Christina, who was extremely strong-willed, was constantly at odds with Oxenstierna. A particular point of contention between them was the Thirty Years' War: Oxenstierna supported it militantly while Christina was one of the prime movers behind the Peace of Westphalia that brought it to an end. Christina was also extremely extravagant and Sweden's finances, already strained from the long war could not support her luxurious court or her grants of crown land to favorites. She eventually had to turn to Oxenstierna to help with Sweden's financial problems.

Sweden may have suffered from Christina's extravagance, but it also benefited from her enlightened rule. She reformed Swedish education, founded colleges, promoted trade and industry, and encouraged science, literature, and the founding of the first Swedish newspaper. However, most of the nobility opposed her policies, continuing in their opposition after she put down their 1651 rebellion and executed its leaders.

An avid scholar, Christina knew nine languages and was particularly interested in philosophy; she invited Rene *Descartes to Sweden to be her teacher. She surrounded herself, and corresponded, with some of the most cultured and knowledgeable minds of the period. The confessor of the Spanish ambassador to Sweden described how she balanced her passion for learning with her conscientiousness towards her duties as Sweden's ruler: "She spends only three or four hours in sleep. When she wakes she spends five hours in reading... She attends her Council regularly... Ambassadors treat only with her, without ever being passed on to secretary or minister." Perhaps it was her rigorous and demanding schedule that undermined her health. Her sexuality has been a subject of debate and she seems to have had lesbian or bisexual proclivities but there is no evidence that any of her many affairs were consummated. When she was seventeen she declared herself against marriage and the thought of childbearing horrified her to the extent that she did not allow pregnant women to approach her.

Seeking a more mystical and ceremonius approach to religion, Christina asked Rome to send Jesuits to discuss Catholic theology with her (1652). Her decision to convert to Catholicism was not an easy one; after all, her father had died for Protestantism. Swedish law, moreover, decreed that only Lutherans could rule Sweden. She decided to convert and was prepared to abdicate her throne, but first entered into lengthy negotiations with the Swedish parliament to secure her future finances and ensure that her choice of a successor (her beloved cousin, Charles Gustavus) was accepted. Finally, in June 1654, a moving abdication ceremony took place, Charles was crowned the next day

---

- Fools are to be more feared than knaves.
- To undeceive men is to offend them.
- Extraordinary merit is a crime never forgiven.
- More courage is required for marriage than for war.
- There is a star which unites souls of the first order, though ages and distances divide them.
- Philosophy neither changes men nor corrects men.

From Christina's *Aphorisms*

---

and Christina left Sweden. Six months later, on Christmas Eve, she abjured Lutheranism.

It took Christina eighteen years to make her leisurely, pleasure-filled way from Sweden to Rome, dressed as armed as a kinght. She was formally converted to Catholicism in Austria, feted by the Italian towns she passed through, and eagerly welcomed to Rome by the pope, although he was to become disillusioned with her shocking actions and masculine attitude. She settled in Rome, but had problems with getting her agreed-upon revenue from Sweden. After pawning her jewels, she was helped by an annuity from the pope. Christina also missed being a reigning monarch her intrigues of the papal court were no substitute,though her attempts to gain a throne failed: her negotiations for Naples' throne fell through during a visit to France when she had one of her retinue put to death for conspiring against her (1657) and her 1668 candidature for the Polish throne was rejected because of her unwillingness to marry. She returned to Sweden twice but was given a cold welcome.

Christina returned to Rome where she spent the last twenty years of her life as a patron of the arts. Her taste in art — reflected in the paintings, statues and art that decorated her apartments (Rome's leading salon) — shaped European culture. She greatly influenced Italian literature, instigated Rome's first opera house, compiled an enormous and valuable collection of books and manuscripts (now in the Vatican library), built an observatory and practiced alchemy. A staunch defender of personal freedoms to the end, she also became active in church politics. She was buried in Saint Peter's.

M. Roberts, *Sweden's Age of Greatness*, 1973.
S. Stolpe, *Christina of Sweden*, 1966.
C. Weibull, *Christina of Sweden*, 1966.

CHRISTOPHE, HENRI (1767–1820), fighter for Haitian independence; king of northern Haiti. Christophe, a liberated slave, was born on the Caribbean island of Grenada to *griffe* (mixed black and mulatto) parents. Little is known about his life prior to the Haitian rebellion, although he apparently traveled in the United States, where he absorbed a sense of revolutionary fervor. Christophe took an active role in the Haitian antislavery rebellion of 1791, thereby coming to the attention of the revolt's leader, *Toussaint L'Ouverture, who appointed him a commander in his army. Christophe so distinguished himself in this role that Toussaint L'Ouverture's successor, Jean-Jacques Dessalines, appointed him general in 1802.

Christophe participated in the conspiracy that led to the assassination of Dessalines in 1806. Although as commander of the northern region of Haiti he expected to succeed Dessalines, Christophe's succession was challenged by the southern commander, Alexandre Pétion. For fourteen years the two men waged an inconclusive civil war, resulting in an unofficial partition of Haiti. Pétion established a republican government in the south; Christophe, a staunch autocrat, declared himself King Henri I of Haiti in the north.

Christophe was a rigid authoritarian who styled his court after that of *Louis XIV. Royal decorum and titles were borrowed from the French and his palace at Sans Souci was modeled on Versailles. Under the guidance of his prime minister, Baron de Vastey, Christophe was a successful but unpopular monarch. A policy of forced labor revived the stag-

Henri Christophe

nant coffee and sugar trade, enriching both king and country. Although great sums were spent on a massive building campaign, which included the royal palace and the fortress of La Ferrire, most of this income was spent in developing an educational and cultural infrastructure. Independent Haiti was regarded by Christophe as a unique opportunity for blacks to prove themselves capable of living as free men; he fervently believed that the state of the blacks in the Americas and Africa (which he regarded as primitive in contrast to Europe) resulted from deficient education. Christophe, therefore, surrounded himself with learned men from Europe and the United States, built numerous schools and theaters, and published books and newspapers. Despite his lack of any formal education, he issued the Code Henri, a legal document forming the basis of his new state's constitution.

> We will make rapid strides towards civilization. Let them dispute, if they please, the existence of our intellectual facilities, our little or no aptness for the arts and sciences, while we reply to these with irresistible arguments, and prove to the impious by facts and examples that the Blacks, like the Whites, are men, and like them are the works of a Divine Omnipotence.
>
> **Henri Christophe**

In matters other than education and culture, Christophe was said to be vehemently antiwhite. At the same time, he declined to involve himself in other local anticolonial revolts, such as that on the eastern portion of the island, then under Spanish rule, or in Simon *Bolívar's struggle for South American independence.

The conflict between Christophe and Pétion in the south remained unresolved, arousing discontent among Christophe's subjects. The harsh measures he had taken to encourage Haiti's development were likened to feudal laws, little better than the slavery he had fought to eliminate. Christophe was paralyzed in his final years, further preventing him from dealing with the crises facing his state. Threatened with a coup d'état, Christophe committed suicide.
H. Cole, *King Henri I of Haiti*, 1967.
B. Winstein, *Haiti*, 1992.

CHURCHILL, SIR WINSTON LEONARD SPENCER (1874–1965), English statesman, war leader, orator, and Nobel prizewinning writer. He was born in Blenheim Palace, Oxfordshire, the eldest son of Lord Randolph Churchill and his American wife, Jennie. His father was a leading Conservative politician who became chancellor of the exchequer but his career ended in ruin after he continually attacked his own government's policies. Churchill had a boundless admiration for his father, taking pride in his achievements, suffering with his political eclipse and, in 1906, writing his biography. The closeness he felt to his mother was not diminished by her hectic schedule of entertaining, leaving little time for her children. When a brother, Jack, was born in 1880, Churchill was delighted and they became inseparable friends. They loved playing with toy soldiers, arraying vast armies of tin against each other.

Churchill's early schooling did not proceed smoothly. He was accepted at the famous public school of Harrow despite poor results in the examinations, as the headmaster recognized his potential. In subjects he enjoyed, like English and history, he excelled, but in those he saw no use for, such as Latin, he made no effort and failed. Having already decided that he wanted to emulate his father and enter politics, he was confident he would suceed; the army offered a means of achieving the fame that would be a springboard to the House of Commons.

The first obstacle was failure in examinations for Sandhurst officer training college. After several attempts, he finally passed. He took well to the arduous training and boisterous social life of the cadets and graduated with an honorable place in his class. Family connections secured a posting as a lieutenant in the prestigious cavalry regiment, the Fourth Hussars. He was eager to see action and get a chance to make his name, but there were no opportunities while his regiment remained in England. He utilized his father's contacts and received permission from the government to travel to Cuba to observe the insurrection against Spanish rule. His reports from the front were published in the *Daily Graphic* and his writing met with acclaim.

Over the next few years Churchill saw action on the northwest frontier of India, in the Sudan, and South Africa. Everywhere he showed himself a capable officer and displayed great heroism, taking part in fierce hand to hand fighting in the Sudan and in South Africa, and making a daring escape from captivity in a Boer prisoner of war camp. His accounts of his experiences were eagerly bought in article and book form.

In 1900 he was elected as Conservative member of Parliament for Oldham on his second attempt. His concern for the plight of the poor and his advocacy of free trade distanced him ideologically from the Conservatives and in 1904 he joined the Liberal party. It was a timely move, for in 1905 the liberals came to power and he attained his first ministerial appointment as undersecretary of state at the Colonial Office. He discharged his duties well and was acclaimed for his role in the negotiations to secure a lasting settlement in South Africa. He served in several different capacities in the Liberal governments of 1905–1916 and played a prominent role in the

| Chamberlain | Greenwood | Halifax | | Sinclair | Duff Cooper | Alexander | Eden | K. Wood |
| Churchill | Attlee | | Bevin | | Morrison | | Amery | |

" ALL BEHIND YOU, WINSTON "

Cartoon by David Low when Churchill formed his National Government in May 1940.

development of its forward-looking welfare program. As home secretary he aroused the wrath of those campaigning to extend the vote to women and was attacked at Bristol railway station by an angry suffragette wielding a horsewhip; she almost pushed him over onto the track.

During his time at the admiralty he encouraged the formation of a fleet air arm and was commended on the readiness of the naval reserve when war began in 1914. In 1915 his enthusiasm for the assault on the Turkish garrison controlling the entrance to the Black Sea (the Gallipoli Campaign) proved a major setback when the attack failed with heavy loss of life. He resigned from the government and went to serve with the army in France. Once more he showed no fear of the enemy's bullets, never ducking and mocking officers who did, telling them that by the time they ducked the bullet was well behind them. He did a wonderful job of restoring the morale of his battle-weary company. Though a strict disciplinarian, he had no taste for giving out punishments and took a keen interest in doing what he could to improve the men's rations and rid the ranks of lice.

In 1908 he had married the beautiful Clementine Hozier, with whom he enjoyed over fifty years of loyal companionship. Financial factors were the cause of numerous differences, with Churchill continually living beyond his means and then writing to cover rapidly accumulating debts. He had expensive tastes in cars, food and drink, and cigars, to list just some of his better known indulgences.

The establishment of a coalition government in 1916 brought Churchill back in the cabinet at the ministry of munitions. He took a dedicated interest in every detail of the ministry's work and again showed a visionary instinct, recognizing the importance of the tank and turning cavalry regiments into tank regiments.

From 1918 until 1929 Churchill held various ministries in several governments. As colonial secretary (1921–1922), he created the emirate of Transjordan and negotiated the Irish treaty of 1921. Disillusioned with Liberal support for the 1924 socialist government, he returned to the Conservative party and served as chancellor of the exchequer for five years. He brought to the office his now well-honed administrative skills, combined with a popular touch exemplified by his broadcasting on the BBC radio, explaining government financial policies in simple, lucid terms.

The Conservative defeat of 1929 led to ten years away from the center of power. He had more time to devote to painting and writing, producing a life of his illustrious ancestor, the Duke of Marlborough and the story of his own early life, among other works. He remained active in the House of Commons, becoming

SAYINGS OF WINSTON CHURCHILL

- It has been said that democracy is the worst form of government except for all those forms that have been tried from time to time.
- Russia is a riddle wrapped in a mystery inside an enigma. (1939)
- I am ready to meet my Maker. Whether my Maker is prepared for the ordeal of meeting me is another matter. (75th birthday)
- Political skill is the art of predicting what will happen in the future and then to explain afterwards why it didn't happen.
- Saving is a very fine thing. Especially when your parents have done it for you.
- In War: Resolution. In Defeat: Defiance. In Victory: Magnanimity. In Peace: Goodwill. (1948)

FROM HIS WAR SPEECHES

- (Battle of Britain) Let us brace ourselves to our duties and so bear ourselves that if the British Commonwealth lasts a thousand years, men will say "This was their finest hour."
- Never in the field of human conflict was so much owed to so few.
- We shall fight on the beaches, we shall fight on the landing grounds, we shall fight in the fields, we shall fight in the hills: we shall never surrender. (1940)

ATTRIBUTED COMMENTS

On Labor leader Clement Attlee

- A sheep in sheep's clothing.
- A typical British under-statesman.
- A modest man who has lots to be modest about.
- An empty taxi drew up and Mr. Attlee stepped out.

On Labor politician Stafford Cripps

- There, but for the grace of God, goes God.

almost a lone voice warning of the growing power of Nazi Germany and calling for rearmament as a deterrent. He fiercely opposed the accepted policy of appeasement, attacking the 1938 Munich accord as a capitulation, a temporary peace at Czechoslovakia's expense. It was "a total and unmitigated defeat...All is over. Silent, mournful, abandoned Czechoslovakia recedes into the darkness."

So strong was the desire for peace at any price that Churchill was excluded from government office out

of fear of offending the Germans. When war came in 1939 and his warnings proved correct, he was invited back into the cabinet as first lord of the admiralty. In May 1940 Prime Minister Neville Chamberlain was forced from office at a dangerous moment, as Adolf *Hitler was advancing through western Europe, and Churchill replaced him, a symbol of the aggressive bulldog spirit the nation felt the crisis demanded. Posters from 1940 showed him in a bulldog guise, fiercely standing guard over the map of Britain. The role he played in building up the nation's morale was crucial. His defiant V-for-victory sign and his speeches in Parliament and over the radio were rallying cries that brought out the very best spirit in his nation. The tone was set on his opening address as prime minister: "I have nothing to offer you but blood, toil, tears and sweat...You ask what is our policy? I will say: It is to wage war, by sea, land and air, with all our might and all the strength God can give us: to wage war against a monstrous tyranny, never surpassed in the dark, lamentable catalogue of human crime...What is our aim? I can answer in one word: Victory — victory at all costs...."

Shortly after Churchill came to power, all Britons had to leave Europe via Denmark and Great Britain was subjected to bombardment by the German air force as Hitler prepared to invade. Thanks to the British air force the invasion never came, but for two years Britain stood alone against Nazi-occupied Europe and Churchill was the symbol and voice, as well as the power, behind fortress Britain.

In addition to offering inspiring words, he also visited bomb-damaged cities and military installations. These "walk abouts" were emotionally charged, both for Churchill and the ordinary citizens he met. He took a characteristic interest in the fine planning of every detail of wartime operations and worked a taxing schedule that many men half his age could not have endured. The warm personal relationship he established with U.S. president F. D. *Roosevelt facilitated close cooperation between the two countries before the United States entered the war. Despite his long record of opposition to communism, Churchill did not hesitate in throwing his full support behind Soviet dictator Joseph *Stalin when the USSR was invaded in 1941. On several occasions Churchill met with Roosevelt and Stalin to plan the course of the war and the face of the postwar world.

When victory came, everyone expected Churchill to be returned to power with a landslide victory at the 1945 election but his party suffered a severe defeat. This outcome was not so much a lack of gratitude for his skills as wartime leader but an expression of the desire to make a fresh start and not return to the depression of prewar years with which his party was associated. He remained in Parliament as leader of the opposition, returning as prime minister in 1951. In these postwar years he warned of the Soviet threat, coining the phrase "Iron Curtain" to describe communist-controlled eastern Europe and seeing the hydrogen bomb as a deterrent to aggression. He also wrote multivolume histories of World War II and of the English-speaking peoples, for which he was awarded a Nobel prize in literature. In 1955 he retired from the office of prime minister and devoted his time to painting; Churchill remained a member of Parliament even during his last, physically debilitated, years.

P. Addison, *Churchill on the Home Front*, 1993.
J. Charmley, *Churchill*, 1993.
M. Gilbert, *Winston Churchill*, 1986.
R. Hough, *Winston and Clementine: The Triumph of the Churchills*, 1990.
W. R. Louis, *Churchill: A Major New Assessment*, 1993.
T. Morgan, *Churchill*, 1982.

CICERO, MARCUS TULLIUS (106–43 B.C.E.), Roman statesman, lawyer, scholar, writer, and orator. Whereas in Rome Cicero was best known as an eloquent proponent of republican values, subsequent generations have acclaimed him primarily for his transmission of classical ideas to the West through his elegant prose and his many translations from the Greek, and have found in his extant letters an unparalleled fund of primary material on antiquity. *Voltaire said: We honor Cicero, who taught us how to think.

Cicero was born to a wealthy family in Arpinium and educated in Rome and Greece. Beginning his practice of the law in 81 B.C.E., he made his reputation with his defense of Sextus Roscius, wrongly accused of murder, in 79 B.C.E.. Thereafter, his legal activities supported him financially; lawyers were not meant to accept money for their services, but handsome payments from grateful clients enabled Cicero to live in the manner he enjoyed.

In 75 B.C.E. Cicero was sent as quaestor (financial administrator) to Sicily, where he remained for several years. There he won his most famous court case, when he successfully prosecuted Gaius Verres, former governor of the island, for extortion, in 70 B.C.E.. Cicero's oratorical style, developed in court, served him equally well in the Senate; it owed something to both prevailing schools of oratory — the Atticist, which stressed directness and simplicity, and the more florid and elaborate Asian. However, his style was distinguished by his erudition and humanity, and by his adherence to the tenets of instructiveness, attractiveness, and emotiveness, which he considered essential to good public speaking. Ciceronian rhetoric long prevailed and molded the style of Renaissance Europe.

Cicero's relationship with *Pompey was the focal point of his political career, but a reversal in his fortunes followed his refusal to join the political alliance of Julius *Caesar, Crassus, and Pompey in 60 B.C.E., on the grounds that it was unconstitutional. In 58, when his enemy Publius Clodius became tribune, Cicero was forced to flee Rome, only to be recalled when Pompey and Milo gained political ascendancy.

Bust of Cicero

When it was apparent that he would be unable to estrange Pompey from Caesar, Cicero joined them. After a year as governor in Cilicia in 51 B.C.E., Cicero sided unequivocally with Pompey and the Republic on the fateful occasion of Caesar's crossing the Rubicon in 49 B.C.E. Despite the eventual defeat of the republican forces, he was allowed to return to Italy in 48 B.C.E. under a guarantee of safety from Caesar. Disillusioned with politics, he turned to writing and contemplation; almost all his philosophical writings were produced in the period between February 45 B.C.E. and November, 44 B.C.E..

Cicero's works were diffuse and sometimes muddled adaptations of various Greek originals, aimed at creating a literature in Latin on the principal questions of philosophy. As he admitted to his friend and correspondent, Atticus, "They are transcripts: I simply supply the words, and I've plenty of those." Their later influence was immense; not only did they foster the use of Latin as a philosophical language but, since their originals are lost, his writings became an irreplaceable source for Hellenistic epistemology, ethics, theology, and political thought, giving to Europe its philosophical vocabulary. His exhortation to study philosophy, *Hortensius*, was instrumental in Saint *Augustine's conversion to Christianity.

Of like significance to historians are Cicero's letters, especially those to Atticus and to his brother Quintus. Even allowing for their subjectivity, they are invaluable in providing a uniquely full account

- Laws are dumb in the midst of arms.
- I prefer the most unjust peace to the justest war ever waged.
- Virtue is its own reward.
- There has never been a poet or orator who thought another better than himself.
- Any man can make a mistake but only an idiot persists in his error.
- No one is so old that he does not think he could live another year.
- Peace is liberty in tranquility.
- A tear dries quickly, especially when it is shed for the troubles of others.
- Persistence in one opinion has never been considered a merit in political leaders.

Cicero

of the significant events of the epoch, with a wealth of circumstantial detail.

With the assassination of Caesar in 44 B.C.E., Cicero attempted a return to the political scene, but badly misjudged the acumen of Caesar's great-nephew Octavian (*Augustus). The triumvirate of Octavian, *Mark Antony, and Lepidus authorized the execution of the great republican, who had held that "the good of the people is the greatest law."

T. A. Dorey, *Cicero*, 1965.
C. Habicht, *Cicero the Politician*, 1990.
W. K. Lacey, *Cicero and the End of the Roman Republic*, 1978.
T. N. Mitchell, *Cicero, The Senior Statesman*, 1991.

CID, EL (Rodrigo Díaz de Vivar; c.1043–1099), Spanish military leader, the hero of Christian Spain's struggle against Islam. He lived in a Spain fragmented into Moorish and Christian kingdoms which subordinated religious differences to political and military expediency. In El Cid's Spain Christians fought Christians, Moors fought Moors, Christians and Moors fought each other, and both Christians and Moors were frequently allies in wars against their coreligionists.

Born into the minor nobility of the Christian kingdom of Castile, El Cid (Arabic for "the noble") resented the great nobles' power and wealth even though it was through his mother's connections with them that he was brought to the royal court, where he befriended the heir to the throne, Sancho II. He gained a reputation for military prowess at a young age; he was only twenty-two when Sancho became king and made him commander of the royal troops. El Cid helped Sancho fight against the Moorish kingdom of Saragossa and negotiate its status as a Castilian tributary. He also helped defeat Sancho's brother Alfonso in war, enabling the king to annex Alfonso's kingdom León. When Sancho died in 1072 and Alfonso inherited Castile's throne,

El Cid found his position at court awkward and his influence declined considerably. Nonetheless he was allowed to remain there and even married Alfonso's niece. However his relationship with the great nobles eventually made his precarious position at court untenable. He deeply resented the nobles' influence over Alfonso and his own dismissal as commander of the royal troops. The nobles, in turn, were offended by his frequently humiliating them in public.

El Cid was finally exiled in 1081 for leading an unauthorized military expedition against one of Alfonso's Moorish allies and retaining part of the tribute collected from another. He was welcomed by the Muslim king of Saragossa, whom he served loyally for eight years, fighting both Moors and Christians and extending its borders at the expense of the Christian kingdom of Aragon.

When Alfonso was defeated by the Almoravid Moors from North Africa in their 1086 invasion which threatened all of Christian Spain, he summoned El Cid back from exile. However, instead of fighting with Alfonso against the Almoravids, El Cid turned his attention to the rich Muslim kingdom of Valencia, making it first his tributary (1089) and then, after the death of its ruler and a year's siege, his own kingdom. He governed Valencia's Christian and Muslim citizens with ability, justice, an iron will, and an understanding of Islamic laws and customs. Valencia became a bulwark against Almoravid incursions which, besieged by Jimema, continued to defend itself for three years after El Cid's death. Although Alfonso came to its aid, he was hard-pressed by Almoravid invaders elsewhere and, unable to spare the troops to continue Valencia's defense, ordered it evacuated and burnt.

The legendary El Cid of hundreds of histories and poems — the idealistic, religiously motivated, indefatigible fighter for Christianity against Islam, which bears so little resemblance to the real El Cid — grew out of the *Poema del Cid,* a romanticized version of El Cid's life (with the less edifying parts falsified or omitted) written sixty years after his death.

R. Fletcher, *The Quest For El Cid*, 1991.

- (Before battle) All I can say is, I shall fight man to man and leave the rest to God.
- You see my sword dripping with blood and my horse sweat. It is thus that the Moors are conquered in the field of battle.
- God has promised me a great victory after my death (last words, prophecying the lifting of the siege of Valencia).
- Enough of brave words; let us settle our differences by arms, like men.

El Cid

CLAUSEWITZ, CARL VON (1780–1831), Prussian general, original and influential writer on the art of war. Clausewitz was born in Burg, near Magdeburg, Germany, of poor but professional middle-class stock. His father was a retired Prussian-army officer; Clausewitz entered the army at the age of twelve, went to war at thirteen, and was commissioned during the 1793–1794 Rhine campaign. He undertook garrison duty for several years, during which time he was able to educate himself, studying philosophy and history as well as the art of war.

In 1801 Clausewitz was sent to the war academy in Berlin, where he came under the influence of the distinguished army theoretician Gerhard von Scharnhorst. He was captured by the enemy during the campaign against *Napoleon Bonaparte and spent the years 1806 to 1808 as a prisoner of war. After his release he was attached to the Prussian general staff with the rank of major. A shy and sensitive individual who largely kept his ideas to himself, he was nonetheless recognized as an outstanding military tactician, was called to lecture at the War Academy, and was made military tutor to the Prussian crown prince. Meanwhile, he was already committing his own theories of war to paper.

Like many other nationalist Prussian military men, he was dismayed by the Franco-Prussian alliance and in 1812 joined the Russian forces against Napoleon as an act of protest, while lobbying for an end to Prussian support for France. With the demise of this short-lived alliance, Clausewitz returned to the Prussian army and participated in the wars of liberation against Napoleon, serving as chief of staff of an army corps during the 1813–1814 campaign.

Promoted to the rank of major general and made director of the War Academy in 1818, Clausewitz held the position until 1830, when he returned to field duty as chief of staff of a Prussian army of observation on the Polish border. There he contracted cholera, from which he died at Breslau.

Although moderately successful as a career soldier, Clausewitz is remembered as an original and influential writer on the art of war. His most famous work, *Vom Kriege (On War)*, was published posthumously in 1833. It has remained in print ever since and is widely recognized as the most important work on the theory of war. In it, Clausewitz propounded a philosophy of war based on his first-hand knowledge of the methods of Napoleon and his study of the campaigns of, among others, his near-contemporary *Frederick II (Frederick the Great) of Prussia.

Unlike many other military works, *On War* does not seek to outline a specific strategy. Rather, it examines the nature of successful military enterprises, and stresses the importance of psychological and accidental factors in determining the outcome of campaigns. Presenting the now-famous dictum that war is an act of violence intended to force our opponent to do our will, Clausewitz delineated the concept of total war aimed at the annihilation of the opponent through any available means. To this end,

- War belongs not to the Arts and Sciences but to the provenance of social life.
- It is better to act quickly and err than to hesitate until the time of action is past.
- Politics begets war. Politics represents intelligence, war merely its instrument.
- Generals have never risen from the very learned or erudite class of officer but have been mostly men who, from the circumstance of their position, could not have attained to any great amount of knowledge.
- Battles decide everything.

From Clausewitz's *On War*

he advocated focusing not just on attacking the enemy's forces, but also on sabotaging its resource base and destroying its will to fight. Military activity was now envisaged as just one means among many to achieve the implementation of one's will.

Another novel aspect of Clausewitz's approach was his definition of war as a mere continuation of policy by other means. It is political goals, he concluded, that determine military aims rather than vice-versa, and the soldier therefore is subordinate to the politician and must accept having his sphere of influence circumscribed by the decisions of the latter. Clausewitz felt that defensive warfare was both militarily and politically preferable to aggressive warfare.

Written over one hundred and fifty years ago, *On War* is still the basis of modern military theory. It has been translated into most major languages and remains required reading for those who would understand the art of war. Moreover, due to its breadth of vision, it has influenced political as well as military thinkers: communist theories of the nature of war are largely derived from Clausewitz.

R. Aron, *Clausewitz*, 1983.
M. E. Howard, *Clausewitz*, 1983.

CLEMENCEAU, GEORGES (1841–1929), French statesman. Clemenceau's family were country squires with pronounced radical sympathies; the father's antigovernment stance had a deep influence on the shaping of the son's attitudes.

Clemenceau studied medicine in Paris, but philosophy greatly interested him too, and he traveled to England to meet the philosopher J. S. *Mill. In Paris he wrote for *Le Travail*, a Republican newspaper, and followed in his father's footsteps by going to jail for organizing a parade to commemorate the revolution of 1848.

With his medical studies completed, Clemenceau went to the United States and worked as a newspaper correspondent during the Civil War. His father was not happy with this adventure and cut off his substantial allowance, so to support himself

Clemenceau also taught French, forming a relationship with Mary Plummer, a student eight years his junior; they married in 1869 and returned to France to live in Vendée, where Clemenceau worked as a doctor. The couple had three children but their personalities were not well matched and after seven years they separated.

Political life in Vendée was limited so Clemenceau moved to Paris, where he was elected mayor of Montmartre. In 1870, as Prussian troops closed in, Clemenceau organized distribution of relief supplies and devoted himself to the welfare of the local children. Though opposed to an armistice with the Prussians, as mayor he was associated with the regime established with Prussian support in Versailles, so he was lucky to be outside the city trying to negotiate a compromise when government troops overwhelmed the Paris commune – both sides in the conflict might readily have killed him. When peace was restored, Clemenceau turned again to medicine, giving free consultations to the poor and paying home visits to their sick; he was shocked by the terrible living conditions he witnessed.

In 1876 Clemenceau was elected a deputy in the Assembly. He had a cutting debating style well-suited to exposing government failures and became a powerful figure in the opposition, responsible for the fall of many ministries. However, in 1892 his career was damaged by association with the financial scandal surrounding a French Panama canal scheme. Following a bitter attack on him from another deputy, a duel ensued, and although neither participant was injured, Clemenceau only narrowly escaped impeachment, while popular feeling against him led to his defeat in the 1893 elections.

Outside the Assembly, Clemenceau achieved success with his writing on social issues but it was the Alfred *Dreyfus case of 1897 that brought his name to the fore again. Initially, he thought that Dreyfus's punishment was too light, but later became convinced of his innocence; he printed Émile *Zola's famous letter, entitled *J'accuse*, in his newspaper *L'Aurore*, which earned them both imprisonment and a fine for criminal libel.

In 1903 Clemenceau was elected to the Senate and in 1906 became prime minister. He angered his radical supporters with repressive policies against strikers and, though he had previously opposed state monopolies, his government nationalized a major railway line. When the government fell in 1909 he accepted responsibility philosophically, noting that "having destroyed every ministry for thirty years, I ended up destroying my own."

Clemenceau was far from finished. During the World War I censors suppressed his newspaper for attacking the poor medical care given the troops. In his capacity as senator, he toured the trenches despite the personal danger, while with his fierce anti-German sentiment he would not even listen to German music. His courage and patriotism made him a popular choice for prime minister in 1917. On taking office he declared, "You ask, what is my policy? I wage war. Foreign policy? I wage war. Everywhere and always I wage war."

Nicknamed "The Tiger," Clemenceau guided France with vitality, authority, and calm determination through the last years of the war. In 1919 he was one of the main architects of the Versailles peace agreement. Having seen German troops devastate his homeland twice in his lifetime, he wanted to ensure that the German war machine would be permanently crippled by heavy reparations and the loss of the Rhineland. He did not get all he wanted and throughout the 1920s prophesied the dangers of a resurgent Germany.

Georges Clemenceau

G. Dallas, *At the Heart of a Tiger*, 1993.
C. L. Mee, Jr., *The End of the Order: Versailles 1919*, 1980.
D. R. Watson, *Georges Clemenceau: A Political Biography*, 1974.

CLEOPATRA VII (69–30 B.C.E.), queen of Egypt. Her family came from Macedonia and although it had ruled Egypt since the time of *Alexander the Great, it had remained Greek in culture, education, and ambitions; Cleopatra was the first to learn the Egyptian language. A native uprising had driven her father, Ptolemy XI, from Egypt in 58 B.C.E. and only Rome's help restored him to his throne. Rome took an increasing interest in Egyptian affairs, frequently dictated Egyptian policy, and stationed soldiers in Alexandria.

Cleopatra was married to her ten-year-old brother, Ptolemy XII, at age seventeen (the marriage was never consummated) and was joint ruler of Egypt at eighteen. Civil war broke out and Cleopatra was banished. When Julius *Caesar arrived in Alexandria (48 B.C.E.), he moved into the palace, started putting Egypt's affairs in order, and sent for Cleopatra. She had herself smuggled into Caesar's chambers in some bedding, captivated him with her liveliness and courage, and was returned to her throne. Ptolemy joined the Egyptian army in a rebellion that was defeated by Caesar, but was drowned in the Nile, carried down by the weight of his armor. Caesar then secured Cleopatra's position as Egypt's supreme ruler by marrying her to another brother, twelve-year-old Ptolemy XIII.

Cleopatra and Caesar's relationship stemmed from a mutual desire for each other's assets: Caesar wanted money and Cleopatra wanted power over Rome. Caesar stayed in Alexandria with Cleopatra for nine months until her son, Cesarion, was born (his paternity is uncertain but Caesar was the presumed father) and placed a golden statue of Cleopatra in his family's temple of Venus. Cleopatra accompanied Caesar back to Rome (47 B.C.E.), and Caesar frequently visited the villa where Cleopatra, Ptolemy, and Cesarion lived for three years until Caesar's assassination in 44 B.C.E., after which she returned to Egypt.

Egypt's trade and industry prospered under Cleopatra's competent financial administration. Her political astuteness led her to entitle herself the daughter of the Egyptian sun god Re, increasing her popularity among the Egyptians. It was her desire to avert Egypt's inevitable subordination to Rome that led to her attempts to gain control over Rome and it was these ambitious — or desperate — attempts that caused her downfall.

*Mark Antony summoned Cleopatra to answer charges (which were untrue) of aiding Caesar's assassins. Cleopatra came dressed as Venus on a barge laden with gifts, which had the desired effect; Antony followed Cleopatra to Alexandria, where he spent the winter of 41 B.C.E. indulging in extravagant debauchery until the Parthian invasion of Syria called him away. Cleopatra gave birth to twins.

Antony made peace with Octavian (the future Emperor *Augustus), sealing it with marriage to Octavian's sister, Octavia. However, he then met Cleopatra in Antioch, married her (37 B.C.E.), and gave her the lands that were once part of her family's empire as a wedding gift. Octavian ignored the marriage on the grounds that it was illegal for Roman citizens to have two wives or marry a foreigner, but it created a rift between them.

Cleopatra provided Antony with troops but would not finance his Parthian campaign; she wanted to save Egypt's treasury for fighting Rome. The campaign (36 B.C.E.) was saved from complete disaster by Cleopatra's bringing food and clothing for Antony's troops after their heroic retreat. Antony waited in vain for Octavian to send the legions he had promised and Cleopatra won him over to her plans.

When Octavia loyally brought the men and supplies Antony needed, he ordered her back to Rome.

Antony awarded himself a triumph and scandalized Rome by celebrating it in Alexandria. The triumph was followed by Antony's declaration that Cleopatra had been Caesar's wife and Cesarion his acknowledged son, which meant disinheriting Octavian as Caesar's heir. Antony then divided the eastern part of the Roman empire between Cleopatra, their three children (another son was born in 36 B.C.E.), and Cesarion.

Cleopatra financed the attack on Octavian, supplying many of the ships, food, and pay. But, she also contributed to its defeat as she was determined to participate in the war and her presence alienated Antony's Roman forces, who were not willing to fight for a foreign queen. Stories of Cleopatra's control over Antony and rumors that she was drugging him spread through Italy.

Antony's formal divorce of Octavia (32 B.C.E.) cost him many supporters, increased Roman resentment against Cleopatra, and infuriated Octavian, who declared war against Cleopatra. Antony was defeated in a naval battle at Actium off the Greek coast (30 B.C.E.) and although he succeeded in escaping with Cleopatra, her attempts to shake his apathy were futile. Octavian ordered Cleopatra to disarm, but she shut herself and Egypt's treasury in a mausoleum, threatening to burn it if her son was not crowned. Octavian was stalemated, as he needed the treasury to keep the support of Italy and his troops.

Rumors of Cleopatra's death led Antony to stab himself. When he learned she was still alive, he asked to be taken to her and died in her arms. Octavian's forces broke into the mausoleum, captured Cleopatra before she could burn the treasury, and imprisoned her in the palace. Octavian killed Cesarion and threatened to kill her other children when she attempted to starve herself to death. Cleopatra tried to seduce Octavian into changing his mind, but when Octavian told her that he planned to annex Egypt and display her in his Triumph, Cleopatra decided to commit suicide. Legend has it that she killed herself with the bite of an asp, the Egyptian symbol of divine royalty. Octavian granted Cleopatra's request to be buried beside Antony. Her children were sent to Rome where they were raised by Octavia.

M. Grant, *Cleopatra*, 1973.
J. Lindsay, *Cleopatra*, 1971.
E. Ludwig, *Cleopatra*, 1937.
H. Volkmann, *Cleopatra*, 1958.

CLIVE, ROBERT (1725–1774), founder of the British Indian empire. Born into a family of Shropshire gentry, he was sent away from home at age three to live with an uncle and aunt in Manchester. It was a happy childhood home, devoted to his well-being, and signs of his bad temper and eagerness for a fight were noted with concern. Sent to school at Market Drayton, Clive supposedly led a gang of hooligans terrorizing local shopkeepers. To help keep him from trouble and find a promising career, his father used his influence to obtain him a posting with the East India Company as a bookkeeper-clerk. At seventeen he embarked for Madras, India. The voyage took more than a year and Clive almost died — the captain saw he had fallen overboard and rescued him.

Clive's first experiences of India were negative; he felt the loneliness of a solitary wretch and was unhappy with poor lodgings and mounting debts — his wages were just five pounds a year plus trading privileges. Depression was so overwhelming that he contemplated suicide but later settled down to life among the European elite; wine, women, and cards somewhat relieved his melancholy.

In 1746 Madras was captured by the French and Clive escaped imprisonment dressed as an Indian. Reaching a company outpost at Fort Saint David, he enlisted as an army officer. He fought with bravery and at times a foolhardiness that cost lives. The company granted a request for promotion and he was appointed steward, responsible for provisioning of the forts, and was able to make a healthy profit from commissions.

Clive's great military success came in the capture of Arcot, taken for a friendly Indian prince from his French-sponsored rival. Clive and his troops marched through a heavy downpour to attack Arcot and the garrison was so astonished by this show of endurance that they lost courage and fled. When a French-supported Indian army mounted a prolonged siege, he led a brilliant night attack, catching the besiegers and their families by surprise and routing them. The enemy's incompetence was a major factor in the collapse of the siege but still Clive had made his name. A leading Indian prince complimented him: "Always victorious over your enemies...a well-known invincible...a complete prudent."

After a break in England, during which he fought an unsuccessful campaign to become a member of Parliament, he returned to India as a lieutenant-colonel and deputy governor of Fort Saint David.

When the nawab of Bengal captured Calcutta and his forces locked up English prisoners in a tiny room (the Black Hole of Calcutta), Clive commanded an expedition to recapture the town. The nawab's forces fled without offering serious resistance. Clive's offensive continued with decisive defeat of the nawab's army at the Battle of Plassey in 1757. In addition to competently managing the military campaign, Clive sponsored a coup against the nawab; many of his troops did not take part in the battle, standing aside to support the British-backed candidate for nawab, Mir Jafar.

Tricks employed by Clive to gather support for the coup were open to criticism. For example, there were two treaties — a fictitious one containing promises of money to a wealthy merchant he did not wish to alienate, and a genuine one lacking these clauses. If these tactics were not in keeping with standards of western chivalry, they were successful and understood in the Orient. Mir Jafar became

nawab and Clive, as governor of Bengal, was the power behind the throne. "Not a man in this part of the world dare send a bale of freight without my permission," he could boastfully claim.

While not cruel, he exercised power with great firmness. Clive took no interest in Bengali language and culture and his view of the people was laced with condescending cynicism. He warned Warren *Hastings to "leave all trickery to the Hindus and Muslims to whom it is natural." He also described his role as "bullying and keeping under the black fellows."

Mir Jafar had to agree to lavish compensation for the attack on Calcutta and Clive emerged with a fortune of over a quarter million pounds thanks to the new nawab's generosity. Later the nawab conferred on him an annual income of £27,000 a year for driving out of Bengal a rival claimant to the principality.

In 1760 Clive returned again to England, to enjoy his wealth and with expectations of a peerage. He was elected to Parliament and support for the government brought him an Irish peerage as Baron Clive of Plassey. His health was poor and there was bitter conflict with Laurence Sullivan, chairman of the East India Company. Clive's allowance from the nawab was challenged, since the nawab was paying it out of rent paid by the company, but after a long struggle Clive emerged triumphant.

When the security situation in Bengal deteriorated, resulting in political instability and bloodshed, Clive was sent for again to be governor and granted full military and civilian power, with three thousand European troops. In 1764 he set sail along with his staff, musicians, and twelve dozen crates of champagne. Once back in India, Clive persuaded the Mogul, the titular ruler of India, to concede to the East India Company the right to collect all the revenues of Bengal, Bihar, and Orissa in return for handsome annuities for the Mogul and his subordinates. This concession represented the legitimization of company rule and the foundation of Britain's Indian empire.

In 1767 Clive finally left India, his health once more broken by malaria, stomach pains, and nervous stress. In England he devoted his energies to the House of Commons and developing his country estates. He also traveled in France and Italy, building up an art collection. Clive's Indian fortune came under increasing scrutiny, and in vicious public attacks he was accused of oppression and venality. Though a parliamentary inquiry largely cleared his name and commended his great and meritorious services to this country, the attacks can only have added to the unbearable pains of the illness that led to his suicide.

M. Bence-Jones, *Clive of India*, 1974.
P. Moon, *The British Conquest and Dominion of India*, 1989.
J. B. Watney, *Clive of India*, 1974.

CLOVIS (Chlodwig c.466–511), king of the Franks. At the death of his father, Childeric I, he inherited the realm of the Salian Franks, which extended over part of present-day Belgium, with its capital at Tournai. He united the Frankish tribes under his rule and in 486 attacked Syagrius, the last representative of Roman rule in western Europe, who had established his rule at Soissons and governed northern Gaul. The defeat of Syagrius and the conquest of Soissons enabled Clovis to annex the territory between the North Sea and the River Loire. He founded the Frankish kingdom, establishing his capital at Paris. Continuing his wars eastward, he absorbed the Ripuarian Franks on the Rhine into his realm and began expanding toward Germany. His quarrel with the Burgundians, who threatened his southern boundaries, ended in 492 with his marriage to Clotilda, niece of the Burgundian king Gundobald. Brought up as a Catholic, Clotilda sought to persuade her husband to convert to Christianity.

Clovis allied himself with *Theodoric the Great, king of the Ostrogoths, who had conquered Italy; Clovis gave Theodoric his sister as wife. This system of alliances allowed Clovis to extend his rule in Germany, where he defeated the Thuringians and fought against the Alamanni in 496 in a struggle so difficult that his victory was attributed to a divine miracle. Clovis's prayer to the God of Clotilda and his promise to convert to the Christian faith in the case of victory is testimony to the great battle. The victory enabled him to annex the Alamanni realm to his kingdom. His subsequent conversion was the result of a combined effort of persuasion by Clotilda and Remigius, the bishop of Rheims, whom Clotilda had brought to the court. Clovis was the first Germanic king to convert to Catholicism; the other rulers were Arians (see *Arius). He thus won the loyalty and support of the Gallo-Roman population, which was Christian. Moreover, religious unity allowed the emergence of peaceful relations between the conquerors and the conquered and created the conditions for their mutual assimilation, leading to the founding of France and the birth of the French people.

Clovis's achievements climaxed with the war against the Visigoths, who ruled southwestern Gaul. In 507 he defeated them at Vouill and undertook the conquest of Aquitaine and Toulouse, the capital of the Visigoths. The Visigoths were defeated in spite of the support of Theodoric.

Clovis is credited with the establishment of the Salic Law, the compilation of the legal traditions of the Salian Franks. In addition to his military and political achievements, he proved his organizational skills by enforcing rigorous discipline in his army, controlling the distribution of booty and rewarding the army chiefs. He also confiscated public lands and gave them as estates to his followers (the *leudes*), who became the new nobility of his kingdom. He did not, however, expropriate private property and was thus able to integrate the Gallo-Roman aristocracy into the ruling class of the kingdom, although they remained subordinate to the Franks.

After Clovis's death, Clotilda retired to the abbey of Saint Martin of Tours, where she was famed for her piety and good deeds. She later became the subject of many legends.

Clovis and Clotilda were buried in Paris, in the church that she and Clovis had built (now Sainte Geneviève church).

G. Kurth, *Clovis*, 1923.
P. Lasks, *The Kingdom of the Franks*, 1971.
F. Lot, *The End of the Ancient World and the Beginnings of the Middle Ages*, 1961.

COLUMBUS, CHRISTOPHER (1451–1506), Italian explorer of the New World. Columbus was born in Genoa, Italy, the eldest son of Domenico Columbo, a weaver. Columbus himself was reticent about his birthplace and nationality, maintaining a discreet silence on the subject of his origins so that they would not impede his ambitions for wealth and position.

He went to see at fourteen, trading in his father's wool. When he was twenty-five his ship was destroyed by pirates and he landed in Lisbon. Since 1453, the Portuguese had been seeking a new route to the Orient, as the traditional route had been closed by the Turks when they captured Constantinople. Expeditions to find a new route had been sent out from Lisbon, and Portuguese sailors had made discoveries in the Atlantic Ocean and along the west coast of Africa. These discoveries fascinated Columbus and were recorded by him and his brother Bartholomeo in the latter's map shop in Lisbon.

Columbus broadened his knowledge of geography by undertaking voyages. He sailed to Iceland and then gained sailing experience in the south Atlantic. His lifelong fascination with gold began with a voyage to Portugal's African gold fields, and he envisioned a new westward route to Asia.

The view of the ancient Greek geographer, *Ptolemy — that ships would run out of supplies long before reaching Asia — remained popular. In contrast, Columbus believed that the Eurasian landmass was much wider than Ptolemy had believed and formulated a plan to reach Asia by sailing west across a narrow Atlantic Ocean. He presented it to the king of Portugal, but was turned down.

Columbus next turned to Spain. He soon won over the devout Catholic Queen *Isabella by emphasizing the number of souls to be converted to Christianity and sharing his vision of recapturing Jerusalem with an army funded by Asian gold. A special commission was set up to study Columbus's proposals. Well aware that many members of the commission were better educated, Columbus tried to hide his ignorance, answering their questions briefly. However, after four years the commission decided against him. It took the euphoria following the fall of Granada in 1492 for King *Ferdinand and Isabella to agree to Columbus's plan.

At that point Columbus stated his exorbitant price for leading the expedition: knighthood, hereditary appointment as admiral, the title of viceroy and governor over any lands he discovered, and a ten percent commission on any commerce with those lands. Ferdinand and Isabella were persuaded to accept these terms (set forth in the Capitulations of Santa Fe) because they were to be fulfilled only if Columbus were successful. The port of Palos was ordered to provide Columbus with two ships or face charges of smuggling and possibly piracy. Martin Alonso Pinzón, a highly respected Palos shipowner, provided the third ship and half the cost of the voyage.

On August 3, 1492, Columbus left Palos with three ships, the *Pinta*, the *Niña*, and the *Santa Maria*. He had the ships loaded with trinkets to trade for gold and took on a crew member who could speak both Hebrew and Arabic. After a stop at the Canary Islands for repairs, they set sail west across the Atlantic, carried by the trade winds

The crossing took thirty-six days. Nervous and doubtful, the crew agreed to continue only if Columbus swore to turn back after seven hundred leagues. Columbus agreed but sailed on, deliberately misinforming them about the distance covered each day. On October 12, 1492, they landed on the island of Guanahani in the Bahamas, taking possession of it in the name of Ferdinand and Isabella; Columbus named the island San Salvador. They sailed on, searching for Japan but finding the Bahamas, Cuba, and Hispaniola. Columbus raised crosses everywhere he went, watching out for material wealth. The Indians they met were peaceful and had some gold, which they traded for Columbus's trinkets, but misled him as to the origin of the gold, directing him to yet another island; he set off in search of an island he never found. The *Santa Maria* foundered and he had to leave thirty-eight men in Hispaniola with provisions for a year — and orders to continue searching for gold.

In 1493 Columbus returned to Spain with gold, tobacco, and Indian slaves. Ferdinand and Isabella showered him with honors. Admired, feted, and rich, Columbus's career reached its peak between his first and second voyages. Ferdinand, a pragmatic man, saw some financial merit in Columbus's idea of capturing and selling Indians as slaves; Isabella, however, insisted that the Indians be made subjects of the Castilian crown and should not, therefore, be enslaved. She persistently ordered Columbus not to bring slaves back with him, but he persistently continued to do so.

His second voyage (1493–1496) theoretically combined colonization, exploration, and missionary activities, but in actuality everything was subordinated to the search for gold. The crew he had left behind in Hispaniola had all been killed; Columbus concerned himself with the gold he believed they might have hidden away. He founded a city named Isabella, whose colonists were mostly sick or busy prospecting for gold. With only two friars, missionary activities were of necessity limited, and were made more difficult by the Spaniards' way of forcibly taking Indian possessions and women. Columbus did succeed in discovering the Lesser

Antilles, Puerto Rico, and Jamaica before returning to Spain. In Hispaniola he was accused of being an incompetent, capricious governor, zealously guarding his power and prerogatives, unable to cope with local needs, and taking off on voyages of discovery when faced with administrative problems. Complaints were laid against him, partly inspired by spiteful jealousy of an outsider's rapid rise. The crown continued to stand behind Columbus, but its faith in him was shaken.

Columbus's third voyage (1498–1500) reached Hispaniola only to find his brother (who governed the island in his absence) confronted with a mutiny, which Columbus solved by mollifying the mutineers before sailing off to discover Trinidad and the coast of Venezuela. Ferdinand and Isabella could no longer ignore the unflattering reports about Columbus and in 1499 appointed Francisco de Bobadilla as governor and chief magistrate of Hispaniola. Columbus refused to acknowledge Bobadilla, who thereupon had Columbus and his brother arrested, put in chains, and sent back to Spain. Insulted, Columbus, the "Admiral of the Ocean Sea," refused offers during the voyage to remove his chains. Shocked at the chains, Ferdinand and Isabella ordered his immediate release and sent him money to come to court. However, their sympathy did not change their opinion regarding his ability to govern.

Frustrated in his dreams of greatness and gold and by reports of new discoveries being made, Columbus turned down offers of compensation and pleaded to be allowed to lead another expedition. The crown agreed, provided that he did not return to Hispaniola. Columbus then sailed straight to Hispaniola where a

Christopher Columbus

fleet of twenty-one ships was preparing to set sail, and warned them of an approaching hurricane. His warning was contemptuously ignored and the fleet set off for Spain, to be destroyed by the hurricane.

On that fourth voyage (1502–1504), Columbus apparently found some gold along the Central American mainland, but it was in an inaccessible location. He remained convinced that his discoveries were part of Asia and at times wavered between clarity and madness. Finally the ships' hulls rotted and Columbus was shipwrecked for nearly a year in Jamaica before being rescued and returned to Spain.

Sick, Columbus spent the last two years of his life attempting to restore his governorship and disputing the amount of money owed him under the Capitulations by which he relinquished his claim to the Governorship of the West Indies. His descendants continued the fight over his legacy in Spanish courts for generations.

S. A. Bedini, ed., *The Christopher Columbus Encyclopedia*, 1993.
H. Davies, *In Search of Columbus*, 1992.
F. Fernandez-Armesto, *Columbus*, 1992.
G. Grangotti, *Christopher Columbus*, 1985.
H. Koning, *Columbus: His Enterprise*, 1992.

COMTE, AUGUSTE (1798–1857), French philosopher, founder of sociology and positivism. The son of a tax-collector in Montpellier, near the Franco-Spanish border, Comte early rejected the staunch royalist Catholicism of his parents, displaying an extraordinary intellectual precocity that earned him a place at the renowned École Polytechnique in Paris when he was sixteen. Once there, he frequently cut classes and encouraged rebelliousness among other pupils, and was expelled from the school shortly before it was closed down by the authorities on the grounds that it harbored republican sympathizers.

Comte chose to remain in Paris, where he eked out a precarious living from teaching and journalism. He devoted most of his time to studies that encompassed not only philosophy and political science but also mathematics, astronomy, physics, chemistry, and biology. His political ideas were strongly influenced by such French political philosophers as Montesquieu, while his theories of the human mind and knowledge owed much to David *Hume and Immanuel *Kant. However, his own philosophical system was to constitute an unequivocal rejection of Kant's idea that one can meaningfully speak of things which are beyond the reach of the scientific understanding.

Probably the greatest single influence on Comte was Claude-Henri de Saint-Simon, French revolutionary activist and founding father of socialism, with whom he was associated from 1816 until 1824. It was from him that Comte got the idea of a scientifically directed society, and his insistence on grounding political visions in historical and social science.

Lonely and isolated in Paris, Comte met and married Caroline Marorin, a young prostitute, in 1821.

However, his hopes for a stable life were dashed when the couple's attempted move to Montpellier foundered on the moral censure of the locals, and Comte was forced to return to Paris once again. There, he endured an increasingly loveless marriage and bouts of debilitating depression until in 1826, just after having begun a series of lectures on his system of positive philosophy, he suffered a breakdown. The lectures were abandoned and Comte lapsed into a despair which culminated in his attempt to commit suicide by jumping into the River Seine. He was saved by a passerby and recovered substantially thereafter. The lecture series was re-attempted in 1829 and was so successful that it was repeated at the Royal Athenaeum that winter.

Comte was slowly achieving recognition as an original thinker, a recognition that grew over the next twelve years as he produced the six-volume *Cours de philosophie positive*. Through this work he earned himself preeminence among those philosophers who sought to provide the basis for a new scientifically-oriented ideology which would replace all that remained of the outlook of medieval Christendom.

Comte aspired to a completely humanistic culture purged of what he saw as the metaphysical equivocations of traditional religion or the idealism espoused by the proponents of G. W. *Hegel and J. G. Fichte. His only standard of rationality was that of science; he also asserted that for a statement to be worthy of belief it must necessarily be verifiable by the methods of empirical science.

Comte traced the development of human thought and society through three consecutive and progressive stages: the theological, characterized by a tendency to animism (the attribution of a soul to natural objects and phenomena); the metaphysical, characterized by a tendency to reify ideas (that is, to think of them as material); and the positive, characterized by systematic collection and correlation of observed facts and abandonment of unverifiable speculation about first causes or final ends.

Although recognizing the study of history as important, Comte argued that there can be no knowledge of the dynamics of history that is not based upon a science of society. He also coined the word sociology to designate such a discipline, in terms of whose laws alone the economic, political, and moral behavior of men might be understood. He hoped that the systematic study of human nature and human needs would provide, for the first time in history, a truly scientific basis for the reorganization of society: "Science from which comes prediction; prediction, from which comes action."

Comte's influence spread to Britain, where his ideas soon found favor with the philosopher J. S. *Mill and his circle. Meanwhile, his marriage finally ended in 1842, and he became increasingly solitary. The death of Clotilde de Vaux, with whom he had enjoyed an intense, albeit platonic, relationship, from tuberculosis in 1846 devastated him and he became increasingly unstable mentally. Nonetheless, he was able to complete the impressive *System of Positive Polity* despite these difficulties; it contained a complete formulation of his sociology.

Comte's last years brought him the acceptance, recognition, and companionship of his many admirers. His bizarre attempts to develop positivism into a religion substitute based on the worship of humanity rather than God may have cost him the support of some of his more serious adherents, but they resulted in positivist societies springing up around the world. His real significance lies in the influence his theories have had on contemporary philosophy, also serving as the basis for the work of subsequent generations of social scientists, not least Émile *Durkheim.

A. Compte, *Auguste Comte and Positivism*, 1975.

A. R. Standley, *Auguste Comte*, 1981.

K. Thompson, *Auguste Comte: The Foundation of Sociology*, 1976.

CONFUCIUS (551–479 B.C.E.), Chinese philosopher and teacher; China's supreme sage and foremost teacher, whose thought has defined and shaped Chinese culture. Born in the state of Lu, in what is now Shantung province, to an impoverished noble family named K'ung, Confucius was named Ch'iu, meaning hill, due to a prominent bump on his head. He was later to use the appellation Chung-ni as his literary name. However, he was most commonly and famously referred to as K'ung Fu-tzu, "Venerable Master K'ung," by the Latinized form of which, Confucius, he became familiar in the West.

Confucius's father died when he was three, so he was brought up by his loving and devoted mother, who was his father's second wife. Nicknamed "long fellow" by his playmates due to his unusual height, he early evinced a liking for practicing many of the rituals that were an integral part of traditional Chinese life and manners. Family circumstances dictated that he had to work from an early age, which he did with diligence, earning praise from the employer who hired him to attend the granaries and flocks of a rich noble.

The boy enjoyed little formal education, but such was his thirst for knowledge and his determination that he became the most learned man of his day. He was later to reflect on his lifetime quest for wisdom: "At fifteen, I set my heart on learning. At thirty, I was firmly established. At forty, I had no more doubts. At fifty, I knew the will of Heaven. At sixty, I was ready to listen to it. At seventy, I could follow my heart's desire without transgressing what was right."

At this time, China was in a state of turmoil and decline. The Chou dynasty had lost power and the empire had disintegrated into a number of warring feudal states. Political dislocations were accompanied by a degeneration in the observance of the time-honored mores, codes of conduct, and ceremonies that gave Chinese society its stability and coherence. Confucius saw these trends as reflections of a deeper moral and spiritual disorder infecting the body politic: its alienation from the natural law that

he regarded as the true foundation of successful human relations. He regarded the pursuit of knowledge as the path to wisdom and a better life for the individual and society. He quickly achieved a reputation as a teacher of outstanding ability, and people from all walks of life came to study under him.

Throughout his life Confucius sought an administrative position that would enable him to disseminate his ideas effectively. He was eventually appointed a high-ranking minister in the state of Lu, but was unable to achieve the reform he promoted due to the jealousy and intrigue of fellow-administrators and neighboring states. He resigned in disgust at the age of fifty-four, and then embarked on a thirteen-year period of traveling and teaching in various states in China. He was received with respect wherever he went, as befitted his reputation as a sage, but was not entrusted with the sort of government post he considered commensurate with his abilities. At the age of sixty-seven he was welcomed back to Lu at the intercession of one of his disciples who was a minister there, and spent his remaining years editing the classical Chinese religio-philosophical texts and continuing his teaching.

Defending the way of the ancients at a time when the old religious imperatives and rituals which regulated all social and political intercourse had lost their force, Confucius invested them with a new moral justification. His way presupposed that the hierarchical structure of the old society corresponded to a natural moral order. It was therefore necessary for each individual to play his proper part and fulfill the moral obligations inherent in his position as, say, son, father, subject, or ruler. This accounts for the stress Confucius placed on the six traditional arts of rituals, music, archery, charioteering, literature, and mathematics: only through a return to the decorum and formality that had underscored the great days of the past could society heal itself. Tradition relates that of his three thousand pupils, seventy-two had mastered the six arts.

SOME THOUGHTS OF CONFUCIUS

- The superior man understands what is right; the inferior man understands what is profitable.
- Fine words and an insinuating appearance are seldom associated with true virtue.
- Learning without thought is labor lost; thought without learning is perilous.
- If a man in the morning hears the right way, he may die in the evening without regret.
- The superior man does not set his mind either for anything, or against anything; what is right, he will follow.
- What you do not want done to yourself, do not do to others.

Confucius meeting Lao Tzu

Despite his emphasis on tradition and manners, Confucius was by no means a conservative. He taught that government must be reformed to make its objective the happiness of its subjects rather than the gratification of the whims of the rulers. Thus he instanced war, often engaged in as a diverting pastime by the ruling class, as a pursuit that rendered the life of the subject onerous and should therefore be avoided if at all possible. He was also in favor of decreasing the severity of punishments for all but the most serious crimes. The key to good government, he believed, was self-rectification on the part of the ruler. Once this had been undertaken and achieved, the state would naturally return to a state of order in harmony with the dictates of nature, and people would be attracted to such a kingdom as a center of peace and justice. Hereditary rulers should have the common sense to delegate all power to ministers selected for their talent and virtue.

Confucius's teaching was not directed solely at the influential and powerful, although many of his pupils were young gentlemen whom he was preparing for government office. An egalitarian who believed that everyone was equally entitled to education, he pursued an open door policy, with enthusiasm and ability rather than wealth or social standing the criteria that mattered: fees were graded, with students paying according to their financial means. Instruction took place through small group discussions conducted in an informal atmosphere. Such an approach was revolutionary; moreover, prior to Confucius, education had been the prerogative of the nobility, with instructors drawn from a caste of petty nobles who were government officials; he was the first private teacher in China, and the first to regard teaching as a vehicle for reform as well as a livelihood.

The cardinal virtue of Confucius's moral and social philosophy was *jen*, usually translated as humanity, "benevolence," or "human-heartedness," and a homophone of the Chinese for "man". *Jen* embraced all the moral qualities of the true man: loyalty, reciprocity, courtesy, friendship, filial and fraternal affection, and dutifulness. Since he held that man had an innate predisposition to goodness, Confucius regarded *jen* as a fundamental human quality, to be developed or revealed rather than learnt.

Confucius appropriated the idea of the *chun-tzu*, or "noble man," to illustrate the ideal type of personality. The word previously had the literal meaning, "son of a prince;" Confucius used it for the individual who was a prince among men, regardless of his nominal social status: virtue was not the exclusive preserve of the high-born. Such a person is characterized by effortless adherence to the virtuous path, rooted in a profound understanding of and sympathy with the dictates of the law that informs creation; he is kind, patient, humble, learned, and generous.

The only reliable source for Confucius's teaching is the *Lun-yu* (Analects), a collection of brief dialogues and sayings recorded by his disciples. As one of the *Four Books*, texts traditionally regarded as written by him or his disciples, it has provided the syllabus for Chinese education at the primary level; secondary-level education in China has long been based on the *Five Classics*, classical texts edited with commentary by Confucius.

Many of his disciples achieved positions of influence in government, so Confucius's ideas took firm root and grew in significance after his death; developed and modified by others, they came to dominate Chinese thought and manners.

H. G. Creel, *Confucius and the Divine Way*, 1960.
I. Eber, *Confucianism*, 1986.
W. Liu, *Confucius*, 1972.

CONSTANTINE I (Flavius Valerius Aurelius Constantinus; died 337), first Christian Roman emperor and founder of Constantinople. He was born in Serbia, and although the month and date of his birth (February 17), is known, as it later became a public holiday, the exact year in which he was born is uncertain (it has been placed between 274 and 288). His father, Constantius, was a native of southern Serbia and an officer in the Roman army. His mother, Helena, was of humble birth.

Constantine was born into a Roman Empire torn apart by the civil wars of rival emperors and under ever-increasing pressure on its borders from both barbarian invaders and the Persian Empire. Local armies all over the empire proclaimed emperors and battled with rival claimants; emperors who succeeded in reigning for more than five years held special celebrations to mark the occasion. Since many of these rival emperors had once been ordinary soldiers, it was said that every soldier carried the imperial purple in his knapsack; Constantine's father was no exception.

In 284 Diocletian became emperor and, in the twenty years of his rule, made administrative reforms which brought order out of chaos. In 285 he instituted a new system of government whereby the empire was ruled by two co-emperors (*augustii*), each of whom had a subordinate emperor (*caesar*). Diocletian appointed Constantinius to be caesar in 293, at the same time insuring his loyalty by taking Constantine to live at court and having Constantius divorce Constantine's mother and marry Diocletian's stepdaughter. Constantine was not to see his father again for thirteen years. Constantius proved an able and loyal caesar and in 305 was appointed augustus for the western provinces when Diocletian and his coaugustus, Maximian, abdicated. When Constantius died in York, Britain, in 306 Constantine was proclaimed augustus in his place. Reduced to the rank of caesar shortly thereafter, Constantine gained the support of Maximian, by divorcing his wife and marrying Maximian's daughter.

Although he received little formal education, the years Constantine spent at Diocletian's court were invaluable training for a future emperor. Diocletian was always on the move — inspecting frontiers, reviewing the administration of provinces, suppressing revolts, and dealing with many of the same problems Constantine would later have to face. The seriousness of the Roman Empire's economic and social problems rivaled that of its military problems, but the reforms that Diocletian initiated and Constantine continued (responding to military threats by greatly increasing the bureaucracy and armed forces; insuring that the army received crucial supplies by making land, trades, and position hereditary) shaped the Roman Empire for centuries to come.

Constantine's feeling that the Christian God was a powerful divinity who must be placated for his own and the empire's continued welfare stemmed from the traditional relationship between the emperor and the multitude of religions in the Roman Empire. One of the emperor's primary tasks had always been maintaining the peace of the gods within the empire. This involved divining and doing what was pleasing to the gods so that they could be worshiped in such a manner as to ensure their continued favor and thus the prosperity and security of the empire.

After Diocletian instituted a persecution of Christians in 303 and then revoked the anti-Christian edicts after becoming seriously ill, Constantine always practiced tolerance toward Christians. In the battles for power among the rival caesars and augustii following Diocletian's abdication in 305 Constantine, according to legend, had a vision in which he saw a cross on the sun before the Battle of the Milvian Bridge (312), against a rival who was anti-Christian. He had the cross emblazoned on all his soldiers' shields and won a victory against all odds. At this point Constantine went beyond mere toleration and began making lavish donations to churches. He wrote letters and edicts on religion, seeing himself as the chosen servant of a divinity who had given him power, and position and victory. The historicity of his Edict of Milan (313), however, which formally made Christianity one of the religions legally recognized within the Roman Empire, is debated by historians.

Beginning in 312 Constantine was sole emperor of the West and in 324 fought and defeated the augustus of the eastern part of the empire, who was anti-Christian, and became the sole ruler of the entire Roman Empire. The following year he summoned and presided over the first general council of the church at Nicaea. In 326 his mother, Helena, visited the Holy Land, identified various sites connected with *Jesus, and discovered what was thought to be the cross on which Jesus was crucified; she was beatified after her death in 330. He rebuilt Byzantium as the Christian city of Constantinople and in 330 made it his new capital.

Constantine tried to strengthen the succession of power by giving each of his sons and one nephew the title of caesar, allotting them parts of the empire to govern starting in 317, and sharing the government of the empire between them. While on an expedition in 337 to defend the eastern frontier against the Persians, Constantine died, officially converting to Christianity shortly before his death.

Constantine's support of Christianity had profound effects on the Roman Empire. An intensely religious paganism had permeated all aspects of life in the empire. Belief in the power of the supernatural and its interest in mankind, expressed through numerous cults, had pervaded all levels of society. The senate, civil service, and army were almost all pagan. Religious tolerance was the norm to which there was one exception, a typical mystery cult with only a few adherents (and those from the unimportant urban middle and lower classes): Christianity. Constantine's sponsorship meant that Christian intolerance of other religions spread to the government. The decorations and wealth of pagan shrines were stripped and given to the new, prestigious Christian churches, leaving the shrines impoverished. Pagans were viewed with disfavor while Christians were promoted. Sunday was proclaimed a weekly holiday and church building was liberally funded, especially at the holy places in Palestine identified by Constantine's mother. He detested and publicly vilified Jews, lavishly subsidizing attempts to convert them to Christianity.

Constantine's personal idiosyncrasies played their part in his major failures with both the church and the empire. Susceptible to flattery, he was easily influenced by the nearest dominant personality. Capricious but easily mollified, he would make threats during outbursts of rage that he usually did not fulfill. His inability to enforce discipline also contributed to his failure to reform the civil service, where corruption and extortion were so prevalent that anything could be accomplished with money and nothing could be accomplished without it.

The Byzantine Empire, which preserved the legacy of the Roman Empire for over a thousand years, owed much to Constantine. He increased the use of barbarian troops in the army and his military reforms, which based the empire's defense on a large, centrally stationed, mobile field army which could be sent where needed instead of a system of reinforced frontier posts that required much more manpower are credited with extending the longevity of the Roman Empire by hundreds of years. He reformed the tax system and stabilized the currency.

His support of Christianity led to the decline of paganism and to Christianity's becoming the official religion of the Roman Empire in 380.

P. Keresztes, *Constantine*, 1981.

R. MacMillan, *Constantine*, 1970.

COOK, JAMES (1728–1779), British explorer. Second son of a Scottish laborer living in the Yorkshire village of Malton, Cook learned to read and write at the local school eventually becoming apprenticed to a grocer. His employer lived close to Whitby on England's east coast and the sight of the sea and the movement of ships opened up an exciting new world for him.

In 1746 Cook enlisted on a collier carrying coal from Whitby to London. He supplemented practical experience with reading while learning the art of seamanship and rapidly became an excellent navigator. In 1752 he became mate of a collier but in 1755 chose to leave the coastal trade and joined the Royal Navy as an ordinary seaman. He saw battle against the French in the Seven Years' War and then enjoyed rapid promotion to the rank of master, giving him responsibility for the ship's navigation and management.

In 1758 Cook served in the expedition that captured and was instrumental in transporting General James *Wolfe's army 120 miles up the Saint Lawrence River to Quebec after the French had removed the river's navigational markers. Quebec was taken by English forces and Cook was awarded £50 for his painstaking work mapping the river (the charts he drew remained in use for over a century), recognition of what his commanding officer termed "Mr. Cook's genius and capacity."

In the mid-1760s Cook was employed as surveyor of Newfoundland, now under the governorship of Sir Hugh Palliser, who, as his former senior officer and friend, made every effort to advance Cook's career. During this survey he observed an eclipse of the sun, and the accuracy of his navigational calculations brought his name to the attention of the Admiralty and the London scientific world. In 1768 Palliser helped Cook secure promotion to lieutenant and obtain command of an expedition to explore the Pacific.

The southern edge of the known world was still shrouded in mystery, with legends of a fabulously wealthy southern continent as large as the known land mass of Eurasia. The competition between Britain, France, and Spain encouraged missions of discovery to lay claim to Australis, as the continent had come to be called. In 1768 there were additional scientific motivations for a voyage south: to observe from both the southern and the northern hemispheres the passage of Venus between the sun and the moon, an opportunity which would not recur for another century.

Cook was instructed to lead an expedition to Tahiti to take observations of the transit of Venus. He was also given secret orders to continue 1,500 miles southward in search of Australis where, after establishing friendship and alliance with the natives, he was to convince them of the benefits of becoming subjects of King *George III.

The ship selected for Cook was the *Endeavour*, four years old and 106 feet long with a width of about thirty-five feet; weighing 308 tons, it was capable of traveling at eight knots. It possessed all the maneuverability needed for shallow waters and had a large storage capacity.

The journey lasted three years and was a resounding success. Leaving Tahiti, Cook took the *Endeavour* two thousand miles around the New Zealand coastline, proving that there were two separate islands and that New Zealand did not form the tip of the undiscovered southern continent.

Cook continued from there to explore and chart the eastern coast of Australia. A vast area of previously unknown territory was now placed on the map and added to the British empire. The scientific information gathered in the course of the voyage was of immense significance; for instance, 1,300 new species of flowers were discovered and numerous observations were taken of meteorological and astronomical phenomena.

In 1772 Cook was promoted to commander and embarked on a second expedition with two ships. The *Resolution* at 462 tons was his flagship, carrying a crew of over a hundred; the smaller *Adventure* carried about eighty men. It was another extraordinary voyage. The Antarctic circle was crossed for the first time in European exploration and the Antarctic continent was almost discovered. In total sixty thousand miles were covered in the course of three years, again adding significantly to contemporary knowledge. Cook's concern on ensuring that his men had airy and clean quarters revealed a humanity not common in naval officers of the period and it also bore dividends in their good state of health at sea; in addition, his innovation of the use of citrus juice as an antidote to the dreaded scurvy earned him praise for the lives thus saved.

Upon return to England he did not permit himself much time with his wife and family. Cook's wife, Elizabeth (they were married in 1762) had a challenging life, with six children to care for and with her husband away for years on voyages. Indeed, in 1776 Cook set out once again, on a futile quest for the fabled navigable passages linking the Pacific and Atlantic Oceans. Sailing via New Zealand and Tahiti, he reached the Arctic Circle between Siberia and Alaska, but failed to discover either of the legendary passages.

Cook had a reputation for excellent rapport with the native populations he encountered. He addressed them in a respectful manner and his natural authority inspired respect in turn. He was ill-prepared, therefore, when a dispute with Hawaiian natives over the theft of a small boat grew into a violent quarrel. Tempers got out of control and a fight ensued in which he was killed.

Cook's final honors came six years later when in 1785 *George III posthumously granted him a special coat of arms bearing the mottoes "Around the globe" and "He left nothing unattempted."

J. C. Beaglehole, *The Journals of Captain Cook*, 4 vols., 1955–1967.

A. J. Villiers, *Captain James Cook*, 1967.

L. Whitney, *Voyages of Discovery: Captain Cook and the Exploration of the Pacific*, 1987.

COPERNICUS, NICOLAUS (Nikolai Kopernik; 1473–1543), founder of modern astronomy. He was born in Thorn (Torun), Poland (then Prussia); his father was a merchant with some social standing. Copernicus studied mathematics under Wojciech Brudewski at the University of Cracow. His graduation in 1494 coincided with the election of his uncle, Lucas Waczenrode, as bishop of Ermeland, who appointed Copernicus a canon at the cathedral of Frauenburg. Assured of financial support, he was able to continue his education in Italy and devote his life to research. He studied all branches of the sciences, in addition to canon law and Greek, and earned a doctor's degree in canon law at Bologna in 1503 and in arts and medicine in 1506. Returning to Frauenburg, he provided medical care for the community's poor and tended to church responsibilities.

Copernicus's primary scholastic interest was in mathematics. His teacher was a follower of the second-century Greek astronomer, *Ptolemy, but Copernicus's doubts led him to make his own measurements of the movements of planets. He unsuccessfully attempted to fit his observed measurements to Ptolemy's theory that the earth was stationary and located at the center of the the solar system with the planets and the sun orbiting around it. Until Copernicus's investigations, Ptolemy's theory had remained unchallenged for 1,400 years. Now Copernicus's measurements cast serious doubt on the Ptolemaic theory. Being able to read recently-published ancient Greek books in their original language, Copernicus discovered that other solar system theories abounded at the time of Ptolemy; there were hints of heliocentric hypotheses even then. The thought of the sun being at the center of the solar system initially seemed absurd to Copernicus, yet when he applied his observations to that hypothesis his mathematical findings and models fit.

By the time Copernicus was thirty-three years old he had formulated his original theory that the sun was the center of the solar system and that the planets orbited around it. The earth rotated daily on its axis, west to east, and also orbited around the sun beyond the orbits of Mercury and Venus. He dismissed Ptolemy's theory and most of the underlying Aristotelian concepts, although Copernicus retained *Aristotle's concept of circular orbits despite the fact that he observed conflicting evidence. To reconcile his findings and theory with Aristotle, he concluded that the sun was located slightly off center of the planets' circular orbits.

Although he published only excerpts of his theory and gave limited lectures about his work, his reputation was renowned enough for him to be invited by the Lateran Council to express his opinion on questions of calendar reform. He did not disclose much of his theory at the Lateran Council. Pope Clement VII approved of Copernicus's first treatise and requested a complete presentation. A printer's proof copy of his six-volume masterpiece, *De revolutionibus orbium coelestium* (Concerning the Revolutions of the Heavenly Bodies), was reviewed

Nicolaus Copernicus

by Copernicus on his deathbed; publication followed shortly after his death in 1543.

Proof of his theory could not be made during Copernicus's lifetime as more sophisticated tools, including the telescope, needed to be developed. Accurate measurements of stellar parallaxes and the exact orbits of the planets were necessary to prove his theory. Copernicus knew what was needed but he could only measure angles of ten minutes of arc, whereas measurements in fractions of seconds of arc were required. Nevertheless, he calculated the radii of the planetary orbits within 99 percent of their actual orbits. Copernicus thought that gravity was not an influence of the whole earth but was a property of its substance. He theorized that gravity extended to the sun, moon, and other stars.

Despite the fact that Copernicus's measurements were made with primitive tools, his published tables of planetary movement remained in use more than one hundred years until replaced by the Danish astronomer Tycho *Brahe's careful measurements.

Johannes *Kepler, a German mathematician, worked with Brahe's records and discovered that the planets traveled around the sun in elliptical orbits, thus solving the problem that Copernicus observed when he concluded that the sun was not located in the center of the planets' orbits. In 1610 *Galileo observed through his telescope that Venus changes from a thin crescent into a full circle. Such phenomena proved that Venus revolved about the sun and that Copernicus's theory was sound. It was Isaac *Newton's work on gravity that finally proved Copernicus correct by discovering the law of gravitation, which explains how every body in the universe attracts every other body.

Copernicus's book was dedicated to Pope Paul III and was financed by a cardinal. The church did not take exception to Copernicus's theory until 1616, when Galileo's work began proving the theory. At that time it was declared false and in conflict with Holy Scripture.

A. Armitage, *Copernicus and the Reformation of Astronomy*, 1950.

M. Harwit, *Cosmic Discovery: The Search, Scope, and Heritage of Astronomy*, 1981.

CORNEILLE, PIERRE (1606–1684), French
dramatist and poet. Corneille was the son of a magistrate in Rouen who was raised to the nobility in 1637. Although the title was made hereditary in 1669, Pierre Cormille declined to take it. Having received a Jesuit education in Rouen, at the time a noted cultural center, he became an advocate in 1624. His posting, advocate to the Admiralty and to the ministry of waters and forests, was not to his liking and he sold it in 1650 for the meager sum of six thousand livres.

The comedy *Mélite*, Corneille's first play, was performed in 1632 and seven others followed in quick succession. An elegy commemorating Cardinal *Richelieu's visit to Rouen in 1634 further enhanced his status because of its mastery of what had become the traditional French style — complicated action and wordy — and his ability to present his ideas lucidly and energetically. So impressed was Richelieu that he had Corneille enrolled among the five poets whose task was to present the cardinal's ideas in drama. Corneille, however, found it difficult to do what was expected of him and soon crossed his employer by altering the structure of a play he was given to prepare.

Corneille continued to concentrate on his own works, producing the grand tragedy *Médée* in 1635. This was followed the next year by his best known work *Le Cid*, a startling and original play which formed the foundation of future French tragedy. Although immensely popular, the play aroused controversy and led to a series of jealous attacks on Corneille from Richelieu's inner circle. It was claimed that *Le Cid* ignored the conventions of composition in that the action was presented poorly, the versification was defective, and some of the more

- Time often serves to justify a deed which seems at first unjustifiable.
- All evils are equal when they are extreme.
- What destroyed one man preserves another.
- To win without risk is to triumph without glory.
- When love is satisfied all its charm is removed.
- What one puts off is half abandoned.
- The fire which seemed extinguished often slumbers beneath the ashes.
- He who cares naught for death cares naught for threats.

Corneille

moving passages had been plagiarized. Unable to get a fair hearing and after leaving the five poets, Corneille retired to Rouen where he remained for the next three years.

Le Cid was the first of several psychological tragedies in which the development of plot was secondary. The publication of *Horace* with a dedication to Richelieu and the intervention of Madame de Combalet (to whom *Le Cid* had been dedicated) finally healed the breach between the two men. Richelieu granted Corneille a pension of five hundred crowns a year, allowing him to continue to produce moving dramas such as *Cinna*. *Le Menteur* proved that Corneille was equally adept at comedy.

In 1647 Corneille was accepted as a member of the French Academy after his application had been twice rejected. He had already produced *Héraclius* (1646), and set to work on *Androméde* and the operatic *Don Sanche d'Aragon* (1650) and on *Nicomède* (1651). The failure of *Pertharite* in 1652 led Corneille to abandon the theater for the next six years, during which time he composed a verse translation of Thomas à Kempis's *Imitation of Christ* (1656), three *Discourses on Dramatic Poetry*, and *Examens*, in which he gave way to the classical rules of drama.

Corneille returned to the stage in 1659 at the urging of French statesman Nicolas Fouquet; his play *Oedipe* was much favored by *Louis XIV. In 1662 Corneille finally moved his residence from Rouen to Paris and a year later was included among the pensioned men of letters with an allowance of two thousand *livres*.

After the production of his next three plays, Corneille met with severe criticism. It was claimed that his writing skills were abating. He stopped publishing in 1674 and during his last decade wrote only a few verses in gratitude to Louis XIV, who ordered the revival of his plays.

Corneille was well known for his brusqueness. The dramatist Jean *Racine commented that Corneille's verses were one thousand times better than his but that he himself was more popular because he made himself more agreeable. Yet Corneille was much admired by many of his contemporaries; later writers openly referred to him as their master and as France's greatest dramatist.

R. J. Nelson, *Corneille, His Heroes, and Their Worlds*, 1963.

P. Yarrow, *Corneille*, 1963.

CORTÉS, HERNANDO (Hernán; 1485–1547), conqueror of Mexico. Cortés was one of many explorers and conquistadors born in the Spanish province of Extremadura, among them Hernando de Soto, Vasco *Núñez de Balboa, and Francisco *Pizarro. Forced to leave Spain because of extensive gambling debts and a penchant for forbidden romances, his first journey to the New World was delayed when, climbing over a fence to meet a married woman, he was attacked by her husband and was nearly killed.

After settling in Hispaniola in 1504, Cortés joined Diego Velázquez's expedition to Cuba in 1511. Many, detested him, and Velázquez agreed to send him to reconnoiter the newly discovered Mexican coast in order to get rid of him. He was ordered to take no risks, never to venture inland, and, in response to his reputation as a philanderer, never to sleep with native women. Having no intention of observing these rules, Cortés loaded his ten ships with horses, muskets, and cannon, but before Velázquez was able to restrain him, Cortés sailed in 1519.

News of strange white men landing at Veracruz was quickly relayed to the Aztec emperor *Montezuma. Montezuma sent ambassadors richly laden with gifts of gold, silver, turquoise, and featherwork. Astounded by the gifts, Cortés could only imagine the wealth of the king who sent them and decided to impress the envoys by charging at them with his horses, and firing cannonballs into the forest. To the Indians, who had never before seen horses or cannon, this only proved that the foreigners must be gods. Cortés then took the chief of the Totonac tribe hostage; under considerable protest the terrified chieftain agreed to install crosses in the temples in return for an alliance against Montezuma. At that, Cortés resigned his commission, sent one ship to Europe to solicit a new commission from *Charles V, ran the remainder of his fleet aground, and declared himself captain-general of the new town of Veracruz, populated by a handful of his men. The rest, accompanied by four thousand Totonacs, marched inland.

After eighty-three days, the Spanish reached the Aztec capital of Tenochtitlan, situated in the middle of a vast lake and connected to the shore by a network of spacious causeways (now the site of Mexico City). Montezuma himself came to greet them on the bridges, bringing gifts more lavish than the Spanish had yet received. He had underestimated their greed, and hoped that Cortés would take the presents and leave Mexico. Instead, Cortés insisted on accompanying Montezuma. For some time, the Spanish were lodged in a capacious palace, where they begged their hosts for gold and other gifts, and persistently tried to persuade Montezuma to forsake his gods. The Spanish ignored the growing animosity toward them until the amount of food they were brought was noticeably decreased, at which point they took Montezuma hostage.

Although Montezuma had long since recognized the Spanish threat to his empire, the outrages he had suffered had broken him and he was no longer able to prevent the Spanish from taking even greater liberties. He was killed by his subjects (or possibly by the Spanish) as he appealed for peace. Although Cortés planned to raze Tenochtitlan, the population had already been decimated by an epidemic of smallpox, unwittingly brought over from Cuba by one of his men. When an enormous meteor crashed into the lake, it was interpreted by the Aztecs as an omen of their inevitable defeat, and in 1521 the city surrendered.

Despite Velázquez's protests to the emperor, Cortés was appointed governor of the new city of Mexico. He proved so unpopular however, that the governor of Jamaica, with whose wife Cortés supposedly had an affair, sent a list of complaints against Cortés to Spain. Cortés sailed to Spain to defend himself, but opposition to him was growing and Charles refused to renew his commission. After a brief visit to Mexico, during which he incurred extravagant debts, Cortés returned to Spain, where he died penniless and forgotten. According to legend, he once passed Charles's carriage and ran to beg the king for alms. Clutching at the door, he called out, "Sir, I gave you more provinces than you had cities, but Charles did not recognize him."

F. L. de Gomara, *Cortés: The Life of the Conqueror*, 1965.

W. W. Johnson, *Cortés: Conquering the New World*, 1975.

CRANMER, THOMAS (1489–1556), archbishop of Canterbury and a chief founder of the Church of England. Born in Aslacton, Nottinghamshire, second son of a minor landowner, he had a brutal schooling at the hands of a severe and cruel schoolmaster, and was then sent to Jesus College, Cambridge, to study for religious orders. He lost his fellowship after marrying the relation of a local innkeeper, but his position was restored when his wife died in childbirth. While at Cambridge, Cranmer came to sympathize with Martin *Luther and the German Reformation.

While tutoring two boys in the town of Waltham, in 1529, he became acquainted with two officials of King *Henry VIII who lodged in the same house. At that time, Henry was grappling with the theological problem of how to divorce his first wife, Catherine of Aragon, who had not produced a male heir, a problem complicated by his wish to marry Anne Boleyn. Cranmer suggested that the king should appeal to the theological faculties of the universities — theologians might find a solution where experts in canon law could not. Henry took Cranmer's advice and found that the majority of the universities in Britain and Europe supported him. Cranmer's reverential attitude to the authority of kings, which he held that no priest had the right to contest, endeared him to his monarch.

In 1532 Cranmer was sent to Germany to muster support for the king's divorce; there he married the niece of the prominent Protestant theologian Andreas Osiander. As he rose to a high position in the church, it became less expedient for his marriage to be known and legend had it that he kept his wife locked in a closet for sixteen years.

In 1533 it occurred to Henry that Cranmer would make a useful archbishop of Canterbury, and he dispatched ten thousand marks to Rome to secure the appointment. When Cranmer took his oath of consecration, he swore to obey the pope but also added an oath that he would do nothing in contravention to the laws of England. In January of that year (1533) Henry secretly married the pregnant Anne Boleyn, and now an act was pushed through Parliament giving Cranmer the power to decide church matters without appeal to Rome. Cranmer presided over a convocation at Dunstable and as papal legate ruled that Henry's marriage to Catherine was invalid in the eyes of God because she had previously been betrothed to his late brother, and that therefore Henry's marriage to Anne was legal.

When Cranmer, who remained the king's favorite clergyman, was accused of heresy by a powerful propapal bloc in the Privy Council, Henry offered him royal protection. Convinced that he could prove his innocence, Cranmer wanted to present his case at trial, but Henry told him that a trial could easily be rigged and gave him his ring as a sign of support. When Cranmer's accusers came to arrest him, he showed them the king's ring and they were forced to make peace with him.

In return for royal patronage, Cranmer was expected to carry out the king's wishes in both religious and in temporal matters. When Henry took a liking to two of the archbishop's palaces at Otford and Knole, Cranmer's reluctance to surrender church property had to yield to the will of his sovereign. Despite the king's dominance, there seems to have been genuine rapport between the two. Cranmer was the clergyman Henry asked for on his deathbed in 1547, and as a sign of mourning Cranmer grew a long white beard.

The period after Henry's death, under the reign of the boy king Edward VI, was in many ways the peak of Cranmer's power. Together with the Protector, the Duke of Somerset, he played a key role in the establishment of the Protestant faith in England. The Catholic mass was abolished, an English book of common prayer introduced, and the Church of England liturgy drawn up. Cranmer formulated forty-two basic articles (later reduced to thirty-nine), which became the foundation of Anglicanism.

Cranmer's reverence for royalty was again demonstrated by his kneeling in the presence of the boy king. He also found an ingenious solution to the problem of royal discipline by introducing the whipping boy. Whenever Edward misbehaved, his playmate Barnaby Fitzherbert was beaten. This was intended to make Edward take pity on his friend and behave properly.

The death of Edward in 1553 and his own error in supporting the claims of the Protestant Lady Jane Grey resulted in Cranmer's downfall when the Catholic Queen *Mary succeeded to the throne. Mary denounced him and he was charged with perjury, adultery, and heresy; he was condemned for treason by Mary's government in 1553. Deprived of his bishopric, he was burned in effigy and imprisoned. At times his treatment in prison was humane and he was allowed to relax with a game of bowls or chess. However, kindness alternated with torture and, after a long trial, the elderly man was forced to issue a recantation of his beliefs in 1556, which he later renounced. When the sentence of death at the stake at Oxford was about to be carried out he plunged his right hand into the fire — punishing the hand that had signed the recantation he bitterly regretted.

G. W. Bromiley, *Thomas Cranmer*, 2 vols., 1956.
J. G. Ridley, *Thomas Cranmer*, 1962.

CROMWELL, OLIVER (1599–1658), parliamentary general of the English Civil War era and subsequently lord protector of the republican Commonwealth. Born in Huntingdon, Cromwell was descended from gentlemen farmers who had acquired wealth and status during the English Reformation. His great-grandfather was the nephew of *Henry VIII's reforming chief minister, Thomas Cromwell, whose surname he adopted. Cromwell grew up in a staunchly Puritan home and, after attending the local grammar school, studied law at Sidney Sussex College, Cambridge.

In 1628 he was elected member of Parliament for Huntingdon, but the king's dismissal of Parliament in 1629 left him politically inactive for eleven years. During that time he inherited a larger estate in Cambridgeshire and began championing the rights of smallholders. Beginning in 1640 he represented Cambridge in the Long Parliament, where his fiery speeches marked him as a leading opposition backbencher. His cousin, John Hampden, was one of the five members whom *Charles I sought to arrest for high treason, only to discover that the "birds had flown." This display of royal contempt for parliamentary privilege led to the outbreak of civil war in August 1642.

Despite his lack of experience in the field, Cromwell was a born tactician and commander. He raised and drilled his own small troop of cavalry and, by October 1643, led units that had outfought the Royalists at Grantham, Newark, and elsewhere. Believing that "honest, godly men" made the best soldiers, he picked "such men as had the fear of

God before them and as made some conscience of what they did." Unlike Prince Rupert's cavaliers, they were trained to ride back into the fray after a charge and not to give any respite to the opposing infantry. In January 1644 Cromwell became lieutenant-general of horse in the Eastern Association army commanded by the earl of Manchester, a supporter of the parliamentary cause. Six months later, on July 2, his "Ironsides" thrashed the Royalists once again at Marston Moor in Yorkshire, turning the battle into a Roundhead victory (a term used to describe the Puritans, who had closely-cropped hair, unlike the monarchists who had long, flowing locks). However, like other conservative Presbyterians, the Earl of Manchester favored a negotiated peace with Charles I and therefore avoided any renewal of hostilities.

In Parliament Cromwell attacked his defeatist superiors and called for the establishment of a unified army. With Sir Thomas Fairfax as its energetic lord general, Parliament's New Model Army was created in 1645 and, thanks to unrelenting pressure by Fairfax, command of the Roundhead cavalry was once more assigned to Cromwell. His Ironsides provided an inspiring example of firm discipline, religious zeal, and wily tactics. In accordance with his strategy — "Put your trust in God, my boys, and keep your powder dry" —, the New Model Army routed the forces of King Charles and Prince Rupert at the battle of Naseby (June 10, 1645). Charles promptly took refuge with the Scots, who handed him over to their English parliamentary allies. While Cromwell led the minority Independents in the Commons, the defeated monarch plotted with Presbyterian sympathizers and tried to win over the Scots. His escape from imprisonment to the Isle of Wight (1647), followed by a royalist uprising in the south and a massive Scottish invasion in the north, plunged the country into a renewal of the civil war.

Having quickly disposed of the southern revolt, Cromwell marched north to intercept the Duke of Hamilton's Scottish army, twice as large as his own, which he shattered near Preston in August 1648. Even though King Charles had repeatedly demonstrated his untrustworthiness, conservative politicians still longed for some sort of accommodation with him. Henry Ireton, Cromwell's son-in-law, drew up a lengthy "Remonstrance" on the army's behalf, insisting that the "Man of Blood" should face trial. On December 5, while the general was besieging Pontefract, Ireton and Colonel Thomas Pride arrested leaders of the (Presbyterian) majority that had voted in favor of continued negotiations. Cromwell accepted Pride's Purge as a fait accompli and an amenable Rump Parliament then authorized the establishment of a court before which the defiant Charles I was arraigned for high treason. As England's lawful king, ruling by divine right, Charles steadfastly denied Parliament's competence to try him, and much pressure had to be exerted before a verdict of guilty was entered, resulting in the death

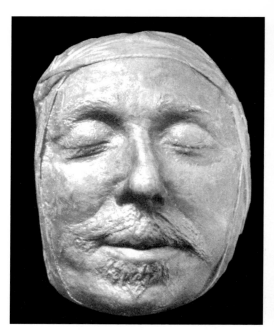

Death mask of Oliver Cromwell

sentence. Cromwell's signature, among others, appeared on the death warrant and, on January 31, 1649, King Charles was beheaded outside the palace of Whitehall. It was an execution which shocked the whole of seventeenth-century Europe.

While a compliant Rump Parliament abolished both the monarchy and the House of Lords, Cromwell undertook three successive campaigns. In Ireland he first avenged the 1641 massacres by ruthless treatment of Catholics at Drogheda and Wexford; next, in Scotland, he replaced Fairfax as lord general and crushed the much larger army of *Charles II, whom the Scots had recognized as the late king's rightful successor, at the battle of Dunbar (September 3, 1650). One year later he trounced the desperate Royalists at Worcester, calling that battle "for aught I know a crowning mercy." With England's treasury drained by civil war, Parliament now sought ways of replenishing it overseas. The Navigation Act of 1651, which prohibited the shipping of English colonial goods in foreign vessels, led to an Anglo-Dutch conflict that ended with the signing of a peace treaty in 1655. Cromwell, whose policies were guided by religious rather than strictly commercial interests, wanted the Dutch Protestants on his side in a war with Catholic Spain and felt that the Rump had outlived its usefulness. When the parliamentarians refused to make way for a more representative elected body, Cromwell brought musketeers into the House of Commons and expelled the "oligarchs" on April 20, 1653, after picking up the mace "What shall we do with this bauble? Take it away!" and ordering the members of Parliament to depart. Someone wrote "This House is to let" over the chamber's locked door.

In succession to the Rump a new Barebones Parliament, comprising moderate reformers as well as zealots, enacted laws — in favor of civil marriage, for example — which Cromwell held to be subversive. Though remarkably tolerant he did not mourn this assembly's collapse and, on December 16, 1653, took office as Lord Protector of the Commonwealth (England, Scotland, and Ireland). A written constitution modified his virtual dictatorship by assigning a balanced authority to the lord protector, the council of state, and triennial Parliaments. In 1655, the Commonwealth was divided into districts controlled by local militia under a number of major-generals; their attempt to enforce Puritan moral legislation encountered so much opposition, however, that the experiment had to be abandoned a year later. Finally, in 1657, Parliament's "Humble Petition and Advice" ventured to offer Cromwell the title of king, which he declined for fear of antagonizing the army. He did accept the prerogative of naming his successor and on June 26 the lord protector was solemnly installed as head of state.

The Protectorate made England a world power. "I would have the English republic respected," Cromwell vowed, "as ever the Roman was." In the space of a year (1655) treaties were signed with France and the Netherlands; a fleet was dispatched to bombard Tunis and root out piracy in the Mediterranean; war was declared on Spain; another fleet sailed to the West Indies; and an English army captured Jamaica. While talking peace, Cromwell sought to extend his nation's might abroad and demonstrated his faith in gunboat diplomacy ("a man-of-war is the best ambassador").

Unlike many Puritans, Cromwell enjoyed good company, food, wine, and music. He was neither vain nor consumed with ambition. Royalists feared and hated the regicide, yet he could be magnanimous toward vanquished opponents and kindly to their families. For a few months after his death his son Richard Cromwell (1626–1712) ruled England. After the restoration of Charles II in 1660 the name of Oliver Cromwell was reviled, his disinterred corpse hung on a gibbet, and his severed head exposed to public insult.

M. Ashley, *Charles I and Oliver Cromwell: A Study in Contrasts and Comparisons*, 1987.
B. Coward, *Oliver Cromwell*, 1991.
A. Fraser, *Cromwell: The Lord Protector*, 1986.
J. Morrill, ed., *Oliver Cromwell and the English Revolution*, 1990.

CURIE, MARIE (Manya Sklodowska; 1867–1934), French chemist. Manya Sklodowska was born in Warsaw, Poland, where her father taught mathematics and physics and her mother directed a school. It soon became obvious that she was both

BY CROMWELL

- A few honest men are better than numbers.
- Necessity hath no law.
- The State, in choosing men to serve it, takes no notice of their opinions. If they be willing faithfully to serve it, that satisfies.

Before the battle of Marston Moor, 1644

- I beseech you, in the bowels of Christ, think it possible you may be mistaken.

Letter to the General Assembly of the Church of Scotland, 1650

- You have sat here too long for any good you have been doing lately.... Depart, I say, and let us have done with you. In the name of God — go!

When dismissing the Rump Parliament, 1653

- I desire you would use all your skill to paint my picture truly like me, and not flatter me at all; but remark all these roughnesses, pimples, warts, and everything as you see me, otherwise I will never pay a farthing for it.

Instruction to the artist Peter Lely

POETS ON OLIVER CROMWELL

He nothing common did, or mean,
Upon that memorable scene,
But with his keener eye
The axe's edge did try.

Andrew Marvell, 1650

Cromwell, our chief of men, who through a cloud
Not of war only, but detractions rude,
Guided by faith and matchless fortitude,
To peace and truth thy glorious way hast plough'd... Yet much remains
To conquer still; peace hath her victories
No less renowned than war...

John Milton, 1652

more intelligent and more ambitious than her fellow students. Distressed that her elder sister Bronia could not continue her education, barred to women in Russian Poland at that time, Manya vowed to work and finance Bronia's studies abroad.

At sixteen she won a gold medal and her father promised her a year's vacation as a reward. She spent that year in the country and upon her return to Warsaw became a teacher, as no other job was available to her. Her sister wanted to study medicine but had only enough money for travel expenses and one year's tuition, room, and board. True to her resolve, Manya worked to earn money to help her sister and persuaded her to go to Paris to study; not long after, she too moved to Paris following a disappointing love affair.

In Paris she entered the Sorbonne and from the start excelled in physics, working day and night and existing on a meager diet. She gained experience in a research laboratory and in 1894 won a second place award in the field of mathematical science.

At the university she met Pierre Curie, who had already established a reputation as a researcher in physics, and they married in 1895; the marriage brought her into the inner circle of physicists. Together, Marie and Pierre Curie discovered how to isolate polonium in 1898, and a short time later they isolated radium. Through their efforts, a new era began in the study of atomic structure.

Seeking a topic for her thesis, Marie Curie devised new experiments and found that the properties which made up uranium were also present in other matter. These experiments led to her discovery of what was later termed radioactivity. At this time, Pierre Curie joined his wife in her work. She concentrated on isolating pure radium in the metallic state and he focused on the physical aspects of the new radiations. As a result of these experiments Marie Curie received her doctoral degree in science in 1903. That year, the couple won the Nobel prize for physics, sharing the award with another physicist for the work done in radioactivity.

Marie Curie had two daughters while continuing her work and was a lecturer in physics at the Ecole Normale Supérieure for Girls in Sèvres. In 1904, she became the chief assistant in the laboratory run by her husband, but in April 1906 Pierre Curie was killed in a motor accident. Marie Curie continued the work they had begun together. In 1909 she was appointed to fill the professorship vacated as a result of Pierre's death, becoming the first woman to teach at the Sorbonne.

In 1910 she published a book describing her work relating to radioactivity and the following year she won the Nobel prize for chemistry in recognition of her achievement in the isolation of radium, as well as for her contribution to chemistry. She was the first person to win Nobel prizes in both physics and chemistry but despite these achievements, she missed election to the Academy of Sciences by one vote.

With the help of her daughter Irène, Marie Curie worked throughout World War I on the development of the use of X-radiography. In 1922 she became a member of the Academy of Medicine and devoted her research to radioactive substances and their medical application.

In 1921 she and her two daughters were invited to America by the U.S. government, where President Warren G. Harding presented her with a gram of radium; following that visit she began an international lecture tour. In later life Marie Curie headed the Pasteur Institute as well as a radioactivity laboratory created for her at the University of Paris. She continued her research to uncover additional sources of radioactivity for purposes of both medicine and nuclear physics. Her daughter Irène (1897–1956) and her husband Frédéric Joliet pioneered the production of radioactive isotopes and received Nobel prizes in 1935. Like her mother, she died of leukemia contracted by lifelong work on radioactive substances.

E. Curie, *Madame Curie*, 1937.
I. Curie and R. Reid, *Marie Curie*, 1974.
E. Doorly, *The Radium Woman*, 1946.
Report of the United Nations on Educational Scientific and Cultural Organizations, *Marie Curie (Sklodowska)*, 1968.

CYRUS II (the Great; c.600–529 B.C.E.), founder of the Achaemenian dynasty and empire. To the Jewish exiles in Babylonia he was the long-awaited savior who enabled them to return to their land and rebuild their temple. His contemporaries depicted him in legendary terms, and it is difficult to distinguish the facts of his reign.

Cyrus was the son of *Cambyses I of the nomadic Achaemenian tribal monarchy, and Mandana, daughter of King Astyages of the Medes. Upon ascending the throne in 559 B.C.E., Cyrus began plotting the downfall of his maternal grandfather Astyages, king of the Medes. With help from Narbonidus, king of Babylonia, he captured the territories surrounding the Median capital of Pasargadae and encouraged many prominent citizens, among them the Median general Harpages, to defect. The city fell soon after and Cyrus declared himself Astyages's heir.

With the Medes subdued, Cyrus's most powerful rival was *Croesus, king of Lydia. Their two armies fought in Cappadocia in 547, but the outcome was indecisive and Croesus withdrew to muster his Greek, Egyptian, and Babylonian allies. This coalition was vastly superior to Cyrus's forces, but Croesus soon sent his allies home, following the advice of his oracles not to fight the Persians in winter. Cyrus responded by attacking the Lydian cavalry with camels. Terrified of these strange beasts, Croesus's horses threw off their riders and fled the battlefield, leaving the infantry unprotected from a Persian onslaught. The few survivors reorganized in their well-protected acropolis, but Cyrus noted that one section of the wall, atop a steep cliff, was poorly

> I am Cyrus, king of the world, great king, legitimate king, king of Babylonia, king of Sumer and Akkad, king of the four rims of the earth, son of Cambyses, great king, king of Anshan, descendant of Teipes, great king, king of Anshan, of a family which always exercises kingship.
>
> **Found on a stele celebrating
> the conquest of Babylonia**

protected, while the cliff was sometimes being scaled by Lydian soldiers who had dropped objects from above. Using this precarious route, Cyrus led his armies into the acropolis and took the city.

Cyrus took advantage of Lydia's fabled wealth to improve communications and administration in his far-flung empire. Lydian stonemasons rebuilt his capital, creating new architectural styles by synthesizing traditional Persian and Greek building techniques, and new roads were constructed enabling messengers to traverse the empire in a week.

To enable his empire to form a single contiguous land mass, Cyrus planned to conquer the territory of his former ally, Nabonidus of Babylonia. Nabonidus, a foreigner, was unpopular with the Babylonian priesthood for his contempt of local gods and his prolonged absences. Important members of the aristocracy defected to Cyrus, among them Gobryas governor of Gutium. To divert the Babylonian armies, he attacked them to the north of the city, leaving Gobryas access through the unprotected and open gates. Babylonia fell without a battle in October 540 B.C.E.; upon entering the city, Cyrus embraced the local gods and adopted the traditional titles of a Babylonian king.

For the remainder of his reign, Cyrus consolidated his kingdom, allowing his subjects considerable autonomy in return for their loyalty, the most notable being his treatment of the Jews whom he allowed to return to Jerusalem and rebuild their temple.

Cyrus's final years were plagued by incursions from the many tribes along his distant borders who resented his attempt to impose Persian rule on them. When Queen Tomyris of the Massagetae advised him, "Rule your own people and try to bear the sight of me ruling mine!" Cyrus crossed into Central Asia to crush Tomyris. The capture and execution of her son however, only provoked her to oppose Cyrus with even greater fury. In the ensuing battle, Cyrus was killed, and his head, brought as a trophy to Tomyris, was dipped in gore as she exclaimed, Have your fill of blood. After considerable efforts, the Persians recovered Cyrus's body and interred it in Anshan. Above the monument, a simple epitaph, "King of Kings," can still be seen.

P. Sykes, *A History of Persia*, 1969.
C. Irving, *Crossroads of Civilization: 3,000 Years of Persian History*, 1979.

D

DAGUERRE, LOUIS-JACQUES-MANDÉ
(1789–1851), French inventor of the daguerrotype,
an early form of photography. After the Napoleonic
War, Daguerre was apprenticed to an architect, but he
was more interested in painting landscapes and portraits than architectural drawings and, overcoming his
father's opposition, he went to Paris to be an artist.

At sixteen, Daguerre began studying theater design at the Paris Opera and at nineteen was made
assistant to the panorama painter, Pierre Prévost.
His skills as an innovator in theatrical design were
revealed in the diorama exhibitions he began in
1822; he placed on stage large transparent and
opaque painted screens depicting views, using a
camera obscura to insure perfect accuracy. By varying the light falling on these screens, he created the
illusion of twilight or daybreak. These lifelike
scenes brought him fame in Paris, and in 1823 he
took the diorama to London's Regents Park, where
his show was an outstanding technical triumph and
financial success.

Daguerre was excited by the possibilities of
recording permanently his camera obscura images.
He was aware of the work of his countryman J. N.
Niepce, who since 1814 had been trying to obtain
permanent pictures from the action of sunlight on
bitumen-coated pewter or glass plates. Daguerre
began a correspondence with him in 1825 but
Niepce was unwilling to share the secrets of his
process until 1829, when the two made an agreement to carry out research together.

The two attempted to find a substance more light-
sensitive than bitumen, which reacted too slowly for
the process today called photography. Niepce died
in 1833 with the search still unsuccessful.

Two years later, Daguerre discovered that silver
iodine was what he had been looking for. He had
put an unsuccessful photographic plate away in the
cupboard with the intention of re-coating it for future use; when he came to take it out after a few
days, he found a strong image registered on it.
Careful investigation of the bottles in the cupboard
showed that mercury from a broken thermometer had
acted as the developing agent on the silver iodine
coated plate. In his excitement he exclaimed, "I
have seized the light! I have arrested its flight! In
the future the sun itself shall draw my pictures!"

Daguerre, along with Niepce's son, agreed to
sell the invention while preserving the secret of
the method; it was a thankless task trying to get
people to invest in an unknown process. Daguerre
then tried to sell the invention to businessmen and
politicians, even starting a rumor that it might be
lost to France if he could not find a buyer. He
eventually found an advocate in the Chamber of
Deputies who convinced the government that both
he and Niepce had made an outstanding contribution to the nation's artistic heritage with their
invention, soon to be known as the daguerreotype.
In 1839 Daguerre and Niepce were voted lifetime
pensions, an award which could not have come at
a better time for Daguerre — his diorama exhibition burned down that year. Nevertheless, although
he was appointed an officer in the Legion of
Honor, he died in relative poverty; his skill as inventor and promoter brought him no fortune.

The daguerreotype had many shortcomings; the
subject had to remain still for a long period and
bright sunlight was needed to register the image.
Moreover, there was no way of reproducing the
picture except by making another daguerreotype of
it. Nevertheless, daguerreotypes for the first time
allowed people of modest means to have their photograph taken.

H. and A. Gernsheim, *L. J. M. Daguerre,* 1968.
B. Newhall, *The History of Photography,* 1982.
J. Szarhowski, *Photography Until Now,* 1981.

DALTON, JOHN (1766–1844), English chemist,
physicist, and meteorologist. Dalton was born in
Eaglesfield, Cumberland, the second son of a
Quaker weaver. He received his early education at
the Quaker village school in Eaglesfield. Dalton's
scholarly aptitude was apparent quite early; when
only twelve he replaced the schoolteacher on the
latter's retirement.

Dalton began his scientific studies in 1787 at the
age of twenty-one. Largely self-taught, he studied

meteorology to learn about the nature and constitution of the atmosphere, observing the aurora borealis and looking for the cause of rain and trade winds. He also wrote essays on the barometer, thermometer, hygrometer, and rainfall as well as the formation of clouds.

He moved to Manchester in 1793 and the following year was elected a member of the Manchester Literary and Philosophical Society, earning his living by tutoring children. One Sunday, his friends happened to remark about the impropriety of his wearing a scarlet coat to a meeting of the Society. Dalton was astonished as he thought the coat was brown. This chance happening led to his study of color blindness and he discovered that he could not see the color red and could recognize only blue, purple, and yellow. In 1798 he published his *Memoirs*, which was the first scientific account of color blindness. Thereafter red-green color blindness came to be known as Daltonism.

One of his most important achievements was his development in 1801 of the atomic theory of matter, which held that all elements are made up of very tiny identical particles (i.e., atoms) that are indestructible. In his theory he assumed that particles of nitrogen and oxygen were of different weights. He determined the relative weights of atoms and developed a technique for calculating the relative weights of the ultimate particles of all chemicals.

He also developed Dalton's law of partial pressures in gaseous systems, which states that the total pressure of a mixture of gases equals the sum of the pressures exerted by each gas independently. He found that gases expand as their temperature is raised. Further experiments demonstrated the rate of diffusion of gases, constancy of the composition of the atmosphere, and the solubility of gases in water.

Dalton received extensive recognition for his work, during his lifetime. In 1822 he was elected a fellow of the Royal Society, from which he received the gold medal in 1826. In 1831 he cofounded the British Association for the Advancement of Science. In 1832 he served as chairman for the chemistry, mineralogy, electricity, and magnetism committee of the Association and continued to be active on various committees. However, his extensive activity came to an abrupt halt in 1837, when he suffered two paralytic attacks that left him a semi-invalid for the rest of his life.

During the period of Dalton's work with the British Association for the Advancement of Science, he was honored by the British government as well as by universities in Britain and abroad. In 1832 Oxford University conferred upon him an honorary degree. In 1833 the British government awarded him a pension of £150, raised to £300 in 1836.

D. S. L. Cardwell, *John Dalton and the Progress of Science*, 1968.

F. Greenaway, *John Dalton and the Atom*, 1966.

A. Thackray, *John Dalton*, 1972.

DANTE ALIGHIERI (Durante; 1265–1321), Italian poet, political thinker, and religious philosopher who created one of the most enduring masterpieces of world literature, *La divina commedia* (*The Divine Comedy*). Dante was born in Florence to a family of noble Italian lineage. By the time he reached adolescence both of his parents had died and he was left in the care of a stepmother. In 1295 Dante married a woman whose family belonged to the Guelph nobility from the house of Donati (a family whose political alliances were in direct opposition to his own); four children were born from this marriage. By the end of Dante's lifetime he had produced a vast corpus of literary, philosophical, and political writings in the Italian vernacular and in Latin. He died of malaria in Ravenna, where he lived his last years in poverty and as a political exile, only shortly after completing the final book of the *Commedia*, the *Paradiso*.

An experience which deeply marked Dante's development as a poet was his meeting at the age of nine with the eight-year-old Beatrice. Dante speaks about his first encounter with Beatrice in his early poetic work, the *Vita Nova*. From this first encounter onward the image of Beatrice became inextricably bound to Dante's highest aspirations as a poet; this can especially be seen in *Commedia,* where Beatrice becomes Dante's spiritual guide in the *Paradiso* and is the embodiment of religious vision and truth. Giovanni *Boccaccio, the first Dante historian and scholar, who lectured and wrote about Dante in the middle of the fourteenth century, said of Beatrice: "...she was the daughter of the noble gentleman and neighbor of the Alighieri, Messer Folco di Ricovera Portinari, who married Messer Simone de Bardi and died at the age of twenty-four in the year 1290." In the *Vita Nuova* Dante writes about the vision that he had of Beatrice after her death: "There appeared to me a wonderful vision wherein I saw things which made me determine to say nothing more of this blessed one until I could more worthily speak of her; for this reason I study all I can, as she truly knows. Wherefore, if it be His pleasure, in whom all things live, that my life endure a few more years, I hope to say of her what has never been said before of any woman."

The years following Beatrice's death were a turning point in Dante's life. He gives an account of this period of his life in his philosophical work, the *Convivio*: "When the first joy of my soul was lost, I remained in such sorrow that no consolation could bring comfort to me. Yet after a certain time...my spirit that longed for healing, found rescue in the way in which other disconsolate persons had found relief before. And I began to read that book of Boethius, which is not known to many, and with which he comforted himself in prison and in banishment." During this period Dante immersed himself in the study of the classics, Christian theology, and the philosophical and scientific knowledge of his times. There are differing views about Dante's formal education; some

Dante, by Luca Signorella

say that he studied under the tutelage of Brunetto La-tini, who was renowned as a great scholar and statesman. Latini was exiled from Florence and lived in France, where he wrote an encyclopedia which was a compilation of the knowledge and philosopy of his time. The *Convivio*, shows Latini's influence. Dante was also connected to a group of Florentine poets, the greatest among them being Guido Cavalcanti, who es-pecially influenced Dante's work, the *Vita Nuova*, and encouraged him to write verse in Italian.

Dante's philosophical and poetic works are insep-arable from his position as a public and political figure. He was very much at the center of the social and political schisms and rivalries which split Flo-rence during the course of his lifetime. At the age of twenty-five he fought in the front line in the Battle of Campaldino. Dante was an important and active member of the guild of physicans and pharmacists, for which he became eligible for priorship (he was elected Prior in the year 1300 and became a member of the government). He was an ambassador to the Republic on two occasions and was a close personal friend of the king of Naples. It is one of the peculiar ironies of history that Dante's poetic genius was al-most overlooked by his contemporaries and that he was known more for his political writings and as a politician than as a poet. Dante's political thinking is expressed in his three-volume treatise, *Monarchia*, which was written in Latin.

In 1308 Dante began to write the *Commedia*. It is a work which reflects in broad scope and depth the knowledge which was of essence to the culture from which it emerged. It is necessary to have some knowledge of the culture of the time in order to grasp its genius and sheer inventiveness. Dante's use

of Italian in the *Commedia* had an impact upon the future of Italian poetry and created a bridge to the Italian of the Renaissance. In a letter to Can Grande, Dante speaks about the allegory and symbolism within the *Commedia,* which he refers to as being polysemeous — that it is to be read or understood on several different levels at once. It is both the use of Christian allegory and symbolism, along with the complex and peculiar meshing of classical motifs, that characterizes the *Commedia* and makes it a para-digm of medieval literature at its greatest height.

The *Commedia* is an epic poem in three books — the *Inferno*, the *Purgatorio*, and the *Paradiso*. The work in its entirety is an allegorical description of man's journey toward spiritual and moral enlighten-ment. The journey begins in this world, and then the reader accompanies the narrator and hero of the poem (Dante himself) into those realms beyond this world where the particular state of the soul is expressed: in the *Inferno* it is the soul's state of sin or moral deprav-ity; in the *Purgatorio*, the expiation or purification of sin; and in the *Paradiso*, the soul's state of grace where the blessed receive the resplendent vision of the divine. Through the realms of the *Inferno* and the *Purgatorio* the classical poet *Virgil is Dante's guide. However, when Dante reaches the *Paradiso*, it is Beatrice who becomes his sole guide and leads the poet to a state of inner illumination and enlightenment. The *Commedia* is at once autobiographical and universal; from it bio-graphical information can be gleaned about Dante's life and it also contains a kind of current chronicle of the social and political personages of Florence — writ-ten with so much candor that one wonders about the scandal that it must have created.

It was one of the great trials and sorrows of Dante's life to have been exiled from his beloved Florence. Dante was a member of the White Guelph party, which was sympathetic to the banished, pro-imperialist Ghilbellines, and in opposition to the Black Guelphs. From about 1302 until his death in 1321 Dante lived in exile. In 1303 he studied in Bologna, a city renowned as a center of philosophy, law, and rhetoric; the *Convivio* and his work *De vul-gari eloquentia* (1304–1305) were written there. In

1306 he was forced to leave Bologna along with other Florentine exiles. In 1308 Dante commenced working on the *Commedia*. His works during these years of exile, until his death in 1321, all bear the mark of his wandering, but it is a credit to the poet's greatness that his works all stand above his own personal suffering. Dante's last home in exile was in Ravenna; inscribed on his monument are the words of Bernardo Canaccio: "Here I am enclosed, exiled from my native country, Whom Florence bore, the mother that little did love him."

W. Anderson, *Dante the Maker*, 1980.
K. Fedren, *Dante and His Time*, 1969.
A. G. Ferrers Howell, *Dante*, 1969.

DANTON, GEORGES-JACQUES (1759–1794), French revolutionary. Born in the small village of Arcis-sur-Aube, about one hundred miles from Paris. His family was originally of peasant stock but through hard work had reached the level of *petit-bourgeois*. Raised in the countryside, he remained attached to the soil and the land. He was a coarse man, with a tendency toward bluntness that verged on the shocking. When he gained power he ruled without the self-discipline and cool detachment mastered by the more practiced aristocrats. He was, for a while, the most popular figure of his time, undoubtedly charming and persuasive, if also volatile and often unpredictable.

He was also somewhat shocking to look at. His face was pockmarked and it bore the scars of being trampled by pigs in the barnyard as a boy and mauled by the horn of a cow whose udders he was sucking. It was said that, "It would be easier to paint the eruption of a volcano than the features of this great man."

At age thirteen Danton was sent to be educated by Oratorian priests, a particularly open-minded, scientifically-oriented sect that inspired in Danton a love of learning, although he was described as a generally lazy student whose innate brilliance appeared only in sudden bursts.

After his education his family met with the priests to determine the further course of his life. It was decided, much to the young Danton's pleasure, that he was to study law. He set out for Paris in 1780 with almost no money and managed, through the sheer force of his personality, to be taken on as a lawyer's apprentice, although he lacked the necessary experience.

During this time he met and fell in love with Antoinette Charpentier, the daughter of the owner of a cafe he frequented. He borrowed money to set up a law practice and married Antoinette two days later. The practice thrived and he took to signing his name D'Anton as if he were an aristocrat. The couple lived somewhat pretentiously, entertaining frequently and often finding themselves stretched financially beyond their means.

They lived in the Cordeliers district of Paris, inhabited by students, printers, journalists, and other unmonied intellectuals. The district became a hotbed of dissent in the early days of the French Revolution, its name becoming synonymous with the Cordeliers movement, of which Danton became the first president after a heroic attempt to protect Jean *Marat, another revolutionary journalist, from arrest. He then joined the Girondins, a movement that, along with the Jacobins, took power in the heat of revolution. They formed a government, the legislative assembly of which Danton was not officially a part, and plotted to overthrow the monarchy.

Danton became minister of justice in the new government and was in part responsible, although it is unclear to what degree, for the September massacres, one of the bloodiest revolutionary purges of the general population. He rallied the nation with the cry "Everything belongs to the country when the country is in danger."

After the massacres it became impossible for Danton to realign himself with the moderate faction of which he was originally a part. He had always been a realist and as the revolution took on a life of its own, political distinctions and groups to which one belonged became increasingly changeable and unclear. Danton was no longer a Girondin or Cordelier; in fact they became his enemies. He was also not a Jacobin but clearly a part of the self-interested and bloody power struggle that characterized the Terror.

Shortly after Danton officially became part of government, personal tragedy struck. He went away for two weeks and returned to discover that his beloved wife had died, leaving him with two young sons. His own downfall can be traced in part, to Antoinette's death. Always immensely popular with the public and famed for his ability to whip up public emotion, he became unable to sutain the level of stamina that had catapulted him to power. The Jacobins and their leader Maximilien *Robespierre grabbed the reigns and held on firmly and brutally. The Girondins, whom Danton saw as the true voice of republicanism, were being slaughtered. Danton became physically and emotionally exhausted and made what can now be seen as his fatal mistake. Claiming illness, he retired for a short while to the countryside to regain his strength. However, in leaving the seat of power for just a brief time he gave his enemies considerable leeway to conspire against him. He returned to find himself accused of plotting to reinstate the monarchy. Danton's revolution, his "war to elevate French people" ended in 1794 when he was tried and imprisoned for crimes againt the Revolution. His execution marked the height of the Terror, one of the most violent periods in French history. On the scaffold he said to the executioner "You must show my head to the people. It is worth showing."

M. Bouloiseau, *The Jacobin Republic, 1792–94*, 1984.
R. Butler, *The French Revolution*, 1975.
S. Loomis, *Paris in the Terror*, 1965.
J.M. Thompson, *The French Revolution*, 1985.

DARIUS I (the Great; 550–496 B.C.E.), king of Persia who ruled from 521 to 486 B.C.E. He was one of three kings of the Achaemenid dynasty called Darius, meaning "possessing good things" in Old Persian. The Achaemenid dynasty began with the reign of Cyrus I (645–602 B.C.E.) and ended with the reign of Darius III in 330 B.C.E.

Darius I was the son of Hystaspes, the head of the younger branch of the Achaemenid dynasty. The older branch ended with the death of King *Cambyses II, *Cyrus the Great's son. According to Darius's own account recorded in the famous Behistun Inscription of 516 B.C.E., he and six other nobles killed the usurper Gaumata the Magian who had pretended to be Bardiya, the brother of King Cambyses. Darius then became king of Persia.

An outstanding administrator and considered the greatest royal architect of the Achaemenid dynasty, Darius I was also a man of military prowess and foresight able to consolidate an empire torn from within by revolt. After the assassination of Gaumata (or as some modern scholars hold, Bardiya himself), groups claiming to belong to the former ruling families set up their own governments. In the Behistun Inscription, Darius records that he defeated nine rebel leaders in nineteen battles. There were three rebellions in Susiana but the most serious was that in Babylon. In 520 B.C.E. Babylon surrendered, enabling Darius to crush the Medean revolt. Babylon rebelled again in the same year, but by 519 B.C.E. Darius's authority was established over the whole empire.

Darius then embarked on a number of campaigns. His conquests extended to Armenia, the Caucasus, India, the Turanian steppes, and Central Asia. In 513 B.C.E. he took eastern Thrace and crossed the Danube into European Scythia. Under his orders the satraps of Asia Minor took all of Thrace, Macedonia, Lemnos, and Imbros. Persia was thus in control of all the approaches to Greece. The conquest of Greece was strategically important to Darius as well as to Persian rulers after him. No military action was taken by Darius against Greece until 499 B.C.E., when he had to put down an Ionian rebellion backed by Athens and Eretria. In 492 B.C.E. a campaign was undertaken against Athens and Eretria by Darius's son-in-law but it was abandoned because of a storm. In 490 B.C.E. another initiative under Datis, a Mede, destroyed Eretria, but was defeated by Athens. A third campaign was planned, but Darius died in 486 B.C.E. before it could get under way.

As an administrator Darius organized the empire into satrapies (provinces), completing the work of *Cyrus the Great. Each province was subdivided, with governors or satraps of each division. The number of satraps and their districts often changed. Thus, according to the book of Daniel, "It pleased Darius to set a hundred and twenty princes over the kingdom," while the book of Esther says that Ahasuerus (perhaps Darius's son, Xerxes I, who ruled 486–465 B.C.E.) "reigned from India even unto Ethiopia over a hundred and seven and twenty provinces." The yearly tribute each satrap had to contribute was fixed by Darius. He standardized the coinage, weights, and measures of the realm, established a system of roads and a postal service, and opened land and sea routes. Perhaps the greatest asset in securing the unification of his empire was his religious tolerance.

Zoroastrianism, the belief in one deity but in dual forces of truth and falsehood, was introduced as the state religion of Persia during Darius's reign. According to his inscriptions, Darius may have been a follower of *Zoroaster, but this is not certain. What is certain is that he continued the example set by Cyrus the Great of respecting the diverse religious beliefs of the peoples of the empire. In Egypt, where he was held in high esteem, he built one temple, supported and restored others, and gave orders to consult Egyptian priests to codify Egyptian laws. He upheld the rights extended by Cyrus to the Greek temples, and in 519 B.C.E. he gave authority to the Jews to rebuild the Temple in Jerusalem.

In 521 B.C.E. Darius made Susa his capital, restored the walls, and built a hall for holding royal audiences and a residential palace. The foundation inscriptions of the palace record how he brought craftsmen and material from all parts of the empire. In his native Persia he established a new royal residence at Persepolis, Darius initiating a style of architecture that lasted until the end of the Persian empire.

A. R. Burn, *Persia and the Greeks*, 1962.
C. Irving, *Crossroads of Civilization: 3,000 Years of Persian History*, 1979
P. Sykos, *A History of Persia*, 1969
D. N. Wilber, *Persepolis, the Archaeology of Parsa, Seat of the Persian Kings*, 1969.

DARWIN, CHARLES ROBERT (1809–1882), English naturalist responsible (along with Alfred Russell Wallace) for the theory of the evolution of organisms through a process of "natural selection." He was born in Shrewsbury; his mother, Susannah, was the daughter of the renowned potter, Josiah Wedgewood, and his grandfather, Erasmus Darwin, was a poet and naturalist who expounded biological theories in verse.

Following the death of their mother when Darwin was eight, his eldest sister, Caroline, brought him up. After attending Shrewsbury school, where Darwin showed no distinction as a pupil, he was sent to Edinburgh University to study medicine, but left without completing his studies (operations sickened him and he spent much of his time collecting marine animals). In 1827 his father dispatched him to Christ College, Cambridge, where he was to prepare to become a clergyman. Once more, Darwin found his studies unappealing and preferred hunting and riding. He did not then "in the least doubt the strict and literal truth of every word in the Bible," but Cambridge academia was a community wracked by the tension between science and religion, where the Old Testament was not taken literally by all.

Darwin was influenced by the astronomer Sir William *Herschel, who held a more liberal view on

- The Old Testament, from its manifestly false history of the earth, and from its attributing to God the feelings of a revengeful tyrant, was no more to be trusted than the sacred books of the Hindoos, or the beliefs of any barbarian.
- The highest possible stage in moral culture is when we recognize we ought to control our thoughts.
- Physiological experiment on animals is justifiable for real investigation, but not for mere damnable and detestable curiosity.
- It is interesting to contemplate a tangled bank clothed with plants of many kinds, with birds singing on the bushes, with various insects flitting about, and with worms crawling through the damp earth, and to reflect that these elaborately constructed forms, so different from each other, and dependent on each other in so complex a manner, have all been produced by laws acting around us.

Charles Darwin

biblical truth, and by John Stevens Henslow, professor of botany, who encouraged his interest in natural history. Henslow recommended Darwin to the Admiralty in 1831 when it sought a naturalist for a voyage led by Captain Robert Fitzroy of the Royal Navy on H.M.S. *Beagle*. The purpose of the voyage was to survey the coasts of Patagonia, Tierra del Fuego, Chile, and Peru, and to visit certain Pacific islands and set up a chain of chronometrical stations around the world. Darwin set sail from Devonport aboard the *Beagle* on December 27, 1831, and returned five years later.

On Herschel's advice, he took with him a copy of Charles Lyell's *Principles of Geology*, and became deeply influenced by this work which expounded the theory that there was an inevitable, gradual change in species, within the context of an overall stability.

The *Beagle* journeyed to the Cape Verde Islands, where Darwin observed a volcano, on to Brazil and its rain forests, and to Argentina, where he saw fossils of mastodons and horses. He experienced an earthquake in Chile, and noted its effects on raising the land's level. He proved adventurous and daring, as he often went (many times alone) on long trips into the hinterland to collect specimens (the sailors nicknamed him "The Flycatcher"). The *Beagle* continued its travels to the Galápagos Islands, Tahiti, New Zealand, Australia, Cocos Keeling Atoll, Mauritius, South Africa, Saint Helena, Ascension Island, back to Brazil, and homeward to Falmouth.

Darwin's initial interest on the *Beagle* voyage had been geology. On that subject he published four important, though overlooked, books that were to form the foundation of his later studies: *Journal of Researches into the Geology and Natural History of the Various Countries Visited by H.M.S. Beagle,* *1832–36* (1839); *Structure and Distribution of Coral Reefs* (1842); *Geological Observations on Volcanic Islands* (1844); and *Geological Observations on South America* (1846). These books described the geology of atolls and reefs, which Darwin concluded must be the result of the subsidence of the sea floor, as the corals grew vertically while their bases fell.

Darwin edited a book on the collection of animals he had made, called *The Zoology of the Voyage of the Beagle* (1840–1843). This work left unanswered many questions on comparative anatomy, classification, and distribution. He wanted to know why, for example, the South American rhea resembled the African ostrich and why the birds and tortoises of each of the Galápagos Islands differed when their environments were apparently the same.

He realized that the answer to these questions was that species could change into other species and maintain common ancestry. This concept of "evolution," which Darwin called his theory of "descent and modification," aimed at solving the problem of how organisms came to be as they were. He did not publish his ideas until twenty years later; he sensed the opposition he would encounter should he be unable to substantiate his theory. He sought his proof in man's careful selection of parents when breeding animals and plants. In Thomas *Malthus's *An Essay on the Principle of Population* (1798), he read that the arithmetical ratio of human food supply could not keep up with the geometrical ratio of the rate of increase in the human population. (This ignored the possibility of artificially increasing food supplies). Darwin applied the basic theory to organisms, showing that the resulting high mortality rate would force the mechanism of selection of parents, and proving that adaptation is a direct consequence of selection pressure. He also showed that modification, i.e., evolution, is correlated to the ecological niches of species, thereby laying the foundation for the science of ecology.

In 1856, Darwin began a massive work about natural selection and evolution, including information on geographical distribution and the role of the wind and sea in dispersing oceanic island populations. He was abruptly jolted from his work in 1858, when he unexpectedly received an essay from Alfred Russel Wallace, a naturalist, who wrote from the Malay Archipelago enclosing the conclusions he had reached on evolution and natural selection. Fearing his life's work would be pre-empted, Darwin consulted his friends, Lyell, Hooker, and Thomas Henry *Huxley, (who advised him to have a joint paper by Wallace and himself read at the Linnean Society of London). In 1858, Darwin published Wallace's idea alongside his own 1844 essay, and then quickly wrote an "abstract" of his ideas, which was published in 1859 as *On the Origin of Species by Means of Natural Selection*, which sold out at once. Darwin never used the word "evolution" in *Origin*, though the last word of the book is "evolved."

He immediately came under a barrage of criticism. Richard Owens, then regarded as the leading biologist, jealously tried to discredit Darwin, his former friend. The Church of England also entered into the fray, since evolution negated the role of divine guidance and design on earth and made redundant the account of creation in Genesis.

Although he was in excellent health during his journey on the *Beagle*, on his return Darwin suffered symptoms which have been described as depressive and obsessional. It is believed that he had suffered the bite of an insect, resulting in lassitude, intestinal malfunction, and heart blockage. Reduced to semi-invalidism, he died at Down and was buried at Westminster Abbey next to Sir Isaac *Newton.

Darwin's sons George, Francis, and Horace were all knighted for their contributions to astronomy, botany, and civil engineering respectively. His son Leonard became an economist and eugenicist.

J. Bowlby, *Charles Darwin*, 1990.

P. J. Bowler, *Charles Darwin*, 1990.

G. De Beer ed., *Darwin and Huxley: Autobiographies*, 1971.

A. Desmond and J. Moore, *Darwin*, 1992.

A. Ellegard, *Darwin and the General Reader*, 1990.

DAVID (c.1037–c.962 B.C.E.), second king of Israel, and its most powerful monarch. His reign spanned forty years, seven of them in Hebron as ruler of Judah and thirty-three in Jerusalem as king of all Israel. The sole source of information on David is the Old Testament (1 and 2 Samuel; 1 Kings: 1–2), which relates that David was the youngest of the eight sons of Jesse of the tribe of Judah, who lived in Bethlehem. According to the lineage recorded in the book of Ruth, David was a descendant of Boaz and Ruth the Moabite.

The prologue to the drama of David's activities is the scene in which the prophet Samuel, who has decided that the succession to the throne will not remain in the family of King Saul, is sent to anoint a replacement from among the sons of Jesse; divine guidance leads him to choose the youngest son. According to one biblical account, David was introduced into Saul's royal household as a musician to soothe the king's frequent bouts of depression. According to another, it was his successful encounter with the Philistine giant Goliath, that brought him to the king's attention and led to his advancement in the army and to his marriage with the king's daughter, Michal. His relationship with Jonathan, Saul's son, has become a paradigm of true friendship.

Saul's suspicious, jealous nature turned him against David, whom he sought to kill when he suspected him of wanting to usurp the throne. David fled and, at the head of a group of misfits and malcontents, found refuge in the service of Achish, the Philistine king of Gath. With an eye to gaining support, David also maintained close relations with the elders of Judah. After Saul's death in battle with the Philistines, David and his band moved to Hebron, where the Judahites appointed him their king. Seven years later he became king of all Israel when a new leader was sought after the death of Saul's son, Ish-baal; the elders of the other tribes of Israel made a covenant with him. David then turned his energies to overcoming Israel's enemies: first the Philistines on the coastal plain of Palestine then, to the east and north, the Moabites, the Arameans, Ammonites, and Edomites. The defeat of the Arameans saw David extend his rule beyond the tribal boundaries of Israel to the banks of the Euphrates. In addition to the sword, he used economic, diplomatic, and political means to assuage his enemies, developing excellent economic relations with the Phoenician, Hiram, king of Tyre.

David's political acumen was put to the test in molding a single nation out of the Twelve Tribes of Israel. One move was to capture Jerusalem — formerly a Jebusite stronghold and hence a neutral area — and make it his capital and center of his well-organized administration. He also turned the city into the religious center of the nation, bringing the Ark of the Covenant there and preparing to build a temple.

While achieving successes on military and political fronts, David did not find domestic peace; having taken wives from different backgrounds he was unable to forge a unified family. Particularly notorious was his plot to kill Uriah the Hittite after he had seduced Uriah's wife, Bathsheba. The two married after Uriah's death, but the adultery was condemned by the prophet Nathan, who foretold the death of the first child of this union. However, Bathsheba remained a powerful figure at court and

Samuel anointing David; detail of a wall painting from the Dura-Europos synagogue, Syria

A PSALM OF DAVID

The Lord is my shepherd; I shall not want.
He makes me to lie down in green pastures;
He leads me beside the still waters.
He restores my soul:
He leads me in the paths of righteousness
For His name's sake.
Yea, though I walk through the valley of the shadow of death,
I will fear no evil;
For You are with me;
Your rod and your staff they comfort me.
You prepare a table before me in the presence of my enemies;
You anoint my head with oil;
My cup runs over.
Surely goodness and mercy shall follow me all the days of my life;
And I will dwell in the house of the Lord for ever.

Psalm 23

eventually played a major role in the intrigue that resulted in their son, *Solomon, becoming successor.

The system of rule established by David was not unopposed, but the king quashed attempts at revolt, including one headed by his son, Absalom. The dynasty founded by David provided the rulers of Judah until the end of the kingdom in 586 B.C.E. He himself achieved a mythic status in Jewish eyes, and it was held that the Messiah would be of the "seed of David." The New Testament traces the genealogy of *Jesus Christ back to him and describes Jesus's birth in Bethlehem, David's birthplace.

Jerusalem, known as the City of David, continues to be venerated by Jews, Christians, and Muslims. As the "sweet singer of Israel," David was regarded in Jewish tradition as the composer of the book of Psalms, seventy-three of which are specifically attributed to him.

R. C. Bailey, *David in Love and War*, 1990.
J. Bright, *A History of Israel*, 1981.
J. W. Flanagan, *David's Social Drama*, 1988.

DAVIS, JEFFERSON (1808–1889), statesman, soldier, and president of the Confederate States of America (1861–1865). Davis was born in Fairview, Kentucky, but soon moved to Mississippi, where his father set up a small plantation. Through the efforts of a Mississippi congressman he received an appointment to the United States Military Academy at West Point, where he developed a love of order and discipline. After graduation, Davis served in the army for some seven years until resigning in 1835 to become a planter in Mississippi.

In December 1845 he was elected to the House of Representatives. At that time abolitionist attacks abounded in the country and Davis, as a congressman who personally owned slaves, remained strongly in favor of slavery. This first stint in Congress was short-lived, as he felt obliged to resign upon the outbreak of the Mexican War in 1846. Once back in Mississippi he commanded a volunteer regiment, known as the Mississippi Rifles, which participated in the celebrated attack on Monterey. By summer of 1847 Davis had apparently again had enough of the army and resigned. He immediately returned to political life and was reelected, this time as a senator from Mississippi; he resigned from the Senate in 1851, but accepted the position of secretary of war in the cabinet of President Franklin Pierce in 1853. In 1857 he again entered the Senate. Although swept along by the secessionist agitation in the South, he indicated in correspondence that he would have preferred something like Canada's status as a dominion in the British empire.

Because of Abraham *Lincoln's antislavery stand and election as president, Mississippi seceded from the Union in 1861. As a dedicated senator from Mississippi, Davis announced its secession in a speech to the Senate and withdrew immediately as senator. On his return to Mississippi he was appointed major general of the state troops and fully expected to become commander of the Southern armies upon the inevitable declaration of war. However, he found himself the compromise candidate at the convention of the seceding states and was appointed president of the Confederacy instead of the military leader he wished to be. "You will see many errors to forgive, many deficiencies to tolerate; but you shall not find in me either want of zeal or fidelity to the cause that is to me the highest hope, and of most enduring affection," he said in his acceptance speech.

Barely two months after his inauguration the Civil War began with the firing on Fort Sumter in Charleston, South Carolina, by Confederate troops on April 12, 1861. Though Davis's own preference would have been to lead the Southern army, he set about organizing the new government and was a

Our present political position has been achieved in a manner unprecedented in the history of nations. It illustrates the American idea that governments rest on the consent of the governed, and that it is the right of the people to alter or abolish them at will whenever they become destructive of the ends for which they were established.

Jefferson Davis's inaugural address as president of the Confederate States, Montgomery, Alabama, February 18, 1861

hardworking executive. He saw it as his duty to win the war and establish Confederate independence. A strict constitutionalist, Davis sought congressional support for his actions, although he usually lost his battles with the states. He lacked finesse in personal politics, was overly sensitive, and viewed political opposition as a personal affront. Davis would often look to religion as consolation and held several days of worship and fasting for the Confederacy.

After the battle of Bull Run in July 1861, Davis thought the South would have an easier time winning the war. In 1862 the South won a series of victories in Virginia, but a lack of coordination did not help it in Mississippi. Davis decided on an offensive in the east instead of reinforcing his troops in Mississippi, but the offensive failed at Gettysburg and the Confederacy was cut in half along the Mississippi. In a last-ditch attempt to turn the tide, Davis dismissed veteran officers and appointed new men. The public reacted angrily, the press denounced him, governors were antagonistic, and his own Congress stopped supporting him. Davis's pride and sensitivity to criticism kept him from making an emotional appeal to the Confederacy.

By April 1865 the Union forces had advanced to Virginia and the Confederate government was forced to flee from Richmond to Danville, Virginia, where Davis gave his last address to the Confederacy. "Animated by the confidence in your spirit and fortitude, which never yet has failed me, I announce to you, fellow-countrymen, that it is my purpose to maintain your cause with my whole heart and soul; that I will never consent to abandon to the enemy one foot of the soil of any one of the states of the Confederacy," he said a day after Richmond fell.

Throughout the Civil War, Davis, always a military man, found himself involved in many disputes with his generals. Even the surrender of General Robert E. *Lee on April 9, 1865, was without his approval. As the war ended Davis fled south, hoping to escape the country, but was captured by federal cavalry.

For two years Davis was a prisoner at Fortress Monroe, Virginia. At first he was placed in irons at the order of the assistant secretary of war; later, after his health failed, he was offered other quarters quite unlike those of a prison. In fact they were so comfortable that his family was permitted to share them. Davis was held in jail for two years without charges being brought against him; government lawyers could find no charge without its technical problems. He was released on bond in 1867 and gradually regained his health but refused to ask for the federal pardon without which he could not serve in the Senate again, although Mississippi wanted him to do so.

In his latter years he was president of an insurance company in Memphis, Tennessee, and wrote *The Rise and Fall of the Confederate Government*. On his gravestone was inscribed, "An American Soldier and Defender of the Constitution. Faithful to all trusts, a martyr to principle. He lived and died the most consistent of America's soldiers and statesmen."

W. C. Davis, *Jefferson Davis: The Man and His Hour*, 1991.
R. H. Sewell, *The House Divided*, 1987.
H. Strode, *Jefferson Davis*, 4 vols., 1955–1966.
S. E. Woodworth, *Jefferson Davis and His Generals*, 1990.

DAVY, SIR HUMPHRY (1778–1829), English chemist. He was born in Penzance, Cornwall, and was educated locally. His wide-ranging interests included writing poetry, making fireworks, and collecting mineral samples.

In 1795, Davy was apprenticed to a surgeon and began the study of moral philosophy, but within a few years discovered that his main interest was in science rather than medicine. He was fortunate in winning the patronage of Davies Gilbert, who found him employment with the "Pneumatic Institute" in Bristol, a research center investigating the potential use of various gases. In 1798, Davy published the results of his investigations on the nature of heat and light.

The work was not without its dangers; in a foolhardy pioneering spirit, Davy acted as guinea pig for his own experiments and nearly killed himself when he discovered the exhilarating consequences of inhaling nitrous oxide the hard way. However, he quickly earned reputations as a scientist of note, and as a gifted conversationalist whose company was much in demand.

In 1801, Davy was appointed assistant lecturer in chemistry at the Royal Institution in London, founded to encourage the application and communication of scientific knowledge for the public benefit. Davy's experiments and a series of very popular lectures brought him to public prominence and he became professor of chemistry at the Institution; in 1803, he was elected a fellow of the Royal Society.

Davy appears to have been the archetype of the absentminded professor, leaving scientific apparatus lying around in a state of great disorder and dipping his fingers in an inkpot whenever he wanted to erase a line of notes. He also had difficulties in restricting himself to a single line of inquiry, often breaking off to take up another research project that had caught his attention. Nevertheless, Davy's work on the chemical composition of electricity broke important new ground. He made significant discoveries about the nature of chlorine and its uses and detected a number of elements, such as sodium, calcium, and magnesium. His teaching skills were widely admired; one of his pupils was Michael *Faraday.

Davy also invented a safety lamp for use in coal mines. Many miners had been killed by explosions of a gas called "fire damp," which could be ignited by contact with a naked flame. Davy's device dramatically reduced this danger and allowed for deeper but safer coal mining.

Davy's name became well known outside England. *Napoleon made a special exception by awarding him the Napoleon Prize while France was still at war with England; he also granted him permission to travel in Europe, where he continued his researches and met leading French scientists.

Davy was knighted in 1812, and later granted a baronetcy. He had refused to patent his safety lamp, sacrificing a potential fortune in order to encourage the rapid adoption of this lifesaver. However, wealth came with his marriage to a rich widow, Mrs. Apreece.

Davy's last important research was on the subject of electro-magnetism, but he also found time to write a book on fly-fishing (illustrated by his own drawings) and become one of the founders of the London Zoo. When he was in his late forties his health seriously weakened and he took up residence in Italy; and died in Switzerland. Through scientific research and teaching he had advanced the wealth of his nation, true to the philosophy he expounded in a letter of 1807: "The wealth of our island may be diminished but the strength of mind of the people cannot easily pass away.... We cannot lose our liberty because we cannot cease to think."

S. Forgan ed., *Science and the Sons of Genius: Studies on Humphry Davy*, 1980.

Hartley, Sir H. *Sir Humphry Davy*, 1966.

D. Knight, *Humphry Davy*, 1992.

A. Treneer, *A Life of Sir Humphry Davy*, 1963.

DEBUSSY, CLAUDE (Achille-Claude; 1862–1918), French composer. He was born in Saint Germain-en-Laye and at the age of ten entered the Paris conservatory, where he studied piano and won second prize at the age of fifteen. Graduating in 1880, he was at once recommended to Nadezhda von Meck, the patroness of Pyotr *Tchaikovsky. He traveled with the baroness as her house pianist, teaching the piano and playing four hands with her children. Debussy traveled all over Italy and Russia with the von Mecks. In Moscow he had an opportunity to study the work of Aleksandr Borodin and Modest Mussorgsky, music that eventually influenced his own creative ideas.

Debussy continued his studies and won several important prizes, including the coveted Grand Prix in Rome in 1884 as a result of his cantata *L'Enfant prodigue.* The composer was not thrilled with the prize: "All my pleasure vanished. I saw in a flash the boredom, the vexations inevitably incidental to the slightest official recognition. Besides, I felt I was no longer free." In the late 1880s Debussy was friendly with a group of French Symbolist poets, especially Stéphane Mallarmé. The composer also became fascinated with the oriental music performed at the Paris Exposition in 1889. His continuous contact with the Impressionist movement and the influence of modern French poetry shaped Debussy's mature style, in which formal structure becomes inferior to mood, atmosphere, and color. In 1890 Debussy wrote what was to become one of his most famous piano compositions, the *Suite bergamasque,* which includes the captivating "Claire de lune." In 1892 Debussy began to compose two of his most important works, the orchestral *Prélude à l'Après-midi d'un faune,* which was premiered two years later in Paris, and the opera *Pelléas et Mélisande.* Of *Prélude* the composer Ferruccio Busoni said, "It is like a beautiful sunset; it fades as one looks at it." Debussy also continued to create in many other musical genres, including chamber and vocal music.

In 1902, a decade after the composer began working on it, *Pelléas et Mélisande* was premiered at the Opéra Comique in Paris. There were many difficulties leading up to the opening night, including the opposition of Maurice Maeterlinck, on whose play the opera is based. The playwright opposed the composer on the choice of the leading soprano. Maeterlinck suggested his own mistress, Georgette Leblanc, while Debussy opted for the American soprano with the less-than-perfect French accent, Mary Garden. After the premiere, with Garden several critics panned the new work for its "decadent characteristics." The opera crossed the Atlantic six years later for its initial New York performance but reached the Metropolitan Opera House only in 1925. Debussy wrote no other complete dramatic work for the stage.

After *Pelléas,* some of Debussy's more important compositions of that period were *La Mer* and the orchestral suite *Images. La Mer,* today a popular French orchestral composition, was not greeted favorably on its appearance. Critics wrote that "for perfect enjoyment of this music there is no attitude of mind more to be recommended than the passive, unintelligent rumination of the typical amateur of the mid-Victorian era." At this time Debussy was conducting his own compositions all over Europe and was about to tour America in 1914. This plan did not materialize, however, because of his deteriorating health, and Debussy eventually succumbed to cancer.

Debussy had many detractors in his time. His new style was not favorably accepted by his peers, by the critics, or by the public. French composer Gabriel Fauré said, for example, after the premiere of *Pelléas,* "If that was music, I have never understood what music was." Francis Poulenc, on the other hand, admitted that "Debussy has always remained my favorite composer after [Wolfgang Amadeus] *Mozart. I could not do without his music, it is my oxygen." Debussy himself said that "a century of aeroplanes deserves its own music. As there are no precedents, I must create anew," which is exactly what he did. He is considered the creator of musical impressionism, in spite of the fact that he himself denied his role in this movement. In the words of musicologist Nicolas Slonimsky, Debussy "like [Claude] Monet in painting and Mallarmé in poetry created a style peculiarly sensitive to musical mezzotint from a palette of half-lit, delicate colors. To accomplish the desired effect, he introduced many novel technical devices. He made use of the oriental pentatonic scale for exotic evocations, and of the whole-tone scale (which he did not invent, however; samples of its use are found in [the works of Mikhail]

Glinka and [Franz] Liszt); he emancipated dissonance, so that unresolved discords freely followed one another; he also revived the archaic practice of consecutive perfect intervals (particularly fifths and fourths). In Debussy's formal constructions, traditional development is abandoned and the themes themselves are shortened and rhythmically sharpened; in instrumentation, the role of individual instruments is greatly enhanced and the dynamic range subtilized."
F. Lesure and R. Nichols eds., *Debussy, Letters*, 1987.
R. Nichols, *Debussy Revisited*, 1992.
A. B. Wenk, *Claude Debussy and Twentieth Century Music*, 1983.

DE GAULLE, CHARLES-ANDRÉ-MARIE-JOSEPH   SEE GAULLE, CHARLES-ANDRÉ-MARIE-JOSEPH DE.

DEMOSTHENES (384 – 322 B.C.E.), Athenian statesman and the most famous of the Greek orators. His father was a well-to-do manufacturer of weapons and his mother was of Scythian stock, evoking the taunts of his political opponents, who called him a barbarian. Demosthenes's father died when he was seven years old and his guardians wasted his inheritance through bad administration. At the age of eighteen Demosthenes set out to recover his patrimony, which proved a difficult task. He studied rhetoric under Isaeus, a famous orator and speech writer. Various stories were later told of Demosthenes's efforts to overcome a stammer and a weak voice. He allegedly would go to the seashore to practice speaking with his mouth full of pebbles, trying to overpower the sound of the waves; or he would run up a hill while reciting poetry to perfect his breathing. He also studied law and history and is said to have copied Thucydides's *History* eight times to improve his language and historical knowledge. Then, after two years of litigation, Demosthenes obtained the very little that remained of his inheritance. He now became a *logographos* (professional speech writer) for litigants, a profession from which he made a handsome income for many years. Sometimes he even wrote the speeches for the accuser as well as for the accused.

Demosthenes entered politics around 355 B.C.E. His first appearance before the *ecclesia* (popular assembly) was in 354 B.C.E., when he delivered a speech on the *symmories* (the naval taxation boards). This was occasioned by the rumor that the Persian king intended to attack Greece. Demosthenes argued that Athens was not prepared for war and advocated the strengthening of its naval power. The following year, he criticized the policy of the financial administrator, Eubulus, who was economizing on military preparations.

The attack by *Philip II of Macedonia (352 B.C.E.) marked a turning point in Demosthenes's political career; from then on he became convinced that Philip of Macedonia was not only the true rival of Athens in the north but also constituted a menace

---

SOME OF DEMOSTHENES'S SAYINGS

- I have a bone in my throat and cannot speak (after being bribed not to speak).
- The easiest thing of all is to deceive oneself; for what a man wishes he generally believes is true.
- Small opportunities are often the beginning of great enterprises.
- The three most intractable beasts: the owl, the serpent, and the people.
- Action! action! action! (on being asked what three things make the perfect orator).
- There is one safeguard known generally to the wise, which is an advantage to us all, but especially to democracies as against despots, and that is suspicion.

---

to freedom and the old political order in Greece. In 351 B.C.E. he delivered his first speech against Philip, the *First Philippic*, and was vindicated in 349 B.C.E. when Philip attacked Olynthus, which only seven years earlier had seceded from the Second Athenian League to ally itself with Macedonia. In his three *Olynthiac* speeches (349 – 348 B.C.E.), Demosthenes urged the dispatch of a strong Athenian force to Olynthus to fight Philip. He argued that the defense of Olynthus was the defense of Athens and that it was better to fight the enemy while it was still far away. However, when a force was eventually sent it was insufficient and too late; Olynthus was captured and destroyed. Demosthenes now became an even stronger opponent of Eubulus. Meanwhile, Philip consolidated his position in central Greece by defeating Phocis.

In 347 B.C.E. Demosthenes served as a member of the *boule* (government council). In 346 B.C.E. he was a member of the ten-member delegation sent to Philip to negotiate peace (another leading member was Aeschines). In the first debate in Athens, Demosthenes supported ratification of the peace treaty but later, when it became known that Philip was in a position to occupy Phocis, he changed his mind. Athens, however, could clearly do nothing to help Phocis, and Aeschines's speech for approval of the treaty carried the day.

Demosthenes was convinced that Philip was unreliable and his policy after 346 B.C.E. aimed at annulment of the peace agreement as well as the destruction of Aeschines. He failed in his prosecution of Aeschines, who countercharged Timarchus, Demosthenes's associate. In 344 B.C.E. Demosthenes demonstrated against Philip in the Peloponnese and when Macedonian ambassadors protested in Athens, Demosthenes delivered his *Second Philippic*. In 343 B.C.E., in his speech *On the False*

Embassy, Demosthenes renewed his attack on Aeschines, whom he accused as being responsible for the disgraceful peace of 346 B.C.E.; Aeschines narrowly escaped condemnation. In his effort to renew the war against Philip, Demosthenes's mission to the Peloponnese in 342 B.C.E. to find allies was a failure. In his *Third and Fourth Philippics* he advocated war with the aid of Persia. It was now quite clear that peace could not be maintained for long; in 340 B.C.E. Philip attacked Byzantium and Perinthus and war was declared. Demosthenes was now in control in Athens. Thebes joined Athens, but the combined Greek armies were defeated by the Macedonians' phalanx at Chaeronea in 338 B.C.E.

Demosthenes's policy had failed and he himself was said to have fled from Chaeronea but he retained his influence and he was chosen to read the funeral oration for the fallen at Chaeronea and served on the committee for the fortification of the city. In 336 B.C.E., Ctesiphon proposed awarding Demosthenes a golden crown for service to the country; Aeschines charged Ctesiphon with making an illegal proposal. However, the death of Philip caused an indefinite delay of the trial. Philip's son, *Alexander (the Great), was quick to show that he surpassed his father. Thebes, in whose revolt Demosthenes was involved, was destroyed and the Greek states were forced to submit to Alexander's will. Not much is known of Demosthenes in these years. In 330 B.C.E. however, Aeschines renewed his attack on Demosthenes, who replied in a brilliant speech in which he surveyed and defended his policy over the previous twenty years. Demosthenes asserted that he had always acted and spoken in the best interests of Greece and Athens; he took full responsibility for the battle of Chaeronea but argued that the outcome was not his fault. His policy had been correct though unsuccessful. Demosthenes's oratory was so impressive that Aeschines secured less than the minimum vote (a fifth of the jury), and he retired to Rhodes.

After Alexander's death, Demosthenes was active in preparations for war against Macedonia but at the battle of Crannon (322 B.C.E.) the Macedonians were again victorious and Demosthenes was subsequently condemned to death. He fled from Athens but, seeing he could not escape his pursuers, committed suicide by taking poison.

Opinion on Demosthenes's policies and significance has changed over the ages; his excellent service to his country was acknowledged within his lifetime. After his death, a statue of him was erected on which was inscribed: "Had his power been equal to his genius, Greece would not have submitted to tyranny." Demosthenes has generally been lauded as a champion of freedom and independence in defiance of tyranny and his orations have served as an inspiration to those pursuing liberty. The wisdom of his policies, however, has been questioned. On the one hand, his advice to oppose Philip in the north was not justified strategically and, on the other hand, his efforts to unite Greece were impractical in view of the intra-Greek feuds. But while opinions vary on Demosthenes the statesman, he has been unanimously recognized as the finest Greek orator. Sixty-one speeches, private and public, have been attributed to Demosthenes but of these, several attributions are spurious. He took great pains in preparing his speeches, which are not bound by any rigid rules; the style employed was simple or lofty as the case demanded, and the narrative and arguments are almost always clear and impressive.

W. W. Jaeger, *Demosthenes: The Origins and Growth of his Policy*, 1938.

G. A. Kennedy, *The Art of Persuasion in Greece*, 1963.

DESCARTES, RENÉ (1596–1650), French philosopher, mathematician, and scientist. Through the application of his definitive method of inquiry, he made contributions to theoretical physics, physiology, and astronomy and invented analytical coordinate geometry.

Descartes was born to a noble family at La Haye in Touraine. Both his father and elder brother were councilors in the *parlement* (law court) of Brittany. His formal education began at the age of about ten when he entered the prominent Jesuit *collège* (secondary school) at La Flèche. It was during his five years at the *collège* that he became enchanted by the conclusiveness and rigor of mathematics, though somewhat skeptical as to the value of existing methods of inquiry.

Descartes was a sickly child, suffering from a pulmonary complaint inherited from his mother. He was always pale and coughing and his Jesuit masters permitted him to study in bed until late morning. He found these early quiet moments so conducive to meditation and focused inquiry that he became an avowed late riser.

FROM THE WRITINGS OF RENÉ DESCARTES

- It is not enough to have a good mind. The main thing is to use it well.
- I must inquire whether there is a God as soon as the occasion presents itself; and if I find that there is a God, I must also inquire whether he may be a deceiver; for without a knowledge of these two truths I do not see that I can ever be certain of anything.
- Thinking is an attribute of the soul, and here I discover what properly belongs to myself. This alone is inseparable from me. I am, I exist. This is certain.
- There is nothing so strange and so unbelievable that it has not been said by one philosopher or another.

He graduated from La Flèche in 1614 and within another two years had obtained a degree in law from the University of Poitiers, in all likelihood to satisfy his father. This was his last association with any academic institution, either as pupil or teacher.

Wanting to experience the world at large, Descartes chose to pursue a career as a soldier, which was not unusual for younger sons of the upper social classes. To his disappointment, he found the routine mostly unstimulating and mainly an excuse for debauchery, though he enjoyed fencing and riding. Indeed he even wrote a text on fencing which, as was his style, examined its theoretical aspects. Then, around 1618, he met and befriended Isaac Beeckman, an eminent mathematician who became his mentor. Descartes ended his military career soon after, evidently never having to draw his sword in battle.

Remaining in Germany, Descartes zealously applied himself to elaborating the concepts that he and Beeckman had generated in their discussions. By the winter of 1619, however, he had closeted himself in a small room in Neuburg, emotionally and creatively exhausted by the intensity of his efforts. There, on the eve of Saint Martin's Day (10 November), he had three dreams that he interpreted as reflecting his inner doubts concerning the worth of his life. The dreams, which he believed were divinely cast, resolved his purpose and revealed to him a holistic and methodical science that it was his destiny to create.

Inspired by these visions, for the next nine years Descartes traveled Europe, observing nature, visiting other men of learning on whom he relied for stimulation, and formulating his method. A man of deep religious convictions, while in Italy he visited the shrine of the Virgin Mary in Loreto to satisfy a vow he had made on the night of his three dreams. Although he wrote little during this period, his reputation in scientific circles grew.

Descartes eventually settled in Holland, where he hoped to avoid the distractions of the frivolous French social life. Entirely devoted to perfecting his method, in 1633 he finished his first book, in which he supported contemporary scientific hypotheses such as the circulation of blood in the body and movement of the earth around the sun. The book was nearing publication when, to Descartes's astonishment, *Galileo was condemned by the Inquisition for similarly reaffirming the Copernican hypothesis. Descartes prudently withdrew his book from the printers.

After a few years' reflection on his near misadventure, Descartes published anonymously his sensational *Discourse on the Method*, taking care to avoid any reference to heretical cosmologies. He wrote with grace and clarity in French rather than Latin, which was the language of learned writing, thereby hoping to make it accessible to all people of intelligence. Over the next decade, Descartes published several other works. To his dismay, however, not all his ideas were welcomed by the religious au-

"Descartes in the Streets of Paris," painting by Chartran

thorities and they never received the official imprimatur for which he longed. Indeed, most of his writings were eventually proscribed by the church.

In 1649 Descartes was invited to Stockholm by Queen *Christina of Sweden to teach her and establish a science academy. At first he was reluctant to live in what he perceived to be a rude and uncivilized society. However, his close friend Pierre Chanut, the French ambassador, eventually persuaded him to accept the invitation. With a sense of foreboding, Descartes tidied up his affairs in Holland and moved north to live with Chanut and his family in the Swedish court. Chanut became ill with pneumonia early in the new year. Descartes, who was weakened by having to instruct the queen at five o'clock in the morning — a detestable hour for someone accustomed to spending his mornings in bed — soon contracted the illness as well. Nine days later, after a course of bleedings recommended by a court physician, Descartes died.

His remains traveled extensively, as he had in life. They were first buried in Sweden but in 1666 they were taken to Paris and reinterred in the Church of Sainte-Geneviève; in 1819 they were relocated to the Church of Saint-Germain. His skull, however, is held in the Musée de l'Homme in Paris.

Descartes is regarded as the founder of modern philosophy. His system was based on a definite method (known after him as Cartesian) and this mathematical method was a clear recognition of the scientific spirit. He pioneered the modern principles of individuality and subjectivity, with the existence of self as the basis of all constructive thought. He posited that the test of truth is the clearness with which it justifies itself to individual reason and formulated the dualistic principle of body and soul moving along parallel lines, with every event in one accompanied by a corresponding event in the other. By this separation he vindicated the purely mechanical nature of physical processes. The basis of his thought is the undeniability of consciousness, exemplified by his most famous dictum, *Cogito ergo sum* (I think, therefore I am), which he considered the basic axiom on which to build certainty. He also reached God through the principle of causality: the existence of God must be postulated as the only explanation for the presence in man of the idea of God, which must have been implanted at birth.

J. Cottingham, *Descartes*, 1986.

M. Grene, *Descartes*, 1985.

P. A. Schouls, *Descartes and the Enlightenment*, 1989.

T. Sorell, *Descartes*, 1987.

DE VALERA, EAMON (1882–1975), Irish nationalist and statesman. De Valera was born in New York City to a Spanish father and an Irish mother. His father died when he was only three and his mother returned to Ireland. Life there was difficult; apart from helping out on the family farm, De Valera often had to walk seven miles to school. Nevertheless he declined his uncle's offer to return to the United States, preferring to complete a degree in mathematics at University College, Dublin, and for a time taught mathematics at schools in Dublin.

Fascinated with the revival of Ireland's native language, De Valera joined the Gaelic League in 1908. He was as yet uninvolved in nationalist politics, but supported the Irish Parliamentary Party, a moderate group advocating self-rule. In 1913, the Gaelic League, along with several other nationally-minded groups including Sinn Féin, merged to form the Irish Volunteers, a vociferous alternative to the Parliamentary Party. Also joining was the Irish Revolutionary Brotherhood (IRB), a republican movement dedicated to armed struggle in attaining Irish independence. The IRB gained rapid ascendancy over the other groups. De Valera was drawn to its uncompromising principles and participated in the abortive Easter Rising of 1916 as battalion commander defending Boland's Mill in Dublin. His cunning military strategy was responsible for over half the British casualties and he was sentenced to death, commuted to life imprisonment only because of his American citizenship. Transferred to Dartmoor prison, he pestered the authorities by organizing his comrades to demand treatment as prisoners of war. A prison strike he organized in 1917 led to his release that same year by the new British government, intent on making a goodwill gesture to the Irish.

At that time, Irish representatives were negotiating terms for a home rule scheme to exclude the predominantly Protestant north. De Valera rejected this and attended a rival Sinn Féin congress demanding total independence. One month after his release he was elected to the British parliament but refused to take his seat, which would have implied acceptance of British rule. He was also elected president of Sinn Féin and of the Volunteers. His proposal that the Irish problem be brought before any peace conference at the end of World War I led to the unfounded suspicion that he was collaborating with the Germans. When papers containing a planned address to the peace conference were found in his possession in 1918, De Valera was returned to prison in England; from there he was re-elected to Parliament on behalf of Sinn Féin. Winning 73 of the 105 seats allotted to Ireland, the Sinn Féin delegates still at liberty chose to form their own parliament, the Dáil. De Valera escaped from Lincoln prison using a master key he received baked in a cake and went in disguise to the United States. Upon returning to Ireland in 1920 he was elected president of the Dáil.

The British government now perceived him as a moderate leader with whom they could negotiate their proposal that the north be separated from the south. De Valera, however, rejected this proposal and again refused to take his seat in Parliament. A new British proposal of dominion status similar to that enjoyed by Commonwealth members was also rejected by De Valera despite exhortations by many of his countrymen to accept. De Valera was unwilling to compromise on two principles: the unity of the island and republican government. He responded with a radical plan of his own, external association, by which Ireland would become an independent state but continue to maintain ties with the Commonwealth.

To provide greater bargaining power for the Irish, the Dáil redefined De Valera's role as president of Ireland. At the same time, Irish Republican Army militants took advantage of a British truce to import arms in case of rebellion. In an attempt to relieve this potentially explosive situation, British prime minister, David *Lloyd George called a conference to negotiate the island's future. De Valera declined to attend, sending instead a team of negotiators that concluded an agreement granting dominion status to Ireland. The treaty was anathema to De Valera, who opposed even the most nominal bonds with the crown, and a heated ratification debate ensued in the Dáil. Even the cabinet was split, and a disgusted De Valera submitted his resignation in order to form a provisional republican government. The treaty's ratification moved the fledgling Irish Free State toward civil war.

A provisional government was formed by De Valera and the *Cumann na Poblachta* (League of the Republic). Although advocating a peaceful resolution to the crisis, he also joined the republican revolutionaries as a soldier as civil war between the factions flared. De Valera was arrested by the Free State government in 1923 but was released the following year. He now realized that a republic could only be realized through parliamentary means and abandoned armed struggle in favor of political activism to form the Fianna Fáil Party (Soldiers of Destiny). He was elected to the Dáil in 1927 but refused to take the oath of allegiance to the British crown. Finally a compromise was reached; De Valera declared in Gaelic that he was signing the oath as a formality, removed the Bible, and covered the text. De Valera was now opposition leader.

As a result of the 1932 elections, Fianna Fáil formed the government, with De Valera (popularly called "Dev") as prime minister and foreign minister. In that year, his international reputation was confirmed by his presidency of the League of Nations Council and in 1938 he presided over the League of Nations Assembly. At home he abolished the oath of allegiance to the British crown and suspended payment of annuities due to Britain, leading to an economic war between the two countries. In 1937 he sponsored a new constitution changing the name of the Irish Free State to Eire (Ireland), to which the constitution applied "pending the reintegration of national territory." In September 1939, he declared the country's neutrality in World War II, leading to frequent tensions with the British. He was the only world leader to offer condolences to Germany on *Hitler's death, but this was the outcome of formalism rather than any identification. De Valera was an austere leader of intellectual bent and founded the Dublin Institute for Advanced Studies. After the war, support for his party seesawed. He was defeated in 1948 but was again prime minister from 1951 to 1954 and from 1957 to 1959, when he resigned to become president, serving until he was ninety-one in 1973.

J. Bowman, *De Valera and the Ulster Question, 1917–1973*, 1983.

F. P. Longford and T. B. O'Neill, *Eamon De Valera*, 1971.

DEWEY, JOHN (1859–1952), American educator, psychologist, and philosopher renowned for his educational philosophy of "instrumentalism," emphasizing "learning by doing" rather than by memorization of material. Dewey was born on a farm in Burlington, Vermont, and initially studied at the University of Vermont, receiving his bachelor's degree in 1879. For the next three years he taught school in Vermont and in Pennsylvania. From 1882 he did graduate work at Johns Hopkins University, receiving his Ph.D. in 1884. He became an assistant professor of philosophy at the University of Michigan and in 1890 he was appointed chairman of the philosophy department until 1894, when he assumed the chairmanship of the department of

John Dewey

FROM JOHN DEWEY'S WRITINGS

- Change as change is mere flux and lapse; it insults intelligence. Genuinely to know is to grasp a permanent end that realizes itself through changes.
- Old ideas give way slowly for they are more than abstract logical forms and categories. They are habits, predispositions, deeply ingrained attitudes of aversion and preference.
- Intellectually, religious emotions are not creative but conservative. They attach themselves readily to the current view of the world and consecrate it.

philosophy, psychology and pedagogy at the University of Chicago, which he held until 1904.

In 1902 he published *The Child and the Curriculum,* presenting his philosophy of education. He believed that the educational process must begin with and build upon the interests of the child, opportunity must be provided in the classroom experience for the interplay of the child's thinking and doing, for which purpose the school should be organized as a miniature community, and the teacher should be a guide and coworker with the child rather than a mere taskmaster.

From 1904 until his retirement in 1930 he taught as professor of philosophy and education at Columbia University in New York City and remained an emeritus professor there until 1951. In 1919 and again in 1931 he was a lecturer in philosophy and education at the University of Peking in China. In the course of his extensive career, he even found time to serve on national organizations. He was president of the American Psychological Association and later president of the American Philosophical Association. In 1915 he was a founder and first president of the American Association of University Professors and helped organize the American Civil Liberties Union in 1920. The latter activity was related to his philosophy of legal realism, which is based on the belief that inasmuch as the judge plays such an active role in the making of the law, he should be aware of the inevitable social consequence of the decisions he makes. This was in keeping with Dewey's feeling that the true function of philosophy was to solve human problems.

His extensive publications included *The School and Society* (1899), *How We Think* (1909), *The Influence of Darwin on Philosophy and Other Essays in Contemporary Thought* (1910), *Essays in Experimental Logic* (1916), *Human Nature and Conduct* (1922), his classic work *Experience and Nature* (1925), *The Quest for Certainty* (1929), *Philosophy and Civilization* (1931), *Art as Experience* (1934),

Experience and Education (1938), *Freedom and Culture* (1939), and *Problems of Men* (1946).

As a philosopher he favored the pragmatism of William James, from which his theory of "instrumentalism" was derived. Dewey favored progressive education and did much to foster its development through the years. His views were adopted by the progressive movement in education, stressing that education should be student-centered rather than subject-centered, i.e., education through doing.

G. Bullert, *The Politics of John Dewey*, 1983.
S. Morganbesser, ed., *Dewey and His Critics*, 1977.
J. E. Tiles, *Dewey*, 1988.
R. B. Westbrook, *John Dewey and American Democracy*, 1991.

DICKENS, CHARLES (1812–1870), British novelist who achieved an unprecedented popularity in his lifetime and a worldwide reputation. He was one of eight children born to John Dickens, a clerk in the Navy Pay House who, though amiable, was incapable of supporting his family. Much of the material for Dickens's novels was furnished by his own youth; it is often said that his father, for whom he had an exasperated affection, was Mr. Micawber, and his mother, Mrs. Nickleby. The family's poverty necessitated several moves, and in 1816 they settled for a six-year stay in Chatham. These years were to provide the material for many of his books — it was there that Dickens had his first experiences with the school system, that he first saw convicts, and first went to the theater, developing a love for it that was to remain with him all his life.

Although he had some schooling in Chatham and an introduction to the world of books, the family's transfer to Camden Town in 1822 seemed to signal the end of his formal education and the beginning of a less formal and less pleasant education as he wandered aimlessly about the streets of London. Worse was yet to come, however, when he was sent to work in a blacking factory in Hungerford Stairs, pasting labels onto bottles at six shillings a week for a twelve-hour day. He worked there for six months, a period of shame, humiliation, and hopelessness about his future prospects. Despite Dickens's contribution to the family finances, his father was arrested for debt and imprisoned in Marshalsea Prison. Most of the family accompanied their father to jail, but Charles lived outside, joining the family only for breakfast and developing a defiant independence which was to characterize many of the children in his novels; prisons and the fear they inspired were also to figure in many of his books.

A small legacy liberated John Dickens from prison and Charles from his hateful employment. He was once again sent to school and remained there for three years until the family's misfortunes required him to resume working in a solicitor's office in 1827. There he acquired an acquaintance with the law that was also to figure negatively in the novels.

Dickens at work; a photograph taken in 1859

Determined to escape the solicitor's office, Charles studied shorthand and used his newly acquired skill to attain a position as a freelance reporter in the law courts. It was at about this time that he fell in love with Maria Beadness, whose father, a banker, was not prepared to let his daughter become involved with a penniless clerk. His idealizing passion for her, which seems to have been somewhat unfounded, was profound and his shock was great when he encountered her thirty years later and found her as spoiled and vain as she had been as a young girl; later she was to resurface as Dolly Varden in *Barnaby Rudge* and as Dora in *David Copperfield.*

In 1831, Dickens became a reporter on the *Mirror of Parliament*, where his father was also employed, and proving an excellent reporter, he also began working for the *True Sun*, and later the *Morning Chronicle.* He acquired a reputation as one of the best shorthand reporters at Parliament, which did nothing to allay his growing contempt for the legislature, which he saw as "the national dustheap."

Wandering about the streets of the city, he amassed a store of observations about the common life of London; in 1834 he took the pen name Boz and submitted his first sketches for publication in various journals. The sketches were successful and were published in book form. Meanwhile Dickens had become friendly with George Hogarth, editor of the *Evening Chronicle,* and had become engaged to one of his daughters, Catherine. His growing success and popularity enabled them to marry in 1836. He also developed a close relationship with Catherine's sister, Mary, who came to live with them after their marriage but died at the age of eighteen.

In December 1836 Dickens was asked to compose the text for a series of humorous sketches by the popular artist Robert Seymour. When Seymour committed suicide Dickens found himself in a position of control over the series, and was able to demonstrate a remarkable talent for comedy and farce, which he based primarily on caricature, eccentricities of speech, and absurd situations. He was an outstanding success, and the publication of the series as *The Pickwick Papers* made him, at the age of twenty-five, one of England's most famous and popular writers. It also established the serial form as the mode of writing for all his future novels. *Oliver Twist* (1838) began to take shape before *Pickwick* was even completed and introduced a feature which was to characterize all of his writings — use of the novel as a vehicle for social criticism. Although he was not a systematic social or political critic, he continued to exhibit a sympathy for the poor and a contempt for the establishment that figures in the caricatures and satires of his writing.

While *Oliver Twist* was an attack on the workhouses and the conditions of relief for the poor, *Barnaby Rudge* (1840), which appeared after *Nicholas Nickleby* (1839), was inspired by a fear of mob violence stirred by the Birmingham riots of 1839. Dickens also began editing a weekly periodical, *Master Humphrey's Clock,* originally intended to publish sketches, essays and short stories, which eventually became a forum for his own serialized novels. The successors to *Master Humphrey's Clock* — *Household Words* and *All the Year Round* — were notable successes; he continued to work on the latter until his death.

In 1842 Dickens visited the United States for the first time. His criticism of American publishers chilled their reaction to him and he was disappointed with what he saw. *Martin Chuzzlewit* (1843), based in part on his reactions to America, was not a commercial success and Dickens's extravagant spending habits soon brought him into debt. He wrote the Christmas books, *A Christmas Carol* (1843) and *The Chimes* (1844), to amend the situation, and moved his family briefly to Marseilles and Genoa in order to save money. He missed London, however, despite his ambivalence toward the city of poverty, crime, and disease; by 1845 he had returned. *Dombey and Son* (1848), written partially in Lausanne, was the first of his books to deal with the evils of society, such as class distinctions, rather than personal sins, such as cruelty or selfishness. It was followed by four successful novels: *David Copperfield* (1849–1850) the partially autobiographical classic which was Dickens's favorite; *Bleak House* (1853), reflecting his legal experience; *Hard Times* (1854), a critique of Benthamite principles; and *Little Dorritt,* inspired by outrage at government malfunctioning and irresponsibility and memories of Marshalsea prison.

It was a shock to the public when, in 1858, the breakdown of their beloved novelist's marriage be-

FROM CHARLES DICKENS'S NOVELS

- I wants to make your flesh creep. (Joe the fat boy)
- "You must not tell us what the soldier, or any other man, said, sir," interposed the judge. "It's not evidence."
- Wery glad to see you sir and hope our acquaintance may be a long 'un, as the gen'l'm'n said to the fi' pound note. (Sam Weller)

Pickwick Papers

- Oliver Twist has asked for more.
- "If the law supposes that," said Mr. Bumble, "the law is an ass."

Oliver Twist

- Barkis is willing
- Something will turn up. (Mr. Micawber)
- Annual income twenty pounds, annual expenditure nineteen nineteen six, result happiness. Annual income twenty pounds, annual expenditure twenty pound ought and six — result, misery. (Mr. Micawber)
- We're so very 'umble. (Uriah Heep)

David Copperfield

- It was the best of times. It was the worst of times.
- It is a far, far better thing that I do, than I have ever done; it is a far, far better rest that I go to than I have ever known.

A Tale of Two Cities

came public knowledge. Dickens had become increasingly estranged from Catherine, notwithstanding the birth of ten children, and his passion for a young actress, Ellen Ternan, signaled the final break.

His last completed novels were *A Tale of Two Cities* (1859), *Great Expectations* (1861), and *Our Mutual Friend* (1864); *The Mystery of Edwin Drood* was left unfinished. During the 1860s Dickens gave public readings of his work, which greatly appealed to his love of theatricality. He participated in three series of readings, the last between 1864 and 1867, during which time he became very ill. Offered an American tour in the winter of 1867–1868, he accepted, despite the dangers to his health and warnings from doctors and friends. Upon his return to England he again became ill but the readings continued to be an obsession and the chronic

nervousness to which they contributed seems to have finally killed him suddenly. He was buried in Westminster Abbey, and his grave was kept open for three days while admirers came to pay their final respects.
P. Ackroyd, *Dickens*, 1990.
F. Kaplan, *Dickens*, 1988.

DIDEROT, DENIS (1713–1784), French encyclopedist, philosopher, satirist, and playwright. Born in Langues, where he received his early schooling from Jesuit priests, he completed his education in Paris (master of arts, 1732). While in Paris Diderot became interested in literature and philosophy and established a friendship with the philosopher Jean-Jacques *Rousseau.

Diderot began translating the works of Anthony A. Cooper, third earl of Shaftesbury, and in 1745 published a free translation of Shaftesbury's *Inquiry Concerning Virtue*. His own original *Pensées philosophiques*, published the following year, contained novel anti-Christian notions and was heavily influenced by Shaftesbury's ideas.

In 1745 the publisher Andre Le Breton asked Diderot to undertake the translation into French of Ephraim Chambers's *Cyclopaedia, or Universal Dictionary of Arts and Sciences*. He began work on this task with the mathematician Jean d'Alembert, but they significantly changed the nature of the publication with the help of the contributors they enlisted. The first of the twenty-eight volumes of the *Encyclopédie, ou Dictionnaire raisonné des Sciences, des Arts et des Métiers*, which was published in 1751, was a wide-ranging revolutionary manifestation of the enlightened philosophy of rationalism; the *Encyclopédie* was ultimately an immense success. In 1758 d'Alembert resigned following Rousseau's attack on his article on Geneva. Diderot continued his work on the *Encyclopédie* despite this and other obstacles, but he suffered a severe blow in 1764 when he learned that Le Breton had secretly censored his proofs.

Throughout the years of his work on the *Encyclopédie*, Diderot produced numerous philosophical writings, only a few of which were published during his lifetime. In these works, Diderot expounded the development of his materialist philosophy and presented his theory of evolution based on superior adaptation. The dissemination of these ideas caused great concern to both church and state, in particular the publication of Diderot's *Lettres sur les aveugles*, with its proposals for teaching the blind to read by touch, which preceded the work of Louis *Braille by a century. This essay emphasized human independence and revealed an underlying doctrine of material atheism which resulted in Diderot's arrest and imprisonment at Vincennes for three months in 1749.

At the same time Diderot wrote short stories, novels, and plays. His novels, such as *Jacques le Fataliste* and *Le Neveu de Rameau*, both of which were published posthumously, were based on his

FROM THE WORKS OF DIDEROT

- What has not been examined impartially has not been well examined. Skepticism is therefore the first step toward truth.
- Only God and some few rare geniuses can keep forging ahead into novelty.
- In order to get as much fame as one's father one has to be much more able than he.
- Posterity for a philosopher is what the other world is for the religious man.
- Anyone who takes it on himself, on his own authority, to break a bad law, thereby authorizes everyone else to break the good ones.
- There is less harm to be suffered in being mad among madmen than in being sane all by oneself.
- Watch out for the fellow who talks about putting things in order; this means getting other people under his control.

personal experiences and vigorously satirized contemporary society. His work analyzing art and artists at annual art exhibitions and the salons of Paris, and especially his *Essai sur la peinture*, established his reputation as a renowned art critic for future generations.

Following the completion of the *Encyclopédie* in 1772, Diderot was dependent upon the patronage of *Catherine the Great of Russia, who bought his library in Paris, appointing him salaried librarian. In 1773 Diderot visited the Russian monarch in Saint Petersburg and remained there for five months. During this period his previous enthusiasm for Catherine's enlightened despotism waned and his revolutionary opposition to such philosophy was evident in his *Observations sur les instructions sur Sa Majesté imperiale aux députés*. Diderot returned to Paris and settled in the house which Catherine had put at his disposal. Here he spent his final years and, old and ailing, he gradually withdrew from society. His final work was published in 1778 bearing the title *Essai sur les règnes de Claude et de Néron*, more popularly known as the *Essai sur Sénèque*.

Diderot is remembered for the originality of contributions in the fields of philosophy, fiction, art criticism, and scientific speculation. His desire to further knowledge and a qualified faith in the progress of the human mind were the motivating forces behind his greatest achievement, the French *Encyclopédie,* which became an influential organ of radical revolutionary criticism in the eighteenth century.

L. Crocker, *Diderot, the Embattled Philosopher*, 1966.
P. N. Furback, *Diderot: A Critical Biography*, 1992.
A. M. Wilson, *Diderot: The Testing Years, 1713–1759*, 1957.

DISRAELI, BENJAMIN, Earl of Beaconsfield (1804–1881), English politician and novelist. Although of Italian-Jewish extraction, Disraeli was baptized into the Church of England, clearing an obstacle barring his entry into English civic life and upper class society.

Disraeli, who supplemented his education through extensive reading in his father's library, was educated at several private schools but felt isolated due to his background and exotic looks. At seventeen he was apprenticed to a firm of attorneys but within a few years turned his back on the legal profession. Differences with his parents, especially his mother, whom he found lacking in affection, and a constant awareness of the social disadvantages of his birth, filled him with a desire for fame and fortune. He bankrupted himself in rash share speculation and helped promote a Tory newspaper that quickly failed.

In 1826 Disraeli attained notoriety with the publication of his novel *Vivian Grey*; deeply hurt by negative reviews, he suffered a mental breakdown soon afterward but recovered by 1830. Known as a dandy in London, he cut a flamboyant figure in fashionable salon society and tried to gain entry into Parliament, standing as a Radical and as a Tory on separate occasions, an adaptability that did not produce a victory. Consolation came in a liaison with Lady Henrietta Sykes.

A line drawing of Disraeli from the 1830's, portraying him as a fashionable dandy

BENJAMIN DISRAELI'S WIT

- Mr. Gladstone has not a single redeeming defect. He is honest in the most odious sense of the word.
- It is well known what a middle man is: he is a man who bamboozles one party and plunders the other.
- Read no history — only biography, for that is life without theory.
- It is much easier to be critical than correct.
- There is no waste of time in life like that of making explanations.
- Youth is a blunder; manhood is struggle; old age a regret.
- It is the fashion to style the present moment an extraordinary crisis.
- Variety is the mother of enjoyment.
- Nature has given us two ears but only one mouth.
- My idea of an agreeable person is a person who agrees with me.

It may have been through Lady Henrietta that his opportunity came to enter the service of leading Tory politician Lord Lyndhurst; once the Tories agreed to support him, election was assured and in 1837 he won a seat.

Having discarded Lady Sykes, Disraeli was free to find a wife able to offer emotional support, money to pay his heavy debts, and a dose of respectability. He found all these qualities in Mary Anne Wyndham-Lewis, widow of a Tory member of parliament. She was twelve years his senior and, as he later admitted, his motives for marrying her were not romantic, yet a singular devotion developed between them. She was not his intellectual equal; but the stability she brought to his life was far more valuable, and in him she found a hero to worship.

Prime Minister Sir Robert Peel disappointed Disraeli by not giving him a ministerial post and he became leader of a small rebel group of Tory members of parliament known as "Young England."

In 1846, in cooperation with Lord George Bentinck, Disraeli orchestrated the downfall of Peel's administration. With Lord George's death a few years later, Disraeli became the most powerful figure in his party. With the help of the Bentinck family he purchased the 750–acre Hughenden estate. He could now set himself up as a country gentleman and acquire a social standing appropriate to the political role he saw himself assuming: defender of the aristocratic principle of government.

In 1852 came the first brief taste of power as chancellor of the exchequer in Lord Derby's government. Although defended with customary brilliance, his budget did not elicit the support of the House of Commons. Disraeli's arguments were de-

molished by W. E. *Gladstone in the first bout of what would become a long, often acrimonious conflict. The government fell and Gladstone took over Disraeli's ministry.

Fame brought him wealth in a surprising way. An eccentric old woman in Torquay began a correspondence with him in 1851; she made him a beneficiary in her will and her death in 1863 brought him £30,000, greatly mitigating the consequences of continual personal financial mismanagement. Fashionable clubs finally decided he was welcome and, most satisfying of all, Queen *Victoria invited him to Windsor Castle, deeply moved by his heartfelt obituary of Prince Albert.

In 1868, Tory leader Lord Derby was forced to retire. Disraeli was fresh from the triumph of having piloted through Parliament a significant extension of the electorate; he had seized upon and made his own one of the opposition's most popular causes. The obvious candidate for prime minister was this time not disappointed. Victoria was especially pleased, as the good impression he had made earlier was reinforced by his chivalrous manner and his flattery of her.

Disraeli's minority government soon fell. He once more confronted Gladstone as leader of the opposition but also found time for writing. In 1870 he published *Lothair*, a best-selling novel set against a background of European religious and nationalist tension, with aristocrats again its heroes.

In 1874 the Tories won a large majority in the general election and Disraeli assumed the post of prime minister. His government's notable achievements included public health and housing legislation and the 1878 Treaty of Berlin, a major foreign policy achievement that defused the threat of war between Britain and Russia. Disraeli showed great foresight in securing Britain's stake in the Suez Canal; the bestowal on the queen of the title Empress of India (1877) was another instance of adroit diplomacy. In 1876 the queen honored him with a peerage and he took the title Lord Beaconsfield.

On the debit side the country became involved in several costly colonial wars. A futile intervention in Afghanistan provided ample ammunition for Disraeli's most hated opponent, Gladstone. Finally, the onset of an industrial slump played a key role in Tory electoral defeat in 1880.

Disraeli retired to Hughenden, while still remaining active in the House of Lords and on the aristocratic social round. He returned to his writing and enjoyed further success; until overtaken by fatal illness, he had even begun a satirical novel portraying Gladstone. In March 1881, sensing the end approaching, he still felt it important to correct proofs of his last speech in the House of Lords for the Hansard record of debates, determined that, "I will not go down to posterity talking bad grammar." He died the following month. Victoria wept when she heard the news, and political friends and foes alike regretted the demise of a man who had made such a substantial and colorful contribution to civic and literary life.

R. Blake, *Disraeli*, 1966.
R. W. Davis, *Disraeli*, 1976
W. F. Monypenny and G.E. Buckle, *Life of Disraeli*, 2 vols., 1929.
J. R. Vincent, *Disraeli*, 1990.

DOMINIC, SAINT (Domingo de Guzmán; c. 1170–1221), Spanish religious founder of the Dominican order. Dominic, probably a scion of the patrician Guzmán family, was born in Calaruega in old Castile, Spain. Before his birth his mother dreamt that she would give birth to a dog bearing a torch that would set the world aflame. Her premonition was interpreted as accurate: Dominic revitalized the church in a critical period during which heretics exploited the unscrupulous behavior of clergymen to their advantage. His teachings and personal example made him the object of universal veneration during his lifetime. Like his two brothers, Dominic attended the college of Palencia, then staffed by the most eminent Spanish theologians. He was a diligent student, who at fourteen already adopted an ascetic regimen, refusing wine and sleeping on the floor. Crowds flocked to the local church to hear him sing in the choir, but he was best known for his charitable endeavors. While he was twice prevented from selling himself to redeem Christians from Saracen slave dealers, he did sell his richly annotated books and donated the money to charity. Upon ordination in 1195 Dominic was appointed a canon of Osma, his native diocese, and rose rapidly in the church hierarchy.

With the appointment of Diego d'Azevedo as bishop in 1200, Dominic became his aide. In 1203 King Alphonso VIII of Castile sent Diego and Dominic to negotiate a marriage for his son. On their way north, the two spent some time in Toulouse, where Dominic first encountered the Albigensians, a heretical sect advocating fanatical asceticism culminating in suicide. Unlike his contemporaries, Dominic rejected force to counter the heretics. Although the clergy acted otherwise, he believed that asceticism was a fundamental tenet of the church and proposed himself as an example of true Christian asceticism. Donning shabby clothes he walked the streets barefoot, flailing himself with a heavy iron chain, yet all the time smiling and singing hymns. Doting crowds eagerly attended his debates with the Albigensians even though these sometimes lasted as long as eight days. Dominic's vast erudition and sparkling humor so unnerved the heretics that they twice threw his notes into a fire. Miraculously these survived the flames, further enhancing Dominic's reputation.

After Diego's death in 1207 Dominic was offered the bishopric. He declined, preferring to engage in missionary work. He grew a beard to disguise himself for a planned mission to Tartary, but because the problems faced by the church at home were no less troublesome the mission was canceled; however, Dominic kept the distinctive beard. He then planned to organize reconverted Albigensians and his rapidly growing following into a monastic order of preachers. While Simon de Montfort organized a brutal crusade against the Albigensians to avenge the murder of a papal legate by the count of Toulouse (they were eventually annihilated, as was the unique troubadour culture of Provence), Dominic favored compassion to draw dissenters back to the fold. Legend depicts him racing through the ravaged streets of Béziers, cross in hand, pleading with Simon's troops for the lives of the apostates.

Dominic's new order was first established in Toulouse and a convent for women was established in Prouille. To prepare his devotees for their mission, Dominic encouraged them to attend university; he also accumulated an extensive library. The Order of Friars Preacher, commonly known as the Dominicans, was officially recognized by Pope Honorius III in 1216. Not content with the narrow confines of Provence, Dominic aspired to extend his mission to the leading intellectual centers of Christendom. Only eight friars were kept in Toulouse; the majority were sent to establish missions in Paris, Bologna, and Spain, where they were similarly successful. In 1219 there were thirty brothers in Paris; by 1224 the number had increased to one hundred and twenty. In a short time Dominican missionaries had spread as far afield as Morocco, Norway, and, nine days after Dominic's death, Oxford. Dominic insisted that his order maintain its poverty, and often ripped up deeds of land bequeathed to it. Rather than have his friars touch money, he proposed the appointment of business managers for each monastery, but in keeping with the democratic spirit of the order, his proposal was rejected. The Dominicans, as zealous defenders of the church, were also prominent in staffing the Inquisition.

Even in his lifetime Dominic was the focus of cultic veneration; legends spread crediting him with numerous miracles, among them the resurrection of the dead. The devotion of the rosary was ascribed to a revelation of the Virgin Mary to him. Dominic was buried in Bologna; his tomb was later adorned by *Michelangelo. At Dominic's canonization (1234), Pope Gregory IX declared that he doubted his saintliness no more than he doubted that of *Peter and *Paul. The feast of Saint Dominic is celebrated on August 4.

B. Jarrett, *Life of St. Dominic*, 1924.
F. C. Lehner ed., *Saint Dominic: Biographical Documents*, 1961.
M. H. Vicaire, *History of St. Dominic*, 2 vols., 1964.

DOMITIAN, TITUS FLAVIUS DOMITIANUS (51–96), Roman emperor; son of Vespasian. Little is known of his youth, but after his father was proclaimed emperor civil war broke out in Rome and Domitian's life was in danger. His father was still in Judea putting down the Jewish revolt, his uncle Sabinus was killed, and he escaped death with difficulty. However, when Vitellius, his father's rival,

ABOUT DOMITIAN

At the beginning of his reign Domitian would spend hours alone every day catching flies — believe or not — and stabbing them with a needle-sharp pen. Once on being asked whether anyone was closeted with the emperor, Vivius Crispus wittily answered, "No, not even a fly."...Domitian presented many extravagant entertainments. Beside the usual two-horse chariot races, he staged a couple of battles, one for infantry, one for cavalry; a sea-fight in the Colosseum; wild beast hunts; gladiatorial shows by torchlight in which women as well as men took part. A lake was dug at his orders close to the Tiber, surrounded with seats and used for almost full-scale naval battles which he watched, even in heavy rain.

Suetonius, *The Twelve Caesars*

was killed Domitian ruled on his father's behalf until Vespasian arrived. During the reigns of his father and his elder brother, Titus, he played no part in government apart from being named consul on a number of occasions. When Titus died childless in 81 Domitian became emperor, determined to secure the frontiers of the empire and win the military glory he had been denied under his father and brother. Domitian's military successes extended the frontier, which he fortified from the river Main to the River Neckar; he took the surname Germanicus and celebrated his triumph.

Late in 85 the Roman governor of Moesia, a country in the newly conquered region, was defeated and killed, and the situation was sufficiently critical to warrant the presence of the emperor himself. Domitian found it expedient to divide Moesia into two provinces, Upper and Lower, and to strengthen his troops there. He apparently thought the war was over and returned to Rome to celebrate a triumph, but sometime later, probably in 87, the Roman army was defeated and its commander killed by Decebalus, ruler of the Dacians, a people in an area corresponding to modern Romania. Domitian was compelled to return and restore order in the Roman army, and in 88 the Romans won a crushing victory over Decebalus, who was given formal recognition as king and received a subsidy. In the following years Domitian conducted several wars in central Europe and, despite a number of reverses, these wars — in which he himself often participated — served to strengthen Roman positions along the frontiers from the Black Sea to the Rhine.

Domitian carried out expensive building operations in Rome, including a palace on the Palatine, a new temple to Jupiter on the Capitol, a temple to Jupiter Custos on the Quirinal, and his own luxurious villa in the Alban hills. Debt continued to increase because of the increase in legionary pay, the prolonged wars, and Domitian's generosity to the people. To make up the necessary funds, Domitian enforced extensive tax collection and instituted efficient provincial administration.

Domitian was consul ten times and allowed himself to be called *dominus et deus*, thus approaching deification. Some of his actions aroused strong senatorial opposition but Domitian ignored them enrolling many new men from the equestrian class and the provinces in the Senate. The revolt by the governor of Upper Germany in 88, though quickly suppressed, was a turning point. Domitian became suspicious, leading to accusations of high treason against innocent persons and real plotters alike. Philosophers, especially Stoics and Cynics, whose teachings on the ideal ruler were directed against the existing regime, were twice banished from Italy. Many of the leading aristocracy were executed, and a reign of terror began.

In 95 Domitian executed Flavius Clemens, whose sons had been Domitian's intended heirs. It now seemed that no one was safe from his suspicions and in 96 two praetorian prefects successfully carried out a plot to have Domitia, the emperor's wife, and Domitian murdered. The Senate immediately expressed its hatred of him with the decree that his official *acti* be annulled, his statues destroyed, and his name erased from inscriptions.

B. W. Henderson, *Five Roman Emperors*, 1927.

DOSTOYEVSKY, FYODOR MIKHAYLOVICH
(1821–1881), Russian writer. Dostoyevsky entered the Saint Petersburg military engineering school when he was sixteen, but upon graduation in 1844 he resigned his commission to devote himself to writing. Two years later his first novel, *Poor Folk*, was published.

Dostoyevsky next published *The Double* in 1846, but this psychological portrait was not as well received as *Poor Folk*. His subsequent writings, in which can be seen the themes and directions of his later works, fared no better until he began writing *Netochka Nezvanova* in 1849. However, no more than three long episodes had appeared when he was arrested for conspiracy against the government and kept in a fortress for eight months before being sentenced. He received eight years hard labor in Siberia, commuted by the Czar to four years, after which he was to serve in the army. But the "conspirators" were informed that they had been sentenced to death, and were led out to face the firing squad in groups. Only when the first group was actually facing the squad were the real sentences read to them. This macabre and cruel torture had an effect on Dostoyevsky that he never forgot.

During the next nine years he completed his sentence and served his four years in the army, also marrying Marya Dmitriyevna Isaeva, a widow with a nine year old son. It was not until 1859 that he received full amnesty and finally returned to Saint

FROM THE WRITINGS OF FYODOR DOSTOYEVSKY

- I have my own idea about art, and it is this: what most people regard as fantastic and lacking in universality, I hold to be the inmost essence of truth. Arid observation of everyday trivialities I have long since ceased to regard as realism... Is not my fantastic *Idiot* the very dailiest truth?
- There is no idea, no fact, which could not be vulgarized and presented in a ludicrous light. There is no object on earth which cannot be looked at from a cosmic point of view.
- A just cause is not ruined by a few mistakes.
- In abstract love of humanity, one always loves only oneself.
- Inventors and men of genius have always been regarded as fools at the beginning (and very often at the end) of their careers.
- There is no subject so old that something new cannot be said about it.
- One can know a man from his laugh, and if you like a man's laugh before you know anything of him, you may confidently say that he is a good man.

Petersburg, where he resumed his literary career. In 1860 he published a collection of his writings and in 1861 began publication of a new literary journal, *Vremya* ("Time") with his brother Mikhail, to whom he was very close. The prison years had had an effect on Dostoyevsky's former radical views, and in publishing *Vremya* he dreamed of reconciling the two main opposing trends in Russian thought, the Westernizing and the Slavophile. The journal was successful and in 1860–1861 he published another novel, *The House of the Dead*, which helped restore him to literary prominence.

In 1862 Dostoyevsky went abroad for the first time. His impressions of Europe led to an essay expressing his horror of the decadent West and his hopes that Russia would avoid its poisonous influence. *Vremya* ceased publication on government orders that year for having published an "unpatriotic" article by another writer, and Dostoyevsky went abroad again. His journey, he claimed, was for the purpose of seeking treatment for epilepsy, but in fact he went to gamble in Wiesbaden, Germany.

After the *Vremya* closure, Dostoyevsky and his brother started a new journal, *Epokha* ("Epoch"), in which he began publishing his *Notes from the Underground*, but his good fortune was short-lived. In 1864 both his wife and his brother died, and *Epokha* closed due to debts. By this time, Dostoyevsky had become addicted to gambling. He went abroad to escape imprisonment for nonpayment of debts, fi-

nancing his journey with an advance from a publisher, but lost everything gaming. Friends in Russia sent him money to help him return to Saint Petersburg in 1865.

Afraid of incurring financial penalties if he failed to meet the deadline set by the publisher whose advance had paid for his journey, Dostoyevsky dictated *The Gambler* to an eighteen-year-old typist, Anna Snitkina. He married her and, in debt again, they immediately left Russia. For the next four years they wandered from place to place, living wretchedly, until returning to Russia in 1869.

From this period date the great novels *Crime and Punishment* (1866), *The Idiot* (1868–1869), *The Possessed* (1872), and *The Brothers Karamazov* (1879–1880), all of which reflect his wrestling with the problem of the existence of God. He also wrote *The Eternal Husband* (1870) and *A Raw Youth* (1875). At the same time, he edited the journal *Grazhdanin* ("Citizen") for a year (1873), resigning to live off the proceeds of his writing, which was, for the first time, profitable. His work on *Grazhdanin* led to his publishing a monthly *Diary of a Writer* in 1876, a forum of his views on a wide range of subjects, from religion to his theory of Russian national uniqueness and panhumanism. This venture, too, lasted one year.

The last years of Dostoyevsky's life were relatively tranquil and happy, unmarred by financial worries. Although by now a celebrity, he preferred to live quietly with his family in a small town outside Saint Petersburg.

Dostoyevsky had an immense influence on world literature and thought, bringing the realm of the subconscious into the novel. Not unlike Dickens, he concentrated his attention on the city; his foggy, squalid Saint Petersburg bears a resemblance to Dickens's London. He exerted enormous, if indirect, influence on Bolshevik political thought both before and after the Russian revolution.

Dostoyevsky's experiences in Siberia led him toward religion, particularly Christian ideals of submission and forgiveness. A complex personality both emotionally and intellectually, he continually sought the meaning of life, suffering, and sin. These themes run through all his works, expressed in their fullest in *The Brothers Karamazov*. Sharp-tongued and spiteful, he himself was not a very lovable character; Ivan *Turgenev commented that Dostoyevsky was the nastiest Christian he had ever met.

A. Gide, *Dostoyevsky*, 1925.
R. Hingley, *The Undiscovered Dostoyevsky*, 1962.

DOYLE, SIR ARTHUR CONAN (1859-1930), British author; creator of the famous fictional detective Sherlock Holmes. Arthur Conan Doyle was born in Edinburgh, the firstborn of an epileptic, reclusive father and a mother who was devoted to teaching her son the ways of a cultured gentleman. At age seventeen he entered Edinburgh University to study medicine under Dr. Joseph Bell, a man admired by the students for his concentration on deductive reasoning. In later years, Conan Doyle claimed that Bell was the inspiration for his most famous fictional character. While still at the university, and then as a young doctor, Conan Doyle began to write short stories to supplement his meager income. These early efforts were romantic tales of heroic adventure.

Nearly a decade passed before the name of Sherringford — soon changed to Sherlock — Holmes appeared in print. Conan Doyle had difficulty in finding a publisher for his first Holmes story, but in 1887 *Beeton's Christmas Annual* accepted *A Study in Scarlet*; it was neither a critical nor a popular success. Not until *Strand Magazine* published six more tales in 1891 did Sherlock Holmes gain public acclaim. Clothed in deerstalker or dressing gown, the enigmatic detective, accompanied by his amiable and gullible companion Dr. Watson, solved puzzles through observation and deduction. Along with the archcriminal Professor Moriarty, these characters delighted Victorian readers with their intrigue and adventure, and with the triumph of intellect over evil.

Conan Doyle, who always considered himself a serious novelist and no mere popular writer, did not intend to write any more detective fiction. His fame meanwhile was growing rapidly in the United States and when his publishers offered him more money he conceded. At the end of the second series of stories, however, Conan Doyle dramatically killed Holmes off, sending him over the Reichenbach Falls locked in the embrace of Professor Moriarty. Conan Doyle was very relieved; he hoped that now his other works, particularly the historical romances which he considered his best, would become popular. However, public demand, boosted by the generous offers of publishers, persuaded him to revive Holmes. In 1901 he reappeared in *The Hound of the Baskervilles*, the tale in which Conan Doyle made most use of the trappings of Gothic literature; it was a huge success. Between October 1903 and December 1904, thirteen more Holmes stories were printed in *Strand Magazine*. The total output of Sherlock Holmes fiction ran to five collections of short stories and four novels.

In all, Conan Doyle wrote more than fifty books, fiction and nonfiction, on a wide range of subjects. Besides the detective stories, most of his works were historical romances, such as *The White Company*, and scientific romances, such as *The Lost World*. He wrote two books on the Boer War and a book exposing the barbaric cruelties practiced on natives in the Belgian Congo. In 1915 he began a six-volume history entitled *The British Campaign in France and Flanders* and from 1918, several books on spiritualism.

Apart from his professional career, Conan Doyle was active in public life. He ran for Parliament twice and, in his rigorous fight for social justice, campaigned to improve the Divorce Law. For seventeen years he championed Oscar Slater, a German

---

FROM THE ESSAY "MR. SHERLOCK HOLMES"

Dr. Conan Doyle's education as a student of medicine taught him how to observe, and his practice, both as a general practitioner and as a specialist, has been splendid training for a man such as he is, gifted with eyes, memory and imagination.... One of the greatest teachers of surgical diagnosis that ever lived had a favourite illustration, which... has made a mark on Dr. Conan Doyle's method: "Try to learn the features of a disease or injury as precisely as you know the features, the gait, the tricks of manner, of your most intimate friend"... [Conan Doyle] created a shrewd, quick-sighted, inquisitive man, half-doctor, half-virtuoso, with plenty of spare time, a retentive memory, and perhaps the best gift of all — the power of unloading the mind of all the burden of trying to remember unnecessary details.

Dr. Joseph Bell, 1893

Jew accused of murder, until Slater was released from prison in 1927.

A lapsed Catholic from an early age, Conan Doyle was converted to spiritualism in 1916, and his faith intensified after his son died in 1918 from injuries incurred during World War I. He spent the last ten years of his life traveling around Australia, North America, South Africa, and Europe, spreading the word of spiritualism.

Today, Conan Doyle's fame rests solely on his creation of Sherlock Holmes and Doctor Watson. Stories of their expoits have been translated into over fifty languages. A Sherlock Holmes fan club was established in England in 1934 and today similar societies exist in many countries of Europe and in the United States.

J. A. Jaffe, *Arthur Conan Doyle*, 1987.
P. Nordan, *Conan Doyle*, 1966.
J. Symons, *Conan Doyle*, 1979.

DRAKE, SIR FRANCIS (c.1540–1596), English sea captain and explorer. He was born in the county of Devonshire in southwest England, the son of Edmund Drake, a seaman and Protestant preacher. In 1549 a Catholic rebellion led to the flight of his family from Devonshire to Chatham in Kent where the Drakes set up house in an old ship moored in the harbor. At the age of thirteen Francis Drake began his apprenticeship in seamanship on a small vessel engaged in the coastal trade along England's eastern coast.

The comparatively peaceful waters of the coastal trade did not provide the challenge he needed and the desire for wealth and an interest in seeing distant lands led Drake to join the fleet of his relative

John Hawkins. By 1565 he was sailing to Guinea and the Spanish Main, trading in slaves. Two unsuccessful voyages to the West Indies brought Drake and his fellow sailors into conflict with the military might of Spain. The hatred for Catholics he had developed during his childhood education and refugee experience now found its focus. Although his private war against Spain had not yet yielded financial returns, he had showed himself a highly capable navigator and commander and this did not pass unnoticed.

In 1572 Drake received royal license from *Elizabeth I to raid Spanish possessions in the Americas. Despite sustaining a wound in an attack on the Panamanian town of Nombre de Dios, his force made a significant haul of booty. Proceeding cross-country he sighted the Pacific Ocean and determined that he would return to challenge Spanish power there, in a sea that they regarded as their own. Drake returned to England with wealth and fame but was denied royal acknowledgment; the conclusion of an armistice with Spain made it politically inopportune for such a welcome.

By 1577 Spanish targets were again in fashion when Drake set off on a historic voyage around the world. The queen told him to do what damage he could to Spanish interests, and there was the added attraction of the lost continent believed to lie in the south Pacific. Drake set sail with 164 men in five ships, the largest being the hundred-ton *Golden Hind,* which he made the flagship. Despite adverse weather conditions and a narrow escape from a mutiny, Drake sailed around Cape Horn and along the west coast of South America, plundering a fortune in precious metals and jewels from the Spanish colonies encountered on route. He continued as far north as Canada in pursuit of the legendary northwest passage into the Atlantic. Unable to continue in the daunting northern climate, he turned south and reached California, claiming this territory for the English crown and naming it New Albion.

Drake returned to England in 1580 after further adventures crossing the Indian Ocean and sailing around the Cape of Good Hope into the Atlantic. Almost half of the crew did not survive the voyage but in those times this did nothing to mar the rejoicing when the *Golden Hind* sailed into Plymouth harbor. The cost of the venture was just £5,000 and the profit was £600,000, excellent returns for the syndicate of courtiers who had invested in it. Beside hauls of treasure, Drake also achieved fame by introducing tobacco to England, a plant he had discovered the natives smoking in the Americas.

Drake received a knighthood in recognition of his exploits and with his fortune he bought himself a comfortable country mansion at Buckland Abbey, where he could assume the role of English country gentleman. Although his broad Devonshire accent and lack of familiarity with the necessary civilities made him an unwelcome intruder among the established noble families, to the people at large he was a national hero.

Civic honor also came with his election as mayor of Plymouth. He discharged his mayoral duties with notable efficiency and is remembered for organizing a water supply for the city that remained in use until the late nineteenth century.

In the mid-1580s Drake was again engaged in attacking Spanish outposts in the New World and caused major financial loss to that kingdom's treasury. In 1586 in a characteristically dramatic exploit, the force under his command destroyed a large Spanish fleet in Cádiz harbor, preventing a planned invasion of England that had received papal blessing. Sir Francis described his victory as "singeing the King of Spain's beard." He became a man the Spaniards feared and at the same time admired for his daring, while winning their praise for the humanity he displayed in his treatment of prisoners.

In 1588 Drake distinguished himself in the defeat of the new Spanish Armada, which this time had reached the English coast. There is a popular story of how Sir Francis, informed of the Armada's approach while he was playing bowls in Plymouth, remarked, "There is plenty of time to win the game and to thrash the Spaniards too." He fought with distinction, and his use of fireships against the Spanish warships that sought refuge in Calais was highly successful. The Armada was scattered and Sir Francis Drake firmly ensconced as one of the naval heroes every schoolboy learns about.

Sir Francis's later years were anticlimactic. Although he still exhibited the seamanship and courage of his younger days, he enjoyed none of the triumph. An expedition against Spain's American colonies ended in disaster when fever broke out on ship and Drake too succumbed, dying off the coast of Panama in 1596 but not before he had used his last strength to put on his armor and meet his death bravely; he was buried at sea.

G. M. Thomson, *Sir Francis Drake*, 1972.
J. A. Williamson, *Sir Francis Drake*, 1951.
J. A. Williamson, *The Age of Drake*, 1965.

DREYFUS, ALFRED (1859–1935), French army captain falsely framed on charges of selling military secrets, whose case became a *cause célèbre*. Son of a textile manufacturer in Alsace who was an assimilated Jew, Dreyfus received a thoroughly French education. The family moved to Paris, where Dreyfus attended the École Polytechnique. In 1882 he entered the military, becoming a captain in 1889. The following year he married the daughter of a diamond merchant.

Dreyfus would have remained an obscure officer, had he not been thrust into the thick of turbulent national events with international implications. In 1894, while with the war ministry, Dreyfus was arrested for selling military secrets to the German military attaché. The anti-Semitic press inflamed the case against him and he was convicted and sentenced to life imprisonment on Devil's Island, a penal colony off the coast of South America. On January 5, 1895, he was publicly demoted in a humiliating ceremony in which his sword was taken away and broken, with the attending mob screaming "Death to the Jews!" All the while Dreyfus proclaimed his innocence. The legal proceedings against him were highly irregular, with insufficient evidence for his conviction, yet it took several years for his cause to be taken up by those not his relatives.

Only with the revelation of proof that the guilty man was apparently Count Ferdinand-Walsin Esterhazy did a number of public figures speak out for Dreyfus's vindication. In 1898, Esterhazy was court-martialed, but acquitted. To protest that verdict, the novelist Émile *Zola wrote his famous open letter to the president, entitled "*J'accuse*," which was published in the newspaper *L'Aurore*. For accusing the army of a cover-up, Zola was prosecuted for libel and found guilty. His conviction was overturned by the Cour de Cassation, but a new trial was then scheduled. Zola fled to England before the verdict. The army intelligence head, Lt. Col. Georges Picquart, was dismissed from office for uncovering the Esterhazy connection, and sent to serve in Africa.

By 1898 the sides in the Dreyfus Affair had crystallized and France was rent in half by the controversy. Reactionaries, supporters of the church's influence on the state, the military, those who yearned for the old order, and outright anti-Semites — insisted on Dreyfus's guilt. Those who supported the rights of the individual, the separation of church and state, parliamentary government, the Third Republic, and full democracy fought to prove Dreyfus innocent.

In 1899 Dreyfus received a second trial at Rennes. By then a basic document which had originally implicated Dreyfus had been proven a forgery; Major Hubert Henry of the intelligence section confessed to having fabricated it, before he committed suicide in prison. Dreyfus's supporters were dismayed when he was nevertheless found guilty again and sentenced to ten years on Devil's Island. They wanted Dreyfus to appeal the verdict, but he accepted the clemency offer of President Émile Loubet in exchange for withdrawing his appeal. In 1904, under a leftist government, Dreyfus requested a new investigation. Only in 1906 did the civil court of appeals finally overturn all previous convictions. Dreyfus was awarded the Legion of Honor and made a major. He retired to the reserves until World War I, when he was recalled to active duty. He led his men bravely in two battles and was promoted to lieutenant colonel.

The Dreyfus Affair had a direct and lasting impact on France and its key participants. Newspaper owner Georges *Clemenceau, by fighting for Dreyfus, won the support of the Republicans and buoyed his political clout. When he became premier of France, he appointed Picquart his minister of war. Esterhazy lived in England for the rest of his life, under various assumed identities. Zola's early death — supposedly due to a faulty flue — was suspected by some of having been caused by the anti-Dreyfusards (although this appears not to have been the case). While attending Zola's funeral, Dreyfus was shot and slightly wounded by an anti-Semitic journalist, who was acquitted on the grounds that it was a "crime of passion."

Greater than these individual effects were the national ramifications of the Dreyfus Affair. The press

Émile Zola's open letter published on January 13, 1898, proclaiming Dreyfus's innocence and accusing his denouncers of libel

proved its influence on political life; as a direct consequence of Dreyfus, in 1905 church and state were declared separate; and the republican forces gained control of France.

J. D. Bredid, *The Affair: The Case of Alfred Dreyfus*, 1986.

M. Burns, *Dreyfus: A Family Affair 1789–1945*, 1991.

N. Halasz, *Captain Dreyfus: The Story of Mass Hysteria*, 1955.

B. Schechter, *The Dreyfus Affair*, 1965.

DU BOIS, WILLIAM EDWARD BURGHARDT

(1868–1963), U.S. social scientist and black activist. Born in Great Barrington, Massachusetts, Du Bois was the child of a racially mixed marriage. His mother's family had lived in New England for 150 years, after an ancestor had been brought over as a slave from West Africa. When Du Bois was one year old his father left in search of employment and never returned, leaving only his mother to ensure that her son received a good education.

Du Bois excelled at school and local parents and teachers, who were white, helped him prepare for college. As a child he did not experience much discrimination and most of his friends were white; Great Barrington had a population of 5,000, with only twenty-five black families. A few incidents made him realize that his color separated him from the other children, but he did not mind at first because "they were the losers who did not ardently court me, and not I, which seemed to be proven by the fact that I had no difficulty in outdoing them in nearly all competition, especially intellectual," he later commented in his autobiography.

During high school, he became the correspondent for the New York black weekly, the *Globe*, and its radical editor, Thomas Fortune, pushed him to encourage blacks to get more involved in politics. This became one of the overriding mottoes in Du Bois's life: blacks would only receive full rights if, acting in concert, they organized themselves as a "race-conscious" bloc. The first black to graduate from his high school, Du Bois gave a commencement speech on the abolitionist and socialist Wendell Phillips. Although he wanted to attend Harvard College, his mother's death in 1885 left him in turmoil. Four white educators took an interest in him and decided to send him to Fisk University, an all-black school in Nashville, Tennessee.

After receiving his bachelor's degree in 1888 he attended Harvard, where he took another bachelor's degree in history and a master's degree, as well as many awards and honors, but he was never able to obtain genuine social equality. In 1892 he traveled to Germany where he studied at the University of Berlin.

Upon returning to the United States, Du Bois taught German and Latin at Wilberforce University in Ohio. His somewhat extravagant dress — high silk hat, gloves, walking cane, and Vandyke beard — shocked most of the campus. While at Wilberforce he finished a doctoral dissertation on the

> The Negro is a sort of seventh son, born with a veil, and gifted with second sight in this American world, a world which yields him no self-consciousness, but only lets him see himself through the revelation of the other world. One ever feels his twoness — an American, a Negro; two souls, two thoughts, two unreconciled strivings; two warring ideals in one dark body, whose dogged strength alone keeps it from being torn asunder.
>
> **W. E. B. Du Bois**

suppression of the African slave trade, which was accepted by Harvard in 1896.

Du Bois soon obtained a position as an assistant instructor at the University of Pennsylvania, where he conducted the first sociological study of American blacks. After his book on the subject, *The Philadelphia Negro*, was published Du Bois went to teach at Atlanta University, where he became known as a leading social scientist of black America. He continued to conduct research and worked to improve black education in the South. At about this time southern states had begun to enact "Jim Crow" laws, segregating streetcars, public parks, and other public areas, and approximately 190 lynchings took place each year. As conditions worsened in the South, Du Bois helped to found the American Negro Academy in 1894, serving as its first vice-president and later president. He soon found himself in a dispute with another prominent black leader, Booker T. *Washington, who told blacks to disavow the struggle against desegregation and to focus on achieving economic advancements; blacks would be a labor force rather than a political force because they were not yet "prepared" to be a political force. Du Bois strongly disagreed with Washington, first in an article in which he did not mention names, and then in an entire chapter of his book, *The Souls of Black Folk* (1903): "So far as Mr. Washington apologizes for injustice, North or South, does not rightly value the privilege and duty of voting, belittles the emasculating effects of caste distinctions, and opposes the higher training and ambition of our brighter minds, we must unceasingly and firmly oppose him."

In 1900 he was a major figure in the first Pan-African conference, held in London, and organized further Pan-African congresses, seeking to unite black people worldwide in the fight for liberty. In 1905, Du Bois helped to establish the Niagara Movement, the predecessor of the National Association for the Advancement of Colored People (NAACP), which was founded in 1910. Ironically, the NAACP founders were mostly white and Du Bois was the only black officer. He became director of publicity and research and began to edit *The Crisis*, the organization's official newspaper. In sometimes controversial editorials Du Bois focused on the theme of the relationship between racism and American democracy and formulated a cultural nationalism encouraging black literature and art. Du Bois continued as editor until 1934, when he resigned from the NAACP as a result of his political differences with the other officers, who he thought were ignoring the masses. In the meantime, Du Bois had continued writing numerous books; he also went on organizing the Pan-African congresses for a few years, thinking these could advance his two favorite goals: Pan-Africanism and socialism. He also began to develop a growing respect for Karl *Marx and the Soviet Union. After his resignation from the NAACP he worked for ten years as the head of the department of sociology at Atlanta University. In 1944 he returned to the NAACP as director of research, working mostly on appeals against racism to the United Nations. Once again, however, Du Bois's socialism and Pan-Africanism made the NAACP vulnerable to being called a Communist organization and he was again dismissed in 1949.

Du Bois became active in various peace movements fighting the cold war, as well as socialist movements, and ran for senator from New York on the American Labor Party ticket. He was indicted for "failure to register as agent of a foreign principal" but received an outpouring of support, including an offer of help from Albert *Einstein. Du Bois was eventually acquitted but was denied a visa to travel abroad and continued to be intimidated by the "politics of fear" that dominated the *McCarthy era.

During the 1950s Du Bois continued to struggle for world peace and good relations with the Soviet Union and wrote about the necessity for a third political party in the United States. In 1958 he was finally issued a passport and traveled to Europe, the Soviet Union, and China. Upon his return his passport was seized again until mid-1960. Du Bois continued to write his autobiography and became director of a project to produce an Encyclopedia Africana, meanwhile traveling to Ghana to work. In 1960 he declared his membership in the Communist party and in Ghana renounced his American citizenship. He became a citizen of Ghana in 1963 and died a few months later at the age of ninety-five.

M. Marable, *W. E. B. Du Bois: Black Radical Democrat*, 1986.

A. Rapersad, *The Art and Imagination of W. E. B. Du Bois*, 1976.

E. Rudwick, *W. E. B. Du Bois: Propagandist of the Negro Protest*, 1968.

DUMAS, ALEXANDRE (1802–1870), French novelist and playwright, known as Dumas père (the elder). His thrilling romances, translated into almost every language, made him the world's best-known and most widely read French writer. Dumas père's father, Alexandre Davy de La Pailleterie (1762–1806), was the natural son of a French marquis and a black Haitian woman, Marie Dumas. He adopted Marie's surname, joined the army of the Revolution, was promoted to the rank of general under *Napoleon, and left his own family penniless when he died. Young Alexandre Dumas had thus to fend for himself. Born at Villers-Cotterêts, near Soissons, he received a mediocre education but his penmanship gained him employment in a law office. Convinced that he was destined for better things, he moved to Paris in 1822 and obtained a minor secretarial post in the household of the duke of Orléans. There he was able to read the many tales of heroism and adventure that sparked his literary ambition. Equally important for the budding writer was the practical experience that he gained from early love affairs and from taking part in the 1830 Revolution, which brought his ex-employer, the former duke of Orléans to the throne as King Louis-Philippe.

Dumas first achieved success with *Henri III et sa cour* (1829), a prose drama that helped to launch the Romantic movement by flouting all classical conventions. *Antony* (1831) was partly autobiographical and *La Tour de Nesle* (1832), a blood-and-thunder historical drama, enjoyed 800 consecutive performances. Around 1839 Dumas turned almost exclusively to fiction, publishing the great historical romances which displayed his true genius and earned him worldwide renown. A team of collaborators, headed by Auguste Maquet, did all the preliminary research and supplied the outline of each book; Dumas then completed the narrative and dialogue, giving them his own personal stamp. He took many liberties with historical data, relying on his creative imagination to people these novels with invented as well as real characters, and showed little regard for psychological analysis. Critics often poked fun at the "novel factory of Alexandre Dumas & Co." but it attracted an enormous and less demanding readership. Like Honoré de *Balzac, Dumas was a pioneer of the *roman-feuilleton* serialized in liberal newspapers, where each episode featured adventures to keep the public in suspense from day to day.

A skillfully woven tale of wrongful imprisonment, daring escape, and revenge, *Le Comte de*

- There is a woman in every case. As soon as they bring me a report, I say: "Find the woman!" (*Cherchez la femme.*)
- All for one, one for all (motto of *The Three Musketeers*).

Dumas père

- Business? That's very simple — it's other people's money.
- All generalizations are dangerous, even this one.

Dumas fils

Monte Cristo (*The Count of Monte Cristo*), is one of the most notable thrillers in world literature. Another great favorite, set in the years 1625–1673 and built around the intrepid D'Artagnan, is the trilogy of romances comprising *The Three Musketeers*, *Twenty Years After*, and *The Man in the Iron Mask*. Different periods of history form the background to novels such as *La Reine Margot* ("Queen Margot"), which includes a chapter describing the Saint Bartholomew night massacre of French Huguenots in 1572; *Le Chevalier de Maison-Rouge* and *Le Collier de la reine* ("The Queen's Necklace"), both of which deal with episodes in the life of Marie-Antoinette; and *Ange Pitou*, in which the fall of the Bastille in 1789 is a dramatic centerpiece.

His staunch republicanism led Dumas into political storms and adventures of his own. As an opponent of Emperor *Napoleon III he had to seek refuge for a time in Brussels (1851–1854); and, as a supporter of Italian unification, he fought alongside Giuseppe *Garibaldi in the early 1860s. Dumas, was enormously prolific and became a rich man, yet he contrived to spend as much as he earned on extravagant projects, a succession of mistresses, and an army of hangers-on. He died bankrupt, "outmoded" by the new literary trends, but his romances have assured him of immortality.

His illegitimate son, the playwright **Alexandre Dumas** (1824–1895), known as Dumas fils (the younger), was the child of a Parisian girl. Although Dumas père made sure that the boy had a good start in life, relations between them were never cordial. Dumas fils, humiliated by the circumstances of his birth, constantly denounced his father's misconduct in the vain hope that he might be persuaded to reform. The younger Dumas was fortunate enough, however, to inherit his father's literary and theatrical skills. He first achieved success with a novel, *La Dame aux camélias* (1848), portraying the sad love life of a courtesan. Reworked for the stage (1852), this work was translated into English as *Camille*, which brought the playwright enduring fame and made him an architect of the new realism's comedy of manners. It also provided a star role for many leading actresses and gave G. F. F. *Verdi the basis for his opera, *La Traviata* (1853).

The masterly dialogue and stagecraft in *Camille* brought further success in *Le Demi-Monde* (1855), which raised the issue of women content to live on the fringes of "respectable" middle-class society. This play again focused public attention on bourgeois hypocrisy and led to the coining of a new term, *demi-mondaine*, for "kept woman."

Although Dumas fils became one of the Second Empire's outstanding dramatists, he was also an outspoken castigator of its declining moral standards. Throughout Europe, he believed, wealth, infidelity, prostitution, and a general disregard for one's lawful responsibilities were corrupting the social order and destroying family life. He was more highly regarded

at that time than his father and was elected to the French Academy in 1874.

A. Craig Bell, *Alexandre Dumas*, 1950.
F. W. Hemmings, *Alexandre Dumas: The King of Romance*, 1980.
A. Maurois, *The Titans*, 1957.

DUNANT, JEAN-HENRI (1828–1910), Swiss pacifist and founder of the Red Cross; first recipient of the Nobel Peace Prize. He was born in Geneva to a wealthy family and for a time worked in banking. A deeply religious man committed to the biblical precept "Love thy neighbor," he was an energetic supporter of the Young Men's Christian Association, for which he lectured and wrote about slavery in Muslim lands and the United States. During one such lecture tour in Italy in 1859, he visited the site of the Battle of Solferino and stared aghast at the carnage. Tens of thousands of casualties lay strewn before him, lacking even the most basic medical attention, heightening the inadequacy of his own feeble attempts to relieve their suffering. To the soldiers, he was the "gentleman in white," an anonymous stretcher-bearer and nurse who waded through blood and mire to save them; to himself, he was incapable of fulfilling the most basic Christian charity to which he was bound.

Immediately after his return home, he wrote *A Souvenir of Solferino*, describing his haunting recollection of the aftermath of war and advocating the establishment of an international network of voluntary relief societies to tend to the sick and injured. Dunant's ideas were discussed throughout Europe and in 1863, the Swiss Federal Council called an international conference to find ways for their implementation. Sixteen states sent representatives to discuss Dunant's *Nine Articles*, calling "for the amelioration of the condition of the wounded in armies in the field." Twelve countries ratified the articles the following year in an international congress held in Geneva. The congress was known as the Red Cross and in recognition of Switzerland's contribution to the gathering, they adopted an inverse Swiss flag as its symbol.

For several years, Dunant was the prime mover behind the Red Cross. The organization grew rapidly, particularly in the wake of the Franco-Prussian War (1870–1871), where it was responsible for saving countless lives. Dunant, however, had neglected his personal affairs and found himself bankrupt. He retired to the resort town of Heiden, where he continued writing pamphlets calling for international disarmament, a world court to arbitrate in international conflicts, and the establishment of a Jewish homeland. But none was as poignant as *A Souvenir of Solferino*, and Dunant soon faded into obscurity. He was rediscovered in 1895 by a journalist who was shocked to find Switzerland's leading humanitarian unacknowledged and impoverished.

Dunant was nominated for the first Nobel Peace Prize, awarded in 1901, despite claims by many, including Alfred *Nobel's private secretary, that if indeed he did deserve the prize it should be for medicine since the Red Cross accepted war as a fact and only worked to ameliorate its effects. After lengthy debates, it was decided that Dunant should share the prize with French pacifist Frédéric Passy. Although poor and sick, Dunant refused to spend the prize money and left it to charity.

Later on, grants enabled him to live out the remainder of his life comfortably as an outspoken advocate of humanitarian ideals and international unity. By the time of his death, forty countries had ratified his *Nine Articles* of the Red Cross. It was only after his death, however, that many of his other ideas — an international ban on slavery, a world court, and a council of nations — were adopted.

V. K. Likhy, *Henri Dunant: Prophet of Peace*, 1967.

D. C. Mercanton, *Henry Dunant*, 1971.

H. N. Pandit, *The Red Cross and Henry Dunant*, 1969.

DURKHEIM, ÉMILE (1858–1917), French sociologist; one of the founders and leading figures of modern sociology. Durkheim was born in Épinal, France, to a Jewish family distinguished by a long line of rabbinical ancestors. Initially he prepared himself to follow in their footsteps, then passed the entrance examination for the prestigious teachers' college, the École Normale Supérieure in Paris. After graduating in 1882 he began teaching philosophy and law at a series of state schools; and later in 1887, after a year's leave of absence in Germany, he was appointed lecturer at the University of Bordeaux, where the first chair in social science was founded in his honor.

One of Durkheim's aims was to formulate a scientific method for the analysis of society. He held that social phenomena could and should be measured and analyzed in the same manner as natural science. A fundamental concept in his writings was the notion of social cohesion in society and the need to understand the basis of social stability. In his earliest major work, *De la division du travail social* ("The Division of Labor in Society"; 1893), he discusses the concept of social cohesion by highlighting the differences between the modern "organically" organized society, epitomized by Western industrialized societies, and the more primitive "mechanically" organized society. Social cohesion in the primitive society is based on a collective conscience while in the modern society, due to the division of labor, cohesion is no longer based on uniformity but rather on the

integration of occupational roles and functions. This change to the more complex form was, according to Durkheim, a result of population growth.

In *Suicide* (1897), Durkheim shows how suicide rates represent differences in the level of social stability. He proposed that societies are separated into three types: altruistic, egoistic, and anomic. The anomic reveals anomie, the lack of standards and values necessary to ensure social integration and stability. The individual in society then feels detached from his social environment. This is often caused by major economic changes such as depressions or periods of great affluence. Furthermore, suicide appears to be less frequent when the individual is more closely integrated within his own society. Thus, what may appear to be an individual's decision to take his own life could be explained through social phenomena and the breakdown in social stability. These early works brought Durkheim considerable fame and influence. However, the revolutionary nature of the work frightened the more conservative thinkers of his day and he was often criticized. Durkheim was also horrified by the Alfred *Dreyfus affair; disturbed by the level of anti-Semitism in a seemingly civilized society, he took an active role in the campaign to prove Dreyfus innocent. During this period he also intensified his efforts with regard to education, seeing it as a means of reforming society. These efforts in educational reform included the preparation of new curricula and methods in an attempt to revitalize the teaching and study of philosophy. Although he was overlooked by the Institut de France despite his stature as a philosopher, he was appointed to the University of Paris in 1902 and made a professor there in 1906.

Durkheim's last major work, *Les Formes élémentaires de la vie réligieuse* (The Elementary Forms of Religious Life; 1915), discusses the totemic system in Australia, again stressing the importance of social stability and cohesion. He saw social cohesion as being dependent on the immutability of both religious beliefs and of practices that are both sacred and secular.

Durkhein was devastated by the news of the death of his son on the Balkan front during World War I and died soon after.

H. Alpert, *Émile Durkheim and His Sociology*, 1961.

S. Fenton, *Durkheim and Modern Sociology*, 1984.

S. G. Mestrovic, *Émile Durkheim and the Reformation of Sociology*, 1988.

EDISON, THOMAS ALVA (1847–1931), American entrepreneur and inventor. He was born in Milan, Ohio, but financial problems led to the family's moving to Port Huron, Michigan, when Edison was seven years old. His childhood was marked by ill health — a bronchial disorder and an attack of scarlet fever that left its mark in a hearing disability that worsened as he grew older. After briefly attending the local school, his education was left to his mother, who had once worked as a teacher. It was she who seems to have kindled his interest in science by giving him a book detailing basic experiments that a curious child could carry out. The work caught his interest in a manner that must have exceeded all her expectations, for at the age of ten he set up a laboratory in the cellar of their home.

Prompted by a desire to purchase more chemicals for his experiments, Edison got his first job at the age of twelve, selling newspapers and candies on a train. He managed to transfer his primitive laboratory to a baggage car and whenever he had the opportunity he would work there, or read to extend his knowledge.

At age sixteen he learned telegraphy; the Civil War was at its height then and the new communications system was proving its worth. There was plenty of work for the young and eager operator and Edison began a nomadic existence, traveling between the telegraph offices of the Midwest. His growing mastery of telegraphy and insatiable appetite for knowledge fueled the desire to improve the equipment he was using and make his own contributions to technological progress. His monthly salary of $120 was greatly depleted by his purchase of more laboratory equipment and books, including Michael *Faraday's Experimental Researches in Electricity*, which helped to initiate new directions in his career. Edison received his first patent in 1868 for an electric vote recorder but he did not find a market for it. His big breakthrough came in 1869 when he succeeded in repairing the telegraphic gold indicator at the Stock Exchange in New York. The feat made his name and he was put in charge of the gold indicator at a salary of $300 a month, a small fortune for the time. The Western Union Telegraph Company commissioned him to produce an improved machine and in 1871 he produced the Edison Universal Stock Printer, capable of transmitting 200–300 words per minute. Edison made $40,000 from this invention and used the funds to set up a factory in Newark, New Jersey, employing eminent scientists. At this factory Edison worked on producing improved telegraph instruments and succeeded in making a telegraph that could send two messages in two directions simultaneously.

The year 1876 can be summed up by two of Edison's oft-quoted expressions: "There is no substitute for hard work," and "Genius is one percent inspiration and ninety-nine percent perspiration." At Menlo Park, New Jersey, he established an industrial research laboratory where he worked on inventions that were to make dramatic contributions to industry and the home. That year also saw him engaged in making an autographic and a speaking telegraph, an electric pen, an electric dental drill,

Edison's drawing and a replica of the original incandescent light bulb

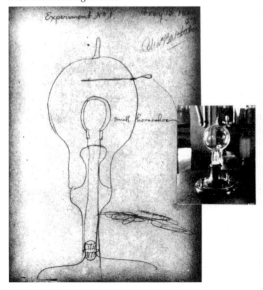

and a sewing machine, among others. Much of his work was based on improving instruments or processes originated by others — his success lay in changing the device to make it marketable.

In 1876 Alexander Graham *Bell invented the prototype of the telephone, with the same apparatus used to transmit and receive. In 1877 Edison produced an improved transmitter using the changing resistance of carbon granules to vary the strength of current in the circuit. The basic pattern of a powered circuit – Edison transmitter and Bell receiver – has remained almost unchanged to this day.

"HELLO"

It was Edison who coined the word "Hello." In a letter in August 1877, a year after Alexander G. Bell patented his invention of the telephone, Edison told a friend that a hearty "Hello" seemed the best way of attracting someone's attention and also for answering when the telephone rang. He apparently adapted the word from the old hunting call "Hulloo" and the British "Hallo," which expressed surprise. When he invented the phonograph, Edison yelled the hunting "Hulloo" into the mouthpiece, but neither "Hallo" nor "Hullo" was yet used as a greeting. Bell had been insisting that any chat on his instrument should be opened with "Ahoy," an utterance he learnt in his Scottish childhood.

When the New Haven exchange opened, the snappy "Hello" prevailed over both "Ahoy" and the official "What is wanted?" recommended by the Connecticut operator's manual.

By the mid-1890s, telephone operators in America and London were known as "hello girls."

Attaching a stylus from an embossing telegraph to a telephone speaker, Edison made what is credited as the most original of his inventions, the phonograph. At first he recorded onto paraffined paper but later found that wax cylinders were more effective. Among the first words in "recorded history" were those of his unique version of a popular nursery rhyme, revealing the inventor's sense of humor: "Mary has a new sheath gown,/ It is too tight by half,/ Who cares a damn for Mary's lamb,/ When they can see her calf!"

The phonograph generated great interest and astonishment; two women fainted when it was demonstrated in 1877 to the National Academy of Sciences.

In 1878 Edison launched himself on the path to even greater fame with pioneering work in electric lighting. Carbon arc lamps had recently come into use for street lighting but their dazzlingly bright light was not suitable for the home. Edison produced an incandescent lamp using a horseshoe-shaped carbon filament in an evacuated glass bulb. At the same time, the English inventor Joseph Wilson Swan, working independently, produced a comparable bulb, and together their inventions laid the groundwork for the introduction of electricity for domestic lighting. Edison foresaw electricity replacing gas as the main form of light in the home; and to this end he even worked on the design of light switches, choosing a turning movement in the belief that potential customers would prefer to operate electricity in the same way they had switched gas appliances on and off. In 1882 Edison's first commercial electric power station was opened in New York.

Edison made $4 million from his electric light bulb only to lose it later in an attempt to mine iron ore magnetically. For all his scientific skills he was a poor businessman, losing control of his own Edison Electric Company in 1892 and not realizing the commercial potential of the electricity supply using alternating current developed by his rival, George Westinghouse (Edison utilized direct current). His losses were recovered through increasing sales of his phonograph and the development of the kinetoscope, using principles he had learned from the phonograph to make the prototype film projector. The kinetoscope, a milestone in the creation of cinematography, was basically a peep show, a series of photographic images projected with such speed that it appeared the subject was moving. The discovery in 1883 of the variation in electrical flow that came to be know as the Edison effect, laid the basis for the production of the first radio waves twenty years later, but Edison was unaware of his discovery's significance and did not pursue it since he saw no commercial potential.

In 1887 Edison established a new laboratory at West Orange, New Jersey, employing 120 research assistants. Around the laboratory there developed the world's first science park, with five thousand workers busy turning out the products of Edison's ingenuity. By the 1890s the most dynamic stage of his inventive career was past but he continued working on an impressively wide variety of projects, ranging from motion picture cameras and dictating machines to batteries and cement kilns.

Edison's witticisms, on subjects scientific and otherwise, were treasured. Commenting on tastes in art he once said, "To my mind the old masters are not art; their value is in their scarcity." In 1929 he was honored by Congress with a gold medal; he symbolized the American dream of a man from a poor background who, through great effort, attains success and great wealth. In 1931 he remarked, "I am long on ideas but short on time. I expect to live to be only about 100." He erred on the side of optimism, for he died that year.

R. Conot, *Thomas A. Edison: A Streak of Luck*, 1986.

E. Hubbard, *Thomas Edison*, 1976.

EINSTEIN, ALBERT (1879–1955), American physicist whose theory of relativity changed the way humankind understands space, time, matter, and energy; in defiance of the contention in classical physics that these concepts are independent and absolute, he unified them into a single theory.

Einstein was born to a Jewish family in Ulm in Württemberg, Germany. As he grew up, there was no evidence of genius — on the contrary, he was a late talker who even at the age of nine was not fluent. Throughout his school years Einstein did, however, show promise at mathematics and physics but his major accomplishments then, as in later years, were outside the framework of school systems, which he found confining and authoritarian. He also studied music from an early age and became an accomplished violinist.

When the family moved to Italy in 1894, Albert was left behind in a boardinghouse in Munich to complete his education, whereupon he deliberately performed poorly in school in order to be expelled so he could join his family. He did not attend school for a year after that. When he was sixteen, his father, who wanted him to become an electrical engineer, arranged for him to take the entrance examination for the Swiss Federal Polytechnic in Zurich despite the fact that he was two years younger than the minimum age requirement. Einstein failed the exam, and was sent to the cantonal school in the nearby town of Aarau for preparation to retake it. After passing the following year, he enrolled in a teachers' training course at the Swiss Polytechnic School in Zürich, specializing in mathematics and physics. Because he did not have Swiss citizenship, however, he was unable to obtain a teaching position on graduation.

In 1902 Einstein managed to obtain both citizenship and a job, and began working in the Swiss Patent Office in Berne, where he was employed for the next seven years. In his spare time he pursued research in theoretical physics and earned a doctorate from the University of Zurich. In 1905 he published three papers for the *Annalen der Physik* that were to revolutionize man's understanding of the physical world. The "special theory of relativity" was outlined in a paper which described the relativistic nature of uniform motion and the interdependence of space and time. Despite its omission of the references and notes found in most scientific articles, it was to rock the scientific world.

Even at the age of sixteen, Einstein had begun questioning Isaac *Newton's law of inertia. Ten years later, he arrived at the conclusion that the principle of relativity was applicable to all of physics, that distance, time, mass, and simultaneity were not absolutes, being dependent on the relative speed of the observer; and that by contrast the speed of light was absolute, and represented, in effect, the greatest speed in the universe.

Using this theory, Einstein arrived at the equation which stated that energy equals mass times the

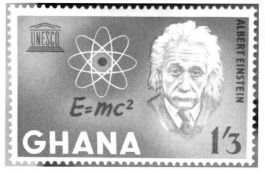

Albert Einstein honored on a Ghanaian stamp

velocity of light squared ($E=mc^2$); in other words, mass is a form of energy, and even a small amount of matter possesses an enormous amount of energy. This theory provided a basis for understanding the energy sources of the sun and stars and, eventually, the atomic bomb. Of the two other papers published that year, one explained the photoelectric effect (emission of electrons from metal surfaces exposed to light) and formed the theoretical cornerstone of quantum theory; it also pointed the way for the invention of television. The other paper, which analyzed the theory of Brownian movement, provided a method of determining the dimensions of molecules.

By 1909 Einstein's work had received significant recognition and he was offered positions at several universities. In 1913 he became a director of the Kaiser Wilhelm Institute for Physics in Berlin and in 1914 he was elected a member of the Prussian Academy of Science, with a yearly stipend so that he could continue his research. He still refused to take back German citizenship, however, and maintained this position until the establishment of the Weimar Republic.

In 1915 Einstein published the *General Theory of Relativity*, extending the principle of relativity to bodies under the influence of gravity and asserting an identity between the law of gravity and the law of inertia. This theory led to several astronomical predictions whose verification in an eclipse of the sun in 1919 confirmed his fame and turned his name into a household word. He received the Nobel Prize for physics in 1921 for his studies on the photoelectric effect, but donated the award to charity.

In 1933 the Nazi regime had him removed from his post in Berlin, revoked his citizenship, and confiscated his property. He decided to immigrate to the United States, becoming an American citizen and accepted a position as professor of mathematics and theoretical physics at the Institute for Advanced Study at Princeton, New Jersey.

In later years Einstein worked toward the development of a "unified field theory" that would combine the concepts of electromagnetic and gravitational fields of force. He hoped to find in this theory a way to interrelate all the forces of the uni-

- When a man sits with a pretty girl for an hour, it seems like a minute. But if he sits on a hot stove for a minute, it seems longer than an hour. That's relativity.
- I simply ignored a maxim.
- Everything that is really great and inspiring is created by the individual who can labor in freedom.
- We should take care not to make the intellect our god; it has powerful muscles but no personality.
- The whole of science is nothing more than a refinement of everyday thinking.
- Science without religion is lame, religion without science is blind.
- Equations are more important for me than politics because politics are for the present, equations for eternity.
- God does not play dice with the world.

Albert Einstein

verse under one set of laws. Although he completed a simplified set of formulas, which were published posthumously, they were not as convincing as his theory of relativity.

A vehement pacifist before the outbreak of World War II, he nevertheless championed the use of force againt the Nazi regime. It was fear of the Nazi menace which impelled him to write to Franklin D. *Roosevelt in August 1939, warning him of the danger to civilization were the Nazis to produce an atomic weapon before the United States. Although the letter helped convince the Americans to develop the nuclear reactor and fission bomb, Einstein was neither involved in, nor even aware of, these developments. After the war he admitted that had he known how little danger there actually was of the Nazis developing atomic power, he would not have written the letter. He became a dedicated advocate for the causes of world government and disarmament. He was also an ardent supporter of the effort to establish a Zionist homeland for the Jewish people as well as one of the early founders and supporters of the Hebrew University in Jerusalem. In 1952 he was invited to assume presidency of the State of Israel but declined, feeling himself unworthy of the position.

His books included *The Meaning of Relativity* (1923), *Investigation on the Theory of the Brownian Movement* (1926), *About Zionism* (1931), *Builders of the Universe* (1932), *Why War* (with Sigmund *Freud, 1933), *The World as I See It* (1934), *Evolution of Physics* (with Leopold Infeld, 1938), and *Out of My Later Years* (1950).

In his will, after disposing of an estate of $65,000 he left his manuscripts and royalties to the Hebrew University, Jerusalem, and his violin to his grandson.

R.W. Clark, *Einstein: The Life and Times*, 1971.
B. Hoffman and H. Dukas, *Albert Einstein: Creator and Rebel*, 1976.
P. A. Schilpp, *Albert Einstein: Philosopher-Scientist*, 1973.

EISENHOWER, DWIGHT DAVID ("Ike"; 1890–1969), thirty-fourth president of the United States and commander of the allied forces that conquered Germany in World War II. He was born in Denison, Texas, and his family moved the following year to Abilene, Kansas. His father, David, never earned more than $100 per month, but he and his wife Ida raised six boys, each of whom achieved success as adults. The Eisenhowers grew almost all of their own food and earned additional cash by selling the surplus. All of the boys worked to earn their own spending money.

Although Eisenhower was only an average student, he was an outstanding athlete in grade school and high school. After graduating from Abilene High School in 1909, he worked in the local creamery, and part of his salary went to help an older brother through college. He took a competitive examination for the U.S. Naval Academy because of the possibility of a free education and the opportunity to play football. After passing the examination, he found he was too old to attend Annapolis, and instead he entered West Point Military Academy in 1911. Here too Eisenhower proved an excellent athlete and during his second year played halfback on the army football team. Sportswriters praised his All-American capabilities, but a twisted knee cut his football career short.

Eisenhower graduated from West Point in 1915 and was sent to Fort Sam Houston in San Antonio, Texas, as a second lieutenant. Two weeks after reporting for duty, he met his future wife, Mamie Geneva Doud, who came from a wealthy Denver family. They were married in 1916 in Denver, Colorado.

Eisenhower was not particularly well read and was never considered an intellect, but he had a sharp, orderly, analytical mind, with the ability to look at a problem, see what alternatives were available, and decide wisely. In 1917 he was promoted to captain just after the United States entered World War I; although he wanted to lead men in battle in France, he was stationed at Camp Colt, a tank training center in Gettysburg, Pennsylvania, where he spent the entire war. Nevertheless, he was awarded the Distinguished Service Medal for his services as an outstanding instructor and trainer. He was promoted to major in 1920 and the following year graduated from the Tank Training School at Camp Meade, Maryland.

In 1922 Eisenhower was transferred to the Panama Canal Zone as the executive officer for the Twentieth Infantry Brigade. There he met General Fox Connor, who spoke to the young officer at length about military history and international problems. Certain that there would be another world war and that George C. *Marshall (then colonel) would command the American forces, Connor suggested that Eisenhower seek an assignment under Marshall.

In 1925 Eisenhower was sent to the Command and General Staff School in Leavenworth, Kansas, finishing first in a class of 275. In 1928 he graduated from the Army War College, gaining the reputation of an outstanding staff officer. From 1929 to 1933 he served as the assistant secretary of war, and in 1933 he was made assistant to the chief of staff (General Douglas *MacArthur), in which capacity he spent the next four years in the Philippines.

In December 1941 General Marshall, now army chief of staff, brought Eisenhower to Washington and put him in charge of the war plans division for the Far East. He was promoted to major general in March 1942, serving as head of the operations division, and in June of the same year, Marshall put Eisenhower in charge of the U.S. forces in the European Theater of Operations (ETO).

On November 8, 1942, with Eisenhower in command, British and American forces successfully landed near Casablanca, Oran, and Algiers and drove the Germans out of North Africa. In July 1943 Eisenhower, now a four-star general, launched the invasion of Sicily and the subsequent invasion of Italy. In December, the combined chiefs of staff sent him to London to take command of the forces gathered for the invasion of France. When he took over Supreme Headquarters, Allied Expeditionary Force, he commanded the most powerful single military force ever assembled. On June 6, 1944, over 156,000 men invaded the beaches of Normandy. During the conquest of Europe, under Eisenhower's command, were General Omar N. *Bradley, General George S. *Patton, as well as British chief of staff Bernard L. *Montgomery. The forces led by Eisenhower, now a five-star general, advanced through France but were held up in Belgium during the winter, until they finally smashed through to Germany in the spring.

The Germans signed an unconditional surrender on May 8, 1945, and Eisenhower headed the occupation forces for six months. He was then reassigned to Washington to succeed Marshall as army chief of staff. After completing the task of demobilizing the American army, he traveled, making speeches to promote national defense. His book *Crusade in Europe* (1948) was a best-seller, and he was urged by both the Democratic and Republican parties to accept a presidential nomination, but declined. In June 1948 he became president of Columbia University, holding that position until January 1953 but on leave of absence from December 1950 when he was appointed by President Harry S. *Truman to be the supreme commander of the North Atlantic Treaty Organization (NATO).

The two major political parties continued to press Eisenhower to accept the presidential nomination. In 1952 he declared himself a Republican and in June of that year resigned his position as NATO supreme commander, returned to the United States,

and began a hectic five-week preconvention campaign. He beat Robert A. Taft by a narrow margin on the first ballot at the Republican national convention.

Basically conservative, Eisenhower advocated a reduction in government controls and taxes, and in the presidential election he received 6.5 million more votes than the liberal Democratic candidate, Governor Adlai E. Stevenson of Illinois (442 to 89 votes in the electoral college). Riding in on the coattails of Ike's popularity, the Republicans captured both houses of Congress. The new president fulfilled one of his campaign promises by halting the fighting in Korea — where South Korea had been invaded by North Korea in 1950 — but the cease-fire led to an uneasy truce rather than a genuine peace.

Eisenhower had a talent for getting people of diverse backgrounds to work together toward a common objective. Although he now drew on this and other capabilities he had shown as a military man, he did not prove to be a strong president. Day-to-day management of the government was left to his staff and he placed foreign policy decisions in the hands of Secretary of State John Foster Dulles. Among the achievements of Eisenhower's administration were the end of the Korean war and the creation of the Southeast Asia Treaty Organization and of the International Atomic Energy Agency.

In 1954 the Republicans lost their majority in both houses of Congress. At first, Congress continued to support the president, but opposition soon grew, and when Senator Robert Taft died, Eisenhower lost his main support in Congress. His attempts to balance the budget took three years, but were reversed shortly thereafter because of mounting expenditures for foreign aid and defense. He tried to end the cold war with the Soviet Union, but despite years of effort was unsuccessful in building mutual trust between the two countries.

Eisenhower was reelected in 1956 by an even greater majority, but his personal popularity did not help the Republican party, which lost in both houses of Congress. During the 1956 Suez crisis Eisenhower and Dulles forced Britain and France to break off their attack on Nasser's Egypt. Subsequently the president proposed the Eisenhower Doctrine, which pledged military help to any Middle Eastern country facing a Communist threat. This policy was put into effect in 1968, when U.S. troops were sent to Lebanon. At home Eisenhower opposed racial segregation and sent federal troops to Little Rock, Arkansas, to enforce desegregation at a local school. In response to the 1957 Soviet launching of Sputnik, the first satellite, he created the National Aeronautics and Space Administration (NASA) in 1958. A planned meeting with the Soviet premier Nikita *Kruschev in 1960 was cancelled by the latter after a U.S. spy plane was shot down over the USSR.

Eisenhower groomed Vice President Richard Nixon as his successor, but Nixon was defeated in the 1960 election. Upon retirement, Eisenhower was treated as a respected elder statesman. President

- It wearies me to be thought of as timid when I've had to do things that were so risky as to be almost crazy. (1944)
- The eyes of the world are upon you. The hopes and prayers of liberty-loving people everywhere march with you. (D-Day Order)
- In the final choice, a soldier's pack is not so heavy a burden as a prisoner's chains. (Presidential Inauguration, 1953)
- I have to speak today in a language that in some sense is new — one which I would have preferred not to use. The new language is the language of atomic warfare. (to the U.N., 1953)
- Peace and justice are two sides of the same coin. (1957)
- There can be no such thing as Fortress America. If ever we were reduced to the isolation implied by that term, we would occupy a prison, not a fortress. (1959)

Dwight D. Eisenhower

John F. *Kennedy frequently asked his opinions on international problems. In his later years, Ike suffered a series of heart attacks, and in August 1965 he ended his active participation in public affairs. He remained a very popular public figure and in the 1968 Gallup Poll topped the list of the Most Admired Americans.

S.E. Ambrose, *Eisenhower* , 1990.
D. Eisenhower, *Eisenhower at War: 1943–1945*, 1986.
R. H. Ferrell, ed., *The Eisenhower Diaries*, 1981.
H. E. Stassen, *Eisenhower: Turning the World Toward Peace*, 1990.

ELIOT, THOMAS STEARNS (1888–1965), British poet, critic, and dramatist. Eliot was born in Saint Louis, Missouri, the youngest of seven children. After receiving his master's degree from Harvard University in 1910, he spent a year in Paris, which was to have a significant influence on his poetry, criticism, and identity.

In 1911 he returned to Harvard. Having left the Unitarian faith in which he was raised, he sought alternatives in the study of mysticism and philosophy. His philosophical pursuits took him to England in 1914, where he planned to concentrate on the study of *Aristotle at Merton College, Oxford. Although he had been expected to return eventually to Harvard to teach philosophy, he turned instead toward a career in poetry. In this decision he was aided by the American poet Ezra *Pound who was also living in England and who helped to get his poem *Love Song of J. Alfred Prufrock* published in 1915.

From 1915 to 1917 Eliot taught at Highgate School in London. In 1915 he married Vivien Haigh Wood, who was often ill and whose medical treat-ment required a reliable income. He worked as a bank clerk from 1917 to 1925, and from 1917 to 1919 was assistant editor of the literary magazine, *Egoist*, which published the works of authors such as James *Joyce, and in which Eliot's own essay "Tradition and the Individual Talent" appeared.

In 1922 Eliot founded *The Criterion*, which he edited until 1939. He saw its purpose as "bringing together the best in new thinking and new writing in its time, from all the countries of Europe that had anything to contribute to the common good." His five-part poem, *The Waste Land*, appeared in the first issue of the magazine.

In 1925 Eliot finally left banking to become director of the newly established Faber and Gwyer publishing house (later Faber and Faber). In 1927, a crucial year in his life, he was baptized in the Church of England and naturalized as a citizen of England.

Eliot's marriage to Vivien was never very happy and eventually the two separated. It was not, however, until 1947, after fourteen years of separation, that the marriage actually ended when Vivien died in a private mental hospital. Eliot's second marriage, to his secretary Valerie Fletcher in 1948, was apparently much more successful. His health, however, had never been good and he was increasingly troubled by emphysema and a double hernia he had endured since childhood. As he got older the English climate became harder to withstand. When he died the words inscribed on his memorial tablet were the first and last sentences of his poem "East Coker": "In my beginning is my end….In my end is my beginning."

Eliot's influence on literary criticism and poetry was profound and lasting. As a poet he abandoned traditional English iambic patterns for the esthetics of the poet's own voice. Content became as open to interpretation as did style, and anything became a viable subject for poetry. As a critic he contended that the critic must have a strong historical sense in order to judge literature from a proper perspective. In *For Lancelot Andrewes* (1928), a collection of essays, he described his critical position as that of a classicist in literature, a royalist in politics, and an Anglo-Catholic in religion.

Eliot's first volume of verse, *Prufrock and Other Observations* (1917), uses the imagery of urban life in a context of poetic intensity, and is notable for its absence of fixed verse or regular pattern and for only occasional rhyme. His *Waste Land* expressed his views on the sterility of modern society as opposed to societies of the past.

Beginning in the 1930s, serenity and religious humility became dominant in his poetry, especially *Ash Wednesday* (1930), *The Rock* (1934), and his first long verse play, *Murder in the Cathedral* (1935). *Four Quartets* was published in 1943. He received the Nobel Prize for literature in 1948, and the U.S. Presidential Medal of Freedom in 1964.

As a playwright, Eliot also wrote *Sweeny Agonistes* (1932), *The Family Reunion* (1939), *The Cocktail Party* (1949), and *The Confidential Clerk*

FROM T. S. ELIOT'S *THE LOVE SONG OF ALFRED J. PRUFROCK*

Let us go then, you and I,
When the evening is spread out against the sky
Like a patient etherized upon a table;
Let us go, through certain half deserted streets,
the muttering retreats
Of restless nights in one night cheap hotels
and sawdust restaurants with oyster shells;
Streets that follow like a tedious argument of
insidious intent
To lead you to an overwhelming question...
Oh, do not ask, "What is it?"
Let us go and make our visit.
In the room the women come and go
Talking of Michelangelo.

(1953). His prose writings included *The Idea of a Christian Society* (1940) and *Notes Towards a Definition of Culture* (1948).

P. Ackroyd, *T. S. Eliot*, 1984.
G. Lyndall, *Eliot's Early Years*, 1977.
R. Tamplin, *A Preface to T. S. Eliot*, 1987.

ELIZABETH I (1533–1603), queen of England and Ireland, the daughter of *Henry VIII and Anne Boleyn; last Tudor monarch. Raised as a Protestant, she grew up amid violent religious changes that threatened her very survival. Both her mother and her childhood playmate Lady Jane Grey fell victim to political intrigue and were beheaded, while the death of her half-brother, Edward VI, at the age of fifteen was followed by the reinstitution of Catholic hegemony in England under her half-sister *Mary Tudor. The latter, suspecting Elizabeth of complicity in Protestant intrigues, had her imprisoned for two months in the Tower of London (1554), and confined to residences outside the capital until Mary's death in 1558.

In her early years Elizabeth received the education of a Renaissance prince, mastering Latin, Greek, and several modern languages; she became an accomplished horsewoman, and excelled as a dancer. At the same time, she learned the virtues of patience and caution, the art of dissembling, and the technique of maneuvering people or turning events to her own advantage. Only a few days after the last Protestant martyrs had been burned at the stake, news reached Elizabeth at Hatfield House of the death of "Bloody Mary" (November 17, 1558). Hearing that she had succeeded the childless queen, Elizabeth is said to have quoted Psalm 118: "This is the Lord's doing; it is marvellous in our eyes."

Her coronation three months later was a signal for nationwide rejoicing and displayed Elizabeth's love of pageantry and rich attire, although, like her grandfather Henry *VII, she would be known for her tightfisted approach to spending money. One of her first acts was to make Sir William Cecil, Lord Burghley, her principal secretary of state. Like the queen a devoted though moderate Protestant, he was a wily politician, resourceful, diplomatic and, if need be, ruthless; he served her faithfully in various capacities for almost forty years. This was no easy task: while a great conversationalist, remarkably well-informed, and kind-hearted at times, Elizabeth was also vain, proud, and dictatorial, given to fits of temper, slow to make up her mind and quick to change it, as well as apt to blame others for the outcome of her own decisions. She could swear like a trooper, slap a councillor's face or threaten to make him "shorter by the head"; she once threw a slipper at Sir Francis Walsingham, the head of her secret service, and warned the Countess of Nottingham: "God forgive you, but I never can."

An issue that long provoked argument between Elizabeth and her ministers was the desirability of a royal marriage for the sake of providing an heir to the throne. Many eligible foreign suitors were suggested, and the queen dallied with each in turn, but no agreement could ever be reached. "I am already bound unto a husband, which is the kingdom of England," she told her councillors, most probably

Elizabeth I

fearing that a prince consort would diminish her own authority. Yet she did have some favorites at court, notably Robert Dudley, the Earl of Leicester (1532–1588), once rumored to be her lover and intended husband, and Leicester's stepson, Robert Devereux, the Earl of Essex (beheaded as a rebel in 1601). Whether by choice or by mischance, Elizabeth remained England's "Virgin Queen."

Throughout her reign, she sought to avoid conflict at home and wasteful campaigns overseas. Disinclined to "make windows into men's souls" and imbued with a hatred of religious fanaticism, Elizabeth approved measures to create a national church broad enough to include loyal Catholics as well as Protestants. This "Anglican compromise," much to the queen's liking, was reached through the Act of Uniformity (1564), which established a Church of England; though doctrinally influenced by Calvinism and prescribing worship in the vernacular, it retained certain Catholic elements in its hierarchy and ritual. Within half a century, however, Anglicanism detached most Catholics from Rome, and England slowly became Protestant.

The tide of events abroad proved unfavorable to Elizabeth's strategy of noninvolvement. Thus, while refusing to support the French Huguenot "rebels," she opposed Spanish efforts to destroy the Reformation and antagonized *Philip II by encouraging the revolt of the Netherlands (1568–1581). Marauding English sea dogs led by John Hawkins and Francis *Drake were another thorn in Philip's side, raiding Spanish colonies in the New World and plundering his treasure-laden galleons. Although Elizabeth protested that these English corsairs were beyond her control, she knighted Drake in 1580 and claimed her own share of the loot. King Philip retaliated by galvanizing foreign hostility toward the English queen and fomenting rebellion among her Catholic subjects.

This mutual enmity and suspicion between England and Spain was exacerbated by the political adventurism of Elizabeth's cousin *Mary, Queen of Scots, whose scandalous domestic life led to her becoming an unwelcome refugee in England (1568). As a great-granddaughter of Henry VII, she had an excellent claim to the English throne; as a resolute Catholic, however, she posed a grave threat, and on Cecil's advice Elizabeth had her placed in protective custody. To Roman Catholics abroad — and to some sharing her faith within the realm itself — Mary was the legitimate queen of England. A short-lived rebellion in favor of Mary (1569), followed by Pope Pius V's ineffectual bull deposing Elizabeth three months later (1570), outraged public opinion but failed to harden the Virgin Queen's attitude toward her royal cousin, whom she treated with indulgence. The rebellious Duke of Norfolk was executed in 1572 and Jesuits celebrating the newly outlawed Mass were hanged, yet it was not until correspondence implicating Mary in a plot to assassinate Elizabeth came to light (May 1586) that royal assent was finally obtained for Mary's execution in February 1587.

> - I know that I have but the body of a weak and feeble woman, but I have the heart and stomach of a king — and of a King of England too — and think foul scorn that Parma, or Spain, or any prince of Europe should dare to invade the borders of my realm....By your valor in the field, we shall shortly have a famous victory over these enemies of my God, of my kingdom and of my people! (to her troops at Tilbury in anticipation of the landing of the Spanish armada).
>
> - Though God hath raised me high, yet this I count the glory of my crown, that I have reigned with your love....There never will Queen sit in my seat with more zeal to my country, care for my subjects, and that will sooner with willingness venture her life for your good and safety than myself (to a Parliamentary deputation in 1601).
>
> - As for me, it shall be sufficient that a marble stone shall declare that a Queen, having lived and reigned for so many years, died a Virgin. (answer to a petition from the House of Commons urging her to marry, 1559).
>
> **Queen Elizabeth I**

The Spanish monarch's fury was now directed against the apostate English and their "doubly accursed heretic queen." While Philip was preparing his "invincible Armada" for an invasion of England, Drake "singed the King of Spain's beard" with devastating naval attacks on Spanish ports and shipping (April 1587). The Armada nevertheless set sail with 17,000 troops aboard on May 30, 1588, prompting Elizabeth to review her land forces at Tilbury, where she was greeted with enthusiasm and then delivered a memorable, rousing speech on August 19, 1588.

By then, Spain's great Armada had already been shattered and dispersed (news of its fate being slow to arrive), yet the anticipated danger had the effect of promoting national unity. Saved by its fleet and proud of its warlike queen, England displayed a patriotic self-confidence that bridged religious and social divides.

Although she could be very difficult in private, Elizabeth gained and retained the affection of her people through her personal charm and sagacity, her many public appearances, and a glorious national image. During the reign of "Good Queen Bess," England replaced Flanders as Europe's center of the wool trade; new markets for English commerce were opened up in distant lands; the East India Company received its first charter (1600), and middle-class prosperity soared. All this foreshadowed the kingdom's emergence as a leading naval and colonial power. There would be far fewer accomplishments under Elizabeth's godson and successor, *James I.

The Elizabethan age witnessed a great renewal of English literature, particularly drama, which attained European stature in the works of Ben Jonson, Christopher Marlowe, and William *Shakespeare. It was to Elizabeth that Edmund Spenser dedicated his *Faerie Queene* (1590), and it was to honor her also that Sir Walter *Raleigh chose the name *Virginia* for England's first colony in North America.

C. Haigh, *Elizabeth I*, 1988.
C. Hibbert, *The Virgin Queen: The Personal History of Elizabeth I*, 1990.
A. Somerset, *Elizabeth I*, 1992.
N. J. Williams, *Elizabeth I, Queen of England*, 1971.

ENGELS, FRIEDRICH (1820–1895), social scientist, writer, philosopher, and revolutionary who, along with Karl *Marx, was the progenitor of modern communism. Engels was born in Barmen, in Prussia, to a moderately liberal family with strong Protestant religious beliefs. His father owned a textile factory in Barmen and was a partner in another plant in Manchester, England. From the time he was eighteen years old, Engels worked in the family business, studying liberal and revolutionary writers in private during his early apprenticeship in business management.

Hegelian philosophy, which integrated all previous philosophical systems into a unity by viewing earlier approaches as different historical stages in the ongoing development of philosophy, particularly intrigued Engels. Many of G.W.F. *Hegel's students went on to write histories of art, religion, and philosophy. Engels and Karl *Marx developed an historically based theory of economics. To the young Hegelians and leftist intellectuals whom Engels met, progress proceeded through a confrontation of opposing ideas, leading into a new synthesis. They wanted to accelerate progress by confronting attitudes they considered to be irrational and outmoded, such as Christianity.

Engels became an agnostic and began publishing his writings under the pseudonym Friedrich Oswald. In 1841 he served for a year in an artillery regiment in Berlin where he attended university lectures and meetings of The Free, a young Hegelian group. After being discharged from the army in 1842, Engels met Moses Hess, who then considered communism the logical extension of Hegel's theories.

Engels was forced to leave Germany because of his revolutionary views. He spent much of his time in England, an industrially advanced country with a massive labor force, or proletariat, which Hess considered ripe for open class struggle. During the day Engels was a successful businessman in his father's cotton plant; at night he studied the economic and political situation of Britain's work force. He also wrote about communism and attended meetings of radicals. Rejecting the institution of marriage, he began living with Mary Burns, an uneducated working-class Irish woman.

Engels and Marx began writing together, attacking moderate Hegelians and socialists who opposed revolution. Engels introduced Marx to the study of economics, and later endorsed his philosophy of a materialist (economic) interpretation of history, according to which religious, cultural, and social values are all determined by economic factors. Two major classes of people were defined: the bourgeoisie, who controlled the means of production and the proletariat which was exploited by the bourgeoisie. In their neo-Darwinian theory of social development, the economically fittest would survive until the underdogs rose up and destroyed them; conflict was inevitable. Ultimately the revolution would come and continue until the means of production were taken from the bourgeoisie and put into communal hands.

In 1847, at the Second Congress of the Communist League, Engels and Marx were commissioned to write a statement on communist philosophy, *The Communist Manifesto*, that would contain a complete theoretical and practical party program. They completed a German version in January 1848; a French translation appeared in the months between the revolution in France of February 1848 and the insurrection there in June. During that time, Engels returned to Germany, where revolution had also broken out, and he and Marx published a Communist daily disguised as being democratic. When the revolution failed they returned to London to reorganize the Communist League. Engels supported himself, Mary Burns, Karl Marx, and Marx's wife and children with earnings from his family's business, in which he became a partner. In 1852 the Communist League was dissolved following the trials of communists in Cologne. Twelve years later, a more broad-based, less radical socialist group called the International Workingmen's Association was set up.

In 1863 Mary Burns died. Engels later lived with her sister, Lizzy, finally agreeing to marry her as she lay on her death bed. In 1869 he sold his partnership in the family business, receiving enough from the sale to sustain himself for the rest of his life and provide a modest annual income to Karl Marx. Engels contributed toward the first part of Marx's *Das Kapital*, and edited the next two volumes after Marx's death in 1883.

Of Engels's other writings, his *The Condition of the Working Class in England* (1844) is a pioneering work of social science. In some economic matters he was prescient; in *Socialism, Utopian and Scientific* (1882), he spoke of economic cycles, of great ups and downs that are built into capitalist economies. His solution was a proletarian revolution leading to the state takeover of the institutions of production "in order to free the means of production from the character of capital."

Engels predicted that after the economic takeover by the state, "the political authority of the state dies out." He had a profound impact on Marxism and on the elaboration of dialectical materialism — the relationship and ensuing struggle between the bourgeoise and the proletariat.

T. Carver, *Engels*, 1991.
M. Levin, *Marx, Engels, and Liberal Democracy*, 1989.
G. Mayer, *Friedrich Engels: A Biography*, 1969.
R. Schmidt, *Introduction to Marx and Engels*, 1987.

EPICURUS (341 – c. 271 B.C.E..), Greek philosopher; son of Neocles, an Athenian schoolmaster; born in Samos. After completing his ephebic service (two years of military training from age eighteen) in Athens, he lived with his family at Colophon, and later taught philosophy at Mitylene and at Lampsacus. In 306 B.C.E. he acquired a house and garden in Athens and established a school of philosophy that took its name (the Garden) from its surroundings. He became a famous teacher and pupils flocked from all parts of Greece and Asia Minor, becoming strongly attached to their master and his teaching. On his death, Epicurus left the property and the school to his friend and pupil Hermarchus of Mitylene.

Epicurus is credited with having written 300 books, all of which are lost; only some fragments of his writings are extant. His ideas are expounded in the *De Rerum Natura* of Lucretius, an important source for his views. Accepting the atomic philosophy of Democritus, Epicurus maintained that the world is a natural result of the combination of atoms, and that worlds are produced and destroyed in a never-ending coming together and separation of atoms. He maintained that the gods are happy and imperishable beings who have no interest in our world and neither punish wrongdoers nor reward the just; they should not be feared. Nor should one fear

---

- When we are, death is not; when death is, we are not.
- When we say that pleasure is the end of life, we do not mean the pleasure of the debauchee or the sensualist, as some from ignorance or ill-will accuse us, but freedom of the body from pain and the soul from anxiety.
- If you want to make Pythocles happy, add not to his possessions but take away from his desires.
- You must think carefully beforehand with whom you are to eat and drink, rather than what you are to eat and drink. For a dinner of meats without the company of a friend is like the life of a lion or a wolf.
- Only the just man enjoys peace of mind.

Epicurus

---

death, which is merely the disintegration of the atoms of soul and body, upon which all senses cease to exist. While man is alive, he should seek the happiness which comes from satisfying his most natural desires. These moral teachings were not simple hedonism, for Epicurus himself led a modest, temperate life. He believed that the most important pleasure is the pleasure of the soul, which is achieved through meditation, when the soul is undisturbed by material or emotional factors (the ideal state of *atarxia*); abstinence from worldly preoccupations is necessary to achieve this state.

Not only men but also women and slaves were attracted by Epicurus's teachings and joined his school, living a communal life. The Epicurean philosophy spread throughout the Hellenistic world and had many followers in Rome. Additional schools were opened in various places (e.g., Antioch and Naples). The school of Epicurus lasted to the fourth century C.E., although Epicureanism encountered much hostility. Epicurean thought rivaled that of the Athenian Academy, for the physical theories of Epicurus were in direct contrast to those of *Aristotle. The Stoics, and later the Christians, abhorred Epicurean doctrines about the gods, ethics, the absence of divine providence, and the nature of the world. Epicureanism fell out of favor, becoming a byword for hedonism and heresy.

N. W. DeWitt, *Epicurus and His Philosophy*, 1954.
J. Rist, *Epicurus*, 1972.

ERASMUS, DESIDERIUS (1466 – 1536), Dutch theologian, scholar, and humanist. He was born in Rotterdam, the illegitimate son of a priest and a physician's daughter. He received an excellent schooling at the austere and demanding Collège de Montaigu (which both Ignatius *Loyola, founder of the Jesuits, and John *Calvin were later to attend).

Erasmus's guardians embezzled his money and cajoled him into joining the Augustinian monastery at Steyn, a move he bitterly regretted in later life, even though he went so far as to be ordained as a monk in 1492; he hated monastic life, the restrictions of which only succeeded in fueling his passion for freedom. Moreover, he found there an abuse of privilege, a complacent ignorance, and an aversion to conscientious study that were to personify for him the failings of the contemporary church throughout his life. He, on the other hand, believed that every domain, including the religious, could be enriched by the application of the intellect and that the word alone should be used as a weapon in religious quarrels.

Erasmus was pleased to accept the post of secretary to the bishop of Cambria in 1494, since it enabled him to escape the tedious round of cloister life. Unsuccessful as a diplomat, he went on to study theology at the University of Paris, where he came into contact with the fledgling humanist movement. Having been influenced at school by "modern devotion," a late medieval lay religious movement stressing education, Erasmus was already deeply suspicious of theological dogmatism, a tendency reinforced by the humanists' arguments. When forced to turn to tutoring to maintain himself, he produced the subsequently celebrated *Colloquies* as a teaching aid.

The search for the patronage that would enable Erasmus to devote himself to study in comfort brought him to England in 1499 at the invitation of Lord Mountjoy. Here he developed lasting and important friendships with John Colet and Thomas *More. His links with the latter were strengthened by their common dislike of scholasticism and religious intolerance. He read and approved More's manuscript version of *Utopia* and was instrumental in persuading him to have it published.

Erasmus has been considered the *Voltaire of the sixteenth century; his chosen targets included the dogmatic theologians of his age. One of his dearest objectives was to encourage the glorification of Christianity in prose as elegant as that of the classical Latin writers. He cited Saint *Augustine and Saint *Jerome to argue that Latinity was quite compatible with true devotion, especially since many of Christ's teachings are echoed in the great classics. His determination to use reason as his touchstone led him to argue for an allegorical interpretation of some aspects of scripture, such as the threat of hellfire.

Despite his frequent complaints about the barbarity of English customs and manners, Erasmus found the country congenial enough to return repeatedly; he found a convivial welcome at the home of More, where he wrote his most celebrated work, *In Praise of Folly*, in 1509. It was dedicated, with a certain playful appropriateness (*moros* means "fool"), to his host. Its blend of humorous irony and bitter invective targeted the many hypocrisies he saw around him; he

Doodles found in the margins of Erasmus's notebooks

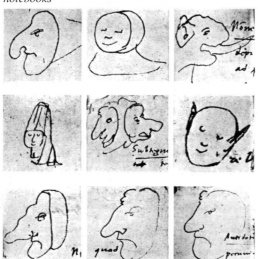

FROM THE WRITINGS OF ERASMUS

- Every definition is dangerous.
- Beware lest clamor be taken for counsel.
- Talk of the devil and he'll appear.
- What do men seek from the saints except what belongs to folly? Among all the votive offerings you see covering the walls of certain churches right up to the very roof, have you ever seen one put up for an escape from folly or the slightest gain in wisdom?
- The philosophers, cloaked and bearded to command respect, insist that they alone have wisdom and all other mortals are but fleeting shadows. Theirs is certainly a pleasant form of madness, which sets them building countless universes.
- Plato's famous saying is often quoted, "Happy are the states where either philosophers are kings or kings philosophers." But if you look at history you will see that no state has been so plagued by its rulers as when power has fallen into the hands of some dabbler in philosophy or literary addict.

---

was unstinting in his ridicule of the church establishment and the monastic orders, whom he called "brainsick fools." He strongly decried ecclesiastical abuses and the wickedness of popes.

The study of Greek that Erasmus undertook in Holland and France after his first departure from England in 1500 was the foundation for his later fame. He was inspired by his discovery of a Greek manuscript criticizing the then unchallenged Latin Vulgate version of the Bible, and determined to undertake a new translation using a method focusing on exact philological exegesis of the original text. He eventually completed his translation of the New Testament into Latin in 1516. The translation was a masterpiece, establishing the critical historical method in the study of scripture and creating new standards in biblical scholarship.

Erasmus's reputation as a scholar and thinker was so great that both sides attempted to recruit his support during and after the Reformation. Erasmus initially supported Martin *Luther, but he came to be disappointed by the reformers, who he felt represented the end of his hopes for the dawn of a golden age of letters: he saw Luther as exactly the kind of dogmatic, violent, aggressive and anti-intellectual theologian he condemned. "Christ I know," he wrote. "Luther I know not. The Roman Church I know and death will not part me from it till the Church parts from Christ."

Erasmus grew increasingly alienated from Luther, even though Luther's supporters could be numbered among his own admirers. Their rift was expressed in his pamphlet of 1524, *Concerning Free Will*, which

Luther roundly attacked in his retort, *Concerning the Bondage of the Will*: "Erasmus is an enemy of all religion, he is the true adversary of Christ: whenever I pray, I pray for a curse on him," he raged.

From 1521 Erasmus lived in Basel, where he wrote on the Church Fathers and argued for a return to their religious values, and maintained an extensive correspondence. Increasingly removed from the sectarian developments of the time, he died with the words "Dear God" on his lips.

C. Augustijn, *Erasmus: His Life, Works and Influence*, 1991.

M. O. Boyle, *Rhetoric and Reform: Erasmus' Civil Dispute with Luther*, 1983.

R. L. Demolen, *The Spirituality of Erasmus of Rotterdam*, 1987.

L. E. Halkin, *Erasmus*, 1993.

ERIKSSON, LEIF SEE LEIF ERIKSSON.

ERIK THE RED (Erik Thorvaldson; c. 950 – c. 1003), Viking explorer and founder of the first European settlement in Greenland. Erik was born in the Norwegian town of Jaeren. Around 960 he and his father Thorvald committed murder and were forced to flee the country. They headed for the prosperous settlement of Iceland, settling in the inhospitable northwest corner of the island. After some time they moved to the more comfortable Haukadale but Erik's fierce temper led to several brawls, ending with the death of a neighbor. Erik moved to the island of Breidafjord but again found himself involved in a local feud, for which he was banished from Iceland for three years.

Rather than risk a return to Norway, Erik decided to explore Greenland. Barely visible from Iceland's west coast, the island had first been mentioned around 900 by Gunbjor Ulfsson, who had approached several outlying islands when his ship was blown off course in a storm. Nevertheless, Icelanders ignored the island for almost eighty years until, in 978, a group of prospective settlers reached the island to escape overpopulation in Iceland; harsh weather conditions led to the abandonment of the colony, however.

Erik took his wife, Thjodhild, two sons, Thorstein and *Leif, and some thirty supporters to Greenland in 981. After exploring the western coast of the island, they settled in a southwest fjord, naming it Brattahlid. Climatic conditions on the island were considerably better than they are today and the small colony flourished. At the end of his term of exile, Erik returned briefly to Iceland to organize a group of settlers to join him in the new land. Twenty-five ships set out to Greenland, but only fourteen survived the four-day sea journey, some deciding to turn back, others being lost at sea. The 350 colonists were exceedingly successful in their first fifteen years, which encouraged more immigrants to join them. In 1002, an epidemic, apparently introduced by prospective new immigrants, wiped out a large part of the colony, including Erik himself. Despite the disaster, the colony recovered and continued to exist until the fifteenth century.

Although Erik remained a pagan, his son Leif Eriksson brought Christianity to Greenland upon his return from a trip to Norway.

H. Ingstad, *Westward to Vinland*, 1969.

F. D. Logan, *The Vikings in History*, 1980.

M. Magnusson and H. Palsson, *The Vinland Sagas: The Norse Discovery of America*, 1965.

EUCLID (365?–300? B.C.E.), Greek mathematician; the father of classical geometry. The date and place of his birth are uncertain and the facts of his life are further obscured by his often being confused by early historians with the Socratic philosopher Eucleides of Megara. The Arabs, who have a long tradition of mathematics, maintain that Euclid was the son of a Greek born in Tyre and living in Damascus. It is known that he founded and taught at a school in Alexandria.

His fame derives mainly from his greatest work, *The Elements*, an elementary geometry text in thirteen books. *The Elements* starts with a list of definitions followed by ten fundamental and self-evident propositions known as the axioms and postulates, from which, it is claimed, all the subsequent theorems contained in the books are logically deduced.

Though credited with the authorship of some of the books, it is believed that Euclid's primary activ-

Euclid, from Raphael's "The School of Athens"

ity was that of editor and compiler, drawing on the body of knowledge developed by his precursors. Nevertheless the design and the organization of the work was enough to merit Euclid's preeminent position in the development of mathematics, for the outstanding feature of *The Elements* is its logical arrangement and systematic approach to reasoning. Until the late nineteenth century, Euclid's work was regarded as the definitive example of deductive theory. However, under the scrutiny of the modern approach to rigorous deductivity, the claim that all theorems in *The Elements* arise logically from the postulates and axioms has been found wanting.

The mathematical quality of *The Elements* is inconsistent, which is a clear indication that it derived from several authors. Euclid as editor, it seems, did not have the mathematical ability to rectify errors in logic and recompose circumlocutive passages. He was described by his contemporary Pappus as a modest and unpretentious person, renowned for his consideration of others and his dedication to his pupils. This seems to fit the character of a man whose major work contains no preamble or other form of self-aggrandizement. Undoubtedly, though, Euclid was an astute educationalist whose textbook, the oldest surviving Greek mathematical work, was used almost unrevised to teach geometry until the beginning of the twentieth century. *The Elements* so completely overshadowed other mathematical books from that period that none of the others survived. Euclid is also known to have written a number of treatises on optics, astronomy, music and mechanics, but many of them have been lost.

Proculus, a Greek philosopher who wrote about Euclid some 700 years after his death, tells how Ptolemy I once asked Euclid if there was not an easier way to learn the discipline of geometry than through studying *The Elements*. Euclid answered the king's inquiry saying, "There is no royal road to geometry."

I. Bulmer-Thomas, ed., *Selections Illustrating the History of Greek Mathematics*, 1957.

T. L. Heath, *History of Greek Mathematics*, 1965.

G. Sarton, *The Study of the History of Mathematics*, 1936.

EULER, LEONHARD (1707–1783), Swiss mathematician. Euler was born in Basel but moved with his family to Rieden, where his father was the Calvinist pastor, and eventually attended the University of Basel, where his impressive mathematical knowledge was noticed by mathematician Johannes Bernoulli. Bernoulli tutored him privately and welcomed Euler into his home, where he became close friends of Bernoulli's sons Daniel and Johann II and his nephew, Nikolaus. At the age of seventeen, Euler took his master's degree.

Euler remained in Basel for several years; in 1727 the young Bernoullis, now living in Saint Petersburg, arranged for Euler to be invited to the Imperial Russian Academy, he readily accepted. However,

the only vacant position was in the medical section, so Euler diligently began learning physiology in preparation for his departure. The study of the ear led him to investigate the mathematical theory of sound, which subsequently suggested theories on the propagation of waves.

The Russian court, due to the death of the empress, had become less indulgent of its scientists, particularly the foreigners among then, but Euler somehow managed to secure a position in the mathematics section. When Daniel Bernoulli returned to Switzerland in 1733, Euler assumed the leading position in the academy.

His existence in Saint Petersburg brightened considerably with the accession of a new monarch, Anne duchess of Courland, in 1730. However, in 1735 he lost the sight of his right eye after spending three days solving an astronomical problem. Euler applied much time to the needs of the court, writing textbooks for schools and reforming the system of weights and measures, but none of these activities prevented him from producing numerous papers on mechanics, geometry, and algebra.

In 1740 Euler gladly accepted an invitation from *Frederick the Great to join the Berlin Academy. However, his fourteen years in the Russian court made him socially inadequate in this new environment. His circumspect character and clumsiness outside of mathematics annoyed the emperor, who was inclined to replace him, but no other mathematician would consider filling Euler's shoes. The emperor made his life intolerable, and after twenty-four years in Berlin Euler once more traveled, at the invitation of *Catherine the Great, to Saint Petersburg, where he was feted like returning royalty.

He began to lose the sight in his left eye, and by 1766 was completely blind. Perhaps through his deep religious faith, Euler approached his blindness with equanimity and, writing in chalk and dictating to his sons, his productivity increased. Defying credulity, he would recall and calculate the most complex formulae in his head. An attempt was made to restore the sight in his left eye in 1776. Although the operation was initially a success, an infection soon set in and after great suffering he eventually relapsed into total blindness.

One afternoon in 1783 he had amused himself by calculating the laws of the ascent of balloons. He played with his grandchild and then while taking his tea suffered a stroke. The man whom his peers dubbed "Analysis Incarnate" died soon after.

E. T. Bell, *Men of Mathematics*, 1961.

H. Eves, *An Introduction to the History of Mathematics*, 1964.

EURIPIDES (c. 484–406 B.C.E.), Greek dramatist. Youngest of the three great tragedians of ancient Greece (the others being *Aeschylus and *Sophocles), Euripides focused his drama on psychological and intellectual issues, making action and plot secondary. His plays are marked by the powerful passions of his characters, particularly the women, and demythologizing the gods and fate.

Born in Salamis, Euripides came from a well-to-do family, though his parents were satirized by *Aristophanes in his play *Frogs,* where his father Mnesarchus was presented as a shopkeeper and his mother Cleito was portrayed as a greengrocer. He spent his time immersed in the study of philosophy and science, and this intellectual propensity colored his approach to drama.

Ancient sources attribute ninety-two plays to Euripides, eighteen or nineteen of which have survived (the play *Rhesus* is of doubtful authenticity). He won the Dionysia prize only five times, his plays and characters apparently being too avant garde for the judges' taste. Nevertheless, he was popular among younger writers and was the most widely-read of the ancients in later generations.

In his earliest plays, Euripides forsook the mainstream myths utilized by Aeschylus and Sophocles as subjects; his earliest work, *Alcestis,* used a folk tale for the plot of this tragedy. A young king, Admetos, doomed to die, is allowed by the powers of fate to offer a substitute. When his wife, Alcestis, volunteers so as to save her husband, no protest is made and Admetos continues to live while Alcestis loses her life. For her valorous selflessness she is restored to life by the gods and in the end her husband regrets his egotism. The couple is then left to contemplate their new knowledge of one another. Contemporary critics found the conclusion inappropriately comic. Euripides next known play, *Medea,* was a work of violence and emotion. Like his first drama, it derived from a folk tale, this time about Medea, the wife of Jason of the Argonauts. Once again, Euripides depicts a woman capable of devotion to her husband, but Medea is driven to unleash her sorceress powers to avenge her husband's unfaithfulness when he tries to leave her for the daughter of King Kreon. Although she struggles to avert disaster and spare those she loves, Medea loses self-control, avenging her husband by murdering Kreon's daughter as well as her own children.

During the early years of the Peloponnesian War, Euripides wrote two nationalistic plays, *The Suppliants* and *The Children of Heracles,* based on the legends of Athens' heroic age, when the state had defeated tyrannical challengers. As the war progressed, Euripides grew disgusted with its violence and produced his play *The Trojan Women* to indict the recent Athenian destruction of neutral Melos. By portraying the sufferings of the Trojan queen Hecuba, he confronted his audience with the misery inflicted on an innocent community through the inhuman frenzy of war.

Euripides's next plays marked a retreat from contemporary events: *Ion* was a romantic tragedy, *Iphigenia in Tauris,* a melodrama, while *Electra* and

> - Account no man happy until he is dead.
> - Whom the gods destroy, they first make mad.
> - Venus, thy eternal sway
>   All the race of men obey.
> - The god of war hates those who hesitate.
> - Misfortune is friendless.
> - Sweet is the remembrance of troubles when you are in safety.
> - What is natural is never disgraceful.
> - A good custom is safer than law.
>
>   **Euripides**

Orestes explore the psychology of legendary murders. In *Electra,* Agamemnon's daughter broods over her dead father, murdered by his wife, Clytemnestra, and her lover, Aegisthus. Sequestering herself in a hut, her need for vengeance cuts her off from life, driving her to murder her mother and Aegisthus. The play's emphasis on fate is a break from the psychological realism of Euripides's earlier plays.

Iphigenia at Aulis was never completed but was later performed after another less capable writer filled in the missing gaps. The play is set at Aulis, where the Greek expeditionary force has been stalled on its way to Troy. Its commander, Agamemnon, feels compelled to sacrifice his daughter Iphigenia in order to propitiate the gods and thereby obtain a strong sailing wind, but he keeps his plans secret to avoid the wrath of his wife Clytemnestra. When discovered, Agamemnon cannot be dissuaded, caught up as he is in the war hysteria of his army. Iphigenia also cannot be saved by her betrothed Achilles, and she finally volunteers to go to the sacrificial altar as a patriotic gesture. The ending remains in doubt — either she is sacrificed or saved by the goddess Artemis.

In 408 B.C.E. Euripides left Athens for Macedonia at the invitation of King Archelaus, who was attracting Greek artists to his court. In Macedonia, Euripides encountered the religious ecstasy of the worshipers of the god Dionysus, an enthusiasm which was absent in Athens. Inspired by the emotionalism of the worshipers, he wrote *The Bacchae,* basing his plot on a Theban legend concerning Pentheus, ruler of Thebes, who met his ruin by resisting the revels of the followers of Dionysus. The play contrasts the repressive attitude of Pentheus with the uncontrolled raptures of the revelers, showing the need for moderation rather than extremes. Euripides died in Macedonia; according to one account he was accidentally torn to pieces by Archelaus's hunting dogs.

A. P. Burnett, *Catastrophe Survived,* 1972.

G. Murray, *Euripides and His Age,* 1965.

T. B. L. Webster, *The Tragedies of Euripides,* 1967.

F

FARADAY, MICHAEL (1791–1867), English physicist and chemist who formulated the electromagnetic theory of light. He was born in Newington, Surrey (now in Southwark), London, where his father, a blacksmith, had moved in search of work. His father suffered increasingly bad health and was never able to provide more than the bare necessities for his family. As a result, Faraday had practically no formal education and was forced to sell newspapers at a very early age to help support the family. At fourteen he was apprenticed to learn the art of bookbinding, but he was soon intrigued by the contents of the books as well, becoming a voracious reader of the books he was binding. His interest in science was first stimulated by a chance reading of the article "Electricity" in a copy of the *Encyclopaedia Britannica* that he happened to be rebinding; he began to study by himself what was then called natural philosophy.

In the course of his seven-year apprenticeship he developed extraordinary manual dexterity, which served him well in his later experimental research. To a large extent the discipline that he exhibited in his studies and his work was derived from his religious faith. His parents were members of the Sandemanian Church, a Protestant sect that believed in the literal truth of the New Testament, stressing love and a strong sense of community (they washed each other's feet). This faith gave him a strong sense of the unity of the universe. Sundays were strictly observed by the sect and Faraday was always in London on Sundays to attend services. When ordered to dine with Queen *Victoria on a Sunday evening, he wrestled with his conscience and then decided to accept her invitation. Although he was an elder of the church, he was suspended from membership for this act and for many years was only permitted to sit in the gallery during services.

Faraday became acquainted with a group of young men who were also interested in science. This group came together as the City Philosophical Society in London and was led by John Tatum, who gave them weekly lectures on scientific subjects and opened his library to them. Faraday became involved with this group in 1810, acquiring a basic scientific education in the process that enabled him to attend lectures on scientific subjects such as electricity, hydrostatics, geology, mechanics, chemistry, astronomy, and meteorology, about which he took meticulous notes. By chance, one of the bookbinder's customers offered him tickets to Sir Humphry *Davy's lectures at the Royal Institution, which he gratefully accepted. Faraday attended all the lectures and took copious notes, as he was honored to have the opportunity to listen to the great chemist. In 1812 Faraday's bookbinding apprenticeship came to an end. His good fortune continued, as he was recommended to be a secretary to Sir Humphry Davy in the latter part of 1812 when Davy was temporarily blinded by an explosion while examining chloride of nitrogen. After working for Davy briefly in this capacity, Faraday sent Davy his carefully bound notes of Davy's lectures, which flattered the chemist; it came as no great surprise when an assistant at the Royal Institution laboratory was fired for fighting and was succeeded by Faraday in 1813. Faraday developed under Davy's tutelage and in 1815, after intensive study of chemistry, he became a journeyman chemist.

In 1821 he discovered the principle of the electric motor and built a primitive model. He was also credited with discovering how to produce electric current by electromagnetic induction, that is, the production of electric current by a change in magnetic intensity. He invented the words *cathode*, *anode*, and *ion*, and discovered benzene, which became the basis of the synthetic dyestuffs industry. Always working on his own, with no collaborator or scientific assistant, he was the first to liquefy chlorine. By the 1830s he had gained recognition as one of Europe's leading scientists. His discovery of electromagnetic induction led to his production of the first dynamo. Faraday is also credited with formulating the basic law of electrolysis. Not only was he an outstanding self-directed and disciplined scientific researcher, but he became a highly regarded lecturer at the Royal Institution. Throughout his life he considered himself, his lectures, and his experiments as simply an instrument for the revelation of truth.

Because his religious faith frowned on acquiring personal profit, Faraday chose not to gain wealth through being consulted in special matters; he remained at the Royal Institution all his working life. In 1862 he resigned his position at the Royal Institution, continuing to lecture from time to time but retiring to a house provided for him by Queen Victoria at Hampton Court, near London, where he lived until his death.

G. Cantor, *Michael Faraday, Sandemanian and Scientist*, 1991.

W. L. Pearce, *Michael Faraday: A Biography*, 1965.

FAULKNER, WILLIAM (1897–1962), American author who fathered the genre of regional Southern literature. Born in New Albany, Mississippi, he moved in early childhood to nearby Oxford, where his father owned a livery stable and where he spent the greater part of his life. It was here that he created the fictional – and often nightmarish – world of Yoknapatawpha County and its inhabitants. He was the son of Murry Faulkner, the unsuccessful offspring of an aristocratic family, and his wife, Maud, who said on her deathbed that heaven would be a place where she did not have to speak to her husband.

Faulkner was a small, weak child, a trait to which he in part attributed his later success writing: "As big as you are, you can march anywhere you want, but when you're little you have to push." A good student as a young boy, Faulkner eventually dropped out of high school to work in his grandfather's bank. He attempted to enlist as a flier in the U.S. Army but was turned down because of his height. Rather than give up, Faulkner passed himself off as an Englishman and joined the Canadian Royal Air Force in World War I.

When he returned to Mississippi he continued his formal education, completing one year at the University of Mississippi. He also continued the habit of recreating himself, presenting himself as a war hero (although he had never flown) and a Bohemian literary figure (although he was as yet unpublished). Faulkner began to spend much of his time with Phil Stone, an older friend who recognized the seeds of talent and took it upon himself to support and educate the relatively untutored Faulkner. It was Stone who got Faulkner the unlikely position of postmaster in Oxford, Mississippi. His brother wrote incredulously of the job, "Here was a man so little attracted to mail that he never read his own being solemnly appointed the custodian of that belonging to others." Faulkner held the job for three years until his indifference became glaringly obvious and he was dismissed for reading on duty. Around the same time, his first book of poetry, *The Marble Faun*, was published. The anthology aroused little interest and most of the 500 copies were remaindered at ten cents each. Faulkner then moved to New Orleans, where he shared an apartment with Sherwood Anderson and wrote his first novel, *Soldier's Pay*, the story of a disfigured

flyer's return after World War I. Discovering that his talents lay in prose, he would nevertheless always consider himself "a failed poet." After a short trip to Europe, where he wrote one of his greatest novels, *The Sound and The Fury*, he married his recently divorced childhood sweetheart.

The *Sound and the Fury* was his first major literary triumph, the strange, disjointed telling and retelling of the Compton family saga through the eyes of a severely retarded man, a student on the verge of suicide, another family member, and a chorus of servants. The novel was critically well received but unfortunately was published on the eve of the Great Depression and, as a result, sold very few copies.

To make money he wrote *Sanctuary* in three weeks. Publication was held up as the publisher said it would land them both in jail. Its publication in 1931 marked a turning point, with one million copies sold by 1951. Critics called it the "peak of American sadism." The theme of the simultaneous destruction of a family and the culture in which they lived appears again in *Absalom, Absalom!*, and *As I Lay Dying*. Again the plotline must be teased out from the backdrop of the land and the voice of the storyteller. The Sutpens of *Absalom, Absalom!* are aristocrats whose characters make them responsible for their fate while, at the same time, hatreds, prejudices, and loves inculcated in them make them wholly the victims of it. The family in *As I Lay Dying* is similarly torn and becomes a model of human endurance.

Perhaps Faulkner's most famous fictional families are the Snopeses and Sartorises of Yoknapatawpha. Coming from all walks of life, they include John Sartoris, modeled after Faulkner's great grandfather, a lawyer, Confederate soldier, and railroad builder, and Flem Snopes, who comes from nothing and works his way up. These families appear over and over, sometimes as the major characters in the story, sometimes only as bit players, as if Faulkner could not bear to part with them.

The tragedy today is a general and universal fear, with the only question "When will I be blown up?" As a result young writers have forgotten the problem of the human heart in conflict with itself, which alone can make good writing because only that is worth writing about. I believe that man will not merely endure, he will prevail. He is immortal because he has a spirit capable of compassion and sacrifice and endurance.

**From William Faulkner's
Nobel Prize award speech**

In his own family life, adjusting to his marriage was more difficult than Faulkner had expected. For one thing, he now had to support his wife, who had grown accustomed to a lifestyle he could scarcely hope to maintain. Although they had known each other for twenty-five years, it seemed the best years of their relationship were over long before their marriage, which drifted; it seemed that a propensity for drinking was the only thing they shared. After the death of his infant daughter Alabama, Faulkner began to drink more frequently, following periods of intense productivity with weekend-long binges. To supplement his income he worked as a Hollywood scriptwriter and the Faulkners moved to California. His film credits include the Humphrey Bogart classics *To Have and Have Not* and *The Big Sleep*. Between 1936 and 1948 he wrote little, but after 1949 his output increased. The rest of his days were marked by great literary success, including the receipt of the Nobel Prize for literature in 1950.

D. Minter, *William Faulkner*, 1980.

P. Nicolaisen, *William Faulkner,* 1981.

L. Thompson, *William Faulkner: An Introduction and Interpretation*, 1967.

FERDINAND I (1503–1564), Holy Roman emperor. He was born in Spain, the son of Philip duke of Burgundy and grandson of Holy Roman Emperor Maximilian I. His mother was Joan the Mad, daughter of King *Ferdinand II and Queen *Isabella. Considered heir to the Spanish throne, Ferdinand was raised in that country, but the throne was inherited by his older brother, Charles

Ferdinand I

(*Charles V), who was crowned Holy Roman emperor in 1520. In the succeeding years, he and Ferdinand divided the empire between themselves and Ferdinand was granted the Habsburg duchies in Austria, Württemburg, Alsace, and Breisgau. He was also appointed head of the government during Charles's frequent absences.

Since Charles had a son, it was unlikely that Ferdinand would succeed to the throne. In the following years, however, Ferdinand broadened his power base. He was a competent administrator of his realms, although he was unable to subdue Austrian regionalism. In 1521 he married Anne, the sister of Louis II, king of Bohemia and Hungary, and they had two sons and eleven daughters. Louis II was childless and upon his death in 1526, Ferdinand was chosen as his successor. Ferdinand was unable to govern his new kingdom adequately. Approximately half the country was under Turkish occupation, while much of the remainder was occupied by János Zápolya, a rival claimant to the throne. In 1529 Ferdinand repelled a Turkish attempt to besiege Vienna; the following year, he signed a truce with Zápolya.

Like his brother Charles, Ferdinand was hostile to the newly founded Protestant religion, but he also recognized the importance of the Protestant princes of northern Germany as allies against the invading Turks. In turn, these princes endorsed Ferdinand as heir to the empire, rather than Charles's own son, Philip. Official sanction for Ferdinand came in 1531, when he was elected king of Rome, the title assumed by imperial successors.

With his authority acknowledged, Ferdinand pressured Charles into signing the Peace of Augsburg in 1555. The treaty recognized Lutheranism (but no other Protestant sect) as a co-official religion with Catholicism in the empire. Princes were given the right to decide which religion their subjects must follow, and all those who declined to conform were required to emigrate. In only a few principalities with a traditionally mixed population were both religions allowed to coexist. Although the Peace of Augsburg favored Catholicism, and declared that the emperor must be of that faith — Ferdinand's own son, Maximilian II, was forced to renounce Protestantism before succeeding to the throne — it was sharply condemned by the Catholic clergy and eventually led to the Thirty Years' War. But Ferdinand had won the admiration of the influential German princes and was chosen King of the German Territories the year the treaty was signed. The next year, Charles abdicated in his favor, and Ferdinand was crowned in Frankfurt in 1558.

Although his reign was brief, Ferdinand had ensured the rise of Protestantism as a legitimate religion in Europe and had absorbed Bohemia and Hungary into the empire.

P. S. Fichter, *Ferdinand I of Austria: The Politics of Dynasticism in the Age of Reformation*, 1982.

FERDINAND II (1578–1637), Holy Roman emperor whose zealous defense of the Counter-Reformation brought about the Thirty Years' War. Born in Graz, Austria, he was the son of Archduke Charles, ruler of inner Austria, grandson of *Ferdinand I, and brother of Emperor Maximilian II. He received a traditional religious education at the University of Ingolstadt, where he was influenced by the Jesuits; throughout his life he maintained a particular fondness for religious literature. He also acquired a knowledge of languages and was fluent in German, French, and Spanish. The Jesuits sought to prepare Ferdinand to rule his father's realm in the spirit of the Counter-Reformation. Upon succeeding his father in 1596 the otherwise good-natured prince adhered to his religious upbringing by embarking on a ruthless persecution of Protestants. Churches were shut, and adherents were given the choice of either reverting to Catholicism or emigrating.

When he was a child it seemed unlikely that Ferdinand would ascend the imperial throne, but Maximilian's sons, Rudolf II and Matthias, were childless. The Habsburg dynasty in Spain favored Ferdinand to inherit the throne in return for future territorial concessions in Alsace and Italy. A secret agreement was reached between Ferdinand and the Spanish Habsburgs in 1615; in 1617 he was elected king of Bohemia, and the next year king of Hungary. In 1619 Ferdinand was chosen to succeed Matthias as Holy Roman emperor.

Bohemia opposed Ferdinand's accession to the throne; the largely Protestant province recalled his harsh measures against their coreligionists and feared similar treatment. When Bohemia elected Frederick V of the Palatinate as king, Ferdinand mustered the support of Bavaria and the Catholic League to suppress the Bohemian insurrection in what became the Thirty Years' War. Bohemia was crushed in the Battle of the White Mountain (1620), and Spain took advantage of the confusion to enter the Palatinate. Within a short time, Protestant northern Europe, led by Sweden, was embroiled in a bitter conflict with Catholic middle Europe. The initial outcome of the war was largely in Ferdinand's favor. His forces, led by General Albrecht von *Wallenstein, conquered Silesia and Moravia. In 1629 Ferdinand enacted the Edict of Restitution, in which all former church lands were restored.

Ferdinand was a temperate monarch who maintained a frugal court. With his favorites, however, his generosity was often excessive. The nobles were particularly alarmed at the favor shown Wallenstein. The general was raised to the highest status in the nobility, with virtual independence in his new realm. At the same time, he was suspected of negotiating with the enemy (he had, in fact, met with France's Cardinal *Richelieu) to support them against the empire. The nobles persuaded Ferdinand to dismiss Wallenstein in 1630, but eighteen months later the emperor was forced to recall him to confront the Swedes. The first battle against Sweden was a resounding victory for Ferdinand's army, but the outcome was not decisive. Wallenstein faced Sweden again in 1632 in one of the fiercest battles of the war at Lützen. Both sides suffered tremendous casualties — the Swedish king *Gustavus Adolphus was killed — but Wallenstein was finally defeated. Ferdinand forced him to resign, and probably had a hand in his assassination in 1634.

Wallenstein was replaced by Ferdinand's son, Prince Ferdinand, who, despite a further victory over Sweden, urged the emperor to sign the Peace of Prague (1635), revoking the Edict of Restitution and assuring religious freedom for local princes. France entered the war shortly after, but Ferdinand was not to witness the outcome. He died in 1637 and was succeeded by his son *Ferdinand III.
C. V. Wedgwood, *The Thirty Years' War*, 1981.

FERDINAND III (1608–1657), Holy Roman emperor; the son of Emperor *Ferdinand II. Like his father, he received a traditional Jesuit education at the University of Ingolstadt. He was elected king of Hungary in 1626 and of Bohemia the following year. In 1636 his father had Ferdinand elected king of Rome ensuring his future right of inheritance to the imperial throne.

Ferdinand first played an important role in affairs of state following the assassination of General Albrecht von *Wallenstein in 1634. He replaced Wallenstein as commander of the imperial armies and led his troops to victory over Sweden at Nördlingen. Ferdinand recognized the damage that the Thirty Years' War was causing Europe and sought to bring an end to the conflict by persuading his father to sign the Peace of Prague (1635), whose terms included the restoration of the rights of Protestant princes and the repeal of the Edict of Restitution enacted in 1629. Although Ferdinand II relinquished all the achievements for which the war was fought, his concessions failed to end hostilities. France entered the war in 1637; a few months later Ferdinand became emperor upon the death of his father.

Ferdinand began his reign in tumultuous times. France's entry into the conflict led to a series of defeats for Ferdinand. His principal ally, Spain, was beset by revolts in Portugal and Catalonia, and the Catholic League of German states was irritated by the indecisive results of a lengthy and costly conflict. In 1644 Ferdinand began negotiations for a settlement of the conflict; the negotiations lasted four years, resulting in the Peace of Westphalia between the Holy Roman Empire and France and Sweden. Spain and the Netherlands soon signed similar accords in the treaties of Münster and Osnabrück. The empire abandoned its ambition to impose Catholicism on Europe and recognized the rights of local princes to considerable autonomy.

The last years of Ferdinand's reign were spent ridding his country of foreign troops. Although the Thirty Years' War had not achieved its goals, Ferdinand left his country with a powerful standing army; the empire was no longer dependent on rallying

troops and allies in times of crisis, thereby securing Austria's role as a leading European power.
C. V. Wedgwood, *The Thirty Years' War*, 1981.

FERDINAND II (1452–1516), king of Aragon. The king most admired by Niccolo *Machiavelli, he was the son of John II of Aragon. His father personally supervised his education, stressing both humanism and statesmanship, and ensured that he learned from personal experience as well as carefully selected teachers. He was nine when his father named him heir apparent and sixteen when he became king of Sicily in an attempt to make him a more acceptable husband for his cousin *Isabella, heiress of the prestigious kingdom of Castile. At seventeen he married Isabella over the objections of her brother, the king of Castile, forging the papal bull necessary to legalize the marriage of cousins when the pope refused to sign it. (A genuine bull was obtained from another pope after they were already married).

When the king of Castile died in 1474 a civil war broke out over his successors: Ferdinand and Isabella, or his daughter Juana and Alfonso V of Portugal. Ferdinand and Isabella won and ruled jointly, although each of their now-united kingdoms continued to be governed through its own institutions. In Castile, for instance, while official decrees were cosigned by both rulers, Isabella remained in charge of internal administration. Castile never really accepted or trusted Ferdinand, only tolerating him for Isabella's sake.

Ferdinand's goal was a strong united Spain and to achieve this he used any means at his disposal: trickery, diplomacy, war, religion. He traveled from kingdom to kingdom, bringing order out of anarchy and powerful nobles under the control of an even more powerful monarchy. As a result of Ferdinand's efforts, his young grandson inherited the strongest kingdom in Europe.

Ferdinand firmly believed that religious uniformity would make a united Spain both stronger and easier to rule. Christian Spaniards regarded church and state as one and the same and gave both their fierce support. They also supported Ferdinand's establishment of the Inquisition in 1478, and with its aim of stamping out all heresy among Christians, especially the greatly resented New Christians (Jews and Muslims who had been converted to Catholicism by force, under threat to their properties and lives, who still clung to their old ways and religions). The Inquisition, Ferdinand's favorite tool in his campaign to unify Spain, was extremely profitable as the crown had the right to confiscate the property of the condemned. From 1482 to 1492 Ferdinand fought against Granada, the last Muslim kingdom in Spain. In 1492 all Jews were expelled from Spain and in 1496 the pope gave Ferdinand and Isabella the honorary titles "The Catholic Monarchs." In 1502 the remaining Muslims were expelled, and Spain became, in theory at least, uniformly Christian.

The newly united kingdom became involved in Italian affairs in 1494 when Pope Julius II asked Ferdinand for help in expelling French forces from Italy. This led to a struggle between France and Spain for control of Italy that would last for over fifty years before Spain was finally victorious. Christopher *Columbus's voyages and the pope's carefully manipulated division of the New World between Spain and Portugal (then more powerful), "gave" most of it to Spain. This led to Spain's eventual conquest of the peoples, lands, and riches of the New World.

Isabella died in 1504 and Ferdinand mourned her, but soon married Germaine de Foix, the niece of the king of France, in an attempt to keep the crown of Castile. He lost it in 1506 when his son-in-law Philip, the husband of his only surviving child, the mentally afflicted Juana, claimed Castile. Philip was welcomed by a kingdom alienated by Ferdinand's quick remarriage.

Ferdinand stayed in his kingdom of Aragon until Philip died three months later, returning to Castile to become regent for Juana. Without Isabella's moderating influence, his rule for the next ten years was vindictively totalitarian and he continued his expansionary policies.

Finally Ferdinand began to age and became suspicious of those around him; he died at sixty-four in the forty-second year of his reign and was buried beside Isabella. During his reign he united the kingdoms of Spain, established the administrative and legal basis for a united Spain and a strong Spanish monarchy, expanded Spain's holdings in Europe, and discovered and claimed a rich new continent. He also sowed the seeds for the eventual destruction of Spain's economy by inaugurating an inquisition and expelling the Jews and Moors.
S. A. Bedini, ed., *The Christopher Columbus Encyclopedia*, 1993.
W. H. Prescott, *History of the Reign of Ferdinand and Isabella*, 1963.

FERMI, ENRICO (1901–1954), American physicist and Nobel Prize winner who directed research that culminated in the first controlled nuclear chain reaction. Born in Rome, Italy, from an early age Fermi enjoyed building electric motors and designing engines. Upon finishing high school, Fermi won a place at an institution for outstanding students in Pisa, where he excelled in his studies and obtained his doctorate.

In 1923 Fermi worked at Max Born's institute in Göttingen for one year, returning to Rome to teach mathematics at the university, then taking an interim post in Florence teaching theoretical mechanics and electricity. He achieved international prominence in theoretical physics with his 1926 paper, "On the Quantification of the Perfect Monoatomic Gas." That same year he was appointed to the newly-established professorship in theoretical physics at the University of Rome, where he tried to introduce

Fermi in his laboratory

modern physics in Italy through the writing of articles and textbooks.

Following Frédéric Joliot and Irène Curie's discovery of artificial radioactivity in 1933, Fermi and his colleagues succeeded in using neutrons instead of alpha particles to bombard atoms, and proceeded to produce artificial radioactivity in the majority of known elements; this discovery was a milestone in atomic physics. He and his team then discovered slow neutrons, finding that the speed at which neutrons impacted with atoms could be reduced if neutron bombardment took place in certain media, such as hydrogen or petroleum; this slowing-down process dramatically increased the rate of atomic activity. The team patented its discovery, which has become fundamental to the production of nuclear power for both civil and military applications.

Fearing for the safety of his Jewish wife after the imposition of anti-Jewish laws in Italy in 1938, Fermi accepted a professorship at Columbia University and emigrated to the United States with his family that year. He went via Stockholm, where he received the Nobel Prize in physics for his work in Rome.

The news of the discovery of fission, which Niels *Bohr brought to the United States in 1939, prompted physicists worldwide to work on developing an atomic chain reaction, and through a letter written by Albert *Einstein on behalf of Fermi's team at Columbia, their work came to the attention of President Franklin D. *Roosevelt. With war raging in Europe, Roosevelt decided to invest seriously in nuclear research with the aim of creating an atomic bomb. Thereafter, all research work was concentrated in Chicago.

Fermi suggested Chicago University's stadium as the test site for the first controlled nuclear chain reaction, which took place in December 1942. Soon after, Fermi and his colleagues developed the thermal column — a graphite block allowing only neutrons to pass through, thus increasing the effect of neutron bombardment. Along with all those involved in the atomic program, Fermi moved to Los Alamos, New Mexico, in 1943, and observed the first atomic test explosion. He was later appointed to a panel of scientists that made recommendations on the use of atomic weapons against Japan.

After the war Fermi became professor in the institute for nuclear studies at the University of Chicago, working mainly on the interaction between pions and nucleons. He stressed the need for international collaboration in nuclear research and opposed the nuclear arms race that followed the onset of the Cold War. In 1954 the U.S. Atomic Energy Commission made its first award to him, for outstanding work in nuclear physics, and these annual prizes subsequently became known as the Fermi Awards.

Fermi, who was outstanding both in theoretical and practical physics, died of stomach cancer before managing to write the course on nuclear physics which he hoped would have been his final contribution to science. The synthetic element Fermium, first identified in 1952, was named after Enrico Fermi.

L. Fermi, *Atoms in the Family*, 1954.

D. J. Keules, *The Physicists*, 1978.

E. Segre, *Enrico Fermi: Physicist*, 1970.

FLEMING, SIR ALEXANDER (1881–1955), Scottish bacteriologist who, along with Howard Florey and Ernst B. Chain, discovered and developed penicillin.

Fleming's discovery led to a revolution in contemporary medical practice, paving the way for the treatment of disease with antibiotics.

At thirteen, Fleming was sent to London, where he attended school. He left at fifteen and went to work for a shipping company, but when, in 1900, an uncle left him a legacy, his elder brother, Tom, an ophthalmic surgeon, suggested he use the money to study medicine. Fleming took some preparatory lessons and sat for the entrance exam for medical school, scoring highest of all the United Kingdom candidates.

Fleming studied at Saint Mary's hospital, specializing in surgery, but in 1906 he joined the research team with which he was to remain until his death.

With the outbreak of World War I in 1914 Fleming and several of his colleagues were stationed in Boulogne, France, where they set up a makeshift laboratory and research center in a fencing school. The war wounded were ravaged by infections, largely due to the deep, jagged wounds caused by explosives. Fleming witnessed the ineffectiveness of antiseptics in the treatment of these wounds and conducted experiments to show that not only was it impossible to sterilize war wounds with antiseptics but that the antiseptics themselves may even have helped to spread infection. Although this research of Fleming's has now been overshadowed by his later discoveries, many experts hold this to have been his most ingenious work.

In 1921, Fleming discovered lys201ozyme, a substance present in human, animal, and vegetable tissues that dissolves bacteria and is part of the body's natural defense system. Fleming's presentation of his findings to the medical establishment met, however, with an indifferent reception.

Fleming went on to study staphylococci bacteria, which he cultivated in agar in petri dishes; often such cultures were accidentally contaminated with airborne spores. As Fleming complained to a colleague one day: "As soon as you uncover a culture dish something tiresome is sure to happen. Things fall out of the air." On saying this, Fleming noticed that on this particular culture, all around the mold that had grown from the spore colonies of staphylococci had dissolved. On further experimentation, Fleming found that this mold inhibited the growth of several bacteria, including diphtheria and anthrax bacteria. He called his mold penicillin.

On presenting his new discovery to the medical world in 1929, Fleming once again met with indifference. He wanted to extract the active ingredient from his mold, but was unable to do so himself and failed to find a chemist who was prepared to, or felt able to extract it. For the next ten years Fleming conducted a series of experiments on penicillin as a local antiseptic, convinced of the importance of his discovery, although few others were. Finally, in 1939, Ernst Boris Chain and Howard Walter Florey

---

- Sport has had a considerable influence on my own career. Had I not taken an interest in swimming in my young days, I should probably not have gone to Saint Mary's hospital; I should not have had Almroth Wright as a teacher, and it is more than likely that I should never have become a bacteriologist.
- Surrounded by all those infected wounds, by men who were suffering and dying without our being able to do anything to help them, I was consumed by a desire to discover, after all this struggling and waiting, something which would kill these microbes (on his experiences in World War I) .
- Never neglect any appearance or any happening which seems to be out of the ordinary; more often than not it is a false alarm, but it may be an important truth.
- All the same, the spores didn't just stand up on the agar and say, "I produce an antibiotic, you know."

Sir Alexander Fleming

---

in Oxford perfected a method of purifying penicillin, and in World War II this was used on the wounded in Egypt with astonishing results.

When, in August 1942, Fleming successfully treated a meningitis sufferer with penicillin, news of the amazing cure spread throughout the medical world and the national press. The big pharmaceutical companies soon began to manufacture the antibiotic. Fleming was elected a Fellow of the Royal Society in 1943 and knighted a year later, following which, he toured the United States and Europe, receiving the Nobel Prize for physiology of medicine jointly with Chain and Florey in 1945.

In 1946 Fleming took over as principal of the institute, working until 1955. He died later that year and is buried in the crypt of Saint Paul's Cathedral, London.
G. McFarlane, *Alexander Fleming*, 1984.
A. Maurois, *The Life of Sir Alexander Fleming*, 1959.

FOCH, FERDINAND (1851–1929), French general. One of four children of a civil servant, Foch was born in Tarbes in the Hautes-Pyrénées department of France. One of his grandfathers had served as an officer under *Napoleon and young Foch eagerly devoured stories of his exploits; military books were from an early age his favorite reading. He enjoyed shooting but, due to a weak right eye, was forced to shoot from his left shoulder.

In view of his interests, the obvious career for Foch was one in the military. In preparation for entry into a military academy, he enrolled in a popular Jesuit school in Metz, absorbing with enthusiasm a strong Catholic education and excelling in mathematics. He was well liked by fellow pupils, regularly winning the prize for good conduct awarded by the students.

In 1870 Foch took the entrance examination for the Ecole Polytechnique in Nancy. It was a fateful year in French history with the Franco-Prussian War raging. Foch left his studies and volunteered as a lieutenant, but the troops in his unit were too young and inexperienced to be exposed to Prussian fire and were never sent into action. France's defeat came rapidly, and Foch felt embittered by the collapse of his country's army and believed the war should have been continued. He found motivation in a resolve to avenge the defeat and regain the provinces of Alsace and Lorraine.

Having passed the army examination with distinction, Foch chose to specialize in artillery and, as one of the best students, was given a choice of posting. Perhaps feeling homesick, he asked to serve in Tarbes. In addition to achieving success at the artillery school, Foch graduated from a course at the cavalry school, and in 1878 was promoted to captain. In 1883 he married and acquired the chateau of Trofeunteuniou. Foch felt quite at home as a landowner: he was fond of gardens and had a special interest in forestry.

In 1885 he was appointed instructor at the Ecole de Guerre. Although he was not an impressive lec-

FOCH IN ACTION

- I have only one merit: I have forgotten what I taught and what I learned.
- My center is giving way, my right is in retreat; situation excellent. I shall attack (at the Battle of the Marne, 1914).
- The edifice begins to crumble. Everyone attack (order of the day, 1918).
- Action is the governing rule of war.
- The most solid moral qualities melt away under the effect of modern arms.

turer, his views on such matters as the importance of using artillery bombardments to clear the ground for infantry were invaluable. By 1895 he was professor of military history and strategy and in 1908 was appointed director of the school. His slow advancement in the army ranks was impeded by his churchgoing, which in the eyes of the anticlerical government made him unreliable.

In 1913 Foch was given command of the Twentieth Army Corps in Nancy, close to the border with German-occupied Alsace-Lorraine. Nearing retirement, he had never fired a shot in war. All this changed with the outbreak of World War I, during which he became an international figure. His first engagement with the enemy, at Morhange, ended in defeat but he managed to slow down the German offensive, giving other French units time to regroup. His natural optimism encouraged his countrymen in the early days of the war when it seemed that all was lost.

Foch's brilliance was recognized in the battles on the Marne and the Yser in 1914, but a failed offensive at Artois in 1915 led to heavy losses of troops and Foch's removal from the front, albeit to a high advisory post in Paris. In 1916 he faced a further setback when seriously injured in a car crash.

Foch still had the capacity to inspire ordinary soldiers and retained the confidence of the French president, Georges *Clemenceau. In 1917 he was appointed minister of war, and in 1918 coordinator of all the Allied armies. Facing a fierce German offensive that once again threatened Paris, Foch held back troops, leaving the British to bear the brunt of the German advance. British generals were resentful but grudgingly took a liking to Foch, who had taken enthusiastically to the British habit of pipe smoking which made him an engaging figure in their eyes.

Trust in his command was justified. In a brave but risky move when faced with a new German offensive in July 1918, Foch prevailed over the opposition of General Philippe *Petain and withdrew reserves defending Paris in order to send them against the German flank at Mangin. The Germans were driven back to their defensive positions and sued for peace.

Foch was honored for his role in the victory and appointed a marshal of France. Recognizing the conclusion of his career, he commented to Clemenceau: "My work is finished, yours is beginning." The provinces of Alsace and Lorraine were returned to France but the attainment of the goal Foch had set himself nearly fifty years previously was no longer sufficient to satisfy him: he now wanted the 1814 French frontier of the Rhine River restored as a security against further German aggression. Throughout the 1920s he was concerned about the threat a resurgent Germany would pose, but to the French government his usefulness was restricted to appearances at patriotic ceremonies which he found wearisome. "I am a mere parcel, I let them push me up. They exhibit me, then store me away again," he remarked. His memoirs appeared in English in 1931, two years after his death.

G. Chapman, *The Third Republic of France*, 1962.
L. Derfler, *The Third French Republic, 1870–1940*, 1966.

FORD, HENRY (1863–1947), U.S. industrialist; the first automobile manufacturer to use assembly line labor-saving devices to produce automobiles more economically and efficiently.

Ford was born to Irish immigrants in Springwells Township, Michigan. As a youngster he already displayed mechanical skills and a knack for innovation and invention, and in 1879 Ford dropped out of school and went to Detroit, where he took a job as a machinist's assistant. When he returned to his father's farm he set up a small machine shop and sawmill, later working for different companies and honing his skills by working on clocks and watches. As an employee of Westinghouse, Ford set up and repaired their steam engines.

Ford moved to Detroit in 1891 and two years later he was made chief engineer of the Edison Illuminating Company. That same year he built his first one-cylinder gasoline motor. Soon after he began to build his first car, a two-cylinder light carriage which he completed in 1896. He did this while working for Edison during the daytime and working on his inventions well into the night.

Ford took his wife and two-year-old son for their first automobile ride the day after he and a friend road-tested the car. During the next week he drove all over Detroit, with a friend bicycling ahead as his flagman. In 1899, Ford quit the Edison Company and started the Detroit Automobile Company. This venture lasted about two years, ending with the company's bankruptcy. Ford's father approved of his son's interest in mechanics but thought Ford was wasting his time working on automobiles, telling Henry, "You'll never make a go of it." Ford then decided to try his hand at making racing cars, more for the purpose of gaining a name than because he supported this use of automobiles. In 1901 he entered his car in a race at the Detroit Fairgrounds, at which the first prize was $1,000 and a crystal punch bowl. It was a twenty-five-mile race, with Ford's major competitor being Alexander Winton, who had an auto-manufacturing company. For more than half

Henry Ford on the racetrack

the race Ford was behind the Winton car but he ended up the winner. When he got out of his car, covered with dirt and visibly shaken, Ford said, "Boy, I'll never do that again! I was scared to death."

In 1903, with the help of a group of backers, Ford organized the Ford Motor Company, of which he owned 25 percent of the stock, and the company began to produce cars that sold well. In 1906 he had a disagreement with Alexander V. Malcolmson, a major stockholder, and bought him out, purchasing 255 shares for $175,000, which made him the majority stockholder. Ford's plans to build an affordable car took off after that. He told one of his employees, "This is a great day. We're going to expand this company, and you will see it grow by leaps and bounds." He began with the low-priced Model N and went on to produce the Model T, which first came out in 1908. The Model T caught the nation's imagination and newspapers praised its virtues. In 1913 Ford introduced the conveyor-belt assembly line and the following year 250,000 Model Ts were sold. Altogether fifteen million Model Ts, also known as Tin Lizzies or Flivvers, were marketed. By manufacturing a large number of the same model, Ford was able to take advantage of mass production, utilizing standardized parts. Although he understood and promoted the benefits of assembly line production, he said, "The idea of repetitive labor — the doing of one thing over and over again and always in the same way — is nothing less than terrifying."

Ford was innovative in rewarding his employees and established an excellent relationship with his workers. Will Rogers said of Ford, "It will take a hundred years to tell whether he helped us or hurt us, but he certainly didn't leave us where he found us."

By 1919 the Ford family had gained complete control of the Ford Motor Company; Ford had become such a powerful force in the company that even key people who disagreed with him were not retained. In 1919 Ford's son Edsel was made president of the company, and he showed a talent for the position. There were differences of opinion between father and son, primarily because Henry Ford failed to see changing trends in automobile styling, color, and manufacture. Although the Model T continued to sell well in the 1920s, General Motors and Chrysler were beginning to make inroads in Ford's sales. In 1927 Ford stopped producing the Model T and it was replaced by the Model A.

Ford dabbled in politics and ran unsuccessfully as a Democratic candidate for the Senate. In World War I he chartered a "Peace Ship," which he sailed "to get the boys out of the trenches by Christmas," but at the same time he was making a fortune in military materiél. In 1918 he bought the weekly *Dearborn Independent* to publicize his political views and published a ninety-issue series of anti-Semitic articles blaming the Jews for the ills of the world, including a reprint of the notorious forgery, *The Protocols of the Elders of Zion*. After being sued for libel by a Chicago Jewish lawyer, Ford issued an apology in 1927 and retracted his attacks on Jews; that same year he closed the *Dearborn Independent*.

Over the years, Henry Ford and his son Edsel had many disputes and the senior Ford again assumed presidency of the company after his son's death in 1943. In 1945 Edsel's son, Henry Ford II, became president of the Ford Motor Company.

In 1936 the Ford Foundation was set up primarily to fund international scientific, educational, and charitable projects.

J. Brough, *The Ford Dynasty*, 1987.

P. Collier and D. Horowitz, *The Fords: An American Epic*, 1986.

A. Nevins and F. E. Hill, *Ford*, 3 vols., 1954-1963.

FOX, CHARLES JAMES (1749–1806), English statesman and orator; a leading advocate of liberal reform. Fox lived in an age when political corruption was rampant in Britain, with parliamentary seats, votes, and even legislation for sale. The aristocracy dominated Parliament, with businessmen playing a small role, albeit one that was growing with the influence of the industrial revolution. King *George III used his position and powers to influence Parliament, rewarding his supporters and punishing those who opposed him; he rewarded Fox's father, Henry, with the title of Baron Holland for helping buy the votes of members of Parliament.

Educated at Eton and Oxford, Fox began his parliamentary career at the age of nineteen, when his father bought him a seat. At twenty-one he became lord of the admiralty, again due to his father's influence, and inherited a fortune at twenty-five when his father, mother, and elder brother died. He became a champion of liberal causes in the great parliamentary battles of the late eighteenth century. These battles had as their subjects the American Revolution, King George III's seeking control of Parliament, the abuses of the East India Company, the slave trade, and the French Revolution.

Fox was a man of contradictions. Though he believed that government should be dominated by the propertied classes, he nonetheless supported the principles of the French Revolution. His mind and memory earned him a reputation as England's most competent orator in an age of great orators. Most of his parliamentary career was spent in opposition and he held office for less than a year in all, yet, despite George III's hatred of him, he was one of the most popular men in England.

Fox opposed British colonial policies both before and during the American Revolution, feeling that they were unjust and that the cost of collecting taxes from far-flung colonies was prohibitive while war would simply interfere with England's profitable American trade; Edmund *Burke felt the same and the two men became friends and allies, fighting for radical causes. The American Revolution's success caused the government to fall and Fox became England's first foreign secretary, but only for a few months: his continued feuding with the king saw to that. Believing that the crown's excessive power was at the root of all England's evils, Fox fought to limit that power. In particular he opposed George's attempts to change England's constitutional monarchy, where the king's power was limited by law and tradition, into a government where the king, not Parliament, shaped policy, made laws, and selected ministers. Fox's friendship with the Prince of Wales, the son whom George detested, was another source of irritation to a king slipping in and out of madness. Fox also endured the continuing hostility of William *Pitt, the prime minister.

The East India company had been misruling India for years. Outraged at the company's history of extortion, cruelty, and slaughter, Fox fought to transfer India's rule to the British government. However, his India Reform Bill of 1783 failed, largely because George made it known that he would regard anyone who voted for it as his personal enemy.

Fox's support for the principles of the French Revolution ended his friendship with Burke, who became the spokesman for Conservative opposition to it. Fox himself spurned the revolution after *Louis XVI's execution, but his opposition party continued to decrease in numbers, especially after war — which he opposed — broke out between England and France in 1793. Welcoming the Peace of Amiens in 1802, he traveled to France, where he was bestowed honors and received by *Napoleon Bonaparte. Again foreign secretary in 1806, he tried to keep peace with the French ruler — even warning him of an assassination plot — and might have succeeded had he not died of dropsy a few months later. Fox was buried in Westminster Abbey next to his perennial opponent, Pitt.

L. G. Mitchell, *Charles James Fox and the Disintegration of the Whig Party*, 1971.
G. O. Trevelyan, *The Early History of Charles James Fox*, 1971.

FOX, GEORGE (1624–1691), English founder of the Society of Friends (Quakers). The son of a Puritan weaver in Leicestershire, Fox was apprenticed to a cobbler who kept sheep. He lived in a time and place very preoccupied with religion; tending sheep gave him time to brood over religious matters. He felt that Christianity had failed if Christians could indulge in excesses and left home to travel the country and seek answers to his spiritual doubts and questions.

Fox turned inward and had a religious revelation that gave him the answers he had been seeking: everyone has a divine light in his heart which will guide him if he but listens; no one is holier than anyone else. Fox felt that his belief revived primitive Christianity after ages of apostasy, and that an individual's revelation from the divine light within is as sacred as the revelation that produced the Bible. He rejected prearranged form, external sacraments, and consecrated buildings.

His gospel of the brotherhood and equality of man led to Quakers becoming fervent social reformers. He advocated reform of the penal code and prison conditions, abolition of capital punishment, education for both men and women (women had equality with men in his organization), payment of a living wage, serving honestly, and treating slaves well. All people were ministers, for "to be bred at Oxford or Cambridge was not sufficient to fit a man to be a Minister of Christ."

Fox began to preach, traveling about on foot, and establishing small local congregations. At first (1648–1652), his followers were few and his attacks on established religious authority and ritual sometimes led to his being stoned and beaten. His insistence on addressing everyone as "thee" instead of using the plural pronoun "you" to people of high rank, his refusal to doff his hat (a gesture of reverence he reserved for God), or take oaths, offended people of authority and rank; they felt it showed a lack of respect, and such actions and omissions led to many beatings and imprisonments for Fox and his followers.

In 1649 Fox was imprisoned for the first time — he was imprisoned eight times between 1649 and 1673 — when he interrupted the minister preaching in Nottingham Church. Fox was accused of blasphemy and imprisoned for a year (1650). For telling the magistrates to tremble at the name of the Lord he received the nickname "Quaker." His jailers were so impressed by his preaching and conduct that he was soon allowed to preach and to attend meetings outside his prison. In one such instance he so impressed a group of soldiers that they offered him captaincy which he rejected on the grounds that war was evil and unlawful and that *Jesus's servants do not fight — earning himself six months in the felons' dungeon. In 1652 he won over large groups in Westmoreland, including Margaret Fell, who became his faithful follower and friend. During the Commonwealth, under Oliver *Cromwell, Fox traveled and preached all over England and Scotland, was imprisoned four times, and had several meetings with Cromwell. A powerful and eloquent speaker, he inspired many men and women to become preachers and set out with missionary zeal to convert others.

The Restoration (1660) led to severe persecutions of the Quakers, who were suspected of plotting against the king. Fox was imprisoned four times, including a sentence of two and one-half years in a cold damp cell that ruined his health. He organized a formal Quaker network of monthly, quarterly and yearly meetings to discuss problems and to meet their business and religious needs.

Fox married Margaret Fell (1669) but, each busy with work for the Quakers, they were seldom together. Worn out, he spent his last fifteen years living with different friends around London, an honored elder who preached, wrote, and was consulted on practical matters, and was overjoyed when the Toleration Act of 1689 brought relief to the Quakers.

V. Noble, *The Man in Leather Breeches*, 1933.
D. E. Trueblood, *The People Called Quakers*, 1966.
H. E. Wildes, *Voice of the Lord, A Biography of George Fox*, 1965.

FRANCIS I (1494–1547), king of France from 1515. The son of Charles of Orléans, count of Angoulême, and Louise of Savoy, Francis's claim to the throne was recognized in his infancy when his cousin Louis XII became king. His position as heir presumptive was further strengthened in 1514, when he married Claude of France, daughter of Louis XII and Anne of Brittany, a union that ensured the eventual incorporation of the duchy of Brittany into the domain of the crown.

A skilled athlete and warrior, Francis received an irregular education, including some classical studies

and much courtly etiquette and chivalry. Women figured prominently in his life: first, his mother, whom he revered and who had brought him up after his father's premature death; second, his learned sister Marguerite d'Angoulême, with whom he spent his childhood; and third, a succession of mistresses, who confirmed his image as a great lover.

Francis's long reign was marked by his interminable conflict with *Charles V. Assuming the crown at the age of twenty amid popular acclaim, he immediately set out to realize his predecessors' unfulfilled ambitions in Italy. The resounding victory of Marignano (1515) put him in possession of Milan and led to an advantageous agreement with Pope Leo X. However, in 1519 he lost his attempt to gain imperial election to Charles I of Spain, who became the Holy Roman Emperor Charles V.

Francis tried to obtain *Henry VIII of England's support in a sumptuous and friendly meeting, known as the Field of the Cloth of Gold (1520). The meeting, held at the Plain of Ardre in France, was conducted in a magnificent manner, accompanied by festivities and games. The French king wanted to draw England to his side in his conflict with Charles V, but Henry VIII continued to support the emperor. In 1521 the war with Charles V began; in 1523 Francis's general, Charles of Bourbon, defected after a quarrel with the king and joined the emperor. The following year Charles of Bourbon drove the French out of Italy and invaded Provence. In 1525 he brought upon Francis his greatest humiliation when, at the head of the imperial troops, he defeated and captured him in the Battle of Pavia. Francis was imprisoned for ten months in Spain, steadfastly refusing to accept terms injurious to France. In the end he signed the Treaty of Madrid (1526) and delivered his two eldest sons as hostages to guarantee its fulfillment.

He was no sooner released than he declared the treaty void. He now laid claim to Burgundy and supported the emperor's enemies in Italy. The war dragged on until concluded with the Peace of Cambrai (the so-called Ladies' Peace), negotiated by Francis's mother and Charles's aunt, Margaret of Austria. Francis left Italy and married the emperor's sister Eleanor (1530); he was given back his sons and retained Burgundy. Hostilities were resumed in 1536. Encircled by the Habsburgs, who now dominated Spain, the Netherlands, Germany, and Italy, Francis did not hesitate to call upon the Ottoman Turks for aid or to support the Protestant Schmalkaldic League (a defensive alliance of the German Protestant states and imperial towns) against Charles V. The pressure of the Turks in Hungary forced Charles to make an accommodation (1538), but conflict broke out again, to be settled by another treaty in 1544. While the borders of France underwent further adjustments, Francis was barred from realizing any of his ambitions in Italy.

Domestically, Francis was more successful in spite of his habitual carelessness with regard to expenditure and administration. A buoyant French economy made possible his costly foreign policies and, for his part, the king organized a more centralized system of tax collection. The machinery of government, especially the council (*conseil du roi*), was similarly reshaped in an attempt to make the secretaries responsible directly to the king, and the French language became mandatory in all legal matters. During the latter part of his reign the Reformation began to have effects in France. Caught between his Catholic ministers and the numerous Protestant sympathizers in his entourage, the king hesitated. In his last years he issued a number of repressive edicts that led to the execution of several prominent Protestants and, in 1545, authorized a wave of persecution and massacres against the old sect of the Waldensians in southern France.

Francis is remembered chiefly as a great patron of arts and letters and a consistent supporter of Renaissance culture. He built numerous chateaux, notably at Chambord, Blois, and Fontainebleau, which signaled a new age in French architecture. At Fontainebleau he established the school of decorative art headed by the Italians Rosso and Primaticcio; among other Italian artists whom he invited to France were *Leonardo da Vinci and Benvenuto Cellini. The printer Robert Estienne, the poet Clément Marot, and the author François *Rabelais were all the recipients of his royal favors. In 1530 Francis founded the Collège de France as an institution of humanist learning to counterbalance the conservative University of Paris.

Continually traveling about his kingdom, being in direct contact with people everywhere, Francis was forgiven his wasteful foreign adventures and remembered affectionately as *le grand roi François*. Succeeding generations were impressed by the fact that he ruled over a unified nation, presenting a much brighter image than the France torn by civil strife of the latter half of the sixteenth century.

F. Hackett, *Francis I*, 1934.
R. J. Knecht, *Francis I*, 1982.

FRANCIS (FRANZ) JOSEPH (1830–1916), emperor of Austria and king of Hungary. Francis Joseph was the last great Habsburg ruler of the vast Austro-Hungarian Empire. The eldest son of the archduke Francis Charles and Sophia, the daughter of King Maximilian I Joseph of Bavaria, he was a devoted, austere ruler who rose at five o'clock each morning and worked well into the night overseeing every detail of the enormous Habsburg administration. During his sixty-eight year reign he consolidated the power of the monarchy through a network of loyal political administrators living in the multinational empire's numerous regions and provinces. Inheriting an empire on the verge of collapse, he created a major power that thrust the continent into the most destructive war the world had seen: World War I.

Francis Joseph succeeded his childless uncle, Emperor Ferdinand I, to the Austrian throne at Olmutz in 1848. Revolution had spread to all the major capitals of the Austrian Empire, and the young Catholic monarch raised hopes of restoring central authority. During the first ten years of his reign, he was determined to establish order in the empire while securing Austria's predominance in Germany. At the Olmutz convention of 1850 Prussia acknowledged Austria's power abroad. One year later, the emperor revoked the constitution, which he had promised only two years earlier.

Francis Joseph's mobilization of Austrian troops on the Russian border in Galicia during the Crimean War alienated the czar, who had helped him quell the 1849 rebellion in Hungary. Then, he hastily led the Austrians into battle against Sardinia and France, suffering a terrible defeat at Solferino in 1859. Rather than put his forces under the command of his allies, the Prussians, he negotiated the Peace of Villafranca, which ceded Lombardy to the kingdom of Sardinia. His defeat abroad now began to erode his power at home and curbed his attempt to establish absolute power.

The congress of princes at Frankfurt in 1863 was a triumph for Francis Joseph. The Prussians, however, did not attend; instead, no longer fearing its Austrian neighbor, Prussia concluded an alliance with Italy, well aware of Francis Joseph's territorial claims against the newly founded state. Hostilities were inevitable, and in the war that broke out in 1866 the Prussian army scored victories against the Austrians, expelling them from Germany. Italy then quickly ousted the Austrians from Venetia and Francis Joseph was soon facing a fatal crisis within his own empire, in Hungary.

The establishment of the Dual Monarchy in 1867 signaled the emperor's move toward internal compromise. Realizing his grave position, Francis Joseph made Austria and Hungary equal partners in the monarchy while the Slavs of Poland, Bohemia, Slovakia, Croatia, and Serbia were left emptyhanded. He continued to pay an inordinate amount of attention to foreign policy while the Hungarians subjected the Croatians and Serbians to Magyarization, thereby making them enemies of the Dual Monarchy. Francis Joseph's foreign policy was highly personal and dynamic. In 1878 the Congress of Berlin approved Austria-Hungary's claims to Bosnia-Herzegovina and an alliance was concluded with Germany a year later, with a Triple Alliance involving Italy following in 1882. The emperor's visits to Russia prevented potential friction and conflict over the empire's treatment of the Slav populations in the south. However, the formal annexation of Bosnia-Herzegovina in 1908 drove a wedge between the two major powers asserting predominance in the region.

Francis Joseph's life was plagued by personal tragedy. His wife, Elizabeth of Bavaria (whom he married in 1854), was not known for her loyalty to her husband and his court's formalities. In 1898, while strolling along the shore of the Lake Geneva, she was fatally stabbed by an Italian anarchist. Ten years earlier the heir apparent, Crown Prince Rudolph, who opposed his father on political grounds, committed suicide with his mistress at the remote hunting lodge of Mayerling. The assassination of the emperor's nephew, Francis Ferdinand, and his wife, by a Serbian student in Sarajevo, provoked the ultimatum to Serbia that drew the European continent into World War I. Francis Joseph supported the ultimatum of 1914 because Germany was there to stand by him. However, it took many lies, mostly by his own foreign minister, to win the emperor's approval.

Francis Joseph died at the height of the war that ushered in modern warfare. At the end of his life, he was a respected ruler who held together a deteriorating empire. Under his successor, Karl, the nephew of the assassinated Francis Ferdinand, the empire would last only another two years.

E. Crankshaw, *The Fall of the House of Habsburg*, 1963.
J. Redlich, *Emperor Francis Joseph of Austria*, 1929.
A. J. P. Taylor, *The Habsburg Monarchy 1866-1918*, 1948.
L. Valiani, *The End of Austria-Hungary*, 1973.

FRANCIS OF ASSISI, SAINT (Francesco di Pietro di Bernardone; 1182–1226), founder of the Franciscan order. Called the seraphic or angelic saint, Saint Francis of Assisi was a leading figure in the movement for church reform in the thirteenth century. He founded three Franciscan orders: the monastic friars for men, the Poor Clares women, and a lay order for those who wanted to follow his teachings while remaining worldly.

His father was a rich textile merchant in Assisi, Italy, and his mother was of cultured French descent; he was educated to read and write in Latin and until age twenty he assisted his father in business. Francis aspired to a martial reputation, and when Assisi entered into a dispute with neighboring Perugia in 1202 he joined the battle, but was captured and imprisoned by the Perugians for several months. After his release he fell seriously ill and this confinement brought him his first opportunity for deep spiritual self-examination.

A cluster of experiences resulting in Francis's conversion occurred at this time. On a pilgrimage to Rome he was moved to exchange clothes with a beggar and spend a day begging for alms. Theretofore disgusted by the lepers, he now gave them alms and kissed a leper's hand, expressing his feelings of universal humanity. Finally, he had a series of visions of Christ. In one of his visions Christ told Francis to "rebuild his house which is in ruins." Francis, who at that time was standing in the crumbling Chapel of Damiano outside Assisi, returned to his father's house. Collecting bolts of cloth, he loaded his father's horse and proceeded to another town, where he sold everything. He then returned to offer the money to the priest of the decrepit church. Francis's father tried to take him to the civil authorities but the youth would not obey. Proclaiming his

Praised be my Lord for our mother the earth, that sustains us and keeps us, and brings forth diverse fruits and flowers of many colors and grass.

Praised be my Lord for all those who pardon one another for his love's sake, and who endure weakness and tribulation; blessed are they who peaceably shall endure, for thou, O most highest, shalt give them a crown.

Praised be my Lord for our sister, the death of the body, from which no man escapes. Woe to him who dies in mortal sin! Blessed are they who are found walking by the most holy will, for the second death shall have no power to do them harm.

Praise ye and bless the Lord, and give thanks unto him and serve him with great humility.

Saint Francis of Assisi

only true father to be in heaven, Francis went off by himself to the wooded area around the city.

Having given up his possessions, Francis nevertheless managed to restore the Chapel of Damiano as well as two others around Assisi. Inspired by the surrender of property proclaimed by Christ to the Apostles, Francis committed himself to a life of poverty and began to preach as a layman to the people of his community. Soon a group of followers gathered around him, attracted by his character and kindness. In 1209 Francis together with a dozen disciples journeyed to Rome and received the verbal approval of Pope Innocent III to establish a new order.

Francis and his friars returned to the area of Assisi, basing themselves in Porziuncola and relying on the alms of the community for their survival. Their preaching followed the basic teachings of Christ and soon attracted many more adherents. Francis taught his followers to utterly deny the self, using whatever they were given to help others. He and his followers kept no possessions for themselves, even as communal property. In 1217 the order was organized by provinces, with supervising ministers.

Saint Francis's material poverty opened the way for a recognition of the common bond of every creature, all united in their dependence upon God. He spoke of every element and experience in creation as his brothers and sisters. Not only "brother sun" and "sister moon" but, toward the end of his life, suffering from a mortal sickness, he even wrote of "sister Death."

Francis set out for the Holy Land but was shipwrecked. During the next years he tried to reach the Moors in Spain in order to convert them but illness incapacitated him. In 1219 he went to Egypt on his way to the Holy Land and entered the camp of the Muslim Saracens. The sultan allowed him to proceed to Palestine, but when he reached the Holy Land he was forced to hurry home as word reached him that

Saint Francis preaching to the birds

the friars in Italy, now numbering some 5,000, were locked in dispute over the direction the order was to take. The simplicity of Francis's rule of life had given but scanty guidance to the friars and he returned to Assisi to expand and clarify the rule of life laid down at the order's inception. This expanded rule was approved by Pope Honorius III in 1223, and with that Francis's involvement in the order waned progressively during the remainder of his life.

In the summer of 1224 Francis removed himself to a mountain retreat at La Verna near Assisi for the celebration of the Assumption of the Blessed Virgin Mary and in order to prepare himself for Saint Michael's Day. He planned a fast of forty days, praying to know how best to serve God. As he prayed he was overwhelmed by a vision of Christ that inflamed his heart and left him with stigmata, wounds on his hands and feet similar to those of crucifixion. He suffered from these wounds for two years, hiding them from his followers, as well as being afflicted by near blindness until his death.

In 1228 he was canonized by Pope Gregory IX. In 1939 Saint Francis was made patron saint of Italy and in 1979 he became patron saint of ecology.

L. Boff, *Saint Francis*, 1982.

A. Fortini, *Francis of Assisi*, 1981.

R. D. Sorrell, *Saint Francis of Assisi and Nature*, 1988.

FRANCO, FRANCISCO (1893–1975), Spanish leader. Born in El Ferrol in northwest Spain, Franco graduated from Toledo military academy in 1910 as a second lieutenant. He was soon sent to join the Spanish Legion in Morocco, where he was seriously wounded. He soon recovered, was repeatedly promoted, and by 1926 was the youngest man to hold the rank of brigadier in all of Europe.

The short, stout man had neither the appearance nor the personality to make him a typical soldier-hero. Nevertheless, his competence as a field commander and skillful, calculating tactician made him a respected figure within the powerful military establishment, and in 1927 he was placed in charge of the prestigious military academy at Saragossa.

Franco's academy was closed down by the Republican government in 1931. The political pendulum swung temporarily to the right in the elections of 1933 and General Franco found employment in brutally and efficiently quashing a rebellion of Communist miners in the Asturias. However, in 1936 a left-wing government came to power, splitting the country between the two political poles. Franco was punished for his role in the suppression of the miners by being sent to command a garrison in the Canary Islands. However, in July 1936 he took a key role in a revolt organized by General Emilio Mola. Franco secured Spanish Morocco for the Nationalist rebels in a move that set the stage for the onset of civil war. The deaths of fellow conspirators and their failure to match his record of military success led to him becoming leader of the right-wing Nationalist, or Fascist, forces. In October 1936 he was formally proclaimed head of the Spanish state, de facto leader of the half of the country that his supporters controlled.

In the three years (1936–1939) of savage fighting and horrific massacres that made up the Spanish Civil War, Franco's forces ultimately got the upper hand. The troops and equipment he received from Benito *Mussolini and Adolf Hitler gave him a qualitative edge, and Madrid and Barcelona fell in 1939. Franco had no inclination to extend clemency to the defeated, whom he characterized as the "anti-Spain" in "the struggle between good and evil" that "never ends, no matter how great the victory..." With executions, long prison sentences, and exile he initiated the "New Order" he had promised the Spaniards three years earlier.

Although Hitler and Mussolini had been generous in their assistance and Franco's sympathies were definitely with their cause, he had never been at ease with his allies, rightly suspecting that they were using his country's struggle to further their own ends. When World War II broke out shortly after the end of the Spanish Civil War, Germany and Italy wanted to see dividends on their investments of men and money, but Franco was unwilling to oblige to the degree they expected. He was determined to keep his war-weary country out of the conflict. He sent the Germans 47,000 men for the campaign against Russia and he granted them naval bases at the start of the war but, to Hitler's dismay, he refused to enter an alliance. Hitler was once kept waiting for half an hour while Franco enjoyed his siesta, only to learn that there would be no Spanish commitment to join the Axis camp. Hitler told Mussolini that he would prefer to have three or four teeth extracted than endure such a futile meeting again. Franco succeeded in maintaining Spanish neutrality throughout the war.

Although he governed a one-party state and gloried in the bombastic title of El Caudillo (the "boss"), Franco was clearly leading a coalition of army, church, and business interests. Voices of dissent in labor and intellectual circles were harshly repressed, yet for all the suffering the regime imposed, Franco never established an all-powerful party apparatus on the Nazi model.

The end of World War II ushered in a period of diplomatic isolation for Spain, which was expelled from the United Nations. Franco took the rebuff in his stride and succeeded in cultivating closer ties with the United States and the Arab world. Spain was readmitted to the United Nations in 1955 and the following two decades saw increasing prosperity, with industrial development and the growth of the tourist industry.

Franco kept his grip on power to the end. Events proved his 1947 description of his rule as merely an emergency interlude before the restoration of a "representative monarchy" to be more than the empty rhetoric it seemed at the time: on his death in 1975 there was a peaceful transfer of power to a constitutional monarchy under King Juan Carlos.

S. G. Payne, *The Franco Regime*, 1987.
J. W. O. Trythall, *El Caudillo: A Political Biography of Franco*, 1970.
J. Yglesias,*The Franco Years*, 1977.

FRANKLIN, BENJAMIN (1706–1790), American author, printer, diplomat, scientist, and inventor. Benjamin Franklin is often held up as an example of the self-made American.

His father sailed to America from England in 1683 and settled in Boston, Massachusetts. His mother was from Nantucket Island. Though he had a demonstrated gift for reading and learning, Franklin attended school for only two years. At the age of ten, he was apprenticed to his father, a candle and soap maker. But despising the work, he was instead apprenticed to his older brother James, a printer.

An avid reader, Franklin decided that he would try his hand at writing. James had begun to publish an anti-clerical newspaper, *The New-England Courant*, and sixteen-year old Benjamin sent submissions of a satiric nature to him under an assumed name: Mrs. Silence Dogood. In all, fourteen "Dogood Papers" were published anonymously.

A series of disagreements with his brother prompted Franklin to leave Boston in 1723. Landing in Philadelphia wet, dirty, and hungry, with nothing but "a Dutch dollar and about a shilling in copper" in his pocket, the industrious youth soon found work with a printer. Impressed with Franklin's work, the governor of Pennsylvania decided to give him a chance to set up his own business. In 1724

Governor Keith, who wished to have at his disposal a printer to spread his political views, sent Franklin to England to make purchases on credit. After a seven-week crossing, Franklin discovered that Keith had no credit in England and as such Franklin was stranded. He found work in printing houses and remained in London until 1726.

About a year after his return to Philadelphia, he set up his own print shop. In 1729 he began publishing *The Pennsylvania Gazette*, which was enormously successful and in time earned him a fortune. Another highly profitable venture was *Poor Richard's Almanack*, an annual publication filled with homey proverbs, satiric verse, and sardonic predictions of the weather and the political climate.

In 1730 Franklin married Deborah Read, a woman he had courted before he left for England. In his absence she had married another, but her husband soon abandoned her. Reports of his death left

---

THE WIT AND WISDOM OF BENJAMIN FRANKLIN

- We must all hang together or we shall all hang separately.
- Without freedom of thought there can be no such thing as wisdom; without freedom of speech, no public liberty.
- If a man empties his purse into his head, no one can take it away from him. An investment in knowledge always pays the best interest.
- Those who would give up essential liberty to purchase a little temporary safety derive neither liberty nor safety.
- Where liberty is, there is my country.
- Who is wise? He who learns from everyone. Who is powerful? He who governs his passions. Who is rich? He who is content. Who is that? Nobody.
- Rich widows are the only secondhand goods that sell at firsthand prices.
- Time is money.
- Snug as a bug in a rug.
- In this world nothing is certain except death and taxes.
- Three may keep a secret if two of them are dead.
- Early to bed and early to rise make a man healthy, wealthy, and wise.
- Necessity has no law and the same applies to some attorneys I know.
- Where there's marriage without love, there'll be love without marriage.
- That man has an axe to grind.
- Never leave to tomorrow what you can do today.

Benjamin Franklin at the royal court of France

her status unclear. Their marriage proved a source of stability and comfort to Franklin.

Franklin's business success and prestige in the community grew and he entered local politics, becoming clerk of the Pennsylvania Assembly and postmaster of Philadelphia. He was soon a leading citizen who left an indelible mark on Philadelphian society. He established the first subscription library in America (1731), a volunteer fire department (1736), the American Philosophical Society (1743), The Philadelphia Academy (1749), later to become the University of Pennsylvania), a militia, and a city hospital (1751).

By age forty-two Franklin was able to retire in comfort and pursue his own interests. One of his passions was science, and through experimentation he invented many practical items, among them the Franklin stove, bifocals, a rubber catheter, and a printing press. He never took a patent on any of these items, saying, "As we enjoy great advantages from the inventions of others, we should be glad of an opportunity to serve others by any inventions of ours." His most famous scientific experiment, one which earned him worldwide renown, proved that lightning was a natural form of electricity. Many are familiar with the image of Franklin, amid a fierce thunderstorm, flying a kite with a key attached to its string. In recognition of his achievements, he was elected to England's Royal Society (1756) and the French Academy of Sciences (1772).

In 1752 Franklin was elected to the Pennsylvania Assembly. The following year he was appointed deputy postmaster general of North America. He made great improvements in the postal system, but perhaps more significantly the position brought him into contact with influential people in all the colonies. Though Franklin firmly believed in the authority of the English Crown in the colonies, he was beginning to see the need for more colonial unity in matters of defense. He communicated his concern to the intercolonial conference that took place in Albany, New York, in 1754. However, the colonies were not ready for a confederation, causing Franklin to cry in despair: "Everybody cries a union is absolutely necessary; but when they come to the manner and form of the union, their weak noodles are presently distracted." In 1757 the Assembly appointed Franklin emissary to London to settle a dispute with the proprietors of Pennsylvania. Accompanied by his son, William, he succeeded in winning some concessions from the Penn family and, by the time he left in 1762, had the satisfaction of seeing his son appointed royal governor of New Jersey. Though Franklin and his son had a close relationship, during the American Revolution the father and son would part ways, William remaining loyal to the Crown and Franklin defending the right of the Americans to declare independence.

Franklin was asked to take a second trip to England in 1764, this time to ask that Pennsylvania's status be changed to royal colony. In America, however, events were taking place that would alter the course of history. Franklin was forced to take sides and slowly came to the realization that what he treasured most was his life as an "American," not as a subject of the Crown. He returned to America in March 1775, served on the Second Continental Congress (May 1775) and helped draft the Declaration of Independence (July 1776).

During the American Revolution, Franklin went to France to persuade that government to aid the American cause. After the American victory at Saratoga (February 1778), the French agreed to an alliance. Franklin made secret contact with London after the British defeat at Yorktown (October 1781) and began negotiations for peace.

In 1785 Franklin returned home in triumph. He completed his *Autobiography*, begun years before, and attended sessions of the Constitutional Convention in 1787. He supported the new Constitution and urged the others to ratify it. Three years later, he died in Philadelphia.

C. D. Bowen, *The Most Dangerous Man in America*, 1987.

W. G. Carr, *The Oldest Delegate*, 1990.

R. W. Clark, *Benjamin Franklin: A Biography*, 1983.

E. Wright, *Benjamin Franklin of Philadelphia*, 1986.

FREDERICK WILLIAM (the Great Elector; 1620–1688), elector of Brandenburg, king of Prussia. Frederick was the eldest son of the Hohenzollern elector George William and Elizabeth Charlotte of the Palatinate. Due to the Thirty Years' War, he left Berlin to study in Kustrin and in 1634 went to the Netherlands, where he attended the University of Leiden. While studying mathematics, Latin, history, and military science he developed a strong admiration for Dutch culture and throughout his life carried this love for the Netherlands as an imposing maritime and commercial power.

George William's rule of Brandenburg was masterminded by Count Adam von Schwarzenberg. Frederick despised him and his attempts to control his father, and even accused the elector's councilor of poisoning him when he came down with the measles. Distrust, paranoia, and enforced inactivity depressed Frederick when he moved to live in Königsberg, Prussia, where he remained until his father's death in 1640.

At the time of Frederick's accession to power in Brandenburg, its fortunes were at an all-time low, with some 50 percent of the population as well as crucial territories being lost in the Thirty Years' War. His father had allowed the nobility, known as the "Estates," to pursue their own interests and to assert power over the central government. Relying upon his mother's political prowess, he reduced Schwarzenberg's power and created a plan to rebuild the army, at the same time negotiating with Sweden, which had taken over Brandenburg territory.

A two-year armistice between Brandenburg and Sweden, concluded in 1641, underlined Frederick's political and military impotence, with Sweden retaining Brandenburg territory. As a Polish duke, Frederick turned to King Wtadstaw IV in order to gain the duchy of Prussia, where he was invested with power later the same year. From an economic point of view, Prussia was more important than Brandenburg because there he could tax directly in order to rebuild the army. In 1646 Frederick married Louise Henriette of Orange, daughter of Frederick Henry of Orange. However, this did not secure Dutch support for the army that Frederick had been building since 1644.

Frederick's ambitions for territorial expansion were stifled in 1648, when the Treaty of Westphalia, officially ending the Thirty Years' War, left him with important lands linking him to his west German territories, but without the prize he hoped for — all of Pomerania. France was on the rise and the Swedes blocked the elector's route to the Baltic Sea. Nonetheless, he retained grandiose plans for the rise of Brandenburg-Prussia as a great commercial and maritime power like the Netherlands.

After a peaceful interlude, the First Northern War (1655–1660) broke out between Poland and Sweden. As a vassal of the Polish king, Frederick was obliged to help, but in 1656, through the treaties of Konigsberg and Marienburg, he allied himself with the Swedes. The Brandenburg army's first victory, in the Battle of Warsaw, gave Frederick full sovereignty over the duchy of Prussia. Turning his back on Sweden, he now signed an accord with Poland and the Habsburgs in 1657. The shift in alliances upset Sweden and hostilities

broke out. Standing at the head of a 30,000-strong army, Frederick expelled the Swedes from Schleswig-Holstein, gaining the much-desired territory of Pomerania. However, the French, as Sweden's allies, amassed an enormous army and forced Frederick to concede the territory in the Peace of Oliva in 1660.

For twenty years, Frederick had ruled in conjunction with some of his closest advisers. Now, after Oliva, he was to become one of the strongest proponents in Europe of princely absolutism. His sense of mission was strengthened by the fact that he was a Calvinist who felt he had to prove himself as a ruler. His scattered possessions lacked physical unity so he used strict economic administration in order to achieve political consolidation. He also utilized terror through the execution of his main opponents in order to demonstrate the strength of the central state over the Estates.

By heavy taxing and subsidies from Austria, Spain, France, and the Netherlands, Frederick laid the foundation of a powerful bureaucracy that was dependent upon him. His foreign policy consisted of maintaining the balance of power in Europe, and he often opted to ally himself with weaker powers in order to preserve the status quo.

Frederick's support of the Spanish Netherlands against the French proved a complete failure, prompting him to join an alliance with Austria, Spain, and Denmark. In 1674 the Swedes invaded Brandenburg and within two weeks Frederick's army was back in Brandenburg, where he defeated the Swedes at Fehrbellin; a poem of the time honoring the victory called him "The Great Elector." Now he saw his chance to gain Pomerania once and for all. The war lasted for five more years with the Great Elector achieving his goal, but once again he was forced by the French to return Pomerania to Sweden (Treaty of Saint-Germain, 1679).

Instead of fighting France, Frederick felt that entering an alliance could gain him what he had sought for so long. The secret pact, established in 1679, lasted as long as Frederick thought he would regain Pomerania. However, France's only interest was obtaining lands along the German border. The alliance was severed and Frederick changed allegiances for the last time in 1685, turning again to his first love, the Netherlands.

While Frederick did not make Brandenburg-Prussia into a major European power, he established a well-organized government that had a respectable army and a functioning economy. He also founded the Berlin royal library, reorganized the universities, opened canals, and developed the city of Berlin. The institutions and administration he founded would become the backbone of the powerful Prussian state developed by his successors.

H. Eulenberg, *The Hohenzollerns*, 1929.

C. A. Macartney, *The Habsburg and Hohenzollern Dynasties in the Seventeenth Century*, 1970.

F. Schevill, *The Great Elector*, 1947.

FREDERICK I (Barbarossa; c. 1123–1190), Holy Roman emperor. As Frederick III, duke of Swabia, he was a member of the influential Hohenstaufen dynasty, led by his uncle, Holy Roman Emperor Conrad III. The Hohenstaufens, also known by the name of their ancestral castle Waibling, were challenged by the rival Welf family of Bavaria (the prolonged feud eventually spilled over to Italy, where the names were altered into Ghibellino and Guelfo), who claimed the imperial throne for themselves. Fearing that his own sons would prove unable to withstand the Welfs, Conrad chose Frederick as his successor. Frederick was both imposing and intelligent; he sported a bushy red beard (*barba rossa* in Latin), and always looked as if he was about to laugh. Furthermore, Frederick's mother was a Welf and Conrad hoped that he would be acceptable to both parties as a compromise. Frederick succeeded Conrad in 1152. For two years he appeased his Welf kinsmen by granting them substantial territory in return for recognition of his ultimate suzerainty. Although no private wars were permitted for personal aggrandizement and the slightest infraction of the agreement was ruthlessly punished, Frederick's measures temporarily mollified the Welfs. Germany was at peace, allowing Frederick to focus his attention on troubled Italy.

The southern half of the empire was plagued with republican and regional sentiment undermining the emperor's ultimate authority. In Rome, Arnold of Brescia, a religious reformer and disciple of Peter *Abelard, had overthrown Pope Eugene III and established a commune. Rome's self-proclaimed independence was imitated by other Italian cities, particularly those of the northern Lombard region. Frederick concluded a pact with the papal aspirant Adrian IV enabling him to recapture Rome and execute Arnold. Once established as pope, Adrian was allowed virtual autonomy in return for recognition of Frederick's ultimate sovereignty. Adrian crowned Frederick as Holy Roman emperor in 1155, but the two soon had a falling-out over Frederick's insistence on his prerogative to reject papal nomination of clergy. Soon after Frederick returned to Germany, Italy reasserted its independence.

Frederick returned to Italy in 1158, this time sparing no measure to dispel any challenge to his authority. Rebellious cities were subject to cruel sieges in which prisoners were often catapulted against the walls. Once defeated, towns were razed and their inhabitants slaughtered. Frederick then lost support even among the clergy he had appointed. Upon the death of Adrian in 1159 the majority of the college of cardinals rejected Frederick's candidate in favor of Alexander III, who enlisted British and French support against the emperor and his lackey, the antipope Victor IV. Following Victor's death in 1164 even the minority of cardinals preferred to transfer their allegiance to Alexander rather than support the new candidate, Paschal III. The German nobility grew uneasy over Frederick's

Frederick Barbarossa and his sons

break with the established papacy — Frederick's proposed canonization of *Charlemagne did little to alleviate the situation — forcing Frederick to defeat Alexander. Rome was conquered in 1167 and Alexander barely escaped to France.

Rome was not the only troubled region of Frederick's Italian realms. That same year the northern cities proclaimed their independence as the Lombard League. Frederick was preparing to face this new challenge when a plague decimated his armies in Rome. The emperor was forced to make a harrowing retreat to Germany, much of the way through hostile Lombard territory.

His vulnerability was eagerly exploited by the German Welfs. Led by Henry the Lion the Welfs reached agreement with Denmark, allowing them to extend their realms beyond the Elbe River along the southern Baltic seacoast. Henry also strengthened his ancestral territories by establishing fortified towns, among them Munich, in strategic locations. With his forces depleted, Frederick resorted to diplomacy and bribery to frustrate Henry's ambitions. A corrupt uncle of Henry's was persuaded to sell much of the new Welf territories to Frederick, thereby confirming him as German overlord. Overly confident, Frederick made the premature decision to return to Italy to defeat the Lombard League.

The German setback in the ensuing Battle of Legnano (1176) was disastrous. Frederick's own shield and personal standard were captured by the rebel Italians. Fearing that another such defeat would signal the end of his empire, Frederick adopted the diplomatic methods that had served so well against

Henry the Lion. After concluding a six-year truce with the Lombards, he agreed to a reconciliation with Pope Alexander. Frederick entered Rome as a penitent; when Alexander approached, he prostrated himself before him. Alexander was moved by Frederick's tears. He lifted him from the ground and embraced him before leading him into church to sign a formal reconciliation.

In 1183, the Treaty of Constance replaced the truce with the Lombards. Frederick recognized their autonomy in return for their recognition of his sovereignty. The empire, once centered around the person of the emperor, had evolved of necessity into a federation of autonomous principalities. Unity had been achieved at the price of imperial power. Frederick's authority, however, could not be slighted. The princes and barons remained his lieges in a newly emerged feudal state. Rivals like Henry were forced to flee; their lands were redistributed among Frederick's loyal retainers such as the Wittelsbachs, who ruled Bavaria until 1918. Peace in his expanded empire fostered a cultural renaissance unparalleled in the medieval period.

Seeking challenges abroad, Frederick led 20,000 men on a crusade against Saladin. He never reached the Holy Land; while attempting to cross the Saleph River in Cilicia, Frederick Barbarossa drowned. Today his place is firmly established in the pantheon of German heroes. According to some legends he is still alive. He sits, sleeping, in a secret chamber in Kyffhauser Castle, his bushy red beard twisted twice around the table before him. Only when it completes its third revolution will Frederick awaken to fight the last battle before the Day of Judgment.

P. Munz, *Frederick Barbarossa: A Study in Medieval Politics*, 1969.

M. Pacaut, *Frederick Barbarossa*, 1970.

FREDERICK II (1194–1250), Holy Roman emperor and king of Sicily. Frederick II was born the day after his father, Emperor *Henry VI, was crowned king of Sicily. Henry schemed to alter the laws of succession in the Holy Roman Empire so that Frederick could succeed him, but his premature death prevented this. Only three years old, Frederick became king of Sicily, with his mother acting as regent. Before her death the following year, she appointed Pope Innocent III as Frederick's guardian and regent of the kingdom of Sicily. Frederick was declared of age in 1208; the following year he married Constance of Aragon, ten years his senior. Constance was genuinely fond of the orphan prince, and in 1211, the couple had a son, Henry.

Sicily's importance as a maritime trading center tempted Emperor Otto IV to conquer the country in 1210. Pope Innocent III regarded this as a challenge to papal authority and urged the German princes to depose Otto in favor of Frederick who, in return, renounced the Sicilian throne in favor of Henry. Frederick accepted and traveled to Germany to assume the imperial throne, avoiding the harassment of troops still loyal to Otto. To ensure his accession, he concluded a pact with Philip II of France. In the Battle of Bouvines (1214), Philip defeated Otto and captured his standard, the golden eagle, symbolic of the transfer of power to Frederick.

However, Frederick also earned the indignation of the new pope, Honorius III, by appointing Henry king of Germany. Hailed throughout Europe as a new Charlemagne, Frederick sought papal approval for his reign by having Honorius crown him emperor in Rome, and agreed to govern Sicily as a dominion independent of the empire. Following his coronation, he returned to Sicily to develop his native realm. Although severe with Christian heretics, he was more favorable toward his Muslim and Jewish minorities. However, the leaders of a Saracen revolt were treated mercilessly; as one prostrated himself before the emperor, Frederick split him in half with the spur of his boot. The Muslim masses were resettled in Apulia, where they enjoyed considerable autonomy. Under Frederick's patronage, non-Christian minorities enhanced the intellectual life of Sicily. In 1224 he inaugurated the University of Naples, which he required all civil servants to attend. This school, staffed by Thomas *Aquinas among others, became a leading academic institution. Important trade routes were secured by the conquest of Djerba off the Tunisian coast. At the same time, Frederick was opposed by both the Lombard League of northern Italy for interfering in its internal affairs and by the new pope, Gregory IX.

Gregory attempted to curb Frederick by persuading him to fulfill his coronation vow to liberate the Holy Land. By marrying the daughter of the titular king of Jerusalem, Frederick attempted to have himself declared king, but an epidemic frustrated his immediate departure on a crusade. Gregory responded by excommunicating Frederick in 1227. The following year Frederick reached the Holy Land and found that the ruler of Egypt, challenged by his brother in Syria, was willing to negotiate control of Jerusalem, Bethlehem, and Nazareth in return for military support against Damascus. Frederick's acceptance resulted in his peaceful acquisition of the holy sites. Bloated by his success, Frederick now considered himself a messiah. Despite his excommunication, he crowned himself king of Jerusalem in the Church of the Holy Sepulcher.

The pope saw Frederick's absence as an opportune time to invade Sicily, but Frederick quickly returned to regain his realm. Peace was finally concluded at the Treaty of San Germano (1230), in which Frederick's excommunication was annulled.

Henry had represented his father in Germany throughout his father's decade-long absence. After conceding demands by local princes for autonomy, he agreed to lead a rebellion against his father. Frederick crushed this new challenge and replaced Henry with his second son, Conrad IV. Henry was imprisoned, never to see his father again; Frederick attempted a reconciliation prior to his death, but Henry misinterpreted his father's intention and committed suicide.

With Germany subdued, Frederick could now suppress the rebellious Lombard League. They were defeated in the Battle of Cortuenova in 1238, but Frederick's demand for unconditional surrender was rejected by the Milanese and tensions continued until his death. The pope again excommunicated Frederick for his supposed claim that *Moses, Christ, and *Muhammad were impostors. Believing that the Romans preferred him to the pretentiously wealthy papacy, Frederick prepared to conquer Rome. However, he underestimated the local population's loyalty to the papal institution. His imprisonment of over one hundred cardinals, bishops, and other church leaders further diminished his popularity. His siege of Rome was only lifted upon hearing of Pope Gregory's death.

The new pope, Innocent IV, was no less hostile to Frederick and officially deposed him in 1245, calling him the Antichrist. Plans to travel to the pope in Lyons were stymied by a revolt in central Italy, the declared neutrality of the German princes in the conflict, and the capture and imprisonment of his son Enzio, king of Sardinia, by the Bolognese. Only by 1249 did Frederick's position improve, but his sudden death the following year left his empire vulnerable.

Although his final years were marked by decline, Frederick's popularity among his subjects never wavered. His uncompromising stand against the church, hated for its wealth and power, led many to believe that the church, not Frederick, was the true Antichrist; Frederick was seen by many as a messianic figure come to restore Christendom. For some time after his death, it was believed he would return from hiding to deliver the final blow against the enemies of the true church, as represented by the pope in Rome.
D. Abulafia, *Frederick II: A Medieval Emperor*, 1988.

FREDERICK II (Frederick the Great; 1712–1786), king of Prussia. He was the third son of Frederick William I of Prussia but after the death of his elder brothers in childhood, he became heir to the throne. His father was a rigid authoritarian who imposed spartan discipline on all his children, particularly Frederick. From his mother, however, Frederick acquired a love of the arts. Throughout his life he spoke French, considering German to be a barbaric language, and spent considerable time playing the flute and composing verse. His father opposed these pastimes, preferring that Frederick devote himself to statecraft. Violent rows ensued in which Frederick was caned or obliged to kiss his father's boots. His animosity toward his father finally led Frederick to contemplate an escape with a close friend, Lieutenant Hans Hermann von Katte, to his uncle, George II of Britain, but his father learned about this attempt and had the two youths arrested. A military tribunal sentenced Katte to two years imprisonment for desertion, but was unwilling to try

Frederick because of his status. Frederick William, however, sought sterner measures against the two, and Frederick was forced to watch from his cell as Katte was beheaded. Although Frederick anticipated a similar fate, his father revoked the sentence and gradually reinstated him. In return, Frederick was compelled to serve in the civil administration to learn the skills demanded of an heir to the throne.

After several years Frederick retired to a country estate, where his artistic inclinations thrived. Through correspondence, he cultivated a meaningful friendship with *Voltaire and other leading intellectuals. In 1733 he married Elizabeth Christina, daughter of the duke of Brunswick-Bevern, but the marriage lasted just three weeks before the couple separated. Frederick had no significant romantic affairs throughout his life, leading to speculation that he was homosexual.

When Frederick acceded to the throne in 1740, it was assumed that Prussia would enter an enlightened period under the guidance of a philosopher king. Artists and scientists were encouraged to settle in Berlin to revive the Royal Academy, long neglected by Frederick William, and Frederick himself published a work, *Antimachiavel*, just prior to his accession, in which he defined the monarch's role as that of a servant of the people. At the same time, his primary objective was personal aggrandizement. He enacted laws abolishing torture, censorship, and religious discrimination, but these reforms were generally not enforced.

Having developed a fascination with the military similar to his father's, Frederick sought an opportunity to demonstrate his prowess. Such an opportunity soon arose: The Holy Roman emperor Charles VI died, leaving his young daughter, Maria Theresa, to inherit the throne of Austria. The European powers sought to exploit the situation by carving the empire up among themselves. Frederick hoped to annex the

---

FROM FREDERICK THE GREAT'S INSTRUCTIONS TO HIS GENERALS

- A perfect general, like Plato's *Republic*, is a figment of the imagination.
- Without supplies, no army is brave.
- If you wish to be loved by your soldiers, do not lead them to slaughter.
- The principal task of the general is mental, involving large projects and major arrangements.
- One should know one's enemies, their alliances, their resources, and the nature of their country in order to plan a campaign.
- The soldier should not have any ready money. If he has a few coins in his pocket, he thinks himself a lord and deserts as soon as a campaign opens.

wealthy region of Silesia, to which Prussia had historical claims. His surprise invasion of that region sparked the War of the Austrian Succession. The planned invasion was a well-kept secret to all but a few trusted advisers. The evening before, as Prussian troops mustered on the Silesian border, Frederick sponsored a ball with his estranged queen.

The invasion of Silesia was an exceptional success – the region was overrun in just seven weeks. Frederick's greatest victory was at Mollwitz in 1741; having little experience in warfare, however, Frederick fled the battlefield, believing defeat inevitable. Not until ten hours after the Austrians were defeated did Frederick learn of his victory. In 1742 Frederick signed the Treaty of Breslau with Maria Theresa. Austria recognized Prussia's claims to Silesia in return for Prussian recognition of Maria Theresa's husband as Holy Roman emperor. The treaty, although beneficial to Prussia, tarnished Frederick's reputation. By signing a separate peace with Austria, Frederick had neglected his ally, France.

Despite the treaty, Austria did not forego its claims to Silesia. A secret coalition of Austria, England, Holland, and several smaller states threatened invasion to check the rising Prussian military might. Frederick recognized the danger to his throne and responded by invading Bohemia in 1744. He succeeded in capturing Prague, but the Austrian army was able to counter any further offensives. At the same time, France invaded Bavaria and Frederick withdrew from Bohemia to concentrate on securing Silesia. After further pointless battles, peace was finally concluded in the Treaty of Dresden (1745). Austria again recognized Frederick's claims to Silesia.

The following ten years were relatively quiet. Frederick devoted considerable effort to improving his military infrastructure. The Treaty of Dresden earned him the title "the Great," and recognition of Prussia as a major European power, but tensions in Europe had not ceased. Austria still yearned to gain Silesia.

France found it expedient to ally itself with Austria to counter Prussia. Russia, too, feared Prussian expansion on the Polish frontier, and Sweden, anticipating an eventual Prussian reverse, wanted a share of the spoils. Only England, for whom France was the sole competitor in the New World, sided with Frederick. Always an advocate of offensive actions to preempt attack, Frederick invaded Austria's ally, Saxony, in 1756, taking the entire army captive and thereby beginning the Seven Years' War. This war, which had little impact on European power politics, was among the bloodiest the continent had seen. It was marked by rapid reversals and events steered by luck more than military might.

Frederick was an aged, broken man by the war's end; he continued to wear his tattered army uniform until his death. For the next quarter century he embarked on a reconstruction program which assured Prussian ascendancy in Europe. He also developed a unified legal system, the *Codex Fredericianus*, promising fair trials for citizens of all ranks. At the same time,

he retained the class system, believing the aristocracy to be a better breed than the peasantry and middle class. All middle-class officers were discharged for possessing "unrefined manners." Although Frederick now disavowed war, his empire was augmented by the annexation of significant segments of Poland following that country's partition in 1772. In 1777 Joseph II of Austria marched into Bavaria. Frederick again led his troops into battle, but after a series of bloodless maneuvers both monarchs retreated.

In 1786, just months before his death, he succeeded in forming a league of German princes, a forerunner of the idea of German unity. Some months later, he went out to inspect his troops despite a raging winter storm. Already an old man, he fell ill and died. Later German nationalists idolized Frederick as the man most responsible for forging Prussia into a major world power. Adolf *Hitler was a fervent admirer of Frederick, to whom he compared himself, and a portrait of Frederick was one of his most treasured possessions.

R. B. Asprey, *Frederick the Great: The Magnificent Enigma*, 1986.

C. Duffy, *Frederick the Great,* 1988.

N. Mitford, *Frederick the Great*, 1988.

FRÉMONT, JOHN CHARLES (1813–1890), American explorer, military officer, and political figure. He studied at Charleston College, South Carolina, and eloped with and married Jessie Benton, the daughter of an influential and powerful senator from Missouri. Jessie Frémont was an author who wrote magazine articles and assisted her husband in writing reports about his expeditions and his memoirs. All three were firm supporters of America's Manifest Destiny and fought for the country's western expansion.

Frémont began his exploring career as an army surveyor on Jean Nicolet's 1838-1839 expedition to the region between the upper Mississippi and the Missouri rivers. Thereafter, he led five western expeditions starting with a trek to the Wind River chain of the Rocky Mountains in 1842, guided by Kit Carson. He mapped the Oregon Trail which was traversed by numerous settlers in covered Conestoga wagons. Frémont's reports caught the imagination of the public and made him a folk hero because of his exploits and courage. As a result of his successful explorations he became known as the Pathfinder. He showed that the "Great American Desert" was a myth and also reported on the fertility of the Great Plains.

President James Polk wanted California to be a territory of the United States and would have paid up to forty million dollars for the land. After the Mexicans refused his offer to purchase it, Polk sent Frémont with supporting soldiers, under secret orders, on a expedition to California. Although Frémont claimed that his expedition was scientific, the Mexicans became suspicious and asked him to leave California. He retreated to Oregon for a short time, resigned his army commission, and returned to California as a private citizen. In June 1846, before news of the outbreak of the Mexican war reached California, Frémont led American settlers in revolt against the Mexicans and established the "Bear Flag Republic" in northern California. Later, separate official American naval forces led by Commodore Robert Stockton, and land forces led by General Stephen Kearny, invaded California and achieved military objectives in the Los Angeles area. Nevertheless it was Frémont, at the head of his privately recruited army, who was able to negotiate the surrender treaty with the Mexicans. Frémont appointed Commodore Stockton as Civil Governor of California, thus provoking the anger of General Kearny who had Frémont arrested and court martialed for leading a military action and accepting an unauthorized surrender. At his highly publicized Washington court trial Frémont was found guilty of doing exactly what he was secretly ordered to do by the president. President Polk immediately granted Frémont a full pardon because of his "meritorious and valuable services" and restored him as an army officer.

In 1850 Californians elected Frémont as one of their first two senators. Following his two-year Senate term, Frémont led another expedition, privately financed by his father-in-law, to find a northern railroad route between the 37th and 38th parallels to the Pacific Ocean. Senator Benton sent Frémont on this quest in reaction to the authorization by the secretary of war, Jefferson *Davis, of expeditions led by southern sympathizers to find southern railroad routes. On that expedition, the Pathfinder became the first explorer to take along and to utilize an official photographer.

The newly formed Republican Party ran Frémont, who was well known from books reporting his adventures, his California accomplishments, and his trial, as their first candidate for president of the United States in 1856. It was a threeway contest among the Democrats, the Whigs, and the Republicans. Frémont ran on the issue of establishing Congressional power to prohibit slavery. The Democratic candidate, James Buchanan, won the election with 174 electoral votes, Frémont came in second with 114 electoral votes, while former president, Millard Fillmore, carried only the State of Maryland, receiving eight electoral votes. That marked the end of the Whigs as a political party.

Major-General Frémont commanded the Union Army's Western Department during the Civil War until he issued a proclamation taking over the property of rebeling Missouri slave holders. President Abraham *Lincoln was not pleased with Frémont's action and transferred him to West Virginia.

Following the war he became involved in various railroad ventures and lost his fortune. His army retirement pay and royalties earned by his wife's writing kept him from dire poverty. His final public service was from 1878 to 1883 as territorial governor of Arizona.

R. J. Bartlett, *John C. Frémont and the Republican Party*, 1970.
A. Nevins, *Frémont: Pathmaker of the West*, 1955.

FREUD, ANNA (1895–1982), child psychoanalyst. The youngest of Sigmund *Freud's children, she was born in Vienna and developed a very special relationship with her father, acting as his secretary, nursemaid, and eventually becoming his successor. The only one of his six children to follow in his footsteps, she became a leading figure in the fields of psychoanalysis, ego psychology, research methodology, and child analysis, all with no formal education in the field.

Her interest in the field may be said to have begun in her youth, for as a fourteen-year old she was to be found "sitting on a little library ladder in the corner" at the meetings of the Vienna Psychoanalytic Society. Nonetheless when she graduated from the Cottage Lyceum, it was to schoolteaching and not psychoanalysis that she turned. She remained close to her father and, as she never married, lived at home with him, caring for him assiduously after he developed cancer of the palate in 1923. In 1918 when she was twenty-two years old, she was psychoanalyzed by him. This seems to have been a turning point in her gravitation toward the field of psychoanalysis.

Anna Freud came to take a particular interest in child analysis after hearing a paper in 1920 by Hermine von Hug-Hellmuth, the first child analyst. That year her father also sent her for analysis to Lou Andreas-Salomé, with whom she was to maintain a lifelong correspondence. Anna Freud also developed a relationship with Dorothy Burlingham, who brought her son to Vienna from America for analysis with Anna Freud, and eventually became a close friend, companion, and colleague.

In 1922 Anna Freud was accepted to the Vienna Psychoanlytic Society and in 1923 established a private practice in Vienna. Two years later she was on the executive committee of the society, and by 1925 she was its chairman. In 1926 she opened a private school in Vienna with Dorothy Burlingham. Her Seminar on Children (1926 and 1927) and a series of lectures on child analysis at the Vienna Psychoanalytic Institute established her as reputation as a leading figure in the field of child analysis, as did her book *Introduction to the Technique of Child Analysis* (1929).

Her investigations into the subject of ego psychology were published in *The Ego and the Mechanisms of Defence* (1936), a seminal work on ego psychology that moved the emphasis of psychology from conflicts in the unconscious toward a study of the mechanisms by which the ego protects itself from anxiety. Such mechanisms (among them repression, projection, sublimation, and rationalization) have remained key concepts in the practice of psychoanalysis.

Adolf *Hitler's rise to power signaled the culmination of Anna Freud's career in Vienna and as the specter of nazism enveloped Europe she insisted that her father leave Austria with her. They moved to London, settling in Hampstead. There she was instrumental in the reestablishment of psychoanalysis after its destruction in Europe. She brought as many analysts as possible out of Europe and opened the Hampstead Wartime Center for the study and treatment of young war victims. The facility, described in *Young Children in War-Time* (1942), *War and Children* (1943), and *Infants Without Families* (1944), eventually developed into the Hampstead Center for the Psychoanalytical Study and Treatment of Children, which she directed until her death. She also helped found and served as editor of *The Psychoanalytic Study of the Child*. After the war she often lectured in the United States and published the classic *Normality and Pathology in Childhood* (1965). Her writings, collected in *The Writings of Anna Freud*, fill seven volumes.

R. Dyer, *Her Father's Daughter: The Works of Anna Freud*, 1983.

P. S. Heller, *A Child Analysis with Anna Freud*, 1990.

J. Sayers, *Mothering Psychoanalysis*, 1991.

FREUD, SIGMUND (1856–1939), Austrian physician and founder of psychoanalysis. He was born in Freiberg, Moravia, but when he was three the family moved to Vienna to escape anti-Semitic discrimination. He lived in Vienna for most of the rest of his life, despite his professed dislike of the city.

A precocious and intellectually gifted child, at the age of seventeen Freud entered the University of Vienna to study medicine, motivated primarily by a deep interest in scientific research, and in his third year he began a study of the central nervous system with Ernst Brücke, which was to delay the completion of his degree by three years. Brücke's determinist philosophy was also to inspire and remain with Freud throughout his life. Even after graduation Freud was reluctant to practice medicine and would have gladly remained permanently in research, but he was eventually persuaded to join the staff of Vienna General Hospital.

Freud's interest in what would become the field of psychoanalysis was sparked by his friend Josef Breuer, physician and physiologist, who in 1884 introduced him to the "talking cure" by explaining that one of his patients was relieved of one of her nervous symptoms when she fully recounted the details of its first appearance. In 1885 Freud received a grant to spend four and a half months in Paris studying with the French neurologist Jean Charcot, who was engaged in pioneering treatments of nervous disoders, in particular hysteria, by hypnosis. When Freud returned to Vienna, he opened a private practice in nervous diseases and attempted to introduce Charcot's views on hysteria and hypnosis. He met with violent opposition from the medical profession, and there followed a ten-year period of almost complete intellectual isolation during which, although he was personally extremely creative and productive, he received no support from the medical community.

Studies in Hysteria, the outcome of his collaboration with Breuer, was published in 1893. On the assumption that hysteria was caused by undis-

charged emotional energy, the therapeutic procedure they advocated involved inducing a hypnotic state in which the patient was to recall fully the traumatic experience and thus cathartically rid himself of the emotions causing the symptoms. Freud eventually abandoned the hypnotic method when he found that although it could help to break down a patient's resistance to repressed material, it was not always an effective cure. He began to substitute the process of free association. This required careful monitoring of the patient's spontaneous flow of speech and thoughts, which would reveal unconscious mental processes and material. Clues emerging from the analysis of dreams and free association would point to unconscious impulses excluded from awareness because of the anxiety they could cause, yet so powerful that they needed to seek expression and thus emerged as neurotic symptoms.

It was during this period that Freud began to find evidence for the mechanisms of repression and resistance; the former was a defense mechanism used to withhold painful or threatening material from the conscious mind; the latter prevented unconscious impulses from coming to awareness and causing anxiety. In 1895 he also undertook undertook self-analysis in order to better understand his own neuroses and improve his ability to understand his patients. He concluded that his own problem, anxiety neurosis, was caused by an accumulation of sexual tension. Much of his analysis was accomplished by consideration of his own dreams. The final product of this intense period of study was the publication of *The Interpretation of Dreams* (1900), in which many of his own dreams were recorded.

Through the study of free association Freud began to develop his theories on the importance of sexuality and the conviction that all neuroses were based on arrested sexual development. It took some time before he came to the conclusion that sexuality existed even at the infantile stage, and that problems in early sexual development could be responsible for neurotic symptoms. When he first made this discovery he assumed that the victims of neuroses had been molested and traumatized by their elders; only later did he come to the conclusion that many of his patients had fantasized rather than actually experienced such encounters, and that their fantasies had assumed a reality for them because as children they had been unable to distinguish between fact and wish.

His work on sexual development and the related assumption that libido, or sexual drive, is a central human drive at all stages of development, led to his identification of the "Oedipus complex," in which a child develops an erotic attachment toward the parent of the opposite sex, and a consequent hostility toward the same-sex parent. During these years Freud also developed the crucial concept of transference, based on the assumption that during therapy the patient necessarily transfers buried emotional responses originally directed at the parent onto the therapist, and thus confronts the emotions anew.

Freud with his sons during World War I

Freud's emergence from isolation was slow. Public hostility was only exacerbated by his publication of *The Psychopathology of Everyday Life* (1904), in which he traced the slightest errors of speech to unconscious causes (from which the term "a Freudian slip" has passed into the language). Nonetheless, in 1902 he was appointed a professor at the University of Vienna. By 1906 his work was beginning to attract the attention of pupils and followers with similar interests, who eventually began meeting regularly in Freud's waiting room. Among the distinguished analysts participating in these weekly gatherings were Alfred *Adler, Wilhelm Stekel, Otto Rank, Abraham Brill, Carl *Jung, Sandor Ferenczi, and Ernest Jones. At a later stage Freud was to break with some of these colleagues, both personally and professionally, when their questioning of some of his theories became unacceptable to him. The split with Jung was particularly bitter. Jung complained that for Freud "the brain is viewed as an appendage of the genital glands," while Freud felt that Jung's action was a classic case of the son rebelling against the father.

The psychoanalytic movement gradually gained recognition; a first congress was held in 1908, and in 1910 the International Psychoanlytic Association was formed. Although the founding group disintegrated, pschoanalysis continued to grow in importance, and in 1909 Freud was invited to Clark University in the United States to receive an honorary doctorate and to introduce his theories to the American community. After World War I he developed a theory of personality structure based on the id, the ego, and the superego. The id, which corresponds to the unconscious and includes sexual and aggressive instinct, attempts to fulfill the pleasure principle — achievement of maximum pleasure and avoidance of "unpleasure." The ego serves as a mediator between the id and the outside world, controlling the demands of the id in accordance with the exigencies of reality. The superego, or conscience, which develops in childhood as the child internalizes the values of the authoritarian figures in his life, strives for perfection. The burden upon the ego of the triple demands of the id, the superego, and reality may become unbearable, thus leading to the activation of the psychological defense mechanisms by which the ego avoids anxiety.

Freud was a hard worker who did much of his writing at night, after seeing patients all day. He was intensely self-critical, yet intolerant of opinions that differed from his, which led to many bitter defections among his colleagues and disciples. He was sixty-seven when he began to suffer from the cancer of the jaw and palate that would torture him for the next sixteen years, requiring thirty-three operations and the use of a prosthesis. (He nevertheless continued to smoke twenty cigars a day.) Notwithstanding his painful impediment, he continued to write and treat patients until the last months of his life. Several of his later works were attempts to apply his theories to the fields of religion, art, and literature in books such as *Civilization and its Discontents* (1930) and *Moses and Monotheism* (1938). He died one year after moving to London to escape the Nazi invasion of Austria. His collected works fill twenty-three volumes.

C. R. Badcock, *Essential Freud*, 1989.
P. Gay, *Freud: A Life for Our Time*, 1988.
E. Jones, *Sigmund Freud: Life and Work*, 1953-1957.

FROEBEL, FRIEDRICH WILHELM AUGUST

(1782–1852), German educational reformer, founder of the kindergarten system. Born to an orthodox clergyman's family in Thuringia, Ernestine Saxony, Froebel he had difficulty learning to read and took scant interest in intellectual pursuits, developing a passionate attachment to the natural world instead. At a very early age he developed a profound personal philosophy regarding the unity of the universe; this influence was to become apparent in the child care theories he later developed.

Froebel evolved the "law of the sphere," which envisaged that shape as the symbol of the divine forces operative in the universe; he was later to assert that balls and circles were an important element in children's play since they could be recognized intuitively by the young as symbols of the unity of the cosmos. He also developed the idea of vitalizing Germany by restructuring its education system. He began to put this idea into practice at the "Universal German Educational Institution," the school he set up in his home village of Thuringia in 1816. Two years later he married Wilhelmine Hoffmeister, a sympathetic and diligent partner who helped him in his work. The school flourished and was moved to the neighboring village of Keilhau: Froebel's book *The Education of Man* (1826) was a philosophical presentation of the principles and methods pursued there.

Froebel conceived of the role of education as that of facilitating the natural "inner unfolding" of the child through spontaneous "self activity," but he often used obtuse quasimystical phraseology to convey his ideas. The role of the teacher was to encourage rather than indoctrinate, and great stress was laid upon cooperative activity between children. The family was considered the true root of human life, and the involvement of parents in their children's education was deemed crucial.

Froebel was suspected of radical tendencies, which meant that he was unable to get government support for his school; eventually he was removed from control on the grounds that he was directing a "nest of demagogues." He left Germany and spent five years in Switzerland; on his return he opened the "Child Nurture and Activity Institute" in Blankenburg, an infants' school soon renamed the "Kindergarten". The institution featured a small boarding school for future teachers. Froebel also founded a publishing firm to produce play aids and other educational material; one of these, *Mother-Play and Nursery Songs*, was immensely popular, and was translated into many languages.

Froebel was very active in his last years, inspired by growing support for his kindergarten movement. In 1851, Prussia outlawed kindergartens as subversive, a ban that was to outlive Froebel himself; it lasted until 1860. However, the Baroness of Mareholtz-Bulow's patronage and promotion of kindergartens in England led to the continued dissemination of Froebel's ideas and the adoption of the kindergarten system throughout Europe.

Often criticized by educationalists for the mysticism with which he leavened his child care theories, Froebel was nonetheless instrumental in creating a flexible system which recognized and was geared to the imaginative needs of its charges, and which persists successfully to this day. Such influential figures as John *Dewey owe many of their ideas to his pioneering approach.

E. M. Lawrence, ed., *Froebel and English Education: Perspectives on the Founder of the Kindergarten*, 1969.

FROST, ROBERT LEE (1874–1963), American poet. Contradictions mark the life of Frost, considered by many in his time to be America's greatest poet. Identified with the New England about which he wrote, Frost was born in San Francisco and moved to New England when he was eleven years old. Though Frost was granted more than a dozen honorary degrees from universities, and though he was a master teacher who taught at Amherst, Michigan, Harvard, and Dartmouth, he never graduated from college. He studied for less than a semester at Dartmouth and at Harvard for two years. This quintessentially American poet published his first book of verse while living in England, and English reviewers gave him his first recognition as a poet.

Frost was thirty-nine years old when he published his first book. Years before, in 1894, he sold his first poem, "My Butterfly." Frost celebrated by privately printing a booklet of six poems, *Twilight*. He printed only two copies, one for himself and one for his fiancée, Elinor White.

Frost's life with White was marked by tragedy. Frost himself suffered from depression; of the couple's four children, a son committed suicide and a daughter suffered a complete mental collapse.

Before achieving fame as a poet, Frost worked at numerous jobs, including teacher, farmer, cobbler, and mill worker. From 1912 to 1915 the Frost family lived in England on the proceeds of the sale of a farm. For the first time Frost worked full-time at writing and the fruits of that period finally brought him acclaim; *A Boy's Will* (1913) and *North of Boston* (1914) were well received on both sides of the Atlantic. The latter had become a best-seller in America when Frost returned to New England to begin the career as poet, teacher, and lecturer that would make him as well-loved as his poetry.

Frost won four Pulitzer Prizes (1924, 1931, 1937, 1943) and numerous awards including a Congressional Gold Medal (1962).

His poetry, like the man himself, abounds with contradictions. Ezra *Pound praised him for his conversational tone and use of natural speech. Despite the aura of simplicity in his works, there is a dark undercurrent to the poetry. In "Desert Places" Frost speaks in a simple voice about loneliness and bleak isolation. "Fire and Ice" and "Once by the Pacific" use simple images taken from nature to evoke a world of rage and destruction. Frost said that in creating poetry he felt the "surprise of remembering something I didn't know I know," and poems such as "Stopping by the Woods on a Snowy Evening," "After Apple-Picking," and "Mowing" reverberate with suggestive undertones, using pictures of winter, of rest, and of silence to express deep unconscious desires and fears.

While Frost was too much of an individualist to get involved with political movements, he admired his fellow New Englander, John F. *Kennedy, and was asked to read a poem at Kennedy's 1961 presidential

---

FROM FROST'S HOMESPUN WIT

- The world is full of willing people. Some willing to work, the rest willing to let them.
- The most terrible thing is your own judgment.
- Hell is a half-filled auditorium.
- Writing free verse is like playing tennis with the net down.
- Poetry is what gets lost in translation.
- If society fits you comfortably, you call it freedom.
- A liberal is a man too broadminded to take his own side in a quarrel.
- A jury consists of twelve persons chosen to decide who has the better lawyer.
- The brain is a wonderful organ. It starts working the moment you wake up and does not stop until you get to the office

inauguration. He wrote an uncharacteristically formal poem for the occasion but could not read it because of the sun's glare. Instead he recited another poem, "The Gift Outright," that describes the early days of America, "still unstoried, artless, unenhanced." "The land was ours before we were the land's," that poem begins, and the works of Frost have played a crucial role in creating for Americans the stories and the art of their own young land.

W. Pritchard, *Frost*, 1984.

L. Thompson, *Robert Frost*, 3 vols., 1966-1976.

FUGGER, JAKOB (Jakob the Rich; 1459–1525), Renaissance financier, businessman, indispensable supporter of royalty and popes. Jakob Fugger was the grandson of Johannes Fugger who founded one of the most influential families in the history of finance. Johannes Fugger, a master linen weaver, settled in Augsburg, Bavaria, in 1367, one year before guilds obtained a share in the management of the city. He capitalized on this new-found political power and developed a successful international business in spices, silk, and woolen materials, with a family branch in Venice. His son, Jakob I, married a daughter of the master of the Augsburg mint. After settling his father-in-law's debts, he moved to Tyrol as a mint master and extended the family business into mining. Jakob II had been destined to work for the church; however, at the age of fourteen, his older brother Peter died and he was called upon to join the family business.

Jakob II displayed great genius for business. The Holy Roman emperor Maximilian I extensively utilized his financial services; as a result, the Fuggers secured interests in silver mines in the Tyrol, copper mines in Hungary, and large tracts of real estate, and controlled the copper market in Venice. Jakob II profitably employed bills of exchange to move large amounts of money for use by the Habsburgs. Without great risk, he skillfully made large profits from the price differential of bills of exchange. The procedure was called *cambiro arbitrio* and is now known as arbitrage.

Historians agree that without the Fuggers' help, *Charles V of Spain probably would not have become Holy Roman emperor in 1519. Jakob II influenced the German princes to support Charles V in return for cash and lines of credit; Charles, in turn, ennobled the family and permitted them to coin their own money.

As a result of Jakob II's business acumen and the financing arrangements made with the extended Habsburg family, the Fuggers became the richest family in Europe. From 1511 to 1527 the Fugger balance sheet showed an increase in equity from 196,796 florins to 2,021,207 florins, an increase of 927 percent or an average annual growth of over 54 percent. Jakob II died childless, leaving his financial interests to his nephews. They and their descendants continued the business until 1607, when bankruptcy occurred. The family made the mistake of extending loans to the Habsburg *Philip II of Spain, who lost his Armada in 1588 in a war with England, and later defaulted on his debts to the Fuggers.

Jakob II was described as being a handsome man of merry disposition and pleasant to all. He gave gala skating and dance parties for society. For the less fortunate he built low-rent housing and established a program to provide bread at subsidized prices. He built many churches and enriched the Church of St. Ann at Augsburg with splendid statues and a family tomb. When the church fell into the hands of the Lutherans he requested that his nephews have him buried elsewhere as he was opposed to the Reformation. His motto was, "I want to gain while I can."

R. Ehrenberg, *Capital and Finance in the Age of the Renaissance*, 1963.

G. T. Mattheus, ed., *News and Rumor in Renaissance Europe: The Fugger Newsletters*, 1959.

J. Strieder, *Jacob Fugger the Rich*, 1966.

G

GALEN (129–c.199), Greek physician, one of the founders of the science of anatomy. Galen's research laid the basis for the development of scientific medicine during the Renaissance. He was born in Pergamon, a provincial capital of the Roman Empire (today in Turkey) renowned for its architectural beauty, where his father was a architect. Exposed to the worship of Asclepius, a healing god whose shrine in Pergamon attracted important personages from throughout the empire, Galen decided to make medicine his vocation. He began his studies at home under the eminent anatomist, Satyros, observing the physician's treatment of injured gladiators who fought at the shrine of Asclepius. He then went to Smyrna where he furthered his knowledge by dissecting animals, since according to Roman law it was forbidden to study human cadavers. In 157 he completed twelve years of medical study in Alexandria, having already written two books on anatomy, now lost.

In 161 Galen cured the well-known philosopher, Eudemus, in Rome and gained entry into the highest circles of the empire's capital city. He became part of the court of the coemperors *Marcus Aurelius and Lucius Verus. His flamboyant pride earned him the resentment of his fellow physicians, who became jealous of his success. Whether it was to escape their ire or the plague that Verus brought to Rome with his returning troops, Galen left the capital suddenly, returning to Pergamon in 166. In 168, after Verus had died, the physician was ordered back to Rome by Marcus Aurelius and entrusted with the care of Commodus, heir to the throne.

His position enabled Galen to study and compose his works on physiology and he wrote his most famous works during this period, including *On the Natural Faculties, On the Use of Parts*, and *On Respiration*. When the Emperor Commodus died in 192, Galen returned to Pergamon and completed his major work, *On the Art of Healing*.

Galen wrote over 300 works on physiology, health, diet, mathematics, ethics, and philosophy. His works on medicine comprise his commentaries on *Hippocrates and attempts to unify medical knowledge within a philosophical framework. His anatomical findings were largely based on the dissection of the Barbary monkey and other lower animals. He assumed the fundamental similarity between primates and humans and based his descriptions of human anatomy on the primates, which he observed with acuity, systematically detailing his findings of muscle and bone structure.

Galen's knowledge of organ function was gained through a series of vivisections. By restricting nerve function he was able to discern the connection of the brain and larynx; by tying the ureters he determined kidney and bladder function, findings unsurpassed for 1,500 years. Through his transection of the spinal cord he gained knowledge of the musculature. He distinguished between the functions of veins and arteries and established that the arteries carry blood, not air, as traditional sources had held. He also explored the workings of the heart and lungs, correctly understanding the lungs' aeration of the blood. His theory of respiration and combustion as well as liver function represented great strides toward the modern understanding of metabolism.

His theory of health was less creative, being derived from Hippocrates theory of balancing the four humors — phlegm, black bile, yellow bile, and the blood — with a subtle material substance, pnemena, carried by the blood. But Galen's writings went beyond medicine to include philosophical treatises that sought the significance of every element of the world, adhering to Aristotle's dictum that, "Nature does nothing in vain."

G. Sarton, *Galen of Pergamon*, 1954.
R. E. Siegel, *Galen's System of Physiology and Medicine*, 1968.

GALILEO (Galileo Galilei; 1564–1642), Italian mathematician, astronomer, and physicist. Galileo's life both shaped and personified the time in which he lived, a time when the Counter-Reformation overlapped with the latter part of the Renaissance. Galileo was born as the artistic period of the Renaissance was coming to an end and a period of objective scientific inquiry was beginning. A devout and loyal Roman Catholic, he was greatly affected by the Counter-Reformation, with its emphasis on strict adherence to Catholic dogma and the uprooting of anything that might be considered heresy by the church.

Born in Pisa to a family in straitened circumstances, Galileo wanted to study drawing and painting but his father's insistence on a better paying profession led to his studying medicine at the University of Pisa.

Although Galileo began what was to be a lifelong study of the phenomenon of the pendulum swing in his first year at university, he did not study mathematics at all until his third year there, when the grand duke's court visited Pisa. The court mathematician gave a lecture on the geometry of *Euclid. Fascinated, Galileo promptly abandoned the study of medicine for that of mathematics.

It was also at the University of Pisa that Galileo first encountered the works of *Aristotle. At that time Aristotle's works (or commentaries on them) were considered the final authority in the study of nature. Any observation or experiment that did not fit in with Aristotle's view of the universe was rejected. Galileo soon became verbally critical of many Aristotelian doctrines and enjoyed making fun of the university's blind devotion to them — even after he began to teach there.

At twenty-five he became a lecturer in mathematics at the university and spent the next three years trying to obtain the chair of mathematics for financial reasons, especially after his father died and he became the main support of his family.

Galileo spent eighteen years at the University of Padua (1592–1610). The Aristotelian view also had its adherents there but there was also an atmosphere of intellectual freedom in which Galileo and his experiments flourished. He was well-liked, with a jovial, lively personality and a sharp, albeit courteous wit. He never married but during this period he entered into a long-term liaison which produced three children.

Galileo was an exceptional teacher, able to communicate concepts and ideas vividly and in a way that illustrated the scientific method he was trying to teach (the study of natural phenomena by observation and the use of repeated experiments for checking hypotheses). His lectures were witty and lively and his popularity grew. Many travelers stopped in Padua to hear his lectures. He also had a clear and persuasive writing style which, along with his insistence on writing most of his works in Italian, meant that he interested and influenced a wide public. All of this contributed to the phenomenal speed with which the news of Galileo's discoveries spread.

Galileo's major scientific achievements in Padua involved the study of motion and astronomy and the construction of mathematical formulations to explain his observations and discoveries. In 1609 he learned about the newly invented telescope. A superb craftsman (this was neither the first nor the last of his inventions), he designed and built a vastly improved model. Being practical, he immediately saw that the telescope's ability to make distant objects clearly visible could be of inestimable value in war and in

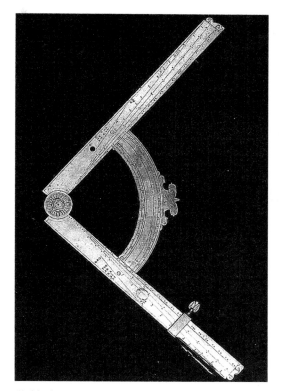

Galileo's geometrical compass

navigation and demonstrated this to an impressed and admiring Senate in Venice. He also did what no one had ever done before — he used a telescope to look at the sky. Suddenly he could see stars no one knew existed because they were invisible to the naked eye. The mountains of the moon, the moons of Jupiter, and the existence of sunspots were some of his astronomical discoveries. Response to his discoveries was mostly favorable, except among scientists, many of whom believed that Galileo's astronomical discoveries were actually optical illusions created by his telescope. However, for the most part scientists did accept his findings after viewing them with their own eyes.

In 1610 a combination of homesickness and a desire to devote himself to his scientific experiments and discoveries led to his seeking posts with no teaching obligations at the University of Pisa and the court of the grand duke. Galileo felt secure enough in the patronage of the Grand Duke Cosimo and the friendship of high ranking clergy to leave Venice, a liberal state which refused to tolerate interference in its internal affairs — even from the church — for Florence, a state whose strong ruling family identified its interests with those of the church.

Galileo had become convinced of the truth of *Copernicus's theory that the earth and the other planets revolve around the sun, which stands still, and began a campaign to convince the church to accept this hypothesis. As a scientist Galileo realized that the discoveries being made about the nature of the physical universe were causing a revolution in man's conception of it, while as a deeply religious and loyal Catholic he did not want the church to take a doctrinal stand about the nature of the universe which it would later have to retract.

The church had not closed its mind against Copernicus's theory until Galileo began his campaign, which was regarded as an outsider's interference in church affairs. Before Galileo popularized it, Copernicus's theory had existed in relative and harmless obscurity for years; Galileo's campaign forced the church to take a stand. It chose to adhere to the traditional Catholic view of the universe (actually Aristotelian doctrine adapted to a Christian format by Thomas *Aquinas) that the universe was divided into two parts — the heavens and the earth. This doctrine holds the earth to be changeable but unmoving while the heavenly bodies are unchangeable, their eternal motion around the earth a reflection of the perfection of God's work and their ultimate purpose the glorification of God.

Charges were brought against Galileo before the Inquisition. In 1615 the Inquisition decreed that he was not to hold, teach, or defend Copernicus's theory. It also put Copernicus's book on its list of prohibited books. For the next three years Galileo obeyed the Inquisition's ruling, continuing with his studies but not publishing. Then in 1618 three comets appeared in the sky. Taking this as a divine sign that he was meant to continue his work, Galileo resumed writing and publishing.

Galileo was further encouraged to hope for the church's acceptance of Copernicus's theory when his old friend and admirer, Cardinal Maffeo Barberini, was elected pope (Urban VIII) in 1623. As a cardinal he had considered himself a philosopher and liked to discuss science with Galileo. As pope he was not particularly open to Galileo's ideas but he did agree that Galileo could write about Copernicus's theory if he presented it as an hypothesis rather than a fact.

Pope Urban VIII was enraged when in 1632 Galileo published *The Dialogue*. Even though the book had been approved and licensed by the Inquisition after Galileo had made all the changes they requested, its refutations of the Aristotelian-church view of the universe were so convincing and the theory that the earth moves around the sun presented so persuasively that it made a mockery of the required statement that the ideas presented were just a theory rather than actual fact.

In 1633 Galileo was brought to trial in Rome for heresy. The trial lasted five months, during which Galileo was constantly pressured to concede that it was his moral duty to submit, as a loyal Catholic, to the authority of the church. He did so on June 22, 1633, and was sentenced to house arrest for the rest of his life.

The eight years of his house arrest were astonishingly productive. It was during this time that he lay the foundation for the science of mechanics. *Two New Sciences*, his greatest contribution to modern science, was published in Holland in 1638. Galileo denied any knowledge of how that book could have reached Holland in defiance of the Inquisition's total ban on his publishing.

Galileo's trial and the church's subsequent prohibition of his works inhibited the development of science in Catholic countries for the next hundred years. Changes in man's conception of the universe gradually did become acceptable, however, and in 1757 Pope Benedict XIV repealed the church's general prohibition against books teaching that the earth revolves around the sun. In 1822 Pope Pius VII approved the printing of books holding that the motion of the earth is an established fact. In 1835 Galileo's *Dialogue* was removed from the church's list of prohibited books and in 1979, Pope John Paul II praised Galileo's views on the relationship of science and religion and admitted that Galileo had suffered at the hands of the church.

In 1992 the Roman Catholic Church issued a statement completely exonerating Galileo.

M. A. Finocchiuro, *The Galilean Affair: A Documentary History*, 1989.

K. Fischer, *Galileo Galilei*, 1983.

GALILEO'S RECANTATION (1633)

I, Galileo, son of the late Vincenzio Galilei of Florence, seventy years of age, arraigned personally for judgment, kneeling before you Most Eminent and Most Reverend Cardinals Inquisitors-General against heretical depravity in all of Christendom, having before my eyes and touching with my hands the Holy Gospels, swear that I have always believed, I believe now, and with God's help I will believe in the future all that the Holy Catholic and Apostolic Church holds, preaches, and teaches. However, whereas, after having been judicially instructed with injunction by the Holy Office to abandon completely the false opinion that the sun is the center of the world and does not move and the earth is not the center of the world and moves, and not to hold, defend, or teach this false doctrine in any way whatever, orally or in writing; and after having been notified that this doctrine is contrary to Holy Scripture; I wrote and published a book in which I treat of this already condemned doctrine and adduce very effective reasons in its favor, without refuting them in any way; therefore, I have been judged vehemently suspected of heresy, namely of having held and believed that the sun is the center of the world and motionless and the earth is not the center and moves.

GAMA, VASCO DA (c.1460–1524), Portuguese explorer. Born to a noble family, Gama grew up in a seafaring Portugal which was exploring more of Africa each year.

Little is known of Gama's early life, but he successfully accomplished royal missions to seize French ships as reprisal for French actions against Portuguese shipping. King Manuel of Portugal then appointed him to head the expedition in search of the sea route to India.

Gama set sail with his fleet of four ships in July 1497. They made their way down the African coast, following the same route as countless other Portuguese ships over the years. Then, off the coast of Sierra Leone, Gama turned west and struck out across the Atlantic to avoid the strong northerly current off the southern half of the west African coast that made traveling southwards so difficult and time-consuming.

Though the distance is thousands of miles greater, it is actually much easier and faster to reach the southern tip of Africa by sailing west across the Atlantic Ocean with the trade winds, down the coast of Brazil with the strong southerly current, and then east across the Atlantic again with the strong easterly Antarctic Current. This is the route that Gama discovered and is still used by sailing vessels today. For ninety-six days he was out of sight of land.

Gama made Portugal's first contacts with the Bushmen, Hottentots, and other natives of southern and eastern Africa. The Portuguese were welcomed at Mozambique, their first port of call, and gained valuable information about trade in the Indian Ocean until the locals realized that these new traders were Christian, not Muslim. Gama had no desire for battle and withdrew from the town.

By the time he arrived at Mombasa, the finest harbor on the east African coast, his reputation as a cruel taskmaster preceded him and he met with profuse protestations of friendship, offers of assistance, and treachery. He tortured two captives by dripping boiling resin on them until they confessed that they had heard that the sheikh of Mombasa was planning to attack if he could catch the Portuguese off their guard; the attempted attack failed.

Gama's next stop was the port of Malindi, Mombasa's rival, where the mariners were welcomed as allies and provided with one of the best and most trustworthy pilots in the Indian Ocean. They arrived in India twenty-three days later, close to the important trading city of Calicut. Muslim traders had turned the friendly ruler of Calicut against him, and tried to prevent his selling Portuguese merchandise or leaving Calicut. Gama finally forced the Calicut ruler to let them leave by seizing hostages and headed back to Portugal, taking five hostages with him.

Gama returned to Portugal after burying his brother Paulo, who was one of his captains, in the Azores. King Manuel was pleased with the results of the voyage, even though the goods brought back were only samples of the spices and jewels available, and rewarded Gama with two annual pensions, two titles, including "Admiral of the Sea of India," import rights, and, provisionally, the town where Gama was born (which he never received). Gama now married Dona Maria da Silva, by whom he had six sons and a daughter.

Manuel sent fleets to India in 1500 and 1501 and then, in 1502, decided to send a large fleet to India to take over the extremely lucrative trade that was being carried by Arab ships and caravans to the cities of Italy and from there to the rest of Europe. He appointed Gama, who brought in his uncle and nephew as subordinate heads of the fleet of twenty ships, to lead the mission, which set sail in February, 1502, proceeding up the east African coast and along the Indian coast. On the way Gama established his first trading base in east Africa, at Sofala (a port which exported gold and hippopotamus teeth). He also lay in wait for pilgrimage ships from Mecca, and when one crossed his path he stripped it of its cargo of spices, set fire to it, and killed all of the hundreds of pilgrims on board, except for twenty boys he saved to become monks.

By the time King John III ascended the throne after Manuel's death in 1521, the Portuguese trading empire in the Indies had become corrupt. Portugal needed someone both strong and feared in India to bring the situation under control, so Gama was appointed Viceroy of India and set sail for the colony of Goa with two of his sons in April 1524. Many welcomed his efforts to restore law, order, and respect for the government but when Gama tried to arrest Goa's corrupt governor, the latter escaped back to Portugal with his ill-gotten gains. Gama also tried to extend his reforms to Cochin but he died there in December of 1524.

G. Correa, *The Three Voyages of Vasco da Gama and his Viceroyalty*, 1964.

H. H. Hart, *Sea Road to the Indies*, 1952.

K. G. Jayne, *Vasco da Gama and his Successors*, 1970.

GANDHI, INDIRA (1917–1984), prime minister of India. As the only daughter of Indian nationalist leader Jawaharlal *Nehru, the life of Mataji (Big Mother) Gandhi paralleled India's struggle to emerge as a modern nation. From her father she learned a deep respect for Western education and ideals; from her mother she came to appreciate the ancient traditions and customs of India. Already as a child in Allahabad, Gandhi contended with the struggle between these two conflicting worlds and with the British colonial power. As a regular meeting place for the Indian National Congress, her home was under constant British scrutiny, and she often watched as her parents were arrested.

After studying Indian poetry and dance at Rabindranath *Tagore's Santiniketan University, in 1937 Gandhi traveled to Oxford to study public administration, history, and anthropology. In England she met a Parsee Indian National Congress activist, Feroze Gandhi (no relation to Mohandas *Gandhi) whom she married, and they returned to India in 1942. The first year of their marriage was spent in prison; between 1943 and 1946, they retired from public life to raise a family. Although doctors warned Gandhi against having children, she had two sons, Rajiv and Sanjay. She could not, however, detach herself from her responsibilities to her father and her country. As India's first prime minister, Nehru needed his daughter's constant presence as his official hostess. She eventually left Feroze and committed herself totally to Indian political activism. In 1959, she was elected party president; she won support not only as Nehru's daughter but as a favorite of younger party activists resentful of the monopoly of older members who had been active in the independence movement.

Gandhi was devastated by Nehru's death in 1964. For several months she was unable to hear her father's name mentioned without bursting into tears. To the Congress party, however, it was crucial that she continue Nehru's legacy and she was invited to join the government as minister of information and broadcasting. Two years later she was chosen to succeed as prime minister; her lackluster performance as minister convinced each of several warring factions that she would be sufficiently malleable to represent their own interests. They were stunned to discover that Gandhi had long considered herself "destined to rule" and already had a well-formulated socialist agenda. Breaking with India's British heritage, she nationalized the banks and reduced the traditional influence of the princely states.

In 1967 her leadership was challenged by Morarji Desai, an elderly companion of her father in the struggle for independence. Gandhi enlisted her traditional base of support among the younger generation of party activists to defeat Desai by a narrow margin in a vicious parliamentary attempt to expel her from the party. An overwhelming victory in the 1971 national election proved that she had the support of the masses. That same year India emerged as a regional superpower because of her support for Bangladesh's bid for independence from Pakistan.

Two years later the Indian economy was ruined by a severe drought, a rapid rise in world oil prices, and corruption in Gandhi's government. Her attempt to blame Western imperialism failed although she toured the country extensively explaining her positions. In 1975 an Allahabad court convicted her of two counts of corruption, for which she forfeited her parliamentary seat and, as a result, the office of prime minister. Gandhi, however, refused to resign and enacted emergency measures, claiming that "democracy has given too much license to the people." In just two months over 50,000 people were arrested, including her archrival and deputy prime minister, Desai. Throughout, Gandhi denied that India was heading toward dictatorship. An election scheduled for 1976 was postponed, while new laws prohibited the press from publishing "objectionable materials." Although she enacted several populist measures such as land reforms and price freezes, the meteoric rise of her son Sanjay was considered to be blatant nepotism and rumors began circulating about an enforced sterilization program to resolve India's overpopulation. Her use of slogans such as "Work More! Talk Less!" failed to curb the mounting public outcry against her both at home and abroad.

In the face of this criticism Gandhi agreed to call a national election in 1977, running at the head of a new Congress-I (for Indira) Party. The opposition, running under the slogan "Dethrone the queen: end dictatorship," succeeded in electing Desai. An investigation of Gandhi's abuses of power was undertaken, and parliament voted to revoke her immunity. For six hours Gandhi refused to leave the parliament buildings, until police were eventually brought to escort her to prison. There, she refused to pay bail and was soon released.

In 1979 Desai resigned and Gandhi reunited her faction with the Congress party. Since she still lacked sufficient support, she endorsed Charan Singh as prime minister, only to overthrow his narrow government and force an election. She was reelected in 1980 by a two-thirds majority. Her final term in office, however, was filled with both personal and national tragedy. Sanjay died in a plane crash and his wife Maneka, a political rival, had to be evicted from the presidential palace. At the same time, militant Sikh nationalists led by Jarnail S. Bhindranwale called for an autonomous Sikh state to be established in the Punjab. Gandhi responded by attacking the Golden Temple of Amritsar, the holiest shrine of the Sikh religion. Over 1,200 people, among them Bhindranwale, were killed in the assault which, once again, provoked an international outcry against Gandhi's rule. Soon after the attack on Amritsar, Gandhi was assassinated by two Sikh bodyguards. She was succeeded by her son, Rajiv, who in turn was assassinated in 1991.

P. Gupte, *A Political Biography of Indira Gandhi*, 1991.

P. Jayaker, *Indira Gandhi*, 1992.

GANDHI, MOHANDAS KARAMCHAND (Mahatma; 1869–1948), Indian political and spiritual leader. Born in Porbandar, the capital of a small principality in Gujarat, western India, where his father was chief minister, Gandhi grew up in a pious Hindu household. Gandhi took the doctrine of *ahimsa* — refraining from harming any living being — for granted; it was later to constitute an integral part of his personal philosophy of social and political action.

Married at thirteen, Gandhi overcame his mother's anxiety and ultraorthodox Hindu condemnation to sail to London to study law in 1888. Separated from his wife and family, the lonely youth was forced to question and justify such personal practices as his vegetarianism; becoming a member of the London Vegetarian Society's executive commitee, he came into contact with such radical figures as Edward Carpenter, George Bernard *Shaw, and Annie Besant. He was also exposed for the first time to the Hindu spiritual classic the *Bhagavadgita*, which was to have a profound and lasting effect upon him.

Unable to make a satisfactory living as a lawyer in India, Gandhi remained there for only two years, sailing to South Africa in 1893 accept a position with an Indian firm. Journeying by train from Durban to Pretoria, Gandhi, despite his elegant Western dress and manner, was expelled from his first-class carriage at the insistence of a white passenger who objected to sharing it with an Indian. In later years, he was consistently to designate this as the single most important formative experience of his life; it moved him to determine to assert his dignity as an Indian and a man in a country where apartheid laws rendered him and his fellow Indians second-class citizens.

Gandhi soon became recognized as a leader of the South African Indian community, staying on to fight for its interests even after his original work was completed. His trip was to have lasted a few months; he remained in South Africa for a quarter of a century.

Founding the Natal Indian Congress, Gandhi organized demands for improved civil rights for the thousands of Indians living in the then-crown colony, most of whom were indentured laborers. In 1899, stressing duties as well as rights, he argued that as citizens of the British Empire, Indians should help defend Natal during the Boer War and formed an eleven-hundred-man Indian volunteer ambulance corps.

Gandhi's life constituted a continuous spiritual quest and in 1904, after reading *Unto This Last*, John Ruskin's avowal of the nobility of manual labor, he gave up his £5,000-a-year legal practice and, with some of his growing band of followers, renounced material possessions and strove to satisfy human needs in the simplest manner, with all labor considered equally valuable and all goods shared. Tolstoy Farm (named after Leo *Tolstoy, whose *The Kingdom of God is Within You* profoundly impressed Gandhi, and with whom he corresponded briefly) near Johannesburg became Gandhi's home and a center for communal living. Throughout his life he was to continue such "experiments with truth," which led him to simplify his diet, renounce sex, spend an hour each morning in careful study of the *Bhagavadgita* (which he came to regard as his "spiritual dictionary"), profess the unity of all religions, dress in the garb of a simple Indian peasant, and even extol the virtues of a daily salt water enema.

The opposition to the Transvaal government's 1906 registration ordinance, which required all Indians over the age of eight to be fingerprinted and carry an identity card, marked the first use of strategies based on the principle of *satyagraha* (literally "truth-firmness," passive resistance) which Gandhi had formulated. His religious convictions had led him to a complete disavowal of violence, but he still received a jail sentence for organizing a boycott of the registration process and peaceful picketing of registration centers.

While in prison, he read Henry *Thoreau's *On Civil Disobedience*, which asserted the individual's

- There is more to life than increasing its speed.
- Prayer is not an old woman's idle instrument. Properly understood and applied, it is the most potent instrument of action.
- Honesty is incompatible with the amassing of a large fortune.
- If blood be shed, let it be our blood. Cultivate the quiet courage of dying without killing. For man lives freely only by his readiness to die, if needs be, at the hands of his brother, never by killing him.
- It is easy enough to be friendly to one's friends. But to befriend the one who regards himself as your enemy is the quintessence of true religion. The other is mere business.
- *When asked his opinion on Western civilization:* It would be a very good idea.

Mahatma Gandhi

right to ignore unjust laws and refuse allegiance to a government whose tyranny had become unbearable; the book acted as a catalyst for his ideas and motivated his strategy for opposing the 1913 decision by the Transvaal government to close its borders to Indians. Thousands of floggings and hundreds of jailings could not break the nonviolent movement, and in the face of international condemnation of its heavy-handed retaliatory measures, Jan *Smuts's government engineered a compromise agreement with Gandhi. "The saint has left our shores, I hope for ever," observed Smuts when Gandhi sailed for India in 1914.

Hailed as "Mahatma" (great-souled) by Rabindranath *Tagore, Gandhi played little active role in Indian politics until 1919, when he organized nonviolent protests against the Rowlatt Act, which sought to repress agitation for Indian freedom. The British authorities' response was nowhere more brutal than in the city of Amritsar, Punjab, where some fifteen hundred unarmed and nonviolent protesters were gunned down by troops. Indians reacted with shock and horror and calls for independence from British rule became even stronger.

Quickly recognized as the undisputed leader of the Indian nationalist movement, Gandhi succeeded in transforming the Indian National Congress from a superannuated body of anglicized Indian gentlemen into a genuinely representative mass organization, using it as the launching pad for a campaign of nonviolent noncooperation against British rule. To the dismay of many of his colleagues, he called off the hugely successful campaign in 1922, when outbreaks of violence convinced him that his followers did not fully understand the importance of the principle of nonviolence. He was arrested shortly thereafter, but was released due to ill health after serving three years in jail.

Mahatma Gandhi with Charlie Chaplin

Convinced that self-sufficiency was an essential prerequisite for successful Indian self-government, he called for a boycott of British goods, a return to the wearing of rough homespun cotton clothing; he himself spent an hour each day at a spinning wheel and homespun soon became the unofficial uniform of nationalist political leaders, In 1930 he marched to Dandi on the Gujarat coast and collected sea salt in defiance of the government monopoly on its manufacture and sale. The wave of civil disobedience this action triggered resulted in 60,000 arrests, including that of Gandhi himself, but the British government was eventually forced to acknowledge Indian nationalist aspirations. The man Winston *Churchill derided as a "half-naked fakir" traveled to London to negotiate with the British government, but negotiations did not yield the timetable for a British withdrawal from India for which he had hoped.

After his return to India, he was increasingly occupied with projects such as the uplift of India's tens of millions of untouchables (economically and socially the lowest of the low, whom he renamed *Harijans*, or "Children of God") and the promotion of village-based economics as opposed to the economics of industrialization and urbanization, which he considered inappropriate to Indian needs. Nevertheless, even after leaving the Indian National Congress in 1934, he remained the spiritual leader of the nationalist movement and the Indian people, exerting a considerable practical and moral influence.

Gandhi's principles led him to staunchly refuse to approve Indian support for the British war effort, despite his acknowledgment that Nazi persecution of Jews meant that "if ever there could be justifiable war in the name of and for humanity, war against Germany to prevent the wanton persecution of a whole race would be completely justified." Meanwhile his 1942 call for the British to "Quit India" led to his imprisonment and that of the entire Congress leadership, but the writing was on the wall for British rule. Five years later, in August 1947, India became an independent state.

Gandhi had consistently struggled against separating the subcontinent into a Hindu India and a Muslim Pakistan, and the sectarian bloodbath that followed partition and claimed a million lives was a realization of his worst fears. He spent the night of the independence celebrations in Calcutta, where his presence successfully prevented the communal violence that had flared elsewhere. When violence did finally erupt there, Gandhi, seventy-seven years old and in poor health, expressed his intention of fasting until the fighting had completely stopped. He had fasted before to achieve spiritual or political ends, but never before had his life been so obviously at risk; within seventy-two hours hostilities in the city ceased.

In early January of the following year Gandhi arranged a truce in the riot-torn capital, Delhi; at the end of that same month he was assassinated by a Hindu fanatic at one of his own prayer meetings. He died with the words *"He, Ram"* ("O! God") on his lips. Among the thousands of tributes to him, none was more moving or heartfelt than Jawaharlal *Nehru's representation of him as "that light that represented the living, the eternal truths, reminding us of the right path, drawing us from error, taking this ancient country to freedom."

The initiator of the twentieth century's struggles against colonialism, racism, and violence, Gandhi has also been an influential symbol of the moral and spiritual resources of the developing world, while his theory and practice of nonviolent direct action influenced many, including the African American civil rights leader, Martin Luther *King, Jr.

L. Fischer, *Gandhi*, 1954.

M. B. Green, *Tolstoy and Gandhi, Men of Peace*, 1983.

C. Kumar and M. Puri, *Mahatma Gandhi*, 1982.

Pyarelal, *Mahatma Gandhi*, 1966.

GARCÍA LORCA, FEDERICO (1899 – 1936), Spanish poet and dramatist who combined rustic imagery with the simple folk rhythms of rural Andalusia. He was a gifted musician who turned to writing when unable to continue his music studies, and an artist influenced by Salvador Dalí. His writing ranges from tender love songs to violent scenes of unrequited passions, paralleling his own brief and troubled life.

After a childhood illness left him unable to participate in most children's games (he could not walk until he was four and had a limp throughout his adult life), García Lorca became preoccupied with his own make-believe worlds. Adults often came to watch as he, pretending to be a priest and wrapped in an old white sheet, demanded that his congregation weep during his sermon. With his first savings he bought a toy theater. Lorca later claimed that his fascination with art originated in this period. A local plowman, he claimed, unearthed an ancient mosaic of Daphnis and Chloe; the bond between love and the soil remained an important theme throughout his writing. Another central theme, the fear of death, may have originated in his witnessing the death and laying out of an elderly neighbor.

THE LITTLE MUTE BOY

The little boy was looking for his voice.
(The king of the crickets had it.)
In a drop of water
the little boy was looking for his voice.
I do not want it for speaking with;
I will make a ring of it
that my silence may wear
on its little finger.
In a drop of water
the little boy was looking for his voice.
(The captive voice, far away,
put on a cricket's clothes.)

Federico García Lorca
(translated by W. S. Merwin)

When Lorca was eight his family moved to Almeria and then to Granada, where he was inspired by the local renaissance in art and literature. His parents anticipated an academic career for him, but Lorca preferred sketching and music to schoolwork. Because he was effeminate he had few friends among his classmates, preferring the companionship of older members of the Granada Arts Club. Although his father insisted he study law at the University of Granada, Lorca concentrated on his musical studies. He became friendly with the composer Manuel de Falla, who encouraged him to collect folk songs. Only the death of his teacher and his father's reluctance to allow him to continue studying music in Paris led Lorca to take up poetry.

His first book, *Impressions and Landscapes* (1918), describes his travels through Spain and his emerging world view. Whereas he had been raised a devout Catholic, he now concluded that Christ's example and sacrifice had been in vain. Nor was he able to reconcile Christian sexual ethics with his emerging homosexuality. In the liberal atmosphere prevalent among Spanish intellectuals, however, Lorca was a rising star.

In 1919 he went to Madrid and entered the Residencia de Estudiantes, an institution of great liberal tradition, where he met many noted poets and other intellectuals. There he produced plays, composed, painted, and wrote poems. He stayed there happily for many years, never finishing his studies.

Lorca's first play, *The Butterfly's Evil Spell*, although not a success, was noted as the work of a great poet. In 1921 he published a *Libro de poemes*, financed in part by his parents, which launched his reputation throughout the Spanish-speaking world. In a short time he was renowned as a poet, dramatist, musician, and lecturer. Always intrigued by the folklore of his native Andalusia, he attempted to revive its traditional puppet theater, while new plays, such as *The Tragicomedy of Don Cristobal* and *Doña*

Rosita la Soltera experimented with local dialect and folk songs. Other important works included the successful *Romancero Gitaero,* love songs rooted in the imagery of the gypsy troubadours of Andalusia. "Although it is called gypsy," he later wrote, "the book as a whole is the poem of Andalusia."

Lorca once told a journalist, "The day one ceases to fight his instincts is the day one truly learns to live." Perhaps he was referring to his homosexuality, which again surfaced after meeting Salvador Dalí in 1923. The two men shared a passion for art, but Dalí rejected Lorca's advances, the unrequited love that appears so often in Lorca's writing. His final rejection by Dalí in 1929, accompanied by political turmoil in Spain, led him to seek sanctuary in America. Although New York did not meet his expectations, he was excited by the black renaissance in Harlem, finding common themes in jazz and his own Andalusian folk music. Only at his parents' insistence did he agree to return to Spain.

The abdication of Alphonso XIII and the ensuing liberal government offered Lorca an opportunity to fulfil his ambition of liberating the educational system from the grip of a reactionary church. Lorca rejected art for art's sake, believing that the theater's most important function was to "assail humanity." His La Barraca theater company roamed rural Spain, presenting both classical and modern drama to the local population. Two of Lorca's most important dramatic works, *Bodas de Sangre* (Blood Wedding, 1933) and *Yerma* (1934), were originally written for La Barraca. The third work of this trilogy, *Le Casa de Benarda Alba,* (*The House of Bernarda Alba,* (1936) was only performed posthumously.

His liberal beliefs, however, earned Lorca the hostility of the fascist Falanges, then threatening to overrun Spain. In 1936 the civil war broke out and a reign of terror began: among its victims was Lorca. In a mock trial he was accused of supporting Russia, possessing and operating a ham radio, homosexuality, and associating with known Republican agitators. He was executed by a firing squad in August 1936.

C. W. Cobb, *Federico García Lorca,* 1967.
H. Cowen, *A Study of Federico García Lorca and Surrealism,* 1982.
I. Gibson, *Federico García Lorca: A Life,* 1989.

GARIBALDI, GIUSEPPE (1807–1882), Italian soldier and revolutionary, romantic hero of the fight to unify Italy. He was born in Nice to a pious mother who hoped that her mellow-voiced, sweet-tempered child would become a priest. However, young Garibaldi had no such desire. Not an intellectual, he studied only what interested him and often escaped from his studies to go hunting or fishing. He became a seaman like his father, sailing the Mediterranean and Black Seas for ten years. An Italian revolutionary's tales of efforts to create a unified, republican Italy fired his interest and indignation.

Garibaldi asked Giuseppe *Mazzini, the leading advocate of the Italian struggle for freedom, how he could help the cause and was told to enlist in the Piedmont's navy and, by spreading propaganda, foster a naval mutiny that would spark a republican revolution. The plot failed, Garibaldi escaped to France, and Piedmont condemned him to death. He was thrilled to read the newspaper stories that appeared afterwards (newspaper reports always embellished his exploits, giving him great pleasure).

Garibaldi sailed for Uruguay, as Mazzini had no other work for him. He stayed in South America for twelve years between 1836 and 1848, fighting in its wars of independence. He also met Anna Maria Ribiero da Silva (known as Anita), a married woman who ran off with him, rode beside him on his campaigns (jealously reluctant to let him out of her sight), bore his children, and married him after her husband's death. Garibaldi's hazardous wartime adventures taught him invaluable skills ranging from how to conduct guerrilla warfare and ride a horse, to how to round up and slaughter livestock to feed his men, or use a poncho as a shield against the elements.

Accounts of Garibaldi's exploits made him famous in Italy, where a liberal pope, *Pius IX, had been elected in 1846. Garibaldi dreamed of saving Italy, in the name of Pius's spiritual leadership, with an army of Italian soldiers he would train, but Pius never responded when he offered his military services. News of the 1848 revolutions sweeping through Italy excited Garibaldi, and he and his army of eighty-five men, two cannons and eight hundred muskets left South America for Italy, where his arrival was greeted with much enthusiasm, but few volunteers. Rejected by Piedmont because of his republicanism and lack of formal military training, Garibaldi marched to Milan where he joined forces with Mazzini. He fought two battles against the Austrians before, heavily outnumbered, he retreated to Switzerland, convinced more than ever that Italy's future lay in independence and unity.

Garibaldi was drawn to increasingly radical Rome, from where Pius had fled after an insurrection in 1848. Although elected to the Roman assembly, Garibaldi was a poor politician, and was impatient with parliamentary procedure. The assembly disregarded his demand for the immediate establishmant of an independent Roman republic. Disgusted, he returned to soldiering, in which capacity he was the mainstay and inspiration of Rome's defense against French forces fighting to restore papal rule. The short-lived republic's administrative incompetence forced its army to retreat from a superior French force mounting in Apulia. The republic's failure caused a great rift between Garibaldi and Mazzini. Garibaldi refused to surrender to the French; during the retreat from Rome his wife Anita died. His international reputation for heroism and patriotism preceded him into his second exile, from 1849 to 1854, to the United States and later Peru.

Piedmont's prime minister, Count Camillo Benso di *Cavour, thought he could make use of Garibaldi and allowed him to return in 1854. Cavour wanted to create an independent Italy ruled by the conservative constitutional monarchy of Piedmont. Public association with Garibaldi could channel republican fervor — that might otherwise turn to revolution — into support for a war to unify Italy. However, it could also make Cavour's careful statesmanship seem a cover for revolution and alienate Piedmont's foreign allies. Cavour solved this problem by making Garibaldi a major-general in a volunteer corps rather than in the regular army. Despite Piedmont's unsuccessful war against Austria in 1859 to gain Italian liberation, Garibaldi was an honored hero.

Garibaldi was romantically involved with several women after Anita: Mrs. Roberts, an English socialite who lionized him; the wealthy Madame Schwartz, who wanted the rights to publish his memoirs; and his housekeeper, who gave birth to a daughter. His marriage in 1860 to Giuseppina, the daughter of the Marchese Raimondi, lasted only a few hours before he left her, having learnt about her lover. It took another twenty years for the marriage to be annulled so that he could marry the peasant woman Francesca Armosino, with whom he had lived since 1866.

Piedmont made use of Garibaldi even though it found him an embarrassment, publicly disavowing him while secretly supporting his military campaigns, which greatly increased its territory. Conservatives were afraid of his socialist ideas and many in the military were jealous of his victories. The church disliked Garibaldi because of his ambition to take Rome (which Cavour thwarted, fearing adverse international reaction) and because he evacuated monasteries and convents to house his soldiers and was a free thinker.

An aged and infirm Garibaldi visits Rome in 1875

Garibaldi's greatest military exploit was his leadership of the expedition of "the thousand heroes," in which his army, the Red Shirts, freed Sicily in May 1860 and then conquered Naples in September, defeating the Kingdom of the Two Sicilies. In 1861 Victor Emmanuel was proclaimed king of Italy. In the war of 1866 Garibaldi again commanded the Red Shirts in Tyrol. He was not with the Italian forces that finally took possession of Rome in 1870, but later that year fought for the French in the Franco-Prussian War.

Garibaldi outlived both Cavour and Mazzini. He spent his last years on the island of Caprera where, crippled by old wounds and rheumatism and visited frequently by admirers, he wrote two novels.

D. Mack Smith, *Cavour and Garibaldi, 1860*, 1985.

D. M. Smith, *Garibaldi*, 1969.

GARVEY, MARCUS

GARVEY, MARCUS (1887–1940), black nationalist and separatist; self-proclaimed first president of the "provisional government-in-exile of Africa." Garvey was born in Saint Ann's Bay, Jamaica. A leading campaigner for social reform on the island, he helped organize the Printers' Union strike of 1907, in demand of higher wages. Appalled by the state of black laborers in Jamaica, he traveled to Central America, where he found the situation on the large banana plantations no better. He returned to Jamaica in 1912, only to set out again shortly thereafter, this time bound for London. There he met several prominent African nationalists, among them Duse Muhammad Ali of Egypt, who became his spiritual mentor. Garvey was also deeply influenced by Booker T. *Washington's *Up From Slavery*, a book that would change his life. Washington's call for black self-sufficiency captivated Garvey and he brought Washington's message back home with him to Jamaica in 1914. There he founded the Universal Negro Improvement Association (UNIA), with the intention of starting an agricultural and industrial school not unlike Washington's own Tuskegee Institute.

Garvey's notions of black pride differed from those of his hero, however. Under the slogan "One God, One Aim, One Destiny," he advanced the causes of black ownership of business and the liberation of Africa from colonialism and its resettlement by the black diaspora; he also advocated black racial purity and total social separation. Having reached the conclusion that he was only marginally effective because of Jamaica's relative isolation, Garvey relocated to Harlem, New York City, in 1916. He founded a newspaper, *The Negro World*, and quickly began attracting adherents to UNIA. Within two months, membership in UNIA had risen to two thousand in New York alone. By 1919 there were thirty branches across the United States, as well as branches in Latin America, the Caribbean, and Africa.

Garvey began realizing his own ideas by establishing a shipping company, the Black Star Line, to sail between New York and the Caribbean. In 1920 he organized the First UNIA International Congress.

> Where is the Black man's government? Where is his king and kingdom? Where is his president, his country and his ambassadors, his army, his navy, his men of big affairs? I could not find them, and then I declared, "I will help to make them!"
>
> **Marcus Garvey**

Twenty-five thousand delegates from around the world filled Madison Square Garden to hear Garvey speak. At the fourth congress, Garvey was declared provisional head of state of the government-in-exile of Africa. A campaign to raise two hundred million dollars for a resettlement program in Liberia failed when the local government, under pressure from Britain and France, banned UNIA supporters from settling in the country.

Garvey's luck continued to decline. Even his personal appeal could not undo the harm done to his movement by the radical direction he was taking. For example, the newly organized African Orthodox Church, affiliated with UNIA, urged its members to use only black Christs and Madonnas in their ritual, and in 1925 he was charged with mail fraud regarding the stock of his floundering shipping company, and sentenced to five years in the Atlanta penitentiary. He received a presidential pardon in 1927, but had to leave the United States. In 1928 he journeyed through Europe, trying to gain support for the establishment of an independent black state in former German African colonies. Garvey returned to Jamaica, only to find that the local branch of UNIA had broken away from the American UNIA. Although he made occasional statements in support of black causes, the most notable being his condemnation of Ethiopian emperor *Haile Selassie for fleeing invading Italian troops, Garvey's importance on the world political scene declined rapidly. After several unhappy years in Jamaica he returned to London, where he died. In 1964 his body was returned to Jamaica and buried in Kingston with full honors.

Garvey was a dreamer whose elaborate plans seemed destined to failure. He was scoffed at by such leading African Americans as W. E. *Du Bois of the National Association for the Advancement of Colored People (NAACP) and publisher Robert S. Abbot. At the same time, Garvey's contribution to the welfare of black men and women around the world is undeniable. He was the first to urge them to take pride in their identity as a distinct ethnic group. Future African leaders such as Ghana's Kwame *Nkrumah stated that Garvey played an important role in the development of their own philosophies of political independence and pan-Africanism.

E. D. Cronon, *Black Moses*, 1981.

A. J. Garvey, *Philosophical Opinions of Marcus Garvey*, 1970.

GAULLE, CHARLES-ANDRE-MARIE-JOSEPH

DE (1890–1970), French general, statesman and first president of France's Fifth Republic. He graduated from the École Militaire of Saint-Cyr in 1912, and in 1913 served in the infantry regiment of Philippe *Pétain. In World War I he was captured at Douaumont during the battle of Verdun in March 1916. While a prisoner of war he wrote his first book, published in 1924, entitled *La Discorde chez l'ennemi,* in which he discussed the relationship between the civil and administrative powers and the military in Germany.

De Gaulle's writing career continued with a series of books that analyzed both military and political leadership: *Le Fil de l'epée,* (1932; *The Edge of the Sword,* 1960), was followed in 1934 by the highly controversial *Vers l'armée de métier* (*The Army of the Future,* 1940) in which he defied existing military and political theories by insisting that France needed a highly mechanized army complete with adequate air power rather than fixed fortifications such as the Maginot Line.

At the outbreak of World War II de Gaulle was colonel of a tank regiment in Alsace, but in May 1940 was promoted to brigadier general and given command of the Fourth Armored Division, which had been formed to halt German advances. Bitterly opposed to surrender, de Gaulle proposed that if the need arose, the government should withdraw to North Africa and continue the war against nazism from there. When Premier Paul Reynaud was replaced by Marshal Pétain, who advocated an armistice with Germany, de Gaulle — although a junior general without an army or money, and with virtually no political experience — declared himself leader of Free France and took his struggle to England. Broadcasting from England, he called on the French to continue their fight alongside England and to resist German occupation, using as his rallying cry "France has lost a battle but she has not lost the war." He thus created an external resistance alongside an internal resistance movement.

Through the BBC, de Gaulle secured both a French and a worldwide audience, insuring his position as leader and symbol of the resistance movement. The use of radio transmitters and receivers enabled both the internal and external movements to coordinate their activities and at the same time made it possible for de Gaulle to concentrate the various groups around himself and his political agenda. Meanwhile, in his absence he was sentenced to death for treason by a French military court.

Despite British government recognition, de Gaulle had not achieved as much support as he would have liked. His relations with Britain were strained by his refusal to implement his promised grant of independence to Syria and Lebanon, former French mandated territories freed from Vichy control by British forces. His hold on the Free French movement was tested further by his troubled relationship with President Franklin D. *Roosevelt and the U.S. government. The United States was fearful

A poster, signed by de Gaulle, calling on the French people to join him in the resistance movement

of his political aspirations and unwilling to damage relations with the Vichy régime. When Allied forces landed in North Africa in November 1942, the United States insisted that de Gaulle take no active role in the operation and he was not told about the successful landings until after they had taken place. De Gaulle moved his headquarters to Algiers in May 1943. He organized the French Committee of National Liberation and appointed himself cochairman. In June 1944 he transformed the committee into a provisional government of the French Republic. Although he was not permitted to land on D-Day, de Gaulle arrived in France a week later and returned to Paris triumphant.

After the war, de Gaulle was unanimously elected president of the French provisional government. As leader of two successive provisional governments he introduced economic programs aimed at the modernization of France. However, he favored the introduction of a constitution that would insure a strong executive and when there seemed to be a stalemate in the debate, he resigned from office in January 1946.

De Gaulle remained opposed to the constitution finally adopted by the Fourth Republic and retired to his country home to write his memoirs. He emerged from retirement in 1947 to form a new

SAYINGS OF DE GAULLE

- I feel not a person but an instrument of Destiny.
- Men are of no importance. What counts is who commands.
- Diplomats are useful only in fair weather. As soon as it rains, they drown in every drop.
- How can you be expected to govern a country that has two hundred and forty-six kinds of cheese?
- Since a politician never says what he believes, he is surprised when other people believe him.
- Every man of action has a strong dose of egotism, pride, hardness and cunning.
- As usual, I have against me the bourgeois, the officers and the diplomats, and for me only the people who take the subway.
- When I want to know what France is thinking, I ask myself.

ABOUT DE GAULLE

- What can you do with a man who looks like a female llama surprised when bathing?

Winston Churchill

- One had the sense that if he moved to a window the center of gravity might shift and the whole room might tilt everyone into the garden.

Henry Kissinger

party, the Rassemblement du Peuple Français (Rally of the French People), a coalition opposed to the existing constitution and the party system. Despite its success in elections, de Gaulle retired once again in 1953. His return to public life was a result of the crisis that erupted in Algeria in 1958; he was recalled as the one person who could steer France out of the mounting political crisis. De Gaulle was named premier and given wide emergency powers, including the power to prepare a new constitution. A new constitution establishing the presidential system was adopted, and de Gaulle was inaugurated president of the Fifth Republic in January 1959.

With the war in Algeria continuing, de Gaulle abandoned his previous stance and advocated political independence for the colony. Faced by revolt by his political supporters, he was forced to use his emergency powers to settle an uprising of the military and settlers in Algeria. Nonetheless, Algerian independence was finally accepted by popular referendum in France in 1962.

Domestically, de Gaulle concentrated on introducing economic reforms with a view to combating inflation while promoting expansion of French industry. He then flexed his muscles in the international arena in an attempt to assert French independence from superpower influence. He constantly blocked Britain's entry into the European Common Market and limited French participation in the North Atlantic Treaty Organization (NATO).

During his second seven-year term he continued his assertive foreign policy and in 1966 announced France's withdrawal from NATO. He sought to enhance French influence in Latin America, Canada, and the Far East, and pursued a policy of détente towards the communist countries in Eastern Europe. During his terms of office he survived a number of assassination attempts.

In May 1968 de Gaulle was faced with student demonstrations and a series of labor strikes. The students demanded reform of the educational system; the workers demanded a greater share in the expanding economy. Taking the issues to the electorate, de Gaulle won a landslide victory in the June elections. With a new mandate to govern, he promised both workers and students a greater role in the decision-making process and a share in the profits of industry. In 1969 he called for a referendum suggesting constitutional reforms to transform the Senate into an advisory body and to give greater powers to regional councils. When his proposals were rejected he resigned the presidency and retired to his home in Colombey-les-Deux-Églises, where he continued to write his memoirs — *War Memoirs* (1955–1960) and *Memoirs of Hope* (1972) — until his death from a heart attack a year later.

De Gaulle was one of the most influential leaders of his time, coming to the rescue of his country in two crucial crises and maintaining France's stature as a major power.

R. Aron, *De Gaulle Triumphant,* 1964.
D. Cook, *Charles de Gaulle: A Biography,* 1987.
A. Crawley, *De Gaulle,* 1969.
B. Crozier, *De Gaulle,* 1973.
B. Ledwidge, *De Gaulle,* 1982.

GAUSS, CARL FRIEDRICH (1777–1855), German mathematician and astronomer. Born in Brunswick, Germany, the son of a bricklayer, by the age of three he demonstrated that he was a mathematical prodigy by finding an error in his father's accounts. The Duke of Brunswick recognized the boy's genius, and over the objection of Gauss's parents sent him to the Collegium Capolinum and later to the University of Göttingen. In college he became known for his unusual intuition in higher mathematics;. his diary discloses that the basis of virtually all his theories and discoveries were thought of in his youth. At age nineteen Gauss demonstrated how to divide a circle into seventeen equal arcs with a simple compass and a ruler.

In 1801 Giuseppe Piazzi accidentally discovered Ceres, the largest asteroid located within the asteroid belt between Mars and Jupiter, but then lost it. Gauss derived a new mathematical procedure which predicted the location of Ceres. Using Gauss's method, other astronomers rediscovered Ceres in 1802. He was appointed the first director of the new observatory at Göttingen in 1807, conducting research and teaching his pupils, the latter not one of his favorite activities. When lecturing he would explain to his students why his right eyebrow was raised higher than the left one. "After all," he would say, "I am an astronomer."

Gauss was conversant with every branch of mathematics. His reputation was established early in his career by his work in the theory of numbers. Among other things he developed a very simple formula to determine the number of prime numbers within a given larger number. From his theory of parallels a new branch of geometry developed. This work was a revolution in the world of mathematics as it ran counter to *Euclid's theories. For example, Euclid stated that the sum of the angles of a triangle equals the sum of two right angles. Gauss and his student Janos Bolyai fashioned a triangle in which the sum of its angles was less than the sum of two right angles. Later another of Gauss's students, Friedrich Riemann, constructed a triangle, the sum of whose angles exceeded the sum of two right angles.

Gauss had developed the theory of surfaces with special attention to the curvature and the conditions for one surface to fit another. His theory of parallels was one of several starting points for Albert *Einstein's theory of relativity. Additionally Gauss proved the basic theory of algebra (already in his doctoral thesis when he was twenty-two) and made advances in higher trigonometry. He himself said, "Mathematics is the queen of the sciences, and arithmetic the queen of mathematics."

T. Hall, *Carl Friedrich Gauss: A Biography*, 1970.
H. W. Turnbull, *The Great Mathematicians*, 1962.

GENGHIS KHAN (1167–1227), Mongol conqueror who united and ruled half of the world as he knew it. A man of immovable will, violent energy, and enormous mental ability, he was merciless toward enemies but lenient and generous with his followers. Although he himself was superstitious, he knew well how to use superstition as a weapon. Above all he was obsessed by the love of power.

Genghis Khan was born to the Mongol chief Yesugai and his beautiful wife Houlun, who had been snatched from her newly-betrothed husband as they were traveling home together. On the day of his son's birth to Houlun, Yesugai returned home with a captive Tartar chief named Temujin. He marked the occasion by naming the newborn boy after his prisoner.

Hunters and nomads, the Mongols gave pride of place at the fire and first choice of food to the warriors. Women and elders came next, leaving the children to fight for warmth and scraps of food. Murder, rape, theft, and clan feuding were a normal part of life, and children grew up quickly. When Temujin was thirteen, he was betrothed to the nine-year-old Bortai and left in the tent of his future bride, as was customary. Temujin never saw his father again; on the way home Yesugai was fatally poisoned, leaving his firstborn to rule as tribal chief.

Most of Yesugai's former followers deserted the tribe. His mother exhorted Temujin to avenge his father's death and regain the old chief's glory. Because his father's former kinsmen saw Temujin as an enemy, they sought his life, and thieves almost stole the eight horses upon which the family's livelihood depended. Temujin prevailed, however, and at the age of seventeen set out to claim Bortai and assume the responsibilites of leadership. His first success was the renewal of an old alliance with his father's former friend Togrul, cemented with the offering of Bortai's dowry — a sable coat — as a gift. Success, however, was followed by defeat, for the Merkit tribe, from whom Houlun had been stolen, now took revenge by kidnapping Temujin's new wife. Invoking his friendship with Togrul, Temujin managed to regain Bortai, but it was never clear whether the son she bore nine months later was his or his enemy's.

- Trustworthy persons have related that the Genghis-Khan, at the time when he came into Kharasan, was sixty-five years old, a man of tall stature, of vigorous build, robust in body, the hair on his face scanty and turned white, with cat's eyes, possessed of great energy, discernment, genius and understanding, awe-striking, a butcher, just, resolute, an overthrower of enemies, intrepid, sanguinary and cruel...He was an adept in magic and deception, and some of the devils were his friends.

Juzjani (Muslim historian)

- Genghis was a man of vast ability and led his armies like a god...Such powers are wonderful and their loss is deeply to be regretted.

Chinese official history

- He was a man of great worth and of great ability (eloquence), and valor.

Marco Polo

- ..ther was nowher in no regiown so excellent a lord in alle thing.

Geoffrey Chaucer

Temujin eventually regained the power his father had lost, and his followers renamed him Chingis (Genghis), which in Chinese means "son of heaven" and "perfect warrior" and may also be derived from the Mongol word for "strong." At this point Genghis was primarily known for keeping order in his tribe, but by 1206, when he was fifty years old, he had come to dominate his subjects and his hostile neighbors by a combination of military genius, superior organization, and treachery. He had conquered most of Mongolia, and his name had been amended to Genghis Khan (Turkish *khan*, "lord").

Fired by his passion for conquest, Genghis Khan began to look beyond the Mongol boundaries. In 1211 he refused to pay tribute to the Chinese emperor, scaled the Great Wall and invaded northern China. Peking fell in 1214, followed by Korea in 1218. His Mongol armies then turned west with relentless fury, looting, massacring, and leaving destruction in their wake. They conquered what is now Iraq, Iran, and the Asian parts of what was later the Soviet Union. Invading parts of India and sweeping through Turkestan, Khan's armies drove the Turks out, preventing the establishment of a Turkish empire in central Asia. In 1222 they reached Russia, expanding an empire that now reached from the China Sea to the Dnieper and from the Persian Gulf almost to the Arctic Ocean.

Uneducated though he was, Genghis Khan demonstrated a remarkable military genius paralleled by an amazing talent for statesmanship. Like his armies, his entire regime was characterized by superb organization and discipline. In Mongolia he had created the Mongol feudal state out of the anarchy of a deteriorating clan system, drawing up a code of law, the *yasak*, to govern it. There were laws on punishment for sexual offenses and rulings on spying and interference, presumably intended to stamp out clan feuds. The *yasak* codified customs of desert hospitality, hygiene, and religious practice, and established codes of behavior and organization for the army.

Genghis Khan organized his empire and united it with great roads, encouraging the growth of trade and providing security. It was claimed that one could travel from one end of the empire to the other without fear of danger. Paradoxically, by destroying everything in his path, he had created the conditions for peace and culture. By founding his empire, he opened up Asia to Europe and made possible a world market and international exchange of ideas. After his death his empire was divided among his four sons, and four of his grandsons — among them *Kublai Khan — became great Mongol leaders in turn.

L. Hartog, *Genghis Khan*, 1989.
P. Rutchnevsky, *Genghis Khan*, 1992.

GEORGE III (George William Frederick, 1738–1820), king of England. Born in London to Frederick Louis, Prince of Wales, and his wife Augusta of Saxe-Gotha, he became heir to the throne at the age of twelve upon the death of his father. George's early years were dominated by the influence of his formidable mother who sought to isolate him from potential moral dangers in the decadent court society around her.

George was not a quick student and did not learn to read until he was eleven. A child of strong emotions, his determination was second to none but this was undermined by feelings of inadequacy. He needed a hero to look up to and found one in his tutor John Stuart, the Earl of Bute, a talented and ambitious politician who soon won George's total confidence.

George acceded to the throne in 1760 and continued to rely on Bute for support and instruction. Bute persuaded the king to put aside all ideas of marrying the young lady he had set his heart on, Lady Sarah Lennox. Apart from the association of her family with Bute's political opponents, she was not of suitable royal stock. George was easily convinced to adopt the safe course and find a Protestant German princess as his queen.

In 1761 he married Princess Charlotte Sophia of Mecklenberg-Strelitz. Although George married out of his sense of duty the marriage was a success, lasting fifty years, with the king's faithfulness to his wife a striking exception to the other monarchs of the house of Hanover. The royal couple had fourteen children between 1762 and 1783.

Duty to his country was a concept deeply embedded in him from his earliest years. Whereas his two predecessors had considered themselves Germans first and English second, King George III declared in his first speech from the throne, "Born and educated in this country, I glory in the name of Britain." He told his subjects, "I do not pretend to any superior abilities, but will give place to no one in meaning to preserve the freedom, happiness and glory of my dominions and all their inhabitants."

His first decade of rule was a difficult period of unstable governments and financial crisis resulting from the Seven Years' War (1756–1763). Although he lacked experience, he handled the shifting alliances of lords and gentlemen well and by the mid-1760s had dispensed with his dependence on Bute and widened his circle of advisers.

King George set for himself a spartan and vigorous routine. Rising at six each morning he worked for an hour or more before taking breakfast and saying his morning prayers. Most of his day was occupied with state business and meals were sparse and eaten hurriedly. During the 1790s, when the wars of the French Revolution caused a rise in bread prices, the king ordered that only brown bread be served at his palace in Windsor. But there were also relaxations, for George was fond of riding and hunting and, along with the queen, he delighted in theater, preferring pantomime and comedies, not tragedies. George was an enthusiastic book collector, favoring books that were educational rather than amusing. In a famous encounter with the writer Samuel *Johnson, George engaged Johnson in literary conversation; Johnson commented afterwards, "They may talk of the King as they will, but he is the finest gentleman I have ever seen."

King George took an active interest in agriculture and did much to popularize the new advances in farming methods, earning the popular nickname of "Farmer George." Under the name of Ralph Robinson he contributed two articles to the *Annals of Agriculture*. Scientific progress also attracted the king's attention. He was fascinated by advances in astronomy and contributed £2,947 towards the cost of William Herschel's forty-foot telescope, which was, at the time the biggest in the world. When he went to view Herschel's telescope with the archbishop of Canterbury, they walked through the huge tube. The archbishop had difficulty keeping his balance and the king extended a helping hand quipping "Come my lord bishop, I will show you the way to heaven."

The king's ability as a ruler was affected by his innate conservatism and obstinately-held prejudices. This was illustrated during the American War of Independence, prolonged several years by George's view of the revolt in terms of a child rebelling against a parent. He put his views forward at the start in the following terms: "The die is now cast, the colonies must either submit or triumph. I do not wish to come to severe measures, but we must not retreat; by coolness and an unremitted pursuit of the measures that have been adopted I trust they will come to submit." With the war ultimately lost and the king's prestige damaged, he showed magnanimity when he greeted John *Adams, the first U.S. minister to England, on the friendliest of terms, saying he wished to be "the first to meet the friendship of the United States as an independent power."

The second half of George's rule was marked by increasing family conflict with sons whose personalities were in direct contrast to that of their staid and frugal father. Two future kings, princes George and William, were particular thorns in his side. Their displays of extravagance and womanizing contradicted the strict upbringing and devotion to public duty he had sought to imbue in them.

The king also suffered increasingly from mental illness resulting from a metabolic disorder thought to have been prophyria. He recovered from a severe attack in 1788, when his eyes looked like black currants and foam poured from his mouth. Popular legend has him dismounting from his carriage to shake hands with an oak tree in Windsor Park, mistaking the tree for King *Frederick the Great. Certainly it is recorded how at one cabinet meeting he concluded each sentence with the word "peacock," to the utter consternation of his ministers.

By 1805 the king was blind and from 1811 his state of mental imbalance necessitated the appointment of his eldest son George as regent. George III, when he was not fastened in a straitjacket or tied to his bed by his ignorant doctors, wandered around

his palace playing on his harpsichord, convinced he was talking to angels.

S. Ayling, *George the Third*, 1972.
J. Brooke, *King George III*, 1972.
H. Butterfield, *George III and the Historians*, 1957.

GERONIMO (c.1829–1909), American Apache chieftain. Originally a medicine man of the Chiricahua Apache tribe of New Mexico, Geronimo — whose native name, Goyathlay, means "One Who Yawns" — terrorized settlers along the Mexican-American border for thirty-five years.

Geronimo's campaign against foreign intrusion into Indian territory began in earnest in 1850. That year, the Mexican town of Janos made overtures to the Indians and invited them to trade. Geronimo and his companions accepted, leaving their wives and children hidden in a secret encampment nearby. In their absence, a Mexican army patrol chanced upon the camp and massacred its inhabitants, hoping to earn cash for each scalp they took. Among the dead were Geronimo's wife, mother, and three children. Only after several days did the unsuspecting braves return to their camp to find the mutilated bodies of their loved ones; fearing that these might be booby trapped, Geronimo and his companions turned away. Geronimo later claimed to have received a prophecy shortly after: sitting alone by a river bank to mourn his family, he heard a voice call his name. "No gun can kill you," the voice told him, "and I will guide your arrows."

Geronimo's revelation was a call to war against all Mexican intruders into the area. Utilizing guerilla

Geronimo on horseback

tactics in the harsh desert terrain he knew so well, he mutilated Mexican soldiers, settlers, and even children (for which he later suffered horrible nightmares) in the belief that they would remain disfigured in the afterworld. Convinced of his invulnerability, he was undaunted by bullets and his startled victims often called out to their patron saint *Jerome in despair. "Geronimo," the Spanish form of the saint's name, soon became the name of the Apache leader.

In 1861 the brunt of the Apaches' attack fell on the Americans for humiliating Cochise, an important chief who was patient and even encouraging of American settlement in the territory. Geronimo and his followers were generally more tolerant of the Americans and, after eleven years of skirmishes, agreed to the establishment of a Chiricahua reservation on their ancestral lands. But by 1872 this accord collapsed when the reservation was dismantled and the Chiricahua were forced to relocate to the territory of their rivals, the Western Apache. A small majority accepted the American offer; about seven hundred Indians, led by Geronimo, protesting the compulsory head count each morning and the growing animosity of the local white population, preferred to escape into the wilderness and resume their guerilla campaign against the whites.

This five-year campaign ended in 1877, when Geronimo agreed to meet Indian agent John Clum to discuss a final arrangement. The meeting was a trap and Geronimo was claped in irons and taken to the reservation, where Clum lobbied for a death sentence. When it became apparent that the government would not hang Geronimo, Clum resigned and Geronimo was released. He returned to the Sierra Madre, but ominous portents and visions seemed to indicate that this time his struggle was doomed.

The Americans began employing scouts from other Apache tribes to track down the Chiricahua, and several members of Geronimo's band were captured. He rushed back to rescue them but was apprehensive about confronting fellow Apaches, who knew his tactics and outnumbered his own band. Instead he decided to send men to befriend them, hoping eventually to inveigle them into a vulnerable position, but the Indian scouts were wary of Geronimo's motives and would not be tricked. His own men were rapidly defecting, and by the winter of 1883 Geronimo too accepted a promise of clemency and settled on the San Carlos reservation.

Although the Apache originally enjoyed considerable autonomy in San Carlos, the following year the American government banned two important Apache practices, the brewing of tiswin, a traditional alcoholic beverage, and wife-beating. In 1885 Geronimo fled again, this time with only 145 Chiricahua. His men longed for their families left behind in San Carlos and Geronimo twice agreed to surrender. On the first occasion, forewarned that he would be hanged, he managed to escape; in 1886, exhausted and left with only sixteen warriors and

twelve women, he finally submitted to the Americans, hoping to spend his final years in San Carlos.

However, Geronimo and his followers were sent to Florida as prisoners of war. Despite countless pleas to President Theodore *Roosevelt, the Chiricahua were forbidden to return to the Sierra Madre until 1913. Eventually, Geronimo settled at Fort Sill, Oklahoma, where he became a farmer and embraced Christianity. He became nationally famous when he appeared in the Saint Louis World's Fair and in Roosevelt's inaugural procession. He died of pneumonia, regretting ever having surrendered to the Americans.

A. Adams, *Geronimo*, 1971.
S. M. Barrett, *Geronimo: His Own Story*, 1970.
O. B. Faulk, *The Geronimo Campaign*, 1969.

GERSHWIN, GEORGE (1898–1937), American composer and pianist who introduced jazz into classical music and was described as a colossus with one foot in Tin Pan Alley and the other in Carnegie Hall. Gershwin was born in Brooklyn, New York, but his Russian Jewish immigrant parents, whose original name had been Gershowitz, soon moved to the Lower East Side. As a very young child he was exposed to jazz concerts and began studying piano at the age of twelve, receiving most of his early musical training in Tin Pan Alley playing the piano for the Jerome Remick music publishing company. Despite his later success as a composer he continued to study music throughout his life, determined to broaden his knowledge and understanding of compositional technique.

At fifteen he dropped out of school and became a song plugger; at sixteen he began to write popular songs, the first to be published being "When You Want 'Em You Can't Get 'Em" (1916). Although not a commercial success it aroused the interest of some popular Broadway composers, the most important of whom, Sigmund Romberg, included Gershwin's "Making of a Girl" in his musical *The Passing Show of 1916*.

Gershwin's first complete score for a musical was for *La, La Lucille*, in 1919, the year in which he achieved his first commercial success with his song "Swanee," popularized by Al Jolson in the revue *Sinbad*. From 1920 to 1924, in addition to a great number of songs, he wrote the scores for several musicals, including all the songs for George White's *Scandals*. For the 1922 production of *Scandals*, he composed a short opera that attracted the attention of Paul Whiteman, the *Scandals*, conductor, who commissioned him to compose a symphonic jazz composition for piano and orchestra; the result was *Rhapsody in Blue* (1924), which became one of his most acclaimed works. The same year marked the start of a lifetime collaboration with his brother Ira (1896–1983), who wrote witty lyrics, beginning with "Lady, Be Good" (1924). Among their most famous musicals are *Oh Kay!* (1926), *Funny Face* (1927), *Girl Crazy* (1930), and *Of Thee I Sing* (1931), a satire of the United States political system and the first musical to win a Pulitzer prize for drama.

While his success in musical comedies blossomed, Gershwin also pursued a career with his more serious compositions, which combined traditional musical forms with jazz and folk themes and rhythms. Following his great triumph with *Rhapsody in Blue*, Gershwin composed the *Piano Concerto in F* (1925), *Three Preludes for Piano* (1926), the symphonic tone poem *An American in Paris* (1928), which incorporated elements of jazz as well as realistic sound effects, the *Second Rhapsody*, for orchestra (1931); and variations on "I Got Rhythm" for piano and orchestra.

His final and most ambitious work, thought by many to be his masterpiece, the opera *Porgy and Bess* (1935), based on the novel by Dubose Heywood about southern black Americans. Before beginning to write the score Gershwin spent a summer on an island near Charleston, South Carolina, in order to become familiar with the customs and music of the people. The final outcome was an opera that broke new ground, combining jazz rhythms, popular song style, and the operatic aria. Although it was considered a failure when it was first produced in Boston and New York in 1935, after the composer's death it received critical acclaim and worldwide performances were given by both touring American companies and foreign opera houses. In 1936 Gershwin and his brother moved to Hollywood and wrote exclusively for films.

C. Schwartz, *Gershwin: His Life and Music*, 1973.
E. Jablonski, *Gershwin Remembered*, 1992.
R. E. Kimball and A. E. Simon, *The Gershwins*, 1973.
G. Peiser, *The Memory of All That*, 1993.

GHAZALI, ABU HAMID MUHAMMAD IBN MUHAMMAD AT-TUSI AL-

(1058–1111), Persian theologian, jurist, and mystic. Within the Muslim world, his championing of Sufi mysticism encouraged its toleration by the religious establishment. He was also responsible for introducing many Greek philosophical conceptions into the Islamic mainstream.

Born in eastern Iran, al-Ghazali rapidly showed himself an able student and was instructed by al-Juwayni, imam of Mecca and Medina. After the latter's death he joined the court of the vizier of the Seljuk sultans, rising to the prestigious and influential position of professor at Nizamiyah college, Baghdad, in 1091. In addition to lecturing, he found time to master Neoplatonism, then the dominant philosophical tradition in Europe, and to produce essays on legal issues.

Al-Ghazali's *The Incoherence of the Philosophers*, completed in 1095, constituted a devastating attack on the speculative reasoning of the Neoplatonist *Avicenna as well as a reaffirmation of orthodox Islamic religious principles; it elaborated twenty propositions against which the careless be-

> - I read the books of sound theologians and myself wrote some books on the subject. But it was a science, I found, which, attaining its own aim, did not attain mine. Its aim was merely to preserve the creed of orthodoxy and to defend it against the deviations of heretics.
> - Public worship is seventeen times better than private worship.
> - Just as it is not a condition of religion to reject medical science, so likewise the rejection of natural science is not one of its conditions. Nature is in subjection to God most high, not acting of itself but serving as an instrument in the hands of its Creator.
>
> **al-Ghazali**

liever was to be on guard and reiterated that the world was deliberately created by God rather than merely emanating from him as Avicenna had suggested. In the same year al-Ghazali experienced the profound spiritual crisis that was to reshape his subsequent life and career; it was also to mark him physically, for he experienced a nervous breakdown and developed a speech impediment as a result. On the pretext of pilgrimage to Mecca, he abandoned wealth, family, and career and adopted the life of a poor Sufi, or Islamic mystic. His autobiographical work, *The Deliverance from Error*, written in 1108, in which he detailed and defended his abandonment of wordly concerns and entry into the life of the mystic mendicant, records his feelings of uncertainty at this time; he said that at the time of his departure he felt that he was "entering Hell."

After extensive travels as far afield as Damascus, Mecca, and Jerusalem, al-Ghazali returned to his birthplace of Tus, where he was soon joined by a group of disciples in a virtually monastic lifestyle. An Islamic tradition states that a renewer of the faith will arise every hundred years, and al-Ghazali had come to believe that he was one such renewer for the sixth Islamic century (corresponding to the twelfth century C.E.). It was during his period in Tus that al-Ghazali wrote his *The Revival of the Religious Sciences*, in which he explained the doctrines and practices of Islam, seeking to show how they can be the basis of a devotional life leading to higher stages of mystical realization. Clearly manifested in this work was his combination of strict orthodoxy with a belief that theology was inferior to mystical experience. This latter view echoed the feelings of many who yearned for a more personal communion with God than was possible within the increasingly arid approach of orthodox medieval Islam.

In 1106 al-Ghazali returned to teaching for a period of four years, finally retiring shortly before his death. Throughout his life he tried to defuse tensions between philosophy and theology, and it was his great achievement to have made theology more philosophical; by using such methods as syllogistic logic to refute Neoplatonism and uphold Islamic dogma he ensured that future Muslim theologians would do likewise. His book *The Aims of the Philosophers*, an erudite exposition of the philosophical schools then current in the Muslim world, was important in making Islamic philosophical ideas known in the West; it was one of the first works ever translated from Arabic into Latin, in the twelfth century.

I. A. Bello, *The Medieval Islamic Controversy Between Philosophy and Orthodoxy*, 1989.

W. M. Watt, *Muslim Intellectual: A Study of al-Ghazali*, 1963.

GIOTTO (Giotto di Bondone; c.1266–1337), chief Italian pre-Renaissance painter, Giotto inspired and laid the foundations of Renaissance painting although he lived and worked at a time when the medieval style was still preeminent. From this medieval context he explored the human form and psychological expression, developed the portrayal of pictorial space to an extent unknown in his time, and led a return to the painting of nature.

Giorgio Vasari, the renowned sixteenth-century historian, was Giotto's champion and contributed to the growth of his legend. He opens his biography of Giotto with an anecdote describing Giovanri Cimabue's discovery of Giotto the shepherd boy, drawing a sheep from life on the surface of a rock. Cimabue, the leading late medieval painter, took Giotto on as a pupil. According to Vasari, the pupil soon surpassed the master and discarded the crude Greek style.

Despite his fame and the significance of his contribution to painting, little is known of Giotto's personal life beyond the fact that he was a prominent businessman who dealt in land and rented looms, a common method of earning money without violating the ecclesiastical prohibition against usury. He became a member of the royal household in 1332 and was honored by being appointed *capo-mastro*, (surveyor) of the Commune of Florence in 1334. The instrument which records the appointment gives him glowing praise: "In the whole wide world nobody is said to be found who is more qualified in these and many other matters... a great master... held dear in the aforementioned city."

Giotto's connections to wealth and commerce are evidenced by his commissions. The Arena chapel was commissioned by Enrico Scrovegni, the heir to the biggest fortune in Padua. This simple, bare chapel serves as a perfect vehicle for Giotto's frescoes, painted between 1304 and 1313. The various biblical narratives depicted around the walls explore the story of man's redemption, culminating in the Final Redemption. As they progress in a spiral around the walls these pictures also reveal Giotto's gradual development as a painter. As work progressed his ambition and skill increased; the later scenes reveal a greater mastery of the human form,

---

> ### EPITAPH ON GIOTTO'S TOMB
>
> I am he by whose undertaking the dead art of painting was restored to life. Nature lacked what was lacking in my art. To no other was it given to paint better or more. But what need is there for words? I am Giotto: my name alone tells more than a long poem.

---

the foreshortening of the monumental figures is bolder, and their draperies more complicated. He achieved a revolutionary level of naturalism, whose roots lay in mid-thirteenth-century French Gothic sculpture. He also used his color range as a decorative device, as did Romanesque artists, although he used a more restricted palette.

Giotto also decorated the chapels of the Bardi and Peruzzi banking families in Arnolfo's church of San Croce in Florence. As with the Arena chapel, he did not paint the frescoes alone; fresco painters of this period generally relied on workshop assistants. His major signed panel paintings, including the *Stigmatization of Saint Francis* and the *Coronation of the Virgin*, were also mainly workshop productions.

In the San Croce frescoes Giotto continued to expand his range. In the *Raising of Druisiana*, in the Peruzzi chapel, painted in the mid-1320s, he created a space which is more than a mere stage for his monumental actors. As the drama is acted out in the foreground, space appears to continue beyond the confines of the fresco itself, beyond the great fortress city in the background. This grand architectural setting is used to create the illusion of three-dimensionality on the flat surface.

While these works mark the emergence of the Renaissance style, Giotto did not attempt to capture the richness of the natural world as did later Renaissance artists. It is the people themselves which generate the power of these works — their facial expressions, gestures, and postures reveal their inner lives. In this respect his frescoes reflect the changes in religion of the thirteenth century, when the emphasis moved to Christ as man, as well as anticipating High Renaissance art, in which man is presented as the center of the universe.

M. Barasch, *Giotto and the Language of Gesture*, 1987.

B. Cole, *Giotto and Florentine Painting*, 1976.

C. Gnudi, *Giotto*, 1959.

GLADSTONE, WILLIAM EWART (1809–1898), English prime minister. Fourth son of a rich Liverpool merchant who had made his fortune from the slave trade, Gladstone was in his own words "brought up to distrust and dislike liberty." Educated at Eton and then Oxford University, Gladstone took first class honors in both classics and mathematics and became president of the student union. His interest in the classics never left him; *Homer became favorite reading matter for "moments of relaxation" (he wrote a three-volume work on Homer and the Homeric Age).

Gladstone's deep religious beliefs were complemented by impeccable Tory principles and oratorical skills devoted to a spirited defense of the religious and social status quo; his attack on the 1831 Reform Bill was a masterpiece of political rhetoric. Gladstone's ambition was to be a clergyman but his father wanted his son to follow him into Parliament. In 1832 the Duke of Newcastle found this great Tory hope a safe seat at Newark.

After a frustrating period during which his potential went unrecognized, prime minister Sir Robert Peel appointed Gladstone to the board of trade in 1841. It was the first step up the ladder of promotion that would take him to chancellor of the exchequer in 1853 and in 1868 to prime minister. By this time his political orientation had taken a sharp turn. Travel in Europe brought him face to face with despotic monarchies; his letter to the prime minister in 1850 denouncing the persecution of political dissidents in Naples showed how the reactionary was turning into a reformer. In economic policy too, Gladstone had become an adherent of free trade, believing that even an income tax of 2.5 percent should be cut further to remove restraints on enterprise. These developing liberal sentiments led to a break with the Tories and alignment with the Liberal party which he led to power in the 1868 general election.

Mrs. Gladstone (née Catherine Glynner, whom Gladstone had married in 1839) shared her husband's religiosity and high moral standards. Their partnership extended to Gladstone's pet project, the rescue of prostitutes from the streets of London and the founding of refuges where they could be rehabilitated. There is little doubt that all he was engaged in in his frequent nightly walks in the streets of London was the attempt to save souls but for the prime minister it was not the most prudent choice of social work. In 1882 one member of parliament enjoyed recounting how he had seen Gladstone talking with a prostitute. When Gladstone was told the story he commented, "It may be true that the gentleman saw me in such conversation but the object was not what he assumed, or, as I am afraid, hoped."

Gladstone held the office of prime minister for thirteen years, between 1868 and 1894. He was never popular with Queen *Victoria, lacking the gift for flattery that secured his rival Benjamin *Disraeli a firm place in the royal affections. The queen said that Gladstone addressed her as if she were a public meeting and described him as a "crazy old man," but to the poorer classes of England he became a folk hero.

Contrary to the normal pattern, as he grew older he became more radical, believing that only major changes in society and governmental policy could correct the injustices that aroused his moral indignation. Thus Gladstone's administrations introduced compulsory elementary education and the secret ballot. The civil service was opened to competitive

- As the British Constitution is the most subtle organism which has proceeded from the womb and the long gestation of progressive history, so the American Constitution is the most wonderful work ever struck off at a given time by the brain and purpose of man.
- A rational reaction against irrational excesses readily degenerates into the rival folly of credulity.
- National injustice is the surest road to national downfall.
- To be engaged in opposing wrong affords, under the conditions of our mental constitution, but a slender guarantee for being right.
- Decision by majorities is as much an expedient as lighting by gas.

William Gladstone

talent and entry to university was open to all. He engaged in a long and ultimately futile campaign to grant self-government to Ireland but found some success in alleviating the persecution and poverty of the Catholic peasantry. Former allies in the Tory party were aghast at a prime minister who could proclaim his philosophy as: "All the world over I will back the masses against the classes." As for the powerful landed interests standing in the way of his reforms, Gladstone heartened his supporters by assuring them: "They cannot fight against the future, time is on our side."

In fiery speeches he condemned injustices outside of Britain, whether committed by the British army in Afghanistan or by Turkish troops on the Bulgarians. His appearances drew vast crowds in the famous Midlothian election campaign of 1879. Standing in firm opposition to the growing tide of imperialist sentiment, he condemned Conservative government policy in Afghanistan, telling his listeners that the lives of villagers in Afghanistan were just as precious as their own. Convincingly placing his party on the side of morality, he won a resounding victory in that year's election.

The Grand Old Man, or G. O. M. as he was affectionately nicknamed, retired from the premiership for the last time in 1894. In 1896 he was still able to deliver a rousing address attacking Turkish atrocities against the Armenians but the strength to continue the crusade to inject morality into politics was nearing its end and in 1898 he died at home, his family kneeling at the bedside.

P. Adelman, *Gladstone, Disraeli, and Later Victorian Politics*, 1983.

P. Guedella, *The Queen and Mr. Gladstone*, 2 vols., 1933.

P. Magnus, *Gladstone*, 1964.

M. J. Winstanley, *Gladstone and the Liberal Party*, 1990.

GOEBBELS, PAUL JOSEPH

GOEBBELS, PAUL JOSEPH (1897–1945), Nazi minister of propaganda. Joseph Goebbels was the son of a poor and pious Catholic family of laborers from the Rhineland town of Rheydt. There are conflicting accounts of his early days; Goebbels, an avid diarist, was also a propaganda genius who later altered his own background in keeping with the political philosophy of the Third Reich. Goebbels's childhood was apparently tainted by his physique: one leg, with a clubfoot, was eight centimeters shorter than the other, causing a pronounced limp. However, his physical handicap was compensated for by his intellect, and Goebbels's parents encouraged him to obtain a classical education in the hope that he would one day enter the priesthood. This dream was shattered when a priest with whom he had an interview commented, "My dear boy, you simply don't believe in God."

Goebbels was rejected from serving in World War I because of his handicap. Like many German youths of his time, after Germany's defeat he turned to radical politics. At first he was attracted to socialism, and he remained an advocate of the socialist platform of the National Socialists until late in his career. Upon completing his doctorate in literature and philosophy at the University of Heidelberg, he planned to become a writer. A semiautobiographical novel, *Michael*, was a failure, and for some time Goebbels wandered from job to job, endlessly submitting articles to the press in the expectation that his "genius" would soon be recognized. He was not yet a rabid anti-Semite, and was engaged for a time to a girl of Jewish descent.

Goebbels claimed to have joined the Nazi party after hearing Adolf *Hitler speak in 1922, but he actually joined in 1924 and found work as managing editor of a biweekly journal published by Gregor Strasser, leader of the party in northern Germany. Sometime that year, Goebbels met Strasser's adversary, Hitler. Apparently, Goebbels was not immediately taken with Hitler, but viewed him as a mere southern agitator for a movement whose future lay with Strasser. Only when the feud between the two leaders came to a head did Goebbels come out in zealous support of Hitler.

Goebbels's reputation as a party spokesman now grew rapidly; his rich baritone voice and expressive hands made him an ideal orator. Unlike Hitler, who relied on his instinctive passions, Goebbels was a practiced speaker who marked his speeches with colored pencils to indicate emotions and tones. Goebbels's passionate advocacy of nazism was noted by Hitler, and he was appointed *Gauleiter* (district party leader) of Berlin in 1926, with the task of winning the capital over to nazism.

Goebbels's activities in Berlin brought the fledgling party to national prominence. In 1928 he was made the Nazi party's propaganda chief. Among the techniques he adopted were the use of blazing red posters (to contrast with the stark Berlin walls), the creation of Horst Wessel, a near-mythical Nazi folk hero, and debates against recordings of political opponents (instituted when Chancellor Heinrich Bruning "refused" to debate with Goebbels — in fact, he was not asked). Goebbels organized heroic funerals for party men who had actually been killed in brawls, and he arranged to have Hitler flown around the country for innumerable speaking engagements. All this time Goebbels dreamed of the possibility of planning and controlling radio broadcasts. Like Hitler, he believed that the spoken word was far more effective than the written word. Goebbels's virulent attacks often brought him into conflict with the authorities; particularly vehement were his attacks on Berlin's Jewish police chief, Bernhard Weiss. Goebbels became a member of the Weimar parliament in 1928 and used his parliamentary immunity to further his cause.

When Hitler was swept into power in January 1933, Goebbels was surprised to find that he was not included in the cabinet; Hitler preferred that he campaign for the upcoming elections undistracted by governmental concerns. Only after the March election was Goebbels appointed minister of popular education and culture — a new ministry that reached into every aspect of German life.

Goebbels was responsible for creating the myth surrounding the Third Reich and its leaders, especially the Führer concept, and he took to his new job with enthusiasm. Having been rejected as a journalist, Goebbels unleashed his resentment against the German press. His often-insipid articles now appeared almost daily, and newspaper censorship became the rule. Even advertisements were victims of government censorship after one drug company advertised, "My Struggle (*Mein Kampf*) Against Flatulence." On May 10, 1933, he instigated the

Goebbels delivering a speech

public burning of "un-German" books. He was now able to take control of the radio, which he made into a powerful weapon, internally and internationally. Always a fan of the cinema, Goebbels encouraged the development of a Nazi film industry whose productions, though mostly banal, included such propaganda gems as the anti-British *Ohm Kruger*, the anti-Semitic *Jud Süss*, and *The Eternal Jew*.,

Goebbels's house was a popular retreat for leading Nazi politicians, especially Hitler, who was particularly fond of his children (six, plus a son from his wife's previous marriage). However, Goebbels was a noted womanizer who enjoyed the company of young actresses. One such affair, with the Czech actress Lida Barova, was only broken off at the insistence of Hitler. Hitler was infuriated by the many crises in Goebbels's marriage to Magda Quandt, which was portrayed to the public as an ideal marriage.

During World War II Goebbels directed Nazi psychological warfare, which had many successes, especially in its early years. He was the father of modern propaganda in a totalitarian state (a term that he coined); it was his theory that the greater the lie, the greater the chance that it would be believed.

Goebbels was an opportunist, unpopular with other leading Nazis, and occasionally with Hitler himself. Throughout the war his position was shaky; it was only solidified after the failed assassination attempt on Hitler's life in July 1944 when, as the leading Nazi in Berlin, Goebbels assured Hitler's hold on power.

Until the end of the war, Goebbels believed in Hitler's infallibility, comparing Germany's increasing number of defeats to those of *Frederick the Great before the decisive Battle of Kolberg in 1760. Even as the Allies encircled Berlin, Goebbels remained with Hitler, spending the final days in his bunker under the chancellery. In reward, Hitler named Goebbels his successor as chancellor, but Goebbels refused to accept. On the day after Hitler's suicide, unwilling to allow his children to survive the fall of the Reich, Goebbels had them poisoned. He and his wife then left the bunker and committed suicide; his charred remains were identified by Russian troops a few hours later.

A. R. Manvell, *Dr. Goebbels*, 1960.
V. Reimann, *Goebbels*, 1976.
R. G. Reuth, *Goebbels*, 1990.

GOETHE, JOHANN WOLFGANG VON (1749–1832),

German poet, scientist, and statesman. Born to an affluent family in Frankfurt-on-Main, he was especially close to his sister, Cornelia; this relationship was later reflected in the numerous intimate sibling relationships in his poetical works. In later years Goethe always praised the middle class social background from which he arose as a perfect breeding ground for the qualities of intellectual excellence.

In 1765 Goethe entered the university of Leipzig to study law, although he was never to practice as a lawyer. He was greatly affected by the bohemian and intellectual nature of the city at that time; he

The Earth Spirit Appears, a drawing by Goethe

discovered the Greek poets and produced his first significant literary work, the *Leipzig Song Book*, a carefree, almost bacchanalian, cycle in praise of love and wine. However he fell seriously ill in 1768, returned home to convalesce, and became increasingly introspective and mystically inclined during his painfully slow recovery. His interest in the occult (most famously manifested in *Faust*) dated from this period. When he went to Strasbourg to continue his studies (he completed his law degree in two years) he was moved to react against the cosmopolitanism of his Leipzig period, asserting a return to Germanic values and an enthusiasm for the Gothic; his contact with the young critic Johann Gottfried Herder resulted in his interest in the development of folk songs and poetry based on traditional regional motifs. The *Sturm und Drang* ("Storm and Stress") movement that developed around him took as its motto "Concerning German Nature and Art." At this time, Goethe also began to produce truly great lyric poetry.

As a pioneer of the discipline of self-consciousness, Goethe was to say that all his works were "fragments of a great confession," and it was his unrequited love for Charlotte Buff that inspired the novel *The Sorrows of Young Werther* which brought him European fame.

The discontent within Goethe was evidenced by his breaking off his betrothal to Liki Schonemann; he fled the fashionable circles he felt were suffocating him and, in 1775, moved to Weimar at the invitation of the reigning duke, Charles Augustus. The duke worshiped Goethe and his arrival was marked by a riot of carnivals, operas, and plays. He was to remain in the tiny dukedom for the rest of his life, and for many years

- Every beginning is cheerful.
- Everything that is wise has been thought already; we can only try to think it once more.
- The first and last thing required of genius is love of truth.
- Law alone can give us freedom.
- The deed is everything; the fame, nothing.
- Insinuations are the rhetoric of the devil.
- Divide and rule is a capital motto; unite and lead, a better one.
- Terrible is he who has nothing to lose.
- Law is mighty, necessity mightier.
- Hypotheses are the lullabies with which the teacher lulls his pupils to sleep.
- There could be no greater torment than being alone in Paradise.
- Who does nothing for others, does nothing for himself. Talent is developed in retirement; character in the rush of the world.
- The eternal feminine draws us upward.
- More light (last words).

Johann Goethe

devoted much of his energy to the task of administering it. As Charles Augustus's minister he dedicated himself to such tasks as inspecting mines, superintending local irrigation schemes, and even arranging the issue of uniforms to the tiny standing army. In 1782 he was ennobled and made president of the Ducal Chamber. He also became devoted to Charlotte von Stein, the wife of a court official; their intense but platonic relationship lasted for some ten years, during which time they met or corresponded daily — he wrote her some fifteen hundred letters. She was the first of Goethe's women to be his intellectual partner as well as a love object, and was able to guide him in the social niceties required of court life.

During this period of intense practical and social activity, Goethe's literary activities were subordinated to the demands of his patron and Frau von Stein; by the mid-1780s, Goethe came to feel that the demands he had placed on himself in Weimar were stifling his muse, and quietly arranged a trip to Italy. Charlotte von Stein was never to forgive him the secrecy with which he veiled the details of this trip, and became his enemy for life.

The Italian journey, undertaken between 1786 and 1788 and described by Goethe as his "return to *Homer*," precipitated yet another emotional and ideological change in a life marked by vivid and deeply felt fluctuations. Writing from Rome in spring 1788 he said that "in these last eight weeks I have enjoyed the greatest contentment of my life and now at least know an extreme point against which I can in future calibrate the thermometer of my existence." Scorning what he now regarded as his previous Gothic follies, he was

again drawn to the literary heritage of the Levant and Italy; works such as the *Roman Elegies*, and the plays *Iphigenie in Tauris* and *Egmont* resulted. Written on his return to Weimar, they also reflected the fulfillment he was finding in his first full-fledged physical relationship with a woman. Christiane Vulpius, a clerk's daughter and maker of artificial flowers, was to bear Goethe several children and, in 1806, became his wife.

Goethe also retained a lively interest in the political and cultural changes that ignited Europe in his day. He accompanied his duke on a disastrous military campaign into France in 1792; a book on the experience resulted. He also realized some of the profound implications of the French Revolution and, like many of his contemporaries, wrote a book expressing his thoughts on this historical turning point. His later meeting with *Napoleon is immortalized by the simple epithet with which the latter described the poet: "Voilà un homme [here is a man]."

In 1794, at a time when he was already a celebrity and the object of literary pilgrimages to Weimar, Goethe was contacted by and developed an intense and close correspondence and friendship with Johann *Schiller, the poet and playwright. These two geniuses of their day were to stay in touch for a decade, and in effect they founded the modern German theater; their daily correspondence is one of the most fascinating presentations available of intellectual intercourse and the genesis of ideas. Although too passionate to wholly accept Schiller's more ascetic vision of the role of poetry, Goethe was influenced by his friend nonetheless; the symbolic content of his work increased perceptibly as a result of Schiller's ideas. This was the time of Goethe's great ballads, and of the completion of his masterwork, *Faust, Part One*.

The last years of his life produced strong works such as *Wilhelm Meister* and *Faust, Part Two*. While he is best remembered for his *Faust*, and as a supreme poet, the sheer range of Goethe's interests and activities was immense. He was apt to rate his scientific researches as more significant than his literary efforts; in his *Theory of Color*, he was presumptuous enough to contradict Isaac *Newton, but more valuable was his botanical work, notably *The Metamorphoses of Plants*. Charles *Darwin was to cite him as an influential forerunner, while his explorations in the field of the philosophy of scientific research were truly pioneering; recognizing the significance of the observer in the experimental equation led him to posit that knowledge of the self must develop with knowledge of the world.

A highly competent draftsman and painter, Goethe was also a keen music critic; here, as in other artistic spheres and, indeed, as in his own being, he sought a fusion between the Dionysian and the more cerebral Apollonian impulses. There was no area of the arts to which he was indifferent; even after retiring from his other administrative duties in Weimar he was happy to continue directing the state theater company for over twenty years.

V. Guenther, *Johann Wolfgang Von Goethe*, 1984.
G. H. Lewes, *The Life and Works of Goethe*, 2 vols., 1965.

GOGH, VINCENT WILLEM VAN (1853–1890),

painter. Van Gogh was born in Groot–Zundert, Holland: his father was a pastor and his uncle a partner in the famous firm of art dealers, Goupil. Both Vincent and his younger brother, Theo, worked for Goupil in the Hague and in Paris; 1873 Vincent was sent to the London office, where he learned English. He collected more than a thousand prints by English, French, American, and Japanese artists and for a time he taught languages and was a lay preacher in England. He became fanatically interested in religion and in 1878 went to work in the Borinage (Belgium), where he lived in utter poverty and tried to teach the miners his religious ideas. In December 1881 Van Gogh went to the Hague, where he studied painting with Anton Mauve and lived on the little money Theo was able to send him. Then for two years he lived with his parents in Nuenen, Holland, painting peasants and weavers in somber earth colors.

In 1886, van Gogh went to stay with Theo in Paris, where he met Camille Pissarro, Edgar Dégas, Georges Seurat, and Paul Gauguin and his palette brightened under the influence of the impressionists and Japanese prints. Although his work was included in a few exhibitions, no one bought it. In February 1888, he went to live at Arles in southern France. He wrote to Theo, "Everywhere — all over the vault of heaven is a marvelous blue, and the sun shade a radiance of pale sulphur, and it is as soft and lovely as the combination of heavenly blue and yellow in a Van der Meer of Delft... As long as the fall lasts, I shall not have hands, canvas, and colors enough to paint the beautiful things I see." But he tried, completing painting after painting, forgetting to eat, subsisting almost entirely on coffee and alcohol.

He invited Gauguin to come and stay with him at Arles. For a long time Gauguin did not respond but Van Gogh persisted, asking Theo to pay Gauguin's expenses and, at last, Gauguin came. The encounter proved disastrous. Gauguin provoked van Gogh into pointless arguments that lasted through the night, adding exhaustion to the ill health caused by his drinking and lack of food.

At Christmas, after one of these quarrels at a cafe, Gauguin took van Gogh home, drunk. Gauguin's story was that the following morning van Gogh cut off his ear and sent it to a prostitute as a gift. Van Gogh was found, bleeding and unconscious, by neighbors, who thought he was dead; the police went to arrest Gauguin for murder. When van Gogh regained consciousness in a hospital the next morning, he remembered nothing. He asked for Gauguin and, upon being told that he had left Arles, his first question was had he taken their money.

Theo hurried to Arles. Depressed, Vincent decided to go to an asylum in Saint Rémy, where the doctor wrote that due to difficulties with his sight and hearing, he had cut off his ear. The doctor diagnosed his problem as incipient epilepsy and advised him to stay for observation. Van Gogh was distressed by his epileptic episodes but his sharp,

Vincent van Gogh, a self-portrait

analytic intelligence remained untouched and he never faltered in his work.

In 1890 an article praising his work appeared in *Mercure de France*, and he sold a painting (the first ever) in Brussels, where he exhibited with The Twenty. In May he left the asylum and went to Paris for three days to visit Theo, his young wife, Johanna Bonger, and their three-month-old baby, Vincent. From there he went to Auvers, to stay with a homeopathic doctor, Paul-Ferdinand Gachet, who was also an artist and whose portrait he painted. On 27 July he took a gun, went out into the fields, stood against a tree, and shot himself. He died two days later, in his brother's arms. Theo, heartbroken, survived him by only six months, and the two brothers are buried at Auvers, side by side.

Johanna van Gogh-Bonger devoted the rest of her life to earning for Vincent's work the appreciation she felt it deserved. She published his correspondence with Theo in Holland and Germany, and translated over six hundred and fifty of the letters into English.

Van Gogh painted for only ten years, but in that short period he produced more than eight hundred oil paintings and seven hundred drawings. In spite of his ill health, malnutrition, and dependency on alcohol, he was a highly disciplined painter. Although he often spent four or five days on one painting, at one period he painted seventy paintings in seventy days. He liked to paint people, but his forthright drawing, his fluid lines, solid forms, and brilliant colors were not flattering to his models, and many refused to sit for him because, they said, he did not know how to draw.

Van Gogh's work (and that of Gauguin) inspired the generation that followed – in particular the group called Les Fauves (the wild beasts), which included Henri Matisse, André Derain, Georges Braque, Georges Rouault, and Raoul Dufy, as well as Chaim Soutine and the German expressionists. Strength, vitality, vibrant colors with a strong touch of decorativeness were the new criteria. These are, to a great extent, still the criteria for contemporary art.

Today van Gogh is one of the best-known and best-loved of all artists and is regarded as the greatest Dutch painter after *Rembrandt. Reproductions of his works can be found in millions of homes, and an entire museum is devoted to him in Amsterdam. He is the subject of books, films, and popular songs, and his paintings — of which only one sold in his impoverished lifetime — now command prices of over twenty million dollars.

A. Krauss, *Vincent Van Gogh, Studies in the Social Aspects of his Work*, 1983.

J. Leymarie, *Van Gogh*, 1968.

C. Nordenfalk, *The Life and Work of Vincent Van Gogh*, 1953.

GÖRING, HERMANN WILHELM (1893 – 1946), Nazi leader; founder of the Gestapo and the Luftwaffe (German air force). Hermann Göring was born to a wealthy family on the fringes of the German aristocracy. Because Göring was an unexceptional but robust student who preferred mountain climbing and hunting in the Bavarian Alps to studying, he was sent to a military academy, where he excelled. In World War I he served as a reconnaissance pilot, winning several medals and citations, and was awarded the Iron Cross First Class for downing an enemy airplane with his pistol. In 1915 he joined the squadron of Manfred von Richthofen, the Red Baron, and even commanded the squadron for a short time after Richthofen's death. In the course of the war he won Germany's highest honor, *Pour le Mérite*, awarded to individuals showing acts of outstanding courage in battle.

With the collapse of Germany, Göring was left penniless. The terms of Germany's surrender proscribed maintaining an air force and like so many of his compatriots, Göring was hard-pressed to find work. He spent some time in voluntary exile in Denmark and Sweden, where he found work as a pilot. Returning to Germany, he was attracted to the Nazi party and admired Adolf *Hitler who, in turn, recognized the value of a decorated war hero to his party and offered him command of the party's private army, the SA. Göring was with Hitler during the abortive Beer Hall Putsch in Munich in 1923. When the troops turned on the demonstrators, Göring was shot in the groin.

After spending some time in Austria, Italy, and Sweden, he returned to Germany in 1927. Hitler had already achieved national renown and Göring, who had many connections among the nobility and industrialists, was sent to Berlin to secure financial support for the party. He persuaded Hitler to have

him represent the Nazi party in the Reichstag in 1928. Although Hitler was at first skeptical, he admitted that Göring was both well-connected and personable, and one of the few party members who could win the support of bankers and industrialists. His social skills were unmatched by any of the Nazi leaders and his military reputation won him entrance into many important houses in Germany, where he was referred to as Hitler's "ambassador."

Göring was appointed president of the Reichstag in 1932. As the highest-ranking Nazi in the country, he was instrumental in bringing Hitler to power by showing total disregard for parliamentary procedure. When Hitler was appointed chancellor in 1933, Göring received several cabinet posts, including minister without portfolio, Prussian minister of the interior, and Reich commissioner for aviation. In 1933 he became prime minister of Prussia and was one of those responsible for forming the Gestapo, which he was later forced to hand over to Heinrich *Himmler. It is probable that he was behind the plot to set fire to the Reichstag in 1933 and to throw the blame on the Nazis' opponents. In 1934 he worked with Himmler to liquidate the SA chief Ernst Röhm and his supporters in Hitler's frantic purge, the Night of the Long Knives. In 1935 he was appointed commander of the Luftwaffe and promoted to *Reichsmarschall*.

In addition to his fascination with aviation, Göring took great interest in economic matters. His involvement led to the resignation of economic minister Hjalmar Schacht and Göring's appointment in 1936 as virtual economic dictator of Germany. Göring amassed considerable wealth and built up an enormous art collection through looting and theft. He was responsible for the confiscation of Jewish property in 1937, and for a time was in charge of the Nazi anti-Jewish policy. He was opposed to war as a threat to Germany's economic recovery and sought

---

- Naturally the common people don't want war... but after all it is the leaders of the country who determine the policy, and it is always a simple matter to drag the people along, whether it is a democracy or a fascist dictatorship, or a parliament, or a communist dictatorship. Voice or no voice, the people can always be brought to the bidding of the leaders. That is easy. All you have to do is to tell them that they are being attacked, and denounce the pacifists for lack of patriotism and exposing the country to danger. It works the same in all countries.
- Guns will make us powerful; butter will only make us fat (usually misquoted as "guns instead of butter").

Hermann Göring

to avoid the invasion of Czechoslovakia and Poland. Only when war in Poland was inevitable did Göring put his air force's full potential into battle. On the day World War II broke out, Hitler appointed Göring field marshal and his heir.

The early years of the war saw Göring's prestige soar, but when the Luftwaffe was unable to quell Britain and protect Germany from Allied air attacks, Göring lost Hitler's approval. He was dismissed from all his posts and the party and spent the final years of the war in semiretirement on his large estate. When defeat was certain, he believed that Hitler had become incapacitated and declared himself Führer, an act for which he was stripped of his rank and expelled from the party. Hitler's final testament contains a harsh condemnation of Göring for this betrayal.

Göring was captured by the Allies and brought to trial at Nuremberg. He was one of the few defendants who did not deny responsibility for the regime's atrocities and, as the leading defendant in the proceedings, seemed, to many observers, to relish having finally attained his goal of succeeding Hitler. Göring was sentenced to death, but two hours before he was to be hanged he poisoned himself in his cell.

R. Manvell, *Hermann Göring*, 1962.
L. Mosley, *The Reich Marshal*, 1975.

GORKY, MAKSIM (Aleksey Maksimovitch Peshkov; 1868–1936), Russian writer. He was born in Nizhny-Novgorod (later renamed Gorky in his honor). His father, died when he was five years old; he was raised by his mother's parents after she remarried, and his book *My Childhood* tells in harrowing detail of the misery and senseless cruelty he encountered from his mother's family. His grandmother, deeply religious but simple, was the only person who showed him love and tenderness, and Gorky later powerfully described the beatings she endured. He was taught to read and write by his grandfather from religious books and all his life retained the unusual square handwriting of the autodidact. Apart from that, Gorky had only two years of technical school, which he did not complete due to "lack of means," as stated in his identity papers.

When his mother died Gorky was sent out to work to help the family's failing finances, and had a variety of odd jobs. At the age of eleven he ran away from home and found work in the galley of a steamship plying the Volga. The head cook there was a dedicated reader who was never without a book, and Gorky became infected with the passion. He continued roaming all over Russia, getting to know the underside of Russian life and becoming acquainted with revolutionary ideas, undergoing much physical hardship in the process. He led this life until the age of twenty-one when, overcome by despair and intellectual confusion, he bought a gun and shot himself in the heart. The bullet missed but caused permanent damage to his lungs. He had written a suicide note in which he claimed that Heinrich *Heine could be held responsible for his death, be-

cause he had invented "toothache of the heart." Gorky also asked that his heart be dissected "to see what kind of devil was in me." After ten days in the hospital he was discharged; the ecclesiastical authorities in Kazan, where he was living at the time, excommunicated him for seven years for having attempted suicide.

Gorky continued his nomadic life until 1890, when he went to Tiflis (Tbilisi), where in 1892 his first story, "Makar Chudra," was published, under an alias that was to become his pen name: Maksim Gorky ("Maksim" from his patronymic, and "Gorky," meaning "bitter"). By the following year friends had helped him obtain a post on a local newspaper, and his literary career was launched. He married his first wife, Yekaterina, at this time. She was later to run the Red Cross organization in Soviet Russia.

Two years later, in 1895, Gorky published a series of stories based on his experiences, which brought him instant celebrity. Moving to Saint Petersburg, he began to write novels and plays, among which *Na Dne* ("The Lower Depths"), dealing with tramps in a flophouse, is the most noteworthy and was produced by Konstantin Stanislavsky at the Moscow Arts Theater in its 1902–1903 season. By this time, Gorky was involved in the illegal activities of the Social-Democrat party and supported its Bolshevik ("majority") faction. He was arrested in 1901 for having published a poem, "Song of the Stormy Petrel" (the magazine in which it appeared was closed down), and exiled to the Nizhny Novgorod district, although he was allowed to spend summers in the Crimea due to his lung problems. It was during one of these summers that he became friendly with Anton *Chekhov and met the woman who was to be his second wife, Maria Andreyeva, an actress with the Moscow Art Theater who was involved in revolutionary work. Chekhov resigned from the Russian Academy of Sciences in 1902 when Gorky's membership there was withdrawn for "political" reasons.

Gorky's next project was the publishing house *Znaniye* ("Knowledge"), intended as a forum for young writers. However, in 1906 he was imprisoned in the Peter and Paul Fortress for having been active in the 1905 revolution. In part due to protests from abroad, he was released and permitted to tour the United States. His visit was spoiled for him when it was discovered that Andreyeva, who had accompanied him, was not his legal wife. The resulting fuss and publicity left Gorky with a jaundiced view of America, which he expressed in a book about New York, *The City of the Yellow Devil* (1906). He spent the next seven years outside Russia. Many of the writers and intellectuals who had fled Russia found themselves at some point in the villa on Capri where Gorky spent most of these years.

In 1913 Gorky returned to Russia. His reputation had diminished somewhat but he was still a popular figure and his next publications restored his name. These were his autobiographical works, *My Childhood* (1913–1914), *In the World* (1915–1916), and

BY AND ABOUT GORKY

- This "search for God" business must be forbidden for a time — it is perfectly ridiculous occupation.
- Only mothers can think of the future — because they give birth to it in their children.
- Happiness always looks small when you hold it in your hand but let it go and you learn at once how big and precious it is.
- One has to be able to count if only so that at fifty one doesn't marry a girl of twenty.
- To an old man, any place that's warm is a homeland.
- When work is a pleasure, life is a joy. When work is a duty, life is slavery.

Maksim Gorky

- If there is something great, boundless, vast, painfully gripping and promising which we have been wont to associate with the name of Russia, then it is Gorky whom we must regard as having best expressed all that.

Alexander Blok

- I think that a time will come when Gorky's works will be forgotten, but it is doubtful that even in a thousand years Gorky the man will be forgotten.

Anton Chekhov

My Universities (finished in 1923, when he was out of Russia). Politically he emerged as controversial, clashing publicly with Vladimir *Lenin until the newspaper he published, *New Life*, was closed on government orders in 1918. Three months later he founded the World Literature publishing house to supply the Soviet reader with the best of world literature in translation. This project enabled him to help many intellectuals during those years of privation, apart from the private aid he gave generously.

In 1921 Gorky left Russia for Sorrento, Italy, the ostensible reason being his health. He wrote *The Artamonovs* (1925) and began the three-volume *Klim Samgin* in 1927 (unfinished at his death). In 1928 he agreed to return for a visit and was accorded a welcome in honor of his sixtieth birthday so overwhelming that in the following year he returned to the Soviet Union for good and threw in his lot with Joseph *Stalin. He emerged as the most prominent of the Soviet writers and was made president of the Soviet Writers' Union upon its founding in 1934. In a notorious pamphlet he praised the construction of the White Sea canal, which had in actuality been built by the inmates of forced labor camps imprisoned on political grounds. Yet now, too, he used his position to help many who would otherwise have starved to death. He also continued to write during this period too, producing plays and the popular *Reminiscences of Tolstoy, Chekhov and Andreyev*.

Among his many projects, literary and political, Gorky took a great interest in occult and other pseudoscientific phenomena, including the theory of "God-building," which had a deep influence on left-wing Bolshevik thought. The main exposition of Gorky's God-building is to be found in *A Confession* (1910). A nonbeliever himself, he nevertheless said, "Christ was the first true people's God, born from the soul of the people like the phoenix from the flames." Gorky held that literature should cultivate optimism among the masses to counteract their natural inclination to passivity. The writer is a theurgist, an "engineer of human souls." The reality he creates will have either a positive or a negative influence on humanity. This, the need to create a political system that would permit the circulation of only "uplifting thoughts" to defend the people from "dark forces," is the basis of Soviet socialist realism.
B. P. Scherr, *Maxim Gorky*, 1988.
H. Trayat, *Gorky*, 1989.

GOYA Y LUCIENTES, FRANCISCO JOSÉ DE

(1746–1828), Spanish painter. He was born in a small Spanish town, the son of an unsuccessful notary and gilder who was forced to take up farming to feed his family. Goya grew up among the peasantry and received very little formal education save the bare rudiments of reading and writing. As a craftsman himself, the elder Goya had little objection to his son's chosen profession, which was at the time little more than a skilled trade like any other. At the age of eighteen Goya set out for Madrid, armed with a notebook from his mother listing rich Spanish families that was meant to be his order book when he gained prominence in his field. Both firmly believed he would achieve his stated goal, to become a "painter of the great." Goya himself said he had three masters: "Velásquez, *Rembrandt, and Nature."

Goya began his training under the tutorship of José de Lujan y Martinez, a devoted teacher whose official title was Reviser of Indecent Paintings, as his main source of income was adding clothing to figures deemed indecent by the inquisition. Martinez gave Goya his first break by passing on a commission to paint a small church.

In 1766 Goya began a work that he planned to enter in the Royal Arts Academy competition in order to win a free trip to Italy; the painting received no mention and the artist scraped up the money to visit Italy himself. The journey, despite a variety of rumors about his scaling the dome of Saint Peter's and kidnapping nuns, was basically unproductive. His work was rejected in another competition and he returned to Spain determined to stifle the originality and creativity that made him unpalatable to the conservative establishment.

At the age of thirty he married Josefa Bayeu, sister of his former master Francisco Bayeu. Bayeu got him a job producing tapestries and assisting in other projects that helped him support himself and his family. It was not, however, until the age of forty that Goya finally achieved success on his own merits. He was given a commission to decorate part of the church of San Francisco el Grande, which, it was rumored, was to be the Christian Parthenon. Though his portion looked much like the others in the church, it was critically well received and this, coupled with his recommendation from a prince who noted that the artist enjoyed hunting almost as much as royalty did, initiated his successful career as a court artist and portrait painter.

Strangely enough, his first period of artistic success also coincided with the onset of periods of artistic block, depression, and paranoia about other artists conspiring against him. The optimism symbolized by his mother's notebook was being realized but his personal life consisted of a series of tragedies, including the death of all his children save one. At the age of forty-six Goya was struck with an undiagnosed illness that brought on fevers and hallucinations and rendered him deaf, which led to his spiritual isolation. From this period, his work changed dramatically. He began to portray subjects that were purely imaginary, often nightmarish, as if he were transcribing hallucinations from his illness. One of the most famous of these is *Caprices*, a series of etchings on women, communication, and social satire that were narrated by the artist with such commentary as "The sleep of reason produces monsters." They were directed against superstition, dandies, ignorance, and hypocritical priests. The subject matter of these etchings and further paintings caused some critics to say they were works produced during periods of insanity, but there is little evidence that Goya was anything but lucid. They annoyed the Inquisition, who ordered their withdrawal, but Goya was protected because the king had accepted a set.

The artist remained married but was also famed for his studio seductions. It was said that whenever he seduced a woman in his studio he covered the statue of the Virgin Mary so as not to offend her. He began a passionate affair with Maria Teresa, the duchess of Alba and one of the outstanding women of her time, whom he depicted in many of his pictures. It was to her that he gave his famous works, the *Maja*, and the *Naked Maja*, whose very existence got him indicted by the Holy Office of the Inquisition, although the matter was hushed up for many years. The *Maja*, was hung in front of the *Naked Maja*, for propriety.

In the years that followed, Goya was appointed first painter to the king and painted portraits of the royal family and the court. He was also, unofficially, the documentarian of the political turmoil Spain was enmeshed in, generated by both the Napoleonic wars and, later, internal strife. From this emerged perhaps his most famous painting, *The Second of May, 1808*, which chronicled the gore and carnage of the Napoleonic wars. His series of etchings, *The Disasters of War*, are among the most powerful visual indictments of war and its horrors. Many of the paintings of his later years are devoted to the dark, wild, and fantastic sides of life, haunted by spirits and demons.

His wife died in 1812 and Goya retired to the country at the age of seventy-three, no longer taking orders and painting only what he wished. He became involved with a woman, Leocadia, who served as both his mistress and his housekeeper, and her young daughter Rosarito, whom he adored.

When the constitutional monarchy was overthrown, Goya, like many others who had supported it, fled to France, where he lived out his remaining days in Bordeaux until he collapsed of a stroke, paintbrush in hand. He was buried in France but was later exhumed; it was discovered that his skull had been stolen, possibly by a group he had befriended while working on *Caprices*, that believed in phrenology, the ability to read a person's character from the bumps on his skull.

O. N. V. Glendinnig, *Goya and his Critics*, 1977.
F. S. Licht, *Goya*, 1979.
J. A. Tomlinson, *Francisco Goya*, 1989.

GRANT, ULYSSES SIMPSON (1822–1885), soldier and eighteenth president of the United States (1869–1877). He was born in Point Pleasant, Ohio, but the year after his birth the family moved to Georgetown, Ohio. Grant showed little academic ability but was very good with horses and preferred to work on his father's farm rather than in his tannery. Against his will, his father sent him to the U.S. Military Academy in 1839. After a short time Grant decided that, "A military life has no charms for me." He graduated in 1843, ranking twenty-first in a class of thirty-nine, his main achievement being in horsemanship. He was commissioned a brevet second lieutenant and assigned to the Fourth U.S. Infantry, which was stationed at Jefferson Barracks near Saint Louis, Missouri.

From 1846 to 1848 Grant served with distinction in the Mexican War, where he was promoted to a full second lieutenant under General Zachary Taylor. In later years Grant copied Taylor's informal dress and lack of military pretension. Grant's regiment was transferred to the army of Winfield Scott, under whom he was promoted, in battle, to first lieutenant and then to captain. For the next four years Grant was stationed in Sachets Harbor, New York, and Detroit, Michigan, but in 1852 he was transferred to the Pacific coast, where he spent two miserable years with an inadequate income and without his family. At that point he had to resign his commission and went to Missouri to try his hand at farming. This attempt proved unsuccessful and he went to work on his father's farm.

In August 1861 President Abraham *Lincoln appointed Grant brigadier-general of volunteers. In January 1862, while in command of the Twenty-First Illinois Volunteers, he achieved the first major Union victory in the Civil War and subsequently participated in many battles as second in command. When his commander was called to Washington in July 1862, Grant led the forces to victory in several impressive battles. In October 1862 he was made commander of the Department of Tennessee and it was his aggressiveness, resilience, independence, and determination that made possible the final victory at Vicksburg, where he succeeded in cutting the Confederacy in half.

His successes brought him to Washington in 1864, where he received Lincoln's personal thanks and was voted a gold medal by Congress. He was promoted to lieutenant general and commander of all the armies of the United States. He then developed a plan of action for the armed forces which, together with their superior numbers, enabled them to defeat the Confederates and on April 9, 1865, General Robert E. *Lee officially surrendered to Grant.

Late in 1865 Grant, who recommended a lenient Reconstruction policy, toured the South, where he was greeted with friendliness. In 1866 he was given the rank of general of the armies of the United States. He became a popular public figure and was the obvious candidate for the presidency, easily defeating Democrat Horatio Seymour; he assumed the presidency on March 4, 1869.

At the time of his election he was forty-six years old, the youngest man to achieve that office. He proved an inept politician; his cabinet consisted of friends, not strong leaders. He had formulated no policy and displayed no leadership in dealing with the Congress, and for the next eight years the coun-

Grant at Cold Harbor, 1864

try was run by his advisers, whose counsel was for the most part poor. During his second term in office, both his domestic and his foreign policies were in such disarray that the Republican party as a whole was discredited and he was defeated at the Republican convention in his attempt to run for a third term.

When he left the presidency Grant went on a world tour, during which he was received not as a discredited president but as the victor of the Civil War. He returned to the United States after two years of traveling and again tried for the presidential nomination. On the thirty-sixth ballot at the 1880 Republican national convention, James A. Garfield was nominated and Grant's political career came to an end.

In 1881 he moved to New York and became involved with an investment firm in which his son was a partner. He invested heavily and encouraged friends to do the same, but a swindle by Ferdinand Ward left him with a debt of sixteen million dollars and a clouded reputation. Grant attempted to recoup some of his losses by becoming a partner in a brokerage firm but like all of his other business ventures, it failed, and in 1884 he was forced into bankruptcy.

He began to write reminiscences of his various battles and to prepare his memoirs. Suffering from throat cancer, he composed in his sickroom in Saratoga, New York, two volumes of his recollections and they remain one of the great war commentaries of all time. These memoirs, published by Mark *Twain, brought the Grant family $450,000 in royalties. In 1885, the family moved to the Adirondacks, where Grant died.

BY AND ABOUT GRANT

- The art is simple enough. Find out where your enemy is. Get at him as soon as you can. Strike at him as hard as you can, and keep moving on.
- Your men must keep their horses and mules. They will need them for the spring plowing.

**Grant to General Lee
at the end of the Civil War**

- I cannot spare this man. He fights.

Abraham Lincoln

- He combined great gifts with great mediocrity.

Woodrow Wilson

His grandiose tomb on Riverside Drive is a well-known New York City landmark.

M. E. Mantell, *Johnson, Grant, and the Politics of Reconstruction*, 1973.

W. S. McFeely, *Grant*, 1981.

J. Y. Simon, ed., *The Papers of Ulysses S. Grant*, 4 vols., 1967–1972.

GRECO, EL (i.e., "the Greek"; Doménikos Theotokópoulos; 1541–1614), painter, sculptor, and architect. Born in Candia, Crete, El Greco's first training was probably with icon painters in Crete at the monastery of Saint Catherine at Candia. The early influence of this Byzantine tradition persisted in his mature painting despite his assimilation of the Italian tradition. He always remembered his Greek origin and signed his works with his Greek name written in Greek letters. It is unclear when he left Crete but he probably arrived in Venice about 1560 and remained in Italy, where he studied the Renaissance and Mannerist masters, until about 1575. During the early years in Venice he painted hundreds of small panels of Gospel scenes in the style of the Byzantine madoneros, the icon painters who formed part of the large Greek colony there.

El Greco soon became a disciple of *Titian although it is not clear whether he actually spent time in Titian's workshop as an apprentice or assistant. He also borrowed motifs and ideas from other Venetians including Parmigianino, Schiavone, and Tintoretto.

El Greco lived in Rome between 1570 and 1572 but was apparently unpopular with the jealous Roman painters. He acquired a reputation as haughty and arrogant after commenting to Pius X that if the Sistine Chapel frescoes were taken away he could paint better ones in their place. He is said to have remarked that "Michelangelo was a good man — a pity he did not know how to paint." Of course, while living in Rome he did study the frescoes of *Michelangelo and *Raphael in the Vatican and he was influenced by Michelangelo's grand vision of the human form. In the 1560s many Italian painters were involved in decorating the Escorial, which was being built in Spain, and the news from Spain probably influenced El Greco to seek his fortune there. He reached Spain in 1577 as a full-fledged Italian master and upon his arrival in Toledo immediately received an important commission to paint the high altar and two lateral altars of the convent church of Santo Domingo el Antiguo. He painted the two huge panels of the *Trinity* and the *Assumption of the Virgin*, and also devised the architecture for the altar, breaking with Spanish tradition by creating a Venetian Renaissance rather than a Gothic design.

By the late 1570s El Greco had gained the admiration of Toledo and, eager to become a court painter of the king, sought to woo King *Philip II, presenting him with a gift of two sketches. The king commissioned El Greco to paint pictures of the *Ado-ration of the Name of Jesus*, and the *Martyrdom of Saint Maurice*. The *Martyrdom*, with its mystical Mannerist mood and dramatic composition was, however, not appreciated by the king and El Greco never again received a royal commission. His wish to become a court painter was never realized but he was very successful as a portrait painter, being favored by church figures and the aristocracy. He received so many commissions that he was forced to collaborate with his disciples, especially in his later years. El Greco's portraiture style — bringing life to the sitter psychologically and physically — was greatly admired in seventeenth-century Spain.

As he grew older El Greco concentrated his efforts on capturing exalted religious feeling and depicting the spiritual realm, utilizing various symbolic motifs. His visionary conception of the real and spiritual world was expressed with supernatural light and flamelike, ethereal forms. His most significant work, *Burial of the Count of Orgaz* (1586–1588), combines mystical and earthly images, portraying the three stages of human existence: life on earth, the grave, and heaven. A modern author has ascribed his characteristic style — a vertical elongation on a slightly oblique axis — to astigmatism, but in fact this was a style familiar in other painters of the time.

El Greco was strongly influenced by Spanish mysticism, and his work is marked by an exalted spiritualism. He was also something of a philosopher and wrote philosophical treatises as well as treatises on art and architecture, but his writings are lost. A self-taught architect, he designed altarpieces for his paintings, developing an individual language of architecture to complement the figures in his paintings. Essentially a painter of religious works, El Greco also painted many fine "psychological" portraits and a number of landscapes. His reputation faded after his death and it is only in the twentieth century that he has been acclaimed as a great visionary artist.

L. Goldscheider, *El Greco*, 1954.

P. Keleman, *El Greco Revisited*, 1961.

R. G. Mann, *El Greco and His Patrons*, 1986.

H. E. Wethey, *El Greco and His School*, 2 vols., 1962.

GREGORY I (the Great; c.540–604), pope. The fourth and last of the traditional doctors of the western church, he invested the papacy with temporal as well as spiritual authority, and is regarded as the father of the medieval papacy. Gregory was the scion of a distinguished Roman family of Christian patricians. His father was a senator but other family members filled important posts in the early church. Gregory's great-great-grandfather was Pope Felix III, and he was also related to Pope Agapetus I. After two years as prefect of Rome, in 574 Gregory abandoned civil administration in favor of a monastic life. He donated his extensive family holdings to the church, enabling the establishment of six monasteries in Sicily and a seventh, Saint Andrew's, on the Caelian Hill overlooking the Colosseum. For five years he led the austere life of a monk, declining promotion in the church hierarchy. Only in 579 could Pope Pelagius II finally persuade him to accept an appointment as papal representative in Constantinople.

For seven unhappy years Gregory defended the religious authority of the Roman church in that city. Constantinople had long been the seat of the empire's temporal authority; the local clergy, led by the patriarch Euchytes, believed that religious authority should also be concentrated there. Gregory's poor mastery of Greek put him at a disadvantage in the resulting theological disputations, nor was he at ease with the pomp surrounding the local church. Much of his time was spent composing the *Moralia*, a commentary on the book of Job, and he was greatly relieved when, in 590, he was recalled to Rome. He longed to engage in his devotions without the distraction of official duties.

This was not to be. That year, Pope Pelagius died in a plague and to his chagrin, Gregory was the unanimously acclaimed candidate of the bishops to succeed him. He spared no effort to dissuade the bishops, even composing a lengthy letter to the emperor Maurice imploring him to reject his candidacy, but nothing he said could alter their decision. Finally Gregory fled to the woods, but unable to escape, he returned to the plague-ravaged city of Rome to arrange penitential processions. Throngs of survivors converged on the basilica of Santo Maggiore, when — according to legend — suddenly an angel appeared sheathing its sword over Hadrian's Mausoleum. The plague abruptly ended and Gregory was anointed pope. Some days later he received a response from the emperor denying his request.

Gregory is often remembered for the Gregorian chants attributed to him, but in fact, these were probably composed at a much later date. The religious reforms dating to his papacy, such as the belief in purgatory and the promotion of celibacy among the clergy, can be safely attributed to his contemporaries, most notably Augustine of Canterbury. Gregory was an outstanding administrator who took advantage of the geopolitical situation of the empire to enhance the church's secular authority. The Italian peninsula had long been neglected by the imperial administration in Constantinople and had been subject to continuous attack by hostile Gothic kings. Since the emperors proved inept in protecting the region, Gregory drafted his own army to protect church lands. His armies were unable to defeat Duke Ariuf of Lombardy but were formidable enough to persuade him to seek a peace treaty. Gregory consulted with Maurice, who immediately rejected the idea, but Gregory was undaunted. An independent peace accord was reached with Ariuf and later with Gothic King Agilulf himself, making the church a vassal of both the Roman Empire and their archrivals, the Goths.

Gregory advocated a philosophy of *patrimonium Petri (*patrimony of Peter), according to which an independent clergy would administer the church's considerable estates directly. Local revenues would enter the church's coffers for both administrative and charitable uses. He believed that the church itself should be responsible for the welfare of Christians, and willingly sold the holy utensils of a Naples church to ransom prisoners. He also asserted that the focus of the church must be in Rome and excommunicated the bishop of Constantinople, John IV Jejunator, for assuming the title of ecumenical, or universal patriarch.

Gregory was intolerant of pagans in his own realm, and encouraged missionary activities abroad. He was tolerant of the Jews and abhorred the use of violence in proselytizing them. Once, when walking in the slave market, Gregory encountered a group of English youths about to be sold. The boys so impressed him with their good looks and courage that he was shocked to discover that their country was still heathen. Remarking that the *Angli* ("English") must become *Angelli* ("Angels"), he sent forty missionaries, including Saint Augustine, later of Canterbury. The conversion of the peoples of Europe became an enterprise encouraged by Gregory.

He was a prolific author; his book laying down the pastoral life of bishops was translated by King *Alfred and became a key work for medieval ecclesiastics. His life of Saint *Benedict was a model of hagiography. He ardently promoted monasticism and in his theological thought followed Saint *Augustine of Hippo.

Although he suffered from a severe case of gout, Gregory was remarkable for the energy and zeal with which he set about transforming the church. Soon after his death he was canonized by popular acclaim. His feast day, formerly celebrated on March 12 (the supposed date of the miracle of Santo Maggiore), has recently been moved to September 3.

G. R. Evans, *Gregory the Great*, 1986.

J. Richards, *Consul of God: The Life and Times of Gregory the Great*, 1980.

GREGORY VII, SAINT (Hildebrand; c. 1020–1085), one of the most powerful medieval popes. He was born in Tuscany at a time when the church had decayed into corrupt depravity. The papacy itself was for sale and the high profitability of a rapid turnover of popes ensured their frequent murder or deposal. Only the Holy Roman emperor prevented the total degeneracy of the institution, disposing of the most blatantly unfit popes and replacing them with competent, sometimes even brilliant men.

Hildebrand served under eight popes before becoming pope himself. He was chaplain to Gregory VI; Leo IX, whose piety and strong stand against immorality singlehandedly restored church prestige and moral leadership, was so impressed by Hildebrand's abilities that he appointed him, at twenty-five, cardinal archdeacon and administrator of the Papal States. Hildebrand's growing influence decided Nicholas II's election, his own appointment as papal chancellor, and Nicholas's reform whereby popes were elected by the College of Cardinals, thereby freeing papal elections from secular interference. Under Alexander II he was made chancellor of the Apostolic See. At first Hildebrand resisted becoming pope, preferring to strengthen and reform the church behind the scenes, but he gave in to popular demand and was consecrated as Pope Gregory VII in 1073.

Gregory denounced anything he felt might damage or indicate disbelief in the church; he was even opposed to the use of medicine rather than faith for the cure of illness. Gregory attempted to deal with the problem of clerics with wives, concubines, and offspring. Large amounts of church property were being lost, willed by priests to their children; mistresses compromised clerical prestige and family demands kept clergy from devoting themselves completely to church matters. Popular opposition had ended Nicholas's attempts to ban clerical marriage; determined to succeed, Gregory renewed Nicholas's decrees excommunicating married clergymen in 1074, a move which met with a violent response. Gregory excommunicated bishops who protected their married clergy and demanded that secular rulers forcibly prevent such priests from practicing. He did not solve the problem, though he did pave the way for later popes to do so.

Gregory's greatest battles involved his attempts to end lay investiture, the practice whereby church officials were appointed by the secular authorities. The underlying issue was Gregory's desire to unify Europe under the papacy instead of individual secular states. Decrees were issued against lay investiture in 1075 and Gregory excommunicated five bishops who were councilors and appointees of *Henry IV, the Holy Roman emperor. Henry responded by keeping them as councilors and appointing three new bishops,well aware of the implications of the loss of state control of church land, which constituted half the land in Germany. Threatened with excommunication, Henry called a synod of German bishops who deposed Gregory and elected their own pope in 1076. Gregory's response was to excommunicate them and pronounce sentences of deposition, excommunication, and anathema against Henry.

Deserted by his supporters because of religious sentiment and the political opportunism of German nobles, Henry was faced with either having the decrees against him lifted or losing his throne; he capitulated, standing in the snow before the gates of the castle in Canossa where Gregory was staying for three days, a humble penitent pleading for forgiveness and absolution. Gregory recanted and accepted him back into the church, whereupon Henry returned to Germany to fight his nobles.

However, in 1080, Gregory supported Henry's rival in Germany's civil war and again excommunicated Henry, who had not fulfilled the promises he had made at Canossa. Henry called another council

of bishops to depose Gregory and seized a large part of Rome in 1084, ruled it for a year, deposed Gregory and appointed a new pope. Norman troops came to Gregory's aid and Henry fled; however, the behavior of the Normans so infuriated the Romans that they turned against Gregory, who fled, first to Monte Cassino and then to Salerno, where he died; he was canonized in 1606. Henry lived to fight for his throne for another twenty-one years.

H. E. J. Cowdrey, *The Cluniacs and the Gregorian Reform*, 1970.
W. Schafer, *The Gregorian Epoch*, 1964.

GROTIUS, HUGO (Huigh de Groot; 1583–1645), Dutch jurist, theologian, diplomat; widely acknowledged as the father of modern international law. By the age of nine Grotius had already composed some Latin poems and at twelve entered the University of Leiden, graduating at fourteen. When he was fifteen, he edited a new edition of the Encyclopedia of Martianus Capella. The same year he accompanied the Dutch statesman Johan van Oldenbarnevelt on a diplomatic mission to the court of Henry IV of France. The king was so impressed with Grotius that he nicknamed him "the Miracle of Holland." Grotius remained in France to study law at the University of Orleans; also in the same year his *Pontifex romanus* was published, comprising six political monologues.

In 1599 Grotius returned to Holland and began to practice law in The Hague. Two years later he was chosen by the states of Holland to be their official historian. Throughout this period Grotius was a prolific writer of poetry and philological works as well as plays with religious content. He also collaborated on a Latin translation of the Greek poet Theocritus.

In 1607 Grotius was appointed attorney general of Holland and became increasingly involved in Dutch political affairs. In 1613 he participated in a diplomatic mission to *James I of England to try to settle a longstanding conflict leading to rivalry between the two nations in the Far East. While in England he met intellectuals who, like himself, were interested in the restoration of Christian unity. Both the diplomatic mission and his theological feelers proved failures. In 1618 Grotius was sentenced to life imprisonment for his support of Calvinist reformers. His wife and seven children were allowed to join him in prison, where he continued to write poetry and also began an introduction to the jurisprudence of Holland. In 1620, with the help of his wife, he made a daring escape from prison hidden in a chest of books and laundry.

Grotius fled to Paris, where he was granted a small pension by Louis XIII. In Paris in 1625 he published his great legal work *De jure belli ac pacis* ("Concerning the Law of War and Peace"). In his book, Grotius examined the idea of the law of nature as a source of rules to be applied to nations as well as individuals. He argued that the law of nations incorporated a concept of just and immutable codes of duties and restrictions. However, the book was not solely a legal treatise; it was also a work of theological and philosophical interest containing many biblical and historical references. Grotius also developed his concept of the distinction between the just and the unjust war, arguing that it was illegal to wage war unless it was to protect rights and property.

In 1625 Maurice of Nassau, who had imprisoned him, died and in 1631 Grotius returned to Holland and began to work as a lawyer in Amsterdam. However, his happy return was shortlived as he again faced arrest, never having been pardoned. In 1632 he went to Hamburg, home of a large community of Dutch exiles. He was greatly admired in Sweden and in 1635 was appointed Swedish ambassador in Paris; lacking the talent of a diplomat, his relations with Cardinal *Richelieu were strained. Nevertheless, he played a role in the negotiations leading to the Treaty of Camineque and held his position for ten years. During this time he edited several works as well as working on his *Historia gotthorum, vandalorum, et langobardorum* (History of the Goths, Vandals, and Lombards). He was offered a membership in the Swedish Council of State but refused to settle in Sweden and on a journey to an unknown destination he was shipwrecked on the coast of Pomerania. He was saved and taken to Rostock, Germany, where he died a few days later. He was buried in Delft.

E. Dumbauld, *The Life and Legal Writings of Hugo Grotius,* 1969.

A. Lysen, *Hugo Grotius: Essays on His Life and Works,* 2 vols., 1925.

GUSTAVUS II ADOLPHUS (1594–1632),

Swedish king and soldier, who transformed Sweden into one of Europe's great powers. He succeeded his father, Charles IX, who had used his brief but unpopular reign to reform Sweden's government, promote industry and commerce, suppress the aristocracy, and make war. Although he had attended the Diet since he was nine, received ambassadors since he was thirteen, ruled a province, and had fought in battle, the nobility, organized as the Estates, would only crown sixteen-year-old Gustavus king if he signed a charter granting them important constitutional concessions subjugating the monarchy to them, to which he agreed.

Gustavus inherited Charles's wars: a dynastic struggle with Poland, a war with Denmark — then one of Europe's strongest states — for control of trade between the North and Baltic seas, and a war with Russia to keep its vacant throne out of Polish hands (the Polish conflict continued to flare up intermittently for almost sixty years). The war with Denmark was clearly a lost cause, and Gustavus ended it in 1613 by promising Denmark a huge indemnity which cost Sweden years of heavy taxation and left a lingering bitterness against the Danes. After a Romanov became czar of Russia, Sweden fought to keep Russia out of the Baltic (1613–1617). Eventually Sweden annexed enough territory to cut Russia off from the Baltic, thereby stopping Russia from becoming a major European power for another eighty years.

Gustavus also concerned himself with much-needed internal reforms. He enjoyed the support of the nobility, which responded to his willingness to observe the spirit of the charter (if not all of its clauses) with a readiness to sacrifice some of their privileges and serve in Sweden's administration as well as its army. He also had the able assistance of his chancellor, Count Axel Oxenstierna, whose phlegmatic personality balanced Gustavus's fiery temperament. Together they promoted commerce, established schools and universities, relieved the poor, developed the mining industry, modernized the army, and reorganized the bureaucracy, giving Sweden the most modern and efficient central administration in Europe.

The Thirty Years' War — a struggle for political and religious domination between Protestant and Catholic powers — was devastating Europe. The major Catholic military force belonged to the Austrian Habsburg Empire, which fought the Protestant northern German kingdoms, the Netherlands, and Denmark. Catholic France, believing that it was more important to check Austria's growing power than to fight Protestantism, formed an alliance against Austria, which Sweden joined, but rivalry among its members soon caused its breakup. Austria conquered Denmark in 1626 and formed an alliance with Poland.

Gustavus believed that "all wars in Europe hang together," and was concerned that Sweden's defeat by an Austro-Polish alliance could turn the Baltic into an Austrian-controlled sea. After the Swedish Diet agreed to support and finance his entry into the war, he collected soldiers, provisions, and allies and marched to Germany in 1630.

The main reason for Gustavus's entry into the Thirty Years' War was his desire to strengthen and save Sweden, but he was also a sincere fighter for Protestantism: his soldiers attended prayer meetings twice a day, heard a sermon on Sunday, and were barred from bringing whores into their camp. Gustavus led his troops into battle personally and fought ferociously, scorning the use of armor; under his command the Protestant forces enjoyed their first victories of the war. He allowed the areas he conquered religious freedom, organized Swedish-type administrations, and proposed the formation of a Protestant League under his direction as the best hope for Protestant security. Jealously resentful, some of the German Protestant princes refused to join the league, thus delaying Germany's unification by two hundred years.

Gustavus was killed in battle at Lützen, after becaming separated from his men while leading a cavalry charge. Oxenstierna became regent for Gustavus's four-year old daughter, *Christina.

M. Roberts, *Gustavus Adolphus,* 2 vols., 1953–1958.

M. Roberts, *Sweden's Age of Greatness,* 1973.

GUTENBERG, JOHANNES (c.1390/1400–1468), German inventor of printing from movable type. Little is known of his life, and the scant information that is available comes primarily from official records of his financial affairs and litigious struggles.

He was born Johannes Gensfleisch in Mainz, but later assumed his mother's family name, Gutenberg. His early career as a goldsmith was cut short when, as a consequence of a prolonged conflict between the craft guilds and the gentry of Mainz, he was expelled from the city. Gutenberg reappeared in Strasbourg, where he established himself anew in the goldsmithing business in partnership with several other craftsmen and investors, one of whom was Andreas Dritzehn. It was during this period that Gutenberg began developing his revolutionary printing process. He worked surreptitiously, fully conscious of the potentially historic value of his efforts. Apparently, his secrecy attracted the attention of his partners, who, when they discovered the nature of Gutenberg's work, demanded that their partnership be extended to cover his new activities. He acceded to their wishes and in 1438 a new contract was prepared for the partners which stipulated, inter alia, that should one of them die, his heirs were not entitled to succeed him in the partnership.

When Dritzehn died only months after the contract was signed, his brothers sued Gutenberg, in spite of the explicit contractual agreement. Court records show that Gutenberg won the case. However, evidence presented during the trial indicates that Gutenberg had been working on a number of secret processes that with hindsight can be assumed to be printing from movable type.

Gutenberg had returned to Mainz by 1448. His printing experiments had progressed and he was able to demonstrate to the satisfaction of Johann Fust, a wealthy lawyer, that printing from movable type was practicable. Fust was sufficiently convinced to invest a considerable sum in Gutenberg's enterprise, against which Gutenberg was required to place his printing equipment as collateral.

Gutenberg was sued by Fust for the recovery of his loans in 1455, accusing Gutenberg of not keeping to their agreement. What actually caused their estrangement is open to speculation.

Interestingly, local legend linked Johann Fust with Dr. Faustus, suggesting a more sinister motivation. Nevertheless Gutenberg was ordered to repay the full amount of the outstanding loans plus accrued interest. Unable to do so, he surrendered to Fust his stock and printing works and abandoned all claim to his invention. Fust continued printing, ably assisted by his own son-in-law Peter Schöffer, who, at Fust's insistence, had been taken on as a copyist and calligrapher by Gutenberg.

About this time the first copies of the Gutenberg Bible (also called the Mazarin Bible because of its discovery in about 1760 in the library of Cardinal Jules *Mazarin) were printed, creating quite a stir. When Fust went to Paris, carrying with him a dozen of these exquisitely executed and immensely valuable works, he reportedly chased out of the city by the scribes, having been accused by them of doing the devil's work in managing to possess so many identical copies of the Bible.

There are forty-seven known surviving copies of the Gutenberg Bible, of which twelve are printed on vellum. They list neither the name of the printer nor the place and date of impression. Consequently historians have been unable to conclusively establish whether or not the Bible was completed before Gutenberg lost control of his press in 1455, although they believe that in all likelihood he was the principal contributor to its production. That being the case, Gutenberg could have averted financial ruin by selling copies of the Bible, and why he did not do so is a mystery. Indeed, the plates for the Bible alone would in all likelihood have been worth considerably more than his debts to Fust. To add to Gutenberg's despair, an exquisite psalter on which he had evidently been working became the first book printed with movable type to carry the name of its publishers; it lists Fust and Schöffer.

The tribulations of Gutenberg were not to end there. With the assistance of a Mainz municipal officer Gutenberg reestablished himself in the printing business. What he did during the next few years of his life is unclear but in 1462, while Mainz was in turmoil, this time caused by a feud between its archbishop and a rival claimant, Gutenberg was once again exiled from the city.

Aging and with failing eyesight, by 1465 Gutenberg was destitute. Moved to compassion and possibly contrition, the archbishop allowed Gutenberg to return to his birthplace and gave recognition to his work as an inventor and craftsman by ennobling him. This afforded Gutenberg various privileges and entitled him to a pension, allowing him to see out his last days in comfort and security.

E.L. Eisenstein, *The Printing Revolution in Early Modern Europe*, 1983.

H. Lehman-Haupt, *Gutenberg and the Master of the Playing Cards*, 1965.

V. Scholdered, *Johann Gutenberg, the Inventor of Printing*, 1970.

Page from the Gutenberg Bible

H

HADRIAN (Publius Aelius Hadrianus; 76–138), Roman emperor. The cousin of the emperor *Trajan, Hadrian was born to an Italian family long settled in Spain. His father died when he was ten and Trajan became his guardian, marrying him off at sixteen to his grandniece, Vivia Sabina. She, in turn, accompanied him on many of his wanderings, occupying herself with founding a Little Senate of Women that decided matters of feminine dress, jewelry, etiquette, and rank, and tolerating his passion for his young Greek page. They had no children.

Hadrian was forty-one years old and the commander of Rome's armies in Syria when he became emperor following Trajan's death in 117. Tall, strong, and elegant, with a full beard (which made beards fashionable for the duration of his reign) he also loved the company of philosophers and scholars. He himself was a musician, architect, the author of several books, and a patron of the arts, preferring Greek to Roman culture.

Among his first acts as emperor was the reversal of Trajan's expansionist policy, to which Hadrian had expressed opposition during Trajan's lifetime, by withdrawing Rome's forces beyond the Euphrates, which then became the empire's new eastern boundary. There was opposition to this policy but it did not last long: the four generals who had led Trajan's forces believed that Hadrian's switch from an offensive to a defensive policy was cowardly and the beginning of the end of the empire; they were executed by the Senate on a charge of conspiring to overthrow the government.

Hadrian devoted himself to the task of reorganizing the empire and carrying out administrative, military, and legal reforms. He supervised every aspect of government, increased the administrative bureaucracy and regulations, and greatly increased tax receipts without raising taxes by appointing an attorney for the treasury to guard against cheating. Eventually his government was so well trained that it continued to function while he toured the empire for years at a time.

Determined to follow a policy of peace, Hadrian felt that the only way to do so was to strengthen Rome militarily so that weakness would not make it a tempting target for its enemies. To this end border defenses, weapons, and supplies were thoroughly inspected and improved, while new, severe regulations improved military discipline and soldiers' legal and economic status.

The codification of Roman law initiated by Hadrian has influenced Western law up to the present day. He commissioned a corps of jurists to codify existing Roman law into a superseding Perpetual Edict. Roman law traditionally protected the person and property of citizens; Hadrian's reforms extended that protection (see inset).

Hadrian spent years visiting every province in the empire. His travels had a twofold purpose. Firstly, he was an indefatigable traveler, eager to view the many peoples and sights in his empire. Secondly, he did not view the provinces as sources of wealth to be drained off to Rome but as integral parts of the empire. He saw it as the emperor's duty to inspect the provinces to determine their needs and how the resources of the empire could best be used to meet them. The supreme authority wherever he went, Hadrian heard petitions and complaints, judged, punished, and rewarded. Cities devastated by earthquake were rebuilt and new cities and roads sprang up. He erected public buildings with imperial funds. In Athens his extensive building program renovated the city while solving its unemployment problem. In Britain he ordered the building of Hadrian's Wall, a seventy-four mile long defensive measure. He beautified Rome with new buildings and renovations (such as the Pantheon), of which many were of his own design, while none bore his insignia. The empire was never so prosperous as during Hadrian's rule.

Having rebuilt many cities during his travels, Hadrian ordered the rebuilding of Jerusalem as the Roman colony of Aelia Capitolina, with a temple to Jupiter on the Temple Mount. That order, and one prohibiting circumcision, resulted in the Bar Kokhba rebellion of 132–135, in which Jewish forces recaptured Jerusalem and destroyed an entire legion. It was a bitterly fought, brutally suppressed war which Hadrian won only by sending in legions from all over the empire. Although it ended victoriously for Rome, Roman casualties were so heavy that Hadrian omitted the customary phrase "I and my army are well" from his report to the Senate.

In 135 Hadrian fell sick with a painful wasting disease. Foreseeing his own death, he adopted Titus Aurelius Antoninus as his successor. Maddened by pain, he accused some of his closest friends of being part of a conspiracy to kill him and had several put to death. Later, crushed by ever increasing pain, he tried desperately but unsuccessfuly to kill himself or to get someone to kill him.

M. T. Boatwright, *Hadrian and the City of Rome*, 1987.

S. H. Perowne, *Hadrian*, 1960.

M. Yourcenaar, *Memoirs of Hadrian*, 1954 (fictionalized, but classic).

HAILE SELASSIE I (Tafari Makonnen; 1892–1975), emperor of Ethiopia. Ras (prince) Tafari was the son of Makonnen, king of Shoa, a cousin and vassal of *Menelik II, emperor of Ethiopia. According to Ethiopian tradition, the family was descended from King *Solomon and the Queen of Sheba through their supposed son, Menelik I. Although he was not expected to succeed to the throne of Ethiopia, the diminutive, pale-skinned Ras Tafari was a great favorite of Menelik II. He was appointed *dejazmatch* (keeper of the door) in Menelik's court when he was only fourteen years old, and at eighteen succeeded his father as governor of Harar. The next year he married Wayzaro Menen, a great-granddaughter of Menelik.

Menelik II was succeeded by his grandson, Lij Yasu, in 1913. Lij Yasu's father was a Muslim who was forcibly converted to Christianity, and Lij Yasu himself flirted with Islam, to the chagrin of the predominantly Christian population of Ethiopia. Ras Tafari therefore led a coup that deposed Lij Yasu in 1916. Menelik's daughter Zauditu assumed the throne, with Ras Tafari serving as regent. He was a popular leader who continued Menelik's policy of modernization, building schools and encouraging outstanding students to further their education abroad. His greatest success was obtaining the international recognition accorded his country upon joining the League of Nations in 1923. The next year, slavery was abolished in Ethiopia, and many additional reforms were instituted after his state visit to Europe, the first by an Ethiopian head of state. In 1928, Ras Tafari assumed the title of *Negus* (king).

Upon Zauditu's death in 1930, Ras Tafari proclaimed Conquering Lion of the Tribe of Judah, Elect of God and King of the Kings of Ethiopia. At his coronation ceremony in Saint George's Cathedral in Addis Ababa, he assumed the name Haile Selassie (Power of the Trinity). The early years of Haile Selassie's reign were characterized by sweeping reforms. He gave Ethiopia its first written constitution, institutionalized taxation, created the Bank of Ethiopia, and formed a parliament, a secretive institution whose infrequent sessions were subject to the whims of the emperor. Nonetheless, local forces favoring rapid modernization saw this as a great step forward.

Despite the changes at home, world events were taking their toll on Ethiopian development. Italy received British support for a sphere of influence in Ethiopia. Despite his pleas at the League of Nations,

Haile Selassie (center) manning an anti-aircraft gun, 1936

Haile Selassie was powerless to prevent Italian incursions into his territory. A clash between Italian and Ethiopian troops over a water hole in the Ogaden Desert resulted in an arms embargo by France and Britain against Ethiopia, while Italy used the dispute as a pretense to escalate tensions. Italian troops, led by Marshal Emilio de Bono and later, Marshal Pietro Badoglio, invaded Ethiopia in 1935. Two hundred and fifty thousand Ethiopian soldiers were killed attempting to repulse the onslaught of the better-armed Italian troops. On May 2, 1935, the royal family fled, and three days later Addis Ababa fell.

Haile Selassie spent the following six years in exile in Europe attempting to muster support for his beleaguered country. Reports reached him of atrocities committed and concentration camps built to subjugate his people. In the five years of Italian occupation, 760,300 Ethiopians are said to have been killed. In 1936, Haile Selassie again turned to the

League of Nations in an impassioned speech, begging the member states to help liberate Ethiopia. This plea by a frail, homeless emperor from an obscure land was considered by many to be the finest speech ever made to the League, but the world governments, on the brink of World War II, were unwilling to risk the fragile peace of Europe for a remote African kingdom. Haile Selassie retired to London, where he remained until 1940.

Only after the outbreak of World War II did Britain and France recognize the strategic importance of Ethiopia to world shipping and trade. Haile Selassie traveled to Khartoum in 1940 to take part in the liberation of Ethiopia; an army of Ethiopian exiles was established in the Sudan and in 1941 British and Ethiopian forces drove out the Italians. Haile Selassie returned to Addis Ababa in 1941.

Once back on his throne, he continued his policy of modernization. The Italian territory of Eritrea was annexed in 1950, to the chagrin of its predominantly Muslim population. In 1955 he granted a new constitution, ceding considerable powers to parliament and even allowing for elections. Despite these reforms, the pace of modernization was considered too slow by some and a failed coup attempt was made in 1960.

Haile Selassie took an active role in world and particularly pan-African politics; the Organization of African Unity was founded in Addis Ababa in 1963. However, the final years of his reign were marked by harsh famine and corruption in the army. The aging emperor was rapidly growing inarticulate and senile; although he was deposed by the military in 1974 and placed under house arrest, Haile Selassie failed to grasp the events taking place and believed that he was still in power. It was claimed that he died in his sleep in 1975.

For many Africans, Haile Selassie represented the suffering of embattled Africa, torn by colonialism and exploitation. He is often regarded as a symbol of Africa's yearning for freedom. One Jamaican-based religious group of pan-African nationalists, the Rastafarians (after Ras Tafari), believe that Haile Selassie was the personification of Christ returned to redeem Africa.

R. Kapuscinski, *The Emperor*, 1983.
H. G. Marcus, *Haile Selassie*, 1986.
L. Mosley, *Haile Selassie*, 1964.

HAMILTON, ALEXANDER (1755–1804), statesman and first secretary of the treasury of the United States of America. Hamilton was born in Nevis, British West Indies. Hamilton began to work, at age eleven, as a clerk in a counting house of a firm of New York merchants who had set up a business on Saint Croix, and by 1772 he had advanced to the position of manager.

He so impressed his friends and associates on Saint Croix that they gathered funds to send him to the mainland to further his education. In 1773 he began studying at King's College in New York (subsequently Columbia University). His student days were shortlived, however, due to his involvement in the revolutionary cause. At King's College he joined a patriotic volunteer group known as the "Corsicans" and drilled in military exercises every morning before classes. In 1774 he made a widely reported speech and wrote a number of pamphlets attacking British policies.

Hamilton's military ability became apparent in 1776 when he received a captain's commission in the provincial artillery. At the second battle of Trenton his talents helped bar General Charles Cornwallis from crossing the Raritan River to attack Washington's main army, and in February 1777 he was made an aide-de-camp to General George *Washington, with the rank of lieutenant colonel. He remained on Washington's staff for four years and even had a command of his own for the Yorktown campaign (September - October 1781).

After the surrender of Cornwallis in 1781, Hamilton, now with a wife and family, proceeded to Albany, New York, to study law, and the following

---

- The sacred rights of mankind are not to be rummaged for among old parchments or musty records. They are written, as with a sunbeam, in the whole volume of human nature, by the hand of the divinity itself; and can never be erased or obscured by mortal power.
- The fundamental source of all your errors, sophisms and false reasonings is a total ignorance of the natural rights of mankind. Were you once to become acquainted with these, you could never entertain a thought that all men are not, by nature, entitled to a parity of privileges. You would be convinced that natural liberty is a gift of the beneficent Creator to the whole human race; and that civil liberty is founded in that; and cannot be wrested from any people without the most manifest violations of justice. Civil liberty is only natural liberty, modified and secured by the sanctions of civil society.

Alexander Hamilton

---

year was authorized to practice in New York. Also in 1782, he was elected to the Continental Congress by the New York legislature. Notwithstanding his extensive involvement in the Revolution, he defended Loyalists in actions brought against them, his strong feelings for justice even leading him to publish pamphlets asking that the Loyalists be treated justly and with moderation. He helped achieve the repeal of laws disbarring Loyalist lawyers and disenfranchising Loyalist voters.

In 1784 he became involved in the founding of the Bank of New York, becoming one of its directors, a move in line with his personal policy favoring a strong banking system.

May 1787 marked the U.S. Constitutional Convention in Philadelphia where Hamilton was a member of the three-man New York delegation. Having always favored a strong central government instead of thirteen small states in a confederacy, Hamilton did his utmost to promote the ratification of the U.S. Constitution. Toward that end he co-authored *The Federalist* together with John Jay and James *Madison, which consisted of eighty-five essays (reputedly two-thirds were by Hamilton) that were to become classics of political literature. These went far in molding U.S. political institutions and concepts of justice, general welfare, and the rights of individual citizens. This presentation of the new federal system and the central government proposed in the new Constitution contributed significantly to securing support favoring replacement of the former Articles of Confederation with the Constitution.

Despite Hamilton's involvement, New York was the eleventh state to ratify and endorse the Constitution. At the New York ratification convention at Poughkeepsie, New York, in 1788, it was only Hamilton's skillful speeches and maneuvering that insured ratification by a vote of thirty to twenty-seven.

In 1789 George Washington became the first president of the United States and named Hamilton as the first secretary of the treasury, an office in which he served from 1789 to 1795. Hamilton realized that the United States must have financial credit for the normal operations of government as well as for commercial functions and industrial development. He believed the government had to arrange to pay off its entire national debt (Revolutionary War debt) as well as the unpaid debts of the several states incurred during the Revolution. However, some officials wanted to repudiate part or even all of the national debt.

Hamilton believed that the functions of paying debts and borrowing money would be helped by the establishment of a national bank of the United States that had the right to set up branches in different parts of the country. On this issue he clashed with the secretary of state, Thomas *Jefferson. Hamilton therefore introduced a bill in Congress to establish a national bank. Jefferson maintained that this was unconstitutional, as the power to do so was not specifically noted in the Contitution and was therefore limited to the several states. Hamilton argued effectively that many powers were implied in such provisions as the one "authorizing Congress to make all laws which shall be necessary and proper" for carrying out such enumerated powers as the levying and collection of taxes, payment of debts, and borrowing of money. Obviously, he argued, a national bank would help such functions tremendously. Congress, in accepting this argument, established the precedent of "implied powers."

Hamilton (right) facing Aaron Burr in their duel

After 1795 Hamilton continued to be a major political voice and for a time served as second-in-command of the army. He was a bitter political enemy of Aaron Burr, thwarting Burr's ambitions on several occasions. After Hamilton criticized Burr at a dinner party, Burr challenged Hamilton to a duel in Weehawken, New Jersey. Hamilton had an aversion to duelling stemming from the death of his eldest son, Philip, three years earlier in a duel on the same site. However, he felt honor-bound to accept the challenge; Hamilton was reported to have shot in the air but Burr killed him.

J. E. Cooke, *Alexander Hamilton*, 1982.
M. B. Hecht, *Odd Destiny: The Life of Alexander Hamilton*, 1982.
R. A. Hendrickson, *The Rise and Fall of Alexander Hamilton*, 1985.
H. C. Lodge, *Alexander Hamilton*, 1981.
J. C. Miller, *Alexander Hamilton: Portrait in Paradox*, 1959.
B. Mitchell, *Alexander Hamilton*, 2 vols., 1957–1962.

HAMMURABI (or Hammurapi; reigned c.1792–1750 B.C.E.), Babylonian king and lawgiver. Hammurabi, the sixth king of the first Babylonian dynasty, was descended from nomadic Amorite tribesmen. Upon ascending the throne, he continued the expansionist policies of his father, Sin-muballit, asserting Babylonian hegemony over the Euphrates basin. Chief among his rivals was Rim-Sin, king of Larsa, who had invaded Isin, a neutral buffer town separating the two kingdoms. In a war against Rim-Sin, Hammurabi freed Isin and captured Uruk (biblical Erech).

Having secured his southern border, Hammurabi proceeded to strengthen his realm. As was customary, each year of Hammurabi's reign was named after the most notable event to take place. This practice allows modern archeologists to reconstruct fourteen tranquil years during which Hammurabi fortified his northern frontier, where powerful city-states such as Asshur, Elam, and Eshnunna were no less threatening than Larsa. He also developed the economic and religious infrastructure of his state. Temples and administrative buildings were restored and rebuilt, and irrigation canals were dug to improve agricultural productivity. It is probable that the well-known Code of Hammurabi, important to scholars studying the development of a secular legal system, was codified at this time.

Three large black steles (stone slabs) containing the Code of Hammurabi were discovered by French archeologists in Susa in 1901–1902. This was the first known legal system predating the Bible and many parallels were identified with later biblical law, as well as significant differences. Future discoveries would show that both Hammurabi's Code and the biblical laws had even earlier predecessors, but it remains the earliest complete legal code so far discovered.

FROM THE CODE OF HAMMURABI

- If a man has stolen an ox or a sheep or an ass or a pig or a boat, the property of a god or a palace, he shall repay thirtyfold; of an aristocrat, he shall replace it tenfold. If the thief lacks the means of repayment, he shall be put to death.
- If a man has broken into a house, he shall be put to death and hanged before the breach he made.
- If a woman has caused her husband's death because of another man, she shall be impaled.
- If a man strikes a free man's daughter, causing her to miscarry, he shall pay two shekels for the fruit of her womb.
- If that woman dies, his daughter shall be put to death.

The Code's 282 laws are indicative of the evolution of power from religious to lay courts. They contain only five prohibitions, other laws being conditional statements ("if a man...he shall be...") and legislation regulating day-to-day affairs, including the fees for a variety of professions. It assumes the existence of a caste system of patricians and slaves. The basis of the law is *talio* (retaliation): the punishment of the accused attempts to parallel the damage caused. Therefore, if a builder's faulty construction of a home results in the death of the inhabitant's daughter, the builder's daughter would be put to death; hitting one's father is punishable by amputation of the hand, etc. Also included is trial by ordeal, particularly for people accused of sorcery or adultery. The suspect was thrown into the Euphrates; survival denotes innocence, drowning is proof of guilt. Legislation also protected the individual. Falsely accusing one's wife of adultery is punishable by branding, while malpractice in selling beer is punished by drowning.

In 1763 B.C.E. Rim-Sin again threatened Hammurabi in the south. Hammurabi, based upstream, simply dammed the river, starving Rim-Sin before suddenly bursting the dam, resulting in devastating floods. He repeated this technique in his war against Zimrilin, king of Mari, two years later. Hammurabi went on to conquer the important city of Sumer near the Persian Gulf and lands to the east of the Euphrates.

Hammurabi was succeeded by his son Samsuiluna. Years of warfare had prevented him from establishing an efficient bureaucracy to govern his realm and the country rapidly disintegrated. Although his empire could hardly compare with the later Babylonian and Assyrian empires, it was an important step in the evolution of city-states into regional states. Unlike his predecessors, Hammurabi did not plan his posthumous deification, which, like his legal system, was important in establishing the role of a secular monarch independent of the priesthood. Previously, scholars identified Hammurabi with the biblical Amraphel, king of Shinar, who defeated Sodom and carried off Lot, but this claim is not supported now.

J. Bottero and E. Cassin, *The Near East: The Early Civilizations*, 1967.

C. J. Gadd, *The End of Hammurabi's Dynasty*, 1965.

HANDEL, GEORGE FREDERIC (1685–1759), composer. Born in Halle, Germany, where his father, who had married for a second time at age sixty-one to a pastor's daughter, was a barber-surgeon and valet to the Prince of Saxe-Magdeburg, Handel was the second child of this marriage. As a child Handel went with his father to Saxe-Weissenfels, where the young boy began to try the organ of the court chapel. Handel then took organ lessons in Halle and soon was able to substitute for his teacher whenever required. At that time he began composing as well. His initial compositions were trio sonatas and motets for the church services on Sundays.

In 1702 Handel entered the University of Halle where he became probationary organist at the Domkirche. Three years later his first two operas, *Almira* and *Nero*, were performed in Hamburg. This was the beginning of a prolific career in which Handel became renowned all over Europe for his orchestral music, operas, and biblical oratorios.

In 1706 he began a long journey to Italy, where he continued to write operas and enjoyed every form of outward success. After four years the composer returned to Germany, where he became Kapellmeister to the elector of Hanover. In 1710 he paid his first visit to England, a country that was eventually to become his home. During his second visit to London Handel wrote, among other compositions, an ode for Queen Anne's birthday, and the piece was performed at Windsor Castle in 1713. The queen conferred a life stipend on Handel.

When Queen Anne died in 1714, Handel's protector, the elector of Hanover, became King George I of England. The composer now settled in England, becoming a British subject in 1726. In London Handel continued to write many operas to Italian librettos. He also wrote, in 1717, one of his most famous nonvocal works, the *Water Music*, composed especially for George I. A huge aquatic celebration took place on the River Thames, with the king's boat followed by a barge on which Handel's fifty musicians played the new composition. In London everyone acknowledged his genius and he lived in comfort, the new king granting him an additional annual stipend.

In 1719 Handel was named director of the newly inaugurated Royal Academy of Music, whose sole purpose was to produce operas at the King's Theater. When the Royal Academy ceased operations in 1728 Handel became associated with the management of the King's Theater. In 1727 George II came to the throne and added to Handel's honorarium for teaching music to the royal princesses. Operatic life in London at the time was filled with intrigue, with many backstage rivalries among singers, composers, and management. Opera companies formed and then folded in a relatively short time but Handel always found an outlet for his works. He wrote many operas, but only a handful remain in the repertoire.

Handel shifted his musical efforts and interests from writing operas to oratorios and his fame grew substantially. For inspiration he now turned to the Bible, using English texts and not foreign librettos. In 1739 Handel premiered his oratorio *Saul* and later that year, *Israel in Egypt*. In 1741 Handel was invited to Ireland where he presented what would become his most famous composition, *Messiah*. It was premiered in 1742 and was first heard in London a year later. The story goes that King George II rose to his feet at the conclusion of the famous "Hallelujah" chorus, with the rest of the audience following suit. Ever since that event, at every performance of *Messiah* the listeners stand up for the "Hallelujah" chorus. *Messiah* was special for Handel as well. After one performance of this crowning achievement of his career he remarked, "My Lord, I should be sorry if I only entertained them; I wished to make them better." On another occasion the composer remarked that when he wrote the *Messiah*, "I did think I did see all Heaven before me and the great God Himself," and in describing the "Hallelujah" chorus he said, "Whether I was in my body or out of my body as I wrote it I know not. God knows."

Handel continued to write many oratorios, alternating between biblical (*Samson, Joseph*) and mythical (*Semele, Hercules*) subjects. Horace Walpole wrote in a letter in 1743: "Handel's oratorios thrive abundantly. For my part, they give me an idea of heaven, where everybody is to sing whether they have voices or not." In 1749 another of Handel's famous nonvocal works was premiered, the *Music for the Royal Fireworks*, written to celebrate the Peace of Aachen. However, not all of his many works succeeded. When the oratorio *Theodora* failed to cause a stir in 1750, Handel quipped: "The Jews did not come because it is a Christian story; the ladies did not come because it is a

---

We have all had our Handelian training in church, and the perfect church-going mood is one of pure abstract reverence. A mood of active intelligence would be scandalous. Thus we get broken into the custom of singing Handel as if he meant nothing; and as it happens that he meant a great deal, and was tremendously in earnest about it, we know rather less about him in England than they do in the Andaman Islands, since the Andamans are only unconscious of him, whereas we are misconscious.

George Bernard Shaw

virtuous one." In the 1750s Handel had to limit his public engagements because of his poor eyesight. His last public appearance in London was at a performance of *Messiah* on April 6, 1759, a week before his death. He was buried in Westminster Abbey, where a monument by Louis Roubiliac marks his grave.

Handel bequeathed most of his manuscripts to his amanuensis, John Christopher Smith, whose son gave them to King *George III. They then became part of the King's Music Library. These manuscripts comprise thirty-two volumes of operas and twenty-one volumes of oratorios, as well as many odes, sacred music compositions, cantatas, and instrumental music. Many of these compositions can be found in critical editions which were published in England and Germany.

W. Dean and J. M. Knapp, *Handel's Operas 1704–1726*, 1987.

C. Hogwood, *Handel*, 1984.

J. Keates, *Handel*, 1993.

HANNIBAL (247–183 B.C.E.), Carthaginian general and statesman, and eldest son of the Carthaginian general, Hamilcar Barca. According to tradition he swore eternal enmity to Rome before leaving Carthage in 237 B.C.E. to accompany his father to Spain. A junior officer under his brother-in-law Hasdrubal, on whose death in 221 B.C.E. Hannibal was elected commander-in-chief. He resumed the aggressive policy of his father, first attacking the Olcades and in 220 B.C.E. the Vaccaei and Carpetani who lived in the north-central part of the peninsula. In 219 B.C.E. he besieged Saguntum (Sagunto) which claimed an alliance with Rome. The capture of that city despite Roman protests led to the outbreak of the Second Punic War.

Hannibal decided to carry the war to Italy. Leaving his brother-in-law Hasdrubal in command of Spain, he set out from Carthago Nova in the early spring of 218. B.C.E. He passed the Pyrenees with an army of some 35,000 infantry and 8,000 cavalry, advanced along southern Gaul, and crossed the Rhone River despite Gallic hostility. Facing many hardships, he succeeded in crossing the Alps in fifteen days with an army and with elephants, and arrived at the Po valley in October 218 B.C.E. with only some 20,000 infantry and 6,000 cavalry, thousands having died in the ice and snow. His first victory was in a cavalry engagement at Ticinus against *Scipio Africanus. At the river Trebia in December he won a great victory over the combined forces of Scipio and the other consul, Sempronius Longus. By these successes he won the support of the Gauls, and was able to allow his army to rest for the entire winter. In 217 B.C.E. he descended to Etruria and destroyed the army of the consul Flamininus at Lake Trasimene. Hannibal was enraged by the Italian cities' refusal to join him and devastated the country around Apulia and Campania. He won his greatest victory at Cannae in 216 B.C.E. where he surrounded and destroyed the larger Roman army. It was then that Capua and other towns in south Italy joined him, and in the next year they were followed by Philip V of Macedonia and Syracuse.

Hannibal brilliant victories and shrewd strategies failed, however, to defeat Rome. The majority of the Italian tribes and cities remained loyal to Rome and Hannibal was unable to besiege those who refused to join him or effectively protect those who joined him. Rome's superiority in manpower, was decisive; in a few years as many as twenty-two legions were recruited, not counting allies. Eventually Hannibal was forced to retreat to the south and in 209 B.C.E. lost Tarentum, which he had captured in 213 B.C.E. In 207 B.C.E. Hasdrubal arrived in Italy with a strong force but was defeated and killed at the Metaurus before he could join his brother. The next year Scipio Africanus completed the conquest of Spain. Finally in 203 B.C.E. after the spectacular victories of Scipio in Africa, Hannibal left Italy, where he had been for sixteen years. He lost the final battle of Zama (202 B.C.E.) to Scipio, who not only employed Hannibal's tactics, but had better troops at his disposal.

Carthage's quick recovery after the war was largely due to Hannibal's reforms in 196 B.C.E. Due to his measures, the oligarchic One Hundred Four Court was to be elected annually by the people; he increased the revenues of the state, not least by making the rich oligarchs pay for the deficits incurred during their administration. His enemies took revenge by accusing him before Rome of contacting Antiochus III of Syria, and so he fled Carthage in 195 B.C.E. for Syria. After the king's defeat by Rome Hannibal found shelter with the Bithynian King Prusias. He committed suicide using poison when Prusias was about to surrender him to the Romans.

Hannibal was a military genius — one of the greatest of all times — and an eminent statesman. At Trebia he prepared an ambush, enticing the Romans to fight on empty stomachs after crossing the cold river. He outmaneuvered the Roman general Fabius, who blocked his path of retreat from Campania in 217 B.C.E, by sending oxen with burning faggots at night in one direction while he led his army to safety. His outflanking tactics are best illustrated by the battle of Cannae where he neutralized the superiority of the legionaries by delaying action in the center while his cavalry routed the enemy and encircled the whole army. He made successful use of reserve forces in battles and was unique in his time in knowing that a commander should not risk his life by personally fighting.

A great leader of men, he retained the loyalty of his soldiers, most of them mercenaries, to the end. The Romans pursued him but could never forget the awe he inspired; with *Hannibal ad porta* ("Hannibal is at the gates") mothers frightened their children and the people were rallied in times of crisis.

G. Charles Picard, *Hannibal*, 1967.

L. Cottrell, *Hannibal: Enemy of Rome*, 1967.

W. J. Jacobs, *Hannibal*, 1973.

J. F. Lazenby, *Hannibal's War*, 1978.

HARUN AR-RASHID (Harun ben Muhammad ben Abd Allah; c.764-809), caliph of Baghdad, made into a legendary figure in the *Arabian Nights*.During his reign the Abbasid Caliphate went into administrative decline and its political disintegration began. He was born in al-Rayy (near modern Teheran), the third son of the third caliph, Mahdi, and Al-Khayzuran, a Yemenite slave girl whom he had freed and married.

Harun spent his youth in the company of eunuchs at the Abbasid court, where he was much influenced by his mother and his secretary-tutor, Yahya ben Khalid. While still in his teens, he led two expeditions against the Byzantines (779-780 and 781-782). In the first, the Abbasid army captured Samalu, and during the second, it reached the Bosphorus for the first and only time in Abbasid history. As a result of these successes, Harun was appointed governor of Ifrikiya (today's Tunisia), Egypt, Syria, Armenia, and Azerbaijan, and was promoted to second-in-line to the throne, while Yahya was put in charge of the administration.

In 786, after a number of court intrigues, Harun succeeded his elder brother al-Hadi as caliph. Yahya was given the right to govern as vizier as a mark of Harun's gratitude for his support and, with his sons al-Fadi and Djafar, remained in power for the next seventeen years; their fall in 803 signaled the end of the prominent role played by viziers as heads of administration and formulators of policy. Harun then found himself increasingly dependent on his eunuchs, who relied on him for their livelihood and were therefore extremely loyal.

Although Harun's rule is remembered as a golden age in Abbasid history, there were many disturbances in the empire. As political instability increased, rival dynasties challenged the Abbasids: the Ummayads of Spain, the Idrisid dynasty of the Maghreb, and the Aghlabi in Tunisia. The tribes of the province of Syria were sympathetic to the Ummayads, and Harun eventually had to despatch his army to quell the unrest there in 796; partly in order to be better placed to control the region, Harun

Harun ar-Rashid dispensing justice

moved to al-Rakka in northern Syria. There were also serious uprisings in Egypt in 788 and 794-795, which in turn affected Abbasid rule in Tunisia, while harsh rule by Harun's governor in Yemen led to the outbreak of a nine-year uprising in 795. Meanwhile, in the eastern parts of the empire, the population was disaffected because of poor economic conditions and the fact that they were only nominally attached to Islam.

Harun's policy essentially constituted a continuation of that of his predecessors, but he was especially severe towards minorities: in 806 he ordered that churches along the Muslim-Byzantine frontiers be demolished and that members of minority groups in Baghdad wear different clothes and ride different animals from those used by Muslims.

A great measure of Harun's fame arose as a result of his wars against the Byzantines. Waging a holy war against the Christians, he personally participated in regular border attacks against this foe. He captured the Byzantine fortress of Safsaf, but eventually concluded a peace treaty with them at the instigation of the Byzantine empress, Irene. However, with the accession of Nicephorus to the Byzantine throne in 802, hostilities broke out again, with Nicephorus eventually capitulating to Harun.

Harun was the first Abbasid to rebuild the Mediterranean fleet after its neglect following the move of the caliph's residence to Iraq. However, although he was successful in his raids on Cyprus in 805 and Rhodes in 807, the net effect was minimal: by the end of his reign, his empire's boundaries were virtually unchanged. Towards the end of his career, he grew increasingly less competent, and his decisions were instrumental in leading his empire towards civil war. He failed to heed warnings of maladministration in Khurasan until a serious revolt had broken out, and was forced to embark upon a campaign there in 808, accompanied by two of his sons, al-Ma'mun and Salih, and a large Iraqi army. Ill-health forced him to halt, and he died near modern Meshed.

Harun made several important errors in his rule which led to the disintegration of the Abbasid Empire. Most notable among them was his apportioning of the empire between his sons al-Amin, al-Ma'mun, and al-Mu'atim. Economically, his empire's far-reaching commercial activities, which encompassed dealings with China, made him known throughout the world and enriched his court, which was a renowned center of art and culture.

N. Abbott, *The Two Queens of Baghdad*, 1946.

A. Cloty, *Haroun al-Rashid and the World of the Thousand and One Nights*, 1989.

A. Joumard, *Haroun al-Rashid*, 2 vols., 1956.

HARVEY, WILLIAM (1578 – 1657), English physician and physiologist; discoverer of the circulation of blood. Son of a successful Folkestone merchant, Harvey was educated at King's School, Cambridge, and in 1593 began studying at Cambridge University. In 1597 he traveled to Padua, Italy, for training in his chosen profession, medicine. Padua was the home of Fabricius of Aquapendente, a leading European anatomist well known for his lectures on the valves in the veins.

Harvey qualified as a physician in 1602 and returned to England, settling in London; in 1604 he married the daughter of Dr. Lancelot Browne, former physician to *Elizabeth I. It is possible that through this marriage Harvey now had some influence at the court of the new king, *James I. In 1609 James supported Harvey's successful application to become physician at Bartholomew's Hospital, one of the most prestigious medical posts in the capital. In 1615 he was elected Lumleian Lecturer to the Royal College of Physicians, a lifetime appointment.

For a number of years Harvey had carried out experiments with the vivisection of coldblooded animals and by 1618 had already made his discovery of the circulation of blood, a major landmark in the advancement of medical science. His stay at Padua had coincided with *Galileo's Galilei tenure there and Harvey was deeply impressed by the Italian's theories. He applied Galileo's science of motion to the biological processes; employing his methods of qualitative calculation of moving objects, Harvey worked out how much blood was pumped by the heart. He calculated that the large amount could only be accounted for if the heart pumped the same blood over and again. He published his conclusions in *Exercitatio de Motu Cordis et Sanguinis in Animalibus*, which can be seen as the foundation of comparative anatomy.

Harvey's opinions were controversial and although by the 1640s some leading scientists had come to agree with him, the majority of doctors opposed his conclusions. Medical practice continued for the rest of the century unaffected by this discovery.

Harvey also became well known as physician to leading noblemen and politicians, including Francis *Bacon, the Lord Chancellor. In 1618 he reached the pinnacle of the profession with his appointment as physician to James I, a position he also held under the latter's son, *Charles I.

Although Harvey's reputation as an anatomist is unchallenged, his skill as a doctor is open to question. The author John Aubrey, who was well acquainted with him, wrote of Harvey as "an excellent Anatomist, but I never heard of any that admired his therapeutic way." It is also curious that despite his understanding of blood circulation he continued to treat patients by the ancient practice of bleeding, to remove "bad blood."

Charles granted Harvey the wardenship of Merton College, Oxford, in 1646; Harvey was present when the city fell to the Parliamentary forces that same year. Harvey was sixty-eight and happy to escape the turmoil of the times in well-earned retirement. As his wife had predeceased him and they had had no children, he lived his last years with his brothers. A friend who visited him in 1650 recorded his saying that "this obscure life and vacation from public cares which would disgust other minds is the medicine of mine."

L. Chauvois, *William Harvey*, 1957.
Sir G. Keyne, *The Life of William Harvey*, 1966.
G. Whitteridge, *William Harvey and the Circulation of Blood*, 1970.

HASTINGS, WARREN (1732–1818), administrator of British India. Forsaken by his clergyman father, Hastings was raised by an uncle. An outstanding student at Westminster School, after just a few months bookkeeping studies, Hastings went out to Bengal as a bookkeeper for the East India Company. Placed in charge of a small rural silk factory, he developed the highest regard for the Indians he dealt with: "They are gentle, benevolent, abhorrent of bloodshed, faithful and affectionate in service." Interest in India's people and culture was reflected in his learning to speak native languages, unlike many compatriots.

Hastings rose to a high position in the company hierarchy, serving as resident (representative of the governor-general of India) to the Nawab of Bengal, forcefully representing company interests at the court of this subjugated Indian prince. Later he sat on the council controlling company activities in Bengal but resigned over policy differences and returned to England in 1765.

Convinced that his future lay in India, Hastings returned in 1769 and despite previous differences his abilities were recognized by superiors in the company administration. In 1771 Hastings was appointed governor of Bengal. He wanted the company to have responsibility for central government, leaving daily administration with the native officials, since the population would suffer less under a corruption they knew than under rule by a tribe of what he called "Europeans of the lowest sort." Land tax and customs were reformed to encourage trade and the native justice system was revitalized; Hastings believed Indians should live under their own laws, not those imposed by England.

From 1774 Hastings was governor-general of Bengal with a new, powerful, independent four-man council appointed by Parliament and comprising British government as well as company representatives. Previously he had enjoyed the cooperation of fellow administrators but this new council was of a different complexion. In particular one of its members, Philip Francis, was a continual thorn in his side, with ambitions to take over Hastings's post.

The new councilors immediately began an investigation of Hastings's activities, especially the employment of company troops in support of the Nawab of Oudh, a war they viewed as unjustified. Hastings refused to hand over relevant correspondence and this exacerbated the rift, since they suspected he had made money through hiring out these soldiers. They also replaced officials he had appointed with men of their own choice. An obliging Indian leader named Nandakumar made allegations of corruption against Hastings but when Nandakumar was arrested and hanged for forgery the plot fell through. Hastings's power base was restored but conflict in the council continued and in 1780 he fought a duel with Philip Francis, who was wounded and left India. Other opponents were removed by sickness and death while he remained in excellent health, going to "bed at ten, abstaining wholly from wine and from every other liquid but tea and water."

The last years of his administration were marked by a series of wars with hostile native princes and the French. The East India Company succeeded in defending its interests against all these threats. Credit was due to Hastings for successful deployment of company forces but methods of financing the war damaged his reputation. He went in person to extract money from the Raja of Benares. The Raja offered him a present and he accepted but gave the money as his own donation to meeting the cost of the war. Then, when the Raja did not reply with sufficient humility to a request for a hefty contribution to the war fund, Hastings had him placed under house arrest. This sparked a rebellion that cost a great deal more money to suppress. He also exerted pressure on the Nawab of Oudh to extract money from the Nawab's mother and grandmother — their palace was blockaded and two of their eunuchs placed in irons and put on short rations.

By 1782 a parliamentary committee censured Hastings's behavior. Philip Francis was busy blackening his name and Hastings sensed he had little support in the British government. He was also for the first time feeling his health weakening, so in 1785 he decided to resign and return to England.

In India, Hastings's rule had been appreciated by the population, who recognized genuine interest in their welfare and saw moderation and respect characterize most of his dealings with them. In England he was viewed differently. His name was associated with the corruption and money-grabbing that characterized the English who went out to India. Impeached by Parliament on charges of corruption and maladministration, he stood trial from 1788 to 1795. The trial ended in acquittal but he had expended all his savings in his legal expenses. However, the East India Company gave him a generous pension. Hastings retired from active public life, living another twenty-three years on his ancestral country estate in Worcestershire, which he had repurchased.

K. Feiling, *Warren Hastings*, 1954.
P. Moon, *Warren Hastings and British India*, 1947.
P. Moon, *The British Conquest and Dominion of India*, 1989.

HEARST, WILLIAM RANDOLPH (1863–1951), American publishing and media tycoon, social reformer, and politician. Hearst was born in San Francisco, where his father, a goldmine owner, was elected to the state legislature in 1865 and later to the U.S. Senate. His mother, who always helped the needy, was the founder of the Parents-Teachers Association.

In 1882, young Hearst enrolled at Harvard College, where, in his sophomore year, he became the business manager of Harvard's humor magazine, the *Lampoon*, which he put on a sound financial footing. He was expelled from Harvard in 1884 after leading a rally and parade which lasted all night following Grover Cleveland's win in the presidential election. He returned to Harvard in 1885, but was expelled again for a Christmas prank, in which he sent each of his instructors a chamber pot inscribed with their names.

In 1887 Hearst took control of the *San Francisco Examiner*, which his father had bought in 1880 for political reasons. He changed the format, hired the best reporters, and sometimes put a sports or feature story on the front page. He crusaded against corruption and privileges and used sensationalism to enliven his pages. He was well connected to politicians through his father and soon made the newspaper profitable.

Breaking into the New York newspaper market in 1895, Hearst purchased the unsuccessful *New York Journal*, bringing several of his reporters from California with him. He was soon able to lure journalists and editors away from rival newspapers and with a one-cent reduction on the price of his paper, bold headlines, and easy-to-read print, Hearst convinced the newsboys to put the *Journal* on top of the other newspapers. Hearst catered to the common people, and was proud of his "yellow" journalistic style. He told his staffers: "The average man in the street wants everything presented to him briefly as well as brightly. If you want to obtain and retain any person's attention you must say something worthwhile and say it quickly." Hearst's newspapers contained daily articles on sports, music, and drama, as well as literary criticism and practical information. They also included crime stories, which his reporters would often help the police solve.

A circulation war broke out between Hearst's *Journal* and Joseph Pulitzer's *World*, during which Hearst succeeded in enticing away Pulitzer's best staff. The 1896 presidential campaign between William McKinley and William Jennings Bryan was a battleground not only for the contenders but also for the newspapers. Hearst supported Bryan, and though not agreeing with him on every issue, believed that "the cause he stood for was the people's cause." Hearst's newspaper was the only major one on the east coast to endorse Bryan, who lost the election.

Both the *Journal* and the *World* pursued news stories vigorously and so were influential in shaping the events upon which they were reporting. For a time, Hearst advocated a noninterventionist policy in Cuba, although he supported the insurgents. However, he was soon pushing the U.S. government to recognize Cuba as an independent nation. Hearst was reported to have encouraged his journalists in Cuba to "furnish the pictures" and he would "furnish the war." Hearst denied sending such a telegram but, real or fictional, it displays his philosophy of presenting the news so as to achieve his desired end.

In 1897 and 1898 the *Journal* whipped up public sentiment against Spain and, following the Spanish sinking of the *Maine* in 1898 with the loss of 266 American lives, he demanded a call to war, thus helping precipitate the Spanish-American War. After William McKinley acquiesced to public pressure and Congress declared war on Spain in April, Hearst chartered a steamship to take him to Cuba, where he served as a war correspondent. He also personally participated in the Battle of Santiago and took twenty-nine Spanish prisoners. During the war the *Journal*'s daily circulation rate soared to 1.25 million, but when the conflict ended, circulation levels dropped.

There is no business in which beauty is more important than journalism. Taste and beauty in makeup and illustration and typography each has its appeal to the public. In fact, a paper which does not excel in these directions has a distinctly cheap and ordinary appearance, and makes conditions difficult for the Circulation Manager and the Advertising Department.

William Randolph Hearst

Hearst now turned to political pursuits, unsuccessfully seeking the office of governor of New York on several occasions. In 1903 he was elected as a congressman from New York, an office which he held for four years. In 1904 he received 263 votes at the Democratic national convention for the presidential nomination. However his political career ended in 1909 after an unsuccessful bid for the mayoralty of New York City. He remained active in politics and in the social reformers' movement but never sought public office again.

Hearst's empire grew as he purchased newspapers in all the major cities; at times he owned up to two or three in one city. He also owned several magazines, including *Cosmopolitan, Good Housekeeping*, and *Harper's Bazaar*. Dabbling in the newsreel and motion picture industries, he financed several movies that starred Marion Davies, his mistress of over three decades. His empire now spanned all aspects of the media industry. At the peak of his career in 1935, Hearst owned twenty-eight major newspapers and eighteen magazines, as well as several radio stations, movie companies, and news services.

During the 1920s Hearst had a castle built in San Simeon, California, on a 240,000-acre area with a fifty-mile oceanfront, at a cost estimated between twenty and fifty million dollars; it also housed his private zoo. Decorating it with art works he had collected in Europe, he resided there with Davies. His wife, Millicent Wilson, whom he married in 1903, refused to give him a divorce, and the two remained married but separated.

The Great Depression and his personal extravagances took a heavy toll on Hearst's financial empire. At the pinnacle of his success, Hearst's assets were worth between $200 and $400 million, but his financial straits caused him to sell a number of his less profitable newspapers and parts of his art collection. By 1940, he had lost control of his empire and after World War II, he was forced to leave his castle in San Simeon and move to a smaller house in Beverly Hills.

Hearst left a legacy of expanded news coverage and a journalistic philosophy that the ends justified the means. Orson Welles's famous film *Citizen Kane* was a thinly disguised portrait of Hearst.

L. Chaney, *The Hearsts*, 1981.
R. Littlefield, *William Randolph Hearst: His Role in American Progessivism*, 1980.
W. A. Swanberg, *Citizen Hearst*, 1971.

HEDIN, SVEN ANDERS (1865–1952), Swedish explorer and geographer. Hedin's lifelong fascination with Central Asia began by chance in 1885 when he accompanied a Swedish engineer to Baku, Azerbaijan, to serve as a tutor for his children. He was immediately enchanted by the rugged landscape and soon mastered Persian so that he could explore the surrounding areas on his own. His first survey of the region took place that same year when, upon completing his duties as tutor, he decided to take a circuitous route on horseback through Iran and Iraq. Upon his return to Sweden he studied geography at the University of Uppsala, but later transferred to the University of Berlin to attend the lectures of Ferdinand von Richthofen, the foremost geographer in Europe.

Hedin graduated in 1899, but he never relinquished the wanderlust of his youth and traveled at every opportunity. Even as a student he was recognized as a competent Persian scholar, and on one occasion accompanied a Swedish diplomatic mission to Teheran as an interpreter; upon completing his duties he set out on a new route from Russian Central Asia to China before returning to Berlin to complete his education.

In the quarter century following his graduation, Hedin made several trips across Central Asia and into Tibet. He often disguised himself as a native and chose only local guides and porters to accompany him, believing that a European-dominated expedition would be considered obtrusive. Over the years Hedin became an adept and experienced traveler, learning from mishaps how to improve future expeditions. On one occasion, while crossing the Takla Makan desert of Sinkiang, he was caught without water. One by one, porters and guides died of dehydration; near death, he and the lone surviving porter crawled to an unmarked watering hole and survived.

In addition to receiving popular attention because of the sense of adventure they evoked, Hedin's reports were of great significance to the scientific community. He was the first person to describe in scientific terms the mysterious wandering Lake of

Lop Nor in the Tarim Basin, which travels across the desert every year, and to determine the source of the Indus and Brahmaputra rivers.

In the 1920s the German airline Lufthansa contemplated establishing an air link between Berlin and Peking, and commissioned Hedin to head a scientific survey of Central Asia to determine an eventual flight path. Sweden and China agreed to cosponsor the survey, and when economic restraints forced Lufthansa to pull out, the expedition was renamed the Sino-Swedish Scientific Expedition. In 1928 Hedin headed a team of European and Chinese specialists, including cartographers, meteorologists, botanists, zoologists, paleontologists, and anthropologists on a scientific survey of the area. The survey lasted seven years, and its findings, not all of which have yet been published, encompass over fifty volumes.

F. D. Scott, *Sweden: The Nation's History*, 1977.

HEGEL, GEORG WILHELM FRIEDRICH

(1770–1831), German philosopher and historian. Although he presented his ideas in a literary style often criticized as so obscure as to verge on incomprehensibly (perhaps inevitable for a man who believed that qualification is the essence of truth), Hegel's influence on subsequent generations of philosophers has been immense. He took seriously *Plato's assertion that the philosopher is "the spectator of all time and all existence," and hence attempted to perform a service for the modern world analogous to that discharged for the ancient world by *Aristotle — to develop a philosophy which as a systematic whole comprehended the entire universe.

The details of Hegel's life are unexceptional and its milestones are his academic appointments and publications. Born to a middle-class family in Stuttgart, he took his Ph.D. in philosophy and classics from Tübingen in 1790 and went on to study theology there, with a view to taking holy orders. His fellow students called him "the old man" due to his diffidence and lack of charisma.

Dissatisfied with the prevailing religious orthodoxy, Hegel never became a priest. Instead he immersed himself further in the study of history and Greek philosophy. It was his subsequent influence that precipitated the renaissance of interest in classical philosophy in the century following his death. He also studied Immanuel *Kant and was moved by the latter to a reinterpretation and reevaluation of the life and teachings of *Jesus and the history of the Christian church. He came to see the Bible as a source of symbolic rather than literal meaning that required considerable philosophical exegesis to be properly understood. "Religion," he said, "anticipates philosophy; philosophy is nothing but conscious religion."

Hegel began teaching at the university of Jena in 1801, lecturing on logic and metaphysics, and was appointed extraordinary professor there in 1805. His irregular style of presentation and poor oratorical powers meant that he was never easy to understand, but nevertheless his reputation grew steadily. His con-

- It is easier to discover a deficiency in individuals, in states, and in Providence, than to see their real import and value.
- The history of the world is the progress of the consciousness of freedom.
- Peoples and governments have never learned anything from history or acted on principles deduced from it.
- Life has a value only when it has something valuable as its object.
- Nothing great in the world has been accomplished without passion.
- Amid the pressure of great events, a general principle gives no help.
- To him who looks upon the world rationally, the world in its turn presents a rational aspect.
- Everything that is, is reasonable.
- Without the world, God is not God.

Georg Hegel

tributions to esthetics and the philosophy of religion were to become part of the Hegelian canon, which has had an impact on almost every area of philosophy.

His first systematic presentation of his theories was published in two parts as *The Science of Logic* (1816) and on the strength of this he first accepted a chair at the university of Heidelberg and then, in 1818, the chair in philosophy at Berlin University. He lectured extensively in the following years, the originality of his ideas belying his diffidence. A strong following now gathered around him and he became rector of the university in 1830.

Hegel conceived of history as a continuous progression toward the spiritual freedom of mankind. He was himself conservative and a firm believer in Prussian values of stateism and bureaucratization, but the revolutionary possibilities of his theory of the inevitability of historical change were recognized and utilized by Karl *Marx; indeed, without Hegel, Marxism is unthinkable.

For Hegel, all ideas and forms of understanding were mutable, the individual was essentially a representative of his age, and reality was a continuous process of becoming rather than a fixed state. Moreover he held that "the truth is the whole," which he called the Absolute. His argument was that any set of propositions that is less than the complete system of propositions will turn out to be self-contradictory; only in the complete system can falsity be removed.

Hegel used his famous dialectic method because he saw contradiction as the medium through which our necessarily imperfect understanding of the Absolute was refined. One starts with an initial proposition, the thesis, which proves to be inadequate and generates its opposite, the antithesis. This in turn proves to be inadequate and the opposites are then subsumed into a synthesis, which preserves what is rational but cancels what is irrational. This triadic process continues, achieving successively closer approximations to the truth.

The 1830 revolution and the prospect of mob rule greatly shocked Hegel, who saw the state as "the embodiment of rational freedom." At the time of his death during the German cholera epidemic of 1831 he was one of Prussia's most influential thinkers.

M. N. Forster, *Hegel and His Critics*, 1989.
M. J. Inwood, *Hegel*, 1983.
P. Singer, *Hegel*, 1983.

HEINE, HEINRICH (1797–1856), German poet and critic. His prose and verse give expression to bitter personal disappointments and also reflect the sociopolitical conflicts of his era. Born in Dusseldorf, he studied law at the universities of Bonn, Berlin, and Gottingen (1819–1825); these studies were financed by his uncle, Salomon Heine, a Hamburg banker. During his student years, he became infatuated with Salomon's daughters, Amalie and Therese, both of whom rejected him in turn; the pangs of unrequited love inspired some of Heine's early verse and left their mark on his subsequent writing.

The reactionary and intolerant atmosphere in Germany made it virtually impossible for Jews to gain advancement; with shame and reluctance, in the summer of 1825, Heine (now Christian Johann Heinrich instead of the original Harry) was baptized a Lutheran so as to obtain his law degree and the "ticket of admission to European civilization." This act never brought him to the governmental or academic posts for which he had hoped, and he often regretted it. However, journalism helped provide Heine with a livelihood while he began publishing the first of his major works, notably the four-volume "Pictures of Travel" (*Reisebilder*, 1826–1831), a mixture of nature poetry, satire, and description. He also published the "Book of Songs" (*Buch der Lieder*, 1827), a bestselling verse collection, with poems such as "Lorelei" and "On Wings of Song," that made Heine an admired European celebrity.

Although popular at home and abroad, Heine found himself increasingly victimized by German censorship and anti-Semitism. In 1831, after welcoming the previous year's liberal July Revolution in France, he left his homeland for Paris, where a more congenial atmosphere prevailed. The Augsburg *Allgemeine Zeitung* engaged him as its Paris correspondent; his friends soon included Hector Berlioz, Ferdinand *Lassalle, Victor *Hugo, and George Sand. He played a leading role in the radical Young Germany movement and endeavored to serve as a cultural mediator between French and German intellectuals, warning both of the threat posed by latent Teutonic savagery. Heine's perceptive, hard-hitting observations were contained in volumes of essays (e.g., "The Romantic School," 1835), as well as newspapers reports and correspondence. German reactionaries, who banned more and more

---

ABOUT HEINE

- I never took his mordant laughter seriously, hearing only the beat of a German heart in songs that will live forever.

Hans Christian Andersen

- Reading Heine's *Intermezzo* is preferable to the wittiest company.

Theophile Gautier

- Heinrich Heine gave me the highest conception of the lyric poet. I seek in vain in all the realms of thousands of years for an equally sweet and passionate music. It will be said one day that he and I have been by far the first artists of the German language — at an incalculable distance from everything that mere Germans have done with it.

Friedrich Nietzsche

- Those conflicts over erecting a monument to Heine, whether in the nineteenth century or under the Weimar Republic, just prove how intolerant leading educated Germans can be when someone dares to hold a mirror up to their faces.

German Federal President Gustav Heinemann, 1972

---

of his works, were especially infuriated by the lines of "Silesian Weavers" and two satirical epics, *Atta Troll* (1843) and "Germany, A Winter Tale" (*Deutschland, ein Wintermarchen*, 1844).

The 1848 revolution's failure in Germany, coupled with the paralysis to which he fell victim three months later, shattered many of Heine's fond hopes and illusions. On his "mattress grave" he was visited by grieving relatives and friends, inspired by a "newly awakened religious feeling," and cared for by Eugénie ("Mathilde"), the affectionate though uneducated Parisian salesgirl whom he had married — after a seven-year liaison — in 1841. His last great verse collection, *Romanzero* (1851), was made up of "Histories," "Lamentations," and three "Hebrew Melodies" based partly on an intensive rereading of the Bible. In accordance with his instructions he was buried in the Montmartre cemetery without church rites.

Heine's expressive works have influenced the writers of many nations and are continually republished in dozens of languages. More than 6,000 *Lieder* and other compositions by Franz *Schubert, Robert Schumann, Felix Mendelssohn, and Franz Liszt (among others) are based on his poetry, and even the violently anti-Jewish Richard *Wagner was indebted to Heine for the themes of *Tannhauser* and *The Flying Dutchman*. One of his prophecies, that "wherever men burn books they will end up burning people" (*Almansor*, 1823), was fulfilled by the Nazis, who tried to convert Heine's "Lorelei" into an anonymous "folksong." Today, however, streets, monuments, postage stamps, and learned societies honor his memory.

F. Futterknecht, *Heinrich Heine*, 1985.

M. Hadas, ed., *Heinrich Heine: A Biographical Anthology*, 1956.

P. Kossoff, *Valiant Heart*, 1983.

R. Robertson, *Heine*, 1988.

J. L. Sammons, *Heinrich Heine: A Modern Biography*, 1979.

HEISENBERG, WERNER KARL (1901–1976), German theoretical physicist who won the 1932 Nobel Prize for the development of quantum mechanics; known for his uncertainty principle.

Heisenberg, the son of a classics professor, was born in Würzburg, Germany. As a student at the University of Munich he showed an aptitude for mathematics and decided to pursue a career in theoretical physics; at the time, physics was facing a philosophical crisis in the wake of the discoveries of quantum theory and relativity.

One school of physics wished to investigate the fundamental nature of matter: the other — to which Heisenberg belonged — was more concerned with describing a functional phenomenological system of nature. Heisenberg determined initially to avoid any attempts to visualize physical processes, and in 1925 developed a primitive quantum mechanics based on matrix manipulations. With the help of his mentor Max Born of Göttingen, by the following

---

BY AND ABOUT HEISENBERG

- Every tool carries with it the spirit by which it has been created.
- Since the measuring device has been constructed by the observer...we have to remember that what we observe is not nature itself but nature exposed to our method of questioning.
- "Heisenberg might have been 'ere, 1969" (graffito on the bathroom wall of the engineering school, Melbourne University, referring to the uncertainty principle!)

---

year his method had been refined into a comprehensive mathematical scheme of quantum theory.

However, this still defied physical interpretation. The search for answers to the seemingly dichotomous behavior of atomic matter as particulate and waveforms brought Heisenberg to Copenhagen in 1927 to study with Niels *Bohr. Noting a spread in the values of the simultaneous position and velocity of electrons, Heisenberg came to believe that in principle at the subatomic level, measurement of certain pairs of variables was limited in accuracy by what became known as "the Heisenberg uncertainty principle." In essence, this principle stated that attempts to observe accurately either the position or the velocity of an electron would interfere with the other variable. Consequently, he affirmed the acausality of quantum mechanics by showing that as we cannot know the present in all its detail, we cannot predict the future.

Heisenberg moved to Leipzig University in 1927, holding the chair in theoretical physics until 1941. In September 1939 he was approached to help the German effort to develop an atomic bomb. In 1941, as it became clear to him that such a weapon was theoretically feasible, he traveled to see his friend Bohr, gravely anxious at the military nature of his work. Bohr, noting that such research was inevitable, left Heisenberg feeling dejected but resolved to accept his part in the atomic project. He was then appointed director of the Max Planck Institute in Berlin to facilitate his investigations. Nonetheless, the German effort to develop the bomb was hardly past the theoretical state when Germany surrendered in 1945. Heisenberg was later stunned by the news that America had successfully exploded an atomic bomb over Japan.

At the conclusion of the war Heisenberg was interned near Paris for several months, along with the other German atomic physicists captured by the Americans. On his release he was reappointed as the director of the Max Planck Institute of Physics, a post he held until 1970, first in Göttingen and then from 1958 in Munich.

P. A. Heelan, *Quantum Mechanics and Objectivity*, 1965.

B. Hoffman, *The Strange Story of the Quantum*, 1959.

M. Jammer, *The Conceptual Development of Quantum Mechanics*, 1966.

HEMINGWAY, ERNEST MILLER (1899–1961), American author. In his early, post-World War I writings, Ernest Hemingway described the sense of chaos and loss of a young generation shattered by the horrors of modern-day warfare. Throughout his life, the Nobel Prize winning author wrote in his distinctly terse and understated style about man's courage and search for meaning in the face of a violent and meaningless reality.

Hemingway was born in Oak Park, Illinois, a well-to-do and conservative suburb of Chicago. His father, a doctor, taught him to hunt and fish and

Hemingway would go on to celebrate these pursuits, in both his life and his works, as part of his masculine code of challenge and endurance.

Hemingway's mother was a strong, independent woman who at first earned far more money teaching music than did her husband who, in addition to attending to an ever-expanding medical practice, took care of most of the household responsibilities. Recent biographies of Hemingway suggest his confusion of masculine and feminine roles, perhaps abetted by his mother's tendency to dress her son in a feminine style: this confusion may lie at the core of the overstated masculinity found in Hemingway's heroes and in his own life. It might explain as well the misogyny some critics find and condemn in Hemingway's depiction of woman characters.

Young Hemingway refused to attend college and began a journalism career as a cub reporter for the *Kansas City Star*. With the outbreak of World War I, Hemingway tried to enlist in the army and was rejected because of an eye injury. Instead, he joined the Red Cross as an ambulance driver and was sent to Italy. Badly wounded at the Austro-Italian front, Hemingway was subsequently decorated by the Italian government for bravery under fire. While recuperating Hemingway fell in love with a young American nurse, who eventually ended the affair. The incident inspired the story of a wounded soldier's romance with a nurse in *A Farewell to Arms*.

After his return home, Hemingway sailed to France in 1921 as foreign correspondent for the *Toronto Star*. He became part of the large, vibrant society of expatriate American artists in Paris that included Gertrude Stein, Sherwood Anderson, Scott Fitzgerald, and Ezra *Pound.

Hemingway's distinctive and influential style arose out of those years as a journalist and aspiring writer in Paris. From his experience as a reporter Hemingway achieved his terse, almost telegraphic style that seeks a sense of immediacy and compression. Gertrude Stein taught him to use rhythm and repetition effectively and Ezra Pound encouraged him to cut out adjectives and adverbs.

In 1925 Hemingway published his first book, *In Our Time*, a series of stories about Nick Adam's youth in northern Michigan, presented alternately with brief vignettes of war and violence. The following year his first novel, *The Sun Also Rises*, appeared, describing the aimlessness and disillusionment of the expatriates of the 1920s, whom Gertrude Stein called "the lost generation." The work, which catapulted the twenty-seven-year-old writer to fame, is a noteworthy example of his style. It tells the story of Jake Barnes, a young soldier rendered impotent by a war wound. The work pares down language to its essentials; sentences are short, descriptions concrete, and the action is described objectively, without narrative interruption or authorial emotion. Hemingway described his style as working "on the principle of the iceberg," with the

- What is moral is what you feel good after and what is immoral is what you feel bad after.
- The first panacea for a mismanaged nation is inflation of the currency; the second is war. Both bring a temporary prosperity; both bring permanent ruin. Both are the refuge of political and economic opportunists.
- They wrote in the old days that it is sweet and fitting to die for one's country. But in modern war there is nothing sweet nor fitting in your dying. You will die like a dog for no good reason.
- A serious writer is not to be confounded with a solemn writer. A serious writer may be a hawk or a buzzard or even a popinjay but a solemn writer is always a bloody owl.
- Cowardice, as distinguished from panic, is almost always simply a lack of ability to suspend the functioning of the imagination.
- Courage is grace under pressure.

Ernest Hemingway

emotion hidden under the surface of the work, for the discerning reader to find, though not directly revealed by the author.

Jake Barnes's sexual impotence became a symbol for the sterility of the postwar generation in a world torn apart by violence and brutality. In the short story "A Clean, Well Lighted Place," Hemingway parodies the Lord's Prayer, stating that all is "nada," nothingness. Hemingway's heroes have all lost their faith — in God, in man, in lofty ideals. The bull-fighting scenes of *The Sun Also Rises* suggest that the peasants of Spain have found in ritual and bravery an answer to life's emptiness. While Hemingway's heroes are too modern and self-conscious to lose themselves in primitive ritual, they find a solution of their own in adhering to a code of honor and endurance.

Hemingway created numerous "code heroes" in his six novels and more than fifty short stories; in a sense he also created himself as such a hero, in his own life. He sought adventure in war as a correspondent on the Loyalist side in the Spanish Civil War, which he later wrote about in *For Whom the Bell Tolls* (1940), and again in World War II, participating in the D-Day landing at Normandy and in the liberation of Paris. His nonfictional works reflect his interest in such pursuits as bullfighting (*Death in the Afternoon*, 1932) and big game hunting (*Green Hills of Africa*, 1935).

Hemingway's 1937 novel *To Have and Have Not* was not a success; he followed it three years later with his most optimistic novel, *For Whom the Bell Tolls*. Even more dramatically, in 1950 Hemingway published *Across the River and into the Trees*, a novel almost universally derided by critics. Just two years later, again undefeated by defeat, he wrote *The Old Man and the Sea*, a moving story of a Cuban fisherman's endurance. The book was awarded the Pulitzer Prize and was crucial in winning Hemingway the Nobel Prize in literature in 1954.

Hemingway's personal life was turbulent; he was married four times, divorced three; and survived numerous illnesses and accidents. In 1945 he settled on an estate near Havana. Forced out by Castro, he began to suffer depression and memory losses. He was hospitalized twice for electric shock treatments until, in one more act of violence, he shot himself.

P. L. Hay, *Ernest Hemingway*, 1992.
K. S. Lynn, *Hemingway*, 1987.
J. R. Mellow, *Hemingway*, 1993.
J. Meyers, *Hemingway*, 1985.

HENRY IV (1050–1106), king of Germany and Holy Roman emperor. Henry, the son of Henry III and Agnes of Poitou, became king at age six. Agnes served as regent during Henry's minority; her inability to maintain control permitted the German nobility to pursue their own personal political ambitions in a country plagued by civil war and conflict. In 1062 a group of nobles led by archbishop Anno of Cologne kidnapped the boy king, intending to rule in his name. Conflict among the new regents thrust the leaderless German kingdom into complete disarray.

Henry began to consolidate control over Germany in 1066. Due to the deterioration of the kingdom under his mother, he was forced to establish his own power, independent of German nobles and clergymen. Upon winning the loyalty of the nobles of the Rhine, Henry concentrated on the restoration of his power in the northern region, Saxony; the ensuing wars in Saxony, which continued intermittently between 1073 and 1088, strongly influenced the struggle for domination between the German king and the papacy. Open rebellion broke out in east Saxony in the summer of 1073. With the pope's blessing, Henry led a combined military force from the duchies in the south and defeated the rebel forces at the river Unstrut in 1075.

In order to offset the power of hereditary nobles, German kings usually depended upon the selection and control of loyal bishops who oversaw administrative functions within their sees. After his victory over the Saxons, Henry invested a new nominee with the sees of Milan, which were crucial to maintaining his power in Lombardy. Pope *Gregory VII, however, contested Henry's power of investiture, and excommunicated him in 1076, declaring him deposed.

Seizing upon the papal excommunication, opponents of the king claimed that he would lose his kingdom if he did not regain the pope's favor within a year and a day of his excommunication. In anticipation of the diet to be called at Augsburg in February 1077, Henry slipped out of Germany to meet the pope at a castle in Canossa, Italy on the eve of Christmas 1076 in order to receive absolution from him. Standing outside the castle gates, bare-

Henry IV (kneeling, center) begs Matilda of Tuscany's intercession on his behalf with the pope

foot in the snow, Henry repented for three days in what was to be an important political victory for the pope, reasserting the church's role in sustaining the German monarchy.

The rebel German nobility, however, deposed Henry and elected Duke Rudolf of Swabia as anti-king. Henry still had strong support among many German bishops and in most of Lombardy, Burgundy, Bavaria and Franconia. He invaded Saxony and divided the Saxon forces. In light of this substantial diplomatic victory, Henry once again broke ranks with the pope, and was once again excommunicated. This time, however, Henry, seen as a martyr, had the power to contest Gregory's tyrannical decision.

Members of a council at Brixen deposed Gregory and installed archbishop Guibert of Ravenna as anti-Pope Clement III. With the death of the anti-king, Rudolf, in battle against Henry in 1080, Gregory turned to the invading Normans and their leader, Robert Guiscard, for support. Meanwhile Henry invaded Rome in 1081; He was crowned Holy Roman Emperor by Clement III. However his victory was shortlived: the Normans destroyed the city on returning from their campaign against the Byzantines in Apulia and Henry was forced to flee.

After Gregory's death, Henry strengthened his power in Germany. He reasserted his authority over the church, in opposition to Pope *Urban II, and had his son, Conrad, crowned as king of Germany in 1087.

The emperor's power and prestige diminished when Urban consolidated his own strength. In spite of the threat of a renewed rebellion in Germany, Henry set off to invade Italy once again. However, when rebellion did indeed break out in Germany, Conrad supported it, believing that Henry's policies endangered the monarchy. Conrad died fighting his father in 1101; secular opposition was quelled, but the rest of Henry's life would be plagued by familial treachery and strife.

Henry's second son (the future Henry V) was crowned king of Germany in his brother Conrad's stead in 1098, but in 1104 he too rebelled against his father. Henry was captured by his son in 1105 and was forced to give up his empire, escaping to Cologne. He died the following year while building up an army to confront his son in battle. He came to be seen as a tragic national hero who opposed the Roman papacy in order to maintain a strong Germany.

E. Boshof, *Heinrich IV*, 1979.

K. Hampe, *Germany Under the Salian and Hohenstaufen Emperors*, 1973.

A. Haverkamp, *Medieval Germany: 1056–1273*, 1988.

B. H. Hill, *Medieval Monarchy in Action; The German Empire from Henry I to Henry IV*, 1972.

HENRY VI (1165–1197), king of Germany and Holy Roman emperor. A member of the Hohenstaufen family, Henry VI was the second son of Frederick *Barbarossa. He was crowned king of Germany in 1169 but did not become the sole ruler of the German kingdom until his father's death while on a crusade in 1190. Henry sought to consolidate his own power in Germany, Italy and the Mediterranean through political maneuvering.

In 1186 Henry married Constance of Sicily. In 1190, he traveled to Rome where he was crowned emperor by Pope Clement III. He immediately set out to purchase the support of cities in northern Italy. When he returned to Rome, the new pope, Celestine II, would not honor the coronation; only after a treaty was signed between the powerful German army and the Romans did the pope crown Henry.

The new Holy Roman emperor met his first challenge when Queen Constance became the legal heiress to the throne of Sicily following the death of William II. Neither the Sicilians nor the papacy wanted the Germans to unite Sicily with the German kingdom. The pope conspired against Henry by supporting the election of Tancred, Count of Lecce and the illegitimate son of Constance's brother, as king in Sicily. Henry, preparing to besiege Sicily, was accused by the pope and the clergy of compliance in the murder of Bishop Albert of Brabant by German knights in 1192, and returned to Germany in order to defend himself.

At this time, the English ruler *Richard I ("The Lionhearted"), returning from a crusade in the Holy Land, was captured by his enemy the Duke of Austria, who summarily handed him over to Henry in 1193. Richard, an ally of the Welfs in Germany and Tancred in Sicily, made a deal for his release that would defuse the imminent rebellion against Henry. He was released on terms favorable to the German monarchy: 150,000 marks' ransom, vassalage of England to the

Holy Roman Empire, reconciliation of the Welfs to the empire, and the abandonment of Tancred.

With nothing now standing in their way, Henry and Constance conquered Sicily, where she assumed the throne in 1194. A few days later, the empress gave birth to Frederick Roger, who was elected king of Germany in 1196 despite Henry's attempts to establish a hereditary monarchy. During his brief rule Henry expanded the empire to its widest boundaries. However, the instability of his alliances and incomplete reconciliation with the papacy left him without a sound political foundation. Thus, by the time of his death he found himself incapable of surmounting the growing opposition of his vassals and a politically powerful pope.

H. Fuhrman, *Germany in the High Middle Ages c. 1050–1200*, 1986.

W. E. Goodrich, *Henry VI and the Decline of the German Monarchy*, 1970.

K. Hampe, *Germany Under the Salian and Hohenstaufen Emperors*, 1973.

A. Haverkamp, *Medieval Germany, 1056–1273*, 1988.

HENRY V (1387–1422), king of England from 1413 to 1422. He was born in Monmouth, Wales. His father, Henry of Bolingbroke, of the House of Lancaster, seized the English throne in a coup in 1399, becoming King Henry IV.

As royal prince, Henry took command of the successful campaign to put down the rebellion of Owen Glendower in Wales. Victory came with the capture of Aberystwyth in 1407 and Harlech in 1408. Relations with his father were strained by Henry's demand for a larger role in government but a reconciliation was effected before Henry IV's death in 1413.

Upon assuming the kingship Henry V turned his back on the wildness of his youth and devoted his energies to the strengthening of his kingdom. Two uprisings were easily put down and he could turn his full attention to recovering lands held by his ancestors in France and to extending his dominion further. War also provided a distraction for the nobility from domestic quarrels.

His first expedition to France in 1415 almost ended in disaster. His army succeeded in capturing the port of Harfleur but was decimated by an outbreak of dysentery. Henry took his depleted forces to Agincourt in the direction of Calais, and where a pursuing French army of some forty thousand caught up with his force of six thousand. Henry's men were positioned in a way that forced the French to approach along a narrow front. He inspired his soldiers to make a courageous stand and the English archers, skilled in the use of the longbow, wrought havoc in the French ranks. It was a famous victory in the Hundred Years' War and helped establish England as a major European power.

Henry returned to France in 1417 and, exploiting deep divisions in the enemy camp, captured Normandy and forced the French to accept him as the legitimate heir to the French throne and to agree to his marriage with Catherine of Valois, daughter of the mentally ill French king, Charles VI. The Treaty of Troyes was a triumph for Henry the soldier king, but it was gained at the cost of neglecting the government of England, which Henry failed to place firmly under his control.

The treaty with France might have afforded Henry more time to enjoy other pursuits. He was fond of hunting but was also a musician of talent and loved to have minstrels accompany him on his expeditions. He was also literate, an advantage over his predecessors, favoring tales of chivalry. After the conclusion of the Treaty of Troyes, however, rather than grant himself a respite from war, he continued his pursuit of military glory. He did not live to enjoy the fruits of victory as his health had been weakened on the battlefield and he died of fever, still at war with France.

C. Allmand, *Henry V*, 1992.

E. F. Jacob, *Henry V and the Invasion of France*, 1963.

D. Seward, *Henry V as Warlord*, 1987.

HENRY VII (1457–1509), king of England 1485–1509, founder of the Tudor dynasty. Henry Tudor was born in Pembroke, Wales; through the House of Lancaster he had an ancestral claim to the English throne, although not as strong as that of other contenders. His mother, Margaret Beaufort, was only thirteen when he was born; his father, Edmund Tudor, had died a few months earlier and the boy was raised by his uncle, the Earl of Pembroke. In 1471, the forces of the House of York brought Edward IV to the throne and Henry took refuge in Britanny. The murder of Henry VI and the death of his son in battle left Henry the leading Lancastrian claimant to the throne.

Edward IV's death in 1483 prompted a seizure of power by his brother, Richard III. The Yorkist party was divided and this gave Henry his opportunity. Landing on the coast of Wales with a small force of mercenaries he marched north and took his army across Wales, defeating Richard's superior forces at the battle of Bosworth. It was a ferocious battle and Richard fought his way to within yards of Henry before he was killed.

Henry married Richard's niece, Elizabeth of York, in accordance with an oath he had made at Rennes Cathedral. This was a strategic alliance that grew into a marriage of deep affection. It also succeeded in ending the War of the Roses, symbolized by the red and white Tudor rose combining the signs of Lancaster and York.

Almost to the end of his reign, Henry was rightfully fearful of coups. One of the best known of these was led by Lambert Simnel, who pretended to be Richard, son of Edward IV. Simnel, a baker's son taught by a priest to impersonate the royal duke, was crowned King Edward VI in Ireland. Henry took mercy upon him after his defeat and found him work in the royal kitchen, appropriate to his background.

The tomb of Henry VII and his wife

A man of religious feelings, Henery was keen to limit bloodshed through mercy to domestic opponents and peaceful policies in Europe. Convenient marital alliances with the French and Scottish royal families also strengthened his position but his last years were embittered by the early death of his eldest son, Arthur, and shortly afterward, of his wife. Heavy taxation caused discontent among the nobles but his dynasty was by this time firmly established and the foundation was laid for a century of relative stability and prosperity in England.

S. B. Chrimes, *Henry VII*, 1972.

J. Ridley, *The Tudor Age*, 1988.

R. L. Storey, *The Reign of Henry VII*, 1968.

HENRY VIII (Henry Tudor; 1491–1547), king of England from 1509. Henry was the second son of King *Henry VII and Queen Elizabeth of York. His father disliked him, and although he granted Henry many impressive titles, denied him any power. Prince Henry was left to wile away his days in sport while his elder brother, Arthur, was groomed for the throne. The death of Arthur in 1502 placed Henry first in line for the succession, and he became king following his father's death in March 1509.

Educated under the direction of the poet John Skelton, Henry had acquired fluency in Latin and French and an excellent grounding in court etiquette. He enjoyed the company of leading intellectuals, including Thomas *More and Desidarius *Erasmus, and delighted in music; composing a number of impressive musical pieces.

A POEM WRITTEN BY HENRY VIII

As holly groweth green,
And never changeth hue,
So I am, ever hath been
Unto my lady true;
As the holly groweth green
With ivy all alone,
When flowers cannot be seen
And green wood leaves be gone,
Now unto my lady,
Promise to her I make,
From all others only
To her I me betake.
Adieu, mine own lady,
Adieu, my special,
Who hath my heart truly,
Be sure — and ever shall.

Henry developed into a fine sportsman and hunter. Six feet four inches high and with fine features, he represented the ideal of the young Renaissance prince. One visitor from abroad wrote of him: "His majesty is the handsomest potentate I have ever set eyes on — above the usual height, with a fine calf to his leg, his complexion very fair and light, with auburn hair, and a round face so beautiful it would become a pretty woman."

Henry's accession was welcomed among the cultural elite, and the ordinary people were pleased that one of his first acts was to order the execution of two of his father's leading ministers, Dudley and Empson, who had been associated with the high taxation of Henry VII's reign. Henry VIII also won popularity with the success of his armies against the French and the Scots, traditional enemies whose defeat the English relished.

Despite inexperience in government, the young monarch displayed from the first a shrewdness and ruthlessness in the exercise of power that was to mark his reign. The daily routine of correspondence and government meetings held little interest for him, but the ultimate authority remained firmly in his hands, albeit exercised through ministers — if all went well he could take the credit and in the event of disaster there were suitable scapegoats.

Henry benefited from the services of a succession of statesmen of competence and international prominence, including Archbishop Thomas *Wolsey, Thomas *More, and Thomas *Cromwell. He utilized their political skills as long as he believed they served his interests. As soon as they were suspected of plotting against him or not working zealously enough to promote his cause (and the distinction he drew was a fine one), he had no scruples about parting them first from their high offices and eventually from their heads.

Henry's appearance had the color and fashionable glamor that demonstrated to all who saw him the English king's wealth and power. In 1515, for example, the Venetian ambassador was impressed by Henry's gold collar with a diamond the size of a walnut. King Henry's famous meeting with the king of France *Francis I, at the Field of the Cloth of Gold in 1520 was a stunning display of royal grandeur — huge palaces of stone, brick, and wood rapidly constructed and their walls lined with expensive gold cloth, a lavishly decorated chapel, and a store of three thousand barrels of the best wine. Henry himself excelled in the jousting tournament and chivalrously let the French king's shield be given the place of honor.

Acting on the request of his father, on becoming king in 1509 Henry married Catherine of Aragon, the wife of his deceased brother Arthur. It was an alliance with great strategic advantages, linking England with countries that could form a front against the traditional enemy, France. Moreover, Henry for years loved Catherine, calling himself "Sir Loyal Heart." When she bore him a son in 1511, he was ecstatic and the city of London celebrated with pageants and bonfires. The child, however, lived only seven weeks; from a succession of pregnancies, Catherine's sole child to survive was a girl, the future Queen *Mary. Henry found comfort with his mistress, Elizabeth Blount, one of Catherine's ladies-in-waiting. She bore him a son in 1519 and he was named Henry Fitzroy. Later his father made him Duke of Richmond and considered making him his legitimate heir, but Fitzroy died at seventeen.

Henry VIII by Hans Holbein

In the mid-1520s Henry fell in love with Anne Boleyn, a woman of noble birth but no great beauty. There was one obstacle to the king's passion — Anne's refusal to be his mistress. His marriage with Catherine had to be dissolved and Henry decided the pope must be persuaded (or threatened) into taking the necessary steps. A the time, Henry was in papal favor for his fierce attack on the Lutheran heresy in a book he had written in 1521. As a token of esteem he had been awarded the title "Defender of the Faith," still today proudly displayed by English sovereigns in their formal title. Nevertheless, granting Henry's request was not such a simple matter, for his queen was not only related to the Spanish royal family but was a relative of the powerful Holy Roman emperor, who represented the secular power of the Catholic church in Europe.

Henry enlisted the help of leading theologians, including *Wolsey and Thomas *Cranmer. He hoped to prove that the marriage was invalid due to the relationship between his wife and his brother; the judicious use of bribes won him considerable support. In the background there remained the threat of making a break from the church of Rome since the exercise of papal power had long been viewed as impinging on English sovereignty and the corruption of the church in England had brought it into disrepute.

The divorce case against Queen Catherine continued for seven years but during that time Henry prevailed upon Anne to become his mistress, separating from Catherine in 1531. In 1533 Anne was pregnant; should this be the long-awaited male heir, their marriage had to be speedily legitimized. The two were secretly married and the break with Rome put into effect. A separate English church was established, with Cranmer as archbishop of Canterbury and Henry as supreme head. At last Henry got his divorce and Anne Boleyn was declared his legitimate wife. The child, however, was a girl, the future Queen *Elizabeth I.

Henry remained concerned for the succession and when he met Jane Seymour in 1535, Anne became an obstacle. She was arrested and charged with adultery; while she awaited her fate in the Tower of London, Henry enjoyed himself at a succession of lively parties. Archbishop Cranmer granted him a divorce and Anne was executed. His marriage to Jane Seymour at last produced a son who survived infancy, the future King Edward VI, but his mother died soon after the birth. Anne of Cleves, Katherine Howard, and Katherine Parr became in succession his last three wives. The first he married for state reasons but never cared for, the second he had beheaded for adultery, and the last outlived him. The break with papal authority opened up to Henry an attractive way of augmenting his power base by dissolving the monasteries, at the time among the major landowners in England and unpopular for the rapacious manner in which they had dealt with their tenants and the immoral behavior imputed to the monks. Dissolution gave Henry access to huge funds and to lands he could apportion out to the nobility and squires. Religious conviction does not seem to have been the major factor; he successively switched his favor between the Catholic and Protestant camps and persecuted both ruthlessly to his own advantage.

In Henry's last years he could no longer walk or even lift his huge frame, which overeating had burdened with a fifty-four-inch waistline. Although physical powers failed him, he retained his grip on government as well as a good measure of popularity.

Among the achievements of Henry's reign were the Protestantization of his realm, accomplished without widespread violence, the upgrading of parliamentary rule, and the building up of the English navy, which was to play such a crucial role in the reign of his daughter, Queen Elizabeth I.

J. Bowle, *Henry VIII*, 1964.
H. Miller, *Henry VIII and The English Nobility*, 1986.
J. Ridley, *Henry VIII*, 1984.

HENRY IV (Henry of Navarre; 1553–1610), king of Navarre from 1572 and king of France from 1589. The son of Antoine de Bourbon and Jeanne d'Albret, queen of Navarre, he was brought up by his mother as a Protestant and at the age of sixteen took part in the Wars of Religion (a series of civil wars in France with foreign intervention) on the Huguenot side. Becoming king of Navarre when his mother died in 1572, he married Marguerite de Valois, the daughter of *Catherine de Médicis and sister of the king of France, Charles IX. The arrival of many Huguenots to Paris to celebrate the marriage led, a week later, to the Saint Bartholomew massacre (August 23–24), in which Henry himself was forced to convert to Roman Catholicism to save his life. In 1576, however, he regained his freedom and rejoined the Protestants, establishing himself at their head. In 1584 the death of the duke of Anjou, brother of Henry III, made Henry of Navarre the heir-presumptive to the crown of France. However, his claim was rejected by the Holy League, the organization of the Roman Catholic party in France formed to combat the Huguenots, and headed by Henry, duke of Guise. In 1580 the seventh War of Religion, known as the Lovers' War, opened with the slaughter of Catholics in Cahors, a town claimed by Henry of Navarre as part of the dowry of his wife. Although Henry of Navarre defeated the royal army at Coutras during the eighth war, the so-called War of the Three Henrys (1585–1587), his prospects of acceding to the throne were as slim as ever. But in 1588 Henry III broke with the Holy League, and finding himself without support against a popular insurrection of militant Roman Catholics in Paris, the king fled to Henry of Navarre's camp and the following year, before he was murdered, the king pronounced Henry his legitimate heir. However, the Holy League, aided by *Philip II of Spain, continued to oppose the new king, and it was not until 1593 that Henry, realizing that he could not remain a Protestant and rule a predominantly Roman Catholic nation, decided to convert, declaring that "Paris is well worth a Mass." In 1594 he was crowned at Chartres and took possession of the capital; in 1596 the opposition of the League came to an end.

Among his domestic policies Henry's most important measure was the Edict of Nantes (1598), which put an end to the Wars of Religion and settled the status of the Protestants, according them religious freedom with certain limitations (freedom of worship with the exception of Paris) and laid the foundation for religious coexistence in France.

During his reign much was done to heal the wounds of the previous fifty years, with the help of well-chosen counselors. In particular, his finance minister Maximilien de Béthune, duke of Sully, did much to rehabilitate France's economy. However, his new tax, the Paulette, made French officeholders into a closed caste: In return for an annual tax, offices were made hereditary and could be passed on or sold at will. The judicial machinery was brought under control, the financial basis of the monarchy reformed, and agriculture and industry were encouraged; the silk industry was introduced, and the manufacture of cloth, glassware, and tapestries encouraged. The army was also reorganized and strongholds were fortified. French architects began to adorn Paris with splendid monuments and palaces (the Tuileries, Place Royale, Pont Neuf, the Hôtel de Ville). France's system of canals dates from this reign.

In foreign policy, Henry terminated the conflict with Spain (1598) and maintained generally friendly relations with England, the Italian states, the United Provinces of Holland, and the Ottoman empire. Henry was instrumental in the truce between Spain and the Netherlands (1609). He believed that the peace of Europe was threatened by the ambition of the Habsburgs, declaring that the greatness of the Habsburg Empire meant the ruin of peace in Europe.

Henry was known for his easygoing manners and his many love affairs. The most famous was with Gabrielle d'Estrées, who wielded a strong influence over the king, made him adopt Catholicism, and bore him three children; and with Henriette de Balzac d'Entragues, whose three children he legitimized. He is remembered as Henry the Great for his political achievements and for his concern for the poor, wishing that every laborer have a *poule au pot* (a chicken in his pot) on Sunday. By his second wife, Marie de *Médicis, whom he married in 1600, he had six children.

Henry IV was assassinated in Paris by François Ravaillac, a Catholic fanatic, thus ending his plan to mobilize an international military coalition against Spain and Austria, and his intention of forming a European confederation.

D. Buisserat, *Henry IV*, 1984.
H. D. Sedgwick, *Henry of Navarre*, 1930.

HENRY THE NAVIGATOR (1394–1460), Portuguese prince. The architect of his country's naval explorations. The third of the five sons of King John the Great of Portugal and his wife, the English Princess Philippa of Lancaster, Henry was born into a Portugal that was still a small, underpopulated, medieval kingdom of landbound peasants. By the time of his death, it had become a powerful seafaring nation, well on its way to acquiring an empire that would span half the world. Henry's life changed with Portugal's capture of the great Moroccan trading city of Ceuta, the first European base in Africa. Henry now came into contact with Africa and people with knowledge of the old African caravan routes. As governor of Ceuta, a position he held until his death, he wanted to find out more about Africa, especially its Atlantic coast. Turning down the offers for his military services pouring in from the kings of Europe, he withdrew from court and settled on the barren, sea-swept headland of Sagres on Portugal's southern Atlantic coast.

From there, Henry launched a systematic and continuous campaign of exploration. He had been appointed grand master of the Order of Christ (a position that demanded a vow of chastity), and as such he sent out exploratory ships from Sagres, paying for them from the order's funds and his own. Expeditions were instructed to reach further south, and Henry would generously reward success.

Henry surrounded himself with cosmographers, astronomers, and physicians and immersed himself in study. He coordinated the expeditions and mapped their results, developing the charts and navigational skills that would eventually enable Europeans to sail over all the world. Scientific curiosity was not the only reason he sent out his ships; he was also motivated by his strong religious beliefs. The desire to search out the heathen and convert them, and the search for allies in Portugal's long fight against the Moors were also strong motivations. Henry sought the legendary Prester John, a Christian king to the south, hoping to join forces with him, encircle the Muslims, and crush them.

The first expeditions were almost paralyzed by superstitious fear of the Atlantic, where monsters were supposed to dwell, seas boiled, and the thundering rush of water carried ships over the world's edge into darkness. Even the Arabs knew very little about Africa's Atlantic coast and accepted that the world ended off the Cape of Bojador (south of the Canary Islands), where the sun was so hot that people were burned black and killed. The first voyage began to dispel these superstitions when a ship was swept out into the Atlantic and discovered the Madeira Islands. Many ships ignored Henry's order to explore, preferring the known and more profitable dangers involved in raiding the Moors. Still, the Azores were discovered thirteen years later and the African coast was slowly revealed. It took just seventeen years of voyages before the dreaded Cape Bojador was rounded.

The early voyages were sailed in the tiny-oared vessels used for coastal sailing in the placid Mediterranean; they were unsuited for sailing in the open Atlantic, with its strong winds and currents. Soon the caravel was developed which, with its shallow bottom, maneuverability, and ability to tack against the wind, could sail the Atlantic, explore coasts and rivers of unknown depths, be manned by a minimal crew if disaster struck, and be easily beached for necessary repairs. It was in caravels that the great exploratory voyages discovered America, rounded Africa, reached the Indies, sailed around the world, and established the first colonies.

King John died in 1433 and was succeeded by Henry's oldest brother, Edward. Henry now pressed for an attack on Tangier to strike a blow at the Muslims and allow his younger brother Fernando to win his knightly spurs; the attack was a disastrous failure in which many died, and Fernando was captured and held hostage for the rest of his life. Henry held himself responsible and secluded himself, mourning, in Sagres; Edward died a year later.

In 1441 the first black slaves were brought to Europe and revolutionized Portugal's view of Henry's explorations. For twenty years he had been generally considered a fanatical monomaniac wasting time, lives, and money. Now the profitable uses for slaves in underpopulated Portugal were immediately obvious. Slavery was not considered immoral but a way to convert heathens into Christians. Private expeditions were sent out and made fortunes with the slaves, gold, and other goods they brought back. Ships began to explore new territories willingly, not just for Henry's rewards, and the pope eagerly granted Henry's request that all new territory beyond Cape Bojador would belong to Portugal. Henry objected to the slavers' violent methods since they hindered his desire to establish peaceful trading relations with Africa, so he established a series of forts along the African coast to regulate and protect trade.

Henry left Sagres in 1449 and unsuccessfully tried to make peace between the new king, Afonso V, and his uncle Don Pedro. When Pedro was killed, Henry returned to Sagres, brotherless and sickened by the world's corruption. In 1458 he led Portugal's successful battle against the city of Alcazar, finally avenging the defeat of Tangier and boosting the morale of a Europe reeling from the shock of the Turkish capture of Constantinople. He died, deeply in debt from the cost of his voyages, in a Portugal enriched by his discoveries. He had initiated the era of exploration although — despite his sobriquet — he himself never sailed further than across the Straits of Gibraltar.

E. D. S. Bradford, *A Wind from the North: The Life of Henry the Navigator*, 1960.
R. H. Major, *The Life of Henry Prince of Portugal, Surnamed the Navigator*, 1967.
E. Sancean, *Henry the Navigator*, 1947.

HERACLIUS (c.575–641), Byzantine emperor. Heraclius was born into an empire of contrasts: between great wealth and dire poverty, between religious piety and brutal corruption. Invasion was responded to by refusing to serve in the military. A centurion, Phocas, had butchered the Emperor Maurice and his entire family in 602, and subsequently led the empire to defeat in every battle he fought against the Persians. Constantinople's aristocracy pleaded with the governor of Africa to come to their aid and save the empire. He sent his son, Heraclius, in his stead.

Heraclius faced tremendous problems after overthrowing Phocas and being crowned emperor in 610. The bureaucracy that had run the empire more or less efficiently for hundreds of years had disintegrated; the treasury was empty and the trade that had once flowed through Constantinople had been disrupted by war and revolution. Repeated defeats had devastated the army's personnel and morale, and the empire's citizens had become unsettled by religious persecutions, high taxes, and fear.

Heraclius's administrative reforms departmentalized the bureaucracy, made Greek rather than Latin the empire's official language, and initiated the military district system, which placed provinces under the rule of military governors and gave land to peasants in return for military service, and to soldiers in lieu of pay. It eventually led to the revival of agriculture and the replacement of unreliable mercenary forces with peasant soldiers. Heraclius's attempt to unify his empire by resolving religious conflict was less successful; his doctrine of monothelitism — that Jesus had one will but two natures — was not accepted.

After the conquest of Syria, Palestine, Egypt, Libya, and Asia Minor by Khosrow II, all that was left of the Byzantine Empire was a fragment of southern Europe and Africa, a few ports in Asia, its navy, and a besieged Constantinople that was left desperate and hungry by the loss of Egyptian grain. The patriarch of Constantinople agreed to lend Heraclius money (at interest) to finance the recapture of Jerusalem, and in 622 Heraclius made peace with the Avars and declared war against the Persians. He set out with his army from Constantinople dressed as a penitent, carrying a sacred image of the Virgin Mary and accompanied by psalm singers. A brilliant military tactician who personally led his men into battle, Heraclius succeeded in pushing the Persians out of Anatolia before attacking Persia through Armenia. The Persians advanced to the Bosphorus, where they planned a joint attack on Constantinople with the Avars, but Heraclius forestalled them by sinking the Avar fleet. He attacked Persia again in 627, and Khosrow fled in the face of the defeat of one Persian army after another. He was deposed, imprisoned, and put to death by his son in 628.

The unusual mercy that Heraclius had shown to the areas he conquered by not enslaving or massacring the population or prisoners of war helped him to make peace quickly with Khosrow's son. He asked only for the return of the True Cross which had been stolen from Jerusalem, and the people and lands Khosrow had captured. Heraclius personally restored the Cross to Jerusalem and returned to Constantinople in triumph.

Heraclius was old and ill when Arabs poured out of Arabia, unified and inflamed by the new religion of Islam. Persia and the Byzantine Empire were defenseless before them, having fought themselves into mutual exhaustion and ruin. The Arabs defeated Heraclius's army (which Heraclius was too sick to lead personally) in 636, captured Jerusalem in 638, and Egypt in 641. However, the Byzantine Empire did not fall, but continued to hold out against the Muslims until 1453, and much of the credit for its ability to do so belongs to Heraclius's administrative and military reforms.

E. Franzius, *History of the Byzantine Empire*, 1967.
G. Ostrogorsky, *History of the Byzantine State*, 1968.

HERODOTUS (c.484 – c.430 B.C.E.), historian known as "the father of history." He was born to a well-to-do family in Halicarnassus, a Greek city in Asia Minor under Persian rule. His family was involved in the political struggle against the tyrant Lygdamis and Herodotus left for Samos, the first station in his extensive travels throughout his life. In his wanderings he visited Egypt and Cyrene, Palestine, Phoenicia and Babylonia, the north Aegean region, the Black Sea, Scythia, and many other Greek places in the Mediterranean area. He undertook these travels expressly to get information for his work; some perhaps for commercial purposes as well. He stayed a long time in Athens, where he composed and read parts of his work to audiences, taking ten talents for a lecture. Herodotus's work is a pioneer of historiography, the first secular narrative history; its subject is the wars between the Greeks and the Persians and their causes. The work was later divided into nine books, each named after one of the Muses. They cover the Greco-Persian wars from 500 to 479 B.C.E. and give an account of the chain of events that led to the invasion of Greece by the Persians, of the Persian conquests, and a survey of the Persian Empire and its peoples. The work contains digressions inserted by Herodotus to explain the main events or to talk about customs or episodes which are of human or historical interest.

Herodotus's work is also the first large and, on the whole, well-planned prose work in Greek; he was the first European to use prose as the medium of a work of art, collecting much material and preparing drafts of the work before he wrote it in its final form. It was an *historia*, that is, an inquiry or research. Geography, ethnography, and religion were for him part of his historical subject. Herodotus presented what he heard, saw, read, and inquired into. His literary sources included poets, travelers, and logographers (the predecessors of Herodotus who wrote prose works with some historical content). Nevertheless, his critical methods were poor; he was prepared to recount a good story and let his reader decide on its reliability rather than drop it. But modern scholarship based on archeological finds and documentary evidence not known to him more often than not corroborate his accounts of Egypt and Babylon. As a

- Men trust their ears less than their eyes.
- How much better it is to be envied than to be pitied.
- Chances rule men and not men, chances.
- Neither could snow nor rain nor heat nor gloom of nights stop these couriers from the swift completion of their appointed rounds (inscribed on the General Post Office, New York).
- One tyrant helps another tyrant.

From the writings of Herodotus

Herodotus invites us to walk by his side, to listen to his voice, to mark on his face the shifts of expression from grave to joyous, from wonder, awe and admiration to incredulity or amusement; it gives us the man himself as he lived among men, noting with unappeasable zest their infinite variety and strangeness, not without a lift of the eyebrow at their odd ways and occasional propensity for telling lies.

Aubrey de Selincourt

historian, he compared one source of information with another if this was possible. However, his interest was in writing the story of what had happened; analyses of politics and strategy were beyond him. This search for the true story was executed with remarkable success. Though a Greek, he wrote with impartiality about the Persians and showed no sign of racial prejudice. His explanations for what happened took account of fate, chance, and divine intervention.

Few historians have equaled Herodotus as writers. He wrote an attractive history with fascinating character portrayals, dramatic passages, and moments of insight into the deep forces of human life. His work was well enough known in Athens by 425 B.C.E. to be parodied by *Aristophanes.

Herodotus took part in the Athenian colonization of Thurii in southern Italy in 443 B.C.E. and probably remained there, completing his history.

J. A. S. Evans, *Herodotus, Explorer of the Past*, 1991.
J. Gould, *Herodotus*, 1989.
D. Lateiner, *The Historical Method of Herodotus*, 1989.

HERSCHEL, SIR WILLIAM (1738–1822), English astronomer and telescope maker. His discovery of the planet Uranus in 1781 was the first such discovery since ancient times. Friedrich Wilhelm Herschel was born in Hanover, Prussia, to a talented musician who taught his children several instruments. Herschel left school at age fourteen to help support his family by playing alongside his father in the Hanoverian Guards Marching Band.

In 1756 he arrived in England as part of a goodwill tour by the band. When war broke out between Prussia and France, Wilhelm decided to return to England, where his first job was as a music copier. Within two years he was fluent in English and had anglicized his name to William. In 1760 he accepted an invitation to travel to Yorkshire as an instructor for a military band, by which time he had become thoroughly English. He composed for the band, performing in many stately homes and making a name for himself even within royal circles.

He traveled frequently, but always managed to take with him a small telescope for observing the stars, a hobby that quickly grew into an obsession. His first observations were with a small refracting telescope, but this was limited in its usefulness. He experimented by mounting lenses in tubes up to twenty feet long, but found them much too unsteady and cumbersome for practical observation. Then he happened upon a small reflector telescope and found its compactness so appealing he set about designing a model of his own. When he tried to purchase the mirrors he needed to construct the telescope he found the price of having a mirror custom-ground prohibitive and concluded he would have to make his own.

Herschel bought a set of optical tools from a retiring polisher in Bath and set about learning the craft of mirror-making. His brothers, sisters, and even music pupils were put to work making larger telescopes. In 1775 he completed a seven-foot reflector with an aperture of 6.2 inches, which was to remain his favorite. The following year he completed a twenty-foot version that he mounted in his garden. In the midst of all this he was offered a post of director of the Bath Orchestra, which he accepted, as he still needed to support his tinkering.

He would often set up his seven-footer outside his home. On one such occasion a passerby by the name of Dr. William Watson introduced himself and inquired what he was doing. The two became close friends, and Watson, a member of the Royal Society, introduced Herschel to the scientific community. However, it was not until 1781 that he won international acclaim. While observing the sky, his sister taking notes, he noticed an object that did not resemble an ordinary star. Subsequent study suggested it was a planet. He communicated his findings to Watson, who immediately notified the Greenwich observatory. Astronomers and mathematicians in Europe were quickly searching the heavens for this new observation, calculating its orbit, becoming increasingly convinced that it was indeed a new planet beyond the six known and observable to the naked eye. It was the most sensational discovery since *Galileo had invented the telescope.

Herschel named the planet Georgium Sidus in honor of the English monarch but Europeans, who objected to this colonization of a planet, renamed it Uranus in keeping with the mythological motif of the solar system.

Herschel was now a celebrity. He was made a Fellow of the Royal Society, yet still earned his living from music. Finally, in 1782 he became a fully dedicated astronomer, accepting a stipend from the king and moving closer to Windsor Castle, where the king could visit him occasionally. Orders began pouring in for telescopes from around Europe. Herschel was still planning the construction of the largest telescope ever conceived and eventually in 1790, after much experimentation, the mammoth forty-foot telescope was completed. On his first gaze through its eyepiece he discovered two new moons of Saturn.

In 1792 Herschel's son John was born and went on to assume a place alongside his father in astronomy. Herschel continued to catalogue stars and identified nebulae for the first time. His theories of the origins of stars paved the way for modern astrophysics.

In 1816 Herschel was knighted, and when the Royal Astronomical Society was formed in 1820, he was persuaded to become its first president, although by that time he was in poor health. That same year he made his last telescope with his son, with which John later mapped the skies of the southern hemisphere.

Sir John Herschel reexamined his father's catalogues of nebulae and clusters, adding another 525 as well as several thousand more double stars. An important chemist, who made discoveries in photography (he coined the terms "positive image" and "negative image"), he also translated part of the *Iliad* into English. William's sister, Caroline Lucretia, also made an independent name for herself as an astronomer, publishing a star catalogue and discovering eight comets and three nebulae.

A. Armitage, *William Herschel*, 1962.

M. A. Hoskin, *William Herschel and the Construction of the Heavens*, 1963.

J. B. Sidgwick, *William Herschel: Explorer of the Heavens*, 1955.

HERTZ, HEINRICH RUDOLPH (1857–1894),
German physicist whose experimental work provided the first proof of the existence of electromagnetic radiation. Hertz was born the son of a successful Hamburg lawyer and parliamentarian, and was raised as a devout Lutheran despite his father's Jewish origins. He excelled at school, exhibiting particular talent in language and natural sciences. By the time of his matriculation, Hertz was beset by uncertainty about a suitable career: his first intention was to study engineering, and in 1876 he enrolled in the Dresden Polytechnic. However, he soon realized that the regulated life of an engineer did not suit his temperament, and after consulting with his father decided to go into academic research.

After completing a year of mandatory military service in 1877, Hertz entered the University of Munich to study applied mathematics. The following year he moved to Berlin, which at the time was a major center of physics research. Although only in his second year of study, his individual research and dedication quickly drew the attention of Hermann von Helmholtz, the noted professor of physics in Berlin. Helmholtz was to fill the role of his mentor and, later, close friend.

Hertz began his doctoral dissertation into electromagnetic induction at the end of 1879, completing it with distinction within just three months. His first salaried position was as Helmholtz's assistant at the Berlin Physical Institute, where he remained for the next three years, publishing diverse papers and building a sound reputation, particularly in the field of electricity.

Transferring to Kiel as a *privatdozent* (lecturer) in 1883, Hertz was pleased to find his lectures popular, both for their content and for his manner of presentation. However, he was frustrated by the lack of a physics laboratory, and when Kiel offered him an associate professorship in 1885, he refused it, preferring to find a faculty that could offer him more than just theoretical experience.

That offer came from Karlsruhe, where he spent the following four years in research that was to make him famous. By the end of 1888 he had demonstrated the existence of finitely propagated electric waves of air and proven that electromagnetic radiation traveled at the speed of light. His work drew immediate acclaim worldwide. At the age of thirty-one Hertz found himself a much sought-after physicist. He could now select a chair that best suited his wish to extend his practical research, and accepted the physics professorship in Bonn.

Hertz began to amass an impressive array of awards and accolades. However, at about this time he began to suffer from a malignant facial bone condition. His first symptom was a mild toothache and by early 1889 he had had all his teeth pulled. He was forced to stop work for some time in 1892, due to the extreme pain he was enduring in his throat and nose. His doctors were baffled and unable to prevent further deterioration. Over the next few months, depressed as much by his forced retirement as by the disease, Hertz underwent several operations to no avail. He intermittently worked on a theoretical study of the principles of mechanics, which he managed to hand to the publishers in December, 1893, dedicating it to Helmholtz. On New Years Day 1894, Hertz died at thirty-six.

The unit of frequency was named "the hertz" to honor his work, though because of his Jewish background that name was dropped in Germany during Nazi rule, when his wife and two children were forced to emigrate to England in 1937 because of their Jewish origin.

N. H. Heathcote, *Nobel Prize Winners in Physics*, 1953.

HERZL, THEODOR (1860–1904), founder of political Zionism, journalist, and playwright. He was born in Budapest, son of a businessman. Although Herzl's paternal grandfather was a traditional Jew,

his father was an assimilated middle-class urban Jew with little interest in things Jewish.

Tutored at home when young, Herzl was an apt pupil. Generally isolated from playmates, his companion was his sister Pauline. His first school was a local Jewish one. But when he showed an intense interest in science, his parents transferred him to a science secondary school, where, however, he proved an indifferent student. Discovering a passion for literature, he moved to the Evangelical high school.

His sister, with whom he was very close, died suddenly shortly before his matriculation exams, and soon thereafter the family moved to Vienna. He studied law at the University of Vienna, receiving a doctorate, but he preferred to pursue his interest in literature.

Although Herzl dreamed of a career as a playwright — one of his plays was produced at Vienna's famed Burgtheater — he earned his livelihood as a journalist, working mainly for the prestigious *Neue Freie Presse* of Vienna. As a foreign correspondent he worked in Paris and was a leading feuilletonist — the highest paid in Europe.

In 1889 Herzl married the daughter of a wealthy Viennese businessman, but the union was strained. Never satisfied with their financial status and unable to get along with his mother, Herzl's wife came to believe that the Zionist movement had deprived her of a husband.

While covering the *Dreyfus affair in Paris in 1894-1895, Herzl came to the conclusion that despite assimilation Jew's would never gain full acceptance in society: Europe's Jews needed their own homeland. Initially he did not have a defined geographical area for that new home, but as his thinking evolved, he focused on the land of Israel, then a backwater state ruled by the Ottoman Empire.

At first unsuccessful in attracting the assimilated Jews of the Western Europe and unable to interest major Jewish philanthropists, Herzl eventually found an audience among Eastern European Jews and Jewish students in many parts of central Europe. When he published the *Jewish State* (1896). His proposals seemed utopian. Nonetheless, Jewish State went through some eighty editions in eighteen languages, and Herzl's call for a state for the Jews resulted in the formation of the Zionist movement.

The plan for achieving a state, as designed by Herzl, was to obtain a charter to Palestine from the Ottoman sultan and then to settle Jews there. Herzl made an unsuccessful attempt to meet with the sultan in 1896, and despite numerous further overtures, which finally resulted in a meeting, was unable to achieve tangible results.

The Zionist movement gained international recognition with the First Zionist Congress, convened in Basel in August 1897. Herzl used the symbols of statehood, including flags, medals, and music, to fire the imagination of Jews who had come from various part of Europe, including Russia, and from America. Herzl was elected president of the movement and held that position until his death.

- If you will it, it will not remain a dream.
- Zionism is the Jewish people on the march.
- All my testament to the Jewish people: Build your state so that the stranger will feel at ease among you.
- Diplomacy is the art of dealing with robbers.
- If we ever get to Jerusalem and I am still able to do anything actively at that time, I would begin by cleaning it up.
- Whoever would change men must change the conditions of their lives.
- Every creed of a man was once a dream.
- The wealth of a country is in its working people.

Theodor Herzl

Although he continued to work as a journalist, Herzl devoted himself body and soul to the Zionist movement, organizing yearly congresses, seeking audiences and support from influential political figures, and trying to keep peace among the various factions in the movement. In 1898 he journeyed to Palestine for an abortive meeting in Jerusalem with Kaiser *William II. In 1902 he published *Altneuland*, a utopian vision of the future Jewish state (which was envisaged as having a culture with much in common with that of Europe). He came to be adored by the Jewish masses, who saw him as a modern *Moses, despite some dissenting voices calling him a madman.

Herzl's physical constitution could not bear the pace demanded by his unceasing efforts on behalf of the Zionist movement; he suffered a fatal heart attack in 1904 and was buried in Vienna. In 1949 his remains were transferred to the state of Israel and reinterred in Jerusalem on Mount Herzl.

A. Bein, *Theodore Herzl*, 1940.
S. Beller, *Herzl*, 1991.
A. Elon, *Herzl*, 1975.
E. Pawel, *The Labyrinth of Exile*, 1989.

HIDALGO Y COSTILLA, MIGUEL (1753–1811), Mexican revolutionary priest in the war of independence. The son of a Creole estate manager, Hidalgo's studies for the priesthood at the Jesuit College de San Francisco Javier were disturbed by the proclamation of King Charles III of Spain banning the Jesuits from Mexico. He continued his clerical studies at the College of San Nicolás Obispo, but also found time to learn local Indian languages and read the proscribed revolutionary literature of France. After his ordination in 1778 Hidalgo served as rector of the college until a scandal over mismanagement of funds led to his resignation.

In his new position as curate of the village of San Felipe, Hidalgo came under the constant scrutiny of the Inquisition. Not only had he abandoned the spiritual welfare of his parishioners in favor of their physical well-being by encouraging forbidden agriculture and industry, but he was rumored to have abandoned important church dogma. In fact, he questioned the Virgin Birth and the authority of the pope, and took a mistress to flaunt his rejection of celibacy. His home was modeled after fashionable French salons, and a theater and orchestra were organized. Among his close friends was a liberal cavalry captain, Ignacio de Allende, with whom he organized a revolutionary society under the guise of a literary club. Together they established a newspaper, *El Despertador Americano*, and signed the first proclamation outlawing slavery in the New World.

Foremost on their minds were plans to overthrow the Spanish regime and declare Mexico's independence. A coup was planned for December 8, 1810, but by September news had leaked out, and the Spanish army came to arrest the conspirators. When, on September 16, Hidalgo and Allende discovered that they were about to be arrested, they decided to act immediately. Hidalgo ran to the church and rang its bell, summoning his parishioners to what they assumed was mass. Instead, he exhorted them to revolt.

The content of this speech, known as the *Grito del Dolores*, is still debated. It is unlikely that he called for "independence," as that term would have been incomprehensible to the peasant masses. He did call for a defensive war against the Spanish, ending with, "Long live Ferdinand VII [the Spanish king imprisoned by *Napoleon]! Long live America! Long live the Catholic religion! Death to bad government!" The crowds cheered wildly.

Adopting the Virgin of Guadalupe, a humbly dressed Indian icon, as his standard, Hidalgo attracted a growing mob of peasants. The entire local militia of San Miguel joined the rebels in their assault on the provincial capital of Guanajuato. Hidalgo was a firm believer in the power of the masses and rejected Allende's warnings that such a mob, now numbering almost one hundred thousand men, could not be controlled without strict discipline. Allende was right; all towns on the road to Guanajuato were pillaged. While Hidalgo was convinced of his oratorical skills in controlling the frenzied masses, stories of atrocities reaching Guanajuato strengthened the locals' resolve to defend their city. Spanish troops fortified themselves in the government granary, but were no match for the waves of angry peasants. Even Hidalgo was forced to fire on his supporters to restore order.

Hidalgo reached Mexico City on November 1, 1810. Allende encouraged him to invade the city but Hidalgo realized that the revolutionary fervor of his supporters had waned. After several days' hesitation, he turned north to Morelia (present-day Guadalajara), chased by Spanish troops. His retreat was fatal. To Allende it seemed that Hidalgo's bloated ego bordered on insanity. As the self-proclaimed "Captain General of America," he insisted upon being addressed as "Serene Highness." Finally, Hidalgo was removed from his command and installed as a figurehead.

In January 1811, the Spanish caught the rebels en route to the United States. The ensuing Battle of Calderón was a disaster for Hidalgo. Again, he had rejected Allende's advice and ordered all his men into battle. The rebels were routed and Allende and Hidalgo captured. Allende was executed immediately and Hidalgo was taken in chains to Chihuahua to face the Inquisition. Although he recanted, he was defrocked and sentenced to death by firing squad. His decapitated head was placed in a cage and suspended from the Guanajuato granary as a warning to all future insurgents. It remained there until 1821.

Today, Hidalgo is considered the "Father of Mexico." September 16, the anniversary of the *Grito del Dolores*, is the principal national holiday of Mexico, celebrating the achievements of a man who died ten years before independence.

H. Hamill, *The Hidalgo Revolt: Prelude to Mexican Independence*, 1966.

M. Lieberman, *Hidalgo, Mexican Revolutionary*, 1970.

HIMMLER, HEINRICH (1900 – 1945), Nazi leader; head of the Schutzstaffel ("Protection Squad" or SS) and of the Gestapo; next to Adolf *Hitler, the most powerful man in the Nazi hierarchy. Himmler was the son of Gebhard Himmler, a Munich schoolteacher, who spent many long evenings sharing Germany's heroic past with his children. One prominent figure in these stories was Gebhard's own father, a mercenary; another was Henry I, the Saxon founder of the First Reich, with whom young Heinrich felt a special affinity, at one point believing himself to be Heinrich's reincarnation. Nothing further was known about Himmler's family origins, a fact that plagued him throughout his life; he feared the validity of rumors that his family was not of pure Aryan stock, and hired a full-time researcher to refute these claims. Himmler was a mediocre student, often overshadowed by his older brother, whom he followed into the army in the last year of World War I. He served as an ensign but was never at the front. With the defeat of Germany he enrolled at the Technical High School for Agriculture in Munich, where he was first introduced to plant and animal breeding.

Like many young Germans, Himmler responded to Germany's loss of the war by joining Ernst Röhm's rabidly nationalist organization, the Reichskriegsflagge ("State War Banner"). Himmler played a minor role in the abortive Munich Beer Hall Putsch of 1923, joining the Nazi party in 1925 and subsequently he served the Nazi leader Gregor Strasser, as secretary. Much of his time was spent collating articles for the party organ, *Der Völkischer Beobachter*, and in amassing information on party rivals, notably communists and Jews. In 1926 he was appointed deputy leader of the SS, then still a small and insignificant organization serving as Hitler's personal bodyguard.

A raise in salary and his marriage to a wealthy woman allowed him to invest in a small farm, where he bred chickens and grew herbs. At this time he befriended Alfred Rosenberg, the philosopher of the Nazi party, who encouraged him to turn his attention to breeding humans. In 1929 he submitted a plan to Hitler whereby the SS would become a breeding ground for racially pure Aryans. Hitler was enthralled and appointed Himmler Reichsführer (State leader) of the SS.

Himmler proceeded to transform the SS into a rival to the Nazi army, the SA. He coined the motto, "Race, Obedience, Sacrifice," and adopted the double lightning bolt symbol, an ancient Teutonic rune for *Sieg*, or victory. Much emphasis was placed on the physical appearance and ancestry of SS men. They and their wives had to be of pure German ancestry and committed to having at least four children. He sought to create an aristocracy of the Aryan master race, which would rule Europe for many centuries to come. Files were assembled on all possible party opponents, including Communists, Jews, Catholics, freemasons, and socialists. To assist him in the building up of the SS, Himmler enlisted Reinhard Heydrich as his lieutenant.

In 1930 Himmler entered the Reichstag (parliament). Although he was disappointed at not being given a post in Hitler's shadow cabinet, Heydrich persuaded Himmler to have Hitler appoint him police president of Munich. Once Hitler assumed power, Himmler set about constructing Dachau, his "school for good citizenship," in fact a concentration camp. Special SS troops, conspicuous by the death's head symbol they wore, were commissioned to run the camp. Another special SS unit was appointed as Hitler's bodyguard; membership required light blond hair and a minimum height of six feet. The impetus for the formation of this unit came after an assassination attempt on Hitler, in which Himmler received a bullet in his arm.

Despite his rivalry with police minister Hermann *Göring, Himmler advanced rapidly in the Nazi party. By 1934 he was chief of police for every province except Göring's own Prussia, in which he was soon appointed Gestapo chief. In the infamous Night of the Long Knives in 1934, Himmler oversaw the execution of Hitler's potential rivals, including Ernst Röhm, head of the SA (Sturmabteilung or Storm Troopers); the SS was now entrenched as the party's police force.

Himmler was among the most brutal advocates of racial purity and an originator of the 1935 anti-Semitic Nuremberg Laws. He despised Jews and Catholics, despite his own Catholic upbringing. His own newspaper, *Das Schwarze Korps*, was well-known for its rabid attacks on the Catholic clergy.

Himmler often received appointments to oversee the party's dirty work. In 1936 he became head of the German police and used his power to terrorize opponents — of the party and of himself. With *Goebbels, he organized the November 1938 anti-Jewish pogrom, and later planned the "reduction of Russia's population" by thirty million. He was responsible for the development and administration of the entire concentration and death camp system. However, he was personally squeamish and when he was taken to witness a mass shooting of Jews he almost fainted and replaced shooting with gassing as the method of killing. He supervised the organization of the deaths of millions of Jews which he considered as a national racial mission. Following Heydrich's assassination in 1942, Himmler organized the obliteration of the Czech village of Lidice, and he appointed Adolph Eichmann to administer the "final solution" of the Jewish problem (i.e., the extermination of the Jews). Always interested in quack science, he encouraged doctors to use concentration camp inmates in horrific pseudomedical experiments.

In 1943 Himmler convinced Hitler to appoint him interior minister and later, chief of the army's home organization, giving him virtual dictatorial powers over Germany. With defeat imminent in 1945, he attempted to negotiate a truce with the Western powers enabling him to pursue the war with the Soviet Union. Hitler was enraged by Himmler's betrayal; in his will he called for his expulsion from the Nazi party. The Allies' refusal to accept Himmler's terms led to his attempted escape, disguised as an ordinary soldier, and arrest. However, Himmler was never brought to trial; shortly after his capture, he swallowed a cyanide capsule he had hidden on his person.

R. Breitman, *The Architect of Genocide*, 1991.
W. Frischauer, *Himmler: The Evil Genius of the Third Reich*, 1953.
R. Manvell and H. Fraenkel, *Heinrich Himmler*, 1965.
P. Padfield, *Himmler*, 1988.

HINDENBURG, PAUL LUDWIG HANS ANTON VON BENECKENDORFF UND VON

(1847–1934), German general and president. He was born in Posen fortress, where his father was aide to the commander, and he entered the officer cadet corps and saw his first fighting in the war against Austria in 1866, during which he won the Order of the Red Eagle. In the Franco-Prussian War of 1870–1871 he was awarded the prestigious Iron Cross and was honored by his regiment with election as their representative at the proclamation of the German empire in Versailles.

Hindenburg was not noted for his brilliance but performed his duties with sufficient efficiency to ensure regular promotions that brought him to the rank of general. He retired in 1911, believing he had gone as far as he could go in the army and that with Europe at peace there was no reason for him to remain on active service at his age; rumors at the time suggested he was forced to retire after allowing the army corps commanded by Kaiser *William II to lose during maneuvers.

World War I rescued Hindenburg from obscurity; he was recalled from retirement and given command of German forces in East Prussia, which was under heavy pressure from a Russian offensive. Although as a general he had shown little initiative and imagination, he had a presence which won him admirers. Heavily built with a square-shaped head, he moved slowly, with a dignified bearing, and possessed the air of authority and superiority that Germans appreciated in their leaders.

Hindenburg and his chief of staff, General Erich von *Ludendorff, succeeded in reversing Germany's fortunes. Though men of completely different temperaments, their partnership was highly effective; within eighteen days of their taking command, the Germans inflicted a crushing defeat on the Russian invaders at Tannenburg.

Although the battle strategy was planned by his chief of staff, Hindenburg took final responsibility and pursued the attack until its victorious conclusion. He received full credit and overnight became a national hero. There were soon Hindenburg cigars, boots, and ties in the shops; dishes were named after him in leading restaurants. Correspondence addressed to "The Most Popular Man in Germany" reached him, old ladies sent him galoshes and young ones, pillows stuffed with their own hair. A battleship was named after him and statues of him were erected throughout Germany.

For all his popularity with the people, the kaiser never held Hindenburg in high regard, perhaps fearing a rival for popular affection, but was forced to concede to demands to give Hindenburg overall command of Germany's army since he was seen as the only general capable of initiating a German breakthrough on the western front. Victories over Rumania suggested that hopes of a German victory were justified but before long the situation again looked poor. Hindenburg was too easily swayed by those serving under him, especially Ludendorff, who persuaded him to support the policy of unrestricted submarine warfare that brought the United States into the war against Germany, and worked for Hindenburg's isolation, restricting access to him to those who believed in continuing the war at all costs. In any case Hindenburg was naturally inclined to side with military men and reject civilian calls for compromise.

Hindenburg pinned his hopes on a last offensive in 1918. After a promising start the attack collapsed and within three months Germany was suing for an armistice. The German Empire collapsed in the midst of civil unrest, the kaiser went into exile in Holland, and Hindenburg retired, avoiding involvement in the serious unrest of the Weimar Republic's first years. Soon the call went out from conservative sectors of society to bring Hindenburg back as a bulwark against the new democratic forces, and he was elected second president of the Weimar Republic.

For the duration of the 1920s, as the German economy boomed, Hindenburg carried out his duties with distinction. His very presence assuaged the fears of conservatives, yet he showed dedication to the Republic. In 1927 he was granted an estate in East Prussia as a measure of public esteem. However, the depression of the 1930s and the rise of the Nazis found him too weak to provide the firm leadership that might have saved his country. He became increasingly a prisoner of advisers, including his own son, Colonel Oskar von Hindenburg. He was persuaded to dismiss Dr. Heinrich Brüning, the legally elected chancellor (who had been instrumental in Hindenburg's re-election in 1932), and the new chancellor, Franz von Papen, eventually convinced him that giving Adolf *Hitler power was the only way to tame the worst excesses of the Nazis.

Hindenburg's last year was spent in seclusion on his East Prussian estate. Protected by secretary of state Dr. August Meissner and other members of his entourage, it seems that he never properly understood the evil of the regime he had helped place in power.
T. N. Dupuy, *The Military Lives of Hindenburg and Ludendorff*, 1970.
W. Maser, *Hindenburg*, 1989.
J. W. Wheeler-Bennett, *Hindenburg: The Wooden Titan*, 1967.

HIPPOCRATES (c.460–c.370 B.C.E.), the most famous physician of antiquity; founder of modern scientific medicine who became known as "the father of medicine." Very little is known with certainty about his life. He came from a family with a tradition of practicing medicine and was born in Cos, off the coast of Asia Minor. There, he founded a school of medicine at the famous temple of Asclepius, the god of healing and medicine. Traveling extensively, Hippocrates taught and practiced throughout Greece. He became so famous that he was consulted by kings — among them King Artaxerxes I of Persia — and his help was requested by the Athenians during a severe epidemic that struck the city-state in 430.

Hippocrates favored prognosis over diagnosis. A good physician, he believed, should learn through observation to foretell the course of a disease; after the initial manifestations of the malady appear, the physician should be able to predict its course. In most cases, he believed, there is a critical stage, the crisis, that indicates the forthcoming end — of the disease or of the patient. The almost mathematical calculation of the day of the crisis was a characteristic element of Hippocrates's theory. If, during the crisis, the natural heat of the body of the patient can overcome the pathological elements and reject them, recovery follows. Nature, that is the constitution of the patient, is always the main healing factor; the physician can only decrease or eradicate the obstacles opposing the natural defenses of the body. That is why Hippocrates did not make much use of drugs; instead, he prescribed fresh air, enemas, emetics, massages, bleeding, cupping, and hydrotherapy. He primarily prescribed a healthy way of life to prevent illness.

Of the extant collection of works related to medicine known as the Hippocratic Collection

HIPPOCRATIC OATH

I will look upon him who shall have taught me this Art even as one of my parents. I will share my substance with him, and I will supply his necessities, if he be in need. I will regard his offspring even as my own brethren, and I will teach them this Art, if they would learn it, without fee or covenant. I will impart this Art by precept, by lecture and by every mode of teaching, not only to my own sons but to the sons of him who has taught me, and to disciples bound by covenant and oath, according to the Law of Medicine.

The regimen I adopt shall be for the benefit of my patients according to my ability and my judgement, and not for their hurt or for any wrong. I will give no deadly drug to any, though it be asked of me, nor will I counsel such, and especially I will not aid a woman to procure abortion. Whatsoever house I enter, there will I go for the benefit of the sick, refraining from all wrongdoing or corruption, and especially from any act of seduction, of male or female, of bond or free. Whatsoever things I see or hear concerning the life of men, in my attendance on the sick or even apart therefrom, which ought not to be noised abroad, I will keep silence thereon, counting such things to be as sacred secrets.

(*Corpus Hippocraticus*), very few can be definitively attributed to Hippocrates. The works cover all fields of medicine: surgery, dietetics, pharmacology, prognostics, therapeutics, and ethics. Presumably they are, in part, remains of the medical literature of the fifth and fourth centuries B.C.E., including that of the Hippocratic school. Among the more important of these writings are the book on epidemics, which includes case studies; the treatise on epilepsy, in which the ailment is explained by natural causes rather than by demonic possession; and the *Aphorisms*, which were used as textbooks until the nineteenth century. Another work, *Airs, Waters, and Places*, can be considered today as a treatise on human ecology, as it stresses the effects of food, occupation, and climate in causing disease.

Hippocrates gained eternal fame as the ideal physician, in part because he ennobled the medical profession by emphasizing medical ethics. In taking the Hippocratic oath (ascribed to him almost certainly incorrectly), physicians down through the ages have sworn to maintain the ethics associated with him and his school.
O. Temkin, *Hippocrates in a World of Pagans and Christians*, 1991.

HIROHITO (1901–1989), Japanese emperor. Hirohito's family had been emperors in Japan since the seventh century B.C.E. However, from the twelfth century onward, Japan's real rulers had been the shoguns (warlords). Hirohito's grandfather, Emperor *Meiji, wrested power from the shoguns and, responding to Admiral Matthew *Perry's naval expedition of 1853, started modernizing his country and opened up to trade with the West. By the time Hirohito was born, Japan had abolished feudalism, established a parliament, adopted a constitution, modernized its navy, and industrialized. In 1905, with its victory over Russia, it became a major power.

Heir to Japan's Chrysanthemum Throne from birth, Hirohito's life was considered too precious to be exposed to the intrigues of the Court. He was separated from his mother when only three months old and sent to a foster home for safekeeping. At age three he was taken to the palace of his father, Crown Prince Taisho, but still only saw his mother once a week and his father even more rarely. A guardian, conscious that he was shaping a future emperor, supervised Hirohito's education and surrounded him with protective and disciplinary restraints. By seven, Hirohito had learned to hide his feelings and was conscious of his responsible position.

According to legend, Japanese emperors were the descendants of a Shinto goddess and were themselves revered as gods. Hirohito began to doubt his family's divine origin as he grew older but was persuaded to keep his feelings private so that Japan might not be denied the unifying symbol of a divine emperor. In return he was allowed to pursue his interest in natural history and to study marine biology: in a small boat at sea he could collect the biological specimens that fascinated him unaccompanied by a retinue of officials.

Meiji died in 1912 and Taisho proved a self-indulgent, dissipated, mentally unstable fop. His advisers were not displeased that Taisho's lack of interest made him disinclined to interfere with them, but they were upset when Hirohito, as prince regent, wanted to become a constitutional monarch. Hirohito envied the comparative freedom and informality enjoyed by Britain's royal family, whom he had visited during his 1921 tour of England and the Continent. Japan's powerful military clique and secret societies were appalled: their unquestioned power derived from their role as the instruments of a divine emperor: a nondivine, constitutional monarchy would be open to public scrutiny and actions could be challenged. Determined to end Hirohito's tentative bids for independence, they pressured his advisers to rebuke him for trying to free himself from some of the stifling Japanese protocol and create a new image by such devices as throwing a party, waving his hand to acknowledge cheers, and smiling in public. Chastened, Hirohito conformed, although he continued to eat an English breakfast of bacon and eggs each morning.

Hirohito was sixteen when his marriage with the Princess Nagako was arranged and twenty-three when it was solemnized. In 1926 he became emperor of Japan upon the death of his father.

Military fanatics were gaining control of Japan through threats and assassination. Disliking their growing influence, Hirohito opposed the army's activities in Manchuria in 1931. He requested that a new prime minister be selected "who has no fascist leanings… who is moderate in thought and who is not militaristic," and expressed misgivings about withdrawing from the League of Nations in 1933. Fanatical young officers mutinied against their more conservative superiors in 1936 and plotted Hirohito's

Emperor Hirohito being greeted by sumo wrestlers

assassination. Bursting into Hirohito's study, the would-be assassin was challenged by an outraged Hirohito: "How dare you come in here? Do you not know that I am your emperor?" The assailant, taught from childhood to revere the emperor as a god, bowed himself out, and committed suicide. The mutineers obeyed Hirohito's orders to surrender and, on Hirohito's insistence, were severely punished for their crimes.

Hirohito was able to assert his will in a crisis but his nature was gentle and reserved rather than dominating. He reverted to being a figurehead immured in the royal palace. When the military seized control of Japan, they kept Hirohito uninformed of their activities, disregarded his stated opposition to Japan's alliance with Germany, brought Japan into World War II (ignoring his desire for peace), and evoked his name in every patriotic speech and proclamation exhorting the Japanese people to greater efforts.

In May 1945 Germany surrendered and Tokyo was in ruins. The Potsdam Conference called for Japan's unconditional surrender, the atomic bombs were dropped on Hiroshima and Nagasaki, yet the Japanese cabinet still could not decide whether Japan should surrender or fight to the bitter end. In desperation, it decided to take the unprecedented step of asking the emperor to decide Japan's fate. He chose to surrender: "I have given serious thought to the situation prevailing at home and abroad, and I have concluded that continuing the war can only mean destruction for the nation and a prolongation of bloodshed and cruelty in the world." The radio broadcast he made informing the Japanese people of his decision to surrender marked the first time that they had heard his voice.

Hirohito was not accused of being a war criminal (even after he accepted responsibility, as emperor, for Japan's wartime actions), but there were still attempts to cut the emperor down to size. Six thousand palace servants were dismissed (in their stead, more than twenty thousand Japanese volunteers a year came to help clean the palace) and the imperial family was given the same rations as other Japanese. Forced by the American occupation forces to deny his divinity in a New Year message and to go out to meet his people face to face, Hirohito became more popular than ever before.

Hirohito's role in postwar Japan was mostly ceremonial and involved attending state functions and various events around Japan. He resumed his beloved research in marine biology and became a recognized authority, writing six books on the subject. The name Showa (Enlightened Peace), given his reign at its start, seemed increasingly prophetic with the growth of Japan's postwar economic power.

E. Behr, *Hirohito*, 1990.

T. Crump, *The Death of an Emperor*, 1991.

T. Kawahara, *Hirohito and His Times*, 1990.

HITLER, ADOLF (1889–1945), German dictator.

He was born in Branau, Austria, the son of Alois Schicklgruber, who had changed his name to Hitler, a variant of the surname of his stepfather, Johann Hiedler. Hitler's mother was twenty-three years younger than Alois, worked for the Hitler family as a maid during Alois's second marriage, and bore him two stillborn children before becoming his third wife. She pampered and indulged Hitler, her first living child. His father, who sternly disapproved of Hitler's poor performance in school (lazy, undisciplined, and convinced that his gift for drawing meant he was an artistic genius, Hitler refused to study anything else), died when he was thirteen.

Arrogant, bad-tempered, and quarrelsome, Hitler had few friends as a boy. At that time he developed his lifelong love for Richard *Wagner's operas and appreciation of the adventure stories of Karl May. The hero of May's seventy Western novels (packed with vivid descriptions of cruelty and violence) was an American named "Old Shatterhand," who massacred Indians because they belonged to an inferior race. Hitler later claimed that May's novels made him aware of "the nature of the world," and called the Russians "Redskins" after invading the USSR in 1941. He left school at sixteen without a diploma.

Claiming that his artistic temperament made regular work hours uncongenial, Hitler refused to get a job. He was shocked and bitterly disappointed when, at eighteen, he failed to be accepted to the Academy of Fine Arts in Vienna. He returned to Vienna to try again after his mother's death from cancer. Rejected also by the School of Architecture, he deteriorated rapidly. He soon ran through his inheritance from his parents and a government orphan's allowance and was reduced to sleeping in doorways, municipal shelters, and on park benches. He supported himself by begging, various odd jobs, painting advertisements, and copying picture postcards, but preferred reading newspapers, discussing politics (dominating every discussion and screaming with rage if contradicted), and concocting get-rich-quick schemes.

The foundations for Hitler's political and social ideas were laid during his five years in Vienna, when he became anti-Semitic and an extreme German nationalist. His interest in the supernatural led him to the Ostrara movement, which combined occultism with anti-Semitism, presented a vision of the world as a struggle of the noble white race against its beastlike inferiors (advocating the inferiors' sterilization, deportation, and murder), and took a swastika as its symbol.

Strong feelings of German nationalism, an increasing distaste for the multinational Austro-Hungarian Empire, and a desire to avoid his compulsory Austrian military service prompted Hitler's move to Munich in 1913. He immediately volunteered for the German army when World War I broke out and found there the sense of security and identification he had hitherto lacked. Now obsessively clean, he spent hours trying to remove every speck of dirt and trace of body odor. He was a good soldier, following all the rules, serving well as a courier, receiving several decorations, and ending up as a corporal. Temporarily blinded in a gas attack, he was in hospital when he heard of the armistice. At that time he decided to enter politics, primarily to fight the Jews.

Hitler remained in the army after the armistice but refused to participate in the revolutions that broke out in Germany. When the revolution in Bavaria was overthrown by reactionaries, Hitler supplied them with information about revolutionary sympathizers that sent hundreds to the firing squads. The new government used Hitler to infiltrate civilian radical groups, which was how he happened to attend a small meeting held by the anti-Semitic German Workers' party in 1919. Finding himself in agreement, he was moved to give a speech of his own, advocating a greater Germany, that was so persuasive that he was invited to become a member of the party's steering committee. Six months later he left the army to devote himself to the party, which, revitalized by his genius for propaganda and oratory, changed its name to the Nationalsozialistische Deutsche Arbeiterpartie — the Nazi party. In 1921 he became its chairman and the Nazis began to take on some of the trappings for which they became famous: Hitler acquired the title "Unser Führer" (Our Leader), instituted the "Heil!" greeting (later "Heil Hitler!"), and designed the Nazi flag — a black swastika on a blood-red background.

The armistice's humiliating terms and huge reparation payments discredited the postwar German government in German as well as international eyes. Germany's postwar economy was devastated by the impossibly high reparations, the occupation of the Ruhr — Germany's major industrial area — by France, and an international economic blockade. Inflation was rampant: the mark fell from 4.20 to 4.2 trillion marks to the dollar between 1914 and the end of 1923. Businessmen made huge profits, people on fixed incomes suffered, and membership in extremist parties grew. By 1923 the Nazi party had a membership of fifty-six thousand and a private corps of fifteen thousand stormtrooper guards (SA) that terrorized the opposition with violence, encouraged by Hitler both for the publicity and fear it engendered and the pleasure it gave him.

The Munich Beer Hall Putsch — Hitler's November 1923 attempt to take over the government by raiding a mass meeting of Bavarian government officials in the beer cellar of a brewery with his stormtroopers — was a complete failure. Hitler was bitterly disappointed and sure that his political career had ended, and threatened to commit suicide. He recovered in time to use his trial as a public forum to advertise his goals and himself, and his skilled oratory combined with extensive newspaper coverage gained him international fame. Sentenced in 1924 to five years' imprisonment in a fortress, he used his lenient prison conditions (comfortable quarters, good food, numerous visitors, and sympathetic guards) to dictate the first volume of his book, *Mein Kampf* ("My Struggle").

Mein Kampf spelled out Hitler's plans for Germany's future — inclusion of all German-speaking

---

- The great masses of the people will more easily fall victims to a big lie than a small one.
- The one means that wins the victory over reason: terror and force.
- The efficiency of the truly national leader consists primarily in preventing the division of the attention of a people and in concentrating it on a single enemy.
- Mankind has grown strong in eternal struggles and will only perish through eternal peace.
- Success is the sole earthly judge of right and wrong.
- The first essential for success is a perpetual and regular employment of violence.

From *Mein Kampf*

Adolf Hitler is a bloodthirsty guttersnipe, a monster of wickedness, insatiable in his lust for blood and plunder.

Winston Churchill

---

areas into Germany, conquest of vast territories to the east, avenging the humiliation of Germany's defeat, wiping out communism, and destroying the Jews, whom he saw as inferior parasites responsible for Germany's defeat. Repetitious and boring, it sold poorly until Hitler became dictator and made possession of a copy obligatory.

By the time Hitler was released (after serving only nine months of his sentence), Germany had stabilized its economy through currency reform, established friendly relations with the rest of Europe, and outlawed the Nazi party. Having decided that power could only be achieved through legal means, Hitler persuaded Bavaria's prime minister to lift the ban.

With the advent of the inflation and unemployment attendant upon the Great Depression, extremist parties flourished, and by 1931 the Nazis and the Communists and were the second and third largest political parties in Germany. The small group of industrialists and financiers that controlled Germany's industry (whom Hitler had courted for years) feared the Communists, wanted a strong right-wing anti-working-class government and therefore subsidized Hitler. With solid financial backing the Nazis became strong enough (although the highest share of the vote that they received in a free election was 37 percent in 1932) that Hitler was appointed chancellor in a minority government in January 1933. In February he engineered the burning of the Reichstag building (Germany's parliament) as an excuse for crushing the Communists and other opponents. In March the Reichstag passed the Enabling Law, the constitutional basis for Hitler's dictatorship. In July

Hitler saluting his triumphant troops in Poland

all other parties were dissolved, leaving the Nazis as the only recognized party.

In 1934 Hitler became head of state and commander in chief of the army, with the title of *Führer* (leader) and Reich Chancellor. The next five years were spent consolidating control: crushing the trade union movement; making education, art, and the media into tools of Nazi indoctrination; and depriving Jews of both rights and property. He won the support of the regular army generals by killing thousands of stormtrooper leaders in 1934, while at the same time getting rid of many of his old enemies. Incomes were low but unemployment was nonexistent as Hitler activated Germany's military industries to rearm Germany and prepare for war. In 1938 he annexed Austria; later that year Europe's leaders consented to his takeover of the Sudeten areas of Czechoslovakia, and in March 1939 he took over the rest of Czechoslovakia. In September he invaded Poland, thus beginning World War II.

World War II changed the map of Europe and brought about the deaths of over thirty million people. Many of those deaths were the direct result of Hitler's attempts to create a "new order" in Europe by eliminating members of what he considered to be inferior races. In the first years of the war, Germany enjoyed a series of successes and by 1941 controlled most of Europe. Hitler fancied himself a military genius, but his many alterations of the design of Germany's new war weapons prevented their being completed in time to play a decisive role in the war while his rejection of his generals' advice, insistence on devising his own military strategy, and inability to alter his plans to meet current realities led Germany to defeat. His greatest mistake was his attack on the Soviet Union in 1941. After spectacular initial victories, the German armies were eventually driven back by Soviet forces in alliance with the United States and Britain.

Germany's dictator had many idiosyncracies. He did not converse with people but rather subjected them to long, repetitious monologues that actually communicated very little (he was always on guard against self-revelation). He tried to give the impression he was amazingly knowledgeable about many subjects by quoting numerous (mostly invented) statistics and avoiding contact with experts who might discover his ignorance. He did not smoke, drink, or eat meat, and often taunted nonvegetarian companions for consuming what he called "corpse juice" and "dead bodies." A hypochondriac who suffered badly from insomnia and nightmares (though he boasted of his ice-cold nerves), he was constantly swallowing and being injected with large quantities of drugs.

Convinced of his infallible genius, Hitler blamed any failure on unworthy followers who deserved to be destroyed. During the war, his destruction of the Jews of Europe was largely achieved, with six million Jews put to death in extermination camps or by mass-shootings and starvation. Hitler ordered his soldiers that "anyone who gives up any ground must be shot" and fell into frenzied rages when informed of retreats and attempts to surrender. When he realized that defeat was inevitable — Berlin was surrounded by the Soviets — he married his long-time companion Eva Braun and they committed suicide together. Germany surrendered a week later in May 1945.

A. Bullock, *Hitler: A Study in Tyranny*, 1974.
A. Bullock, *Hitler and Stalin*, 1992.
J. C. Fest, *Hitler*, 1974.
W. C. Langer, *The Mind of Adolf Hitler*, 1972.
W. Maser, *Adolph Hitler*, 1989.
J. Toland, *Adolf Hitler*, 1976.

HO CHI MINH (1890–1969), Vietnamese political leader. Born Nguyen That Than in Annam, central Vietnam, Ho was raised in a nationalistic household; his father, a minor government official, was dismissed from his job for activities against the French colonial regime. Ho grew up a committed anticolonialist, the first of his many pseudonyms being Nguyen Ai Quoc ("Nguyen the Patriot"). After working as a teacher in his home district, he began traveling in 1911, working as a kitchen helper aboard a passenger liner and later on the staff of the Carlton Hotel in London. Toward the end of World War I he settled in France, where he became a member of the French Socialist party. At the 1920 Tours congress he sided with the left of the party, which split off from the socialist mainstream to join the Communist International (Comintern). As a founding member of the French Communist party, he often criticized it for its lack of interest in the colonial question.

Ho was early recognized as a gifted theoretician and polemicist. He edited *Le Paria* ("The Outcast"), a monthly anticolonialist journal, and in 1923 was chosen to study in Moscow at the Communist University of the Toilers of the East, which had been set up by the Russian Communist authorities as a center for training Asian Communists. He played an active role in the Fifth Congress of the Communist International in 1924, and in 1925 the Soviet authorities entrusted him with the task of promoting Communist revolution in Indochina.

While acting as translator for Mikhail Borodin, the official Soviet adviser to *Sun Yat-sen's nationalist Kuomintang in Canton, China, Ho devoted most of his energy to recruiting and training young fellow-Vietnamese expatriates for the revolutionary anticolonial war he envisaged for the future. The organization that he founded at this time, the Association of Revolutionary Annamite Youth, was the forerunner of the Indochinese Communist party of 1930, which in turn spawned the Vietnam Workers' party.

After leaving China in 1927, Ho embarked on an extensive and often dangerous mission through southeast Asia, disseminating Marxist teachings, establishing Communist organizations, and advocating armed resistance to colonialism in Malaya, Siam (now Thailand), and the Dutch East Indies (Indonesia), as well as in Indochina. With the failure of the 1940 uprising against the French in Indochina, he was forced to flee back to Southern China, where the League for the Independence of Vietnam — commonly known as the Viet Minh — was set up at a congress in Kwangsi in 1941. Ho now took the *nom de guerre* with which he achieved international fame: Ho Chi Minh ("He who enlightens").

With World War II raging in Europe, the fall of France to the Axis forces in 1940 had allowed the Japanese to establish their authority in Vietnam — which they ruled through the existing French administrators — by setting up Emperor Bao Dai as their puppet in the southern capital of Saigon. In 1944 Ho and his close associate, Vo Nguyen Giap, organized Viet Minh strongholds over a wide area of northern Vietnam, leaving them well placed to take advantage of the power vacuum that was created by the 1945 Japanese arrest of the French administration. Within a month of Japan's surrender to the Allied forces in August 1945 the Viet Minh, in alliance with other nationalist groups, formed a provisional Vietnamese government based in Hanoi. Ho, announcing the creation of an independent Democratic Republic of Vietnam by virtue of his position as prime minister, foreign minister, and president of the new administration, echoed the sentiments of the American Declaration of Independence by saying: "All men are born equal: the Creator has given us inviolable rights, life, liberty, and happiness."

Vietnamese street mural of Ho Chi Minh

Subsequent French attempts to reassert control over their former colony led to an anticolonial war fought and won under Communist leadership. Supported and supplied by *Mao Tse-tung's Chinese Communist regime, the nationalist forces held out against the French, and their victory over France's last surviving northern stronghold, Dien Bien Phu, in 1954 signaled Viet Minh control over the whole of northern Vietnam. The international community recognized the Vietnamese right to self-determination through the Geneva Agreement of 1954 which provided for the establishment of a demarcation line between northern and southern Vietnam until free elections could be held to choose a representative national government.

Those elections never took place. Frightened that free elections might result in a Communist victory, the United States prevailed upon Bao Dai to appoint Ngo Dinh Diem, an anti-Communist, to rule South Vietnam. In response, the North Vietnamese government undertook the training of southern Vietnamese Communists, who then infiltrated the south to encourage insurrection. These men and women, the South Vietnam National Liberation Front, or Viet Cong, spearheaded the movement that politically and militarily challenged Diem, who was overthrown and assassinated in 1963.

As early as 1955 Ho had surrendered his premiership of North Vietnam, but his appointees and disciples continued to fill the key places in the North Vietnamese administration — in particular the all-important positions of leadership of the Communist party — so his influence remained significant. Small and seemingly fragile, he dressed simply and lived austerely, and was widely revered as a patriot and liberator, and as the elder statesman of the Vietnamese revolution. Even the increasingly repressive and totalitarian nature of a poor, isolated, and embattled North Vietnamese regime propped up by Chinese food aid and Soviet arms could not undermine the popularity of "Uncle Ho," as he was known by the people.

Direct American military intervention in Vietnam prompted Ho to assert that "we will never agree to negotiate under the threat of bombing." Recognized worldwide as one of the prime movers of the post-World War II anticolonialist movement, he did not live to see the conclusion of the war that ravaged Vietnam from the mid-1960s. When North Vietnamese troops finally captured Saigon in 1975, it was renamed Ho Chi Minh City in his memory.

D. Halberstam, *Ho*, 1971.
N. Khac Huyen, *Vision Accomplished? The Enigma of Ho Chi Minh*, 1971.
J. Lacouture, *Ho Chi Minh*, 1968.
D. O. Lloyd, *Ho Chi Minh*, 1986.
C. P. Rageau, *Ho Chi Minh*, 1970.

HOKUSAI, KATSUSHIKA (1760–1849), Japanese artist. Born in a countrified quarter of Edo (today Tokyo) that belonged to the district of Katsushika, he was adopted as a child by a functionary in the court of the shogun and his name changed, as was the custom, from Tokitaro to Tetsuzo. He showed an early talent for drawing, but his adopted father saw no future in it and apprenticed him to a bookseller when his schooling was completed.

The woodcuts and other works of art he saw in his master's shop influenced Tetsuzo, and when he was fourteen he became an apprentice to an engraver of plates for colored woodcuts. After four years, during which he acquired technical skills, he was taken on in the studio of Katsukawa Shunsho, a famous painter of the day. A disagreement with Shunsho led Tetsuzo to leave. He continued to study with other painters and to support himself. He wrote, painted, and printed booklets of novels and poetry; when these efforts failed to produce income, he became a vendor in the market.

His luck turned when he received a commission to paint a picture to be used as a flag for a national holiday. He returned to his own work with new energy and began to paint *surinomo*, colored sheets of paper decorated with pictures, which were used for invitations, announcements, and greetings. Within a few years his work had become extremely popular and he had begun publishing books of colored woodcuts.

It was at this time that he settled on the name under which he was to become famous both in Japan and in the West; he selected Katsushika (after the place he had been born) Hokusai, or "artist from the north."

Copies of his many books reached Europe and ensured his popularity there. The Japanese government banned the export of one of his books of sketches of Japanese life on the grounds that it was too revealing. However, the most famous of his works is the

> Since the age of six I have felt a desire to paint everything I see around me. Only now, at the age of seventy-three, have I partially understood the real shape and character of birds, fishes, and plants. At the age of one hundred and ten everything I shall create, every point and every line I draw will be life itself
>
> **Hokusai**

"Thirty-Six Views of Fuji," later increased to forty-six, a series of woodcuts depicting Mount Fujiyama.

Hokusai never lost his interest in experimenting with innovative methods of painting. He was the leading member of the Ukiyo-e school of painting which sought to portray everyday life realistically, in contrast to other more stylized schools. Toward the end of his life he signed his drawings "An Old Man Mad-On-Drawing." It is estimated that he produced thirty-five thousand pictures and illustrated 169 books issued in 437 volumes.

R. Lane, *Hokusai, Life and Work*, 1989.

HOLMES, OLIVER WENDELL (1841–1935), American jurist and legal scholar; son of the famous Boston writer and physician Oliver W. Holmes, known for his essays in *The Atlantic Monthly* column, "The Autocrat of the Breakfast Table."

Holmes studied at Harvard College from 1857 to 1861, when, with the advent of the Civil War, he enlisted for a three-year term, serving initially as a lieutenant in the twentieth Massachusetts Regiment of Volunteers and advancing to the rank of captain. From 1864 to 1866 he attended Harvard Law School and received his law degree, following which he worked for a Boston law firm and was subsequently admitted to the bar in 1867. After working for the firm until 1870, he was determined to try his hand at solo practice. At the same time, he wrote for one of the few legal journals of the time, the *American Law Review*, and served as its coeditor as well as lecturing at Harvard College. Continuing his legal writings, he became sole editor of the *American Law Review* in 1872.

While involved in other work, in 1869 he began editing *Kent's Commentaries on American Law* and by 1873 had completed what was to be its twelfth edition. Immediately following this publication, he became a partner in a new law firm, Shattuck, Holmes and Munroe. This last period in private practice, primarily on the appellate level, continued until 1882. His writings over the years culminated in the Lowell Lectures (1880), published as *The Common Law* (1881), which became a legal classic reprinted to this day.

In 1882 he left private practice to accept an appointment as a professor of law at Harvard. However, a few months later he became an associate justice

CLEAR AND PRESENT DANGER TEST

We admit that in many places and in ordinary times the defendants in saying all that was said in the circular would have been within their constitutional rights. But the character of every act depends upon the circumstances in which it is done.... The most stringent protection of free speech would not protect a man in falsely shouting fire in a crowded theater and causing a panic.... The question in every case is whether the words are of such a nature as to create a clear and present danger that they will bring about the substantive evils that Congress has a right to prevent. It is a question of proximity and degree. When a nation is at war, many things that might be said in time of peace are such a hindrance to its efforts that they will not be endured...and that no court could regard them as protected by any Constitutional right.

Shenck v. U.S. **249 U.S. 47 (1919)**

TEST OF TRUTH AND POWER OF IDEAS

In this case sentences of twenty years imprisonment have been imposed for the publishing of two leaflets that I believe the defendants had as much right to publish as the Government has to publish the Constitution of the United States...To allow opposition by speech seems to indicate that you think the speech impotent....But when men have realized that time has upset many fighting faiths, they may come to believe even more than they believe the very foundations of their own conduct that the ultimate good desired is better reached by free trade in ideas — that the best test of truth is the power of the thought to get itself accepted in the competition of the market....

Abrams v. U.S. **250 U.S. 616 (1919)**

grand total of more than 2,000 signed opinions and innumerable unsigned memorandum opinions.

Not only was Holmes one of the greatest jurists on the U.S. Supreme Court, but he was also the author of countless legal opinions that were literary gems as well. These included his famous opinions in the Schenck case (unanimous court, early 1919) and the Abrams case (dissenting opinion, late 1919), which were the beginnings of modern First Amendment (freedom of speech) law. The Schenck case involved leaflets mailed by the then-secretary of the Socialist party to men about to be inducted during World War I calling the draft unconstitutional. On the other hand, the Abrams case involved leaflets in Yiddish dropped on Broadway by a few zealous anarchists who did not oppose World War I with the Germans, but opposed intervention in Russia.

Holmes was a Washington institution. In the words of Walter Lippmann in the *New Republic* in 1916, when Holmes was a mere seventy-five: "When you enter [the home of Justice Holmes], it is as if you have come into the living stream of high romance. You meet the gay soldier who can talk of Falstaff and eternity in one breath, and tease the universe with a quip... A sage with the bearing of a cavalier; his presence is an incitement to high risks... He wears wisdom like a gorgeous plume, and likes to tickle the sanctities between the ribs."

C. D. Bowen, *Yankee from Olympus: Justice Holmes and His Family*, 1944.
M. de W. Howe, *Justice Oliver Wendell Holmes*, 2 vols., 1957–1962.
M. Lerner, ed., *Mind and Faith of Justice Holmes*, 1943.
S. M. Novick, *Honorable Justice: The Life of Oliver Wendell Holmes*, 1989.

HOMER (ninth-eighth century B.C.E.), the most famous of the Greek poets, believed by the Greeks to have composed the great epics the *Iliad* and the *Odyssey*. Details of his life were disputed even in antiquity. He was variously dated to the periods of the Trojan War, the Ionian migrations, the middle of the ninth century B.C.E., and 500 years after the Trojan War! Seven cities claimed to be his birthplace. By extant accounts he was blind and poor, came from Ionia, and wandered throughout Greece. The discrepancy among the ancient authorities and the critical analysis of the poems have, in modern times, resulted in the denial of his very existence, but this hypercritical attitude has been rejected. Logical considerations, the Ionic dialect of the poems, and their internal evidence suggest that he lived in Ionia (the traditional belief), specifically in Chios (the place of the Homeridae) or in Smyrna (Pindar's view). That he lived in the eighth century B.C.E., that he was very much like one of the bards described in the *Odyssey* (he never mentions himself in the poems), and that he may well have been blind seem to be true.

on the Massachusetts Supreme Judicial Court, where he served until 1902 (as chief justice from 1899). In 1902 Holmes was appointed an associate justice of the U.S. Supreme Court by President Theodore *Roosevelt. He continued to serve for a period of some thirty years until his retirement in 1932, just before his ninety-first birthday.

During his tenure on the U.S. Supreme Court, Holmes published some 975 opinions, of which 873 were for the full court (more than any other justice) as well as some 72 dissenting opinions that earned him the title of the Great Dissenter. Including the twenty-year period he served on the Massachusetts Supreme Judicial Court, he was credited with a

Earliest known portrait of Homer, fourth century B.C.E.

The subject of the *Iliad* is war, the war of the Greeks against Troy (Ilium), or more precisely, the wrath of Achilles, the best-known hero of the Greeks. Insulted by Agamemnon, who has taken Briseis, his beautiful captive, Achilles sulks in his tent and refuses to take part in the war. As a result the Greeks suffer defeats and even the active support of Patroclus, Achilles's friend, does not help; Patroclus is later slain by the Trojan hero Hector. Overcome by grief, Achilles sets out for battle; again he is motivated by anger and the desire for revenge. Almost maddened with fury, he pursues Hector, slays him, and for days abuses the corpse. Finally he lets Priam take the body of his son for burial. There are only four days of actual fighting in the poem, and the whole plot takes place during a few weeks at the last stage of the war. By way of allusions and flashbacks the story of the war, which lasted ten years, is skillfully told. By relating the exploits of the main heroes on both sides and the part taken by the gods above, as well as various episodes (such as the funeral competitions for Patroclus) and portrayals, the poet composes a rich and broad narrative, the essential quality of epic poetry. From first to last, however, the unity of the action is maintained and dominated by the tragic figure of Achilles, the hero who knows he is doomed to die.

The *Odyssey* narrates the ten-year adventures of Odysseus on his voyage home from Troy after its sack by the Greeks. In this respect it is a sequel to the *Iliad*. Here again the narrative begins in the last stage, some six weeks in all, and other events are related in retrospect. It starts with Odysseus's departure from Calypso; he manages to reach Sicheria, the island of the Phaeacians, after his raft is wrecked by Poseidon. Simultaneously his son Telemachus is induced to go in search of news of his father in Pylos and Sparta; the first four books are devoted to this journey. At Scheria, Odysseus narrates his adventures to Nausi-

caa and her parents at a banquet, a model followed by *Virgil in his *Aeneid*. He is then taken to Ithaca, where his faithful wife Penelope has been delaying suitors for years. He comes disguised as a beggar, recognized only by Eurycleia, his old nurse, and by his dog. Finally he kills all the suitors. Here, too, there is one central figure, unity of theme with interwoven episodes, a full account of the other characters and many allusions — the Wooden Horse, the Sack of Troy, the murder of Agamemnon, among others.

The charm of the Homeric poems is in the simplicity of the narrative, the nobility of the characters, and the reality of the action; unity of plot is maintained throughout, combined with rich and varied episodes. The digressions provide broadness and do not delay the development of the action in the climaxes. The language is rich and artfully employed to fit all moments and situations; a distinct feature are the similes, many more in the *Iliad* than in the *Odyssey*. Short or long, they are made to match the occasion, and are often pieces taken out of the world of nature or the familiar surroundings of the poet's own life and as such add vividness and variety.

The Homeric poems purport to describe the Achaean world at the time of the Trojan War, a world of heroes and heroines, of great warriors, great palaces filled with treasures and spoils of war. However, in their final form they reveal that they were composed several centuries later. While retaining some of the features characteristic of the old civilization, such as chariots and arms, they give evidence of changed conditions, customs, and social institutions.

A critical approach to the poems began with some ancient scholars who argued that the two poems had separate authors. Modern critics collected inconsistencies, emphasizing different attitudes and differences in style and vocabulary. The extremists claimed that they were collections made in the sixth century B.C.E. out of several earlier works. All the arguments can be answered, firstly by assuming that the *Odyssey* was the work of the same poet who wrote the *Iliad* at an earlier stage of his life. Research shows that there are similarities in structure and technique between the two poems. Still, it is true that the poems were preceded by a long tradition of oral epic poetry. The earlier bards told the old tales using conventional phrases and episodes; hence the appearance of formulas and the same lines or passages in the poems. It is equally true that the poet, or poets, who composed the *Iliad* and the *Odyssey* using the old material achieved remarkable works, consistent in many aspects, with a distinct touch of originality in design, structure, character portrayals, and language — which all show the genius of their author.

The poems, composed around the eighth century B.C.E., were probably transmitted orally for about two centuries. It is believed that with their introduction to Athens for recitation in the Panathenaea under Pisistratus, a written text was prepared. However, the poems spread in the Greek world in different versions. The Alexandrian scholars, notably *Aristophanes of Byzantium and Aristarchus, did painstaking research to establish a correct text, but they were not able to establish it as the definitive version.

The Homeric poems had a unique place in Greek culture. They were learned by children, recited at festivals, cited in political disputes, and used as historical sources. Though criticized by *Plato on moral grounds, they were admired by Aristotle as masterpieces of epic poetry. Romans also admired them, and Virgil modeled his Aeneid on the Homeric poems. Throughout the ages they have continued to influence critics, poets, writers, artists, and ordinary readers.

W. A. Camps, *An Introduction to Homer*, 1980.
J. Griffen, *Homer*, 1980.
G. C. Kirk, *Homer and the Epic*, 1965.

HOOVER, HERBERT CLARK (1874–1964), thirty-first president of the United States (1929–1933), who earned recognition in four major areas: engineering, reform of governmental bureaucracy, international relief work, and politics.

Hoover was born in West Branch, Iowa. Orphaned at the age of nine, he went to live with an uncle in Oregon. In 1895 he graduated from Stanford University as a mining engineer, then worked as an engineer in Colorado and was hired in 1897 by a British firm as chief engineer. He worked for them in western Australia and within a year was offered a position by the Chinese government. The Boxer Rebellion took place while he was in China and Hoover had his first taste of war, refugees, and war relief.

For the next twelve years Hoover worked in various countries, forming a business firm of consulting engineers and building up a personal fortune. During World War I in London, Hoover, who was a Quaker, became chairman of the American Relief Committee, coordinating worldwide efforts to provide relief for starving civilians. After the United States entered the war in 1917, he was appointed National Food Administrator. He served in the cabinets of Presidents Harding and Coolidge; Harding appointed him secretary of commerce "and assistant secretary of Everything Else." As chairman of the Colorado River Commission, he was responsible for the construction of Boulder (later called Hoover) Dam. Hoover documented his personal philosophy in *American Individualism*, published in 1922, while together with his wife he published a translation of an ancient work on minerals.

When Coolidge announced that he would not run again, the Republicans approached Hoover to be their presidential candidate and he carried the election against Al Smith by more than six million votes. At the beginning of his term, things went well as there was a Republican-dominated Congress. However, the economy was declining and within a few months the stock market collapsed. In his efforts to deal with the economic crisis of the country, Hoover tried a number of forceful solutions. Loans were extended to banks and large businesses to generate a revival, but the country was reeling under the depression and Hoover was heavily defeated in his

---

FROM THE WRITINGS OF HERBERT HOOVER

- Prosperity cannot be restored by raids on the public treasury.
- The sole function of Government is to bring about a condition of affairs favorable to the beneficial development of private enterprise.
- Rugged individualism.
- We in America today are nearer to the final triumph over poverty than ever before in the history of the land....We shall soon be in sight of the day when poverty shall be banished from this nation (acceptance speech in 1928).
- Older men declare war. But it is the youth who fight and die.
- Blessed are the young for they shall inherit the national debt.

bid for reelection in 1932 by the Democratic candidate Franklin D. *Roosevelt.

After he left office Hoover often wrote about and spoke in behalf of isolationism. He did, however, spend a great deal of time during this period working for the relief of famine, having gained experience in China and London, and he was very successful in devising workable programs, notably for humanitarian relief during and after World War II.

When Harry S. *Truman became president, he utilized Hoover's abilities, often seeking his advice. In July 1947 the Hoover Commission was created to investigate inefficiency and to recommend reorganization of the executive branch of government. Hoover was the chairman, serving in that capacity until 1949, and again from 1953 to 1955. His library of World War I documents was deposited at Stanford University, where it forms the basis of the Hoover library.

M. L. Fausold, *The Presidency of Herbert C. Hoover*, 1985.
E. A. Rosen, *Herbert Clark Hoover: President*, 1977.
R. N. Smith, *Herbert Hoover*, 1984.

HUDSON, HENRY (1565–1611), English explorer and navigator. Little is known of his early life. In his later years, between 1607 and 1611, he led three exploratory voyages for the English and one for the Dutch, with the object of finding a shorter route from Europe to Asia, "to the islands of spicery." In 1607, as part of his search for a northwest passage to Asia, Hudson, his son, and ten companions attempted to find the route to Japan and China by way of the North Pole. They reached the edge of the polar ice pack and followed it as far as the Svalbard Archipelago. As a result of their discovery, the Spitzbergen whale fisheries were established.

The following year his sponsor, the Muscovy Company, again sent Hudson out to sea. This time the target was to go beyond Svalbard to the islands of Novaya Zemlya. Once again he failed in his attempt to find the desired northwest passage. After his return to England the Dutch East Indies Company sent him to investigate two possible channels to the Pacific across North America. Hudson's curiosity was aroused and he wanted to continue further, but was bound by contract to return to Amsterdam. He and his crew decided to ignore the contract and set off in a different direction to seek the northwest passage. In 1609 they sailed on the ship *Half Moon* one hundred and fifty miles inland from the site of New York City along a large river, later named after Hudson.

The English government discovered that Hudson was engaged in exploration for the Dutch and ordered him to stop working for other governments. His ship's logs and papers describing the voyage and discoveries were sent to Holland, where they were published. Back in England, Hudson was asked to make a voyage to America and under the sponsorship of the British East Indies Company, the Muscovy Company, and eighteen private backers, he set sail in 1610 in the vessel *Discovery*.

After a brief stop in Iceland, Hudson continued the voyage, sailing through what later became known as Hudson Bay (which had been previously discovered). From there he continued along the east coast to James Bay. Again, his mission to find an outlet to the Pacific Ocean failed and, due to weather conditions, he and his crew were forced to spend the winter at James Bay. While there, Hudson and his crew had a falling out. Hudson demoted one of his men and accused another of stealing and hoarding provisions. These two men conspired to call a meeting of the rest of the crew and claimed that Hudson was hoarding the provisions for himself. The meeting turned into a mutiny; Hudson, his son, and seven others were cast adrift in a small boat on the open seas. Although the *Discovery* returned to England, the two ringleaders of the mutiny were not on board; they had been killed in a battle with the Eskimos. Hudson and his party were never heard of again.

The discovery of Hudson Bay was of great importance to navigators and explorers who followed Henry Hudson to the area. In 1670 the Hudson Bay Company was established for fur trading. Although Hudson never found the easier route to the Pacific, his four dangerous voyages laid the groundwork for future explorers. His discoveries extended knowledge of the Arctic and enabled the Dutch to colonize the Hudson River, while the British were able to lay claim to a huge portion of land in Canada.

G. M. Asher, *Henry Hudson the Navigator*, 1963.
L. Powys, *Henry Hudson*, 1928.
S. Purchac, *Henry Hudson*, 1966.

HUGHES, WILLIAM MORRIS (1864–1952), Australian prime minister. He was born and educated in Wales, working briefly as a student teacher before drawn by the lure of Australia in 1884. He settled in New South Wales and worked intensively for the unionization of maritime workers in Sydney.

In 1894 Hughes was elected to the New South Wales legislature as a Labor member. He worked to achieve the federation of the several independent Australian states and when the federal government was established in 1901 Hughes entered the first federal parliament as a Labor representative. In 1904 Australia had its first Labor government, in which Hughes was minister for external affairs. He served in subsequent Labor cabinets and from 1908 until 1915 was attorney general, helping to establish a national system of defense and also closely involved in establishing a judicial arbitration system for labor disputes.

Hughes became prime minister in 1915, holding the position until 1923. Shortly after becoming prime minister he visited England and became convinced of the value of wartime military conscription. In 1916 he proposed conscription, which the Australian Labor party rejected, causing a split in the party. Rising above party politics, Hughes helped establish the new Nationalist party, at the head of which he continued as prime minister in a coalition government.

Under his leadership, Australia was actively involved in World War I. This, in turn, led to its participation in the Paris Peace Conference of 1919, where Hughes strenuously pushed Australia's interests in the Pacific, especially against Japan. His achievements included gaining control over German New Guinea. Hughes also successfully opposed the Japanese-sponsored racial equality clause for inclusion in the League of Nations.

Hughes suffered defeat in the elections of 1922 at the hands of the so-called Country party but maintained his seat in parliament until his death at eighty eight. He served from 1934 to 1941 in an Australian cabinet under the United Australian party. During World War II Hughes sat on the Australian Advisory War Council, serving as minister of the navy in 1940–1941.

This dynamic political figure was affectionately known as "Billy" or "the little Digger." He perfectly expressed the temper of the Australian Labor movement and the nationalistic feelings during a key developmental era of the country.

W. F. Whyte, *William Morris Hughes*, 1957.

HUGO, VICTOR-MARIE (1802–1885), French poet, playwright, and novelist. Hard-working, versatile, and prolific, he brought a new freedom to poetry and drama and raised satire to unequaled heights in both verse and prose. Hugo wrote novels that became enduring best-sellers and enriched the poetic culture of his native land with powerful imagery and metaphor, subtle coloring, a distinct personal note, and the brilliant development of themes such as nature, childhood, love, sorrow, and death. Hugo also championed the downtrodden, advocating universal suffrage, state-supported compulsory education, and minority rights.

Born at Besançon, Victor Hugo had an unsettled childhood resulting from the tensions between his parents. While his mother was a confirmed royalist, his father — Count Sigisbert Hugo (1774–1828) — served as one of *Napoleon's generals and took the family with him to Corsica, Italy, and Spain. After a separation in 1812 the couple agreed on a divorce (1818) and his mother retained custody of her three sons. Young Victor displayed a gift for poetry in his teens, winning praise from the French Academy (1817) and publishing *Le Conservateur littéraire* with his brothers (1819–1821). His pro-royalist verse gained him awards from the crown and in 1822, a year after his mother's death, he married Adèle Foucher, who bore him five children. She then took the critic Charles Sainte-Beuve as her lover while her mortified but still devoted husband found solace in the arms of other women.

Odes et ballads, incorporating all his earlier poems, and *Bug-Jargal*, a novel about Santo Domingo's black uprising, both appeared in 1826, when Hugo had started to shed his literary and political conservatism. This change of direction, manifested in the preface to his first drama, *Cromwell* (1827), came to a head in the famous battle over *Hernani* (1830), when noisy objections to that romantic play were overcome by Hugo's well-organized supporters. The development of his social conscience may likewise be gauged from the temporary banning of *Marion Delorme* (staged in 1831) and from statements in *Le Dernier jour d'un condamné* (1829), a novel inveighing against capital punishment and public executions.

However, until the disastrous failure of *Les Burgraves* (1843), Hugo's ambitions were set on the theater. *Le Roi s'amuse,* a story of tragic revenge, provoked even the mild censors of King *Louis-Philippe and was banned soon after its premiere in 1832. *Hernani* was later turned into an Italian opera by Giuseppe *Verdi, who borrowed the plot of *Le Roi s'amuse* for his *Rigoletto*. *Lucretia Borgia* (1833) was also transformed into an opera by Donizetti, while Felix Mendelssohn composed an overture for the German stage version of *Ruy Blas* (1838). Juliette Drouet (1806–1883), who played one of the minor roles in *Lucretia Borgia,* became Hugo's mistress, secretary, and constant companion over the next fifty years, many of his love poems being dedicated to her.

Outside France, Victor Hugo's renown stems largely from translations of his great novels, usually in condensed form. *Notre Dame de Paris* ("The Hunchback of Notre Dame") inspired by the romances of Sir Walter *Scott, is a gripping evocation of fifteenth-century Paris, with its Gothic cathedral as an eerie focus of the plot. Its unlikely hero is the deformed bellringer, Quasimodo, who tries vainly to save the gypsy dancer Esmeralda from his villainous master, Archdeacon Frollo, and a besieging mob. *Les Misérables* (1862), set in the Bourbon restoration period, describes at length the continual efforts made by Jean Valjean, a victim of social injustice, to lead an honorable life and help fellow unfortunates while evading the police inspector who relentlessly shadows him. Like *The Hunchback of Notre Dame*, this prose epic has often been filmed and has also served as the basis for a successful musical.

Hugo was elected to the French Academy on his fourth attempt (1841) and raised to the Chamber of Peers in 1845. Social issues and a growing belief in the poet-prophet's role as the torchbearer of mankind helped to thrust him into politics. After the 1848 revolution he strongly supported Prince Louis Napoleon's election as president of the Second Republic, then outraged the Party of Order with his indictment of reactionary moves at home and abroad. Denied high office, Hugo sensed the prince-president's real ambition and, as chief architect of the Napoleonic legend, was chagrined to find it

QUOTATIONS FROM VICTOR HUGO

- Popularity? It's glory's small change.
- Slaves would be tyrants if the chance were theirs.
- Dark Error's other hidden side is Truth.
- No one should expect me to give a moment's thought to an "amnesty"... I will share freedom's exile to the very end. When freedom returns, so will I (1859).
- Perseverance is the secret of every triumph.
- If we must suffer, let us suffer nobly.
- Because we have had Napoleon the Great, must we have Napoleon the Little? (speech, July 1851).
- The greatness of a people is no more affected by its number than the greatness of an individual is measured by his height. Whoever presents a great example is himself great (speech at Geneva, 1862).
- Homer and the Bible — the only two books which the poet need study. In a sense one finds in them the whole of creation under a dual aspect: the genius of man in Homer, the spirit of God in the Bible.
- It is through brotherly action that liberty is saved (speech in Paris, 1870).
- We love our children far more than they love us.
- I decline the funeral rites of any church; I request a prayer from every soul; I believe in God (last will and testament, 1883).

helping to enthrone his treacherous ex-ally as *Napoleon III. Hugo's efforts to organize popular resistance after the coup d'état of December 2, 1851, met with failure and a week later he fled in disguise to Brussels. In answer to a decree of expulsion, he wrote *Histoire d'un crime* (which only appeared in 1877) and *Napoléon le petit*, a scathing satire published in London (1852).

Compelled to leave Brussels for a safer haven in the Channel Islands, Hugo and his oddly assorted household (wife, children, and mistress) initially took up residence on the island of Jersey, where they dabbled in spiritualism. Few poets in world literature can match the invective of *Les Châtiments* (1853), which reaches its height in "Ultima Verba" and "L'Expiation" — a savage account of Napoleon's retreat from Moscow and defeat at Waterloo. *Les Contemplations* (1856) appeared after an enforced move to Guernsey, which became Victor Hugo's permanent base in exile (1855–1870). He sought to establish himself as a deep thinker in his *Contemplations,* switching from lyrical to elegiac verse and then proceeding on a mystical journey into the unknown.

These years of exile were extraordinarily productive. Having rejected an imperial amnesty in 1859, Hugo published the first series of his *Légende des siècles*, which traced the history and strivings of mankind from the expulsion from the Garden of Eden to the nineteenth century and onward into the future. This epic (completed in 1883) stresses man's duty to resist tyrants and constitutes the zenith of Hugo's creativity as a poet. It was followed by another huge output of verse, while his prose works included *William Shakespeare* (1864), interpreting Hugo's favorite dramatist, and the novels *Les Travailleurs de la mer* ("Toilers of the Sea") in 1866, a Channel Islands tragedy, and *L'Homme qui rit* ("The Man Who Laughs"), an eccentric view of seventeenth-century England.

A few days after Napoleon III's resounding defeat by the Prussians at Sedan in 1870, Hugo arrived in Paris to find that nineteen years of self-imposed exile had made him an almost legendary hero. The horrors that he witnessed during the Prussian siege and the Commune were recorded in *L'Année terrible* (1872) and, when the Third Republic was established on the ruins of the Second Empire, he attempted a political comeback. No one took his utopian, humanitarian brand of socialism very seriously, nor did his efforts to rehabilitate the Communards prove successful, but his immense cultural prestige led to his appointment to the French Senate in 1876. During his last years he concentrated on his manuscripts, publishing *Quatre-vingt-treize* ("Ninety-three") in 1874, a novel about divided family loyalties and guerrilla warfare in the Revolutionary era, and *L'Art d'être grandpère* ("The Art of Being a Grandfather," 1877), poems compensating for the fact that all of his children had predeceased him. These and other works revived and enhanced his popularity. The death of Hugo brought a national outpouring of grief that Paris had rarely seen. During a state funeral his remains were conveyed from the Arc de Triomphe and laid to rest in the Panthéon.

V. Brombert, *Victor Hugo and the Visionary Novel*, 1984.

E. M. Grant,*The Career of Victor Hugo*, 1945.

R. B. Grant, *The Perilous Quest: Image, Myth and Prophecy in the Narratives of Victor Hugo*, 1968.

A. C. Haggard, *Victor Hugo: His Work and Love*, 1979.

A. Maurois, *Victor Hugo*, 1956.

HUMAYUN (Nasin-ud-Din Muhammad; 1508–1556), second Mogul emperor. Humayun, the son of *Babur, ascended to his father's throne in 1530. Rather than dispute his accession with his brothers, Humayun chose to divide the empire among them. While Humayun kept the bulk of northern India for himself, his younger brother, Kamrun, received suzerainty over the areas surrounding Kabul. Although the terms of the division of the empire stipulated that Humayun would have ascendancy over Kamrun, this was not to be.

Immediately upon ascending the throne, Humayun's authority was challenged. Local kings, led by Sher Shah, leader of the Indian Afghans of Bengal, were unwilling to support a dynasty they considered to be headed by foreign usurpers, and saw Babur's death as an ideal opportunity for them to assert their own independence. At the same time, Kamrun attacked the Punjab region belonging to Humayun. Kamrun occupied Lahore in 1531 and defeated Bahadur Shah of Gujarat soon after. Rather than attack his brother, Humayun preferred to acknowledge his conquests so that he could focus his attention on the local uprising led by Sher Shah.

The struggle against Sher Shah was a failure from the start. Humayun, an opium addict, spent much of his time delving into mysticism and astrology and reorganizing his court accordingly. His entire court was divided into twelve ranks, represented by arrows. Humayun himself receiving the highest rank. The court was further divided according to the four "elements": the military was represented by fire, the kitchen and stable staffs by air, irrigation by water, and agriculture and construction by earth. Officials received special uniforms in the color of their specific element. Court was held only on Sundays and Tuesdays, in keeping with advice Humayun received from his astrologers. An admirer of pomp and court ceremonies, Humayun instituted unusual salutations and the beating of drums on official occasions, ceremonies later adopted by his son, *Akbar. Despite Humayun's excesses, Mogul art and ingenuity flourished during his reign. Splendid boats were constructed and set afloat on the river Yamura; they contained lush gardens and elaborately decorated apartments, and were used by the emperor on ceremonial occasions.

Spending so much time cultivating his court prevented Humayun from governing his country effectively and he was defeated by Sher Shah at Jaumpur in 1532 and Bihar in 1533. In 1535 he was defeated in the east by Bahadur Shah of Gujarat, and after ten years of incessant warfare, Humayun was forced to flee his empire. His brother Kamrun refused to give him sanctuary, forcing him to flee to Persia. On his way to exile, Humayun passed through Sind; his son, Akbar, was born there in 1542.

Humayun never relinquished his hope of one day recovering his empire. In 1545 he joined Persia in an attack on his brother's realm in Kabul. The battle was a success and marked the turning point in Humayun's career. Sher Shah was killed in the storming of Kalinjar that same year, allowing Humayun to attempt to regain his lost domain. The ensuing battles lasted ten years; only after defeating the Surs at Sirhind in 1555 was Humayun able to reenter Delhi and Agra.

Humayun did not live to reap the fruits of his success. In 1556 he died after falling from a parapet in his palace and was succeeded by his son Akbar. Humayun's tomb in Delhi is one of the finest examples of Mogul architecture in India.

W. Erskine, *India under Babur and Humayun*, 1972.
B. Gulbadan, *Humayun-Nama*, 1972.

HUMBOLDT, ALEXANDER (1769–1859), German naturalist and explorer born in Berlin. In 1790 he accompanied George Foster, Captain *Cook's companion on his second voyage, on a visit to England, beginning a series of journeys which were to shape his life and thinking.

In 1792 Humboldt was given the position of assessor of mines in Berlin, quickly made his way up to the highest post in his department and was given important diplomatic assignments. At the same time he published, in 1793 a paper entitled *Florae Fribergensis Specimen*, based on his research of the flora of the Freiburg mines, and in 1794 published another paper on the results of lengthy experiments on muscular irritability.

In 1796, following the death of his mother, Humboldt left his work to devote himself to travel. Accompanied by the French botanist Aimé Bonpland, he journeyed to Madrid and unexpectedly received the patronage of the Spanish minister d'Urquijo. As a result, he and Bonpland set out on an exploration of Spanish America, a voyage which was to form the foundation of Humboldt's greatest meteorological and geographical discoveries.

The two set sail from Corunna in 1799 and landed at Cumana in Venezuela. On the night of November 12–13, 1799, Humboldt observed a meteor shower, which led him to begin the study of the periodicity of meteors. In 1800 he charted the course of the Orinoco river; after traveling 1,725 miles in four months, he successfully discovered where the Orinoco and the Amazon divided. He and Bonpland continued their lengthy journey, traveling to the sources of the Amazon on their way to Lima. Humboldt noted the fertilizing properties of guano and published his findings on the subject, leading to the importation and use of guano as a fertilizer in Europe. After spending a year in Mexico, he and Bonpland returned to Europe in 1804.

Humboldt's findings on the expedition, published in thirty volumes, devised ways to show that climatic conditions in countries could be compared. He investigated the rate of decrease in mean temperature with the increased elevation above sea level, and through his research into the origin of tropical storms, was able to deduce one of the main laws on atmospheric disturbances in higher altitudes. He also published an essay about the correlation between the distribution of organic life and physical conditions. He also discovered that the earth's magnetism decreases from the poles to the equator. Through his studies of the New World's volcanoes, he showed that they fell into pattern of linear groups that probably corresponded with underground fissures. He also debunked many previously held theories on rocks thought to have aqueous origins when he proved their igneous properties.

In Europe Humboldt visited Italy with Joseph Gay-Lussac to investigate the law of magnetic declination, and stayed for two years in Berlin. He settled in Paris in 1808 and, supported by Paris' scientific circles, spent the next twenty-one years working on the information he had gathered on his voyages. His fame had spread through Europe and America and academies all over the world sought to have him as a member. But it was in Paris that Humboldt felt most at ease, and when he received a summons to join the court in Berlin, he made a point of traveling to Paris as often as possible. In 1827, he settled permanently in Berlin.

In Berlin Humboldt began to study "magnetic storms" — a term he invented for abnormal disturbances of the earth's magnetism. In 1829 he made a request to the Russian government to set up a line of magnetic and meteorological stations across northern Asia; he also obtained the cooperation of the British Empire for his project. By so doing, he established the basis of the first international scientific joint effort, believing that science should be supra-national.

Humboldt did not resume his journeys until he was sixty. In 1829, he crossed the Russian Empire in twenty-five weeks, covering 9,615 miles from Neva to Yenesei. As a result of this trip, Humboldt was able to correct the exaggerated estimate then held of the height of the central Asian plateau; he also discovered diamonds in the gold areas of the Ural.

Between 1845 and 1847, Humboldt published the first two volumes of his greatest work, *The Cosmos.* The third and fourth volumes appeared between 1850 and 1858 and the fifth was published in 1862, after his death. Humboldt died at ninety and was honored by a state funeral. He never married and left his entire estate to his loyal servant Seifert. He was remembered not only for his scientific discoveries,: but also for fighting for improved conditions for the miners of Galicia and Franconia. He was also an outspoken opponent of slavery.

Humboldt's brother, Karl Wilhelm von Humboldt (1767–1835), was an educationalist and scholar of languages. He pioneered in ethnolinguistics and more particularly in the study of the Basque language, and also worked on the languages of the East and the South Sea islands. From 1809 he was Prussia's first minister of public instruction and founded the university in Berlin, now known by his name. He was also a noted diplomat, serving as Prussian ambassador to Vienna from 1812.

A. Bayo, *Humboldt,* 1970.
H. Beck, *Alexander Von Humboldt,* 1971.
D. Botting, *Humboldt and the Cosmos,* 1973.

HUS, JAN

HUS, JAN (1372–1415), Czech religious reformer. Born of peasant parents in Husinec, Southern Bohemia (hence the name "Hus"), he first wanted to become a priest "to secure a good livelihood and dress and be held in esteem by men." While studying at the University of Prague he earned a living first as a choirboy, then as a teacher at the university; he was awarded his M.A. in 1396 and was elected dean of the university's philosophy faculty in 1400.

Ordained as a priest in 1400, Hus became a preacher at the Bethlehem Chapel in Prague in

Hus burning at the stake, a contemporary illustration

1402; the chapel was at that time the center of the Czech reform movement, which advocated moral reform and religious teaching in Czech. Although he was held in sufficient esteem to be appointed preacher to the Prague Synod in 1405, his use of the pulpit as a platform for denouncing of clerical vices and abuses alienated him from the religious establishment.

This was the period of the Great Western Schism, when three conflicting contenders declared themselves pope: Gregory XII of Rome, Benedict XIII of Avignon, and Alexander V of Pisa. The Czech reformers briefly benefited from their support of Alexander, since King Wenceslas of Bohemia was also allied to that camp and therefore favored them. However, the archbishop of Prague, Sbinko von Hasenburg, belatedly declared his allegiance to Alexander, whereupon he was empowered to proceed against the reformers and persuaded Alexander to place a ban on chapel preaching. When Hus, who had become rector of the university in 1409, refused to abide by this, he was excommunicated.

Hus might have continued to enjoy royal support had he not, in denouncing a papal bull issued by Alexander's successor, John XXIII, also criticized the sale of indulgences in Prague, thereby infuriating Wenceslas, who was a beneficiary of these sales. Charged with explaining his opposition to the bull, Hus failed to appear at his hearing and was excommunicated for a second time in 1412. Public feeling ran high in Prague, with the population rising against indulgences and staging a mock burning of papal bulls. Hus left the city to save it from the possibility of ecclesiastical retaliation and found refuge with supporters among the Czech nobles.

Hus's insistence on according supreme authority to the life of *Jesus and personal conscience rather than the fiat of the pope threatened the authority of the church. He was brought to trial on a charge of heresy; his prosecutors so misrepresented his views that Hus refused to address the charges brought against him. He was duly pronounced guilty and martyred at the stake, chanting prayers until the flames engulfed him completely. The University of Prague declared him a martyr and fixed the date of his execution as his feast day.

The spirit of Hussite reform lived on. In Czechoslovakia public outrage prompted a huge pro-reform movement, which was only suppressed after its army had won many victories. The Czech national church continues the Hussite tradition to this day and his statue stands in Prague's main square. Moreover, Hus was an inspiration to generations of later reformers, including Martin *Luther and John *Calvin, who were instrumental in the Reformation of the sixteenth century.

H. Kaminsky, *A History of the Hussite Revolution*, 1967.

M. Spinka, *John Hus*, 1968.

HUSAYN IBN ALI (c.1854–1931), king of the Hejaz and Grand Sharif of Mecca. Husayn was born in Istanbul, a Hashemite descendant of *Muhammad. Part of his youth was spent in the Hejaz and part in Istanbul, and he was bilingual in Arabic and Turkish. He quickly distinguished himself in local society, and his appointment to the Ottoman council of state gave him access to the highest court and official circles.

After the Turkish revolution of 1908 the emir of Mecca went into exile, leaving the way clear for a new emir; Husayn was appointed by Sultan Hilmi Pasha to the post. Nurturing his growing ambitions, he made contact with Arab secret societies in Syria and Egypt and supporting home rule for the provinces. He even sent his second son, *Abdullah, to hold talks with the British in Egypt.

At the outbreak of World War I in 1914, Husayn strengthened his contacts with the British and deliberately failed to raise troops in the holy cities for the caliph's holy war. After negotiations with the British, letters were exchanged between the British high commissioner in Egypt, Sir Henry McMahon, and Husayn, which came to be known as the "McMahon Letters." Although seemingly an expression of a broad Anglo-Arab agreement, they were ambiguously worded and caused much controversy later. In the summer of 1916, encouraged by British promises of aid and the increased suppression of the Arabs in Syria, Husayn proclaimed the Arab revolt against the Turks, and succeeded in expelling the Turks from the whole of the Hejaz except Medina. He then proclaimed himself "King of the Arab Countries," which Britain, France, and Italy scaled down to "King of the Hejaz."

Unable to understand the events that followed or to control the West's' growing role in the Middle East, he remained in Mecca, where he became more and more isolated. Allied military occupation of geographical Syria and Iraq and the arrangements they made in the Sykes-Picot Agreement of 1916 defining the Allies' imperial schemes, precluded real Arab rule. Husayn found himself unable to influence the course of events. He could no longer control his four sons, Ali, Abdullah, Feisal, and Zeid, whom he had previously dominated and used as his private emissaries to the British and Arabs. After 1918, his role in Arab affairs, much to his bitterness, became restricted to the Hejaz. He could only listen to reports on the Versailles peace talks, where Arab claims were given little consideration.

Husayn's own kingdom suffered from his maladministration. He was unable to extend his rule over other parts of Arabia and refused to ratify the peace treaty because of the mandates applied to Arab territories. He aggravated relations with Egypt by disputing arrangements for the pilgrimage to Mecca and more seriously, with Abdul Aziz *Ibn Saud over control in central Arabia. He made his greatest mistake when, in Amman in 1924, he proclaimed himself caliph, although that office had been abolished by the Turks. The Arabs strongly opposed him and that further diminished his standing.

Six months later, the Wahhabi followers of Ibn Saud, offended by Husayn's assumption of the title of caliph, invaded the Hejaz and forced the king to abdicate. His eldest son, Ali, took the throne, while Husayn retired to Nicosia, Cyprus. He is said to have carried his personal fortune of several million pounds sterling as gold coins in petrol tins.

Husayn died of a stroke at his son Abdullah's court in Amman and was buried in the Haram al-Sharif (area of the Great Mosques) in Jerusalem.

G. Antonius, *The Arab Awakening*, 1938.

R. Baker, *King Husain*, 1979.

E. Kedourie, *England and the Middle East 1914–1921*, 1956.

Z. N. Zeine, *Arab-Turkish Relations and the Emergence of Arab Nationalism*, 1958.

HUXLEY, THOMAS HENRY (1825–1895), English naturalist, writer, lecturer, and proponent of Charles *Darwin's theory of evolution. He was born at Ealing, London; at ten he went to Coventry, where he was introduced to medicine by his elder sister's husband. By age sixteen he had become an assistant to a medical doctor, despite a professed interest in becoming a mechanical engineer.

In 1842 Huxley moved to London where he entered Charing Cross Hospital's medical school. He received his M.B. three years later at London University and had his first medical paper published, "On a Hitherto Undescribed Structure in the Human Hair-Sheath." He later said of himself on becoming a natural scientist instead of an engineer: "I am not sure that I have not, all along, been a sort of mechanical engineer... Physiology is the mechanical engineering of living machines." Later critics did, in fact, fault his mechanistic view of human evolution.

Huxley was assigned to Haslar Hospital in 1846 as lieutenant, R.N. Medical Service; that winter he sailed as assistant surgeon to survey Australasian waters. "On the Anatomy and Affinities of the

> - There is the greatest practical benefit in making a few failures early in life.
> - The great end of life is not knowledge but action.
> - The thief and murderer follow nature just as much as the philanthropist.
> - If individuality has no play, society does not advance; if individuality breaks out of all bounds, society perishes.
> - If a little knowledge is dangerous, where is the man who has so much as to be out of danger?
> - Irrationally held truths may be more harmful than reasoned errors.
>
> **Thomas Huxley**

Medusae" was written during this time, based on his research at sea. Upon his return from this four-year voyage on H.M.S. *Rattlesnake* he discovered that it had been published by the Royal Society.

Huxley was frustrated at first in his attempts to have the rest of his work published and to find a suitable position, despite receiving the Royal Medal of the Royal Society in 1852. Two years later he was offered the post of paleontologist and lecturer on natural history at the Government School of Mines. He refused the former, not caring for paleontology (the study of fossils), and agreed to lecture on natural history only until he could find a position in physiology; "But I held the office for thirty-one years, and a large part of my work has been paleontological," he later wrote. He had another paper published, "On the Educational Value of the Natural History Sciences."

In 1856 Huxley went on an expedition to Switzerland to study the structure of glaciers. He continued to publish papers and in 1859 his review of *The Origin of Species* appeared in *The Times*. The 1860 meeting of the British Association for the Advancement of Science was a victory for Darwin's theories. Deeply committed to the advancement of the scientific method, a firm believer in rationality and "the development and organization of scientific education,"

Huxley was, in his own words, in an "endless series of battles over evolution." He considered religion to be "that ecclesiastical spirit...[which is] the deadly enemy of science." Huxley saw religion and science as inimical and questioned any belief in God or in the spiritual world that could not be objectively proven, coining the term "agnostic" to describe this view. Huxley also introduced the term "biogenesis" to describe his view of the origins of life — that life only arises from another life — in juxtaposition to the description in the Book of Genesis (where life is created by God *ex nihilo*). Huxley spoke of having "helped that movement of opinion which has been called the New Reformation." Yet this "New Reformation," as its name implies, itself became a kind of secular, unprovable religion. One of the dogmas of Huxley's new creed was a belief in the dominance of the strong over the weak, the survival of the strongest.

During the next decade, Huxley's *Evidence as to Man's Place in Nature* and *Lectures on the Elements of Comparative Anatomy* were published, among other works. In 1871 he was appointed secretary of the Royal Society. A breakdown in his health soon followed, but a sizeable gift from his friends enabled him to take a complete rest. In 1880 his book *The Crayfish* appeared. Huxley was elected president of the Royal Society in 1883 and appointed to the Privy Council in 1892. He was awarded the Darwin Medal of the Royal Society in 1894. Altogether he wrote one hundred essays, two hundred scientific papers, and twenty books.

Three of Huxley's grandsons made notable achievements, two of them in scientific endeavors. Sir Julian Sorell Huxley (1887–1975), a noted biologist, helped establish the United Nations Educational, Scientific and Cultural Organization (UNESCO), of which he was its first director general; Andrew Fielding Huxley (born 1917) shared the Nobel Prize for physiology in 1963; and Aldous Leonard Huxley (1894–1963), was a famous novelist who protested the excesses of scientific thought and deplored the tendency toward the mechanization of life in the modern age.

C. Bibby, *Scientist Extrordinary: The Life and Experimental Work of Thomas Huxley*, 1972.
G. de Beer, ed., *Charles Darwin and T. H. Huxley, Autobiographies*, 1983.

I

IBN KHALDUN (Abu Zayd Abd ar-Rahman ibn Khaldun; 1332–1406), Arab historian, sociologist, and philosopher. Born in Tunis into an Arab political family, he obtained a broad classical Islamic education. After the Marinid invasion (1347–1349), he studied with the many excellent theological and literary scholars who came to Tunis, concentrating on philosophy and problems of Arabo-Muslim thought. The Marinid rule ended in bloodshed and, soon after, the Black Death which swept through Tunis claimed the lives of his parents.

He left Tunis to continue his studies in Fez, the capital of the Muslim West. Under the new sultan, Abu Salim, Ibn Khaldun was appointed secretary of the chancellery, but further disturbances and a new sultan found him forced to change allegiances once again. Ibn Khaldun must be regarded as a man of his time who, like his contemporaries, had to switch sides time and again as law and order crumbled.

Eventually, from 1375, he was able to live for four years in the castle of Ibn Salama in present-day Algeria. There at last he could devote himself to study, and there he wrote his most important work, the *Mukaddima* ({Introduction [to History]), which was the basis of his philosophy, and *Kitab al-Ibar*, his massive history of Muslim North Africa.

Later he returned to Tunis and became a teacher and scholar, but his past was not forgotten and in 1382 he decided to leave the Muslim West for Cairo. He was well received at the Mamluk capital and his courses at Al-Aznar University were extremely popular. However, his success was mixed with hardship. In 1384 his family was drowned in a shipwreck off Alexandria. Appointed a *kadi* (religious judge), he was resented for insisting on wearing his Maghribi dress (a dark burnoos). Six times he was appointed *kadi*, then dismissed.

Ibn Khaldun drew on his traditional Muslim education and political experiences when writing his *Mukaddima*. He is considered the founder of the science of history and of other disciplines, including sociology and economics. He was a realist and set laws for the reliable criticism of history. As an empiricist he based criticism on evidence and the probability of facts. In analyzing the evolution of history he saw a need to discover underlying laws. He developed his argument in a defined plan, stating a broad outline in six chapters on general human society (including the influence of the environment on human nature, i.e., an anthropological study); rural and primitive societies; different forms of government, states, and institutions; urban civilizations (the most sophisticated forms of society); industrial and economic affairs; and finally scholarship, literature, and culture.

He concentrated on the cause of the decline of a civilization, utilizing only examples from Arabo-Muslim history as he had witnessed and experienced its disintegration in North Africa. He denounced speculative reasoning and agreed with the cyclic system of historical interpretation through which he was able to develop other sciences, especially sociology and economics. Ibn Khaldun identified the basic causes of historical evolution in economic and social structures, the most significant of which he regarded as the common bond uniting members of a family, a tribe, or a nation, which drives them to corporate action on behalf of the community. He was also interested in the influence of the way of life and production methods on the development of social groups.

He discovered that the laws governing human society organized into political entities were as unalterable as those of human nature, and therefore became the first thinker to include the whole of society into a scientific inquiry. He noted that to found and maintain a state can be done quite independently of any religious content. On this point Ibn Khaldun was attacked for his unorthodoxy, but for him the Islamic state was nonetheless superior to a political state because the former had man's happiness in the future world at heart, while the latter only cared for man's material well-being in this world.

Ibn Khaldun also wrote an autobiography, *Ta'arif*, and several other works, including a treatise on arithmetic and an outline of logic. He had no Arab successors and it was Europeans who discovered his works and realized his significance.

A. Al-Azmeh, *Ibn Khaldun*, 1982.

F. Baali, 1988. *Society, State and Urbanism*, 1988.

W. J. Fischel, *Ibn Khaldun in Egypt*, 1967.

IBN RUSHD, MUHAMMAD SEE AVERROES

IBN SAUD, ABD AL-AZIZ (Abd al-Aziz ibn Abd ar-Rahaman ibn Faysal ibn Turki Abd Allah ibn Muhammed Al Saud; 1880–1953), warrior-statesman who united the tribes and emirates of the Arabian Peninsula into the kingdom of Saudi Arabia. Ibn Saud was a Wahhabi Muslim of the Saudi dynasty, a tribe whose roots can be traced to the mid-1700s. His ancestor, Muhammad Abd al Wahhab, was chased from his village by relatives after his conversion to strict Hanbali Sunni Islam. He and his protector, Muhammad ibn Saud, teamed up and converted nearby Arab tribes. Known as the Saudi dynasty, and teaching what became called the Wahhabi doctrine, they and their followers extended their influence throughout much of northern Arabia, taking control of the holy cities of Mecca and Medina in the early nineteenth century; they eventually lost power to the Ottoman-backed Rashid clan.

Ibn Saud was born in Riyadh but his family was driven out of the city ten years later by the Rashids and took refuge near the Rub' al-Qali, the Empty Quarter, of the Arabian Peninsula. There, among poor beduin tribes, Ibn Saud learned to ride and shoot expertly, and became accustomed to dealing with tribal Arabs. In 1902 he and a band of loyal Wahhabi tribesman retook Riyadh from the Rashids, thus beginning thirty years of conquests that would unify the peninsula under his rule.

In 1906, after subduing the Rashid clan, Ibn Saud defeated tribes in the central and eastern parts of the peninsula. During World War I the British made a treaty with him recognizing him as ruler of an independent Najd and Hassa, and were content with his benevolent neutrality. His conquests attracted foreign notice when he took the Hijaz and the holy cities of Mecca and Medina in 1926, thereby becoming the most respected leader in Arabia. Ibn Saud strictly adhered to the teachings of Wahhabi Islam and enforced them among his troops, using religious beliefs to temper the beduin tribesmen's love of battle and loot.

In addition to his martial skills, Ibn Saud used marriage as a way of cementing tribes' loyalty, marrying daughters of newly subdued tribes. To remain within the Koran's limit of four wives, Ibn Saud frequently divorced his wives after a brief marriage and sent them, laden with gifts, back to their guardians.

A decisive factor in Ibn Saud's ability to unify Arabia was his formation of the religious organization the Ikhwan (the Brothers), which required beduin to give up their nomadic lifestyle in favor of an agricultural one. This made the men easier to control, more willing to heed Wahhabi religious teachings, and more easily disciplined when they were needed for military service. Without the Ikhwan, it is doubtful that Ibn Saud would have been able to unite Arabia within one generation. However he disbanded the Ikhwan in 1930 when members began conducting raids on Iraqi tribes. After conquering Asir in 1932 and creating the

King Abd al-Aziz Ibn Saud

kingdom of Saudi Arabia, Ibn Saud ceased his conquests. He also, after a brief war in 1934, relinquished all claims to Yemen, a wise move since the residents of Yemen were Zaydi Shi'ites and would have bitterly resisted conquest by Wahhabi Sunni Muslims. By the 1940s Ibn Saud was widely regarded as the Arabs' elder statesman.

Until the late 1930s, the Saudi kingdom was desperately poor, relying on trade in dates and camels, and the revenue brought in by the approximately one hundred and fifty thousand tourists who visited the holy cities on the annual Haj (pilgrimage). It was believed that Arabia had mineral wealth and oil, but the harsh climate, fierce beduin tribes, and religious fanaticism discouraged foreign prospectors until the American Charles Crane and his partner Karl Twitchell began prospecting for oil in 1931.

Crane and Twitchell found nothing but two years later Twitchell returned as an employee of Standard Oil of California, which had obtained exploration rights in eastern Arabia. For a $300,000 loan, an annual rent of $30,000 and a small royalty, Ibn Saud gave the Americans a sixty-year concession to search for and export oil. Within five years, crude oil was being exported and refineries were being built; a "little America" had sprung up in Dharan, where the American oil workers lived, complete with lawns, swimming pools, and a commissary that sold American food.

At the time, Saudi Arabia had no modern government framework, and no division was made between the king's personal fortune and state wealth, which was kept in wooden chests in the palace; no state bank existed. Each of King Ibn

Saud's subjects could approach him personally to air grievances. Wahhabi Islam was strictly enforced, with religious leaders going from house to house to ensure that Muslims prayed five times daily. Justice was administered according to the Koran — thieves' hands were chopped off, murderers beheaded. Alcohol, tobacco, Western clothes, movies, and dancing were forbidden.

In this atmosphere, the effect of the "little America" of the oil workers was revolutionary. It was, for nearly all Saudis, their first exposure to the Western world, although Ibn Saud himself had learned the value of technology in helping him to maintain his power, owned a car, and introduced the telegraph and telephone into Saudi Arabia.

Ibn Saud had forty-seven sons by twenty-two different women, and approximately the same number of daughters. They were required to marry into one of a few well-respected families. Each member of the royal family had his own palace, a state income, and held some public office. Eventually the royal family became corrupted by the tremendous oil wealth and the aging, lame, half-blind king was unable to understand the change or comprehend modern economics. When he died, his eldest son, Saud, took over and quickly ran up $300 million of debt before being deposed and replaced by King Faisal.

M. Almana, *Arabia Unified*, 1985.
J. Goldberg, *The Foreign Policy of Saudi Arabia*, 1986..
J. Teitlebaum, *The Saudis and the Hajj*, 1916–1933, 1988.

IBN SINA SEE AVICENNA

IBSEN, HENRIK JOHAN (1828–1906), Norwegian poet and dramatist. He was born in Skien to a wealthy family and when he was four the family moved into a large house where they entertained lavishly. By the time he was six his father had gone bankrupt and all that was left of the family fortune was the farm they lived in, outside Skien.

The second child of a large family, Ibsen used to escape to an unused pantry to get some peace. There he would lock himself in and draw caricatures of the members of the family. He felt no real warmth for any of them, with the exception of his sister Hedwig, and when his father died, some thirty years after he had left home, he learned about it from a newspaper.

As a youth he dreamed of becoming a doctor but his father could not afford to finance his schooling. In lieu of a formal education he apprenticed himself to an apothecary in the town of Grimstad, where he lived for the next six years. Although he was not particularly happy sharing cramped quarters with the apothecary's small children, his life there was not all bad; he wrote poems, drew caricatures, and spent time with his friends Christopher Due and Ole Schulerud.

In 1849 Ibsen wrote his first full-length play, *Catalina*. When publishers turned it down,

---

GEORGE BERNARD SHAW ON HENRIK IBSEN

- Ibsen's morality is original all through; he knows well that the men in the street have no use for principles because they can neither understand nor apply them; and that what they can understand and apply are arbitrary rules of conduct, often frightfully destructive and inhuman, but at least definite rules enabling the common stupid man to know where he stands and what he may do without getting into trouble.
- Ibsen supplies the want left by Shakespeare. He gives us not only ourselves but our situations. One consequence is that his plays are much more important to us than Shakespeare's.

Schulerud paid for its publication and the two left immediately afterward for the university in Christiana (Oslo). There they lived in a garret, waiting to get rich from Ibsen's playwriting ability, but all they received for his talents was the money a greengrocer gave them for the 205 copies of *Catalina* they sold to him as wrapping paper.

That winter his play *The Warrior's Tomb* was staged. The following summer he took his entrance exams for the university and failed in Greek and mathematics. Instead of a place at the university he took the position of resident poet at the Bergen Theater, which essentially meant acting as assistant to the assistant stage manager. He stayed there for seven years, writing verse plays based on old Norse folk ballads and legends. Of these only *Feast at Solhuag* was a success, and it got him an invitation to the home of Paster Thoresen, whose daughter he married in 1858.

In 1857 he was offered a much more lucrative post at the National Theater at Christiania, which had been founded for the purpose of developing a national Norwegian style of drama. During the five years he spent there he wrote two of his more important early plays, *The Warriors at Helgeland* (1858) and *Love's Comedy* (1862). The theater, however, was unsuccessful, and closed in 1862, leaving him and his family poverty-stricken.

With a grant for foreign travel, Ibsen left Norway for Copenhagen in 1863. There, stirred by the Danish efforts in their war with Prussia, he tried to rally Scandinavian support for the Danes, but Sweden and Norway remained neutral. When the Danes were defeated he felt ashamed and betrayed by his country. The years 1864 to 1891 were spent mostly abroad, in Italy and Germany. In 1866 he wrote the dramatic poem *Brand*, a vision of his countrymen as they should have been, about the duty of the individual to be true to his best characteristics. His poem touched the Norwegian national conscience and was a huge success — finally he had become the national poet of Norway.

For Ibsen the highest goal was self-realization and he saw failure as a rejection of the individual call that each person has from God. As a writer he saw his role as going beyond the visible to the essence. His best works were his angriest, railing against dishonesty, apathy and indifference, and giving his audiences deep psychological insight into societal and personal conflicts. The plays he wrote between 1866 and 1890 were essentially about two themes: the importance of the individual and the need for a society which would allow the individual full opportunity for self-development; and the evils caused by the denial of love. They included the dramatic poem *Peer Gynt* (1867), about the degeneration of an individual who has no moral fiber and shirks his responsibility; *The League of Youth* (1869); *The Pillars of Society* (1877), calling for truth and freedom to replace hypocrisy and lying in society; and *A Doll's House* (1879), about a marriage that is not based on love and respect for the individual, which created a sensation when the "new woman" walked out of her home and marriage, slamming the door behind her. These were followed by *Ghosts* (1881), a play which caused a scandal by showing a son suffering from hereditary venereal disease, the consequence of his father's misdeed, *An Enemy of the People* (1882), about social hypocrisy, and *The Wild Duck* (1884), which suggests the need on occasion to lie when the truth would lead to tragedy.

Ibsen's social and psychological themes aroused criticism in Europe and Norway and shocked audiences who saw drama as entertainment rather than serious commentary. He was warmly championed, however, by critics such as George Bernard *Shaw in England and Georg Brandes in Denmark, and in time his plays were accepted. When he returned to Norway in 1891 it was as its greatest living writer. The plays have been translated into many languages including Japanese. His later works include *The Lady from the Sea* (1888) and *Hedda Gabler* (1890), which again anticipated modern feminism, *The Master Builder* (1892), *Little Eyolf* (1894), a tragedy of children seeking to break away from their parents to lead their own lives, *John Gabriel Borkman* (1896), and *When We Dead Awaken* (1900). With all of these works Ibsen ushered in modern, naturalistic, social drama.

B. F. Dukore, *Money and Politics in Ibsen*, 1980.

A. Ganz, *Realms of the Self*, 1980.

G. E. Rieger, *Henrik Ibsen*, 1981.

M. M. Levesen, *Ibsen, a Biography,* 3 vols., 1967–1971; 1 vol., 1991.

INNOCENT III (Giovanni Lotario de' Conti; c. 1160–1216), one of the most powerful popes of the Middle Ages. He was born into a noble Italian family, the counts of Segni, who provided him with all the advantages of birth and education. His commanding presence, influential connections, and tactful diplomacy enabled him to advance rapidly in ecclesiastical circles: at twenty-six he was ordained a subdeacon, at twenty-nine a cardinal deacon, and at thirty-seven he became pope. His pontificate was the climax of the temporal and spiritual supremacy of the Roman see.

Innocent was determined to dominate both the church and the world. He believed wholeheartedly that the pope's spiritual power made him lord of the world and its ruler, and so forsook the traditional papal title of "Vicar of Peter" for "Vicar of Christ, Successor of Peter, Anointed of the Lord, God of the Pharaohs, less than God but greater than man."

Innocent was determined to reform the church, which had become corrupted by widespread selling of church offices, services, fraudulent relics, and indulgences, as well as by clerical immorality, drunkenness, and violation of laws of chastity. He tightened the church chain of command, gave the impetus to Saint Dominic's mission, and approved the founding of the Franciscan and Poor Clare monastic orders (he met Saint *Francis of Assisi twice; the first time ejecting him as a beggar, the second to officially authorize the Franciscan Order).

His sincere belief in the righteousness of his cause and cool support of any means by which his goals were to be achieved caused numerous clashes with secular rulers. Innocent had no scruples about using his powerful religious weapons of interdict, excommunication, and deposition, which could bring the strongest kings to their knees. He succeeded in making the church more powerful than it had ever been — giving rise to the fear of a church-dominated Europe that eventually brought about the Protestant Reformation.

Innocent's fight to stop heresy and spread Christianity gave fresh impetus to the Inquisition; he forced the Jews to wear distinctive badges and inaugurated three more crusades; the Fourth Crusade (1202), the Albigensian Crusade (1209), and the Children's Crusade (1212). Innocent placed the direction of the Fourth Crusade in the hands of the Venetians, who did not want to damage their lucrative Egyptian trade by following Innocent's plan for attacking the Holy Land through Egypt. Instead they made use of the Crusaders to subjugate a rival port city and conquer Constantinople. Innocent rejoiced at the unification of Orthodox and Catholic churches under his rule while deploring the sack of Constantinople. The Albigensian Crusade, directed against a Christian sect in southern France that denied the Church's authority, was marked by widescale robbery, murder, and seizure of land belonging to heretics and the faithful alike. Innocent had not called for the Children's Crusade, as he had the other two crusades, but rather tried to discourage this pathetic episode led by a French peasant boy who had experienced a vision, gently telling the children to go home.

By the Fourth Lateran Council (1215) Innocent's control was so absolute that his decrees were passed without change or comment. The Council condemned clerical marriages, trial by combat, trial by ordeal, and the Jewish people for crucifying *Jesus. Exhausted, Innocent died soon after.

S. R. Packard, *Europe and the Church under Innocent III*, 1968.

J. M. Powell, *Innocent III: Vicar of Christ or Lord of the World*, 1963.

H. Tillman, *Pope Innocent III*, 1980.

ISABELLA I (1451–1504), queen of Castile. She was the daughter of John II of Castile and his second wife, Isabella of Portugal. John died when Isabella was three and she was brought up away from court by her mother, whose extreme piety had a great influence on Isabella's character. John's successor, Isabella's half-brother Henry, was known as "Henry the Impotent" because of his wastefulness, incompetence, and childlessness. Dissatisfied nobles searched for a competent heir, so Henry brought Isabella to court at thirteen to watch over her. Henry did claim to have a daughter, Juana, but the nobles doubted that Henry the Impotent was really her father and forced Henry to acknowledge Isabella as his heiress when she was seventeen.

Isabella had a number of suitors but chose at eighteen to marry her cousin *Ferdinand, king of Sicily and heir to the kingdom of Aragon. The nobles helped to contrive the match over her brother's disapproval; a Jewish lawyer loaned them enough money to get married. Henry's death precipitated a war of succession against Juana and her husband, which Ferdinand won in 1476.

Ferdinand and Isabella made an extremely effective team. Though officially joint rulers of their kingdoms, Castile's internal administration remained in Isabella's hands. With Ferdinand's cooperation she restored order in Castile, subduing powerful nobles, ending highway robbery, and reforming the legal system. Interested in education, she studied Latin, encouraged scholars, and patronized the arts. Publicly extravagant and privately frugal, she spent her spare time making embroideries for churches.

Entitled "the Catholic" by the pope, Isabella demonstrated extreme piety and selected the sternest, most intolerant priests as her confessors and spiritual guides. She tried to reform the morals of both clergy and laity and even criticized the immorality of some popes. She refused to accept several papal appointers to positions in Spain on the grounds that their moral standards were not high enough and that such appointments infringed on royal rights. Intensely interested in the war against Granada (the last Muslim kingdom in Spain), she courageously kept her court with the besieging army for years and was personally responsible for improving military supply lines and establishing a military hospital. The lure of potential new souls for Christianity led her to overcome Ferdinand's lack of interest and send Christopher *Columbus off on his voyages of discovery. Loyal to her friends and tender to her children, she was cruel to heretics. Although loved by her Christian subjects for her warmth and kindness, she was responsible for instituting the Inquisition and expelling both Jews and Muslims from Spain.

Isabella suffered much from the tragedies of her private life. Ferdinand was frequently unfaithful, seven of her ten children died young or were stillborn, and her only son died childless in 1497. Her ambitions to unify Spain and Portugal ended when the queen of Portugal, her own daughter Isabella, died in childbirth in 1498 and, further, with the death of her grandson Miguel in 1500. Her only surviving child, Juana, went mad. In 1990 conservative Catholic circles proposed that she be beatified during 1992, the five hundreth anniversary of Columbus's voyage. The proposal was contested within the church, which thought that aspects of her zeal — such as her devotion to the Inquisition and cruel attitude to Muslims and Jews — made the suggestion untimely, and it was shelved.

M. Lunenfeld, *Keepers of the City*, 1987.

W. H. Prescott, *History of the Reign of Ferdinand and Isabella*, 1963.

ISAIAH (eighth century B.C.E.), one of the greatest prophets of ancient Israel. Isaiah spoke out against social injustice and idolatry among the people and advised the Hebrew kings to rely on God rather than political and military alliances that compromised the nation's ability to fulfill its divine covenant.

The book of Isaiah has been divided by scholars into at least two sections. The first division, chapters 1–39, is attributed to Isaiah, son of Amos, who prophesied in the late eighth century B.C.E. The second part dates from 540 B.C.E., nearly two hundred years later, when Israelites in the Babylonian exile hoped to return to Zion when the Persian king *Cyrus conquered Babylonia. Scholars have attributed this later part of the book to an unnamed author referred to as Deutero-Isaiah (Second Isaiah).

Isaiah, the son of Amoz, came from a noble family and was advisor to the kings of Judah. His wife was also a prophet, and their sons were given symbolic names: Shear-Jashub ("a remnant shall return"), referring to the part of Judah that would survive the onslaught of Syria and the northern kingdom, and a second son, Maher-Shalal-Hash-Baz ("the spoil speeds, the prey hastens"), perhaps foretelling the defeat of Syria and the northern kingdom by the Assyrians.

Isaiah lived during the reigns of four Judean kings: Uzziah, Jotham, Ahaz, and Hezekiah. The years preceding Uzziah's death were peaceful and prosperous, the kingdom of Judah having been fully transformed into an agricultural and urban nation. Under Uzziah, the distribution of wealth in the

A fragment from the first century B.C.E. scroll of Isaiah, found in Qumran

kingdom was equitable and it became the most stable and powerful state in the region. Conditions began to change under Jotham, and by the time Ahaz came to power the dominance of wealthy landowners and merchants had reduced many people to a state of dependence.

While social inequity grew, the kingdom came under military threat from Assyria. It was at this time that Isaiah received his prophetic commission. It began at the temple in Jerusalem, according to chapter six of the book of Isaiah, in the year of King Uzziah's death. In his prophetic pronouncements Isaiah railed against inequality in the society, attacking the indifference of the rich as well as criticizing those who carried out ritual sacrifices in the temple without sincere intention to mend their ways. He urged the Israelites to set aside the idols they had adopted from surrounding nations and return to their original covenant with the monotheistic and moral God revealed at Sinai.

When the northern kingdom of Israel, which was also prepared for an imminent attack from Assyria, urged the new king, Ahaz, to join an anti-Assyrian alliance, Isaiah advised against it. He felt that Judah's only security lay in fulfilling its covenant with God; an alliance with the northern kingdom and Syria would only weaken its independence and commitment to fulfilling the divine commandments. This linking together of contemporary history included Isaiah's view that Assyria was the rod that would be the instrument of God's punishment of Judah should it fail to return to its covenantal obligations. When people failed to heed his call for change, Isaiah began to forecast doom — the overthrow of the kingdom by Assyria. When Jerusalem was besieged it looked as though his prediction would be fulfilled, but to the amazement of all Assyria suddenly and unexpectedly withdrew. Isaiah refused to be comforted, warning that the judgment had merely been postponed.

When Jerusalem was again threatened, Isaiah returned to his theme that obeying the moral commands was the only means to security, while the generals turned to an alliance with Egypt to help fend off the Assyrians. Although the people were oblivious to his warning, Isaiah predicted that a remnant would survive the destruction of the kingdom. The year of the Assyrian *Sennacherib's siege of Jerusalem, 701 B.C.E., marks the last year of Isaiah's known activity.

The approach taken in chapters 40–66 of the book of Isaiah presumes the fall of Jerusalem, which occurred in 586 B.C.E., and the exile to Babylonia. Apparently written in Babylonia, it predicts that the Persian king Cyrus will soon conquer Babylonia and redeem the Hebrew exiles. In contrast to the harsh

FAMILIAR QUOTES FROM ISAIAH

- They shall beat their swords into plowshares and their spears into pruning hooks: Nation shall not lift up sword against nation, neither shall they learn war any more.
- The wolf shall dwell with the lamb and the leopard shall lie down with the kid.
- How art thou fallen from heaven, O Lucifer, son of the morning.
- Let us eat and drink; for tomorrow we shall die.
- All flesh is grass.
- There is no peace, saith the Lord, unto the wicked.
- A man of sorrows and acquainted with grief.
- Comfort ye, comfort ye my people, says thy God.
- Can the Ethiopian change his skin or the leopard his spots?
- The fathers have eaten a sour grape and the children's teeth are set on edge.
- He is brought as a lamb to slaughter.

warnings contained in the first chapters of the book of Isaiah, it brings a message of comfort to the Jewish nation, speaking of its reconciliation with God and a renewal of the covenant. Israel is seen as a suffering servant of God, bringing God's message to the nations of the world even while it is persecuted by them.

Isaiah was an uncompromising monotheist, exalting God's transcendence as well as His involvement in the mundane affairs of man. He rejected dualism and attributed everything that occurs, whether good or bad, to God's providence. He believed in the universality of God rather than a narrow nationalistic view of the divine and held that Israel's duty was to communicate God's teachings to the rest of the nations. This would inevitably cause Israel suffering, and its trial would come at the hands of the nations that rebelled against these teachings. Isaiah predicted that in spite of these trials Israel would triumph in its task by accepting even its persecutions in order to fulfill the divine will.

The book of Isaiah proved a rich source for Christianity, as many of its sayings were seen as foretelling the events and beliefs of the New Testament. In particular, the "suffering servant" was identified with *Jesus.

S. B. Freehof, *The Book of Isaiah*, 1972.
J. L. McKenzie, *Second Isaiah*, 1968.

ISHMAEL (Heb., "may God hear"; lived c. nineteenth century B.C.E.), traditional progenitor of the Arab peoples. The eldest son of the patriarch *Abraham (born when his father was eighty-six), Ishmael's mother was Hagar, the Egyptian handmaiden of Sarah, Abraham's wife. Fearful of Abraham's heirless state and believing herself to be barren, Sarah gave him Hagar as his wife. However, when Hagar conceived Sarah became jealous, believing that Hagar despised her for her infertility. At Sarah's request, Abraham gave Hagar into her hands. To escape Sarah's harsh treatment, the pregnant Hagar fled to the wilderness, where she was found by an angel of God who commanded her to return to her mistress and told her that God would "multiply her seed exceedingly" (Gen. 16:10). He also told her that she would bear a son and call him Ishmael, "because the Lord has heard your affliction" (Gen. 16:11). Ishmael would be a "wild man; his hand will be against every man, and every man's hand against him" (Gen 16:12).

In response to God's command, Abraham had Ishmael circumcised when he was thirteen. Abraham himself was ninety-nine years of age when he was circumcised. God promised him a son from Sarah with whom he would establish a covenant, but Abraham said: "O that Ishmael might live before thee!" (Gen. 17:18). To console him, God promised to make Ishmael a great nation and father of twelve princes.

When Sarah gave birth to Isaac, her fear for her own son's birthright and inheritance caused her to force Abraham to send Hagar and Ishmael away into the wilderness. The Bible relates that Sarah saw

Ishmael mocking her at the feast Abraham had prepared to celebrate Isaac's weaning, upon which she went to Abraham and insisted that he send away the handmaid and her son. Abraham was reluctant to do so, but God promised him again that Ishmael would be a great nation because he was Abraham's seed.

The following morning Abraham rose early to send Hagar and Ishmael away with a jar of water and a loaf of bread. They wandered in the wilderness near Beersheba, where Abraham was encamped, until these supplies were gone, and Hagar left Ishmael under a bush in order not to watch him die of thirst. In response to her weeping, an angel opened her eyes and she saw a well of water.

Ishmael became a hunter and later married an Egyptian woman who bore him twelve sons and a daughter, whose names are listed in the book of Genesis (23:13–15). The books of Judges and Chronicles also mention individuals as well as tribes identified as "Ishmaelites." Genesis relates that they were traders in spices who went by camel from Gilead to Egypt. Like their father Ishmael, they were nomads who wandered the desert.

Ishmael is last mentioned in Genesis in connection with the death of Abraham, whose burial in the cave of Machpelah he and his half-brother Isaac supervised jointly. Ishmael was 137 years of age when he died. In Islamic tradition, Abraham, the father of Ishmael, is referred to as the Friend (of God) and is considered the first Muslim, i.e., the first to have submitted unquestioningly to the will of Allah.

N. M. Sarna, *Understanding Genesis*, 1966.

ITO, HIROBUMI (1841–1909), Japanese statesman; father of the Japanese constitution. Under Ito's aegis Japan became the only Eastern nation to integrate successfully into the modern Western world of the time.

Ito was born in Choshu at a time when Japan was still governed by the Tokugawa shogunate, which was intent on maintaining the country's isolationism. The son of a low ranking samurai, Ito could not have expected to rise higher than the middle reaches of the civil service.

By 1857 Japan was suffering the death throes of the shogunate as restless feudal domains attempted to reinstate the powers of the emperor. At this time, Ito entered the Shoku Sonjuka Academy, where he was imbued with a proimperial, anti-Western ideology.

Ito departed for England in 1863 as part of a Choshu delegation studying naval affairs. En route, in Shanghai, he witnessed for the first time the sight of Western naval fleets at anchor and realized that Japan would be better served by conciliation with the West (which he had hitherto deemed barbaric); this would enable it to build a strong industrial base and subsequently become a regional power in its own right.

The shogunate was overthrown in 1867 in what became known as the Meiji Restoration. Ito received a low ministerial job in the new government, quickly demonstrating his special skills of negotiation and compromise. A few years later he was appointed to a team selected to tour the West headed by Okuba Toshimichi, the home minister and most powerful figure in the government. Ito quickly caught Okuba's eye and in 1877 Okuba appointed him minister of public works. When Okuba was assassinated the following year, Ito replaced him as home minister and, almost overnight, became one of the most senior councilors in Japan, though still not forty years of age.

Ito had a precise vision for Japan, involving both political and industrial modernization. With this in mind, in 1882 Ito headed a delegation to Europe to study models for a constitution for Japan. He was elevated to the peerage in 1884 with the title of marquess. By 1885 he had reorganized the government around a cabinet structure and became Japan's first modern prime minister, and one of only a few in pre-World War II times to have achieved this status without a blood relationship to the imperial household. He began drafting the constitution in 1886, basing it on the Prussian model, and finally publicized it in 1889. Though Ito was revolutionary for his time, he was nonetheless steadfastly loyal to the emperor; the new constitution stressed supreme monarchic virtues. When the first Diet sat in 1890, Ito became president of the House of Peers.

In 1892 Ito once again became prime minister, achieving two notable successes in this term. First, he gained a partial revision of the unequal treaties that operated between Japan and the Western powers. Then in 1895 he oversaw Japan's decisive military defeat of China. However, Western intervention on behalf of China led to diplomatic humiliation, and Ito reluctantly resigned from office. He again served as prime minister in 1898, and then again for seven months in 1900 after forming his own political party, the Seiyumai, the first to control the lower house of the Diet in its own right.

The following year Ito retired to the House of Peers. After Japan's stunning victory over Russia in 1905 he was appointed the first resident general of Korea. His rule there, though absolute, was moderate by Japanese standards, although in the end it failed because he was unable to win the confidence of the local population. Ito was made a prince of Japan in 1907 for his services to the country, but in 1909 he was shot dead by a Korean assassin.

T. K. Gikai, *Ito Hirobumi*, 1979.

Y. Oka, *Five Political Leaders of Modern Japan*, 1985.

ITURBIDE, AGUSTIN DE (Agustin I; 1783–1824), emperor of Mexico. Born in the Mexican town of Valladolid (now Morelia), he joined the Spanish colonial army when only fourteen years old and quickly rose through the ranks. He supported the colonial power against independence-minded rebels and was responsible for the capture of Jose María Morelos, a prominent leader of the independence movement.

Fearing the collapse of Ferdinand VII's regime in 1820, Mexican conservatives sided with the independence movement in a bid to ensure the continuation of favorable local policies. Iturbide was chosen to lead them. At first the liberals, suspicious of Iturbide's abrupt turnabout, were reluctant to meet with him, but eventually, liberal rebel leader Vicente Guerrero agreed to coordinate policy between the two movements. Early contacts with the liberals were doomed by Iturbide's insistence on dictating a conservative agenda for independence, but in 1821 the two produced the Plan of Iguala, a compromise allowing the divided factions to join forces against Spain. The plan contained three guarantees: independence agreed upon by both parties; recognition of the official status of the Roman Catholic Church (a gesture to the conservatives), and racial equality for all Mexicans (a gesture to the liberals). Another thorny issue was the nature of the future government; the conservatives were avowed monarchists, while the liberals were republicans. The final compromise envisioned a constitutional monarchy with Ferdinand or another European prince as head of state.

The already demoralized Spanish troops were easily defeated by the combined liberal and conservative forces. On August 24, 1821, Viceroy Juan de Donoju initiated the signing of the Treaty of Córdoba recognizing the Plan of Iguala as the basis for immediate Mexican independence. The Treaty of Córdoba, however, contained one significant deviation from the Plan of Iguala, initiated at Iturbide's behest. A new clause was inserted stating that should no European prince be willing to accept the kingship, that role would be assumed by a native Mexican.

Iturbide joined a five-man junta appointed to govern Mexico until a king was chosen. Already the conservative favorite for the role, his supporters ensured his preeminence over other junta members by having him appointed commander in chief of the Mexican army with the pompous title *Generalissimo de Tierra y Mar* (Commander of Land and Sea). Knowing that his support among the liberals, who had not abandoned the idea of a republican government, was abating, Iturbide began campaigning on his own behalf as the most suitable candidate for king. A massive demonstration was organized to march from the Congress buildings to his own home demanding his acceptance of the throne. As the mob stood chanting his name in the street, Iturbide appeared on the balcony and proclaimed his acceptance. He told the crowd that he sought no self-aggrandizement, but would not venture to insult them by rejecting their offer. He then joined the mob and led them back to Congress, where he was voted emperor although the necessary quorum for congressional proceedings was lacking. That afternoon, Iturbide was sworn in as Emperor Agustin I.

Agustin I reigned only ten months, but in that short time he managed to ruin the Mexican economy, already in shambles after twenty years of civil war. Congress ignored pressing economic and social issues to deliberate on matters of imperial etiquette and protocol. Among the issues discussed were whether the motto on the new currency should be in Latin or Spanish; whether newly appointed nobles should be required to kiss the emperor's hand at the coronation, and whether the coronation should be preceded by a three-day national fast (determined as impractical to enforce). The coronation ceremony itself was modeled on that of *Napoleon.

Iturbide's despotic regime lost all support when he dissolved congress in favor of his own absolute rule. Former revolutionary comrades, including Guerrero and Antonio López de Santa Anna, plotted in Vera Cruz to oust Iturbide and proclaimed a republican government in that city. The rapid growth of the republican cause led to Iturbide's abdication in February, 1823. He was forced into exile in Italy, but was provided with a sizable pension in recognition of his contribution to Mexican independence.

Noting from exile how the republican revolution exacerbated rather than resolved Mexico's problems, Iturbide plotted to regain his throne. He returned to Mexico but was arrested, imprisoned, and executed by a firing squad. Mexico remained a republic until *Maximilian assumed the throne in 1863.

T. E. Anna, *The Merxican Empire of Iturbide*, 1990.
W. S. Robertson, *Iturbide of Mexico*, 1952.
J. E. Rodriguez (ed.), *The Independence of Mexico and the Creation of the New Nation*, 1989.

IVAN III VASILYEVICH (Ivan the Great; 1440–1505), grand prince of Russia and founder of the Russian Empire. Born in Moscow, he was to become a pawn in the civil war between his father, Grand Prince Vasily II of Moscow, and members of his father's family who sought the predominance of Novgorod, Moscow's rival as guardian of Orthodox Christianity. When Vasily's fortunes were at an ebb (he was arrested and blinded), his supporters spirited Ivan, age six, out of Moscow; they then betrayed Vasily by giving Ivan up to Vasily's enemies. On Vasily's return to power, he cemented a political alliance with Tver by having his son, still six years old, betrothed to the daughter of that city's grand prince.

From 1446 until his father's death in 1462, Ivan was groomed for the throne. At the age of twelve he married the princess to whom he had been betrothed and took command, at least in name, of a troop sent out by Vasily to the far north to eliminate the last of his enemies. At eighteen Ivan distinguished himself against the Tatars in the south of Russia. On his father's death he became grand prince, and the next five years passed relatively quietly.

In 1467 Ivan's wife died. Having only one son from this alliance and wishing to secure the succession, he decided to remarry. After a long period of indecision, in 1472 he married the niece of the last Byzantine emperor and ward of Cardinal Bessarion of Rome, Zoë Paleologus. During these years, having succeeded in annexing both Novgorod and Tver by a mixture of Machiavellian religious intrigue and straightforward fighting, he

had sent out parties of explorers to the new regions that had come under his power, especially in the northeast as far as the Arctic.

Zoë, whose name had been changed to Sophia upon her marriage, escaped from the Kremlin in 1480, the year in which Ivan's two younger brothers rebelled against him and the Tatars invaded his territory. Ivan, using bribery and intrigue, had tried to avoid outright battle, but in 1480 he was forced to face the Tatars, who had crossed the Don and reached the Oka, menacing Moscow. He waited for weeks before ordering his army to retreat to Moscow; this battleless campaign of 1480 was later seen as marking the end of Tatar oppression of Russia. It was in fact typical of Ivan's policy and the means by which Moscow slowly and relatively bloodlessly absorbed its neighbors and possible rivals.

When Ivan's heir, his son by his first wife, died in 1490, the problem of succession became more serious. He hesitated until 1497, unable to decide between Dmitri, his nephew or Vasily, his own eldest son by Sophia. His decision was made harder by his need to cement relations with Moldavia, his ally in the ongoing conflict with Lithuania; Dmitri's mother was the daughter of Moldavia's ruler. In 1497 Ivan chose Dmitri, who was then fourteen years of age, and had him crowned grand prince in 1498 after uncovering a plot against him concocted by Sophia and Vasily, then nineteen.

In 1500 Vasily defected to the Lithuanians, and after two years of indecision, Ivan deposed Dmitri and had him imprisoned, nominating Vasily as his heir instead. Despite the various successes and innovations that marked his reign, including the introduction of compulsory military service to be rewarded with a grant of land, on his death three years later Ivan left many political, ecclesiastical, and territorial problems unsolved.

J. L. I. Fennell, *Ivan the Great of Moscow*, 1961.
Presniakov, Aleksandr Ergen'erich, *The Tsardom of Muscovy*, 1986.

IVAN IV VASILYEVICH (Ivan the Terrible; 1530–1584), czar of Russia who completed the formation of the Russian Empire. Born in Moscow, he was three years old when his father died and he was proclaimed grand prince. His mother, Princess Yelena Glinskaya, ruled as his regent until 1538, when she too died, possibly having been poisoned. The target of much intrigue at court, he spent most of his time studying religious works under a tutor, the monk Sylvester, author of the *Domostroi*, a book setting out rules covering every aspect of Russian domestic life. Ivan was possessed of a cruel streak that led him to take advantage of his autocratic powers, ordering the execution or punishment of anyone he considered to have committed lèse-majesté against his person. At the age of thirteen he had the leader of one of the court factions executed; he imprisoned the noble who had assisted his mother during the period of her regency, and sent the man's

ιιсонишениси ѕьмихилаопленлιεпιιτι
ιйиьεικοй ·

Ivan the Terrible being showered with gold coins at his coronation

sister, who had been his nurse, to a nunnery. One of the few people who had an influence on him was the metropolitan Makary, who was instrumental in saving some, although not all, of the courtiers the young Ivan wished to punish, and who later served as regent when Ivan was absent from Moscow during his campaigns against the Tatars.

In 1547 Ivan was crowned czar, ending *boyar* (aristocratic) rule. Shortly afterward he married, on Makary's advice, after selecting his bride, Anastasiya Romanovnan, a member of the Romanov family, from hundreds brought to Moscow for this purpose in a Cinderella-like episode. During this period Makary prevailed upon Ivan to work toward shaping the conglomeration of cities and territories that made up his domain into a state based on religious ideals. Ecclesiastic assemblies in 1547 and 1549 ratified Ivan's church reforms. A new legal code was drawn up, and a national assembly consisting of representatives of local administrations convened in 1549. Together with a faction of court favorites known as the "chosen council," the assembly served Ivan in an advisory capacity.

In 1552 Ivan achieved the final subjugation of the Kazan Tatars and in 1556 that of the Astrakhan Tatars, the latter without bloodshed. In the years be-

tween these two successes, despite — or perhaps in part due to — the reforms he had introduced, internal tension ran high. In 1553 Ivan, sick at the time with a fever contracted during his Kazan campaign, succeeded in having his son Dmitri, then a child, named as heir to the throne after a struggle that split the court, which was divided between Ivan himself and his cousin Vladimir. On gaining the upper hand, Ivan took no immediate steps against his rival, but Vladimir was to die in 1569 by Ivan's hand.

In 1565 Ivan divided his realm into two. Due to the lack of documentation from this period his reasons for taking this step are not clear, although they were probably connected to his mistrust of his advisors and military functionaries. He himself administered an extensive personal territory known as the *oprichnina*, or "widow's share," backed up by a brotherhood of 1,000 black-garbed men known as *oprichniki*, his personal troop who helped him institute a reign of terror. The other territory was administered by the various councils of boyars, and this arrangement continued until 1572 when the people of Moscow, tired of the chaos it caused, petitioned Ivan to return.

In 1556, two years after subduing the Tatars, Ivan had set out to solve a problem that would tax Russia until the time of *Peter the Great. Seeking an outlet to the sea, he embarked on the useless, costly Livonian War with Poland and Sweden which was to continue for twenty-four years. In 1581, a year before the war ended, Ivan quarreled with his heir (Ivan, not Dmitri, who had died) and killed him in a fit of rage, thus bringing to an end his own dynasty. His remorse, which may have contributed to his death, led him to buy prayers for his son, as well as for over 3,000 men he had had executed, mainly during his *oprichnina*, when his cruelty had apparently had no restraint. He was also apparently married seven times, doing away with his wives when he felt necessary by murder or consignment to a nunnery.

Although he was an autocrat with an overriding belief in the divine right of kings, and a tyrant with an uncontrollable, paranoid temper, Ivan was also a devout Orthodox Christian. He loved music and wrote at least two hymns. An educated man who read widely, he introduced the printing press into Russia. Under his direction, Makary completed an encyclopedia that included world as well as Russian history. Ivan expanded Russian art and built a lavish cathedral in the Kremlin (legend has it that Ivan had the architects blinded when the work was finished so that they would never build anything more beautiful).

B. Bobrick, *Ivan The Terrible*, 1990.

F. Carr, *Ivan The Terrible*, 1981.

W. P. Hansen and T. Haney, *Ivan The Terrible*, 1987.

H. Troyat, *Ivan The Terrible*, 1986.

J

JACKSON, ANDREW (1767–1845), seventh president of the United States (1829–1837), famed general in the war of 1812, and statesman. He was born in Waxhaw, South Carolina, to an Irish farmer who died before Andrew's birth. His mother, unable to manage alone, moved the family to the nearby home of her invalid sister.

As the youngest of eleven children, Jackson was given to excessive and wild behavior. In school he was taught to read and write, but little else; his grammar and spelling were atrocious throughout his life. His behavior was often violent and unpredictable, and he was not a particularly happy child.

During the War of Independence Jackson helped his mother tend to the wounded and dreamed of being a soldier like his brother Hugh, who was later killed in action. Jackson eventually had his chance to serve his country, but in the spring of 1781, he and his brother Robert were captured by British forces. In captivity they developed raging fevers, and though they escaped after a few weeks, Robert died from smallpox two days after they were liberated. His mother was sent to care for other sick cousins and she, too, became ill with fever and died.

Once over the illness, Jackson discovered he had inherited a small fortune of 400 pounds from his grandfather. After claiming it, however, he wasted it on a spending spree. He soon convinced himself that his life had been spared so that he could lead a life his mother would be proud of — a life of honor, courage, and order.

After moving from one set of relatives to another, Jackson decided to be a lawyer. He studied in Salisbury, North Carolina, and gained permission to practice law in 1787. He found a job as a prosecutor in a western district superior court on the frontier. Before arriving in Nashville, Tennessee, in 1788, he tried to establish a reputation for himself as a "civilized" man by buying a slave and fighting a duel.

Jackson aspired to be a judge but first he became a politician. Through the patronage of William Blount, the first governor of the Southwest Territory, Jackson was one of a five-member delegation to the constitutional convention in 1796 that promoted statehood for Tennessee. Blount, his patron,

Andrew Jackson

became the first U.S. senator from Tennessee, and Jackson became the first representative in the House. The beginnings of his political career were uneventful, and he soon resigned in 1798. He distrusted central government and was a great believer in personal loyalty, of which he did not see much in national politics.

In 1798 he returned to Tennessee, where he finally became a judge. In 1801 he was appointed major general of Tennessee, though he had little formal military training. He soon became embroiled in the Burr conspiracy, in which former vice president Aaron Burr visited him and asked him to build boats for a possible military excursion against Spain. Burr was accused of attempting to divide the union and, though he was later acquitted in court, the incident tarnished Jackson's reputation.

In the war of 1812 Jackson still held the position of major general of Tennessee. He proved himself to be an excellent military leader, developing the nickname Old Hickory because hickory was the hardest wood that the soldiers knew. The war was a disaster for the Americans, bringing into question the young nation's independence. In the battle of New Orleans on January 8, 1815, Jackson's troops repelled the invading British soldiers. Over two thousand enemy troops were killed or wounded, while less than a dozen Americans fell. "Through Andrew Jackson, the American people were vicariously purged of shame and frustration. At a moment of disillusionment, Andrew Jackson reaffirmed the young nation's self-belief; he restored its sense of national prowess and destiny," wrote John William Ward, one of his biographers.

In 1824, Jackson ran for president. He was regarded as the symbol of democracy and later, people spoke of Jacksonian democracy. Though he received more popular votes than his opponents, he did not obtain the necessary electoral votes, and the House of Representatives eventually chose John Quincy *Adams. For the next four years Jackson devoted his time to becoming president, promising to rid the government of corruption.

In 1828 he received 56 percent of the vote, although he had not promised specific programs. The era came to be known as the Age of Jackson, and it stretched from his inauguration to the Civil War. Jackson brought in many of his own people to run the government, which his opponents called the spoils system.

During his first term he advocated the "voluntary" removal of the Indians, promising them a home in the southwest if they would relinquish their tribal lands in the east. Other events marking his presidency included his war against the Second Bank of America, in which he vetoed the bank's recharter, and his vast expansion of presidential powers. He was reelected in 1832 by 55 percent of the popular vote.

Shortly after his reelection, he faced the greatest challenge of his presidency. South Carolina was threatening to secede because it perceived existing tariff laws as a northern conspiracy. A long congressional fight ensued and finally in May 1833 a compromise bill was passed that settled the crisis.

The remainder of Jackson's term was not as successful and his health began to fail. In February 1837 he left office, succeeded by Martin Van Buren, who was Jackson's personal choice. He lived at his home, the Hermitage, near Nashville, Tennessee, for the rest of his life.

J. C. Curtis, *Andrew Jackson and the Search for Vindication*, 1976.
R. V. Remini, *The Revolutionary Age of Andrew Jackson*, 1985.
R. V. Remini, *The Legacy of Andrew Jackson*, 1988.

JAMES I (1566–1625), king of Scotland as James VI and of England as James I from 1603. James VI became king of Scotland when only eighteen months old, after his mother, *Mary Stuart, queen of Scots, was deposed over her alleged role in the as-

---

SAYINGS OF JAMES I

- I can make a lord, but only God can make a gentleman.
- I will govern according to the commonweal, but not according to the common will.
- No news is better than evil news.
- He was a bold man who first swallowed an oyster.
- Smoking is a custom loathsome to the eye, hateful to the nose, harmful to the brain, dangerous to the lungs, and in the black stinking fume thereof nearest resembling the horrible Stygian smoke of the pit that is bottomless (from his *Counterblast to Tobacco*).

God gives not kings
the style of gods in vain,
For on His throne,
His scepter do they sway.

From the introductory sonnet of James's *Basilikon Doron*

IMPRESSIONS OF JAMES

- The wisest fool in Christendom.

Sully

- He was made up of two men — a witty, well-read scholar, who wrote, disputed, and harangued, and a nervous, driveling idiot, who acted.

Thomas B. Macaulay

---

sassination of her husband and James's father, Henry Stewart, Lord Darnley. Much of Scotland's animosity toward Mary was the result of her fervent Catholicism. In contrast, James received an austere Calvinist education, stressing subjects' rights as against the powers of the monarchy. James repudiated this doctrine in *The Trew Law of Free Monarchies* and *Basilikon Doron*, expounding his philosophy of the divine right of kings.

With James's early reign plagued by civil war, his safety was of concern. He was constantly surrounded by armed troops, generating a phobia of weapons throughout his life. The danger was, however, real; three regents met violent deaths between 1600 and 1602.

In 1579 James, whose sexual preference was for members of his own sex, fell in love with Esmé Stuart d'Aubigny, a relative raised in Roman Catholic France. As James began assuming royal authority,

Stuart d'Aubigny was named duke of Lennox. Another favorite was Captain James Stewart, later earl of Arran. Lennox's involvement in a plot to restore Mary led to a Protestant coup in which James was captured and imprisoned by the earl of Gowrie for ten months. Lennox was banished from Scotland, but with Arran's help James escaped to assert his rule.

James recognized the necessity to accommodate all factions to avoid insurrection. Arran was deposed as James began centralizing authority in his own hands as the self-proclaimed "Universal King." At the same time, he coveted the English throne of *Elizabeth I, who was without heir. Elizabeth never officially recognized James as her heir, but granted him a sizeable pension in return for peace between the two countries. James, in turn, did much to placate her; even the death sentence passed against his mother was answered with only a mild threat. In 1589 James married Anne of Denmark, who bore him three children to survive infancy: Henry, Charles (later *Charles I), and Elizabeth. Having heirs increased his eligibility to succeed Elizabeth, and James corresponded with English secretary of state Robert Cecil to that effect. When Elizabeth died in 1603, James was summoned to the English throne. Before leaving Scotland, he promised his subjects to return regularly — in fact, he did so only once.

Poets described his dramatic journey south from the bleak Scottish highlands to the fertile plains of England. En route he was greeted by cheering crowds unaware of James's intention to implement the divine right of kings. This animated reception soured rapidly, however, upon James's entry into London, then in the throes of a plague. His coronation was delayed, but James immediately assumed his new throne with ardor. He convened a synod to define the role of the church under his reign, and alienated both Catholics and Puritans with caustic witticisms and his claim to be the supreme religious authority. Presbyterian Scotland was also perturbed by his assertion, "No bishops, no king," by which he professed the need for an established episcopacy. Many disgruntled Puritans eventually left for the New World, as the Pilgrims did in 1620, but James did concede to their request for a new English translation of the Bible, the Authorized, or King James, Version, completed in 1611.

English Catholics proved more militant. The queen herself was a devout Roman Catholic who refused Anglican communion at the coronation. In 1605, Guy Fawkes was caught attempting to blow up the House of Parliament. Under torture he revealed the names of other eminent Roman Catholics plotting to overthrow James. Roman Catholic historians later claimed that the Gunpowder Plot was actually fabricated by James and Cecil (now earl of Salisbury) to discredit the Catholic gentry.

James's popularity also waned with Parliament because of his insistence that full authority be delegated to his privy council, a collection of favorites, several of them lovers. Some were promoted to the nobility,

among them: James Carr, earl of Somerset; George Villiers, later duke of Buckingham; and the Spanish ambassador, the Count of Gondomar, responsible for the death of Sir Walter *Raleigh. James summoned Parliament only once during his reign, in 1614. Known as the Addled Parliament, it refused to sanction his self-styled title, King of Great Britain (it was only in 1707 that England and Scotland were formally united). Sir Edward Coke, England's first chief justice, asserted Parliament's independence and denied James's claim to be head of the judiciary.

Under such celebrities as Ben Jonson and William *Shakespeare, England continued the literary renaissance begun under Elizabeth. James was an intellectual who wrote verse as well as studies on witchcraft, politics, and religion. However, the common folk despised the king with the thick Scottish accent who had squandered England's wealth gambling and bestowing exorbitant gifts on favorites. It was suggested he be granted a state salary, but compromise over an acceptable sum was never reached. Instead, he took to selling honors; all propertied men were expected to pay thirty pounds to obtain a knighthood, or compensation should they decline. The country anticipated the succession of Henry, but his premature death placed the inept Charles in line to the throne.

By the time of his death in 1625, the flamboyant James had alienated both his English and Scottish subjects, allowing Parliament to assert its ascendancy.

C. Bingham, *James VI of Scotland*, 1979.
C. Bingham, *James I of England*, 1981.
J. Goldberg, *James I and the Politics of Literature*, 1983.

JANSEN, CORNELIUS OTTO (1585–1638),

Flemish theologian, founder of the Roman Catholic reform movement known as Jansenism. Born in Acquoi, Jansen entered the university of Louvain in the Spanish Netherlands in 1602 to study theology. Louvain was the site of a struggle between the Jesuits and the supporters of the theological doctrines of Michel de Bay, whose works were condemned by Pope Pius V in 1567.

Bay had held that everyone was marked by the original sin of Adam, and hence salvation could not be achieved through good works but only through the grace of Christ. His rigorous interpretation of the theory of predestination led him to assert that those who would be saved represented a small number of elect chosen in advance by God and hence irrevocably destined to enter the Kingdom of Heaven. These conclusions had been based on certain writings of Saint *Augustine. Jansen was deeply influenced by Bay's teachings and therefore opposed the Jesuits.

While continuing his theological studies in Paris, Jansen became friendly with Jean Duvergier de Hauranne, later Abbé de Saint-Cyran. The two dreamed of reviving theology, which they believed the scholars of the University of Paris had been reduced to vain disputations that alienated the faithful from the humble and simple *Jesus of the Bible.

Jansen remained in France as director of the episcopal college in Bayonne (located near the home of Saint-Cyran's parents), a position he occupied from 1611 to 1614. Thereafter, he embarked on an intensive course of study of the early church fathers.

Returning to Louvain in 1617, Jansen was made director of the College of Sainte-Pulchène, which was created for Dutch students. In addition to his administrative duties, he further immersed himself in private study, concentrating particularly on Augustine's anti-Pelagian works (Pelagius had asserted that man remains free to do good and can attain salvation by merit).

Jansen lived out his life as an eminently respectable churchman. He wrote commentaries on the evangelists and the Old Testament, as well as a number of anti-Protestant tracts. In 1635 he became rector of Louvain University, and in 1637, bishop of Ypres. Jesuit opponents alleged that he received the latter post as a result of the direct intervention of Philip IV of Spain in recognition of his tract *Mars Gallicus,* which criticized Cardinal *Richelieu for contracting an alliance with Dutch Protestants against Spain.

It was only after his death from the plague that Jansen's friends arranged the publication of the *magnum opus* upon which he had been working for some twenty-two years: the three-volume *Augustinus* represented the fruits of Jansen's researches on Augustine's teachings (he claimed that he had read the entire corpus of Augustine's writings ten times) and reasserted the Augustinian refutation of Pelagius. Ever the humble servant of the pope, Jansen recorded in his epilogue that "I leave my work to the judgment of the Roman Church. I retract all that she will decide I ought to retract." Jesuit opposition convinced Pope Urban VIII to issue a bull in 1642 charging that the work was based on the already-condemned doctrines of Bay and forbidding its being read.

In 1653 Pope Innocent X picked out five specific propositions in *Augustinus* for special condemnation. They were that: certain of God's commandments cannot be observed by righteous men if grace is lacking; a sinner cannot resist grace when it is granted; man is free only insofar as he is not constrained to commit sin; man's will of itself can neither obey grace nor resist it; Christ did not die for all men but only for the elect. Despite Pope Alexander VII's reiteration of this condemnation, the nuns of the abbey of Port-Royal in France (who had been taught the doctrines by Saint-Cyran) continued to subscribe to Jansenist tenets and acted as a focus of popular resistance to Jesuit attempts to suppress them. Furthermore, despite having suffered repeated papal condemnation, Jansenism continued to receive the support of notable Catholic intellectuals, including Antoine Arnauld and Blaise *Pascal.

In 1713, *Louis XIV had the abbey of Port-Royal razed, its nuns moved to other convents, and even its graveyard emptied in an effort to end the movement's influence in France. Jansenists in the Netherlands broke with Rome and established an independent church; the church slowly declined, until today the Jansenist faithful number only a few thousand, mostly located in the Netherlands.

Jansenism had a slight influence in northern Italy in the eighteenth century. The term "Jansenist" is sometimes used to signify extreme rigidity in matters of morality, dogma, customs, and discipline.

N. J. Abercrombie, *The Origins of Jansenism,* 1936.
M. Escholier, *Port-Royal,* 1968.

JEFFERSON, THOMAS (1743–1826), third president of the United States (1801–1809). Known for his political sophistication, he authored the Declaration of Independence and the Virginia Statute for Religious Freedom. To this day he is regarded as the outstanding champion of political and spiritual freedom and, together with Benjamin *Franklin, is viewed as the closest American approximation to the "universal man." He was a brilliant conversationalist and was regarded as one of the best-educated men of his time. He was also an inventor whose inventory included a reclining chair and a stick that unfolded into a chair.

Jefferson was born in Shadwell, Virginia, where his father, a man of legendary strength, was a successful planter, surveyor, explorer, and mapmaker. His mother, Jane Randolph, was a member of one of the most famous families in Virginia. Having grown up in a wealthy family, Jefferson was well-educated, attending small private schools where he was taught the classics. He attended the College of William and Mary and had many exceptional instructors in mathematics, science, and law. He graduated in 1762 and until 1767 was an associate and read law with some of the finest legal minds of the time. He was admitted to

Thomas Jefferson

BY AND ABOUT THOMAS JEFFERSON

- Science is my passion, politics my duty.
- I have sworn upon the altar of God eternal hostility against every form of tyranny over the mind of man.
- The tender breasts of ladies were not formed for political convulsions.
- I tremble for my country when I think that God is just.
- Delay is preferable to error.
- We hold these truths to be self-evident, that all men are created equal, that they are endowed by their creator with certain unalienable Rights, that among these are Life, Liberty, and the Pursuit of Happiness.

Declaration of Independence

- I think this is the most extraordinary collection of talent, of human knowledge, that has ever been gathered in the White House with the possible exception of when Thomas Jefferson dined alone.

John F. Kennedy, at White House dinner honoring Nobel Prize winners

the bar in 1767 and practiced law until 1774, when the courts were closed due to the American Revolution.

As a young lawyer, he worked toward the emancipation of the slaves, but was not successful. Even though he had a flourishing law practice, he did not depend on his income for maintaining his lifestyle, as he had inherited a considerable estate from his father.

Jefferson's interest in architecture grew out of his desire to build his own home at Monticello in central Virginia, a project he began in 1769. Private homes such as the one he wanted did not exist at the time, and he did much research before beginning construction. He was responsible for both design and construction, and when it was finished, he was considered an authority on house building.

Jefferson's emphasis on local government came from his own experiences. He had served as a magistrate and as county lieutenant of Albemarle County. When he was only twenty-five he was elected to the colonial House of Burgesses, serving from 1769 to 1775. There he proved his effectiveness as a committee member and drafter of legislation, but he was not an able orator.

He entered the revolutionary scene in 1769 and seven years later wrote the credo of the new nation. From the beginning of the struggle with England, he stood together with the most ardent patriots, and his knowledge of English history and political philosophy served him well. His best known early contribution to the House was his powerful pamphlet, *A Summary View of the Rights of British America*, pleading for colonial self-government, which he wrote in 1774.

As a member of the second Continental Congress, Jefferson was chosen to write the Declaration of Independence (1776). He once said that his writing of the declaration and the Virginia Statute for Religious Freedom (1786) were more memorable than his presidency of the United States.

Because he wanted to be closer to his family he left the Congress in 1776, and served instead in the Virginia legislature until he was elected governor of Virginia in 1779. He remained as governor until 1781, and when the British overran Virginia, he galloped away ahead of them. This led the legislature to investigate charges of cowardice which ended with his vindication. From 1783 to 1784 he once again served in the Continental Congress, where his proposal for a decimal monetary system was adopted.

In 1784 Jefferson became the minister to France, serving for five years, during which he won many concessions from the French. He welcomed the advent of the French Revolution and was sympathetic to the moderate revolutionaries. When he returned to the United States in 1789, he was informed that President George *Washington had nominated him to serve as secretary of state. A letter from Washington followed, and after four days of soul-searching Jefferson decided that he could not refuse the president and accepted the offer. Before leaving for Washington he returned to his home at Monticello, where he was afforded a hero's welcome by his slaves, friends, and relatives. As secretary of state, a position he held from 1790 to 1793, he was in conflict with Alexander *Hamilton, secretary of the treasury. Hamilton supported the British and Jefferson was pro-French. Washington mainly relied on Hamilton, and Jefferson resigned.

In 1794 he returned to Monticello and spent three years remodeling his beloved home. He wanted to retire to private life and spend his remaining years reading and studying, but this was not to be. In 1796 he ran for president but was defeated by John *Adams by only three electoral votes. He automatically became vice president and in 1797 he was elected president of the American Philosophical Society.

Jefferson disagreed with Adams in many areas, which resulted in his running against Adams for the presidency in 1800, defeating him on the thirty-sixth ballot. The election campaign was based on Jefferson's contention that he was a stronger supporter of the U.S. Constitution than his opponent, and his victory marked the first time that the federalists were defeated by a Republican. He was inaugurated as president on March 4, 1801, with Aaron Burr as vice president.

The most notable achievement of Jefferson's first term was the Louisiana Purchase. As secretary of state he had recognized the importance of free navigation down the Mississippi River and was determined to incorporate the area, especially after it had been transferred from Spain to France.

Throughout his lifetime Jefferson had his detractors, particularly regarding his attempts to separate church and state. He was quoted as saying, "I have no ambition to govern men. It is a painful, thankless office." This sentiment was proven when Aaron Burr's attempts at conspiracy were foiled.

Reelected and inaugurated on March 4, 1805, Jefferson began his second term with George Clinton as vice president. During this term, the Lewis and Clark expedition, that explored the territory of the Louisiana purchase and the country beyond as far as the Pacific, was concluded.

Jefferson continued his efforts to acquire west Florida, which turned out to be an "exercise in futility." His relations with Congress were good and remained stable until shortly before he completed his second term of office. When he left the presidency he was a discouraged man, and spent the last seventeen years of his life at Monticello. From there he continued to exert a strong influence on the government. He said, "The happiest moments of my life have been the few which I have spent in the bosom of my family."

Those final years were among his most productive. He founded the University of Virginia and held the position of first rector, and also designed its buildings. William Howard Taft once said that Jefferson was still spoken of there as if he were sitting in the next room.

Jefferson died at Monticello on July 4, 1826, just hours after the passing of John Adams, and on the fiftieth anniversary of the Declaration of Independence. The Jefferson Memorial in Washington was dedicated on the two hundredth anniversary of his birth.

H. S. Commager, *Jefferson, Nationalism and the Enlightenment*, 1975.

R. M. Johnston Jr., *Jefferson and the Presidency*, 1978.

D. Malone, *Jefferson And His Times* 5 vols., 1948–1975.

F. McDonald, *The Presidency of Thomas Jefferson*, 1988.

JENNER, EDWARD

JENNER, EDWARD (1749–1823), English physician who discovered the vaccine against smallpox, an often fatal disease that in former times was epidemic worldwide. Born to a family of landed gentry in Berkeley, Gloucestershire, Jenner was orphaned at age five and brought up by his three sisters. In 1757 he was sent to the local grammar school as a boarder, and while there was inoculated against smallpox through the primitive and risky method of variolation, an arduous process that consisted of inoculating the patient with a small amount of smallpox lymph, and which sometimes proved fatal. This traumatic experience gave Jenner insomnia as a child, and he was persistently plagued by imaginary noises. While at school, he also developed an interest in fossil collecting, a hobby he maintained for the rest of his life.

At age twelve, he was accepted as an apprentice surgeon to John Ludlow, with whom he remained for the next six years. He then enrolled as a student at Saint George's Hospital, London, where he lodged with John Hunter, the most eminent surgeon of his time. Hunter's wife, Anne Home, was a Scottish poet who hosted an artists' salon which Jenner, a fair poet and musician, frequented.

In 1771, when Captain James *Cook returned from a voyage of scientific discovery aboard the ship *Endeavour*, Hunter recommended Jenner for the task of classifying the thousands of natural specimens, never before seen in Europe, which had been collected. Pleased with Jenner's work, the ship's chief botanist invited the young man on Cook's next trip, but Jenner turned down this and other offers of work abroad due to his deep attachment to Gloucestershire and his family.

Jenner returned to Berkeley, where he lived in his brother's house, and worked as a country doctor. In 1783, after the Montgolfier brothers launched the first balloon flight in history, Jenner organized the first flight of a hydrogen balloon in England, assisted by the earl of Berkeley.

In 1785, Jenner bought Chauntry Cottage and began work on a paper on the breeding habits of the cuckoo, the publication of which led to his acceptance as a member of the Royal Society in 1788.

As a country doctor, Jenner regularly inoculated against smallpox using the variolation method. However, finding some patients to be resistant to smallpox, he discovered that they had all previously had cowpox, corroborating the old wives' tale that cowpox provides immunization against smallpox. Jenner distinguished between two forms of cowpox, only one of which provides protection against smallpox and only when the lymph extracted from vesicles is administered when still fresh.

In 1796 Jenner inoculated James Phipps, the eight-year-old son of a landless laborer who had often worked for the Jenners, with cowpox lymph extracted from a vesicle from a milkmaid's arm. James was subsequently inoculated with smallpox, but the disease did not manifest itself. This led to Jenner's publication in 1798 of *An Inquiry into the Causes and Effects of the Variolae Vaccinae*, in which he coined the word "virus." Had Jenner decided to keep the nature of his findings to himself, he could have profited handsomely. Instead, he shared his findings and the practice of vaccination spread, with cowpox lymph being transferred from arm to arm. Jenner stood by his findings in the face of sometimes fierce opposition.

Jenner discovered that cowpox lymph could be kept for up to three months if preserved in dried form, thus facilitating the worldwide distribution of the vaccine. The success of vaccinations in Moscow prompted the dowager empress Maria to send Jenner a diamond ring, while in the United States, President Thomas *Jefferson wrote to Jenner: "Mankind can never forget that you have lived." After personally sending pamphlets about the vaccine to the Abenaqui tribe of Canadian Indians, Jenner received a reply with an address of thanks from ten chiefs, communicated by a string of wampum. *Napoleon Bonaparte had a medal struck in Jenner's honor, made vaccination compulsory in the French army and, in response to Jenner's request in 1813 for the release of an English captain, is said to have replied: *"Ah, Jenner, je ne puis rien refuser à Jenner."*

Jenner, who vaccinated the poor free of charge, was awarded two separate grants from the British Parliament, amounting to £30,000, in recognition of his work, and the Royal Jennerian Society was established in 1802, leading to a widespread program of inoculation.

In 1817 Jenner was appointed to serve as mayor of Berkeley. From then until the end of his life, he resumed his inquiries into the migration of birds, and continued to collect fossils.

In 1980 the World Health Organization announced the worldwide eradication of smallpox as "an unprecedented event in human history," and with it the fulfillment of Jenner's dream.

R. B. Fisher, *Edward Jenner*, 1991.

D. Fisk, *Dr. Jenner of Berkeley*, 1959.

JEROME, SAINT (c.347–c.420), saint, translator, and teacher. Also known as Eusebius Hieronymus, Jerome is revered as the most learned of the Latin church fathers; he and his two contemporaries, Saint *Ambrose and Saint *Augustine, are, along with Pope *Gregory the Great, traditionally known as the four doctors of the Western church. His enduring monument is his translation of the Bible into a Latin comprehensible to the common people of his age, known as the Vulgate version, which became the authoritative translation in the Roman Catholic church. Also of great significance is the impulse to monasticism that he engendered in the church. Many of his letters have been preserved so that, in addition to his literary legacy, there remains a volume of detailed personal information.

Born to affluent parents in Stridon, near Ljubljana in Slovenia, Jerome was a precocious student in his youth; at twelve he was sent to Rome to study grammar, rhetoric, and philosophy. He leavened his scholastic duties with liberal doses of the pleasures of the flesh; his sins were to return to haunt him in his years of asceticism. In Rome he was baptized by Pope Liberus. After his studies, he spent the next twenty years in travel; this was the period when he first became attracted to the monastic way of life. He also developed links with an Italian ascetic elite grouped round Bishop Valerius and hence formed a friendship with Rufinus; both men greatly admired the writings of the Alexandrine scholar, Origen, who had done much work in establishing the text of the Old Testament.

A naturally passionate man of robust appetites as well as a lover of the classical authors, Jerome was to find the ascetic life a great trial. He relates in one of his letters how hard it was to cut himself off from his friends "and — harder still — from the dainty food to which I had become accustomed." The Greek and Roman authors he loved were pagan and considered inappropriate reading for the faithful; nonetheless, he admits that "miserable man that I was, I would fast only that I might afterwards read *Cicero," after whom the style of the prophets seemed "rude and repellent."

The revelation, beloved of early church literature, that led to his renunciation of pagan writers occurred in Antioch in 374: he beheld the Last Judgment, where *Jesus asked him who he was; upon his answering that he was a Christian, the reply descended that "thou liest, thou art a follower of Cicero and not of Christ." Thereafter he seems to have avoided the temptations of paganism, although references to *Virgil, *Horace, and *Ovid would reappear in his letters on occasion. During his lonely years as a hermit in Chalcis from 375 to 377 Jerome learned Hebrew from a Jewish convert, but he left when the place became suspected of harboring heretical views. He agreed to be ordained a priest in 378, on condition that his monastic aspirations not be prejudiced and that he be allowed to continue his studies.

As secretary to Pope Damasus between 382 and 385, Jerome was able to progress in his translation of many key early Christian texts. He also held classes for pious gentlewomen, to whom he was fond of extolling the virtues of virginity. The erotic mysticism with which he praised the joys of convent life is apparent in his letters to Eustochium, daughter of his most devoted disciple, the widow Paula, preparing her for her chosen vocation as a nun: in them, he used the now-familiar description of nuns as the Brides of Christ and cited the Song of Solomon as the biblical text celebrating this marriage.

His success in persuading some of these aristocratic ladies to adopt the ascetic life made him unpopular among many of his peers, and also with the pope who succeeded his patron Damasus. Jerome's tirades against the lax lifestyles of monks and clergy further increased resentment against him and in 386 he left Rome for the Holy Land, vehemently decrying the papal city as "Babylon"; he remained in Bethlehem until his death, grieving at the barbarian invasion of the Roman Empire and ruing the hypocrisy that plagued the priesthood: "Our walls shine with gold...yet Christ dies before our doors naked in the person of His poor," he lamented.

It was in the monastery financed by Paula (who had accompanied him to Bethlehem) that, between 391 and 406, Jerome undertook and completed his translation of the Bible on the basis of the original text. While always anxious to remain strictly orthodox, Jerome did not allow this determination to cloud his conclusions as to the authenticity of his sources. Thus, although Christians had traditionally maintained that the Jews had falsified the Hebrew text where it seemed to predict the Messiah, Jerome dismissed this view outright as incompatible with the findings of scholarship. He even took the help of rabbis to clarify textual difficulties for him. His acceptance of the text endorsed as correct by Jews ("Let him who would challenge aught in this translation ask the Jews," he proposed) led to his translation initially receiving a hostile reception; Saint Augustine's championing helped it win approval.

Strong-willed and temperamental, Jerome was sometimes involved in petulant dispute: he argued with Saint Augustine over the behavior of Saint *Peter; he was moved to break with his friend Rufinus when he found it prudent to disavow his own youthful espousal of Origen, whose doctrines had fallen out of favor; he was so vehement in his opposition to the Pelagian heresy of questioning the doctrine of original sin that his monastery was attacked by a mob; he penned savage attacks on the married state in response to Jovian.

In his homilies to his monks, however, his depth of learning as a scholar is evident; it was as a scholar rather than as a thinker that he accomplished his greatest achievements, not least in transmitting Greek thought to the West.

H. Friedmann, *A Bestiary for Saint Jerome*, 1980.
J. N. D. Kelly, *Jerome, His Life, Writings and Controversies*, 1975.

JESUS CHRIST (Jesus of Nazareth; c.4 B.C.E – 30 C.E.), founder of Christianity. Regarded by Christians as the universal messiah or savior, Jesus (the Greek form of the Hebrew name, Yehoshua) was a Jew who lived in Judea during the Roman occupation. He taught a message of forgiveness of sins, love of neighbor, and the reign of the Kingdom of God.

The Gospels of the New Testament, all written by the first part of the second century C.E., are the main source of information about Jesus. Gathered from various traditions after his death, they trace the genealogy of his parents, Joseph and Mary, back to King *David, from whose descendants the Messiah (or "christ" in Greek) was traditionally expected to originate. The couple lived in Nazareth, in the Galilee region of northern Israel, but because of a census they traveled to Bethlehem where Jesus was born in a stable. Joseph was a carpenter and Jesus seems to have practiced this trade as well. Not much is known of his early life; the Gospels tell of his encounter with *John the Baptist when he was already an adult. In about 26 B.C.E, John, following the words of the prophet *Isaiah, "to make a way for the Lord in the wilderness," had left the towns of Judea to dwell in the desert, baptizing adherents to his prophetic message in the waters of the Jordan River. John preached that the present age was corrupt and that a heavenly judgment was imminent that would cleanse the world through fire. Those who wished to live in the new age that he prophesied were enjoined to repent of sin and do good deeds as well as be baptized by immersion. This was a period of intensive messianic anticipation among the Jews, precipitated by the curtailment of their independence by the Roman rulers of their country.

SOME FAMOUS PHRASES OF JESUS

- Blessed are the meek, for they shall inherit the earth (Matthew 5:5).
- You are the salt of the earth. (Matthew 5:13).
- You are the light of the world (Matthew 5:14).
- Resist not evil; but whosoever shall smite thee on thy right cheek, turn to him the other also (Matthew 5:39).
- Let not your left hand know what your right hand does (Matthew 6:3).
- No man can serve two masters (Matthew 6:24).
- Consider the lilies of the field, how they grow; they toil not, neither do they spin; And yet I say unto you, that even Solomon in all his glory was not arrayed like one of these (Matthew 6:28:29).
- Take therefore no thought for the morrow: for the morrow shall take thought for the things of itself. Sufficient unto the day is the evil thereof (Matthew 6:34).
- Neither cast ye your pearls before swine (Matthew 7:6).
- Seek, and ye shall find; knock, and it shall be opened unto you (Matthew 7:7).
- Beware of false prophets, which come to you in sheep's clothing, but inwardly they are ravening wolves (Matthew 7:15).
- Let the dead bury their dead. (Matthew 8:22).
- He that is not with me is against me (Matthew 12:30).
- It is easier for a camel to go through the eye of a needle, than for a rich man to enter into the kingdom of God (Matthew 19:24).
- All they that take the sword shall perish with the sword (Matthew 26:52).
- The sabbath was made for man, and not man for the sabbath (Mark 2:27).
- For the poor always ye have with you (Mark 14:7).
- If the blind lead the blind, both shall fall into the ditch (Luke 6:39).
- What shall it profit a man if he gain the whole world and lose his own soul (Mark 8:36).

Jesus' own sense of destiny was catalyzed by John's teaching, but before he began to preach he underwent a period of trial, tempted with spiritual and material power. After surviving these tests he began to travel throughout Galilee, preaching his message in the towns and villages there, gathering around him numerous disciples and an inner group, the Twelve Apostles: *Peter, James, John, Andrew, Philip, Bartholomew, Matthew, Thomas, James the son of

A sixth-century portrait of Jesus, the oldest known hand-painted icon in existence

Alphaeus, Thaddaeus, Simon the Cananite, and Judas Iscariot (later replaced by Matthias). The Apostles accompanied Jesus on his mission, with Peter given authority above the rest and being privy to miracles and teachings the other Apostles did not witness.

Jesus' first miracle was changing water into wine at a marriage feast in Cana in Galilee. Thereafter, he cast out demons, healed the blind and leprous, and raised the dead. He also walked on the waters of the Sea of Galilee, and fed the multitudes in the wilderness. In his Sermon on the Mount, Jesus preached the love of God and man and taught that salvation rested on fulfilling the inner meaning of the law and not its outward performance. A healer in the tradition of Elijah and Elisha, his works attracted crowds of people who had heard of his deeds. Without claiming to be the Messiah, Jesus spoke of the coming of the Kingdom of Heaven, teaching in parables that contained spiritual insights veiled in everyday stories. He proclaimed that God was forgiving, as in the parable of the prodigal son, but could also be wrathful, as in the parable of the unmerciful servant. Both these attributes became more accentuated in Jesus' teaching than they had been in Jewish tradition. He offered a threat of damnation if God's will was not obeyed, a promise of salvation if it

was. The kingdom of God was not a temporal reality that would mean salvation from the Roman enemy, but a new reality of which Jesus was the sign.

While he sometimes set aside the Jewish law in order to accomplish a pressing task, he insisted that his message was to his fellow Jews and that they should adhere strictly to the Law. He spent a year in the north of Israel, healing the sick and curing people of demons before heading south for Jerusalem, which he had prophesied would be the place where he would die.

Jesus arrived in Jerusalem in the spring, the season of the Passover festival. By this time, the radical nature of his teachings had produced many enemies antagonized by his attacks on the religious establishment, which he accused of injustice and hypocrisy. At his last meal, known as the Last Supper, he blessed and gave out bread and wine to his Apostles, instituting the sacrament of Communion. Jesus' preaching of the forthcoming destruction of the Temple angered the Sadducees, the priestly caste. While he was in the garden of Gethsemane on the Mount of Olives, he was arrested by the Temple guard — who had been led there by one of the Apostles, Judas Iscariot — and brought to the high priest. The Sanhedrin, the Jewish court, was convened and Jesus, suspected of being a false messiah, was condemned as a blasphemer and was handed over to Pontius Pilate, the Roman procurator of Judea, on the grounds that he claimed to be king of the Jews. Pilate, initially finding no fault with Jesus, relented to pressures from the Sanhedrin and ordered Jesus to be crucified, the usual form of execution. On a hill called Golgotha outside the city walls, Jesus was crucified and, after a three-hour ordeal, died and was entombed. Three days later his tomb was discovered to be empty. His disciples recorded Jesus' appearances before them during the next weeks, until on the fortieth day after the Resurrection they declared that he had ascended to Heaven. Following this the his disciples began their own mission of proclaiming his life and establishing communities in Jerusalem and throughout the Mediterranean region.

C. H. Dodd, *The Founder of Christianity,* 1970.

M. Grant, *Jesus,* 1977.

D. Flusser, *Jesus,* 1969.

A. Schweitzer, *Quest of the Historical Jesus,* 1954.

JINNAH, MUHAMMED ALI (1876–1948), founder and first governor general of Pakistan. Muhammad Ali Jinnah Poonjah was the son of a wealthy Karachi merchant. Raised and educated in Karachi and Bombay, he was a difficult student who preferred beaches and horses to his studies. He attracted the notice of a British trader who arranged for him to work as an apprentice in his London firm. Arriving in London in 1893, he found that sitting over a ledger all day bored him. He was attracted to the big city, its sounds (English became his preferred language) and its fashions (Jinnah wore expensive clothes throughout his career, once boasting that he never put on the same silk cravat twice). He quit his job to study law and — after a brief acting career — passed the bar in 1896. The dour but urbane advocate shortened his name to Jinnah, meaning "thin man." Over six feet tall, he weighed only 120 lbs.

Upon his return to Bombay, Jinnah became the first Indian advocate in the Bombay high court. A skilled, if humorless, orator, his reputation thrived. Only twenty-three, he declined a permanent judicial post at fifteen hundred rupees per month, claiming he would soon make that per day.

Jinnah had begun his political career while in England as secretary to Dadabhoy Nauroji, who became the first Indian member of the British Parliament. In India he also served on the Imperial Legislative Council representing the Muslim community from 1910 to 1919. Although as a member of the Indian National Congress he was committed to Hindu-Muslim unity, he joined the Muslim League in 1913, insisting that his sponsors pledge that "his activities would not hinder or bring about his dissociation from the larger national cause to which he dedicated his life." As a champion of communal cooperation he was twice chosen president of the Muslim League, in 1916 and 1920.

Jinnah supported Indian participation in World War I in return for constitutional reforms. By 1919, however, the situation in India had deteriorated: mass arrests, secret trials, and the suspension of habeas corpus were a matter of course. To protest the situation, Jinnah resigned from the Indian legislative council, but he rejected Mahatma *Gandhi's policy of noncooperation, fearing that it would bring more harm than good. This was the first sign of a growing rift between Jinnah and the Congress. It ended with his resignation from that body in 1921 over the Congress's rejection of his proposal for separate elections for the Hindu and Muslim populations for any future Indian legislative bodies as undemocratic and antinationalist. Although Jinnah was by no means a religious Muslim, he gradually adopted increasingly extremist Muslim positions, favoring separate Muslim negotiations with the British over the future of India.

It was in this capacity that Jinnah participated in the debates of the Reform Inquiry Committee and the Sandhurst Committee over India's future. He also attended the Round Table Conference in London in 1930–1931 but became bitter at the lack of results and decided to retire from public affairs. The Muslim community, however, refused to let the Qaid-e-Azam, or "great leader," abandon them. He was elected to the Central Assembly of the Muslim League in absentia, and chosen its permanent president in 1934, returning to India as the undisputed leader of his community.

While at first the British supported Jinnah as a counterbalance to the extreme nationalism of the Congress, he proved no less opposed to colonialism than his rivals but, unlike Congress, willing to accept British constitutional proposals granting self-rule to the provincial legislatures based on separate elections. The program soon failed and despite Gandhi's goodwill the Muslim minority remained subject to Hindu discrimination. The two communities drifted further apart during World War II, when Congress opposed aiding the war effort and resigned en masse from the legislative council. Jinnah, who supported the Allies, called Congress's resignation the "Day of Deliverance" of India's Muslim community.

Jinnah's community, as well as the world, was shocked when, at the 1940 Lahore Conference of the Muslim League, he declared that the Hindus and Muslims of India were two separate nations and that any solution other than partition would lead to civil war. He proposed the creation of a Muslim state to encompass Western India and East Bengal and Assam in the east. The state would be named Pakistan, meaning "land of the pure" in Urdu. It was also an acronym for the various areas that would make up Western Pakistan (P — Punjab; A — Afghan tribes of the Northwest Frontier Province; K — Kashmir; S — Sind; and TAN from Baluchistan). In return for a promise of partition, the Muslims would support Britain's war effort. "Pakistan" soon became the rallying cry of the Muslim communities, although in 1941 the partition proposal was temporarily dropped so that a popular government in India could be formed during the war.

The 1942 mission of Sir Stafford Cripps on behalf of the British government rejected Jinnah's proposal, but Jinnah eventually succeeded in convincing both Jawaharlal *Nehru and the British viceroy, Lord Mountbatten of its feasibility in the face of mounting popular approval. On 3 June, 1947, the partition of India was accepted and the Dominion of Pakistan was created on 15 August, with Jinnah as governor general and president of the legislative assembly. Shortly after, he suffered a nervous breakdown from overwork and from the stress of the intercommunal strife which developed into a full scale war with India. Although he soon returned to office, he never fully recovered and died shortly afterwards.

A. Saeed, *The Green Titan: A Study of Quaid-i-Azam Mohammad Ali Jinnah, 1976.*
S. A. Wolpert, *Jinnah of Pakistan, 1984.*

JOAN OF ARC (Jeanne d'Arc; c.1412–1431), French national heroine of the latter phase of the Hundred Years' War, known as La Pucelle d'Orleans, "the Maid of Orleans." The daughter of a peasant family of the village of Domremy on the Meuse river, in the Vosges, she was a taciturn, very pious girl, who could neither read nor write. Her fascination for military life worried her father and he tried to frighten her by threatening to drown her if she ran away with the soldiers, and ordered her brothers to drown her if he were not on the spot. From about the age of thirteen she had visionary experiences in which voices, that she identified as belonging to Saint Catherine, Saint Marguerite, and Saint Michael, urged her to assume the task of saving France from the English and see that the dauphin (Charles VII) was crowned.

She is the notable Warrior Saint in the Christian calendar, and the queerest fish among the eccentric worthies of the Middle Ages. Though a professed and most pious Catholic, and the projector of a Crusade against the Hussites, she was in fact one of the first Protestant martyrs. She was also one of the first apostles of Nationalism, and the first French practitioner of Napoleonic realism in warfare as distinguished from the sporting ransom-gambling chivalry of her time. She was the pioneer of rational dressing for women, and, like Queen Christina of Sweden two centuries later, to say nothing of innumerable obscure heroines who have disguised themselves as men to serve as soldiers and sailors, she refused to accept the specific woman's lot, and dressed and fought and lived as men did.

As she contrived to assert herself in all these ways with such force that she was famous throughout western Europe before she was out of her teens (indeed she never got out of them), it is hardly surprising that she was judicially burnt, ostensibly for a number of capital crimes which we no longer punish as such, but essentially for what we call unwomanly and insufferable presumption...

**Preface to *Saint Joan*
by George Bernard Shaw**

France was in a critical situation at the time: the northern part of the kingdom was occupied by the English allied to the Burgundians. The French crown was contested: the dauphin's insane father, Charles VI, had declared his son illegitimate and had designated *Henry V of England regent and future heir. Yet after Charles' VI death, his son was recognized as king by southern France. Five years after his father's death the dauphin Charles had not been crowned at Rheims, where the French kings were traditionally consecrated, as the town was within the occupied territory.

In 1428 Joan of Arc tried and failed to convince the commander of the French troops at Vaucouleurs, Robert of Beaudricourt, of the genuineness of her mission. However in 1429, when some of her prophecies had been fulfilled, she was allowed to come before the dauphin (the future Charles VII) who was at Chinon with his court. To test her, the dauphin disguised himself as one of his courtiers, but Joan recognized him immediately. Joan was submitted to the examination of a commission of theologians and her views were found untouched by heresy. In view of the desperate situation of Orleans, besieged by the English army, she succeeded in convincing the dauphin and was sent at the head of a small expedition to lift the siege of the town (April-May 1429). Wearing white armor and

carrying a banner, she succeeded in inspiring the French troops who finally entered the town. Thanks to the popular national movement inspired by the young woman, the French king was able to recover the occupied territories and the way to Rheims was opened. On July 17, 1429, Joan, holding her white banner, was present at the coronation of the king at the Cathedral of Rheims. In September she was wounded during an attempt to recapture Paris. She rejoined the French army in the spring of 1430 but on May 24 was taken prisoner near Compiegne and in November was sold to the English by the duke of Burgundy. Charles VII did nothing to rescue her. Imprisoned at Beaurevoir Castle she attempted to escape by jumping from a tower and recovered from her fall after fasting for several days. She was taken to Rouen in an iron cage where she was tried for heresy and witchcraft in February 1431 by a court of French ecclesiastics headed by the bishop of Beauvais, Pierre Cauchon. After a long trial, she was found guilty on seventy counts; among these was the accusation of blasphemy since she claimed the authority of divine revelation; of prophesying the future; of immodesty since she wore men's clothing. She was also accused of daring to say that the saints who spoke to her spoke in French and not in English! Joan answered with simplicity and courage. The charges were reduced to twelve. Pressured to recant under threat of torture, she did so. She was condemned to life imprisonment but a few days later Joan declared that Saint Catherine and Saint Margaret had condemned her abjurating. She was then condemned to be burnt at the stake and handed over to the English secular authorities at Rouen for execution of the sentence. As the flames engulfed her she maintained that the voices she had heard were sent from God and were true.

Her sentence was revoked by Pope Calixtus III in 1456. She was beatified in 1909 by Pope Pius X, and canonized in 1920 by Pope Benedict XV. Her status as France's national heroine is a comparatively modern phenomenon, stimulated by French Catholics of the late nineteenth century.

Joan of Arc has been the subject of a great number of literary works, notably by *Voltaire, Johann *Schiller, Mark *Twain and Bernard *Shaw.
M. Waldman, *Joan of Arc*, 1985.
M. Warner, *Joan of Arc*, 1987.
C. T. Wood, *Joan of Arc and Richard III*, 1988.

JOHN XXIII (Angelo Roncalli; 1881–1963), pope, the initiator of far-reaching reforms in the Roman Catholic church during his short pontificate. Roncalli, son of poor tenant farmers, was born near Bergamo, Italy.

He was ordained in Rome at the age of twenty-two. In 1905 he became secretary to the archbishop of Bergamo, with whom he had a close relationship. He served as spiritual director at the Bergamo seminary until the new pope, Benedict XV, called him to Rome to take charge of missionary activities and elevated him to the rank of monsignor.

In 1925 Pope Pius XI removed Roncalli from the Vatican by promoting him to archbishop and sending him to Bulgaria as an apostolic vicar, where only 1 percent of the population was Catholic. Lonely and hurt by the Vatican's treatment, Roncalli visited Bulgaria's impoverished and scattered Catholic communities, ordered communal prayers to be said in the vernacular (the Vatican refused or ignored his requests for other changes), and developed his diplomatic skills. His diplomacy was based on the motto "see everything, ignore a good deal, improve things where possible"; he optimistically believed that time, opportunity, and patience improved almost any situation. He accomplished his goals by generating good will through friendly gestures and using his warmth and good humor to defuse antagonism caused by individual or ideological differences.

When Roncalli was transferred to Istanbul in 1934, these skills helped him overcome the hostility of different Christian denominations, the anti-Italian Orthodox Greeks, and the secular anti-Western Turks. During World War II, he maintained relations both with Nazi occupiers and the local community in Greece and negotiated grain shipments to alleviate the 1941 famine. Roncalli's friendliness with Germany's ambassador in Istanbul ensured German noninterference with attempts to save Jews (in which he was involved), while his peace keeping activities within Istanbul's divided French community influenced his appointment as papal nuncio to France in 1944.

The new French government had dismissed Roncalli's predecessor from France and demanded that thirty-three bishops be removed from office for their acquiescence in the Viehy regime. However, Roncalli's tenure as papal nuncio was so effective that the French president insisted on attending his investiture as a cardinal in 1953, when he was appointed patriarch of Venice.

In 1958, aged seventy-six, Roncalli was elected pope, taking the name John XXIII. He was a compromise candidate because it was believed that as an elderly man he would not be too active in introducing innovation. He however, called for *aggiormento*: the updating and renewal of the church in the modern world.

In 1959 Pope John proposed three undertakings: a diocesan synod for Rome, the revision of the code of the canon law, and the calling of an ecumenical council — the first in nearly a century. He attributed his inspiration for convoking the Second Vatican Council The council issued decrees on religious freedom and conscience, the liturgy, the church as the people of God, and on was and peace, unequivocally condemning the arms race. He invited non-Catholic observers and established a Secretariat for Promoting Christian Unity. In 1963 he issued his encyclical *Pacem in Terris,* calling for peace among nations based on justice, charity, and the right organization of society, and calling for an end to the arms race, a ban on nuclear weapons, and eventual disarmament.

Pope John was warm and friendly, a kind of father-figure; he was accessible and often walked through Rome talking to the people. He became a voice for unity and peace, appealing to "all men of good will" to learn to live together. Pope John died before the council's second session but in his short reign he had revitalized the church, raising its moral prestige to unprecedented heights and becoming the most popular pope of modern times.

P. Johnson, *Pope John XXIII,* 1975.

JOHN III (John Sobieski; 1629–1696), Polish king who saved Europe from the Turks. He was born into the lesser Polish nobility and educated at the University of Cracow. As was customary for one of his rank, he also traveled extensively in Europe. At this time, Poland's real ruler was its powerful Catholic nobility, which elected the king, controlled the Polish parliament, and weakened the country with its extensive and shortsighted use of the right of all nobles to veto any parliamentary act. The nobles' attempts to establish feudal conditions and obstruct Orthodox religious worship in Ukraine resulted in Bohdan *Khmelnytsky's destructive Cossack rebellion of 1648. When news of his father's death and the Cossack rebellion reached John, he cut his travels short, returned to Poland, and joined the Polish army.

Occupied with fighting a Russian-Cossack alliance, Poland offered little resistance to Sweden's 1655 invasion (which was actually welcomed by John and most of the other Polish nobles who opposed Poland's king, John II Casimir). John served in the Swedish army for a year but became a leader in the successful fight to expel the Swedes from Poland after the Protestant Swedish forces ran wild, massacring people and despoiling church property in violation of the Swedish king's promises of religious toleration.

The love story of John and the widowed Maria Casmire de la Grange d'Arquien (Marysienka) has become a Polish legend. Raised in France and Poland, of royal French blood, classically beautiful, courageous, intelligent, extravagant, and unscrupulous, Marysienka began scheming to have John elected king immediately after their marriage in 1665. John was promoted to grand marshal that same year, to field commander of the Polish army in 1666, and — after defeating the Tatars and Cossacks — to commander in chief in 1668, but Michael Wisniowieski was still elected king when John Casimir abdicated. John plotted with other nobles to depose Michael, claiming he was a coward unable to defend Poland, and demonstrating his own fitness for the position by his victories over the Cossacks and Turks. John's famous letters to Marysienka were written during the frequent separations caused by his military duties and her trips to France, where she worked to gain the support of *Louis XIV for his election. Her efforts were aided by Michael's pro-Habsburg policies, since France was the bitter rival of the Holy Roman Empire and its Habsburg rulers. John's defeat of the Turks the day Michael died made him a prime candidate for king and, in 1674, he clinched his election with French money and six thousand troops.

King John faced a complicated international situation. The conquering armies of a revitalized Ottoman Empire posed a serious threat to Christian Europe, which was unable to unite to counter it because of conflicting political and religious interests. Catholic Austria (the Holy Roman Empire) fought the Turks while partially-Protestant Hungary (desiring freedom from Austria's religiously repressive rule) welcomed them, and Catholic France was their ally. France wanted Poland to become its ally against Austria, while Austria wanted Poland to fight the Turks, freeing Austria to annex territory that Poland also claimed!

In 1675 John defeated the Turks, recovered western Ukraine, freed Poland from Turkish claims for tribute payments, and signed a treaty with France promising to fight Austria after making peace with the Turks. However, his initial pro-French policy was gradually altered by Louis's unwillingness to recognize Marysienka's French relatives as French nobility, Louis's refusal to support the succession of John's son to Poland's throne, the opposition of the nobles who feared Louis would help John become an absolute ruler, and John's growing realization that France's allies, the Turks, were Poland's greatest enemies.

John felt that it was essential to drive the Turks out of Europe or at least to prevent them from making further conquests. He tried to form a Christian alliance against them, but Leopold, the Austrian emperor, refused to fight the Turks in the east lest Louis seize the opportunity to attack Austria in the west. Louis refused to promise not to attack Leopold while the latter's forces were fighting the Turks. French attempts to bribe Poland's parliament backfired. John revealed Louis's machinations, and anti-French feeling swept Poland. In 1683 John and Leopold became allies, sworn to each other's aid in the event of a Turkish attack.

When a Turkish army of 250,000 besieged Vienna, Leopold fled and sent word to John, begging him to save the city: "Your name alone, so terrible to the enemy, will ensure a victory." Vienna was about to fall, its defenders stricken by starvation and disease, when John led his army of 60,000 against the Turks. They fought with an almost Crusader-like fervor, the Turks fled, and John entered Vienna to be greeted as a savior. Leopold returned some time later, coldly thanked John for his services, and refused to allow the marriage of John's son to Austria's archduchess. John set off in pursuit of the Turks, defeated them again, and returned to Poland. In 1684 he failed to conquer Moldavia which he wanted as a kingdom for his son.

Widely read, John made his court the center of Poland's cultural revival, patronizing French and Italian artists and encouraging the erection of baroque palaces and churches. Although he used his position to increase his own wealth, on many occasions he paid Poland's soldiers with his own money, even selling his property to buy them weapons. Obstreperous nobles limited his power and prevented implementation of his policies of helping the peasants, forcing the rich to pay taxes, creating a standing army, and forcing the nobles to fight the Turks rather than each other.

John's last years were plagued by illness, his failure to secure his son's succession, and futile conspiracies by his wife and children to determine who would become king when he died. After his death the Polish parliament sold the crown to Frederick Augustus of Saxony.

J. Stoye, *The Siege of Vienna*, 1965.

JOHN THE BAPTIST (died c.29), prophetic leader of an apocalyptic sect in the Judean Desert; according to the New Testament, the forerunner of Christ and considered by Christians a saint. John abandoned his Jewish priestly heritage, condemning corruption of the priesthood and prophesying imminent divine cataclysm and the beginning of a new providential era. His baptismal rite, a single immersion in the waters of the Jordan River, was the culmination of the penitence and purification that his followers carried out through prayer and charity. *Jesus of Nazareth viewed John as surpassing all previous prophets, bringing his message of the coming kingdom of god on earth. Jesus' ministry developed from John's beginnings and many of John's followers became disciples of Jesus after John was put to death.

From the priestly lineage of Aaron, John the Baptist's parents, Zechariah and Elizabeth (a kinswomen of Mary, mother of Jesus), lived in poverty in a Judean town (not named but later identified with the village of Ein Kerem near Jerusalem). According to New Testament sources, the Baptist's birth came after a series of events that typically precede the birth of a preeminent biblical figure. Zechariah, while carrying out his priestly function in the Temple received a vision that his wife, who was barren, would give birth to a son who should be kept away from worldly pleasures and would eventually become a great leader of his people. Nothing certain is known regarding John's early years, but it has been suggested, given his parents' home in Judea as well as John's later religious practices, that his family were members of the Essenes, an ascetic and apocalyptic group of Jews.

New Testament sources first recount John's life when he was already active as a prophetic preacher in the southern Jordan valley near Jericho. He remained in the wilderness, attracting followers from the nearby cities while avoiding the populated centers, in light of the prophecy of *Isaiah: "The voice of one crying in the wilderness, 'Make ready the way of the Lord, Make his path straight.'"

John's diet of locusts and honey and his abstinence from wine probably indicate he kept lifelong vows as a Nazirite. This asceticism was strengthened by his manner of dress — a garment of camel hair. With the Jewish nation in a spiritual and historical crisis, John proclaimed the need for repentance together with the acceptance of God's impending judgment of the world through fire. John's call for repentance was not like that of the Essenes who stressed strict adherence to Jewish law. Indeed, many of the Baptist's followers came from the disenfranchised poor or persons whose lives were lived outside of Jewish law. John exhorted these followers to prepare for God's wrathful judgment of the world by overcoming their sinful ways and engaging in good acts. John also announced that he would be followed by one even greater than himself. It is not clear whether he was referring to an angel, a human messiah or God Himself, but his words were taken by the early Christian community as pointing to Jesus of Nazareth. The baptismal rite utilized by John represents the one-time purification undergone by his adherents accepting the new era of divine justice that the Baptist prophecied for the immediate future.

John's heralding the new era set the stage for the ministry of Jesus, who went to John in the desert to receive baptism. This encounter marks the start of Jesus' public ministry carried out in the towns and villages of Galilee, in contrast to John's retreat to the wilderness. The Gospels of the New Testament grapple with John's preceding Jesus in announcing the coming of the Kingdom of God and cast him in the role of Elijah who, according to biblical prophecy, was expected to announce the advent of the Messiah.

John's demise is recounted in two different sources, the New Testament as well as the *Antiquities of the Jews* of the Jewish historian Josephus. According to the former, the Baptist was beheaded in order to avenge Herodias, the second wife of the tetrarch (governor), Herod Antipas. When John attacked as incestuous this new marriage of Herod Antipas to his step-brother's wife, Herodias had her daughter by a previous marriage, Salome, entice Herod Antipas to promise her the head of John on a platter, a promise Herod felt compelled to carry out although it went against his wishes.

Josephus gives a different account. He presents John as a teacher of morals and gives a geopolitical explanation for his execution. In order to marry Herodias, Herod Antipas divorced his first wife, daughter of the Nabataean king, Aretas IV. The region of this tribe bordered Perea where John was preaching, and Herod feared that a revolt inspired by John's verbal attacks might combine with an assault of the Nabataeans. John was apparently beheaded in 29 C.E. just before Herod suffered a crushing defeat of his army by Nabatean forces, a fact which the common people attributed to Herod's execution of the Baptist. After John's death many of his followers became adherents of Jesus, and the new Christian sect adopted the Baptist's rite of submersion in water for their own ritual purposes.

C. H. Kraeling, *John the Baptist*, 1951.
C. H. H. Scobie, *John the Baptist*, 1964.
W. Wink, *John the Baptist in the Gospel Tradition*, 1968.

JOHNSON, LYNDON BAINES (1908–1973), thirty-sixth president of the United States (1963–1969). He was born in Johnson City, Texas, and his family ran a farm in poor, hilly country. He attended public school and graduated from Johnson City High School in 1924, after which he worked at various jobs. At his mother's urging he enrolled in Southwest Texas State Teachers' College in San Marcos. It was during this period that he began to show his potential and develop his skills. Even though he participated in the debating society, edited the school paper, and spent a year teaching away from school, he managed to graduate in three and a half years. His first job out of college was teaching public speaking and debate at a Houston high school.

His father had served five terms in the Texas legislature and was friendly with Congressman Sam Rayburn. Johnson inherited his father's interest in politics and in 1931 campaigned for Democratic Congressman Richard M. Kleberg. Kleberg rewarded Johnson's efforts by appointing him as his secretary. This was his first opportunity to see where the power lay and how to use the machinery of government. The friendships he developed with colleagues of President Franklin D. *Roosevelt and Vice President John N. Garner, along with his personal friendship with Sam Rayburn, proved politically beneficial to him in later years. While working as congressional secretary for Kleberg, Johnson met Claudia Alta Taylor, better known as Lady Bird, and after a whirlwind courtship they were married in 1934.

Lyndon Johnson tossing out the opening pitch

Johnson was an admirer of Roosevelt's New Deal policies. In 1935, he became administrator of the National Youth Administration in Texas. This position enabled him to utilize the power of government to obtain educational and job opportunities for young people, and thousands of young voters remembered and were grateful to him. In 1937 he felt ready to move up the political ladder: he ran for a vacated seat in Texas's tenth congressional district. He was opposed by five people who challenged the New Deal policies of Roosevelt, but won easily. In Washington he quickly received good committee assignments.

Johnson appreciated the power of the public, and worked diligently on behalf of flood control, land reclamation, and public housing. When it became apparent that the United States was going to be involved in World War II, he supported President Roosevelt's foreign policy. Johnson did not forget his humble beginnings. Much of the legislation that

---

LYNDON JOHNSON'S POLITICS

- Never trust a man whose eyes are too close to his nose.
- While you're saving your face, you're losing your ass.
- A Great Society — a place where the meaning of a man's life matches the marvels of man's labors.
- Doing what is right is not the problem. It's knowing what is right.
- Patriotism often means concealing a world of error and wrong judgment beneath the flag.

The bill is the latest, and among the most important in a long series of victories. It is the beginning of freedom; and the barriers to that freedom are tumbling down. Freedom is the right to share fully and equally in American society — to vote, to hold a job, to enter a public place, to go to school. It is the right to be treated in every part of our national life as a person equal in dignity and promise to all others.

But freedom is not enough. You do not wipe away the scars of centuries by saying: "Now you are free to go where you want and do as you desire." It is not enough just to open the gates of opportunity. All our citizens must have the ability to walk through those gates.

This is the next and more profound stage of the battle for civil rights. We seek not just freedom but opportunity. We seek not just legal equity but human ability, not just equality as a right and a theory but equality as a fact and equality as a result (from his commencement address at Howard University, 1965, on the voting rights bill safeguarding black voters).

---

he proposed for the little man resulted from his early upbringing and the hardships he witnessed as a child. His experiences with poverty and educational disadvantages served as a foundation for his endeavors to create change.

In 1941 he suffered a political setback when he was defeated in his race for the Senate, even though he had the backing of Roosevelt. He joined the navy in December 1941 and saw action in the Pacific. However, he was only in service for eight months when Roosevelt ordered all congressmen on active duty to return to Washington. He remained in Congress for the better part of eight years and in 1948 again attempted to win a seat in the Senate. Out of 900,000 votes cast in the Democratic primary, he won by only 87 votes, earning the nickname of Landslide Lyndon, but he had no difficulty beating his Republican opponent in the general election.

Shortly after entering the Senate he became a member of the Armed Services Committee, where he defended and supported President Harry S. *Truman's decision to intervene in Korea, but did not approve of the way in which the war was being waged. In 1951 Johnson became the party whip, and was elected party leader in 1953. He was the majority whip when the Democrats regained the majority in the Senate. Since the Democrats controlled Congress during both of Dwight D. *Eisenhower's presidential terms, Johnson's position was extremely important, and he carried it out with devotion and dedication.

In 1960 Johnson decided to run for president, but he stayed out of the primaries and hoped his good work in the Senate would propel him to the White House. Instead, John F. *Kennedy's primary victories and other factors gained him the Democratic nomination; Kennedy then asked Johnson to be his running mate. Johnson helped Kennedy defeat Republican candidates Richard *Nixon and Henry Cabot Lodge and became vice president in 1961. In this position he was very active, and his legislative background greatly helped Kennedy, even though he himself felt that his abilities were not sufficiently utilized by the White House staff. He chaired the National Aeronautical and Space Council and the Committee on Equal Employment Opportunities.

When Kennedy was assassinated on November 22, 1963, Johnson was dramatically sworn in as president in Air Force One, the presidential plane. Shortly after assuming office, Johnson was able to persuade Congress to enact far-reaching proposals on civil rights and taxes, areas in which he had been very active when he was majority whip. He proposed a large-scale fight against poverty and sought to establish what he called the Great Society. Much legislation was passed during his first year in office, and with Senator Hubert H. Humphrey as his running mate, he soundly defeated Senator Barry Goldwater in the 1964 presidential election, in which he also carried a big majority in both houses of Congress. Historic legislation provided for Medicare, safeguards for black voting, and antipoverty bills.

However, it was not long after that Johnson began to be criticized for the increasing American involvement in Vietnam. America began to increase its armed forces initially sent simply as "advisers," in Vietnam considerably. At one point Johnson said, "I can't get out. I can't finish it with what I have, so what the hell can I do?"

Opposition to the war spread as the youth in the United States grew more and more disenchanted with the increased American involvement in what seemed to them to be a no win situation. At one point there were over five hundred thousand American troops in Vietnam, and South Vietnam was insisting on more and more military aid. Neither President Truman in Korea nor Johnson in Vietnam were able to put a stop to the wars to which they had committed troops.

On March 31, 1967, Johnson announced that he would not seek reelection. When he left office in January 1968 he retired to his ranch near Johnson City, Texas, where he wrote his memoirs, entitled *The Vantage Point* (1971).

V. D. Bonnet, *The Presidency of Lyndon B. Johnson*, 1983.
R. Dallek, *Lone Star Rising*, 1991.
R. J. Donovan, *Nemesis: Truman and Johnson in the Coils of War in Asia*, 1984.
Lady Bird Johnson, *A White House Diary*, 1970.
M. Miller, *Lyndon: An Oral Biography*, 1980.

JOHNSON, SAMUEL (1709–1784), English writer and wit. Johnson was born in Lichfield, son of a secondhand bookseller and stationer. A melancholy, overweight boy inclined to indolence, his idea of sport was having another boy pull him across a frozen pool by his garter.

If his body was not in the best of shape, intellectual abilities raised him to preeminence at school. Growing up surrounded by books awakened literary interests at an early stage. He had a remarkable memory and an excellent command of the classics and entered Oxford University with a head start over his contemporaries. After a year, his father's business went bankrupt and poverty forced him to leave without completing the degree.

Johnson turned to teaching for a livelihood but it did not suit him and he could not decide if it was more disagreeable for him to teach or his pupils to learn. His inclination was toward literature and his first work of note was published in 1733, the translation from French of a book describing a voyage to Ethiopia. Johnson was living in Birmingham at this time and here he met his wife, Elizabeth Porter, widow of a good friend. He feared his humble background would lead her to reject him — he frankly admitted one of his uncles had been hanged. He need not have worried, for the portly Mrs. Porter was not easily put off and told him that she had fifty relatives who deserved hanging! They were married in 1735; at forty-five she was twenty years his senior.

In 1737 Johnson moved to London, attracted by the greater prospects for a man of letters. He experi-

THOMAS B. MACAULAY ON JOHNSON

That strange figure which is as familiar to us as the figures of those among whom we have been brought up, the gigantic body, the huge face, the black worsted stockings, the grey wig with the scorched foretop, the dirty hands, the nails bitten and pared to the quick. We see the eyes and the mouth moving with convulsive twitches; we see the heavy form rolling; we hear it puffing; and then comes the "Why, Sir!", and the "What then, Sir!" and the "No Sir!" and the "You don't see the way through the question, Sir!"

enced bitter poverty but found employment writing for *The Gentleman's Magazine* and wrote a biography of Richard Savage, a London rake whose story proved most popular. In 1747 he published a plan for the book destined to win him fame — *The Dictionary of the English Language*. Several booksellers combined to offer the huge sum of 1,575 pounds sterling for this momentous work. He employed six copyists to help prepare the dictionary for the press. Definitions were made with a good dose of subjectivity and wordiness. "Pension" for example was explained: "in England it is generally understood to mean pay given to a state hireling for treason to his country." It is interesting that despite this cynicism Johnson accepted a pension from King *George III in 1761.

Oxford University awarded him a doctorate and in 1755, when the dictionary was finally published, the compiler was named as Dr. Johnson. Although a popular book, it did not make much money, and when his mother died in 1759 he hurriedly wrote the novel *Rasselas* to cover the expenses of the funeral. In later years he published an edition of Shakespeare with comments, as well as *Lives of the Poets* among other well-known books, including volumes of poetry.

In 1763 Johnson met his future biographer and most enthusiastic disciple, the dissipate Scottish lawyer James Boswell. Johnson's fame as a writer, conversationalist, and character attracted a wide circle of friends and acquaintances and Boswell aspired to join them. Despite Johnson's low opinion of the Scots ("The noblest prospect which a Scotchman ever sees is the high road that leads him to England"), they struck up a lasting friendship. During late night dinners and meetings of Johnson's literary club, Boswell was able to enjoy, and at times feel, the sharp end of Johnson's barbed wit in good company — the painter Sir Joshua Reynolds, the author Oliver Goldsmith, and the actor David Garrick were also club members.

In 1773 Boswell and Johnson made the tour of the Scottish Highlands and Hebrides that became famous through the account Johnson wrote of the journey. Despite prejudices to the contrary, Johnson was pleased with his Scottish travels and the hospitality shown him by his hosts. He saw that rumors of scarcity of food in Scotland were nonsense, though this did not dispel his confidence in England's superiority. When Boswell asked him if he had found sufficient meat and drink in Scotland, Johnson responded "Why yes, Sir, meat and drink enough to give the inhabitants sufficient strength to run away from home." The Americans came off little better in the doctor's eyes, for he was a firm believer in the justice of the English cause and commented, "Had we treated the Americans as we ought, and as they deserved, we should have razed all their towns and let them enjoy their forests."

In 1783 Johnson suffered a stroke and the death he feared drew near. He had always taken a deep interest in religious matters and came to dread going to the place "where we shall receive no letter." The following year he died and was honored with burial in Westminster Abbey. Boswell's biography — which covered the last third of his life — was immediately recognized as a classic and made Johnson one of England's most famous characters, conversationalists, and wits.

J. Boswell, *The Life of Samuel Johnson*, 1991.

J. Hawkins, *The Life of Samuel Johnson*, 1962.

E. P. McCaughey, *From Loyalist to Founding Father*, 1980.

J. Wain, *Samuel Johnson*, 1974.

JONES, JOHN PAUL (1747–1792), American naval hero of the War of Independence, whose indomitable courage and brilliant seamanship won him the title of father of the U.S. Navy.

Jones was born John Paul, son of a gardener in Scotland, where he inherited the doggedness and cavalier attitude that were to serve him well at sea.

After briefly attending school in the local parish, he was apprenticed to a shipowner out of Whitehaven, England. His first voyage, at the age of thirteen, was to Virginia, where his brother had established a tailoring business. In Virginia, Jones stayed with his brother for a short period, but eager to continue at sea, soon found a berth aboard a slaver. Taking jobs where he could find them, by the age of nineteen he had advanced to the rank of first mate.

Jones received his first command at the age of twenty-one, of a small merchant vessel, the *John,* in which he made several voyages to Tobago. On one such voyage he flogged the ship's carpenter for neglect of duty; several weeks later, after a bout of malaria, the man died while on board another ship. Jones was charged with murder and briefly imprisoned. Although he subsequently proved his innocence, he earned a reputation as a harsh master.

On a later command in 1773, Jones killed the ringleader of a mutiny. According to Jones, the man had rushed onto his sword. Advised by his friends to leave Tobago because of the hostility of the witnesses in the case, Jones traveled incognito to Virginia. At this time he attached "Jones" to his name. He passed the next two years in quiet obscurity, running the estates of a dead brother in Virginia.

The impending War of Independence was an opportunity for the young seaman to show his mettle. He traveled to Philadelphia and made the acquaintance of a number of eminent congressmen, who were impressed with this small, intense Scotsman. In 1775 he received his first commission as a lieutenant on the frigate *Alfred* the first ship to fly the continental flag. The following year he was given command of the *Providence,* with overall command of a small fleet and promotion to the rank of captain soon following. He quickly established an unrivaled reputa-

A French medal showing John Paul Jones with the Bonhomme Richard *in action on the reverse*

tion for skill and strategy, achieving several resounding victories for the fledgling U.S. Navy. However, his common background rankled the naval establishment and, despite his obvious talent, Congress ranked him low on the captains' list. However, in clear deference to his ability, he was given command of the *Ranger*, and ordered to head for France.

The *Ranger* itself was a rather insubstantial ship when compared to the British man-o'-wars. Nevertheless Jones was determined to inflict serious punishment on the enemy in its own waters. His first attack at Whitehaven, a port he knew well from his youth, was not the total success he had sought. The most notable event of his first cruise was the capture of the *Drake*, the first British naval ship captured by the Continental navy. After twenty-eight days Jones returned triumphantly to port in Brest. The British for their part were rightly alarmed by the presence of an obviously formidable raider near their own territory. Jones was dubbed a renegade Scot pirate and a price was offered for his capture.

Jones was eager to continue his adventures, hoping that after his early successes he would be given command of a more significant ship. What he received was an old and slow refitted merchantman, which he named the *Bonhomme Richard*. After several false starts, he set sail accompanied by a number of other smaller ships all under his command. Jones's squadron had captured seventeen small vessels around the coast of Great Britain when, in September 1779, they encountered the Baltic trade fleet of forty-two vessels being escorted by two British ships of war, the small *Countess of Scarborough* and the forty-four-gun *Serapis*. The *Scarborough* soon surrendered, leaving the *Richard* engaged in a tremendous battle with the *Serapis*, which carried more than twice its firepower. Hopelessly outclassed, Jones saw his only hope of victory in close quarters action. He skillfully maneuvered the *Richard* alongside the *Serapis* and lashed the two ships together. For hours the two crews savaged each other's vessel. The *Richard* was set on fire and began taking on water so badly that a British officer asked Jones if he would surrender, to which he made the famous retort "Sir, I have not yet begun to fight!" After some three hours of desperate skirmishing, the *Serapis* struck its colors. The unlikely victory of the *Richard* was credited wholly to Jones's valor and skill. The *Richard* sank the following day, its colors still flying.

Returning to Paris, Jones was feted as a national hero. He enjoyed his time ashore, plunging into French society wholeheartedly. This harsh seafarer even composed poetry for his lady friends, of whom there were many. Eventually, Jones set sail for America in 1781. There too he was paraded and lauded for his heroic efforts, yet still his rank was not raised, due to objections by other senior officers. By way of compensation, Jones was given command of the soon-to-be-completed ship of the line *America,* which conferred on him the *de facto* rank of rear admiral. However, before he took com-

mand, the vessel was given to the French government as a gift.

Jones marked his time, writing on naval warfare and observing the maneuvers of the French fleet. He traveled to Europe for a few years where he negotiated the return of the booty he had captured from Britain. Returning to America in 1787, he was awarded a gold medal by Congress for his valor and service, but still had no place in an America at peace. In 1788 he received an offer to command a fleet for the Russian navy against the Turks, which he accepted, hoping to keep his hand in for future service in America. However, from the first his position was untenable. The other Russian officers were not happy to have this adventurer in their midst, and despite some notable battles his successes were credited to others. Then a scurrilous rumor was circulated that he had violated a young girl, and he unceremoniously returned to France in 1789. His disappointment in Russia affected his health badly. He took up comfortable lodgings in Paris, keeping company with a few close friends, his heroic days over. In 1792 the U.S. government appointed him commissioner to Algiers, but before the letter detailing the appointment reached him, he died, prematurely aged by his years at sea.

He was buried in a lead coffin, filled with alcohol and ready for shipping, in the hope that he would be accorded a hero's burial in the United States. However, over the years the cemetery was closed and forgotten. Only in 1905, after an intense search, was the coffin discovered, opened, and Jones's body positively identified. It was taken for its final interment at the U.S. Naval Academy in Annapolis, Maryland.
L. Lorenz, *John Paul Jones,* 1969.
Morison and Eliot, *John Paul Jones,* 1964.

JOSEPH II (1741–1790), Holy Roman emperor. Joseph was the fourth child and eldest son of *Maria Theresa and the Holy Roman emperor Francis I. He was an "enlightened" despot who was at once a militarist and absolutist as much as he was a liberal humanitarian. Cold and calculating, he personally claimed that "a great king did not need to be loved, he only needed to be right." Maintaining that the empire required transformation, he introduced unpopular reforms to that end. His attempt to modernize and unify the ethnically diverse Habsburg Empire ultimately met with failure.

As a child, Joseph was difficult and reserved, concentrating endlessly on his studies. His marriage to Isabella of Parma in 1760 brought considerable, albeit short lived, joy into his life: three years later his wife died of smallpox. His second wife, Maria Josepha of Bavaria, also died of smallpox in 1767, two years after their marriage. His father died in 1765, and Joseph was then elected Holy Roman emperor and coruler, with his mother, of the Habsburg lands.

Dressing simply, usually in military uniform, Joseph was not interested in the ceremonial pomp of royal power. He perceived himself as the leader of a secular state, not the head of a divinely sanctioned empire. As an austere and dutiful statesman, he was committed to bureaucratic efficiency and meticulous organization. In 1768 he wrote to his brother Leopold, grand duke of Tuscany: "Love of country, the welfare of the Monarchy, that is genuinely the only passion I feel, and I would undertake anything for its sake."

Until the death of his mother in 1780, Joseph concentrated his attention on foreign affairs, aiming to strengthen imperial power. His attempts to rejuvenate his kingdom were thwarted by the aristocracy supported by Austria's chief enemy, *Frederick II (Frederick the Great) of Prussia. A nominal alliance with France gained him no leverage, and he temporarily solved the conflict of interest between Prussia, Russia, and Austria at the expense of Poland. The civil war in Poland (1772) provided for its partition, with Joseph acquiring Galicia and Bukovina.

The death of Maria Theresa gave Joseph absolute power in both the domestic and foreign spheres. In 1781, he concluded a significant alliance with *Catherine the Great of Russia. Freed from worry about the east, the Austrians broke their treaty with the Dutch and pressed for the opening of the Scheldt River to benefit the Austrian Netherlands, giving them a route to the sea. The Dutch, however, protested, forcing Joseph to retract.

Joseph's first complete failure in foreign policy was his bid to exchange the Austrian Netherlands for Bavaria. Prussia protested and marched into Bohemia, a domain of the Habsburg Empire. Concurrently, Frederick the Great was persuading numerous German princes in the League of Princes to oppose Joseph's power. In response, Joseph was forced to strengthen his alliance with Russia, and was propelled into the Russo-Turkish war of 1787 as a result. The campaign of 1788 was a disaster and Joseph's military prestige was damaged: open rebellion broke out in the Austrian Netherlands, and sporadic unrest in other parts of the empire.

Joseph's domestic policy called for increased centralization and despotic absolutism. Continuing his mother's policies, he sought to base his rule in a sound bureaucratic apparatus. In 1782 he concentrated his entire administration in two main offices in Vienna and Budapest. He imposed a system of districts according to population density, without regard to ethnic diversity, and attacked "regional peculiarities" by making German the official language of law and commerce throughout his lands: the link between Germanization and centralization was now forged.

In the economy and the area of civil law, Joseph sought to resolve problems that existed between the landowners and the peasants. Serfdom was abolished in the edicts of 1781 and 1782, restricting patrimonial justice and giving the peasants the right to move, marry, and change occupations. In return, they had to obey the state, pay taxes, and serve in the army. In compensation to the landed nobility, Joseph promoted mercantilist economic policies through free trade and moderate protectionism.

Joseph's secularization of the empire caused the most unrest, leading to a breach in relations with the Roman Catholic church. He felt it was necessary to reform the church within his domain because it diminished the state's ability to rule absolutely. First, he introduced the Statute of Toleration (1781) which emancipated the Jews and gave greater freedom to Protestants. Then, he dissolved monastic orders and closed seven hundred monasteries. He went on to restrict the issuance of papal bulls, reorganized various dioceses, and placed seminaries under state control in 1783. Finally, he consolidated the educational system, limiting the church's role.

Foreign setbacks and domestic problems threatened to split the Habsburg Empire apart. The landed nobility in places like Hungary, Germany, and the Austrian Netherlands, remained strong enough to oppose reforms that were not to their liking. Lying on his death bed, Joseph was forced to renounce most of his reforms. In his policies, as in other despotic systems of the Enlightenment, new forms of freedom went hand in hand with new forms of restraint.

D. Beales, *Joseph II*, 1987.

P. P. Bernard, *The Limits of Enlightenment: Joseph II and the Law*, 1979.

S. K. Padover, *The Revolutionary Emperor: Joseph II of Austria*, 1967.

JOYCE, JAMES AUGUSTINE (1882–1941), Irish novelist and poet and one of the greatest writers in twentieth century literature. His books, once banned as obscene by the United States and Britain, are today required college reading. He was born in Dublin to a genteel but penurious father, and was educated in Jesuit schools and at University College, Dublin, but later broke with Catholicism, which he felt was strangling freedom of expression in Ireland. In 1902 he went to London to study medicine, but soon returned home because of his mother's fatal illness. Finding the atmosphere in Ireland too constricting, he left again for Europe in 1904 with Nora Barnacle, with whom he lived and had children but married only in 1931, and settled eventually in Trieste, Italy. During the rest of his life he briefly returned to Ireland only twice.

As well as being a quick reader and extremely well versed in classical and modern literature, Joyce was a fount of popular science and general knowledge and had a gift for languages; he was fluent in Italian, French, and German, and had a working knowledge of Dano-Norwegian and Latin. In Europe he initially made his living (a rather poor one) as a teacher of languages.

Joyce published his first volume of verse, a collection of thirty-six love poems called *Chamber Music*, in 1907. *Dubliners*, his first work of fiction, consisting of fifteen short stories, followed in 1914 and dealt with various aspects of life in Dublin throughout childhood, adolescence, and adulthood.

For many years Joyce and his family lived in poverty. In 1915 he moved to Zurich, Switzerland,

FROM JAMES JOYCE'S WORKS

Stately, plump Buck Mulligan came from the stairhead, bearing a bowl of lather on which a mirror and razor lay crossed. A yellow dressinggown, ungirdled, was sustained gently behind him by the mild morning air. He held the bowl aloft and intoned: *Introibo ad altare Dei.*

Opening of Ulysses

Riverrun, past Eve and Adam's, from swerve of shore to bend of bay, brings us back by a commodius vicus of recirculation back to Howth Castle and Environs.

Sir Tristram, violer d'amores, fr'over the short sea, had passencore rearrived from North Armorica on this side the scraggy isthmus of Europe Minor to wielderfight his penisolate war.

Opening of Finnegans Wake

From Justice John M. Woolsey's decision in New York District Court lifting the ban on James Joyce's Ulysses (1933)

Joyce with astonishing success has shown how the screen of consciousness with its ever-shifting kaleidoscope impressions carries, as it were on a plastic palimpsest, not only actual things about him, but also in a penumbral zone of past impressions, some recent and some drawn up by association from the realm of the subconscious...Whilst in many places the effect on the reader is somewhat emetic, nowhere does it tend to be aphrodisiac.

James Joyce (right) discussing his work

presented in a different way. Interior monologue is developed to the full into a unique and insightful method of character portrayal. On its publication, the book ran into immediate censorship problems and was banned in the United States and Britain (and, inevitably, in Ireland) but appeared in France. A landmark legal decision in 1933 permitted its publication in the United States as a recognized literary masterpiece. It has become one of the seminal works of twentieth-century literature.

Joyce worked for the next seventeen years on *Finnegans Wake*, published in 1939. Attempting to embody a synthesis of all existence, it takes the form of a broken series of dreams in a single night in the life of Humphrey Chimpden Earwicker, the representative of all humanity (his initials also stand for "Here Cometh Everyman"). In this novel, Joyce took linguistic experimentation to the extreme, coining portmanteau words, puns ("freudened while jung," "one man's fish is another man's poisson"), and inventing a polyglot language drawing on his vast knowledge, with sources ranging from Finnish to Hebrew.

Joyce remained in Paris until the early years of World War II and left France after its fall to the Nazis in 1940, fleeing to Zurich, where he died of a perforated stomach ulcer the following year.

Joyce was interested in psychology and mythology, and though he was skeptical about Freudian psychoanalytic treatment, Freudian symbols and Jungian myths are evident, particularly in *Finnegans Wake*. J. G. Frazer's *The Golden Bough*, a compendium of magic and ritual, also played a part in the making of *Finnegans Wake*. His greatest mentors in literature were Gustave *Flaubert and H. J. *Ibsen. While he adopted naturalistic techniques from the French author, from Ibsen he acquired the myth of the artist as tragic hero.

One of the crucial events in Joyce's writing was the "epiphany." Joyce's secular interpretation of the religious experience was a moment of revelation which overcame his central characters, infusing a commonplace object with a sense of sudden radiance.

and lived there until 1919. It was with the publication of *A Portrait of the Artist as a Young Man* in 1916 that he began to gain fame in literary and artistic circles. This was a semiautobiographical novel dealing with the youth and home life of Stephen Dedalus, his alter-ego, and was characterized by considerable use of the stream of consciousness technique, which recreates all the thoughts, feelings, and sensations of a character.

In 1920 Joyce moved to Paris, where he was to make his home for the next twenty years. *Ulysses*, begun in 1915, was completed during those years and published in 1922. The entire action takes place in Dublin on a single day — June 14, 1904 (the day Joyce met Nora). The two central figures are a converted Jew, Leopold Bloom (after whom June 14 has come to be known as Bloomsday) and Stephen Dedalus. The book is divided into eighteen sections, each inspired by an episode in the *Odyssey*. It is written in a dazzling variety of styles, each episode

His other works include the play *Exiles* (1918) and two collections of poetry, *Pomes Penyeach* (1927) and *Collected Poems* (1936).

R. Adams, *James Joyce, Common Sense and Beyond*, 1971.

P. Costello, *James Joyce: The Years of Growth, 1882–1915*, 1992.

R. Deming, *James Joyce: The Critical Heritage*, 1971.

R. Ellmann, *James Joyce*, 1983.

M. Hodgart, *James Joyce, A Students' Guide*, 1978.

JUÁREZ, BENITO PABLO (1806–1872), Mexican leader. Born in San Pablo Guelatao near Oaxaca, Mexico, the son of poor Zapotec Indians, he was orphaned at age three and left to the care of an uncle. In his youth he worked as a household servant for a religious bookbinder in Oaxaca. Exposed to a multitude of books, he studied Spanish. Later, under the influence of his religious employer, Juárez began to study for the priesthood, but changed his mind.

He enrolled in 1829 at the Oaxaca Institute of Arts and Sciences, studying law and science. Three years later he became a member of the state legislature. Always driving himself, he was admitted to the Mexican bar in 1834 and began his practice immediately. Desirous of helping people, he often represented poor Indians with legal problems and found himself becoming involved in politics as a strong supporter of liberal views. In 1842 he was appointed a civil court judge. By the age of thirty-seven, with the improvement of his social and economic position, he was finally able to marry the daughter of a well-known family.

In 1846, Juárez served a term as deputy to the national congress. He was elected in 1847 governor of Oaxaca where he proved himself a good administrator. Ever mindful of his humble beginnings, he always defended the interest of Indians. After his term as governor, he returned to the practice of law as well as to teaching at his alma mater.

Shortly thereafter, in 1853, the conservatives returned to power with Antonio de Santa Anna as president. One of Santa Anna's official acts was to imprison Juárez, because Juárez had refused to grant Santa Anna sanctuary in Oaxaca during his term as governor when Santa Anna was fleeing from the troops of the American general Winfield Scott during the Mexican War. Juárez, mindful of the power of the United States, preferred not to antagonize it.

Juárez managed to escape from prison and went into exile in the United States (1853-1855), finding sanctuary in New Orleans, Louisiana, where he supported himself with an assortment of menial jobs. He also joined other exiles to plot the overthrow of the military dictator, Santa Anna. His chief associates were Juan Álvarez and Ignacio Comonfort, men of integrity and liberals like himself. Their revolt succeeded, driving Santa Anna into exile; they established a reform movement. Juan Álvarez became president of Mexico, Ignacio Comonfort minister of war, and Juárez minister of justice.

The new liberal regime desired to establish a constitutional government, which would abolish the special privileges of the clergy and the military as well as stimulate the economy through the expedient of selling the vast property holdings of the church. They reorganized the judicial system and limited the jurisdiction of military and ecclesiastical courts. The "Juárez Law" ended judicial immunities enjoyed by the clergy and the military in civil cases, provoking a tremendous uproar leading to Áplvarez's resignation and his replacement by the more moderate Comonfort.

Progress was not halted and in 1856 the Lerdo Law was adopted to do away with large property holdings, especially those of the church, and mandated public auction of such agricultural tracts. In 1857 a liberal constitution was adopted and Comonfort was elected president. He named Juárez governor of Oaxaca, a position he held from 1855 to 1857. A bitter civil war ensued, incited by the church, causing Comonfort to resign and flee the country. Now Juárez became the de jure president. By 1859 the U.S. government recognized him and his government, providing them with some aid. It took until 1861 and a bitter war before Juárez's conservative opponents were finally defeated. The government was practically bankrupt and Juárez's solution — a two-year moratorium on payment of all foreign debts — was not appreciated by foreign creditors.

Armed intervention followed by France, Spain, and Great Britain, to protect their investments. The United States then occupied with its own civil war, could not get involved in a further war to enforce the Monroe Doctrine (enunciated in 1823 to oppose any European intervention in the Americas) against the European invaders. Without any meaningful opposition, the French , by 1862, had marched on Mexico City forcing Juárez and his government to flee northward.

*Napoleon III, king of France, installed *Maximilian, the Austrian prince, as king of Mexico. In the battles that ensued, many Mexicans who fought against the French invasion were captured and in 1865 Maximilian ordered their execution. By 1867 the United States finally induced the French troops to withdraw from Mexico. Maximilian was captured, given a military trial, and executed.

In July 1867 Juárez triumphantly returned to Mexico City and was reelected to the presidency. The period following his return was difficult, with uprisings and factional opposition, including the split of his Liberal party in 1871 into three. This resulted in Porfirio Díaz and Sebastián Lerdo de Tejada running against Juárez for the presidency, but Juárez was reelected. As the turmoil was coming to an end in 1872, Juárez died.

Juárez was the most prominent personality in Mexico and Mexican history during the turbulent period of 1856 to 1872. It is only after Juárez that one can truly speak of a Mexican nation — one that he brought out of feudalism and welded into a democratic republic.

I. E. Cadenhead, *Jr., Benito Juárez*, 1973.

R. Roeder, *Juárez and His Mexico*, 2 vols., 1968.

C. A. Smart, *Viva Juárez*, 1975.

C. A. Weeks, *The Juárez Myth in Mexico*, 1986.

JUNG, CARL GUSTAV (1876–1961), Swiss psychiatrist and analytical psychologist. A highly original thinker, his central theoretical concept was that of the collective unconscious, which has significantly enriched psychological thought and saved it from the barrenness of a purely individualistic psychology. Jung never restricted himself solely to the dry discipline of academic psychology, believing rather that in order to establish an understanding of the links between the individual personality and the symbolic field it inhabits, it was necessary to undertake wide-ranging socio-cultural studies. A talented linguist and a scholar of sufficient ability to read medieval Latin texts in the original, it was he who elucidated the important relations between religion and psychology.

As a child, Jung had remarkably striking and unusually intense dreams and fantasies, which he was in later years to posit came from the area of the mind he called the collective unconscious. The son of a pastor, he was expected to follow the family tradition and become a clergyman. However, his observation of his father's failing belief and his own inability to communicate his experience of God to the elder Jung led him to reject the expected course and opt to study medicine in Basle. He also read widely in the field of philosophy. Following a Ouija board session where a young girl adopted a variety of roles suggested to her in the course of the seance, Jung determined to take up psychiatry that he might discover "the intruders of the mind."

After completing his studies at the universities of Basel and Zurich, he joined the Bergholzli Asylum in Zurich in 1902. There he made his name through his outstanding success in using association tests as an indicator of hidden emotional activity. For the constellation of activity within the unconscious mind he coined the term "complex," now a familiar usage in everyday speech. Many of his findings led him to champion the then hotly disputed theories of Sigmund *Freud. For a period of some five years, from 1907, the two men collaborated closely, even engaging in mutual analysis.

Jung was widely expected to succeed Freud as the leader of the psychoanalytic movement headquartered in Vienna, and was elected president of the International Psychoanalytic Society in 1911. The two came, however, to disagree significantly on certain matters: Jung could not accept Freud's insistence on the sexual bases of neurosis, while Jung's views on symbolism conflicted sharply with Freud's more formalized approach. The formal break occurred in 1912; resigning from the Psychoanalytic Society, Jung founded a new school based in Zurich.

Disturbed by the break with Freud, Jung studied the reasons for it and was led to conclude that a constitutional difference in type inevitably led each to approach clinical and other problems from different angles. From these findings he evolved his differentiation of people into two attitude types: extroverted (outward looking) and introverted (inward looking). He went on to posit four basic mind functions —

thinking, feeling, sensation, and intuition — one or more of which predominated in any given person. This outstandingly important — albeit controversial — theoretical development was delineated in his work *Psychological Types* (1923), which also manifested the breadth of his scholarship.

Jung believed that the free association technique used by Freudian analysts lead away from the complexes of which we need to become aware. He also believed that the types of neuroses that could be adequately dealt with in Freudian terms were characteristic of the earlier part of life. He stressed that a neurotic symptom cannot be explained solely through reference to the patient's past: it also represents an attempt to deal with the present problems confronting the patient. He called the process by which patients could discover their own balanced synthesis of the competing demands of their drives and circumstances "individuation."

Due to his interest in the unconscious, unapprehended, background of conscious life, Jung stressed the importance of dreams. The appearance in the dreams of many of his patients of apparently ancient material, which he could not explain in terms of the personal history of the dreamer, led him to the study of ethnology and comparative religion with special emphasis upon religious symbolism. He conducted field research in Africa and the Americas and launched an extensive study of world religions. He was to discover that the same symbols and themes recurred in widely different times and places in mythologies and religions, as well as in art. He concluded that the mind, like the body, had a long ancestry and that just as the traces of our mammalian descent are plain on the physical level, so the mind too bears archetypal patterns, inherited tendencies of psychic functioning common to the species, through which the collective unconscious reveals itself.

Jung believed that people have a strong need for religious beliefs and experiences since it is through these that they are able to encounter and accept the contents of the collective conscious, a process he deemed necessary to psychological health. In addition to his fascination with alchemical symbolism, he was especially interested in Chinese thought, meeting the noted Sinologist Richard Wilhelm and contributing commentaries to his translations of the *I Ching* and *The Secret of the Golden Flower*, two of the most noted Chinese religious-philosophical works.

Jung held that the increase in scientific understanding had led to a dehumanization of the natural and social worlds and a corresponding lack of awareness of the powers of human nature; to this he ascribed the increased propensity to psychological disorder in modern society. He dated this process of disorientation as beginning with the original Christian break with paganism and accelerating after the Enlightenment.

This approach helped make him a pioneer in the psychotherapy of the middle-aged and elderly, in whom he was able to reinstate a sense of the value of their lives in the context of the sequence of history.

Jung was in demand as a skilled lecturer, often visiting the United States and Great Britain; he was awarded numerous honorary degrees. A chair of medical psychology was created for him by Basle University in 1943. By the time of his death in his eighty-sixth year, institutes teaching Jungian methods were well established, most notably the famous C. G. Jung Institute in Zurich.

L. Donn, *Freud and Jung*, 1988.
P. Stern, *C. G. Jung, the Haunted Prophet*, 1976.
L. Van der Post, *Jung and the Story of Our Time*, 1975.

JUSTINIAN I (Flavius Petrus Sabbatius Justinianus; 483–565 C.E.), Byzantine emperor. Although Justinian was born into an Illyrian peasant family, his illiterate uncle, Justin, was a senator who brought Justinian to Constantinople and provided him with a good education. Justin usurped the throne of Emperor Anastasius after his death and enjoyed the prerogatives of his position, leaving the management of the empire to Justinian. When Justin died in 527, Justinian became emperor. For the entire thirty-eight years of his reign, he was sensitive to the weakness of his claim to the throne and encouraged the concept of the divine right of kings, demanding whoever came into his presence to kneel and kiss his toes or the hem of his robe.

The historian Procopius, intimately acquainted with Justinian, wrote a biased book describing him: "insincere, crafty, hypocritical, dissembling his anger, double-dealing, clever, a perfect artist in acting out an opinion which he pretended to hold, and even able to produce tears… to the need of the moment… He was a fickle friend, a truceless enemy, an ardent devotee of assassination and robbery." This might have been true, but he was also abstemious, amiable, accessible, generous, hard-working, eager to learn, merciful, and religious.

Justinian was deeply attached to Theodora, daughter of a bear master, whom he made first his mistress, then his wife, and finally empress. He granted her power equal to his own which she sometimes exercised in opposition to him. She was capable of both murder and mercy and her love of worldly pleasures moderated Justinian's monkish ways. A controversial version of Theodora's early life holds that she was a prostitute. This story may have stemmed from the fact that, as empress, she founded a convent of repentance for reformed prostitutes, banned brothel keepers from Constantinople, and became a strict moralist in her old age.

The response of Justinian and Theodora to the serious revolt they faced in 532 reveals much about their characters and their relationship. Justinian responded to the murderous, burning and looting mobs rampaging through the streets by hiding and trying to flee. Theodora called on the army, which mercilessly quashed the rebellion. Justinian then showed mercy to the rebels and their families.

Justinian's passion for unity shaped his reign. Militarily, he wanted to drive out the barbarians and restore one rule within the Roman Empire's old borders. He also wanted to end religious divisions, particularly the disagreements between the Eastern and Western churches. He sought to create an updated, uniform

Justinian and his court; sixth-century mosaic at San Vitale, Ravenna

code of law for the entire Roman Empire, to replace the existing, often conflicting, jumble of laws from the multitude of nations within the empire.

The military achievements of Justinian's reign were due to his generals, notably Belisarius and Narses. His own contributions to his wars were diplomatic — he never fought in an actual battle. He would forge an alliance with potential foes, allowing him to concentrate his forces on one war at a time. The end of one war would mean the creation of a new alliance so he could freely attack his old ally. Despite a serious lack of both funds and soldiers Justinian succeeded in doubling his territory. North Africa was to remain Roman until the Arab conquest and Italy was so devastated from eighteen years of war that it did not recover until the Renaissance. The empire would prove incapable of defending its expanded territory, and within a hundred years the rest of Justinian's conquests were lost and the Roman Empire was smaller than when his reign began.

He was responsible for an ambitious building program, the jewel of which was the Constantinople church of Saint Sophia (Hagia Sophia). To finance his projects he exacted heavy taxation and if the people rose up in protest, they were savagely massacred.

Justinian's legal reform, the Code of Justinian, was essentially rigid and conservative. It decreed severe punishment for heresy and sexual deviation, the inalienability of church property, the supreme authority of the emperor, and legalized serfdom. Justinian wanted to forbid divorce but was persuaded that that would increase the number of poisonings, so divorce laws remained quite liberal. The code was too severe to be widely enforceable, but it remained the law of the Byzantine Empire until its end and became a cornerstone of the Western legal system.

Justinian's efforts to resolve certain theological controversies failed. He was devastated by Theodora's death when he was sixty-five. He lost all interest in government after that and immersed himself in theology. Justinian ruled for seventeen more years, but rarely dealt with any of the series of disasters ranging from earthquake to an invasion of the Huns that plagued his empire. His theological studies took some strange turns, and he was considered a heretic when he died at eighty-three.

J. W. Barker, *Justinian and the Later Roman Empire*, 1966.

R. Browning, *Justinian and Theodora*, 1971.

K

KAFKA, FRANZ (1883–1924), Czech author. A master of German prose, Kafka created a narrative fiction simple yet subtly surreal that expressed his personal alienation and that of his age. Almost unknown in his lifetime, he has won posthumous acclaim as one of the greats of twentieth century European literature.

Born into a middle-class Jewish-Czech family living in Prague, the young Kafka felt overpowered by his father, a domineering man who had built a successful business as a merchant. While Kafka was fond of his mother, her subservience to her husband left him feeling isolated and contributed to the loneliness of his childhood.

Kafka attended a Prague high school, known for its harsh regime, and upon graduation obeyed his father's wishes and enrolled in the German University of Prague to study law, despite his personal indifference to the subject. During his years in law school Kafka was involved in literature: he joined a literary association and expressed characteristic views against the fashionable writings of Oscar *Wilde with his doctrine of "art for art's sake," preferring the morally and socially conscious views of Thomas *Mann and Gustave Flaubert.

While at university, Kafka met Max Brod, who became his lifelong friend, intellectual and spiritual companion, and ultimately the posthumous savior and editor of his writings. While he was still a student, Kafka's first published work appeared in the Viennese literary journal *Zeit*. In June of the same year, 1906, he received his doctorate and began to work for an Italian insurance company, which he left in 1908 to join the quasi-governmental Workers' Accident Insurance Institute for the Kingdom of Bohemia. He remained in this post for nearly ten years until illness made him unable to continue. During these years working as a lawyer, Kafka was torn by the conflict between the need to "earn one's living or to live one's life." While he was an excellent worker, becoming his firm's most trusted employee, he would return home in the afternoon to begin his other life, writing for the remainder of the day and often on into the night without a break for food or sleep.

In 1913 Kafka's story, *The Judgment*, was published in Brod's journal, *Arkadia*. The narrative describes a father-son relationship involving an inconceivably unjust sentence of punishment that results in the youth's suicide. These themes of law, the tyrannical father, and the unbridgeable gap between the hero and his environment are found throughout Kafka's works. The story had been written during Kafka's passionate courtship of Frauline F. B., a relationship that initially released Kafka's creative powers, but later foundered when his lover married another man, leaving him devastated. A second unsuccessful relationship evidenced Kafka's ambivalence toward marriage: although drawn into deep relationships, he was unable to commit himself to the worldly responsibility he so highly idealized. Instead, his life's energies were poured into his writing.

The outbreak of World War I made Kafka's difficult life even more miserable, causing shortages of food and heating coal essential to maintaining his fragile state of health. He tried to join the battle at the front but was unable to because of his weakness

Kafka (left) with friends at the Vienna amusement park

and returned to Prague. During this period his writing progressed; few outside an intimate circle were privy to the content of these masterworks, although in 1915 his story *The Stoker* won the Fontane Prize.

Kafka's mature years were not solely a time of suffering. He traveled to Switzerland, Paris, and Weimar, and took part in the intellectual life of Prague's salons, discussing German idealism, science, and psychoanalysis. His works reflected these vanguard ideas, particularly the dream reality probed by Sigmund *Freud's psychoanalytic theory. Kafka's novels project inner fantasies and states of mind as though objectively real with uncanny lucidity and detail, bringing the reader into another realm both familiar and utterly foreign. This style enabled Kafka to explore modern feelings of anxiety and absurdity that had hitherto lacked a thoroughgoing literary expression.

Was help at hand? Were there some arguments in his favor that had been overlooked? Of course there must be. Logic is doubtless unshakable, but it cannot withstand a man who wants to go on living. Where was the High Court, to which he had never penetrated? He raised his hands and spread out all his fingers. But the hands of one of the partners was already at K.'s throat, while the other thrust the knife into his heart and turned it there twice. With failing eyes K. could still see the two of them, cheek leaning against cheek, immediately before his face, watching the final act. "Like a dog!" he said: it was as if he meant the shame of it to outlive him.

From the conclusion of *The Trial*

In his short story, *The Metamorphosis*, the fantastic is clearly evident but only as a means to express the writer's alienation from his family. The main character of the story awakens one morning to find that he has become a cockroach, and dreads his father's reaction of anger now that his reputation is endangered by his son. In his novel, *The Trial*, Kafka tells the story of a bank bureaucrat dedicated to his job, suddenly victimized by an ephemeral yet deadly legal authority. The impossible conundrums in which Kafka's characters are cast have been variously interpreted as symbolizing the problems of original sin and existential guilt, as well as constituting psychological studies, political attacks, and prophecies of Nazism.

After 1917, when Kafka left his work in the insurance company, he moved from sanitorium to sanitorium, writing whenever his health permitted. In 1923 he met Dora Dymont, a Polish Jew still in her teens. Kafka, then forty and ailing from tuberculosis, found his relationship with Dora the most fulfilling of his life. Dora's affectionate ministrations allowed him additional time to create and he wrote his most optimistic story during this period, *A Little Woman*.

Before Kafka succumbed to his disease he had completed a number of short stories and three novels: *The Trial, The Castle*, and *America*. Disappointed by his own creations, he directed his friend Max Brod to destroy his works after his death. Fortunately for posterity, they were preserved. With their publication, he became one of the most discussed writers of his time, striking a chord with his reflection of the angst, malaise, and anxieties of modern society; his frustration with labyrinthine modern bureaucracy brought the term "Kafkaesque" into everyday parlance.

M. M. Anderson, *Kafka's Clothes*, 1992.
P. U. Beicken, *Franz Kafka*, 1974.
P. Citati, *Kafka*, 1990.
H. Politzer, *Kafka: Parable and Paradox*, 1962.

KANT, IMMANUEL (1724–1804), German philosopher. He was born in Königsberg and his parents, influenced by the Pietist religious movement, instilled in him a respect for work and duty. He studied classics at the Collegium Fredricianum and physics and mathematics at the university in Königsberg. When his father died he had to stop studying and earn his living as a private tutor, but in 1755 a friend helped him to resume his studies and obtain a doctorate. For the next fifteen years he taught at the university, first science and mathematics, later branching out to all aspects of philosophy. He received a chair in 1770, and was made professor of logic and metaphysics. For the next twenty-seven years he taught at the university. Such an extensive period of teaching may have taken its toll. While his early lectures were lively and inspiring, in later years they were, according to the young J. G. Fichte, soporific.

His teachings, which were unorthodox and based on rationalism rather than revelation, brought him into conflict with the Prussian government and in 1792 the king forbade him to teach or write on religious subjects. Kant accepted the restriction until the death of the king, five years later, and in 1798, one year after retiring, he published a summary of his religious views. Toward the end his life, his health declined seriously. He became blind, weak, confused, and slowly lost all of his formerly immense intellectual powers.

Kant was one of the most influential philosophers of all times; his most important German successors were Fichte, F. E. Schelling, and G. W. F. *Hegel. His thinking was the basis for the Hegelian version of Kantian philosophy, on which Marxist socialism was based, while the dialectical method, founded on his method of reasoning, was used by both Hegel and Karl *Marx. The late nineteenth century neo-Kantian reaction to Hegel, which reflected a return to Kant's philosophy, was espoused by thinkers such as Hermann Cohen and Ernst Cassirer.

A transcendental idealist, Kant distinguished between noumenon, the object of purely intellectual intuition, and phenomenon, the object of perception or experience, and argued that the latter exist not in themselves, but only in relation to the mind. Essential to Kant's philosophy was his concept of the *a priori* (i.e., that which is universal and necessary and whose validity is both independent of and a condition of experience). One of his greatest contributions to philosophy was the argument that the *a priori* is a condition for the structures of both knowledge and morality.

Kant achieved fame only with the publication of his main work, the *Critique of Pure Reason* (1781), when he was fifty-seven. This work, which had occupied his mind for twelve years before he began writing but was written in four to five months, was the keystone of his thought. In it he examined the structures of human knowledge and its limitations, and then attempted to show how reason is driven to transcend these limitations and with what results. He believed that antinomies, contradictions arising from opposing statements about the same fact, grew out of this drive to transcend knowledge. Antinomies are characterized by the equal necessities of asserting both a proposition or thesis and the contrary proposition or antithesis. One such basic antinomy suggested by Kant was the question of whether the world began at a certain point in time and is limited in space, or has always existed and is unlimited in space. As one is compelled to accept both the thesis and its antithesis, the only resolution of the conflict seems to be to transcend the limits within which both propositions are valid, and assert that neither is correct, which according to the theory is an inevitable process of reason. Philosophic investigation shows, however, that the questions and propositions are logically unsound and based on false propositions, thus causing reason to enter into conflict with itself.

Kant formulated four such antinomies dealing with inferences about the nature of the soul, and examined various alleged proofs of the existence of God, which he saw as outgrowths of the illusion of reason. All were characterized by the facts that they were inferences about things which experience could not verify or falsify, dealt with metaphysical propositions about the world, the soul, and God, and that they were invalid because of fallacies basic to the nature of reason itself. Kant was inspired by this feature of reason — its compulsion to state propositions which are incompatible — to enter into the critique of pure reason. He concluded that there are certain fundamental a priori categories of understanding that have a fundamental validity and without which there could be no knowledge. With the assistance of these categories we can understand what we perceive with our senses. Thus these categories are the conditions for all empirical knowledge. They are concerned with four groups: unity, plurality, and totality deal with quantity; reality, negation, and limitation deal with quality; substance and accident, cause and effect, and reciprocity deal with relation; and possibility, existence, and necessity deal with modality.

Kant's main ethical work was *Critique of Practical Reason* (1781), although *Foundation of the Meta-physics of Morals* (1785) may offer a better introduction to his ethical thought. For Kant, morality was identified with practical reason and the supreme cause was a moral one. He believed that morality could not be subjective because it is determined by pure reason and the truth of reason is *a priori*. For him the purely moral act was one motivated by the understanding that duty compels one to perform it. Thus it is not only the consequence of an act which has moral value, but the motive behind it; an act performed for the sake of expediency or in conformance to law is not moral.

According to Kant, two types of commands were given by reason. The hypothetical imperative proscribes a given course of action in pursuit of a specific end. The categorical imperative, which demanded that a course of action must be followed because of its rightness and necessity, stated: "Act as if the maxim of your action were to become through your will a general natural law." The latter was an absolute unconditional command, universally binding on every rational will.

On a personal level his own attitude to morality pervaded his existence — living the moral life, that is, according to duty, was imperative. His daily schedule was almost obsessively regular and left no time for a family, and he remained single all his life. He would rise at five, drink a cup of tea and smoke a pipe of tobacco, dress in a robe, nightcap, and slippers, and spend the next two hours preparing his morning lectures. After the lectures he would again don the robe, and work until dinner. The later part of the day was occupied in a daily walk on his own, and work until bedtime at ten o'clock.

Kant's health was frail and because of his belief that he had a duty to preserve it so that he could work to the best of his ability, he took immense care of it. Apparently, to avoid the sedentariness of spending his life writing, he kept his handkerchief on a distant chair in the room so that he had to walk over every time he needed it.

Kant's ethical ideas grew out of his belief in the fundamental freedom of the individual as stated in *The Critique of Pure Reason*. He saw this freedom as the right to self-government, that is, the freedom to obey the laws of the universal as revealed by reason. He saw the welfare of each individual as an end in itself, and believed the world was progressing toward an ideal society governed by reason and laws which sprung from the united will of the people. In *Perpetual Peace* (1795) he advocated a world federation of republican states in order to avoid war.

Kant's collected work filled twenty-seven volumes. Other works included *Prolegomena* (1783), *Metaphysic of Nature* (1786), and *Of Judgment* (1790).

G. Buchdahl, Kant and the Dynamics of Reason, 1992.

T. F. Godlove, *Religion, Interpretation and Diversity of Belief*, 1989.

R. Kennington, ed., *Philosophy of Immanuel Kant*, 1985.

S. Koerner, *Kant*, 1990.

K. Rossman, *Immanuel Kant*, 1979.

KASTRIOTI, GEORGE SEE SKANDERBEG

KEATS, JOHN (1795–1821), English poet. Born in London, Keats was the eldest of four. His father, a prosperous coachman, was killed in an accident when Keats was eight years old, and six years later his mother died of tuberculosis, having already left her young children in the custody of several unscrupulous guardians. Apprenticed to a surgeon, Keats was sent to medical school at the age of sixteen and eventually received a certificate permitting him to practice medicine. It was during these years that Keats, in spite of the time constraints imposed on him by his medical training, developed the genuine poetic voice which would become his true calling.

Like his contemporaries *Byron and *Shelley, Keats was influenced by the grandeur of *Milton and the Romantic principles of *Wordsworth. Feeling compelled to create a work that would match the scope of the Miltonic epic and the innovative doctrines of Wordsworth, Keats wrote his first long poem, "Endymion," in 1818. Despite the unenthusiastic reviews of this work, Keats continued to explore in his writing the intricacies of human life and perception. His letters, as well as his poetry, reveal an independent mind of extraordinary sensitivity and intelligence. In a letter written to his brothers, Keats presented the concept of "negative capability — that is when man is capable of being in uncertainties, mysteries and doubts, without any irritable reaching after fact and reason," a doctrine reflecting Keats's unique talents of detachment and objective perception.

During the fall of 1818 Keats nursed his tubercular brother Tom, who died in December, and the following year, he himself exhibited the first signs of the disease, caught from his brother. It was at this time that Keats made the acquaintance of Fanny Brawne, the young woman with whom he fell hopelessly in love and who was the inspiration behind many poems, including "The Eve of St. Agnes."

Most of his major work was written in 1818–1819. In April 1819, Keats began writing works reflecting the self-awareness of his imaginative life. "Ode to Psyche" and "La Belle Dame sans Merci" were followed by the composition of the great odes "On a Grecian Urn," "On Melancholy," and "To a Nightingale." This year of concentrated creative effort culminated in the writing of "The Fall of Hyperion" and "To Autumn."

By February 1820 Keats realized that he had only a year to live and that he would never marry Fanny Brawne. In September he sailed to Italy, where he remained in the hope of improving his health. A year later, though, he died in Rome at the age of twenty-five. At his request no name appeared on his gravestone but only the line "Here lies one whose name was writ in water."

Keats was one of the great poets of the Romantic School. He wrote much of the contrast between the striving for an ideal and the disillusionment of reality. The intensity and precision of his descriptions influenced many poets of the Victorian era such as

---

Late one night, John Keats wrote to his brother George, 'the fire is at its last click — I am sitting with my back to it with one foot rather askew upon the rug and the other with the heel a little elevated from the carpet... These are trifles — but... Could I see the same thing done of any great man long since dead it would be a great delight: as to know in what position Shakespeare sat when he began "To be or not to be."'

SOME OF KEATS'S BEST-KNOWN LINES

- A thing of beauty is a joy for ever.

Endymion

- Charmed magic casements, opening on the foam
  Of perilous seas, in fairy lands forlorn.

Ode to a Nightingale

- Heard melodies are sweet, but those unheard are sweeter.
- Beauty is truth, truth beauty — that is all
  Ye know on earth or need to know.

Ode on a Grecian Urn

- Then I felt like some watcher of the skies
  When a new planet swims into his ken:
  Or like stout Cortes when, with eagle eyes,
  He stared at the Pacific — and all his men
  Looked at each other with a wild surmise —
  Silent, upon a peak in Darien.

On First Looking into Chapman's Homer

Alfred *Tennyson. The aesthetic school of writers of the late nineteenth century idolized Keats' poetry which remains classic and popular.

M. J. Middleton, *Keats*, 1955.
S. M. Sperry, *Keats the Poet*, 1973.
C. T. Watts, *A Preface to Keats*, 1985.

KELLER, HELEN ADAMS (1880–1968), American author and lecturer. A native of Tuscumbia, Alabama, at the age of nineteen months she became ill with acute congestion of the stomach and brain and lost the senses of sight and hearing, and was also rendered mute by her new disabilities. Until the age of seven she was totally dependent on her parents, who loved her but had no idea how to educate her and who let her run wild. When Anne Sullivan from the Perkins Institute for the Blind, herself a former victim of blindness, was hired as her tutor in 1887, she found that her first task was to teach Helen obe-

Helen Keller and Indian poet Rabindranath Tagore

dience. It was a difficult battle but Anne (who came to be called Annie) triumphed and so opened the door to Keller's initiation into the joys of language.

"We walked down the path to the well house.... Someone was drawing water and my teacher placed my hand under the spout. As the cool stream gushed over one hand she spelled into the other the word water, first slowly, then rapidly. I stood still, my whole attention fixed upon the motions of her fingers. Suddenly I felt a misty consciousness as of something forgotten — a thrill of returning thought; and somehow the mystery of language was revealed to me. I knew then that "w-a-t-e-r" meant the wonderful cool something that was flowing over my hand. That living word awakened my soul, gave it light, hope, joy, set it free!"

Sullivan was a dedicated and talented teacher and Keller was a bright pupil. She quickly learned to read by the Braille system and to write with a typewriter. In 1890 she learned to speak. She wrote in her autobiography that the impulse to utter audible sounds had always been strong in her, and before her illness she had already been learning to talk. Once she learned to communicate it did not take her long to realize that other people communicated differently, and a determination to speak like them began to prevail in her. Despite discouragement from her friends she was determined to try, and engaged the assistance of Sarah Fuller, principal of the Horace Mann School. Within a brief period she had begun to realize her ambitions.

In 1900 Helen entered Radcliffe College, graduating in 1904 with honors. She served on the Massachusetts Commission for the Blind and lectured all over the world. After World War II she visited wounded veterans in hospitals and spoke throughout the United States and Europe on behalf of the physically handicapped. In 1964 she received the U.S. Presidential Medal of Freedom. Her books include *The Story of My Life* (1902), *The World I Live In* (1908), *Out of the Dark* (1913), *Mid-stream — My Later Life* (1930), *Let Us Have Faith* (1940), *Teacher: Anne Sullivan Macy* (1955) and *The Open*

A TEACHER BRINGS LIGHT

The most important day I remember in all my life is the one on which my teacher, Anne Mansfield Sullivan, came to me. I am filled with wonder when I consider the immeasurable contrasts between the two lives which it connects....

On the afternoon of that eventful day, I stood on the porch, dumb, expectant. I guessed vaguely from my mother's signs and from the hurrying to and fro in the house that something unusual was about to happen, so I went to the door and waited on the steps. The afternoon sun penetrated the mass of honeysuckle that covered the porch, and fell on my upturned face....

Have you ever been at sea in a dense fog, when it seemed as if a tangible white darkness shut you in, and the great ship, tense and anxious, groped her way toward the shore with plummet and sounding line, and you waited with beating heart for something to happen? I was like that ship before my education began, only I was without compass or sounding-line and had no way of knowing how near the harbor was. "Light! give me light!" was the wordless cry of my soul, and the light of love shone on me in that very hour.

Helen Keller

Door (1957). *The Miracle Worker*, a play by William Gibson based on her life, was produced in 1957.

M. Gins, *Helen Keller or Arakawa*, 1992.

L. Markham, *Helen Keller*, 1993.

KELVIN, WILLIAM THOMSON, BARON

(1824–1907), British physicist. Kelvin was born in Belfast, son of a professor who was appointed to the chair of mathematics at the University of Glasgow in 1832. His mother died when he was six; along with his brother, James, he was educated by his father. A gifted pupil, at the age of ten he was studying in the University of Glasgow, where he emulated his father as a mathematician but also showed a talent for physics. In 1840 he was awarded the university medal for an essay entitled "On the Figure of the Earth."

Kelvin did not graduate from Glasgow but transferred to Cambridge University where he again demonstrated his proficiency as a scientist. He also displayed an interest in nonacademic pursuits, winning a "blue" for rowing in a boat race in 1844, cofounding the Musical Society, and playing the French horn in university concerts. He also enjoyed the sport of curling, but in 1860 this led to his suffering a serious injury in a fall that left him with a permanent limp.

In 1846, aged twenty-two, Kelvin was appointed professor of natural philosophy at Glasgow University, a post he held for fifty-three years. He established a pioneering physics laboratory and engaged in research into electric measurement and the electrodynamic properties of matter. He had the ability to communicate his enthusiasm to his students, both the dedicated assistants in the laboratory and those attending his lectures; the use of mechanical models was an important element in his teaching.

Kelvin was never satisfied with theoretical studies alone, believing that "the life and soul of science is its practical application." In this spirit, he investigated the oscillation of electric current and electric telegraphy. In 1856 he became director of a company formed to lay a transatlantic cable, supervising the laying of the cable in 1858. After carrying a small number of transmissions, the cable ceased to function. The problem was caused because Kelvin's advice concerning voltage was ignored, but nevertheless the failure was a blow to him. He did not despair but continued his association with the project, and in 1866 the cable was at last laid successfully and Kelvin received knighthood. As an accomplished sailor who for many years kept a yacht, Kelvin was also interested in the study of the motion of waves.

Kelvin brought the Bell telephone to Britain from the United States in 1876 and in 1881 pioneered the introduction of electric lighting in Glasgow. He was instrumental in the adoption of international standards for electrical measurement and became a major figure in the development of precision measurement instruments, going into partnership with a Glasgow instrument maker and becoming closely involved in supervising production at the factory.

Kelvin held many views in advance of his time. A convinced advocate of the use of the metric system, he described British imperial measures as "absurd, ridiculous, time-wasting, brain-,destroying." In 1881 he suggested the harnessing of the Niagara Falls to produce electricity, anticipating the future use of hydroelectricity.

Kelvin's studies strengthened his deep religious convictions as he saw clear design in the natural phenomena he investigated. He did not allow his achievements to go to his head and on the fiftieth anniversary of his professorship commented that "I know no more now than I knew and tried to teach to my students in my first session." He was honored with a peerage in 1892. His name remains well known today, primarily through the Kelvin scale for measuring temperature.

D. K. C. MacDonald, *Faraday, Maxwell and Kelvin*, 1965.
H. I. Sharlin, *Lord Kelvin: The Dynamic Victorian*, 1979.
S. P. Thompson, *Life of Baron Kelvin*, 1910.

KENNEDY, JOHN FITZGERALD (1917–1963),

thirty-fifth president of the United States. He was the youngest person elected to the presidency, the

Kennedy on the campaign trail being greeted by admiring crowds

first Roman Catholic elected, and the youngest president to die in office. Kennedy was born in Brookline, Massachusetts, a suburb of Boston, to Joseph Patrick Kennedy and the former Rose Fitzgerald. He was the second of nine children in this warm, close, but competitive Irish-American family. Both of John Kennedy's grandfathers had had active political careers. His mother's father, John Fitzgerald (known as Honey Fitz), had been a popular Boston mayor as well as a member of Congress. His paternal grandfather, Patrick J. Kennedy, had been a state senator and a ward boss. Kennedy's father, was at age twenty-five, already a successful bank president.

As the Kennedys prospered they moved first to Riverdale and then to Bronxville, New York. Kennedy attended Choate in Connecticut; when he graduated in 1935 he was nominated by the students as "most likely to succeed." He did not expect success to come, however, via the political path of his grandfathers. While political arguments dominated the family's dinner table discussions, it was intended that his older brother would make his mark in politics. Kennedy entered Princeton University, but due to illness had to leave college for a time. In 1936 he went to Harvard University to study government and international relations. The spring and summer of 1939 he spent in Europe interviewing statesmen and politicians on the prospects of war; he reported his findings to his father, then U.S. ambassador to England. His senior thesis, later published under the title *Why England Slept*, ana-

SAYINGS OF JOHN F. KENNEDY:

- Sure, it's a big job, but I don't know anyone who could do it better than I can.
- Those who make peaceful revolutions impossible make violent revolutions inevitable.
- The New Frontier of which I speak is not a set of promises — it is a set of challenges.
- Let us never negotiate out of fear, but let us never fear to negotiate.
- The supreme reality of our time is our indivisibility as children of God and the common vulnerability of this planet.
- All free men, wherever they may live, are citizens of Berlin. And therefore as a free man, I take pride in the words "Ich bin ein Berliner."
- The one unchangeable certainty is that nothing is certain or unchangeable.
- Failure has no friends.
- When written in Chinese the word crisis is composed of two characters — one represents danger, the other opportunity.
- There are risks and costs to a program of action. But they are far less than the long-range risks and costs of comfortable inaction.
- The great enemy of truth if often not the lie but the myth.
- We must never forget that art is not a form of propaganda; it is a form of truth.

lyzed England's lack of preparedness for the coming onslaught. Kennedy graduated cum laude in 1940; his book received critical acclaim.

He entered Stanford University's Graduate School of Business but stayed only six months. On his return home, after an extended trip through South America, he enrolled in the Navy; three months later the United States entered the war.

Kennedy was ensign of a PT boat when, on 2 August, 1943, it was cut in two by a Japanese destroyer. Two crew members were killed instantly, Kennedy and ten others clung to the wreckage through the night and then, despite injury to his back, he towed one of the disabled to a nearby island, ordering the others to swim there also. He spent most of the next four days in the water looking for assistance, which he obtained with the intervention of friendly Cross Island natives. Kennedy received the Navy and Marine Corps Medal and Purple Heart. Due to back pain, he was in and out of military hospitals for the next few years. In between his hospitalizations he served as an instructor in the navy.

His brother Joseph was killed in a bombing mission during World War II. Later, explaining his own entry into politics, Kennedy said, "Just as I went into politics because Joe died, if anything happens to me tomorrow, my brother Bobby would run for my seat in the Senate, and if Bobby died, Teddy would take over for him." In 1946, with the support of his siblings and his parents, he won the nomination from his district Massachusetts for the U.S. House of Representatives against a field of nine other Democrats. In the election he won against the Republican candidate easily; this was the first of his undefeated political candidacies.

In 1952 he ran for a seat in the Senate against Henry Cabot Lodge, a popular and experienced Republican senator. Although Dwight D. *Eisenhower carried Massachusetts in the presidential election, Kennedy beat Lodge.

In September 1953 Kennedy married Jacqueline ("Jackie") Lee Bouvier, daughter of a wealthy Wall Street broker. She had attended Vassar College and the Sorbonne and had studied at George Washington University. More hospitalizations for Kennedy followed as he required spinal surgery. While recuperating he wrote *Profiles in Courage*, which received the Pulitzer Prize in 1957. The book details eight great American politicians who displayed leadership by following their conscience.

In the mid 1950s Kennedy was still a moderate regarding Joseph *McCarthy's anticommunist excesses. During the late 1950s, his views grew increasingly liberal. At the 1956 Democratic Convention he narrowly missed becoming Adlai Stevenson's running mate. In 1958 Kennedy made a strong showing in the Senate race and was thus in position to make a run for the presidency.

In the early months of 1960 Kennedy defeated the extremely popular Senator Hubert H. Humphrey in the presidential primaries. At the Democratic national convention he was nominated on the first ballot despite competition from Adlai Stevenson, Stuart Symington, and Lyndon B. *Johnson. In his acceptance address he said, "We stand today on the edge of a New Frontier," which became the theme of his presidency.

He named Johnson the vicepresidential nominee, although there were claims that his request was half-hearted and would not be repeated were he to run for a second term. His race against Richard M. Nixon was determined by the television debates. Whereas the glare of the television lights made Nixon, who was suffering from a leg injury, look sallow and drawn, Kennedy presented a vigorous appearance. Although Kennedy led by only a tiny margin in the popular vote, he received a clear electoral majority because of his standing in the larger states with heavy urban populations, including the working class, and blacks.

Kennedy's idealism, expressed in his inaugural speech, "Ask not what your country can do for you. Ask what you can do for your country," held promise that the ills at home and abroad could be healed. Many of the liberal goals for which he fought during his brief tenure as president, however, were only achieved after his death. Three months after taking office, in April 1961, the Bay of Pigs fiasco occurred. CIA-trained Cuban refugees attempted to take a beach head in Cuba; their exploits ended in disaster. Kennedy accepted "sole responsibility" and engaged in a test of wills with the leader of the Soviet Union, Nikita *Khrushchev. They met in Vienna in June 1961 with little achieved. In August of that year East Germany erected a wall dividing Berlin between East and West.

In October 1962 the Cuban missile crisis, which nearly precipitated a nuclear conflict, was settled by Kennedy's display of resolve. The U.S.S.R. had placed missiles in Cuba, prompting Kennedy to establish an aerial and naval blockade of the island. Soviet ships, rather than confront the blockade, turned around in the waters and headed back for the Soviet Union. The missiles were later removed.

A nuclear test ban treaty was at first unsuccessful. The Soviets went on with atmospheric tests of their weapons, but by August 1963 the U.S.S.R. joined the United States and Great Britain in signing the treaty, and by October they agreed to ban nuclear arms in outer space.

Kennedy initiated the Alliance for Progress, a foreign aid package that strengthened the weaker economies of Latin America. In South Vietnam, Kennedy, hoping to prevent communist expansion in Asia, in fact planted the seeds for the Vietnam War. He increased the number of military advisers there from seven hundred to fifteen thousand.

One of Kennedy's finest achievements, combining his idealism and pragmatism, was his establishment of the Peace Corps in March 1961, which encouraged large scale volunteering to bring assistance to developing countries. Kennedy's appointment of his brother, Robert, as attorney general strengthened the hands of those battling for civil rights. While Kennedy's support for civil rights and medicare legislation did not win Congressional approval during his lifetime, his successor, Lyndon B. Johnson, did push through these liberal programs.

Kennedy and his wife were closely watched by the press and public. Mrs. Kennedy's bouffant hairdo and her pillbox hats were copied by young women across America. Family sorrows and joys, including the progress of their daughter Caroline and son John, were eagerly followed. Under Mrs. Kennedy the White House became a center of artistic activities.

In November 1963 Kennedy traveled to Texas to mend some political fences, and his wife joined him. She was seated beside him in the car, with Governor John B. Connally of Texas and his wife in the front seat. As the motorcade drove through Dallas on the way from the airport, when shots were fired from the Dallas public school book depository building. Connally was seriously injured; Kennedy died of his wounds shortly after. Lee Harvey Oswald was apprehended as the assassin but during his transfer to a second prison the following day, he was fatally shot by Jack Ruby, a man in the crowd overcome by passion at the death of President Kennedy. The nation, and indeed much of the world, was shocked and grieved.

President Johnson, in one of his first presidential acts, appointed a commission of seven members under Chief Justice Earl *Warren to investigate the murder. The commission concluded that there was no proof that either Oswald or Ruby was part of any conspiracy. However, this issue has never been totally laid to rest.

Tragedy continued to haunt the Kennedy family. Robert F. Kennedy was assassinated while running for the presidency in 1968, while the younger brother, Edward, a liberal senator, endured a series of scandals, undermining his hopes for attaining the presidency.

After his death, the mystique of John Kennedy waned. He was associated with the beginning of the Vietnam debacle, while in private life he as well as his brothers were shown to be incorrigible philanderers. However, his youthful vigor and liberal image continue to conjure widespread affection. After his death, his wife commented, "Now he is a legend when he would have preferred to be a man."

T. Brown, *J.F.K.: History of an Image*, 1989.
N. Hamilton, *J.F.K.*, 1992.
W. Manchester, *The Death of a President*, 1967.
A. M. Schlesinger Jr., *A Thousand Days: John F. Kennedy in the White House*, 1965.

KENYATTA, JOMO (c.1894–1978), African nationalist and first leader of independent Kenya. A member of the Kikuyu tribe, Kenyatta's given name was Kamau wa Ngengi, and from an early age he was assigned the duty of looking after his family's livestock; he also often accompanied his grandfather, a prophet and magician, on his travels around Kikuyuland. At about age thirteen Kenyatta left home for the Church of Scotland Mission, where he received treatment for a spinal disease and remained for five years, studying and assisting with the first translation of the New Testament into Kikuyu.

On being baptized he changed his name to Johnstone Kamau, and in 1914 moved to Nairobi, where he began working as an interpreter at the Supreme Court, and later as an inspector of water supplies, a post that gained him status among Africans. He adopted the name Kenyatta from "Muibi wa kinyata," the name of a beaded belt he wore, and became involved in politics, joining the Young Kikuyu Association. In 1928 he was elected general secretary of the Kikuyu Central Association (KCA) and edited the party newspaper, formulating the African case against exclusive European occupation of the Kenya Highlands.

Kenyatta visited London in 1929, and again in 1931 on behalf of the KCA. Interested in communism, he made a four-month visit to Russia in 1933, returning to London where he worked as an assistant in phonetics and taught Kikuyu at London University. He represented Kikuyu grievances against colonialism and campaigned for his people's right to self-determination, by presenting petitions to government officials and voicing his opinions in the British press. He studied social anthropology under Bronislav Malinowsky at the London School of Economics, publishing his thesis in 1938 in the form of a book, *Facing Mount Kenya*, which, as well as being a pioneering work of anthropology, was also a perceptive criticism of British colonialism.

Through the Workers' Educational Association, Kenyatta lectured on Kenya and imperialism, and met his second wife. With the outbreak of war the couple moved to a small village in Sussex, where Kenyatta worked as a farm laborer, adopting the forename "Jomo" from the nickname "Jumbo," which the villagers called him on account of his stature. In 1945 he helped to form the Pan-African Federation and the following year organized the fifth Pan-African Congress in Manchester.

Leaving his English family behind, Kenyatta returned to Kenya in 1946, where he was made president of the KCA — by now banned by the British — and of the Kenya African Union (KAU), and campaigned for independence through peaceful means, emerging as a much loved national figure.

In 1952 he was arrested by the colonial authorities and charged with managing Mau Mau, the violent nationalist movement opposing colonialism. Although no evidence was found linking him to this cause, he was nonetheless convicted and imprisoned at Lokitaung. His arrest sparked off bloody rebellion and unrelenting pressure for his release, until he was finally freed in 1961.

In 1962 he was elected to the legislative council, becoming Kenya's first prime minister in May 1963, and then president upon the declaration of Kenya as a republic in December 1964.

As a proponent of African socialism, Kenyatta believed that traditional tribal values of individual responsibility and cooperation within the extended family could serve as a model for the governance of and organization within the nation-state, and, under the slogan of "Harambee" ("pulling together"), called upon all Kenyans, regardless of race or tribal affiliation, to cooperate in developing Kenya. Black Kenyans were allowed rights to purchase land that had formerly been reserved exclusively for whites, improvements were made in education, the econ-

omy grew rapidly, and agriculture, industry, and tourism were expanded.

Fostering resentment toward colonialists for past wrongs was futile, Kenyatta felt; he allowed white settlers to stay on their farms and kept British advisers within his government. He rejected Soviet communism as just another form of imperialism, and his maintenance of ties with the West brought an inflow of investment; he came to be thought of by Western countries as an important source of stability within Africa.

Other Kenyans resented Kikuyu predominance both in government and in society at large; the Luo tribe in particular resented the dismissal of one of its members, Oginga Odinga, from his post as vice president, after he adopted a communist stance; the assassination of their leader, Tom Mboya, in 1969 almost led to tribal warfare between the Kikuyu and Luo. Kenyatta, however, refrained from using violence to suppress hostilities and the atmosphere eventually calmed.

Kenyatta was instrumental in forming the East African Community in 1965, which operated mainly as a customs union between Kenya, Uganda, and Tanzania. The refusal of Julius Nyerere, President of Tanzania, to continue relations with Uganda after General Idi Amin's coup in 1971, led to a near state of war between the two countries; Kenyatta's mediation was a crucial factor in resolving the conflict.

Toward the end of his life, "Mzee," or "Father of the Nation," as Kenyatta was fondly known, confined himself largely to ceremonial duties.
G. Arnold, *Kenyatta and the Politics of Kenya*, 1974.
J. Murray-Brown, *Kenyatta*, 1973.

KEPLER, JOHANNES (1571–1630), German astronomer who developed the laws of planetary motion at a time when Europe was constrained by the Ptolemaic system. Kepler was born in Weil but spent most of his early life in Lewenberg. His father was a roving soldier who frequently abandoned his family. His mother, a rather garrulous woman, was forever plunging into troubles, and at a later date only her son's renown saved her from being burned as a witch. When still a small child Kepler was critically ill with smallpox, which resulted in a permanent awkwardness and poor eyesight, making it all the more remarkable that he should choose to study the heavens. Happening to live in a state that maintained a system of free education, he was able to matriculate at Tübingen University, despite his impoverished upbringing. He was an exceptional scholar, enthusiastic and original, seemingly destined to become a theologian. While at Tübingen he was introduced surreptitiously to the controversial theories of Nicolaus *Copernicus. Kepler at once embraced the Copernican system and for the rest of his life tried to expound and prove it.

He was an unpopular boy among his peers until he discovered that by using his mathematical genius he was able to plot the horoscopes of his classmates who began to seek him out for counsel. The distinction between astronomy and astrology at the time

> If we unite now, each and every one of us, and each tribe to another, we will cause the implementation in this country of that which the Europeans call democracy. True democracy has no color distinction. It does not choose between black and white. We are not worried that other races are here with us in our country, but we insist that we are the leaders here, and what we want, we insist to get ... Remember the old saying that he who is hit with a club returns, but he who is hit with justice never comes back.
>
> **Jomo Kenyatta**

was nonexistent, and indeed most royal courts employed a mathematician to provide them with essential advice on matters of state. Kepler himself was to say, "Astrology is the foolish and disreputable daughter of astronomy, without which the wise old mother would starve."

It became clear to his superiors that this was a young man unsuited to ecclesiastical duties, and in 1594 Kepler was dispatched to Graz to teach mathematics. Nonetheless religion remained a motivating factor in his life's work, which he faithfully believed was ordained. He was later to say, "I may have to wait one hundred years for a reader, but the Creator also had to wait six thousand years for the observer of his works."

His first paper appeared two years later, a somewhat mystical treatise that described the structure of the cosmos as a geometrical construct derived from the five perfect solids of *Euclid. While this concept was inane, it was also the first paper published in defense of Copernicus. Its imaginative development and complex mathematical analysis attracted wide attention, and when the imperial astronomer *Tycho Brahe needed an assistant, he offered the position to Kepler. Kepler accepted and had been in Prague barely a year when Brahe died. Kepler, a Protestant, now became the imperial mathematician in the Catholic court of Rudolph II. He inherited the task of calculating new astronomical tables, which involved incredibly tedious manipulations, and his first project was the orbit of Mars. As his work progressed, he began to notice irrefutable discrepancies between Mars's motion and the fundamental principle held at that time that planets move at constant speed in circular orbits. After a further six years of patient observation his book of tables was published. It contained his first two laws of planetary motion, which described orbits as elliptical with the sun at one of the foci, and noting that equal areas of the elliptical plane are swept in equal time.

In 1610 Kepler received a copy of *Galileo Galilei's book *Message from the Stars*, which inspired him to begin experimenting with lenses; at that time he began corresponding with Galileo. Kepler provided the first correct theory of the eye and coined the term "focus" (of a lens). He compiled his findings in the book *Diotropics*, the founding text on the science of refraction.

Throughout this period Kepler was constantly beset by troubles. His health was failing, Rudolph II was avoiding paying him, and his first wife had died. When the emperor died, the political situation in Prague became untenable for a Protestant and Keplar accepted a position in Linz. Although he had hoped to spend much of his time on research, he was once again required to occupy many hours casting the fortunes of his benefactors. Nevertheless, during the next fourteen years he managed to complete a number of major works, which introduced his third law of planetary motion.

With the Thirty Years' War raging around him, Kepler left Linz in 1626 without prospects for him-

- So long as the mother, Ignorance, lives, it is not safe for Science, the offspring, to divulge the hidden causes of things.
- Oh God, I am thinking Thy thoughts after Thee!

Johannes Kepler

self or his family. He refused offers to return to the imperial court as it required his conversion to Catholicism. Despite his failing health he decided to petition the emperor in Regensburg personally for payment of the past debts he was still due. Several days after his arrival there, he died.

A. Beer and D. Beer, eds., *Kepler: Four Hundred Years*, 1974.
M. Caspar, *Johannes Kepler*, 1962.
A. Koestler, *The Watershed: A Biography of Johannes Kepler*, 1961.
C. Meier-Herr, *Kepler's "Phisica Caelistis,"* 1991.

KEYNES, JOHN MAYNARD, BARON (1883–1946), British economist. The son of an economist, Keynes was born in the university city of Cambridge. Raised in a prosperous home in an atmosphere imbued with the accepted Victorian ethics of moral endeavor and resolution, he received a traditional schooling at Eton. In 1902 he began a scholarship in classics and mathematics at Cambridge University. Here he began to associate with writers and artists from the Bloomsbury group, whose work and lives represented a permissive artistic reaction against perceived Victorian cultural values.

Following graduation he entered the civil service and worked for the India Office. He also for a time taught economics at Cambridge and worked on a philosophical treatise dealing with probability, which was finally published in 1921.

During World War I Keynes served in the Treasury dealing with the budgeting of the war and trying to panic prime minister Lloyd George with visions of imminent national bankruptcy. The huge spending on armaments provided a moral dilemma for the pacifist Keynes. He was more at ease after the war as a British representative at the Versailles peace conference dealing with the economic ramifications of the postwar settlement. The heavy burden of reparations the victors insisted on placing on Germany was, in Keynes's opinion, a major error,and led to his resignation. He returned to England and set out his views in a book entitled *The Economic Consequences of the Peace*. It met with a favorable response from the public and gave him the high profile that would last for the rest of his life.

His marriage in 1925 to a Russian ballerina, Lydia Lopokova, who knew no English, surprised his social circle. The marriage was successful and his wife's artistic interests enhanced a lesser-known side of the famous economist — his interest in and support of the arts. Keynes was a believer in government funding for the arts and in 1946 was appointed to the newly established Arts Council. In 1936 he had been a founder of the Cambridge Arts Theatre, which offered his wife a new opportunity to continue her career on stage.

In 1926 Keynes paid a visit to Russia along with his wife and over the following decade made two further trips. He was not attracted by the Russian economic experiment and turned politically towards the Liberal party, becoming a skilled propagandist for their cause in the 1929 election. Britain was already suffering from the heavy unemployment that was to characterize the 1930s. In a Liberal election pamphlet Keynes advocated the use of public works to tackle mass unemployment.

Keynes wrote a number of books and pamphlets in the 1920s and 1930s culminating in the 1936 *General Theory of Employment, Interest and Money*. In this monumental and influential work he dealt with the key role of consumer demand in the wellbeing of the economy. A deficiency of demand led to rising unemployment. The answer to this problem was to increase investment which Keynes found to have a "multiplier effect," its benefits in economic growth far exceeding the original amount invested. Although the investment could come from private sources as easily as government, the theory posed a major challenge to conventional economic thinking that advocated wage cuts as the answer to unemployment and saw downturns and upturns in trade in similar terms to the weather — you have to make the best of it since you are powerless to alter it.

Keynes was confident that government investment in public works and construction could reverse the Great Depression. He even suggested humorously that government finance pyramid building rather than display passivity in the face of the millions out of work, though he added that investing in housing would be a somewhat more worthwhile way of tackling the problem.

The return to full employment with the massive spending of World War II proved to many the wisdom of Keynesian theory. During the war he served as a director of the Bank of England and a government financial adviser once more, his economics having already gained a wide measure of acceptance. After the war he was involved in such projects as the setting up of the World Bank and the International Monetary Fund. Keynesian economic planning became a cornerstone of the economic policy of the Western world but he was not to live to see it. He had been in weak health following a heart attack in 1937 and died in 1946

M. Blaug, *John Maynard Keynes; Life; Ideas; Legacy,* 1990.

D. E. Muggridge, *Maynard Keynes: An Economist's Biography,* 1992.

R. Skidelsky, *John Maynard Keynes,* 2 vols., 1983.

KHAYYAM, OMAR SEE OMAR KHAYYAM

KHMELNYTSKY, ZINOVY BOHDAN (c.1595–1657), Cossack leader. Khmelnytsky (also Khmielnicki) was the son of a Ukrainian Cossack landowner. The factors contributing to the growing Ukrainian hatred of the Poles in his time were national (Ukrainian versus Polish), religious (Orthodox versus Catholic), social (serfs versus nobles), and economic (only six thousand Cossacks were maintained by the Polish government as salaried solders during peacetime). After the disastrous Cossack rebellion of 1637, the Cossacks lost their traditional rights and autonomy and Ukraine was administered by Polish governors.

Khmelnytsky married, had five children, farmed his estate, and grew wealthy. It was only as a vigorous widower of fifty, in love with his beautiful housekeeper, Helen, that he was motivated to rebel against Polish rule. Czaplinski, the Polish governor's assistant, wanted Khmelnytsky's estate. He raided it, burned the Khmelnytsky's mill and granary, flogged Khmelnytsky's youngest son to death, and married Helen, justifying his actions by claiming that Khmelnytsky did not formally own his land. After unsuccessfully seeking Helen's and justice return from the Polish governor, courts, Diet, and king, Khmelnytsky took his case to his fellow Cossacks. His agitation for rebellion led to war with Poland after the Cossack general assembly elected him their leader in 1648.

Khmelnytsky initial military victories sparked a peasant uprising. Led by Cossack officers, Ukrainian peasants burned noblemen's mansions, Catholic monasteries, and Jewish towns, massacring the inhabitants. Khmelnytsky qualms about killing his fellow gentry did not extend to Jews; more than one hundred thousand were killed and three hundred Jewish towns were burnt. The peace terms Khmelnytsky dictated to Poland included provision for the expulsion of the Jews from Ukraine. Having defeated Poland and won back Helen (he promptly remarried her after annulling her marriage to Czaplinski), he set about forging an effective fighting force from the mixture of Cossacks, peasants, and adventurers who flocked to his standard.

Wars with Poland — interspersed with brief periods of peace beginning with King John Casimir's acceptance of Khmelnytsky's peace terms at the Compact of Zborów in 1649 and ending with their rejection by the Diet — marked the next three years. Khmelnytsky was continually pressed to make war by his ally, the Crimean khan, who considered peace an unprofitable waste of time that could be better spent plundering. Powerful states sent envoys to negotiate with Khmelnytsky, who discovered a gift for statesmanship (thus, he first aided Moldova's ruler, Basil Lupul, then ravaged Moldova with Cossack and Tartar forces until Lupul agreed to marry his daughter to Khmelnytsky's oldest son). In 1651 Khmelnytsky discovered that his wife, in correspondence with Czaplinski, had been plotting his murder. Khmelnytsky had her hanged and began indulging in bouts of drunkenness. After the Cossacks were defeated by Poland, he regrouped his forces, though his position was weakened. Thousands of Cossack peasants emigrated to Russian lands. However, Khmelnytsky was still able to keep Lupul from marrying his daughter to a Polish noble with the message "Do please, my lord, give your daughter in marriage to my son, and everything will be well with you; otherwise I shall smash you into dust."

Khmelnytsky's search for the strong protecting power he felt was needed if Ukraine was to remain independent of Poland ended in 1654 with his long-desired alliance with Russia. He soon came to doubt Russia's intentions and was trying to form an international coalition against Poland to safeguard Ukrainian autonomy when he became seriously ill. He called a general assembly of the Cossacks and insisted they appoint his successor. Lack of a more suitable candidate made them elect Khmelnytsky's weak fourteen-year-old son, whose power was quickly usurped after his father died. The usurper allied the Cossacks with Poland in 1658
G. Vernadsky, *Bohdan Hetman of Ukraine*, 1941.

KHOMEINI, SAYYID RUHOLLAH MOUSSAVI

(c.1900–1989), Iranian Islamic fundamentalist leader. Khomeini, a Shi'ite Muslim, was born in Khomeyn, and later adopted the name of his hometown in accordance with the customary practice among Shi'ite religious heads. A descendant of religious leaders, he was raised by his brothers after the death of his father, killed on the orders of a local landlord. Khomeini believed that the landlord had acted on the orders of the shah of Persia (Iran), Reza Pahlavi. This prompted his lifelong opposition and resistance to the shah. A son and a grandson of Khomeini are also believed to have been killed by the shah's secret police.

Khomeini was educated in religious schools and knew the Koran by heart by the time he was six years old. In 1917 he began studying theology with his eldest brother, completing his studies in 1926 and beginning his career as a cleric. He wrote on religious philosophy, law, and ethics, and quickly became known as a brilliant theology teacher. In the early 1940s he published his first book, *The Key to Secrets*. He became an ayatollah (a major Shi'ite religious leader) in the 1950s, moving in 1962 to the Iranian religious center of Qom.

Meanwhile, Khomeini had become politically active through involvement in campaigns against many of the shah's proposals and reforms, such as allowing non-Muslims to run for local councils and allowing women to vote. During anti-government riots in 1963, Khomeini spoke out against the shah and was imprisoned, but the following year he was released into exile in An Najaf, a holy city in Iraq. In 1977 he began calling himself imam, the highest sacred title in Shi'ia Islam, and one which had not been used in hundreds of years. He encouraged an escalation of the Islamic revolution and continued his attacks on the shah until the latter requested that Iraq, too, exile Khomeini. Asked to leave Iraq in 1978, he went to Paris, where he continued his anti-shah activities, including the smuggling of cassettes with his anti-shah message into Iran. Such activities contributed to the overthrow of the shah in January 1979. Two weeks after the shah's departure, Khomeini returned to Teheran, Iran's capital, acclaimed as the religious leader of the revolution. He appointed a government and moved back to Qom.

In December 1979 Khomeini was elected Iran's religious and political leader for life, ushering in an age of fundamentalism. He proclaimed an Islamic republic, based on Islamic law as interpreted by him and his followers, which he promoted as a cure for all society's ills. He crushed all opposition, real or potential. He began by executing hundreds of individuals who had worked for the shah and later killed hundreds of people who constituted the moderate opposition to his regime. He saw religious leaders as the sole legitimate rulers and gave them control over affairs of state.

The shah's pro-Western foreign policy was replaced by a vehement anti-Western policy that regarded the United States as the "Great Satan." The taking of the U.S. embassy in Teheran in November 1979 and the holding of hostages by Iranians enjoyed his sanction. Under his regime Iran became an important sponsor of Islamic fundamentalist groups involved in hostage-taking and terrorist activities around the world.

Khomeini's authority in Iran was absolute, despite considerable suffering for the Iranian people. He consistently refused to seek a peaceful solution to the bloody Iran-Iraq War, which started in 1980 and resulted in well over a million casualties and immense economic hardship. He was seen as a premier spiritual leader well beyond the confines of his homeland. His issuing of a death sentence against British writer Salman Rushdie, whose book, *The Satanic Verses*, he considered blasphemous, drew widespread condemnation from governments around the world, but inspired sufficiently serious anti-Rushdie rhetoric from a wide spectrum of Muslim communities for the author to go into hiding to thwart attempts on his life.

Khomeini was virulently antinationalist, considering nationalism an "imperialist plot" to divide the Muslim world. He advocated the spread of his traditional Islamic society and fundamentalist revolution to other countries, by force if necessary; many embraced his fundamentalist vision. His death was the occasion for massive demonstrations of grief and defiance by his distraught followers.
M. M. Milani, *The Making of Iran's Islamic Revolution,* 1988.
A. Taheri, *The Spirit of Allah: Khomeini and the Islamic Revolution,* 1985.

KHOSROW I

(Khosrow the Just, or Chosroes; died 579), Persian emperor. The facts of Khosrow's early life are shrouded in legend and conjecture. He is said to have been the child of a liaison between his father, King Kavardh I, and a peasant girl, and emerged victorious from the struggle for power that followed his father's death by having his brothers slain. This bloody beginning ushered in a reign later regarded as epitomizing the cardinal kingly virtues of justice and wisdom.

After swiftly quelling the social unrest and disorder attendant upon a religious revolt launched by the Mazdakite sect, Khosrow initiated widespread changes within the Sasanid Empire. Reversing the process of decentralization of authority away from the monarch, he strengthened the power of the lower aristocracy — who were dependent on his patronage — at the expense of the great feudal lords whose influence had threatened to rival his own. His reforms of the hitherto cumbersome bureaucracy of the empire included the introduction of a system of ministries answerable to his prime minister, Bozorgmehr, a talented and faithful subordinate.

The system of taxation Khosrow inherited, which involved a tax that varied with land yield, was inequitable and resulted in large and unpredictable fluctuations in the revenues available to his exchequer. To combat this, he oversaw a fiscal review based on the Roman system inaugurated by Diocletian, which involved a fixed-sum tax and resulted in the stabilization of state income. As a consequence he was able to engage in effective long-term planning; many of his innovations were so effective that they lasted well into Islamic times.

Khosrow's subsequent fame rested as much on his reputation as a conqueror as on his domestic reforms. His reign saw an extended campaign by his forces against the Byzantines, which culminated in the capture of Antioch in 540. Khosrow joined forces with the newly emergent Turks against the Hephthalites, to such good effect that they were crushed and by the end of his reign the eastern frontier of his empire stretched as far as the Amu Darya (Oxus River). To the south, his armies conquered Yemen.

Khosrow's military successes were based on a combination of diplomatic skill and superior force, the latter augmented by a thoroughgoing overhaul of the military. He jettisoned the traditional practice of conscription through feudal levies, creating instead a well-trained standing army of professional soldiers led by hand-picked officers. He also had defensive walls built to protect the empire's boundaries, and appointed four chief commanders, each of whom was responsible for protecting one of the frontiers.

The emperor was a notable patron of the arts and sciences, including astronomy. His renown was such that when the academy of Athens closed in 529, many philosophers migrated to Khosrow's court, where they received a warm welcome from him. He ordered the codification of the sacred book of Zoroastrianism, the *Avesta*, and also arranged for the translation of Indian medical texts from the original Sanskrit. His patronage resulted in a previously unparalleled blossoming of Persian poetry and literature: Ferdowsi's classic *Shah-nameh* (Book of Kings) was based on a literary canon established in Khosrow's day. The sovereign also promoted the game of chess, which traders had brought from India.

In the early Islamic era, Khosrow came to be seen as a model ruler to be emulated by Muslim princes. Became factual details about his reign were relatively sparse, virtually all unassignable developments and reforms were ascribed to him; among the common people in particular, he enjoyed an unrivaled reputation for justice and wisdom

R. N. Frye, *The Heritage of Persia*, 1963.
P. Sykes, *A History of Persia*, 1968.

KHRUSHCHEV, NIKITA SERGEYEVICH

(1894–1971), Soviet leader. Born in Kursk to a family of workers, he received some schooling through the parish church and went to work in a factory in Yuzovka in the Don basin at the age of fifteen, which earned him exemption from military service in World War I. He joined the Bolshevik party in 1918 and served in the Red Army from 1919 to 1921. In the following year he began a quest for education that led him to political positions within the Communist party. In 1925 he gave up his factory work and became party secretary of a district in Yuzovka. At about this time he met Lazar Kaganovitch, a colleague of Joseph *Stalin, who headed the Ukrainian party organization. Becoming more prominent as a party organizer, Khrushchev served in Kharkov and Kiev before receiving permission in 1929 to study in Moscow.

From the time of his arrival in Moscow, Khrushchev continued his steady climb in the Communist party. In 1934 he was elected a full member of the Central Committee and in the following year, having supervised the final stages of Kaganovitch's construction of the prestigious Moscow subway, he was nominated secretary of the Moscow party organization. As a supporter of Stalin, other promotions followed until he achieved candidate membership of the Politburo in 1937 and secretaryship of the Ukrainian party organization in 1939.

Following the Nazi-Soviet pact on the eve of World War II, Khrushchev supervised the Soviet takeover of the Polish territories ceded by Germany as part of the agreement, which included the forced evacuation of their populations. After the German invasion of the Soviet Union in 1941 his responsibilities included the evacuation of Ukraine's vital industries and various positions as political adviser in the army. Immediately after the war, Ukraine, already devastated, suffered a catastrophic famine. Khrushchev had experience of famine,himself: his first wife had died in 1921 during a famine in Yuzovka, but his efforts to solve Ukrainian problems were unsuccessful. Stalin demoted him in 1947, but in 1949 he was recalled to Moscow and took up his previous position (equivalent to mayor) in the Moscow party organization and also became first secretary of the All-Union Central Committee.

From 1949 until Stalin's death in 1953, Khrushchev trod the tightrope of ensuring his survival of Stalin's purges of party leaders while building his own power bases. He spent some time on his specialty, agriculture, setting up the groundwork for the agricultural towns with which he proposed to replace the system of collective farms. On Stalin's death, he managed to patch up his differences with Georgy Malenkov, Stalin's declared successor, long enough to have Lavrenty Beria, the chief of state security, arrested and executed. A few months after Stalin's death Khrushchev had enough power to take over from Malenkov as first secretary. In 1955 he replaced Malenkov as premier with his own man, Nikolai Bulganin. His policy at the time veered toward the conservative.

The first sign of a change in Khrushchev's attitude toward Stalin came in 1955 when, visiting Marshal *Tito of Yugoslavia, he apologized for the cessation of "fraternal relations" decreed by Stalin in 1948. In that year, too, a treaty was signed with Austria, West Germany was granted diplomatic recognition, a summit meeting was held in Geneva with the United States and Great Britain, and Khrushchev visited India, Burma, and Afghanistan with Bulganin.

However, it was at the Twentieth Party congress, held in February 1956, that Khrushchev made his boldest move yet. In a four-hour speech delivered before a closed session he denounced Stalin and recited the list of his crimes. At the Twenty-Second congress held in 1961, he called for the removal of Stalin's body from the Lenin Mausoleum. It was a daring step, and he could not have taken it had his power base not been firmly established.

The process of de-Stalinization thus set in motion caused political difficulties for Khrushchev, but he crushed the Hungarian revolution and weathered the Polish crisis of 1956 to emerge in 1957 as the unchallenged leader of the Soviet Union. He displaced Bulganin in the following year as premier and now held the two top Soviet posts. This period was characterized by a slight thaw. Amnesties were declared, freeing hundreds of thousands of political prisoners; thousands more were posthumously rehabilitated. Writers, artists, and other members of the intelligentsia experienced a certain slackening of official control.

Having firmly established himself in power, Khrushchev turned to foreign relations. His policy of peaceful coexistence with the West led to an easing of cold war tensions, but caused increased difficulties with China. He visited the United States in 1959, but the summit conference held in Paris in the following year broke up when the U.S.S.R. announced that a U.S. plane had been shot down over Soviet territory and Khrushchev walked out in protest of U.S. espionage. In 1961 he held an abortive conference in Vienna with President John F. *Kennedy, and in 1962 the two leaders had another confrontation, this time over Cuba. Khrushchev's handling of this crisis,

SAYINGS OF NIKITA KHRUSCHEV

- To recognize as unsuitable the continued retention in the Mausoleum of the sarcophagus with J. V. Stalin's coffin, since the serious violations by Stalin of Lenin's behests, the abuses of power, the mass repressions against honest Soviet people, and other actions in the period of the cult of the individual make it impossible to leave the coffin with his body in the V. I. Lenin Mausoleum (resolution of the Twenty-Second Party congress, 1961).
- Tonight the mice have buried the cat (remark attributed to Khrushchev on the night Stalin died).
- If you cannot catch a bird of paradise, better take a wet hen.
- Politicians are the same everywhere. They promise to build a bridge even where there is no river.
- We offer the capitalist countries peaceful competition.
- Those who wait for that must wait until a shrimp learns to whistle (on speculation that the USSR might abandon communism).
- In a fight, you don't stop to choose your cudgels.
- If we should promise people nothing better than only revolution, they would scratch their heads and say, "Isn't it better to have good goulash?"

which apparently averted war between the superpowers, led to a greater split in Soviet relations with China, and the 1963 nuclear test-ban treaty did nothing to repair matters.

On the home front, despite the steps he took to solve the problems of domestic supply, his agricultural policies failed. His attempts to reorganize the unwieldy centralized bureaucracy also proved impossible to enforce and thus strengthened his internal opponents. The continuous and shifting struggle for power that characterized the Soviet political system gave his opponents their opportunity, and Khrushchev found himself maneuvered into resigning from the leadership in 1964. From then until his death seven years later, he lived in obscurity, emerging briefly in 1970 when his purported memoirs were published in the West. Despite his denials, they were generally accepted as genuine.

Khrushchev was the first Soviet leader to lean toward the West both politically and personally. Acts such as his appearance at the General Assembly of the United Nations, when he took off his shoe and rapped the table with it, contributed to his notoriety — some called him a buffoon. Khrushchev was not accorded a state funeral, nor was he buried in the

Kremlin walls with other leaders. Ernst Nezviestny, a sculptor who had been denounced by Khrushchev as decadent and whose works were banned, was asked to design his tomb, which can be seen in the Novodevichye cemetery

G. W. Breslauer, *Khrushchev and Brezhnev as Leaders*, 1982.

E. Crankshaw, *Khrushchev: A Career*, 1966.

M. Frankland, *Khrushchev*, 1966.

R. A. and Z. A. Medvedev, *Khrushchev: The Years in Power*, 1976.

S. Talbot, *Khrushchev Remembers* 2 vols., 1970, 1974.

KIERKEGAARD, SÖREN AABYE (1813–1855), Danish philosopher and theologian. Although little known in his own lifetime and for many years after his death, Kierkegaard has come to be regarded as the founder of modern existentialism and a revolutionary in the field of Protestant Christianity. His stress on the importance of the "existing individual," together with his analysis of such features of religious consciousness as faith, choice, despair, and dread became key parameters for his successors. He was a brilliant intellectual satirist who was to reserve his bitterest invective for Georg *Hegel's idealistic rationalization of the Christian tradition. For him, philosophy was not a matter of constructing systems or analyzing concepts, but of authentically expressing one's individual existence. The epitaph he composed for himself was simple: "That individual."

Born in Copenhagen, Kierkegaard inherited from his austere and melancholy father a deeply emotional pietist devotion. In addition, he somehow felt a guilty involvement in his father's having solemnly cursed God when a young man. This intensified Kierkegaard's interest in the question of how man can be rescued from despair. He was forever seeking "a truth which is true for me, to find the idea for which I can live and die." By the time he was twenty-one, three of his sisters and two of his brothers had died.

From 1830 to 1840, Kierkegaard studied theology at Copenhagen's university but never took holy orders. After breaking off his engagement to a charming young woman called Regine Olsen — an act of great symbolic importance to him since he felt that the married state was incompatible with his vocation — he lived a withdrawn life as an author, although still to be seen around Copenhagen in the cafés. His father's death in 1838 left him with a comfortable income and he was able to devote himself to his writings. His renunciation deepened his sense of a special relationship with Divine Providence. A troubled, moody man, he twice achieved some local notoriety, first through his public quarrel with a popular Copenhagen satirical paper and then with his condemnation of the established Danish Lutheran church when the Hegelian Hans Martensen became its head in 1854.

He published his first book, *Either-Or*, in 1843, followed by many other works. His influence was long restricted by the fact that his writings were in Danish. The posthumous publication in the twentieth century of his *Journals* shed much light on his life and thought.

Kierkegaard's works are less a coherent doctrine than a radically subjectivist presentation of a particular sensibility. The problem of being takes precedence over that of knowledge and cannot be made the subject of objective inquiry; rather, it is revealed to the individual by reflection on his or her own circumstances. Moreover, since according to Kierkegaard no individual has a predetermined place in some rational system, everyone is compelled to assume the responsibility for making his own choice.

Kierkegaard hated the hypocritical, comfortable, bourgeois world in which he lived. His study of the Greeks and the medieval monastics led him to characterize his own age as sadly lacking in the passion they had felt. He asserted that only through confrontation with supremely difficult psychological and spiritual situations can individuals progress toward an understanding of their own significance; thus, any way of life or doctrine designed to buffer people against having to face up to the pressing need to find an authentic means of self-expression was anathema to him.

His particular hatred of Hegelian views sprang from his belief that they constituted just such a doctrine, a gospel for those who have betrayed their own individualism and are content to live

Kierkegaard

> - Life can only be understood backwards; but it must be lived forwards.
> - A man must get out of the poetical and into the existential and ethical.
> - Truth is subjectivity.
> - When the passions of a young man run wild, two powers can save him: a loving woman and God in heaven. If he is saved by a woman, he is reduced to finitude. If he is not saved by a woman's love but is nevertheless saved, then it is by God and his existence will have significance.
> - Christianity does not lie in the sphere of the intellect.
> - Truth is a snare; you cannot have it without being caught. You cannot have truth in such a way that you catch it, but only in such a way that it catches you.
>
> **Sören Kierkegaard**

merely as functionaries of the state. Kierkegaard saw anxiety and existential dread as an inevitable concomitant of the realization of one's necessary freedom of choice, ignorance of the future, and manifold options.

Since human existence is irredeemably finite, argued Kierkegaard, its standpoint is incorrigibly partial and hence speculative system-building falsifies human existence by suggesting the possibility of an absolute, objectively correct viewpoint. Kierkegaard viewed all truth as subjective, valid only for the person who discovered its relevance to his or her own situation. His antirationalism was even manifested in his habit of writing his works under different pseudonyms and attacking the views he expressed under one name when writing under another. Nonetheless, he saw his central task as the explanation of what is involved in being a Christian. He identified Christianity with suffering and felt the Christian revelation to "express something which man has not given to himself...something that would never have entered any man's mind even as a wisp or an idea."

Not until after World War I did Kierkegaard's numerous works attract the attention of European philosophers. Then, his vision resonated strongly with intellectuals who saw the demise of the world order based on the complacent certainties engendered by the philosophical systems builders of the nineteenth century. The new age of uncertainty and individualism found its voice through him and hailed him as the precursor and begetter of a new movement.

P. Gardiner, *Kierkegaard*, 1988.
N. Lebowitz, *Kierkegaard: A Life of Allegory*, 1985.
P. P. Rohde, *Sören Kierkegaard: An Introduction to His Life and Philosophy*, 1963.

KING, MARTIN LUTHER, JR. (1929–1968), American Baptist minister, leader of the U.S. civil rights movement and winner of the Nobel Prize for peace. Born the son and grandson of Southern Baptist preachers, King was originally christened Michael Luther, but his father changed both their names in honor of the sixteenth-century religious reformer, Martin *Luther. When fifteen he went to Morehouse College, Atlanta, under the auspices of the special program for gifted students. Despite an early interest in medicine and law, he decided to follow in his father's footsteps and enter the ministry. In 1951 he was awarded his Bachelor of Divinity degree from Crozer Theological Seminary, where he was first exposed to the ideas of Mahatma *Gandhi and modern Protestant theologians such as Paul Tillich who brought existentialism, depth psychology, and neo-Scholastic ontology to bear on their religious thinking. King himself was always to see God as an active personal entity and salvation as resulting through faith in God's guidance.

In 1955 King received his doctorate from Boston University. Two years earlier, he had met and married Coretta Smith; the young couple moved to Montgomery, Alabama, where King took up his pastoral duties. When, in December 1955, Rosa Parks was arrested for refusing to surrender her seat on a bus to a white passenger, King who was chosen to head the Montgomery Improvement Association to oppose the segregated transport system. Although he was from a comfortable middle-class black family and had therefore been cushioned from the worst excesses of racial discrimination and prejudice that were the common experience of many black people, King identified passionately with the cause of black liberation.

King immediately avowed his commitment to the principle of nonviolence in thought as well as deed: "We will not resort to violence. We will not degrade ourselves with hatred. Love will be returned for hate." He and his supporters faced violent opposition, his family was threatened and his home dynamited, but a year later the protesters achieved the desegregation of both inter and intrastate transportation and King was launched to national prominence. He immediately organized the Southern Christian Leadership Conference to unify those forces working for black civil rights; this gave him a national platform for the dissemination of his views. A magnificent and emotive speaker, he fused the rhetoric of a Southern preacher with the cogency of a philosopher, expressing his nonviolent philosophy of social justice in lectures throughout the country.

While continuing to organize, agitate, and educate for change, King also traveled widely, winning worldwide support for both his cause and his methods. In India, which he visited in 1959, he was warmly welcomed by Jawaharlal *Nehru and became even more convinced of the potency of nonviolent resistance methods as a weapon for the oppressed through his meeting with Gandhian work-

Martin Luther King receiving the Nobel Peace Prize

ers. He returned to his home town of Atlanta convinced that "the psychological moment has come when a concentrated drive against injustice can bring great, tangible gains."

In October 1959 King was arrested while leading a demonstration protesting the segregation of an Atlanta lunch counter. The charges were dropped, but a national outcry resulted when he was imprisoned for having violated the terms of his probation on a minor traffic offense some months previously. He was eventually released through the personal intervention of Democratic presidential candidate John F. *Kennedy; the latter's slender victory in the presidential election a few days later has been attributed to the swing in the black vote which his support for King occasioned.

King, still only thirty-one years old, was now undisputed leader of the civil rights movement, which succeeded in attracting the support of many black and liberal white supporters and of successive Democrat administrations under Kennedy and Lyndon B. *Johnson. Reactionary white retaliation against the movement could be brutal, however. In spring 1963, police in Birmingham, Alabama, turned dogs and fire hoses on peaceful demonstrators led by King; he and hundreds of his supporters, including schoolchildren, were jailed. At the same time, a local black church was bombed and four girls attending Sunday school there were killed. King's open letter from the Birmingham jail constituted an eloquent rejoinder to those more conservative elements within the black establishment who questioned his confrontational tactics.

The acme of the civil rights campaign was the August 1963 march on Washington, the largest peacetime demonstration ever seen in the United States, in which a peaceful multiracial crowd of over two hundred thousand people marched to the Lincoln Memorial in support of the equal rights platform. There, they heard King give a moving oration, part vision, part statement of intent: many were moved to tears by the power of his words. The Civil Rights Act passed the following year authorized the federal government to enforce desegregation of public housing, and outlawed discrimination in publicly owned facili-

SAYINGS OF
MARTIN LUTHER KING, JR.

- We have no alternative but to protest. For many years we have shown an amazing patience. . . . But we come here tonight to be saved from that patience that makes us patient with anything less than freedom and justice (at the first meeting of the Montgomery Improvement Association, 1955)..

- You may well ask: "Why direct action? Why sit-ins, marches and so forth? Isn't negotiation a better path?" You are quite right in calling for negotiation. Indeed, this is the very purpose of direct action. Non-violent direct action seeks to create such a crisis and foster such a tension that a community which has constantly refused to negotiate is forced to confront the issue (open letter from Birmingham jail, 1963).

- I have a dream that one day this nation will rise up, live out the true meaning of its creed: "We hold these truths to be self-evident, that all men are created equal." I have a dream that one day on the red hills of Georgia, the sons of former slaves and the sons of former slave-owners will be able to sit together at the table of brotherhood. I have a dream that one day even the state of Mississippi, a state sweltering with the heat of oppression, will be transformed into an oasis of freedom and justice. I have a dream that my four little children will one day live in a nation where they will not be judged by the color of their skin but by the content of their character (at the Washington rally, 28 August 1963).

- I don't know what will happen now, we've got some difficult days ahead. It really doesn't matter with me now, because I've been on the mountain top. I won't mind. Like anybody I would like to live a long life. Longevity has its place. But I'm not concerned about that just now. I want to do God's will and he's allowed me to go up to the mountain, and I've looked over and I've seen the Promised Land. I may not get there with you, but I want you to know that we as a people will get to the Promised Land. Well, I'm happy tonight. I'm not worried about anything. I'm not fearing any man. Mine eyes have seen the glory of the coming of the Lord (Speech shortly before his assassination, 1968)..

ties and employment. In 1964 King was awarded the Nobel Peace Prize for his work.

Despite the achievements of the civil rights movement under his leadership, the lack of greater substantive progress led to increasing frustration with King's nonviolent methods among younger radicals. Thus, an incident at Selma, Alabama, in 1965, when demonstrators demanding a federal voting rights law turned back to avoid confronting a police cordon, led to accusations that King had struck a deal with the state authorities. Increasingly, it became apparent that the strategy that had broken segregation laws was not adequate to deal with some of the more complex racial problems, such as the disadvantaged socio-economic position most blacks occupied within American inner cities.

King's response was to seek to broaden the scope of his nonviolent vision to address other concerns that had a bearing on the black cause. Thus, a year before his death he came out against the war in Vietnam, despite strong opposition from many within the civil rights camp. His plans for a Poor People's March on Washington were interrupted by a trip to Memphis, Tennessee, in support of a strike by city sanitation workers. There, he was shot and killed while standing on the balcony of his motel room. Countrywide rioting followed the news of his murder, and a massive hunt was launched for his killer. James Earl Ray was eventually apprehended in London and pleaded guilty to the crime.

Since 1986, the third Monday in January has been a federal holiday marking the anniversary of King's birth.

G. Presler, *Martin Luther King, Jr.*, 1984.

S. B. Oates, *Let the Trumpet Sound*, 1982.

KING, WILLIAM LYON MACKENZIE

(1874–1950), Canadian prime minister. He was born in Berlin (now Kitchener), Ontario, and named after his maternal grandfather, William Lyon Mackenzie, a fiery orator and rebel who agitated for home rule for British North America. King's childhood has been the subject of much speculation and study. He was remarkably insecure and appears to have been inordinately connected with his domineering mother. A diligent rather than bright student, he studied at the University of Toronto and the University of Chicago and received a doctorate in economics from Harvard.

King's reputation as a competent negotiator resulted in his appointment as deputy minister in the new department of labor when he was only twenty-six. He entered Parliament as the Liberal representative for Waterloo in 1908 and the next year, prime minister Sir Wilfred Laurier appointed King minister of labor. Although King lost his seat after the Conservative sweep in the election in 1911, the Conservatives were unable to remain in power for long. Upon the outbreak of World War I, prime minister Robert Borden enacted a conscription law, supported by English Canada but condemned by the French minority unwilling to take part in a European war on behalf of Britain. Laurier's opposition to conscription resulted in a split in the Liberal party. Many members hurried to join Borden's union government in 1917; King remained faithful to Laurier.

The Liberal party met to choose a new leader in 1919; King, a dark-horse candidate, was not expected to succeed against party veterans. His candidacy gained momentum, however, after a speech in which he outlined a revolutionary social platform including old-age pensions, an eight-hour work day, and unemployment insurance. Furthermore, King was recognized as an accomplished economic theorist because of his book, *Industry and Humanity*, which enhanced his reputation and led to his victory. Two years later, King led his party back to power.

Although King was forced to form a coalition government with the Progressive party, his government saw Canada prosper as never before. He enacted radical social and economic legislation to absorb war veterans returning from Europe. Canada in the 1920s was torn between former colonial and cultural bonds with Britain and the enormous attraction of the United States. During his term of office, King sought to establish a separate Canadian identity and although he was not entirely successful, he was instrumental in forming the Canadian Broadcasting Corporation to compete with American radio, and in bringing the recognition of hockey as the national sport. The Conservative party made a significant comeback in this period, and King's coalition began to crumble. The Liberals lost a vote of confidence in 1925 and King was forced to call an election, which resulted in a resounding Liberal victory, ensuring the continuation of King's policies until the stock market crash of 1929.

A firm believer in the supernatural, King often consulted with mediums before making any important decision. One such medium advised him to call the 1930 election in which he was defeated by the Conservatives. However, this defeat was actually advantageous to King; it left the Conservatives to contend with the depression. King was involved in several financial scandals, but managed to retain the support of his party; in the election of 1935, under the slogan, "King or Chaos," he returned his party to power despite its lack of any significant platform. Once returned to office, he concluded a treaty with the United States, furthering the close ties between the two countries.

To Britain's chagrin, King followed an isolationist policy prior to World War II; he was unwilling to forego support of French-speaking Canadians. Nevertheless King joined the war in 1939, leading to vociferous protests by French speakers. Canada braced for civil war as Quebec prepared for a provincial election. The danger was only averted when the French-speaking members of King's cabinet threatened to resign, leaving an English-speaking government, if Quebec refused to support King. King continued to oppose conscription, but sent a volunteer army to Britain. Only when Germany threatened to overrun Europe did King enact the National Reserve Mobilization Act, enabling conscription for home defense units; no conscripts were sent to Europe.

> The Dominions are autonomous communities within the British Empire, equal in status, in no way subordinate one to another in any aspect of their domestic or external affairs, though united by a common allegiance to the Crown, and freely associated as members of the British Commonwealth of Nations.
>
> **From a declaration initiated by King at the Commonwealth Conference, 1926**

Canada's war economy boomed and the country was even able to loan Britain one billion dollars. Canadian volunteers fought bravely, but until preparations for D-Day began, they were relegated to a minor role in the battlefield. King managed to avoid the thorny issue of conscription until 1944, when he proposed a national plebiscite. He explained his support of laws enabling conscription as, "Not necessarily conscription, but conscription if necessary." King won the plebiscite at the cost of traditional support of French speakers. In the 1945 election he led the Liberals to a narrow victory but lost his own seat and resigned as prime minister in 1948.

King was important in establishing Canada as a state distinct from Britain. He led the country into the League of Nations, and after World War II was instrumental in the formation of the North Atlantic Treaty Organization (NATO). As an individual, he was an eccentric, obsessed with Victorian sexual morality (he never married), and the occult. Nonetheless, his contribution to asserting Canadian independence led to Canada's becoming one of the leading nations of the Western world.

J. E. Esberey, *Knight of the Holy Spirit*, 1980.
J. L. Granatstein, *Mackenzie King: His Life and World*, 1977.
B. Nolan, *King's War*, 1988.
J. W. Pickersgill and D. F. Forster, *The Mackenzie King Record*, 4 vols., 1960–1970.

KNOX, JOHN (1514–1572), Scottish theologian and preacher. Little is known of Knox's background and early years; he came from Haddington in the East Lothian district of Scotland, where his family may have been farmers. He probably studied at Saint Andrew's University and was ordained by 1540. His involvement with Protestantism began when he was tutor to the sons of two prominent East Lothian proponents of reform. He soon became the leader of the reformers, despite his personal misgivings about accepting such a role; however, he came to believe that this was the will of God, especially since it ran so contrary to his own desires.

In 1547, when Knox was preacher in Saint Andrew's, the Scottish governor called in the French to help put down the reformers' agitation (they had occupied the castle of Saint Andrew's in Edinburgh). Knox and his followers then spent nineteen months as slaves in the French galleys; English intervention secured their release, but Knox never fully recovered his health.

Moving to England, Knox pursued a massively successful itinerant ministry; his passionate and earnest preaching and leadership pacified the factious border town of Berwick-on-Tweed, and, in 1551, he was made chaplain to Edward VI; however, he refused the offer of a bishopric due to his distrust of the duke of Northumberland's regency. He was one of the shapers of the articles of the Church of England and was responsible for important insertions in the *Book of Common Prayer*, including a refutation of the principle of transubstantiation (the belief that the communion bread and wine become the body and blood of Christ).

With the accession of the Catholic *Mary I to the English throne in 1553, Knox, to escape persecution, fled to the Continent, where he formulated his idea that citizens could rightfully resist an unjust monarch. To promote this view he wrote his *Faithful Admonition* in 1554, but its extreme and intemperate style alienated many who felt that he hypocritically underestimated the hardships faced by dissenters under Mary. Knox's ministry to the Protestant refugee congregations of Frankfurt-on-Main and Geneva was, however, inspirational: it was said that a sermon from him could do more for the spirit of his listeners than ranks of rallying trumpets echoing in their ears.

Geneva, where Knox lived between 1556 and 1558, was considered by him as "the most perfect school of Christ on Earth since the days of the Apostles." It was there that he wrote the *First Blast of the Trumpet Against the Monstrous Regiment of Women*, which argued that women should be excluded from political power and led to the newly enthroned *Elizabeth I of England barring him from ever entering her realm.

When, in 1559, the French-born regent of Scotland, Mary of Guise, sought to overthrow Elizabeth I and unite the whole of Britain under Francis II and *Mary Stuart, Knox returned to Scotland to rally and inspire a Scottish Protestant force to hold out against Mary's French troops until Elizabeth I consented to English action against the French threat. With the French defeated and Mary of Guise dead, Knox masterminded the hasty composition of the *Scottish Confession;* lauded as the "warm utterance of a people's heart," it denounced the papacy and mass and, alongside the *First Book of Discipline*, defined the essential elements of Scottish Presbyterianism, including its austere moral tone, democratic format, and Calvinist rather than Anglican bent. Knox was also responsible for compiling the *Book* *of Common Order*, adopted as the book of worship of the Scottish church.

Knox and Mary Stuart (Mary, Queen of Scots) — who succeeded to the Scottish throne — hated each other. While vehemently opposing the Catholic Mary's proposed marriage to Don Carlos of Spain, Knox further outraged the monarch by himself marrying her distant cousin, Margaret Stewart (his previous wife had died in 1560). On Mary's abdication in 1567, Knox's old friend James Stewart, earl of Moray, became regent; Knox was bitterly distressed when the latter was murdered, and was seeking to rally the reformers' cause once again when he died in Edinburgh. His leadership, and legacy of writings and teachings earned him the title of the father of the Church of Scotland, whose genesis he recorded memorably in his *History of the Reformation in Scotland*.
S. Lamont, *The Swordbearer: John Knox and the European Reformation*, 1992.
J. S. McEwen, *The Faith of John Knox*, 1962.
J. G. Ridley, *John Knox*, 1968.

KOCH, ROBERT (1843–1910), German physician recognized as the principal founder of modern bacteriology for his discoveries of the tuberculosis and cholera bacteria; recipient of the Nobel Prize.

Koch was the son of a mining official in Clausthal, Germany. His parents were industrious and disciplined Lutherans who encouraged Koch in his natural inquisitiveness. The young Koch was particularly attracted to the natural sciences, collecting insects and plant specimens, and identifying and dissecting them meticulously.

In 1862 Koch was admitted to Göttingen University to study sciences, but after one year transferred to medicine. One of his first teachers, Jacob Henle, who had twenty years previously proposed theories on bacteriology, influenced profoundly the course of Koch's life. Koch was not a brilliant student, but his insatiable curiosity and unparalleled thoroughness — which characterized his career — were evidence of a different type of genius. He graduated in 1866 with the highest honors.

Koch's preferred career was to travel the world as a ship's doctor or to join the military, but his recent marriage mitigated against such choices. After several moves, he finally settled in Rakwitz to establish his own practice, and his earnest manner and efficiency won him a good reputation and a fair income. During the Franco-Prussian War (1870–1871) Koch volunteered for work in a field hospital, and on his return he received an appointment as the district physician for Wollstein. There, in what little spare time he had available, he established a small laboratory at the rear of his home, and began the bacteriological research that was to make him famous.

Koch first investigated anthrax, which at the time was ravaging his district's herds. He traced the cause of the disease to rodlike microorganisms and went on to study techniques of culturing them, developing an effective methodology to determine their life cycle and formation. His reputation in the field was established almost overnight, and his self-confidence grew. He became very much a man of the Second Reich; pugnacious, arrogant, quick to condemn, and unwilling to admit error or acknowledge the ability of others. He spent the next few years improving his methods for fixing, staining, and photographing bacterial cultures as well as investigating the cause and nature of surgical infections.

In 1880 Koch was appointed to the imperial health ministry office in Berlin, where he continued his work with the assistance of his own research team. The bacteriological methodology he developed and published at this time became the basic instructional text in this subject for many years. He demonstrated in-vitro pure culture techniques, using aniline dyes for staining and gelatin, and later agar, as the solidifying agent. Using these techniques he successfully isolated the small tuberculosis bacteria and proved its transmissibility. Paul Ehrlich, on seeing a spellbinding demonstration of this by Koch, improved the staining method overnight. He presented the results to Koch, and the two great researchers became close professional and personal friends. At the same time Koch began a decade-long rivalry with Louis *Pasteur, which was exacerbated by nationalistic pride and professional jealousies.

In 1883 Koch traveled to India, where a cholera epidemic was raging. He identified the source of the epidemic as water infected with a particular comma-shaped bacillus. However, he was unable to induce the disease in experimental animals with this bacillus, so was uncertain as to whether it was indeed the direct cause of cholera. Nevertheless he returned triumphantly in 1884 to Berlin where he became the chief adviser on state hygiene and was appointed director of the Berlin Hygiene Institute the following year.

At the end of a routine lecture in 1890, Koch announced that he had "hit upon a substance which had the power of preventing the growth of tubercle bacilli." People flocked to his institute for inoculation. He was lauded by governments, and even Pasteur praised his efforts, but his vaccine proved ineffective. Koch had ignored his years of meticulous attention to detail and for the first time in his career prematurely made a claim founded on insufficient data, a fault he often found in others.

Koch was shaken by the debacle, but was redeemed by his tireless drive to help Hamburg through a cholera epidemic in 1892. He instituted treatment of the city's water supply after showing a direct correlation between the dispersion of victims and infected water. In 1905 he was awarded the Nobel Prize in medicine for his discovery of the tuberculosis bacillus.
C. and P. Barlow, *Robert Koch*, 1971.

KOSCIUSZKO, TADEUSZ ANDRZEI BONAWENTURA (1746-1817), Polish nationalist statesman and soldier. Born into a noble family in the village of Mereczowszczyno, Kosciuszko early developed a fierce love for his native country and a wish to see it free from foreign interference and domination. He opted for a career in the army, beginning his military education in the Warsaw Corps of Cadets, where he specialized in military architecture and the construction of fortifications. Outstandingly talented, he was chosen to go to Paris to further develop his skills as architect and draftsman. In 1772, during his absence, Austria, Russia, and Prussia cooperated in a tripartite partition of Poland.

Kosciuszko returned to Poland in 1774, but was forced to flee the country two years later to escape the wrath of General Josef Sosnowski, with whose daughter he had unsuccessfully attempted to elope after being engaged to act as her art teacher. He traveled to America, where he was inspired by the aims and ideals of the American revolutionaries, with whose desire for sovereign statehood he sympathized, and offered his services to the U.S. forces in their war against Britain. Between 1778 and 1780 he was able to put his theoretical training to good practical use, supervising the fortification of West Point military academy. He later served as an engineer and cavalry officer, and by war's end he had risen to the rank of brigadier general, being granted U.S. citizenship in recognition of his contribution to the American independence movement. Despite having acquired a substantial estate in the United States, as an ardent Polish nationalist he chose to go back to his homeland, which continued to suffer the depredations of the land-hungry great powers that surrounded it.

On his return in 1784 Kosciuszko was unable to secure a position in the Polish army due to his association with antimonarchist elements, and was reduced to living in near-poverty on his small country estate, awaiting the opportunity to participate in the struggle to reassert Poland's independent statehood. At this time, he demonstrated his liberal convictions by freeing his own serfs from part of their villein duty despite the additional hardship this caused him.

The institution of liberal reforms in Poland in 1789 coincided with the French revolution (many of whose aims Kosciuszko heartily endorsed), and heralded his return to military service, assisted by the patronage of his old sweetheart, Ludwika Sosnowski, who was now married to the influential Prince Lubomirski. He rose to fame through his spirited leadership of Polish troops opposing *Catherine the Great's Russian forces, who invaded Poland in 1792 in an effort to suppress the reformist constitution adopted there in 1791. However, despite his defeat of the invading forces pitted against him at the Battle of Dubianka, he was unable to resist the Russians' superior forces indefinitely: Catherine's troops completed the occupation and, with King Stanislaw II forced to renounce his reform program, Kosciuszko went into exile in France, from where he plotted insurrection to restore Polish sovereignty.

The 1794 Polish uprising, which Kosciuszko returned to lead and organize, enjoyed great popular support but was hampered by lack of adequate weapons in the face of well-equipped professional opponents. Kosciuszko showed great ingenuity in developing new battle tactics designed to maximize the greater numerical strength of the nationalists and managed to inflict a defeat on the Russians at Raclawice with a force consisting largely of hurriedly-recruited peasants brandishing a motley assortment of agricultural implements in lieu of proper arms. Later, leading the defence of a besieged Warsaw, he was able to enlist the aid of the civilian population in resisting the enemy by building defensive earthworks. At all times his personal example was of crucial importance: not content merely to formulate policy, he further demonstrated his leadership qualities by heading the most dangerous charges against the opposing soldiers. Even during such a period of crisis he found time to institute liberalizing reforms: his Polaniec Proclamation declared Poland's long-indentured serfs free.

The nationalists' acts of great valor not withstanding, the confrontation between an ill-equipped rabble and the army of one of Europe's most powerful and populous states could only admit of one conclusion. Despite the desperate heroism of his Polish men, Kosciuszko was for a second time faced with having to bow to superior might; the defeat of Poland's nationalists at Maciejowice and Kosciuszko's capture signaled the collapse of the rebellion and the final partition of Poland.

In 1797, on his release from the Peter-Paul fortress in Saint Petersburg, Kosciuszko sailed to the United States. He was made welcome there, moved freely in the society of like-minded intellectuals, and developed a lasting friendship with Thomas *Jefferson. Here too he evinced his humanitarianism, setting free his black slaves and using some of the revenues from his estate to fund their education. However, despite his comfortable position in American society, he retained his deepseated desire to live to see a free Poland and, judging that *Napoleon's rise in France could bode well for nationalist Polish aspirations, returned to the Continent to negotiate with the French leader. However, his expectations remained unfulfilled, Bonaparte being uninterested in Poland's fate. He subsequently attempted to interest other European leaders, including Czar Alexander I, in his plans for the establishment of a liberal independent Polish state, but his ideas were rejected.

Kosciuszko eventually retired, disappointed, to Switzerland where he lived out his few remaining years. Although his nationalist dreams were not realized, his crusade had struck a responsive chord among the Polish people, and he was idolized in his homeland. After his death his remains were transferred to Cracow cathedral, where they were buried alongside those of Poland's kings.

M. Haiman, *Kosciuszko, Leader in Exile*, 1946.

M. Haiman *Kosciuszko in the American Revolution*, 1971.

KOSSUTH, LAJOS (1808–1894), Hungarian statesman, patriot, and revolutionary hero. His family was of old noble stock but landless and penniless. His father worked as a lawyer protecting the interests of local landowning families. Although the family were Lutherans, religion played almost no role in his upbringing. Graduating in 1821 from a Calvinist law school, he practiced law and served as a junior official in his native country between 1824 and 1832.

In 1832 Kossuth was sent by his employer, Countess Andrassy, to the National Diet in Pozsany to appear as a substitute delegate for one of her relatives. At the Diet Kossuth was captivated by the liberal ideas of Hungary's new reformers, who aimed to overthrow the absolutist system under which Hungary was ruled from Vienna. It was in this atmosphere that he developed his own liberal and nationalist program. Although not entitled to participate in Diet debates, he devised his own method of influencing Hungarian politics, developing the idea of issuing bulletins on the Diet's meetings. These bulletins were not verbatim reports but overt political messages which were circulated throughout Hungary. They were greeted with instant success and after the end of the Diet session in 1836 Kossuth was invited to report on Hungary's county assemblies. However, he was no longer protected by parliamentary immunity and, judging him seditious, the authorities had him sentenced to four years in prison in 1837. Freed three years later, he became editor of *Pesti Hirlap* and created Hungary's first political newspaper. His articles and political radicalism angered the authorities, who eventually engineered his dismissal from the newspaper.

Kossuth attempted to continue his struggle through other means and sought to create several associations for the development and protection of Hungary's industry, with the aim of achieving greater economic independence for the country. Although doomed to failure, his associations allowed him to maintain a public profile as a populist hero. In 1847 he was elected to the Diet at Pozsany as leader of the National Opposition. Inspired by the French and Italian revolutions of 1848, the Hungarian reformers conducted a bloodless revolution in March of that year. They demanded and received civil rights, emancipation of the peasantry, and the abolition of privilege, as well as independence from Austria. Kossuth, with his legal knowledge and fiery oratory, played a decisive role and when in April Hungary was granted a separate government, he was appointed minister of finance in Hungary's first constitutional cabinet.

Kossuth continued and intensified his anti-Austrian campaign. His principles were liberal but his nationalism was opposed to the fulfillment of the ambitions of the Slavic, Rumanian, and German minorities in Hungary, and he was particularly resented in Croatia.

When the Austrians encouraged the Croat army to prepare to move against Hungary, Kossuth became head of the Hungarian government of national defense. Before the advance of the Austrians, his government withdrew to Debrecen, where he organized the brilliant spring campaign that drove the Austrians out of Hungary. In April 1849 the Hungarian parliament declared Hungary an independent republic and acclaimed Kossuth as governor-president.

Victory was, however, short-lived. Russian troops intervened in favor of Austria and Kossuth was forced to resign the government to General Artur Gorgey, his arch-rival. Two days later Gorgey surrendered to the Russians and Kossuth fled to Turkey. He visited England and the United States and was received as a champion of liberty, addressing a series of mass meetings in English, which he had learned during his internment in Anatolia. However, he could not raise official support for his cause. Returning to western Europe, he spent the rest of his life plotting a new revolution in Hungary, but his plans collapsed with Hungary's compromise with Austria in 1867. On the eve of the conclusion of the compromise Kossuth wrote an open letter opposing the move, but the letter's controversial and provocative tone could not prevent adoption of the measure.

Kossuth spent his last years in impoverished exile, having refused an offer of amnesty in 1890. He died in Turin, Italy; his body was returned to Budapest and he was buried in state. After his death Kossuth remained a popular hero, his name forever linked with the struggle for national independence and civil rights.

J. Deak, *The Lawful Revolution: Louis Kossuth and the Hungarians*, 1979.

F. A. Pulszky, *White, Red, Black*, 2 vols., 1970.

D. Zarek, *Kossuth*, 1970.

KRUGER, STEPHANUS JOHANNES PAULUS (generally known as Paul Kruger, or by the sobriquet "Oom Paul," i.e., Uncle Paul; 1825–1904), South African Boer leader and president of the Transvaal Republic. Kruger is the acknowledged builder of the Afrikaner nation in South Africa. He was born in the Cradock district of the British Cape Colony, the child of farmers of Dutch descent. His education was limited, but following his parents, he became a devoted adherent of the strict Calvinist Dutch Reformed Church.

The first great event in his life, and one which influenced his future thinking, took place when Kruger was ten years old. He accompanied his family on the Great Trek, a mass migration of frontier Afrikaner farmers from the British Cape Colony to the northern interior, in an attempt to establish their own independent state.

During this momentous pioneering period, the young Kruger gained a reputation as a fighter against native African tribesmen, wild animals, and even rival Boers. Before he had reached the age of twenty, Kruger was already participating in public affairs, occupying a post of combined civil and military duties. He began his long political career at the

Sand River Convention of 1852, when Great Britain formally recognized the independence of Transvaal, the new republic established by the Boers of the Great Trek. In 1856 he was instrumental in drawing up the new republic's constitution.

When civil disturbances and black tribal attacks broke out in the mid 1860s, Kruger was promoted to commandant general and was largely responsible for pacifying outbreaks and further strengthening the unity of the republic.

Independence did not last long in Transvaal, for it was occupied and annexed by the British in 1877. At this time Kruger began to emerge as the leader of the Afrikaner resistance movement, and he traveled to Britain twice in an attempt to regain his country's independence. When the missions failed, Kruger returned home undeterred and organized passive protests against the British administration. These protests turned forceful in 1880 and after a series of victories, which ended in British defeat at Majuba Hill in 1881, Kruger was able to negotiate the restoration of independence to the Transvaal.

Kruger's political rise culminated in his election to the presidency of the Transvaal, a post he held until the Boer defeat in 1902. Essentially a conservative man with ideas based upon those of the frontier Boers of the Trek, Kruger's extended terms of office were highlighted by struggles to avoid British encroachment and by efforts at preserving the character of the rural Boer society. He would sit on the "stoep" (veranda) of his beloved farm, Boekenhoutfontein, top-hatted, pipe in hand, gazing out into the vast empty spaces he had worked so hard to possess, a figure held in veneration by his fellow Boers.

In 1886, the discovery of gold in the Witwatersrand area of the Transvaal quickly saw the establishment, only forty miles from the republic's capital, Pretoria, of a new sprawling city, Johannesburg, which soon attracted thousand of foreigners, "outlanders," mainly of British background coming to seek their fortunes. Kruger saw this new "Anglo" community as a clear threat to the national identity of his Boers, whom he fondly called "God's People" and began to institute tough mining and residential regulations on the outlanders. He also taxed the mines heavily and promoted economic and railway policies aimed at protecting his administration and republic. The results were higher gold production costs.

These actions brought Kruger into direct confrontation with Cecil *Rhodes, the Cape premier, who besides having his own gold interests also entertained ideas of a grand British African empire, which included a united South Africa. Angered and provoked by Kruger, Rhodes sponsored an ill-fated raid to overthrow Kruger's government.

Having survived the Jameson raid of 1895 intact and with increased prestige, Kruger rallied his people and overwhelmingly won the 1898 election. With the departure of Rhodes and the arrival of the new governor Sir Alfred Milner, Kruger attempted to compromise with the Cape government and the outlanders by offering to soften the tough regulations he had earlier imposed. His proposals were rejected and tensions again rose. On 11 October 1899, following months of confrontation and exchanges of ultimatums, Kruger declared war on Britain.

Kruger was obstinate but forceful and fully believed in his cause. By not compromising earlier, however, he ultimately gave Britain the pretext to subjugate the Boer republics and establish British rule all over South Africa. Despite early successes, Pretoria was captured on 5 June 1900, and the Boer army forced into retreat. The aged Kruger, unable to keep up with the army, escaped to Holland where he tried to enlist Dutch support for the war until its end in May 1902. He died in 1904 in Clarens, Switzerland, and was finally buried in Pretoria later that year.

His name is commemorated in the world-renowned Kruger National Park in the eastern Transvaal (established through his efforts), the town Krugersdorp in the Transvaal, the gold Kruger coins, which brought the Republic of South Africa prosperity in the latter half of the twentieth century, as well as streets, squares, and statues in towns and cities throughout the country.

S. Cloete, *Against These Three*, 1979.
J. Fisher, *Paul Kruger, His Life and Times*, 1974.
J. S. Marais, *The Fall of Kruger's Republic*, 1961.

KUBLAI KHAN (1216–1294), Mongol emperor of China. Kublai was born in the year that his grandfather, *Genghis Khan, took Peking. His connection with China took a more tangible form when he was granted lands there in 1236. The inhabitants fled but were induced to return when they realized that the young Mongol was implementing agrarian policies in the area, not the traditional nomadic policies of his forefathers. From 1251 to 1259 he led military campaigns in southern China and in 1260 succeeded his brother as head of the empire founded by Genghis Khan.

Kublai was elected supreme leader of the Mongols by a *khuriltai* (convention) of Mongol leaders in K'ai Ping, in northern China. This choice of location was to cast a shadow of illegitimacy over his reign since the *khuriltai* had traditionally been held in the Mongol homelands, and opposition to him was bitter. In the first year of Kublai's reign, his brother Arigh Boke was elected supreme ruler of the Mongols at a *khuriltai* convened in Karakorum, the Mongol capital. After several clashes, Arigh Boke surrendered in 1264, and was pardoned. However, those Mongol nobles who had supported him, especially Kaidu (who eventually became the de facto ruler of the Mongol homelands), remained hostile to Kublai's rule, considering it a dilution of the glorious Mongol nomadic tradition.

Since adaptation to agrarian and urban policies was seen by Kublai as the key to effective administration in China, his response to such accusations took the form of an aggressive foreign policy, aimed both at the Southern Sung dynasty, which ruled in the south of China, and at China's Indo-Chinese and Japanese neighbors. In addition, Kublai abandoned the Mongol capital of Karakorum, and replaced it with Beijing, called T'aitu by the Mongols. The Turks called the town Khan-Balik, Marco Polo and the Italians called it Kanbalu or Cambulac, and Samuel Taylor Coleridge made Kublai's capital famous as Xanadu, site of the pleasure dome in his poem "Kubla Khan."

Early on in his rule, Kublai achieved a diplomatic coup in Korea — which had been conquered in 1258 by the previous Khaghan, his brother Mongke — by marrying his daughter to the Korean crown prince. Kublai's sobriety and thriftiness in his early years was manifested in his distaste for the Korean craftsmen who used pure gold in decorations on ceramics, a practice he declared to be unnecessary and wasteful.

Kublai's successes in China in terms of administration of a large and diverse area were remarkable. He gathered about him an extensive court, relying heavily on the advice of his Chinese advisers in the management of Chinese affairs, although senior administrative positions were open only to Mongols and foreigners. His main deviation from Chinese practice was in the abolition of the civil service examinations. In addition, he divided the population into four main groups: Mongols, other foreigners, northern Chinese, and southern Chinese. There was clear racial segregation, and the Chinese were forbidden to learn the Mongol language, to marry Mongols, or to carry arms.

Several new government institutions were established, including a secretariat to deal with most civilian matters, a privy council responsible for the supervision of military affairs, and a censorate, essential for the inspection of and reporting on all major officials and thus for the control of Kublai's huge domain.

A countrywide system of three types of paper currency was instituted, one based on silk and the other two backed by a silver reserve. The system of transport was greatly improved, tree-lined avenues were built, and postal stations established to facilitate delivery of mail. Merchants were among those who benefited greatly from the Mongol regime: *Marco Polo and members of his family reached Kublai's court in 1275 in search of trade and were warmly welcomed. In line with Kublai's policy of giving foreigners key positions in the administration of China, Marco Polo acted as governor of Yangchow, near Nanking, for three years. He writes of the support given to merchants and artisans, to physicians, astronomers, geographers, and mapmakers. Theater blossomed under Kublai's rule, and colloquial language was encouraged, which strengthened the development of the novel.

Kublai's elaborate court was enhanced by his second wife Chabi, who exerted great influence on imperial decisionmaking. It was she who persuaded him to leave the assault on the Southern Sung until after he had dealt with the threat posed by Arigh Boke's counterclaim to supremacy over the Mon-

gols, a decision that strengthened Kublai's position in subsequent campaigns. Chabi was inventive, resourceful, and frugal. Ever practical, she designed hats with a rim to be worn against sunshine, and a sleeveless garment for Mongol soldiers to wear in combat. She saw herself as a Chinese empress and encouraged her husband in his emulation of Tang Tai-Tsung, the great seventh-century emperor of the Tang dynasty. Her death in 1281 presaged the onset of Kublai's physical and political decline.

Despite the efficient administration of the country and the Pax Mongolica, which enabled merchants to trade freely throughout Asia and Eastern Europe, the Chinese hated their foreign masters and resented their exclusion from the army and from high-ranking positions in the civil service.

In Japan, Kublai suffered a resounding defeat. Several delegations urging the Japanese to bring tribute to the Mongol court were ignored, and Kublai's ambassadors were often executed. Expeditionary forces were repelled by bad weather and by effective Japanese defenses in 1274 and 1281. The seizure of Champa's capital in 1283, the invasion of Tonkin (which was halted at Hanoi in 1285), and the defeat of the king of Annam in 1288, drained Kublai's finances, supplies, and manpower.

Kublai, aided by the famous general, Bayan, was more successful in his campaigns against the Southern Sung. The fall of Hangchow in 1276 signified the end of the Sung dynasty, and the last Sung emperor, aged nine, drowned near Canton in 1279. However, despite Kublai's economic support for the south following the conquest, Chinese scholar-officials refused to cooperate with him.

Following the death of his wife, Kublai's health deteriorated. He became obese, drank to excess, and suffered from gout, which he tried to alleviate by wearing special slippers made of fish skins. He was in financial difficulties, which, according to Chinese sources, were due to his three chief ministers during that period, each of whom was eventually dismissed or executed. Anti-Muslim edicts were enacted after Muslim merchants refused to eat meat that had not been ritually slaughtered that was served at a banquet hosted by Kublai. This added to the atmosphere of civil unrest. His designated successor, Chabi's son the Crown Prince Chen-chin, died in 1285. Depressed and despondent, Kublai died in his eightieth year. The exact site of his burial is unknown. The Mongol regime in China collapsed some seventy years after his death.

M. Rossabi, *Kublai Khan, His Life and Times*, 1988. J. J. Saunders, *The History of the Mongol Conquests*, 1971.

KUTUZOV, MIKHAIL ILIARONOVITCH,

prince (1745–1813), Russian field marshal. Born in Saint Petersburg, he attended the engineering-artillery college for two years, becoming a corporal in the artillery at the age of fourteen. Two years later, in 1761, he was commissioned, carrying on his father's

Kutuzov at the time of the Battle of Borodino

tradition (the senior Kutuzov had been a lieutenant general under *Peter the Great). From 1764 to 1769 he served in Poland and in 1770 was sent to Turkey.

Kutuzov fought brilliantly in the Russo-Turkish wars, where he served under two of *Catherine II's most outstanding military leaders, A. *Suvorov and P. Rumyantsev. He was badly wounded in 1774, losing an eye, but continued his military career. By 1784 he had risen to the rank of major general.

He went through Catherine's second major war with the Turks (1787–1792), serving with distinction on most of its fronts, especially Odessa, and sustaining another serious wound. As a result, the next five years of his life, from 1793 to 1798, were spent in a number of diplomatic and military posts in Turkey and Finland (ambassador and governor general, respectively); he was also director of the Saint Petersburg cadets corps and military governor of that city.

In 1802 Kutusov retired from public life until *Alexander I, who had acceded to the throne in 1801, summoned him back to assume command of the Russian army, which, with England and Austria, was facing *Napoleon.

The Battle of Ulm (October 1805), in which Napoleon defeated Austria, took place before Kutuzov could join the Austrians. In November he defeated the French at Durrenstein and retreated, suffering only minor losses. Alexander rejected his plan to withdraw to the Russian frontier; however, this did not stop him from blaming Kutuzov for the defeat Napoleon inflicted on the combined Russian and Austrian armies at Austerlitz, in December.

Once again Kutuzov was removed from active duty and served as military governor of Kiev and of

Lithuania (his second term in Vilna). The long standing Russo-Turkish conflict had broken out again, and in 1811 Kutuzov was reinstated by Alexander and appointed commander of the army in Moldova. Kutuzov trounced the Turks and gained Bessarabia for the Russians. Alexander rewarded him with the title of count.

Shortly afterwards, in June 1812, Napoleon invaded Russia with his Grand Army of six hundred thousand men. The Russians suffered a number of defeats as Napoleon advanced. After the bitter rout of Smolensk, Alexander was forced to replace the commander in chief of the Russian army, Prince Mikhail Barclay de Tolly. On the recommendations of his military advisers, Alexander reluctantly gave the post to Kutusov, who made it a condition that he would not have the czarevitch (Alexander's son and heir to the throne) under his command because he would be unable to punish him if he made a mistake and unable to reward him if he did well. Kutuzov was also named prince of Smolensk on assuming command of the army.

Under Kutuzov the Russians retreated from Napoleon, burning and destroying as they went, and harassing the French with a small party of Cossacks who penetrated French lines. When the Russians reached Borodino, a village sixty miles from Moscow, Kutusov made his stand against Napoleon. In the ensuing carnage there were eighty thousand casualties. Kutuzov then retreated again, resuming Barclay's waiting tactics. A week later the French occupied Moscow, and the city was set on fire by its inhabitants to deprive Napoleon not only of booty but also of the stores he had counted on to replenish his own diminished supplies. Cut off from his own supply lines and unable to find other sources in the devastation created around him, Napoleon ordered a retreat. As the French fled, "General Winter" made its slow approach. The harsh conditions of the Russian winter, combined with Kutuzov's relentless harassment, proved deadly as any battle field. Of the six-hundred thousand men who made up his Grand Army, only forty thousand returned from Napoleon's campaign in Russia.

Kutuzov pursued the remnants of the French army into Poland and Prussia in January of the following year, after having nearly crushed them in November at the Berezina River, where thirty-six thousand French corpses were reported to have been found. He himself died in April in Germany.

Known as the "Fox of the North," Kutuzov was immortalized in Leo *Tolstoy's *War and Peace* where, in accordance with Tolstoy's theories at the time, Kutuzov is portrayed as a passive and determined in contrast to Napoleon, ambitious but petty. "Patience and time" was Kutuzov's well-known motto. He was buried in the newly built cathedral of Kazan.

M. G. Bragin, *Kutuzov,* 1970.
R. Parkinson, *The Fox of the North*, 1976.

L

LAMARCK, JEAN-BAPTISTE-PIERRE-AN-TOINE DE MONET, CHEVALIER DE (1744–1829), French botanist and zoologist. Since three of his brothers had been sent to the army, Lamarck — one of eleven children of an aristocratic army officer, lord of the manor of Bazantin in Picardy — was to be trained in that other profession suitable to a man of high birth: the priesthood. It was a plan he found disagreeable and as soon as his father died in 1759, he left his Jesuit college and enlisted in an infantry regiment fighting in the Seven Years' War.

Mounted on an old horse and attended by a boy from Bazantin, he reached the lines on the eve of battle and insisted on taking a place in the front line. All the officers around him were killed in a heavy artillery bombardment and he was thrust into a position of command. He refused stubbornly to withdraw his men until he received orders to that effect; for this bravery he was appointed lieutenant. In 1768, while his regiment was stationed in Monaco (where his interest in botany was first kindled), he was injured in the neck while horsing around with his comrades and was forced to leave the army. He went to Paris and found employment in a banker's office.

In 1778 Lamarck wrote a guide to French flowers with his own identification key, considered an improvement on the work of Carolus Linnaeus. That the guide was written in French rather than Latin was an important factor in its popularity. Lamarck attracted the patronage of the Comte de Buffon, a leading French botanist with high social connections who obtained for him appointment as royal botanist. With Buffon's son as his student, Lamarck traveled extensively through Europe in 1781–1782, augmenting his knowledge of flora and fauna. His discoveries provided material for a botanical dictionary (part of a major encyclopedia project), which also helped make his name well known.

In 1788 Lamarck was offered a post in the Royal Botanical Gardens and continued working there through the French Revolution. The reorganization that followed this upheaval brought him a new position: in 1793 he was asked to serve as professor of zoology specializing in insects and worms. Invertebrates had been neglected by Linnaeus, and Lamarck carried out pioneering work in their classification, drawing a division, for example, between six- and eight-legged insects. It was he who first used the term "invertebrate" and described the study of living things as "biology," both words in common usage ever since.

In 1809 Lamarck publish his *Zoological Philosophy,* considered the most significant of his works since it offered a theory of the evolution of life on earth. His thesis was based on observations that species of animals developed according to the characteristics they found most useful in sustaining their existence. He instanced the giraffe, which had only recently been discovered by Europeans, suggesting that it had developed from antelopes that stretched their necks out to eat leaves higher up on trees and that over the generations this stretching had resulted in a lengthening of the antelopes' bodies.

Lamarck came to believe that through inheritance the elements in the animal's composition that prove most useful are preserved and less useful elements phased out. These ideas of "the inheritance of acquired characteristics" were mistaken but their ingenious presentation was sufficient to start the debate later associated with the work of Charles *Darwin.

In addition to botany and biology, Lamarck carried out extensive research in chemistry, meteorology, and geology, subjects he considered as interconnected, but in none of these did he achieve comparable renown.

Lamarck married several times and had eight children, six by his mistress Marie Delaporte, whom he married in 1792 as she was dying; he had been living with her since 1777. He himself began to suffer from failing vision in 1809, and by 1818 was completely blind. He continued work on his books by dictating to one of his daughters. In 1829 he died in poverty, having outlived his era and receded into oblivion. His family did not even have enough money to pay for his funeral and had to appeal to the French Academy of Science for help.

R. V. Burkhardt, *The Spirit of System: Lamarck and Evolutionary Biology,* 1977.
P. Corsi, *The Age of Lamarck,* 1988.
H. L. McKinney, *Lamarck to Darwin,* 1971.

LAO-TZU (c. sixth century B.C.E.), Chinese sage. Lao-tzu himself would probably have been satisfied with the confusion and mystery that have surrounded attempts to uncover hard evidence about him. It was said of him that "he strove towards self-concealment and remaining without name." He has been variously identified as a court scholar who was an historical contemporary of *Confucius; as the great astrologer Tan; as a chimerial personification of what was in fact a group of sages and scholars working independently and at different times during the fifth to third centuries B.C.E.; as the immortal personification of the Tao; as the *Buddha incarnate. The significance of this mysterious personality rests on his composition of the *Tao te Ching* (translatable as "The Way and its Power" or "Life and its Meaning"), a treatise that has had a fundamental and lasting effect on Chinese thought for over two thousand years. The work is a poetic celebration of the Way (Tao) of the primordial forces of nature, and describes how the man of virtue identifies himself with these forces through his conduct. It is the fundamental Taoist text.

Alternative suggestions notwithstanding, Lao-tzu (this epithet is best translated as "the Old One") is most credibly identifiable as an archivist at the imperial court of the Zhou dynasty in Luo-Yang, in what is now the province of Henan in central China. The family name of the scholar in charge of the sacred books of the royal court was Li, his proper name Erh, and his appellation Tan. What little is known about him is inextricably entangled with myth and legend.

Lao-tzu is said to have met Confucius when the latter visited the royal court. Much has been talked and conjectured about the meeting of these two giants of Chinese letters: the schools they founded, Taoism and Confucianism respectively, represent the two most significant strands of Chinese philosophy. All reports agree that Lao-tzu spoke in rather a deprecatory manner about Confucius's honored idols, the heroes of ancient times, and tried to convince Confucius of the futility of his cultural pursuits. Confucius, on the other hand, expressed his respect for the sage's wisdom, comparing him to a dragon who rises up to the clouds (unlike their counterparts in European mythologies, Chinese dragons represent powerful and beneficent forces).

Chinese society was experiencing uncertainty, civil strife, and change in Lao-tzu's day. The period is known as the time of the Warring States, and lasted for some two hundred years. Lao-tzu is said to have left the court when political conditions had deteriorated beyond hope of repair. Traveling westward, he arrived at the Hsien-ku pass (riding, some say, on the back of a black ox) where he was confronted by its legendary guardian, Yin Hsi. Yin Hsi begged the sage to leave him some written record; without further ado, Lao-tzu composed the *Tao te Ching* on the spot, handed it over, and disappeared into the west.

Lao-tzu

Lao-tzu's weariness with the world of current affairs is suggested by the fact that there is not one historical reference in the *Tao te Ching*. However, the text is not simply a mystical treatise unrelated to worldly considerations; it does implicitly address issues of government and society. Faced with the hypocrisy and moral turpitude that characterized the latter days of the Zhou dynasty, he felt that all forceful attempts to put things right were inevitably corrupted by the prevailing malaise. Hence the *Tao te Ching* indicates that conventional moral, political, and social standards need to be discarded because they are based on value judgments and lead people to undertake activities that alienate them from nature. Rather, the individual should seek to pursue the way of the Tao, a path beyond praise or blame that conforms to cosmic principles.

The Tao is perhaps best understood as the universal force that animates the cosmos, an ineffable reality experienced in ecstasy, empty of inherent qualities but manifest in everything. It is the unchanging unity that underlies the transient plurality of appearances. If this force is allowed to flow smoothly and uninterruptedly, harmony will be achieved through the balancing of opposing forces. Lao-tzu's superior man empties himself of desires, preconceptions, and goals so that the Tao can work through him unobstructedly. By so doing he reaches a state where his actions are

> The Tao (Way) of Heaven is not to contend
> and yet be able to conquer.
> Not to declare its will and yet to get a re-
> sponse,
> Not to summon but have things come spon-
> taneously,
> To work very slowly with well-laid plans.
> Heaven's net is vast, with wide meshes:
> Yet nothing is lost.
> Let me do nothing and the people will trans-
> form themselves.
> Let me love quiescence and the people will
> put themselves right.
>
> **Lao-Tzu**

so completely in accord with the proper and natural harmony of things that no trace is left of the author of the action. Lao-tzu denominates such action as *wu wei*, or nondoing, and equates it with the behavior of the ideal leader, who effectively becomes the personification of the Tao itself.

While the influence of Taoism and the *Tao te Ching* grew, so too did the legend of Lao-tzu. It was widely believed that the Old One had discovered the secret of immortality through his world-shunning practices, and he came to be revered as a cosmic force himself, a physical manifestation of the Tao. By the time of the later Tan dynasty (23–220 C.E.), he was even worshiped by the emperor himself. Other tales of the period credited Lao-tzu with a miraculous childhood akin to that traditionally ascribed to the Buddha — his mother was supposed to have borne him in her womb for seventy-two years, for instance. Any historical evidence about the individual was thus buried beneath the welter of supposition and legend.

Western interest in Taoism and the *Tao te Ching* is of more recent origin. However, Leo *Tolstoy acknowledged his indebtedness to the sage for the doctrine of nonaction, closely related to *wu-wei*, while Carl *Jung was also fascinated by Taoist teachings. Lao-tzu's work has been through innumerable translations in the west in the course of the last one hundred and eighty years, while the upsurge of interest in Eastern philosophy and religion has rendered the Old One's teachings accessible to a wider audience than ever before.

M. Kaltenmark, *Lao-Tzu and Taoism*, 1969.
A. Waley, *The Way and its Power*, 1956.
R. Wilhelm, ed., *The Teaching of Lao-Tzu*, 1985.

LASSALLE, FERDINAND (1825–1864), German socialist and founder of the German labor movement. He was born in Breslau, Germany (today Wroclaw, Poland). His father was a well-to-do Jewish merchant and town councilor who had germanized the family name to Lassal and supported German enlightenment while his mother adhered to the traditional precepts of Orthodox Judaism.

After attending a business school in Leipzig, Lassalle went to the University of Breslau, where he fell under the spell of the Young Hegelians (see Georg *Hegel). He studied philosophy, history, and philology. His diaries and letters from this period show his romantic and melodramatic views. To widen his horizons, and perhaps also to avoid expulsion on political grounds, he continued his education in Berlin. It was at this time that he visited France (1845–1846), where he met and became friendly with the German poet Heinrich *Heine. Heine was engaged in a battle with his family regarding a pension, and Lassalle enthusiastically joined forces to help him. While in France, Lassalle gallicized his name to that of a French revolutionary general.

In 1846 Lassalle found another cause to champion: that of Countess Sophie von Hatzfeldt. Under the laws of the time, she was unable to obtain a divorce despite her husband's mistreatment of her. Lassalle threw himself into the case with typical enthusiasm. For eight years he waged legal battles on her behalf until she was awarded her divorce, garnering much publicity and renown for himself in the process, and ending by achieving his own financial independence when the countess granted him a permanent annual income in 1854.

Before that, in 1848, Lassalle had moved to Dusseldorf where he took part in the revolution of that year and was eventually imprisoned for six months for fomenting violence. His justification of his actions, printed under the title *Meine Assisen-Rede* (1849), enhanced his fame. During the early 1850s Lassalle and Karl *Marx were in regular correspondence as Lassalle sought to help Marx in various practical ways. However, the differences between the two were too deeply rooted for their association to continue. Lassalle was the flamboyant political personality, the financially secure frequenter of Berlin literary salons; these qualities helped him to secure the support of the working classes in the 1860s, but drove a wedge between himself and Marx, the stateless refugee writing in poverty-stricken exile. The

---

ENGEL'S LETTER TO MARX ON SEPTEMBER 4, 1864, FOLLOWING THE NEWS OF FERDINAND LASSALLE'S DEATH

What an extraordinary way to die. This would-be Don Juan really falls in love with the daughter of a Bavarian ambassador and wants to marry her. Then comes up against a rejected suitor of the lady — who incidentally is a swindler from Rumania — and gets himself shot dead by his rival. This could only happen to Lassalle, with his unique character, part Jew, part cavalier, part clown, part sentimentalist. How could a politician of his caliber let himself be shot dead by a Rumanian adventurer?

growing differences in their political and philosophical doctrines were too great to be bridged. Friedrich *Engels had despised Lassalle almost from the outset, referring to him as a "greasy Jew."

Lassalle's reputation was greatly enhanced by the publication of his work on the Greek philosopher Heraclitus and his dramatic epic, *Franz von Sickingen* (1858). He was now a lion of Berlin society. His understanding of the need for style in politics, as much as his political aims and views, even attracted Otto von *Bismarck. It was also of great use to him in disseminating his ideas for integrating the workers into a united and strong Germany. Arousing the political awareness of German workers, he organized an army of workers to agitate for universal suffrage. In 1863 he founded and was elected first president of the ADAV (Allgemeiner Deutscher Arbeiterverein, or General Association of German Workers), the first workers' political party in Germany. The ADAV became the channel through which Lassalle disseminated his political ideas. Its members idolized their authoritarian and charismatic leader.

In 1864 Lassalle embarked on what was to be his last love affair (which inspired George Meredith's *Tragic Comedians*). Having proposed to a lady in Switzerland, he claimed that her family disapproved of him because of his Jewish origins and offered to be baptized. He then challenged her father and her former fiancé to a duel. The fiancé accepted and Lassalle was shot dead at their encounter. He was buried in the Jewish cemetery in Breslau. Paradoxically, it was this romantic, ambitious, and grandiose personality, who had promised his fiancée that he would one day enter Berlin as president of the German republic in a chariot drawn by six white horses, who had through his hard work and political insight laid the foundations for the future German Socialist Democratic party.

D. J. Footman, *The Primrose Path: A Life of Ferdinand Lassalle*, 1969.

LAURIER, SIR WILFRID (1841–1919), Canadian statesman. Born in Saint-Lin, Quebec, then a part of British North America, he completed a law degree in 1864. He worked as both a lawyer and as editor of the French-language newspaper *Le Défricheur*. British North America was then in the process of uniting as an independent dominion within the British Empire. Laurier, as a supporter of the liberal Parti Rouge, advocated the incorporation of the territory into the United States. He believed that an enduring bond with the British crown would disenfranchise the sizeable Francophone minority. Confederation, nonetheless, was legislated by the 1867 British North America Act. The Parti Rouge evolved into the Canadian Liberal party.

Laurier represented the Liberal party in the Quebec provincial legislature, but resigned in 1874 over indifference to regional problems. That same year, he was elected to the Canadian House of Commons, where he felt he could make a more marked impact on the true problems facing the new nation, notably on the relations between the French and English communities. In 1877 he joined the Liberal cabinet of Prime Minister Alexander Mackenzie, defeated by the Conservatives the following year.

In 1879–1884 the Métis, a people of mixed French and Indian blood, carried out an abortive revolt against incorporation into Canada. Laurier vehemently protested the execution of the Metis leader Louis Riel; although his bid to save Riel failed, Laurier was the subject of national interest and a recognized leader of the Liberal party. He was elected opposition leader in 1881, despite the protests of more veteran party members. His support for economic reciprocity with the United States was opposed by the government as threatening traditional bonds with Great Britain. Faced with an impending election, Laurier successfully transformed his party into a national force. In 1896, he was elected Canada's first French prime minister.

Despite his ethnic origins, Laurier refused to favor any community. He resisted the establishment of a separate Roman Catholic school system for French inhabitants of Manitoba (and later for the new provinces of Alberta and Saskatchewan, which joined Canada in 1905), but similarly opposed the integration of British dominions as farflung as England, Canada, Australia, and India into a single state. He refused to send troops to fight in the Boer War, but did provide financial assistance. Laurier favored compromise in the interest of Canadian independence. To assert Canadian sovereignty, he enacted the Naval Service Bill establishing a token Canadian navy of five cruisers and six destroyers. But by 1911 Laurier had annoyed the French by denying their right to separate education in the west, and the English by favoring America over Great Britan with his Treaty of Reciprocity. After losing the 1911 election to Conservative Robert Borden, Laurier returned to the opposition.

His final years as opposition leader were marred by harsh debate surrounding Canada's entry into World War I. The French community opposed any support of Britain, which they still mistrusted as a former colonial power; the English remained loyal to the mother country. Although Laurier supported Britain in the war, he opposed conscription in favor of a volunteer army. His suggestion of a referendum on conscription was rejected by Borden. Laurier also opposed Canadian financial assistance to Britain, particularly the grant of $35 million to the British navy. As the war progressed, the status of the Liberal party dwindled. Many Liberal parliamentarians defected to Borden's wartime union coalition, leading to a second Liberal defeat in the 1917 election.

Only after his death in 1919 was Laurier recognized as the true heir to Sir John A. MacDonald, the father of confederation. During his term of office he had forced compromise on two communities, both fiercely protective of their own interests, and helped transform Canada from a British colony into an independent na-

tion. The sturdy ties between the United States and Canada are the product of Laurier's administration.
R. T. Clippingdale, *Laurier*, 1979.

LAVOISIER, ANTOINE-LAURENT (1743–1794), French chemist and experimental genius as well as social reformer and economist; founder of modern chemistry. His father, a Parisian solicitor, gave his son a fine education. At the age of eleven he was enrolled at the College des Quatre Nations, or Collège Mazarin, reputedly the best school in France, for a nine-year course of study.

At age eighteen, Lavoisier transferred to the Faculty of Law, in keeping with family tradition. He received his baccalaureate in law in 1763 and his license the following year. While pursuing his legal studies, he did not abandon his scientific interests, especially geology, but continued them on an extracurricular basis. Recognition of his work came early. In 1766 he received a Gold Medal from the Academy of Sciences for an essay on street lamp urban lighting. At this time Lavoisier wrote on thunder, the aurora borealis, congelation as well as an analysis of gypsum. In 1768 he was nominated associate chemist at the Academy of Sciences and rose rapidly in this prestigious institution, for which he prepared two hundred reports on subjects ranging from the steam pump to mesmerism.

In 1771 he married Marie Anne Pierrette Paulze, the only daughter of a farmer-general. While Lavoisier was twenty-eight years of age at the time of his marriage, his bride was not yet fourteen. Although the marriage was childless, it was happy and harmonious. Lavoisier's wife trained herself to be her husband's collaborator as well as a skilled draftsman and engraver. In the process she learned English, which Lavoisier did not know, and studied art.

In 1772 he made an important scientific discovery regarding the gain or loss of weight of substances when burned or reduced with charcoal, describing the changes occurring due to absorption or loss of air. In the same year his father purchased a title of nobility for him.

In 1768 he became a full member of the Ferme Générale, the main agency for collecting taxes, and in 1775 he was appointed commissioner of the Royal Gunpowder Administration, serving as its scientific director. He equipped a fine laboratory for that purpose at the Paris Arsenal and took up residence there. In 1778 he started a model farm at Frechines. By 1785 he had been nominated to the committee on agriculture and served as its secretary, drawing up numerous plans for proper cultivation of crops and other agricultural proposals.

Also in 1785 Lavoisier became director of the Academy of Sciences. Two years later, as a member of the provincial assembly of Orleans, he was responsible for social and economic reforms.

In 1790 he was appointed secretary-treasurer of the commission that determined uniform weights and measures throughout France. In the process of this endeavor, the metric system was established. He attacked the widespread belief in a entity called "phlogiston" which he castigated as "the *deus ex machina* of the metaphysician, a term which explains everything and explains nothing." He looked for experiments that could be understood without phlogiston and discovered the process of oxidation. He coined the name of oxygen or "acid producer" for "dephlogisticated" air. By 1783 he announced to the French Academy that water was produced by the combination of hydrogen and oxygen (as already discovered by the English chemist, Henry Cavendish). This led to the start of quantitative organic analysis in the study of chemical reactions, as well as early thermochemical investigation. His 1789 treatise on chemistry represents the foundation of modern chemistry with its distinction between elements and compounds.

He maintained a rigid schedule in order to carry out all his public responsibilities without neglecting his scientific endeavors. He rose at 6 a.m. and worked at science until 8 a.m., resuming this work at 7 p.m. and continuing until at least 10 p.m. The rest of the day was devoted to the business of the Ferme Générale, the Gunpowder Administration, and meetings of the Academy of Sciences and its many committees. One complete day a week, however, was devoted solely to scientific experiments.

Despite his many accomplishments, Lavoisier was an object of suspicion during the French Révolution, partly a result of his membership in the hated Ferme Generale. In May 1794 he was arrested as a result of accusations by Jean *Marat, whose own scientific pretensions had been rebuffed by Lavoisier. After a brief trial he was condemned to death. He and his father-in-law and other members of the Ferme were guillotined at the Place de la Revolution (Concorde). The day after his execution, Joseph Lagrange, the French-Italian mathematician who had worked with him on the commission to reform weights and measures, said, "It took only a moment to sever that head, and perhaps a century will not be sufficient to produce another like it."
S. French, *Torch and Crucible*, 1941.
H. Guerlac, *Lavoisier: The Crucial Year*, 1966.
D. McKie, *Antoine Lavoisier: Scientist, Economist, Social Reformer*, 1962.
R. B. Marcus, *Antoine Lavoisier and the Revolution in Chemistry*, 1964.

LAWRENCE, DAVID HERBERT (1888–1930), English novelist and poet. The son of a miner, he was born in Eastwood, Nottinghamshire, and completed a two-year teachers' certificate course at Nottingham University college. In 1901 he began a friendship with Jessie Chambers, who was to serve as the model for Miriam in *Sons and Lovers* (1913). He was, however, abnormally close to his mother, and his love for her so much overshadowed his relationship with Jessie that he finally ended it in 1911. His most famous masterpiece, *Sons and Lovers*, is based on this triangular relationship. It is ironic that this pioneer of open writing on sex discovered sex late and, when he was twenty-three, refused to believe that women had pubic hair.

His career as a schoolteacher came to an end with an illness that was eventually to be diagnosed as tuberculosis. In the same year, 1911, *The White Peacock* was published, just weeks after the death of his mother. The following year he met Frieda Weekley, the German wife of his former modern languages tutor, and six weeks later eloped with her to Germany. They walked over the Alps to Italy and settled at Gargnano, returning to marry in England in 1914, when Frieda's divorce was granted.

Lawrence began his first book, *The White Peacock*, when he was twenty, working at it for four years and digging it out, as he later said, "in inchoate bits from the underground of my unconscious." He rewrote it at least four times, but even when it was finally published he found it necessary to excuse it as a book he had begun when he was very young.

Lawrence lived precariously from his writing. As one of the earliest of modern English novelists to employ the principles of psychoanalysis in fiction and to write openly about sexual impulses, his work was often banned in England and the United States. *The Rainbow*, completed in 1915, was suppressed, while for *Women in Love*, completed the following year, he could not find a publisher. *Lady Chatterley's Lover* (1928) stirred up immense controversy and was banned as obscene in the United Kingdom until 1960. Lawrence believed in the importance of emotion and sexual impulse, which he saw as expressions of creativity and true human nature.

Lawrence's illness and a need to find a more benevolent climate, as well as a desire to discover a lifestyle more fulfilling than that which the industrial West had to offer, took him all over the world. The time he spent in Italy, Sardinia, Australia, Mexico, and New Mexico gave him material for his travel books and background for other fiction.

He was gifted with incredible energy and worked at a headlong pace. Many people seemed to have disliked him for his tendency to engage in moral bullying. His wife attributed this to his disappointment over people's failure to overstep the bounds of conventions and relate to him at a deeper human level. Aldous Huxley blamed the erratic nature of his relationships on the essential solitude to which his gift condemned him. Yet he also wrote that as a companion Lawrence was never bored or boring. No task was too humble for him or lacked interest, whether it was cooking, sewing, milking a cow, or lighting a fire. His high spirits, moreover, wrote Huxley, were infectious, even during the last years of his life, when his illness was clearly gaining the upper hand.

Lawrence had a passionate dislike of science, believing that too much knowledge diminished human

---

FROM THE WRITINGS OF D. H. LAWRENCE

- My great religion is a belief in the blood, the flesh, as being wiser than the intellect. We can go wrong in our minds. But what the blood feels, and believes, and says is always true.
- No absolute is going to make the lion lie down with the lamb, unless the lamb is inside.
- In the dust where we have buried the silent races and their abominations, we have buried so much of the delicate magic of life.
- Freedom is a very great thing. But it means, above all, freedom from lies.
- Be a good animal. True to your animal instincts.
- If a woman hasn't got a tiny streak of a harlot in her, she's a dry stick.
- And Hamlet, how boring, how boring to live with. So mean and self-conscious, blowing and snoring. His wonderful speeches, full of other folks' whoring.
- Men must develop their poetic intelligence if they are ever going to be men.

---

sensitivity to the great mysteries. His esthetic principle was that art be totally spontaneous and, like its creators, imperfect, limited, and transient. Thus, rather than correcting his work, and so reducing its spontaneity, he rewrote his novels. He abandoned the conventions of character portrayal for his own theory, a philosophy which cared not so much about what a person feels as what that person is. As he wrote in a letter in 1914, "You mustn't look in my novel for the old stable ego of the character. There is another ego, according to whose action the individual is unrecognizable, and passes through, as it were, allotropic states which it needs a deeper sense than any we've been used to exercise to discover are states of the same single radically unchanged element."

In addition to novels he also published several volumes of poetry as well as miscellaneous works such as *Twilight in Italy* (1916), *Psychoanalysis and the Unconscious* (1921), and *Studies in Classical American Literature* (1923).

J. T. Boulton and M. H. Boulton, eds., *The Letters of D. H. Lawrence*, 6 vols., 1991.

J. Chambers, *D. H. Lawrence, A Personal Record*, 1980.

F. von Richthofen, *Not I, But the Wind*, 1983.

J. Worthen, *D. H. Lawrence: The Early Years 1885–1912*, 1991.

LAWRENCE, THOMAS EDWARD (Lawrence of Arabia; 1881–1935), British soldier and author. Lawrence was the second of five sons born to Sir Thomas Chapman and Sarah Maden. Chapman, a former land-owning Irish noble, fled Ireland with Maden, the governess to his daughters. Although the couple never married, they lived in Wales as Mr. and Mrs. Lawrence. In 1896, the family moved to Oxford, where Lawrence attended high school and Jesus College, Oxford University, where he studied medieval military architecture.

After traveling to France to study Crusader castles, Lawrence went on to Mesopotamia, where, from 1911 to 1914, he participated in an archeological expedition on the Euphrates River. While working on the dig, he learned fluent Arabic. Immersing himself deeply in the local culture, he adopted Arab dress and manners (retaining them even after his return to England) and became so well accepted that the people of the area often turned to him for advice on topics ranging from legal matters to marital matchmaking.

In 1914 Lawrence accompanied a map-making expedition to the northern Sinai desert, and was then drafted into military service, first as a map-maker for the British war department, later as an Arab affairs expert for the intelligence service in Cairo. In 1916 he was sent on an expedition to Arabia with Sir Ronald Storrs, entrusted with the mission of encouraging Arab revolt against the Ottoman Turks.

Persuading Faisal Husseini, a son of the emir of Mecca, to lead the revolt, Lawrence became its organizer and military technician. He proved himself a master of hit-and-run guerilla tactics, specializing in blowing up trains and railroads and in mining bridges; his bands made the Damascus-Medina railway inoperable. The Arabs succeeded in capturing Aqaba in July 1917 by attacking through the desert after a dangerous crossing on camels. The Turks, expecting an attack from the sea, had all their heavy artillery facing the wrong way and were completely wrong-footed. Lawrence was captured and tortured by Turkish officers, but was not recognized, which was fortunate for him as by this time he had a price on his head and would have been killed if his identity had been revealed.

Upon his release Lawrence led the Arabs to Damascus, the ultimate target of their campaign, in October 1918. Lawrence, who had been promoted to lieutenant colonel, soon returned to England. There, he was nominated for the Distinguished Service Order, a decoration he turned down in order to express his disapproval of British government treatment of its Arab allies.

Demobilized in 1919, Lawrence attended the Paris Peace Conference to lobby for the Arab cause. Throughout the conference, at which he served as an adviser and interpreter to Faisal, he wore Arab dress. Disillusioned with the treatment of the Arabs by the British and French, he returned to England. After a period spent teaching and beginning work on his book *The Seven Pillars of Wisdom* (published in 1926), he became an adviser on Arab affairs in Cairo to the then-colonial minister Winston *Churchill. Many of his contemporaries were surprised that such a restless adventurer would accept a desk job, asking of Churchill: "What! Wilt thou bridle the wild ass of the desert?"

As Churchill had anticipated, Lawrence performed well in the position, earning the praise and admiration of his minister. He proved a good team member and made a significant impact on the developing British policy in the Middle East, realizing some of the goals he had failed to achieve in Paris. When he considered his job well done, he left, telling his colleagues that "all you will see of me is a small cloud of dust on the horizon." He returned to England to finish work on *The Seven Pillars*. Churchill considered the work "unsurpassed as a portrayal of the Arabs," adding that "it ranks with the greatest books ever written in the English language."

At the beginning of the *Seven Pillars of Wisdom*, the publisher incorporated Lawrence's replies to queries from the book's proofreader.

Proofreader: There are many inconsistencies in the spelling of proper names.

Lawrence: I spell my names anyhow to prove what rot the systems are.

P: Jeddah and Jidda used impartially throughout. Is this intentional?

L: Rather

P: You use Ruwalla, Rualla, Rueli?

L: Should also have used Ruwala and Ruala.

P: Jedha, the she-camel, was previously spelled Jedhah.

L: She was a splendid beast.

P: "Meleager, the immoral poet." I have put "immortal" poet, but the author may mean immoral after all.

L: Immorality I know. Immortality I cannot judge. As you please: Meleager will not sue us for libel.

P: Sherif Abd el Mayin becomes El Main, el Mayein, el Muein, el Mayin, and Muyein.

L: Good egg. I call this really ingenious.

T. E. Lawrence in Aqaba, 1917

In later years, Lawrence sought privacy and anonymity through a return to the military, enlisting in the British Royal Air Force as a private under the alias John Hume Ross. However, after a London newspaper found him out and published his story, he was released from the air force. He then enlisted in the tank corps in 1923, calling himself T. E. Shaw (which legally became his name in 1927). In 1925 he rejoined the air force, from which he was discharged in 1935. He died in a motorcycle accident a few months later.

His idiosyncracies notwithstanding, Lawrence combined a rare blend of outstanding qualities: archeologist, scholar, philosopher, soldier, statesman, and writer. He was also a man who consistently backed up his strong beliefs with determined action.

B. H. Liddell Hart, *T. E. Lawrence: In Arabia and After*, 1964.

J. E. Mack, *Prince of Our Disorder: The Life of T. E. Lawrence*, 1978.

M. Yardley, *T. E. Lawrence: A Biography*, 1986.

LAYARD, SIR AUSTEN HENRY (1817–1894), British diplomat and archeologist who excavated Nineveh. He was born in Paris and educated in Italy, France, England, and Switzerland. He early developed a desire to travel but this was frustrated when his parents sent him to work in a solicitor's office in London, where he remained for six years. In 1839, when a relative offered to find him a job in the Ceylon civil service, he set out on a lengthy overland journey that turned out to be a series of adventures, especially in the Middle Eastern countries, where he

was enchanted by his visits to antiquities and ruins. He especially fell in love with Mesopotamia (modern-day Iraq) writing that "the huge mounds of Assyria made a deep impression on me." He decided not to proceed to Ceylon but returned to Constantinople, where he managed to get a job on the staff of the British ambassador to Turkey, Sir Stratford Canning, who was as fascinated with potential archeological discoveries as Layard.

In 1845 Canning agreed to provide initial financing for Layard to dig at the site of the ancient city of Nimrud, promising that if the excavations proved successful, he would get more money from the British government. En route, in Mosul, Layard put off the suspicious Turkish governor of the region with the pretext that he was on a hunting expedition, and made his way to the deserted mound of Nimrud, where he employed Arab workers from the vicinity.

On the first day of digging Layard discovered ruined buildings as well as many cuneiform inscriptions. In those days archeological methods were crude and he was unable to excavate each chamber he encountered, but by the end of the first day had found the remains of a royal palace. Word soon got back to Mosul and the governor, convinced that Layard was looking for treasure, stopped him. Layard had to go to Constantinople to have the governor's orders countermanded; on his return, he continued to make impressive discoveries, including sculptured bas-reliefs, inscriptions, and large sculptures, among them one depicting a magnificent human-headed bull.

The following year, Layard continued his work and uncovered the chambers of the palaces of the famous rulers of Assyria. His finds were moved on rollers across the desert and shipped from the Persian Gulf to London, where they remain the basis of the British Museum's magnificent Assyrian collection. Back in London in 1848, he published an immensely popular account of his work.

Returning to Iraq in 1849, he turned his attention to a mound which he identified as ancient Nineveh, and located the palace of *Sennacherib, the Assyrian king mentioned in the Bible; on the walls was a vast relief depicting Sennacherib's siege of Lachish in Palestine (described in 2 Kings 19). His greatest find at Nineveh was the royal library containing some twenty-six thousand tablets covering a wide variety of subjects from historical, literary, and religious compositions to scientific and medical documents. The ancient world of Assyria came alive as scholars studied and published these invaluable texts. In 1851 Layard returned to London, his archeological career completed.

In 1852 Layard became a member of parliament for Aylesbury, and for a few weeks held the post of under-secretary for foreign affairs. He left this post after openly criticizing the government, especially on matters concerning army administration. He was in the Crimea during the Crimean War, and was made a member of the committee appointed to investigate the British expedition there. In 1855 he was elected lord rector of Aberdeen University.

After failing to keep his seat at Aylesbury in 1857, Layard went on a visit to India to look into the causes of the mutiny. He was elected member of parliament for Southwark in 1860, and from 1861 to 1866 held the post of under-secretary for foreign affairs, first under Lord Henry John *Palmerston and then under Lord John Russell. In 1866 he became a trustee of the British Museum, and in 1868 was made chief commissioner of works in William *Gladstone's government. Layard retired from parliament in 1869 after being chosen as envoy extraordinary to Madrid. In 1877, Lord Beaconsfield appointed him ambassador at Constantinople, where he remained until 1880 when he retired from public life. He lived out his retirement in Venice, where he collected paintings from the Venetian school and wrote on Italian art.

A. C. Brackman, *The Luck of Nineveh,* 1978.

LE CORBUSIER (pseudonym of Charles-Edouard Jeanneret; 1887–1965), Swiss architect, painter, and writer. Born in La Chaux-de-Fonds in the Swiss Jura, Jeanneret became an apprentice engraver at the local art school when just fourteen. Four years later, he was working with an architect, René Chapallaz. In 1908 he went to Paris where he worked with Auguste Perret, who was experimenting with reinforced concrete and the uses of glass in architecture. The following year, Jeanneret traveled through Europe and went to Berlin, where he worked with Peter Behrens, and met Ludwig Mies van der Rohe and Walter Gropius who based their architecture on function and materials..

During World War I, Jeanneret planned what he called the "Dom-Ino" system of building to replace the devastation of Flanders, but the continuing war made rebuilding impossible. Still, the designs were innovative and effective: six stanchions, with slabs of concrete projecting over them, supported the walls, which could be made of glass, or any other desired material.

Jeanneret moved to Paris in 1917 and lived there for seventeen years. With Amédée Ozenfant, he published a declaration of "purist" principles called "*Après le Cubisme.*" For five years he and Ozenfant published a magazine, *L'Esprit nouveau,* in which they called for a halt to decadence, and for "order after the chaos of war." Jeanneret started calling himself "Le Corbusier," a family name he felt was more in character with his artistic personality than "Jeanneret." In partnership with his cousin, Pierre Jeanneret, he built homes for people who were advanced enough to accept his idea of a house being a "machine for living in." His homes for workers, which he called "Citrohan houses," were very successful, because they were adaptable to the necessities of the individual families. He was then asked to make a model of a city for the Paris autumn Salon To be built of concrete and steel, with glass skyscrapers, parks, and a central transportation complex with many levels, his city was rejected as too radical for the 1920s..

After the Germans invaded France in World War II, the Vichy government issued an edict allowing le Corbusier to continue his work, and in 1942 Phillipe *Pétain appointed le Corbusier director of housing and real estate. Because of his ties to the Vichy government, he found it difficult to find people to work for him, so he concentrated on painting and writing.

After the war ended, le Corbusier reorganized his office, hiring part-time workers at low wages. In Marseilles, he built what he called "the universal solution to mass housing" for the French government. The handsome concrete building itself was a huge framework, into which could be fitted twenty-one varieties of prefabricated apartments. The building stands on huge supporting stilts that allow passage underneath. It accommodates sixteen hundred inhaitants, and has a pool, a track for running, and children's playgrounds. Its size, however, made it difficult to emulate in already existing neighborhoods.

During the postwar period, Le Corbusier was active in painting and sculpture; he went to the United States, where traveling shows of his artwork originated at the Walker Art Center in Minneapolis, and at the Boston Institute of Contemporary Art. In 1951, when Jawarhalal *Nehru planned a capital city, for the state of Punjab in newly independent India, he asked Le Corbusier to design it. Le Corbusier tried to emulate the delicacy and grace of Mogul architecture, while his buildings were planned to epitomize the new democracy. He worked on this city of Chandigarh until 1964, spending two months a year in India.

During the same period, he built his famous chapel and monastery of Notre-Dame du Haut, at Ronchamps, using the remnants of the previous chapel, which had been destroyed during the war. Light entered the interior through apertures in the heavy concave and convex walls; the east wall was designed as an outdoor chapel, where pilgrims could pray. The complex was built over a slope, the monastery soaring over the hill on stilts, with walks at different levels available from the monks' cells.

Le Corbusier completed his book, *Mise au Point,* in 1965. That year, on 27 August, he was drowned in an accident while swimming at Cap Martin in the south of France. A man of ideas, he wrote copiousl, and left thousands of architectural plans and sketches. His work has been and still is influencing architecture in all continents. Simplicity and the spirit of the times; were his artistic concerns. The most important element, he believed, was the intention governing the methods, the materials, and the final result. Construction was taking materials and building a house or even a palace — but architecture, consists of making something beautiful, touching the heart.

His reinforced concrete vertical stanchions supported the buildings, freeing the interior from the necessity of being determined by the walls, and per-

FROM THE WRITINGS
OF LE CORBUSIER

- Architecture is the magnificen,knowledge-able, and correctplay of volumes under light.
- The esential joys are sun, space, and ver-dure, which should be the foundation of machine-age town planning in every conti-nent.
- The four essentials of urbanism are dwelling, working, cultivating mind and body, and cir-culating.
- A great architecture must not only express a manner of living; it must inaugurate and im-pose one… in an ailing society,it is the duty of the artist to build.

mitting "picture" windows and glass facades. With his use of stilts, he lifted his buildings into the air. He admired the pure line of a flat roof against the sky, but also saw it as living space, a roof garden, for instance. The buildings that Le Corbusier created were designed to make the most of their sites and to function according to the needs of their inhabitants Jacques Guiton, ed., *The Ideas of le Corbusier on Architecture and Urban Planning*, 1981.

LEE, ROBERT EDWARD (1807–1870), general of the Confederate army in the American Civil War. Best known for his role as an almost–legendary Civil War general, Lee is one of the few military geniuses who gained fame mainly through his actions in de-feat. He was born in Westmoreland County, Virginia, the son of a famous American Revolution cavalry officer, Henry "Lighthorse Harry" Lee. Lee was raised as a Southern gentleman, albeit in near poverty because his father had squandered his and both his wives' family fortunes, even spending some time in prison because of his debts. After his father's death when he was only eleven, Lee took over fam-ily responsibility, caring for his mother and sisters. He was a pious and honest man, never smoked or drank and was friendly and even-tempered, his pri-vate life untouched by any hint of scandal.

At the age of eighteen Lee entered West Point, where he graduated second in his class, never having received a single demerit. He entered the army's pres-tigious Corps of Engineers and distinguished himself through his service in Mexico in 1846. Meanwhile, in 1831 Lee had married Mary Anne Randolph Custis, the daughter of George *Washington's adopted son. The couple had seven children; their three sons all later served as Confederate soldiers. In 1857 Mary's father died, and the Lee family took up residence at her family estate in Arlington, Virginia.

After the Mexican War, Lee took charge of the construction of Fort Carroll in Baltimore Harbor. Following this assignment, Lee became superinten-dent of West Point in 1852. He soon tired of acade-mic life and, in 1855, transferred to the Second Cavalry Division, serving in Missouri, Kansas, and Texas, where the cavalry protected settlers from rov-ing bands of Indians.

Home on leave in Arlington in 1859, Lee was ap-pointed to lead the troops that put down abolitionist John Brown's raid on Harper's Ferry. He then went back to Texas, remaining until February 1861. On his return to Arlington, Lee realized that the grow-ing tension between North and South meant that he would have to decide whether he owed greater loy-alty to his country or to his native state. Lee disapproved of slavery and had freed his own slaves years before the war. He was deeply distressed by the thought of the dissolution of the Union, but nonetheless decided that his primary duty lay in loy-alty to his home state. Therefore in April 1861, when Lee was offered field command of the United States Army, he declined the position and resigned his commission in the army. He intended to remain a private citizen and wrote to his brother that, "Save in defense of my native state, I have no desire ever again to draw my sword." Soon after the governor of Virginia offered him command of that state's army, which he accepted.

In the field, Lee eschewed the privileges generally taken by officers. Not wanting to displace civilians from their homes, he lived in a tent and kept a mini-mum of aides-de-camp and servants. Lee's first field test came in June 1862 when, after he took over command from the wounded General A. E. John-ston, the army of Northern Virginia forced General George B. McClellan's Union troops to withdraw from their siege of Richmond. In August of the same year Lee, aided by Generals Thomas J. "Stonewall" Jackson and James Longstreet, faced the Union's General John Pope at Second Bull Run. Lee devised a bold plan for his greatly outnumbered troops, di-viding the army and sending Jackson, with three divisions, around Pope's army to a point twenty-four miles behind the line of battle. Lee's daring strategy gained him his first decisive field victory.

Lee then moved his troops into Maryland and at-tempted to gain Marylanders' support for the South; the response was less enthusiastic than he had hoped. In a further stroke of bad luck, Union soldiers found a copy of Lee's orders for the invasion of Maryland, giv-ing McClellan a valuable edge in the upcoming confrontation at Antietam (Sharpsburg). Despite that setback, Lee swiftly and elegantly maneuvered his troops in what historians call his most brilliant perfor-mance ever. The Antietam campaign, which included "the bloodiest single day of the war," on which over twenty-three thousand soldiers were killed and wounded and over twenty-seven hundred were missing (on both sides), could have resulted in the destruction of the Confederate army and the end of the war. But Lee's brilliance, coupled with McClellan's indecisive-ness, turned what could have been annihilation into a mere defeat, with Lee withdrawing to Virginia.

BY AND ABOUT LEE

- Men must be habituated to obey or they cannot be controlled in battle, and the neglect of the least important order impairs the proper influence of the officer.
- Well, well, General, bury these poor men and let us say no more about it (order, after the Battle of Bristoe Station).
- Never mind, General, all this has been my fault, it is I that have lost the fight, and you must help me out of it the best way you can (order to General Wilcox after the Battle of Gettysburg).
- It is well that war is so terrible — we would grow too fond of it.

Robert E. Lee

- Lee is the only man I know whom I would follow blindfold.

General Thomas J. Jackson

- If I were on my deathbed and the President should tell me that a great battle was to be fought for the liberty or slavery of my country, and asked my judgment as to who should be commander, I would say with my dying breath, let it be Robert E. Lee.

General Winfield Scott

- One of the greatest captains known in the annals of war.

Winston Churchill

His next two engagements, against General Ambrose E. Burnside at Fredericksburg in November and at Chancellorsville in May 1863, brought victories to the South. Lee then decided to invade the North and drove his troops up the Shenandoah Valley, through Maryland and into Pennsylvania, where his next major battle took place at Gettysburg in July 1863. Bad judgment and delays by Lee's subordinate officers in carrying out his orders cost him severely. The end of the first day's fighting saw a decided Confederate victory, with Union troops retreating in disarray and panic. It was here that the Confederacy could have won the battle and, possibly, the war. Lee saw that the Union troops were beaten and tired and he knew that they could not withstand another assault. He also understood that whoever controlled the hills would command the battle. Knowing this, he told General Richard Ewell to "take that hill if at all practicable," but Ewell had made the fateful decision to

wait until morning, giving the Union army all night to receive reinforcements and build barricades. On the second day of the battle Lee tried to crack the Union flanks. By then, however, they were well anchored and fortified and the assaults failed. On the third and final day Lee, feeling that he had no alternative, took a big gamble, sending 15,000 men in a charge, (Pickett's Charge) against the Union center. The men broke through briefly but, to Lee's horror, the surviving gray troops soon came wearily down the hill and Lee conceded, "this is all my fault." The Southern forces retreated to Virginia to regroup, expecting a counterattack, which never came. Casualties at Gettysburg numbered more than one third of the Virginia army's troops. Lee accepted blame for the defeat and offered his resignation, which was refused.

Lee's troops were severely lacking in supplies and rations throughout the rest of 1863 and early 1864 but resumed fighting in May 1864, sparring with General Ulysses S. *Grant in the battle of the Wilderness and forcing the Union troops to a standstill. The Petersburg campaign began in June and dragged on for months, wearing down the poorly fed and badly equipped Confederate troops. In February 1865, Lee became general-in-chief of all Confederate armies, by then an almost meaningless title. In April, as Federal troops closed in, Lee ordered the evacuation of Petersburg and Richmond. He remained in retreat until his surrender to Grant at Appomattox Court House.

Lee had lost his United States citizenship because he had served as a Confederate officer and, after the war, was indicted for treason, but the case was allowed to lapse. Lee urged his troops and all Southerners to accept the Union victory and help to rebuild their country. He applied for the restoration of his citizenship and swore a loyalty oath before a notary, but by accident his citizenship was not restored until an act of Congress in 1975 corrected the oversight.

After the war Lee accepted the presidency of Washington College (later renamed Washington and Lee University) in Lexington, Virginia. He rebuilt and revitalized the war-ravaged college and after his death on October 12, 1870, was buried in the university chapel.

B. Davis, *Gray Fox: Robert E. Lee and the Civil War*, 1956.
P. Earle, *Robert E. Lee*, 1973.
F. Lee, *General Lee*, 1961.
R. Wheeler, *Lee's Terrible Swift Sword*, 1992.

LEEUWENHOEK, ANTON VAN (1632–1723), Dutch biologist. Born in Delft, Holland, son of a basket maker, Philips Thoniszoon, who died when his son was six years old. The surname by which he became famous was taken from a house named "Lion's Corner" which his father owned.

Leeuwenhoek was educated at Warmond grammar school and in 1648 commenced an apprenticeship to an Amsterdam cloth merchant. He returned to his native town and opened a draper's shop in 1652. In 1660 he obtained a sinecure position as an usher at Delft town hall, a post he retained for the rest of his life. In 1677 he was made chief warden and in 1679 winegauger. His business was prosperous and the additional income from municipal office meant he could afford to give time to scientific experiment.

Leeuwenhoek was familiar with the glasses used to inspect the quality of cloth. He experimented with grinding glass and mounting the lens on a specimen holder that could be revolved in three planes: the result was an effective microscope. He was not the first person to make such a device but the lenses he ground were of greater mathematical accuracy and power than any previously known. Although these lenses were tiny and of short focus, they provided almost two hundred times magnification. In the course of his life he ground 419 lenses, attaining as much as five hundred times magnification. With this powerful microscope an exciting new world of biological observation opened up. Within a few years of commencing his experiments in 1671, Leeuwenhoek discovered that microorganisms are living creatures and was the first to reveal the single-celled organisms now called protozoa. Leeuwenhoek investigated the life cycle of the flea and found "this minute and despised creature...endowed with as great perfection in its kind as any large animal." He even found tiny parasites living on fleas and this find brought him the distinction of inspiring the poet Jonathan *Swift to write:

So naturalists observe, a flea
Has smaller fleas that on him prey;
And these have smaller still to bite 'em;
And so proceed ad infinitum.

Taking samples from such varied sources as ditch water, tooth scrapings, and sperm, Leeuwenhoek made significant contributions to man's knowledge of bacteria. He developed a method for measuring such minute creatures, using for a scale such tiny objects as a hair from his beard and a grain of sand.

Leeuwenhoek's research extended understanding of the fertilization process in animals and plants. It had been believed for many years that certain tiny creatures like fleas or weevils in grain were generated spontaneously or somehow developed out of the decay of natural matter. He demonstrated conclusively that they were really little creatures with reproductive processes comparable to those in larger animals. In the same way he refuted the widespread belief that eels developed from dew: his studies showed that they had an ordinary process of generation.

A Dutch correspondent of the Royal Society of London initiated a correspondence between Leeuwenhoek and the society in 1673. At first members were skeptical concerning his work but he sent to London twenty-six microscopes so they could make their own investigations to confirm his conclusions. Contact with the Royal Society was important in disseminating this new knowledge since he did not publish his findings until 1684 and he wrote mostly in Dutch, a language not widely read outside Holland. In 1680 he was elected a fellow of the Royal Society and in 1697 he was similarly honored by the Paris Academy of Sciences.

His discoveries brought Leeuwenhoek international fame and he was visited by many of the great figures of Europe, including King James II of England and Czar *Peter the Great of Russia. In Delft his achievements were not properly understood and he was annoyed to find many townsmen considered him a magician. The municipality, however, did show appreciation to their most eminent citizen, awarding a pension. He was able to continue his work into a ripe old age.

C. Dobell, *Antony van Leeuwenhoek*, 1960.
A. Schierbeek, *Measuring the Invisible World*, 1959.

LEIBNIZ, GOTTFRIED WILHELM (1646–1716),

German philosopher, mathematician, scientist, courtier, diplomat, and man of letters. A man of universal attainments, Leibniz contributed to logic, mathematics, jurisprudence, history, linguistics, theology, and metaphysics. Leibniz has also been characterized as a man of meaner moral than mental stature. Bertrand Russell considered that "he had the virtues that one would wish to find mentioned in a testimonial to a prospective employee: he was industrious, frugal, temperate, and financially honest...but he was wholly destitute of the higher philosophic virtues." One of his problems was that he had no independent source of income and had to retain the approbation of his employers; as a result, he was moved to conceal that of his work which he considered might offend them. Only in the last century, as more of his voluminous papers have been brought to light, has the full scope of his activity been revealed.

Born into a pious Lutheran family in Leipzig, Leibniz was largely self-taught in the extensive library of his father, a professor of moral philosophy. A precocious and ambitious student, he left Leipzig for good in 1666 when he was not allowed to study for his doctorate in law there, on the grounds that he was too young. This marked the beginning of Leibniz's lifelong peregrinations: ever after he remained an indefatigable traveler. In contrast, Altdorf, the university town of the free city of Nuremberg, not only allowed him to pursue his doctoral studies but also offered him a professorial chair. This Leibniz declined, on the grounds that he had "very different things in view."

In 1667 he entered the political service of the powerful archbishop elector of Mainz and as his emissary Leibniz sought to deflect the predatory *Louis XIV's attentions away from the Holy Roman Empire and toward Egypt. The four years that he spent in Paris in pursuit of this goal were of great significance to his intellectual development, since the city was at that time the philosophical and mathematical center of the western world. It was here that Leibniz developed the foundations of integral and differential calculus, which he was to publish in

1684, in ignorance of Isaac *Newton's previous but unpublished work on the same subject. The subsequent dispute over the authorship of the ideas was bitter and was one of the reasons he did not accompany his patron, George Louis of Brunswick, to England when the latter was declared George I in 1714: the country was hostile to him for he had crossed her intellectual hero. The fact that he had seen various unpublished papers by Newton while making his way back to Hanover in 1676 (at which time he had also met and compared notes with Baruch *Spinoza) only further increased suspicions that his brilliantly original mathematical work had been a plagiarism.

Leibniz became an employee of the house of Brunswick in 1676, when John Frederick was duke, and served it faithfully for the rest of his life. Only an individual of phenomenal energy — he was a workaholic — could have pursued so many disparate interests: although deeply immersed in the realpolitik of the petty German dukedoms, he continued to invent, write, and correspond prodigiously (maintaining contact with some six hundred individuals through his letters). In addition to perfecting binary numeration and developing topology, he invented a mining pump that significantly ameliorated conditions in mines while, through his genealogical researches, he helped John Frederick's successor, Augustus, to inherit another electorate. George Louis's boorishness encouraged Leibniz to spend as much time outside Hanover as he could after the former's succession in 1698; between 1711 and 1714 he acted as the emperor's adviser in Vienna. He had wished in 1714 to attend his patron's coronation but was ordered to remain in Hanover and continue his work on the history of Brunswick. George I's displeasure with Leibniz increased after he became king of England, possibly due to the influence of Newton's friends. Leibniz spent his last two years neglected, in virtual house arrest, and his death aroused no interest in Hanover, London, or Berlin. Only his secretary attended his funeral. However, in Paris a memorial oration was pronounced by Bernard de Fontenelle, the distinguished president of the Academy of Sciences.

In his philosophy, substances must be real unities and cannot be affected by anything outside themselves. The essence of material substance is not extension, nor even motion, but force, a character inside things that is presupposed by solidity and motion. The universe consists of an infinity of substances, which Leibniz called "monads." These are only apparently interactive insofar as God has so arranged that the behavior and movements of individual monads will correspond to create a semblance of causally related actions and events; in fact, this causal interrelatedness is wholly contingent since it simply represents a whim of God. At the same time, there is a prearranged harmony that gives the universe its unity; without this there would

Queen Sophie Charlotte of Prussia entertaining Leibniz

be a chaotic and absurd plurality. Reality is governed not by mechanical laws but by laws of reason. His pious doctrine that this is the best of all possible worlds led to his being ferociously satirized (as Dr Pangloss) by Francois-Marie *Voltaire in *Candide* and was later to inspire W. H. Bradley's retort "and everything in it is a necessary evil."

Leibniz's grasp of the importance of mathematical logic was far ahead of its time while his assertion that (contrary to the view expounded by Newton) space is not an absolute is still of great relevance in relating perception to physics. In the history of philosophy he is recognized as one of the greatest of system-builders and is one of the fathers of modern philosophical thought, chiefly through his influence on Immanuel *Kant.

S. C. Brown, *Leibniz*, 1984.
N. Jolley, *The Light of the Soul*, 1990.
B. Mater, *The Philosophy of Leibniz*, 1986.
G. R. Ross, *Leibniz*, 1984.

LEIF ERIKSSON (d. 1020), Viking explorer, widely considered to be the first European to explore North America. "Leif the Lucky," younger son of *Erik the Red, was apparently born in Iceland but emigrated to Greenland with his family when his father was exiled following a murder charge. Eriksson traveled to Norway in the early 990s to serve as a retainer at the court of King Olaf Trygvasson. There he adopted Christianity, which he brought back to Greenland on his return. That journey, however, was marked by harsh storm winds, causing Eriksson's ship to lose course. After sighting the coast of North

America he managed to return to Greenland, where he reported on the new lands.

Although other Greenlanders, notably Bjarni Herjulfsson, had spotted the North American coastline, no one had set out to explore the region or examine settlement possibilities. In 1001, leading a crew of thirty-five, Eriksson sailed south from Greenland. The first land he encountered was an inhospitable mass of glaciers and rock slabs, generally identified as Baffin Island; he called the area Helluland ("Slab Land"). Sailing south, Eriksson discovered sandy beaches leading to dense forest. This area, apparently on the Labrador coast, he called Markland ("Forest Land"). The explorers then discovered an island described as having the "sweetest dew we have ever tasted."

Eriksson spent the next day sailing around the opposite headland until he found a suitable harbor. The site, with lush pastureland and abundant salmon fishing, was chosen as a good place to make camp and the crew disembarked. According to the writer of the saga, in the commotion of making a campsite, they failed to notice that one of their members, Tyrkir, was missing. Just as Eriksson had organized a search party, a drunken Tyrkir staggered into the camp, explaining that he had eaten some wild grapes. After confirming Tyrkir's claim, Eriksson decided to call the country Vinland. In fact, Vinland comes from the old Norse meaning "meadow land" but was later misinterpreted.

Archeologists and scholars have argued over the precise location of Vinland. Claims range from as far north as Labrador and Newfoundland to as far south as Florida, and as far west as Minnesota. A number of clever forgeries of Viking remains and runic script were exposed in the 1960s, but the debate continues. Two possible locations are Quebec and Virginia.

After spending a year in Vinland, Eriksson returned home to Greenland. Attempts to settle the new lands failed, although the Greenland settlers apparently traveled to Vinland frequently to fish and harvest timber. Eriksson remained in Greenland until his death in 1020.

E. F. Gray, *Leif Eriksson*, 1972.

H. Ingstad, *Westward to Vinland*, 1969.

F. D. Logan, *The Vikings in History*, 1980.

M. Magnusson and H. Palsson, *The Vinland Sagas: The Norse Discovery of America*, 1965.

LENIN (ULYANOV), VLADIMIR ILYICH

(1870–1924), Russian Communist leader. Talk of revolution was commonplace for the children of a respectable mathematics teacher named Ulyanov. His elder son, Alexander, was executed in 1887 for plotting to kill the czar, and his younger son, Vladimir Ilyich, only lasted one month at university before being expelled for taking part in a demonstration. In an early display of resilience in the face of setbacks, Vladimir Ilyich completed his law studies on his own, and in 1890 got a degree from the University of Saint Petersburg. Although he now entered legal practice, illegal activities remained his chief interest; from an early age he believed in the propagation of Marxist philosophy as the panacea for the ills of oppressed Russia.

Vladimir Ilyich traveled around Europe making connections in revolutionary circles and returned to Russia loaded with subversive literature; the police caught up with him and he was exiled to Siberia. It was not a harsh imprisonment: he had time to pursue his studies and write pamphlets in milk — the words only became visible after the paper was dipped in tea and warmed. He could also relax with a little snipe hunting, and courted his fellow exile Nadezhda Krupskaya, whom he married 1898.

In 1900 Vladimir Ilyich started a newspaper that was printed in Switzerland and smuggled into Russia; he now assumed the name "Lenin." In 1903 he initiated a split in the Russian Socialist party between those favoring his revolutionary approach and others more inclined to social democracy; his majority faction became known as "Bolsheviks," his opponents "Mensheviks." For many years Lenin and his wife led a peripatetic life, traveling round Europe, busy with party intrigues and with organizing a series of terrorist acts, ostensibly to provide funds for the organization. Their income was low and their living quarters and diet were basic but they were totally absorbed in the dissemination of their ideology and material comfort was not a high priority.

Lenin did not join in the popular Russian uprising of 1905, biding his time for the revolution he was awaiting. In the relatively prosperous years that followed, Bolshevik fortunes suffered a downturn. However, the onset of World War I saw a series of serious military setbacks that led to growing civil unrest in Russia. In February 1917 liberal democrats overthrew the czarist government. Lenin was in Switzerland at the time, and might have died in obscurity but for the fact that the German government wanted to encourage unrest in Russia to cripple the Russian war effort. It therefore had Lenin transported across Germany in a sealed railway carriage, and on into Russia. He became a popular speaker at antigovernment rallies, also attacking the Socialists who supported the government. He was soon forced to leave in the face of popular hostility, the provisional government denouncing him as a German agent.

Undaunted, Lenin soon returned in disguise, wearing a wig and with his beard shaven. Working in unison with Leon *Trotsky and using the slogan "bread, peace, and land," he organized the relatively bloodless coup that toppled the provisional government and gave him the long-awaited opportunity to introduce the dictatorship of the Communist party with himself in the position of president. One of the first acts of the new government was to sue for peace with Germany, yielding up a quarter of the Russian Empire to achieve this end. Russian troops were in no mood to continue the czar's war but were, in Lenin's words "voting with their feet" for

Left: Lenin addressing a crowd on Sverdlov Square, May 5, 1920, with Trotsky and Kamenev beside him

Right: The same scene (retouched under Stalin), minus the presence of Trotsky and Kamenev

peace on any terms. Besides, Lenin was sure that the Communist party would soon come to power in Germany, too, so Russia's loss of land need only be a short-term one.

Peace was achieved rapidly, but the application of communist theory to the economy was difficult: the abolition of private trade was unpopular, and when party officials organized the seizure of crops from the peasants, they cut back their production, adding famine to the long list of the country's afflictions. Resistance to the communist takeover was supported by foreign military intervention and bitter civil war raged. In 1921, the Red Army defeated the last of the invading armies but at the cost of a country laid waste.

Lenin's response to opposition was the initiation of the violent crackdown on dissent that became a characteristic of the new state. Arguing that "the cruelty, which the conditions of our life make necessary, will in the future be understood and vindicated," he did not hesitate to eliminate brutally all who might threaten the new order, exemplifying the belief that the end justifies the means. However, although his hatred for him was strong, Lenin opposed the shooting of the czar on the grounds that it would damage Russia's already poor international relations, while he was against the killing of the rest of the royal family on humanitarian grounds; the execution subsequently was initiated and organized by others.

Meanwhile, the man who had inherited the czar's dictatorial powers did not assume a lifestyle commensurate with the office: Lenin would only accept the wages of a skilled worker and slept on an iron bedstead in an uncarpeted room in the Kremlin, continuing to live the life of an impoverished exile.

In 1919 Lenin established the Third International to foster world revolution. The unpopularity of the new regime was reflected in an attempt on his life in 1918, and in 1921 the sailors at the Kronstadt naval base, who had been key supporters of the 1917 revolution, now rose in revolt against their new masters. Lenin at last took note and decided that the path to a socialist Russia had to be taken more slowly. He allowed a return to private trade and

agriculture under the auspices of the New Economic Policy, launched in 1921. Lenin did not live to see the success of these reforms. In 1922 he suffered a paralytic stroke; two other strokes followed over the next two years, creating the power vacuum that was filled by Stalin. In his last days, Lenin tried to prevent Stalin's succession, but by then it was too late.
H. Draper, *"The Dictatorship of the Proletariat" from Marx to Lenin*, 1987.
L. Fischer, *The Life of Lenin*, 1964.
P. Leblanc, *Lenin and the Revolutionary Party*, 1990.
L. Schapiro, *The Communist Party of the Soviet Union*, 2nd ed., 1970.
D. Schub, *Lenin*, 1966.

LEONARDO DA VINCI (1452–1519), Italian painter, sculptor, architect, scientist, military engineer, and inventor; the embodiment of universal genius known as a Renaissance man. The illegitimate child of a notary and a peasant girl, he was brought up on his father's estate in Vinci, a Tuscan village between Florence and Pisa. As a boy he was talented in writing and music, but painting was his greatest interest, and he was placed in the studio of Andrea del Verrocchio, the Florentine sculptor, whose intellectual curiosity and pursuit of knowledge were inspiring to his young assistant. He worked with Verrocchio until 1478. At twenty da Vinci became a member of the guild of artists. While he was working with Verrocchio he was arraigned on a charge of sodomy and imprisoned for two months, but the case was dismissed because of lack of evidence.

In 1481 he started work on the *Adoration of the Magi* and a *Saint Jerome*, but left for Milan before they were completed. In Milan he applied to Duke Ludovico Sforza for a commission to sculpt an equestrian statue of the duke's father, saying that he was also competent as a military engineer. He received the commission and worked on the statue for sixteen years. Although he had interested himself in the process of casting in bronze, he had never learned the requirements of the process for sculpting. "The Horse" was therefore never cast and the clay model was eventually destroyed by French soldiers.

In addition to designs of canals and artillery pieces for the duke, Leonardo designed pageants and masquerades for the duchess's entertainments. He painted the duke and duchess and many of their courtiers and was rewarded with expensive gifts and a good salary. He also painted the beautiful *Madonna of the Rocks* for the Confraternity of the Immaculate Conception, but sued for the return of the painting when they paid him a meager sum. The suit dragged on for years.

Duke Ludovico ordered the artist to paint the *Last Supper* on the refectory wall of the convent of Santa Maria della Grazie. The artist worked very slowly, making many studies for the heads of *Jesus and the disciples, and spending much time just looking at what he had done before he took up his brushes again. Unfortunately, Leonardo's compulsion to experiment resulted in the use of a medium that was not compatible with the ground. He completed the painting but twenty years later the paint had begun to flake off.

In 1497 the duchess died, and with her death Leonardo's salary stopped. The duke was forced to leave Milan, which shortly afterward was captured by the French; by that time Leonardo had already left.

In the spring of 1500 the painter was in Florence, where he was inspired by the atmosphere. He did more work in his six years in Florence than in all the years he had worked in Milan. It was there that he painted the *Mona Lisa*, one of the world's most famous portraits. He worked on it for four years; it is said that he used a compass to construct the famous "enigmatic" smile. The model was Lisa Gherardini, wife of a wealthy merchant. The critic Giorgio Vasari reported that da Vinci engaged musicians, singers, and jesters to keep her merry "and remove that melancholy which painting usually gives to... portraits." King *Francis I of France bought the painting, and it found its home in the Louvre.

He was commissioned to paint an altarpiece for the church of Santissima Annunziata. His first cartoon, on the subject of the Virgin and Child and Saint Anne, was rejected because it was "only beautiful," not instructive. The second, however, showed Saint Anne with the Virgin in her lap, both rising to support the Child, who is reaching for a lamb (the symbol of sacrifice). This version was accepted and the painting was highly acclaimed.

Leonardo left Florence to work on military projects for Caesar Borgia (see *Borgia Family), who was campaigning in the Romagna, but when Borgia ordered the assassination of Leonardo's good friend Vitellozzo Vitello, who was one of Caesar's own officers, Leonardo returned to Florence. There he received a commission to make a fresco mural for the Sala di Gran Consiglio in the Palazzo della Signoria. *Michelangelo received the commission to do a mural for the opposite wall. The rivalry of these

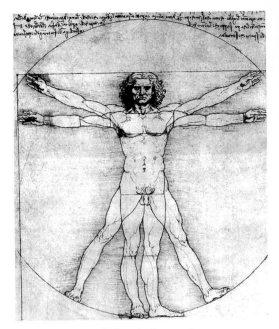

The Proportions of Man, *by Leonardo*

two giants divided the city into two camps. The two cartoons were made and exhibited — much visited and copied. However, neither Leonardo nor Michelangelo finished his fresco. Leonardo, as usual, experimented. The new plaster which he used did not set; he started the work but soon gave up.

In May 1506 he went to Milan for nine months to work for the French king Louis XII and painted the king's portrait. Although he was the official architect and engineer for the French government in Milan, Leonardo spent much time designing pageants and studying various branches of life sciences and geology. In 1509 he wrote his *Trattato de Divina Proportione*, for which he made sixty geometric designs.

Da Vinci met a handsome young artist, Francesco Melzi, and visited him at his family's home in Vaprio for two months. When Giovanni de' Medici (see *Medici Family) became Pope Leo X, Leonardo, with Melzi, went to Rome. The pope's brother, Giuliano de' Medici, Leonardo's patron, arranged for Leonardo to occupy an apartment in the Vatican.

Leonardo was now over sixty years of age and not too pleased with his new situation. His neighbors complained to the pope about him because he studied anatomy by dissecting cadavers. He lived quietly and modestly, tending to be withdrawn and antisocial; his neighbors intruded on his privacy and got on his nerves. Nevertheless, he continued with his studies and writings and completed several paintings.

After Giuliano de' Medici died, *Francis I, who had ascended the throne of France the previous year

(1515), invited Leonardo to come to live in France, appointing him First Royal Painter, Architect, and Engineer. Francis sincerely admired Leonardo for his artistic genius and his intellect and gave him a liberal pension, as well as the castle of Cloux near the royal residence at Amboise. He appointed Melzi to the position of Gentleman of the Chamber, and often visited Leonardo.

To the great grief of King Francis, Leonardo died at Cloux. He left his manuscripts, his drawings, and his books to Francesco Melzi. None of his writings — several thousand pages, all written in his left-handed "mirror-writing" — had been published. These included his many notebooks, and treatises on the art of painting, on harmony, optics, and aeronautics (he designed a flying machine). There was nothing that did not interest him. If there were phenomena that puzzled him he devised experiments to help him understand — experiments which often resulted in important contributions to the field he was exploring. He also left thousands of pen and ink and chalk sketches on a wide range of subjects.

Leonardo's powerful mind and the diversity of his accomplishments have remained an object of wonder and admiration. He is appreciated as much for his contributions to knowledge and thought as for his artistic genius.

S. Bramly, *Leonardo, the Artist and the Man*, 1992.
K. Clark, *Leonardo da Vinci*, 1989.
R. L. Douglas, *Leonardo da Vinci: His Life and His Pictures*, 1944.
J. Wasserman, *Leonarde da Vinci,* 1992.
V. P. Zubov, *Leonardo da Vinci*, 1968.

LERMONTOV, MIKHAIL YURYEVICH

(1814–1841), Russian poet and novelist. He was a descendant of George Learmont, a Scottish mercenary who settled in Russia in the early 17th century. Lermontov's mother, of a more aristocratic background than his father, died when he was very young and he was brought up by his wealthy grandmother. He first attempted poetry when he was thirteen and under the spell of the *Byron cult. At sixteen, following an unhappy love affair, he wrote his first cycle of love poems.

In 1830 he began studying at Moscow University but was barred from taking an examination for "riotous conduct" — in his own words, "poetry, drowned in champagne." He went to Saint Petersburg but instead of entering the university there, he enrolled in a military academy and in 1834 received a commission in the Guards.

In 1837 the death of Alexander *Pushkin in a duel aroused Lermontov's wrath, and he wrote a poem expressing his despair and anger at the circumstances surrounding Pushkin's untimely death. Castigating the "greedy servility about the throne" that "hide[s] behind the law's corrupted name," the poem was too politically dangerous to be published, but was circulated privately and came to the attention of Czar Nicholas I. As a result Lermontov was court-martialed and sent to a regiment stationed in the Caucasus.

After less than a year he was pardoned and restored to his previous rank in the Guards, but the short time spent in the Caucasus had revived his old Byronic leanings and in 1838 he returned to Saint Petersburg, this time with a growing reputation as a poet.

In 1837 and 1838 he published more poetry and in 1839 he began publishing frequently in *Notes of the Fatherland*, a magazine founded by a friend of his. In 1840 a selection of his poems and the short novel *A Hero of Our Times* appeared in book form, to immediate acclaim. The book was a tale-within-a-tale of military and romantic adventure in the Caucasus.

During these years Lermontov shunned literary circles but was interested in political questions; in 1836–1837 he belonged to a secret debating group. He also had no great liking for fashionable society. A duel with the son of the French ambassador, fought on a trivial pretext, led to another court-martial and a second exile to a Caucasus-based regiment. This time he saw active duty and was recommended for awards, which were not, however, approved by the authorities. In 1841 he visited Pyatigorsk, a Caucasian spa, where he was challenged by a Major Martynov, a former school friend. The two were rivals for a lady's affections and Martynov took exception to Lermontov's public taunts. The duel took place on July 15 and Lermontov was killed on the spot by a bullet in his heart. A few months before his death he had written a poem in which he described his own dead body with a bullet in its heart lying in a "valley of Dagestan at noon."

His first formal publication was *Hajji Abrek*, a Caucasian tale of revenge in verse which appeared in 1835, but his official literary career is considered to have begun with his poem on Pushkin. After his death, collections of his juvenilia were published; his output between the ages of fourteen and eighteen included three hundred lyrics, fifteen long narrative poems, three prose plays and one prose tale. These works, while not of high literary quality, already display the themes that Lermontov was to employ in the last five years of his life as he moved from romanticism to a form of realism. His creativity was original in its technical details, depth, caustic wit, and in its simple, clear style. His influence on the development of Russian literature was great and can be seen in the works of the great Russian writers of the nineteenth and twentieth centuries.

B. M. Erkhenbaum, *Lermontov*, 1981.
C. E. L'Ami and A. Weliktory, *Mikhail Lermontov: Biography and Translation*, 1967.
J. Lavrin, *Lermontov*, 1959.

LESSEPS, FERDINAND MARIE, DE

(1805–1894), French diplomat and engineer who promoted and executed the Suez Canal project. Born in Versailles, son of a distinguished diplomat who represented *Napoleon Bonaparte's interests in

Egypt and later in Italy, Lesseps spent his early childhood in Italy but attended school in France. He was a promising scholar yet only just passed his exams, being more interested in sport than study. He enjoyed fencing and was a strong swimmer; once, rather than take the ferry with the other schoolboys, he swam across the river Seine for a dare.

In 1825 family connections obtained for him the vice consulship in Lisbon, where his father was serving as consul, and in 1832 he was appointed vice consul in Alexandria. He took to his new posting with enthusiasm, since he was attracted to the desert and a boy's taste for adventure had not left him. He studied Arabic and Islam and cultivated excellent relations with the viceroy, Muhammad Ali, a man his father had helped to put in power. Lesseps gained the confidence of the viceroy's son, Said, whom he taught fencing and, in contravention of the strict diet imposed by the viceroy, fed generously on macaroni.

Lesseps found out that during Napoleon's campaign in the Middle East plans had been drawn up for a canal linking the Mediterranean and the Red Sea. The project fired his imagination: it would advance international commerce and might bring him enduring fame. However, in 1839 he was posted away from Egypt and in the following years served in Spain, Holland, and Italy. In 1849 he was censured by his government and placed on public trial for failing to negotiate the surrender of the Roman Republic to French forces. He felt he had been made a scapegoat and resigned from the diplomatic corps. For a period, he was employed as land agent to his mother-in-law and wrote of how "I pass my days among cattle, pigs and sheep."

The inactivity did not last long. Said became viceroy of Egypt and remembered the kindness shown him years before. He warmly welcomed Lesseps back to Egypt and gave him a position of honor at his side. Lesseps soon convinced Said of the glory and wealth the Suez Canal would bring and was authorized to build it, subject to the approval of the sultan in Constantinople. He formed a company, guessing that the British would want a large share in the project, and convinced British businessmen to back him. However, he faced opposition, as the British foreign minister, Lord Palmerston, suspected a plan to increase French influence in the Middle East.

British pressure on the sultan and French government ambivalence were constant obstacles; at one point even the viceroy withdrew his support. Throughout, Lesseps refused to give way to despair and, when the Egyptians withdrew their conscripted workers, he found laborers on the free market and made increasing use of steam-powered machinery. Much of the capital for the building work was raised in France, where the canal became a patriotic venture and Lesseps was able to use friends in high places — he was a cousin of the Empress Eugénie and the patron of his company was Jerome Bonaparte, heir to the throne.

Lesseps personally began the excavations in 1859 and ten years later he saw the grand ceremonial opening of the Suez Canal in the presence of Empress Eugenie. He was now a much-admired figure and happily married for a second time (his first wife had died of scarlet fever in 1853), to Helene de Bragard, forty-four years his junior. The couple had twelve children, the last when de Lesseps was aged eighty.

In the 1870s Lesseps began a disastrous involvement in the launching of a Panama Canal company, which collapsed in 1889 in the midst of scandals over heavy losses and the bribery of government ministers. In 1893 he and his son Charles were put on trial and sentenced to five years imprisonment for bankruptcy fraud. Only Charles was imprisoned, and later in the year the verdict was reversed. Lesseps died senile and isolated, yet still honored and respected.

C. Beatty, *Ferdinand de Lesseps,* 1950.
C. L. Longfield, *Ferdinand de Lesseps,* 1956.
J. S. Pudney, *Suez: de Lessep's Canal,* 1960.

LINCOLN, ABRAHAM (1809–1865), sixteenth president of the United States. He was born in a log cabin in the slave-owning state of Kentucky, but when he was small the family moved to Indiana, and then he settled in Illinois (first New Salem, then Springfield). Lincoln's father was a hardworking man, but lacked money sense and was always moving his family to another, supposedly better, farm further west. Lincoln's mother died when he was eight and he was cared for by his elder sister until his father remarried. His stepmother encouraged his studies, but even so he was able to attend school for a total of only twelve months, accumulated during the times they happened to live near a school. Ambitious and extremely intelligent, he taught himself reading, writing, arithmetic, and later law, spending every spare moment reading.

Lincoln was very tall, thin, and extremely strong. He became known for amazing feats of strength, an attribute he needed as many of the jobs on the frontier (and young Lincoln worked at different times as a store-keeper, casual labourer, rail-splitter, waterman, and soldier) required great physical strength. In many ways the frontier had a life-long influence on him. His everyday speech and sense of humor, though witty, at times were coarse and homely — typical of the time, place, and people with whom he lived as a boy and young man. Yet his morals and character were atypical. For example, although hunting was common on the frontier, he never hunted again after shooting a turkey when he was eight. He never smoked or drank.

At the age of thirty-three he married Mary Todd, an ambitious, supportive woman with a temper and a gift for graceful hospitality. She faced their poverty with spirited resolution but disliked his uncouth appearance and ways. Their relationship was marked by a common love for their children, a lack of serious quarrels, and his avoidance of conflict, which sometimes meant an avoidance of her.

At twenty-five he was elected to the Illinois state legislature, where he served for three undistinguished terms. He did, however, present a pioneer statement endorsing female suffrage. In 1847 he was elected to the U.S. House of Representatives. He never ceased working as a lawyer and had an excellent reputation for kindness and honesty as well as ability. One of the shrewdest, most experienced politicians in Illinois, he knew how to turn situations to his political advantage. Lincoln tried twice to run for the U.S. Senate. He withdrew from the first race in 1856 to ensure the victory of a third, antislavery candidate from a different party. His second attempt was unsuccessful and the next public office he held was that of president of the United States. Previous to that, in 1858, he won a great reputation in his seven public debates with the proslavery senator Stephen A. Douglas, in which he contended that slavery, apart from being morally wrong, threatened all workers.

In 1860 Lincoln was elected president. At first the new president did not make a favorable impression on the government in Washington. While it was never suggested that he was untrustworthy or motivated by personal aims, Lincoln did not inspire confidence in anything but his good intentions. His peculiar appearance and eccentric ways were regarded by many with embarrassment or condescending amusement. Idiosyncracies such as his tactlessness, his insistence on standing back to back with other tall men to see who was tallest, and his way of beginning a conversation by telling a little story, were regarded with affection by those who came to know and appreciate the inner Lincoln. For many that knowledge, appreciation, and affection came only after his death.

The South extolled the beauty and virtue of the Southern way of life based on slavery, which they wanted to see extended into the territories. Lincoln was the candidate of the Republican party in 1860. The Republican Party, founded in 1854, believed that while slavery had to be tolerated where it already existed to maintain the Union (it was constitutional), it was nevertheless fundamentally wrong and should not be extended. Lincoln's election was the first time that a united North succeeded in outvoting the South. The South considered Lincoln's antislavery stand a threat to its way of life. The first steps toward secession were taken shortly after the November elections. In his inaugural address Lincoln assured the Southerners: "The Government will not assail you. You have no conflict without yourselves being the aggressors."

Secession changed the basic issue between North and South from slavery to unity. The North viewed secession as outright rebellion, holding that the national government, the Union, had authority over the states. The South held that the Union was merely an agreed-upon alliance of the individual states, with states' rights (including withdrawal from the Union) having priority over those of the national government. Once the war began, slavery ceased to be an issue in the South: Southerners were fighting for their freedom and nothing else. Most Northerners, on the other hand, were willing to fight a war to preserve the Union but not to end slavery (four of the states on the Northern side were slave states).

This shift in issues presented Lincoln with a dilemma. He had hated slavery ever since he first encountered it as a young man on a visit to New Orleans. Yet he would have continued to tolerate an institution he hated, to preserve one he loved —

- As I would not be a slave, so I would not be a master. This expresses my idea of democracy. Whatever differs from this, to the extent of the difference, is no democracy.
- If I could save the Union by emancipating all the slaves I would do so; if I could save it by emancipating none of them I would do so; if I could save it by emancipating some and not others I would do that too.
- With malice towards none; with charity for all; with firmness in the right, as God gives us to see the right, let us strive to finish the work we are in; to bind up the nation's wounds, to care for him who shall have borne the battle, and for his widow and his orphan — to do all which may achieve and cherish a just and lasting peace among ourselves and with all nations.
- Government of the people, by the people, for the people, shall not perish from the earth.
- That I am not a member of any Christian church is true; but I have never denied the truth of Scriptures.
- Among free men there can be no successful appeal from the ballot to the bullet.
- No man is good enough to govern another man without that other's consent.
- A nation may be said to consist of its territory, its people, and its laws. The territory is the only part which is of certain durability.
- Capital is only the fruit of labor and could not have existed if labor had not existed first.
- You can fool all the people some of the time, and some of the people all the time — but you cannot fool all the people all of the time.
- Let us have faith that right makes might.
- He reminds me of the man who murdered both his parents, and then when sentence was about to be pronounced, pleaded for mercy on the grounds that he was an orphan.
- The Lord prefers common-looking people. That is why he makes so many of them.

Abraham Lincoln

Abraham Lincoln with his troops

the Union. Afraid that turning the war into an anti-slavery crusade would split the North, Lincoln resisted emancipating the slaves and let the individual generals decide the status of runaway slaves fleeing to Union forces. He favored a gradual emancipation that provided compensation for owners and opened ways for blacks to advance, such as education of black children or resettlement in Africa. He encouraged bills for gradual emancipation in the Congress and state legislatures, but none of them passed. The Emancipation Proclamation of 1863 ended slavery only in the South; it did not affect the Northern slave states. Two more years were to pass before, in January 1865, Congress voted for a constitutional amendment prohibiting slavery in the United States, with Lincoln putting a great deal of pressure on certain congressmen to ensure a sufficient number of votes. When Lincoln was inaugurated for the second time as president in March, 1865, he had a battalion of black soldiers in his escort. His reelection had not been easy; radical elements, feeling he was too moderate, had talked of dumping him. Lincoln called on the nation not to "swap horses while crossing a stream," and won the election.

Lincoln's greatest task was to preserve Northern unity. His handling of the powerful men in his cabinet (only Lincoln could have brought them to work so long and well together) illustrates how he accomplished this. Happy to delegate authority to men whose capabilities and judgment he trusted, Lincoln intervened very little unless he was unhappy with results (as with the Northern generals before Ulysses S. *Grant). It was said that Lincoln's was the only real vote in his cabinet, but he preferred to bring his cabinet to agree on the best course of action rather than dictate to them. Sometimes he deferred to its superior knowledge of a subject or to public opinion, and there were also occasions when he made important decisions on his own, without consulting anyone. Lincoln used whatever methods he felt necessary to keep the North united sufficiently to fight the war until the end. No one else could have done it.

As the Civil War drew to a conclusion the question of the treatment of the defeated rebel states was debated. Lincoln wanted reunification, not revenge, and he might have got it but for a plot to kill important government figures by a small group of fanatical Southerners. Only one of their attempts succeeded: on Good Friday, April 14, 1865, Abraham Lincoln was assassinated by a Confederate sympathizer, the actor John Wilkes Booth, while watching a play at Ford's Theater in Washington. The Confederate forces had surrendered at Appomattox Court House just five days before.

B. Catton, *The Civil War*, 1987.
J. Duff, *A. Lincoln, Prairie Lawyer*, 1960.
S. B. Oates, *Abraham Lincoln*, 1984.
R. Painter Randall, *Mary Lincoln: Biography of a Marriage*, 1953.
C. B. Strozier, *Lincoln's Quest for Union*, 1982.

LINDBERGH, CHARLES AUGUSTUS (1902–1974), aviator who made the first nonstop solo flight across the Atlantic Ocean in May 1927. He was born in Detroit, Michigan. His father served as a member of Congress for Minnesota from 1907 to 1917 and held a unique set of principles: stoic self-reliance, opposition to the Eastern banking system, opposition to American entrance into World War I, and affirmation of the anti-Catholic Free Press Defense League. Although these values cost him the governorship of Minnesota in a rowdy campaign in 1918, they were inherited by his son.

Charles A. Lindbergh, Jr., early displayed mechanical skills. He began college studies in engineering at the University of Wisconsin in 1920, but dropped out after two years to do stunt flying. In 1924 he joined the U.S. army to train as an army air service reserve pilot, graduating the next year as the best pilot in his class. Lindbergh was hired to fly the mail between Saint Louis and Chicago, giving him the opportunity to develop his initial, limited reputation as a serious pilot.

A prize was offered for the first aviator to fly nonstop between Paris and New York by Raymond Orteig, a New York City hotelier, in 1919 and again in 1926. Although a number of men had sought it and had been either injured or killed in the attempt, none had succeeded. Lindbergh decided to try for the prize and on May 20 1927, upon suddenly hearing a good weather report, he prepared to take off from Roosevelt Field, New York. Two other planes were also on the runway, ready to compete for the prize, but the pilots let Lindbergh go ahead. His plane, the *Spirit of Saint Louis*, was manufactured according to Lindbergh's own specifications, costing $10,580, which was paid for by nine Saint Louis businessmen. Lindbergh landed in Paris, a distance of thirty-six hundred miles, after a flight of 33.5 hours, some of it through treacherous sleet an ice cloud — to the greetings of an exuberant crowd of 20,000. He said his experience with the mob was the most dangerous part of the flight.

His feat made him a popular hero and spawned a love-hate relationship between the handsome aviator and the public that idolized him. Reticent by nature, he spent subsequent years avoiding reporters and photographers. President Calvin Coolidge presented him with the Congressional Medal of Honor and the first American Distinguished Flying Cross. As a result of his popularity, he was sent on a goodwill mission to Latin America. In Mexico he met and fell in love with Anne Spencer Morrow, the daughter of the U.S. ambassador, Dwight M. Morrow. Their courtship, engagement, wedding, and honeymoon were all spent in an intricate game of hide-and-seek with a persistent press. The young Lindberghs wore disguises, wrote in code to each other, and tried various escapes from the public eye, often to no avail.

Lindbergh taught his wife to fly and they went on a number of expeditions together. They inaugurated the transcontinental air passenger service and flew over Alaska to Siberia, Japan, and China. At each stop along the way they were quoted and photographed.

Anne Morrow Lindbergh was pregnant with her second child in Hopewell, New Jersey, when on March 1, 1932, their twenty-month-old son was kidnapped from the family home. The national press hounded the couple during the ten weeks of police investigation before the baby's body was found. The Lindbergs received an outpouring of compassion from the nation via thousands of letters during and after their ordeal. Two years later the police arrested Bruno Richard Hauptmann, a carpenter, who was tried, convicted, and executed for the murder. From diary entries and letters she wrote from 1929 to 1932, Anne Lindbergh described the early years of her marriage, both the romance and the suffering, in *Hour of Gold, Hour of Lead* (1973).

Their desire for privacy now became an obsession and the Lindberghs relocated to Europe for the rest of the 1930s, moving from place to place. They had five more children. While on the continent, Lindbergh toured the French and Nazi German aircraft industries, and was impressed by the latter. In 1938 he accepted a German medal of honor from the Nazi leader Hermann *Goring, which brought the Lindberghs severe criticism upon their return to the United States in 1939. Lindbergh's advocacy of the America First Committee and his open criticism of "the three most important groups which have been pressing this coun-

In the spring of '27 something bright and alien flashed across the sky. A young Minnesotan who seemed to have nothing to do with his generation did a heroic thing, and for a moment people set down their glasses in country clubs and speakeasies and thought of their old best dreams.

F. Scott Fitzgerald on Charles Lindbergh

try toward war... the British, the Jewish, and the [Franklin] *Roosevelt Administration," did nothing to alleviate his image as a Nazi sympathizer.

Lindbergh was denied reenlistment during World War II, although he did serve as a civilian consultant in the Pacific zone and as such flew a number of combat missions. After the war he retired from public view. Anne Morrow Lindbergh, a poet and essayist, published several books in the 1950s and 1960s. Lindbergh, who became a consultant for Pan American World Airways and helped design the Boeing 747, took an interest in the conservation movement during the last years of his life. He died at his home on the Hawaiian island of Maui. His book, *The Spirit of Saint Louis* (1953), received the 1953 Pulitzer Prize. *An Autobiography of Values* was published posthumously in 1978.
L. H. Kennedy, *The Airman and the Carpenter*, 1985.
L. Mosley, *Lindbergh*, 1976.

LINNE, CARL VON, (Carolus Linnaeus; 1707–1778), Swedish naturalist, of whom it was said, "God created, Linnaeus set in order." His father, Nils, was a country parson in Stenbrohult, southern Sweden, who laid out a beautiful flower garden around the parsonage and instilled in his son his passion for botany.

Linne was a mediocre student at school; plants were all he really cared to learn about. Botany might be a hobby, but Nils Linne doubted it could provide his son a livelihood; poor progress at academic studies ruled out holy orders. In 1726 he considered apprenticing him to a tailor or shoemaker, but Dr. Johan Rothman, one of Linne' teachers, persuaded him that Carl could be usefully employed in medicine.

In 1727 Linne began medical studies at Lund University, but the instruction available there was of poor quality. However, it proved to be a good place for botanical studies: he had at his disposal an extensive library and collection of specimens, and he explored the surrounding countryside, augmenting his knowledge of plant life. He gained his medical degree and meanwhile also attracted the sponsorship of fellow botany enthusiasts, Professor Rudbeck and Olaf Celcius. With the latter, he undertook field trips investigating the flora of the region.

Charles A. Lindbergh

By 1730 Linné had developed his theory of plant classification based on sexuality. That year he was appointed lecturer on botany at Uppsala University and gave demonstrations in the botanical gardens. In 1732, on behalf of the university, he made a historic forty-six hundred mile four-month tour through Lapland, recording its flora and the customs of the natives. He discovered one hundred new species of plants, and described the small plant *Linnaea borealis* as "lowly, insignificant, flowering for only a short while, named after Linné who resembles it." It was he who showed that any species of plant — or, indeed, of any other living being — could be described in two words, denoting it and its relationship. The first word, a Latin noun, gives the genus, the second, a Latin adjective, the organism. His best known definition is *Homo sapiens*.

Linné left for Holland to take a doctorate at the University of Harderwijk in 1735, when he also published his *Systema Naturae*, a pioneering classification of the animal, plant, and mineral kingdoms. Originally it consisted of just seven folio leaves, but by the tenth edition had expanded to twenty-five hundred pages. It marked Linné' emergence as the leading European botanist and he drew many patrons willing to finance his books. In 1737 he published a book on his travels in Lapland and *Genera Plantarum*, an important reference work describing all 935 plant species then recognized.

In 1738 Linné returned to Sweden and started practicing as a physician in Stockholm, where he was appointed physician to the Admiralty. In 1742 he returned to Uppsala university, this time as holder of the chair of botany and medicine. The rest of his life he devoted to development of the university's botanical garden and to teaching enthusiastic students who flocked to Uppsala from many different countries. His students sent him plants from their own regions and he proceeded to cultivate these in the garden at Uppsala. The Swedish parliament also commissioned him to travel around the country surveying natural resources.

In his later years Linné developed his views on a natural order in which every component filled a set role. He was amazed at the smooth working of all the interlocking components in this world, writing of "seeing the infinite, all-knowing and all-powerful God from behind." In all creation he sensed "an eternal wisdom and power, an inscrutable perfection."

Linné took pride in his fame and was intolerant of other botanists challenging his work. He said of himself that God had bestowed on him the greatest insight into the knowledge of nature, more than anyone had hitherto enjoyed. As a teacher he was a gifted communicator, a charismatic figure inspiring devotion. He sent pupils on study trips to America, China, Japan, and other distant lands. These expeditions made significant contributions to botanical knowledge but were so dangerous that an estimated one-third of the students sent out never returned.

Linné' field studies around Uppsala were outstandingly popular. Two to three hundred students at a time, clad in light linen garments and equipped with collecting tools, would set off with him into the surrounding countryside, all marching in formation to the accompaniment of French horns and drums.

Linné was a welcome visitor to the Swedish court and in 1747 was appointed Royal Physician. In 1761 he was ennobled. An attack of apoplexy forced him into retirement in 1774. His only son (also called Carl) succeeded him in the professorship. Sir James Smith bought his botanical collection for 900 guineas and removed it to Burlington House, London, where in 1788 the Linnaean Society was founded.

N. Gourlie, *The Prince of Botanists: Carl Linné*, 1953.

LI PO (or Li-T'ai Po; 701–762 C.E.), Chinese poet, perhaps the greatest and most influential Chinese poet of all time. His poetry, simultaneously simple and complex, often describes his innermost dreams. It is wonderfully descriptive of his own stormy life as a wandering minstrel, court poet, and suspected rebel. Li Po's well-earned reputation as an adventurer, womanizer, and alcoholic is also reflected in his poetry. In China, his reputation is that of a "fallen immortal" — his poetry is considered to have been written in a state of divine inspiration.

Li Po was born in western China, near the present-day Tadzhikistan-Afghanistan border. Few facts are known about his family's origins; biographies of Li Po are generally based on legends and gossip. The family claimed descent from Li Erh, thought to be *Lao-Tzu, the founder of Taoism. Li Po's poetry was, in fact, influenced by Taoism rather than by the more common Confucianism.

Some modern scholars have suggested that Li Po was not actually Chinese but Turkish. By his own admission he was able to compose equally poignant poetry in another language, probably a Turkish dialect spoken in Central Asia. Even for an ethnic Han Chinese his poetry was unusually cosmopolitan, displaying both Turkish and Persian influences. Li Po was the first Chinese poet to mention the rose, an image that did not achieve popularity until contact was resumed between China and Europe hundreds of years later.

When he was five years old his family, apparently traders, settled in Szechuan, in China proper. Li Po began studying swordsmanship at age fifteen and soon afterward took to the road. An impulsive, boastful wanderer with flashing eyes and a shrill voice, he used his sword to redress wrongs. Many of Li Po's poems were composed during his travels as payment to his hosts. He put down no roots, often referring to many places where he traveled as home.

Although he was appointed court poet to T'ang Emperor Hsuang Tsung, for some unknown reason Li Po did not take the imperial examinations that would have assured him a government position. Between the years 742 and 744 he did, however, serve as a member of the prestigious Hanlin Academy, a

> ## QUIET NIGHT THOUGHTS
>
> Before my bed
> There is bright moonlight
> So that it seems
> Like frost on the ground:
> Lifting my head
> I watch the bright moon,
> Lowering my head
> I dream that I'm home.
>
> **Li Po**

gathering of Chinese artists and intellectuals. He also studied physics and alchemy, apparently in an attempt to discover the elixir of life.

When rebels in the city of An Lu-shan threatened the T'ang dynasty in 757, Li Po joined the emperor's son, Prince Lin, in suppressing the revolt, not realizing that the prince's true intention was to usurp power from his father. The coup was swiftly crushed and its leaders were executed. Li Po's death sentence was commuted to banishment; he was pardoned three years later but died on his return from exile. According to legend, Li Po drowned while leaning out of a boat, trying to kiss the reflection of the moon's image in the water. It is more probable that he died of pneumonia (in Chinese, death by drowning is a euphemism for pneumonia).

Li Po's poetry is impulsive. It plays on the reader's imagination by hinting at meanings rather than stating them explicitly. Li Po rejected the stiff formal rules of verse and meter adopted by his contemporaries, preferring older, looser styles. He composed several ballads, called *yueh fu*, as well as drinking songs inspired by his beloved cabarets and his own drunkenness. He was well versed in other Chinese poets but loved the works of Meng Hao-jan (689–740) best of all. His poems often condemn war and other evils he considered to be the result of people's stupidity. Some poems reflect his love of women; Li Po himself was married four times. Two wives died, one he divorced, and the last outlived him. Today the works of Li Po and those of his contemporary *Tu Fu are considered to be the epitome of Chinese poetry.

A. Cooper, *Li Po and Tu Fu*, 1973.
A. Waley, *Poetry and Life of Li Po*, 1950.

LISTER, JOSEPH, BARON (1827–1912), British surgeon who developed the use of antiseptics in medical practice. Born to Quaker parents in Upton, Essex, Lister inherited a fascination for natural history from his father, a successful businessman who had won membership to the Royal Society for his discoveries in the field of optics. From an early age Lister expressed a desire to enter surgery, but as the universities of Oxford and Cambridge were barred to him on religious grounds, he entered the nonsectarian University College, London, in those days popularly known as the "Godless College in Gower Street."

Lister boarded in London with other Quaker students, but soon fell victim to a nervous breakdown induced by his austere lifestyle combined with the rigor of studies and an attack of smallpox. He resumed his education later that year and received his medical degree in 1852, along with a fellowship in the Royal College of Surgeons.

In 1853 Lister began work under James Symes, professor of clinical surgery at the University of Edinburgh, and the two became good friends. Lister became resident house surgeon in 1854, marrying Symes's eldest daughter, Agnes, in 1856. Marriage to a non-Quaker compelled Lister to resign from the Society of Friends, much to the consternation of his family, who nevertheless maintained their close ties with him.

Upon returning from a lengthy tour of Europe, Lister took up the post of assistant surgeon at Glasgow's Royal Infirmary, and worked as an extramural lecturer at the medical school. He accepted a professorship at the University of Glasgow in 1860 and was elected to the Royal Society. His lectures were held in a dim, dusty operating theater where students sat in semicircles around the kitchen table at which he operated and behind which hung a blackboard.

After taking charge of the surgical wards at the Royal Infirmary in 1861 Lister contributed to the rapid progress being made in surgery — following the advent of anesthesia — through his invention of several instruments. He was remarkably deft in surgery and his innovations included radical mastectomy for breast cancer and the pinning together of fractures. In those days hospitals were filthy and infection was rife; 40 percent of patients died from septicemia following limb amputation. Lister, who insisted upon scrupulous cleanliness in order to prevent infection, was mocked by colleagues for being overly fastidious.

As only external wounds were subject to infection, Lister postulated that the festering of wounds was a form of decomposition produced by something in the hospital air. On reading of Louis *Pasteur's discovery that airborne microorganisms on contact with an appropriate medium cause fermentation or decomposition and multiply, he deduced that these airborne microbes might cause the infection of wounds and began to search for a chemical destroyer. Carbolic acid, which destroyed entozoa when spread on polluted fields could, he thought, act as an effective antiseptic on wounds.

Between 1865 and 1867 Lister successfully used carbolic acid to prevent infection in cases of compound fractures and created an antiseptic putty for use on abscesses. He constantly modified and improved upon his techniques, which were based on methodical and thorough testing, and began to use carbolic acid in surgery. Many fellow surgeons, however, were skeptical of Lister's findings, published in *The Lancet* in 1867.

In 1869 Lister was appointed professor of clinical surgery at the University of Edinburgh, and devoted himself to the perfection and promulgation of the antiseptic system. He left Edinburgh in 1877 to take up the professorship of the newly created chair of clinical surgery at Kings College, London, where he encountered a hostile reception. His ideas were, however, received enthusiastically abroad, and the following year Lister was appointed surgeon-in-ordinary by Queen *Victoria. He carefully followed developments in aseptic surgery in Germany in the 1880s, appreciating its importance in view of the fact that antiseptics can damage the body's natural healing processes but stood by his conviction that antiseptics still had an important role to play in medical treatment.

Lister retired in 1892 and was made president of the Royal Society in 1895. In his final years he suffered from rheumatism and lived with his sister-in-law in a small town on the coast of Kent. In accordance with his own wish he was buried alongside his wife in West Hampstead cemetery. A funeral service was held at Westminster Abbey where a marble medallion now hangs in his honor.

Lister's antiseptic system transformed the ancient craft of surgery into an enlightened profession. His work resulted in a huge reduction in deaths following surgery, and made possible abdominal, chest, and later brain operations, which had formerly been inconceivable. Lister received many honors and in 1897 was raised to the peerage.

L. Farmer, *Master Surgeon: A Biography of Joseph Lister*, 1962.
Sir R. J. Godlee, *Lord Lister*, 1918.
I. Noble, *The Courage of Dr. Lister*, 1960.

LIVINGSTONE, DAVID (1813–1873), Scottish explorer of Central Africa. He was one of seven children of a poor Scottish peddler from the mill town of Blantyre; the family lived in a room measuring ten by fourteen feet. At ten David was sent to work a twelve-hour day in the mill, but his ambitions lay elsewhere. With his first week's wages he bought a Latin primer. While working he committed sentences to memory, and studied intently for a few hours in the evening. He avidly read science and travel books, and spent his infrequent holidays investigating local flora and fauna.

Around the age of twenty he decided he wanted to be a missionary in China. Livingstone's upbringing was devoutly Christian and the travel stories he enjoyed stirred his imagination with colorful images of distant lands and peoples. The London Missionary Society accepted him in 1837; although his preaching skills were poor, they were impressed with his honesty and courage, among other outstanding qualities. War in China thwarted his plans to travel there, but Africa was also an appealing option. In 1840, newly ordained, he embarked on the long voyage to Cape Town.

Not content with the relative comfort of an established mission station, he lived with a local tribe, learning the language and customs. Then, accompanied by two native converts, he embarked on the first of many expeditions seeking out tribes no missionary had reached. Traveling on ox-back seven hundred miles and living off locusts and honey, Livingstone experienced the wildness of Africa to the fullest. Savaged by a lion, he was left with a crippled left arm and returned to the mission station, where he was nursed by a missionary's daughter, Mary Moffatt, whom he married in 1845.

With his wife and children, Livingstone resumed his journeying, seeking out a place to establish a new mission deep in the heartland. He was helped by Sechele, an African chief and the only convert he ever made; most tribesmen were attracted by his medicines but not his religion. In 1852 he sent his family back to England to save them the ordeal of further hazardous journeys. However, he made poor provision for their support in England and they endured grinding poverty.

Livingstone traveled across southern and central Africa from the west coast to the east to open up the country to European Christian civilization and commerce, which he hoped would put an end to the slave trade. He endured many hardships along with the party of African tribesmen who devotedly followed him; attacks from hostile tribes and being thrown from an ox were among the lesser hazards. The trek was a momentous achievement and was crowned in 1855 by the discovery of the waterfall he found "the most wonderful sight I had witnessed in Africa"; he named it after Queen *Victoria.

Following a successful tour of England, where the now-famous explorer became a best-selling author with an account of his travels, he returned to Africa as British consul in Mozambique with an assignment to explore more of east and central Africa. Livingstone urged his fellow explorers to have every respect for chiefs and witch doctors and not to kill animals unnecessarily. As for the ordinary Africans, "We come among them as members of a superior race and servants of a Government that desires to elevate the most degraded portions of the human family."

His expedition was beset with difficulties from the start. The specially-built steam launch performed poorly, and illness was rife, adding to the tensions. Livingstone's rapport with Europeans never matched the relationships he established with Africans. Before the British government put an end to the costly project, Lake Nyasa and a nearby area suitable for European settlement were discovered. Although one aim was to put an end to slavery, opening up new routes into the interior had the opposite effect — slave dealer followed close on the heels of explorer. Conflict was inevitable, but Livingstone's expedition freed any gangs of slaves they encountered.

After another visit to his family in England, Livingstone left on his final expedition to find the source of the great African rivers. By this time his health was broken and he had little control over his party. Many porters deserted and one ran away with the medicine chest. Another spread rumor that Livingstone had been killed. A journalist employed by an American newspaper, H. M. *Stanley, set out to find him, and their meeting at Ujiji, opening with the famous words "Dr. Livingstone, I presume," has gone down in folklore. He was the last European Livingstone saw. Within a year he succumbed to his final illness and died in a remote village, thirty thousand miles of African exploration behind him.

E. Huxley, *Livingstone and His African Journeys*, 1974.

T. Jeal, *Livingstone*, 1993.

G. Seaver, *David Livingstone: His Life and Letters*, 1957.

LLOYD GEORGE, DAVID (1863–1945), British
politician. Born in Manchester, he was raised in the cottage of his uncle, Richard Lloyd, a shoemaker in the Welsh village of Llanystumdy after his father, a Welsh schoolmaster, died during his infancy. His uncle was committed to nonconformist Christianity and radical liberal politics. The boy eagerly absorbed this outlook and became sensitive to the inequalities of the society around him.

Richard Lloyd tutored his nephew for a legal career and after passing the exams, Lloyd George set up practice as a solicitor. He made a reputation brilliantly defending poachers and small farmers in disputes with their landlords. Success and eloquence made him a natural choice for Parliament and in 1890 he became a radical Liberal member of parliament for Caernarvon, a seat he held for fifty-five years. On being elected he redoubled his attacks on the power of aristocratic society "where idleness is regarded as a badge of nobility... [by those who] live luxuriously upon the labor of others."

In 1888 he married Margaret Owen but was soon notorious for infidelities, earning the nickname of "goat." His magnetism attracted women and he delighted in their company. He had a long liaison with his secretary, Frances Stevenson, whom he married in later life after the death of his first wife.

Patriotic sentiment swept the country, but Lloyd George sacrificed popularity for the sake of opposition to the Boer War (1899–1902): "Money that would have built comfortable homes for hundreds of thousands of our fellow-men has gone to dig graves in South Africa." In Birmingham, where he was addressing an antiwar meeting, half bricks were sold at three a penny to hurl at him; he was forced to make his escape disguised as a policeman.

Lloyd George became a minister in the Liberal administration of 1905–1914, serving as president of the Board of Trade (1905–1908) and chancellor of the exchequer (1908–1915). He was responsible for much progressive welfare legislation, including old age pensions and unemployment insurance, which put in motion a social revolution. The ire of the wealthy was aroused by increased taxes to finance welfare reforms. Resulting conflict with the

David Lloyd George as chancellor of the exchecquer

House of Lords, which he was keen to provoke, resulted in a historic limitation of their powers.

War with Germany in 1914 brought a dramatic switch in his position. The pacifist now became an archpatriot, urging men to volunteer to fight and calling for great improvements in the army's equipment. As minister of munitions (1915–1916) and of war for a few months in 1916, his characteristic dynamism breathed fresh life into the indolent Whitehall bureaucracy, resulting in more supplies reaching the front.

In 1916 Lloyd George succeeded Herbert Asquith as prime minister; the division this coup provoked was to destroy the Liberal party. As prime minister he provided the decisive leadership the war demanded. Working tirelessly, at times twenty-one hours a day, he established a small, effective war cabinet and initiated new strategies, such as convoys to protect shipping. However, swept along by his own patriotic rhetoric, he blocked secret peace overtures that might have ended the slaughter far sooner.

With victory in 1918, Lloyd George retained his position as prime minister, vowing to make Britain a "land fit for heroes to live in." Another promise, of retribution against the Germans, helped him win an election, although at the Versailles peace conference his stance toward Germany was moderate. In 1921 a peace treaty setting up the Irish Free State was achieved. The following year, with Britain on the brink of war with Turkey, his government fell following accusations of knighthoods sold to fund his party. Lloyd George never returned to power, although he continued to sit in Parliament as a Liberal

M.P. He published his *War Memoirs* (1933) and shortly before his death he received an earldom.

B. B. Gilbert, *Lloyd George: A Political Life*, 2 vols., 1989–1992.

R. Lloyd George, *Lloyd George*, 1960.

M. Pugh, *Lloyd George*, 1983.

LOCKE, JOHN (1632–1704), English philosopher and political scientist; founder of the British empirical tradition in philosophy. He was born at Wrington, Somerset, where his father was an attorney and small landowner. During the Civil War his father commanded troops in the Parliamentary army. The upheavals of the war caused Locke to study at home until the age of fifteen, when he went to Westminster public school. From there he proceeded to Oxford University and commenced a long-standing connection as student and later teacher. From 1658 he was a Senior Student (equivalent to today's Fellow) and from 1660 lectured in Greek and philosophy.

Although his family held firm Puritan convictions, John Locke welcomed the Restoration in 1660, an event also pleasing to most of his colleagues at Oxford. His politics at this time were described as "extreme authoritarian," but he had already become disillusioned with the philosophical abstractions and speculations then in fashion at the university. He decided it would profit him more to study medicine and science and he became a student of Robert Boyle. He also traveled abroad to Germany and broadened his horizons. In 1667 he stopped tutoring at Oxford and moved to London where he had been offered a position as physician to the earl of Shaftesbury. He had learned his medicine well and performed a successful operation on his patron around 1668.

Although he might have had the skills, Locke did not have the inclination to make medicine his career. The same year he accepted this position he wrote a treatise in favor of religious tolerance, a marked change in the views he had held only seven years previously. London provided him with the intellectual stimulation that Oxford could no longer offer.

The earl of Shaftesbury rose to a position of power in the government of England and so Locke came into contact with leading political figures and was even secretary to the Board of Trade. It was an exciting period and saw a widening of his interests in many directions. He became a fellow of the Royal Society, wrote a treatise on the rate of interest, drafted a constitution for the colony of Carolina, continued his medical practice, and most significant of all began the first drafts of his major work of philosophy, *Essay Concerning Human Understanding* (begun in 1671 but not published untill 1690). The work sprang from a discussion with several friends on the deep moral questions that were troubling them and Locke chose to set his ideas down on paper.

In 1681 Shaftesbury hatched an ill-fated plot to overthrow the government and had to flee to Holland. Locke came under suspicion and the Crown even had a librarian at his Oxford college keep an eye on him; he reported back that Locke steered clear of all rebellious statements. In fact, Locke was writing material that royalist circles would have found profoundly disturbing. In his *Treatises on Government* (1690) he attacked the concept of the divine right of the king to rule as he saw fit and justified the right to rebel against the abuse of royal authority. Locke realized the wisdom of voluntary exile and soon moved to Holland. Even there he could not feel completely secure for the British government viewed him as a threat and tried to have him extradited. For a time he went under the name of Dr. Van der Linden but he need not have feared so greatly since the Dutch authorities had no intention of yielding to extradition requests.

- New opinions are always suspected, and usually opposed, without any other reason, but because they are not already common.
- No man's knowledge can go beyond his experience.
- It is one thing to show a man that he is in error, and another to put him in possession of the truth.
- We should have a great many fewer disputes in the world if words were taken for what they are, signs of our ideas only, and not for things themselves.
- There cannot any one moral rule be proposed whereof a man may not justly demand a reason.

John Locke

The five years spent in exile were highly productive. He published an essay called *Thoughts on Education* (1693) and at last completed *An Essay Concerning Human Understanding*, designed "to survey our own understandings, examine our own powers, and see to what things they were adapted." It is primarily on this work that his reputation as a great philosopher has come to rest. Yet as he wrote, "New opinions are always suspected and usually opposed without any other reason but because they are not already common," and so it was with his writings which aroused great controversy, especially in ecclestiastical and government circles.

England's 1688 Glorious Revolution found its intellectual rationalization in the philosophy of Locke. He returned to England in noble company, sailing in the flotilla of Queen Mary. Locke was granted lucrative state office and was a Commissioner of the Board of Trade, but his health was not up to coping with the burden of the work; the climate of London was especially hard on his asthma.

Locke had never married, and the doyen of Europe's philosophers lived out his last years as a guest of the Masham family in Essex, content to be surrounded by the books and scientific instruments around which his life had revolved.

He was the father of philosophical empiricism. In a common sense approach, he rejected the theory that there are innate ideas and principles, insisting that all ideas must be derived empirically from our own experiences. As a political scientist, his *Two Treatises on Government* had an important influence on the American Declaration of Independence and Constitution. He advocated the separation of church and state and helped to formulate the principle of "no taxation without representation."

M. Cranston, *John Locke: A Biography*, 1957.
J. J. Jenkins, *Understanding Locke*, 1983.
J. D. Mabbott, *John Locke*, 1973.
J. O'Connor, *John Locke*, 1952.

LONGFELLOW, HENRY WADSWORTH

(1807–1882), the most popular American poet of the nineteenth century. Longfellow was born in Portland, Maine, to an established family. His father was a member of both the state legislature and the U.S. Congress, and Longfellow's maternal grandfather was General Peleg Wadsworth, who served in the American Revolution. As a child, Longfellow was educated in private schools, and in 1822 he entered Bowdoin College as a sophomore, joining the same class as the writer Nathaniel Hawthorne. During his college years, he wrote to his father: "I most eagerly aspire after future eminence in literature; my whole soul burns most ardently for it, and every earthly thought centers in it." While he was at Bowdoin, many of his poems were published in national magazines, and his translating was so good that he was offered the college's newly established professorship of modern languages, on condition that he first study in Europe. After three years visiting Spain, Germany, France, and Italy, Longfellow returned to teach in 1829. He remained at Bowdoin for five years, during which time he wrote and published his own textbooks. In 1836 he took up a professorship at Harvard.

Although Longfellow was a good teacher, liked by his students, he did not enjoy academic life. He longed to be a creative writer and in 1838 "A Psalm of Life" became his first significant success, prompting him to publish his first volume of poetry the next year. Over the next twenty years he achieved international fame for what he called his "National Ballad." These narrative and dramatic poems were based on local New England legends and history. Among them are some of Longfellow's most famous poems: "Evangeline," "The Song of Hiawatha," and "The Courtship of Miles Standish."

Determining that "I shall win this lady or I shall die," Longfellow finally married Fanny Appleton in 1843 (his first wife had died after a miscarriage),

---

SOME FAMOUS LINES OF LONGFELLOW

- Tell me not in mournful numbers,
  "Life is but an empty dream,"
  For the soul is dead that slumbers,
  And things are not what they seem.

  A Psalm of Life

- Lives of great men all remind us
  We can make our lives sublime,
  And, departing, leave behind us
  Footprints on the sands of time.

  A Psalm of Life

- Under a spreading chestnut-tree
  The village smithy stands.

  The Village Blacksmith

- The shades of night were falling fast,
  As through an Alpine village passed
  A youth who bore, 'mid snow and ice,
  A banner with the strange device,
  Excelsior!

  Excelsior

- I shot an arrow in the air,
  It fell to earth, I know not where.

  The Arrow and the Song

- The cares that infest the day
  Shall fold their tents, like the Arabs,
  And silently, steal away.

  The Day is Done

- Thou too, sail on, O Ship of State!
  Sail on, O Union, Strong and great.

  The Building of the Ship

- Then the little Hiawatha
  Learned of every bird its language,
  Learned their names and all their secrets.

  Hiawatha

- Ships that pass in the night.

  Tales of a Wayside Inn

---

having waited seven years for her to consent to marry him. During this time he wrote *Hyperion*, an autobiographical novel that described his passion for Fanny and also embarrassed her greatly.

Fanny was from a very wealthy family and her father gave the new couple the Craigie House, a mansion in Cambridge, Massachusetts. They had six children; Fanny gave birth to their third child under anesthesia in 1847, becoming the first woman in the Western world so to do.

In 1855, bored with teaching, Longfellow resigned from Harvard; he has been credited with establishing modern languages as a basic part of American education during his eighteen years there.

One summer day in 1861, Fanny Longfellow's dress caught on fire; the flames enveloped her and she died the next day. Longfellow was so severely burned from trying to save her that he could not attend the funeral. From then on, unable to shave due to the burns on his face, he grew a thick, white beard. He continued to be a loving and devoted father, although he was tormented: "The terrible days go by and bring no relief." His writing became more serious and personal, and less popular. His translation of *Dante Alighieri's *The Divine Comedy* and his *Michael Angelo* are among the most important works written after the death of his wife.

Longfellow was popular in Europe as well; on his last trip to Europe in 1868–1869, Oxford and Cambridge universities gave him honorary degrees and after his death, Britain honored him with a memorial bust in Westminster Abbey.

Many twentieth-century critics have criticized Longfellow's poetry for its moralizing. However, he believed that "to oppose error and vice, and make mankind more in love with truth and virtue....[is] a far higher motive than mere literary ambition."

E. S. Sutherland, *Life of Henry Wadsworth Longfellow*, 1972.
E. Wagenknecht, *Henry Wadsworth Longfellow: His Poetry and Prose*, 1986.
C. B. Williams, *Henry Wadsworth Longfellow*, 1964.

LOPE DE VEGA, FELIX SEE VEGA CARPIO, LOPE DE

LORCA, FEDERICO GARCIA SEE GARCIA LORCA, FEDERICO

LOUIS XI (1423–1483), king of France from 1461. The son of *Charles VII and Mary of Anjou, he had an austere upbringing and was married in 1436 against his wishes to Margaret of Scotland. When he was seventeen he joined the Praguerie, a movement of the nobility directed against the king and, in 1446, was exiled by his father, whom he never saw again, to Dauphiné. There Louis strengthened his position as a semiindependent ruler. After his wife died he married Charlotte of Savoy in 1452, who gave him five daughters and a son. In 1456, when his father approached Dauphiné with his army, Louis took shelter at the court of Philip the Good of Burgundy, with whom he remained until he succeeded his father in 1461.

As king Louis pursued from the start a policy designed to strengthen the monarchy in alliance with the urban middle classes. Of his father's councillors he retained those of lowly origins who were known for their antifeudal attitudes. His policies estranged him from his former protector Philip the Good, and provoked the formation of the League of the Public Weal, a movement among the higher feudal French nobility supported mainly by Burgundian forces, who opposed Louis. The League overcame the royal troops at the Battle of Montlhery (1465) and besieged Paris.

The king had to make concessions to the rebels but soon regained much of his losses. However, he found himself confronting the powerful alliance of England and Charles the Bold, duke of Burgundy. Louis scored the first victories. Then, in a meeting between the king and Charles the Bold (1468), the duke accused Louis of encouraging sedition among his subjects in Flanders, kept him captive, and released him only after he had signed a humiliating treaty. Louis responded by intensifying his repressive measures against the high nobility and by aiding the Lancastrians against Edward IV of England (1470). Not until two years later, when his own brother's death weakened the internal coalition against him, was Louis able to make real progress. He then forced the duke of Brittany to make peace and crushed the powerful house of Armagnac. In the meantime he continued successfully to wage war in the south, as a result of which the Pyrenees became France's southern boundary.

The struggle against Charles the Bold took longer and necessitated cooperation with foreign allies. In 1474 Louis formed the Union of Constance against Burgundy, with the Swiss and Sigismund of Austria. On his side, Charles called for help from Edward IV, who invaded France, but Louis met the king of England and bought him off with a substantial sum of money and the promise of an annual pension. The Swiss defeated the duke of Burgundy, who finally met his death at Nancy in 1477. Rid of his strongest adversary, Louis continued his successful repression of the recalcitrant French nobles and pursued his goal of suppressing feudalism and achieving the unity of France. He added to the royal domain Roussillon, Cerdagne, Anjou, Maine, and Provence, and took over Burgundy and Picardy (1482).

Louis XI was the true architect of the centralized French monarchy. He made the *taille*, a property tax paid by all except the nobles and the clergy, the main source of government revenue, to which were added the *gabelle*, the salt tax, and other indirect taxes. He expanded the economy by introducing the silk industry to Lyons, and encouraged the production of textiles in the north of France. Traveling constantly around the kingdom, he ran the government while being in direct contact with his people. He was, however, resistant to any restraint on his personal authority and was continually at odds with the *parlement of Paris*. A brilliant diplomat, a compulsive talker, and totally unscrupulous, Louis's brand of Machiavellianism was tempered by religious piety. He built shrines, endowed many churches, and prayed often, and went on pilgrimages, but this behavior may have been designed to keep the support of the church.

Louis XI is described as a tireless worker, though physically weak and ugly, with a long hooked nose. He dressed simply and was recognized by his old felt hat. Yet the "Spider," as he was nicknamed, was the greatest European monarch of his time.

P. Champion, Louis XI, 1929.
C. Hare, The Life of Louis XI, 1941.
P. M. Kendall, Louis XI, 1974.

LOUIS XIV (1638–1715), the longest-reigning and most magnificent king of France. Known as the Sun King and as the Great Monarch, he was the builder of Versailles and his reign marked the climax of monarchical absolutism in France. He was born in Saint-Germain-en-Laye and was nicknamed le Dieudonné, "the gift of God," because the marriage of his father, Louis XIII, and Anne of Austria had been barren for more than twenty years and many had given up hope of an heir to the Bourbon throne.

He was only four years old when his father died. His mother served as regent, but it was her adviser, Cardinal *Mazarin, who really ruled. In 1648, when Louis was nine years old, the nobles and the Paris parlement (law court) rebelled against the crown, beginning the civil war known as the Fronde (1648–1653). His experiences during these turbulent years taught Louis that divine authority was not enough to rule a kingdom, but that he also needed a powerful army. As a result, his reign was marked by a distrust of the Paris parlement, the nobility, and his capital city. In 1653 Mazarin proved victorious over the rebels and continued in his task of creating a strong administration and teaching Louis the art of statehood. Although Louis had now been proclaimed of age, he did not dare to dispute Mazarin's right to govern.

In 1660 Louis married his cousin, the Spanish Infanta Marie-Thérèse. For this political alliance he sacrificed his true love for Marie Mancini, the niece of Mazarin. This attempt to ratify peace between Spain and France later gave France a legal claim to a portion of the Spanish inheritance, Louis claiming that the dowry, in consideration of which Marie-Thérèse had renounced her rights to the Spanish inheritance, had never been paid. This marriage was Mazarin's last act of state, for he died the following year.

Louis now declared his intention to assume all responsibility for governing the kingdom. His statement, "L'etat, c'est moi," ("I am the state") aptly personifies his reign, for without his permission nothing could be signed, "not even a passport."

In taking power into his own hands Louis profited by inheriting experienced ministers from Mazarin. Jean-Baptiste Colbert developed industry and commerce on mercantilist principles and opened up colonial trade. The war minister, the Marquis de Louvois, built up the army and the navy. With their assistance Louis laid the foundations for absolute monarchism. In 1665 he ordered the parlements to register royal edicts without discussion. A police system was created in Paris and intendants (executive agents) were established permanently in the provinces.

In his foreign policy, Louis sought to achieve ultimate power and control. When Philip IV of Spain died in 1665, Louis used his marriage as an excuse for the War of Devolution (1667–1668), as a result of which he received part of Flanders, although the Dutch then established the Triple Alliance (England, Holland, and Sweden) to oppose him. In 1672 Louis attacked the Dutch, which resulted in his annexation of Franche-Comté but brought on financial problems. Louis now abandoned war for diplomacy and sought legal grounds to lay claim to various cities, which he then annexed. He seized the German town of Strasbourg in 1681, securing it by treaty three years later. Europe now feared him and he was faced with a broad coalition when he attacked the Holy Roman Empire in 1688. This war ended in the Treaty of Rijswijk (1697), through which Louis forfeited most of the territories he had gained since 1679, except for Strasbourg. His last war, the War of Spanish Succession (1701–1714), had to be fought in the Netherlands and in Italy, and Louis suffered a series of defeats. It left France in debt and deprived of colonies, but Louis's grandson did obtain the Spanish throne. Louis, however, had brought France to the verge of ruin.

Louis's other attempts at achieving glorification of the crown involved the building of a lavish palace on a swamp at Versailles. As well as adding to his own sense of importance, this served as a means to remove the court and administration from the politically unstable capital. In addition, Louis used the creation of a magnificent new court as the means to distract the court nobles by luring them into a hedonistic lifestyle, thus ensuring that they could not be plotting against him elsewhere. His reign was an era of great culture: the period of Jean *Racine, Pierre *Corneille, and Jean-Baptiste *Moliere. However, the heavy taxation he imposed for his luxury and ostentation almost bankrupted France.

In his personal life the king had a series of mistresses, among them Louise de la Vallierè and Madame de Montespan, the wife of the prince of Monaco. The queen died in 1683, leaving behind only one living child (out of six), the grand dauphin, born in 1661. With her beauty vanishing and rumors of witchcraft and poisoning affecting her reputation at court, Madame de Montespan was replaced by Madame de Maintenon, the former governess of the Montespan children, as the object of Louis's affections. After the death of the queen, Louis secretly married her and under her influence adopted a more pious lifestyle. However, with advancing years and the result of over-indulgence, Louis's health began to suffer and between 1684 and 1686 he had three operations.

With the onset of failing health combined with his newfound sense of piety, Louis turned his attention to religious affairs. Although at the outset he was tolerant of dissent, he now wished to impose religious uniformity. His persecution of the Huguenots led to the revocation of the Edict of Nantes in 1685, causing the emigration of half a million Protestants from France. Many of them were merchants and skilled artisans and their departure further crippled the economy. His actions also alienated the Protestant powers, eventually costing France its supremacy.

Louis died at the age of seventy-seven and his body was taken to the abbey church of Saint-Denis. The grand dauphin and his son, the duke of Burgundy, had already died (1711 and 1712, respectively), and the latter's only surviving son, Louis's five-year-old great grandson, was not expected to live (but recovered, to succeed him as Louis XV). Louis had distrusted his nephew, the duke of Orléans, and had wanted to leave the task of governing to his son by Madame de Montespan. Toward this end Louis had written a will detailing his intentions, but after his death the will was annuled by the Paris *parlement*, anxious to regain powers lost during Louis's reign. In a famous scene the dying king bade farewell to the future Louis XV and warned him, "Do not imitate my wars and my love of building."

P. Burke, *The Fabrication of Louis XIV*, 1992.

W. F. Church, *Louis the Fourteenth in Historical Thought*, 1976.

V. Cronin, *Louis XIV*, 1974.

P. Goubert, *Louis XIV and Twenty Million Frenchmen*, 1972.

D. Ogg, *Louis XIV*, 1967.

LOUIS XVI (1754–1793), king of France 1774–1792, third son of the dauphin Louis and his consort Maria Josepha of Saxony, grandson and successor of Louis XV. In 1770 he married Marie-Antointette, an Austrian archduchess and daughter of Maria Theresa and the emperor *Francis I. In 1774 Louis acceded to the throne totally devoid of the personal qualities necessary to govern France at a time of social and political turmoil. Lacking in self-confidence, shy and awkward, he was easily subject to the political agenda of his court intimates.

Faced with an ineffective king, reforms introduced by the finance controller, Anne-Robert-Jacques Turgot, were easily resisted by the court alliance. In 1787, unable to ward off bankruptcy, the king convoked the Assembly of Notables to ask their consent to tax the privileged classes. A few minor reforms were accepted but the assembly refused to consent to taxation, referring the matter to the Estates-General (the representative assembly of the three "estates": the nobility, the clergy, and the people). In 1789 Louis finally summoned the Estates-General, but his resistance to the combined meeting of the estates resulted in the third estate proclaiming itself a national assembly. Undeterred, Louis ordered the estates to assemble but to vote as

separate bodies, but on June 27, 1789, he was forced to capitulate and allow the estates to sit together and vote as individuals. Suspicious of the French guards, he sent troops to Paris in the hope of suppressing any pro-assembly sentiments. This action combined with the dismissal of his finance minister, Jacques Necker, was seen as an attempt by the king to subvert the assembly and prompted the storming of the Bastille on July 14, 1789. Faced with such violent opposition Louis was forced to withdraw his royal troops, retain Necker, and accept the new national red, white, and blue cockade, symbol of the revolutionaries.

Despite outward appearances to the contrary, and encouraged by his wife and court intimates, Louis continued to oppose the revolutionaries. In August he refused to approve the abolition of feudal rights and as a result of his persistent refusal to accept populist demands, a mob marched on Versailles on October 6, 1789, and forced the royal family to return to Paris where they were confined in the Tuileries palace.

Louis's fate was finally sealed when in June 1791 the royal family attempted to escape. Disguised as a servant of his children's governess, Louis was detected and apprehended by the mayor of Varennes and an inkeeper from a neighboring village. The attempted escape was seen as proof of Louis's treasonable contacts with emigre circles and he was forced to accept the constitution of 1791.

Following his return, Louis concentrated his efforts on the intervention of foreign powers. During this period, he was in constant communication with Austria and Prussia, imploring them to intervene on his behalf. In 1798 the outbreak of the war with Austria, combined with the duke of Brunswick's threat to destroy Paris if the royal family were harmed, enraged the revolutionaries and on August 10 the Tuileries was captured by the people of Paris and the provincial militia. The royal family was imprisoned, the king's powers suspended, and on September 21 the first French republic was proclaimed.

In November documents discovered in an iron chest in the Tuileries after the fall of the king proved his correspondence with the emigrés and his desire to subvert the constitution. Louis was indicted on December 11, charged with plotting against the nation, with paying troops raised by the emigrés abroad, and with attempting to overthrow the constitution. Once he appeared before his judges, the members of the Convention, his conviction for the high political crimes of which he was accused was assured. His stubborn refusal to recognize the authority of the evidence against him created a bad impression. The chief plea of his leading defense counsel, that the king was inviolate under the terms of the constitution of 1791, proved useless. A unanimous verdict of guilty was returned against the king and he was condemned, 387 votes to 334. As twenty-six of the majority had been in favor of an amendment for suspending the death sentence, a fresh vote was taken on the deferment of execution and the final decision to execute Louis was taken by a majority of seventy. On January 21, 1793, he was guillotined in what had formerly been the Place Louis XV, now renamed the Place de la Revolution. Marie-Antoinette suffered the same fate in October.

As France's final monarch preceding the revolution of 1789, Louis XVI proved incapable of responding to the demands of his position. With his easy-going temperament and slow-witted approach, he was easily manipulated by the court reactionaries. This complete subservience caused him to adopt a policy of sheer inaction, the consequences of which sealed his fate.

V. Cronin, *Louis and Marie-Antoinette*, 1974.

J. Hardman, *Louis XVI*, 1992.

S. K. Padover, *Life and Death of Louis XVI*, 1963.

LOYOLA, SAINT IGNATIUS OF (1491–1556),

leader of the sixteenth-century Catholic reformation; founder of the Society of Jesus (the Jesuits). Born at a critical juncture in the history of the Roman Catholic church, when its spiritual life had deteriorated, plagued by impiety, simony, and laxity, Loyola, from a noble and wealthy background, helped to renew the life of the church, setting an example of poverty, devotion, and loyalty to the pope.

Baptized Iñigo Lopez de Loyola in the Basque country of Spain, Loyola had an aristocratic upbringing. When he was twelve, his parents arranged a position for him in the household of Juan Velázquez de Cuellar, King *Ferdinand's treasurer. Velazquez educated Loyola to be his page in the royal court, grooming him impeccably and teaching him courtly manners as well as martial arts. Loyola read the chivalric tales that were popular at the time, seeing his own life on the way to high accomplishments.

By 1507 both his parents were dead. In 1517, when Velazquez died, Loyola left Cuellar for Navarre, also in northern Spain, pledging his loyalty and military services to the duke of Nájera. In the revolt of the Comuneros, Loyola fought to put down the rebellion, but withdrew for reasons of conscience when the troops began the traditional plunder of the defeated town. In 1521 the French attacked the Navarre region at Pamplona, its capital. Loyola hid out, refusing to surrender with the rest of the town. He took refuge in the city's fortress, convinced that he would be killed by the French army which greatly outnumbered Navarre's forces. In the battle that ensued, he was hit by a cannonball, injured in both his legs. When the Spanish forces surrendered, the French treated Loyola's wounds; he was left limp and deformed from his injuries. He refused to accept his fate, suffering through excruciatingly painful surgery to correct his condition so that he could return to his chivalrous lifestyle. The period of his convalescence turned out to be the beginning of a spiritual revolution in his life. During this time his readings of the life of Christ and the saints led him to turn away from his martial pursuits toward a devout life of Christian spirituality.

In 1522 he left Navarre to go on pilgrimage to the Holy Land. In transit he stopped at Monserrat, a pilgrimage site in northeastern Spain. Here he divested himself of his wealth, taking the rough clothes of a beggar and discarding the weapons of his military career. He then continued to Manresa where he stayed for eleven months doing penance, dwelling in a cave, begging for food, breaking his bodily strength, and formulating what would become his great devotional work, *Exercitia Spiritualia*, Spiritual Exercises.

The *Exercises* was based on Loyola's own experiences of transformation, intended as a guide, leading the believer through a process of Christian self-examination, penitence, recommitment of faith and strengthening. Accordingly, the *Exercises* was divided into four weeks, each week concentrating on another stage of the process of restoring Christian commitment. Although formulated during these critical months at Manresa in 1522, the work did not reach its completed form until 1541.

From Manresa, Loyola went on to the Holy Land, leaving from the port of Barcelona to sail to Italy before finally arriving on foot in Jerusalem. Denied permission to stay there, Loyola returned to Barcelona in 1525 after making pilgrimages to various sites in the Holy Land. Back in Spain he studied Latin and philosophy, while also counseling those who sought his wisdom in spiritual matters. Gaining followers, many of whom were women, he was accused of heresy and imprisoned for a period of time.

When he gained his freedom, he went to Paris where he resumed his study of philosophy, receiving a master's degree in 1534. That same year, six men joined him in taking vows and studied his *Spiritual Exercises*, performing the prayers and meditations under his direction. Soon Loyola attracted more followers, increasing the group's number to ten before they departed for Jerusalem. On the way, in Venice, seven of the pilgrims were ordained as priests.

In 1539 the group became the Society of Jesus, and Loyola sent the principles of the Society to Pope Paul III, who confirmed it the next year. Loyola became general of the order, leading it until his death. His pleas to resign his duties during his last years when he suffered severe illness went unheeded by his followers, who looked to him for guidance. By the time of Loyola's death there were one thousand members of the Society spearheading the church's Counter-Reformation against the Protestants while working within the Catholic church for its spiritual revival.

Loyola set a precedent of strong central authority for the Jesuits and this has continued throughout their history. They combated the trend in the sixteenth century away from religion — a move that had been accompanied by the study of classical texts — by teaching theology with rigorous scholarship and preaching the gospels. In addition the Society continued to emphasize education, good works, and helping the underprivileged. Al-

Saint Ignatius of Loyola

ready during Loyola's lifetime, the Jesuits were active in Asia, Africa, the New World, and throughout Europe. By 1626 their membership numbered over fifteen thousand and one hundred years later this number had grown to twenty-two thousand.

The *Spiritual Exercises* became one of the church's most influential writings. In 1548 it received high praise from Pope Paul III and this was just the first of the book's accolades, reaffirmed again and again by the church through the centuries. Loyola's concept of spiritual retreat has sometimes been a subject of controversy, criticized because of the influence of the Jesuit leader over the practitioner in directing his prayer and spiritual life. Others focusing on the private nature of the meditations have criticized them for encouraging an inappropriate individuality in spiritual life. Loyola himself aroused differing appraisals. For some he was a militaristic leader of an authoritarian, secretive group. For others, he was a paternal figure whose strictness was a natural and necessary response to the Reformation as well as the need for reform within the church itself. Through Loyola's combination of pragmatism and spiritual rigor and sincerity, he became one of the major figures that rescued the Catholic church from one of its worst crises.

J. Brodrick, *Ignatius Loyola: The Pilgrim Years*, 1956.
P. Caraman, *Ignatius Loyola*, 1990.
P. Dudon, *Saint Ignatius of Loyola*, 1949.
W. W. Meisner, *Ignatius of Loyola*, 1993.
J. C. Olin, ed., *The Autobiography of Saint Ignatius Loyola with Related Documents*, 1974.

LUDENDORFF, ERICH FRIEDRICH WILHELM (1865–1937), German general. Ludendorff was born in Posen. As a boy he was lonely and reserved, and obsessive about cleanliness. He showed little aptitude for sports, but excelled in his studies, especially mathematics, showing great self-discipline in keeping at his books. Aged twelve, he entered the cadet school at Plon, and in 1880 moved to the military academy at Lichterfelde, near Berlin.

After five years at the academy, Ludendorff received his commission as second lieutenant and served in different areas of the Prussian army over the following eight years. In 1893 he was chosen to attend the Kriegesakademie in Berlin for further training and was promoted, reaching the rank of colonel by 1911. The turning point in his career came when he was ordered to Berlin to serve in the general staff under Alfred von Schlieffen, architect of the Schlieffen plan for the simultaneous conquest of France and control of the Russian front. Ludendorff, like many of his colleagues, became committed to the concept of an inevitable two-front war. He fell out of favor in Berlin when he resorted to political maneuvering, anathema to the aristocratic Prussian military elite, in order to try to obtain more manpower for the war, and was dismissed in January 1913, being posted to Dusseldorf for routine regimental duties.

Ludendorff had already begun developing his theories of total war, which he later expounded in his book *Der Totale Krieg*, published in 1936, in which he rejected Carl Von *Clausewitz's principle that it is the purpose of war to serve the goals of the political leaders, instead defining the politicians' role as the support of military objectives.

In early 1914, Ludendorff was posted again, this time to Strasbourg for organizational duties. Soon after the outbreak of World War I, he earned the adulation of the German people for his prowess in the field, especially for heroic activities such as his single-handed capture of the citadel in Liege, and his victory at Tannenberg (Stebark). Although brusque and abrasive, with tendencies to sudden rages, Ludendorff was well liked by his soldiers, who even called him "Father" on occasion. His transfer to the eastern front marked the beginning of his relationship with Field Marshal *Hindenburg, under whom he served as chief of staff.

During the years 1916–1918 Ludendorff, with the more aristocratic Hindenburg as his figurehead, held undisputed power in Germany and in the areas occupied by the German armies and ruled over both military and domestic affairs. He orchestrated the German offensive on the western front, which culminated in the second battle of the Marne in 1918, but backed down under the pressure of the major Allied-U.S. counteroffensive later that year, suffering, according to some, a nervous breakdown. His popularity reached an all-time low following the end of the war, and he fled to Sweden. He had been completely opposed to the unconditional surrender forced upon Germany by the allies, believing that

Ludendorff with Hitler after the Beer Hall Putsch

the German armies should have preserved the honor of the fatherland through a suicidal offensive rather than accept such humiliating terms. He developed the theory that Germany had been betrayed by the politicians, Catholics, and Jews in the Versailles peace negotiations.

During the period immediately after the war, Ludendorff's home became a meeting place for right-wing elements. He was heavily involved in the ineffectual Kapp putsch, which tried to establish a right-wing dictatorship in March 1920, and in Adolf *Hitler's Munich putsch of November 1923 but swiftly became disillusioned with Hitler when he realized that his actions were more for self-aggrandizement than for the glory of Germany. In 1926 he divorced his wife and married Dr. Mathilde von Kemnitz, with whom he proceeded to produce a series of eccentric and extreme pamphlets and books filled with polemic and invective against Jews, Catholics, and Freemasons. He became totally estranged from Hindenburg due to the latter's alliance with Hitler, and when Hindenburg, as president, offered the chancellorship to Hitler in January 1933, Ludendorff accused him of placing the safety of the fatherland in the hands of one of the greatest demagogues of all time. He died in a Catholic hospital in Munich. Despite his estrangement from the Nazi party, he was given a state funeral with Hitler walking behind the coffin.

D. J. Goodspeed, *Ludendorff,* 1966.
M. Kitchen, *The Silent Dictatorship,* 1976.
R. Parkinson, *Tormented Warrior,* 1978.

LUMIÈRE AUGUSTE (1862–1954) **and LOUIS** (1864–1948), French photographic and cinema entrepreneurs, credited with the invention of cinematography. Born in France, near Lyons, the sons of a prosperous manufacturer of photographic plates, Lumière and his older brother Auguste

(1862–1954) studied at the Martinier School of Industry and Commerce. Both brothers joined their father in the family business and quickly showed signs of the ingenuity and business acumen that was to become their trademark. Before he was twenty, Lumière had perfected his father's production techniques to the point where their factory was a leader in this new field. Within fifteen years the Lumière brothers had become important industrialists; they kept up to date with the latest developments in photography and soon became interested in the development of motion pictures, a field very much in its technological infancy a that time.

In 1894 the Lumière brothers came into contact with Thomas *Edison's Kinetoscope, a primitive contraption by which a short sequence of moving images could be viewed by one customer at a time. They were immediately inspired with the idea of projecting moving images onto a screen in front of an audience and within a year they had developed an elegant machine that combined camera, processor, and projector. Its original contribution was a system of claws that moved the film. Patented under the name *Cinématographe,* from which the word *cinema* is derived, this machine was used to shoot one-minute films that were first shown privately throughout 1895. Confident of their technique, the brothers premiered their films to the paying public on December 28, in a basement of the Grand Café in Paris. The ten films totalled twenty minutes, and there were twenty screenings a day. Each film was limited to a physical length of fifty feet, which was the capacity of the spool box holding the negative.

Not only did the Lumière brothers' *Cinématographe* produce high quality images, it had the added advantage of being portable, so that for the first time the cameraman was able to leave the studio and record the outside world at work and play. The Lumiere's films were short, lively documentaries that presented a warm, secure image of bourgeois life at the turn of the century. Initially, the Lumières made use of family and friends in their films. Their first production, *Workers Leaving the Factory,* shows their own employees leaving the family photographic factory. Another early work, *Baby's Tea,* is a charming sequence that features Louis Lumière, his wife, and their baby daughter. From the beginning, Louis also showed a lively comic talent and produced many popular comic sketches.

The Lumières started to send cameramen all over the world to cover international events and satisfy audience's curiosity about foreign lands and cultures. People queued up for hours to be astounded by the Lumières' lifelike moving images. One of their most famous films, *The Arrival of the Train,* caused an uproar when it was first shown as many people thought that the approaching train on the screen was actually going to hit them. Despite the fact that none of the Lumières' works lasted more than a few minutes, they were skillfully organized in terms of time and space, testifying to Louis Lumière's experience as a stills photographer.

The Lumière brothers set out to market their films internationally and jealously guarded the secret of the *Cinematographe*, employing their own cameramen and projectionists. However, imitators proliferated and the brothers soon found themselves in competition with English and American filmmakers. Despite considerable financial success, they never had the resources of their rivals and as a result grew discouraged. Louis Lumière gradually wound down his production of films and by 1903 had returned to photography and developing the production of color plates. During World War I the company diversified its production, working on ways of heating aircraft, and in 1920 Louis Lumière abandoned direction of the factory to concentrate on technical inventions. In 1934 he returned to the cinema with three-dimensional films, which were premiered in Paris in 1936. Meanwhile Auguste Lumière had directed his energies to medical research and published many respected articles.

Louis Lumière was the first person to recognize the cinema as a profitable form of public entertainment, and the artistic excellence and sound marketing of his films ensured that the cinema would be more than just a passing technological novelty. The irony is that Louis Lumière himself never believed that the cinema had a long-term future or that it could ever do more than represent everyday life; it was left for others to exploit the narrative and aesthetic properties of the medium. The Lumière factory in Lyons is now a museum and archive, and the gates featured in his first film are still in place.
G. Sadout, *Louis Lumière*, 1958.

LUTHER, MARTIN (1483–1546), German theologian, ecclesiastical reformer, founder of Protestantism. Luther was born in Saxony, where his father worked in the copper mines and rose to a position of some authority and affluence. Somber piety and strict discipline characterized the family's home life. The elder Luther wished for his son to better himself and the family, and it was therefore decided that he should study for a career in law. To this end he entered university, where his manner earned him the nickname "the Philosopher" among his fellow students; he graduated with a master's degree in 1505.

To his father's chagrin, Luther was destined never to pursue a legal career. At an early age he had come into contact with the Brethren of the Common Life, one of the most pious and spiritual of late medieval religious movements, and was much influenced by them. His heightened religious sensibilities drew him inexorably toward the life of the spirit; then, on experiencing a ferocious thunderstorm near Stotterheim while on his way to university, he vowed to become a monk if he should survive. He was as good as his word, and entered the Augustinian (See *Augustine) monastery at Erfurt and was ordained in 1507.

His diligence and talent marked him out as a fine scholar, and in 1508 he was sent by his order for further studies at Wittenberg. During a visit to Rome in 1510, on a mission to present the viewpoint of the German Augustinians in debate, he was shocked and disillusioned by the worldliness of the clergy there and the apparent absence of genuine spiritual values; this was to exacerbate his increasing alienation from the church of Rome.

The peculiarities of Luther's complex personality are a central component among the factors that precipitated his revolutionary theological formulation. Standing as he did at the gateway between the medieval and modern ages, he heralded the latter while manifesting the temperament of the former; the road to revolt was not an easy one for him, and his spiritual dilemmas can be seen to represent those of his age. Alternating between bouts of ecstasy and depression, and constantly and painfully oppressed by a sense of guilt at his own sinfulness, Luther increasingly came to feel that the established church could offer him little spiritual succor. The angry God of the Old Testament aroused in him no love, only fear. Moreover, he came to feel that human acts of repentance and good works were insufficient to expunge the burden of sin that each individual carried and accreted from cradle to grave. Salvation depended entirely on the grace of God rather than on human merit, he concluded; faith, therefore, became the cornerstone of his theology. He stressed the need for each man to minister to himself in the sovereign solitude of his conscience.

In 1512 Luther gained the title of doctor of theology; thereafter, regardless of the momentous religious controversies in which he became embroiled, his chief function remained lecturing in the chair of biblical theology at Wittenburg, while from 1514 he pursued an influential teaching ministry from the pulpit. He was vehemently anti-philosophical, characterizing himself as the northern barbarian storming the strongholds of the effete southern papists; in his autobiographical *Table Talk* he rued the time spent "on philosophy and all that devil's muck, when I could have been busy with poetry and legend and so many good things." Through his influence, Wittenburg forsook the study of *Aristotle and the Scholastics for direct study of the Bible in a humanist framework: "Our theology, and that of Saint Augustine, reign," he declared triumphantly.

If a single date can be identified as signaling the advent of Protestantism, it is October 31, 1517, when Luther nailed his ninety-five theses to the door of All Saints' Church in Wittenburg, roundly attacking the practice of selling indulgences (the remission of sins under certain conditions). The theses were a declaration of the inward nature of Christianity, a criticism of the corruption rife in the established church, and an attack on papal policies. Luther outlined his "theology of the cross," which stressed the need of each Christian to share the temptation

Martin Luther and Jan Hus giving communion

and suffering of Christ and argued that a person's communion with God requires no intermediary.

In the ensuing furor, Luther was supported by the chapter of his own Augustinian order, but nonetheless there were calls for his condemnation. In his debate with the theologian Johann van Eck in 1519, he was maneuvered into casting doubt on the findings of the General Council of Constance (1414–1418) and into supporting some of the doctrines of Jan *Hus; within a year a papal bull had been issued against him and his works were publicly burned. However, Luther enjoyed strong popular support within Germany, and reacted combatively to church condemnation with two of his most influential tracts: his *Address to the Christian Nobility of the German Nation*, which protested the need for the secular powers in Germany to intervene to ensure reform within the church, and his *Prelude Concerning the Babylonian Captivity of the Church*, which argued for the reduction of the seven sacraments to just three — baptism, the Lord's Supper, and penance — on the ground that only these were sanctioned by Scripture. This latter stance was consistent with his belief in "sola Scriptura": that is to say, that Holy Scripture, not the word of the pope, is the supreme authority and guide for the true believer. His rejection of the established ecclesiastical order was now complete.

Following his public burning of the papal bull against him, Luther was formally excommunicated in January 1521. Nonetheless, such was the popular support for him within Germany that Emperor *Charles V, despite his pro-Catholic and antireformist

sentiments, agreed that Luther should be allowed to present his own case to the Diet of Worms. Apocryphally uttering "Here I stand; I can do no other," Luther evidenced his undisputed moral courage and rectitude by saying that he would not recant unless convinced of his error by Scripture or evident reason. The diet marked him as an outlaw whose works were proscribed; spirited away by influential supporters to Wartburg Castle, he remained in hiding for a year; many presumed him kidnapped or dead.

An emotionally turbulent individual, Luther found his period of enforced retreat difficult; he plunged into deep depression and put on weight. He did not, however, remain wholly inactive, for this was the time in which he commenced his translation of the Bible into German, which was completed in 1534. The poet Heinrich *Heine was to say that the creator of the German language was Luther: the foundation of a common German literary experience did not exist until Luther provided it. His biblical translations and political and theological pamphlets were written in a language of unprecedented lucidity and richness, with a vigor and flexibility of expression equally suited to the requirements of exposition and argumentation, of satire and humor. When the new printing presses made them available throughout the German states, they transformed the tongue which his adversary Charles V had described as fit only for speaking to horses. His noble hymns were a major contribution to the German language and to Protestantism, and encouraged the congregation to participate in religious services.

Returning to Wittenburg in March 1522, Luther joined in the administration and control of the expanding movement he had initiated. His aims were political as well as purely spiritual: "Our manner of life is

> - Eve got into trouble when she worked in the garden alone. I have my worst temptations when I am by myself.
> - Don't argue with the devil. He has had five thousand years of experience.
> - A mighty fortress is our God,
>   A bulwark never failing.
> - Faith is a living and unshakeable confidence, a belief in the grace of God so assured that a man would die a thousand deaths for its sake.
> - Music is one of the greatest gifts that God has given us; it is divine and therefore Satan is its enemy. The devil does not stay where music is.
> - A Christian is no one's servant, subject to none, and he is everyone's servant, subject to all.
> - To pray well is the better half of study.
>
> **Martin Luther**

as evil as that of the papists," he admitted, "but when I can show that their doctrine is false, then I can easily prove that their manner of life is evil." He accepted the concept of the division of church and state, and his assertion that a citizen must obey the laws of the latter paved the way for the increase in the power of kings that was seen in the succeeding century.

Luther's quarrelsome nature involved him in many arguments: he accused the radical reformers who flocked to his cause of being more interested in honor and glory than the salvation of souls. During the 1524 Peasants' War his brutal *Against the Murdering and Thieving Hordes of Peasants* drove many of those unfortunates into the Anabaptist fold, and once he realized the Jews would not convert, he advocated persecution of them. He also alienated many humanists by his vindictive personal assault on Disadrus *Erasmus, whose views on free will conflicted with his own, and he disputed vigorously with the Swiss reformer Huldrich *Zwingli over communion.

The Edict of Worms was suspended in 1526, and in 1530 Luther's assistant Philipp Melanchthon produced, in the *Augsburg Confession*, the great document of the reform movement. In 1525 Luther married a former nun and watching his baby son, Martin, at his mother's breast, he commented, "Your enemies are the Pope, the Bishops, Duke George, Ferdinand and the Devil. And there you suck and take no heed." Luther's preoccupations in his last years turned increasingly toward consolidating Protestant gains through education.

M. Edwards, *Luther, a Reformer of the Churches*, 1983.

E. W. Gritsch, *Martin, God's Court Jester*: *Luther in Retrospect*, 1983.

H. G. Haile, *Luther: A Biography*, 1980.

D. C. Steinmetz, *Luther in Context*, 1986.

LUTHULI, ALBERT JOHN MVUMBI (c. 1898–1967), South African black leader awarded the Nobel Peace Prize in 1960 for his sustained non-violent fight against the white supremacist National party's oppressive and discriminatory policy of apartheid. Luthuli was born in Rhodesia (now Zimbabwe) and raised at the Groutville Mission (Umvoti), Natal, where his grandfather, chief of the Abasemakholweni Zulu, had been the first convert to the Methodist church, and his father a missionary. Luthuli himself was a devoutly religious man and Methodist lay preacher throughout his life. In 1917 he qualified as a primary school teacher and taught for fifteen years.

In 1936 he was elected tribal chief of the five thousand member Abasemakholweni tribe in Groutville, a post that afforded him a good opportunity to promote the economic and social position of his people. He presided over the councils, put down disturbances in the sugar fields, arbitrated disputes, and imposed laws. He also strengthened his ties with organized Christianity.

In 1946 he joined the ineffectual, government-sponsored Native Representatives Council. He was already a member of the African National Congress, then still a small organization of some one thousand members devoted to achieving equality for South Africa's blacks. The legal aspects of apartheid were only then being formulated by Daniel Malan's government, and the black majority responded with a vocal defiance campaign, patterned after the nonviolent protest of Mahatma *Gandhi. In the course of the campaign, Luthuli, a soft-spoken moderate, quickly rose to national prominence. He was dismissed from his state-appointed position as tribal chief and briefly arrested. Rather than prosecute him, however, the government enacted the Criminal Laws Amendment Act, calling for severe penalties for anyone breaking the law in protest of government policies. In another protest, Luthuli challenged the government over the unequal division of land between blacks and whites, contrary to the Group Areas Act. In response, the government legitimized its discriminatory policies in the Separate Amenities Act.

In 1952 Luthuli was elected president general of the African National Congress. He held the post until his death, at which time membership was over one hundred thousand. Although he was regularly banned, he played an active role in black politics and helped formulate the Freedom Charter of 1956 declaring South Africa the inheritance of all its inhabitants regardless of race. The government regarded the charter as a serious threat, and Luthuli, along with 155 others, was arrested and tried for treason. He was soon acquitted; no proof could be found that he had plotted the violent overthow of the white government.

- I am no racist. South Africa is large enough to accomodate all people if they have large enough hearts.
- I pray to the almighty to make our beloved Union of South Africa a true democracy and a true union, in form and spirit, of all the communities in the land.
- In a strife-torn world, tottering on the brink of complete destruction by man-made nuclear weapons, a free and independent Africa is in the making, in answer to the injuction and challenge of history: "Arise and shine, for thy light is come."(Nobel Prize speech)
- Who will deny that thirty years of my life have been spent knocking in vain, patiently, moderately, and modestly, at a closed, barred door.

  Albert Luthuli

Just prior to the 1960 Sharpeville massacre, Luthuli was restricted to his tribal reservation for five years. He nonetheless burned his passbook, the document which, under the policies of Apartheid, South African blacks had to carry on their persons at all times and which severely restricted their movements within the country. For this he was arrested and fined. Other black leaders were calling for armed violence against the oppressive white regime, but Luthuli remained dedicated to nonviolence. In 1960 he was awarded with the Nobel Prize for Peace, the first black African to win the award. At first, the government was reluctant to permit him to attend the prize ceremony in Oslo, but finally agreed to allow him one week abroad. Money from the prize was used to establish shelters in Swaziland for political exiles.

In 1964 the ban on Luthuli was extended for another five years. Although he was forbidden to publish, his impassioned autobiography, *Let My People Go*, appeared in 1962. Luthuli died in 1967 when he was struck by a train while crossing a railroad track near his home.

M. Benson, *Chief Albert Luthuli of South Africa*, 1963.

E. Callan, *Albert John Luthuli and the South African Race Conflict*, 1965.

M

MACARTHUR, DOUGLAS (1880–1964), U.S. military leader, commander of the Allied Pacific Forces during World War II and the U.S. Army during the Korean War. His father, who had been awarded the Congressional Medal of Honor for exceptional bravery during the Civil War, constantly reminded his son that he received the award for an assault he led without having received an order to do so, and encouraged his son to take similar initiatives. MacArthur's mother saw her two older sons die prematurely, perhaps explaining the curious bond she maintained with MacArthur until her death. She even followed him to West Point Military Academy, keeping a hotel room near the campus to support her son's diligence and to remove any external distractions, notably women, that might interfere with his progress. His father, Arthur, was a haughty and often flamboyant commander who served in such prestigious military positions as military attaché to China and commander of the Philippines. Douglas MacArthur excelled at West Point, finishing with a record average. He graduated with the rank of second lieutenant and chose to serve in the Philippines to be close to his father.

He found the Philippines alluring and befriended many prominent local leaders, including Manuel *Quezon, later first president of that country. On the family's return to the United States, Douglas Macarthur studied engineering. He distinguished himself in the Spanish-American War for several daring assignments. In one, according to his own account, he single-handedly killed seven enemy gunmen. He was startled to discover that his bravery would not be rewarded since there was no verification of his feat and that the story, if true, was dismissed as an "error in judgment." He later served as military adviser to President Theodore *Roosevelt.

During World War I MacArthur reached the rank of colonel and got the opportunity to command the Rainbow Division, formed, at his instigation, of National Guardsmen. In his two years in Europe he was the recipient of numerous medals and decorations. His troops fought in eight major battles. Yet despite his acknowledged bravery, MacArthur was regarded as an eccentric. He refused to wear a gas mask or helmet and carried no weapon but his riding crop. After a mission, he returned to base one night leading a high-ranking German officer with his crop.

After returning to America MacArthur was appointed superintendent of West Point, but was soon removed. Officially, his dismissal was attributed to the radical changes he had made in that institution, but he always ascribed his removal to the mutual distrust between himself and the commander of the army, General John J. *Pershing. MacArthur was returned to the Philippines with the rank of major general.

In 1930 he was appointed army chief of staff. The depression-era posting saw enormous cuts in the military budget, including a cut in military pensions. Disgruntled veterans marched on Washington but were dispersed with considerable violence by MacArthur. Presidential candidate Franklin Delano *Roosevelt responded to the attack on unarmed veterans by calling MacArthur, "one of the most dangerous men in the country."

Rather than settle for a lesser post, MacArthur accepted the position of military adviser to his old friend Quezon, soon to be president of an independent Commonwealth of the Philippines.

General MacArthur accepting Japan's surrender

In return for his encouraging Quezon to assert full independence for the Philippines, MacArthur was appointed field marshal of the Philippine army, a force whose creation had been the result of his own devoted efforts in the face of official American opposition. Roosevelt came to detest MacArthur who, in turn, took every opportunity to deride the president. In 1937, two years before his tour of duty in the Philippines was to end, MacArthur was finally convinced to retire from active service. He remained in the Philippines at the request of President Quezon, who continued to employ him as adviser, but the relationship between the two men degenerated and Quezon sought unsuccessfully to have MacArthur replaced by his rival and former aide, General Dwight D. *Eisenhower. MacArthur was, however, still recognized as an authority on East Asia; with the rising threat of Japan to the region, Roosevelt requested MacArthur to remain in Manila.

Following the Japanese occupation of French ports in Indochina, the new chief of staff, General George C. *Marshall, persuaded Roosevelt to appoint MacArthur supreme commander of the armed forces in the Far East. MacArthur encouraged the American administration to abandon its original plan to defend only Manila and Subic Bay in favor of a comprehensive defense policy for the entire archipelago. The islands soon had the largest force of fighter planes outside the United States. When the Japanese invaded the Philippines in 1942, the local army crumbled in just two days. MacArthur evacuated Manila and moved his troops to the Bataan Peninsula and Corregidor Island. He defended the area for five months until, upon realizing that the Americans had chosen to abandon the front, he too made plans to retreat. His own

---

- It's the orders you disobey that make you famous.
- There is no substitute for victory.
- I have come through, and I shall return.
- A good soldier, whether he leads a platoon or an army, is expected to look backward as well as forward, but he must think only forward.
- It is fatal to enter any war without the will to win it.
- Like the old soldier of the ballad, I now close my military career and fade away.

Douglas MacArthur

The best and the worst things you hear about MacArthur are quite true.

General Sir Thomas Blamey

---

press releases from the embattled island had already assured his entry into the pantheon of American heroes. After accepting a $500,000 gift from Quezon as a token of their friendship, MacArthur led his family and troops to Mindanao, where a plane took them to Australia. Arriving in Darwin, he issued his famous statement, "I shall return!"

Despite his growing fame among the masses, MacArthur's popularity waned in the administration. It was said that some would have preferred, "to see MacArthur lose a battle than America win the war." He differed with the administration over wartime priorities and questioned the emphasis placed on the European rather than the Pacific front, claiming that life under the Nazis would be "tolerable; after all, the Germans are a civilized people."

Shortly before the Allied assault on Japan, MacArthur was appointed general of the army, empowered to lead the ground assault on Japan. To his dismay, this opportunity was "stolen" from him after the nuclear attacks on Hiroshima and Nagasaki. He did, however, conclude the armistice treaty with Japan and served as military governor of the country, overseeing its transformation into a democratic society. He showed great respect for Emperor *Hirohito, and rejected all attempts to try him as a war criminal. His new constitution for Japan, drawn up in just six days, rejected militarism and redefined the role of the emperor. Although he was their conqueror, MacArthur won the esteem of the local population. From Japan MacArthur ran an unsuccessful bid for the Republican presidential nomination in 1948, but was defeated in the first two primaries and abandoned the race.

The Korean War in 1950 returned MacArthur to the forefront of American life. It was MacArthur who encouraged President Harry S. *Truman to place American troops in combat and who planned the successful invasion of the port of Inchon, behind enemy lines. MacArthur was skeptical of the Chinese threat to enter the war, and when three hundred thousand Chinese troops swept down against American advances, he attributed it to faulty intelligence and refused to assume responsibility. MacArthur's support of an invasion of Communist China ran contrary to the plans of the American administration. His threat to disobey orders and carry out his plan forced Truman to recall him to the United States. It was there he made his last important public appearance, a farewell address to Congress interrupted by thirty ovations.

Three years before his death he made a last visit to the Philippines as the guest of honor at Independence Day celebrations.

D. MacArthur, *Reminiscences*, 1964.
W. Manchester, *American Caesar*, 1978.
M. Schaller, *Douglas MacArthur*, 1990.

McCARTHY, JOSEPH RAYMOND (1908–1957), U.S. senator who emerged at the beginning of the 1950s to become the most strident spokesman for the Republican campaign against communism. His name has come to represent this period of witch hunts against alleged communists and those merely suspected of "un-American" activity. The term "McCarthyism" describes the ruthless partisan exploitation of the climate of anticommunist suspicion that flourished after World War II.

McCarthy's personal campaign, together with government measures such as the House Committee on Un-American Activities and anti communist legislation, inflamed existing suspicions to a fever pitch. As a result, a mass audience was convinced that communists and subversives occupied positions of power in the government, serving as agents of a Soviet-led conspiracy.

McCarthy was born to a hardworking Irish Catholic family in Grand Chute, a small township near Milwaukee, Wisconsin. He left home at an early age to work and went on to study law, at Marquette College, Wiisconsin, graduating in 1935.

After starting to work as an attorney in 1936 he began in earnest to nurture his real passion, which was politics. His first involvement was with the Democrats but he switched loyalties in 1939 after going into partnership with an attorney who was associated with the Republican party. McCarthy then embarked on a journey up the political ladder, first running in the 1939 Republican primary for the position of judge in the Wisconsin tenth circuit (which he secured) and eventually winning a Senate seat in 1946 for Wisconsin on the strength of the nationwide popularity of the Republicans.

In his early years as a senator he did not have a particularly distinguished record nor was he heavily involved in fighting communism. He sprang to prominence as a "Red hunter" in 1950 in a speech made in Virginia, where he claimed to have a list of 205 communists who had infiltrated the State Department and who were actively shaping government policy. He also charged that the secretary of state was aware of their presence in the department. These charges received national media coverage and provoked denials from the president and the State Department. Over the next few years he delivered a continuing barrage of similar charges. In 1954 his target was General George *Marshall who he claimed was linked to a "Red" plot. In 1952 it was Adlai Stevenson who was accused of aiding communists.

McCarthy had strong popular support, particularly among small businessmen, the nouveaux-riche, and some Catholics, all of whom were traditionally hostile to liberalism and big business. To this sector of the population he represented the ordinary man who overcame modest origins to achieve success in a world of old money and power. Despite his moralistic cause, McCarthy's public persona was that of a rugged fighter who loved women and alcohol. He typically described his critics as "squeaking left-wing bleeding heart phoney liberals." He toured the country, particularly the Midwest, making speeches and spreading his gospel of the "Red menace."

In his speeches denouncing communism he tapped into the mood of intense patriotism and the sense of cultural superiority that then prevailed in the United States. In a speech made in 1950 he stated that "the great difference between our Western Christian world and the atheistic communist world is not political — it is moral. The real, basic difference lies in the religion of immoralism." He characterized communism as an ideology which repudiated justice and freedom, whereas America was the intellectual and moral leader of the world. Ironically, his campaign against the domestic threat of communism was launched when the heyday of communist politics had passed. It was during the 1930s that the trade union movement and intellectuals were most influenced by communist ideology. However, McCarthy still believed that "the communists within our borders have been more responsible for the success of communism abroad than Soviet Russia."

In 1953–1954 McCarthy, as chair of the Senate Permanent Investigating Committee, presided over a sensational series of hearings on the role of communism in government and other areas of life. The hearings climaxed with the investigation of alleged subversion in the Signal Corps. The hearings were controversial and the committee was accused of exerting improper pressure on the army and War Department, resulting in a recommendation that McCarthy be censured for contempt by the Senate. In December 1954 he was "condemned" rather than "censured" but his tactics were also attacked by President Dwight D. *Eisenhower, who denounced "book burners" and "thought control," and McCarthy's influence diminished quickly. His prominence was shortlived but it had a devastating impact on the American system of democracy.

D. Caute, *The Great Fear*, 1978.
R. M. Fried, *Nightmare in Red*, 1990.
Allen J. Matusow, ed., *Joseph McCarthy*, 1970.

MACHIAVELLI, NICCOLO (1469–1527), Italian statesman, author, and political scientist. Niccoló Machiavelli grew up in Florence, where his father had a minor government position as well as some property. He provided Machiavelli with an education that left him well versed in Latin and was the source of his life long interest in Roman history. When France invaded Italy in 1494, the *Medici were expelled from Florence, and Machiavelli was employed by Florence's new, republican government as a clerk in the Second Chancery of Commerce (which controlled Florence's departments of War and the Interior).In 1498 Machiavelli was appointed secretary of the chancery, a position he was to hold for fourteen years. His first mission ended in failure as he was completely outmaneuvered by older, more experienced and devious diplomats. His second mission was successful, and thereafter he was often sent to

FROM THE WRITINGS OF MACHIAVELLI

- Though a prince need not possess all the virtues, to seem to have them is useful.
- Whoever wishes to found a state and give it laws, must start with assuming that all men are bad and ever ready to display their vicious nature whenever they find occasion for it.
- Where it is an absolute question of the welfare of our country, we must admit of no considerations of justice or injustice, of mercy or cruelty, of praise or ignominy: but putting all else aside we must adopt whatever course will save the nation's existence and liberty.
- War should be the only study of a prince. He should consider peace only as a breathing-space, which gives him leisure to contrive and furnishes ability to execute military plans.

foreign powers and other Italian states. These missions gave him intensive, first hand experience of diplomatic machinations. With Spain and France invading Italy, he was convinced that Italy needed a strong, ruthless ruler to unite it and maintain its independence. He admired Cesare *Borgia's efficient if unscrupulous techniques, and the latter became his model for an ideal ruler. Machiavelli believed that military security was best guaranteed by a trained citizens' army rather than by hired mercenaries, who might easily succumb to a more tempting offer from the enemy. He suggested this to the government of Florence and was put in charge of establishing such a force. However, this militia was put to flight by Pope Julius II's trained mercenaries and the Medici were restored to power in 1512. Surrounded by personal and political enemies who either resented his militia's failure or his important position in the former republican government, Machiavelli's advances to the Medici were fruitless: the militia was dissolved, he was removed from office, and then tortured and imprisoned on accusations of plotting against the Medici.

After his release from prison, Machiavelli spent the next fourteen years in restless poverty with his wife and children in internal exile on his family estate, indifferent to the great art and discoveries of the Renaissance; his whole life had revolved around political intrigue. His feverish attempts to fill his empty days with study, writing, and dissipation resulted in his political, historical, and literary works.

Machiavelli's first work, *Discourses on the First Ten Books of Livy*, was an attempt to apply classical principles of government to political analysis. He hoped that his dedication of this work to the Medici would restore him to favor and political activity. When it became clear that a work of the length he initially envisaged would take too long to complete, he produced a summary of his ideas in *The Prince*, which revolutionized political science through its advice to rulers about how to acquire and keep power. Its cool disregard of moral considerations and stress on the welfare of the state over the individual offended many, and also added a new word, *Machiavellian* (meaning characterized by cunning and duplicity) to the world's vocabulary. However, it has been noted that while posterity may have condemned Machiavelli, it also practiced his doctrines.

The dedication to the Medici failed in its desired effect, and Machiavelli was forced to continue to write. *The Art of War* expressed his view that a state must fight the occasional minor war to keep its vital military skills honed; *Belfagor Arcidiavolo*, one of Italy's most popular novellas, satirized marriage; *Mandragola*, the outstanding drama of the Renaissance, satirized Renaissance immorality and led to his being commissioned to write a history of Florence, *Itorie florentine*, which revolutionized historiography. His vividly pornographic correspondence has not been published.

Machiavelli's ambitions to reenter the political arena seemed destined to be realized in 1526 when the Medici chose him to serve on a board for Florence's defense and sent him on diplomatic missions. However, the restoration of the republic and the expulsion of the Medici the following year put an end to his hopes. His request to be restored to his old post rejected, he died a broken man twelve days later.

P. S. Anglo, *Machiavelli*, 1970.
U. Dotti, *Niccolo Machievelli*, 1964.
P. Villari, *Life and Times of Niccolo Machiavelli*, 1973.

A contemporary caricature of Machiavelli

MADISON, JAMES (1751–1836), fourth president of the United States (1809–1817) and one of its founding fathers. Born in King George County, Virginia, he was taken as an infant to Orange County, Virginia, which was to be his home throughout his life. Little is known about his childhood. His early education came from local clergymen. In 1771 Madison received his bachelor of arts degree from the College of New Jersey at Princeton.

After graduation Madison became one of the principal writers of the Whig party. From 1774 to 1776 he served on the Orange County Committee for Safety and during this period wrote papers defining and defending the concept of religious liberty. His writings also sought to define the authority of the king of England.

In 1776 he was elected to represent the Orange County Committee at the Virginia Convention. His drafting of the guarantee of religious freedom was a pioneering document in modern history and became the model for other states. The convention had a lasting effect on Madison, becoming the foundation of the beliefs he adhered to for the rest of his life. However, he was not reelected because he failed to provide the electors with free whiskey.

In 1776 he was involved in the drafting of the Declaration of Independence; a delegate to the Continental Congress in 1780, he became one of its leading figures. A plan he introduced in Virginia became the basis for the Constitution of the United States and was adopted by the national government, giving it the power of taxation and law enforcement. Madison became known as "the father of the Constitution" and was co-author of *The Federalist,* the essays on the Constitution that played an important role in its adoption by the States.

When he was forty-three he married the widow Dolly Todd, a lively Washington hostess, whose magnificent entertaining became legendary and whose personality often overshadowed that of her quiet husband.

From 1789 to 1797 he was a member of Congress, where he was responsible for the first ten amendments to the Constitution. Madison worked closely with Thomas *Jefferson, whom he helped gain the presidency in 1800. Jefferson appointed Madison his secretary of state and he served through both of Jefferson's terms, becoming heavily involved in the negotiations and agreement which enabled the country to make the Louisiana Purchase. He was instrumental in the enactment of the Embargo Act and obtained American ownership of the Gulf coast between Florida and New Orleans.

Madison was Jefferson's own choice as successor and was easily elected president in 1808. For three years he tried to negotiate rather than go to war over English attacks on American shipping but on June 12, 1812, war against Great Britain was declared. He was reelected the same year although this time the election was more closely contested by the Federalist party. In the war the United States at first

> - I believe there are more instances of the abridgment of freedom by gradual and silent encroachments of those in power than by violent and sudden usurpations.
> - The personal right to acquire property, which is a natural right, gives to property, when acquired, a right to protection as a social right.
> - If we advert to the nature of republican government, we shall find that the censorial power is in the people over the government and not in the government over the people.
> - I always talk better lying down. (His last words)
>
> **James Madison**

sustained a series of defeats culminating in the burning of the White House in 1814. He was the only American president to have faced gunfire while in office: when the British entered Washington, Madison took command of an artillery battery for a time but as the situation deteriorated he returned to his carriage and drove off in the other direction. However, the tide of war turned somewhat and when neither side found it could gain the advantage, the 1815 Treaty of Ghent ended the fighting. During the remaining years of Madison's presidency he was immensely popular and many of his domestic programs were passed into law.

He spent his last years in retirement on his Virginia farm, supervising its operations and introducing various agricultural innovations. He also served as rector of the University of Virginia.

R. Allen, *James Madison,* 1986.

D. R. McCoy, *The Last of the Fathers,* 1989.

W. L. Miller, *The Business of May Next*, 1992.

R. A. Rutland, *James Madison: The Founding Father*, 1987.

MAGELLAN, FERDINAND (1480–1521), Portuguese explorer. At the age of twelve Ferdinand Magellan became a page in the royal court (his family belonged to the lesser Portuguese nobility); at sixteen he became a clerk in the Marine Department responsible for equipping ships bound for Africa and the Indies.

The ownership of all newly discovered lands had been divided between Spain and Portugal by the pope with the Treaty of Tordesillas. Riches from the Indies poured into Lisbon, and many saw the region as a quick route to wealth and advancement; Magellan and his friend Francisco Serrao sailed there in 1505, serving bravely and well. Investing his savings in spice shipments, Magellan lost everything when shipwrecked on the return voyage. He tried to recoup his losses in India but was not successful and returned to Portugal in dire financial straits in 1513.

Ferdinand Magellan

Unaccustomed to inactivity, Magellan volunteered for a military expedition to Morocco, where he was accused of corruption. A man of great personal integrity, he was outraged at the unfounded accusation (he was eventually cleared) and embittered when condemned to idleness by the king's refusal to give him a hearing and the captaincy of a ship. He left Portugal for Spain in 1515. One thing of value remained from his years in the Indies: knowledge of the location of the Spice Islands, which his shipwrecked friend Serrao had described to him in letters from there. Magellan mistakenly concluded that they were close to America and developed a plan to reach them by sailing west.

In Spain he swore loyalty to King Charles, who agreed to finance such an expedition, giving Magellan his complete support against those who opposed his leadership because he was Portuguese. Portugal, for its part, did its best to sabotage the expedition by playing on Spanish-Portuguese rivalry, offering Magellan leadership of a Portuguese expedition, pressuring Charles, and sending fleets to intercept Magellan.

Magellan sailed in 1519, with five ships (*San Antonio, Trinidad, Concepcion, Victoria, Santiago*), two years of supplies, trinkets for trading, two hundred thirty-seven men of various nationalities, and three Spanish captains who boasted they would mutiny and murder Magellan if he angered them. Because currents and winds made it practical to follow the Portuguese trade route, Captain Juan de Cartagena doubted Magellan's loyalty and mutinied off the African coast. Magellan tricked Cartagena into coming aboard his ship and arrested him, ending the mutiny.

Faced with an American continent much larger than expected, and failing to find the passage between the Atlantic and Pacific oceans, Magellan wintered in South Africa. Realizing that his maps and theories were incorrect, he became withdrawn, his men lost confidence in him, and Cartagena led the Spanish officers in another mutiny. Magellan put down the mutiny and continued his voyage in August 1520 minus a shipwrecked *Santiago* and Cartagena.

The passage, later named the Strait of Magellan, was discovered in October. Gomes, a pilot, then mutinied and sailed the *San Antonio*, containing most of the fleet's food and water, back to Spain to get credit for the discovery. Realizing that the Pacific might also be larger than theorized (it was in fact several thousand miles wider), Magellan nonetheless sailed into it despite his now inadequate supplies. His plight became desperate: water was putrid and his sailors were reduced to eating worms, rats, sawdust, and leather; many died.

The survivors reached the Mariannas and the Philippines in March. Magellan's conduct there contrasted sharply with prevailing Spanish and Portuguese colonial practices of destruction, massacre, rape, and enslavement: he preferred the establishment of peaceful trade relations to conquest, and kept his men under tight control. He had become fervently religious, and much more interested in Christianizing natives than exploiting them. His preaching and personal conduct led to mass conversions and, indirectly, to his death: he fell fighting on behalf of a converted king who faced rebellion.

With Magellan gone, the crews' rapaciousness alienated the natives who attacked them, leaving them so undermanned that they abandoned the *Concepcion*. After six months of piracy, aimless wandering, and starvation, another mutiny gave them a capable and disciplined leader. They reached the Spice Islands, found Serrao and the others dead bought cargoes of spices, and prepared to return to Spain. The *Trinidad* was left behind for repairs and captured by the Portuguese. The *Victoria* sailed around Africa into the Atlantic, with starvation and disease rife on board. It arrived in Spain eight months later with just eighteen men left; the survivors were to spend years waiting to get paid. Ironically, a subsequent negotiated settlement acknowledged Portugal's claim to the Spice Islands on the basis of the Treaty of Tordesillas.

A. Pigafetta, *Magellan's Voyage*, 1975.
E. Roditi, *Magellan of the Pacific*, 1972.

MAHAVIRA (Vardhamana; c. 549–477 B.C.E), Indian religious reformer, Jain prophet. Tales and legends of Mahavira abound, but there is little indisputably factual material to corroborate them. Sources relate that he was born near what is now the city of Patna, in the northern Indian province of Bihar. The stories concerning the young Mahavira are sufficiently similar to those woven around the youth of Gautama *Buddha to suggest that they constitute elements of a conventional hagiography of the time rather than representing an accurate reflection of actual events. Thus, like Buddha, Mahavira is said to have been of noble birth, while the details and significance of his conception were foretold to his mother (as they were to Buddha's) in a series of dreams. He enjoyed a princely education; his compassion and love for his parents led to his delaying his renunciation of worldly affairs and concerns until their deaths, by which time he was thirty years old. Some legends relate that they starved themselves to death; in theory, this remains the most impeccable manner for a Jain of the requisite level of spiritual development to die, since once one has no further use for one's body as a vehicle for the quest for enlightenment, one abstains from the harmful practice of consuming other living things simply to sustain it.

Mahavira is commonly regarded as the founder and systematizer of Jainism as it is now practiced; within the Jain pantheon, he is revered as the twenty-fourth and last of the *Tirthankars* ("finders of the path"), mythical prophet-reformers of Jainism. Living the life of a naked ascetic in the eastern region of the Ganges valley, he attained to *kevala-jnana* ("the highest knowledge") after twelve years; he vowed to refrain from violence, stealing, lying, unchastity, and owning possessions. After his full spiritual awakening, he proved himself an able administrator as well as an enlightened teacher, successfully revitalizing Jainism by organizing his followers into groupings of monks, nuns, and male and female laity. His reforms laid the foundations for a dynamic and successful Jain community that continues to thrive more than two millennia later.

Mahavira's Jainism holds that the universe is infinite and was not created by a deity, and believes in reincarnation according to the law of *karma*, or cause and effect; eventual spiritual salvation and liberation from the endless cycle of rebirths *(moksha)* is achieved through following the path of the *Tirthankars*. Mahavira stressed and practiced *ahimsa*, reverence for all life and the avoidance of injury to any living thing, as an indispensable component of the spiritual life. Due to this belief Jains are strict vegetarians and monks often cover their mouths with a piece of cloth to avoid accidentally swallowing even the tiniest insect. Mahatma *Gandhi was greatly influenced by Jainism and adopted the doctrine of *ahimsa* as an integral part of his concept of *satyagraha* ("truth force").

Mahavira was one of the first Indian spiritual leaders to challenge the ritualistic orthodoxy of the Brahmin-dominated Hinduism of his day and to replace it with an ethical and metaphysical system stressing individual responsibility and equality. Today, there are some four million Jains in India; the high levels of education and commercial success they enjoy mean that they have an influence disproportionate to their numbers.

P. S. Jaini, *The Jaina Path of Purification,* 1979.

B. C. Law, *Mahavira, His Life and Teachings,* 1936.

M. Nagaraja, *Contemporaneity and Chronology of Mahavira and Buddha,* 1970.

MAIMONIDES, MOSES (Moses ben Maimon; 1135–1204), Spanish philosopher, legal codifier, rabbi, and physician. He was born in Córdoba, Spain, to Rabbi Maimon, a rabbinical judge, scion of a long chain of rabbis. The family left Córdoba in 1148 to escape religious persecution. After wandering in Spain and North Africa, they settled in Fez in 1160. Maimonides had begun writing even before then; his first compositions, written in Arabic, included one on the terminology of logic and metaphysics and a work on the Jewish calendar.

During this period, many Jews faced with forced conversion adopted Islam but in name only, remaining secretly loyal Jews. This phenomenon prompted Maimonides to write a "Letter on Forced Conversion," in which he concluded that a Jew must not remain in any country where he is subject to forced conversion.

In about 1165 Maimonides left Fez with his father and brother, heading for the Holy Land, where they stayed for five months. They went from there to Egypt, where they settled in Fostat, the old city of Cairo. Supported by his brother David, a dealer in precious stones, Maimonides was free to write and serve as religious and lay leader of the Jewish community, of which he became the head around 1177. His brother's death in 1169 — he was lost at sea in the Indian Ocean, along with the entire family fortune, while on a business trip — made it necessary for him to find a livelihood, and he chose the medical profession. He attained prominence in this field with his appointment as one of the physicians to al-Fadil, a powerful vizier, while his medical writings became classics that were studied for centuries.

In the early 1170s Maimonides wrote an open letter to the Jews of Yemen, who had turned to him for guidance when faced with a false messiah as well as forced conversion to Islam. His response gave them courage to withstand the pressure toward conversion and reject the attraction of the would-be messiah. Maimonides's *Commentary on the Mishnah* (one of the basic rabbinical lawbooks) was finished in 1168. It included thirteen principles expressing the fundamental beliefs of Judaism, which represent the first formulation of a Jewish creed. His *Book of the Commandments* defined and categorized the traditional 613 commandments identified in rabbinical law. This was a preparatory step toward the *Mishneh Torah* ("Repetition of the Law"), a fourteen-volume code of Jewish law compiled by him and written in clear Hebrew. His goal was to codify all literature on Jewish law in the Talmud and post-Talmudic works according to subject matter. Previously, the vast corpus of Jewish law had been diffuse and unsystematic. This was one of the first attempts at such a compilation, but it drew widespread criticism through its very success, the more so because Maimonides had cited neither his sources nor his authorities.

Maimonides completed his *Guide for the Perplexed*, aimed at showing that reason and revelation are compatible, in about 1190. It was written in Ara-

TEACHINGS OF MAIMONIDES

- Astrology is a disease not a science.
- Nobody is ever impoverished by the giving of charity.
- A gambler always loses. He loses money, dignity, and time. And if he should win, he weaves a spider's web around himself.
- One whose belief depends on miracles is of imperfect faith since miracles can be wrought by magic and sleight-of-hand.
- There are nine degrees in giving charity:

    Giving a person a gift or a loan or entering into a partnership or procuring him work to enable him to become self-sufficient.

    Giving to the poor in such a way that the giver and the recipient are unknown to each other.

    Donating money to the community charity-fund.

    Where the donor is aware to whom he is giving alms but the recipient does not know from whom he receives them.

    Where the recipient knows the donor but not vice-versa.

    The man who gives to the poor before he is asked.

    The man who gives after being asked.

    The man who gives less than he should — but with good grace.

    The one who gives grudgingly.

bic using Hebrew letters, and a Hebrew translation was completed by Samuel ibn-Tibbon before Maimonides's death. This translation and a subsequent one were the source for the Latin translation through which Maimonides became know to Christian philosophers, and deeply influenced Scholastic philosophers such as Thomas *Aquinas and Albertus Magus. Maimonides set medieval Jewish philosophy on an Aristotelian basis, seeking to reconcile Jewish revelation with *Aristotle's rationalism. His target audience was those among the Jewish intellectual elite who were wavering in their faith, and he couched his text in such terms that only persons with an adequate intellectual background would be able to ascertain its true meaning. The result led to immense controversy in parts of the Jewish world, leading in some places to a ban on his works. Eventually, however, his views were universally accepted as authoritative.

Although Maimonides's literary output ceased after *The Guide,* he continued his energetic letter writing. The many letters that have survived exhibit a human warmth which complement the dispassionate, rational nature of his serious works.

Maimonides married rather late and had one son, Abraham, who also became a well-known Jewish scholar and succeeded him to leadership of the Egyptian Jewish community, a position which, as a mark of respect to Maimonides, remained hereditary among his descendants for two centuries. Maimonides's reputation was so great that when he died public mourning was declared by Jews wherever they lived. He was buried in Tiberias with a tombstone reading:

"From [biblical] *Moses to Moses [Maimonides], there was no other like Moses."

L. E. Goodman, *Rambam: Readings in the Philosophy of Moses Maimonides,* 1976.
M. Fox, *Interpreting Maimonides,* 1990.
A. J. Heschel, *Maimonides,* 1982.
O. Leaman, *Moses Maimonides,* 1990.

MAKARIOS III (1913–1977), archbishop and first president of Cyprus. Archbishop Makarios III was born to a family of Greek shepherds in Ano Panayia, Cyprus, and he was christened Mikhail Khristodolou Mouskos. At age thirteen, he entered a monastery of the Orthodox Church of Cyprus; it was there that he adopted the name *Makarios,* meaning "blessed." After his ordination he studied law and theology at the University of Athens, and then traveled to America in 1946 to study at the Boston University School of Theology. He returned to Cyprus in 1948 to assume the position of bishop of Kition.

Upon the death of Archbishop Makarios II in 1950, Makarios was chosen to succeed him as archbishop of Cyprus, a position both political and religious. Cyprus was then ruled by the British; the majority Greek population favored *énosis,* a political union of the island with Greece which the Turkish minority opposed. As temporal and religious leader of the Greek population, Makarios led the resistance to British rule and the struggle for *énosis.* The island erupted into violence and in 1956 Makarios, considered by the British authorities to be the principal agitator, was exiled to the Seychelles Islands. He was released a year later and settled in Athens.

Increasing acts of terrorism prompted the British to agree to independence for the island, provided that Makarios and the Greeks abandon their goal of *énosis.* An agreement on independence was reached in 1959 and Makarios was elected president; independence was declared in 1960.

Despite preindependence agreements dividing political power between Greek and Turkish inhabitants of the island, civil war immediately erupted. Greece and Turkey intervened in 1963 and a peacekeeping force was sent to the island the following year.

In 1967 a military junta seized power in Greece; Makarios did not favor the new Greek government and relations between the two countries cooled. To the dismay of many of his compatriots, Makarios rejected the idea of *énosis* as a desired political objective. Pro-*énosis* forces finally overthrew him in a 1974 coup and the archbishop fled to England.

Regarding the new government as a threat to the Turkish minority, Turkey invaded Cyprus, occupying about 40 percent of the total land mass although the Turkish minority constituted only about 18 percent of the population. Makarios appealed to the United Nations Security Council to restore peace to the troubled island. Despite failure to find a satisfactory solution to the crisis, Makarios received a hero's welcome on his return to the Greek sector of the island on December 7, 1974. He was reelected president, a position he held until his death in 1977.

M. Attalides, *Cyprus*, 1979.

P. N. Venezis, *Macarios*, 1976.

MALCOLM X (Malcolm Little; Muslim name, el-Haj Malik el-Shabazz; 1925–1965), U.S. black leader, one of the founders of the Nation of Islam and voice of black discontent with white society. He was born in Omaha, Nebraska: his mother was West Indian, and his father, Earl Little, a preacher devoted both to baptism as well as to the secularist nationalist teachings of Marcus *Garvey.

The Little family was driven out of Omaha by a group of white vigilantes who complained about Earl Little "spreading trouble" by teaching the "back to Africa" messages of Garvey to the "good Negroes" of Omaha. They moved to Milwaukee and then to Lansing, Michigan, but it was not long before local antiblack activists started threatening the Littles. One night in 1929, when Malcolm was four, they burned down the house and the family barely managed to escape before the building collapsed. A few years later, in 1931, the Black Legion, a local antiblack group, caught up with Malcolm's father for the final time. Beating him senseless, they left him to die under the wheels of a streetcar. Malcolm was only six. The family then disintegrated. After the insurance money ran out, even the small wages their mother and older brother earned were not enough to feed the family, and the children often went hungry.

After Malcolm was caught stealing he was placed in the care of a white family. He dropped out of school in eighth grade and ran east to Boston and later to the Harlem district of Manhattan. After a series of menial jobs he began dealing and using drugs, burglarizing homes and stores, and steering white customers to black brothels. He was given an eight-to-ten-year sentence by the state of Massachusetts for burglary.

While in prison he began to read the teachings of Elijah Muhammad, the founder of the Nation of Islam, who maintained that the white race was the race of devils created to torment the black sons and daughters of Allah.

When he was released from prison in 1952 Malcolm made his way to Detroit, where he met Elijah Muhammad and began to recruit young blacks to the fold. He soon received his "X" from the Muslims, which symbolized the true African family name he would never know. "For me," he wrote in his *Autobiography*, "my 'X' replaced the white slave-master name of 'Little' which some blue-eyed devil named Little had imposed on my paternal forebears."

> - I can capsulize how I feel — I'm for the freedom of the twenty-two million Afro-Americans by any means necessary. By any means necessary. I'm for a society in which our people are recognized and respected as human beings, and I believe that we have the right to resort to any means necessary to bring that about. So when you ask me where I'm headed, what can I say? I'm headed in any direction that will bring us some immediate results. Isn't anything wrong with that.
> - Sitting at the table doesn't make you a diner, unless you eat some of what's on that plate. Being born here in America doesn't make you an American.
> - You show me a capitalist and I'll show you a bloodsucker.
> - Power never takes a backstep — only in the face of more power.
> - Be peaceful, be courteous, obey the law, respect everyone; but if someone puts his hands on you, send him to the cemetery.
>
> **Malcolm X**

Over the next few years, Malcolm X concentrated on recruiting young blacks from the streets, trying to bring Allah and Elijah Muhammad into their lives. Beginning in 1953 the minister of Malcolm X's temple in Detroit, recognizing his gift for oratory, urged him to speak. His passionate speeches inspired countless people, and each time he would give a speech his voice would get hoarse. The central object of his life became to rid blacks of their shame of the past, to give them self-esteem. He began to see that rage could provoke people to action and he toured the country speaking, opening new mosques, and starting a newspaper called *Muhammad Speaks*. Soon the media caught on and he was invited to appear on several talk shows.

As his fame grew, some of his fellow Muslims became jealous and Malcolm X felt hurt when he heard that Elijah Muhammad had been spreading rumors that Malcolm X was becoming dangerous. At the same time, reports began to crop up that Muhammad had fathered children by some of his former secretaries, and though Malcolm X did not want to believe it, he was eventually convinced. He felt that he needed to "inoculate" other Muslims against the "epidemic" which would soon catch the Nation of Islam by surprise and destroy it. But the Muslims to whom he expressed these fears turned on him, saying he was only fanning the flames of the fire. When John F. *Kennedy was assassinated in 1963 and Muhammad spread the word to his followers to express "no comment," Malcolm X did not listen and said he saw the assassination as a case of the "chickens coming home to roost." Officially for that speech, and unofficially for the internal tensions in the Nation of Islam, Mal-

Malcolm X

colm X was dismissed from the ministry and the Nation of Islam in 1963.

Forming his own group, Muslim Mosques, Inc., Malcolm X began taking tutorials in orthodox Islam. He made a pilgrimage to Mecca where, for the first time, he came in contact with white Muslims. He embraced Sunni Islam, adopted the name El-Haj Malik el-Shabbaz, and returned to the United States a changed man. He denounced his former guru as a racist and changed his own theories on white people, saying he would now judge them on their behavior and not by the color of their skin.

By 1965 Malcolm X had begun to receive death threats from his former Nation of Islam followers. His house was firebombed, and he knew he was marked for death. On February 21, while addressing a crowd of the Organization of Afro-American Unity at the Audubon Ballroom in Harlem, he was shot and killed by a group of Black Muslims, who were angry that he had insulted Elijah Muhammad. Three men were tried, convicted, and sentenced to life imprisonment. Malcolm X received further recognition after his death, and his message of black power and pride continue to influence thousands of black Americans.

D. Gallen, *Malcolm X: As They Knew Him*, 1991.

C. E. Lincoln, *The Black Muslims in America*, 1961.

Malcolm X, and Alex Haley, *TheAutobiography of Malcom X*, 1964.

MALTHUS, THOMAS ROBERT (1766–1834),

British economist. He was born near Dorking, Surrey, to wealthy and highly educated parents. His father was a friend of the philosopher David *Hume

and a keen disciple of Jean-Jacques *Rousseau, and had an optimistic utopian outlook. Prior to his entry to Jesus College, Cambridge, in 1784, Malthus's schooling was provided in this highly intellectual home environment.

Malthus developed into a dedicated student, setting academic success as a key goal. He won prizes in Latin and Greek and graduated in 1788, continuing his studies for a master's degree, which he attained in 1791, subsequently becoming a fellow of his college in 1793. Four years later he took holy orders and became curate at Albury, Surrey.

Inspired by the French and American revolutions, philosophers speculated with ideas of a utopian existence being at last within man's reach. Malthus's contribution to the debate was in direct opposition to such views. In 1798 he published (initially anonymously) his famous *Essay on the Principle of Population*. His thesis was that man's capacity to reproduce is greater than his power to produce subsistence, i.e., population growth was outstripping the food supply. He saw population increasing in a geometric progression whereas the food supply was increasing only arithmetically. The consequences of this pattern would be expressed in human disaster if population growth was not curbed. A golden age, such as his father envisioned, was an impossibility.

Malthus saw the checks of poverty, famine, war, disease, bad nursing, and large towns as impeding population upsurge, but the danger was such that one could not count on the operation of these balances alone. Restraint was needed; in particular the poorer classes, who lacked the means to support large families, should exercise control over the number of their children. He opposed contraception, advocating moral constraint.

In 1805 he was appointed professor of history and political economy at the college of the East India Company in Haileysbury. It was a new post — he was the first person in England to be professor of political economy — and signified the growth of interest in the economic studies he was so effectively promoting. Little is known of his private life, but he was known as being kindly, placid, and cheerful.

In 1819 he became a fellow of the Royal Society. In 1820 his *Principles of Political Economy* foreshadowed late twentieth-century economic theories by advocating public works and private investment as an antidote to periods of trade depression.

Malthus, who had a profound influence on Charles *Darwin's theory of natural selection, was a highly respected and honored figure in the academic world, albeit a target of abuse for radicals like William Cobbett, who was violently opposed to the harsher attitude toward the poorer classes that Malthusian economics appeared to promote.

W. Peterson, *Malthus*, 1979.

D. Winch, *Malthus*, 1987.

J. Ronar, *Malthus and His Work*, 1924.

MANET, EDOUARD (1832–1883), French painter whose work profoundly influenced the direction of modern painting. Manet was born in Paris, where his father was a high official in the ministry of justice. Expected to become a lawyer, at sixteen he announced that he had decided to be an artist. His family encouraged him in an abortive attempt at a naval career, but he was soon back in Paris studying art with Thomas Couture (and piano with a young Dutch woman, Suzanne Leenhoff, with whom he lived and eventually married). In 1853 he traveled to Italy, where he visited Venice and Florence and painted copies of the Renaissance masters, and Spain, where he copied Velasquez.

Manet's early original compositions, such as *The Absinthe Drinker*, won praise from fellow artists, including Eugène Delacroix, but were too radical for the conservative artistic sensibilities of the Salon of the French Academy, but in 1863 his work *Déjeuner sur l'herbe* ("Luncheon on the Grass") was hung in the Salon des Réfusés, a gallery sponsored by *Napoleon III to accommodate pictures rejected by the academy. Crowds flocked to the Salon to laugh at the "outrageous subjects and inept techniques" of the exhibits; they considered Manet's contribution scandalously shameless. In it, a lightly draped woman kneels over a little brook; two men are seated on the ground, conversing. In front of them, stark against the black of their clothes, is a nude woman, painted as only Manet painted, with not so much as a shadow or a nuance to soften the brilliance of her flesh.

Manet's painting, *Olympia* (1863), showing a reclining nude staring boldly at the viewer, aroused such vehement public outrage that the painting was rehung in a spot in the salon where it was hoped that no one would see it. Manet's exhibition of his own work at the 1867 Paris World Fair promised its viewers "not flawless, but sincere" works, true to his dictum "instantly paint what you see."

Between 1862 and 1868 Manet made over a hundred prints, experimenting with different techniques. Many of these prints were based on works of old masters as well as his own paintings. He also used photographs as studies for portraits.

Returning to Paris in 1871, after military service in the Franco-Prussian War, Manet found his studio vandalized; luckily, he had stored his canvases safely. The city was controlled by the Communards, and Manet was elected to the artists' federation of the Commune. He made many sketches of the Paris of the Commune.

In 1875, refused by the salon once again, Manet decided to exhibit his paintings in his studio for two weeks. Thousands came and the occasion was so noisy and elicited so many complaints from the neighbors that he was evicted from his studio when the lease expired.

In 1878 a pain developed in Manet's left foot, the first sign of syphilis manifesting itself in a relentlessly progressive locomotion-ataxia. By 1883 he was bed ridden. His gangrenous left leg was amputated, but after ten days of high fever, delirium, and great pain, he died.

Manet has been called "the first modern painter." His friend, Emile *Zola, said that every time he placed his canvas on the easel, he departed for the unknown. His reality had nothing to do with "realism," his truth was not of flesh and blood or lace and velvet, but of paint and painting. One must paint the truth regardless of adverse criticism, he believed. He had a revolutionary impact, even though his own goal had always been to achieve official recognition.

P. Courthion, ed., *Portrait of Manet by Himself and His Contemporaries*, 1962.

J. Dufwa, *Winds from the East*, 1981.

P. Florence, *Mollarme, Manet, and Redon*, 1986.

MANI (Manes; c. 216–c. 276), Persian founder of the religion of Manichaeism. He was born in southern Babylonia (present-day Iraq) at a time of widespread tendencies to eclecticism and syncretism. Through his mother he was related to the Parthian royal family, while his father was a spiritual seeker who joined a religious community that practiced baptism, abstinence, purification, and the acquisition of liberating knowledge in its quest for salvation. When only twelve years old, Mani had a vision of an angel, *al-Tawm* ("the Twin"), but was unclear what was expected of him; when the angel appeared a second time twelve years later, in 240, it was to urge the young man to go forth and preach the true religion that was revealed to him.

Mani's proselytizing ministry was characterized by his dauntless energy and absolute confidence in the truth of his revelation. He first traveled to India, where he made many converts, among whom may have been members of the Christian community established by Saint Thomas the Apostle in the first century. In later centuries the Christian church was to consider Mani the greatest of heretics, even though Manichaeism constituted a separate religion rather than a Christian heresy.

On returning to Persia, Mani was favorably received by the Persian king, Shapur I, who permitted him to preach his doctrines throughout the Persian Empire for the duration of his reign: the date of Shapur's coronation in 243 was adopted as a Manichean holy day. Manichaeism proved immensely successful. Mani was innovative in his use of the pictorial arts to help in spreading his message and was also instrumental in initiating many improvements in the written form of Persian languages. His writings achieved canonical status among his followers. A prolific author, his works included the *Living Gospel*, the *Treasure of Life*, the *Mysteries, Treatise, Book of Giants*, and *Epistles*, as well as collections of psalms and prayers.

Revered as the "Apostle of Light" and the "Illuminator," Mani viewed himself as the final successor in a long line of prophets that included *Buddha, *Zoroaster, and *Jesus. Each of these, he taught, had offered an incomplete revelation; only

Mani's teaching represented the complete and definitive explication of the path to salvation.

The core of Mani's message was a type of gnosticism that promised salvation through special knowledge of spiritual truths. His radically dualistic philosophy envisaged the world, and especially human life, as a struggle between the totally independent principles of good (associated with light and spirit) and evil (associated with darkness and matter). The role of the righteous was to take the side of light and, through rigorous asceticism, strive towards ultimate freedom from the darker, material elements in human nature. In so doing, they would assist in the coming of the universal "moment" wherein the principles of good and evil were once again separate, as they had been in the past. Life in this world was seen as unbearably painful and inescapably evil; the reward of righteousness was Paradise, while the souls of the fallen were condemned to successive reincarnations into the material world.

The death of Shapur signaled an immediate reversal in Mani's fortunes. Shapur's successor, Bahram I, was unsympathetic to the prophet, and the Zoroastrian priests of the religious establishment took the opportunity to have him imprisoned, tortured, and, after twenty-six days, killed — according to legend — by crucifixion. Their action could not prevent the rapid growth of Manichaeism after Mani's death. His teachings spread west into the Roman Empire and North Africa (Saint *Augustine was a convert in his pre-Christian days), reaching Spain and southern Gaul by the fourth century. To the east, it established itself in China and Turkistan. Manichean communities stressed asceticism and sexual continence, separating themselves into the "elect," who practiced rigorous self-discipline, and "hearers," who supported the elect through work and alms. Reviled by Christian, Muslim, and Zoroastrian alike, the Manicheans suffered greatly from persecution. Mani's beliefs later influenced such heretical medieval European Christian sects as the Bogomiles, the Catharists, and the Albigenses, all of whom were suppressed by the established church.

L. Ort, *Mani: A Religio-Historical Description of His Personality*, 1967.
G. Widengren, *Mani and Manichaeism*, 1965.

MANN, THOMAS (1875–1955), German novelist and essayist. Mann was born in Lübeck and, after his father's death in 1891, moved to Munich, where he lived until 1933. He began writing, following the career of his brother Heinrich, and produced his first novel, *Buddenbrooks*, in 1900. His early work was influenced by the philosophies of Friedrich *Nietzsche and Arthur *Schopenhauer and the music of Richard *Wagner. The two novellas *Tonio Kröger* and *Tristan*, written in 1903, were partially autobiographical studies in which Mann investigated the nature of German bourgeois culture and the relation of the creative artist to society.

FROM THE WRITINGS OF THOMAS MANN

- There is a way of being an artist that goes so deep and is so much a matter of origins and destinies that no longing seems to it sweeter and more worth knowing than longing after the bliss of the commonplace.

From *Tonio Kroger*

- Whatever profits man, that is the truth. In him all nature is comprehended, in all nature only he is created, and all nature only for him. He is the measure of all things, and his welfare is the sole and single criterion of truth.
- The friend of humanity cannot recognize a distinction between what is political and what is not. There is nothing that is not political.

From *The Magic Mountain*

- What the collectivist age wants, allows, and approves is the perpetual holiday from the self.

In 1905 Mann married Katja Pringsheim, the daughter of a professor of mathematics at Munich university. Two of the six children of the marriage, Erika (1905–1969) and Klaus (1906–1949), achieved distinction as writers and journalists in the United States and became active critics of Nazi Germany. In the years preceding World War I Mann published a number of works, notably *Königliche Hoheit*, (1909; *Royal Highness*, 1909) and *Der Tod in Venedig*, (1912; *Death in Venice*, 1928), in which he dealt with the complexities of spirituality, eros, and death, themes that were to recur in his novels and short stories.

During World War I Mann asserted his staunch patriotism, conflicting with his brother Heinrich, who maintained a critical attack against German authoritarianism. Mann published his *Reflections of an Unpolitical Man* in 1918 in the spirit of German nationalism, defending the concept of a totalitarian state; however, the rise of nazism in the postwar Weimar Republic led Mann to reconsider his views. He acknowledged his new stance in the novel *Der Zauberberg*, (1924; *The Magic Mountain*, 1927), in which he communicated a fateful awareness of the threatened disintegration of his society and the precariousness of the situation in Europe.

When Adolf *Hitler came to power in 1933 Mann expressed a growing concern over the fanaticism of the National Socialists and his criticism of Nazi ideology was illustrated in his essays and in the lectures he gave in many European cities during the 1930s. In 1936 Mann expressed his aversion to German anti-Semitism and the Nazi persecution of the Jews; he was deprived of his German citizenship the same year.

Mann left Germany for the United States, where he lived until 1952, becoming an American citizen in 1944. At the beginning of World War II he broadcast regularly to Germany, decrying the atrocities of the Nazi regime and calling for the assertion of humanity and reason by the German people.

Throughout this period Mann was working on various compositions that elucidated his perception of the contemporary social and political catastrophe. His prose epic *Joseph und seine Bruder* (*Joseph and His Brothers*) was completed in four volumes in 1943 and was a profound treatment of this biblical theme, evoking individual responsibility out of the collective community and appealing to man's power of reason. In a similar vein, Mann wrote *Lotte in Weimar* (1939; U.S. title: *The Beloved Returns*, 1940), in which he borrowed the theme from J. W. von *Goethe's *The Sorrows of Young Werther*, elaborating upon it to determine the fundamental principles of humane civilization. The most overtly political of his novels, *Doktor Faustus* (1947), was begun during the war in 1943. In this work Mann depicts the tragic collapse of German culture and humanism in the preceding decades and its subjugation to a savage but sophisticated barbarity.

After the war Mann visited Germany on several occasions but refused to settle there again. In 1952 he left the United States for Switzerland and lived in Zürich until his death. During these last years Mann produced a number of imaginative novels written in a more relaxed style than his previous works, including *Der Erwählte* (1951; *The Holy Sinner*, 1951), *Die Betrogene* (1953; *The Black Swan*, 1954) and *Die Bekenntnisse des Hochstaplers Felix Krull* (1954; *The Confessions of Felix Krull, Confidence Man*, 1955). His last major essays, on Goethe (1949), Anton *Chekhov (1954) and Johann *Schiller (1955), record Mann's impressions of the social and ethical responsibilities of writers.

Mann is considered the greatest German novelist of the twentieth century and the leader of Germany's anti-Nazi intellectuals. He was awarded the Nobel Prize for literature in 1929 and received many public honors in postwar Germany. His literary works and essays have maintained the status of classics both within Germany and, in translation, throughout the world.

H. Buergin and H. Mayer, *Thomas Mann: A Chronicle of His Life*, 1969.

H. Goldman, *Max Weber and Thomas Mann*, 1988.

E. Mann, *Thomas Mann: Autobiographisches*, 1968.

MAO-TSE TUNG (1893–1976), Chinese Communist revolutionary leader. He was born in Hunan province in the interior of China to a peasant farmer who had managed to fight his way from poverty to relative prosperity

- In a class society everyone lives as a member of a particular class, and every kind of thinking, without exception, is stamped with the brand of a class.
- We Communists are like seeds and the people are like the soil. Wherever we go, we must unite with the people, take root and blossom among them.
- All reactionaries are paper tigers.

From the *Thoughts of Chairman Mao*

All the scenery of the North
Is enclosed by a thousand *li* of ice
And ten thousand *li* of whirling snow.
Behold both sides of the Great Wall!
There is only a vast confusion left.
On the upper and lower reaches of the Yellow River
You can no longer see the flowing water.
The mountains are dancing silver serpents,
The hills on the plains are shining elephants.
I desire to compare my height with the skies.

From Mao's poem "The Snow."

for himself and his family. As a child, Mao worked in the rice fields like everyone else in the peasant community, but when he was eight his father sent him to the local primary school, where he was educated in the basics of the Confucian classics (see *Confucius). At the age of thirteen Mao was forced to return to farm work. He was rebellious by nature and idolized great warrior emperors in Chinese history and Western heroes such as *Napoleon Bonaparte and George *Washington.

Moa rebelled against paternal authority from an early age, attempting an escape from home when ten. As he grew older, tensions with his father increased. At sixteen he left home to attend the Tungshan academy, which offered a higher primary education and introduction to more modern subjects, and in 1911 moved on to a secondary school in the provincial capital of Changsha, where he first encountered Western ideas and for the first time in his life read a newspaper. It was the *Peoples' Strength*, put out by a secret society of exiles and their supporters, the Alliance party, who believed that national revolution and toppling the monarchy would save China. Its leader was Dr. *Sun Yat-sen.

In October 1911 fighting against the Manchu dynasty broke out and spread to Changsha, where Mao, caught up in the revolutionary fervor, enlisted as a soldier. After six months of the military life the rebellion ended and Mao was released. He now decided to become a teacher and entered the First Provincial Normal School in Changsha, which offered a high standard of education in both Chinese and Western studies. He impressed his fellow students with his intelligence and application and

Mao

their soldiers on the epic six-thousand-mile Long March to Shensi Province in northwest China, where they formed a base of operations against the KMT.

After Japan attacked China in 1937, China entered into an uneasy alliance with the U.S.S.R. and Mao proposed a truce between the Communists and the Nationalists, offering Chiang the full military cooperation of the Chinese Red Army. The agreement lasted until the end of World War II when Chiang and Mao met to discuss a coalition government but parted in disagreement, signaling a resumption of civil war.

The Red Army relentlessly drove Chiang's armies south and when they finally fled the mainland in 1949, Mao proclaimed the establishment of the People's Republic of China with himself as chairman of the republic and of the Communist party. During Mao's visit in 1949 to Moscow (his first time outside China), Joseph *Stalin canceled a previous treaty with Chiang Kai-shek and signed a thirty-year Sino-Soviet treaty. China soon found its loyalty to the treaty tested when it was dragged into the Korean War in support of the Moscow-supported regime in Pyonyang.

Mao's attempt to transform China into a socialist state involved purging landlords and collectivizing the land. In 1956, in an attempt to win over the intellectuals to his cause he introduced the policy of permitting criticism, which he called "letting a hundred flowers bloom." This policy, however, had alarming consequences including criticism of the country's leadership by the Communist party. Mao soon backtracked with an announcement that "all who help to build socialism belong to the people and all who resist it are enemies." In 1958 he launched the Great Leap Forward, a largely unsuccessful attempt to accelerate China's economic policies by local initiative rather than capital-intensive programs. For the next several years he was less in the public eye and, though retaining the post of chairman of the Communist party, resigned from his position of chief of state. In 1966, however, together with Lin Piao he launched the purge known as the Great Proletarian Cultural Revolution, initiating a period of massive violence and disorder in which the Mao personality cult was fostered in order to counteract political opposition.

His writings and speeches were summarized in a book of quotations, known as the *Little Red Book*, which became (after the Bible) the most distributed book in the world, in which Maoism was identified with faith in the Communist party and in the transcendance of personal desires to serve the people as a whole.

As Mao reached the end of his life he became increasingly feeble. His third wife, Chiang Chi'ing, and three other of his intimates ("The Gang of Four") were accused of trying to seize power after his death and were imprisoned.

became active in student affairs, serving as secretary of the students' society and helping to establish several student organizations, among them the New Peoples' Study Society, some of whose members were to become prominent in the Communist party.

After graduating in 1918, Mao went to Beijing University where he worked for half a year as a library assistant. He founded a Marxist study circle and came under the influence of the two men who were to figure prominently in the foundation of the Chinese Communist party: Li Ta-chao and Ch'en Tu-Hsiu. This was the period of the May Fourth Movement when students were rebelling against the Paris Peace Conference's decision to give former German concessions in Shangtung to Japan instead of China. Mao himself was active in organizing merchants, workers, and students in demonstrations against Japan. His belief in the power of the peasantry to serve as a revolutionary force was to develop later.

In 1921 Mao helped to found the Chinese Communist party (CCP) and in 1923 when the party established an alliance with *Sun Yat-sen's Kuomingtang (KMT), he joined the KMT and served on its central executive commitee. Illness from overwork caused him to return to his native village for a rest, and it was while there that he began to become aware of the revolutionary potential of the peasant population.

With Sun Yat-sen's death in 1925, *Chiang Kai-shek took over the KMT and in 1927 began to purge both the party and the army of communists. Mao and Chu Teh, commander in chief of the Chinese Communist armies, initiated a peasant revolution and formed the Fourth Chinese Red Army from the peasant masses. In 1930 Chiang Kai-shek launched a campaign against the provinces dominated by the Red Army and by 1934 had driven them out of southern Kiangsi. From 1934 to 1936 Mao and Chuh Teh led

J. Dunster, *Mao Zedong and China*, 1980.

J. Mh'en, *Mao and the Chinese Revolution*, 1956.

H. E. Salisbury, *The New Emperors: Mao and Deng*, 1992.

S. R. Schram, *Mao Zedong*, 1983.

MARAT, JEAN-PAUL (1743–1793), French physician, journalist, and politician, leader of the Montagnard faction during the French Revolution. Born to poor parents in Boudry, Switzerland, he left home at sixteen in search of a career. After moving to Bordeaux, and later to Paris, he settled in England in 1765. He studied medicine, acquired some repute as a doctor in London and Paris, and published books on both scientific and philosophical subjects. However, his most famous thesis, *Philosophical Essay on Man* (1773), was attacked by the French philosopher *Voltaire for its extreme materialism.

Marat returned to France in 1774 and secured an appointment as physician to the personal guards of the comte dArtois, *Louis XVI's youngest brother (later Charles X). Despite an increasingly lucrative practice among the wealthy aristocracy, Marat was obsessed with obtaining a reputation for himself as scientist and philosopher. However, when he submitted a book of theory and experiments claiming to have toppled Isaac *Newton's sacrosanct science of optics, the French Academy of Sciences categorically denounced it as a sham. Marat, thoroughly convinced that powerful enemies had conspired to persecute him and prevent his election to the academy, nursed his grievances and later had his revenge when in 1793 he was instrumental in bringing about the abolition of France's corporate academies.

At the beginning of the Revolution he publish a pamphlet entitled *Offering to Our Country,* in which he expressed the view that the monarchy was still capable of solving France's social and economic problems. However, the experiences of the early months of the Revolution soon transformed Marat into one of the most radical of revolutionaries. In September 1789 he became the editor of the propagandist paper *L'Ami du Peuple,* which he used to vent his bitter hatred and suspicion of those in power. He denounced those he suspected of treason and demanded that repressive measure be taken against counter-revolutionaries. "Blood must flow," he proclaimed.

From October 1789 to the fall of the monarchy on August 10, 1792, Marat was frequently arrested. Outlawed, he twice fled to England, in 1790 and the summer of 1791, and during the interval between these two flights he hid in the sewers of Paris, this exacerbating a skin disease he had previously contracted which required constant treatments in a warm bath. During this difficult period he continued to publish his journal in secret and to attack Jacques Necker, the king's finance minister, and such moderate revolutionary figures as the Marquis de *Lafayette, Comte *Mirabeau, and Jean Sylvain Bailly, mayor of Paris. He also continued to warn against the émigrés who were urging foreign powers to restore the monarchy. These inflammatory articles helped to foment the August 10, 1972, uprising and the September massacres.

Entering public life again in August 1792, his popularity ensured him a seat in the National Convention, which was empowered to draft a new constitution. In the convention, as a member of the Jacobin Club, and in his journal, Marat continued to call for the execution of counterrevolutionaries but appears to have had no direct involvement in the massacres that followed. Popular with the Parisians, Marat soon became one of the most influential members of the Convention. When, in the spring of 1793, France suffered further defeats in the war against Austria and internal rebellion brewed, Marat blamed the crisis on the Girondins, the dominant political group in the Convention. His constant attacks against the Girondins made him a symbol of the radical Montagnard faction and in April the Girondins had him arraigned before the revolutionary tribunal of Paris for sedition. However, his popularity among the Parisians assured his acquittal and guaranteed the beginning of the fall from power of the Girondins.

His triumph, however, was shortlived. On July 13, 1793, seriously ill and tormented by his skin disease, he was at work preparing the Bastille Day issue of his newspaper in his bath when Charlotte Corday, a twenty-four-year-old Girondin supporter from Normandy, gained admission and stabbed him to death with a six-inch butcher knife. Marat's violent murder had a profound impact on the political scene. The Girondins were immediately hunted down and executed and his death served to consolidate and intensify the Terror. Marat was exalted to the position of martyr and became the object of a revolutionary cult. The Engragés claimed to be Marat's heirs and successors and founded their own newspaper, with the same title as Marat's journal. Twenty-one French towns were named after him and until the reaction of 1795 Marat was considered the "friend of the people and martyr for liberty." He was initially buried in the Panthéon but when the moderate countereaction gained the upper hand, he body was removed.

J. Douxois, *Charlotte Corday*, 1989.

L. G. Gottschalk, *Jean Paul Marat: A Study in Radicalism*, 1927.

MARCION (died c. 160), Roman founder of an independent Christian church. Born around the end of the first century in Sinope, a city on the Black Sea, Marcion was a wealthy shipowner. His religious unorthodoxy was quickly evident and he was expelled from the Christian community of his home town (where, some sources suggest, his father was the bishop). In western Asia Minor, too, he was ostracized because of his ideas, so he traveled to Rome, where he found acceptance in the city's more cosmopolitan congregation. However, as his own ideas developed after contact with the teachings of Cerdo, a Christian teacher from Asia, he ran into conflict with the church of Rome as well. He was excommunicated and the two-hundred-thousand sesterces donation he had made to the church was returned.

In 144, after his split with Rome, Marcion founded his own church, which spread rapidly through the Roman Empire and even came to rival the Catholic church itself. He proclaimed a God whose sole attribute was goodness and denied any relationship between Judaism and Christianity. To his mind, the God of the Old Testament bore no connection to the God of Christ. He argued that the scriptural basis for such a message was the teachings of Saint *Paul, whom he believed to have been alone among early Christian leaders in understanding *Jesus' message.

Consistent with Marcion's repudiation of a Jewish basis for Christianity was his firm rejection of attempts to see the coming of Christ as having been the fulfillment of ancient prophecy. He therefore abandoned the entire Old Testament and abbreviated the New Testament to conform to his teachings. The Marcionite church adopted as its bible Marcion's version of the Scriptures, which consisted of an edited version of the Gospel of Luke and ten of Paul's Epistles.

Marcion was often characterized as a gnostic, and his ideas did indeed have many similarities to gnosticism. Thus, like the gnostics, Marcion contrasted the creator God of the Old Testament with the high God without wrath or judgment who is the father of Christ. His deprecation of the material world as inherently evil, his dualism, and his view that Christ did not have a real human body are also consistent with gnostic views. However, Marcion did not believe in the attainment of salvation through *gnosis* (knowledge), and he also rejected the gnostic contention that there is a "spark of light" placed in human beings by the God of Christ. Rather, he considered human beings to be wholly the work of the creator God.

Such a set of beliefs inevitably meant that Marcion's interpretation of the significance of the life and death of Jesus diverged widely from church orthodoxy. Where the conventional view was to consider Christ's sacrifice as a vicarious atonement for human sin, Marcion envisaged it as a legalistic act that canceled the creator God's claim on man. He identified the words "Christ redeemed us" (Galatians 3:13) as constituting scriptural evidence for his view, and they became a key Marcionite text. Marcion's work *Antitheses,* which presented contradictions between the creator God and the God of Christ, also came to assume creedlike status as a confession of faith for the Marcionite congregation.

Marcion's views aroused widespread condemnation from the established church. He was vilified as "the firstborn of Satan," and his ideas were attacked by such distinguished figures as Tertullian and Origen. Nonetheless, the Marcionite church persisted until the middle of the third century. It was founded on strict asceticism, with marriage forbidden and the consumption of wine and meat discouraged. Women were admitted to the priesthood. Since its members practiced chastity, the church's membership increased only through people coming to embrace Marcionite doctrines; this, allied to its emphasis on asceticism, meant that it was never destined to be a mass movement. By the end of the third century, most Marcionite communities had been absorbed into Manichaenism (see *Mani), but small numbers continued to exist for some time longer.

Marcion had a significant impact on the development of the established church, which, in the face of Marcionite competition, was encouraged to examine and establish its liturgical and scriptural foundations from among the welter of available material. All his writings have been lost.

E. C. Blackman, *Marcion and His Influence,* 1948.
R. J. Hoffman, *Marcion and the Restitution of Christianity,* 1984.
J. Knox, *Marcion and the New Testament,* 1942.

MARCO POLO   SEE POLO, MARCO

MARCONI, GUGLIELMO (1874–1937), Italian inventor of wireless telegraphy and Nobel prize winner. Marconi was born in Bologna, where the differences between his Irish mother and Italian father made his childhood insecure and unstable. His strict, disapproving father condemned Marconi's boyhood fascination with dismembering electrical devices and constructing new gadgets from the pieces as a nonsensical waste of time better spent in study. He felt that Marconi would never amount to anything, especially after he failed the naval academy's entrance exams. However, his doting mother got him into a technical institute, where his scientific interests found an outlet and he became an avid student of practical physics and electricity, although he still failed to get into the University of Bologna.

By then, an extensive telephone and telegraph system had been developed, information on electricity was readily available, and Heinrich *Hertz had just discovered that electrical energy could be radiated through space. Marconi read about Hertz's experiments with electromagnetic waves and, becoming obsessed with the idea of creating a system of wireless telegraphy based on them, began experimenting with homemade equipment.

Marconi's ability to tinker with equipment, modifying it until it achieved good results, was always one of his greatest assets. After two years of experimentation, he developed a model, which he first offered to the Italian government; when it rejected it, he went to England where he patented his device and demonstrated it to the British post office, which was extremely impressed and sponsored a further series of tests that brought Marconi international fame.

Marconi's flair for staging dramatic, attention-getting, and successful demonstrations contributed to the phenomenal speed with which his inventions were developed and adopted. The scientific community continually criticized his dramatics as an unseemly, unscholarly, and unethical means of grabbing credit for the scientific discoveries of others. However, Marconi himself never claimed to have discovered the principles upon which his inventions were based; he was just the first to make use of them for practical applications.

Italy became interested in Marconi's invention and criticized him for having taken it to England, and for avoiding his obligatory Italian military service. He turned the criticism to acclaim by accepting the nominal position of a naval cadet attached to Italy's London embassy — which allowed him to continue his work uninterrupted — and giving an extensive demonstration of his invention for the Italian navy. From then on, Italy was his most consistent supporter. Marconi's good relations with the British post office never recovered from his decision to form a company (1897) for commercial exploitation of his patents — the British expected favored treatment because they had helped him get started.

Marconi hoped to use his invention to solve the problem of communicating with ships at sea. He successfully demonstrated it to the British, Italian, and French navies, but his demonstration to the American navy failed because rival companies' broadcasts interfered with his transmissions (Marconi soon worked out how to fine-tune his transmitters and receivers to exclude such interference). The intense rivalry between wireless companies involved Marconi's company in many legal battles over patent rights, kept it short of money, and necessitated constant innovation on Marconi's part, to keep ahead of the competition.

Marconi attempted to establish his company's clear superiority over its competitors by achieving commercially viable transatlantic wireless communication. Using powerful generators and tall antennae to transmit and receive the hundreds-of-meter long electromagnetic waves then thought necessary, transatlantic transmission was achieved in 1901 (thanks to the existence of a previously unidentified reflective ionosphere encircling the earth). However, this achievement resulted in a temporary loss of customers when, despite Marconi's own objections, the Marconi Company announced that transatlantic commercial wireless communication was available before it had been sufficiently perfected.

Marconi continued to improve and demonstrate his wireless, receiving a Nobel Prize in physics in 1909 for his work. The following year he lost his right ear in a car accident. Marriage to the young Irishwoman, Beatrice O'Brien, had little effect on his preoccupation with his work and his traveling, or on his enjoyment of high living and other women. He was a very proud and private person, and the association of his name with the Marconi scandal (the 1912 revelation of financial speculation in Marconi stock by British government figures) outraged him, especially since he was not even involved in it

His patriotism led Marconi to spend World War I serving Italy by inspecting and improving mobile wireless stations, procuring military equipment, checking the uses of wireless in airplanes, experimenting with short-wave (about fifteen meter-long) communication, and participating in a goodwill mission to the United States. Marconi was also an Italian emissary to the Paris Peace Conference, where he signed the peace treaties with Austria and Bulgariaι.

Marconi continued his work on short-wave communication after the war. He persuaded the British government to try short-wave stations for the imperial wireless scheme linking the British Empire. The contract he received contained stiff penalties for failure, which were never enforced since short-wave communication was a success, and Marconi's great ambition of creating a worldwide wireless network was realized.

Beatrice and Marconi were divorced in 1923 after living increasingly separate lives for years. His role in his company decreased as it became less involved with research and innovation. Italy bestowed on him many honors, including a life membership in the Senate. After his marriage to Cristina Bezzi-Scali of the Roman nobility in 1927, his interests were increasingly Italian.

Marconi refused to stop working or even slow down, despite a series of heart attacks. He continued his research in microwaves (waves under a meter long) that led, after his death, to the development of radar and television. He also did extensive public relations work abroad for Fascist Italy (having become a member of the Fascist party in 1923). He suffered a fatal heart attack in 1937, and wireless stations worldwide observed two minutes of silence.
W. P. Jolly, *Marconi,* 1972.
D. P. Marconi, *My Father, Marconi,* 1962.

MARCUS AURELIUS (Marcus Annius Verus; 121–180), Roman emperor and Stoic philosopher. Aurelius was raised by his rich grandfather after his father's death when he was three months old. Well educated (he had seventeen tutors), he grew to love philosophy, while his ascetic ways (e.g., sleeping on straw strewn over the floor) almost ruined his already weak health. Administrative offices tempered his philosophic and religious beliefs with realism. Yet acceptance of other people's seamy sides did not lower his expectations of himself: "self-government, and not to be led aside by anything; cheerfulness in all circumstances, and a just admixture of gentleness and dignity, and to do appointed tasks without complaining."

Emperor *Hadrian, a frequent visitor to Aurelius's grandfather, took a fancy to Aurelius and recommended to his adopted successor, Antoninus Pius, that he in turn adopt Aurelius (seventeen years old) and a certain Lucius Aelius Verus (eleven years old) as his successors. Antoninus became Aurelius's mentor and had a tremendous influence on him (as emperor, Aurelius would live simply and unostentatiously, occupied with official duties and the study of philosophy — like Antoninus). Lucius, meanwhile, spent his time pursuing pleasure. In 146 Antoninus adopted Aurelius as his sole heir and kept him privy to his counsels and actions.

Aurelius became emperor upon Antoninus's death in 161 and immediately made Lucius his coruler and son-in-law, fulfilling Hadrian's wishes despite Lucius's demonstrated unfitness. Lucius abandoned himself to hedonism and left Aurelius to run the empire.

As emperor, Aurelius tried to realize his "idea of the state in which there is the same law for all, a polity of equal rights and freedom of speech, and the idea of a kingly government that most of all respects

FROM MARCUS AURELIUS'S *MEDITATIONS*

- Nowhere can man find a quieter or more untroubled retreat than in his own soul.
- A man does not sin by commission only but often by omission.
- A man's worth is no greater than the worth of his ambitions.
- Anything in any way beautiful derives its beauty from itself and asks nothing beyond itself. Praise is no part of it, for nothing is made worse or better by praise.
- Do not waste time arguing what a good man should be. Be one.
- A man's happiness is to do the things proper to man.
- Reject your sense of injury and the injury disappears.
- The art of living is more like wrestling than dancing.
- Our life is what our thoughts make it.

Equestrian statue of Marcus Aurelius, second century

the freedom of the governed." He respected the rights of the senators and made himself into a public servant. He spent large sums of public money on gifts, games, and the corn dole, while waiving unpaid taxes and tribute. He extended Hadrian's legal reforms administratively (more court days and shorter trials) and socially (legislating protection for the weak against the strong, wards against dishonest guardians, debtors against creditors, provinces against governors).

Barbarians and rebels interpreted Aurelius's reputation as a peaceful, kindly philosopher-king as weakness. In 162 revolt broke out in Britain, barbarians invaded the North, and Parthia declared war. Aurelius sent capable generals to deal with the revolt and invasion, but sent Lucius to fight Parthia. In Antioch, Lucius made love rather than war while Parthia overran Syria. Aurelius sent a plan of action with which Lucius's second-in-command defeated Parthia.

Lucius's troops returned to Rome, bringing plague as well as victory. Infection spread everywhere they went. Syria, Mesopotamia, Asia Minor, Egypt, Greece, Italy, and Gaul were devastated. Corpses lay in heaps. So many died that famine followed plague as farms lay empty and transportation of goods was disrupted.

Attracted by Rome's weakness, northern barbarians invaded en masse in 167, laying waste to northern Italy. Rome's plague-decimated legions met defeat when sent against the invaders. Aurelius took charge of the war, financing it by auctioning off objects from his palaces. He enlisted anyone, even slaves and barbarians. He trained and led his new army to rout the barbarians skillfully, ending the First Marcomannic War (167–168). Then he fortified the border and returned to Rome to rest, his frail body overstrained.

Rumor credited Aurelius's pretty, lively wife, Faustina (daughter of Antoninus Pius), with many lovers. True or not, Aurelius treated her with affection and respect, promoted her rumored lovers to high offices, and deified her when she died. Of their four children, one girl died young, one married Lucius, and one of their twin boys died at birth. The much doted-upon surviving son, Commodus, rejected both morals and education, preferring gladiator sports and cruelty to philosophy. Aurelius chose to ignore his son's true nature, hoping that Commodus's promotioon to high office would have a salutary effects resulted in his appointing Commodus as his heir in 176. He justified his decision with the belief that Commodus would be less harmful to Rome as emperor, than as a potential insurgent in a civil war.

Aurelius spent the rest of his life fighting the barbarians (his famous book, *Meditations*, a distillation of Stoic thought, was written on campaign). He planned to extend the empire to the Carpathian Mountains, a more defendable border against the barbarians. However, the Second Marcomannic War (169–175) ended in a hasty peace and withdrawal after the barbarian's defeat because of the rise of a rival emperor in Egypt. Aurelius died during the Third Marcomannic War (178). Commodus had promised to continue fighting until he reached the mountains; instead he immediately made peace with the barbarians and returned to Rome to enjoy himself.

A. Birley, *Marcus Aurelius*, 1961.
R. B. Rutherford, *The Meditation of Marcus Aurelius*, 1989.

MARIA THERESA (1717–1780), archduchess of Austria and queen of Hungary and Bohemia. When his only son died, Holy Roman Emperor Charles VI promulgated the so-called Pragmatic Sanction, which asserted the right of female issue to succeed to Habsburg domains, thus clearing the way for his daughter Maria Theresa to become his heir. In 1736 Maria Theresa married Francis Stephen, duke of Lorraine, who gave up his ancestral duchy in exchange for the grand duchy of Saxony. The union was a love match and the couple had sixteen children, ten of whom survived to maturity.

On her accession to the throne in 1740, Maria Theresa faced the invasion of her territory by land-hungry neighboring states, who chose to reverse their acquiescence in the terms of the Pragmatic Sanction. Her naive courage in weathering the eight year War of Austrian Succession won her many supporters in her previously factious Hungarian estates, and in 1745 she succeeded in installing Francis Stephen as Emperor Francis I, while the 1748 Treaty of Aix-la-Chapelle ratified her rights of succession. However, she suffered the loss of her most wealthy and populous region, Silesia, to *Frederick the Great of Prussia.

Surrounded by potentially or actually hostile states, Maria Theresa decided that the establishment and maintenance of an effective standing army was essential to the security of her kingdom. Friedrich Wilhelm Haugwitz, the first in a series of gifted advisers, recommended that in order to raise the money required to fund such a force she institute wide-ranging fiscal changes designed to reduce the power of her dominion estates to control the purse strings of the empire. As a result, she abolished the tax exemptions of the great landowners.

Administering the new tax system meant introducing complementary social reforms and increasing central government intervention in the running of the empire. Maria Theresa had little formal education herself, but she had the common sense to understand that an effective system of higher education was necessary if the state was to produce men competent to staff the expanded bureaucracy and judiciary necessitated by her reforms. She pioneered the introduction of textbooks to secondary schools, and the linking of the University of Vienna medical school with the embryonic public health service, while establishing the sovereign's right to veto the election of deans by the university faculties.

While Maria Theresa's reforms led to some real improvements in the welfare of the empire's citizens, these were largely incidental to her main purpose, which was the creation of an Austria rich and strong enough to resist foreign aggression. Like most rulers of her time, she had no sense of duty to maintaining the welfare of the population at large. Thus it was only when peasant riots in Bohemia threatened the stability of her domains that she limited the use of forced labor. Similarly, she introduced compulsory primary education in an effort to strengthen the human resources available to the state rather than because of any desire to enrich the lives of her subjects. A curious mixture of pragmatism and piety, Maria Theresa was a strictly observant Catholic and intolerant of religious dissent; nonetheless, reasons of state prompted her to allow control of education to be taken out of the hands of the Jesuits whom she revered.

In an attempt to respond to the growth of Prussia's power in the European arena, and in the hope of winning back Silesia, Maria Theresa initiated a radical political realignment by jettisoning Austria's traditional ally, England, in favor of agreements with France and Russia. However, when Austria still emerged on the losing side of the Seven Years' War (1756–1763), she quickly became a proponent of peace, realizing that her debt-ridden exchequer could not finance another major conflict.

Maria Theresa was devastated by Francis I's death in 1765, but found some solace in renewed legislative activity. Her government evolved a new public-debt policy, oversaw the settlement of unpopulated areas of Hungary, and drafted a unified penal code to supersede the plethora of local systems.

While she had reason to look on her reforms with satisfaction, her own family life gave Maria Theresa less reason for pride. She personally supervised the education of her children but was generally disappointed with the results, being particularly alarmed by her willful eldest son Joseph (later the Emperor *Joseph II), who was fascinated by the new philosophy of the Enlightenment. Four of her daughters were married to princes of the House of Bourbon, thus cementing the Franco-Austrian alliance; Maria Theresa railed against their frippery and warned them of the dire consequences that might follow from such behavior (in light of the fate of one of them, Marie Antoinette, who married the future *Louis XVI and was eventually guillotined, her fears seem to have been prophetic).

As Joseph took an increasingly active role in government, Maria Theresa often found herself in opposition to his policies. She bemoaned the immorality of participating in the 1772 partition of Poland — when Austria, Russia, and Prussia resolved their differences at Poland's expense by dividing its territory among them — and was hurt when her attitude was taken as hypocritical in many of the courts of Europe. She still retained the authority to prevent full-scale involvement in the 1778–1779 War of Bavarian Succession, but her last years were spent in increasing isolation in her palace at Schönbrunn. Despite her disappointments, the successes of her reign meant she was remembered as one of the greatest rulers of the House of Habsburg.

E. Crankshaw, *Maria Theresa,* 1970.
R. Pick, *Empress Maria Theresa,* 1966.
P. Reinhold, *Maria Theresia,* 1977.

MARK ANTONY

MARK ANTONY (Marcus Antonius; 82–30 B.C.E.), Roman general. Antony was born into a noble Roman family at a time when the empire was torn by civil wars over who would control the Senate (and therefore the empire) — the nobility or merchants and lower classes. As the death throes of the Republic convulsed the empire the Forum was adorned with the heads of the losing side.

Antony spent a dissipated youth but his kinsman, Julius *Caesar, appointed him to responsible positions in Rome. Caesar's lieutenant in Gaul, Antony was a strong and courageous general. Spirited and vigorous, knowing that his handsome head might soon decorate the Forum, he divided his time between army camps and the pursuit of pleasure. He kept a harem of both men and women, acquired wealth and possessions by dubious means, and wallowed in good food and wine. He was appointed commander in chief of Italy and played a key role at the Battle of Pharsalia in 48 B.C.E. when Caesar defeated *Pompey.

Antony reacted to Caesar's assassination in 44 B.C.E. by collecting as much of Caesar's papers and money as he could, "finding" among them appointments and decrees beneficial to his friends and himself. He convened the Senate, agreed to a general amnesty wherein the conspirators could safely flee to the provinces if the Senate ratified Caesar's acts and appointments, and delivered Caesar's funeral eulogy. Much to Antony's chagrin Caesar's will made his eighteen year-old grandnephew, Octavian (the future emperor *Augustus), his adopted son and heir. Invited to Rome by a Senate anxious to curb Antony's growing power, Octavian was determined to continue Caesar's work and avenge his death. Antony planned to lead an army against Brutus, one of the conspirators who had killed Caeasar, to gain the income from his prosperous province. When Antony delayed distribution of Caesar's bequests, Octavian paid them and organized his own army. Antony charged Octavian with attempted assassination and civil war broke out, with Octavian and the Senate defeating Antony.

Octavian discovered that the Senate, which had just been using him as a tool against Antony, was now his enemy. He made peace with Antony, forming the Second Triumvirate to share the entire Roman Empire (43–33 B.C.E.). Eager for vengeance and money, the Second Triumvirate started a reign of terror. Wealth became punishable by death; exits from Rome were guarded and rewards offered for the heads of thousands proscribed by the triumvirate for both personal and political reasons (Antony's wife Fulvia had a neighbor proscribed for the "crime" of refusing to sell her his mansion). Meanwhile the conspirators raised a large army in the East which was defeated by Antony in the battle of Philippi (42 B.C.E.).

The triumvirate divided up the empire, with Antony getting the richest part: Egypt, Greece, and the East. Antony ruled with occasional good judgment and mercy and frequent sensual excess. He pardoned everyone who had fought against him except those who had actually conspired to kill Caesar. He was particularly susceptible to women's pleas and offers for mercy.

The Egyptian queen, *Cleopatra, was summoned to Antony on charges of aiding the conspirators. She sailed to him, dressed as Venus in transparent silks. She invited Antony first to dinner and then to Alexandria for the winter. Infatuated, he wound up presenting her with part of the empire and neglecting the rest. Cleopatra saw in Antony a way to become queen of a Roman-Egyptian empire, an ambition she had failed to realize with Caesar.

Fulvia and Antony's brother tried and failed to overthrow Octavian. Fulvia died and Antony would have fought Octavian but their armies refused to fight and they had to make peace. Antony married Octavian's sister, Octavia, and lived with her in Athens, attending philosophers' lectures. This peaceful, virtuous existence was shattered by Parthia's invasion. Antony sent Octavia to Rome, returned to Cleopatra and asked her to finance his unsuccessful attempt to conquer Parthia (36 B.C.E.).

When Antony divorced Octavia and married Cleopatra (32 B.C.E.), Octavian was furious at Antony's treatment of his sister. Octavian read the Senate Antony's supposed will that declared his children by Cleopatra his sole heirs and ordered his burial beside her in Alexandria. Convinced that Cleopatra was scheming to take over the empire through Antony, the Senate declared war against her.

Octavian defeated Antony in the naval battle of Actium and Antony fled with Cleopatra. Both Antony and Cleopatra tried unsuccessfully to negotiate with Octavian: Antony offered first peace, then suicide if Octavian would spare Cleopatra. Antony attacked Octavian's forces desperately until he heard a false rumor of Cleopatra's death, stabbed himself, and died in her arms. Cleopatra killed herself after failing to charm Octavian. Antony and Cleopatra were buried side by side and their children sent to Octavia, who raised them as her own. Antony's great-grandsons, Caligula and *Nero, became emperors.

J. M. Carter, *The Battle of Actium*, 1970.

E. G. Huzan, *Mark Anthony, A Biography*, 1978.

A. E. Weigall, *The Life and Times of Cleopatra*, 1968.

MARLBOROUGH, JOHN CHURCHILL, FIRST DUKE OF

MARLBOROUGH, JOHN CHURCHILL, FIRST DUKE OF (1650–1722), English general. Son of Winston Churchill, a Devon gentleman and Royalist who found refuge in the Civil War at the home of his mother-in-law, Lady Drake, a supporter of Parliament, John Churchill was born in her mansion and raised in genteel poverty; the family could not afford to repair war damage to the house. In 1660 *Charles II became king and Winston Churchill became a member of Parliament. John's sister Arabella was the duke of York's mistress and probably used her influence to get John appointed as page. His interest in soldiering was appreciated by the duke and soon a commission was found for the young man.

Churchill saw his first fighting in Tangiers against corsair pirates. Later he fought with the French in a British-supported war against Holland. Slightly wounded at a siege, he was publicly thanked by *Louis XIV. The handsome and gallant young officer won the affections of King Charles's former mistress, Barbara Villiers. They lived together for several years and a daughter was born. Villiers was an excellent contact at court, with access to funds and appointments; in 1675 Churchill was appointed a gentleman of the bedchamber to the duke of York.

He now became attracted to Sarah Jennings, a beautiful fifteen-year-old maid of honor to the Duchess of York. Although she had no money and was therefore a poor match for a man of ambition, he pursued the courtship against family objections and in 1678 they married. Sarah became a faithful, if quarrelsome, wife and a ferocious promoter of her husband's interests. In turn, as numerous love letters testify, his devotion was equally strong. In later years he would write from the scene of battle, "Your letters are so welcome to me that if they should come in the time I was expecting the enemy to charge me, I could not forbear reading them."

The duke of York's espousal of Roman Catholicism led to his exile from London and the Churchills dutifully followed him. In 1685 James II became king. Although loyal to him, Churchill was a committed Protestant whereas the king was a Catholic. When a son was born to James in 1688 and the Protestant succession looked doomed, Churchill, now a major-general, took a prominent part in the Glorious Revolution that brought *William of Orange and Mary over from Holland to the throne of Britain. Churchill was much criticized for treachery but he felt he was following his convictions.

William made him earl of Marlborough and entrusted him with the reorganization of the army. Sale of commissions from dismissed Catholic officers as well as wise investments put the Marlboroughs well on the way to a fortune.

The new reign saw Marlborough gaining further glory by leading the king's armies in the Low Countries and Ireland, but he also had his share of troubles. His rapid rise aroused jealousies and he was accused at court of plotting to restore James II. At one point he was imprisoned in the Tower of London for treason. His wife did not help matters, alienating Queen Mary with her outspoken, quarrelsome nature. In time Marlborough recovered his position and in 1701 was given command in an anti-French alliance in the War of the Spanish Succession. In 1702 William died and Anne came to the throne. The duchess of Marlborough was her most intimate friend; the Marlboroughs' position could not have been stronger.

Marlborough brought to war a revolutionary change in military tactics, believing in decisively defeating the enemy in open battle instead of wearing him down in piecemeal sieges conducted with all the traditional formalities. He also had a sincere regard for the welfare of his troops, another departure from the usual practice. He went out of his way to see that they were fed and lodged properly and in the middle of one long march was thoughtful enough to order a supply of new boots. Soldiers responded to his concern with intense loyalty bordering on hero worship. He was merciful to captured enemy troops, making sure that their wounded received the same treatment as injured English.

Marlborough had the ability to ascertain quickly the layout of a battlefield and decide the best positions for his forces. He repeatedly misled enemy commanders as to his intentions. The initiative was invariably his, even if it meant fast-marching forty thousand soldiers three hundred miles across Europe without the French knowing his plans. Overcoming the cautiousness of his Dutch allies, he never tasted defeat but in brilliant battles such as Blenheim (1704), which saved Vienna from the French, Ramillies (1706), Oudenarde (1708), and Malplaquet (1709), his armies delivered devastating blows to France and her allies. French generals were afraid to confront this fearless general on a white horse who enjoyed a succession of narrow escapes from death.

The great hero was rewarded with the grant of fifteen thousand acres of land near Oxford where a splendid palace, named Blenheim, was to be built at the nation's expense. He was at the peak of his fame but soon discovered how fickle royal favor could be.

Following the early death of their son, the duchess had withdrawn from society, including that of Queen Anne. She furthered the break by continually arguing with Anne over politics. Anne's affections were transferred to her chambermaid, Abigail Hill, a distant relative of the duchess, who was furious over her displacement and even wrote to Anne several times accusing her of a lesbian infatuation with Abigail.

The enmity of Abigail Hill and, through her, of Queen Anne, became combined with the intrigues of crafty politicians desirous of concluding a separate peace with France at the expense of the allies. Marlborough stood in the way of these ambitions; accordingly trumped-up charges of financial irregularities with army funds led to his dismissal; Sarah also was discharged from the queen's service. The accession of George I in 1714 led to their rehabilitation but not long afterwards Marlborough was incapacitated by a stroke. He died in 1722 and was buried in Westminster Abbey. His wife lived until 1744, overseeing the completion of Blenheim, feuding continually with her remaining daughters, and leaving a fortune of three million pounds.

V. Cowles, *The Great Marlborough and His Duchess*, 1983.

W. S. Churchill, *Marlborough: His Life and Times*, 6 vols., 1933–1938.

D. Chandler, *Marlborough as Military Commander*, 1973.

MARSHALL, GEORGE CATLETT (1880–1959),

U.S. general and statesman. He was born in Uniontown, Pennsylvania, to a family of Virginia settlers; by the time Marshall entered Virginia Military Institute in 1897, his father, a coal merchant, had lost most of his money. He graduated in 1901 and was commissioned a second lieutenant in the cavalry.

After graduation, Marshall was sent to the Philippines for a year and a half. Early in his military career, he developed the habit of rigid self-discipline, and his attitude toward command soon won him the respect both of his soldiers and of civilians. His quiet self-confidence brought out the best in those under his command.

Marshall attended school at Fort Leavenworth, Kansas, at that time the center of the army's advanced educational program, and graduated first in his class. He then served there as an instructor from 1908 to 1910. In 1913 Marshall was sent back to the Philippines, where he remained until being called, in 1916, to serve in San Francisco and on Governor's Island in New York Harbor. During World War I Marshall was sent to France as the chief of operations. From 1919 to 1924 he was General John *Pershing's senior aide, and then assistant commandant in charge of instruction at the infantry school.

Although Marshall was by then a lieutenant colonel, Pershing felt that he had not been promoted quickly enough and said of him, "He is the best goddamned officer in the U.S. Army." In 1933 Marshall was promoted to full colonel. He was made the senior instructor of the Illinois National Guard and served as a brigade commander in Vancouver Barracks for two years.

In 1938, Marshall moved to Washington and served as chief of war plans and then deputy chief of staff. President Franklin D. *Roosevelt then nominated him as the head of the army and on September 1, 1939, the day the war began in Europe, Marshall took full command, a position he held for six years. Under Marshall's command, the army grew from two hundred thousand to almost eight and a half million. When President Harry S. *Truman, considering an alternative to dropping the atomic bomb, was weighing the possibility of a blockade coupled with heavy bombing of Japan, Marshall pointed out that similar action in Germany had not brought about an end to the war in Europe.

Marshall attended all the great conferences and was deeply involved in directing Allied strategy during the invasion of Europe. Paying tribute to his efforts in planning, training, and supplying the Allied troops, Britain's Winston *Churchill said, "General Marshall was the true organizer of victory."

Marshall resigned as chief of staff on November 21, 1945, and Truman appointed him ambassador to China, where he served from 1945 to 1947. Despite his lack of success in mediating the Chinese civil war, he had proved himself an able statesman and was appointed secretary of state in January 1947. In a speech delivered at Harvard in June of that year he

George Marshall

outlined what came to be known as the Marshall Plan for the economic recovery of Europe, based on his belief that Russia was taking advantage of Europe's economic problems to control the area. During this period, representing the United States, he worked diligently in the United Nations and spent time in South America developing greater cooperation between Latin American countries and the United States. Marshall resigned as secretary of state in 1949 due to ill health.

Unwilling to let Marshall retire, Truman appointed him secretary of defense in 1950, when Marshall was almost seventy. This position gave Marshall the freedom to criticize General Douglas *MacArthur's statements and actions. He opposed MacArthur in controversy between Truman and MacArthur.

The Korean War had begun. Marshall again enlarged the United States army and helped to develop the North Atlantic Treaty Organization (NATO). As secretary of defense, Marshall strove to stop the expansion of the Korean conflict. While he obviously favored a strong America, he still sought peaceful solutions in Asia. In December of 1953 he was awarded the Nobel Peace Prize, after which he returned to private life.

In recognition of his service to the American people, the George C. Marshall Library was dedicated in Lexington, Virginia, in 1964, five years after his death. President Lyndon B. *Johnson and former president Dwight D. *Eisenhower both spoke at the dedication ceremony.

G. Catlett, *George C. Marshall*, 1982.

R. H. Terrell, *George C. Marshall*, 1966.

MARSHALL, JOHN (1755–1835), third chief justice of the United States. Marshall was born in a log cabin on the Virginia frontier in Prince William (now Fauquier County), Virginia. From 1776 until 1779 he served with distinction as an officer in the American Revolution, first as a lieutenant, and later captain. His war service included the critical battles of Brandywine, Valley Forge, Monmouth, and Stony Point. When he left the army in 1779 he went to live in Yorktown. While there, his interest in law developed, an interest that began with his reading William Blackstone as a teenager. In 1780 he was admitted to the bar and in 1783 began to practice law in Richmond, Virginia and also in Fauquier County, Virginia, the county of his birth. While in practice he periodically served in the Virginia House of Delegates; in 1788 he was a delegate to the Virginia state convention that ratified the Federal constitution. Despite his involvement in politics, from 1795 through 1798 he was obliged to turn down, for financial reasons, appointments as attorney general of the United States, ambassador to France, and even associate justice of the U.S. Supreme Court.

By 1799 he could no longer keep out of national politics and was elected to the House of Representatives, followed in 1800 by his appointment as secretary of state in John *Adams's cabinet. Shortly thereafter he was the beneficiary of a lame duck appointment by President Adams as chief justice of the United States, an appointment made on January 20th, 1801, just a few months before the end of Adams's term as president. Such an unusual opportunity presented itself due to the physical condition of the then chief justice, Oliver Ellsworth, who had become too ill to continue in office any longer. Since Adams was a Federalist and the Senate majority was then Federalist as well, approval of Marshall's appointment was almost automatic and came just in time for Chief Justice Marshall to administer the oath of office to newly elected president Thomas *Jefferson.

Marshall, a Federalist, served as chief justice of the United States during the successive terms of Presidents Thomas Jefferson, James *Madison, James *Monroe, and Andrew *Jackson who were of the opposition party, the Republican party, later called the Democratic party. During his thirty-four years on the bench, Marshall's compelling arguments and integrity won over his colleagues most of the time; his court rendered some eleven hundred opinions during that period. Of these opinions, Marshall himself wrote 519 and dissented a mere eight times. It was Marshall who really breathed life into the Constitution; his decisions were the first to find that the Constitution was not constrained by the bare meaning of the text.

Marbury v. Madison (1803) was one of Marshall's earliest constitutional decisions of great consequence. Today, however, Marshall would probably have disqualified himself from sitting on the case as it arose from a matter before the secretary of state when he was serving in that office.

MARSHALL IN
MARBURY V. MADISON **(1803)**

The Constitution is either a superior paramount law, unchangeable by ordinary means, or is on a level with ordinary legislative acts, and, like other acts, is alterable when the legislature shall please to alter it.

If the former part of the alternative be true, a legislative act contrary to the Constitution is not law: if the latter be true, then written constitutions are absurd attempts, on the part of the people, to limit a power in its own nature illimitable.

Marbury, the plaintiff, had been appointed a justice of the peace in the District of Columbia by President Adams just before he left office. In his haste to assume his position on the Supreme Court, Secretary of State Marshall forgot to issue Marbury's commission. So, Marbury brought action against Marshall's successor in office, James Madison, to issue the commission under an act of Congress that gave the Supreme Court original jurisdiction in such matters. Here too there were political reasons why Madison dawdled, among them that the appointment in question was that of a former president of a different political party. In any event, Marshall succeeded in turning this would-be debacle into a judicial triumph. In a unanimous decision, he found that a member of the executive branch of government has the duty to obey the law just like anyone else, that a citizen has a right to judicial redress against an illegal action by a member of the executive branch, that Marbury, a private citizen, had the right to his commission as justice of the peace, and Madison as secretary of state had a duty to deliver it, as this commission had been signed by Madison's predecessor but merely not delivered. However, since the Constitution specifically limited cases in which the Supreme Court could assume original jurisdiction and since the appointment of justices of the peace in the District of Columbia was not one of them, the Supreme Court could not officially act in this matter but had to send it to a lower court. Yet the Supreme Court was able to render a decision here that an act of Congress giving additional original jurisdiction to the Supreme Court is inconsistent with a constitutional provision that limits the jurisdiction of the Supreme Court primarily to appeals cases and strictly limited types of original jurisdiction cases; therefore, the U.S. Constitution was recognized as a superior, paramount law.

In *McCulloch v. Maryland* (1819), the Supreme Court ruled that Congress may exercise powers that can be implied from its authority enumerated in Article I of the Constitution, as well as that the Constitution and laws based upon it are superior to conflicting state laws. Another memorable decision by Marshall was *Gibbons v. Ogden* (1824), in which he ruled that the Commerce Clause power in Article I of the Constitution includes intrastate as well as interstate commerce since it includes anything affecting "commerce among the states."

Upon Marshall's death on July 6th, 1835, the Liberty Bell in Philadelphia cracked as it was rung, popularly believed to be an expression of mourning for his loss.

E. Corwin, *John Marshall and the Constitution*, 1919.
J. Cuneo, *John Marshall, Judicial Statesman*, 1975.
F. Stites, *John Marshall, Defender of the Constitution*, 1981.

MARTÍ Y PÉREZ JOSÉ JULIAN (1853–1895),

Cuban nationalist; founder of the Modernist movement in Spanish literature. The son of a Spanish colonial soldier, Martí was born in Havana, Cuba. An impressionable, bookish child, he later recalled that among his earliest memories was the sight of black slaves being beaten for some minor infraction. Although this was commonplace in Cuba, it made a lasting impression on the boy and sparked his awareness of a need for true social justice.

Martí was enrolled at the Havana Municipal School for Boys, headed by Rafael Mar!a de Mendive, a poet and vociferous advocate of Cuban independence. Martí considered Mendive his second father and spent many evenings absorbing literary and political discussions held in Mendive's parlor. He also acted as Mendive's private secretary, transcribing his poetry and translations. In return, Mendive paid Martí's tuition.

Like his fellow students, Martí engaged in anticolonial activities, which gained impetus following Mendive's arrest for sedition in 1869. The next day, Martí's first underground newspaper, *La Patria Libre*, was published. Two months later the school was shut down, but Martí's clandestine activities continued.

The turning point in Martí's career followed a parade of Spanish soldiers, watched by several of Martí's friends from a window. They jeered the passing soldiers, but elicited no immediate reaction. That night the soldiers returned, bursting into the house and arresting Martí's friends. A search revealed several copies of *La Patria Libre* and a letter that Martí had sent to a schoolmate, castigating him for enlisting in the colonial army. Although only fifteen, Martí was arrested and charged with treason. At his trial, he refused to succumb to parental pressure and delivered a stirring address defending his activities. The courthouse was stunned by the intelligence and courage of the young man who faced serious punishment; whereas Martí's friends received only light sentences, Martí was sentenced to six years imprisonment with hard labor.

He spent only six months in prison as his family succeeded in having the sentence commuted to exile on the Isle of Pines. The short time spent in jail furthered his awareness of the injustices inherent in colonial rule. Many of his fellow inmates had been imprisoned for merely joking about the regime; they lived in subhuman conditions and received frequent beatings. Martí himself suffered several such thrashings; throughout his life he had medical problems from the scars he received in prison. During his exile he overcame the trauma of prison life but now felt that he was achieving nothing for Cuba. His literary skills were atrophying, as well. With the support of the local governor he requested permission to travel to Spain. Since it was believed that this would prevent him from fomenting trouble on the island, his request was granted and he was deported in 1871.

Martí impressed the Cuban expatriate community in Spain by his moving account of prison life. While a student in Madrid and Saragossa, he produced several nationalist pamphlets which received wide circulation; the atmosphere in Spain was charged with a revolutionary spirit. The short-lived first Spanish republic (1873–1874) seemed promising to the Cuban expatriate community, but their hopes were soon dashed. Although the republic offered considerable social changes in Spain, little was done to improve the lot of the colonies. Martí supported the republicans in the civil war; with their defeat, he hastily completed his studies and traveled to Mexico.

Martí felt comfortable in the liberal atmosphere of Mexico. He won renown as a journalist and his play, *Amor con Amor se Paga* (Love is Repaid with Love), was a success. But Mexico was also plagued by internal strife. The liberal government of President Lerdo was overthrown by Porfirio Díaz. Having declined citizenship, Martí was now an undesirable alien whose liberal opinions were opposed to those of the new regime. Despite his misgivings about leaving the country he had grown to love, he returned to Cuba.

Although Martí wanted to start a career in education or law, the authorities would not recognize his Spanish diploma. Furthermore, his continued agitation for independence was unpopular with the regime, which was threatened by a new outbreak of violence. Martí was imprisoned and deported to Spain, but after a brief stay, news reached him of a Cuban community prospering in New York and he moved there.

Martí was based in New York for the last fifteen years of his life. Always able to attract a following because of his considerable talents, he supported himself as a journalist and as honorary consul for several Latin American states. It was in New York that he published some of his most memorable poetry, including *Ismaelillo* and *Guantanamero*. Much of the time he journeyed through Latin America seeking support for an independent Cuba. His activities resulted in the formation of the Cuban Revolutionary party, opposed to any concessions to the Spanish as envisioned by the failed Peace of Zanjón, and advocating armed revolt as the sole feasible means of attaining independence. Encouraged by the Montecristi uprising, he sailed for Cuba to take part in the revolt.

Martí and his companions reached Cuba on April 11, 1895. The apostle of Cuban nationalism was named a major general in the rebel army. For one month his troops wandered the mountainous countryside, attempting to join the main rebel army but he was not to succeed; Martí was killed in his first skirmish.

The collected writings of Martí, comprising seventy-four volumes, were published 1936–1953.

J. M. Kirk, *José Martí: Mentor of the Cuban Nation*, 1985.

F. Lizaso, *Martí*, 1953.

MARX, KARL (1818–1883), German social and political philosopher; founder and ideologist of communism. Born in Trier, Germany, to a family descended from rabbis, he was six years old when his father had the family converted to Lutheranism. The elder Marx had himself been converted in 1817 in order to practice law, which was forbidden him as a Jew. Marx's mother was baptized only in 1825 after the death of her father, a rabbi.

His Lutheran schooling notwithstanding, Marx later became an atheist (possibly the most quoted of his remarks is the famous "religion is the opium of the masses"). With German as his mother tongue, he studied French and Latin at school and later taught himself Spanish, Italian, Dutch, the Scandinavian languages, Russian, and English. He first attended the University of Bonn in accordance with his father's wish that he become a lawyer, but later transferred to the University of Berlin where the undergraduate debauchery that had marked his career at Bonn was altered on his becoming part of the Young Hegelian (see Georg *Hegel) circle. He was awarded a doctorate in philosophy in 1842 from the University of Jena. In the following year he married Jenny von Westphalen, daughter of an aristocratic Trier family, whose father had been Marx's spiritual mentor, and accepted the editorship of a journal founded by Hegelians in Cologne.

Marx ruthlessly attacked the Prussian government in print, even advocating that citizens resist tax collectors with arms, until his paper was suppressed a year later. He moved to Paris, where he met Friedrich *Engels, with whom he was to have a lifelong friendship and collaboration.

In 1845 the Prussian government pressured France to expel Marx and he went to Brussels. A short visit to England exposed him to working-class organizations and encouraged him to put socialist theories into practice rather than on paper. He founded the German Workers' party and was active in the establishment of the Communist League where in 1847 he presented the forty-page *Communist Manifesto* (published in 1848) in which he and Engels defined the principles of communism. The pamphlet foretold that when capitalistic private ownership prevents the proper exploitation of the means of production, the working class will achieve power, and called on them to use force to "overthrow existing social conditions." Over the next

Marx's favorite chair in the British Museum library

century it was translated into over one hundred languages and sold fourteen million copies.

In 1848 the Belgian government expelled Marx for radicalism and he moved back to Cologne to continue working as a journalist. Less than a year later his paper was suppressed and he was exiled from Prussia. He returned to France but was soon expelled again. At long last his nomadism came to an end when he settled in London although even there he was denied citizenship. Marx worked as a journalist, writing for the *New York Daily Tribune*, but it was Engels who sent him money for his support, while he devoted most of his energy to promulgating his theories of communism (his mother, who died in 1863, reportedly remarked that Marx wrote so much about "capital," but had never been able to make a living). In 1864 Marx helped to found the International Workingmen's Association, which was dissolved in 1872 due to internal intrigues and political disagreements.

In 1867 the first volume of his *Capital (Das Kapital)*, appeared. One of its basic premises was the "materialist conception of history," reversing the Hegelian doctrine that history is determined by a universal idea that shapes institutions. According to Marx, history is regulated and determined by the evolution of economic institutions. Dialectically, the process is one of thesis, antithesis, and synthesis. The evolution of communism was to be achieved by the interaction of precapitalism, the thesis, and capitalism, its antithesis, which would result in communism, the synthesis. Put another way, the working classes would be involved in a class strug-

FROM THE WRITINGS OF KARL MARX

- A specter is haunting Europe — the specter of Communism.
- The history of all hitherto existing society is the history of class struggle.
- Hegel says somewhere that all great events and personalities in world history reappear in one fashion or another. He forgot to add: the first time as tragedy, the second as farce.
- Capitalist production begets, with the inexorability of a law of nature, its own negation
- In proportion as the antagonism between the classes vanishes, the hostility of one nation to another will come to an end.

The Communist Manifesto — with Engels

- The proletariat have nothing to lose but their chains. They have a world to win. Workers of the world, unite! (The Communist Manifesto)
- From each according to his abilities, to each according to his needs.

Critique of the Gothe Program

Marx once stated that the aim of philosophy should be to change the world and probably no other philosophy has had such an impact, although not necessarily always as he would have hoped. His system enabled a consistent attitude to the social world, with practical implications. It made an enormous appeal to a secular public living in an industrial and scientific age, which believed that man could control history. Economic forces were supreme and the history of man dictated his conformity to the forces of production. The economic establishment would resist change and it was up to the proletariat to overthrow them and assume hegemony. He promised the working man a future of hope, maintaining that the adoption of his economic program would end economic scarcity and class antagonism. Marxism became a new secular religion that brought hope to millions but when applied on a large scale, as in the U.S.S.R. and communist China, led to distortions (which its opponents claimed to be inevitable) and disillusionment.

S. Avineri, *The Social and Political Thought of Karl Marx*, 1968.

I. Berlin, *Karl Marx: His Life and Environment*, 1963.

D. McLellan, *Karl Marx: His Life and Thought*, 1978.

F. Mehring, *Karl Marx: The Story of his Life*, 1962.

MARY I (Mary Tudor; 1516–1558), queen of England and Ireland from 1553. Born to *Henry VIII and his first wife, Catherine of Aragon, she initially enjoyed a warm relationship with both parents, her father proclaiming her princess of Wales in 1523; but when Catherine fell out of favor with Henry after failing to produce a male heir, so did her daughter. Mary was further estranged from her parents owing to the influence of Anne Boleyn, whom the king married in 1532. Henry's claim that his previous marriage had been invalid implied that Mary was illegitimate, and so without rights to succession.

Later that year, when Anne gave birth to the future queen, *Elizabeth I, Mary was ordered to dismantle her household and take up residence with Elizabeth's entourage; but when called upon to abandon her title, she refused. Anne Boleyn conducted a vehement persecution of Mary, who fell victim to bouts of hysterical illness. She retained a deep affection for her mother, despite being denied any contact with her from 1532 onwards, and was deeply distressed at her death in 1536.

Anne Boleyn was executed later that year, and Mary enjoyed far better relationships with her father's subsequent wives, and also grew very fond of her brother Edward.

Mary, despite her own devout Catholicism, finally gave in to her father's pressure and signed an act of submission, acknowledging Henry as Supreme Head of the Church of England, renouncing the authority of the pope, and acknowledging Henry's marriage to her mother as having been unlawful. She was thereafter reconciled with her father and was reinstated in the succession in 1544.

gle to establish a proletarian dictatorship, which would evolve into communism.

In 1874, at the age of fifty-six, Marx contracted a liver ailment that sent him all over Europe in search of treatment. His beloved wife's death from cancer in 1881 was a serious blow, as was that of one of his three surviving daughters two years later. He died of lung trouble and was buried in Highgate Cemetery in London, where his grave became a site of Communist pilgrimage. At his funeral Engels said, "Before everything else, Marx was a revolutionist. Few men ever fought with such passion."

Marx was a prolific writer, but only five of his books were published during his lifetime, among them the *Critique of Political Economy* and the first volume of *Capital*. Engels published the second and third volumes of *Capital*, consisting of works written by both of them, after Marx's death. A fourth volume of *Capital* was published after Engels's death.

A painstaking scholar, Marx spent much of his working time in London at the British Museum, carefully checking every source he used — before writing *Capital* he read every available work on economic and financial theory and practice. After his hours at the museum he would return home to write, often until four in the morning. He smoked very heavily while he wrote, remarking once that *Capital* would not even cover the cost of the cigars he had smoked writing it.

Generous by nature, Mary enjoyed bestowing gifts upon friends and regularly gave alms to the poor. She was not very interested in learning or the arts but, like her father, had a passion for gambling.

Edward VI succeeded Henry in 1547 and, under the influence of his protectors, tried to induce Mary and her household to adopt Protestant rites. Mary refused and as Edward's health failed, John Dudley, duke of Northumberland, who was, in effect, ruling the kingdom, arranged a marriage between his own son and Lady Jane Grey, a royal claimant. Edward was persuaded to change the order of succession, so that precedence was given to Lady Jane Grey. In July 1553, Mary, en route to visit her dying brother at Northumberland's request, got wind of the latter's plans to capture her, and took flight to Sawston Hall. She left in disguise, narrowly escaping an arson attack on the building by a group of her opponents.

Mary proclaimed herself queen on July 9, and, in response to her pleas, vast numbers rallied to defend her from Northumberland's advancing forces. She entered London victoriously in August, and was crowned the following month, sending Northumberland — and later Lady Jane Grey — to the scaffold.

Following her accession, Mary was primarily concerned with finding a husband, in order to reestablish and perpetuate the Catholic line. She accepted a marriage proposal from Prince Philip of Spain (*Philip II), a man ten years her junior, but fear of a Catholic restoration, and, more pertinently, a Spanish marriage, provoked plans for popular rebellion which, in most parts of the land, failed to ignite. In Kent, however, Sir Thomas Wyatt and his men crossed the Thames and advanced on the capital. Against the advice of her ministers, the queen rode into the city and called upon her subjects to resist the insurgents. Wyatt and his followers were subsequently crushed, and Elizabeth was arrested for suspected complicity, and held in the Tower of London, saved from the executioner's axe by Wyatt's admissions, after prolonged questioning.

Philip received a cool reception upon his arrival in England in 1554, and the couple, who shared no common language, were duly wedded. Mary lost no time in embarking upon a program of complete Catholic restoration, naively assuming that this was what most of her subjects desired. Eminent Protestants, including one quarter of the country's clergymen, were deprived of their living, some being sent to prison, and several bishops were deprived of their sees. Parliament would not, however, pass a bill punishing people failing to attend church services.

Reginald Pole, a staunch Catholic, who had been living in exile in Padua for the past twenty years, returned to England in 1554, with the task of restoring Catholicism by overseeing the abolition of all ecclesiastical legislation passed in England since 1529, so that the nation could be reconciled to papal authority. Mary renounced the title of Supreme Head of the church, but Parliament managed to evade the highly explosive issue of the return of lands confiscated from papal dominion under Henry VIII.

From 1555 until the end of Mary's reign, nearly three hundred Protestants — including the outstanding churchmen Latimer, Ridley, and Thomas *Cranmer, the archbishop of Canterbury — were executed, a legacy which has earned the English queen the epithet "Bloody Mary."

Although Mary succeeded in bringing France and Spain to negotiate peace, Philip's invasion of the Papal States the following year led to a renewal of war. Mary wished to remain neutral, but pressure from her husband, along with provocation from France, compelled her to join forces with Spain and declare war in June 1557. The English navy was successful in removing all French shipping from the Channel, and English troops prevented an invasion by the Scots, who were allied to France; but a temporary halt in hostilities allowed the French to replenish their forces, and launch a surprise attack on Calais, the loss of which dealt a severe blow to English morale. With the war proving ever more costly, and Protestants continuing to burn in intolerable numbers, the queen once more fell ill, while Philip abandoned her for a lover in Brussels. Mary, who had had several false pregnancies in the past, developed a swelling in her belly, and yet again believed that she was with child. She made a will bequeathing the throne to her offspring, but finally accepted the truth, acceding to a request from Philip, delivered by one of his council, to acknowledge Elizabeth as heir. Popular legend related that she died with the words "Philip" and "Calais" etched on her heart.

D. M. Loades, *The Reign of Mary Tudor*, 1979.
R. Tittler, *The Reign of Mary I*, 1984.
M. Waldman, *The Lady Mary*, 1972.

MARY STUART (Mary, Queen of Scots; 1542–1587), queen of Scotland. The only surviving child of King James V of Scotland and Mary of Guise, she was heir to the Scottish throne and, as the great-granddaughter of *Henry VII of England, could lay claim to that throne also.

When news arrived that his wife had given birth to a baby girl James V, already in a state of despair at his battle losses to the English, cried out (in reference to the Stewart dynasty): "Adieu, farewell, it came with a lass, it will pass with a lass." Within a few days he was dead, leaving the six-day old Mary Stuart as queen, the Earl of Arran acting as regent.

On hearing of the Scottish king's death, *Henry VIII of England temporarily ceased hostilities and was eager to see an eventual marriage between his own son, Edward, and Mary, thus uniting the two kingdoms under English rule. Two treaties relating to this union were drawn up, but fear that Henry VIII might attempt to kidnap the baby queen prompted Mary of Guise to head north with her child to the relative safety of Stirling castle, where Mary Stuart was crowned at the age of nine months. Meanwhile the Scottish parliament denounced the

Mary, Queen of Scots

treaties and an enraged Henry VIII launched a full-scale attack on his northern neighbors.

While Mary was growing into a clever, charming, and energetic child, her troubled kingdom floundered under unrelenting attacks from the English. In despair, the Scots looked to France for help. The French king, Henry II, offered support in return for a marriage alliance between Francis, his sickly son, and Mary. The Scots agreed and in August 1548, Mary, age six, set sail for France accompanied by a small entourage, but without her mother. The French court was charmed by the beautiful child queen, Henry II describing her a "the most perfect child that I have ever seen." Despite the great distance between them, Mary of Guise took great interest in her daughter's upbringing and Mary Stuart was raised a devout Catholic, remaining so until her death.

In 1558 Mary, age sixteen, and Francis, a year younger, were married, and the following year Francis ascended the French throne. The death of her mother in 1559 threw Mary into a state of grief, accompanied by physical collapse. Six months later she lost her husband also, and grieved deeply for him. Now that she was only dowager queen of France, the influence she had been able to exert in Scotland through the French crown, and through her Guise relations' direction of French foreign policy, was no longer secure. Amidst an array of propositions to remarry, Mary, age eighteen, decided to return to her native Scotland to rule.

She arrived in Scotland in 1561, welcomed by subjects who approved of their young and beautiful ruler. From the outset, Mary showed remarkable

SPEECH GHIVEN BY THE ARCH-BISHOP OF BOURGES MARCH 12, 1587, AT THE REQUIEM MASS FOR MARY STUART AT NOTRE DAME CATHEDRAL, PARIS

Many of us saw in the place where we are now assembled to deplore her, this Queen on her bridal day, arrayed in her regal trappings, so covered in jewels that the sun himself shone not more brightly, so beautiful, so charming withal as never woman was. These walls were then hung with cloth of gold and precious tapestry; every space was filled with thrones and seats, crowded with princes and princesses, who came from all parts to share in the rejoicing. The palace was overflowing with magnificence, splendid fetes and masques; the streets with jousts and tourneys. In short it seemed as if our age had succeeded that day in surpassing the pomp of all past centuries combined. A little time has flowed on and it is all vanished like a cloud. Who would have believed that such a change could have befallen her who appeared then so triumphant, and that we should have seen her a prisoner who had restored prisoners to liberty; in poverty who was accustomed to give so liberally to others; treated with contumely by those on whom she had conferred honors; and finally, the axe of a base executioner mangling the form of her who was doubly a Queen; that form which honored the nuptial bed of a sovereign of France, falling dishonored on a scaffold, and that beauty which had been one of the wonders of the world, faded in a dreary prison, and at last effaced by a piteous death. This place, where she was surrounded with splendor, is now hung with black for her. Instead of nuptial torches we have funereal tapers; in the place of songs of joy, we have sighs and groans; for clarions and hautboys, the tolling of the sad and dismal bell. Oh God, what a change! Oh vanity of human greatness, shall we never be convinced of your deceitfulness.

tolerance toward her mainly Protestant subjects but, a Roman Catholic herself, was persistently maligned by John *Knox, the Presbyterian leader. Under her influence, the royal court at Holyrood Palace, Edinburgh, soon became a center of learning, peopled by painters, musicians, and poets. Mary herself loved music and poetry and was a graceful dancer. From time to time she enjoyed dressing in men's attire to wander in the streets of Edinburgh incognito.

Mary finally married her handsome but self-centered English cousin, Henry Stewart Lord Darnley, in 1566, but her passion for him soon cooled, and Darnley, along with several other nobles, began to resent the favor Mary showed her Italian secretary and confidant, David Rizzio, also a Catholic. Darnley, encouraged to believe that his wife was Rizzio's lover, became party to his bloody murder, which was committed in front of the pregnant queen. Mary was now aware of the possibility of Darnley making an attempt on her own life.

Mary gave birth to a son (the future James VI of Scotland and *James I of England) in 1566 and sent him to Stirling castle to be brought up by relatives. Apart from a few brief visits with her son during his infancy, Mary was never to see him again.

The queen's intention to divorce Darnley was pre-empted by his murder in 1567, committed by several lords including James Hepburn, earl of Bothwell. The queen's marriage to Bothwell three months later incensed her subjects, and she was suspected of having been party to Darnley's murder, especially after the appearance of the incriminating Casket Letters, claimed to have been written by the queen to Bothwell, but whose authenticity has never been proven.

Three weeks after their wedding Bothwell took Mary from Holyrood to the castle of Borthwick, which was soon surrounded by insurgents. Bothwell fled the country, leaving Mary in the hands of rebel lords who held her captive in the castle of Lochleven in the middle of the vast lake of that name (1567). Mary was forced to abdicate and in July of that year, James VI, aged thirteen months, was crowned king, and Mary's half-brother, James, the earl of Moray, proclaimed regent.

After more than ten months in captivity, Mary managed to escape and made her way to England. Far from being welcomed there, *Elizabeth I decided to hold her captive, fearful that the Scottish queen might try to overthrow her. Mary had been publicly blamed for Darnley's death and this provided the excuse for her prolonged confinement. For the next eighteen years Mary was held prisoner, transferred from castle to castle, her health failing, her youth and beauty ravaged. Despite Mary's constant pleas, virtually all communication with her son was prohibited, while James VI was brought up to believe that his mother had murdered his father so that she could marry her lover. In Europe, Mary gradually came to symbolize the martyrdom that Roman Catholics underwent in England.

When, in 1586, Mary was found guilty of conspiracy in a plot to murder Elizabeth and take the English throne from her, she was sentenced to death. As her death warrant was read to her, Mary replied calmly, "I thank you for such welcome news. You will do me great good in withdrawing me from this world out of which I am very glad to go." She was beheaded in February 1587.

A. Fraser, *Mary, Queen of Scots*, 1970.
R. K. Marshall, *Queen of Scots*, 1986.
G. M. Thomas, *The Crime of Mary Stuart*, 1967.

MASARYK, TOMÁS GARRIGUE (1850–1937), founder of Czechoslovakia. The son of a Slovak coachman and a Czech domestic servant, Masaryk was born in a small town close to the present Czech-Hungarian border. His mother was determined her son would receive a secondary education even though boys from poor families were under great pressure to start work as early as possible. After a short period working as a blacksmith's apprentice, Masaryk was enrolled in the German high school in Brno in 1865. He justified the hopes placed in him, excelling at his studies. He graduated with a doctorate in philosophy in 1876 from the University of Vienna. That same year he married Charlotte Garrigue, an American music student he met while studying in Leipzig, and in honor of her American family he added their surname to his own, hence Garrigue Masaryk.

By 1881 Masaryk was lecturer in philosophy at Vienna University; in 1882 he became philosophy professor at the Czech University in Prague. Many men might have been satisfied with such a successful academic career, but Masaryk's nobility of character and his passion for the true and the moral impelled him to look beyond the confines of the university to the injustices in the society around him.

From his experiences in his home town and in Vienna, Masaryk was well acquainted with the national and ethnic tensions underlying the Austro-Hungarian Empire. A strong interest in the revival of Czech culture provided the subject for some of his earliest works. He achieved a measure of fame in his unmasking of two literary forgeries: these poems had been presented as priceless relics of medieval Czech culture but he exposed them as early nineteenth century fakes.

Masaryk once said that "a lie has short legs," and throughout his life he sought to prove the truth of this statement, even at the risk of personal unpopularity. A prime example of this was his defense of a Jewish butcher accused of the ritual murder of a gentile child in 1899. Masaryk showed that the butcher's innocence was beyond doubt and that the old blood libel was a wicked lie. It was a courageous moral stand given the anti-Semitic climate of the time and led to student demonstrations against him. Masaryk was not disturbed by such personal hostility as long as "the truth prevails."

Masaryk's quest for justice and the spread of democratic values in national life found expression in political activity. He was first elected to the Austrian parliament in 1891, at which time he associated with the Young Czech movement. In 1900 he founded his own Realist party; they won only a few seats in the new parliament but their leader's influence far exceeded the number of votes at his call. He was a powerful advocate of minority rights within the empire and spoke out against the imperialist policies that paved the way for World War I. While a member of the imperial parliament, he again achieved renown through the discovery of forgeries, this time documents manufactured by the government to discredit the leaders of the Slavic minorities.

During World War I, Masaryk went into voluntary exile in London, where he chaired the Czech National Council, a pressure group campaigning for an independent, democratic Czech-Slovak state. Viewing the war as a struggle between Western liberal values and German totalitarian ones, he understood its implications for the minorities within the Austro-Hungarian empire who sought an opportunity to break free of rule from Vienna.

Besides Masaryk's credentials as a moral philosopher and sincere democrat, the fine performance of a Czech battalion fighting against the Russian Communists did much to win support for the Czech cause, especially in the United States. Czechs and Slovaks who had made their home in America were also vocal in advocating the cause. In June 1918 Czechoslovakia was recognized as an Allied power in the war against Germany, with frontiers as proposed by Masaryk. A convention with Slovak representatives resulted in agreement on a large measure of autonomy for Slovaks within the republic, and this helped win their support.

Masaryk returned to his homeland and was elected president in November 1918, an office to which he was reelected in 1920, 1927, and 1934. He worked tirelessly to mold the new state into a strong liberal democracy; he was inspired by the freedom and tolerance he had seen in the United States. He faced a daunting struggle in creating an outpost of democracy within a Central Europe that came to be dominated by totalitarian regimes violently opposed to all the values he held dear.

Within Czechoslovakia ethnic tensions among Czechs, Slovaks, and Germans generated continual friction; the autonomy agreement with the Slovaks proved a recurrent source of dispute. Masaryk's approach to the country's ethnic problems was clearly stated in a 1918 letter in which, referring to problems with the German minority, he wrote to his chief disciple and eventual successor, Dr. Eduard Benes: "We shall have to negotiate with our Germans so that they will accept our state, which is not going to have a nationalist structure but will be genuinely a modern democracy."

Masaryk lived long enough to see and decry the rise to power of the Nazis in Germany. He resigned from the presidency in 1935. During forty years of Communist rule after World War II, the name Masaryk was officially reviled and his works unavailable. With the reestablishment of democracy in 1989, he again became a national hero.

Z. Anthony, *The Masaryks*, 1976.

G. J. Kovtun, *The Spirit of Thomas G. Masaryk 1850–1937*, 1990.

S. B. Winter, ed., *T. G. Masaryk 1850–1937*, 1990.

MATTHIAS CORVINUS (1443–1490), king of Hungary.

Matthias was the second son of Hungary's greatest hero, János Hunyadi, who spent his life fighting the Turks and finally defeated them so conclusively that Hungary was spared their attacks for sixty years. Matthias campaigned with his father at nine, was knighted at eleven, married at twelve, and, with his father's death when he was thirteen, condemned to death by his enemies. His life was spared because of his youth, and the governor of Bohemia kept him for a time in hospitable captivity, betrothing Matthias to his daughter (Matthias's first wife had died). At fifteen, Matthias was elected king by a majority of Hungary's nobles.

A fine general, Matthias quickly secured his precarious hold on Hungary, defeating the Turks, invading Serbia, and driving out the Holy Roman Emperor who had been crowned king of Hungary by a group of rebellious nobles (including Matthias's uncle). His powerful nobles subdued, he proceeded to centralize his government, becoming a tireless administrator and a fair judge whose attempts to shelter the weak and the peasants from aristocratic rapaciousness even involved disguising himself and going out among his people to inspect conditions at first hand. He displayed a machiavellian skill at diplomacy and was not averse to displaying generosity or achieving his goals with the use of gold rather than force.

Matthias is not remembered primarily for his military accomplishments — notable as they were — but for being a true Renaissance prince and patron of the arts. His art collection was extensive (*Leonardo da Vinci painted a Madonna for him, having been assured that "he is able to value a picture as few men can.") His magnificent court, which welcomed and supported artists and scholars, had a choir rivaling that of the pope. Matthias's personal taste was more literary than artistic: he stayed up reading half the night, collected vast quantities of books (particularly illuminated manuscripts), and established Budapest's first printing press. His library was the finest outside Italy, holding some ten thousand volumes by the time of his death. He was able to write sincerely: "O scholars, how happy you are! You strive not after blood-stained glory, nor monarch's crowns, but for the laurels of poetry and virtue. You are even able to compel us to forget the tumult of war."

Matthias's wife died in 1464 and he then joined a league against his former father-in-law, who had become king of Bohemia. He invaded Bohemia, where he was crowned king by a group of nobles in 1469 and fought off other contenders for the crown for nine years before being forced to surrender it.

Matthias's third marriage, to Beatrice of Aragon in 1476, strengthened his already strong cultural ties with Italy; however, it did not produce any children and Beatrice's vehement opposition to Matthias's making an illegitimate son his heir meant that Matthias had no successor when he died unexpectedly at the age of fifty. The nobles seized the opportunity to elect a king they could dominate. Their unbridled excesses led, in a relatively short time, to the conquest of Hungary by the Turks, who pillaged Matthias's art collection and library.

C. Csapoki, *The Corvinian Library*, 1973.

MAXIMILIAN I (1459–1519), Holy Roman emperor. Maximilian was the eldest son of the emperor Frederick III and Eleanor of Portugal. In 1477 he married Mary, the daughter of Charles the Bold, duke of Burgundy. He acquired considerable tracts of land in Flanders and on the eastern border of France. As a result, the French, under *Louis XI, invaded, but were defeated at the battle of Guinegate in 1479. With the death of his wife in 1482 he had to assert his right to retain power by defeating the armies of the Netherlands States General who challenged his rule.

With the Treaty of Arras (1482) Louis recognized Maximilian as the regent of Flanders until his young son, Philip, could assume control. The possession of the Netherlands would later become so well established that they remained loyal to the Habsburgs for nearly three hundred years. Maximilian was crowned king of the Romans (heir to his father) in 1486. He went on to forge an alliance with Spain, England, and Brittany in order to continue his war against France and insurgent Flemish towns. During a campaign in the Netherlands he was captured and imprisoned by the burghers of Bruges. As a result, his father had to collect an army and release his son personally.

At the diet of Frankfurt in 1486 Maximilian perceived the dangers of a disunited Germany facing powerful military neighbors, among which were France, Spain, and the Ottoman Empire. In order to consolidate power, he sought imperial reforms that were in his own interest. His plan included the cessation of private wars, improvement of imperial justice, establishment of an imperial army paid for by imperial tax, and allowing the Estates (local representative assemblies) to share power. The reforms faced opposition from local rulers, who contested a centralized form of government that would compete with them for power within their own domains. Maximilian's inability to gauge the political environment was to make his reign a frustrating one, with many disappointments and failures.

In 1490 Maximilian married by proxy the duchess Anne of Brittany in an anti-French move. This came at a time when he had recently reestablished his family's control in Austria and was busy asserting his claim to the throne in Hungary. Charles VIII of France subsequently rejected the hand of Margaret, Maximilian's eldest daughter, and succeeded in making Anne of Brittany break her alliance with Maximilian and become his wife in 1491. While tensions with France heightened, Vladislav II of Bohemia was elected to the Hungarian throne. Despite inadequate resources, Maximilian attacked and, through the Treaty of Pressburg (1491), assured that if there were no male heir to the throne in Hungary, it would pass to the Habsburgs.

The Peace of Senlis in 1493 confirmed German control of the Low Countries and increased Maximilian's popularity on the eve of his succession to the sole rulership of the kingdom with the death of his father. In the summer of that year the Germans drove the Turks from the southeastern borders of their country, and Maximilian married Bianca Maria Sforza of Milan in order to contest control of Italy with the French. However, the French invaded Italy in 1494, forcing the Germans to join the Holy League with the pope, Spain, Venice, and Milan. The alliance with Ferdinand of Spain led to a double marriage between Maximilian's children Philip (now duke of the Netherlands) and Margaret, and Juana and Juan of Spain. This alliance would help to establish Habsburg control over half of Europe.

At the meeting of the Reichstag at Worms in 1495, the German princes weakened Maximilian's centralizing policies and limited his power. The subsequent defeat of the Holy League's forces and the German king's unsuccessful bid to consolidate his own authority crippled Germany. In a speech at Freiburg in 1498, following the death of Charles VIII and the succession of Louis of Orleans to the throne in France, Maximilian claimed that: "By the Lombards I am betrayed. By the Germans deserted. But I will not let myself again be bound hand and foot as at Worms... I must and will make war... This must I say, even should I have to throw the crown at my feet and stamp upon it."

In 1499 the Germans were defeated by the Swiss confederation in a war that the king did not want and which forced him to grant Switzerland de facto independence. At the same time, the French moved further into Italy, while in 1500 the princes of Germany created a supreme council to diminish the king's power.

Maximilian strengthened his position by coming to an agreement with France and securing funds from various south German business firms. With the revival in his fortunes he campaigned, in 1506, to assure his succession to the Hungarian crown in spite of Vladislav's male heir. He now felt the time was right to be crowned officially by the pope as Holy Roman emperor. However, he was kept out of Italy by the Venetians and his campaign against them failed miserably. The roads to Rome were blocked, and he was forced to content himself with the title of "Emperor-elect" bestowed on him in Trent in 1508 with the consent of Pope Julius II. He was never formally crowned and decided to wage an unpopular war of revenge on the Italian peninsula. Joining the League of Cambrai, with his daughter (now regent of the Netherlands), Spain, and the pope, he unsuccessfully renewed his fight against Venice. His attempt at conquering Venice being futile, he betrayed his agreement with the French and pursued their expulsion from Italy.

Maximilian was never successful in establishing German control in Italy, while Germany itself was plagued with private wars and anarchy. He continued to pursue his plans for peripheral expansion (into Poland, Bohemia, and Hungary) to the benefit of the Habsburg family, all the while neglecting the ambitions of a unified Germany. He died a poor and broken man who did not live to see how the Habsburg family's possessions would, indeed, spread from the Iberian peninsula to the plains of Hungary and Bohemia.

Personally, Maximilian was charming, congenial, and talented, with a passion for athletics, the hunt, and the arts, of which he was a great patron. He was the author of two chivalric allegories in verse, and planned to write his autobiography in Latin. His many admirers dubbed him "the last of the knights."
G. Benecke, *Maximilian I: An Analytical Biography,* 1982.
C. Dericum, *Maximilian I,* 1979.

MAXIMILIAN (1832–1867), emperor of Mexico. Archduke Ferdinand Maximilian Joseph, younger brother of the Austrian emperor *Francis Joseph I, was born in Vienna. He assumed command of the Austrian navy in 1854, and married Charlotte, daughter of King Leopold of Belgium in 1857. That same year, he was appointed governor of the Lombardo-Venetian kingdom.

After a devastating war against the United States in which Mexico lost half its territory, the country was in severe debt. While the Mexican president Benito *Juárez's moratorium on debt repayments angered the European powers, the French emperor *Napoleon III was already attempting to reestablish France's presence in the New World. He invaded Mexico in 1863 and imposed a conservative junta of notables to govern the country with French military backing. Seeking to establish a Mexican monarchy, the junta offered Maximilian the throne in 1863.

At first, Maximilian hesitated. A liberal and Freemason, he insisted that a plebiscite be held to determine whether the majority of Mexico's population favored a monarchy. He failed to realize that most Mexicans were illiterate peasants who did not understand what they were voting for. When the anticipated results, an overwhelming victory, were presented to Maximilian the following year, he eagerly accepted the throne. He also agreed to repay all debts and maintain a sizable French military presence.

Crowned emperor in 1864, Maximilian was sincere in his desire to govern effectively. He studied Spanish, and Charlotte became known as Carlotta. Their castle was opened to the public once a week, and Maximilian set out on an exhausting tour of the provinces. He was shocked to discover the degree to which the church was ignoring the needs of the peasants and called on the clergy to practice charity. Not only did he refuse to restore expropriated church property or to enfranchise Catholicism as the state religion, he also ordered the church to lend money to the government for much needed rural development. Most liberal demands were accepted as legitimate and a general amnesty was granted to all political prisoners sentenced to under ten years in prison. The junta suggested that an arch be constructed in honor of Carlotta, but Maximilian countered that an arch celebrating Mexican independence would be more appropriate.

Although he was now opposed by the conservatives, he did no better in appeasing the liberals, who were appalled by the idea of a foreigner ruling the

The Execution of Maximilian of Mexico

country. Juárez ignored imperial overtures and began a guerilla war with American support. Meanwhile, Napoleon decided to withdraw his troops. Maximilian contemplated abdication but was persuaded by Carlotta to keep his throne, saying she would travel to Europe to win him French and papal support. The conservatives then falsely informed Maximilian that Juárez had been defeated and had fled to the United States and urged Maximilian to issue a death sentence on any of Juárez's supporters caught with arms.

Carlotta's visit to Europe was a failure. Napoleon refused to commit troops and the pope was angered by her husband's hostility to the church. Depression kept her from returning to Mexico, and she eventually went insane.

Maximilian's lack of military support enabled Juárez to increase his offensive. Maximilian fled the capital and fortified himself in Queretaro, but surrendered after one hundred days. Juárez refused to forgive Maximilian for his proclamation demanding the summary execution of his supporters and demanded the death penalty. Maximilian was tried before six judges, three of whom favored exile and three execution by firing squad. The president of the court cast the deciding vote for execution. International protests poured into Mexico, but to no avail. Maximilian was brought before a firing squad and with his last breath prayed that his blood be the last shed for Mexico (May 15, 1867).

Some time before he was deposed, Maximilian smuggled his fortune to Texas hidden in flour barrels. A guard accompanying the caravan became suspicious of the elaborate security precautions for a shipment of flour and discovered the barrels' secret. He attempted to steal the treasure but was killed in a skirmish. After several more adventures, the convoy decided to bury Maximilian's gold somewhere in the mountains surrounding El Paso. It has never been found.
E. Corti, *Maximilian and Charlotte of Mexico,* 2 vols., 1968.
J. Haslip, *The Crown of Mexico,* 1971.

MAXWELL, JAMES CLERK (1831–1879),

Scottish physicist whose electromagnetic theory was one of the fundamental concepts that led to Albert *Einstein's theory of special relativity. Maxwell was born in Edinburgh. His father, a lawyer, engaged a tutor for him at a young age. The tutor found his student dull. However, at Edinburgh Academy, when he was only fourteen, Maxwell had his first scientific paper published, describing a series of elliptic curves that could be traced with pins and thread. At age sixteen he entered the University of Edinburgh where he had two more scientific papers published. In 1850 he enrolled at Cambridge University, and for the next five years distinguished himself in mathematics and mathematical physics.

His father's failing health prompted Maxwell's return to Scotland. In 1856 he was appointed professor of natural philosophy at Marischal College in Aberdeen, and in 1858 he married the daughter of the college principal. From 1860 to 1865 he was professor of natural philosophy at King's College, London, and during this period he did his groundbreaking work in the field of electrodynamics.

In 1871 Maxwell was elected to the Cavendish professorship at Cambridge. He knew the work of Michael *Faraday and William Thomson (Lord *Kelvin) and was in correspondence with both. Faraday had suggested that electric and magnetic phenomena do not act directly on distant objects, but through a medium. Maxwell was to name this medium electric and magnetic fields. Thomson had started the task of putting Faraday's ideas into mathematical form, but it was Maxwell who developed the complete electromagnetic theory. In the preface to his *Treatise on Electricity and Magnetism* (1873), Maxwell stated as his main task the work of transposing Faraday's physical laws into mathematical form. In 1861 he had formulated a set of partial differential equations that represented electromagnetic phenomena. In considering his equations, however, Maxwell found something wanting. According to some, he saw a lack of symmetry, while others say he drew an analogy from hydrodynamics. In any case, he added a term to the equations called "the displacement current" and from this adjustment, he made an enormous discovery. Calculating the velocity of the transverse waves produced by the displacement, he found they were exactly the velocity of light in vacuum. He concluded that light was made up of the same waves that caused electric and magnetic currents. Then, based on his equations, he stated that other electromagnetic waves of different frequencies must also exist.

In 1881, twenty years later, Heinrich *Hertz confirmed the existence of these waves experimentally, leading to the development of the radio industry. On Maxwell's history-making discovery, Einstein wrote: "Imagine his feelings when the differential equations he had formulated proved to him that electromagnetic fields spread in the form of polarized waves and with the speed of light!"

In developing his kinetic theory of gases, Maxwell already knew of the second law of thermodynamics discovered in 1850 by Rudolf Clausius. Originally stated, the law said that heat cannot go from a colder to a warmer body without some other change taking place. In finding a statistical distribution of gas molecule velocities both above and below their mean free path (the average distance it takes before one molecule collides with another), Maxwell was the first to state that the second law of thermodynamics is a statistical law. Maxwell's "demons" (so named by Thomson) were tiny finite beings who could control individual gas molecules, thus leading to the realization that individual or small groups of molecules were not subject to statistics. In a letter written in 1868, Maxwell stated the purpose of his demons: "to show that the second law of thermodynamics was only a statistical certainty." The concept of statistical certainty in contradistinction to absolute certainty and the concept of the indeterminacy of matter on a microscopic level overturned the strictly mechanical view of the world previously held by science.

While still a young man, Maxwell proved that the rings of Saturn were not made up of continuous matter but consisted of multitudes of small satellites orbiting the planet, a discovery confirmed over a century later by the first Voyager space mission to reach Saturn. His contribution to the kinetic theory of gases was essential to the concept of the atomic and molecular composition of matter. He also made significant contributions to the field of color theory, color vision, and color photography; to geometric optics; and to the theory of structures. His work on speed governors is considered the foundation of cybernetics.

Albert *Einstein named Maxwell as one of his true precursors and paid tribute to him by referring to the revolution in scientific thinking that his work had ushered in. "The lion's share in this revolution was Maxwell's... Since Maxwell's time, physical reality has been thought of as represented by continuous fields...This change in the conception of reality is the most profound and the most fruitful that physics has experienced since the time of [Isaac] *Newton."

Maxwell died in Cambridge and was buried in a small village in his native Scotland.

L. Campbell and W. Garnett, *The Life of James Clerk Maxwell*, 1969.

C. W. F. Everitt, *James Clerk Maxwell: Physicist and Natural Philosopher*, 1975.

M. Goldman, *The Demon in the Aether*, 1983.

R. A. R. Tricker, *The Contribution of Faraday and Maxwell to Electrical Science*, 1966.

MAZARIN, JULES (1602–1661),

French cardinal who succeeded Cardinal Armand-Jean *Richelieu as chief minister of France, consolidating the rule of the monarchy and establishing France's primacy in Europe.

Mazarin was born Giulio Mazarini in Peiscina, Italy, to a notable yet poor family. He learned early in life the advantages of nurturing well-connected friends, and through the good offices of family connections he received a sound basic education at a Jesuit school in Rome and then studied law in Spain. Returning to Italy in 1624, he received a commission in the papal army. He was not especially devout in his Catholicism until the following year, when he experienced a mystical conversion on Christmas Eve. He subsequently left the army and joined the papal diplomatic service.

In 1630 Mazarin was dispatched by the pope to negotiate with Richelieu over France's war with Spain. He was immediately enthralled by Richelieu, henceforth seeking every opportunity to travel to his court. He in his turn made a favorable impression on Richelieu after successfully brokering a peaceful settlement to the dispute at hand.

In 1634 Mazarin was appointed nuncio to France to negotiate a lasting peace between Spain and that country. He adored the French and was welcomed into their realm, so it was with great disappointment that he saw Richelieu bring France into the Thirty Years' War against Spain soon after his arrival. His mission a failure, he returned to Rome, where he nonetheless did his utmost to further French interests. The king of France, Louis XIII, at the urging of Richelieu, gratefully bestowed on Mazarin French citizenship in 1639 and nominated him for a cardinalcy. Although Mazarin had little theological training and was not even a priest, Pope Urban VIII raised him to cardinal the following year, citing his efforts toward achieving peace.

Mazarin returned to France in 1640 at the invitation of the king. When Richelieu died in 1642, he found himself unofficially filling the great man's shoes. When Louis XIII died the following year with his heir *Louis XIV still an infant, the mother of the heir, Anne of Austria, turned to Mazarin for counsel. He successfully installed her as regent, spoiling the machinations of various other nobles, while building a strong and trusting relationship with her. Mazarin, a handsome and charismatic character, was accused of maintaining an illicit relationship with Anne, a claim which, though quite possible, remained unsubstantiated. Anne confirmed his appointment as first minister. He brought to Paris his seven nieces, all of whom married into the nobility.

Mazarin hoped initially to bring to an end the conflict between the great Catholic kingdoms of Europe, although recognizing that he was no longer a papal mediator and his principal duty was to France. His first task was to end the Thirty Years' War, which led to the favorable peace of Westphalia in 1648. However, the general conflict with Spain was to continue for another decade.

The cost of the hard-fought peace settlement was internal division. Mazarin had financed the years of war by imposing stern fiscal measures on all classes of society, selling public offices and manipulating the economy. His edicts were enforced by royal agents whose strong-arm methods enraged the pop-

ulation. Eventually, the first of the revolts known as the Fronde broke out in 1648, led by the judiciary of the Paris parliament, and quickly drew in factions of the nobility, even attracting many provincials. Mazarin and Anne were forced to flee the capital in 1649, but he succeeded in maintaining a modicum of control over state affairs. The initial successes of the Fronde led to other local rebellions against the state, which by this time was so fractured that it was unable to quell effectively the turmoil. Spain, trying to profit from French disarray, offered support to a noble faction of the Frondeurs and invaded the Netherlands. Mazarin seized on the general mayhem in the ranks of the Frondeurs and in 1653 returned to Paris to reimpose the authority of the crown. The early gains of the Fronde were all lost and the rebellious nobles were banished from the court.

Louis XIV was enthroned the same year, and spent much of his reign drawing the strings of power ever more tightly together, heeding Mazarin's lessons on statesmanship and absolutism. The war against Spain still flared intermittently, until Mazarin managed to maneuver Spain into diplomatic isolation through carefully extracted treaties with Austria and England. Spain finally signed a peace with France in 1659, ceding large tracts of land, and sealing France's domination in Europe. Mazarin left an immense fortune and a magnificent library bequeathed to the College Mazarin.
R. Briggs, *Early Modern France, 1560–1716*, 1977. A. Hassall, *Mazarin*, 1970.

MAZZINI, GIUSEPPE (1805–1872), Italian nationalist leader. His father, a professor of anatomy, supported the democratic ideals of the French Revolution, and Mazzini was to inherit many of his political sensibilities from him. A sickly and stubborn child, he could not speak until the age of five, but could already read at four. He was taught by Jansenist priests who inspired in him an abiding love of religion. As a young man, Mazzini saw refugees fleeing from the failed Piedmontese revolution of 1821: this event moved him to put on a black suit in mourning for Italy's misfortunes, and he dressed in such somber hues for the rest of his life.

Studying law at the University of Genoa, Mazzini did not neglect his first love, literature. His essays on writers such as Johann Wolfgang von *Goethe, Lord *Byron, Sir Walter *Scott, *Dante Alighieri, and Alessandro Francesco Manzoni eventually filled some one hundred volumes. However, he quickly set aside his passion for literature in order to commit his life to the unification of Italy.

In 1827 Mazzini joined the clandestine Carbonari revolutionary society and was imprisoned for three months for his involvement with it. It was in prison that he decided to found his own organization, dedicated to attaining national independence through education and insurrection. Upon his release, Mazzini went into exile in France where he established Young Italy, which was based on belief in the exis-

Giuseppe Mazzini

tence of God, the unity of humanity, and the necessity of progress. His principle of association stressed the duties of men to each other and society. Forced to leave France, he went to Switzerland, where he tried to instigate a mutiny in the Piedmontese army. The insurrection failed miserably and Mazzini's influence began to diminish. He remained in Switzerland until he was expelled, whereupon he eventually found a home in liberal England in 1837.

Mazzini remained in London for more than a decade, and returned for an even longer period of time after the defeat of the Roman Republic in 1849. In London he lived in poverty while occasionally working as a journalist. Between 1840 and 1844 he published a journal called *Apostolato Popolare* and opened a school for Italian exiles. During this time he stayed in a dilapidated one-room apartment, where his many canaries flew free. Nonetheless, despite the personal difficulties he faced, he was quickly becoming an important spokesman for nationalism and its expression through the modern nation-state.

In March 1849 Mazzini returned to Italy in order to fight alongside Giuseppe *Garibaldi, and eventually was elected a member of the triumvirate of the Roman Republic after the flight of the pope. Ruling Rome for just over three months, he was tolerant and enlightened. A man of integrity, he did not receive a salary and lived a modest life. He abolished the death sentence, granted clemency to imprisoned French priests, and employed prostitutes as nurses, attempting to reconcile freedom, order, and justice with effective rule. Eventually, the shortlived republic was defeated by the French in spite of Mazzini's concerted defense. With the help of the U.S. consul, he escaped to London once again.

Mazzini was not one to compromise his political ideals. His friends now began to desert him as he attempted two more unsuccessful rebellions in Mantua (1852) and Milan (1853). During this period, he displayed his religious fervor by couching nationalist propaganda in spiritual rhetoric. He claimed that God spoke through the people and that the only way to achieve national unification was through popular initiative. He continued to organize uprisings throughout the 1850s but was not directly involved in Italy's declaration of statehood in 1861. More moderate political forces in Italy were able to persuade *Napoleon III of France and Victor Emmanuel II of Sardinia that Mazzini's visionary revolution was undesirable.

While Mazzini's dream of a unified Italy was being realized, he refused to accept the form it assumed. The unification of the country through its annexation to Piedmont, under Count Camillo Benso di *Cavour, at the initiative of foreign forces was unacceptable to him. Upon the final capture of Rome by Italian forces in 1870, Mazzini asserted: "I had thought to revive the soul of Italy, but all I find before me is its corpse."

Mazzini was elected to the new parliament as a representative of Messina, Sicily. However, he was not allowed to fill his position due to a political dispute. He never accepted united Italy, but frequently traveled there from his exile. On one visit, as he set out for Sicily, he was imprisoned for several months for violating his exile. He died at Pisa, in disguise as an English doctor, a stranger in the country he helped to build.

G. O. Griffith, *Mazzini*, 1970.

G. Salvemini, *Mazzini: Prophet of Modern Europe*, 1956.

MEDICI FAMILY (1434–1737), rulers of Florence. The growing prosperity of Florence began to attract members of the Medici family around 1200 and by the end of the thirteenth century some of Florence's leading merchants were Medici. Nominally a republic, Florence was actually a merchant oligarchy where only guild members could be elected city officials or spokesmen. By 1300 Medici had served terms as both. They gained a reputation as friends and champions of the people and by the beginning of the fifteenth century, through their merchant and banking interests, had acquired one of the greatest fortunes of the day. **Cosimo de'Medici** (1389–1464), the first Medici to rule Florence, had certain characteristic Medici traits: civility, graciousness, aversion to violence, interest in the arts and humanities, and a particularly painful gout. Though prominent as Florence's richest banker, Cosimo was not at first part of the ruling clique. Carefully trained in both business and politics (in Florence the two were intertwined), he had served in the government but was essentially a merchant. He rose to power when Florence's unofficial ruler, Rinaldo delgi Albizzi, mismanaged Florence's war against Lucca (part of Florence's long-term policy of conquering and unifying Tuscany). Threatened by criticism, Rinaldo arrested Cosimo and his brother Lorenzo and called a parliament to exile them. The parliament, a device to dispose of inconvenient opposition, was supposedly an assembly summoned to determine the people's will so that it could be acted upon. In fact, parliaments were well-orchestrated, prearranged, supporters-only farces. Their exile revoked by another parliament, the Medici brothers returned in 1434 to Florence, which Cosimo ruled unofficially for the next thirty years.

A moderate, humane man, who recorded with satisfaction that during his three terms as a spokesman "no one was exiled or suffered ill-treatment," Cosimo further corrupted Florence's already crooked electoral system to ensure that he stayed in power. Preferring to work behind the scenes to avoid offending republican sensibilities, he controlled Florence's finances and foreign affairs. A patron of arts and scholarship, Cosimo established an academy of Platonic studies and several libraries, including the first public library in Europe, and commissioned buildings and works of art. In 1453, realizing the need for a peaceful, united Italy, he instigated a defensive-wars-only policy under which Florence and the Medici prospered.

Piero (1416–1469), who succeeded his father Cosimo in 1464, continued Cosimo's patronage of the arts and libraries and his discreet behind-the-scenes style of government. A merchant by education and inclination, he married into one of Florence's leading banking families and strengthened the family bank, which prospered under his guidance. He reigned only five years before dying from gout.

Lorenzo ("the Magnificent"; 1449–1492), eldest son of Piero, was only fifteen when Piero became ruler of Florence. He had to represent his bedridden father who discussed political problems with him as an equal. The elevated status of the Medici family affected both Lorenzo's education and his choice of wife: his education was humanistic and religious, not commercial; his bride came from one of the oldest aristocratic families. Of his accession to power Lorenzo wrote: "On the second day after my father's death, although I, Lorenzo, was only twenty-one years old, the leading men of the city and state came to my house to condole with me and at the same time to request that I assume charge of the city and state as my father and grandfather had done before me. Owing to my youth, I accepted the responsibility with reluctance and solely in the interest of our friends and their fortunes, since at Florence one lives insecurely without the control of the state."

Lorenzo's reign was shaped by his outstanding traits of energy, enthusiasm, and mercy. His failures came from abandoning Medici policies and practices. He increasingly delegated business responsibilities, but many of his representatives were incompetent and unreliable. Medici bank and business interests declined, and Lorenzo was unable to continue aiding Florence financially; persistent rumors accused him of using state funds to help his bank. Militarily, his aggressive challenge to the pope's attempts to strengthen the papal states led to

a serious threat to Lorenzo's rule, the assassination of his brother, and war throughout Italy, and eventually increased Medici respect for the pope's power.

Himself an artist and poet, Lorenzo continued the family tradition of patronage of the arts and was considered the epitome of a Renaissance man. He enlarged the university of Florence, establishing a branch in Pisa, and encouraged the development of Italian literature. He discerned the genius in *Michelangelo, giving him a place in his household, and was the early patron of *Leonardo da Vinci. Lorenzo made his rule both official and highly visible by calling a parliament to change Florence's form of government. The increase in Medici status and Lorenzo's respect for the papacy effected the marriages he arranged for his six children: Lorenzo's heir, Piero, married into an aristocratic Roman family, and his second son, Giovanni, was made a cardinal at age thirteen.

When the family gout killed Lorenzo in 1492, **Piero** (1471–1503) began his reign. His haughtiness, political incompetence, and indifference to Florence's republican traditions engendered opposition to his rule. Piero was overthrown and the Medici family driven into exile in 1494. Despite several attempts to reconquer it with mercenaries by Piero (who later drowned in a shipwreck), the restored republic was a French client state until 1512. Meanwhile **Cardinal Giovanni** (1475–1521) had achieved prominence in the papal court, which requested Spain's help in forcing France out of Italy. He arranged that Spain's victory should include restoration of Medici rule to Florence. Returning to Florence in 1512, Giovanni replaced his opponents with supporters, rather than exiling or murdering them, and used parliament to restore the Medici constitution. In 1513 Cardinal Giovanni was elected pope. As Leo X his energy and will were increasingly subjugated to a hedonism he no longer sought to control. His attitude was: "Now that God has given us the papacy, let us enjoy it." A worldly, cultured, almost completely unreligious politician, he was incapable of dealing with the Protestant Reformation, which began during his papacy, being neither willing nor able to understand its religious or moral motivations and implications. He first scornfully ignored it, then fought it with diplomacy and force. Caught in the struggle between Spain and France for the control of Italy, Leo finally excommunicated Martin *Luther and promised to support *Charles V of Spain if he brought Luther to trial.

Leo's main interest was the advancement of the Medici family. He raised them to the rank of royalty by arranging his brother's marriage to a French princess. Although he appointed **Lorenzo** (Piero's son; 1492–1519) as Florence's titular head, Leo remained the real ruler, receiving daily reports and sending frequent advice. Leo deposed the duke of the papal state of Urbino and conferred his rank on Lorenzo (1516). In 1518 Leo married Lorenzo to a French princess who later died giving birth to

Catherine (see *Catherine de Médicis). Lorenzo died soon after and **Cardinal Giulio de'Medici** (1478–1534) became Leo's representative in Florence. Leo had made Giulio, the illegitimate son of Lorenzo the Magnificent's brother, a cardinal. Giulio's excellent administration of Florence, which he continued after Leo's death in 1521, increased Medici prestige and popularity. The lack of a male Medici successor was a problem he solved after becoming Pope Clement VII (1523) by revealing the existence of two bastard Medici boys, Ippolito and **Alessandro** (1511–1537; certainly Clement's favorite and possibly his son). He sent them to live in Florence as its future rulers.

Clement was not a successful pope because of his indecisive character and the overwhelming problems he faced. His conspiracy with France led to the ferocious sack of Rome by Spanish forces in 1527. Florence took advantage of this to get rid of the Medici youths and restore the republic. When king and pope quickly came to terms Florence fought bitterly against the return of the Medici but could not prevent it. Alessandro was twenty-one when he returned to Florence and immediately ordered the death or exile of the rebellion's leaders.

In 1532 Clement abolished Florence's old constitution and appointed Alessandro hereditary duke. With that Florence became a duchy and the old republic came to an end. Clement had a moderating influence on Alessandro, but when he died in 1534, Alessandro became a vicious, corrupt tyrant. His close companion was Lorenzino ("little Lorenzo") of the younger branch of the Medici (descended from Cosimo's brother Lorenzo). The two branches had been estranged for years but now the two young Medici were inseparable, until Lorenzino murdered Alessandro in 1537, supposedly to rid Florence of a tyrant. Alessandro's successor, seventeen-year-old **Cosimo** (1519–1574), of the younger Medici branch, was his closest male relative. Cosimo's first act was to outlaw Lorenzino, thereby negating Lorenzino's superior claim to Alessandro's throne. Powerful and intelligent, Duke Cosimo I reigned from 1537 to 1574 during which time he reorganized Florence under Medici to rule, lasting until 1737.

J. Claugh, *The Medici: Tale of Fifteen Generations*, 1976.

D. Kent, *The Rise of the Medici*, 1978.

G. Pottinger, *The Court of the Medici*, 1978.

F. Schevill, *The Medici*, 1970.

MEHEMET ALI (Muhammad Ali Pasha; 1769–1849), ruler of Egypt. He was the son of Ibrahim Agha, the commander of the small provincial force maintained by the governor of Kavala, Albania, a part of the Ottoman Empire. Mehemet's father died while he was still a child and he was then adopted by the governor, growing up as a member of his family and, when eighteen years old, marrying one of his daughters. An active and ambitious young man, he became a successful businessman involved in the tobacco trade.

When *Napoleon Bonaparte invaded Egypt in 1798, its Ottoman rulers organized an expeditionary force to oppose him, of which Mehemet was a part. The three-year French occupation completely disrupted the traditional Egyptian political and economic structure; Mehemet used the upheavals to further his own ends and maneuvered so skillfully in the aftermath of the occupation that by 1805 he had, by dint of charm, guile, and native wit, secured appointment to the position of viceroy (with the rank of pasha) to the Ottoman sultan. As the ruler of Egypt, he was now in a position to continue the revolutionary social changes initiated by Napoleon.

Mehemet was ruthless and brutal in the measures he took to safeguard and increase his own authority. In 1811 he had the Mamelukes, who were the ruling military oligarchy, massacred, and subsequently transferred the property of the old landowning classes to his control, subordinated Egypt's religious class to the state, and restricted the activities of native merchants and artisans. When peasant disaffection with the new measures led to protests, Mehemet crushed the nascent rebellion.

By 1815 the extent of the reforms introduced by Mehemet meant that most of the agricultural land in the country had passed into the hands of the state; Mehemet then pioneered the introduction of new crops, such as cotton, which ensured high cash returns and bolstered state income from farming, and oversaw the development of improved methods of irrigation. Meanwhile, Egypt's administrative structure was reorganized to allow for stricter centralized control of the economy.

The armed services were also comprehensively restructured and expanded, with a conscript army replacing the mercenary force that Egypt had hitherto deployed. Mehemet's efforts at modernization even encompassed attempts to set up a modern industrial infrastructure for the processing of Egypt's wealth of raw materials.

Mehemet had no real vision beyond that of self-aggrandizement, his policies being implemented to serve the interests of him and his family (he fathered ninety-five children by many different wives) rather than to create a new society. As a result, he proved incapable of providing an ideology able to motivate the nation to support his reform program, which foundered due to mismanagement, excessive taxation, and an inadequate human and resource infrastructure. Military conscription of the peasantry led to a fall in agricultural output, while the state monopoly on trade had a stultifying effect on the economy and individual enterprise.

Mehemet's early deference to his Ottoman masters (he helped to suppress rebellions against them in Arabia and Greece) later changed to rivalry as he pursued his own territorial ambitions. As his campaigns (including the invasion of the Nilotic Sudan in pursuit of fresh conscripts for his army) prospered, the Ottomans sought to pacify him by granting him possession of Crete in 1830, but he progressed to open war against them, winning control of Syria as far north as Adana by 1833. His forces' decisive defeat of the Ottoman army at the Battle of Nizip in 1839 was followed by the defection to him of the Ottoman fleet. However, his hopes of winning total independence from Constantinople were dashed by the intervention of the great powers: Britain, Prussia, Russia, and Austria could not stand by and watch the international balance of power being threatened, and in 1840 stepped in to end Mehemet's rule in Egypt.

The Ottoman sultan therefore retained suzerainty in Egypt, and Mehemet had to be content with his family being given the hereditary right to rule there in his name. His last years were marked by his decline into feeble-mindedness, and he was succeeded by his son Ibrahim Pasha in 1848, a year before his death. His native wit and great charm had compensated in great measure for his limited knowledge and narrow-mindedness, but few of his reforms survived the disappearance of his commanding personality. Nonetheless, the dynasty he founded survived to shape modern Egypt until the nationalist takeover of the 1950s.

M. Abir, *Modernisation, Reaction, and Muhammad Ali's Empire*, 1977.

A. L. Al-Sayyid, *Egypt in the Reign of Muhammad Ali*, 1984.

H. Dodwell, *The Founder of Modern Egypt*, 1967.

MEHMED II ("The Conqueror"; 1432–1481), Ottoman emperor, conqueror of Constaninople. As the third son of Emperor Murad II, born to a Christian slave girl, Mehmed had little chance to inherit his father's throne. However, when he was only eight years old his eldest brother Ahmed died prematurely and Mehmed was appointed governor of the influential province of Magnesia. Three years later, his second brother Ali was assassinated, leaving Mehmed as heir. Murad insisted that Mehmed, as future emperor, concentrate on his previously neglected studies and ordered his tutor to beat him if he slacked. Turning diligently to his studies, Mehmed became attracted to the writings of a heretical sect promoting the affinity between Christianity and Islam. Although he later abandoned these beliefs, it was probably this youthful flirtation with the church that inflamed him to attempt to subdue Constantinople.

Murad abdicated in 1444, thinking that Mehmed could do little harm to the empire. During a seven-year reign, however, Mehmed made plans to take Constantinople, much to the chagrin of the Janissary troops who feared that an assault on the city would undermine Murad's tenuous European conquests. As the threat of war became real, Murad deposed his son and exiled him to Adrianople but recalled him in 1451 to assist in a final assault on Kosovo.

Mehmed II, "The Conqueror"

When news reached Mehmed later that year that Murad had died, he summoned his troops and exclaimed, "Whoever loves me, let him follow me!" Reaching Bursa, the capital, he was pleased to see the mother of his younger brother, a potential rival claimant to the throne, coming to congratulate him on his ascension. Nevertheless, the boy was strangled in his bath as his mother kissed Mehmed.

Mehmed was an imposing figure, with sharp, aquiline features and a penetrating gaze. With little respect for human life, he often walked among his troops disguised as a common soldier, butchering anyone who dared to recognize him. He entered into a pact with *Constantine of Constantinople, assuring integrity of Constantine's territory, but when his father's vizier Halil came to visit with a rich gift of gold, Mehmed threw the coins in his face and cried, "The only gift I want is Constantinople." Churches were razed for building materials as Mehmed began erecting fortresses along the Bosphorus, and Europe, realizing Mehmed's true intentions, regarded him as the anti-Christ.

Although Constantinople's might had been declining sharply, it was still considered the last bastion of Christendom. Constantine had sent for gigantic bronze cannons from Europe but was unable to pay; the cannons were bought by Mehmed. Mehmed's army consisted of over one hundred thousand men; Constantinople had only seven thousand, but the city was well fortified and prepared to withstand a lengthy siege. Surveying the city, Mehmed guessed that the weakest link was along the sea and organized an impressive naval force to attack from there. However, Constantine blocked the entrance to the bay, and even after six weeks of heavy bombardment, the city would not surrender. After careful consideration, Mehmed found a means of bringing his ships into the bay. A road was built across the Golden Horn and his ships were transported overland on greased rollers. The inhabitants of Constantinople shuddered at the sight of an entire flotilla with sails extended rolling down the hills, but after seven weeks, even Mehmed's navy could not defeat Constantinople's resolute defenders. Mehmed decided to make one last assault. He gathered the Janissaries and offered them three days to pillage the city unhindered; only the buildings and walls were to be left for him. After three failed assaults, a soldier noticed that a gate had been accidentally left open and led his companions surging through it. In the ensuing fracas, Constantine perished, with no one knowing how he died. On May 29, 1453, Mehmed proceeded to the Church of Saint Sophia to declare himself the new Kaisar-i-Rum ("emperor of Rome"), but to his soldiers, he was Mehmed Fatih (Mehmed the Conqueror).

Whereas Europe was startled by the fall of Constantinople, it was soon rumored that Mehmed was flirting with Christianity. He spared the local population and allowed them to practice their religion freely. A new patriarch, Gennadius, was appointed for the Greek Orthodox church, and a local Christian, Lucas Notaras, was discussed as a possible minister. In fact, Mehmed found neophyte Muslims to be more loyal than the established Ottoman aristocracy and favored Lucas more because of his attractive fourteen-year-old son than for any of his administrative skills. When Lucas finally refused to hand his boy over to Mehmed, the entire family was exterminated.

Constantinople flourished under Mehmed. By encouraging Greek and Italian scholars and Jewish merchants to immigrate, he quadrupled the population within a few years. Around his new Topkapi Palace, he built bazaars, mosques, hospitals, and religious colleges, to make Constantinople the major commercial center of the world and the link between Europe and the Orient.

Mehmed now turned his attention to Europe where the rulers of Hungary, Serbia, Albania, and Venice were undermining his authority. He reconquered Serbia in 1456 but was unable to capture Belgrade. He also seized Trebizond on the Black Sea where the Comnenids, the last remaining claimants to the Byzantine throne, ruled.

Mehmed's most notorious European foe was Vlad Dracul of Walachia, well known in folklore as Count Dracula. When Mehmed marched into his territory to suppress a revolt, he was greeted with the sight of twenty thousand Ottomans impaled or crucified. Vlad Dracul was deposed and replaced by his brother Radu who, having been raised in the Ottoman court, was Mehmed's favorite sexual partner. After two years, Radu was deposed by the rulers of Moldavia and Hungary. Bosnia was also persuaded to revolt but

surrendered to Mehmed as he approached its borders. Mehmed agreed to grant the local nobility a general amnesty, but soon recanted and had them beheaded, claiming that a vow made to an infidel need not be kept. Seeking to appease Mehmed, most Bosnians eventually converted to Islam.

In 1467 Mehmed received news that his most pernicious rival, George Kastrioti *Skanderbeg of Albania, had finally died. "At last, Europe and Asia belong to me!" he rejoiced; "Unhappy Christianity! It has lost both its sword and buckler." A planned expedition against Venice was temporarily delayed to crush revolts in Anatolia and Albania, but by 1477, Ottoman troops could be seen from the roofs of Venice. A truce was arranged and Mehmed turned to the south, occupying the town of Otranto in the heel of Italy. Eight hundred people were massacred; they were later canonized for refusing to convert to Islam. He also attacked the island of Rhodes but the siege was lifted after his troops nearly mutinied over orders not to loot.

Since he was generally in the battlefield, the task of government was left to his viziers. A sophisticated court hierarchy was established, marked by different colored boots, cloaks, and turbans for each rank. From Constantinople he borrowed the practice of remaining aloof from his subjects and was the first Ottoman to eat only with members of his immediate family. As every member of the Ottoman aristocratic hierarchy was required to have a craft, Mehmed was a gardener and took great pride in his vegetables. Once, when a particularly large cucumber he was fond of showing off disappeared, he had a fellow gardener cut open to look for its remains in his stomach. Yet, despite his potential for acts of extreme cruelty, Mehmed was a patron of the arts; he was the first emperor to have his portrait painted.

Toward the end of his reign, Mehmed became sickly. He probably died from an overdose of opium administered by his son *Bajazet.

F. C. H. Babinger, *Mehmed the Conqueror and his Time*, 1978.
T. Beg, *The History of Mehmed the Conqueror*, 1978.

MEIJI SEE MUTSUHITO

MEIR, GOLDA (Myerson, née Mabovitch; 1898–1978), Israeli prime minister and political leader. She was born in Kiev, Russia, but in 1906 the family emigrated to the United States to escape persecution and poverty. They settled in Milwaukee, Wisconsin, where, after graduating from high school, she enrolled in a school for teachers. Still affected by memories of pogroms in Russia, she became a Zionist, proving to be an excellent public speaker for the cause in both Yiddish and English.

In 1921 she and her husband, Morris Myerson, emigrated to Palestine, where they joined *kibbutz* Merhavyah. Meir left the *kibbutz* in 1924 to participate in Labor politics. From 1934 she was a member of the executive committee of the Trades Union Federation. From 1946 she headed the Jewish Agency's political department and took a leading role in the events that culminated in the establishment of Israeli independence in 1948. Thus, in November 1947 and May 1948 she met secretly with King *Abdullah in an unsuccessful effort to convince him to keep out of the war brewing between the Arabs and the new Jewish state.

After the state was proclaimed, Meir became Israel's first minister to the Soviet Union (1948–1949). Her appearance in Moscow galvanized Russian Jewry into open pro-Israeli demonstrations. On being elected to Israel's first Knesset (parliament) on the Labor ticket in 1949, she was appointed minister for labor and immediately launched an ambitious housing and road-building program. In 1956 she became Israel's foreign minister, a post she held until 1965.

Meir maintained a high profile on the international scene, often appearing in the United Nations, especially during the 1956–1957 Suez crisis. One of her most notable achievements was the establishment of friendly relations with Africa's newly-independent countries. On resigning from the foreign ministry in 1966 she was elected secretary-general of the Israel Labor party.

Meir left this post in 1968, but returned to politics as Israel's fourth prime minister in 1969, after the death of Levi Eshkol. A popular premiere, she proved a political hard-liner. She retained her post in the general elections of 1969, leading a broad-based "national unity" coalition that had been established just before the Six-Day War of 1967.

The outbreak of the Yom Kippur War in 1973 was the greatest crisis that Meir faced. Taken surprise by the Egyptian-Syrian attack, the Israeli armies had to fall back in the early days of the campaign, and for a time the outcome appeared uncertain. The war ended in a decisive Israeli victory, but the country demanded that there be an investigation of the causes of the initial unpreparedness. Meir was exonerated by a commission of inquiry, but chose to resign in 1974, thereby accepting part of the overall responsibility for the failure of intelligence sources. In the last months of her term, she signed the disengagement agreements with Egypt and Syria. She spent her last years writing her memoirs, *My Life* (1975).

P. Mann, *Golda*, 1971.
M. Syrkin, *Golda Meir, Israel's Leader*, 1969.

MENCIUS (Meng-tzu; c.371–289 B.C.E.), Chinese philosopher. In many ways, the life of Mencius parallels that of his master, *Confucius — their relationship is often compared to that of *Plato to *Socrates. Both traveled throughout the warring states of China trying to implement their philosophies; both eventually gave up in despair at their rejection. Like Confucius, Mencius was born in the kingdom of Lu and lost his father at an early age.

Mencius lived with his mother opposite a cemetery until she noticed him imitating the rites associated with death. She moved to the marketplace, only to discover him mimicking the merchants' haggling. Determined that he be exposed to a positive influence, she finally settled opposite a school, so that Mencius imitate the scholars. Some years later, fearing that her son was neglecting his studies, she suddenly broke a thread she was spinning. Mencius asked her why, to which she answered, "Just as spinning creates a thread, education is the act of spinning the thread of life."

Having studied for many years under Confucius's grandson, Mencius rejected the contemporary philosophies of Mo-tzu and Yang Chu. Mo-tzu's philosophy was legalistic and utilitarian and emphasized the love of all men equally; Yang Chu taught that each man was for himself. The former ignored the special relationship between children and their parents; the latter not only degraded the role of the sovereign ruler, but offered no solution to the dichotomy of rich and poor. In describing the contemporary influence of these outlooks, Mencius complained, "Wise kings are no longer, and foolish princes give reign to their hearts." What he did learn from these schools, however, was the use of logical arguments to advance his position. "I am not fond of arguments," he explained, "I simply have no alternative."

After several years in the kingdom of Ch'i, where he hoped to implement Confucian principles, Mencius realized that King Hsian merely sought his intellectual company. The nobles were still motivated by greed and power, and even Hsian admitted that he was overwhelmed by lust. Although he believed that lust is acceptable as long as it does not interfere with other people's pleasures, Mencius realized that he must move on if his beliefs were ever to become effective. In order to entice Mencius to stay, Hsian offered him and his students a home and ten thousand measures of grain, but Mencius was determined to leave. He left Ch'i at a slow, lugubrious pace explaining that although he could not remain in such circumstances, he believed that Hsian was good at heart and would one day call on him to return.

At his first stop, Wei, the local prince asked Mencius what benefit he could bring to the country. His reply, "Do not look to sages for profit, utility, or material benefit," expressed his belief that philosophy, rather than serving a utilitarian objective, strove to bring man to the greatest possible good. The heir to the throne of T'eng was impressed by Mencius and asked him to accompany him home, only to discover that there was no suitable position for him there.

Mencius taught that "one does not succeed in bringing peace and order to subjects by remaining in a lower position and not being picked by a superior," and was therefore excited that one of his disciples, Yo Ching, was appointed government administrator in Lu. Expecting finally to have an opportunity to see his philosophy flourish, he traveled to Lu, only to discover that an indifferent king

> To dwell in the broad house, which is the whole world;
> To stand upright, which is the whole world;
> To travel the main highway, which is the whole world;
> When ambition is attained, to exercise it in cooperation with your subjects;
> When it is not attained, to travel one's road alone;
> To be uncorrupted by riches or honors;
> To remain firm when poor and in low estate;
> To be unflinching even when threatened with war...
> This is to be a mighty man!
>
> **Mencius**

refused to meet him. Complaining that "Heaven does not yet want that the empire should rejoice in tranquility and good government," he retired to the country to write his thoughts. His maxim, "Man's possession of excellence, intelligence, specific arts and devices, or knowledge, constantly depends on his having suffered misfortunes," echoes the disappointments of his own life. He is said to have died as the peasants were celebrating the summer solstice.

Mencius's philosophy emphasizes that the natural goodness of humanity (*jen*) is innate in all men. Since *jen* embraces knowledge and morality, anyone can be a sage, provided that his education encourages an awakening of these natural attributes. "The great man is he who never loses the heart of a child." Politically, Mencius comes closest to the modern perception of democracy: "The people are the most important element in a country. The ruler is the least." Once, when asked whether the ancient Prince Wu was right in assassinating the king of Chao, Mencius explained that one who commits an outrage against benevolence is a robber; against righteousness, is a hooligan. Wu's victim was a robber and a ruffian — not a king. Mencius also condemned an abstemious and celibate lifestyle, holding that producing offspring is man's foremost responsibility. He enjoyed fine food (particularly bear's paw), archery, hunting, poetry and the arts.

Mencius's popularity declined until the neo-Confucianist school noticed the similarity between his philosophy and the Buddhist belief that the Buddha is present in each individual. To them, Mencius was Ya Sheng (Second Sage), the foremost expounder of Confucian thought.

Shu Cheng, *Meng-Tzu Tzu I*, 1990.

A. F. Verwilghen, *Mencius: The Man and his Ideas*, 1967.

MENDEL, GREGOR JOHANN (1822–1884), Austrian monk, first discoverer of laws of heredity. Born in Heinzendorf, Austria, he early showed an interest in the natural sciences. He attended the Philosophical Institute at Olmutz for two years and entered the Augustinian monastery at Brno in 1843; he was ordained there in 1847. Throughout this period he taught himself science.

In 1851 Mendel's abbot sent him to the University of Vienna, where he studied physics, chemistry, mathematics, zoology, and botany. In 1854 he returned to Brno, where he taught natural sciences at the technical high school. In 1868 he was elected abbot of his monastery and ceased teaching.

As early as 1856, Mendel had begun to work in the small monastery garden, conducting experiments that were to lead to his discovery of the basic principles of heredity and to the founding of the science of genetics. Mendel found support among the other teachers at the high school, several of whom were active in the sciences and had helped found the Natural Science Society in Brno in 1862. Mendel participated in the society's meetings and often borrowed books from its library, as well as that of the monastery, concentrating especially on agriculture, horticulture, and botany — subjects with which he was already familiar, since his father owned an orchard and farm.

Mendel also bought his own books and was aware of Charles *Darwin's publications of the 1860s and 1870s. He had already started his experiments before Darwin published his first book and before heredity was widely regarded as the basis of evolutionary change. Reporting his findings, which he called "plant hybridization," to the Natural Science Society in 1865, he stated that his experiments went further than any others in the subject "to make it possible to determine the number of different forms under which the offspring of hybrids appear, or to change these forms with certainty according to their separate generations, or definitely to ascertain their statistical relations." Hence Mendel for the first time defined the imperatives for studying heredity through experimentation and provided the data that fulfilled these imperatives; these established the foundations for understanding heredity and evolution as well as biological processes.

Mendel carried out his experiments on garden peas, which he crossed to gather data on single alternative characteristics: tallness, dwarfness, presence or absence of color in the blossoms and leaf axils, alternative differences in seed color and seed shape, position of flowers on the stem, and the pod's shape. He found that each cross exhibited a "dominant character" for one of the alternative types in the hybrids (e.g., tallness over dwarfness). Yet when these crosses reproduced by self-fertilization, the second showed both grandparental types in the same constant proportion: approximately three-quarters exhibited the dominant type, and one quarter the recessive type. Mendel also proved that when the second-generation hybrids were individually tested, about one quarter of them resembled one of the pure parent varieties in the single character being observed, one quarter the other pure variety, and half resembled in appearance and behavior the first generation hybrid.

The essential part of his hypothesis was that paired elementary units, now known as genes, caused the occurrence of visible alternative characters in the plants in the constant varieties and in their descendants. These units he symbolized by letters; he assumed that they occurred in alternative forms *AA* and *aa* in the constant parent variety and *Aa* in the hybrid. Where the "dominant" feature — such as tallness — appeared, he labeled it *Aa,* resembling *AA.* The other, "recessive," feature — in this example, dwarfness — was to be found in *aa* individuals.

Mendel showed how his findings were based on a simple statistical law whereby the reproductive cells of one hybrid transmitted half the unit, *A,* and the other transmitted the other half, *a.* The separation of alternatives in the reproductive cells (or the principle of segregation) came to be known as Mendel's first law and could be used in predicting the occurrence of features in living organisms. Mendel went further and showed how a range of combinations of features could be obtained by crossing several pairs of alternative characters. He observed this when he crossed peas with seven pairs of differentiating characters and found that they recombined randomly, governed by the law of independent assortment. More is now known of this phenomenon: this law or principle applies only to units, or genes, which are transmitted in different linkage groups, now called "chromosomes," where genes are organized.

The publications of Mendel's results in 1866 had little effect at the time. He continued his experiments on other plants and maintained a lifelong interest in botany, bee culture, and meteorology, but could not devote much time to them due to his increasing administrative duties as abbot. It was not until 1900, well after his death, that he was rediscovered when other scientists obtained results similar to his.

H. Iltis, *Life of Mendel,* 1932.
K. R. Lewis, *The Matter of Mendelian Heredity,* 1964.
R. C. Olby, *The Origin of Mendelism,* 1966.

MENDELEYEV, DMITRI IVANOVICH

(1834–1907), Russian chemist, famed for his work on periodic law. He was the first to determine that "the properties of the elements are in periodic dependence upon their atomic weights." This statement, found in his best known textbook, *The Principles of Chemistry* (two volumes; 1868–1870), was the first to assert that the atomic weights of elements reflect the connections between the elements themselves and their properties. Mendeleyev went on to state that this law of nature could be used to determine new classifications and facts about the elements.

Mendeleyev was the fourteenth child in a family from Tobolsk, Siberia. His father was blind, and his mother, who directed a glass factory, looked after the family. In 1848 she traveled thousands of miles to Moscow in order to enroll Mendeleyev in the university. However, at that time no Siberians were allowed to enter that institution, so they set out again, this time for Saint Petersburg. In 1850 Mendeleyev was admitted to a training college for teachers; his mother died soon after, but his love and devotion to her memory remained with him all his life.

Receiving his degree in chemistry, in 1856 Mendeleyev became a *privatdozent* (official but unpaid lecturer). In 1859 he spent two years in Heidelberg working out his own theories and ideas. Upon his return to Saint Petersburg he became a professor at the university, where he remained until 1890, when he resigned after a dispute with the administration over his liberal views. From 1893 he directed the bureau of weights and measures.

In Saint Petersburg, Mendeleyev investigated the periodic law, the composition of solutions, and the nature and origin of petroleum. His first periodic table (developed in 1869), which contested accepted atomic weights, became an extensive paper presented in German in 1871. His new finds led him to believe that three previously unknown elements existed. He assigned these elements and their compounds specific structures, terming them boron, eka-aluminum, and eka-silicon. Chemists took an interest in his findings when they were confirmed within fifteen years: the discovery of gallium, scandium, and germanium earned him considerable respect throughout the scientific community.

Mendeleyev also undertook extensive research on the nature of solutions and the thermal expansion of liquids. His work in this area, conducted in the early 1860s, predated the findings of Thomas Andrews on the critical temperature of gases. Independently, they both defined the absolute boiling point of a substance as "the temperature at which cohesion and heat of vaporization become equal to zero and the liquid changes to vapor, irrespective of the pressure and volume."

The Royal Society honored Mendeleyev with the Davy medal in 1882, and the Copley medal in 1905.
D. Q. Posin, *Mendeleyev: The Story of a Great Scientist,* 1948.

MENDELSSOHN, MOSES

(1729–1786), German Jewish philosopher, writer, Bible translator and commentator, community leader, and foremost figure of the Jewish Enlightenment in Germany. Mendelssohn was born and raised in Dessau, Germany; his mother came from a distinguished family while his father was a humble Jewish religious scribe of limited means.

He received a traditional Jewish education and was so faithful a disciple of his teacher, Berlin-born Rabbi David Fraenkel, that when he returned to his native city, young Mendelssohn, aged fourteen, followed him there. Mendelssohn, however, did not qualify for any of the categories allowing Jews to reside in Berlin at that time and was permitted to enter and remain there only as a student of Talmud supported by the Jewish community.

Moses Mendelssohn

Although he did continue his Talmudic studies, it was not long before Mendelssohn felt the need to expand his intellectual horizons. He saw that languages would be his key to general culture, along with mathematics, philosophy, and sciences. With the aid of young Jewish intellectuals such as Abraham Kisch and Aaron S. Gumperz, he learned French, Greek, and Latin, but above all, German, which he ultimately acquired to perfection. He had studied *Maimonides and other medieval Jewish philosophers but now also mastered Christian Wolff, John *Locke, and Gottfried W. *Leibniz.

In 1750 Mendelssohn became tutor for the family of Issak Bernhard, a successful silk manufacturer. In 1754 Bernhard made him a clerk in his company and in 1761 manager of his ever-increasing business, providing Mendelssohn with a permanent livelihood. All of his literary and communal activity had to be done outside of work hours.

Through Gumperz he was introduced to liberal, tolerant Gotthold E. Lessing in 1754, originally as a chess partner, but it was a match that lasted a lifetime, personally and intellectually. Lessing helped Mendelssohn improve his German style and encouraged him to publish his writings and in 1755 his first works appeared: *Philosophische Gespräche* ("Philosophical Speeches"), in praise of Leibniz, and *Briefe ueber die Empfindungen* ("Letters on the Sentiments") — neither under his own name. It was only after his essay in the competition for the prize of the Prussian Royal Academy of Sciences on the question of whether metaphysical truths are susceptible of the same evidence as mathematical truths had won first place that he began to publish under the

name Moses Mendelssohn. (Immanuel *Kant, not famous at the time, was given a special honorable mention for second place in that contest.)

In 1762 he married a Hamburg Jewess, not known for beauty or learning, but who helped make their home a magnet for intellectuals, Jews and non-Jews alike, who came to hold discussions with Mendelssohn. King *Frederick II granted him "right of residence" in Berlin only in 1763.

In his own time his most acclaimed work was the dialogue *Phäedon* (1767), on the immortality of the soul. The work was widely successful, selling out within four months, and going through numerous reprints and translations. It earned for him the accolades of German society.

In 1763 Mendelssohn met the Swiss Christian theologian Johann Lavater with whom he became friends. In 1769, however, Lavater sent him his translation of a work by Charles Bonnet that he felt had incontrovertibly proved the truth of Christianity. In Lavater's dedication he called upon Mendelssohn to convert if he could not refute Bonnet's proofs. The ensuing controversy, which Mendelssohn entered reluctantly, wreaked havoc on his physical condition. By 1771, still firmly entrenched in Judaism, Mendelssohn was in such a state that for several years he could not deal with the demands of philosophical pursuits.

From that time on, most of his literary efforts dealt with Jewish themes. He also aided Jewish communities facing various difficulties with the authorities.

Mendelssohn was greatly interested in spreading German culture, especially among Jews so they could make their way into German society as equals. To assist them in the acquisition of the German language, he translated the Old Testament into German — written with the Hebrew alphabet — completing the task in 1783. He accompanied his translation with a commentary reflecting the spirit of the Enlightenment. In his *Jerusalem* he called for the separation of church and state and for religious tolerance.

While Moses Mendelssohn could remain an observant Jew and straddle the Jewish and general worlds, reaching distinction in both, four of his six children converted to Christianity.

A. Altmann, *Moses Mendelssohn: A Biographical Study*, 1973.
E. Jospe, *Moses Mendelssohn: Selections from His Writings*, 1975.
H. J. Schoeps, *Moses Mendelssohn*, 1979.

MENELIK II (1844–1913), emperor of Ethiopia; founder of the modern Ethiopian state. Menelik was the son of King Haile Malakot of Shoa, a vassal of the emperor of Ethiopia. Menelik's grandfather, Sahla Selassie, was the first emperor of Ethiopia. Nothing is known about his mother and it is possible that he was illegitimate. Haile Malakot died when Menelik was only a boy; much of his youth was spent under the shadow of the Emperor Theodore, who regarded Menelik as a rival claimant to the throne and curbed his movements. Upon Theodore's death Menelik made a bid for the imperial throne but was defeated by John IV, whom he later recognized as emperor. In return, John granted Menelik the southern part of the empire and named him his heir. John was killed in battle in 1889; Menelik, not only the emperor's named heir but, as a result of his extensive conquests, the most powerful individual in Ethiopia, assumed the throne.

The greatest problem facing Menelik's reign was European colonialism in the horn of Africa. The British occupied the Sudan and the Italians were making inroads on the coast. Shortly before assuming the throne Menelik signed the treaty of Uccialli, thereby recognizing Italian control of Eritrea. Since Menelik's expansionist policy centered on the Muslim and pagan areas of the south, the northern territories, although containing Ethiopia's only outlet to the sea, were not considered as vital in importance as European recognition of his kingdom. Yet despite his concessions, a mistranslation of the treaty led to a conflict with the Italians. They understood the treaty to recognize their ultimate sovereignty over all of Ethiopia; Menelik assumed it to include only the area surrounding the port of Asmara. The dispute broke into full-scale war in 1896. At the Battle of Adowa Menelik's army of seventy thousand troops defeated seventeen thousand Italian soldiers, killing over twelve thousand. Following Italy's defeat, a new accord was signed recognizing Ethiopian sovereignty. Nonetheless, the Italians kept Eritrea.

His empire secure, Menelik was free to embark on sweeping reforms aimed at bringing Ethiopia up to the level of those European countries whose colonies surrounded her. The French were commissioned to build a railroad connecting the new capital of Addis Ababa with the port of Djibouti. Although Menelik maintained absolute power, he created a panel of ministerial advisers to counsel him on affairs of state. New ministries included justice, commerce, and foreign affairs, indicative of Menelik's objective of bringing Ethiopia into the family of nations. Laws were also passed banning slavery, but these were largely ignored.

Throughout his reign Menelik was influenced by his empress, Taitu. A young woman of remarkable beauty, Taitu had several influential husbands. Her sway over the emperor was such that she retained the title of empress although she bore him no heir. As she aged Taitu lost much of her beauty, but she remained popular with the people because of her devotion to the empire. In one battle against insurgents, she herself led a successful cavalry charge; at the battle of Adowa, she prostrated herself before the troops and had a large stone placed on her back. Remaining in this position, she prayed until the battle was concluded.

In the last years of his reign, Menelik became increasingly feeble and suffered from frequent memory lapses. Since no heir had been named, leading contenders schemed vigorously to succeed him.

Rival claimants included Ras Mekonnen, father of *Haile Selassie, and Menelik's daughter Zauditu (Taitu's choice). The succession was finally awarded to Lij Yasu, a grandson of Menelik and the son of a southern king who had opposed Menelik's ascension to the throne after the death of John IV. Menelik died after five years of illness.

R. H. Kofi Darkwah, *Shewa, Menilek, and the Ethiopian Empire*, 1975.

H. G. Marcus, *The Life and Times of Menelik II: Ethiopia 1844–1913*, 1975.

C. P. Rosenfeld, *Empress Tayto and Menilek II*, 1975.

METTERNICH, KLEMENS (1773–1859), Austrian statesman. Born in Coblenz in the German Rhineland, he was the eldest son of Count von Metternich-Winneburg and the Countess Beatrix Kagenegg. As members of a noble Rhenish family, they enjoyed relative freedom in the management of their estates, which were held in direct line from the Holy Roman emperor. The family also benefitted from the count's position as the emperor's representative to the archbishop of Trier.

Hoping to follow in his father's footsteps, the young Metternich enrolled at the University of Strasbourg in 1788; it was there that he developed his forthright conservative views. His fear of liberalism and the threat posed by revolutionary forces were given further emphasis by his personal experiences of the French Revolution; while studying in Strasbourg, Metternich witnessed the rioting there, and when France took over the Rhineland his family's entire estate was seized. In 1794 the family sought refuge in Vienna and later received the abbey of Ochsenhausen in Swabia as compensation for loss of their estate in Germany.

In 1795, Metternich married Eleonore von Kaunitz, granddaughter of the former chancellor, Wenzel Anton von Kaunitz. As a result, Metternich gained not only the benefits of his wife's vast land holdings but also a foothold into royal circles. For the next few years, he managed his wife's estates and cultivated his interests in scientific and medical studies, while biding his time for the best opportunity to enter politics. This career began in 1797, when he became the representative of the Westphalian counts at the Peace Congress of Rastatt (1797–1799).

After the signing of the Treaty of Campo Formio in 1797 — it formalized the compensation payable to those German princes who, like the Metternich family, lost their property when the French took over the Rhineland — Metternich entered the diplomatic corps. His first postings were as Austrian ambassador to Saxony in 1801 and to Prussia in 1803. *Napoleon I was said to have been so impressed with Metternich's work in Berlin that in 1806 he requested his presence in France as Austria's representative. While in Paris, Metternich, who always had a reputation as a ladies' man, lived for a time with Napoleon's sister, Caroline.

Sensitive to France's hegemony in Europe, Metternich spent his time there obtaining information on French foreign affairs and developing his understanding of Napoleon's complex personality. Mistaking the military importance of the success of Spanish guerrilla forces against Napoleon's troops, Metternich encouraged the new Austrian foreign minister, Johann Philipp, to declare war on France. Austria suffered a bitter defeat and Metternich was enlisted to conduct the peace negotiations but was saved the humiliation of the signing of the Treaty of Schönbrunn.

In 1809 Metternich was appointed foreign minister and, concerned with Napoleon's increasing territorial ambitions, sought to protect a severely weakened Austria from a French offensive. One of his first acts of state was to arrange the marriage between Napoleon and Marie-Louise, daughter of Emperor Francis I. This cleverly arranged political alliance provided Austria with an element of protection from Napoleon's hostility. In 1812 Napoleon invaded Russia and Metternich committed Austrian troops and supplies to the French offensive. However, in 1813, when French defeat appeared inevitable, Metternich attempted to achieve a balance of power between the two sides by undertaking an armed mediation between France and Russia. Napoleon remained recalcitrant and when no progress was made at the peace congress in Prague, Austria entered the war against France. In 1813 the Quadruple Alliance of Russia, Great Britain, Sweden, and Austria was formed; Metternich was made a prince; and, following the allied victory at Leipzig and Napoleon's abdication, the first Treaty of Paris was signed on May 30, 1814. Using his political influence, Metternich included terms for the establishment of a European peace congress to be convened in Vienna in the following months.

The 1815 Congress of Vienna proved to be Metternich's diplomatic coup to such an extent that the period following the congress up until 1848 has been called the Age of Metternich. Indeed, the very concept of a multipower congress to discuss common problems was an innovation. Although he was unsuccessful in his aim of forming two confederations, one German, the other Italian, in which Austria would maintain the balance of power, he managed through brilliant negotiating skills to bring about a German Confederation whose role was to provide a balance of power between France and Russia. Furthermore, Metternich managed to block the harsh settlement demands of Russia and forced Prussia to compromise on its demands regarding the fate of Saxony. As head of the confederation, with the support of Great Britain and a secret agreement with the kingdom of the Two Sicilies, Austria became the bulwark of the European balance of power, a position not commensurate with its fundamental weakness. In a show of gratitude, Francis I gave Metternich a castle and vineyard.

Metternich hoped to consolidate gains made at the Vienna Congress by a system of congresses at which the great powers would coordinate their actions and, in the case of rising revolutionary forces, intervene to maintain the peace. In 1815 he created the Holy Alliance, a conservative association of monarchs. However, following the congresses of Aix-la-Chapelle in 1818, Troppau in 1820, Laibach in 1821, and Verona in 1822, Metternich's influence began to wane. With revolutionary activity brewing in Europe and the departure of Great Britain from the alliance, Austria became increasingly dependent on Russia, forcing Metternich to accept Czar *Alexander I's principles regarding prior authorization of the congress before intervention against revolutionaries. However, for a brief period following Alexander's death in 1825, and in light of the spate of revolutionary insurrections sweeping Europe, an alliance was formed between Austria, Prussia, and Russia with the aim of protecting the powers from revolutionary attack.

Although Metternich had been appointed state chancellor in 1821, his influence in Austrian affairs was weakened by his rivalry with the minister of state, Franz Kolowrat. Metternich's increasing tendency to push his forthright views made him a symbol of repression and when revolution erupted in March 1848 he was forced into exile and lived in London. He returned to Vienna in 1851 and died there eight years later.

A. J. May, *The Age of Metternich, 1814–1848*, 1963.

A. Milne, *Metternich*, 1975.

MICHELANGELO BUONARROTI (1475–1564),

sculptor, painter, architect, poet. Born in Caprese in Tuscany, he was sent to school in Florence and at age thirteen was apprenticed to Domenico Ghirlandaio, who introduced him to the works of the Italian and Flemish masters. He lived in the home of Lorenzo de' Medici (see *Medici family) who supported him. With Lorenzo, Michelangelo went to hear Girolamo *Savanorola preaching against the corruption of Florence, a campaign that ended in the expulsion of the Medici from Florence in 1494. Michelangelo fled to Bologna but returned to Florence the following year. In 1498 his great sculpture *Pietà* was commissioned for Saint Peter's; it took two years to complete.

In 1501 he signed a contract with Cardinal Piccolomini — the first of several commissions he was unable to fulfill and which therefore made his life miserable. His great creative imagination was inspired by the proposed projects but he often failed to execute the monuments before a new and more enticing proposal came along. Because his patrons were cardinals, popes, and dukes, the commissions were as difficult to refuse as to complete. Cardinal Piccolomini (the future Pope Pius III) ordered fifteen statues of apostles for Siena Cathedral; Michelangelo finished two and had three others made according to his design, but sixty years later the contract had still not been fulfilled. Similarly, in 1503 he agreed to produce twelve statues for the Cathedral of Florence; only one was ever blocked out, and even this was never finished. In 1501, however, Michelangelo received a block of marble that had been given to another artist years before for a statue of a prophet; by 1503 he had completed the fifteen-foot-high *David*, an early example of his heroic, young male nudes.

Pope Julius II summoned Michelangelo to Rome to design a monument — forty statues and bas-reliefs surrounding the sarcophagus — for his tomb in Saint Peter's. Michelangelo purchased the marble but the pope decided instead to rebuild Saint Peter's, postponed the project, and refused to reimburse the sculptor for the money he had laid out. Furious, Michelangelo left Rome for Florence but the pope sent five messengers with threats and entreaties; Michelangelo returned to Rome, where the pope now commanded him to make a gigantic statue of himself. The statue was eventually erected in Bologna but a few years later, when the fortunes of war had turned against the martial pope, it was removed and melted down to make a cannon.

Meanwhile, however, the pope had given Michelangelo his greatest commission — the Sistine Chapel ceiling in the Vatican. Work began in 1508 and was completed five years later, shortly before the pope's death. Perched on a scaffolding high above the floor, Michelangelo labored to create his depiction of the Creation and other biblical scenes and figures that have become one of the world's best-known masterpieces. Time dimmed the magnificence of the colors but restoration work has brought back the splendid brightness of the original.

Before Julius died he arranged for work to begin on his tomb, although on a somewhat smaller scale than the original plan, and Michelangelo worked on it for the following three years. Among the statues he completed for it was his famous *Moses*.

However, Julius's successor Leo X had other plans: he forbade the sculptor to continue work on the tomb and ordered him to begin creating the façade for the Church of San Lorenzo in Florence. The contract, which included twenty figures, was to be completed in nine years. Michelangelo, working under tremendous deadline pressures, secretly tried to continue his work on Julius's tomb at night. The tomb was eventually finished in 1545 and placed in the Church of Saint Peter in Vinculi.

In 1529 Michelangelo enthusiastically supported the republic which had been established in Florence and, during its short life, was in charge of the city's fortifications. When the republic was overthrown the following year the pope pardoned the sculptor on condition that he work on the new Sacristy of San Lorenzo. Michelangelo agreed without enthusiasm and finished three tombs there over the next two years.

- Painting is the music of God.

    Michelangelo

- No one who has not seen the Sistine Chapel can have a clear idea of what a human being may achieve.

    Goethe

- God took pity on humankind and, seeing their attempts to discover true nature were floundering and futile and to show them how to achieve perfection in all these arts and in moral philosophy, He sent them Michelangelo.

    Vasari

In 1532 he met Tommasso dei Cavalieri, to whom he wrote passionate love poems; the handsome young Roman gentleman remained Michelangelo's close friend for the rest of his life. He also had a deep friendship based on religious feelings with Vittoria Colonna and wrote many beautiful sonnets for her.

Paul III became pope in 1534 and the following year appointed Michelangelo architect, sculptor, and painter of the Apostolic Palace, giving him the task of painting the *Last Judgment* on the altar wall of the Sistine Chapel. When the top part was completed the pope brought his master of ceremonies, Biagio de Casena, to see it. Biagio was shocked by the nude figures and said the painting belonged in a tavern or brothel. Michelangelo promptly painted Biagio in the lower region as a legendary judge in Hades. Later popes had the nude figures clothed.

Following the completion of this project Pope Paul III had Michelangelo paint frescoes in his Pauline Chapel. He completed two but suffered severe illnesses when working on them and never painted another fresco. He then began another major task, the rebuilding of Saint Peter's, working on a model and designing a great dome that was the most important element viewed both from within and outside. Michelangelo refused all remuneration, saying that it was God's will that he build Saint Peter's and that he was doing it for the love of God. His plan was almost completed when he died at age eighty-nine. His successors lengthened the nave (compromising its harmony with the dome) and added a colonnade.

In his will Michelangelo consigned "his soul to God, his body to the earth, his substance to his nearest relatives." His body was taken to Florence and buried in the sepulcher of the Medici family.

Michelangelo had burst upon the art world like a comet and his impact was historic. No preconceived idea was sacred to him; he shattered accepted crite-

Michelangelo, a self portrait from the Pietà

ria and pointed the way to be followed by future generations. The laws of perspective so diligently worked out by his predecessors were swept aside as he discovered his own. His perspectives did not create a three-dimensional "illusion" — they were three-dimensional and his use of architectural details in his paintings enhanced this feeling. Innovative in his use of materials, bringing new ideas even to the building of bridges, Michelangelo left behind a completely fulfilled body of work.

H. Hibbard, *Michelangelo: Painter, Sculptor, architect,* 1979.

R. Lieberts, *Michelangelo,* 1983.

R. Schott, *Michelangelo,* 1966.

F. de Tolnay, *Michelangelo: Sculptor, Painter, Architect,* 1975.

MILL, JOHN STUART (1806–1873), English political philosopher, logician, political economist, and politician. Mill was born in London, where his father, an author and historian of British India, and a friend and disciple of the philosopher Jeremy *Bentham, was his sole teacher, teaching him Greek from the age of three. By the age of eight, Mill had studied *Plato and *Herodotus, and by the age of twelve he had read more classics than most college students. His father was stern, unrelenting, and exacting in his supervision.

At age fourteen he traveled to France, where he studied French, chemistry, zoology, metaphysics, logic, and mathematics, and after enjoying French culture and the "genial atmosphere of continental life," returned to England, where he continued his studies, this time of English philosophers. Chiefly influenced by Bentham's works, Mill adopted the "principle of utility" as a religion. By the age of sixteen, he and his friends saw reason and rationalism as their creed and formed a society which earned them the title "The Utilitarians."

The next year, Mill entered India House in London, where he worked as assistant examiner and then the chief examiner, responsible for the company's relations with the native states. Though he worked at India House for thirty-five years, he found time to pursue his academic and analytical interests. He published several articles in the *Traveller* and the *Westminster Review,* in which he set out his political creed. Mill later edited the *London Review* from its founding in 1835 to 1840, continuing to write many important essays. At the age of twenty Mill fell into a deep depression, which he later attributed to the "destructive effect upon the emotional life of the analytical process." Though supremely interested in reason and rationalism, Mill also had a love for the arts, and it was William *Wordsworth's poetry that helped him out of his depression.

A primary influence was his friendship with a married woman, Harriet (Hardy) Taylor. She helped give his work a humane touch and made him realize that such works could only be truly practical if they contained elements of the human experience. After her husband died, nineteen years after she and Mill first met, they were married.

Mill published *The System of Logic* (1843), *Essays on Some Unsettled Questions in Political Economy* (1844), and *The Principles of Political Economy* (1847), which was very successful. Throughout his life this was revised and his changing viewpoints can be seen in the revisions. Though he originally was a strong supporter of individualism, he eventually supported extensive state regulation and control for activities which he felt were detrimental to human beings. Although he wished to control what he felt to be destructive behavior, his philosophy of personal human freedom remained the steady doctrine of his life. These themes can be seen in most of his works on his theory of government, including *Essay on Liberty and Thoughts on Parliamentary Reform* (1859), *Considerations on Representative Government* (1861), and *The Subjection of Women* (1869). His autobiography was published posthumously in 1873.

From 1865 to 1869, Mill fulfilled an old ambition of sitting in Parliament, where his actions and attitudes reflected the greater themes in his life, of reason and utility. Refusing to spend money on his constituency or cater only to parochial interests, Mill spoke out with candor on almost every issue. Benjamin *Disraeli called him a "political finishing governess," and some of his speeches made a deep impression. He helped to found one of the first women's suffrage societies, the National Union of Women's Suffrage Societies, in 1867.

Retiring at the age of sixty-two, Mill lived in England and then in the south of France, where his

FROM THE WRITINGS OF JOHN STUART MILL

- The concessions of the privileged to the unprivleged are seldom brought about by any better motive than the power of the unprivileged to extort them.
- Customs are made for customary characters and customary circumstances.
- Eccentricity has always abounded when and where strength of character has abounded; and the amount of eccentricity in a society has generally been proportional to the amount of genius, mental vigor, and moral courage which it contains.
- The liberty of the individual must be thus far limited; he must not make himself a nuisance to other people.
- If all mankind, minus one, were of one opinion and only one person were of the contrary opinion, mankind would be no more justified in silencing that one person than he, if he had the power, would be justified in silencing mankind.
- Unquestionably it is possible to do without happiness; it is done involuntarily by nineteen-twentieths of mankind.
- He who knows only his own side of the case knows little of that.

wife died in 1858. He found comfort in the company of her daughter, Helen Taylor, and enjoyed reading, writing, and botany. He was happy to be in Avignon to see the spring flowers and even went on a botany excursion a few days before his death.

S. Holland, *The Economics of John Stuart Mill*, 1985.
J. Skorupski, *John Stuart Mill*, 1989.
C. Smith, *John Stuart Mill*, 1989.

MILTON, JOHN (1608–1674), English writer of poetry, epics, and prose. Although his reputation has suffered from radical fluctuations as critical thought about him has changed over the years, Milton was one of the greatest writers in the English language.

Born in London, Milton acquired his religious beliefs from his father, who was disinherited by his Catholic father when he became a Protestant. Milton credits his father, a composer of some repute in his day, with instilling in him his love for music. In *Ad Patrem*, an early poem in Latin, young Milton rejects the practical dream of a lucrative career, choosing instead the more noble calling of a poet. In that poem, dedicated to his father, Milton writes, in the exalted language that marks his later works, that his gift for the arts as well as the tremendous learning that he brought to his writings are all legacies of his father. "Phoebus, wishing to divide himself between us twain, gave one half of his gifts to me, the other half to my father, and so we, father and son, possess the god in shares," he writes.

Milton studied Latin, Greek, and Hebrew in school and later with private tutors. A voracious reader, he blamed his love for literature for the blindness that afflicted his later years. From the age of twelve onward he rarely stopped reading before midnight, a strain on the eyes at that time when nights were illuminated only by candlelight.

Milton spent seven years studying at Cambridge, receiving the bachelor's and master's degrees. His college career was not without its problems. He was once sent home after a disagreement with a tutor and was nicknamed "the Lady," possibly because of his delicate features, possibly because of his delicacy of mind. Although he ultimately gained the respect of the dons and the students, he kept his dislike of the cold scholasticism of the university curriculum and denounced it years later in his pamphlet *Of Education* (1644).

After college, Milton spent six years studying at home, followed by a year-long European tour. He may well have been the most educated poet of English literature, although the very erudition of his style, which uses sophisticated allusions from classical mythology and from the Old and New Testaments, perhaps prevented him from being more widely admired and loved.

Milton's life as a writer divides naturally into three stages. In his earliest years, he wrote in English, Latin, and Italian, gaining mastery in different poetic forms and rhythms. His earliest poem is an elegy, "On the Death of a Fair Infant," written after the death of his niece (1628). This was followed by "On the Morning of Christ's Nativity," a mature, complex poem written by the twenty-one-year old poet that foreshadows the religious themes central to his later works. Soon afterwards he wrote two companion poems, "L'Allegro" and "Il Penseroso," celebrations of mirth and melancholy. A brief tribute to William *Shakespeare that he had written was printed in the second Folio edition of the works (1632), and a masque, *Comus*, a classical fable with religious overtones, was performed before the earl of Bridgewater. In addition, at this early stage Milton wrote and published his elegy, "Lycidas," regarded by many as his first great work and one of the most complex elegies in the English language.

In the middle stage of his life, Milton ceased writing poetry, turning instead to politics and using his talents to write political and religious prose. Paradoxes abound in Milton's political and religious stances. As a Protestant, this most religious poet fought the power of the state religion and clergy. Often called an elitist because of the difficulty and inaccessibility of his work, Milton was actually a strong supporter of individual liberties and an opponent of the monarchy. Perhaps his most famous political tract is *Areopagitica*, an eloquent call for freedom of the press (1644).

John Milton

Milton married seventeen-year old Mary Powell in 1642. The marriage was a mistake from the beginning, and Powell returned to her family shortly after the wedding. In his numerous tracts on divorce Milton argued, probably from his own experience, that incompatibility should be grounds for divorce. In a society in which only adultery could be admitted as such grounds, his position gave Milton his first notoriety, and this serious and moral spokesman for the Puritans was accused of being a libertine.

Mary Powell returned to live with Milton for a few years, bearing him three daughters and a son who died in infancy. She herself died in 1652, a few days after childbirth. Milton was married twice more, his second wife also dying in childbirth.

In 1649 Milton became a secretary for foreign languages for Oliver *Cromwell's government. That year he wrote *Eikonoklastes*, a defense of the execution of *Charles I. Milton sacrificed the last of his fading eyesight for Cromwell's cause, straining his eyes fulfilling his official writing and translating duties and becoming completely blind in 1652.

After the Restoration in 1660, Milton was in danger of losing his life. However, perhaps because of his blindness, or perhaps because of the intercession of powerful literary friends, he was only briefly imprisoned, fined, and then allowed to retire.

In his retirement, the exiled writer who had lost power and vision found, at last, the power of his own voice. For in this third stage of his literary life, Milton wrote the works to which he had aspired all his life. *Paradise Lost*, the epic tale of Adam's "fortunate fall" that opened for mankind the doors to divine forgiveness and grace, was composed in the poet's head and dictated to his secretaries, to his daughter Deborah, and to the nephews and friends who surrounded him. The work was finished in

---

FROM MILTON'S POETRY

- Of Man's first disobedience and the fruit
  Of that forbidden tree, whose mortal taste
  Brought death into the world, and all our woe,
  With loss of Eden.

  Opening of *Paradise Lost*

- Thick as autumnal leaves that strow the brooks
  In Vallombrosa.
- Who overcomes
  By force, hath overcome but half his foe.
- Just are the ways of God,
  And justifiable to men;
  Unless there be who think not God at all.
- Hence, vain deluding joys,
  The brood of Folly, without father bred.
- Tomorrow to fresh woods and pastures new.
- Peace hath her victories
  No less renowned than War.
- Come and trip it as ye go,
  On the light fantastic toe.
- The world was all before then, where to choose
  Their place of rest, and Providence their guide.
  They hand in hand, with wand'ring steps and slow,
  Through Eden took their solitary way.

  Conclusion of *Paradise Lost*

1665. Milton compares himself to the other great blind poet, *Homer, and his use of the images of light and darkness, of order and of chaos, resonates dramatically, coming from the voice of a blind poet who survived a bloody civil war. *Paradise Lost*, written in blank verse, is epic in scope, its twelve books spanning the heavens and the earth, depicting a universe vast enough to include the demonic Satan and his followers in its ultimate plan for man's salvation.

Paradise Regained was published together with *Samson Agonistes* in 1671. The former is a brief epic in the style of the Book of Job, describing *Jesus' temptation in the wilderness. Critics argue over when *Samson Agonistes* was actually written, with some claiming it was an early work and others viewing it as the culmination of Milton's career. The work itself is a powerful rendering of the Hebraic tale of Samson, a combination of the traditions of Jewish mythology, Greek drama, and Christian theology. In this last published masterpiece Milton creates a hero whose blindness becomes part of

God's plan, a fitting tribute from a blind poet whose life and work reverberate with a desire to celebrate the ultimate order as well as the grandeur of God's universe.

C. Hill, *Milton and the English Revolution*, 1977.
L. L. Martz, *Poet of Exile*, 1980.
W. R. Parker, *Milton: A Biography,* 2 vols., 1968.
A. N. Wilson, *The Life of John Milton*, 1983.

MIRABEAU, COMTE DE (Honoré-Gabriel Riqueti; 1749–1791), French revolutionary and political leader; eldest son of the economist Victor Riqueti, marquis de Mirabeau. His early years were characterized by wild excesses that ruined his health and caused him to be repeatedly jailed — several times on the request of his father, with whom he carried on a public feud. On returning home from cavalry service in Corsica, he was reconciled with his father and in 1772 married Emilie de Marignane, a Provençal heiress. Family harmony was short-lived and following an adulterous involvement with the marquise de Monnier, Mirabeau, arrested and disgraced, was forced to renounce the aristocratic society into which he had been born.

Following his release from jail and estranged from his family, Mirabeau lived the life of an adventurer. While in London, he moved in influential Whig circles and in 1786 was sent on a secret mission to Prussia. However, he betrayed his government's trust by publishing unedited reports to Paris containing accounts of scandal and intrigue in the Prussian court.

In May 1789 the estates-general, an assembly of the three estates (the clergy, the nobility, and the commons) was summoned in the hope of introducing much needed reforms into French society. As the author of numerous pamphlets violently denouncing abuses of the *ancien regime*, Mirabeau was elected in 1789 as a delegate of the third estate for Aix-en-Provence. With his fiery eloquence, his clear and practical ideas, and his terrifying yet imposing appearance, Mirabeau became the spokesman of the third estate, particularly when, on June 23, *Louis XVI ordered the estates-general to leave the hall after the day's session had been declared closed. In reply to the marquis de Dreux-Breze, who had announced the king's order, Mirabeau declared (his words have been variously reported): "Return to those who have sent you and tell them that we shall not stir from our places save at the point of the bayonet." His historic reply strengthened the resolve of the deputies to disobey and to establish the National Assembly. In the heady days of July 1789 Mirabeau's speeches contributed to inspire the assembly to demand the removal of the troops concentrated around Paris.

However, despite such revolutionary outpourings, Mirabeau's overriding political objective was to create a strong constitutional monarchy modeled on that of Great Britain, which would permit him to play a decisive role as a minister. His political ideal

was a free but limited monarchy possessed of sufficient strength to restrain the excesses of revolutionary radicalism and to defeat the misguided intrigues of the counterrevolutionaries. To this end he opposed the assumption of national sovereignty by the third estate, criticized the expediency of drawing up a Declaration of Rights, and vigorously advocated granting the king an absolute veto over legislation.

In October, after the Parisians had marched on Versailles and taken the king back to Paris, Mirabeau, concerned about rumors that he was plotting against the king, cast himself in the role of savior of the monarchy. Notwithstanding his eloquent debates, hounded by rumors of his disloyalty and his involvement with the court, Mirabeau's concern was to know how to juggle his machiavellian pursuits. The ambiguity of his position became more pronounced in December 1790. In that month, he held office as president of the Jacobin club and at the end of January 1791 was elected a member of the administration of the department of Paris, and acted, with great personal success, as president of the Constituent Assembly. Constantly troubled by reports in newspapers accusing him of treason, he was increasingly criticized in the Assembly, particularly by the Jacobins, who opposed his moderation. His political position gradually became untenable.

Plagued by ill health since his ascendancy to the presidency of the Assembly, Mirabeau died on April 2, 1792, amid impressive manifestations of public sorrow and respect, for he had never lost his popularity with the masses. In his honor the new church of Sainte Genevieve was converted into the Pantheon, for the burial of outstanding Frenchmen. His body was later removed when papers proving his dealings with the court were found in an iron chest in the Tuileries palace.

Although he failed to achieve his political objective, Mirabeau is renowned for being the most formidable orator and one of the greatest political minds in the National Assembly which governed France in the early phases of the French revolution.

B. Luttrell, *Mirabeau*, 1990.
O. J. G. Welch, *Mirabeau: A Study of a Democratic Monarchist*, 1951.

MIRANDA, FRANCISCO DE (1750–1816), Venezuelan soldier and patriot. Born in Caracas, Miranda purchased a captaincy in the Spanish forces at the age of twenty-two and went on to serve with them in North Africa. A wayward and self-willed individual, he was imprisoned for disobedience, but avoided a discharge and, in 1780, was sent to Cuba to fight the British. His subsequent involvement in the American Revolution included the defeat of British crown forces at Pensacola, Florida, and cooperation in the capture of New Providence in the Bahamas.

While in the army, Miranda became increasingly angry at the attitude of peninsular Spaniards towards those, like himself, of colonial origin. When, in 1783, he was accused of the misuse of funds, he protested his innocence vehemently but fled to the United States nonetheless. Because of his wartime exploits, he was welcomed and became acquainted with all the important U.S. leaders. While there, he first formulated his project to win freedom from Spanish colonial rule for the whole of Latin America; he envisioned an independent empire running from the Mississippi south to Cape Horn, headed by a hereditary emperor from the royal house of the Incas and governed through a two house legislature. He turned to his erstwhile opponents, the British, for support in realizing this ambitious dream.

Miranda sailed to England and agitated for the cause of Latin American freedom. He managed to get some support and protection from prime minister William *Pitt, who thought that Miranda might help Great Britain in her strategy of weakening Spain's hold on her lucrative overseas possessions. He also traveled widely on the Continent, where his charm won him the favors and support of the Russian empress, *Catherine the Great.

Judging that the time was not yet ripe for revolution in his homeland, Miranda remained on the Continent to fight for the French revolutionary armies. He served during the victories at Valmy and Antwerp, but manifested his usual flair for finding trouble by being charged with treachery after the French defeat at Neerwinden; he was narrowly acquitted, however. Once it became clear that Napoleon had won control in France, Miranda returned to London, where he became the leader of all the exiled plotters against the Spanish colonial power.

Miranda's 1806 attempt at an invasion of Venezuela was a pathetic failure condemned to futility at an early stage by its inability to win peasant support; he returned dispirited to London. However, Napoleon's invasion of the Iberian peninsula in 1808 triggered a succession of anticolonial uprisings in Spanish America, and, after the patriotic forces in Venezuela established a revolutionary government in Caracas in 1810, Simon *Bolivar persuaded Miranda to return there. Venezuela declared itself a republic (the first in South America) in 1811, with Miranda as generalissimo and, as royalist armies threatened, virtual dictator.

The new republic's defenses crumbled rapidly. In 1815, after a disastrous earthquake and the fall of the fortress of Puerto Cabello, Miranda chose to surrender to the royalists rather than risk the bloody rout of his troops. Once again, his actions were misjudged: the other revolutionary leaders considered his capitulation treasonable and thwarted his attempted escape. He was captured by the Spanish and transported to Cadiz, where he died in prison a year later. Often reviled and misunderstood during his lifetime, he came to be reckoned "the Precursor," the first Hispanic American nationalist whose vision anticipated and informed the views of his more successful successors.

J. F. Thorning, *Miranda: World Citizen*, 1952.

MITHRIDATES VI EUPATOR (Mithradates; c.132 B.C.E. -63 B.C.E.), known as Mithridates the Great, son of Mithridates V Energetes, king of Pontus, descendant of a noble Persian family claiming descent from *Darius I. After the death of his father, his mother and guardians wanted to kill him in order to seize the throne but he escaped from the palace, disguised his identity, and for seven years lived and hunted in the woods clothed in animal skins. In 115 B.C.E. his mother was deposed during a coup and he regained his throne, following which he killed his brother and married his sister Laodice. As with all Oriental monarchs he was at risk of assassination so he took the precaution of drinking a small amount of poison each day to acquire immunity from most of the poisons in use at the time. From this experience he learned about many antidotes to poisons, thus awakening an interest in medicine, and he recorded some of his findings. It is reported that the Roman general *Pompey had them translated into Latin. Thanks to his life in the woods he acquired great physical strength and spiritual endurance; it is told that he could run as fast as a deer and drive a sixteen-horse chariot. Mithridates could outeat and outdrink anyone who dined at his table and kept a large harem. A student of Greek literature and music, he never required an interpreter, maintained Greek philosophers and artists at his court, and collected works of art.

Embarking on an expansionist policy, Mithridates organized a strong army trained in Greek fashion. His first conquests included the northern country of the Black Sea (the Bosporan kingdom), eastern Pontus and Colchis. He thus gained large revenues, the control of a corn supply, and extensive military manpower. He also extended his rule to Armenia Minor and, but for Roman intervention, would have controlled Asia Minor. As it was, his incursions into Cappadocia and Paphlagonia after 105 B.C.E. were opposed by Rome; in 96 B.C.E. *Sulla compelled him to evacuate Cappadocia. The First Mithridatic War started in 88 B.C.E. after Nicomedes of Bithynia, incited by Roman businessmen and senators to whom he was indebted, invaded Pontus. Mithridates quickly overran Asia Minor, generally without opposition because of the population's hatred of the Romans and Italians who had been exploiting them. It is reported that on his orders eighty thousand Italians were killed in one day. He also conquered most of the Aegean islands and Greece. To show his scorn for the Romans, whom he accused of being stingy, he poured gold powder down the throat of one of his prisoners. However, in 86 B.C.E. Sulla defeated his armies and drove him from Greece, concluding a peace treaty at Dardanus (85/4 B.C.E.) in which Mithridates surrendered the territories he had conquered.

The Second Mithridatic War (83–81 B.C.E.), which started when Murena, the governor whom Sulla had left in Asia, invaded Pontus, was brief as Mithridates successfully defended himself and peace was restored.

> There was a king reigned in the East:
> There, when kings will sit to feast;
> They get their fill before they think
> With poisoned meat and poisoned drink.
> He gathered all that springs to birth
> From the many-venomed earth,
> First a little, thence to more,
> He sampled all her killing store;
> And easy, smiling, seasoned sound.
> Sate the king when healths went round,
> They put arsenic in his meat
> And stared aghast to watch him eat.
> They poured strychnine in his cup;
> And shook to see him drink it up:
> They shook, they stared as white's their shirt:
> Then it was their poison hurt.
> — I tell the tale that I heard told.
> Mithridates, he died old.
>
> **A. E. Housman**

In 74 B.C.E. Mithridates started the Third Mithridatic War after Rome received Bithynia left to it by Nicomedes as an inheritance. Again Mithridates won victories at first; Bithynia was occupied and he advanced to the Aegean. But Licinius Lucullus destroyed his army at Cyzicus and conquered Pontus (72–71 B.C.E.). Mithridates escaped and sought help from Tigranes I of Armenia, his son-in-law, who too was defeated by Lucullus. By then Mithridates was able to regain control of a large part of his kingdom after a mutiny in Lucullus's army. In 66 B.C.E. Pompey was invested with the command of the Roman army against him and defeated Mithridates, who fled to the Crimea, where he planned to raise an army and proceed to Italy. Confronted with strong opposition, including that of his son Pharnaces, he attempted to commit suicide by taking poison but he had made himself immune and did not die, and had to order a mercenary to kill him.

Mithridates was the greatest opponent met by Roman generals in the East. Energetic, of great physical strength, ambitious and brave, he lacked political wisdom. Overpowered by his ambitions and impulses, he overestimated his power and misunderstood Rome's determination. Nevertheless he was one of the few men that were a threat to the Romans. His downfall is the subject of the play *Mithridates* by Jean *Racine.

B. C. McGing, *The Foreign Policy of Mithridates VI Eupator King of Pontus*, 1986.

D. Magie, *Roman Rule in Asia Minor*, 2 vols., 1950.

MOLIÈRE (Jean-Baptiste Poquelin; 1622–1673), French playwright and actor. He was born in Paris, where his father was a supplier of furnishings to the royal household, and received a fine education at the College de Clermont. His father wished him to go into trade, but Poquelin sought a career on the stage. He was forced to abandon his early hopes of becoming a successful tragedian, since he was too big and too swift in his movements to play tragic roles as custom required; he also had a slight speech impediment. He therefore turned to comedy, then the poor cousin of theatrical styles. In 1643 he cofounded the ten person Illustre Théâtre comedy company — which performed on a Paris tennis court — and took the stage name Molière to avoid embarrassing his father.

Unable to survive economically in the face of stiff competition in Paris (Molière was twice imprisoned for debt in 1645), the company left the city to tour the French provinces for some thirteen years in what was to prove a rigorous apprenticeship in the art of actor-managing for Molière. His ability to succeed after returning to Paris in 1658 owed much to the qualities of tenacity, persistence, quick wittedness, and flexibility that he developed during the company's years on the road. His first two plays, *L'Étourdi ou les contretemps* (The Blunderer) and *Le Dépit amoureux* (The Amorous Quarrel), date from this period.

In 1658 the company's performance at the Louvre of Molière's own composition, *Le Docteur amoureux* (The Amorous Doctor), won them the approbation of *Louis XIV and the patronage of the duke of Orleans. However, it was Molière's next comedy, *Les Précieuses ridicules* (The Affected Young Ladies), produced in 1660, that first won him widespread acclaim. In 1661 the company, now called the Troupe du Roi, moved to what was to be its permanent home, a hall at the Royal Palace built as a theater by Cardinal *Richelieu. Here they performed *L'École des femmes* (The School for Women), which both scandalized and delighted Parisian theatergoers on its opening in 1662. The tale of Arnolphe, the woman-fearing pedant who determines to marry a girl entirely unacquainted with the ways of the world and then falls in love with her, offended many people's sensibilities but came to be recognized as a comic masterpiece, the first of many created by Molière.

That same year Molière married Armande Béjarte, a relative (possibly the daughter) of Madeleine Béjarte, a friend who had first encouraged Molière to form a theater company. Armande was an actress and was to appear as the female lead in many of Molière's plays, but the couple's private life was not a happy one: there were frequent rumors that Armande had affairs with other men. In any case, it was to the stage that Molière was inseparably wedded; he worked ceaselessly, writing, producing, directing, and acting in the plays that made his troupe the most successful in the cutthroat theatrical world of Paris. Borrowing the rhetoric of movement and gestures from the Italian *commedia dell'arte*, he created a form that dominated theatrical comedy for three centuries and elevated comedy to the status of high art.

THE WIT AND WISDOM OF MOLIÈRE

- We die only once, but for such a long time!
- The more we love our friends, the less we flatter them; it is by excusing nothing that pure love shows itself.
- Anyone may be an honorable man and yet write verse badly.
- Good Heavens! For more than forty years I have been speaking prose without knowing it.
- That conflicts with common sense. But it is so, for all that.
- *Géronte:* I think you are putting them in their wrong places. The heart is on the left and the liver on the right.
  Seganarelle: Yes, that was so in the old days. But we have changed all that.
- Pure reason avoids extremes, and requires one to be wise in moderation.
- Love makes people inventive.
- Men are all alike in their promises. It is only in their deeds that they differ.

With the production of *Dom Juan* and *Tartuffe*, Molière incurred the wrath and permanent opposition of the church. *Dom Juan*, a cynical and witty retelling of the tale of the Spanish libertine, was banned shortly after its first performance. *Tartuffe*, Molière's hilarious and mordant play about the hypocrite who dupes a naive householder by posing as an inhuman ascetic when he is in fact an outrageous lecher who seduces the daughter of the family, suffered a five-year ban after its 1664 premiere. Through his ridiculing of hypocritical self-interest masquerading as religious sensibility, Molière constituted a permanent irritant to the ecclesiastical hierarchy.

By the time he was forty-five, Molière's successes as a dramatist had made him a rich man. His later plays include classics such as *Le Misanthrope, L'Avare* (The Miser), *George Dandin, Le Médecin malgré lui, Le Bourgeoise Gentilhomme*, and *Le Malade imaginaire* (The Imaginary Invalid). In the last, Molière created comedy out of the tragedy of his life, playing the leading role of a hypochondriac who fears death and doctors even as he himself succumbed to illness exacerbated by the exhaustion brought on by a lifetime's unflagging dedication to the exigencies of his chosen *métier*. Special royal dispensation meant that church opposition could not prevent his being buried in consecrated ground, but the interment took place by night. However, the torchlight procession was attended by thousands of admirers.

No cohesive philosophy informs Molière's dramatic works, although his plays' humorous contraposition of acquired and natural human qualities undoubtedly owes something to the influence of the work of the essayist and philosopher Michel de *Montaigne, by whom he was deeply affected. However, Molière's first concern was always dramatic and comic effect: he wrote for the stage, not for posterity or publication. Working at great speed (he was the author of thirty-one of the ninety-five plays his company performed in fourteen years in Paris, writing as many as five in a single year), he took little care over the accuracy of the published form of his plays, and never read or corrected proofs of his works. Indeed, he only published in order to avoid being exploited (as it was, two of his plays were pirated) and left seven of his plays unpublished. Given his apparent indifference to the literary impact of his compositions, the fact that he is widely lauded as one of France's greatest ever writers is testament to the extraordinary force of his genius.

Although the plays he wrote were unabashedly popularist, Molière was a great theatrical innovator. His *L'Impromptu* made theatrical history by reproducing the backstage world of rehearsals, while his entire canon was testament to his great energy and the intensity of his dramatic vision. As an individual he was not a great talker but he had uncanny abilities as a mimic, which he put to use in producing characters who were recognizable living types, a process he considered essential to his comic enterprise. Although wary of theoretical pontification, he did reveal his belief that "incongruity is the heart of the comic," and that "to know the comic, we must know the rational, of which it denotes the absence." By the juxtaposition of wise and foolish, right and wrong, fantasy and reality, he explored the tension between human impulses and the tyranny of convention to erect a memorable dramatic monument.

M. Bulgakov, *The Life of Monsieur de Molière*, 1988.

W. D. Howarth, *Molière: A Playwright and His Audience*, 1982.

A. A. Tilley, *Molière*, 1968.

MONROE, JAMES (1758–1831), fifth president of the United States (1817–1825), best known for the drafting of the Monroe Doctrine. Monroe was born in Westmoreland County, Virginia, carrying on the tradition of American presidents whose place of residence was the state of Virginia. In 1776 he dropped out of William and Mary College to serve in the Continental army, rising to the rank of major. Harlem Heights, White Plains, Trenton, Brandywine, Germantown, and Monmouth are some of the battles in which he fought.

Monroe left the army in 1780 to study law under Thomas *Jefferson, who was then governor of Virginia and who became a close friend and political adviser to Monroe. Although not an equal intellectually with Jefferson and James *Madison, Monroe worked well with both of them. He studied with Jefferson for three years and in 1782 became a member of the House of Delegates of Virginia and served in the Continental Congress from 1783 to 1786.

Monroe left the army in 1780 to study law under Thomas *Jefferson, who was then governor of Virginia and who became a close friend and political adviser to Monroe. Although not an equal intellectually with Jefferson and James *Madison, Monroe worked well with both of them. He studied with Jefferson for three years and in 1782 became a member of the House of Delegates of Virginia and served in the Continental Congress from 1783 to 1786.

In 1788, as a member of the Virginia House of Delegates, Monroe opposed the proposed state constitution. Politically aligned with Jefferson, Monroe became involved in the organization and advancement of the Republican party.

President George *Washington, although representing an opposing political party, appointed Monroe minister to France in 1794, where he spent two years. His work was considered less than satisfactory and he was recalled. From 1799 to 1802 he served as governor of Virginia and in this position demonstrated an aptitude as an administrator.

In 1803 Jefferson sent Monroe back to France, this time to negotiate the Louisiana Purchase, and Monroe established himself as a person with future presidential capabilities. From 1803 to 1807 he served in various posts abroad.

Despite their political differences, President Madison, who defeated Monroe in his first presidential bid, appointed him to serve as secretary of state, and for a six-month term as secretary of war. Monroe held both positions during the War of 1812, doing an excellent job and winning the respect of Congress.

In 1816 the Federalist party was in a state of collapse. Monroe was easily elected president as the Democratic-Republican candidate, inaugurating the "era of good feelings" between the Republicans and the Federalists. His major cabinet choices were wise selections and continued to serve during both of his terms. He was reelected to his second term, winning all but one electoral vote.

Foreign relations was Monroe's strong point. The Monroe Doctrine, introduced in 1823 as part of a

James Monroe

presidential message, sought to establish the autonomy and independence of the New World, rejecting European intervention and proclaiming that the United States would not intervene in European politics. During Monroe's term of office, Florida was acquired from Spain (1819–1821) and the Missouri Compromise of 1820 paved the way for the state of Missouri to join the Union.

After completing his presidency in 1825, Monroe served as the presiding officer of the Virginia Constitutional Convention.

H. Ammson, *James Monroe: The Quest for National Identity*, 1971.

S. G. Brown and D. G. Baker, eds., *The Autobiography of James Monroe*, 1959.

W. P. Cresson, *James Monroe*, 1971.

F. Merk, *Monroe Doctrine and American Expansionism*, 1966.

MONTESSORI, MARIA (1870–1952), Italian physician, scientist, and originator of the Montessori method of education and philosophy of human development. Born in Chiaravelle in the province of Ancona, Italy, she displayed, from a very early age, a keenness for learning and received opportunities that at the time were not usually open to women. She attended a hitherto all-male technical school and expressed an interest in the field of engineering; however, she was not encouraged in this direction and turned her attention to biology in the hope of becoming a doctor. She attended the University of Rome, and in 1894 became the first woman in Italy to graduate in medicine. She then practiced surgical medicine and sought to encourage other women to

- There is every reason to believe that our system will soon attain the highest degree of perfection of which human institutions are capable.
- The American continents are henceforth not to be considered as subjects for future colonization by any European powers.
- In the wars of European powers in matters relating to themselves we have never taken any part, nor does it comport with our policy to do so. It is only when our rights are invaded or seriously menaced that we resent injuries or make preparations for our defense.

James Monroe

further their education and to demand equal rights in all aspects of society.

While still involved with the surgical wing of the hospital, Montessori began to teach in the psychiatric clinic attached to the university. There she became interested in the education of mentally retarded children and arranged to teach some such younger children on a regular basis. She based her teaching on the works of Jean Itard and Edouard Seguin, and within two years some of the children had progressed so quickly that they managed to pass the regular school examinations. In 1899 she was appointed director of the State Orthophrenic School in Rome, where she developed her methods for teaching mentally handicapped children, using her classroom as a type of laboratory in which to observe children and test her ideas of ways to help them achieve their greatest potential.

In 1901 she returned to the University of Rome for further study in educational philosophy, anthropology, and psychology and in 1904 was appointed professor of anthropology. Throughout this period she continued her medical studies and published articles on childhood nervous conditions.

In 1909 Montessori was given the opportunity to work with ordinary children. The housing authorities in Rome had established a children's day nursery in the poverty-stricken area of San Lorenzo and needed a director to be in charge of over fifty three- to six-year old children. Marie called the nursery "Casa dei Bambini" (Children's House); and it was there that she fully developed her teaching method. Initially she used teaching methods and materials similar to the ones she had applied when teaching mentally handicapped children. She discovered that although the children appeared to enjoy these exercises, they preferred to be left alone to achieve the tasks independently. By carefully monitoring the children's attitudes and approach to new challenges, she developed an educational method based on the ideas of freedom and self-motivation, encouraging children to develop their own skills and capabilities.

To enable children to best achieve their potential, Montessori devised a classroom setting utilizing a variety of multisensory learning materials, including three-dimensional geometric puzzles, beads for use in mathematical equations, and the presence of plants and animals, which the children learned to care for. She observed that in such an environment children between ages three to six could work with these materials for extended periods of time with concentration and yet display an inner calmness and self-discipline that obviated the need for an external authority figure. The teacher's role was to prepare the necessary environment and provide initial guidance but then to remain unobtrusive, allowing the children to work with the material at their own pace.

Her success in San Lorenzo led to the opening of several other Montessori schools throughout Italy and later in the United States. After two decades of working with children, she began to publish her findings and observations, writing over fifteen books and numerous articles on education. Her later years were spent traveling throughout Europe and the United States lecturing educators and establishing teacher-training programs. In 1922 she was appointed inspector of schools in Italy but left her native country in 1934, unwilling to live under a Fascist dictatorship. She eventually settled in the Netherlands and died in Noordwijk.

D. Gettman, *Basic Montessori*, 1988.
R. Kramer, *Marie Montessori*, 1983.
P. Lillard, *Montessori*, 1973.
R. C. Orem, *Montessori*, 1978.

MONTEZUMA II (1466–1520), Aztec emperor whose death precipitated the Spanish conquest of Mexico. Montezuma was the grandson of Montezuma I, founder of the Aztec empire. He was born in Tenochtitlán (present-day Mexico City), where he served as a high priest until succeeding his uncle Ahuitzotl to the throne. The empire Montezuma inherited, consisting of Tenochtitlán, Texcoco, and Tlacopán, contained five million inhabitants and controlled most of central America.

Aztec records show that in the early years of Montezuma's reign certain unusual incidents foretold the decline of his empire. Eight omens were reported during the ten years prior to the arrival of the Spanish conquistadors in Mexico: a column of fire was seen in the late night skies; the temple of the god Huitzilpochtli was mysteriously consumed by fire; a lightning bolt, unaccompanied by thunder, struck the Tzonmolco temple; a comet was seen in the skies during the day; sudden waves on a clear, windless day caused serious flooding in Tenochtitlán; a woman's voice was heard weeping, "Oh my sons, we are lost. Oh my sons, where can I hide you?"; an odd bird with mirrorlike eyes was caught and when peering into the mirrors Montezuma saw strange men landing on his shores; and people with several heads but one body were seen walking the streets of Tenochtitlán. Furthermore, the soothsayers of Nezahualpilli, lord of Texcoco, foretold that the empire would soon crumble. Montezuma rejected Nezahualpilli's warnings and the two made a bet to determine the truth. So certain was Nezahualpilli of his soothsayers that he was willing to gamble his realm for three turkeys. The bet was decided by a series of ball games. Montezuma's team won the first two games; Nezahualpilli's team won the next three in succession, supposedly proving the veracity of his statement. Montezuma came to expect the arrival of fair-skinned gods, as foretold in ancient prophecies, who would come to rule over the empire in his stead.

The arrival of the Spanish was, therefore, no surprise to Montezuma. Despite the advice of many of his prominent advisers he accorded them a royal welcome, showering them with expensive gifts and even offering human sacrifices to them so that they could partake of the flesh. The Spanish commander, Hernando *Cortés, was believed to be the great god Quetzalcoatl and his followers lesser gods. Yet despite his respect and fondness for Cortés, Montezuma refused to abandon his ancient gods and accept Christianity. Spanish soldiers, numbering only a few hundred, began to feel threatened in Tenochtitlán and after some consideration Cortés conceded to their demand that Montezuma be arrested and kept in captivity to assure the allegiance of his subjects. Montezuma was invited to a dinner where, to his surprise, he found himself placed under house arrest. Although he continued to govern his kingdom, he now did so jointly with Cortés.

The human sacrifices offered at the celebration of the Aztec festival of Huitzilpochtli appalled the Spanish troops. Since Cortés had left for the coast at this time, the acting commander put an end to the festivities, angering the Aztec leadership. Upon his return, Cortés found the Aztecs in open revolt against the Spanish. A large body of Aztecs had surrounded the Spanish troops, forcing them to retreat to the palace where Montezuma was held prisoner. Despite his disillusionment with the Spanish, Montezuma went to the balcony to implore his subjects to retreat. A shower of stones and darts rained down on him and to this day it is uncertain whether Montezuma was killed by his own subjects or by the Spanish, but his death did not end the Aztec revolt. Two emperors, Cuitlahuac and Cuauhtemoc, succeeded Montezuma, but both were defeated that year (1521), allowing the Spanish to control Mexico.

B. Diaz, *The Conquest of New Spain*, 1963.
M. L. Portilla, *The Broken Spear: The Aztec Account of the Conquest of Mexico*, 1962.
G. C. Valliant, *The Aztecs of Mexico*, 1950.

MONTGOMERY, SIR BERNARD LAW,

(1887–1976), British general. Family background might have inclined the young Montgomery to a career in the Church of England: his father was a bishop and his grandfather, dean of Canterbury Cathedral. Al-

though he greatly admired his father, he did not want to be the next Montgomery to hold high clerical office. He opted instead for the other profession considered suitable for sons of the upper classes: the army.

After completing his education at Saint Paul's School in London, Montgomery entered the Royal Military College at Sandhurst. During his training there he gained a reputation for sadism with fellow cadets. An incident is recorded where he burnt another cadet and in 1906 he was almost dismissed from the army. Although his behavior was an embarrassment to the army and presumably his family as well, to balance the account strongly in his favor, he was top of the musketry course, excelled at bayonetry, and was a fine hockey player. Montgomery was commissioned into the First Royal Warwickshire Regiment and posted to the northwest frontier of India in 1908.

During World War I, Montgomery was given a command on the western front. He was soon in a situation for which his parade ground skills left him singularly ill-equipped. Confronted by a German soldier taking aim at him, Montgomery was armed only with his ceremonial sword, which he was not trained to use in combat. There was no time to consider the situation, and he hurled himself at the enemy, kicking him in a sensitive area. The German collapsed to the ground, screaming out in pain, and in this heroic manner Montgomery captured his first prisoner.

In 1914 he took part in the retreat from Mons, fought at the Battle of Le Cateau, and then was seriously wounded at the First Battle of Ypres. Awarded the Distinguished Service Order and the croix de guerre, he recovered to return to the front in 1915 as a brigade major. His bravery in combat and proven capabilities as a leader of men worked to advance his promotion and by the end of the war he was appointed chief of staff of the Forty-seventh (London) Division.

General Montgomery

During the inter war years Montgomery served in a variety of capacities. In 1920 he held an appointment at the Staff college at Camberley, later he served in Ireland, and then returned to his post at the College. In 1931 he wrote the official British army manual on infantry training. In 1938 Montgomery was a major general in charge of the northern region of the Palestine Mandate dealing with the suppression of a serious Arab insurrection.

In his personal life he enjoyed ten years of happy marriage but these years ended with his wife's early death in 1937. He was devastated and his personal bitterness was reflected in his dealings with fellow officers. Although this affected Montgomery's popularity, he retained many friends in high places and the ordinary soldiers held him in high esteem.

At the outbreak of World War II, Montgomery was given command of the Third Division of the British Expeditionary Force in France and Belgium. The disasters that befell his army did not damage his reputation; rather he emerged from the Dunkirk evacuation with distinction as the most competent of the British generals. As a tactician he had many failings and these were compounded by his abrasive personality which made it hard for other commanders to work well with him. As an efficient organizer of huge armies he had few equals and was usually well aware of the extent of the human and material resources under his command.

Montgomery's greatest moment came in October 1942 with his decisive defeat of Erwin *Rommel's North Africa Corps at the Battle of El Alamein in Egypt, regarded as the turning point in Allied fortunes. After first defeating a German offensive he held back his counterattack until he felt confident of success. Then the British Eighth Army managed to rout the Germans and begin the campaign that would soon drive the Germans out of North Africa. Montgomery continued the battle against the Germans through Sicily and Italy but here he was under the overall authority of General Dwight D. *Eisenhower; he had serious disagreements with the Americans over tactics.

In 1944 Montgomery was commander in chief of all land forces for the invasion of Normandy. He insisted that the landing be made with five divisions as opposed to the three in the original plan. D-Day was a great victory but afterwards, departing from his characteristic caution, he committed men to an ill-planned attempt to seize quickly the Rhine bridges, which led to a serious Allied defeat at Arnhem. He redeemed himself by leading American troops in pushing back the German counterattack at the Ardennes, but Montgomery was most reluctant to implement the Allied agreement to transfer to Eisenhower overall command.

Montgomery was known as a strict disciplinarian but he had a talent for gaining the admiration and affection of ordinary soldiers, who developed a fierce loyalty to the commander they affectionately nicknamed "Monty." His personal life showed the same regularity he liked to see in his battles. He would always go to bed at 9.30 P.M. and even a visit of King George VI could not persuade him to alter his plans. He turned to the king one evening at this time and apologized, saying, "If you will excuse me, Sir, we have the battle to win and I must go to bed."

In 1945 he led the crossing of the Rhine and accepted the surrender of German forces in northern Europe on Luneburg Heath. He was made Viscount Montgomery of El Alamein in 1946 and as late as 1958 was still serving as Deputy Supreme Allied Commander in Europe.

A. Chalfont, *Montgomery of Alamein*, 1976.
N. Hamilton, *Monty: The Making of a General, 1887–1942*, 1981.
R. Lamb, *Montgomery in Europe 1943–1945, Success or Failure?*, 1983.

MORAZÁN, FRANCISCO (1792–1842), advocate of Central American unity; president of the Federation of Central America. He was born in Tegucigalpa, Honduras, and received little formal education. Self-taught as a lawyer, he worked for the local municipal government, where he advocated liberal policies opposed by the aristocracy and the church. Similarly, he resisted incorporating the Central American states (Costa Rica, Guatemala, Honduras, Salvador, and Nicaragua) into Augustin de *Iturbide's Mexican empire and commanded the local militia in a failed attack on the Honduran capital of Comayagua.

Iturbide was toppled in 1823 and the Central American states seceded soon after. Like most states of the new Central America Federation, Honduras elected a liberal government, with Morazán as secretary general and as president of the state legislature. The federal government and Guatemala, however, continued to be dominated by conservatives. Conflict was inevitable. To institute more like-minded local administrations, the federal gov-

- You can't run a military operation with a committee of staff officers in command. It would be nonsense.
- Leadership which is evil, while it may temporarily succeed, always carries within itself the seeds of its own destruction.
- I've got to go to meet God — and explain all those men I killed at Alamein.

Viscount Montgomery

- In defeat, unbeatable; in victory, unbearable.

Winston Churchill on Viscount Montgomery

ernment did not hesitate to use its army. Morazán recruited his own small band of supporters in Tegucigalpa, but, lacking ammunition, they were no match for the well equipped federal troops. Morazán was undeterred and after a brief spell in prison began recruiting a new army.

Morazán's new army originally consisted of only five hundred men but by routing the federal army at La Trinidad, their cause was adopted by thousands more. Tegucigalpa fell in 1827, and Morazán was declared chief of state of Honduras. His first act was the official establishment of the "Protector of the Laws Army," dedicated to overthrowing the conservatives in neighboring states. El Salvador fell in 1828; Guatemala in 1829.

Elections confirmed Morazán's claim to popular support. As president of the Federation of Central America, he embarked on nationwide ecclesiastic, economic, educational, and judicial reforms. At the same time, he failed to gauge the growing support for the conservatives and regional separatists, who were drawing from his original supporters. Stability could only be maintained at great expense, a burden borne grudgingly by tax payers. Antigovernment propaganda exploited even the most banal events, such as a cholera epidemic among the Indians, to demonstrate the government's ineptitude. The 1834 elections further tested Morazán's popularity. In fact, he lost, but kept power after the death of his opponent before assuming office.

Morazán was not despotic; even as conservative rebels, led by Jose Carrera, threatened to topple his government, he refused to assume dictatorial powers. Finally, in 1840, Morazán fled to Peru. Although given the choice between the ministry of war or command of an army against Chile, Morazán refused to abandon his dream of a united Central America under a liberal regime. He returned to Costa Rica in 1842.

Carrera immediately responded to news of Morazán's return by sending an army, under General Vicente Villase or to capture him. Villase§or, however, was so impressed by Morazán's determination and vision for Central America that he reached an agreement with him, the Pacto del Jocote, recognizing Morazán as president of Costa Rica. Still, Morazán refused to relinquish his dream of a united Central America and invaded El Salvador before even asserting control over Costa Rica. His own army deposed him shortly after and planned his execution.

Tied to a post in the main square of San Jose, Morazán was informed that, in deference to his position as head of state, he would be allowed to command his own firing squad. He gazed at the troops and sighed, "Very well, then...Fire!" Slowly raising his head, he called out, "I am still alive!" A second volley ended his life. One hundred and fifty years later, Central American intellectuals still cherish the dream of unity espoused by the man many call the "George *Washington of Central America."

R. S. Chamberlain, *Francisco Morazán: Champion of Central American Federation*, 1950.

MORE, SIR THOMAS

MORE, SIR THOMAS (1478–1535), humanist, author of *Utopia*, statesman, and chancellor of England; executed for opposing the reformation of the Church of England; canonized by the Roman Catholic church in 1935. More's father was a lawyer who was knighted and appointed a judge on the king's bench. Thomas was educated at Saint Anthony's Hospital in Threadneedle Street, but was soon transferred to the household of Cardinal Morton, archbishop of Canterbury and lord chancellor. The sophisticated prelate was so impressed with his young charge that he predicted that "this child, whoever shall live to see it, will prove a marvellous man." At the age of fifteen More began a two-year course at Oxford which, aside from enabling him to study Greek under John Linacre, also introduced him to the intellectual challenges of the new learning that was then being imported from Europe.

In 1494 More's father withdrew him prematurely from the university and, deciding that he should pursue a legal career, entered him as a student at New Inn in London. More's thirst for knowledge, his capacity for work, and his great intelligence enabled him to study for admission to the bar, transferring to Lincoln's Inn in 1496 and qualifying in 1501, without neglecting his literary and philosophical pursuits. During this period he began his lifelong friendship with the Dutch humanist Desiderius *Erasmus and remained an avid reader of holy scripture and the classics of the ancient world.

More may have acquiesced to his father's will regarding the study of law, but he harbored doubts as to its suitability as a career. For about four years he lived in the Carthusian house next to Lincoln's Inn, immersing himself in the rigors of ascetic life and testing the idea of vocation in the priesthood. He passed long hours in prayer, mortified his body with fasting, and wore a coarse hair shirt next to his skin. Eventually, on the advice of Thomas Linacre and others, he renounced his clerical ambitions, though not his severe practices. Although he was elected to Parliament in 1504, More's clash with *Henry VII over fiscal matters impeded his progress in public life and even led to the fining and brief incarceration of his father. However, the accession of *Henry VIII removed all obstacles to success; More became an undersheriff of London in 1510, and rose to distinction as an impartial judge and "general patron of the poor. In May 1515 More traveled to Bruges as a member of a diplomatic delegation and during visits to the Low Countries began his masterpiece, *Utopia*. Utopia, a Greek name which More devised, means "no place" and the work describes an ideal society, a city-state governed entirely by reason where the evils of poverty and misery have been eliminated. Part satire on the wretched, selfish policies of the European Christian kingdoms and part blueprint of a model society, Utopia embraces com-

SAYINGS OF SIR THOMAS MORE

- The Utopian way of life provides not only the happiest basis for a civilized community, but also one which, in all human probability, lasts for ever.
- Male priests are allowed to marry — for there is nothing to stop a woman being a priest, although women are not often chosen for the job and only elderly widows are eligible. (Utopia)
- Both the raven and the ape think their own young the fairest.
- He should be able to prove the moon is made of green cheese.
- No more alike than chalk to coals.

Now it is something — now it is rhyme; previously it was neither rhyme nor reason.
**To a friend who had put
into verse an indifferent book**

- Farewell my dear child and pray for me, and I shall for you and your friends that we may merrily meet in heaven (letter to daughter on eve of execution).
- See me safe up; for my coming down, I can shift for myself (on ascending the scaffold).

munism, constitutional monarchy, religious pluralism, euthanasia, and women's rights. The entire community regards itself as one family and there is no private property. Religion enjoins a belief in God and toleration for all creeds. It was an immediate success with the intellectual elite upon publication in 1516, and became the model for much subsequent Utopian writing. To some extent More tried to implement his principles within his own household, in which ongoing education was prescribed for men and women, the children learned the Greek alphabet by shooting with bow and arrow at the letters, gardening was compulsory for all, physical punishment was barred, and gaming and idleness forbidden. Erasmus came from Holland to stay with him and reported on being taken into the garden to see the rabbits, fox, ferret, weasel, and monkey (which can be seen in Holbein's painting of More's household). He was even visited there by King Henry VIII. For the rest of his life More remained at the center of Renaissance scholarship. According to the playwright Robert Bolt (who wrote the play and film *A Man for all Seasons* about More), "a visitors' book at his house in Chelsea (to which he moved in 1524) would have looked like a sixteenth-century *Who's Who*: Holbein, Erasmus, Colet, everybody." In public life More quickly distinguished himself as one of the king's most favored advisers, or possibly his most accomplished apologist. He became undertreasurer and a knight in 1521, helped Henry VIII compose an attack on Martin *Luther, and following Luther's counterattack, published in 1523 the scurrilous *Responsio ad Lutherum*. In the same year he was appointed speaker of the House of Commons.

Though doubting Henry VIII's biblical proofs that his marriage to Catherine of Aragon was void because it had failed to produce a male heir, and incestuous because of her former marriage to Henry's brother, he retained the king's favor, and in 1525 gained the powerful position of chancellor of the duchy of Lancaster. The clash between humanist tolerance and religious doctrine was resolved in favor of the latter, and More accepted a commission to refute heretical texts written in English, publishing seven polemical work between 1529 and 1533. Finally, he submitted to Henry's wish: "First look up to God and after God to me." More became lord chancellor in 1529, the first commoner ever to hold the position.

More took an oath of admission to office which included a clause that he would "use his power to destroy all manner of heresies." Loyalty to the law and fidelity to doctrine made him a ferocious adversary of religious reform. During his chancellorship he sentenced reformers to death, torture on the rack, and severe corporal punishment. These acts, and the intolerance of More's diatribes against heresy, are difficult to reconcile with his Utopian pluralism, as well as with Samuel *Johnson's view that "he was the person of the greatest virtue these Islands ever produced."

When England and its king moved toward reform, More stood still. He was distraught when the clergy acknowledged the king as supreme head of the Church of England and begged Henry to free him from office in 1532 when the clergy promised never to legislate or convene without royal permission. He refused to attend the coronation of Anne Boleyn a year later. In 1534 he was summoned to agree under oath to the Act of Succession, which stated that Anne was queen and validated her marriage to Henry. More could not deny that Anne was indeed the queen, but he refused to take an oath that negated papal supremacy and was confined to the Tower of London, where he wrote *A Dialogue of Comfort Against Tribulacyon*.

More was tried for treason in 1535. The evidence against him relied largely upon false testimony, but nothing could save him when he objected that "no temporal man may be head of the spirituality." He was convicted and sentenced to be "drawn, hanged and quartered," which Henry changed to beheading. Upon reaching the scaffold More conducted himself with great dignity, blindfolding himelf, reassuring the executioner, and quipping before the ax fell: "Stay till I have moved my beard; that at least has not committed treason". He was mourned by Erasmus as "a man whose soul was more pure than any snow, whose genius was such that England never had and never again will have the like."

A. Fox, *Thomas More: History and Providence*, 1982.
J. A. Guy, *The Public Career of Sir Thomas More*, 1980.
E. E. Reynolds, *The Field is Won: The Life and Death of Saint Thomas More*, 1968.
T. Stapleton, *The Life and Illustrious Martyrdom of Sir Thomas More*, 1984.

MORTON, WILLIAM THOMAS GREEN

(1819–1868), American dental surgeon, pioneer of anesthesia through the use of ether. He was the son of a Massachusetts farmer whose family was among the earliest settlers in New England. He went to Boston to work as a salesman, but the commercial life did not satisfy him for long and in 1840 he enrolled at the College of Dental Surgery in Baltimore, finding a profession more appropriate to his talents and interests.

Morton opened a practice in Farmington, Connecticut, and later in Boston. He did not succeed financially and felt that he lacked sufficient medical training, and so enrolled in Harvard Medical School in 1844. This was also the year of his marriage, and his new responsibilities led to financial difficulties: leaving Harvard without completing his degree, he returned to working as a dentist.

A Harvard professor, Charles T. Jackson, had demonstrated to his chemistry class that the inhalation of sulfuric ether caused loss of consciousness. Jackson gave Morton the idea of using this as a local anesthetic for dental fillings. Previously Morton had investigated narcotics, intoxicants, and even mesmerism in order to remove the pain from dental surgery, but none of these had worked satisfactorily.

Morton carried out his tests of the power of ether on his own body. Initially, he mixed it with opium and was encouraged by the numbness produced by prolonged inhalation. Further experiments followed at the family farm, where he etherized a hen and then cut off its comb without the bird showing any signs of discomfort. Encouraged, he returned to Boston and gave himself a heavy dose of sulfuric ether, even though the effects of this inhalation were then unknown. He lost consciousness for eight minutes without ill-effect.

When a patient named Frost arrived at the surgery with a painful toothache, Morton told him he had something much more effective than mesmerism to remove the pain of the extraction. He administered ether from a handkerchief and the patient was soon unconscious. The tooth was removed without reaction, Frost remaining, as Morton later described it, "still and motionless as if already in the embrace of death." For a moment he feared he had killed his patient but Frost revived when he threw a glass of water over him. Frost could not believe the tooth had been extracted, for he had felt nothing.

Morton chose to publicize his discovery through a demonstration in the Massachusetts General Hospital. The operating theater was crowded with doctors eager to see the new process. As the doubting medical men looked on, Morton administered the ether and the patient lapsed into unconsciousness. A tumor was removed without any sign of pain and all sensed a historic step forward in medical practice had just been witnessed.

Morton did not want to have to share the rewards for the discovery with Professor Jackson, and refused to accept an award from the French Academy of Medicine since Jackson was named as joint discoverer. He refused to disclose the ingredients of the ether and named it "letheon," suggesting a new, previously unknown substance. He allowed certain charity hospitals to use this free of charge.

The last twenty years of Morton's life were spent on his farm at Wellesley. He was awarded medals from Russia and Sweden, but at home there was a long legal struggle both for recognition as discoverer of the anesthetic and for appropriate financial reward. Although he maintained his temper and did not seek to retaliate against his opponents, it was a bitter fight and reduced him to abject poverty. His death was ascribed to an apoplectic attack that occurred while driving in New York's Central Park reading an article by Professor Jackson attempting to impede efforts by Morton's supporters to raise a testimonial subscription for him.

B. MacQuitty, *Victory Over Pain*, 1971.
G. S. Woodward, *The Man Who Conquered Pain*, 1962.

MOSES

(c. thirteenth century B.C.E.), Israelite prophet and lawgiver; the outstanding personality in the foundation of Judaism and the emergence of the Jewish people. According to the Book of Exodus, Moses was born during a time when the burgeoning population of Hebrews in Egypt was subject to growing repression. Pharaoh, the ruler of Egypt, decreed that all newborn Israelite males should be drowned in the Nile River. Jochebed gave birth to Moses and, after hiding him for three months, secreted him in a basket which she placed among the bulrushes on the banks of the Nile, where he was found by Pharaoh's daughter, who had gone to bathe in the river. She brought him to the palace and gave the child the name Moses, explained as meaning "drawn from the water" (a folk etymology).

Moses was raised within the royal household, but when he reached manhood he still identified with the Israelites and found their suffering under slavery intolerable. When he witnessed an Egyptian taskmaster abusing an innocent slave, he killed him and, on realizing his deed was known to the authorities, fled from Egypt to Midian, in the northwest part of the Arabian peninsula. After intervening when shepherds harassed the daughters of Jethro, the priest of Midian, he became a part of Jethro's

Moses holding a scroll; fresco from the Dura-Europos synagogue, Syria, third century C.E.

Moses and Aaron assured the Hebrews that the time for liberation had come. But after their first meeting with Pharaoh, not only did the bondage continue, but the Israelites were denied the straw they formerly received to accomplish their task of making bricks, creating terrible hardship. The refusal of the Egyptian ruler (who has been identified with *Ramses II) to set the Israelites free resulted in the series of ten plagues which proved that Moses had indeed been commissioned by God. Pharaoh remained unconvinced until the last plague, when the firstborn of Egypt were slain and the Egyptians, in panic, pressured the Israelites to leave. As Moses led the people in the Exodus out of Egypt to the shore of the "Red Sea" (the exact location is uncertain), Pharaoh changed his mind and pursued his former slaves; Moses now raised the staff that God had given him at the burning bush and split the waters, enabling the Israelites to escape. As Pharaoh and his chariots pursued them into the depths of the sea, the Israelites gained the far shore and Moses again raised his staff, drowning the Egyptian pursuers in the tumultuous waters.

From the Red Sea, Moses took the people to Mount Sinai and, on the fiftieth day after leaving Egypt, ascended to the top of the mountain, while the entire nation heard the Ten Commandments spoken by God. Coming down from Sinai later than the people expected, Moses found them worshiping a golden calf which they had created as an idol during his absence. Angered by this lapse into idolatry, Moses broke the tablets of the covenant he was carrying and destroyed the calf. On Moses' order, the tribe of Levi killed the idolaters (numbering some three thousand), and a period of mourning and supplication followed. Moses asked that God forgive the people and reascended the mount to receive a second set of tablets, which he then delivered into the camp. He began to teach his disciple Joshua and the elders the divine doctrine, which was then transmitted to the people. The teachings incorporated an extensive

household, tending his flocks and marrying his daughter, Zipporah.

After many years, as Moses led Jethro's sheep in search of grazing land, he came to Horeb, another name for the Sinai region, and there experienced a theophany — God revealing Himself in a burning bush that was not consumed. God commanded Moses to go with the elders to demand that Pharaoh free the Jewish people for a three-day journey into the wilderness in order to sacrifice to Him, knowing that Pharaoh would not grant such a request. To aid him in convincing the children of Israel that he was sent by God, Moses was given three miraculous signs; because he stammered, his brother Aaron was to act as his spokesman.

MOSES TO THE ISRAELITES

Hear O Israel, the Lord our God, the Lord is one.

You shall love the Lord your God with all your heart and with all your soul and with all your might.

These words which I command you this day you shall take to heart. You shall teach them diligently to your children. You shall recite them when you are at home and when you are away, morning and night. You shall bind them as a sign on your hand, they shall be a reminder above your eyes, and you shall inscribe them on the doorposts of your home and upon your gates. Deut. 6:4–9.

religio-legal-ethical code to regulate all aspects of life, which became the basis of the Jewish religion. Moses also supervised the construction of a portable cult center (the Tabernacle), which accompanied the Israelites through the desert and centuries later found a permanent home in the Jerusalem Temple.

The Israelites remained in the desert region between Egypt and the Promised Land for forty years, covering a large tract of land even though the distance to Canaan could have been traveled much more quickly by taking a direct route. During this time Moses forged them into a people with a homogenous culture and religious practices. They stopped at forty-two resting places and underwent a series of tests, sometimes lacking for food and water, but for most of the period they were based in one oasis — Kadesh Barnea. Moses reprimanded the people for their protests and finally, moved to anger, struck — instead of addressing — a rock at Meriba in order to produce water, for which he was punished by not being allowed to enter the Promised Land. Because of their having idolized the golden calf, the entire generation that witnessed the revelation at Mount Sinai was condemned to die in the desert, with a few exceptions. Joshua, Moses' disciple, was one, spared because of his faith. Moses established a judicial system to distribute the burden of adjudication, which was too much for a single leader to cope with alone.

In the fields of Moab on the border of Canaan, Moses addressed the people for the last time, summarizing the Sinaitic legislation and renewing the covenant with God. He passed his leadership to Joshua when he had finished, and then ascended Mount Nebo to view the Promised Land before his death. When he died, Moses was 120 years old, and his powers had not diminished. His burial place is unknown. Joshua led the people in conquering Canaan.

D. M. Beegle, *Moses, the Servant of Yahweh*, 1972.
M. Buber, *Moses*, 1969.
G. W. Coats, *Moses*, 1988.
M. and M. Roshwald, *Moses: Leader, Prophet, Man*, 1969.

MOSES BEN MAIMON SEE MAIMONIDES

MOZART, WOLFGANG AMADEUS (1756–1791), Austrian composer and pianist. Born in Salzburg, he was baptized Johannes Chrysostomus Wolfgangus Theophilus Mozart. His father, Leopold, was a busy and well-respected musician, who wrote a treatise on violin technique and was responsible for his children's initial music studies. Leopold himself was a composer, but his greatest contribution to the world of music is the music lessons he gave his young son.

Leopold Mozart taught his two surviving children, Wolfgang and his sister Maria Anna or Marianne ("Nannerl"), to play the piano. Mozart began his music studies at age four and a year later was composing. When he was six and his sister eleven, the family traveled to Munich. The three weeks in

Wolfgang Amadeus Mozart

Bavaria were far from successful, but the next "celebrity tour" to Vienna was astonishing. The entire city took notice of the two small children who performed wonders on the keyboard, including a recital for royalty at Schönbrunn Palace, and heralded by the Viennese aristocracy.

The Mozarts continued to tour, reaching Munich, Paris, and London. In London they were billed as "Miss Mozart of Eleven and Master Mozart of Seven Years of Age, Prodigies of Nature," and King *George III tested Mozart with improvisations. At times they were quite desperate but, on the whole, Europe took to the prodigies. After four years of touring, the Mozarts returned in 1766 to Salzburg, no wealthier than they had set out, but Mozart was kept busy with commissions from the archbishop of Salzburg and others (the archbishop had first doubted reports of Mozart's genius, and had him confined while he composed a cantata). Soon Mozart received an appointment as concertmaster to the archbishop.

As a child, Mozart had a quick tongue, which he never lost. His many letters to all the members of his family, written during his many tours, tell much about the boy and his character. They convey a sense of drama and of fun, sometimes obscene, and mirror his precocity. He twice went on visits to Italy and often to Vienna, where he was greatly influenced by Joseph Haydn, whom he called "master" and who regarded Mozart as a consummate composer. In Salzburg his father insisted on his studying the vio-

ON MOZART

Mozart's father, returning from church one day with a friend, found his son, aged five, busy writing. "What are you doing there, my little boy?" he asked. "I am composing a concerto for the harpsichord, and have almost got to the end of the first part." "Let me see your fine scrawl." "No; I have not finished it yet." The father, however, took the paper and showed his friend the sheet full of notes, which could hardly be deciphered for the blots of ink.

The two friends at first laughed heartily at this scribbling; but after a little time when the father had looked at it with more attention, his eyes were fastened on the paper and, at length, overflowed with tears of joy and wonder. "Look, my friend," he said, "look. Everything is composed according to rule. It is a pity that the piece cannot be made any use of; but it is too difficult. Nobody would be able to play it." "It is a concerto," replied his little son, "and must be studied until it can be played properly. This is the way it should be played." This was the beginning of Mozart's composition.

lin, believing he would be the greatest violinist in Europe and, although he never made a reputation as a violinist, his familiarity with the instrument enabled him to compose five sublime violin concertos. Mozart, however, preferred to concentrate on the pianoforte, which had been only recently invented.

Growing increasingly discontented with life in Salzburg and with his position, he set out in 1777 on another journey, this time with his mother because the archbishop would not grant his father leave. He visited various German cities and Paris but was eventually summoned back to Salzburg where he had been appointed organist; he spent much time pouring out his compositions that included symphonies and music for the church. He also wrote an opera, *Idomeneo*, for the Munich carnival of 1781, which enjoyed a brief success. Increasingly angered by the archbishop, he eventually resigned and moved to Vienna, where in 1782 he married Constance Weber, a singer and daughter of a music copyist, a match of which his father disapproved. He was soon in financial difficulties, despite the success of his comic opera *The Abduction from the Seraglio*, which was patronized by the emperor. A hoped-for court appointment did not materialize and his money worries increased as his wife gave birth regularly at annual intervals (only two children survived, one to become an Austrian official, the other a musician of no significance). While the marriage was happy, Constance hardly appreciated him and he suffered from loneliness. He found great solace in Freemasonry, and his letters contain many Ma-

sonic allusions, as does his last great opera, *The Magic Flute*. For years he struggled in Vienna; Joseph Haydn was indignant that he received no court appointment, despite the emperor's enjoyment of his music. Only in 1787, after the performance of some of his greatest works, was he appointed chamber musician and court composer to the emperor, but the meager salary barely covered his rent.

His great operas resulted from a happy collaboration with the libretto writer Lorenzo da Ponte, an Italian Jew who had become a priest. *The Marriage of Figaro* was premiered in Vienna and *Don Giovanni* in Prague from where the commission had emanated.

His last years were spent with ongoing financial problems, partly due to his wife's inability to manage the household practically. Despite being continually beset by money worries he could divorce himself from all his troubles when he was composing and produced a series of masterpieces — operas, symphonies, and concertos, chamber and piano works that have become great treasures in the world's musical heritage. His famous last three symphonies were composed within two months. His opera *Don Giovanni* failed to please the public, and the emperor commented, "It is divine but not meat for my Viennese," to which Mozart responded, "We must give them time to chew it."

After the emperor, *Joseph II, died in 1790, his successor, Leopold II, failed to renew Mozart's appointment as Kapellmeister, later making him only the assistant. Mozart's discouragement was accentuated by the ill-health of himself and his wife. His last triumph was *The Magic Flute*, but the excitement it engendered came too late.

Mozart was offered a generous payment by a mysterious stranger "dressed all in grey" to compose a requiem mass, on condition that he should not try to discover his patron's identity. Mozart became convinced that the stranger was the angel of death presaging his own demise. He fell sick and on what was to be his deathbed worked feverishly at the requiem. He fell unconscious after singing the opening bars of the "Lacrymosa." He was buried in a pauper's grave, which within a few weeks was no longer identifiable. The mysterious stranger proved to have been the steward of a nobleman who after Mozart's death had the work performed as his own composition.

A. Einstein, *Mozart*, 1946.
B. Hastings, *Wolfgang Amadeus Mozart: A Guide to Research*, 1989.
I. Keys, *Mozart: His Music in his Life*, 1980.
S. E. Schenk, *Mozart*, 1975.

MUHAMMAD (c. 570–632), founder of Islam. Muhammad was born in the city of Mecca in Arabia, to a merchant family of the Quraish tribe. Mecca was then an important religious center for the local peoples, housing the Kaaba shrine, with the maintenance of which the Quarish were involved.

Since the earliest biographies of Muhammad date from more than one hundred years after his death, there is little substantial information about the prophet's life: much of the material available is of an apocryphal nature. Sources agree that Muhammad's was orphaned at an early age and was raised by his uncle, Abu Talib. A successful merchant by the age of twenty-five, he married Khadija, a widow fifteen years his senior.

Contact with the many Christian and Jewish inhabitants of the region caused Muhammad to question the pagan beliefs of his tribe. He came to believe that a new religion, based on divine commandments, was needed to unite the warring Arab tribes. This idea was not unique to Muhammad; many Christian and Jewish leaders had predicted the coming of a new prophet — according to some legends, rabbis, monks, and magicians were already pointing to Muhammad as the longed-for teacher.

As Muhammad neared forty his preoccupation with religious matters intensified. He would spend long days fasting and praying in the deserts outside Mecca. During one such vigil, later referred to as the Night of Destiny, the angel Gabriel appeared to him, telling him that God (Allah), who had "created man of a blood clot," was now calling Muhammad to be His messenger.

Muhammad later explained that he was only a channel through which God or Gabriel spoke. Khadija, who was the first to believe in the veracity of her husband's visions, encouraged him to declare himself the prophet of Allah. She is therefore considered the first convert to Islam. As Muhammad attracted a following, his revelations were transcribed. Many were later collated to form the Koran — the holy scripture of Islam, universally regarded as a masterpiece of Arabic poetry and prose — while others, known as hadiths (a record of Muhammad's words and deeds) were similarly transmitted and form the basis of much of Islamic law and tradition.

Members of Muhammad's native tribe were hostile to Muhammad's new faith. His opposition to their traditional idolatrous beliefs threatened the revenues they enjoyed from stewardship of the pagan sanctuary in the Kaaba. With the death of Abu Talib in 619, Muhammad was deprived of a powerful protector and felt increasingly insecure in Mecca. Meanwhile, small groups of Muhammad's supporters had introduced the new religion to the city of Yathrib (Medina), whose faithful now offered him sanctuary. In Mecca, the new head of the Quraish had threatened to kill him. On the evening of July 16, 622, Muhammad entered the Kaaba, smashed the idols, and began his flight to Medina, known as the *hejira*. This date marks the beginning of the Islamic calendar.

In Medina, Muhammad formalized his religion's creed, basing it on five articles of faith: belief in the One God, Allah; belief in benign and wrathful spirits (angels and *jinn*); acceptance of the Koran as the authenic word of God; acceptance of the revelations

---

THE WORDS OF THE KORAN

- God — there is no god but He, the Living, the Self-subsistent.
- Slumber does not seize Him nor sleep. To Him belongs whatsoever is in the Earth. Who is there that shall intercede with Him save by His Will? He know what is present with men and what shall befall them, and nought of His knowledge do they comprehend, except what He wills. His Throne is wide as the Heavens and the Earth, and the keeping of them does not weary Him. And he is the High, the Mighty One....

---

of the prophets and of Muhammad, the apostle of God; and belief in reward of the righteous, punishment of the wicked, and a future Day of Judgment. While he preached tolerance of other monotheistic religions, true believers, known as Muslims were commanded to make a profession of faith (the *shahada,* consisting of the formula, "There is no God but Allah and Muhammad is his prophet"), conduct a series of prayers and obeisances five times daily, pay the *zakat* tithe, fast during the month of Ramadan, and make the *haj* (pilgrimage to Mecca) at least once. Many of his revelations were concerned with even the most mundane secular matters, covering specific social, moral, and political issues and he enjoyed the unquestioning obedience of believers.

As converts flocked to Medina, there were severe food shortages. Raids, some under Muhammad's leadership, were conducted against the passing caravans of his Quraish rivals. One fifth of the spoils were set aside for religious and charitable purposes; raiders were promised paradise if slain.

At first, Muhammad anticipated that the local Christian and Jewish population would embrace his religion eagerly. Their reluctance to do so led to strained relations between the communities and the abandonment of many rituals (such as facing Jerusalem when praying) adopted from these rival faiths.

With a strengthened grip on the Medina area and the conversion of many influential Meccans to Islam, Muhammad was in a position to negotiate a ten-year truce with the Quraish enabling his followers to make the pilgrimage to the Kaaba. Many of his followers, however, adopted a more bellicose attitude and encouraged him to seek a pretense to take Mecca. An opportunity was provided by the Meccans in 630, when they broke the pact by abandoning their neutrality in a local dispute. Muhammad marched on the city, which surrendered without a fight. As the city's new ruler, he declared a general amnesty and swept the Kaaba clean of everything but the Black Stone, consecrating Mecca as the holy city of Islam. Soon, all of Arabia accepted Muhammad's religion and rule. For the remaining two years of his life, Muhammad governed justly, his severity leavened by frequent acts of mercy.

Even as ruler of all Arabia, Muhammad continued to practice a simple, austere lifestyle. The absence of a male heir (all but two of his wives were barren), led many to believe that Muhammad was immortal, although he made no such claim. As news spread that the prophet was dying, the faithful crowded around his home. News of his decease was broken to them by *Abu Bakr with the words: "If you are worshipers of Muhammad, know that he is dead. If you are worshipers of God, know that God is living and does not die."

Within a century of Muhammad's death, armies sweeping out of Arabia initiated the process of converting the Middle East, northwest India, North Africa, and Spain to Islam. Succeeding centuries saw Islam become the dominant religion in Malaya, Indonesia, Turkey, and the Balkans. Today it remains a vital and fast-growing religion, set to overtake Catholicism as the world's largest by the end of the century. Muhammad is now the most popular boy's name in the world.

T. Andrae, *Mohammed, The Man and His Faith*, 1971.
K. Armstrong, *Muhammad*, 1992.
M. A. Cook, *Muhammad*, 1983.
J. B. Glubb, *The Life and Times of Muhammad*, 1970.

MUSSOLINI, BENITO (1883–1945), Italian prime minister, first of Europe's Fascist dictators, who called himself *Il Duce* ("the Leader"). Mussolini would often exaggerate the degree of poverty he had to suffer as a child; in fact he grew up in a middle-class home in his birthplace of Romagna, where his father was a blacksmith and socialist journalist and his mother a school teacher. Nonetheless, his father's drinking and extravagant spending on his mistresses often caused the family hardship.

An aggressive and unruly child, who was twice expelled from schools for knifing fellow-pupils, Mussolini was also very intelligent; he easily passed his final examinations and qualified as a schoolteacher. He soon, however, realized that he was wholly unsuited to such a career and left for Switzerland, where he spent several months living a hand-to-mouth existence financed by a succession of temporary jobs.

Mussolini had inherited his father's socialist tendencies, and while in Switzerland sought to further his own political education through voracious, albeit superficial, reading of a wide variety of philosophers and political scientists. While he was particularly influenced by the existentialist philosophy of Henri *Bergson, he turned toward an eclectic mélange of sources to buttress a radical socialist philosophy that advocated violent change. His magnetism and charisma, allied with his burgeoning rhetorical talents, made him an arresting speaker

and political journalist; he was already well known (and marked as a troublemaker by the authorities) by the time he returned to Italy in 1904.

Mussolini's trade union activism and political extremism led to his arrest and imprisonment in his native country but also earned him considerable kudos among his political peers. As early as 1908 he was calling for the amalgamation of the working classes "in one formidable bundle [*fascio*]." His journal *La Lotta di Classe* (The Class Struggle) was so successful that he was soon called to edit *Avanti*, the flagship broadsheet of Italian socialism. When World War I broke out, he opposed Italian involvement, in line with socialist policy. However, he broke with the mainstream of the socialist movement and came to advocate and support Italy's entry into the war. Undeterred by his expulsion from the socialist party, he launched the paper *Il Popolo d'Italia* and went on to serve in the Italian army. Wounded in action he became vehemently antisocialist.

By now, Mussolini was openly advocating the emergence of a dictator, "a man who is ruthless and energetic enough to make a clean sweep." In 1919 he founded the organization of Fasci de Combattimento, taking as its symbol the *fascinae* of the lictors, the ancient Roman symbol of authority — the Fascist movement was born. Mussolini's superb oratory and macho bombasticism, and the regimented militarism of the Fascist blackshirts (Mussolini took the idea for their uniform from the dress of anarchists) attracted many supporters in an Italy traumatized by postwar economic depression. In 1922 a Fascist-organized march on Rome to protest the calling of a general strike led to the fall of the government and King Victor Emmanuel III's call on Mussolini to head a new government; he was soon installed as Italy's youngest prime minister.

The Italian elections of 1924 confirmed Mussolini in power. The Fascists used ballot-box fraud to make sure of the result, but Mussolini and his movement were genuinely popular in Italy anyway. He tackled widespread unemployment by initiating a series of massive public works (such as the draining of the Pontine marshes), while also managing to improve the conditions of workers. Under his leadership a hitherto moribund Italy achieved some notable economic successes (quickly exaggerated by party propagandists), and Il Duce was regarded as a superman both at home and by his many admirers abroad.

Between 1925 and 1929 Mussolini's dictatorial regime devised its "corporative state." Fascist party labor unions gradually replaced existing socialist and Catholic unions, using a mixture of brutal physical coercion and incentives to ensure support, and were eventually recognized as the sole legitimate representatives of the workers. These unions were then grouped into nationwide federations, alongside which there were national employers' federations. A ministry of corporations (of which Mussolini was minister for many years) oversaw the whole structure, in which strikes were

Fascist political poster of 1934, featuring a mask of Mussolini

outlawed and all disputes settled by arbitration based on the 1927 Labor Charter defining the rights of workers. This system enabled the dictatorship to regulate the economy and maintain rigid control over industry, while the Fascist party's auxiliary organization the Opera Nazionale Dopolavoro (National After-Work Organization) provided a variety of social and recreational leisure-time activities for the workers. Even so, Italy, too, suffered the effects of the economic depression that hit Europe in 1930.

The attempt to impinge upon all aspects of citizens' lives and the widespread use of propaganda techniques characterized the regime. Moreover, in the course of a series of conflicts within his party, Mussolini had managed to prevent the Fascist party from becoming a rival power to himself, in the process converting the Fascists from a hooligan mob to a collection of time-serving careerists fit for little more than the execution of his will. Party secretaries of low caliber succeeded each other with ever-increasing frequency, leaving Mussolini as the only constant power in the Fascist and state apparatus, with party members dependent for their continued power and influence on him alone. His 1929 concordat with the Vatican gained him the full recognition of the papacy, further consolidating his prestige and authority.

Had Mussolini confined himself to domestic affairs he might have retained the sympathy and support of the world community, but his popularity foundered on his desire for foreign conquest. He believed that a rejuvenated Italy needed overseas dominions if it was to reascend to the glorious heights attained by the Roman Empire of antiquity, the Italian golden age he sought to re-create. Therefore, in October 1935 the Italian army invaded Abyssinia (now Ethiopia); in 1936 Mussolini was able to announce that Italy once more had an empire. The League of Nations condemned the aggression but took no action. Mussolini was later to admit that had Italy been embargoed, as some had advocated, he would have been unable to retain Abyssinia for more than a few months.

Mussolini's support for General Francisco *Franco's Fascist Nationalists in the 1936–1939 Spanish civil war ended any possibility of reconciliation with Britain or France. Il Duce's new ally was Germany's Nazi chancellor, Adolf *Hitler. Anti-Jewish legislation was enacted in Italy in 1938 and the Rome-Berlin Axis was formalized in the 1939 Pact of Steel, just months before German aggression against Poland precipitated World War II.

Mussolini did not wish to enter the war, rightly believing that Italy's chances of economic recovery depended upon peace, and hoped that Hitler would quickly fulfill his territorial ambitions, but in 1940 he felt that he had no option but to launch an attack on Greece through Albania. The campaign resulted in a humiliating defeat for Italian forces, who had to be extricated by their unwilling allies.

Mussolini became the ineffectual puppet of the Nazis and faced opposition and unpopularity at home; the July 1943 Allied invasion of Sicily heralded the defeat of Italy. Mussolini was dismissed by the king and imprisoned on Gran Sasso in the Abruzzi mountains. The Germans managed to rescue him and set him up as head of their puppet administration headquartered in Salo in northern Italy, where he became increasingly estranged from reality and belatedly returned to his earlier socialist and collectivist ideals. As the Axis forces crumbled, Mussolini and his mistress were captured and shot to death by Italian Communist partisans as he tried in vain to head for the Valtellina mountains and a last defense. The man who had been a popular hero in his homeland died unmourned by a nation he had led into a costly and unnecessary war.

R. Collier, *Duce*, 1971.

A. J. Joes, *Mussolini*, 1982.

D. Mack Smith, *Mussolini*, 1981.

MUTSUHITO (Meiji; 1852–1912), Japanese emperor. During his forty-five-year rule, Japan emerged from two hundred and fifty years of cultural and economic isolation to become a major world power. Mutsuhito was a hardworking, austere and sincere ruler who ordered the sweeping reforms which would modernize Japanese society under one central government in a remarkably short period of time.

The second son of Emperor Komei, Mutsuhito took the throne at the age of fourteen, upon his father's death. The following year he was formally enthroned and, in a Shinto ceremony, selected a slip of paper that bore the Chinese characters "bright" and "rule": taken together these read "Meiji," which was the name (which may be translated as "enlightened rule") subsequently used to designate his reign. Mutsuhito, unlike his father, was dedicated to Japan's modernization. In order to achieve this task he first sought to consolidate his power under one central government. For this it was necessary to subjugate the Tokugawa Shogunate which had long ruled the country. When the emperor established three ministerial posts, Yoshinobu Tokugawa, leader of the shogunate, lead his forces against the loyalists in the Battle of Fushimi-Toba (1868). His defeat, and the unwavering commitment of the subsequently-assembled council to the restoration of imperial power, marked the beginning of the era known as the Meiji Restoration.

Later in 1868 Mutsuhito took the "Charter Oath of Five Principles," which launched the country on its course of Westernization. The charter claimed that a council chamber would be established, that all classes would achieve their "just aspirations," that wisdom would be sought throughout the world, and that strange customs of the past would be discarded. The shoguns, having surrendered to the emperor, gave him their capital, Edo. Mutsuhito's move to Edo and his proclamation that it would be the capital of all Japan, under the name Tokyo, was a sign of the triumph of the forces of modernization.

From his new residence in Tokyo, the emperor passed the laws which ushered Japan into the modern era. In 1871 the country was divided into prefectures and the feudal system was officially abolished. The imperial army was expanded and the first railroad was built between Tokyo and Yokohama. A new educational system was implemented in 1872, Japan adopted the Gregorian calendar, and a senate was instituted in 1875. In 1877 the government successfully faced its first test of power when the Satsuma Rebellion broke out: retaliating against Mutsuhito's attempts to do away with them, the ancient order of the Samurai led a forty-thousand-man army into battle against imperial forces numbering sixty thousand, but were defeated.

In 1881 Mutsuhito promised a constitution within ten years. By 1885 a cabinet system had been established to replace the previous oligarchical system, with the constitution being promulgated in 1889; the following year a national assembly was instituted. The constitution declared that the emperor was "sacred and inviolable" and that legislative power would be exercised in conjunction with the national assembly. However, the emperor was to maintain absolute command of the army and navy, and retained the sole right to declare war, make peace, and confer all ranks and titles.

Under Mutsuhito's control of the armed forces, Japan gained territory and commanded respect abroad. The emperor played a crucial role in Japan's victories in the Sino-Japanese War (1894–1895) and the Russo-Japanese War (1904–1905).

After the Anglo-Japanese Alliance of 1902, the British prince, Arthur of Connaught, visited Japan and conferred upon the emperor the Order of the Garter, making him the first Oriental monarch ever to receive this decoration. As a result of Japan's victories in war, Mutsuhito acquired the beginnings of an empire. The annexation of Korea to the Japanese Empire in 1910 was a significant accomplishment for a country which had emerged from feudalism less than fifty years earlier.

P. Akamatsu, *Meiji 1868: Revolution and Counter-Revolution in Japan*, 1972.

W. Beasley, *The Meiji Restoration*, 1972.

H. Bolitho, *Meiji Japan*, 1977.

R. W. Bowen, *Rebellion and Democracy in Meiji Japan*, 1980.

H. A. Yunesuko, *Meiji Japan through Contemporary Sources*, 1970.

N

NANAK (Guru Nanak; 1469-c.1538), Indian religious reformer and teacher (*guru*); founder and propagator of the Sikh religion. Nanak was born in the Punjab village of Talwandi. His father, Kalu, was a member of a caste of traders and merchants. Because of Nanak's reputation as a holy man and prophet it is difficult to distinguish fact from legend about his life. It seems that at a young age he was already given to religious contemplation; his questions may have prompted one of his libertine school teachers to become a *sadhu*, or Hindu ascetic. Much to his parents' distress, Nanak often sat in the forest meditating. Kalu attempted to cure his son's lack of interest in worldly affairs by giving him twenty rupees with which to conduct business. Setting out to buy salt, Nanak encountered a group of *sadhus*. After spending many long hours discussing religion with them, the young man discovered that they had not eaten for four days and promptly used his money to provide them with food.

Nanak was subsequently sent to Sultanpur, where his father had arranged for him to be a storekeeper in a royal granary. There he received a good salary, married, and had two sons, but he spent most of his money on the poor, keeping only what he needed to survive. He spent most nights praying in the forest. At the time, India was torn by religious rivalries between Hindus and Muslims. Once, after spending three days secluded in prayer (during which time he was thought to have drowned), Nanak emerged from the forest bearing a message from God that "there is no Hindu and no Muslim." Taking only one companion, he returned to the forest to become a *sadhu*. There he wrote the devotional hymns comprising the *Adi Granth*, the sacred book of the Sikh religion.

Nanak's new religion attempted to merge Hinduism and Islam. It spoke of the equality of man before God and denounced the priests and Brahmans, who presumed to be intermediaries between man and God. Despite his father's objections, Nanak set out on four missionary journeys, traveling to Benares, Gaya, Dharmasala, and Delhi. Legend states that he was imprisoned by the Mogul emperor *Babur while on this expedition. The latter, however, upon hearing of Nanak's wisdom, asked to

---

FROM THE WRITINGS OF NANAK

- Pilgrimages, penances, compassion, and almsgiving bring a little merit, the size of a sesame seed.
- There is one God, eternal truth is his name, Creator of all things, and the all-pervading spirit. Fearless and without hatred, timeless and formless, Beyond birth and death, self-enlightened.
- Thou art part and parcel of all things equally, O Creator; Thou must feel for all men and all nations.
- He cannot be installed like an idol, Nor can man shape his likeness.
- Thou watchest all creation, Where sounds of musical melodies,
  Of instruments playing, minstrels singing,
  Are joined in divine harmony.

---

see the prisoner; after several hours of conversation, Babur granted Nanak royal protection. On his second voyage Nanak traveled south, possibly reaching Ceylon; on his third journey he went to Kashmir. Nanak's final trip took him to the west. He may have reached Mecca where, it is reported, he came into conflict with local religious officials. On being asked at a Muslim shrine how he dared put his feet in the direction of the House of God, Nanak retorted, "How can you not?"

Upon completing his voyages, Nanak settled in the town of Kartarpur, where he continued to preach but renounced the life of a *sadhu*, claiming that moderation was the true way to achieve holiness. The remainder of the *Adi Granth* was collated by his successors Baba Angad and Arjun, who continued to propagate the Sikh religion after Nanak's death.

Nanak attracted both Hindu and Muslim followers, each group promoting its own religious values in the new religion. Nanak foresaw that upon his death the two camps would be at odds over whether to cremate or bury his body and so bade them stand at opposite sides of his bier and spread flowers over both sides; they were to follow the tradition of the side whose flowers did not wither. Upon his death, the two groups remained by the body throughout the night to await the outcome. Tradition has it that they woke the next morning and found that the body had disappeared.

C. H. Payne, *A Short History of the Sikhs*, 1970.

J. Singh, *The Religious Philosophy of Guru Nanak*, 1983.

NANSEN, FRIDTJOF (1861–1930), Norwegian explorer and humanitarian; Nansen was an active, curious boy who loved sports, especially skiing. He won Norway's long distance skating championship once, Norway's cross-country ski race often, and broke the world's mile skating record. He also enjoyed hiking through Norway's forests and mountains ("I used to pass weeks at a time alone in the forest. I disliked having any equipment for my expeditions. I managed with a crust of bread and broiled my fish on the embers. I loved to live like Robinson Crusoe up there in the wilderness."). All these extracurricular interests kept him from doing his best scholastically, but by concentrating on his studies at examination time he was accepted at university.

Nansen was interested in science and decided to study zoology "as that promised more fun, more shooting, and out-of-door life." In 1882 he sailed on a sealing ship to pursue zoological research in the Arctic. This voyage was a precursor to his own exploration expeditions in several respects: it introduced him to the Arctic, it aroused his interest in Greenland, and it demonstrated his ability to work well with others, who liked him for his good humor, sporting abilities, and willingness to work. After his return, Nansen became a curator in the Bergen Museum. For the next six years he worked on microscopical anatomy, publishing two important scientific works. Sometimes his active nature chafed against this sedentary way of life, but his father, whom he greatly loved and respected, was not well and Nansen did not try to form an expedition to explore Greenland until after his death.

Nansen's plans to explore Greenland's interior on skis was greeted with skepticism and derision, and the Norwegian government refused to finance the scheme. His 1888 expedition's route from Greenland's unoccupied east coast to its occupied west coast was determined by Nansen's personal philosophy which he later expressed as "to burn my boats and demolish the bridges behind me. Then one loses no time in looking behind when one should have quite enough to do in looking ahead. Then there is no choice for you or your men but forward. You have to do or die!" Nansen's care in selecting the expedition's members and provisions enabled it to cross successfully Greenland's inland sea of ice and prove that it contained no habitable oases. Nansen

returned, famous, to Norway in 1889. He married, went on an international lecture tour, and wrote a book about his Greenland expedition, which was published in 1891.

The North Pole expedition was based on Nansen's theory that over several years a ship would naturally drift across the North Polar basin to Greenland. Nansen's 1893–1896 polar expedition — in a special ship, the *Fram*, designed to resist the pressures of Arctic ice — proved the correctness of this theory and discovered most of what is known about the Arctic basin. During the expedition's second year Nansen and a comrade set out by dog sled for the North Pole and approached 160 miles nearer to it than any previous explorers.

Appointed professor of zoology at Oslo University after his return, Nansen occupied himself with his family, writing books, scientific research, international lecture tours, and advising Arctic and Antarctic explorers. He also played a key role in Norway's liberation from Swedish rule by influencing public opinion in its favor, persuading Prince Charles of Denmark to become Norway's king, and serving as Norway's first minister to England.

Norway was neutral during World War I and Nansen carried out crucial wartime negotiations with the United States to ensure the country's food supply. Appalled at the tremendous suffering and upheaval caused by the war, Nansen used his energy and personal prestige to organize the postwar repatriation of prisoners of war (succeeding — with a budget of £400,000 — in repatriating four hundred thousand), and relief for Russian, Greek, and Armenian refugees. He firmly believed that the League of Nations was the world's hope for the future, but when it — and individual governments — rejected his appeals for help to fight the famine in Russia, he personally campaigned for famine aid throughout the world; the response saved millions from starvation. He was awarded the Nobel Peace Prize in 1922 for his humanitarian efforts, which continued until just before his death. After he died, the Nansen International Office for Refugees was established in Geneva. The documents it issued to the stateless were known as "Nansen passports."

L. Nansen Hoyer, *Nansen: A Family Portrait*, 1955.

A. de Selincourt, *Nansen*, 1957.

P. Vogt, *Nansen: Explorer, Scientist, Humanitarian*, 1962.

NAPOLEON I (Napoleon Bonaparte; 1769–1821), French emperor. Napoleon Bonaparte was born in Corsica but his father, a small landowner who originally supported Pasquale di Paoli's fight for Corsican independence, became pro-French in return for French recognition of his claims to nobility. This made Napoleon eligible, at ten, for acceptance into French military academies for aristocrats, where his schoolmates' scorn for his poverty, Corsican origins, and unfamiliarity with French (Italian was his native tongue) made him an ardent Corsican patriot.

Napoleon I in his coronation robes

ship's leader, Paul François de Barras. When Napoleon married Barras's widowed former mistress — the lazy, unfaithful, but kind opportunist, Josephine de Beauharnais, with whom he was passionately in love — Barras gave him command of France's Italian campaign as a wedding present.

Napoleon's Italian campaign was a resounding success even though he had no previous experience in large scale military operations. He reveled in being greeted as a liberator by an Italian population rejoicing at the defeat of their Austrian masters; negotiated a peace treaty; and founded a new Italian Republic on his own initiative (massive shipments of booty reconciled the French government to his independence). He also made sure his family shared in his victory: his brother Joseph became rich supplying Napoleon's army.

Despite the debacle of his 1798–1799 Egyptian expedition against the British, which aimed at blocking Britain's lucrative India trade but ended with Napoleon abandoning his troops and escaping back to France, France's bourgeoisie welcomed the 1799 coup that made Napoleon First Consul, feeling that only he was strong enough to bring France peace and stability. In 1801 his second Italian campaign forced the Austrians to make peace and his concordat with the papacy gave the blessing of the church to his rule, while the 1802 Treaty of Amiens ended the war with England. Highly intelligent and hard working, Napoleon instigated much-needed administrative reforms, established the Bank of France, centralized civil administration, reorganized education, reformed the legal system, completing the codification of civil law (the Napoleonic Code), stabilized the currency, and founded a bureaucracy. He also imposed strict censorship, and 90 percent of political newspapers ceased publication.

In 1802 Napoleon became "consul for life" with the right to choose his successor; he crowned himself emperor in 1804. Meanwhile, Britain ended the uneasy peace between the two countries by declaring war in 1803. The British naval victory at Trafalgar in 1805 reasserted British control of the seas and ended Napoleon's hopes of invading England. However, the stunning French victory over Austria at Austerlitz (1805) convinced Europe of the invincibility of Napoleon's army and of the need to accede to his wishes. By 1808 he controlled the Continent, having defeated its armies with his combination of military genius, phenomenal luck, and swift decisiveness. He reshaped the political map of Europe by installing puppet rulers (often members of his own family) and implementing republican governmental frameworks in conquered territories; in theory, Europe remained closed to British trade.

It little concerned Napoleon that this control and blockade existed more on paper than in reality. What did bother him was that his empire — his bid for immortality — had no heir. His love for Josephine had long since faded into mutual infidelity but he appreciated the benefits derived from her popularity and

When his father died, leaving his family in desperate financial straits, Napoleon became the real head of the household, supporting them with his salary after entering the army at sixteen, when he became a second lieutenant and was assigned to the artillery. Peacetime garrison duty was undemanding and he spent much of his time with his family in Corsica, immersing himself in books about political philosophy.

The French Revolution in 1789 ended Paoli's exile from Corsica, but he was only interested in an independent Corsica and had no use for republican principles or Napoleon. In 1792 Napoleon returned to Corsica to oppose him openly. Napoleon lost his army commission because of his prolonged absence, and he and his family had to flee to France when his attempt to seize Ajaccio failed.

A known supporter of the revolution, Napoleon made his name during the wars of the French Revolution (1792–1802); his brilliant use of artillery played a key role in the 1793 siege of Toulon. The Thermidor coup d'état, which ended the Reign of Terror, however, saw a temporary decline in his fortunes: he was even imprisoned briefly in 1794. The ability and expediency with which he suppressed the mobs that threatened the Thermidoreans' corrupt rule, however, made him a favorite of the dictator-

NAPOLEON IN HIS OWN WORDS

- Power is my mistress. I have worked too hard at her conquest to allow anyone to take her away from me.
- What is history but a fable agreed upon?
- From the sublime to the ridiculous is but a step.
- Treaties are observed only as long as they are in harmony with interests.
- England is a nation of shopkeepers.
- In order to have good soldiers, a nation must be always at war.
- It is worse than a crime — it is a blunder.
- You must not fight too often with one enemy or you will teach him all your art of war.
- It is the cause, not the death, that makes the martyr.

skills as a hostess. She was barren, however, so Napoleon divorced her and married the Austrian princess Marie Louise in 1810. France rejoiced with him at the birth of his only legitimate child.

Napoleon's insatiable ambition led him to look for more battles to fight and more lands to bring under his control. France was war-weary, tired of the unending conscriptions. Deserters and draft evaders abounded, while the sale of government bonds dropped with news of renewed hostilities. Napoleon was indifferent to the needs of his soldiers for food, clothing, pay, and medical attention, regarding them as so much cannon fodder. Defeat began to shatter the myth of his invincibility. Spain was the first to stand up to him and he became involved there in a long guerilla war, in which the Spanish were supported by British troops. Then the Austrians rose against him, followed by the Russians.

Napoleon's defeats were distinguished by military blunders, misfortune, and indecisiveness in battle; inadequate supplies and/or supply lines; disdain for the wishes of allies (including relatives or subordinates he had rewarded with a throne); emphasis on the collecting, guarding, and transporting of booty rather than military matters; abandonment (on four separate occasions) of his defeated army to escape back to France.

Napoleon's Grand Army was depleted by his disastrous invasion of Russia in 1812. The Russians pulled back beyond Moscow, destroying everything as they retreated, and when Napoleon in desperation sought to withdraw, his army was destroyed by the Cossacks and the wintry conditions. His regime collapsed after the Grand Army's defeat at the Battle of the Nations (1813), and he was deposed by the Allies in 1814. He was granted the island of Elba in the Mediterranean as a principality, given a lavish annual income, and allowed to keep the title of emperor, but a Bourbon king, Louis XVIII, mounted the French throne.

The new Bourbon rule was much more liberal than Napoleon's, but it delegitimized the Revolution. Resentment of this was behind France's enthusiastic acceptance of Napoleon's return after ten months' exile in Elba. The army went over to him without a fight, the Bourbon king fled, and once again Napoleon was in control of the country. However the France he ruled was once again a republic, not an empire, and he chafed under the strict limitations placed on his powers. A new anti-Napoleon international coalition was determined to overthrow him, and he was eager to fight it, convinced that victory in battle would restore his absolute rule. Instead, his second reign ended after one hundred days with his defeat at Waterloo in 1815. He abdicated and was taken, at the age of forty-six, to the South Atlantic island of Saint Helena where he stayed, a British prisoner for the rest of his life.

One of history's great figures and a military and organizational genius, Napoleon emerged at the beginning of his career with a message of hope and liberation, spurred by the noble ideals of the French Revolution. However, these were discarded under the urge for power that led him to unbridled expansionism and caused Europe to unite against him, eventually achieving his downfall. Inside France, he introduced much-needed reforms that determined the nature of modern France and long outlived him, with the Napoleonic Code inspiring lawmakers in many lands. In the words of Johann Wolfgang *Goethe, "he went forth to seek Virtue, but since she was not to be found, he got Power." Of small stature but charismatic personality, he has never ceased to fascinate.

L. Bergeron, *France Under Napoleon*, 1981.
A. Guerard, *Napoleon I*, 1969.
J. H. Kirchberger, *The French Revolution and Napoleon*, 1989.

NAPOLEON III (Louis-Napoleon; 1808–1873), French emperor. Charles-Louis Napoleon Bonaparte; the son of *Napoleon I's brother Louis and stepdaughter Hortense, lived his whole life in Napoleon's shadow. Born during his father's brief reign as king of Holland, he was the first Bonaparte to be a prince from birth. His father lost his throne when his determination to be more than Holland's puppet king displeased Napoleon. The restored Bourbon regime banished all Bonapartes from France in 1815 and Louis-Napoleon's mother Hortense (estranged from her husband) spent years traveling Europe seeking a country that would withstand French pressure and grant her refuge. She was finally allowed to settle in Bavaria (where her brother was the king's son-in-law).

Louis-Napoleon's character was shaped by his Bavarian childhood, and he became much more German than French, speaking French with a German accent all his life. Other childhood influences were his sternly republican private tutor, his extremely religious (after the loss of her lover) mother, and prolonged visits to his Bonaparte relations who instilled in him an admiration for Napoleon's genius.

The 1830 insurrections that flared through Europe (toppling the Bourbons from the French throne and replacing them with the Orléans) threw Italy into turmoil. Vitally interested in the dream of a united Italian nation, Louis-Napoleon participated in the abortive Romagna rebellion and only Hortense's daring ingenuity and the help of the future Pope *Pius IX saved him when it failed.

Louis-Napoleon became the Bonapartist pretender for the French throne after Napoleon I's only legitimate son died in 1832, and embarked on an extensive public relations campaign to restore credibility to Bonapartism. His 1832 pamphlet, asserting that France could only combine glory and liberty under an emperor, publicized both his name and his cause (he was an accomplished political writer); complimentary copies of his knowledgeable Artillery Manual were sent to members of the French military, establishing courteous relations with them.

Louis-Napoleon's farcical attempts to stage coups by winning over the French army (in Strasbourg in 1836, and in Boulogne in 1840) were unsuccessful: he was not sufficiently dashing or stylish to capture soldiers' imagination and loyalty. Exiled to America after Strasbourg, he might have sunk into obscurity if the French king, Louis-Philippe, had not imprisoned him in the Castle of Ham when he returned to Switzerland to be with his dying mother, thereby winning him international sympathy and publicity; after six months he escaped to England in 1846.

Louis-Napoleon went to Paris at the outbreak of the Revolution of 1848, but the provisional government sent him back to England. However, his name and his disassociation from the failed attempts of the various French factions to gain control of the government and maintain order led to his election to the constituent assembly a few months later. He returned to Paris and prepared to run for the presidency, supported by the Catholic-royalist Party of Order, which considered him a harmless nonentity it could use.

Louis-Napoleon was a modern politician in terms of his regard for public opinion, use of propaganda, and his election campaigns. His campaign for the presidency of France was masterly: evoking the Napoleonic legend, he promised to bring back the days of national glory while keeping the peace, and give the bourgeoisie order and prosperity while helping the poor. His victory was overwhelming, winning the support of the vast majority of the French people, and when the assembly voted against amending the constitution to enable him to run for president a second time, he overthrew the government in a bloody coup d'état, brought in a new constitution, restored the empire, and became Napoleon III.

As emperor, he seldom used the police and military to suppress rioting and civil disorder, not because he had any compunction about so doing but because, except for a brief period in 1851–1852 and again

---

THOUGHTS ON NAPOLEON III

- Because we have had Napoleon the Great, must we have Napoleon the Little?

Victor Hugo

- A great unrecognized incapacity.

Otto von Bismarck

- Copies never succeed.

Lajos Kossuth

---

after an 1858 assassination attempt by an Italian radical, there was no need. Political meetings were prohibited throughout most of his reign because they contributed to factional strife, but he instituted almost universal suffrage and men of every political persuasion participated in his government. The arts flourished; in the Second Empire there was freedom of speech, press and ideas — but not of action.

Describing himself as a socialist, Napoleon III used his government to enhance French prosperity and the welfare of the French people, promoting industry and agriculture, improving the transport infrastructure, and establishing credit institutions and mutual assistance societies. His concern for the welfare of the poor expressed itself in a variety of ways, from lowering the price of bread to constructing hygienic houses for laborers.

Louis-Napoleon married the Spanish countess Eugènie de Montijo in 1853, and they had one son. Eugènie was beautiful, fashionable, capricious, virtuous, and haughty — but not very wise or intelligent. She was devoted to her son, worked hard at being empress, conducting a brilliant court, and sought power to compensate for the pain of her husband's many infidelities. Feeling guilty and physically weak (he was incapacitated by repeated bladderstone attacks after 1860), Louis-Napoleon let Eugènie have power. Staunchly Catholic and determined to preserve her son's inheritance, her influence on France's foreign policy was catastrophic. She encouraged the preservation of the pope's rule over Rome, France's disastrous part in Archduke Maximilian's attempt to create a Mexican empire, and the territorial pretensions that led to France's defeat at the hands of Prussia and the consequent end of the empire in 1870.

Louis-Napoleon's interest in innovative military technology (modern artillery, armored warships, and military use of captive balloons) evidenced his interest and promotion of modern technology in general. He had mixed motives for his foreign military involvements — he firmly believed in the national right to self-determination and the use of international arbitration to solve Europe's problems, but to keep the support of French Catholics he helped restore the pope to Rome in 1849, withdrew his support of Piedmont in its war against Austria in 1859, and even preserved the pope's rule over Rome with French troops between 1860 and 1870.

The French army was badly in need of reform, but Louis-Napoleon's attempts to achieve this aroused enormous opposition, since the French did not want to admit that their army could not conquer Europe, while the bourgeoisie did not want to be subject to a general draft. Sick and weak, Louis-Napoleon could not control the territorial ambitions that led the country headlong into the Franco-Prussian War and his empire's fall in 1871. He went to live in England, where he continued to study technical and social problems, publish articles defending his politics, and suffer from bladderstones. He died between operations two years later.

J. Bierman, *Napoleon III and His Carnival Empire*, 1988.

W. H. Smith, *Napoleon III*, 1972.

J. M. Thompson, *Louis Napoleon and the Second Empire*, 1983.

NASSER, GAMAL ABDEL (1918–1970), Egyptian officer and statesman, president of Egypt (1956–1970).

Born in Bani Mor, Asyut district, son of a postal clerk, he graduated from secondary school in Cairo in 1936 and from the military academy in 1938. He served in Sudan and from 1941 was an instructor at the military academy. After advanced training at the military staff college he commanded a battalion in Egypt's expeditionary forces in the 1948 Palestine war and, with his battalion, was besieged in the "Faluja Pocket." In 1951 he was promoted to the rank of colonel and appointed lecturer at the military college.

Nasser was a leading member of a clandestine group, the Free Officers, conspiring to remove Egypt's old leadership, whom they held responsible for both the humiliating defeat of 1948 and all the rest of Egypt's ills. On July 22, 1952, they mounted a successful coup and took power, overthrowing King Farouk. General Muhammad Nagib was appointed to head the Revolutionary Council; according to some, he was a figurehead only, while its real leader was Nasser. In September Nagib took over the premiership and rivalry soon developed between Nagib and Nasser. In June 1953 Nasser became deputy premier and minister of the interior (while Nagib became president and retained the premiership).

In February 1954 the struggle between Nasser and Nagib came to a head. Demonstrations and counter-demonstrations took place and rival army units moved into position. In April the struggle was resolved and Nasser became prime minister. He now took action against the remnants of the old political parties, seen as potential sources of opposition, by

Gamal Abdel Nasser

conducting a series of purges and trials. An attempt on Nasser's life in October 1954 was ascribed to the Muslim Brotherhood and they in particular were severely suppressed; their leaders were put on show trials and some of them were executed.

From 1955 to 1956 Nasser's policies were presented as a new doctrine of Arab Socialism. He also set about to reshape Egypt's political system. In January 1956 a new constitution was proclaimed which made Islam the state religion and gave women the vote. In a referendum the same year, Nasser was elected president for a six-year term. Following the merger of Egypt and Syria in February 1958 he was elected president of the United Arab Republic (UAR); after the dissolution of the UAR in September 1961 he insisted on retaining for Egypt the official name of UAR and remained its president. Nasser convened a congress of so-called popular forces in 1962, founded a new ruling party — the Arab Socialist Union — and formulated a national charter as the basic Arab-Socialist doctrine of the party and the nation. In 1965 Nasser was elected president for a second six-year term.

In their first years of power, Nasser and his team had appeared moderate and pragmatic in their foreign and inter-Arab policy. In 1964 they reached a final agreement with Great Britain that had eluded all previous governments for some eight years, obtaining the abolition of the Treaty of 1936, the evacuation of British forces, and the termination of any special privileges for Britain. They also conceded (1952–1953) to the Sudan the right of self-determination, which all former rulers had denied.

In the mid-1950s Nasser began adopting increasingly activist, extremist-revolutionary policies. His growing inclination toward the Third World and a neutralist position led him to oppose the Baghdad Pact, a plan for a Middle East defense alliance linked to the West. The ensuing confrontation with the West coincided with Nasser's first appearance — at the 1955 Bandung Conference of Asian leaders — as a leading figure on the international scene and his emergence as one of the architects of a neutralist bloc. The confrontation also induced him to conclude an arms deal with Czechoslovakia in 1955, marking a budding alliance with the Soviet bloc. In 1956 the United States retaliated by denying Egypt aid (and inducing the World Bank to do likewise) for the Aswan High Dam, Nasser's pet project. This step led Nasser to obtain the aid denied by the West from the USSR. He then dramatically announced the nationalization of the Suez Canal, which had effectively been under British control since 1875. Western countries feared for their vital route through the canal for oil supplies; negotiations dragged on and showed little progress. Finally in October 1956, Britain and France took military action against Suez while, according to a prearranged plan, Israel invaded the Sinai peninsula, which it occupied in six days. The British and French, however, made no headway and after a few days of heavy pressure from the United Nations — and especially from the United States — had to call off their attack and withdraw from Egyptian soil.

From that crisis of 1956 Nasser emerged triumphant as the leader of a newly independent nation that had successfully withstood imperialist aggression, and his international standing was greatly enhanced. In December 1957 the first Afro-Asian solidarity conference was held in Cairo; in 1961 Nasser participated in the founding conference of the Casablanca Bloc and in a neutralist summit meeting in Belgrade. In 1963 he attended a summit conference founding the Organization for African Unity, which held its second congress in 1964 in Cairo. In 1958 Nasser paid his first visit to the Soviet Union.

From the mid-1950s Nasser took an increasingly activist line toward the Arab countries. Egypt had always seen itself as the center of the Arab world. In his booklet *The Philosophy of the Revolution* (1954) Nasser himself described its position at the center of three circles: Arab, Islamic, and African. But gradually Nasser's policies tended toward domination by fostering "Nasserist" pressure groups in the Arab countries, by direct Egyptian pressure, by subversion and, if needed, by force. In 1962 Nasser decided to intervene in a civil war that had broken out in Yemen, sending an expeditionary force to support the republican camp. It was a disastrous decision as Egyptian forces were bogged down there until 1966.

Even in countries with Arab-Socialist leanings, such as Algeria, Syria, Iraq, and later Libya, national self-interest and particularist tendencies soon prevailed. Thus, after the debacle of the Yemen ex-

pedition and the general failure to subvert Arab governments and create regimes in the Nasserist image, from the early 1960s Nasser toned down his interventionist statements and policies and cooperated with these conservative regimes in renewed efforts at pan-Arab cooperation.

While preparing in 1966–1967 for war against Israel Nasser revived and reinforced his alliance with Syria and in May 1967, after making war inevitable by proclaiming a blockade of the Straits of Tiran and ordering the UN Emergency Force to withdraw from Sinai, he imposed a close alliance on Jordan, too, compelling King Hussein to toe the line. The frenzy of the Six-Day War (June 1967), orchestrated by carefully built-up mass enthusiasm, brought Nasser to the pinnacle of his all-Arab leadership; every Arab country fervently backed him and many sent troops or equipment to aid Egypt. When the war turned into a stunning defeat Nasser, taking personal responsibility, resigned, but stormy mass demonstrations — seemingly spontaneous but in fact carefully staged — "forced" him to retract the resignation. Thus he turned even that day of bitter defeat into a personal victory.

Subsequently his policies, though less flamboyant, remained unchanged and the contradiction between his pragmatic position at the center of the inter-Arab status quo and his radical inclinations (which included occasional interventionist sallies) was never resolved. For instance, Nasser supported the Palestine Liberation Organization's (PLO) buildup of its state-within-a-state in both Jordan and Lebanon and prevented the governments of the two countries from taking effective measures against it, imposing a precarious coexistence embodied in agreements with the PLO that were formulated under his sponsorship (and never kept by the PLO). When that coexistence broke down in Jordan and King Hussein confronted the PLO in desperate battle in 1970 Nasser mediated, but in fact sided with the PLO and acted to discredit and ostracize King Hussein. Nasser also led Egypt into an ever-increasing dependence on the Soviet Union, with thousands of Soviet civil and military technicians and advisers working in Egypt.

Nasser's attitude toward Israel and to the prospects of an Arab-Israel settlement also remained ambivalent. He accepted Security Council Resolution 242 of 1967 calling for peaceful coexistence of Israel and the Arab states (interpreting it, as most Arabs did, as providing for Israel's total withdrawal from all territories occupied in 1967) and did not join the hawkish Rejection Front (Syria, Iraq, the PLO, Algeria) that refused in principle to coexist with Israel in any form. Yet he always refused to negotiate with Israel and seldom spoke of the possibility of peace with her. It was Nasser who formulated the "Three No's" — no peace with Israel, no negotiations, no recognition — of the 1967 Khartoum summit. In numerous speeches he stated that he would not be satisfied with the "removal of the results of the aggression of 1967" (i.e., Israel's withdrawal from the territories occupied), but would continue to struggle for the "removal of the results of the aggression of 1948," i.e., for the destruction of Israel's very existence. He repeatedly declared, "What was taken by force, can be regained only by force," and he continued, in his last years, conducting a "war of attrition."

Nasser died suddenly in September 1970 and his image dimmed somewhat after his death. His successors kept their distance from him, allowing previously hidden aspects of his rule to be revealed. The failure of his economic policies, particularly the state enterprises, the all-pervading corruption, and especially the police state he created through suppression of freedom of speech, organization and the press, through unlawful detention and torture of adversaries, were all made public. There is no doubt, however, that Nasser was endowed with unusual charisma and wielded an immense, if controversial, influence throughout the Arab world.

J. Gordon, *Nasser's Blessed Movement*, 1992.

T. Y. Haso, *The Struggle for the Arab World: Egypt, Nasser, and the Arab League*, 1985.

D. Hofstadter, *Egypt and Nasser*, 3 vols., 1973.

P. J. Vatikiotis, *Nasser and His Generation*, 1977.

NEBUCHADNEZZAR (Nebuchadrezar; c.630–562 B.C.E.), Chaldean king. The eldest son of Nabopolassar, the founder of the Chaldean (Neo-Babylonian) Empire, his name is from the Akkadian Nabukudurri-Usur, "O Nabu, protect my boundary-stone," the "boundary-stone" referred to being the line of kingly succession. While his father had disclaimed royal descent, Nebuchadnezzar sought to further legitimize his rule by claiming the third-millennium B.C.E. ruler Naram-Sin as his ancestor. The true facts of his career are liberally spiced with legend: the only available sources of information about him are a number of cuneiform inscriptions and the later writings of Jewish and classical authors.

Nabopolassar ensured that his son had a reverence for the gods of his kingdom instilled in him from an early age: one of Nebuchadnezzar's first tasks was working as a laborer in the restoration of the temple of Marduk, the national god of Babylonia. He was also trained from an early age in the arts of war and kingship, becoming a military administrator by 610 B.C.E. and taking command of an army in the mountains north of Assyria in 607 B.C.E. After the empire's armies were defeated by the Egyptians in 606 B.C.E., he took his father's place as military commander-in-chief and demonstrated brilliant generalship in routing the Egyptian forces at Carchemish and Hamath, victories that signaled the beginning of the end of Egypt's power in West Asia. Shortly thereafter his father died, but so firm was Nebuchadnezzar's grip on power that he was able to return to campaigning just three weeks after ascending the throne.

Nebuchadnezzar pursued an expansionist territorial policy throughout his reign, engaging in regular military expeditions. His 604 B.C.E. expedition in Syria and Palestine led to the submission of local states including Judah, but his gains were reversed when his heavy losses in clashes with the Egyptians in 601 B.C.E. triggered defections among his vassal states. He then retreated to Babylonia to rebuild his forces, only returning to campaigning in 598 B.C.E. By 597 B.C.E. Jerusalem had fallen to him, and he deported its king, Jehoiachin, to Babylonia. When Zedekiah, his appointed successor to Jehoiachin, rebelled, Nebuchadnezzar besieged and then destroyed Jerusalem (586 B.C.E.), carrying many Jews into captivity in what the Old Testament refers to as the Babylonian Exile. Despite his sack of the holy city, the Biblical prophets Jeremiah and Ezekiel regarded him as an appointed instrument of God. Subsequent campaigns saw him capture Tyre, after a thirteen-year siege, in 573 B.C.E., and attempt an invasion of Egypt in 568 B.C.E.

His military accomplishments notwithstanding, Nebuchadnezzar was proudest of being "the one who set into the mouth of the people reverence for the great gods." He achieved this by completing the rebuilding of Babylon in a manner commensurate with its status as the religious center of the empire, and scorned those of his predecessors who had built palaces elsewhere. He extended the fortifications begun by his father, built canals, a moat, and an outer defensive wall, and embellished the principal temples.

A thoughtful and loving spouse, Nebuchadnezzar tried to ease the homesickness of his Median wife by creating a system of terraces, watercourses, and exotic trees to simulate the hills of her native land. These Hanging Gardens of Babylon were classified by the Greeks as one of the seven wonders of the ancient world. Even more visually striking was the ninety-meter high ziggurat, a series of tiers and stairways.

Nebuchadnezzar is an important figure in the Old Testament, where he is represented as a majestic, just, but troubled ruler, who is moved to recognize the god of the Jews as a result of repeated evidence of his might. However, the tale of his seven years of madness following the prophecy of Daniel that "thy dwelling shall be with the beasts of the field, and they shall make thee to eat grass as oxen," is apparently apocryphal, the result of an exaggerated recounting of events that actually took place under a later ruler, Nabonidus, who quit Babylon to live for a decade in the deserts of Arabia.

At his death, Nebuchadnezzar was able to bequeath to his son and successor, Amel-Marduk, an empire bigger than that of any Assyrian or Babylonian predecessor.

D. J. Wiseman, *Chronicles of Chaldean Kings*, 1956.

NEHRU, JAWAHARLAL (1889–1964), Indian statesman, first prime minister of independent India. He was born in Allahabad, north India, where his father was a high court advocate and an influential member of Anglo-Indian society, mixing easily and familiarly with the country's British rulers. Nehru was educated by a succession of English tutors and sent to complete his studies in England where he received an education befitting an English gentleman: he studied successively at Harrow, Trinity College, Cambridge, and the Inns of Court in London, where he qualified as a lawyer.

Nehru loved England and his time there profoundly affected him, as he quickly absorbed many of its manners and values: he was later to say, "I have become a queer mixture of the East and the West, out of place everywhere, at home nowhere." Equally at home and elegant in English suits as in the English language, he was in many ways to be a strange figure for a nationalist revolutionary, especially in the country of the *dhoti*-clad Mahatma *Gandhi. He subsequently eschewed western dress in favor of the homespun cloth more appropriate to his political convictions, but always retained his appreciation of the literature and arts of the Occident.

On his return to India in 1912, Nehru discovered the limits of his de-Indianization when he was refused entry to the local all-white British club. Despite his Anglicization, he was drawn to the growing Indian independence movement and joined the Congress party, where his activism in the noncooperation campaign led by Gandhi soon landed him in jail. In all, Nehru was to spend almost nine years in prison between 1921 and 1945. He described prison as "the best of universities"; the maturation of his political philosophy and much of his best writing can be credited to the periods of enforced inactivity and reflection he endured there. His travels among the common people in India in 1920 and 1921, later documented in his *Discovery of India*, had already given him a deep respect and sympathy toward them, although he always remained opposed to the centrality of religion in India, believing that it impeded the country's progress. Then, in 1926, while based in Geneva seeking treatment for his wife's poor health, Nehru traveled extensively in Europe and Soviet Russia. He came into contact with socialist and anti-imperialist groups there and returned to India in 1927 a confirmed socialist and believer in the necessity of industrialization in India. Although never communist, his economic yardstick was consistently Marxist thereafter, and he always remained a supporter of the U.S.S.R.

He was elected to succeed his father as president of Congress the Indian National in 1929, and was the obvious candidate for the premiership when India became an independent nation on August 14, 1947. A superb orator, he commemorated that moment in his speech to the nation: "Long years ago we made a tryst with destiny, and now the time comes when we shall redeem our pledge, not wholly or in full measure, but very substantially. At the stroke of the midnight hour, while the world sleeps, India will awake to life and freedom. A moment comes which comes but rarely in history, when we step out from the old to the new, when an age ends,

and when the soul of a nation long suppressed finds utterance." There followed a difficult period as Nehru faced a succession of problems at home and abroad, beginning with the refugee problem and bloodshed in the aftermath of partition. The attempted Pakistani invasion of the predominantly Muslim state of Kashmir in October 1947 marked the onset of a territorial dispute that persists to this day. Gandhi's assassination in January 1948 seemed to mark the end of an era and Nehru's grief at the loss of his mentor was tangible in his words: "The light has gone out of our lives and there is darkness everywhere."

Nehru's achievements were considerable and made a lasting impression on the subcontinent. The complexity and variety of conflicting problems and interests facing India at that time often seemed to find correspondence in the character of Nehru himself, a man with an intricate complex of traditional values and contemporary attitudes. He emerged as an internationally respected statesman, always eager to persuade rather than coerce, and India's place in the international community was closely shaped by his vision.

Nehru sometimes had to compromise in the interest of political expediency. He was criticized for calling for massive Western aid to finance the five-year plans (which increased India's industrial output by 50 percent by the end of the 1950s) at the same time as he was promoting anticolonialism and nonalignment as à vis the United States and the Soviet Union to other developing nations in Asia and Africa.

The friendly relations with China that he coveted never recovered from the Chinese invasion of Tibet. In October 1962 a brief war ensued over Chinese incursions into the Brahmaputra valley and Nehru's hopes of an Indo-Chinese axis in Asia floundered. An opponent of the use of force, he often needed to resort to it in the troubled years of the early 1960s, as border squabbles with Pakistan also escalated and India forcibly integrated Portuguese Goa into the Indian republic.

Nehru was proudest of his achievements in social reform at home, where he promoted a civil code granting equal rights of inheritance to women and outlawing casteism, as well as making some inroads into the intractable problems of rural education and agrarian reform. When India became a republic in 1950, it was Nehru's model of a secular, federalized state with a strong center that had prevailed. The Indian people revered and trusted him, as evinced by his comprehensive electoral victories. One of his last significant acts was to sign a nuclear test ban treaty.

He died in May 1964 and according to his wishes his ashes were scattered from an aircraft "over the fields where the peasants of India toil so that they might mingle with the dust of the soil of India and become an indistinguishable part of her." India's faith in the house of Nehru persisted: his daughter Indira *Gandhi was prime minister from 1966 to 1977 and again from 1980 until her assassination by Sikh militant separatists in 1984. Her son, Nehru's grandson Rajiv, followed her as premier. He too was assassinated, by Sri Lankan Tamil separatists, during the 1991 Indian election campaign.

S. R. Bakshi, *Nehru and His Political Ideology*, 1988.

M. Edwardes, *Nehru*, 1971.

S. N. Nadan, *Paradoxical Nehrus and Indian History*, 1988.

NELSON, LORD HORATIO (1759–1805),
British admiral. Born in Burnham Thorpe, Norfolk, Nelson, whose mother died when he was eight years old, was one of the eight children of a parson. Horatio (he preferred to call himself Horace) often went to view vessels plying the Norfolk coastal trade. At twelve, he enlisted as a midshipman on the warship *Raisonnable*, captained by his uncle Maurice Suckling — a veteran of many battles and a figure young Horatio looked up to.

Nelson learned to handle the ship's boat ferrying men and supplies to and from his uncle's man-of-war. Still in his teens he sailed in the *Carcass* on an exciting expedition to discover the northeast passage through the Atlantic to the Orient. His ship was trapped in ice flows and Nelson almost lost his life in a foolhardy attempt to get a polar bear skin for his father.

After his return, Nelson did not stay in the safety of England long but was soon off on a voyage in a warship to India. He caught malaria and had to return to England. During the voyage he had a mystical experience sighting a "radiant orb," a vision that inspired him with a heroic mission to serve king and country. While he was abroad, his uncle Maurice had been promoted to naval comptroller and could use patronage to advance his nephew's career, but it was rather Nelson's more proven skills as a ship's officer that won him a commission as lieutenant at the age of eighteen.

Nelson served in several theaters of conflict. He took part in an ill-fated attempt to seize territory in Nicaragua, aimed at dividing Spanish America in two. Transporting troops up river through the jungle was a severe test of his resourcefulness and the monkey stew cooked by the Indians, a test for his stomach.

During service in the Caribbean Islands, he made enemies by vigorously pursuing ships from rebel America illegally trading with Britain's colonies. The colonists resented interference in their business, and Nelson and fellow officers were excluded from the plantation social life that was their chief diversion. Despite unpopularity with merchants, he received a hospitable reception from the president of Nevis, John Herbert. He was attracted to Herbert's niece, a young widow named Frances Nisbit, and they were married in 1787.

Following the wedding the Nelsons returned to Norfolk. His activities against illegal trading had also made enemies in London, thus he had to settle down to the quiet life of a gentleman farmer on land around Burnham Thorpe. Efforts to get a naval command met with failure until the outbreak of war with France.

Nelson embarks at Portsmouth for his last campaign

In 1793 Nelson was assigned to the Mediterranean where the siege of Toulon and the capture of Corsica offered ample opportunity for the initiative and gallantry that became his trademark. In an attack on Calvi he suffered serious injury to his right eye. In 1797 a battle with the Spanish off Cape Saint Vincent brought him national fame. Ignoring naval regulations, he broke from the squadron and succeeded in capturing two Spanish warships after broadsides disabled them; Nelson personally led a boarding party, sword drawn.

Honored with appointment as a rear admiral and a knighthood, he was in a confident mood and underestimated the strength of the Spanish garrison of Tenerife in the Canary Islands. The landing party he was courageously leading was ambushed and Nelson shot in his right arm; the wound necessitated amputation with a cold knife and opium to dull the pain. The attack was repulsed but Nelson still returned to England with a hero's welcome. Besides being an honored guest in homes of aristocrats, he had won a place in the hearts of ordinary sailors, showing concern that they should be promptly paid and families compensated in the event of a death. Although a strict disciplinarian not averse to the use of floggings, sailors knew he never asked of them anything he was not prepared to do himself; he would challenge nervous trainee officers to a race up the mast head, encouraging them not to fear one of the most daunting of the sailor's duties.

In 1798 Nelson pursued the French fleet around the Mediterranean. In August he caught up with them moored in the Nile estuary and with skillful

> May the Great God, whom I worship, grant my Country, and for the benefit of Europe in general, a great and glorious victory; and may no misconduct in anyone tarnish it; and may humanity after Victory be the predominant feature in the British Fleet.
>
> For myself, individually, I commit my life to Him who made me, and may his blessing light upon my endeavors for serving my Country faithfully. To Him I resign myself and the just cause which is entrusted to me to defend. Amen. Amen. Amen.
>
> **Nelson's last writing**
> **before the Battle of Trafalgar**

maneuvering the British squadron placed themselves in a position from where they destroyed or captured almost all the enemy ships. This sensational victory left *Napoleon's army stranded in Egypt with the Royal Navy controlling Mediterranean sea lanes.

Nelson delighted in his own praises, and the British government's were usually not sufficiently generous to satisfy his ego. In Naples he received a grand welcome. Most enthusiastic was the famous courtesan Emma Hamilton, wife of the British ambassador; she wore a ribbon round her forehead proclaiming "Nelson and Victory." He was soon infatuated with her and was delighted when she bore him a daughter. Her husband, Sir William Hamilton did not seem in the least perturbed but Mrs. (now Lady) Nelson was understandably averse to her husband's new affection. When the Nelsons and Hamiltons met in London, the confrontation between the women left his marriage to Fanny extant on paper only. Nelson set up home with Emma and Sir William, in a house Emma found for them in Merton outside London. Nelson's behavior provided abundant material for gossip writers and cartoonists and distanced him from his elderly father. When his father died in 1802 he did not go to the funeral in order to avoid his wife who had remained close to her father-in-law.

The end of the short-lived peace with France in 1802 increased fears of invasion. For several years Admiral Nelson chased the French fleet round the Mediterranean and across the Atlantic engaging in skirmishes, trying to bring them out into a full-scale battle, convinced he would break their power once and for all.

On October 21, 1805 the long-awaited confrontation came off Cape Trafalgar. He signaled to his captains the famous message "England expects that every man will do his duty" and they did; the superiority of British gunnery and seamanship won the day, effectively ending French naval power and leaving Britain in command of the seas. Nelson knew of the triumph but did not live to celebrate. Ignoring his colleagues' advice he remained at his command post on the deck of H.M.S. *Victory* wearing numerous shiny medals on his uniform, an obvious target for the French sniper who cut him down. His last words were "Thank God I have done my duty." Nelson's greatest glory came posthumously. He was buried under the cupola of Saint Paul's Cathedral and became a legend. His statue stands on a high pillar in London's Trafalgar Square, although a similar pillar which long stood in Dublin's main street was blown up by Irish nationalists.

R. Hattersley, *Nelson*, 1974.
T. Pocock, *Horatio Nelson*, 1988.
O. Warner, *A Portrait of Nelson*, 1958.

NERO (Nero Claudius Caesar; 37–68 C.E.), Roman emperor. His mother, Agrippina, was an ambitious, ruthless woman. Married and widowed three times, she got her son Nero, from her first marriage, great wealth from her second, and a crown from her third. She played on the extreme susceptibility to women of her uncle, Emperor Claudius, to become his fifth wife. Claudius was unfortunate in his choice of wives: one died, two he divorced, one he had killed, and the last one, Agrippina, murdered him.

Marriage to Claudius did not satisfy Agrippina's ambitions. She wanted Claudius to adopt Nero as his heir over the rival claims of Claudius's own son, Britannicus. Nero was eleven when his mother married Claudius and sixteen before she succeeded in persuading Claudius to adopt him and marry him to Claudius's daughter, Octavia (aged thirteen). Meanwhile Agrippina had become powerful and feared, using the weapons of exile and death, and the power of the Praetorian Guards headed by her friend, Burrus. Claudius finally realized what Agrippina was doing and threatened to end her power and name Britannicus as his heir. Agrippina killed him before he could make good his threats and Nero became emperor at seventeen (54 C.E.). The new emperor accepted the crown but had little interest in government. What he loved was sports (gymnastics, chariot racing, and so on), and what he really wanted to be was a great artist. He set about learning music, art, drama, and poetry and surrounded himself with artists and musicians, holding private competitions with them to see whose work was best. He took their compliments and his successes in these contests at face value, choosing to ignore the idea that the punishments meted out to anyone who beat him might have prevented his work from being judged on merit alone.

At first Agrippina administered the empire for Nero, but the philosopher Seneca (Nero's old tutor) and Burrus persuaded Nero that they should replace her. Furious, Agrippina threatened Nero by announcing that Britannicus was the real heir, whereupon Nero had Britannicus poisoned and Agrippina retired to her villa.

Seneca and Burrus encouraged Nero to occupy himself with indulging his appetites to prevent his interference in governmental matters. As a result Nero

NERO AND MUSIC

Music formed part of his childhood curriculum and he early developed a taste for it. He studied and practiced and conscientiously undertook exercises for developing and strengthening his voice. He would lie on his back with a slab of lead on his chest, use enemas and emetics to keep down his weight, and refrain from eating apples and other fruits regarded as harmful to the vocal cords. Eventually, though his voice was feeble and husky, he was pleased enough with his progress to nurse theatrical ambitions. His first stage appearance was at Naples where, disregarding an earthquake which shook the theater, he sang his piece through to the end. So captivated was he by the rhythmic applause of some Alexandrian sailors from a fleet which had just put in that he sent to Egypt for more. He chose more than five thousand youths to learn the Alexandrian method of applause and provide it liberally whenever he sang. In Rome when the crowd clamored to hear his heavenly voice, he obliged them in his palace gardens. Colonels of the Guards carried his lyre as he went up to play. When the title of his song was announced it was the whole of the opera *Niobe* and he sang on two hours until dusk. He also appeared in operatic performances, taking the part of gods and heroes, sometimes even of heroines and goddesses wearing masks either modeled on his own face or whatever woman was his current mistress.

Suetonius: *Lives of the Twelve Caesars*

build. According to legend he ordered the famous fire that destroyed most of Rome while he played on his lyre. He did in fact, respond to the emergency with strenuous efforts to control the fire and alleviate suffering, while he blamed the Christians for setting it. Then he had the pleasure of rebuilding the improved Rome of his dreams — at the cost of thousands of lives and many priceless buildings, manuscripts, and works of art.

In his twenty-eighth year he began giving public performances as a musician, singer, and actor. His performances increased his popularity with a populace flattered at an emperor's begging for their applause. Large crowds that gathered did not stop him from ensuring a captive audience by forbidding anyone leaving alive before he finished performing — even women in labor. His wife Poppaea died that year, pregnant with his longed-for heir. Rumors of Nero's responsibility for her death did not prevent his eulogizing her or finding, castrating, and marrying a boy who resembled her. The discovery of a plot to overthrow him led to many deaths (including Seneca's) and exiling many others.

Nero spent the next year in Greece, participating in the Games as both athlete and performer. Carefully obeying all the rules, he "won" every contest he entered (including the chariot race he did not complete), rewarding Greece with an exemption from paying tribute and his opponents with Roman citizenship.

In 68 Gaul rebelled against Nero and was soon joined by the Roman army in Spain, headed by Galba, which marched against Rome. Threatened with the defection of the Praetorian Guard, the Senate declared Galba emperor and Nero fled — to commit suicide a day later.

M. T. Griffin, *The End of a Dynasty,* 1970.
M. T. Griffin, *Nero,* 1984.
A. Weigall, *Nero, Emperor of Rome*, 1950.

ran wild while Rome thrived under Seneca's wise guidance: frontiers were well guarded, corruption and oppressive taxes were reduced, sea travel was made safe, the empire expanded, and peace made. The young emperor recognized no moral or temporal authority other than his own immediate desires. He wandered the streets of Rome from brothel to tavern, committing robbery, murder, and mayhem. Poppaea Sabina, a married woman, agreed to become his wife if he divorced Octavia. At twenty-two he murdered his mother for opposing the divorce. Three years later he divorced Octavia and married Poppaea, then exiled and murdered Octavia.

His excesses drained the treasury. To replenish it he stripped temples and confiscated the estates of those who "plotted" against him or did not leave him enough in their wills. Degenerate, uncontrollable — Burrus was dead and Seneca dismissed — Nero declared himself a god.

Nero dreamt of redesigning and rebuilding a Rome too crowded for the palace he wanted to

NESTORIUS (c.381–c.451), Persian prelate. Although he was to give his name to one of the major heretical Christian movements, Nestorius came to prominence as a zealously orthodox churchman. Born of Persian parents in Germanicia, Cilicia (modern-day Turkey), he distinguished himself by his asceticism and skill as a preacher in Antioch, Syria. In 428, when the clergy of Constantinople were unable to agree over who should succeed the patriarch Sisinius, the emperor invited him to accept the appointment. As patriarch, he was vigorous in his persecution of Arianism and Novatianism (the former, the belief that Jesus was only semidivine, and the later, a belief in the doctrines of the antipope Novatianus), but unwittingly laid himself open to the charge of heresy through his acquiescence in the ideas promulgated by his assistant Anastasius, who had come with him from Antioch.

Anastasius criticized the use of the Greek word *theotokos* (God-bearer) to denominate the Virgin Mary, preferring to refer to her as *christokos*

(Christ-bearer). Nestorius concurred with this position, the significance of which in the ensuing schism was that it could be interpreted as demonstrating that Nestorius denied the unity of Christ and God. In fact, the doctrinal difference between Nestorius and his critics was small: where orthodox teachings regarded *Jesus as having two separate "natures," one divine and the other human, Nestorius held that these same two aspects represented two separate "persons" in Christ.

Nestorius was not the originator of such opinions: they had first arisen among thinkers in east Asia Minor, most notably Diodore of Tarsus and Theodore of Mopsuestia. During this period, they came to represent an important characteristic of the Antiochene school of Christian thought (to which Nestorius became sympathetic during his time in Antioch), which criticized the rival Alexandrine school's traditional stress on Christ's unity with God as jeopardizing the integrity of his human nature. They cited Luke 2:52 ("Jesus increased in wisdom and stature, and in favor with God and man") as being very difficult to interpret if one does not allow for the possibility of genuine human growth in Christ, which a belief in the indivisibility of his divinity seems to deny.

The dispute became grounds for a test of strength between the rival schools. It was Cyril, ambitious patriarch of the see of Alexandria, who initiated proceedings against Nestorius, motivated by a desire for ascendancy within the church hierarchy as well as by genuine opposition to the Nestorian doctrinal position. Use of the designation *theotokos* had become a mark of doctrinal orthodoxy, so Pope Celestine found against Nestorius, who had already aroused the pontiff's ire by receiving into his congregation some of the followers of Pelagius (who denied the doctrine of original sin), whom Celestine had condemned.

Nestorius was anathematized by the Council of Ephesus (431), deposed from his patriarchate, and, after several years in a monastery in Constantinople, exiled to Upper Egypt. During his exile, he composed the pseudonymous *Bazaar of Heracleides of Damascus*, which constituted his life story and a justification of his teachings. The exact date of his death is unknown, but it is possible that he lived to hear the conclusions of the Council of Chalcedon in 451, which his supporters hailed as a vindication of his views and a repudiation of Cyril.

Nestorius's memory came to be revered by the Nestorian church, a once-thriving body (by 451 most of the eastern part of the Church of the East was Nestorian), which now exists almost solely in the form of a small community in the Kurdistan mountains and one of Armenian origin in Chicago in the United States.

F. Loofs, *Nestorius and His Place in the History of Christian Doctrine*, 1914.

R. V. Sellers, *Two Ancient Christologies*, 1940.

A. R. Vine, *The Nestorian Churches*, 1937.

NEVSKY, ALEXANDER SEE ALEXANDER NEVSKY

NEWTON, SIR ISAAC (1642–1727), English mathematician and scientist whose prodigious genius discovered the law of gravity, the laws of motion, and the differential calculus, and who made significant contributions to the study of optics.

Newton was born prematurely and frail on Christmas Day in Lincolnshire and was not expected to live. His father had died a few months before he was born, and his mother became the central force in his early life. As a young child he did not display any exceptional abilities. At grammar school in Grantham he seemed more interested in devising mechanical contraptions than studying — including a small windmill worked by a mouse. At the age of fourteen upon the death of his stepfather, his mother brought him home to help with the management of their estate. She realized the futility of this course when he was constantly found poring over whatever books he could lay his hands on, and a year later he was returned to school to prepare for university.

He was admitted to Trinity College, Cambridge, in 1661. The education was classical and he progressed initially at an ordinary pace. Having enrolled in a course in optics, Newton read the prescribed texts and by the first class had a better grasp of the topic than the tutor. He was attracted to astronomy and taught himself René *Descartes's text on analytical geometry. He formed a close friendship with his professor, Dr. Isaac Barrows, who by 1664 was asking Newton to criticize and revise his manuscripts. Later that year Newton received his bachelor degree in arts. Trinity College was closed in 1664 because of the plague, and Newton returned to a secluded life in Lincolnshire. The next two years were to be the most crucial in Newton's life, during which time his powers of scientific creativity were at their zenith and the groundwork for all of his future discoveries was laid. Newton himself referred to this period as his miracle years.

He began by writing a series of papers on a new mathematical technique he called fluxions (calculus). In a matter of months Newton proceeded to determine the composite nature of white light and, by all accounts, around this time noticed an apple fall from a tree in an orchard while out on an afternoon stroll. This unexceptional event inspired him to discover the law of gravity and the laws of motion. He did not publish any of this for many years. Newton suffered from an intense insecurity that manifested itself both in his academic life, where he was reluctant to publish his works, and in his private life where he was unable to form a lasting friendship with any woman other than his mother, and later in life with his niece to whom he was a guardian.

Returning to Cambridge in 1667 Newton was elected a minor fellow of Trinity College, and the following year made a master, an esteemed position for such a young man. By 1669 Barrow was so impressed with Newton that he stood aside to allow

Sir Isaac Newton

- If I have seen further it is by standing on the shoulders of giants.
- To every action there is an equal and opposite reaction (Third Law of Motion)
- I seem to have been only like a boy playing on the seashore and diverting myself in now and then finding a smoother pebble or prettier shell than ordinary, while the great ocean of truth lay all undiscovered before me.

Isaac Newton

Nature and Nature's Laws lay hid in night;
God said, Let Newton Be! and all was light.

Alexander Pope's epitaph to Newton

Newton to assume his chair as Lucasian Professor of Mathematics. His first few years in the professorship were spent extending his research in optics where he identified the phenomenon of chromatic aberration. This was his first published work and attracted some criticism. His most ardent critic was Robert Hookes, the curator of the Royal Society; a lifelong animosity between the two men ensued. Newton, ever anxious and introverted, was infuriated by the response to his paper and decided that in future he would not publish or involve himself in public discussion of his theories.

In 1678 Newton's mother died, bringing on the first of a series of nervous collapses, which together with his rampant paranoia led many of his friends to question his sanity. On recovering his health Newton threw himself into the study of the transmutation of elements, known as alchemy, applying rigorous scientific technique to this hitherto mystical pursuit. This was but part of his lifelong attempt to reconcile his understanding of nature with God. Newton compiled a sizable body of theological work that attests to his deep faith but bespeaks a contempt for the traditional orthodoxies.

Newton's crowning achievement was his work *Philosophiae Naturalis Principia Mathematica*, published at the behest of his friends in 1687, in which he expounded for the first time the laws of motion and gravity. Robert Hookes once again charged Newton with plagiarism, basing this on the evidence of letters he had written to Newton some eight years earlier containing an outline of his own gravitational theory. Though Hookes could fairly claim he was due some acknowledgment for his contribution,

Newton was so enraged by the accusation he deleted almost all reference to Hookes's work in subsequent editions of *Principia*.

Principia was immediately acclaimed as a remarkable treatise. It was to lay the foundations and determine the direction of modern science. Newton was acclaimed the pre-eminent scholar of his day. In 1699 he relented to join the Royal Society, which to this time he had scorned, and then in 1703 after the death of Hookes he was elected president, a post he held until his death. Through the society Newton despotically dominated English science over the next few decades, manipulating its influence to his favor in the many controversies that embroiled him.

By this time he had become more worldly. He had been appointed warden of the Royal Mint in 1696, then master of the mint in 1699, and in 1701 had entered Parliament, resigning his positions at Cambridge and moving permanently to London.

Newton's reluctance to publicize his work occasioned his acrimonious dispute with the German mathematician G. W. *Leibniz over the prior discovery of calculus. Newton had developed the calculus early in his career and used it in his own subsequent works, but it was Leibniz who first published an outline of the method in 1684. By the time Newton presented his version of calculus in an appendix to his *Opticks* in 1704, the priority controversy (as it became known) was set to dominate the last years of his life. Disparaging rumors quickly turned into inflammatory charges of plagiarism against Leibniz by Newton and his minions from the Royal Society. It is now accepted that Leibniz developed the calculus independently from Newton, but the episode besmirched both their reputations.

In his final years Newton occupied himself with revising his works and presiding over the Royal Society. He was buried in Westminster Abbey.

E. N. Andrade, *Sir Isaac Newton*, 1965.

A. R. Hall, *Isaac Newton*, 1992.

F. E. Manuel, *A Portrait of Isaac Newton*, 1968.

> - The wine is poured; and we must drink it (order to advance before the Battle of Jena).
> - People who think of retreating before a battle has been fought ought to have stayed at home.
> - Soldiers, when I give the command to fire, fire straight at my heart. Wait for the order; it will be my last to you (last words before his execution)..
>
> **Michel Ney**

NEY, MICHEL (1769–1815), French soldier, famous for his bravery and daring in battle. He rose rapidly through the ranks of the revolutionary army and was nicknamed "the bravest of the brave" by *Napoleon. Ney was born in Saarlois, the son of a barrel cooper and blacksmith. He was apprenticed to a local lawyer, but ran away and enlisted in a hussar regiment. He soon distinguished himself with acts of bravery, displaying great physical courage. Despite his military successes and his leadership skills, Ney showed an unwillingness to accept higher ranking but he was promoted to general and won a crucial victory at Hohenlinden (1800).

In May 1801 Ney was presented to Napoleon Bonaparte, who had declared himself First Consul. Initially suspicious of Ney as a potential rival, Napoleon was soon convinced that Ney would become one of his greatest generals and staunchest supporters. In 1802 Napoleon had his wife Josephine arrange Ney's marriage to Aglaé Aguié, one of her maids of honor and daughter of a high official. In 1804, the day after Napoleon declared himself emperor, he made Ney marshal of the empire.

The following year, Ney distinguished himself once again by leading a daring attack against the Austrians at Elchingen. He fought at Jena and Eylau and commanded an army at Friedland, where the French defeated the Russians in 1807. Ney was made duke of Elchingen and was sent to Spain where he fought first under Napoleon and then under Marshal Massena. He continued to prove himself a brave and daring soldier but at the same time was also known to be temperamental and insubordinate. Although he had conducted a brilliant campaign in Portugal, he was eventually dismissed by Massena for refusing to maintain his already crippled army in Portugal.

In 1812 Ney led the charge against the Russians at Borodino and was honored with the title Prince de la Moskowa. During the retreat from Moscow he fearlessly protected the rearguard. Napoleon and Joachim Murat left the army after its defeat and hastily returned to France, but Ney remained with the Great Army during the disastrous retreat. His force of ten thousand men was constantly attacked by Cossacks and faced savage weather conditions. The army's ability to resist and eventually elude the superior Russian army was due largely to Ney's leadership. Ney himself was the last to cross the Niemen River with the few hundred of his soldiers who survived. He fought courageously in the campaign of 1813 and in France's defense in 1814, but he was one of the first generals to persuade Napoleon to abdicate after the Battle of Leipzig. When Louis XVIII succeeded Napoleon, Ney retained his titles and took an oath of allegiance to the Bourbon dynasty.

On 1 March 1815, when Napoleon returned from Elba, Ney reaffirmed his allegiance to the monarchy and promised to "bring back that man to Paris in an iron cage." However, after receiving messages from Napoleon, Ney changed his mind and decided to join him in the march on Paris. The king fled and Napoleon returned to the Tuileries. Ney led the last French charge at Waterloo in 1815 but his role there remains controversial. Although he showed tremendous bravery his temperamental personality and sometimes ill-conceived charges possibly contributed to the French defeat.

After the return of the house of Bourbon, the ultraroyalists demanded that Ney be charged with treason. Attempting to flee the country, Ney was recognized and arrested. The House of Peers condemned him to death, and he was executed by firing squad in the Luxembourg Gardens.

H. Kurtz, *The Trial of Marshal Ney, His Last Years and Death*, 1957.

J. B. Morton, *Marshal Ney*, 1958.

NICHOLAS II (1868–1918), last czar of Russia. The son of Czar *Alexander III, he was born in Tsarskoye Selo outside the Russian imperial capital of Saint Petersburg. He received the standard education accorded to the Russian heir to the throne, including foreign languages, diplomacy, and his favorite subject, military science. One tutor, an Englishman named Charles Heath, taught him English and imbued him with the love of sports that would remain with him throughout his life. In addition to receiving military training Nicholas developed a fondness of military pomp and ceremony; he was always attracted by uniforms and loved parades. His most influential tutor, however, was Konstantin Pobedonostov, an ultranationalist reactionary and bigot who remonstrated with Nicholas against reform, particularly after the assassination of Nicholas's reform-minded grandfather, *Alexander II, when Nicholas was thirteen years old.

After completing his education, Nicholas toured the Middle East and Far East but his journey was cut short following an assassination attempt in Japan. Nicholas never forgave the Japanese people for the attempt on his life, which left him with a scar.

Alexander III died suddenly in 1894 and Nicholas, then twenty-six, ascended the throne. Despite his friendly features, he often appeared shy and even sad. He looked very much like his cousin, George V of England, and was sometimes mistaken for him.

Although he was an obdurate autocrat, Nicholas was often plagued by doubt as to the wisdom of his decisions as czar. He was weak-willed and allowed himself to be dictated to by his mother, the Empress Dowager Maria Fyodorovna, and later by his wife, the Czarina Alexandra. Although there was much excitement and an air of expectation at his coronation (three thousand people were crushed to death at his coronation festivities), Nicholas's subjects soon came to pity the czar and even regarded him with contempt. Nicholas himself commented on his ascension, "I am not prepared to be a czar. I never wanted to be one. I know nothing of the business of ruling. What is going to happen to me — to all of Russia?" Nicholas's words were ominous. At his coronation the Imperial Chain fell from his chest to the ground, an omen perceived by the people as suggestive of upheavals to take place during his reign.

Immediately after his ascension to the throne, Nicholas married Princess Alix of Hesse-Darmstadt, a minor German princess who was a granddaughter of Queen *Victoria. Princess Alix or, as she became known, the Czarina Alexandra, was a strong-willed woman who manipulated her husband. She bore Nicholas four daughters: Marie, Olga, Tatiana, and Anastasia, before she finally produced in 1904 an heir to the throne, Alexei, a sickly child who suffered from a rare form of hemophilia. The royal family sought the aid of *Rasputin, a mystic monk and faith healer who seemed able to relieve the boy's suffering. Rasputin soon wielded a remarkable influence over the empress and through her, over the czar.

Nicholas sincerely tried to govern Russia well. He was a dedicated autocrat who claimed that, "Certain people...have let themselves be carried away by the senseless dream of participation by elected regional representatives in internal government. Let all know that in devoting all my strength on behalf of the welfare of my people, I shall defend the principles of autocracy as unswervingly as my deceased father." He dreamed of a Russian superpower and was urged by Kaiser *Wilhelm II of Germany, as well as by his own military and economic advisors, to assert Russian influence in China and Korea. No one believed that Japan would respond to Russian inroads in that region but the Russians misread the mood of Japan; the Russo-Japanese War of 1904–1905 ended in a humiliating defeat for Russia.

Revolution was fomenting throughout Russia. In January 1905 a group of citizens led a peaceful march on the Winter Palace in Saint Petersburg to present a petition for democratic reform. The palace guards opened fire, injuring and killing hundreds. Although Nicholas was away at the time of the massacre, he was blamed. His position became increasingly precarious as several attempts were made on his life and on the lives of leading government officials. To ensure the safety of the royal family, two identical trains were built to carry the imperial household from destination to destination. It was hoped that the uncertainty as to which train actually held the royal family would thwart would-be assassins.

Nicholas II and Alexandra in their coronation robes

Nicholas was forced to respond to growing pressures for democratization. In 1905, under the influence of Prime Minister Serge de Witte, Nicholas issued the October Manifesto, promising civil liberties and democratic elections to a national body of representatives, the Duma. Nicholas retained the power to dissolve the Duma, and did so twice.

Although some authorities have argued that Nicholas did not comprehend the scope of reforms promised by the October Manifesto, others claim that he simply did not agree to any reforms which would limit his authority as autocrat, a title Nicholas insisted on keeping. In 1907 Nicholas led a coup d'état against the Duma and installed a more compliant body of representatives. This third Duma enacted a more conservative electoral law, disenfranchising many of the voters. With his authority assured, Nicholas then withdrew from politics to his family. In 1909 he made a state visit to England; in 1912 Kaiser Wilhelm II of Germany visited Russia. In 1913, amid great pomp, Nicholas and Russia celebrated the tercentenary of the accession of the Romanov dynasty.

Nicholas regarded himself as a protector of the smaller Balkan States. He tried to prevent the outbreak of World War I but when the Balkans were threatened by Turkey's territorial ambitions, particularly in the Dardanelles, Nicholas saw the need to maintain Russia's warm water port and decreed a general mobilization. Forty-eight hours later, on August 1, 1914, Germany declared war on Russia. At first the war received wide popular support but increasing defeats and four million Russian deaths destroyed any remaining support for the war and the czar. Nicholas was under pressure from strikes and from protests in the Duma to form a Government of National Confidence but urged on by Alexandra, he used the opportunity to turn against Rasputin's enemies in the government. Rasputin's influence had reached the point that it was whispered that he, rather than Nicholas, was the true ruler of Russia. Alexandra herself was a stern autocrat who wrote to her husband that, "Responsible government...would be the ruin of everything," and Nicholas responded in a letter signed, "Your poor, little, weak-willed hubby." He fired the commander of his armies, his uncle Grand Duke Nikolai Nikolayevich, and assumed command himself. His absence from the capital allowed Alexandra and Rasputin to assume total authority over the country. Even Rasputin's assassination in December 1916 by a group of aristocrats who saw him as the greatest threat to the monarchy could not stem the growing tide of opinion opposed to a monarch totally removed from the people. Unemployment was rampant, the cost of living rose 300 percent, and food was scarce. Nicholas was shocked by the February revolution in 1917. He attempted to make his way from army headquarters to the capital, only to find his way blocked. Finally, on March 15, 1917, he abdicated in favor of his brother, Grand Duke Mikhail. Immediately after signing away his crown, Nicholas returned to the book he was reading, *Julius Caesar*. Mikhail himself renounced the crown the next day and a provisional government was formed.

The Romanov family was kept under house arrest in their palace at Tsarskoye Selo. Nicholas tore up the lawns and planted a vegetable garden, content with the calmer turn his life had taken. Although many revolutionaries called for the czar's execution, Alexander Kerensky, leader of the provisional government, refused to hand over Nicholas. With the arrival of Vladimir *Lenin and Leon *Trotsky in Russia, Kerensky sent the czar to Tobolsk, Siberia, for his safety.

The royal family was installed in the governor's mansion but with the rise of the Bolsheviks to power following the October Revolution, the palace soon became a prison. Eight months later, the family was moved to Ekaterinburg in the Urals. The Bolsheviks feared Menshevik and royalist threats to save the royal family. Some time on July 16–17, 1918, the royal family was awakened from sleep and brought to a dark room, where a death sentence was passed against them. Nicholas rose to protest as his judges pulled revolvers from under their coats and shot the royal family to death. Their bodies were burned and thrown in a mine shaft; only the slightest remains identified the bodies as those of the royal family.

Since the circumstances of the murder of the Russian royal family remained obscure (no one would take credit for ordering their execution), several individuals have claimed to be surviving members of the Romanov family. Nicholas was reportedly seen in London in the 1920s. Nicholas's youngest daughter, Anastasia, was reported to have survived the massacre and over the years several women have claimed to be Anastasia, but the evidence shows that the entire family was indeed shot. Nicholas and his family have been made saints of the Russian Orthodox Church.

M. Ferro, *Nicholas II: The Last of the Tsars*, 1992.
R. K. Massie, *Nicholas and Alexandra*, 1967.
E. Radzinsky, *The Last Tsar*, 1992.
A. Summers, and T. Margold, *The File on the Tsar*, 1976.

NIETZSCHE, FRIEDRICH (1844–1900), German philosopher and poet. Now recognized as one of the most original and important figures in modern philosophy, Nietzsche's reputation has fluctuated widely since his death. Variously interpreted and often misunderstood, he was characterized as the forerunner of the irrationalist ideologies of power that reached their apotheosis in nazism and fascism; indeed, many of his sayings were wrenched out of context to buttress the crude philosophical base of German National Socialism. Later and more sympathetic readings have pointed out that such a view of Nietzsche is partial and inadequate. Instead, he has been conscripted to the contemporary causes of existentialism, depth psychology, and linguistic analysis. What remains undoubted is his status as one of the very greatest poets and prose stylists Germany has produced, whose effect on twentieth-century literature has been incalculable.

Friedrich Nietzsche with his mother

SAYINGS OF FRIEDRICH NIETZSCHE

- People demand freedom only when they have no power.
- Woman understands children better than man does, but man is the more childlike.
- Only he who is man enough will release the woman in woman.
- Wherever Germany extends her sway, she ruins culture.
- Man is a rope connecting animal and superman. What is great in man is that he is a bridge not a goal.
- Woman was God's second mistake.
- Is man one of God's blunders or is God one of man's blunders?
- God is dead; but considering the state the species Man is in, there will perhaps be caves for ages yet in which his shadow will be shown.
- Body am I entirely and nothing else; soul is only a word for something about the body.
- It was subtle of God to learn Greek when he wished to become an author — and not to learn it better.
- All idealism is falsehood in the face of necessity.
- Blessed are the sleepy for they shall soon drop off.
- The thought of suicide is a great consolation; by means of it one gets successfully through many a bad night.

Nietzsche's dramatic and unabashed subjectivism allied to the well-known fact that he went mad have led to attempts to search his life for clues that might become the key to an understanding of his often difficult writings. Misinterpretations have been legion, not least because Nietzsche's sister Elizabeth was to falsify, control, and suppress much of the material available after his death. (She married a man who tried to found an anti-Semitic colony in South America.) What remains fairly constant is a picture of a brilliant but progressively more lonely and estranged man, obsessed by the absurdity of human existence and deeply conscious that he was living "at the end of the world," a time when the old certainties that had bolstered European culture and society since the Enlightenment were breaking down. Nietzsche's work can be seen as both reaction to and exegesis of this condition.

Christened Friedrich Wilhelm (in honor of Friedrich Wilhelm IV of Prussia) by his father, a Lutheran minister, Nietzsche was later to shed his family's patriotism and religion along with his middle name. His father became mentally ill in 1848 and died shortly thereafter. Brought up in an overpoweringly female-dominated environment, Nietzsche was to develop an almost pathological misogynism. Although he was to propose to several women whom he barely knew, his proposals were really desperate attempts to relieve his terrible solitude. They were rejected and he lived the life of a sexual ascetic. The only woman he felt for deeply was Lou Salome (later the beloved of the poet Rainer *Rilke and friend and disciple of Sigmund *Freud), but his sister's intrigues ended their relationship in 1882 and left him more isolated than ever.

Nietzsche received an excellent classical education at his first school and went on to study at the University of Bonn. Moving to Leipzig University in 1865, he discovered Arthur *Schopenhauer and Richard *Wagner, the two greatest influences on his early thought; the will to power, the root metaphor of Nietzsche's philosophy, is a Darwinian modification of Schopenhauer's will to live, with the desire for ascendancy superseding the desire for mere survival. It is probable that this was also the time at which he contracted the syphilis which, untreated, is the most plausible explanation of his tragic slide into madness.

Nietzsche was so outstanding that he received the chair of professor of classical philology at the University of Basel in 1870 at the age of twenty-six. He also became a Swiss subject, although he received leave to volunteer as a medical orderly in the Franco-Prussian War, returning with his health shattered; in 1879, he was to resign his post at the university on grounds of ill health. In later life he suffered appallingly from migraines and near blindness, living in almost constant pain and driven only by the urgent need to write. His great works were written between 1879 and 1888, a period he spent as a lonely wanderer in Italy and southern France, living in second-class boarding houses, usually dieting and often on drugs.

Although his friendship with the composer Wagner meant much to him — and the Nietzschean Superman parallels Wagner's Siegfried in some respects — Nietzsche became progressively more disillusioned with what he saw as the older man's hypocrisy, especially his deference to Christianity in the opera Parsifal, which sealed their break in 1878. After 1879 Nietzsche devoted himself to his writing and in the next ten years produced the dazzlingly original and memorably aphoristic works that later made him famous. His mental breakdown took place in June 1889 — he vegetated until his death in 1900. Thus his mind did not survive to witness the repute that was his by the end of the century.

The reason that so many different schools of thought have been able to assimilate Nietzsche is that he was not interested in formulating a coherent system of philosophy: his ideas were complex and ambiguous and ranged over a number of subjects, although certain salient features remained relatively constant. Among them are his stress on the primary importance of the individual; his perspectivist analysis of truth — "facts are precisely what there are not, only interpretations"; his suggestion that all reasoning is mere rationalization based on "physiological demands for the preservation of a certain type of life"; his rejection of conventional social mores as the road to uncreative conformism and complacent hedonism; and his belief that language necessarily falsifies reality.

"God is dead" declared Nietzsche. Individuals must work out their own salvation here on earth unfettered by ideological constraints. Nietzsche is the most extreme anticollectivist in the history of modern philosophy. His habitual symbol for the masses was "the herd," and he supported the overthrow of the ethics of service on which he saw society as based.

His hostility to historical Christianity was unremitting: he saw it as the epitome of the dualistic, weak, and "life-denying" outlooks that posit an objective reality and moral order in an unconscious ideological attempt to stifle the fundamental drive — the will to power — of exceptional individuals, the Supermen. The otherworldliness of Christianity is seen as the will to power of the weak who despair of fulfillment in this life. "Remain faithful to the earth and do not believe those who speak unto you of superterrestrial hopes," conjured Nietzsche. His theory of the eternal recurrence of the same events at gigantic intervals went some way to fulfilling the need he felt for a belief in personal immortality after his rejection of the conventional theological notion of eternal life.

His best-known works are *The Birth of Tragedy* (1872), *Thus Spake Zarathustra* (1883–1891), and *Beyond Good and Evil* (1886). *Zarathustra* is written in a prophetic biblical style; his other books consist of loosely connected maxims.

P. Bergmann, *Nietzsche: The Last Anti-Political German*, 1987.

R. J. Hollingdale, *Nietzsche*, 1965.

L. P. Thiele, *Friedrich Nietzsche and the Politics of the Soul*, 1990.

NIGHTINGALE, FLORENCE (1820–1910),

English nurse and health reformer. She received her first name from the Italian city her wealthy parents were visiting when she was born. Nightingale's upbringing was privileged and comfortable, imbued with the earnest humanitarian, cultural, and Christian religious commitments of her family. Her parents could not find a tutor for their daughters who matched their exacting standards and consequently the father undertook the task of educating them. The range of subjects they were taught was broad, embracing the classics, French and Italian, history and philosophy.

In 1837 Nightingale felt the first of four divine calls to dedicate herself to holy works but initially she did not know in what field. She was free meanwhile to continue a busy social life and made an excellent impression on Paris society as a cultured and well-bred young lady. The social round continued with her presentation at Queen Victoria's court in 1839 and participation in all the other events that a lady of marriageable age was expected to patronize. She even had two suitors during the early 1840s, but neither won her favor. She had decided her mission demanded total commitment and that she must forgo marriage for she was taking upon herself the devotion of the Roman Catholic nuns whose medical missions she studied and admired.

By 1844 Nightingale had decided that nursing was to be her vocation. She had some experience from looking after sick family, friends, and some of the local villagers and wanted to get training working at Salisbury Infirmary. Her parents thought this was no place for a young lady of her class; hospitals in their view, were unhealthy places and nurses had a poor moral reputation. Frustrated by family opposition, she toured Europe, visiting a model hospital at Kaiserswerth, Germany, where there she found an institution run on high moral principles, though staffed by nurses who were "only peasants — none of them gentlewomen." Eventually, persistence met with success and her father granted her an allowance of five hundred pounds a year and did not oppose proposals to make her superintendent of the Institution for the Care of Sick Gentlewomen in Distressed Circumstances in London. With typical enthusiasm she began to make improvements in hospital organization, saving a considerable sum of money.

In 1854 the Crimean War began and the British public was dismayed when it learned of the incompetence with which the war was being managed. Disease was a far greater danger to the troops than Russian bullets: a fifth of the expeditionary force went down with cholera. There was a national outcry and Nightingale was approached and volunteered to lead a party of nurses to the Crimea under War Office sponsorship. However, her arrival was unwelcome to the army medical establishment who resented female interference in their traditional preserve. The nurses were housed in cramped and insanitary quarters without the most basic amenities. To complete the unpleasant reception there was a Russian general whose dead body nobody had bothered to remove from the nurses's living quarters!

Nightingale was deferential toward the authorities and made do with the appalling living conditions. The state of the hospital was even worse, and following the Battle of Inkerman (1854) an influx of wounded overwhelmed the primitive facilities and the army medical men were forced to turn to Nightingale and her nurses for help. She was not intimidated by the dreadful conditions but found herself moved by the character of the ordinary soldiers, who had long been considered the lowest of the low. She recorded how "these poor fellows bear pain and mutilation with unshrinking heroism and die without complaint. Not so the officers."

The task was daunting. Nightingale ensured that the patients had clean linen and were bathed regularly, not just once in eighty days as had been the norm. Other innovations including scrubbing the floors of the wards and the distribution of literature and lectures for the wounded soldiers, as well as facilities for sending money home. Where necessary equipment was not forthcoming from the govern-

Florence Nightingale

ment supplies, she drew on a fund raised by the British public and used her own personal allowance toward these purchases. To the nurses working under her she could appear as a harsh, intimidating figure, convinced nobody had a right to oppose her will. For the soldiers, as she toured the hospital at night with her lantern, she became a comforting figure — the legend of "the Lady with the Lamp" was born.

When the war ended in 1856, Nightingale returned to Great Britain a national heroine. Physically and emotionally exhausted, she took to her bed as an invalid, which she remained for the rest of her long life. Incapacity did not prevent her from using her considerable influence to press for further reforms in the army medical services. She met Queen Victoria and Prince Albert and enlisted their support for a thorough investigation of military hospitals to prevent the "scene of '54" from ever being reenacted. Queen Victoria commented of her: "Such a *head*! I wish we had her at the War Office."

Nightingale also took a deep interest in improving sanitary and medical conditions for the troops in India and invested a vast amount of time in promoting the development of professional training for nurses and the betterment of treatment of the sick in the workhouse infirmaries of London. Some of her attitudes became outdated — she refused to accept the germ theory of the spread of disease — but in other ways her views were in advance of the time.

She argued that the sick in the workhouses were not the indolent poor to be punished but merely "poor and in affliction" and that every step necessary to their recovery should be taken.

In 1907 this elderly blind lady became the first woman to be awarded the Order of Merit by the king.
M. Baly, *Florence Nightingale and the Nursing Legacy*, 1986.
M. Vicinus and B. Nergaard, eds., *Ever Yours: Florence Nightingale, Selected Letters*, 1989.
C. Woodham-Smith, *Florence Nightingale, 1820–1910*, 1964.

NKRUMAH, KWAME (1909–1972), African nationalist; first president of Ghana. Kwame Nkrumah was born in the town of Nkroful in the Gold Coast (now Ghana). He was named Francis Nwia Kofi at birth. Although his mother, a trader from the Nzima tribe, later claimed that he was born in 1912, the parish register records his baptism as having taken place in 1909. He attended the local Catholic mission school and continued on to the Government Training College in Accra, the first college on the continent specifically geared for native students. After graduating in 1930 he worked as a teacher.

Because the educational opportunities open to Africans were limited at that time, like so many of his compatriots, Nkrumah was forced to travel abroad to further his education. He sailed to America in 1935 to study at Lincoln University, from which he graduated in 1939. He then did graduate work at the University of Pennsylvania but returned to Lincoln to lecture in political science. Nkrumah was also active in various African-American causes. He was president of the African Student Organization of the United States and Canada and helped W. E. B. *Du Bois found the National Association for the Advancement of Colored People. Traveling to England in 1945, Nkrumah continued his studies and while there helped to organize the Fifth Pan-African Conference.

His reputation as an ardent African nationalist and competent organizer reached his native Gold Coast and in 1947 he agreed to return to the territory as general secretary of the United Gold Coast Convention. Nkrumah's demand that the Gold Coast receive immediate independence led to a rift between himself and the more established party leaders. He quit that party in 1949 to form his own Convention People's Party (CPP). The CPP was a pan-Africanist party that regarded Ghanaian independence as a prerequisite for pan-African independence and the emergence of a United States of Africa.

Nkrumah's platform called for "positive action" to attain independence. Other leaders heeded his call, sparking a year-long boycott of European and Syrian businesses as well as increasing protests and violence. In order to quash the growing unrest the British authorities arrested Nkrumah in 1950 but this action did not diminish his increasing popularity. Despite his detention the CPP won the 1951 election for self-government; Nkrumah was released from prison to assume the role of prime minister of the Gold Coast and used his position to further his demands for total independence.

FROM NKRUMAH'S ADDRESS TO THE FIRST PAN-AFRICAN CONGRESS, MANCHESTER, ENGLAND, 1945

We believe in the rights of all peoples to govern themselves. We affirm the right of all colonial peoples to control their destiny. All colonies must be given the right to elect their own government, a government without restrictions from a foreign power. We say to the peoples of the colonies that they must strive for these ends by all means at their disposal.

In 1957 the Gold Coast became the first black African state to achieve independence. The country was renamed Ghana and Nkrumah was elected its first prime minister. Upon Ghana's becoming a republic in 1960, Nkrumah was appointed president for life. He continued to pursue a radical pan-African policy which envisioned his country as the foundation for a United States of Africa. Believing that political integration of the emerging states must take priority over economic integration, Nkrumah attempted to unite his state with other African countries. In 1958 Ghana nominally united with Guinea and in 1960 Mali joined the union. At a conference of African states held in Casablanca, Morocco, in 1961, Nkrumah urged African leaders to form a Council of Heads of State, a Committee for Political Affairs, an African Consultative Assembly, and a military High Command. Although these specific plans were rejected, Nkrumah's ideas informed the underlying beliefs of the Organization of African States. His neutralist policy in international affairs was severely criticized during World War II and he was accused of being a communist. He replied "It is very unfair to be accused of being a communist on the basis of anti-colonialism." In order to promote the ideal of pan-African unity in a personal manner Nkrumah married an Egyptian woman, Fathia, whom he largely neglected in favor of his many mistresses.

Another goal of Nkrumah's was the introduction of socialism to Africa. He forged strong ties with the eastern bloc but failed in cultivating socialism at home, later noting that, "Socialism cannot be built without socialists."

Nkrumah was a flamboyant leader who stifled dissent and jailed his opponents. Two assassination attempts, in 1962 and in 1964, were made on the man who styled himself *Osagyefo* (Victor). Other names and titles used to describe Nkrumah ranged from Showboy to Messiah. Although his popularity waned at home, world leaders thought of him favorably. He traveled extensively, preaching his message of anticolonialism and pan-Africanism, for which he was awarded the Lenin Peace Prize in 1962.

While Nkrumah was visiting China in 1966 his government was overthrown in a coordinated police and military coup. Because of Nkrumah's ties with the eastern bloc it was later speculated that the coup was sponsored by the United States Central Intelligence Agency. Unable to return to Ghana, Nkrumah was granted asylum by his old friend and fellow pan-Africanist, Sékou Touré, president of neighboring Guinea. Nkrumah died in Romania in 1972 while undergoing cancer treatment; his body was returned to Ghana for burial.

K. B. Hadjor, *Nkrumah and Ghana*, 1988.
C. L. R. James, *Nkrumah and the Ghana Revolution*, 1977.
K. Nkrumah, *Autobiography*, 1957.

NOBEL, ALFRED BERNHARD (1833–1896), Swedish inventor of dynamite and philanthropist. Born in Stockholm, he spent many of his younger years in Saint Petersburg, Russia, a year in Paris, and four years in the United States. From 1859 he lived in Sweden and spent his final years in San Remo, Italy. Nobel was a frail and sickly child who required constant care by his attentive mother. As an adult Nobel wrote the following poem in memory of early childhood: "My cradle looked like a deathbed and for years /A mother watched with ever anxious care / Though little chance to save the flickering light."

He was devoted to his mother his entire life, foregoing marriage. Because of this, unfounded rumors abounded that he was a homosexual. The Nobel Foundation abetted the rumors by keeping his love letters secret for fifty years following his death. It then transpired that Nobel had hired prostitutes and had one eighteen-year love affair in the autumn of his life. Nobel's father, Immanuel, was a chemist who began experimenting with explosives in 1837. His experiments led to the development of land mines for the Russian army and an interest in the subject by his three eldest sons. At Immanuel's insistence Alfred conducted research with nitroglycerine, which had been developed by an Italian, Aslanio Sobero, in 1847. Sobero mixed nitric acid with sulphuric acid and glycerine to yield an oily liquid that was very powerful but very unstable.

Alfred Nobel initially succeeded in taming the violent explosive in underwater experiments. Later his older brother Oscar discovered a granular powder that could soak up the liquid nitroglycerin, thereby making the material less volatile. Nobel devised a method of securely sealing the explosive material in a cylinder that could accommodate a primary charge and fuse in order to be safely detonated on land. After patenting "Dynamite" in 1862, he built mass production factories to meet the great demand by mining and excavation companies and by the mili-

ALFRED NOBEL'S WILL

The whole of my remaining realizable estate shall be dealt with in the following way:

The capital shall be invested by my executors in safe securities and shall constitute a fund, the interest on which shall be annually distributed in the form of prizes to those who, during the preceding year, shall have conferred the greatest benefit on mankind. The said interest shall be divided into five equal parts, which shall be apportioned as follows: one part to the person who shall have made the most important discovery or invention within the field of physics; one part to the person who shall have made the most important chemical discovery or improvement; one part to the person who shall have made the most important discovery within the domain of physiology or medicine; one part to the person who shall have produced in the field of literature the most outstanding work of an idealistic tendency; and one part to the person who shall have done the most or the best work for fraternity among nations, for the abolition or reduction of standing armies and for the holding and promotion of peace congresses.

The prizes for physics and chemistry shall be awarded by the Swedish Academy of Sciences; that for physiological or medical works by the Caroline Institute in Stockholm; that for literature by the Academy in Stockholm; and that for champions of peace by a committee of five persons to be elected by the Norwegian Storting. It is my express wish that in awarding the prizes no consideration whatever shall be given to the nationality of the candidates, so that the most worthy shall receive the prize, whether he be a Scandinavian or not.

Paris, 27 November 1895

One morning in 1888 Alfred was shocked as he read his own obituary in a French newspaper. In fact, his brother had died but the reporter erroneously thought that the deceased was the inventor of dynamite. The negative article centered on the "Dynamite King" becoming extremely wealthy over bodies of soldiers whose deaths were caused by his weapons of destruction. Nobel was obsessed with the idea that the public would only remember him in terms of war when in fact he had developed dynamite to serve mankind. As a result, he decided to leave his fortune to a foundation that would distribute its earnings in equal prizes to individuals in five fields for their preceding years' work. Alfred Nobel bequeathed the then-princely sum of $9,200,000 to establish his foundation, but he was also generous during his lifetime. "As a rule," he wrote, "I'd rather take care of the stomachs of the living than the glory of the departed in the form of monuments." From his letters we learn about a case in which the pastor of the Swedish Church in Paris turned to him with a request for aid on behalf of a needy Swede. Nobel wrote, "I always feel happy to be able to help honest and industrious people in difficulties against which they struggle in vain. Mr. B. felt he could get along with 600 francs, but since I know very well that inadequate help and no help at all are not very far apart, I increased the amount on my own accord to 1,000 francs.

N. Halasz, *Alfred Nobel: A Biography*, 1938.

H. Schuck et. al., *Alfred Nobel: The Man and His Prizes*, 1950.

NÚÑEZ DE BALBOA, VASCO (1475–1519), Spanish explorer; discoverer of the Pacific Ocean. He was one of the adventurers who came to the New World in search of fame and fortune. Born to a noble but impoverished family in Xeres de los Caballeros, after a dissolute youth he joined an expedition exploring the southwest Central American Caribbean coast (1502). He learned much that was helpful to him later, such as when to fight Indians and when to make peace, and which Indians used poison-tipped arrows. He tried being a planter in Hispaniola (Haiti) but was unsuccessful and in 1509 had to escape his creditors by stowing away on a ship financed and commanded by Martin Fernández de Enciso.

Enciso lost his ship and supplies in a shipwreck and would have lost most of his men to Indian attacks if Balboa had not led them to a village where the inhabitants did not use poison arrows. They drove off the Indians and settled in the village, naming it Santa María de la Antigua, in Darién (eastern Panama). Enciso did not know how to handle men, especially the fortune-hunting adventurers sailing with him. They rebelled when he insisted that only he could trade with the Indians for gold. Balboa ousted Enciso from power, earning his undying enmity. Enciso returned to Spain, determined to turn King *Ferdinand II against him.

tary around the world. Nobel would personally demonstrate that dynamite was safe to use by throwing sticks, dropping sticks onto rocks, and by burning them. Then he would attach the primary charge and detonate the dynamite from a safe distance.

His development of dynamite was not without personal cost. His younger brother was killed, along with three other people, when nitroglycerine in the Stockholm laboratory unexpectedly blew up. Nobel concluded that the nitro, which was not mixed with granular power, exploded when the temperature inside the laboratory building exceeded thirty degrees centigrade. While saddened by the death of his brother, he bore no moral guilt as he believed that the power of explosives would ultimately serve humanity.

Balboa's personal strength and calm assurance enabled him to outmaneuver peacefully all opposition and become the leader of the new colony of Darién. The colonists faced many hardships: disease, hunger, and hostile Indians whom they fought, defeated, and stripped of food and gold. Balboa made allies of other Indians, married a chief's daughter, traded with them for gold, and listened to their tales of a great sea (the Pacific Ocean) and gold-rich lands on the other side of the mountains.

A ship arrived at Darién bearing a royal commission appointing Balboa temporary governor of Darién but there were also rumors of the effect Enciso's spiteful lies were having on the court. Balboa felt that his only chance lay in performing some great deed. He set off in September with guides provided by his father-in-law on the first expedition to penetrate the interior of America, en route either killing off the Indians who opposed him or converting them into allies. Balboa discovered the Pacific Ocean in September 1513 and claimed it for Spain. By the return trip many of the men, including Balboa, were sick and exhausted and had to be carried by their new allies.

Meanwhile Ferdinand II had been turned against Balboa and sent out the cruel, narrow-minded Pedrarias Dávila as governor of Darién (1514). He arrived several months after Balboa's return, laden with gold and pearls. Pedrarias expected a recalcitrant rebel and was not prepared for Balboa's welcome and formal submission to his authority. He became jealous of Balboa and began to use petty, backstabbing tactics against him, despite the fact that he betrothed by proxy his daughter, who was in Spain, to Balboa.

Meanwhile Balboa built the first ships ever constructed in the New World. Many people died in the monumental effort required to transport the wood across the mountains to the Pacific. Balboa sailed two ships to the Pearl Islands and then one hundred miles south down the coast. Pedrarias's jealousy flared at the news and he was determined Balboa would neither escape his jurisdiction nor beat him to the gold of Peru. He had Balboa swiftly arrested, tried, sentenced, and beheaded, and took possession of his ships.

C. L. G. Anderson, *Life and Letters of Vasco Núñez de Balboa*, 1971.

O. Garrison, *Balboa: Conquistador*, 1971.

K. Romoli, *Balboa of Darien*, 1953.

O

O'CONNELL, DANIEL (1775–1847), Irish politician known as "the Great Liberator." O'Connell was born in the family mansion of Derrynane Abbey in County Kerry in southwest Ireland. Income from the ancient O'Connell lands supplemented by the proceeds of smuggling supported a comfortable upbringing and schooling in Saint-Malo, France, a school in fashion with Irish Catholic gentry. He was influenced by the libertarian ideas of the late eighteenth century and supported the Irish rebellion of 1798. The violence of the revolt made a deep impression on him and he decided that violent protest was no solution to Ireland's woes and that the struggle should be confined to the political arena, with the threat of force used only as a last resort.

Catholics did not enjoy the same civil liberties available to Protestant citizens. This was especially irksome to men of O'Connell's class who felt their social position entitled them to a share in political power. Only in 1793 were Catholics in Ireland first allowed to serve as jurors, as army officers, or as lawyers; it was the latter profession that O'Connell chose. He possessed a natural talent with words; ambitious and determined, he became very wealthy from his legal practice.

In pursuit of Catholic emancipation, O'Connell sought to galvanize the Irish masses in one of the first examples of a popular political campaign. The Chief Secretary for Ireland, Sir Robert Peel, described him as an "eloquent and vulgar speaker," the kind of man who could soon have a large crowd at his command. O'Connell was a lover of ceremonies at which bands, uniforms, and shamrocks were all utilized in what the ruling establishment viewed as rabble rousing; he has been called "the greatest agitator of all time."

O'Connell was also proud and hot-tempered, not one to take an insult, perceived or actual, lightly. Sir Robert Peel soon fell foul of his wrath after quoting him in a manner O'Connell found offensive. In 1815 O'Connell challenged him to a duel; he had already shot another political opponent dead in a duel that same year. It was probably Peel's good fortune that O'Connell was arrested on the way to the duel in Ostend (dueling was illegal in England). In later years there was a bungled attempt at reconciliation between the two men but their continuing dislike for each other became a real factor in British politics as both came to occupy positions of power.

In 1823 O'Connell formed the Catholic Association, which attracted mass support for its program of removing Irish political disabilities. Its low subscription of a penny a month allowed it to develop into a popular political organization. O'Connell was quick in realizing the potential of a body that could raise £20,000 in less than a year and draw the support of the Catholic church and peasantry. The association became a powerful force in Irish politics, registering supporters and electing candidates favorable to emancipation. The struggle culminated in the election of O'Connell as a Member of Parliament for Clare in 1828. He could not take his seat since it involved making an oath objectionable to Catholics, but the government, aware of his strong following, decided concession was the safest course. In 1829 the Act of Catholic Emancipation was passed by the British Parliament.

O'Connell became a key figure in Westminster politics, entering into alliance with the Whigs, whom he considered most likely to favor Irish advancement. Disraeli, the great opponent of the Whigs called O'Connell "an incendiary and a traitor." O'Connell retaliated by calling his opponent a "miscreant" and another duel was in the offing; this time it was O'Connell's opponent who was arrested and fined and the contest thus averted.

In the 1840s O'Connell initiated a campaign of "Monster Meetings" to press for the repeal of the 1800 union between Ireland and England; again pageantry and a quasi-military discipline was brought to bear. At the most famous of the meetings at Tara (associated with early Irish kings) he addressed some seven hundred and fifty thousand people (almost 10 percent of the country's population) and told them that "the strength and majority of the national movement was never exhibited so imposingly." His forecast of the closeness of repeal of the Union was premature. This time the government viewed the price of concession as too high: a future meeting was banned and O'Connell arrested, and his goal took the best part of a century to achieve.

O'Connell died in Genoa in 1847 while on his way to an audience with the pope. He asked for his heart to be buried in Rome and the rest of his embalmed body to be returned to Ireland. In his lifetime he had become a popular legend, the Liberator who had brought to fruition the potential political power of the Irish masses. He raised the Irish people from their torpor and educated them to political technique and action. He defined the nature of modern Ireland and in defining it, created it.

A. Macintyre, *The Liberator: Daniel O'Connell*, 1965.

OMAR (Umar ibn al-Khattab; 586–644), second Muslim caliph; father-in-law of *Muhammad. Omar was an early opponent of Muhammad who once planned to kill the prophet. Met by a cousin, he was warned that Muhammad's followers would not hesitate to avenge him; he would do better if he would first restore his sister Fatimah and his brother-in-law to their family's religion. Omar arrived at Fatimah's home as she and her husband were being taught a newly revealed fragment of what would become the Koran. The teacher hid himself, and Omar's sister Fatimah concealed the manuscript in her bosom. When his brother-in-law confirmed that they had adopted the new faith, Omar attacked him. Fatimah threw herself between the two men, and was wounded by her brother. Staring at the blood streaming down her face, Omar was appalled by what he had done. His cowardly attack in which his own sister was injured contrasted sharply with the couple's conviction. Omar asked his sister to teach him about Islam. The teacher then came out and began to read from the manuscript. So deeply moved was Omar by the text that, in the sixth year of Muhammad's mission, he too became a Muslim.

Omar was soon a favorite of the prophet. When Muhammad married his daughter Hafsa, it was expected that Omar would succeed him. He himself refused to accept that Muhammad was mortal; when told that Muhammad had died, he responded, "The prophet is not dead, but only swooned away." No one could convince Omar that the prophet could have died before every nonbeliever and heretic had been rooted. Only when *Abu Bakr made his famous statement, "O you believers! Know that the Prophet Muhammad is dead. But you who have faith in God, know that God is alive and can never die," did Omar accept Muhammad's demise. Omar was a zealous supporter of Abu Bakr in the caliphate. Although their temperaments were different — Abu Bakr was calm and sedate; Omar was often rash and violent — the two men became close. Othman, an early follower of Muhammad, questioned Abu Bakr's announcement that Omar was his heir but was rebuffed: "What is hidden is better than what is revealed."

Despite his severity, Omar was a just man with no pretensions to glory. He succeeded Abu Bakr as caliph in 634 amid questions of his ability to govern fairly if his own son was known to engage in lecher-

ous activities. Omar asked what the penalty for lechery was; when told it was eighty lashes, he proceeded to beat his son. He often wandered the market, whip in hand, seeking out religious offenders. "Omar's whip is more terrible than another's sword," was a common saying. At the same time, Omar was frugal; when military leaders reported to him in all their splendor, he threw gravel at them. He was willing to go to extremes to help his subjects, once providing and cooking an entire meal for an indigent widow and her family. He could be cruel to his foes, and often demanded that all prisoners be killed, but was tolerant of Christians and Jews, allowing them to practice their religion beyond the boundaries of the sacred Arabian peninsula.

The two greatest feats accomplished by Omar were his vast conquests and his civil innovations. His many generals, led by Abu Obeid and Amr ibn al-As, conquered Syria, Iraq, Persia, Egypt, Libya, and Palestine. Omar's conquests would have extended even farther were it not for his insistence, against the advice of his generals, that no new conquests be made until Islamic law was enforced in the newly captured territories. Omar also planned a naval invasion of Abyssinia (Ethiopia) but abandoned any further attempts at naval conquest when the expedition met with disaster. Among the civil innovations begun by Omar was the adoption of a new lunar calendar dating from Muhammad's flight from Mecca to Medina in 622. He also started the *diwan*, a census of Muslims, so that spoils of war could be distributed among the believers. Omar planned that the distribution of wealth be carried out on a fixed scale based on three factors: priority of conversion, affinity to the prophet, and prior military service.

The most prized of Omar's conquests was Jerusalem, the city from where Muhammad — according to tradition — had ascended to heaven to receive the Koran. The city was besieged by Amr ibn al-As, whom Omar joined personally, bringing four thousand horses. When he arrived at the encampment, his attendant was riding a camel while Omar walked alongside. Everyone hailed his attendant as the caliph, unaware that the real caliph was the person guiding the camel. The Greek patriarch Sophronius's request for a truce was accepted, but Omar first asked Sophronius to lead him to the rock from which Muhammad ascended to heaven. First, Sophronius took him to the Church of the Holy Sepulcher. Omar immediately realized that the site did not fit the description of Muhammad and asked to be taken to the rock. Sophronius then brought him to another church, this one on Mount Zion, but the site still did not fit the description, so Sophronius took him to another church, then another, until they had seen all the churches in the city. Finally Omar was brought to a sewer, but realizing that the site finally fit Muhammad's description, he crawled on his knees until he reached the sacred rock.

Omar was tolerant of both the Jewish and Christian communities of Jerusalem. Jews had served in his armies and were therefore granted the right to settle in the city and even to rebuild their Temple (this was revoked immediately after Omar's death). His relationship with the Christians can be understood from his visit to the Church of the Holy Sepulcher. The call for prayer was suddenly sounded, so Sophronius invited the caliph to pray in the church. Omar responded that for him to do so would sanctify the site to Muslims as well as Christians and future wars would be fought over its possession. Instead, he would pray elsewhere; the Mosque of Omar was later erected on the site he chose.

Omar's prolific career was cut short by an assassin. In 644, he was murdered for personal reasons by a Persian slave. The caliphate was inherited by Othman, the zealous Muslim who had questioned Abu Bakr's choice ten years earlier.

F. Gabrieli, *Mohammed and the Conquests of Islam*, 1968.
W. Muir, *The Caliphate*, 1924.

OMAR KHAYYAM (died c.1123), Persian poet, mathematician, astronomer, and scientist. Little accurate information on the life of this mysterious but evidently brilliant man is available. Khayyam (meaning "tentmaker") is most probably a nickname referring to the profession of his ancestors, although the similarity of the Persian word for "tents" and for "verses" has suggested to some an intriguing alternative. Today he is remembered almost exclusively as the composer of the verses which, when presented in English translation by Edward FitzGerald, took the Victorian world of letters by storm.

In his own time, Khayyam was recognized a preeminent man of science. A supporter of *Avicenna's theories, he was a scholar of philosophy, history, and jurisprudence. However, he was not a prolific writer, although it is known that he produced works on physics, existence, and being and obligation. Under the auspices of the sultan Malik Shah he collaborated in the 1074 reform of the Persian calendar; the result was substantially more accurate than its predecessor and constituted an impressive work of mathematical astronomy.

Omar Khayyam was in addition one of the great mathematicians of medieval times. His work on algebra is widely considered as the most notable contribution of his country and his age to the subject. He was one of the first to make a scientific attempt to classify equations of the first degree, or to consider cubes from the standpoint of the general equation, while his *Difficulties of Euclid's Definitions* was a pioneering medieval essay on the Greek mathematician. As a physicist, Khayyam concentrated on researching the specific weight of silver and gold; this had a useful practical application in assessing the quantities of these valuable materials in objets d'art and jewelry.

Such was Khayyam's renown that Malik Shah offered him preferment at the Seljuk court, but this did not meet the poet-philosopher's needs. Instead, he requested the means to live in retirement and oc-

Omar Khayyam, by Max Beerbohm
1 The Book of Verses. 2 Bough. 3 Loaf of Bread
4 Jug of Wine. 5 Thou. 6. Wilderness

cupy himself with learning. The arrangement was duly made, and he received a pension enabling him to pursue his mathematical and astronomical studies uninterruptedly.

The subject matter of Omar Khayyam's *Rubaiyat* serves to indicate that, in addition to his pursuit of knowledge, Khayyam was also an avid pursuer of more hedonistic interests; the work is a frank admonition to enjoy life's fleeting pleasures to the full before the inevitable unknown of death and contains many verses praising the virtues of love and wine. It is written in quatrains, four-line verses in which the first, second, and fourth lines rhyme. FitzGerald's version, *The Rubaiyat of Omar Khayyam*, is in fact far more than a simple translation, for the quatrains he brought together and ordered into a coherent whole were in reality disparate fragments from the poet's corpus (while some of the verses cannot be definitively ascribed to Omar Khayyam at all). Moreover, in translating, FitzGerald sought to render the spirit rather than the letter of the original,

> ## FROM THE *RUBAIYAT*
>
> - A Book of Verses underneath the Bough
>   A Jug of Wine, a Loaf of Bread — and Thou
>   Beside me singing in the Wilderness —
>   Oh, Wilderness were Paradise now.
> - The Worldly Hope men set their Hearts upon
>   Turns Ashes — or it prospers; and anon
>   Like Snow upon the Desert's dusty Face,
>   Lighting a little hour or two — is gone.
> - The Moving Finger writes; and having writ,
>   Moves on; nor all your Piety nor Wit
>   Shall lure it back to cancel half a Line,
>   Nor all your Tears wash out a word of it.

being prepared to sacrifice pedantic rigor where it clashed with the demands of euphony.

The *Rubaiyat*'s arresting mix of sarcastic pessimism, epicurean hedonism, and mystic inquiry has intrigued as well as entertained. Critics have discerned a symbolic significance in the work that points to Khayyam's affinity with the Sufis, the Muslim mystics whose interpretation of Islam often deviated from that of the orthodox and who craved ecstatic communion with God. Yet Khayyam's verses also criticize quasi-mystical pretentiousness, showing the author to have been free from clear-cut religious affiliations.

The publication of FitzGerald's second edition of the verses in 1868 heralded the onset of the *Rubaiyat* enthusiasm that was to catapult both the self-effacing Victorian translator and the medieval Persian sage to fame. To this day Khayyam's quatrains remain favorites, one of the most oft-quoted and more idiosyncratic collections to have gained a place among the undisputed classics of world literature.
A. J. Arberry, *Omar Khayyam*, 1952.

O'NEILL, EUGENE GLADSTONE (1888–1953), first great American playwright and a Nobel prizewinner for literature (1936). He wrote more than sixty plays, entering the dramatic scene at a time when American theater was groping for its own identity. His American drama was characterized by stories of sorrow, tragedy, and despair, not as the result of catastrophic occurrences, but rather the tragedy of everyday life — twisted relationships, wrong choices, unfulfilled dreams. The son of a distinguished, romantic, but alcoholic Irish-American actor, James O'Neill, Eugene was born into the life of the theater. He had a Catholic upbringing, which he later rejected, and from the age of eight attended boarding schools; the tragic family relationships of his youth are reflected in many of his plays. Ten months after he entered Princeton University he was expelled for throwing a brick through the window of the stationmaster's home.

In 1909 O'Neill traveled to Honduras to prospect for gold. He also sailed as a seaman on several voyages to Buenos Aires and Portuguese East Africa. These experiences were to provide him with the background for a number of one-act plays, including *The Long Voyage Home.*

After returning to the United States, O'Neill worked as a journalist for the *New London Telegraph* in Connecticut but developed tuberculosis and was hospitalized in a sanatorium for five months.

During that time O'Neill began to read the plays of August Strindberg, which greatly influenced him to begin writing his own plays. While recuperating over the next fifteen months, O'Neill wrote eleven one-act plays and two longer ones. Only six of them survived his scrutiny. His father paid for the publication of five of those plays in a volume entitled *Thirst* in 1914 and sent his son to the year-long Workshop 47 playwriting course at Harvard University.

O'Neill's first real break came in 1916, when a summer stock theater troupe, the Wharf Theater in Provincetown, Massachusetts, produced *Bound East for Cardiff.* At season's end the troupe moved to New York, becoming the Provincetown Players, and continued to produce O'Neill's works. In 1920 *Beyond the Horizon* won him his first Pulitzer Prize. He was awarded two more Pulitzers, for *Anna Christie* (1922) and *Strange Interlude* (1928), the latter employing the stream-of-consciousness technique.

Other plays of the 1920s and 1930s included *The Emperor Jones* (1920), an expressionist play for a single actor; *The Hairy Ape* (1922); *Desire under the Elms* (1924), the first of his plays directly inspired by Greek tragedy; *The Great God Brown* (1926), which experimented with the use of masks; *Marco Millions* (1928); and his only comedy, *Ah, Wilderness!* (1933). His outstanding trilogy, *Mourning Becomes Electra* (1931), tells the story of a family in New England in the period after the Civil War while retelling the ancient Greek tragedy of Clytemnestra, Agamemnon, and their children.

After *Days without End* (1934), O'Neill was silent for twelve years, making his comeback in 1946 with the powerful *The Iceman Cometh*, set in a New York bar. During this time he began work on a nine-play cycle about the "rise and fall" of the American family from 1775 to 1932, *A Tale of Possessors Self-Dispossessed*, but very little of it was completed before his death.

With the onset of World War II, O'Neill sank into despair and was unable to work for a time. However, from this low point he went on to write a series of plays inspired by his early family life. His most famous work, *Long Day's Journey into Night*, produced posthumously in 1956, revealed a family secret. His mother had become a morphine addict at his birth; she was given the drug by a doctor to ease her pain and then became addicted. Many attempts to wean her from the drug were made but none succeeded. The play was not to have been produced, by O'Neill's request, for twenty-five years after his death, but it was released by his widow and staged in 1955. He was posthumously awarded another

FROM O'NEILL'S WRITINGS

- The theater to me is life — the substance and interpretation of life. And life is struggle, often — if not usually — unsuccessful struggle, for most of us have something within us which prevents us from accomplishing what we dream and desire.
- None of us can help the things life has done to us. They're done before you realize it, and once they're done they make you do other things until at last everything comes between you and what you'd like to be, and you've lost your true self forever.
- When men make gods, there is no God.

Pulitzer for the play. Other plays with a family background were *A Moon for the Misbegotten* (1947) and *A Touch of the Poet*, produced posthumously in 1958.

His last years were marked by tragedies which sometimes seemed to be reenactments of his own dramas. Two of his three marriages ended in divorce; his eldest son committed suicide, and he never saw or spoke to his daughter, Oona, after she married Charlie Chaplin, who was her father's age. In 1947 he was stricken with Parkinson's disease; his hands trembled so much that he could no longer write. Dudley Nichols, a close friend, critic, and Hollywood writer, offered to write for him but he would not agree: "His handwriting was a part of his mind, almost a part of his imagination....His hand stopped, his work was stopped, and he knew it."
A. and B. Gelb, *O'Neill*, 1973.
J. Martine, *Critical Essays on Eugene O'Neill*, 1984.
L. Sheafer, *O'Neill*, 2 vols., 1968–1973.

OPPENHEIMER, J(ULIUS) ROBERT

(1904–1967), theoretical physicist and scientific administrator responsible for organizing the development of the first atomic bomb.

Oppenheimer was the son of a cultured and successful German-Jewish immigrant family in New York City. As a young child he displayed a prodigious genius and eclectic curiosity. He spent a brief period at a boarding school in Los Alamos, New Mexico, where he developed a love for its dramatic vistas and rugged terrain. It was no coincidence that he would return to this place later in his life to complete his greatest achievement.

His three years at Harvard University were spent mostly in the library. He first majored in chemistry, then switched to experimental physics, and finally after taking on a course load equal to seven normal undergraduate requirements, graduated in 1925 in theoretical physics. He also had an extraordinary knowledge in other fields: he could quote the sonnets of Donne and the wisdom of oriental philosophers and was fluent in several languages.

In 1926 Oppenheimer, a gangly youth with a rattling cough, traveled to Europe, first to Cambridge where he began his doctoral studies under Ernest *Rutherford, and then on to Göttingen in 1927 to work under Max Born. He dazzled his peers and professors with his erudite and eloquent dissertations, and his easy manner won him many friends. In 1927 he was awarded his doctorate, moving on to Leyden in Holland where he lectured for several months.

By this time he was becoming homesick and made inquiries about academic positions in the United States. His growing reputation had preceded him, and he was courted by several universities. He eventually settled on an assistant professorship at the University of California, Berkeley, giving as his reason his enchantment with the collection of French Renaissance poetry in the university library. An inspirational and dedicated teacher, he arranged his teaching calendar to allow him to spend alternative semesters lecturing at the California Institute of Technology, Pasadena. His students would frequently follow him from institution to institution, and despite his youth, he soon became the master of the new generation of American physicists. His pupils would even imitate his mannerisms, coughing occasionally and tilting their heads slightly when talking, as he did, Ironically, Oppenheimer's persistent cough was discovered not to be an affectation but a symptom of tuberculosis. The disease, which was not diagnosed for several years, never seemed to impede his immense energy or activity. Despite his remarkable success as a teacher, Oppenheimer never mad a fundamental contribution to physics. His work mostly refined and elaborated the discoveries of others.

Oppenheimer, like most intellectuals of his age, was deeply distressed by the rise of fascism in Europe, especially when members of his own family fell victim to Adolf *Hitler's policies. His interest in politics remained dormant, however, until 1936, when he began dating Jean Tatlock, a psychiatry student. She was a committed communist, and through her Oppenheimer became peripherally involved in the Left. After his father's death in 1937, Oppenheimer even began using some of his large inheritance to finance a number of anti-Fascist causes. The couple were close to marriage when, in 1940, Oppenheimer fell in love with and married an attractive laboratory assistant, Katharina Puening. At the same time he severed all connections with the communists after hearing disturbing reports about conditions in the Soviet Union.

In 1942 Oppenheimer was selected to head the Manhattan Project, the Allied effort to develop the atomic bomb. The knowledge that the Nazis were trying to produce a similar bomb prompted him to accept. Searching for a suitable remote location to assemble his team, he remembered his old boarding school at Los Alamos, which was well inland and isolated. Thus, in March 1943 the first atomic scientists ascended the New Mexico Mesa to begin their research.

Robert Oppenheimer

His appointment necessitated that he pass a security screening, which revealed his previous association with the Communist party. The chief security officer for the project subsequently recommended against the appointment, bus his recommendation was rejected by the military head of the project, General Groves. Nonetheless, the security services continued to amass information on Oppenheimer over the next decade.

Despite his young age and relative lack of scientific credentials, Oppenheimer's brilliant leadership soon became apparent. With the help of his personal charisma, which was described by one of his recruits as "intellectual sex appeal," he managed to cajole or persuade many great scientists, including several Nobel laureates, to work in a cooperative effort to develop the bomb. The first atomic bomb was tested under the code name "Trinity" on 16 July, 1945. Its explosive power shocked even its inventors and gave them a new dread of what they had created. Oppenheimer was heard to quote from *Bhagavad Gita* "I am become Death, the destroyer of worlds." The news three weeks later that a bomb had been used on Hiroshima led Oppenheimer to say later that "physicists have known sin." Oppenheimer was, to his discomfort, embraced by a frenzied American public as the heroic father of the atomic bomb. Although perceiving that nuclear rivalry would now escalate between America and the Soviet Union, practical political concerns probably stopped him from joining the growing scientific chorus of warnings. This caused him to lose many of the friends who had idolized him for years.

In October 1945 Oppenheimer resigned as director of Los Alamos, initially intending to return to his academic duties. The war years, however, had irreversibly transformed him from an eager theorist into an extremely successful planner and politician. He was promptly co-opted onto numerous government committees and in 1947 became the director of the Institute for Advanced Study at Princeton. He was also appointed chairman of the general advisory committee to the newly established Atomic Energy Commission.

Around 1949 the military and a number of atomic scientists headed by Edward Teller began promoting the development of the hydrogen bomb. Oppenheimer and his committee felt that such an action would only accelerate the arms race, so when the project was approved by the government Oppenheimer immediately resigned his chairmanship of the committee. The cold war had begun and anti-Communist feeling was running high. Oppenheimer was stunned when in 1953 his security clearance was revoked on advice from Edgar J. Hoover, head of the F.B.I., that he was probably a spy. Not only were his previous Communist alliances resurrected, but his opposition to the hydrogen bomb project was brought as evidence of his disloyalty. Refusing to step down from the Atomic Energy Commission, loyalty proceedings were initiated against him in 1954. He was duly found a loyal citizen but not a good security risk, and he was dismissed from all public offices. Edward Teller was the only scientist to speak against Oppenheimer at the hearing, and for his actions was ostracized from the scientific community for many years.

In 1963, by way of an apology, the Atomic Energy Commission awarded Oppenheimer its highest honor, the Enrico Fermi Award. He remained the director at Princeton until 1965, lecturing with profound insight about the world in the atomic age. He died a year later of throat cancer.

R. Jungk, *Brighter Than a Thousand Stars*, 1958.
L. Lansing, *Day of Trinity*, 1965.
H. F. York, *The Advisors*, 1976.

OSMAN I (1258–1326), founder of the Ottoman Empire. Much of what is known about Osman is shrouded by legends perpetrated by later Ottoman historiographers to confer a stately lineage on the imperial family. They claim that Osman's father Ertugrul led four hundred nomadic Seljuk horsemen through Anatolia where they encountered Sultan Aladdin of Konya besieged by Mongols. His men favored siding with the Mongols, but Ertugrul admonished them that justice demanded they support the weaker Aladdin. The Mongols were defeated, and Ertrugul was rewarded with Eskishehir and Sugut, where Osman was born. When Osman succeeded Ertugrul, Aladdin granted him a banner and drum, traditional symbols of sovereignty.

Osman was originally a pagan, but while residing at a Muslim's house, he noticed how his host cherished a well-worn Koran. When told that the book contained the word of God, Osman studied it throughout the night until, just before dawn, he began to doze. God appeared to him in a dream and said, "Since you have honored my word, so too your descendants will be honored forever." Inspired by his vision, Osman converted to Islam, which he studied with the *kadi* (Muslim religious judge) Edebali. He fell in love with Edebali's daughter Malkatun, but the *kadi* was hesitant about giving her to Osman. After two years of courtship, Osman had another dream. In it, a full moon rose from the sheikh's breast and entered his own. A tree then grew from his loins, bearing branches that shaded the world. He then saw four mountain ranges: the Balkans, the Caucasus, the Atlas, and the Taurus, watered by four rivers: the Tigris, the Euphrates, the Nile, and the Danube. The land contained noble cities in which the cry to prayer mingled with the singing of nightingales. Suddenly, the leaves of the tree became swords, pointing to Constantinople. The city was a diamond ring, mounted between two emeralds and two sapphires. Just as Osman was about to put the ring on his finger, he woke up. Edebali interpreted the dream as meaning that from the union of Osman with Malkatun, a great empire would emerge and so allowed them to marry.

Osman was an imposing figure who radiated a natural sense of superiority to his subjects. As a neophyte, he had a well-developed sense of Islamic justice but insisted on peaceful relations with his Christian neighbors, many of whom later embraced Islam. In return, he adopted their administrative and mercantile practices, and did little to harass the cities of Nicaea, Nicomedia, and Bursa, blocking his way to Constantinople. The Byzantine emperor, however, was wary of Osman's mounting strength and unsuccessfully endeavored to enlist Mongol assistance in constraining him. Only after the Byzantines attacked Osman in 1301 was he persuaded to launch his own assault. In 1308 he conquered the fortress of Ak Hisar, controlling the descent of the Sakarya River to the Black Sea, enabling him to sever the land route between Bursa, Nicaea, and Nicomedia. Determining that Bursa was the weakest link in the defense of Constantinople, he lay siege to the city. For seven years, the local governor Evenros waited for troops from Constantinople to relieve him. Finally, as Osman lay dying, Evenros surrendered the city and converted to Islam. At his death, Osman left just a salt cellar, a spoon, a robe, and a number of sheep. He was succeeded by his son Orhan. In later Ottoman (a word derived form "Osman") tradition, new emperors were girded with Osman's sword and blessed, "May he be as good as Osman."

M. A. Cook, *The History of the Ottoman Empire to 1730*, 1976.

H. A. Gibbons, *The Foundations of the Ottoman Empire: A History of the Osmanlis up to the Death of Bayezid I*, 1968.

Lord Kinross, *The Ottoman Centuries: The Rise and Fall of the Turkish Empire*, 1978.

OTTO I (Otto the Great; 912–973), German king and Holy Roman emperor. The son of King Henry I, Otto, a strong and practical leader, sought to bring order and justice to the newly developed German Reich. His vassal dukes feared him more than they loved him. In spite of a failed rebellion led by his half brother and supported by his younger brother, Henry, Otto continued to rely on family alliances in order to control his kingdom. However, loyalty and trust within the duchies quickly began to deteriorate under the corrupt feudal system.

Hereditary feudalism posed a serious threat to Otto's monarchy. In response, he began to appoint trusted, celibate church officials who could not distribute fiefs among their relations. The monarchy's alliance with the church became crucial to Otto's own consolidation of power; the mores of Christianity and German security were used to justify the ensuing wars against the Slavs in the east.

After subduing the Slavs through the conquest of Bohemia in 950, and increasing his political influence among weak kings in France, Otto invaded Italy in 951. His bid to restore the empire of *Charlemagne appeared feasible as he tried to control a route to the East while reinforcing his alliance with the church through closer relations with the papacy in Rome.

Otto assumed the Lombard crown in Pavia, where he married his second wife, Adelaide. In the midst of his military campaign to establish control over the Italian peninsula his son Liudolf, from his first wife, led a revolt in Germany. However, the rebel forces were weakened by the Magyar invasion of Bavaria in 954. Liudolf and the rebelling dukes submitted their armies to Otto, who defeated the Magyars in the Battle of the Lechfeld, near Augsburg, in 955.

Otto's consolidation of power in Germany was complete with the crowning of his son, Otto II, as king of Germany in 962. Otto once again invaded Italy, conquered the Papal State and was crowned Holy Roman emperor by Pope John XII in 968, recreating the Empire of the West which had existed under Charlemagne. A few days after the coronation, a treaty, the *Privilegium Ottonianum*, defined the roles of the emperor and the pope in an empire that was to be the central ruling power of Europe for centuries. Problems, however, arose in Rome, where Pope John XII was unwilling to cede control over the Papal States to Otto. Otto deposed him and nominated Leo VIII as pope. After Leo VIII's death in 965, his successor, John XIII, was expelled by the Romans. Otto marched into Italy for the third time, to reestablish his control over the region and reinstate John XIII as pope.

The appointment of John XIII and the creation of new Latin archbishoprics in the south brought Otto's empire into conflict with the Byzantine Empire of the East. Otto attempted to exacerbate the conflict through military confrontation but eventually initiated negotiations with the Byzantine

Emperor Nicephorus Phocas. The resulting marriage of Otto II with the Byzantine princess, Theophano (daughter of Romanus II), in 972, reinforced the Holy Roman emperor's sovereignty over a reunited Europe. Otto I spent six years in Italy before returning to Germany, where he died.

Otto's reign as Holy Roman emperor revived and reunited the Western world after its near collapse following the demise of the Carolingian Empire. While the resurrected empire was not quite as spectacular as that of Charlemagne, it was more firmly based on contemporary social and cultural forces, which stimulated literature, language, and art in a more civilized Europe.

J. Bryce, *The Holy Roman Empire*, 1961.

J. Fleckenstein, *Early Medieval Germany*, 1978.

J. J. Gallagher, *Church and State in Germany under Otto the Great*, 1938.

K. J. Leyser, *Medieval Germany and its Neighbors*, 1982

OVID (Publius Ovidius Naso; 43 B.C.E.–17 C.E.), prominent Roman poet; native of Sulmo (a Paelignian town in central Italy). Of a noble family, Ovid studied law at Rome and began a government career. He was helped by Messala Corvinus and was acquainted with other poets of his time; having close ties with Propertius and Tibullus. In the midst of his literary and social success, *Augustus banished him to Tomi (Constanta) on the Black Sea in 8 C.E. Ovid only alludes to the reasons for his banishment: a poem he wrote and an error; what this error was has never been satisfactorally. The poem was his *Ars Amatoria*, and apparently this *Art of Love* so offended Augustus that public libraries in Rome were not allowed to keep his works. Tomi was an inhospitable place for Ovid, with a population only partially Hellenized, bad climate, and frequent attacks by Scythian tribes. In his *Tristia* and *Epistulae ex Ponto* he often expresses his feelings about these hardships. Time and again he asked to be pardoned but was rejected both by Augustus and *Tiberius and he died in exile.

The extant poems of Ovid are numerous. *Amores*, love poems, originally comprising five books (c. 20 B.C.E.), were edited to three volumes. These are forty-nine short poems addressed mainly to one Corinna, an imaginary beloved. *Heroides* are verse love letters by mythical women (Penelope, Deianira, Helen, and Ariadne, among others) to their husbands or lovers. To the original fifteen letters (that of *Sappho is suspected of not being genuine) Ovid later added another five poems (letters and replies). The letters are more like monologues and Ovid's rhetorical training is clear in them. Only one hundred verses remain of *Medicamina faciei Femineae*, a poem on cosmetics. *Ars Amatoria*, a three-book didactic poem, gives instructions how to win and retain a lover. The first two books are for men; Ovid added the third for women in response to a request ("to provide amazons with arms"). Original, witty,

and accomplished, this work parodies didactic literature. *Remedium Amoris*, a sequel of the former work, teaches how to end a love affair.

While all of his other poems are written in elegiac couplets, Ovid's *Metamorphoses* is an epic written in hexameters. Here he drew on the vast mythological material in Greek and Roman literature relating to changes from one form into another and presented them within one poem. He succeeded in giving unity to the different stories by providing ingenious ties between them (including a story within a story) and by using chronological sequence. The last change is that of the transformation of Julius *Caesar into a god. The material was so vast that the poem fills fifteen books. It was incomplete when Ovid was banished and he reacted by burning it; but his friends had copies. The epic remains extremely popular even in modern times and has had extensive influence on writers and artists.

In *Fasti*, a verse account of the calendar of Roman religion, each month was assigned one book, but Ovid was banished after completing only six books. For such an erudite poem there was no appropriate library for him to complete his research in Tomi and so he was never able to finish it. *Tristia*, comprising five books of elegies written in exile, also described his journey to Tomi and his new experiences and conditions, and *Epistulae ex Ponto* (four books) contains elegies with the same mood and motifs as the *Tristia*. *Ibis* is a curse in verse on an unknown enemy. Ovid's other works, including a tragedy, *Medea*, are not extant.

If his main theme is the passionate emotions of the heart, Ovid is too much of a cynic to treat it with complete seriousness; irony, reason, and ease govern his erotic poetry. Erudite, witty, and inventive, master of language and meter, Ovid wrote poems for enjoyment, both his own and his readers'.

B. Otis, *Ovid as an Epic Poet*, 1966.

L. P. Wilkinson, *Ovid Recalled*, 1955.

OWEN, ROBERT (1771–1858), British social reformer. A native of Newtown, Wales, his father was a saddler, ironmonger, and local postmaster in one. Owen was an outstanding if precocious student and at age seven was already assisting the local schoolmaster. His interests were wideranging, including history, nature, travel, and religion, although at the age of ten he decided none of the established religions met his ideals.

In 1781 he began an apprenticeship with a draper in Stamford. Owen earned a reputation as a hard worker and then succeeded in finding better paying jobs in London and, in 1788, in Manchester. He was appointed supervisor of a cotton mill employing five hundred. He initiated marked improvements in productivity; the owner was impressed and took him into partnership.

In Manchester Owen witnessed the Industrial Revolution in its key formative phase; the employment of power driven machinery in large factories and the emergence of a proletariat living in appalling housing and sanitary conditions — life expectancy was just nineteen. He saw both the potential and the dangers in these radical changes and for the rest of his long life, much of his effort was invested in trying to improve conditions for factory workers. While in Manchester, Owen joined the influential Philosophical and Literary Society, finding the courage to deliver the first of many public addresses.

Marriage took him away from Manchester to New Lanark in Scotland, where he married the daughter of David Dale, a mill owner and merchant. In partnership with his associates in Manchester he acquired a share in the New Lanark mills established by Dale.

The Scottish peasantry were reluctant to exchange the natural rhythms of farm work for life regulated by the clock. Therefore the workforce was formed from pauper children sent from Edinburgh workhouses and unruly adult operatives drawn from the lowest section of society. Owen described their "living in idleness, in poverty, in almost every kind of crime; consequently in debt, out of health and in misery." The children were well housed but they began work at six years old and a thirteen-hour working day left many deformed.

Owen's takeover was resisted by workers resenting their employer not being a Scotsman and fearing he would tighten Dale's lax discipline. Gradually he overcame suspicions, convincing them that the mill community could be reorganized to their advantage. Instead of punishments, checks were introduced, cutting down opportunities for theft. Owen stressed that the rewards of honest industry would from now on far exceed those of stealing. By reducing the number of drink retailers and an effective propaganda campaign, alcoholism was much reduced. A sixtieth of workers' wages went toward a fund for sick benefit, compensation for injury, and pensions. Free education was provided for children from age five until they began work at ten. Attention was also given to improving housing and a cheap grocery store was established.

The experiment created a contented industrial community under Owen's paternal guidance and New Lanark cotton mills produced healthy profits for the owners. The inhabitants demonstrated their new regard for him by unharnessing his carriage and drawing it themselves through the village.

In 1813 Owen set out his views in *A New Society*. New Lanark had demonstrated that by improving work and living environments and extending the benefits of education to working class children, great advantages accrue to all.

Many people of rank and consequence visited New Lanark and were impressed with the prosperity of his business and the condition of the inhabitants. The intelligence and happiness of the children was often noted; the infants' school was governed on the principle of making lessons interesting — not the more traditional reward and punishment approach.

Owen's philosophy remained highly controversial, particularly his advocacy of secular schooling, which angered the church. Factory owners also expressed hostility when he began pressing for legislation to reduce the working day. They saw their profits threatened, and some were concerned how workers might misuse additional leisure time.

Owen came to believe the solution to society's ills lay in the replacement of the capitalist system by one based on cooperative communities. Modern machinery could reduce the hours of work necessary to make a livelihood and hence everyone would have time to get a good education and throw off the vices of the ignorant. He circulated tens of thousands of newspapers carrying his proposals and stopped at nothing to ensure their distribution, even delaying the departure of the Royal Mail stagecoach from London. He traveled in Europe, trying to persuade princes and politicians of the merit of a drastic socioeconomic reform. *Napoleon was among these men of renown from whom Owen sought support.

In 1825 he purchased twenty thousand acres in Indiana in the United States and established a model community named New Harmony. For a period it flourished under his guidance but the economic basis was weak. Owen did not select members but accepted all who responded to his newspaper advertisement for "rational and well-intentioned" people; there were enough who did not answer the description to sow the discord in which New Harmony collapsed. Owen lost £40,000, the bulk of his fortune. Later, other Owenite communities were established in England, Ireland, and America but all proved short-lived.

Owen attracted a mass following from the English working- class. In the mid1830s he led a national trades union called the Grand National Consolidated Trades Union and saw the foundation of labor exchanges where artisans could barter their products. The union drew workers from many trades and they tried through a succession of strikes to advance the cause of labor. Determined employer and government opposition soon undermined it, but a landmark in the growth of the union movement had been passed.

During the 1840s Owen was as active as ever publicizing a philosophy that was now often termed socialist. Cooperative wholesale societies founded by Owen's followers proved highly popular. The society founded in Rochdale in 1844 marked the foundation of the still thriving Co-operative Wholesale Society. In his last years Owen turned to spiritualism, sure that in this way he would be able to succeed where he had failed in convincing the world of the need for radical change.

His son, **Robert Dale Owen** (1801–1877), settled in the United States, where he was also a social reformer. The first person to advocate publicly birth control in the United States, he helped to found the Smithsonian Institution and worked for the emancipation of slaves. He was U.S. minister to Naples, 1853–1958, and like his father, an avid spiritualist.

G. Claeys, *Citizens and Saints*, 1989.

G. D. H. Cole, *The Life of Robert Owen*, 1965.

P

PAINE, THOMAS (1737–1809), political writer and analyst; advocate of democratic principles. Thomas Paine was born in Thetford, Norfolk, England, the son of a Quaker corset maker. He lived a rather unsettled life, trying a great variety of occupations for brief periods. These included attempts as a sailor, teacher, tobacconist, grocer, and even customs inspector. In 1774 he decided, at the suggestion of Benjamin *Franklin, to try his fortune in America. Soon thereafter he found his vocation as a writer and editor of the *Pennsylvania Magazine*.

In 1776 he published his influential *Common Sense* pamphlet containing practical and persuasive arguments in favor of American independence from England. This sold one hundred and twenty thousand copies within three months and total sales reached half a million including four editions that were published in Europe. During the period of the revolutionary war (1776–1783) Paine not only served in the Continental army but published sixteen *Crisis* papers as well. The opening passage of the first *Crisis* paper published in 1776 was so stirring that General George *Washington ordered it to be read to the troops at all revolutionary encampments. The simple eloquent patriotism of this work allayed the fears and hesitation of many in, and even outside, the army.

From 1777 to 1779 Paine served as secretary of the Committee for Foreign Affairs and in 1779 was clerk of the Pennsylvania Assembly. By 1781 there was a need to negotiate aid from France, and Paine was sent to Paris to assist in this task. Apparently looking for new challenges after the revolutionary war, Paine left the United States and lived in Europe from 1787 to 1802. In 1791, while in England, he wrote and published his *Rights of Man* as his answer to Edmund *Burke's *Reflections on the French Revolution*, only to have the work suppressed for containing seditious passages. The English authorities then tried him for treason, but he managed to escape to France. Once in France, he was elected to the revolutionary National Convention, probably on the basis of his *Rights of Man*, which contained such passages as, "My country is the world, and my religion is to do good." However, his French triumph was short-lived due to the advent of Maximilien *Robespierre to power. In 1793 Paine was arrested, imprisoned, and stripped of his French citizenship.

In November 1794, through the efforts of the U.S. minister to France, James *Monroe, Paine was released from prison after a year of incarceration. While in prison, Paine wrote his famous work, *Age of Reason*, advocating moderate deism. In this work he attempted to develop a system of religion based upon science and morality, by applying principles of natural reason to religion. This work contained another of his oft quoted phrases: "The sublime and the ridiculous are often so nearly related that it is difficult to class them separately. One step above the sublime makes the ridiculous, and one step above the ridiculous makes the sublime again."

In 1796, probably after considerable thought but without proper investigation of the circumstances, he wrote a letter to President George *Washington

Bust of Thomas Paine, by John Wesley Jarvis

> - These are the times that try men's souls. The Summer soldier and the sunshine patriot will, in this crisis, shrink from the service of their country, but he that stands it *now* deserves the love and thanks of man and woman. Tyranny, like Hell, is not easily conquered; yet we have this consolation with us, that the harder the conflict the more glorious the triumph. What we obtain too cheaply we esteem too lightly; it is dearness only that gives everything its value. Heaven knows how to put a proper price upon its goods; and it would be strange indeed if so celestial an article as *freedom* should not be highly rated.
>
> **The Crisis** (first paper), 1776
>
> - Character is much easier kept than recovered.
> - My own mind is my own church.
> - Where there are no distinctions there can be no superiority; perfect equality affords no temptation.
> - Society is produced by our wants and government by our wickedness.
> - He that would make his own freedom secure must guard even his enemy from oppression.
>
> **Thomas Paine**

accusing him and Gouverneur Morris, Monroe's predecessor as minister to France, of deliberately plotting to keep him in jail in France. Paine had indeed languished in prison in France without any apparent action on his behalf by Morris, but for good reason. Morris knew that Paine's early release would have resulted in the reopening of his case. Such a reopening could easily have resulted in a death sentence. All that Paine accomplished with his famous letter was to alienate the American public.

In 1797 he published his *Agrarian Justice*, a proposal for a broad government welfare program to benefit youth as well as old age. By 1802 upon his return to the United States, he found no welcome — he had become a forgotten man due to his radical free thinking which upset people of all parties. He spent the last seven years of his life in poverty, ill-health, and obscurity. An obituary gave the assessment "He lived long, did some good, and much harm." In 1819, William Cobbett removed his remains to England intending to give him an appropriate burial but the bones were lost and never found.

A. Aldridge, *Thomas Paine's American Ideology*, 1984.
H. Fast, *Citizen Tom Paine*, 1943.
D. Hawke, *Paine*, 1974.
M. Philp, *Paine*, 1988.

PALMERSTON, JOHN HENRY TEMPLE, VISCOUNT (1784–1865), British statesman. Born in London to an Irish viscount, John Palmerston spent a large part of his early years with his family in Italy. He was then educated at Harrow and spent three years in Edinburgh studying under the famous philosopher Dugald Stewart. At seventeen he inherited the viscountcy, and a year later entered Cambridge University; politics interested him more than the classics and he made several unsuccessful attempts to become a Tory member of Parliament.

Through the patronage of Lord Malmesbury, a family friend, Palmerston entered government without having to win an election; in 1807 he was appointed a junior admiralty lord. Soon afterwards a seat was found for him at Newport, a borough under the control of Sir Leonard Holmes, who was so jealous that another might exercise influence there that he stipulated that Palmerston should not even visit his constituency.

Palmerston was not a gifted orator: his speeches were full of awkward pauses, but a determined, commanding manner revealed his leadership qualities. As early as 1809, Prime Minister Spencer Perceval offered him the post of chancellor of the exchequer. Palmerston thought this was an office "above his proper level" and reluctantly declined, but when it was suggested he might like to be secretary of war instead, he agreed, holding this position until 1828.

Although dedicated to his work, he was not neglectful of his pleasures. He enjoyed the customary circuit of country house parties, developing a model village on his Irish estate and managing his race horses. Palmerston's fondness for female company was well known and earned him the nickname "Cupid."

Early in his career Palmerston was a Tory who favored flogging in the army and a supported the slave trade, but his experiences in Ireland helped convince him to liberalize his opinions. By the late 1820s, when the duke of *Wellington's hard-line Tory government came to power, Palmerston was already out of sympathy with their opposition to parliamentary reform and Catholic emancipation, so he resigned his office and switched allegiance to the Whig party.

In 1830 he returned to the cabinet as foreign secretary, and once more enjoyed a long tenure. Skilled at languages and with many contacts in Europe, he was well suited for the job and served with distinction. He gave his support to newly emerging liberal regimes, played a crucial role in the creation of an independent Belgium, and demonstrated a sincere commitment to the suppression of the slave trade.

From 1841 to 1846 Palmerston was in the opposition. His return to the Foreign Office in 1846 was unpopular with Queen *Victoria and Prince Albert. They were opposed to his stand against Europe's absolute monarchies and never forgave him for an incident that had occurred in 1839 when he had tried to rape one of the queen's ladies while their guest in Windsor Castle. They longed for his resignation even though Prime Minister Lord John Russell assured them that Palmerston, now in his mid-sixties, was unlikely to trouble the court ladies again.

The hostility of royalty was counterbalanced by popularity with the public. He demonstrated his sympathy for Hungarians involved in a revolt against Austrian rule and when a visiting Austrian general was attacked in London he condoned the act. The attack on the home of Don Pacifico, a British subject from Gibraltar, who lived in Athens, led to his ordering the seizure of Greek ships in compensation. The originator of "gunboat diplomacy" believed the British government should intervene wherever its citizens were threatened or mistreated, and that they should always be free from indignity and could say like the ancient Romans "*Civis Romanus sum*" ("I am a Roman citizen"). Britain's parliamentary system was a model he wished to encourage other nations to adopt, stating "I hold that the real policy of England is to be champion of justice and right." His belligerency echoed the mood of the public and the press, contributing to his image as popular patriot.

In 1851 Palmerston went too far, by welcoming Louis *Napoleon's coup in Paris without first consulting the prime minister or Queen Victoria; he was forced to resign. His strong following in the country and in Parliament soon led to his return to office as home secretary and he turned his attention to measures to improve public health in Britain's cities.

In 1855 Lord Aberdeen's government collapsed in a scandal over mismanagement of the Crimean War. Popular opinion favored bringing in Palmerston to cope with the crisis and the queen had reluctantly to accept him as prime minister. For most of the next ten years he remained in power. The Crimean War was successfully ended, the Indian mutiny suppressed, and Great Britain enjoyed a period of comparative peace and tranquillity.

Palmerston remained hale; at the age of seventy-nine he could still cover twelve miles in an hour's ride and he celebrated his eightieth birthday on a strenuous tour of south coast defenses. A few weeks before he died, his wife saw him jump over some railings when he thought nobody was looking. There were lapses of memory, but he kept his firm grip on power and popular sentiment to the end. His last words before his death, were "Die, my dear doctor? That's the last thing I shall do!"

K. Bourne, *Palmerston: The Early Years*, 1982.

J. G. Ridley, *Lord Palmerston*, 1970.

C. Webster, *The Foreign Policy of Palmerston*, 2 vols., 1969.

PANKHURST, EMMELINE (née Goulden; 1858–1928), British suffragette. Her father, Robert Goulden, was a Manchester textile manufacturer and a friend of the political radical, Dr. Richard Pankhurst, who had drafted the first women's suffrage bill in the late 1860s. Goulden and Dr Pankhurst were campaigning together in 1875, when the doctor met Emmeline, recently returned from college in Paris. They were married the following year.

During her early married life, Mrs. Pankhurst was occupied with bringing up their four children. When she returned to public activities, she became increasingly involved with her husband's parliamentary work, and in 1889 they established the Women's Franchise League.

Beginning in 1895, Mrs. Pankhurst held several municipal posts in Manchester, but when Dr Pankhurst died suddenly in 1898, she retreated from active politics. It was her eldest daughter, Christabel, who led her back into the suffrage campaign, and in 1903 she founded the Women's Social and Political Union. The WSPU gained widespread recognition in 1905 when two of its members were thrown out of a hall where the prime minister and several cabinet ministers were holding a meeting. These two demonstrators were arrested in the street for technical assault on the police, and after having refused to pay a fine, the Suffragettes — a name coined by the press — were imprisoned.

A year later, when Mrs. Pankhurst moved to London, the campaign intensified. Neither the Liberal government nor the Labour opposition were taking the suffragettes' cause seriously. "Votes for women would do more harm than good," said Prime Minister Herbert Asquith, "Parliament is not elected on the basis of universal suffrage — children are not represented there." Reluctantly, the WSPU resorted to militant tactics. At first they were not violent, merely vociferous and obstructive. Nevertheless, in the year 1908–1909, Mrs. Pankhurst was imprisoned three times.

In 1909 the WSPU began using hunger strikes as a political weapon. A truce was called a year later, but when the government blocked a franchise bill, the suffragettes launched a period of violent militancy. Arson attacks, directed from Paris by Christabel Pankhurst, were making the headlines. Under the notorious Cat and Mouse Act of 1913, Emmeline was arrested, released, and rearrested twelve times in one year.

It was a surprise to her colleagues when, at the outbreak of World War I, Emmeline Pankhurst immediately called off the campaign and urged the suffragettes to stand loyally with the government and England. She traveled around the country advocating national service for women, and wrote her autobiography, *My Own Story*, in 1914.

By 1915, there were severe problems keeping the factories open and producing and David *Lloyd George, the minister of munitions, asked Mrs. Pankhurst to organize a march which would demonstrate women's readiness to fill men's placesat work. Thousands marched under the slogan "We Demand the Right to Serve," and consequently a national register of women was compiled.

The war years gave women the chance to exercise their vital social power; finally, after the war, they were afforded the political power they had demanded for over five decades. An act in 1918, allowing women over thirty to vote, gave the franchise to women for the first time.

During the postwar years, Mrs. Pankhurst lived in the United States, Canada, and Bermuda. She returned to England in 1926 and was immediately chosen as a Conservative candidate for a London constituency. Her declining health prevented her from being elected. She died in 1928, only a few weeks after the Representation of the People Act extended the vote to women on terms equal to male suffrage.

Her two daughters were also leaders of the women's suffrage movement. The fiery **Christabel Pankhurst** (1880–1958) was a militant suffragette who won an adoring following. Thrown out of the House of Commons, she screamed at a policeman, "I shall assault you, I shall spit at you!" For a time beginning in 1912, she was responsible for an arson campaign for which she was imprisoned. She became an evangelist and eventually was recognized by the establishment when created a dame of the British Empire in 1936.

Sylvia Pankhurst (1882–1960) opposed the institution of marriage and defended the right to be an unmarried mother (she was one herself). In the 1930s she was active in behalf of Ethiopian independence.

D. J. K. Mitchell, *The Fighting Pankhursts*, 1967.

E. S. Pankhurst, *The Life of Emmeline Pankhurst*, 1935.

E. Pankhurst, *My Own Story*, 1914.

A. Raeburn, *The Militant Suffragettes*, 1973.

PARNELL, CHARLES STUART

PARNELL, CHARLES STUART (1846–1891), Irish leader. A surprising figure to emerge as leader of the predominantly Catholic Nationalist movement, Charles Parnell was a wealthy Protestant landowner, with five thousand acres in County Wicklow. His family had links with the ruling Protestant landed elite and Parnell's upbringing had been in keeping with the privileged position he stood to inherit. He gave the impression of a perfect English gentleman in speech and bearing but his background was subtly different from that of others of his class and this was to help shape the dramatic course of his life.

An ancestor of Parnell's had been vocal in opposition to the union of Ireland with England and banners from the conflict still decorated the Parnell mansion at Avondale; his mother's father was an American admiral who had defeated the British navy in the War of 1812. It has further been suggested that the deep anger Parnell channeled into his politics sprang from his distress at his parents strange decision to send him to a girls' boarding school in England where he was the sole boy!

Parnell went on to Cambridge University but was sent down after four years for involvement in a nasty street fight; a judge also fined him twenty pounds for participating in this affray. Back home in Ireland, he could not stay out of trouble. He got into a fight in a County Wicklow hotel, but there he had family friends in high places and it was his opponent who got fined. Parnell's aggression at this time was rooted in frustration: he did not know what to do with his life; money was not a problem but boredom was.

PATRIOTIC PARNELL POETRY

Parnell's sister, Fanny, founded a separate Land League for women. She wrote patriotic poems, such as:

Now, are you men or are you kine, ye tillers of the soil?
Would you be free, or evermore the rich man's cattle toil?
The shadow on the dial hangs that points the fatal hour —
Now hold your own; or branded slaves for ever cringe and cower.
Oh, by the God who made us all — the seignior and the serf —
Rise up and swear this day to hold your own green Irish turf;
Rise up and plant your feet as men where now you crawl as slaves,
And make your harvest fields your camps, or make of them your graves.

Becoming a politician offered a good opportunity for a man of means to make his way in the world, so Parnell stood for Parliament on a platform supporting home rule for Ireland and was elected member for Meath in 1875. He did not take long to make his reputation as a fiery exponent of Irish autonomy and land reform, becoming the leader of the Irish members in the House of Commons in London. In 1879 he became president of the Land League, an organization campaigning for reform in the relationship between landlord and tenant in Ireland and an end to the widespread evictions that had caused bitter distress in many rural areas. Parnell told a tenants' meeting in that year: "I hope that on those properties where the rents are out of all proportion to the times a reduction may be made. If not, you must help yourselves, and the public opinion of the world will stand by you, and support you in your struggle to defend your homesteads."

In his public statements Parnell abhorred the use of violence but these words were mainly for English consumption. He was well aware that the leading officials of the Lane League had backgrounds in the Fenian Brotherhood, a violent organization, forerunner of the Irish Republican Army (I.R.A.). Moreover, his inflammatory speeches further aroused the passions of his supporters, encouraging the very actions which this astute politician thought prudent to condemn.

One tactic of the Land League Parnell felt free to encourage openly was the boycotting of particularly unpopular landlords or those who took over land from evicted tenants. Indeed, the word 'boycott' dates from this period, for Captain Boycott was one of the unlucky Anglo-Irish landlords to whom the policy was applied, "isolating him from the rest of mankind as if he was a leper of old" in Parnell's words.

The Liberal government was moving toward reform of the Irish land laws, if only to remove a major cause of unrest, but its first priority was to quieten the country through the application of the appropriately named Coercion of Ireland Bill. Parnell and his colleagues tried to block the bill's passage through a forty-one-hour filibuster but were suspended from the House of Commons.

When Parnell undertook a tour of America he made no pretence about the ultimate aim of his crusade: "None of us will be satisfied until we have destroyed the last link which keeps Ireland bound to England." On his return he was viewed as too dangerous an agitator to be at large. Prison, however, only raised him to the status of martyr for the Irish cause and he emerged from custody an even more powerful force to be reckoned with.

The Liberal government needed the support of Irish M.P.s and so even while Parnell was still in prison they entered negotiations with him. The process was set back by the murder of the Chief Secretary for Ireland in Dublin in 1882, which Parnell was charged with having encouraged, but by the mid 1880s the majority of the Liberal party was committed to home rule. Although Parnell aroused English suspicions with his famous statement that "no man has a right to fix the boundary to the march of a nation," his support for the more limited Home Rule Bill was seen as genuine.

When he was at the height of his political power, Parnell's career collapsed around him. In 1889 he was cited in the divorce proceedings of a fellow Irish M.P., Captain William O'Shea, against his wife Katherine. Parnell had been introduced by the captain to Katherine in 1880 and had been carrying on a liaison ever since, renting apartments under assumed names in resort towns on England's south coast. A daughter was born to them but soon died. When Captain O'Shea discovered the inheritance he expected his wife to bring him would not materialize, he sued for divorce.

The case produced a wave of anti-Parnell sentiment among his Irish Catholic supporters and among the Nonconformists, who formed a major block in the Liberal party's constituency. Parnell's colleagues deposed him from leadership, splitting the Irish party in the process. Election results in Ireland showed how his power base had been undermined and his health broke under the strain. Within four months of his marriage to Katherine O'Shea, Parnell took ill after addressing a meeting in Galway and soon died. To this day Irish people will say of a woman suspected of an adulterous relationship: "A right little Kitty O'Shea, that one."

F. Callanan, *The Parnell Split*, 1993.
F. S. L. Lyons, *Charles Stewart Parnell*, 1978.
R. E. Foster, *Charles Stewart Parnell: The Man and His Family*, 1976.
R. B. O'Brien, *The Life of Charles Stuart Parnell*, 2 vols., 1968.

PASCAL, BLAISE (1623–1662), French mathematician, philosopher, scientist, and writer. Pascal was born at Clermont-Ferrand but after the death of his mother in 1626, the family moved to Paris. His father, a tax administrator, was an eminent mathematician and under his instruction Pascal displayed mathematical genius from an early age. In 1640 he completed an analytic study of the work of Girard Desargues on synthetic projective geometry, and wrote an essay on conic sections based on his analysis. During the years 1642–1644 Pascal worked on the construction of a calculating device, originally designed as an aid for his father's tax computations. The mechanism was acclaimed in mathematic circles and Pascal's work was noted by René *Descartes, the illustrious philosopher and mathematician.

There followed an intense period of scientific work. He corresponded with the leading scientist Marin Mersenne and began to test the theories of *Galileo and Evangelista Torricelli (the Italian physicist who invented the barometer) by means of experiments using mercury barometers to measure air pressure. His experiments led to further studies in hydrodynamics and hydrostatics and during the course of this work Pascal developed an improved version of Torricelli's barometer and also invented the syringe. His major success at this time was the invention of the hydraulic press, which was based upon a formula that came to be known as Pascal's law. This theory states that in a fluid at rest in a closed container, a pressure change in one part is transmitted undiminished through the liquid to the walls of the container in all directions, regardless of the area to which the pressure is applied. A modern application of the principle is its utilization in hydraulic brakes. Pascal also published a number of essays and treatises during this period (1646–1654) dealing with the problem of the vacuum, the equilibrium of liquid solutions, the weight and density of air, and the arithmetic triangle, in which he formulated the foundations for the modern theory of probabilities.

As a young man Pascal embraced the theological teachings of Jansenism, a religious movement centered at the abbey of Port Royal. Contrary to classical Jesuit principles, Jansenist doctrine accepted predestination and rejected free will: it held that divine grace alone was capable of restoring man to true freedom. Under Pascal's influence, his entire family turned to Jansenism in 1646 as an expression of spiritual and religious life. Pascal himself experienced a mystical revelation in 1654 which he interpreted in terms of "conversion." He kept his account of it sewn in his coat for the rest of his life: "From about half past ten at night to about half after midnight, Fire. God of Abraham, God of Isaac, God of Jacob, not of the philosophers and the wise. Security, security. Feeling, joy, peace. Righteous Father, the world has not known you but I have known you. Joy, joy, joy, tears of joy."

In 1655 Pascal joined the Port-Royal solitaries, those who without taking vows undertook a reli-

FROM PASCAL'S *PENSÉES*

- The last function of reason is to recognize that there are an infinity of things which surpass it.
- Nature has some perfections to show that she is the image of God and some defects to show that she is only His image.
- Men despise religion; they hate it and fear it is true.
- Faith embraces many truths which seem to contradict each other.
- Physical science will not console me for the ignorance of morality in the time of affliction. But the science of ethics will always console me for the ignorance of the physical sciences.
- The eternal silence of infinite space frightens me.

gious life outside the convent under the direction of its leaders.

Pascal's writings during the subsequent year, in particular *Lettres écrites par Louis de Montalte à un provincial*, better known as *Les Provinciales* ("Provincial Letters"), and *Pensées* ("Thoughts"), established him as a master of French prose. The *Provinciales* were written in defense of Antoine Arnauld, a Jansenist who had been expelled by the faculty of theology in Paris for his controversial religious works opposing Jesuit interpretation of Roman Catholic orthodoxy and adherence to dogma. Pascal vigorously attacked the lax moral teachings and ethical code of the Jesuits and advocated a more spiritual approach emphasizing the soul's union with the body of Christ. The *Provinciales*, written in brilliant rhetorical style, replaced the vituperative monotony of conventional French writers with a brevity and sarcasm that proved immensely popular among French literary critics. Pascal's other major work of this period was his *Apologie de la religion chrétienne* ("Defense of Christianity"), which he began as a composition of Christian apologetics based on his meditations on the proofs of Christianity and intended to vanquish skepticism. He insisted upon a sharp separation of theology from philosophy, maintaining that much of the spirit of Christianity conflicted with the requirements of human physiology and reason and concluded that there is a continuous "guerre intestine de l'homme entre la raison et les passions" (internal war in human beings between reason and passion). The work, comprising a collection of fragmented notes, remained unfinished at his death; it was edited by his executors and published under the title *Pensées*.

Following a severe illness in 1659, Pascal spent his final years devoted to spiritual concern and care of the poor. He remained periodically active in the controversy over the formulary, the church document that called for universal condemnation of Jansenism, but withdrew from the dispute as a result of a disagreement with the school of Port-Royal.

Pascal's achievements in the realms of mathematics and science constitute important developments in these areas; however, as a religious philosopher Pascal firmly believed that the scientific approach could never yield certainty in its own right: he maintained that experience of God was to be attained through the heart and rejected the "truths of fact" and reason in an almost existentialist fashion, doctrines that influenced later philosophers such as Jean-Jacques *Rousseau.

A. J. Krailsheimer, *Pascal*, 1980.
P. Maynard, *Pascal*, 1991.

PASTEUR, LOUIS (1822–1895), French chemist and biologist, founder of modern bacteriology. Pasteur was born at Dole in France, the son of a tanner. He was a careful boy who liked to spend his free time painting. When he was nine, a rabid wolf attacked his village, and he witnessed the attempts to prevent its victims from catching rabies by cauterizing their wounds; weeks later he heard their screams of agony as they died.

The character traits that shaped Pasteur's career — the ability to work extremely hard and make others do the same and determination to accomplish great achievements — began to appear during his college years. However, when he took his science degree in 1842, his chemistry performance was classed as mediocre. At twenty-six he made his first discovery (that certain chemical compounds could split into components that were mirror images of each other).

In 1849 Pasteur was made professor of chemistry at the University of Strasbourg, where he married the rector's daughter. His enthusiasm for his experiments and long working hours led him frequently to neglect her, but her love and support for him was constant and their marriage a happy one. On becoming dean of the new science faculty at the University of Lille, where he served from 1854 to 1857, he put his research to practical uses. Thus, when the industry for producing alcohol from sugar beets faced difficulties due to the imperfection of its fermentation process, Pasteur was asked to help. He discovered that yeast turned sugar into alcohol and deduced that the fermentation process was not working in some of the vats because of the presence of certain microbes. He now set out to investigate these microbes.

As director of scientific studies at the Ecole Normale Supérieure in Paris (1857), Pasteur tried to continue his fermentation experiments. He was not put off by the small, rat-infested attic where he had to set up his laboratory, or by criticism from some of the biggest names in the scientific world for his disproving of accepted tenets such as the theory of spontaneous generation. His stubborn conviction that he was right caused him, at times, to gloat when he proved other scientists wrong, and on occasion even to engage in shouting matches with his colleagues.

Pasteur saved France's endangered wine and vinegar industries by examining the different kinds of spoiled wine and discovering the microbes that caused them to spoil. He invented the process of pasteurization — heating a liquid rapidly to just below the boiling point — to kill those microbes without spoiling the wine, and later used it to kill microbes in beer and milk. He also examined the vinegar-making process, discovering the microbe that turned wine into vinegar, and teaching the vinegar industry how to tend it.

Despite the fact that as a chemist he knew nothing about moth larvae, Pasteur was asked to try to cure diseased silkworms. Although he knew he risked the public failure he dreaded, he moved his family south to France's silk country and started examining parts of silkworms under his microscope. Fifteen days later he announced his method of distinguishing healthy silkworm eggs, persuaded silkwork growers to accept it, and faced their scorn and attacks after his method failed. It was two years before he saved France's silk industry by discovering the parasite causing the disease and how to counter it.

Meanwhile the demands of his research had caused Pasteur to give up his administrative and teaching responsibilities. In 1868, just as a laboratory of physiological chemistry was being built for him with *Napoleon III's support, Pasteur was almost killed by a stroke. Partially paralyzed for the rest of his life, he walked with a limp, but resolutely continued his work.

A patriotic Frenchman, Pasteur was determined to get revenge on Germany for France's defeat in the Franco-Prussian War (1870) by making French beer better than German beer. He succeeded in improving French beer, but his dislike of the taste of any beer eventually forced him to abandon the project.

When Pasteur began researching disease-causing microbes, he succeeded in isolating the microbes causing the chicken cholera and anthrax that were then devastating France's livestock and discovered that those diseases could only be caught once. His system of vaccination, which gave lifelong immunity from a disease by artificially inducing a mild case of it with weakened microbes, made him a national hero. His image, however, became slightly tarnished when some of the vast quantities of vaccine he was obliged to produce to meet farmers' demands proved defective.

In 1882 Pasteur was elected to the French Academy and embarked on the research for which he was most famous — the prevention of rabies. He developed a series of shots to prevent an animal infected with rabies from developing the disease but was reluctant to use them on people until a boy who had been bitten by a rabid dog was brought to him in 1885. As a result of his treatment, the boy lived and Pasteur became internationally famous. People in-fected with rabies rushed to him for treatment, among them nineteen Russian peasants who had been mauled by a mad wolf. In gratitude for their cure, Czar Alexander III sent money to finance the building of the now-famous Institut Pasteur in Paris, which was inaugurated in 1888, and headed by Pasteur until his death.

J. Nicole, *Louis Pasteur: The Story of His Major Discoveries*, 1961.

R. Vallery-Radot, *Life of Pasteur*, 1960.

PATRICK, SAINT (fifth century), British Christian missionary to Ireland. Ireland's patron saint was born in Britain (the location has not been identified) into a Christian family of good standing; his father was affluent enough to own a villa, from which, at the age of sixteen, Patrick was carried away into slavery by Irish pirates, who pressed him into service as a herdsman for six hard years, in the area of modern Killala, County Mayo. Although previously he had not been particularly pious, Patrick's Christian devotion deepened in captivity: "In a single day I would say as many as a hundred prayers, and almost as many at night," he later recalled. He also experienced dreams and visions which he took to be divinely inspired. In one of these, it was revealed to him that a ship was waiting to take him home; he duly escaped and boarded the vessel and, saving himself and the crew from starvation when his prayers for food were answered through the miraculous appearance of a herd of wild pigs, returned to his parents.

Despite his parents' protestations, Patrick was now determined to return to Ireland to carry the word of God to his heathen erstwhile captors. He dreamt that he was given a letter representing "the voice of the Irish," stating that "we beseech thee Holy Youth to come and walk once more among us." To this end, he acquired an ecclesiastical training and was duly appointed bishop for the mission to Ireland; his episcopal see was probably sited at Armagh. There, despite his self-avowed "rusticity," he was deeply beloved by the people and by the end of his life had succeeded in establishing Christianity firmly on the island; the Irish church was later to be very influential in the evangelization of Western Europe, the preservation of the monastic tradition, and, through successive waves of emigration from Ireland, in the development of Catholicism in North America.

Legends concerning the saint abound. He is reputed to have driven out the snakes from Irish shores, which have remained serpent-free to this day. He is also remembered for having used the shamrock, with its three leaves on a single stalk, to explain the mystery of the Holy Trinity as three aspects of a unity to one of his simple converts. The shamrock is now Ireland's national flower and is traditionally sported on the saint's feast day, 17 March.

Early in his career, Patrick was hindered by the jealousy and rivalry of others; he was initially refused the episcopacy when a supposed friend of his revealed to the religious authorities a sin that he was alleged to have committed. Despite his subsequent installation in the post, Patrick was deeply hurt by this evidence of treachery. In his *Confessions*, written as a vindication of his own life and conduct in the face of his ecclesiastical opponents' charges that he sought office for its own sake and was uneducated, Patrick left a moving testament which reveals his disarming honesty and modesty, his deep pastoral concern, and his sense of unworthiness for the task which God had been gracious enough to bestow upon him.

Confusion reigns over what dates can authentically be ascribed to the saint. Some scholars have suggested that he was a legendary figure, a synthetic character based on a combination of Palladius Patricius, the bishop sent by Pope Celestine to minister to the Irish between 432 and 461, and the author of the *Confessions*, whose date of death is given as 492. However, a more likely explanation is that, given Patrick's immense proselytizing success, it was tempting to ignore the relatively feeble attempts of his predecessor Palladius and to regard him as Ireland's first missionary. However, the actual dates of Patrick's ministry in Ireland remain a subject of controversy.

L. Bieler, *The Life and Legend of Saint Patrick*, 1949.

J. Carney, *The Problem of Saint Patrick*, 1961.

R. P. C. Hanson, *Saint Patrick*, 1968.

PATTON, GEORGE SMITH, (1885–1945), U.S. general. Born in San Gabriel, California, to a family steeped in military tradition, George Patton from a very early age showed a keen interest in history; papers that he wrote in grade school clearly express his desire to gain recognition, fame, and glory through heroic acts. Academic learning did not come easily to him, but he had a good sense of humor and a great love of the military. He worked conscientiously to improve himself in order to be accepted to military school.

To prepare himself for a military career, Patton first attended the Virginia Military Academy, where he proved himself an outstanding athlete. He set the school record in the 220-yard hurdles, won the 120-yard hurdles, and placed second in the 220-yard dash. He expressed his philosophy: "By perseverance, study, and eternal desire, any man can be great." When he left the military academy, he went on to West Point, graduating in 1909, forty-sixth in a class of one hundred and three. Commissioned a second lieutenant in the cavalry, he remained deeply interested in the battles and history of the American Civil War.

Patton's first assignment was at Fort Sheridan in Illinois. In 1911 he was transferred to Fort Meyer, Washington, D.C., and was selected to compete in the fifth Olympic Games, which were held in Sweden. He was entered in the modern pentathlon, which involved shooting, swimming, fencing, cross-country steeplechase, and cross-country running, and finished fifth. This was a remarkable achieve-

- We shall attack and attack until we are exhausted, and then we shall attack again (before invasion of North Africa).
- The most vital quality a soldier can possess is self-confidence, utter, complete and bumptious.
- Practically everyone but myself is a pusillanimous son of a bitch.
- Never tell people how to do things. Tell them what to do and they will surprise you with their ingenuity.
- All very successful commanders are prima donnas and must so be treated.
- Wars may be fought with weapons but they are won by men. It is the spirit of the men who follow and of the man who leads that gives the victory.

George S. Patton

ment, as he had not participated in sports competitions for over two years prior to beginning his training for the pentathlon.

In 1913 Patton was assigned to Fort Riley, Kansas, where he remained for two years. He was then transferred to Fort Bliss, Texas, and while he was there, Pancho Villa raided Columbus, New Mexico. Under General John J. *Pershing, Patton became involved and remained in Mexico until February 1917. In appraising Patton, Pershing said, "Lieutenant Patton is a capable, energetic officer, and would perform the duties of a field officer of volunteers with credit to himself and the government."

With the onset of World War I, General Pershing brought Patton to France, where he served with distinction and was promoted several times. Returning to the United States in 1919, he served at Camp Meade, Maryland, and in 1920 was transferred back to Fort Meyer but this time as the commander of the cavalry. In a letter to his father, Patton wrote, "Some day I will show them. I fear that I will never be a general."

Between World War I and World War II Patton served at forts Riley and Leavenworth, both in Kansas, in Boston, and in Hawaii. His field of expertise changed from cavalry training to tanks, and he went on to prove his genius in tank warfare.

With the threat of war imminent, Patton was assigned to the Second Armored Division at Fort Benning, Georgia, promoted to divisional commander, and commanded what became the army's toughest outfit. He then took command of the First Armored Corps, a much larger unit; he and his troops were sent to fight in the North African Campaign, and he was promoted to lieutenant general.

Under General Dwight *Eisenhower, Patton was placed in charge of the Tank Force Troops and commanded the Seventh Army during the invasion of Sicily in 1943, capturing Palermo the following year.

Known for his quick temper and impetuousity, Patton created an incident that was to mark a reversal in his career. While visiting wounded soldiers in a military hospital, Patton struck a soldier who was suffering from battle fatigue because he felt that the man was malingering. Reprimanded by General Eisenhower, Patton was forced to make a public apology. This action delayed his promotion, and he lost his command; it was not until August 1944 that he was promoted to major general.

In March 1944 Patton assumed command of the Third Army and prepared it for the invasion of Normandy, where his brilliant sweep across the base of the Breton peninsula led to the liberation of Metz. The Germans then launched their Ardennes counteroffensive, and Patton turned his forces quickly northward against the German southern flank and helped contain the enemy. General Omar N. Bradley said later, "Patton accomplished one of the most astonishing feats of generalship of our campaign in the West."

Patton, together with his troops, caused the breakthrough in the Battle of the Bulge and went on to speed across Germany, cutting the country in half. "Old Blood and Guts," as Patton was known, proved himself to be one of the great tactical commanders of all times. However, he got himself into trouble once more, this time as military governor of Bavaria, when he made statements criticizing the "denazification" policies; it was felt he was too lenient with Nazis and was removed from his command. Patton was then assigned a lesser post and toward the end of 1945, was involved in a fatal automobile accident.

M. Blumenson, *The Patton Papers*, 1972.
L. Farego, *The Last Days of Patton*, 1981.
P. B. Williamson, *Patton's Principles*, 1984.

PAUL, SAINT (Saul; died 67 C.E.), apostle of *Jesus and founder of numerous Christian communities. His letters (epistles) to these communities in the Roman empire (the Pauline Epistles), account for about one fourth of the New Testament. Born in the city of Tarsus in Cilicia, Asia Minor, the son of a Pharisee, Paul was both a Jew and a Roman citizen, and by profession a tentmaker. Surrounded by the Greek culture of the day, but educated in the Jewish tradition, he completed his studies in Jerusalem at the feet of the Jewish teacher of the law, Gamaliel, becoming a thoroughgoing and zealous Pharisee, a sect that strictly adhered to the letter of the Law.

By his own admission, Paul was the most pious kind of Jew. "Circumcised on the eighth day [according to the Law of *Moses], of the stock of Israel, of the tribe of Benjamin, a Hebrew of Hebrews; as touching the law, a Pharisee; concerning zeal, persecuting the church; touching the righteousness which is the law, blameless" (Phil. 3:5–6). Paul devoted

---

SAYINGS OF PAUL THAT HAVE PASSED INTO EVERYDAY USAGE

- There is no respect of persons with God.
- Who against hope believed in hope?
- The wages of sin is death.
- Vengeance is mine; I will repay, saith the Lord.
- Love is the fulfilling of the law.
- A little leaven leaveneth the whole lump.
- It is better to marry than to burn.
- I am become all things to all men.
- Now abideth faith, hope, and charity; but the greatest of these is charity.
- Fallen asleep in Christ.
- Let us eat and drink, for tomorrow we die.
- O death, where is thy sting? O grave, where is thy victory?
- Whatsoever a man soweth, that shall he also reap.
- And they two shall become one flesh.
- The peace of God that passeth all understanding.
- Drink no longer water but use a little wine for thy stomach's sake.
- The love of money is the root of all evil.
- Fight the good fight of faith.
- Rich in good works.
- Unto the pure, all things are pure.

---

himself to seeking out and arresting those Jews who believed in Jesus, and minded the cloaks of those who stoned Stephen. So great was his hatred of these people that he obtained letters from the high priest and elders in Jerusalem to permit him to travel to Damascus in order to extradite Jews who believed in Jesus and to return them to Jerusalem for judgment.

On the road to Damascus, however, he experienced a stunning revelation. It was midday, when "suddenly there shone from heaven a great light." Saul fell to the ground and "heard a voice saying to me, 'Saul, Saul, why are you persecuting Me?' And I answered, 'Who art Thou, Lord?' And He said to me, 'I am Jesus the Nazarene, whom you are persecuting.' And those who were with me beheld the light, to be sure, but did not understand the voice of the One who was speaking to me" (Acts 22:7–9).

Saul arose from the ground but could not see and was therefore led away to Damascus. Three days later Ananias, a devout Jew and believer in the Way (as it was called), came to Saul and prayed for him, and he regained his sight. From that point on life was radically different.

His "conversion" was not well received. The Jews who already believed in Jesus were highly suspicious of Paul at first, for they knew with what purpose he had come to Damascus. In the synagogues the news was received even more violently.

Saint Paul, from a tenth century Byzantine cross

Jews in both Damascus and Jerusalem were so enraged that on separate occasions they sought to kill Paul. In Damascus he was forced to escape under cover of night by being lowered outside the city walls in a basket.

Paul was not deterred. The same unwavering commitment to the Law of God that had driven him to persecute the Christians now spurred him in his profession that Jesus was indeed the long-awaited Jewish messiah and had brought salvation through grace.

Paul's dramatic transformation took place about 33 C.E.. He spent some time in the Arabian desert and returned to Jerusalem three years later. He spent the next ten years in Tarsus and Antioch until he set out on his first journey — lasting some two years — to proclaim the gospel. Within approximately a twelve-year period Paul completed three missionary tours of areas in the Roman Empire, bringing the Christian message of salvation. In 45 C.E. he set out from Antioch accompanied by Barnabas and John Mark, who left them after visiting Cyprus. The book of Acts records that in Cyprus and the cities of Asia Minor their preaching was often accompanied by signs and wonders, such as healing the sick and casting out demons. On Paul's third journey a young man was raised from the dead.

As was his custom, upon entering a new city Paul went first to the synagogue with his message. He and Barnabas were often well received with many, both Jews and Gentiles, accepting their teaching. However, many times those who did not believe, both Jew and Gentile, incited the city residents to chase the two out of town. In Lystra Paul was even stoned and left for dead, but revived and completed his journey in 48 C.E.

During his second journey, which lasted for about five years, Paul was accompanied by Silas. In Lystra Timothy joined them and the three continued through Troas, Macedonia, and finally into Europe. On this trip Paul and Silas were beaten and thrown into prison.

Paul's third journey from about 54 to 57 C.E. took him mainly to Ephesus but also to Greece. During this time it is thought that Paul wrote the Epistles of I Corinthians, Galatians, II Corinthians, and Romans. Through his endeavors Christian centers were established in most cities in Asia Minor and Greece.

After the completion of his third journey, Paul went to Jerusalem. With him he carried a large offering from the Gentile Christians in the Roman Empire to the Jewish Christians in Jerusalem. He reported to the elders all that was happening among the Gentiles and was informed that there were many thousands of Jews in the city who believed and were all zealous for the Law of Moses. However, he was told that many Jews believed Paul was teaching Jews in the Diaspora to forsake the Law of Moses. In order to disprove this accusation, the elders suggested that Paul shave his head and join other Jewish Christians in the temple who were fulfilling a vow.

Near the end of the seventh day other Jews in the temple recognized Paul and accused him of preaching against the Law of Moses as well as of having brought a Gentile into the Temple. He was dragged from the temple and beaten but was rescued by Roman guards. He was arrested and through a series of appeals was granted an audience in Rome.

In the spring of 61 C.E. Paul arrived as a prisoner in Rome after an eventful voyage ending in shipwreck on Malta. His incarceration was unusual — for two years he lived under guard in his own hired house, able to receive visitors. There he wrote the letters to the Ephesians, Philippians, Colossians, Philemon, and perhaps to the Hebrews (authorship is uncertain).

Most scholars believe he was acquitted and released from prison. He may have journeyed to Spain then but within two years he was arrested again and taken to Rome. At that time the Roman empire was ruled by *Nero, who, most historians agree, set Rome alight because he wanted to rebuild a finer city. However, he needed a scapegoat on which to pin the blame for the blaze and the Christians provided the outlet. It may have been in this framework that Paul was re-arrested and beheaded in about 67 C.E.

The focus of all of Paul's writing is Jesus, through whom God has effected redemption for all people regardless of ethnic or social background. Paul's interest in Jesus is selective, taking little notice of how he lived or what he taught, focusing instead on who he was and what his death and resurrection accomplished. For Paul, Jesus is God's son in a unique and absolute sense, who by his death made possible the reconciliation of sinful man with his holy Creator and took on all the sins of the world. Once this redemption was accomplished, God set his seal on it by raising Jesus from the dead. Paul's personal revelation of the risen Jesus permeates his thinking. The living, ascended Jesus sent the Holy Spirit as a guarantee of the sure fulfilment of all of God's promises to the believer. Just as man fell from the image of God through sin, so Jesus took on humanity in order that men might be re-formed into the image of God's son. Paul always identifies Jesus with the church, and foresees the day when Jesus will return to take that church to himself.

L. E. Keck, *Paul and His Letters* , 1982.
E. P. Sanders, *Paul*, 1991.
H. J. Schoeps, *Paul*, 1961.
K. Stendahl, *Paul Among the Jews and Gentiles*, 1976.

PAVLOV, IVAN PETROVICH (1849–1936), Russian physiologist and pioneer in the field of conditioned reflexes, winner of the 1904 Nobel Prize in physiology. Born in Ryazan, Russia, the son of a poor priest, Ivan Pavlov loved to work with his father in gardens and orchards and his interest in botany lasted all his life. Each spring he planted flowers in his home and then transplanted seedlings to formal gardens at his Estonia dacha. During the famine years of the Russian Revolution, he grew food in space allotted to the staff of the institute of experimental medicine in Saint Petersburg. His godfather, the head of an abbey, influenced him spiritually, instilled in him a pride for work, and expanded his mind by giving him reading assignments.

Upon completion of schooling at the ecclesiastical seminary in Ryazan, Pavlov attended the University of Saint Petersburg. His graduation was delayed a full year because of his involvement in his first experiment on the nerves of the pancreatic gland. Scientific research and experimentation was to become his life work. Graduate work was at the military-medical academy, where he became a professor in 1890, holding the chair of pharmacology and, from 1895, the chair of physiology. He made innovative changes in teaching methods by introducing demonstrations within lectures. As a rule, he would lecture sedately from a chair behind a table until he began to conduct a demonstration, at which time he would become very animated. His teaching talents, however, did not extend to creating good illustrations on the blackboard. His crude drawings were a constant source of amusement to the students.

During his years of teaching he continually conducted and supervised experiments. Visiting his laboratory assistants to inspect their progress, he usually carried a mug of tea, which he sipped while nibbling cubes of sugar taken from his pocket.

In 1904 Pavlov won the Nobel Prize in physiology and medicine for his research on digestion and the nervous system, which disclosed how nerves control the flow of digestive juices of the stomach and pancreas. Upon being informed of the prize he was in a state of shock, partly because his book *Lectures on the Works of the Digestive Glands* had not been well received. Following presentation of the prize by the king of Sweden, sales of the book improved. He deposited the prize money, approximately thirty-six thousand U.S. gold dollars, with the Saint Petersburg branch of Nobel's Russian firm. Following the Russian revolution of 1917, he lost all his money because the Bolsheviks liquidated all stocks and bonds of value.

Pavlov was a man of integrity, principle, and personal courage. In 1922 Vladimir *Lenin refused his request to relocate his laboratory outside the country but, as a consolation, offered him the same food rations as an honored Communist. Pavlov refused on the grounds that his colleagues were excluded. In 1924 he voluntarily and publicly resigned from the military-medical academy because the authorities did not permit children of clergy to receive higher education. As the son of a clergyman, he felt that it was an injustice arbitrarily to deprive a portion of the population of university education. In addition, he wrote to Joseph *Stalin in 1927 stating, "You are depriving and annihilating the intelligentsia to such an extent that I am ashamed to be called a Russian." Upon returning to Russia from a visit to the United States in 1929, he publicly denounced Communism.

Although Pavlov won the 1904 Nobel Prize, he is best known for his later development work in the field of conditioned reflexology, and his famous experiment with salivating dogs. That experiment involved bringing food, accompanied by a ringing bell, to hungry dogs. The normal physiological reaction of the dogs was to salivate upon smelling the food. In time Pavlov was able to get the dogs to salivate only upon hearing the bell, an artificial stimulus, even when the food was withheld. Pavlov believed that conditioned reflexes controlled all acquired habits. He continued to work in his laboratories until his death at age eighty-seven.

B. P. Babkin, *Pavlov, A Biography*, 1968.
M. Kaplan, ed., *Essential Works of Pavlov*, 1966.

PEARY, ROBERT EDWIN (1856–1920), American Arctic explorer who was the leader of the expedition that is generally credited with being the first to reach the North Pole. Robert Peary was born in Cresson, Pennsylvania. His father, a barrel maker, died when he was only three, after which his family moved to Maine. He attended the local schools and in 1877 earned a civil engineering degree from Bowdoin College. He was a competitive athlete, which undoubtedly stood him in good stead for the rigors he would endure later in his life.

His first job was as a county surveyor in Fryeburg. In 1881 he enlisted in the naval civil engineering corps with the rank of lieutenant. A few years later he was posted as assistant engineer on the team sent to survey the proposed Nicaraguan shipping canal, returning to the United States in 1885.

About this time, Peary came across a magazine article on Greenland and the Arctic wastes. He began to read voraciously on the subject, becoming increasingly consumed by the idea of being the first man to cross the polar ice cap. To this end, he secured a brief leave of absence from the navy in 1886, and set off on a whaler for Greenland. Along with him went Matthew Henson, his African American servant, who would accompany him on all his subsequent expeditions. Peary found this small taste of the northern reaches beyond his wildest expectations. He was unabashed in stating that his desire was for glory and fame, not for scientific achievement for the betterment of humanity.

Peary was once again posted by the navy to Nicaragua in 1887, this time as chief engineer. The following year, upon his return to the United States, he married, and devoted most of his spare time researching the Arctic and lobbying extensively among various scientific and geographical societies for support for his planned adventures. In 1891 he once again took a leave of absence from the navy, and with a team of six, which included his wife, Henson, and Dr. Frederick Cook, headed for Greenland on a small sealer, the *Kite*. His wife's presence was intended as a publicity exercise, as she was the first white woman to withstand the Arctic winter. The mission began badly when Peary broke his leg as the *Kite* was smashing its way through the pack ice, but Cook, the team's surgeon, set the break so well that Peary was back on his feet within a few weeks.

After the long winter night, the team moved inland, assisted by Eskimos, who proved invaluable in teaching Peary about Arctic survival. Peary now began studies of the Eskimo culture, which he continued on later visits. He also fathered a number of children by Eskimo women and took part in the local custom of wife sharing. He crossed Greenland and proved for the first time that it was an island.

Peary's success brought him a modicum of fame and renewed offers of support. His next expedition set off in 1893 with a larger team, and his first legitimate child was born in Greenland late that year. This time, however, he was plagued by bad weather and returned home in 1895 without much more to show for his years of effort than three large meteorite specimens he had discovered, including one that weighed over ninety tons.

Peary realized that he required a new approach and decided he would push as far north as possible in a ship and then strike out with sleds to reach the Pole in the summer. His plan received the support of the British, who presented him with the *Windward*, a ship that had previously served their own Arctic expedition. By 1897 public interest in the Arctic was at its peak, each "farthest north" making the headlines. Peary judged the time was right for a fresh attempt, but the navy was not inclined to grant him further leave despite the appeals of his backers and many prominent scientists. Only the personal intercession of President William McKinley made the navy yield. Yet despite all his preparations, this expedition, beginning in 1898, also failed to reach the North Pole. Peary returned to the United States in 1902 minus eight toes, which he had lost in 1899 to frostbite. He still believed his strategy for reaching the North Pole was correct, but now concluded that he needed a custom built ship that could break much farther north than the *Windward*.

In 1905 he returned to Greenland with his new vessel, the *Roosevelt*. This time his expedition reached a new farthest north record of 174 miles from the Pole. He returned to New York the following year, by now over fifty years of age, feeling that his next expedition would likely be his last. By 1908 he was ready once again. The *Roosevelt* reached within four hundred miles of the Pole, a record in its own right for a ship under its own power. The winter was spent gathering scientific data and making preparations for the summer dash for the Pole, building igloos, and storing supplies along the intended route. Early in 1909 the party set off from the base camp with twenty-three men (seventeen of them Eskimos), nineteen sleds, and one hundred and thirty-one dogs. As they proceeded, groups peeled off, leaving more supplies for the lead party's return journey. The final leg to the Pole was to be attempted by Peary, Henson, and four Eskimos pulled by forty dogs on five sleds. By early April a desperately weary Peary reckoned he was within three miles of the Pole, after traversing treacherous pack ice flows for many miles. To be sure they did not miss the Pole, the party deliberately pulled out in several directions. Peary broke through the ice where he believed the Pole to be and confirmed that it was in fact in the midst of a vast ocean. He planted five flags — the United States, the U.S. Navy, the Daughters of the American Revolution, the Red Cross, and his college fraternity. Assisted by favorable weather, he made it back safely to base by late April, cabling his wife "I have the old Pole."

The jubilant Peary, however, was shocked by the news that his erstwhile team surgeon, Cook, had claimed to have reached the North Pole in 1908. Whereas Peary had undertaken a well-planned, well-financed expedition, Cook claimed to have achieved the same goal almost singlehanded. Cook's bravado immediately captured popular attention, and official doubts as to the veracity of Cook's claim were dismissed by the press as attempts to discredit an independent explorer. Indeed, the press turned on Peary, accusing him of sinister motives and deceit in his own claims. Nevertheless, Peary was awarded the rank of rear admiral by Congress and received numerous awards from learned societies worldwide. He retired from the navy in 1910, although he served as chairman of the National Committee on Coast Defence by Air in World War I.

Cook's priority claim looked even more suspect when his supposed ascent of Mount McKinley in 1906 was alleged to have been an outrageous fraud. Today it is generally accepted that Peary and Henson were the first to reach the North Pole.

W. R. Hunt, *To Stand at the Pole*, 1981.

D. B. MacMillan, *How Peary reached the Pole*, 1934.

PEDRO I (Dom Pedro IV of Portugal; 1798–1834), first emperor of Brazil. Pedro I was the son of John VI of Portugal. In 1807 the Portuguese royal family fled to Brazil to escape the

Napoleonic wars. By 1815, with Rio de Janeiro serving as the temporary capital of the Portuguese empire, Brazil was elevated to the status of a kingdom coequal with Portugal. King John left Brazil following the Oporto revolts (1820) but his son Pedro, who in 1817 had married Archduchess Leopoldina of Austria, remained behind to supervise the internal affairs of the country.

Soon after John's return to Portugal the attitude of the Cortes (Portuguese parliament) toward Brazil began to change. Many of the privileges earlier granted Brazil were rescinded as its former colonial status was slowly restored. Although Pedro was instructed to return to Portugal he rejected the decrees of the Cortes and sided with the local nationalists. Pedro was in Ipiranga on September 7, 1822, when news reached him that troops had been sent to take him back to Portugal. He rushed out to the balcony before a crowd of supporters, unsheathed his sword and declared, "Independence or death!" On 1 December, in a lavish ceremony, Pedro was crowned and anointed constitutional emperor and perpetual defender of Brazil.

The early years of Brazilian independence were troubled; regional tensions nearly tore the country apart. Some regions, notably the north, favored continued association with Portugal or a republican regime in place of the monarchy. During a war with Argentina in 1825 the southern Cisplatine province seceded, declaring itself the independent Republic of Uruguay. Pedro was able to overcome the threats to his regime's stability thanks to the enlightened advice of Lord Chamberlain Jose Bonifacio de Andrada e Silva, who was able to keep the radicals at bay. Pedro was, however, unable to secure the world's recognition his country longed for; European powers were reluctant to upset the Portuguese by recognizing the new state and the United States hesitated over recognizing a monarchy in the western hemisphere.

Pedro's popularity soon faded. He nurtured an absolutist policy and often rejected the legislature in favor of his own political initiatives. In 1824 he ignored the national legislature and appointed ten people to write a constitution for Brazil, completed in 1889. Following the death of his wife in 1826, he married Princess Amelia of Leuchtenberg. At the same time he carried on a series of illicit but well-known romances. His most prominent affair was with Domitila de Castro, whose children he recognized and whom he raised to the nobility. At the same time Pedro carried on another affair with Domitila's sister, Maria Bendita. Finding his cavorting unpopular with the people, Pedro rejected Domitila. She, thinking that the emperor simply preferred her sister, shot at Maria Bendita.

Pedro remained interested in Portuguese affairs throughout his reign. Following the death of his father in 1826 Pedro favored his infant daughter Maria to succeed as queen of Portugal. His absolutist tendencies and increasing involvement in European affairs finally led prominent officials and

military men to petition the emperor in 1831 to change his attitude toward the throne. He responded, "I will do everything for the people but nothing by the people." Seeing the empire had reached a stalemate, Pedro abdicated in favor of his young son *Pedro II. Pedro I, now known as the duke of Braganza, sailed for Portugal to further his daughter's claims to the throne. Maria was crowned queen of Portugal in 1834; Pedro died shortly after.

In 1972 his remains were returned to Brazil. They were interred in the cathedral of Ipiranga, the city where he had declared Brazilian independence 138 years earlier.

R. J. Barman, *Brazil, The Forging of a Nation; 1798–1852*, 1988.

N. Macaulay, *Dom Pedro: The Struggle for Liberty in Brazil*, 1986.

PEDRO II (Dom Pedro de Alcantara; 1825–1891), second and last emperor of Brazil. Dom Pedro de Alcantara John Carlos Leopoldo Salvador Bibiano Francisco Xavier de Paolo Leocadio Miguel Gabriel Raphael Gonzago was the son of King *Pedro I of Brazil and his consort, the Archduchess Leopoldina of Austria. Pedro ascended the throne when only five years old following the abdication of his father. Regents governed in his stead until 1840; Pedro's coronation took place on 18 July, 1841. During his lengthy reign he proved to be a capable and popular monarch who modernized and industrialized Brazil. He was an intellectual who spoke twelve languages and corresponded with other leading intellectuals of his day, and a liberal who gradually abolished slavery, a mainstay of the Brazilian economy. He brought an end to the regionalism of Sao Paulo, Minas, Geraes, and Sao Pedro do Rio do Sul, which threatened to divide the country, and established democratic principles in the empire. It was often said that, "Brazil under Dom Pedro is the only real republic in South America." It was his longing for modernization and democratization that eventually brought about the downfall of the Brazilian monarchy and the establishment of a republic in its stead.

The long reign of Pedro II was generally quiet until the final years. Despite several revolts, notably in Pernambuco in 1849, and wars, such as one with Argentina in 1852, the empire prospered and developed. The turning point of Pedro's reign seems to have been the War of the Alliance (1864–1870) in which Brazil, Argentina, and Uruguay fought Solano López, dictator of Paraguay. Although the Alliance won the war, victory proved costly. At the same time, the military attained unprecedented power in Brazil, becoming a force to be reckoned with in the following years. In the four years following the abolition of the monarchy Brazil was under military rule.

Pedro made gradual steps to abolish slavery in Brazil, a move which brought him into conflict with the powerful planters whose livelihood depended on indentured labor. The slave trade was banned in 1850; emancipation of slaves was begun in 1870, following the victory of the Alliance. The first slaves freed were those who had fought for Brazil in the war. Emancipation slowly gained pace until slavery was totally abolished in 1888.

Pedro's experiments in economics and political structure were regarded as incompatible with a monarchy. The Republican party, founded in 1876, was allowed to grow, gaining support from the army and those classes Pedro had alienated in his bid for modernization. At that time, Pedro sought to separate church and state in Brazil, curbing the authority of the influential Roman Catholic church. Although this alienated Pedro from the church he gained the support of the Republicans — support soon lost when his attempt to curb the church's power failed. By the mid-1880s Pedro had lost support from all segments of society. The conservatives saw him as endangering the traditional structure of Brazilian society; the liberals as an anachronism unwilling to go far enough to modernize the country. Although Pedro considered abdicating in favor of his daughter, Isabel, growing tensions made this impossible.

On 15 November, 1889, Pedro was deposed in a republican military coup led by Marshal Manuel Deodoro da Fonseca. The royal family was exiled from Brazil. Pedro settled in Paris, spending his remaining days touring the libraries and museums of that city; he died two years later. In 1920 his body was returned to Brazil and interred in the cathedral of Petrópolis, the summer capital he had built years earlier. His descendants returned to Brazil, where they continue to promote the cause of a Brazilian monarchy.

R. J. Barman, *Brazil; The Forging of a Nation; 1798–1852*, 1988.

H. Bentsen, *Dom Pedro II*, 1973.

C. W. Simmons, *Marshall Deodoro and the Fall of Dom Pedro II*, 1966.

M. W. William, *Dom Pedro the Magnanimous, Second Emperor of Brazil*, 1966.

PENN, WILLIAM (1644–1718), British Quaker (Society of Friends) and founder of Pennsylvania. William Penn was the son of Admiral William Penn, a wily old salt who managed to serve both King *Charles I and Oliver *Cromwell and had little time to spare for his son, whose interests and convictions diverged sharply from his own.

While studying at Oxford University, Penn came under the influence of the Quaker minister Thomas Loe. The university administration was intolerant of deviation from Church of England practice and Penn was expelled. His father gave him a sound beating and threw him out for disgracing the family name. He sent him to Paris in the hope that secular attractions would divert his mind from all religious speculations.

Penn returned, seemingly a changed man, and was sent to manage the family's Irish estates. Unfortunately for Admiral Penn, Thomas Loe was active in Ireland and Penn again heard him speak. He came

William Penn trading with the Indians

home inspired once more as a fervent Quaker. When he appeared in front of his father wearing a hat, as was the Quaker custom, he was once more thrown out.

The government held Penn's propagation of Quaker beliefs to be disruptive and he was imprisoned several times. Once he defended himself so ably in court that the jury refused to deliver a guilty verdict. The judge threatened that they would be locked away and deprived of food and drink until they delivered the correct, that is, guilty, verdict. They did not bow to the pressure and an important legal precedent of the independence of English juries was established. Admiral Penn was moved by his son's fighting spirit and paid a heavy fine imposed on him, and by the time of Penn's father's death in 1670, the two were reconciled.

Persecution drove Quakers to seek refuge in America. Two of them had acquired land in New Jersey but quarreled over ownership and when Penn was called in to mediate, he saw the area's great potential. King *Charles II owed the late Admiral Penn a substantial sum of money and, to settle this claim, the son petitioned for a land grant. In 1680 Charles agreed, subject only to Penn's fealty to him and the payment of two beaver skins per year. Penn wanted to name the land Sylvania but Charles added the prefix Penn in honor of the admiral and Pennsylvania was born. William Penn was dismayed with such vanity and even offered a twenty-guinea bribe to the royal secretary to alter the name; it was refused.

Penn was an excellent publicist and wrote persuasively of the attractions Pennsylvania offered: a warmer climate than England, sweet and clear air, and good grape-growing. Even the Indians (with whom Penn cultivated close relations) were, in his words, transformed into remnants of the Lost Tribes of Israel, which added to the appeal for the religiously minded.

Five-thousand-acre blocks of land were on sale for just one hundred pounds. Liberty of conscience was guaranteed and although Penn was granted supreme authority as governor, in practice there was a strong measure of representative government. The penal code of the colony, in sharp contrast to that of

> - The Humble, Meek, Merciful, Just, Pious and Devout Souls are everywhere of One Religion; and when Death has taken off the Mask, they will know one another, tho' the divers Liveries they wear here makes them Strangers.
> - Never give out while there is hope; but hope not beyond reason, for that shows more desire than judgement.
> - Never marry but for love, but see that thou lovest the lovely.
> - Seek and ye shall find, I testify for God. But then ye must seek aright with your whole heart, as men that seek for their lives, yea, for their eternal lives, diligently, humbly, patiently. O, it is a travail, a spiritual travail let the carnal, profane world think and say as it will. And through this path you must walk to the City of God that has eternal foundations, if ever you will come there.
>
> **William Penn**

England, only used the death penalty for cases of murder and treason.

Penn had a manor house built at Pennsburg and rode round the colony a great deal, though he preferred a six-oared barge for journeys to the chief town, Philadelphia. Pennsylvania prospered and many Quakers emigrated there or invested in it. Penn's initial stay was for only two years. In 1684 he went to England to settle a boundary dispute with Lord Baltimore and to assist the persecuted Quakers. In 1686 he was responsible for the release of all persons imprisoned for their religious convictions. He did not return to Pennsylvania until 1699, by which time the state suffered ill repute as a haven for pirates, and internal friction was threatening stability. The British government wanted to assert stronger royal control.

Penn felt Pennsylvanians owed him respect and deference to his wishes in the administration, but they felt otherwise. While he was occupied in America, Philip Ford, steward of his English and Irish estates, was busy forging the account books and eventually persuaded him to sign away Pennsylvania as security for an imaginary debt. Adding to Penn's worries was his son William's spendthrift and drunken behavior, the opposite of the Quaker ideal. These bitter last years saw Penn in debtors' prison for nine months, and in 1712 he had a mental breakdown — a "poor, shallow, half-crazed creature" as described by the nineteenth century British historian Macaulay.

M. B. Endy, Jr., *William Penn and Early Quakersism*, 1973.

W. I. Hull, *William Penn: A Topical Biography*, 1937.

C. O. Peare, *William Penn: A Biography*, 1957.

PERICLES (c.495–429 B.C.E.), Athenian statesman. Pericles was born into one of Athens's most prestigious families. His father, Xanthippos, was a successful general and politician; his mother was from the House of Alkmeonidai, an aristocratic family claiming descent from King Nestor of the Trojan War. Education, philosophy, culture, and politics (especially the blossoming of Athenian democracy) dominated Pericles's upbringing. When still young, he was urged to enter politics and speak at the assembly, but he chose a military career instead, distinguishing himself as a soldier in Greece's long war with Persia.

Thereafter, Pericles rose rapidly to power as leader of the Athenian democracy; there are only a few minor documents recording details of his early career. It appears that while Pericles the politician insisted that Athenians live by a stringent code of moral values, he lived by his own standards. It was said that when young, he planned the assassination of his own party leader in order to succeed him; rumor hinted that he seduced his son's wife and poisoned his close friend, Pheidas, in order to suppress damaging testimony against himself.

Pericles ignored the rumbling of rumors and concerned himself with issues concerning the welfare of Athens. He spearheaded an anti-Persian naval alliance with other Greek city-states called the Delian League, which led to the defeat of Persia at the battles of Marathon and Salamis. Buoyed by military victories, Pericles developed Athens politically by stressing the importance of citizenship. He served as the central figure of Athenian intellectual, military, and political life, and surrounded himself with Athens's cultural elite: the great philosopher *Socrates; the playwrights *Sophocles, *Euripides, Anaxagoras, and *Aeschylus; the philosophers Zeno and Protagoras; *Phidias the sculptor; and Damon the musician. At the pinnacle of his career, Pericles succeeded in rallying Greece around the Athenian flag, and the glorious days of Athens were called the "Periclean Age."

As self-proclaimed leader of the Greek city-states, Pericles decided to use Delian League funds to embellish the Acropolis and construct the Parthenon —

FROM AN ORATION BY PERICLES

Our constitution is called a democracy because power is in the hands not of a minority but of the whole people. When it is a question of settling private disputes, everyone is equal before the law; when it is a question of putting one person before another in position of public responsibility, what counts is not membership of a particular class, but the actual ability which the man possesses. No one, so long as he has it in him, to be of service to the state, is kept in political obscurity because of poverty.

the Greek world's most expensive temple. To further his desire for a greater Athens, Pericles tried to turn his allies into subjects not only by imposing Athenian-style democracy, but also by impressing the usage of Athenian coinage, weights, and measures.

Pericles envisioned a tribune-paying Athenian empire founded on the Delian League, a possibility the city-state of Sparta was determined to prevent. Sparta's revolt against Athenian imperialism led to the devastating Peloponnesian War of 431–404 B.C.E. While Pericles believed that the war would be in the best interest of Athens, its citizens disagreed and, in 430 B.C.E., they ousted him from office and forced him to pay heavy fines. Although he was reinstated in office a year later, Pericles shortly afterwards died of the plague that had enveloped Athens. Pericles's critics asserted that he had abused the powers invested in him and had had a devastating influence on the state, bringing Athens into a war it could never win and setting the stage for the collapse of its empire. Others, like the thinker *Thucydides — the only historian to write about Pericles from personal acquaintance — saw him as an unequaled politician, orator, and policymaker.

C. M. Bowra, *Periclean Athens*, 1971.
D. Kagan, *Pericles of Athens and the Birth of Democracy*, 1991.
R. Sealey, *The Athenian Republic: Democracy or the Rule of Law*, 1987.
C. G. Start, *The Birth of Athenian Democracy: The Assembly in the Fifth Century B.C.E.*, 1990.

PERON, JUAN (1895–1974) and **EVA** (1919–1952), Argentinian rulers. Juan Peron was raised on the expansive, treeless, plains of the Argentinian pampas. As a youth, he lived the life of a gaucho (South American cowboy) on his family's small ranch. Sent off to miliary college at sixteen, he proved to be a poor student, but was a tough soldier and a brilliant sportsman. Tall and handsome, he was also witty and charming, with a compelling, persuasive personality and the gift of winning the support of people of diverse political beliefs by convincing them that he shared their convictions and goals.

A military attache in Fascist Italy in the 1930s, Peron came to idolize Benito *Mussolini. In 1940 he convinced his fellow-officers in a rural Argentinian garrison to form a military political organization (called the GOU for its slogan "Government! Order! Unity!") dedicated to reducing governmental corruption by increasing the military's role in political affairs. Almost all of Argentina's army officers had become members of the GOU by 1943 when it came to power in a military coup, with Peron becoming head of the newly-created secretariat of labor and welfare.

Evita (as she became known) also came from the pampas, where her mother, Juana Ibarguren, was the mistress of a married man, Juan Duarte. Duarte rented her a one-room house where she brought up their five children (Evita was the youngest). Ostra-

Juan and Eva Peron

cized as bastards by their neighbors, the children were even refused permission to attend their father's funeral. Juana supported them after Duarte's death by cooking for rich ranchers, whose kitchens provided Evita with her first glimpse of the lifestyle of the rich, which contrasted starkly with her own. She was thirteen when her mother found a new protector who moved them to a bigger house and town, fourteen when participation in a school play fired her ambition to become a famous actress, and fifteen when she ran away to Buenos Aires with a young tango singer.

Evita had the will to work, learn, and suffer deprivation in her search for fame, but was neither talented nor especially attractive. She owed her acting jobs to her stubborn tenacity and a series of carefully chosen lovers in the theatrical business. When she was twenty-three, a wealthy lover's sponsorship started her career in radio. Featured first in radio soap operas, then on magazine covers, she became a well-known figure throughout Argentina. Her acting was not destined to improve, but when she became the mistress of the new military government's minister of communications, her employer raised her salary substantially in the hopes that it would prevent his radio station from being closed down. Her salary was increased yet further when she became Peron's mistress in 1944.

Peron was taking steps to secure his hold on the government. He quelled union leaders who opposed him with jail or threats; countered the attempts of the president (who had been installed as a puppet) to acquire real power by replacing him with someone more amenable and making himself vice-president; and seized control of the military establishment after some generals sought to restore civilian rule.

Peron had announced that the government's goal was to "strengthen national unity by securing greater social justice and an improvement in the standard of living of Argentine." Evita had the idea of broadening Peron's power base to include Argentina's working class. Declaring that "the unrestricted ambitions of the conservative classes to keep everything for themselves blinded them to the evidence: whoever wishes to keep everything will lose everything," Peron ignored the objections of employers and passed laws providing workers with decent living accommodation, guaranteed minimum wages, paid holidays, sick leave, protection from arbitrary dismissal, and a salary bonus at Christmas. For the first time Argentinian workers also benefitted from Argentina's prosperity. He united all the trade unions into a single, giant, vociferously pro-Peron organization.

A military coup forced Peron to resign as vice-president in 1945. Fired from the radio station, Evita refused to let Peron give up. She called on her contacts and Peron's supporters in the army, police, ministry of communications, and unions. Anti-Peron newspapers were closed down, pro-Peron street demonstrations broke out, and radio stations broadcast Peron's farewell speech live, but these activities only resulted in his arrest. Ordered to arrest Evita too, the police had to leave her behind, unable to cope with her hysterical screaming, tears, and threats to attack them. She immediately began organizing massive worker demonstrations that frightened the military into releasing Peron. Taken from jail, Peron addressed a crowd of three hundred thousand from the balcony of the presidential palace with a speech resigning from the army and dedicating himself to the cause of Argentina's poor, "the shirtless ones (descamisados)." He married Evita the next day.

Peron won the 1946 election for president with the help of promises to the descamisados and dirty tricks which sabotaged his opponents' campaign. Once in power, he quickly seized control of the bureaucracy, the supreme court, and the universities. His refusal to take sides in the Cold War did not deter American businessmen from making deals with his regime. He took advantage of post-war food shortages to charge much higher prices for Argentina's grain and beef, then bought Argentina's foreign-owned utilities and railways and nationalized them. He extended Argentina's influence over other Latin American countries with loans, and increased the standard of living of most Argentinians with a massive program of public works, benefits, and wage increases.

Evita's frequent public declarations of love and faith, ruthlessness with enemies, exploitation of radio and newspaper for propaganda purposes, and care for the descamisados were integral elements of Peron's rule. Huge pictures of the Perons and copies of Evita's sayings were plastered on billboards, and photographs of her appeared constantly in the newspapers. Educated Argentinians were as appalled by her emotional rhetoric (which radio stations were forced to broadcast) as the descamisados were appreciative, but had to be extremely careful about anyone overhearing their criticism. Evita never forgot or forgave an insult (real or imaginary) and either jailed or harassed her enemies. She replaced a prestigious society charitable organization which refused to accept her as a member with her own charity, the Social Aid Foundation, which built hospitals, homes for unmarried mothers, old age homes, parks, recreation centers, schools, a working girls' hotel, workers' holiday resorts, orphanages, and a model children's village; trained nurses; and operated clinics. Evita also embezzled funds from it to pay for her priceless collection of jewels and fill her Swiss bank accounts.

Opposition to Peron's rule grew as Argentina's economy suffered from inflation and declining foreign reserves. Deprived of Evita's energy, guidance, and ruthlessness by her death from cancer in 1952, Peron cut back his working hours drastically, preferring to spend time with his thirteen-year-old mistress. His attacks on the Catholic church and increasing dependence on force rather than reforms to silence criticism alienated many of his supporters. In 1955 he was overthrown by a military coup that revoked most of the economic benefits that his rule had brought to the descamisados.

Peron was gone, having settled in Madrid and married a night-club singer, Isabel, but Peronism remained. Argentina's rulers tried to get rid of it by purging Peron's followers, destroying monuments honoring the Perons, hiding Evita's embalmed body — everything except raising the living standard of the workers. Finally, in 1972 Argentina's military government invited Peron to return. He was elected president, with Isabel vice-president, but his ineffective leadership failed to solve Argentina's problems. When he died, the military tried to keep the Peronists' support by making Isabel president and bringing Evita's body back to Argentina, but after annual inflation approached 1000 percent and civil war almost broke out, Isabel was deposed by a coup and Evita was quietly buried.

J. Barnes, *Eva Peron*, 1978.
R. D. Crassweller, *Peron and the Enigmas of Argentina*, 1987.
J. A. Page *Peron*, 1983.

PERRY, MATTHEW CALBRAITH (1794–1858), father of the U. S. steam-powered navy and leader of the 1853–1854 expedition to Japan that opened up the Far East to the United States. He was born in Newport, Rhode Island, and at age fifteen he began his long career in the U.S. Navy as a midshipman on the *Revenge* under the command of his brother, Oliver Perry.

Perry was wounded in the first action of the 1812–1815 war with Britain, when a "bow-chaser" cannon exploded upon firing. While his ship was blockaded in New York harbor Perry married Jane Slidell, a daughter of a New York soap and tallow merchant. The Slidell family consented to the marriage partly because of the glory of Matthew's older brother Oliver, who won the battle of Lake Erie. They were married in 1814 and had ten children.

In 1819 Perry escorted a group of freed blacks to Liberia and cruised the Guinea coast in search of slave traders. Returning in 1821 to the African coast in command of the *Shark*, he achieved some success in freeing and returning Africans. A year later the *Shark* was deployed to the West Indies squadron to rid the Caribbean of pirate ships flying the Jolly Roger. Sailors under his command nicknamed him "Old Bruin" because he conveyed commands in a loud, gruff voice.

While captain of the Brooklyn Navy Yard (1833–1842), he was placed on the editorial board of *The Navy Magazine*. Perry deplored the fact that the U.S. Navy was only the eighth strongest in the world, ranking after Egypt, and his magazine articles and key position as captain of the yard provided him with the means to influence the development of the navy.

Favoring the incorporation of steamships into the navy, Perry utilized an old appropriation to build the *Fulton II* at the navy yard, but it consumed excessive fuel and had steering difficulties. At one time she inadvertently rammed and damaged another ship, thereby giving Perry the idea of restoring the Roman ramming technique as a modern weapon. He sailed the *Fulton II* to Washington and entertained President Martin Van Buren on board to prove that steam power was the future for the U.S. Navy. In 1839 Congress authorized the construction of three improved steamships equipped with shell guns, the *Mississippi*, the *Missouri*, and the *Union*. The *Mississippi* was active in the Mexican War, and was part of the expedition to Japan led by Perry.

In 1845 President Polk gave Vice Commodore Perry command of the Gulf Squadron, and Perry fought in the Mexican War on the *Mississippi*. His service was notable for his energy, intelligence, and military accomplishments, which included capturing many ports and conducting upriver expeditions.

Prior to being given command of the Japanese expedition by President Millard Fillmore, Commodore Perry had served as diplomat to the king of the Two Sicilies and the sultan of Turkey. He interviewed New England whaling captains and read every available book on Japan before making his first Pacific Ocean voyage, selecting specific gifts for the Japanese shogun (military dictator) to demonstrate United States culture and technology. The gifts included copies of Audubon's illustrated books, champagne, Colt arms, mirrors, perfumes, clocks, farm implements, stoves, a camera, telegraph instruments, and a one-quarter scale steam locomotive with tender, coach and sufficient track to make a 350-foot diameter circle.

Perry sailed into Tokyo Bay on 8 July, 1853 at a speed of nine knots with two steamships, each towing a sailing vessel. The Japanese had never seen steamships and were impressed by their speed on a windless day. While Perry was out to break Japan's isolation by a show of force, he truthfully told the Japanese officials, "I have come here as a peacemaker," and delivered a letter from President Fillmore. He knew that a show of strength would favor a successful mission so he deliberately delayed the arrival of six other ships until his return visit in February 1854. At that time he distributed all the presents, which were accepted with great interest, and negotiated a trade treaty, signed 31 March, 1854 which paved the way for other agreements between Japan and western nations. Perry was the first westerner to be received with dignity by the Japanese.

S. E. Morison, *Old Bruin: Commodore Matthew C. Perry 1794–1858*, 1967.

R. Pineau, ed., *The Japan Expedition: The Personal Journal of Commodore Matthew C. Perry*, 1968.

A. C. Walworth, *Black Ships of Japan*, 1946.

PERSHING, JOHN JOSEPH (1860–1948), U.S. general. John Pershing was born near Laclede, Missouri, to a family of modest means. While still in his teens, he taught in a country school. He won an appointment to the United States Military Academy after taking a competitive examination, and graduated in 1886. He then served in the cavalry, fighting in wars against the Indian chief *Geronimo (1886) and the Sioux (1890–1891).

While a military instructor at the University of Nebraska, he earned a law degree. In 1897 he was a tactical officer at West Point and fought in the Spanish-American War, where he was awarded a Silver Star for gallantry in action.

Between 1901 and 1903 he fought in the Philippines and was commended by President Theodore *Roosevelt for his leadership ability. In 1905 Pershing was sent to Manchuria as a military attaché during the Russo-Japanese War. In 1906 Roosevelt promoted him to brigadier general over the objection of eight hundred senior officers. He then had another tour of duty in the Philippines after which he was sent to Mexico (1916) to crush the band of Mexicans led by Pancho Villa, who had made a surprise raid on the U.S. Cavalry garrison in New Mexico.

While in Mexico, Pershing learned that his wife and three daughters had perished in a fire and only his son had survived. However, six days later, he led his troops into Mexico and dispersed Villa's guerrillas, although Villa himself was never captured.

When the United States declared war on Germany in 1917, Pershing was appointed commander of the American Expeditionary Forces and sent to France to review the situation. Upon his arrival in Europe, he was told that the Allies saw America's role as limited to supplying more troops for their depleted ranks. Pershing rejected this view and gained approval for his plan to build a large army in Europe. Within two months he completed plans for a full scale offensive against Germany. He frequently feuded with French, British, and Italian commanding officers, and at one heated session he pounded his

Pershing (center) with Marshal Foch in Normandy

fist on the table and shouted, "Gentlemen, I have thought this program over very deliberately and will not be coerced!" The Allied commanders continually requested that Pershing be replaced, but U.S. secretary of war Newton Baker had faith in him. His newly formed United States First Army was used very effectively in September 1918 in the Saint Mihiel salient in which sixteen thousand prisoners were taken. On 25–26 September, Pershing launched his second offensive and in forty-seven days the American Expeditionary Force had broken through to the outskirts of Sedan. On 11 November, 1918, an armistice was signed, marking an end to the war.

In eighteen months Pershing had established himself as a great military leader, having assembled an army of two million men who in two hundred days played a large role in defeating a German army hardened by four years of fighting experience. President Harry *Truman, who served under him in World War I, said, "He was a great general and the only one without political ambitions."

In 1919 Pershing was made general of the armies, a rank unheard of prior to that time, and served in that capacity until he retired from the army in 1924. The following year he was sent to South America to settle a dispute between Peru and Chile. Upon his return to the United States, Pershing spent the rest of his active life as the chairman of the American Battle Monuments Commission. He wrote his memoirs, *Final Report* (1919) and *My Experiences in the World War* (two volumes, 1931). In 1937 he headed the U.S. delegation to the coronation of King George VI.

F. Palmer, *J. J. Pershing, General of the Armies*, 1948.
D. Smythe, *Guerrilla Warrior: The Early Life of John J. Pershing*,1973.
F. E. Vandiver, *Black Jack: The Life and Times of John J. Pershing*, 1977.

PESTALOZZI, JOHANN HEINRICH

(1746–1827), Swiss pedagogue and educational theorist, promoter of education for the poor. Johann Pestalozzi was born in Zurich, and as a young man became concerned at the miserable neglect of the poor in Europe. He considered entering the church, then decided to study law at the university of Zurich,

but, in 1769, abandoned his studies, frustrated by his inability to be of service to those in need. He established a farm, Neuhof, near the river Aare, wishing to discover for himself the fundamental essence of education by being near nature. He had decided that only by enriching the poorer classes with knowledge could he hope to break their poverty cycle.

Pestalozzi was very impressed by the educational ideas of Jean-Jacques *Rousseau, although after applying some of Rousseau's theories to his own children he found them too abstract. This spurred him to develop new educational methods, and in 1774 he took in a group of poor, ill-treated children and began developing them into able adults through an integrated program of formal education, physical activities, and group recreation in a familial, supportive environment. Despite the school's collapse in 1779 due to lack of funds, Pestalozzi was convinced that he had managed to devise a relevant educational framework.

Unable to secure an outlet for his ideas, Pestalozzi spent the next few years committing them to paper. His first novel, *The Evening Hour of a Hermit*, in which he described his educational doctrine, was completed in 1780, and established the concept that education should be natural, building on the abilities of the pupil and gradually progressing at the pupil's own developmental rate. His second work, *Leonard and Gertrude*, was concerned with rural German life. This moralistic tale promotes the values of the family through the purity and steadfastness of its main protagonist, the humble peasant woman Gertrude. The novel successfully influenced the pedagogical perception of the importance of the family environment in early education.

Pestalozzi believed that through the implementation of his educational system, people could realize their full potential as God had intended. Unlike many of his predecessors, including Rousseau, he attributed much of a person's character and abilities not to nature, but to nurture. All these themes conflicted with orthodox educational views and consequently for many years Pestalozzi's ideas went unheeded. However, he held unwaveringly to his own beliefs, living quietly at Neuhof with his family, writing on politics, economics, and education.

Finally, in 1798, Pestalozzi received an opportunity to build a school when the Helvetian Republic in Switzerland asked him to organize its higher education system afresh. He, however, chose to focus on the roots of the system, opting to establish a school at Stans, where he gathered orphans from the Napoleonic wars, hoping to rejuvenate their humanity in a caring, warm environment. Although he stayed there only a few months, they were the most rewarding of his life.

Pestalozzi's radical views began to attract other progressive teachers, and he established a teachers' training institute. In 1805 he moved to a boarding school in Yverdon as a director and remained there for the next twenty years. Yverdon became internationally renowned, attracting visitors and pupils from all over Europe, and many pedagogues were influenced by their brief visits there. Pestalozzi was even able to use the school's success to fund another institution for helping the poor, still his most cherished aim.

By 1825 Pestalozzi had ceased his teaching activities to focus his remaining strength on perfecting his ideas. Tragically, in his last years he saw his life's work crumble around him. Infighting among his teachers led to Yverdon's losing its reputation and many of its pupils. His school for the poor was forced to close its doors. Disappointed by the outcome of his efforts, Pestalozzi retired to Neuhof, where he died.

R. B. Downe, *Heinrich Pestalozzi, Father of Modern Pedagogy*, 1975.

K. Silber, *Pestalozzi: The Man and His Work*, 1973.

PÉTAIN, HENRI PHILLIPE OMER
(1856–1951), French marshal, hero of World War I, head of state of the collaborationist Vichy régime during World War II. Henri Pétain was born into a farming family in Cauchy-e-la-Tour and attended a local village school. After graduating from a religious secondary school, he was admitted to the prestigious French military academy at Saint Cyr in 1887. He also attended the Ecole de Guerre, where he later taught. At the outbreak of World War I he was still only a colonel at age fifty-eight, set to retire from military life. His advancement had been hampered by his disagreements with the military establishment regarding tactics. The official army policy favored full infantry attacks while Pétain's lectures at the Ecole de Guerre promoted the concept of defensive resistance.

In the early stages of the war Pétain fought well and advanced in rank, being promoted to the rank of full general in command of the Second Army in 1915. His reputation and popularity among the rank and file was high and he was regarded as a general to be trusted, as he did not waste men's lives in futile battle maneuvers. In February 1916 Pétain was ordered to defend the fortress of Verdun; the German attack lasted six months and the defense was seen as hopeless. However, with Pétain's skillful use of supplies and troops, the attack was foiled and Pétain emerged a popular hero, while his vow "They shall not pass" passed into popular speech.

In 1917 he was called upon to restore morale following the mutinies that had erupted as a result of the ill-conceived spring offensive; he replaced General Robert Nivelle as commander in chief of the French army. In order to reestablish discipline Pétain ordered the execution of twenty-seven mutineers; he, however, responded to soldier's complaints by improving living conditions. In November 1918 he was made marshal of France.

Between the wars Pétain was sent to Morocco where he was responsible for the success of the French and Spanish campaign against the rebel Abd-El-Krim. In 1934 he acted as war minister and in 1939 was named ambassador to Spain. It was, however, as vice president of the French general staff (1920–1930) that Pétain enjoyed his most important pre-World War II role. Convinced that France must not wage an offensive war, he encouraged the construction of the defensive Maginot Line, thus neglecting sorely needed offensive weaponry and tactics.

In World War II when France was on the brink of collapse after the German blitzkrieg, Premier Paul Reynaud recalled Pétain from Spain and appointed him vice premier in the hope that his presence would restore French pride and hope. On 16 June 1940, at the age of eighty-four, Marshal Pétain was asked to form a new ministry. Pétain argued in favor of an armistice and on 25 June most of France was occupied by the Germans. On 10 July 1940 the constitution of the Third Republic was suspended and Pétain was made head of state at Vichy, in unoccupied France.

As head of the Fascist Vichy government and head of state Pétain appointed Pierre Laval as his vice premier. In October he met with Adolf *Hitler at Montoire to offer his cooperation. After the war he claimed in his defense that his cooperation was the only means of protecting French lives until after the war and the defeat of the Nazi régime. However, throughout the occupation Pétain continued to offer his government's cooperation in exchange for nonpunitive peace with Germany. To placate increasing German demands he allowed his government to pass legislation dissolving Masonic lodges and excluding Jews from certain professions. Hitler, however, offered nothing in return, powerful in the knowledge that Pétain would not resist his increasingly harsh requests for money, supplies, and eventually mass deportation of Jews for extermination.

After the Allied invasion of North Africa in November 1942 and the German occupation of all of France, Pétain's role became that of a political puppet serving German interests. When in December 1943 Pétain tried to retain control by dismissing Laval, Hitler ordered him to keep Laval and to stay in office. Pétain continued to practice a policy of cooperation and when the Allies landed in Normandy in June 1944, Pétain ordered the French people to be "quiet and orderly" but not to assist the Allied forces.

After the Allied invasion of France, Pétain was taken by the Germans first to Belmont and later to Germany. In 1945 he returned to France and was indicted on charges of treason. His trial (July–August 1945) resulted in a death sentence, but this was commuted by General Charles de *Gaulle to solitary life imprisonment. He was imprisoned on the Ile d'Yeu, off the coast of Brittany, where he died at the age of ninety-five.

R. Aron, *The Vichy Regime, 1940–1944*, 1958.

S. Huddleston, *Pétain: Patriot or Traitor*, 1951.

H. R. Lottman, *Pétain, Hero or Traitor: The Untold Story*, 1985.

PETER, SAINT (original name: Simon; died c.64 C.E.), one of the twelve Apostles of *Jesus. Peter emerged as the most prominent among Jesus' disciples and was singled out for a position of leadership. After Jesus' death, Peter became the head of the Christian community in Jerusalem and in later times bishops of Rome claimed succession from Peter, proclaiming him the first pope of the Roman Catholic Church.

Peter's family originated in Bethsaida, on the northern shore of the Sea of Galilee. By the time of Jesus' ministry, Peter was married (according to later legend, with children), and lived by the Sea of Galilee in Capernaum, where he and his brother Andrew were fishermen together with two others who would become disciples, James and John, the sons of Zebedee.At the Sea of Galilee, Peter began his apostleship and was the first to proclaim Jesus as the Messiah (Matt. 16:15–16).

Peter was, with James and John, among the inner circle of Jesus' followers (termed "the pillars") permitted to accompany Jesus in his ministry. When Jesus taught the crowd at the Sea of Galilee, he stood in Peter's boat; Peter, James and John accompanied Jesus when he raised the daughter of Jairus from the dead; the same group was also present at the Transfiguration and the critical moments in the Garden of Gethsemane. The New Testament records that it is Peter who first witnessed the Resurrection and, in the Gospel of John, Peter is told by Jesus to "tend my sheep" and "feed my lambs," references to providing spiritual instruction to the faithful in Jesus' absence. In listing the Apostles, Peter is always mentioned first and sometimes he is the only one named.

Peter's position of responsibility for the Christian community accounts for his change of name from the Hebrew, Simon, to Peter, derived from the Latin, *petros*, meaning "the rock." In the New Testament (Matt. 16:15–19), Jesus says to him, "I tell you, you are Peter, and on this rock I will build my church, and the powers of death shall not prevail against it. I will give you the keys of the kingdom of Heaven, and whatever you bind on earth shall be bound in heaven, and whatever you loose on earth shall be loosed in heaven." The church here refers to the early followers of Jesus, and Peter is given unique authority within the community, "the keys of the kingdom." The power to "bind" and "loose," indicating the authority to legislate and to determine the members of the community, was given singly to Peter as well as in common with all of Jesus' Apostles.

Despite his responsible role, Peter does not appear to have been particularly educated, either in Hebrew or Greek, and in his apostleship he erred many times. Thus, he first ate with the gentiles at Antioch but later refused, and the mission to the gentiles was taken over by Paul at that time. It was Peter who declared that he would be faithful to Jesus unto death and then denied his apostleship when confronted by the Roman authorities.

In spite of these failings, the sincerity of Peter's love for Jesus was always clear and once invested with responsibility, he carried out his role with the qualities of leadership. Indeed, Jesus prophesied that Peter's betrayal would be followed by his strengthening of the other Apostles. Thus, after Peter spoke against the Passion that Jesus foresaw, he was first severely rebuked by his master but then received a revelation and made a confession that led to his becoming the foundation of the future church. Likewise, Peter's witness of the Resurrection is said to guard the church from the possibility of future death.

After Jesus' death, Peter led the community for the next fifteen years, disciplining its members, making Matthias the twelth Apostle in place of Judas, leading the church's expansion by going to such groups as the Samaritans, performing miraculous healings, and fulfilling a pastoral role at the gatherings of the faithful. In 44 he was imprisoned by Herod Agrippa after the beheading of James, the son of Zebedee. Miraculously freed, he fled to safety and, while ceasing to play a role in the Jerusalem community he proselytized according to the instructions of James, a cosin or brother of Jesus and the new leader of the Jerusalem church. It is not clear where Peter went after his escape but possibilities include Antioch, Corinth, and Rome. The later years of Peter's life are shrouded in uncertainty; according to tradition he was twenty-five years in Rome as bishop, perhaps a late interpolation designed to lend credence to the claim that papal authority stemmed directly from him. It appears that Peter was martyred during the reign of *Nero, somewhere between 64 and 67; traditional sources record that he was crucified upside-down. The great basilica of Saint Peter is built over the traditional site of his tomb, where human remains have been uncovered, dating from the first century C.E.

R. Brown, *Peter in the New Testament*, 1973.

C. C. Caragounis, *Peter and the Rock*, 1990.

O. Cullman, *Peter*, 1962.

O. Karrer, *Peter and the Church*, 1963.

PETER I (Peter the Great; 1672–1725), Russian czar. His father, Czar Alexei, died before Peter's fourth birthday and was succeeded by Peter's sickly half-brother, Fedor. A few years later Fedor died without issue and Peter, at the age of ten, became czar together with his half-brother Ivan (1682). However, his half-sister Sophia, backed by a revolution of the palace guard (the Streltsy), took power and ruled as regent. Peter and his mother left Moscow for the countryside where he enjoyed much more freedom than was usually allowed members of the royal family. He amused himself planning military maneuvers with boys of his own age, eventually forming regiments of six hunded youths. He spent time learning the crafts of carpentry, masonry, printing, and smithery. He also developed a passionate love of boats. This unorthodox education served as the base for his later effort to force Russia into the contemporary post-Renaissance world.

Toward the end of 1689 Peter challenged Sophia's regency, aided, and to some extent encouraged, by the failure of her second Crimea campaign, and backed by the Streltsy troops, loyal to him as the anointed czar. He assumed power (Ivan, and a figurehead died in 1696) and sent Sophia to the Novodevichy monastery outside Moscow where she spent the rest of her life in luxurious imprisonment. Some of her supporters were executed. Peter himself showed sadistic traits and enjoyed watching people being tortured. At the beginning of 1689 he married Eudoxia, his mother's choice, twenty-three years his senior, who bore him two sons.

Peter now set out to achieve the Westernization of Russia and expand his borders toward the Baltic and the Black Seas, Russia possessing at the time only one seaport on the White Sea. In Moscow there was a small settlement of foreigners, almost a ghetto, known as the "German Suburb." They were not all Germans, but were almost all of wider education and experience than the Russians they lived among, a fact which attracted Peter to their company. Together with Russian friends, they formed a convivial group that remained in existence with Peter at its head until his death. Their orgies and buffoonery, including drunken celebrations held on religious festivals, scandalized many and led church dignitaries to see Peter as the antichrist, especially after the reforms he was later to force on them.

In 1696 Peter made his second and successful attempt (the first had ended in a costly retreat) to take Azov from the Turks, founding a navy in the process. After his victory, he sent twenty-eight Russians, most from the nobility, to Venice and twelve others to Holland and England to learn the crafts of navigation and shipbuilding. He also sent a "Great Embassy" (1697–1698) to travel in Western Europe, accompanying it himself incognito, and spent four months in Amsterdam as a ship's carpenter. He visited England and lived for three months in the writer John Evelyn's house in Deptford; after the Russians left, Evelyn was horrified to see the damage they had done (he received £350.0s.9d in compensation from the English authorities).

Peter visited Dresden and Vienna, but his grand tour was cut short by a letter bringing him news of a military revolt — four Streltsy regiments were marching on Moscow. Halfway home he received news that the revolt had been put down, but decided not to resume his tour.

Almost his first action on returning to Moscow was to shave the beards of the boyars who came to greet him. Peter believed that their beards made Russians ridiculous in the eyes of the West. Eventually he was to tax those who did not want to shave (except for clergy and peasants); the church was shocked by what it saw as a godless act. Later that same winter (1698) he cut off the boyars' traditional

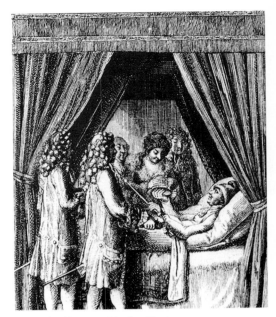

Peter the Great on his deathbed

wide sleeves, and later still decreed the compulsory changing of Russian for Western-style clothes. Not long after his return Peter sent his wife Eudoxia, to whom he had never been close, to a convent, putting his sister in charge of his son Alexei, then nearly nine years of age.

He set in motion a series of startling reforms, some designed to displace the church. A partial list includes universal taxation and the emancipation of women from their lowly status and the *terem* (the Russian equivalent of a harem); he abolished the Moscow patriarchate and established a holy synod in its stead, with himself at its head; he reformed the calendar and the alphabet, at least for nonchurch purposes (the Bible and other church writings were still printed in the church Slavonic alphabet). He built hospitals and founded a new upper class of civil and military administrators. He encouraged trade by minting a new Russian currency to replace the foreign coins in circulation. While he was beginning his reforms, he had the rebellious Streltsy troops sadistically tortured and executed.

With his victory in the Battle of Poltava (1709) during the Northern War with Sweden (1700–1721), Peter gained access to the Baltic Sea. In the midst of the war he built the city of Saint Petersburg, "a window on Europe,"where the river Neva flows into the Gulf of Finland. Constructed on swampland, far north enough to have a summer of very short nights, the city became his capital in preference to Moscow despite its damp, unhealthy climate (*neva* is Finnish for "swamp"). He peopled the city in the same way he had Westernized Russian dress: by force.

Peter's attempts to prepare Alexei, the surviving son of his first marriage, for his future role proved frustrating for both father and son. Alexei, a weak character, fled from Russia and eluded Peter for several months. He was found by Peter's envoys and brought back to Russia. Humiliated by his son's public defection and fearing that Alexei might serve, unwittingly, as a focus of discontent within Russia, Peter first made Alexei sign away his rights to the throne; later, fearing a plot, he questioned his son about his "fellow conspirators." (One of the most famous of nineteenth century Russian paintings, by Nikolai Gai, depicts Peter's interrogation of his son.) A number of courtiers, including senators, military officials, Eudoxia herself, and Alexei's tutor, were arrested and imprisoned, exiled, or executed. As the "evidence" grew, Alexei was arrested and two courts, civil ecclesiastical, were convened. Alexei was tortured and sentence to death; however, he died on the following day before Peter had ratified the sentence. The cause of death is not known.

Peter declared himself emperor ("Father of the Fatherland, Peter the Great, Emperor of All Russia") in 1721 and in 1724 he made his second wife, Catherine I, a woman of peasant origin and dubious early history, empress. They were formally married in 1712, a private wedding having been performed in 1707. They had twelve children, of whom only two daughters survived.

Peter was a strange and enigmatic character. His capacity for self-discipline and hard physical work was as great as his capacity for pleasure, and his demands of himself were as ruthless as his demands on others. He suffered from convulsions, the exact nature and cause of which were never diagnosed.

I. Gray, *Peter the Great, Emperor of All Russia*, 1960.

R. K. Massie, *Peter the Great*, 1981.

P. B. Putnam, *Peter, the Revolutionary Tsar*, 1973.

PETRARCH, FRANCESCO (1304–1374), Italian

poet and scholar. Petrarch's poems, scholarship, and philosophy ushered in the Renaissance, while his life embodied its major themes: passionate interest in the glories of ancient Rome, the revival of classical scholarship, a Humanist synthesis between Christian ethics and the ideals of the pagan classics, and the combination of scholarship and creativity with active interest in worldly affairs.

Petrarch's father was a lawyer who was forced to leave his native Florence for political reasons and was drawn to Avignon — where the exiled papal court had become medieval Europe's center of patronage and diplomacy — by its employment possibilities. There, Petrarch had access to the growing collection of classical manuscripts in the papal library. Petrarch's father insisted that he study law at the University of Montpellier, burnt his copies of classical manuscripts to keep them from distracting him, and then sent him to medieval Europe's greatest center of legal studies, the University of Bologna. Petrarch, however, spent much

of his time there studying classical literature (he was particularly influenced by the works of *Cicero and *Virgil) and becoming acquainted with Italian lyric poetry. He abandoned his law studies completely after his father died in 1326.

Always deeply and sincerely religious, Petrarch took lesser ecclesiastical orders upon returning to Avignon. This provided for his financial needs without demanding much from him and left him free to pursue his studies and enjoy the life of a court dandy. It was during this period of dissipation that Petrarch first saw a woman called Laura in the Church of Saint Clare in Avignon. His deep and chaste love for her lasted a lifetime and inspired his most famous creations, the Italian love poems dedicated to her. Considered the father of modern poetry, he perfected the sonnet form.

Restlessness was one of Petrarch's lifelong traits. His frequent travels, which brought him into contact with the cultures and foremost personalities of Europe, were undertaken not only for business and diplomatic purposes (although he was in great demand as a diplomat up until his death), but also to satisfy his curiosity and passion for exploring new places and the sites of antiquity, and out of a desire to seek out new manuscripts for his library. While still in his twenties, his scholarly philological analysis of the manuscript fragments he discovered enabled him to correct and piece together the most complete available text of Livy's *History of Rome*.

Petrarch's works showed the influence of the classical writers he loved, identified with, and strove to imitate (Livy's history inspired his *Lives of Famous Men*, while he modeled his letters on those of Cicero). The only non-classical author to have such an effect on him was Saint *Augustine, himself greatly influenced by the classics. A copy of Augustine's *Confessions* accompanied him everywhere and was responsible for his later interest in the writings of the church fathers.

Petrarch intensely admired the glories of the past, and longed to recreate them. His account of his first visit to Rome in 1337 describes many of its monuments as they once were, not as the barely identifiable, overgrown ruins he saw. His idealization of the government, heroes, and achievements of ancient Rome motivated much of his political activity. The corruption of Avignon seemed unbearable to him in comparison and he found a retreat at Vaucluse that gave him the solitude and tranquillity he craved. There, surrounded by his friends and the beauties of nature, with a garden he planted with laurel and beech trees to encourage the presence of Apollo and his muses, he pursued a life of contemplation and writing.

In 1341 Petrarch became poet laureate in Rome, although most of his famous poems were as yet unwritten. Extremely conscious of how the world viewed him, he used his writing to create an image of himself for posterity. He constantly rewrote and revised his works.

Several factors contributed to Petrarch's decision to move to Italy permanently in 1353. Many friends (including Laura) had died from the plague, he had supported an attempt to revive the Roman Republic that had alienated his patrons, and he disliked the new pope. In Italy he continued his writing and revising, and was involved in politics and diplomatic missions for his patrons. He lived happily with the family of his daughter, Francesca, for some years. In his last years he enjoyed widespread fame, which grew even greater after his death.

N. Mann, *Petrarch*, 1984.

E. H. Wilkins, *Life of Petrarch*, 1961.

PHIDIAS (c.490–430 B.C.E.), Greek sculptor. Phidias learned painting and sculpture from the master artist Hegias. Later, as the foremost sculptor of ancient Greece, he perfected the idealized style of representing the human form that came to characterize Hellenic art. Although all that remains of Phidias's original works is a few statuettes and coins minted after his design, there are Roman copies and the accounts of ancient writers that provide a fuller knowledge of his accomplishments.

His greatest achievements were the three carvings of the goddess Athena created for the Parthenon and his monumental sculpture of the seated Zeus for Olympia. These works were commissioned by the Athenian ruler *Pericles in 447 B.C.E., with Phidias also overseeing the building of Athens's national shrines. Pericles' projects were extensive and included a series of temples erected on the Acropolis and at Olympia aimed at proclaiming the greatness of Athens and its gods during this period of Athenian ascendancy.

Working in bronze, marble, gold, and ivory, Phidias created forms that revealed lifelike contours of the body while achieving a magnificent grandeur absent in the later periods of Greek sculpture. Two all-bronze statues, the Apollo Parnopios and the Athena Promachos, stood on the Acropolis. The Athena Promachos was Phidias's first statue, completed around 456 B.C.E., and stood ten meters high. The Amazon at Ephesus, done in marble, was probably the basis for the Amazon Mattei in the Vatican. The Athena Lemnia on the Acropolis was done completely in bronze, a thanks-offering commissioned by the Athenian colonists sent to Lemnos around 450 B.C.E. There are Roman copies of this statue in marble in collections in Bologna and Dresden.

Phidias also created works from gilded wood and set with ivory — the Athena at Pellene and the Aphrodite Ourania at Elis.These smaller chryselephantine works were dwarfed by two others done by him in the same style. The Athene Parthenos was completed in 438 B.C.E. and placed in the Parthenon, where it stood some twelve meters high: Roman and Greek copies of it are extant in Berlin and Athens. Phidias's Zeus was in this same style. This statue of the god sitting on his throne was made for the shrine at Olympia and reached to a height of fourteen meters. Zeus's skin is ivory, his tunic gold and the god is shown holding Nike (the Greek goddess of victory) in one hand and a staff in the other. Ancient sources speak of it as Phidias's greatest work. His inspiration for the Zeus was *Homer's descriptions, and the statue became one of the Seven Wonders of the world.

Phidias's statues on the Acropolis reached to such a height that they could be seen, reflecting the sun, by boats passing out at sea. Phidias's status in the ancient world is suggested by the saying that only he knew the true rendering of the gods; the forms he gave them were universally adapted.

Little is known about Phidias's last years. The enemies of Pericles accused Phidias of stealing the gold provided for his work, a charge he successfully denied. It appears, however, that he was subsequently jailed for the impious act of copying his own image and that of Pericles onto the shield of the Athene Parthenos. He went into exile at Elis where molds have been found in a studio thought to have been used for his creation of the Zeus at Olympia.

G. Richter, *Sculpture and Sculptors of the Greeks*, 1970.

PHILIP II OF MACEDONIA (382–336 B.C.E.), conqueror of Greece and father of *Alexander the Great. Philip was the youngest son of the ruling family of Macedonia, the largest and most populous state in the Greek world. Powerful neighbors were quick to take advantage when internal strife weakened Macedonia, and Philip spent three years of his youth as a hostage in Thebes. During that time he came to appreciate Greek culture and learn the newest military tactics. On his return to Macedonia he was appointed governor of a province, becoming an able statesman and administrator.

This experience stood him in good stead when, at twenty-three, he began to rule — as his nephew's regent — a Macedonia threatened by invading neighbors, powerful and rebellious barons, and rival claimants for the throne. He bought off his neighbors, won over his nobles, and drilled Macedonia's independent mountaineers into the most effective fighting force of its time. He then sealed his first political alliance by marrying the Molossian princess Olympias. He declared himself king of Macedonia — having ousted his nephew — after Alexander's birth in 356 B.C.E..

A man of jovial good humor who liked wine, women, and laughter, Philip combined a violent temper with the ability to wait patiently for the best opportunity to achieve his goals. The athletic strength and handsome appearance that he enjoyed at the beginning of his reign were steadily eroded by battlefield injuries, but the brave craftiness of his military strategy remained and his diplomacy continued to be distinguished by his affability, his moderate treatment of the defeated, and his capacity for treachery.

Philip expanded his borders, gained an outlet to the sea, and conquered the rich gold mines of Mount Pangaeum to fund further military campaigns. He used the Third Sacred War of 356 B.C.E. (caused by Phocia stealing the treasury of the temple at Delphi) to gain complete control of northern and central Greece, win increased support in Athens, be recognized as official protector of the Delphi shrine, and obtain a peace treaty recognizing his conquests. He gathered money to finance future military campaigns by selling off thousands of war captives as slaves.

The Athenian orator and statesman *Demosthenes's attempts to unite Greece against Philip were foiled by the apathetic pacifism current in Athens, an attitude that became more popular thanks to Philip's liberal bribes. Philip's obvious and real admiration for Greek culture also had its effect. He asked *Aristotle to educate Alexander in Greek philosophy "so that he may not do a great many things of the sort that I am sorry to have done." He also respected Greek customs. Greece's city-states agreed to suspend their usual belligerence for the monthly duration of the annual Olympic games, and when a fine was imposed on Philip for his soldiers' conduct toward someone en route to the games, he meekly paid it.

The Fourth Sacred War of 339 B.C.E. broke out over a sacrilege committed against the shrine of the Oracle at Delphi. As the guardian of the shrine, Philip accepted the task of punishing the guilty. The presence of the Macedonian army a scant three days march from Athens woke the city from its apathy, and Demosthenes's eloquence persuaded Thebes to ally itself with Athens. The defeat of their joint armies on the plain of Chaeronea in 338 B.C.E. completed Philip's conquest of Greece. Thebes was occupied by a Macedonian garrison but Philip demonstrated his respect for Athens with his lenient peace terms. Although it had to become his ally, it was allowed to keep its fleet, and he never set foot in it.

Philip's ambition was not satisfied with the defeat of Greece and bringing most of the Balkans under Macedonian rule. He also wanted to defeat the Persian Empire, but knew that for this he needed Greek help. To this end, he tried to unify the Greek city-states into a federation under his hegemony. Delegates from every city but Sparta accepted his invitation to the assembly in Corinth (one of the three Greek cities where a Macedonian garrison was stationed). When he revealed his plans to liberate the Greek cities of Asia and completely defeat Persia, the assembly gave him their unanimous support and appointed him to lead the attack, happy to have been given a way to be rid of him so easily. The assembly created the League of Corinth, in which member states kept their autonomy, pledged to supply Philip with men and arms, and were forbidden to attack each other. Essentially conservative, Philip also prohibited revolution, social change, or constitutional amendments within the league. This stimulated business stability and trade and won the support of the propertied classes.

Philip's love for women made sealing political alliances with marriage particularly appealing for him, and he did so as often as he could. Olympias did not have the temperament to take kindly to polygamy and she began indulging in wild Dionysian rites. They became estranged (he did not care for sharing a bed with both Olympias and a snake, even though she assured him that the snake was really a god). Olympias tried to hurt her husband — who was extremely proud of Alexander — by telling both of them that he was not Alexander's real father: rather, Alexander had been begotten by a thunderbolt from Zeus-Ammon. Olympias finally left Philip, taking Alexander with her. In 338 B.C.E., Philip married Cleopatra of Macedonia; two years later during his daughter's marriage celebration he was murdered. His assassin was supposedly motivated by Philip's failure to redress an insult from one of Cleopatra's relatives, but there is a strong suspicion that he was urged on by Olympias.

G. Cawkwell, *Philip of Macedon*, 1978.

D. G. Hogarth, *Philip and Alexander of Macedon*, 1971.

S. Perlman, *Philip and Athens*, 1973.

PHILIP II (1527–1598), Spanish king. Philip was the only son of *Charles V, who as Holy Roman emperor ruled over more territory than any of his predecessors. In 1543 Philip married his cousin, Maria of Portugal, who died in 1545 while giving birth to Don Carlos. Upon his second marriage to *Mary I of England in 1554, he received the kingdoms of Naples and Sicily, followed by the Netherlands in 1555. He became king of Spain and its overseas dominions in 1556, when his father abdicated in his favor.

Philip's marriage to Mary served as a pretext for England's entering the conflict between Spain and France on the Spanish side in 1557. In the same year Spain won an important victory over the French at San Quentin, and in honor of San Lorenzo, on whose feast day the battle was won, Philip commissioned the building of El Escorial palace north of Madrid, where he conducted and orchestrated affairs of state. Suspicious of his court intimates, Philip refused to delegate even the simplest of administrative tasks, which resulted in bureaucratic stagnation and bickering between rival court factions. In 1558 Mary died leaving no heir and a year later Philip signed the peace treaty of Cateau-Cambresis that ended the war with France and sealed his marriage to Elizabeth of Valois, daughter of Henry II of France, with whom he had two daughters. Elizabeth died in 1568, and in 1570 Philip was married for the fourth and last time, this time to his cousin Anne of Austria; their son was to become his successor as Philip III (Don Carlos, whom he hated, having died in prison).

Philip became increasingly obsessed by a grandiose plan to defeat Protestantism and to con-

Philip II

tinue the work of unification. Spain was enjoying a golden age, with accomplishments in literature and painting, and Philip believed that it could and should become the moral voice of Catholicism. In his quest for political hegemony, resistance was quashed by force: the suppression of rebellion of the Moriscos (1568–1570) was an attempt to secure religious unity in Spain; the conquest of Portugal in 1580, an attempt to increase Spanish dominion. However throughout the latter part of his reign, Philip was confronted with rebellion from the Netherlands, which only ended when the Seven United Provinces achieved independence in 1579. He also faced a revolt by the Aragonese in 1591–1592.

English and French support of the Dutch rebellion and constant attacks by England on Spanish shipping vessels led to Philip's building and equipping of the Spanish armada. However, his plan to invade England in 1588 failed and his "invincible" Armada was crushed, with less than half of the 130 ships reaching home. In 1590, continuing his campaign to restore the power of the Roman Catholic church, Philip sent troops and funds to France to aid the Catholic League in its fight against the Protestant ruler, Henry of Navarre (*Henry IV). After failing in his attempt to seize the throne in the name of his daughter, Isabella Clara Eugenia, Philip was forced to accept the accession of Henry of Navarre to the French throne, but had the consolation that Henry had become a Catholic.

On Philip's death, the debts of the Spanish government were estimated at around one hundred million ducats, and interest payments on this sum

alone constituted almost two-thirds of all Spanish revenues; the Spanish government never recovered from the excessive spending during his reign and faced bankruptcy throughout the seventeenth century. Philip had remained indifferent to these problems, concerned only with his political and religious quest. His dreams were not totally unfulfilled and — despite his losses with respect to England, Scotland, and Holland — he had managed to maintain Spanish rule in Belgium, beat off the Ottoman challenge to the east at the battle of Lepanto (1571) and add Portugal to the Catholic crown. Furthermore, he had strengthened the position of the Catholic church in what he saw as its fight against the rising tide of Protestantism.

M. A. S. Hume, *Philip II of Spain*, 1970.
G. Mattingly, *The Defeat of the Spanish Armada*, 1959.
R. B. Merriman, *The Rise of the Spanish Empire in the Old World and the New*, 1962.

PICASSO, PABLO (Pablo Ruiz y Picasso; 1881–1973), Spanish artist. Picasso was born in Malaga where his father, José Ruiz Blasco, was a drawing master. His mother was Maria Picasso from Andalusia and from the age of twenty, he was, following a Spanish custom, known by his mother's name. At first his father readily encouraged his son's artistry but became resentful of his obvious ability. At fifteen Picasso was admitted to La Lonja, Barcelona's school of fine arts. A year later he entered the Real Academia de Bellas Artes de San Fernando in Madrid, but left soon after, unable to tolerate methodical training. In 1900 Picasso chose to visit Paris, unlike many of his contemporaries who followed the *Jugendstil* (decorative style) and went to Munich.

Already strongly influenced by the Spanish painters Isidro Nonell y Monturid and El *Greco, in Paris Picasso became fascinated by the works of Vincent van *Gogh and especially of Henri de Toulouse-Lautrec. Living in poverty, Picasso was strongly attracted by Montmartre's bohemian street life. His paintings, then done in an ethereal blue, were dominated by wretched scenes of beggars and prostitutes, evoking moods of melancholy and despair (*Celestine*, 1903; *The Old Guitarist*, 1903). During this Blue Period, he traveled between Paris and Barcelona.

Picasso finally settled in Paris in 1904 and took lodgings in the so-called Bateau Lavoir, a building in Montmartre. It became the center of an avante garde circle that included the poets Max Jacob and Guillaume Apollinaire and the painter Marie Laurencin. Picasso also knew Henri Matisse, with whom he maintained a friendly rivalry, and Gertrude Stein, who had a great liking for his works. Fernande Olivier, Picasso's mistress, related that his jealousy, with its tragic Spanish overtone, led him to confine her to his studio with no shoes. Their relationship brought a new tenderness to his paintings, and although he liked attending bullfights and being considered a local tough, his works took on subtle rose tones. Sculpturelike figures, family groups, and circus scenes, especially those depicting harlequins, were often portrayed during the Rose Period (1904–1907). Picasso began sculpting for the first time and became interested in African sculpture and Paul *Cézanne's work. He simplified form in this African Period (1907–1909), as in his revolutionary painting *Les Demoiselles d'Avignon* (1906–1907, now in the Museum of Modern Art, New York). As the Fauve painters rebelled against the impressonist use of color, so this work made a statement against the impressionst use of form. *Les Demoiselles* was not exhibited until 1937, at which point art critics considered it the most significant turning point in contemporary painting and the forerunner to Cubism.

Between 1910 and 1916 Picasso worked in close association with Georges Braque, then with Juan Gris, in developing analytical and synthetic Cubism. They introduced the use of collage, *papier collé,* and real elements, as in Picasso's first constructed metal sculpture, *Guitar* (1912).

In 1917 Picasso began designing scenery and costumes for Sergey Diaghilev's Ballets Russes. The first ballet he worked on, *Parade,* was an adaption from a book by his friend Jean Cocteau and brought together the music of Erik Satie and cubism. From 1918 to 1925 Picasso was married to Olga Koklova, a dancer with the Ballets Russes. A social climber used to luxurious living, she introduced Picasso to the fashionable resorts of Biarritz and Juan-les-Pins.

Pablo Picasso

PICASSO ON ART

- I never tried to please the public.
- People don't buy my pictures, they buy my signature.
- One does not paint in order to decorate apartments (on Guernica).
- Sculpture is the best commentary that a painter can make on his painting.
- Art is a lie that makes us realize the truth.
- Taste is the enemy of creativeness.

Picasso continued painting in the Cubist manner while also producing large classical nudes, notably *Two Seated Women* (1920), as well as *Three Musicians* (1921). Although Picasso stated he was not a surrealist, André Breton, the author of surrealist manifestos, considered him the initiator of surrealism. Picasso exhibited *The Three Dancers* (1928) at the surrealist exhibition at the Galerie Pierre Loeb in Paris and illustrated the cover of the movement's first journal, *Minotaure.* It was then that he started producing studies of the minotaur, a mythological image, and of the *Dying Horse* and *Weeping Woman.* In 1930 he began concentrating more on sculpture which was different from his Cubist "constructions." In 1936 he returned to Madrid as director of the Prado Museum but his anger at Francisco *Franco's Fascism led him shortly after to a self-imposed exile for the rest of his life.

After the outbreak of the Spanish Civil War in 1936 and the bombing of the Basque capital, Guernica, Picasso produced his great political masterpiece entitled *Guernica.* This large composition was commissioned for the Spanish Republic pavilion at the Paris World Exhibition of 1937. For many years it was exhibited in New York as Picasso, while feeling his natural home was in Spain, refused to have it shown there under Franco's dictatorship. Only after the redemocratization of Spain was it finally displayed there.

During World War II Picasso remained in Paris, though he was forbidden to exhibit by the German occupying forces. He often hid members of the Resistance in his flat, and during the liberation of Paris he sang aloud as he painted to drown out the sound of gunfire. Emerging from the war a declared communist, Picasso designed the sign of a dove for the Paris Peace Congress of 1949.

In 1946 Picasso met the painter Françoise Gilot and settled in Antibes and in 1947 the couple moved to Vallauris, where he took up pottery, often producing anthropomorphic designs. An intense and obsessional man, when he began his relationship with Gilot, Picasso made ten portraits of her in one day, no two of which were alike. However, after a bitter breakup with her in 1953, Picasso, then seventy-two, did 180 drawings in four months featuring the ravisher minotaur. Considered autobiographical, they portrayed the themes of age and love. That year he met Jacqueline Roque and in 1955 they went to live in La Californie, a villa he purchased in Cannes. In 1958 they married and settled in the Chateau de Vauvenargues near Aix. There Picasso continued investigating new techniques and materials for painting, sculpture, pottery, and, especially, lithography.

Picasso outlived most of his friends, including Matisse, which made him constantly aware of his own mortality. He was a prolific artist whose inventiveness influenced many of his contemporaries, including Jean Metzinger and Fernand Léger and the sculptors Aleksandr Archipenko and Jacques Lipschitz. Many important retrospective exhibitions were held in his later years, most notably that at the Louvre in 1971 commemorating his ninetieth birthday.

M. M. Gedo, *Picasso*, 1980.

J. Richardson, *A Life of Picasso*, vol. 1, 1992.

W. Rubin, ed., *Pablo Picasso: A Retrospective*, 1980.

PIKE, ZEBULON MONTGOMERY

(1779–1813), American soldier and explorer. A native of Lamberton, New Jersey, and son of a captain in the Revolutionary Army, aged fifteen he joined his father's old regiment. After five years' service he became a lieutenant and was posted to the western frontier. In 1805 General John Wilkinson, governor of Louisiana, sent Pike on a mission to find the source of the Mississippi. The project had political purposes, serving to inform Indians and others in this newly acquired territory that they were now under American authority.

Pike embarked from Saint Louis with twenty men and traveled up the Mississippi in a seventy-foot-long boat. He showed himself guileful in dealings with the Indians, purchasing 100,000 acres of land from the Sioux tribe for $200 plus 60 gallons of liquor — the estimated value of this bargain was $200,000! He also prevailed upon British fur traders to accept American sovereignty, but as soon as he moved on, they again hoisted the British flag.

Pike spent eight months on this journey. He had mistakenly identified Leech Lake in Minnesota as the source of the Mississippi, but in charting the new territory and establishing American control, he fulfilled his assignment. Governor Wilkinson soon decided he could use Pike again, this time to explore the southwestern corner of the country, find the source of the Red River, negotiate with native tribes, and assess Spanish defenses.

Pike set off in July 1806 with twenty-three men. In November they sighted a small blue cloud — the Rocky Mountains seen from a distance. Pike made a treaty with the Comanches and discovered the mountain in Colorado that now carries his name. He led his group on a two-and-a-half day march to climb Pike's Peak but it was further away than he imagined. The ascent was abandoned, yet they climbed high enough to see how "the unbounded prairie was overhung with clouds which appeared like the ocean in a storm."

Pike reached the Rio Grande but his location was betrayed to the Spanish, by one of his own party or, as some alleged, by a treacherous General Wilkinson. A force of six hundred Spanish troops arrested Pike and his men and took them to Santa Fe. He argued that he had strayed into Spanish territory by mistake, thinking the Rio Grande was the Red River. He was put on trial but then released after his papers and maps were confiscated. He used this time to spy on Spanish defenses and managed to get information smuggled over the border in rifle barrels.

Pike published his account of his explorations in 1810. It was the first dependable account of these regions to appear, arousing much interest. Soon afterwards he turned to more conventional army duties. During the war of 1812 he was advanced to the rank of brigadier general. He led a successful attack on York (Toronto), Canada, but was killed in the explosion of a powder magazine.

W. H. Goetzmann, *Exploration and Empire*, 1971.

L. R. Haften, W. E. Hollon, and C. C. Rister, *Western America*, 1970.

W. E. Hollon, *The Lost Pathfinder: Z. M. Pike*, 1949.

PILSUDSKI, JOSEF KLEMENS (1867–1935),

Polish revolutionary and dictator. Pilsudski came from an old Polish-Lithuanian family. Although the once-powerful kingdom of Poland and Lithuania had disappeared — partitioned among Austria, Prussia, and Russia in the eighteenth century — the desire for an independent Poland was still alive. Having suppressed a revolt in Polish Lithuania three years before Pilsudski was born, Russia attempted to prevent further uprisings by prohibiting the teaching of the Polish language, literature and history. Nonetheless, Pilsudski's mother continued to teach her children their Polish heritage in secret.

The Pilsudski family manor burned down and they moved to Wilno (Vilnius). Life in cosmopolitan Wilno was the source of Pilsudski's religious tolerance and his firmly-held convictions that different peoples can live together. The contempt and ridicule for Polish culture expressed by the teachers at the Russian high school he attended deepened his feelings of patriotism towards Poland and resentment towards Russia. He later wrote: "For me, my time at the gymnasium was a sort of penal servitude — the unceasing, humiliating provocations from our teachers and the degradation of all that I had been accustomed to respect and love. Although I have since passed through jails and Siberia, and have had to do with a variety of Russian officials, it is still one of my Wilno schoolmasters who plays some part in every bad dream."

Pilsudski's medical studies were permanently interrupted when he was charged with participating in a plot to assassinate the czar. His trial made it clear that he was innocent, but as a known Polish nationalist with socialist sympathies he was considered potentially dangerous and sentenced to five years in Siberia. His Siberian exile gave him the leisure to study history and socialism, experience the Russian empire from within, and meet with other exiled revolutionaries. He returned to Wilno with his socialism confirmed.

Poland had two socialist parties, one seeking to incorporate Poland into Russia for economic reasons, and the other, the Polish Socialist Party, wanting an independent Poland. Pilsudski joined the latter, becoming one of its leaders and the editor of its newspaper. Imprisoned for his activities, he faked insanity and escaped from a Russian military hospital. During the 1904 Russo-Japanese War he tried to persuade Japan that supporting revolution among Russia's subject nationalities was the best way to weaken Russia. His efforts failed because a rival from Poland's pro-Russian socialist party convinced Japan that Pilsudski's plan would only waste their time and money. Pilsudski returned to Poland to take an active part in the 1905 Russian Revolution. However his time in Japan had aroused his interest in military matters.

A European war was clearly on the horizon. Pilsudski studied military strategy, organized a secret Union of Military Action in 1908 (paid for with money he had stolen from a Russian mail train), and by 1914 had over ten thousand trained Polish soldiers. World War I found Poland divided over which side to join. Convinced that only the collapse of the Russian, Austrian, and German empires would give independent Poland a chance to be reborn, he commanded a brigade in the volunteer Poland Legion fighting for the Central Powers (the Austrian and German empires) against Russia.

Germany proclaimed the creation of a Polish protectorate (hoping a Polish army would solve its manpower shortage) and appointed Pilsudski Head of its Military Commission (1916). Courageous, stubborn, with a gift for influencing people, Pilsudski refused to make Polish troops swear a special oath of allegiance to the Central Powers. He was imprisoned and the Polish legions were dissolved, but his prestige and popularity in Poland increased as a result of his stand.

By 1918, when Germany's defeat freed him, Pilsudski was a national hero. He returned to Poland and became provisional head of state and commander-in-chief. Poland was in chaos: war devastation, starvation, and lawlessness were widespread; Poles had become accustomed to resisting authority; prolonged unemployment and inflation had radicalized the working class; after the Russian Revolution socialist leftists had formed a strong communist party advocating union with Russia; and the Russian Red Army was advancing into lands vacated by the Germans.

Pilsudski attempted to solve Poland's problems with domestic reforms (most of which were accepted), fighting the Red Army (with mixed success), and trying to create a federated state that would be strong enough to resist Russia or Germany from the small Baltic territories. He failed to create a Polish federation because of Polish nationalists' refusal to have large minorities in the new Polish state, the growing nationalism and fear of Polish domination on the part of other Baltic peoples, and the powerful vested interests of Polish landowners who wanted an expanded Poland rather than a federation.

In 1921 Poland adopted a democratic constitution and held elections. Pilsudski became chief of the general staff, but resigned when a right-wing government came to power in 1923. His retirement lasted only three years before conditions in Poland led him to topple the government with a military coup; although he refused the presidency, his position as minister of defense meant that he was Poland's real ruler.

As dictator, Pilsudski mercilessly suppressed a 1930 center-left plot to overthrow his government. He wanted to take military action against Germany when Hitler came to power, but France (with which Poland had a defense treaty) refused. Although Pilsudski signed a ten-year non-aggression pact with Germany in 1934, he refused to meet Hitler or form a Polish-German anti-Soviet alliance.

M. K. Dziewanowski, *Joseph Pilsudski: A European Federalist*, 1969.

W. F. Reddaway, *Marshal Pilsudski*, 1939.

PITT, WILLIAM

PITT, WILLIAM (the Younger Pitt; 1759–1806), British prime minister. Born in Hayes, Kent, he was the second son of the prime minister whose name he shared, hence the appellation Pitt the Younger. Pitt the Elder was crippled with ill health and for a long while lived the life of a recluse, yet he saw in his son an extension of himself capable of again placing the name of Pitt foremost among the nation's leaders.

Because young William was considered too weak for the rigors of traditional schooling, a private tutor was engaged. He excelled at studies, encouraged by the affection and interest of his father. At fourteen Pitt was sent to Cambridge University where, although a serious student, as a son of a noble he graduated at seventeen without having to sit for exams.

Young Pitt's chief interest was his father's political career and he would go to the House of Commons to learn from him the orator's art. He accompanied Pitt the Elder on his final appearance in 1778 and within weeks was leading mourners at his father's state funeral in Westminster Abbey. In 1780 Pitt was called to the bar but the life of an obscure lawyer was not his aim and he soon succeeded in getting elected to Parliament.

Pitt's opening performance in the Commons was rapturously received; colleagues saw the dignity and eloquence of speech that had characterized his distinguished father. Younger Pitt's recipe for fine oratory: "It is with eloquence as a flame; it requires fuel to feed it, motion to excite it, and brightness as it burns."

Within a few years he was offered the vice-treasureship of Ireland, a lucrative sinecure, but he declined, determined to wait for the cabinet seat he desired; and it was not long in coming. The Earl of Shelburne had noted his potential and offered the chancellorship of the exchequer and

William Pitt

leadership of the Commons; Pitt was only twenty-three at the time.

The collapse of Shelburne's administration led to King *George III calling on Pitt to form his own government as prime minister. Pitt refused repeated requests and returned to his legal practice, having apparently calculated it was not yet the appropriate time to take over these reins of power.

He made a brief tour of France and received the warmest of receptions at the court of King *Louis XVI. Upon Pitt's return to England the king again requested him to be prime minister, and this time he agreed. At twenty-four he took on leadership of a government that the majority of the Commons opposed but which the king and people enthusiastically supported; the opposition was associated with the disaster of the American war and elicited little sympathy.

Pitt held the office of prime minister for seventeen years. Of tall and slender build, described by contemporaries as "cold and stiff," he rarely smiled but won admirers with felicity of expression and clarity and conciseness in the delivery of speeches. In the early days of his government he gained a reputation for honesty by not awarding himself another lucrative sinecure, giving it instead to a faithful supporter of his father who had become blind in old age.

In the period leading up to the French Revolution, Pitt pursued a range of liberal policies aimed at encouraging commerce and making political adjustments in line with rapidly changing times. He was a keen supporter of William Wilberforce's efforts to abolish slavery and also proposed a mild measure of parliamentary reform and Roman Catholic emancipation. The latter measure was opposed by the king and eventually Pitt abandoned it, fearing this violent

opposition might lead to another bout of royal insanity. Pitt's commitment to free trade embraced even the traditional enemy, France, and was linked with intense efforts to maintain peace in Europe.

The French Revolution and the Reign of Terror resulted in a dramatic switch in emphasis. Determined at all costs to save England from a similar fate, Pitt's administration vigorously persecuted groups fighting for parliamentary reform and civil rights. At the same time, the military campaign on the Continent, where England was fighting France was grossly mismanaged, with a succession of serious defeats and continual wasting of funds necessitating increased taxation. A tax placed on windows was particularly loathsome, with the poor driven to block up what few windows their homes possessed in order to avoid paying.

Despite his losing popularity with radicals, Pitt always retained the support of the large segment of the population who identified themselves with king and church; he was the patriotic leader around whom they could rally. A grateful king and the city of London both offered him huge gifts of money to pay off heavy personal debts accumulated in reckless fashion throughout his lifetime.

Pitt never married. House was kept for him by his sister and finally by a favorite niece, Lady Hester Stanhope; it was his niece he asked for on his death bed. The strain of his last years in office, coupled with the crowning disaster of *Napoleon's great victory at Austerlitz, broke his weak constitution. His final words are disputed, some saying he exclaimed, "Oh! my country, how I leave my country." Others claim a more prosaic request — "I think I could eat one of Bellamy's veal pies."

J. Ehrman, *The Younger Pitt, the Years of Acclaim*, 1969.

E. Royston Pike, *Britain's Prime Ministers From Walpole to Wilson*, 1968.

Lord Roseberry, *Life of Pitt*, 1969.

PIUS IX (Pionono; 1792–1878), pope. Giovanni Maria-Mastai-Ferretti, who as Pope Pius IX shaped the Roman Catholic church's determined opposition to liberalism from the mid-nineteenth to the mid-twentieth century, started his papacy as a liberal reformer. He came from an enlightened family, believed in the ideas of Catholic liberalism, and until his death was popular for his extensive charity, piety, simplicity, eloquence, and sense of humor.

As archbishop of Spoleto (1827–1832) Pius helped the future *Napoleon III escape to Switzerland after the failure of Romagna's 1831 revolution against papal rule. As bishop of Imola, he was outspokenly critical of the church's failure to deal with conditions in his diocese. As a cardinal, he continued to be both independent and liberal, albeit more discreetly.

Elected pope in 1846 on the basis of his liberal reputation, Pius became both spiritual head of the Roman Catholic church and temporal ruler of the central Italian Papal States. International opinion of the time displayed a rare unanimity in its condemnation of the Papal States for their inefficient, undemocratic, and church-administered government and judicial system, as well as for being technologically and economically backward. Pius immediately began reforming the administration of the Papal States, making it more modern, efficient, and popular. He declared a general political amnesty, established agricultural institutions, planned rail routes and street lighting, lifted censorship, revised the criminal code, reformed tariffs, and instituted limited representative government. An ardent Italian patriot, he dreamed of an Italy free of Austrian dominance, of presiding over an independent federation of Italian states that would allow each state to maintain its own customs while pursuing a common financial and foreign policy. He began working toward this goal by ordering the withdrawal of Austrian troops from Ferrara and negotiating the creation of an Italian customs union.

Pius was appalled when the 1848 revolutions spread through out Europe including Italy, with revolutionaries cheering his liberal inspiration and patronage. He did not want to be identified as a revolutionary: his reforms had been liberal, not radical, and he had always put the interests of the church first. Forced to grant Rome a constitution and a parliament with full legislative powers, Pius tried to remain neutral during the Italian kingdom of Piedmont's short war with Austria; there after he was considered a reactionary. His prime minister was assassinated. Revolutionaries declared the end of papal rule and established a democratic republic in Rome; foreign ambassadors helped Pius escape. He then appealed to Europe's Catholic rulers for aid, and Austria and France overcame the revolutionaries, whereupon he was restored to Rome in 1850.

The events of 1848 led Pius to conclude that liberalism invariably led to revolution — which was usually anticlerical — and that political power was a necessary bulwark against attack on his spiritual power. He retained most of his initial reforms and continued to support the technological modernization of the Papal States, but for the rest of his papacy he refused to allow constitutional government, opposed nationalism, and fought any attempt to diminish his temporal power.

Liberal Piedmont's 1855 anticlerical law (closing many monasteries and nunneries), turned Pius against its expressed ideal of a free church in a free state and made him wary of Piedmont's ambition to unite Italy under its rule. Unwilling to take a stand against a Catholic ruler who had helped him return to Rome, Pius remained neutral during Piedmont's 1859 war against Austria, and as a consequence lost the Papal States to Piedmont's new kingdom of Italy. He was able to continue ruling Rome for another ten years only because it was guarded by French troops sent by Napoleon III. When Italian troops occupied Rome during the time of the Franco-Prussian War of 1870–1871, Rome became part of an Italy in which church and state were separated; Pius refused to have anything to do with the Italian government and incarcerated himself in the Vatican until his death, losing all temporal sovereignty.

Pius was responsible for the Catholic church's 1854 declaration of the dogma of the Virgin *Mary's Immaculate Conception, leading the growing movement in the church toward devotional religion and away from intellectualism, and the restoration of independent Catholic hierarchies in England and Holland. He also derived conservative church doctrines from the political exigencies he faced: after losing the Papal States in 1861, he published an encyclical denouncing all modern political doctrines on the grounds that they undermined the church's authority. After France and Italy came to an agreement about withdrawing the French garrison defending Rome, Pius issued an encyclical in 1864 with his famous Syllabus of Errors attached, listing the eighty concepts he felt were "the principal errors of our times." Pius became a strong advocate of ultramontanism (belief in the concentration of church authority in the pope's hands).

The doctrine of papal infallibility was the primary issue for the First Vatican Council (1869–1870). Pius made it quite clear to the council that he wanted that doctrine accepted. The council refused to make the syllabus official church doctrine, but it accepted the papal infallibility, allowing Pius to imprint his conservative image on the church. During the remaining eight years of his life, the church became increasingly alienated from secular political forces and anticlericalism spread throughout Western Europe. Pius was the first pope whose pontificate exceeded the twenty-five years traditionally ascribed to Saint *Peter.

E. E. Y. Hales, *Pio Nono*, 1954.

PIZARRO, FRANCISCO (1475–1541), Spanish conquistador. Born at Trujillo, Spain the illegitimate son of an army captain and a young woman of humble birth, Pizarro's grew up in poverty and ignorance. Raised in the home of his grandparents, he received no formal education and worked for a time as a swineherd before becoming a soldier at an early age. In 1502 he travelled to Hispaniola (modern Haiti), but discovered that the settled life of the colonizer was not to his liking and turned to adventuring. He accompanied Alonso de Ojeda on his Columbian expedition, and later participated in Vasco *Núñez de Balboa's expedition that marked the European discovery of the Pacific Ocean. In the course of these adventures he gained a reputation as a reliable, if uncouth and brutal, companion-at-arms.

By 1519 Pizarro had risen to the position of governor of Panama, a post that enabled him to accumulate a small fortune for himself. However, he retained his lust for adventure and booty, and was greatly excited by the tales of the explorer Pascual de Andagoya, who reported an immensely wealthy Indian kingdom to the south. Fired by the story, he

Francisco Pizarro

and two compatriots, Diego de Almagro and the priest Hernando de Luque, organized a voyage of conquest and discovery down the west coast of South America. Setting out in 1524, they suffered many hardships before reaching Atacamas in northern Ecuador in 1528. Faced with apparently hostile local Indians, they sent back to Panama for reinforcements; when the new governor refused this request, Pizarro drew a line on the ground with his sword and enjoined all those who wished for wealth and glory to cross it and continue their quest unaided. The "famous thirteen" who did so were able to return to Panama later that year with distinct accounts of a great Indian empire in the region they had named Peru; the gold, llamas, and Indians they brought with them served to corroborate their assertions.

In the face of the indifference of the local colonial authorities, Pizarro sailed to Spain to try and convince the emperor, *Charles V, to give his approval for conquest of the region. Charles was in dire need of revenues from his colonies so the request was granted, with Pizarro being given the prerogatives of a viceroy and made governor and captain general of the putative new colony. While all the "famous thirteen" won considerable rights and privileges in the new territories, Almagro was always resentful of the special powers granted to Pizarro.

Pizarro returned to Panama and set off from there to Peru in 1531 with a force of 180 heavily-armed men, thirty-seven horses, and two cannons. The Inca Empire was in the throes of civil war at the time, and this situation was cunningly exacerbated by the Spanish. Pizarro sent an ambassador to Atahualpa,

who was then the incumbent of the disputed Inca throne, promising to acknowledge him as the legitimate emperor.

When Atahualpa deigned to meet the Spaniards at Cajarnarca he was persuaded to leave his army of thirty thousand behind and arrived at the parley with an escort of just three thousand men. If, as the Spaniards claimed, he later admitted that his plan had been to take them unawares, capture them. and sacrifice some to the sun god while castrating the rest for service as eunuchs, then he had seriously misjudged the strength of the adversaries he faced.

At the meeting, Atahualpa was peremptorily ordered to embrace Christianity and accept Charles V as his sovereign lord. Unimpressed by the Spaniards' bullying, he flung to the ground the Bible that had been thrust into his hand: the response was a sudden and sustained onslaught on the defenceless Incas by cannon and horse, which left most of them dead. Pizarro led the squad that snatched Atahualpa from his litter while the Spanish soldiers butchered the surviving Incas.

Despite enduring a ceremony of baptism and paying the enormous ransom demanded by Pizarro, Atahualpa was not released; instead, he was put on trial on a trumped-up charge of having ordered the execution of a rival claimant to the Inca throne. After his murder by strangulation in 1532, the tiny Spanish force installed his rival, Huascar, as emperor; the latter belatedly realized the danger presented by those who offered him the throne and rallied his troops to revolt, but the gesture came too late to prevent Pizarro's men from occupying the Inca capital. They proceeded ruthlessly and brutally to suppress the native population: the wealth of the Incas was now wholly at the disposal of Spain. A further uprising led by the Inca Manco Capac II in 1534 met with a similar fate.

With the completion of the occupation, the rivalry between Pizarro and Almagro escalated. Pizarro, installed as undisputed ruler according to the powers granted him by Charles, tried to buy off Almagro by granting him the concession to exploit Chile. However, the latter was disappointed by the paucity of plunder in that region and returned to Peru to challenge Pizarro; on Almagro's capture in 1538, Pizarro rejected pleas for clemency towards his erstwhile comrade and had him publicly garrotted and decapitated.

Pizarro himself died as he had lived, by the sword. He was hacked to death in his palace in Lima, the city he had founded in 1535, by a band of Almagro's supporters. Lima was to become the capital of the Spanish colonial power in South America.

J. Hemmings, *The Conquest of the Incas*, 1970.
H. Innes, *The Conquistadors*, 1969.
A. Marrin, *Inca and Spaniard*, 1989.

PLANCK, MAX KARL ERNST LUDWIG (1858–1947), German physicist, originator of quantum theory, and winner of the Nobel Prize. Born in Kiel, where his father was a distinguished jurist and professor at the university, Max Planck was an out-

> Planck is one of the few worshipers in the Temple of Science who would still remain should an angel of God descend and drive out of the temple all the lesser scientists, who under different circumstances might become politicians or captains of industry.
>
> **Albert Einstein**

standing student at the Maximilian high school in Munich, where his family moved when he was nine years old. Talented in a variety of subjects, he eventually chose to specialize in physics rather than classical philology or music because he believed that it afforded him his greatest chance of originality.

He graduated from the University of Munich in 1879 and became a lecturer there the following year. Elected to an associate professorship at the University of Kiel 1885, he achieved a full professorship in 1892, at University of Berlin, where he remained for the rest of his life.

Planck's original approach to physics demonstrated his conviction that "pure reasoning can enable man to gain an insight into the mechanism of the world." In his researches, he pursued the ends and methods of a theoretical physicist before theoretical physics was even recognized as a separate discipline. He was moved by the conception of the outside world as something independent of man, and absolute. He instanced the first and second laws of thermodynamics (the law of conservation of energy and the law of entropy, respectively) as examples of absolute physical laws; the second law was the subject of his doctoral dissertation at Munich and lay at the core of the researches that led him to the discovery of the quantum of action in 1900.

The discovery for which Planck is famous and which originated quantum theory — thereby revolutionizing scientific understanding of atomic and subatomic processes — grew out of his research into the properties of "black bodies," objects that reemit all of the radiant energy incident upon them (that is to say, objects that are perfect emitters and absorbers of radiation). His accomplishment was to find a single equation describing the distribution of radiation emitted by a black body; previous attempts had adequately described only the longer and shorter wavelengths.

Planck's results led him to the conclusion that, contrary to the universal assumption before this time, energy exists not as a continuous substance but in the form of discrete packets, which he called "quanta." He further concluded that the size of quantum for any particular form of electromagnetic radiation was in direct proportion to its frequency; the ratio between quantum size and frequency is known as Planck's constant, denominated in scientific notation by the sign h, and constitutes one of the fundamental quantities of the universe. The value Planck calculated for this constant was very close to the most precise modern calculation of 6.626×10^{-27} erg-second.

These results were not immediately accepted, but in 1905 Albert *Einstein made use of Planck's theory to explain the photoelectric effect, which could not be explained adequately by the laws of classical physics; Planck in his turn was the first prominent physicist to champion Einstein's special theory of relativity. After Niels *Bohr incorporated quantum theory into his development of the theory of atomic structure, the importance of Planck's findings became increasingly evident to the scientific community as a whole, and in 1918 his contribution was acknowledged with the award of a Nobel prize.

Planck's quantum theory and Einstein's relativity theory constitute the fundamental theories of twentieth century physics, while quantum mechanics, which developed out of Planck's ideas, remains the indispensable basis of modern theoretical physics. While making his findings, Planck was forced to acknowledge that the second law of thermodynamics was a statistical rather than an absolute law, and that the microphysical world could not in principle be described by ordinary classical mechanics. These conclusions undermined the very beliefs that he had cherished, of a universe governed by absolute laws, so Planck has been described as a reluctant revolutionary, struggling for the retention of the classical theories that he had helped render obsolete.

While Planck regretfully accepted the need to jettison many classical ideas, he was, like Einstein, extremely resistant to the indeterministic, statistical worldview developed by Bohr, Max Born, and Werner *Heisenberg during the late 1920s; he particularly disliked the relativistic idea that the observer and the observed are so intimately linked that the physical universe cannot, even in principle, be described in absolute, objective terms.

His qualities of integrity, reliability, wisdom, academic excellence, and devotion to church and state made Planck a respected figure worldwide and a natural leader of the scientific community in his own country. He held the position of permanent secretary of the mathematics and physics section of the Prussian Academy of Sciences from 1912 until 1938, and was president of the Kaiser Wilhelm Society (now the Max Planck Society) between 1930 and 1937. His presence attracted Einstein and other physicists of international repute, such as Erwin Schrödinger, to Berlin University, which became an unparalleled center for theoretical physics until the Nazis came to power in Germany in 1933.

Although none of his subsequent work could compete in significance with quantum theory, Planck continued to make important contributions in a variety of scientific fields, including optics, thermodynamics and statistical mechanics, and physical chemistry. In his later years, he became increasingly interested in philosophical, religious, and aesthetic questions.

A succession of family tragedies beset Planck. The death of his first wife in 1909, after twenty-two years of happy marriage, was followed by the death of his elder son, Karl, in 1916, in World War I, and the death of both his daughters in childbirth shortly thereafter. His sense of duty led him to choose to remain in Nazi Germany; however, he was unequivocally opposed to Nazi racial policies and approached Adolf *Hitler directly in an unsuccessful effort to have them reversed. The house in which he had lived for years was destroyed by Allied bombs in 1944; his younger son, Edwin, was implicated in a plot to kill Hitler, and his capture and horrible death at the hands of the Gestapo in 1945 finally destroyed Planck's will to live.

Rosenthal-Schneider, *Reality and Scientific Truth: Discussions with Einstein, von Laue, and Planck,* 1980.

PLATO (c. 428–348 B.C.E.), Greek philosopher; one of the key thinkers of the Western world. The twentieth-century philosopher A. N. *Whitehead has asserted that "the safest general characterization of the European philosophical tradition is that it consists of a series of footnotes to Plato." Plato and his student *Aristotle are the two most important philosophers of antiquity and subsequent philosophical developments have inevitably built upon the foundations that they had laid. Of the two, Plato's influence has probably been more pervasive, while he is also notable as a master of Greek prose: his written works have a literary greatness independent of their significance as philosophical treatises.

Plato came from one of the most distinguished Athenian families, his father Ariston claiming descent from the old kings of Athens and even from the god Poseidon. His uncle was Charmides, a leader in the brief anarchic regime of 404 B.C.E. Already as a boy, Plato knew *Socrates, although it is unlikely that he was ever of the inner circle of Socrates's disciples. He was apparently prevented by illness from being present at Socrates's death; nonetheless, he considered Socrates the inspiration for the greater part of his own teachings, if not their actual architect. The works of his own philosophical maturity were frequently presented as dialogues centering around Socrates.

Since it is impossible to determine where Socrates's actual teachings end and Plato's ascriptions to him begin, no definitive answer is available to the question of who originally formulated the fundamentals of Plato's philosophical approach. Certainly, Plato's preoccupation with ethical issues and the centrality of the concept of "the Good" in his works shows the hand of Socrates, but it was Plato who first presented these ideas lucidly argued in written form and it seems likely that they are in great part his own thought, even if they did develop out of an existing philosophical tradition. Also evi-

Plato (left) and Aristotle, from "The School of Athens," by Raphael

dent in the Platonic system are the influences of *Pythagoras's Orphic mysticism; Parmenides's belief that reality is eternal and that all change is illusory; and Heraclitus's doctrine that there is nothing permanent in the world perceptible by the senses. The combination of the last two led Plato to the conclusion that knowledge is not to be derived from sensation but can only be achieved by reflection on the objects of pure thought.

Plato seems to have quickly foregone any political ambitions he harbored in his youth, concluding (as had Socrates before him) that active politics was no place for a man of conscience. He was however, sufficiently close to Socrates and other anti-democratic elements to consider it expedient to absent himself from Athens after Socrates's trial and execution in 399 B.C.E.; he spent several years traveling in Greece, Egypt, and Sicily before returning to the city.

In Syracuse he met and formed a firm friendship with Dion, brother-in-law to the tyrant of Syracuse, Dionysius I. It was this friendship that was later to lead Plato into his one significant — and ill-fated — involvement in public affairs. After Dionysius I's death, Plato, then aged sixty, was asked by Dion to return to Saracuse and act as tutor to the young Dionysius II. It was hoped that the great philosopher would be able to engender in the youth the virtues necessary to a statesman and ruler. Syracuse was at that time a great commercial city engaged in desperate wars with Carthage, and Plato, although reluctant to fulfill the request, felt honor-bound to

PLATO'S GREAT DIALOGUES

Lysis: The nature of friendship
Charmides: The nature of temperance
Laches: The objects of education
Gorgias: The nature of rhetoric: right as the rule of life
Meno: The nature of virtue
Protagoras: Principles of morality: can virtue be taught?
Euthyphro, The Apology, Crito: Trial and death of Socrates
Phaedo: Belief in immortality, the world of eternal truth, the theory of forms
Symposium: Highest form of spiritual love
Phaedrus: Logical method as a source of rhetoric
The Republic: The nature and government of the ideal state: Theory of Forms
Parmenides: Relations between the one and the many, between unity and being
Theaetetus: Definition of knowledge
Sophist: Nature of nonbeing
Statesman: Advocacy of constitutional government, in form of limited monarchy
Philebus: Is the Good a feeling of pleasure or the exercise of intelligence?
Timaeus: Cosmology and physical sciences
Laws: Practical nature of ideal state, its ethics and jurisprudence

extend his services. He undertook the arduous journey from Athens in 367 B.C.E. but the venture was not a success. Dionysius II may not have been an apt pupil; at any rate he was fearful of his uncle's influence and expelled Dion. Plato suffered a like fate and left Syracuse at some personal risk. Dion returned to capture Syracuse in 357 B.C.E.; after his murder in 354 B.C.E., Plato wrote an exoneration and justification of the former's actions.

Plato asserted that the vocation of philosopher had not always appealed to him. Only after reflecting on the treatment meted out to Socrates at the hands of the state he had sought to serve was he moved to view the realm of ideas as his metier. Together with the mathematician Theaetetus, he was responsible for the founding of the Academy in Athens around 385 B.C.E. This famous institution was in effect the first university and had an important influence on the development of mathematics and jurisprudence as well as general philosophy, stressing pure science as the source of wise political action. Its most illustrious student was Aristotle.

The pedagogy of the Academy emphasized dialogue between master and students as the most effective means of transmitting and developing knowledge. Plato himself considered his written works as of less philosophical value than his oral discourses. Like Socrates, he believed that the practical ends that his philosophy pursued involved knowledge as understanding and revelation rather than mere book learning. This can explain why the Socrates of Plato's dialogues seems to hold conflicting views at various times. He is attempting to goad his opponents out of complacency and into the self-inquiry and doubt that Plato considered a necessary prerequisite of philosophical development.

Over two dozen dialogues are attributed to Plato. Most of the early ones are concerned with excellence of character and its development. Plato views knowledge and virtue as synonymous, saying that "all virtue is one thing, knowledge," with the former leading inevitably to the latter. Everyone pursues the Good, so once one has the knowledge to understand what is truly good, one will invariably pursue the course of action that leads to it.

The mystical elements of Plato's doctrines are more evident in his middle and late period works, in which he became increasingly involved in expounding a system of doctrine rather than confining himself to the refutation of erroneous views. According to his theory of Forms, there exist eternal transcendent realities answering to every significant general or abstract term (such as goodness, justice, maleness, table-ness, or whatever), and these realities (Forms, or Ideas) are apprehended only by pure thought. So, when we say something has a certain quality, this is because it partakes of the relevant Form. Indeed, Forms are the only truly real things: the objects presented to the senses are in fact real only insofar as they partake of the reality of the Forms ascribed to them. From this, Plato was led to conclude that the soul is immortal (because its essential character is to partake of the Form of life) and that knowledge consists of recollection; we can know things in this life because our soul was acquainted with the Forms of knowledge before confinement to the body. He saw the aim of the philosopher as being to so love wisdom and learning that he would be drawn through contemplation to an ever closer communion with the realm of Forms; in contrast, he characterized the state of average people as akin to that of bound prisoners in a cave, who believe that the shadows cast upon the wall in front of them by the fire behind them are real, since they have no conception of the real objects to which they are due.

The philosopher, then, is he who escapes the bondage of the cave into the sunlight of Truth, the inhabiter of the realm of Mind. Plato does not present him as a dry, emotionless dialectician. It is the unreason and madness of the lover, he asserts, that are the first signs of the soul's strivings to return to its higher estate; through falling in love one is being drawn closer to the recognition of the Form of beauty. Philosophy is born of passion as well as reason.

Plato was not a democrat. His great work, *The Republic*, which has been called the "first Utopia," envisages the ideal state, a society in which justice holds sway, presided over by the philosopher-king, in which each person knows his place. According to

Plato, each person has a specific contribution that he can make to a rational society; morality and justice consist of discharging that vocation, for living otherwise constitutes spiritual disease. Reports of the circumstances of Plato's death vary: some say he died at a wedding feast, others, while writing. He was about eighty years old and was buried at the Academy. Aristotle said of him that he was a man of such wisdom and character that "it is blasphemy even to praise him."

R. M. Hare. *Founders of Thought: Plato*, 1991.
D. J. Melling, *Understanding Plato*, 1987.
A. E. Taylor, *Plato: The Man and His Work*, 1960.

PLINY THE ELDER (Gaius Plinius Secundus; 23–79 C.E.), Roman writer and administrator. Pliny the Elder's distinguished career as a soldier and administrator in the Roman Empire did not prevent him from indulging his love of learning or from writing the encyclopedic works for which he became famous. He came from northern Italy, being born on his family's estates in Novum Comum (Como). During his twelve years of military service (mostly on the Rhine), Pliny wrote a monograph on cavalry tactics and started his extensive history of Rome's German wars. He also managed a number of scientific tours of various parts of central Europe. Upon returning to Rome in 57 or 58 he studied and wrote about rhetoric, prudently withdrawing from public life during most of *Nero's reign. Toward the end of this period, Nero appointed him procurator in Spain, and he combined the demands of his procuratorship and his subsequent position as counselor to both Vespasian and Titus with the writing of his *History of the Times*, which he discreetly arranged to have published only after his death. He was editing his *Natural History* when in 79, as commander of the western Roman fleet, he went onshore to observe Vesuvius's famous eruption from close at hand and was killed by the fumes.

Only the thirty-seven books of Pliny's *Natural History* have survived, although both *Tacitus and *Plutarch acknowledge using his other histories as source material. The *Natural History* is a comprehensive description of the knowledge of his day. It contained (according to Pliny) twenty thousand facts derived from his study of over two thousand books by 473 authors. Some of its information (usually the most reliable) came from Pliny's personal research and observation. He occasionally enlivened his generally dull writings with philosophical comments reflecting his personal — stoic — views on man and the world: pessimism about humanity, condemnation of the corrupting influence of luxury and money, and rejection of belief in gods (though he appreciated the salutary effect of belief in divine retribution). Pliny published the first ten books himself in 77 and the other volumes appeared posthumously, with their repetitions, contradictions, and mistakes edited.

His nephew described how Pliny managed to accomplish so much: "He had a quick apprehension,

---

PLINY THE ELDER

- It is ridiculous to suppose that the great head of things, whatever it is, pays any regard to human affairs.
- Man is the only animal that at the very moment of his birth gives vent to cries and lamentations.
- If your ear burns, someone is talking about you.

---

incredible zeal, and an unequaled capacity to go without sleep. He would rise at midnight or at one, and never later than two in the morning, and begin his literary work. Before daybreak he used to wait upon Vespasian, who likewise chose that season to transact business. When he had finished the affairs which the emperor committed to his charge, he returned home to his studies. After a short light repast at noon, he would frequently, in the summer, repose in the sun; but during that time some author was read to him. He read nothing without making extracts; he used even to say that there was no book so bad as not to contain something of value. Thereafter he generally went into a cold bath, took a light refreshment, and rested for a while. Then, as if it were a new day, he resumed his studies till dinner, when again a book was read to him and he made notes. In his journeys a stenographer constantly attended him in his chariot or sedan chair. In short, he deemed all time wasted that was not employed in study."

P. Turner, *Selections from the History of the World*, 1962.
H. N. Wethered, *The Mind of the Ancient World: A Consideration of Pliny's Natural History*, 1937.

PLINY THE YOUNGER (Gaius Plinius Caecilius Secundus; c.61–113 C.E.), Roman author and administrator; nephew and adopted son of *Pliny the Elder. Pliny the Younger was born in the village of Como. Orphaned young, his studious and orderly habits were greatly influenced by Pliny the Elder, whose adopted son and heir he became at eighteen. He studied rhetoric under Quintillian (Rome's first professor of rhetoric), philosophy under the Stoic Euphrates, and modeled his oratorical style on *Demosthenes and *Cicero.

Pliny's career advanced under *Domitian, who nominated him quaestor at twenty-eight, tribune at thirty, and praetor at thirty-two. However, he withdrew from public affairs when Domitian became paranoid and started using the Senate for trying and executing his victims. Pliny was chosen to deliver the address welcoming the new emperor, *Trajan, to Rome, was elected consul and became one of Trajan's hardworking administrators, serving as augur (103–104), curator of the Tiber River (105), and governor of Bithynia (111). Pliny lived when many forms of Roman literature were reaching their zenith

PLINY THE YOUNGER

- Individuals can deceive and be deceived; but no one can ever deceive everybody, nor has everybody ever deceived anyone.
- Glory ought to be the consequence, not the motive, of our actions.
- Objects which are usually the motives of our travels are often overlooked or neglected if they lie under our eye.

(17–117 C.E. is traditionally called the Silver Age of Roman culture) and writing and rhetoric were fashionable. He composed a Greek tragedy, a few poems (which have since been lost), and some rather long-winded speeches (of which only his panegyric to Trajan has survived). It is the nine volumes of his letters, describing the Roman aristocracy at work and play, howere, that brought him lasting fame.

Pliny's descriptions were somewhat idealized. Rome's aristocracy might not have been as elegant and courteous, as full of loving parents, warm friends, good marriages, and luxurious country estates as he would have it. He himself was, after all, a rich and propertied citizen of a prosperous and expanding empire, a member of the new aristocracy (most of them recent arrivals from the provinces who worked in the empire's administration and had not yet become infected with Roman decadence), and happy in his loving relationship with his third wife, Calpurnia.

Pliny's descriptions of people were generous and charitable. When he wrote about Martial, for instance, he only hinted at the real nature or work of a man who lived off a talent for creating obscene poems and insulting epigrams: "He was a man of wit, piquant and mordant, who mixed in his verse salt and honey, and not least of all, candor." He was equally generous with his time and money, helping his friends, dispensing charity, and liberally endowing his birthplace, Como, with public buildings.

Pliny's correspondence with Trajan, about problems encountered during his governorship of Bithynia, and Trajan's replies, have also survived. Although Pliny appears to be unusually dependent on Trajan's advice the correspondence still provides an excellent picture of the relationship between a conscientious provincial governor and the central authority in Rome. His last letter explains using the imperial post's coaches to send his sick wife home.

N. Adrian, *Letters of Pliny: A Historical and Social Commentary*, 1966.

PLOTINUS

PLOTINUS (205–270 C.E.), philosopher and mystic; founder of Neoplatonism. He was born in times both nihilistic and superstitious that saw the revival of Platonic (see *Plato) teachings within the Roman Empire. He participated in this movement, creating a new philosophy rooted in Platonism and synthe-

sized from his own lifelong experiences of mystical union with the "Source" of creation. Plotinus's writings are considered the beginnings of the school of philosophy known as Neoplatonism, which remained influential down to the seventeenth century. His thought guided the philosophies of such disparate thinkers as Saint *Augustine, the preeminent church father of the fourth century, and Giordano *Bruno, the Renaissance philosopher who was burned at the stake for heresy.

The facts of Plotinus's biography are subject to dispute and there is no definitive source of information for his early years. It appears that he was born in Upper Egypt in 205, into a family of either Greeks or Hellenized Egyptians, his native language and education — as attested by his writings — having been classical Greek. At age twenty-eight, restless to deepen his knowledge of philosophy, Plotinus sought a teacher in Alexandria but found no one who spoke to his needs. Finally he was introduced to Ammonius Saccas, a former Christian, a philosopher who left no writings but bestowed a vast legacy to European thought through his students, Plotinus, Origen, the influential Christian theologian, and another important philosopher, Longinus. Plotinus was a disciple of Ammonius for eleven years before leaving Egypt for Persia, joining a Roman military campaign. His intention in going with the expedition was to probe more deeply the Eastern religions to whose wisdom he had been introduced by Ammonius. When the emperor, who was leading the expedition, was killed, Plotinus's life was threatened and he fled to Rome where he subsequently established his own school of philosophy. In 244 he gathered a group around him to study the works of Plato, *Aristotle, and the *Pythagoreans, discussing and critiquing the writings of his Greek predecessors with insight and rigor.

In 263 a new student arrived at Plotinus's school, Porphyry, later to become Plotinus's biographer and transmitter of his teachings. A philosopher in his own right, Porphyry organized the notes of his mentor into six sections, each consisting of nine expositions. As the Greek for nine is "ennea," the work is known as the *Enneads of Plotinus*.

Porphyry, in his biographical preface, describes Plotinus as a contemplative who at the same time played an active role in society, arbitrating disputes for fellow citizens; and a man of stainless reputation, his house filled with Roman youth whose parents had named Plotinus as guardian for their children. Plotinus's life in these later years was lived in comfortable surroundings combined with an austere self-discipline.

Ten years after opening his school, Plotinus began his writings. Although attributing motives to Plotinus is speculative, it is possible that his new project undertaken at the time of the rise of Gallienus as emperor of Rome was linked to the new ruler's attempt to revive the grandeur of philosophy and pagan religion at a time when Christianity threatened old

> But if it is to the Soul that the gods owe their divinity, the Soul itself must be a God higher than the gods. Now our Soul is of one form with the universal Soul; and if you remove from it all that is adventitious, and consider it in its state of purity, you will see how precious the essence of the Soul is, far more precious than anything bodily. Since then the Soul is so precious and divine a thing, be persuaded that by it thou canst attain to God; with it raise thyself to Him. The Soul owes its perfecting to Spirit, as it owes its existence — a son less perfect than his father. Its substance proceeds from Spirit. and when it looks upon Spirit, it has within itself, and as its own, what it sees and does. These are, indeed, the only activities of the Soul, properly speaking, which it performs spiritually and itself; the inferior operations come from elsewhere.
>
> **Plotinus**

traditions and social chaos was on the rise. Plotinus at one point petitioned the emperor to build a new city based on Plato's *Republic* and *Laws* to be called Platonopolis, but these plans were scuttled by opposing political forces. This opposition may explain the dispersal of Plotinus's school and his removal from Rome in 268 when Emperor Gallineus was assassinated. Two years later, Plotinus died on the estate of a friend, probably from leprosy.

Like his predecessors Plato and Pythagoras, Plotinus studied, taught, and wrote philosophy as sacred tradition — intellectual, moral, and mystical. In his philosophy, the higher stages of metaphysical contemplation only become possible after the most arduous course of moral purification. The student who takes the philosophical path not only learns about ideas, but his life becomes fused with all souls in the One, the Source of creation, even as he maintains his unique identity. Such a seeming paradox is parallel to Plotinus's notion of creation, the Source of emanation, in no way diminished or affected by the spiritual and material worlds created. Thus, the highest and lowest in creation reflect one another when man accomplishes the philosophical task. The role of moral discipline in achieving the mystical union is explained in Plotinus's metaphysical teachings.

For Plotinus there is an ultimate reality that is beyond being, inaccessible and ineffable, nevertheless the Source of all good and the "object" of man's highest desire, and true intellectuality. The original creative act, an outpouring or emanation from the Source, in no way diminishes it. This emanation, creating worlds with separate souls and intelligences, is considered by the philosopher to be necessary for the Source of all good, even as the Source is considered to be utterly free.

The first reality to come into being is "Intellect" or "Spirit," *nous* in the original Greek. In one sense the intelligences that occupy the realm of *nous* are objects similar to Plato's ideal forms. However, for Plotinus they are also active beings contemplating the whole while remaining discrete entities, interacting in reciprocity with the lower realms they create. Like the One above, which produced the multiplicity of intelligences, the intelligences in turn are the source of realities on lower levels: the realm of souls and the realm of bodily forms.

Soul is midway between intellect and materiality and it is because of this that man has a choice whether he will become mired in sensuous reality below or, through discipline, ascend to Intellect through the higher aspect of Soul. This in turn allows him to merge with the One, beyond multiplicity, the Eternal Real. For Plotinus, philosophy was the realization of man's highest desire, uniting him with the Source that is in everything, a religious experience without a personal God, and Plotinus's teachings are in sum a blueprint of the moral and intellectual discipline necessary to participate in this mystical union.

E. Brehier, *The Philosophy of Plotinus*, 1958.

G. J. O'Daly, *Plotinus*, 1967.

J. M. Rist, *Plotinus's Philosophy of the Self*, 1972.

PLUTARCH (c. 46–120 C.E.), Greek philosopher, diplomat, and biographer, mainly known for his extensive and readable biographies of prominent Greek and Roman figures of the classical world. His main work was his collection of forty-six *Parallel Lives*, a matching of biographies of famous Greek and Roman public figures. Through Plutarch's biographies, the reader receives both a glimpse of the individuals who made history in Plutarch's time, and more character-oriented histories of those who had lived before his time. His prolific writing did not extend to autobiography, however, so much of what is known of his personal history has to be culled from hints scattered throughout his work, and from the writings of contemporaries.

Plutarch believed that outstanding men determine the course of historical events; he wrote only of men of action and thus his work is closely connected with historiography. He himself makes a sharp distinction between history and biography in his *Life of Alexander the Great*, where he states categorically that "We are not writing histories but lives; it is not always the case that virtue or badness is disclosed by the most glorious actions. Indeed it often happens that a minor incident, a saying and a jest show up character more clearly than battles with numerous casualties, armies facing each other and cities under siege." Plutarch's great sense of drama inspired Michel de Montaigne and William *Shakespeare, the latter basing some of his classical heroes on Plutarch's *Lives*.

Plutarch was born to an ancient Theban family and raised in Chaeronea, in the westernmost corner of Boeotia, Greece, in luxury and affluence. Throughout his life, his main ties were with the city of his birth and with Delphi, the home of the oracle, where he be-

SOME OF PLUTARCH'S SAYINGS

- When the candles are out, all women are fair.
- We are more sensible of what is done against custom than against nature.
- Nature without learning is blind, learning apart from nature is fractional, and practice in the absence of both is aimless.
- Rest is the sauce of labor.
- It is a great thing to be well descended, but the glory belongs to our ancestor.
- Character is simply habit long continued.
- I live in a small city and prefer to dwell there that it may not become one smaller still.
- The best things are most difficult.
- The conduct of a wise politician is ever suited to the present posture of affairs. Often by foregoing a part he saves the whole and by yielding in a small matter secures a greater.

came one of the two permanent priests at the shrine. Although Plutarch's ancestors were not renowned for academic or intellectual achievement, his descendants, from his nephew Sextus, who taught *Marcus Aurelius, through to the third century Nicagoras, holder of the rhetorical chair at Athens, and the fourth century sophist Himerius, were to pride themselves on the noble intellectual lineage his name conferred. His fame is further evinced by the increasing use of the name Plutarch after his death.

In his youth, Plutarch studied philosophy in Athens under the great Platonist, Ammonius. He was also a passionate student of mathematics.By his late twenties he was already recognized as a philosopher and had made a start on his diplomatic career. He grew up at the time of *Nero and despite the latter's high-handed attitude to his subjects, Plutarch saw him as an essentially good man. In principle, he was in favor of firm rule and hated faction, and Nero's form of rule may have appealed to him for this reason.

He was not so generous with the Flavians who ruled during his maturity, especially following Domitian's expulsion of philosophers from Rome and Italy in 93 or 94 C.E. Plutarch traveled extensively at this time, visiting Alexandria and Rome, both in the interests of diplomacy and for academic reasons due to his standing as a philosopher. However, he wrote very little during this period, especially since any work might have been interpreted by this repressive regime as traitorous and inflammatory.

Plutarch reached the peak of his abilities during his latter years under Nerva and his successors. He was granted consular rank by *Trajan, his fame as a philosopher increased, he received many visitors of the highest intellectual rank, and was appointed procurator of Greece by *Hadrian.This last position was most probably an honorary one. It was during this period that he produced the bulk of his work. He died in his late seventies, probably in Delphi, after a painful illness.

C. P. Jones, *Plutarch and Rome*, 1971.
D. A. Russell, *Plutarch*, 1973.
Alan Wardman, *Plutarch's Lives*, 1974.

POE, EDGAR ALLAN (1809 – 1849), American. poet, short–story writer, and critic. Born in Boston, Massachusetts, Edgar Allan Poe never knew his alcoholic father, who disappeared shortly after he was born, while his actress mother died of consumption before he was three years old. He was brought up in Richmond, Virginia, by a wealthy merchant, John Allan, and his wife, who acted as foster parents and whose surname Poe took for his middle name.

He was educated partly in England and then in 1826 went to the University of Virginia. Despite his brilliance as a student, his stay there was brief and stormy: his fiancée Sarah Elmira Royster married another man when she thought she had lost Poe's affections. A gambler with a shortage of funds and a taste for drink, Poe amassed considerable debts. Allan withdrew his financial support and Poe was forced to leave the university.

Bust of Edgar Allan Poe from the New York Hall of Fame

> ## "ALONE"
>
> From childhood's hour I have not been
> As others were — I have not seen
> As others saw — I could not bring
> My passions from a common spring.
> From the same source I have not taken
> My sorrow; I could not awaken
> My heart to joy at the same tone;
> And all I lov'd, *I* lov'd alone.
> *Then* — in my childhood — in the dawn
> Of a most stormy life — was drawn
> From ev'ry depth of good and ill
> The mystery which binds me still:
> From the torrent or the fountain,
> From the red cliff of the mountain,
> From the sun that 'round me roll'd
> In its autumn tint of gold —
> From the lightning in the sky
> As it pass'd me flying by —
> From the thunder and the storm,
> And the cloud that took the form
> (When the rest of Heaven was blue)
> Of a demon in my view.
>
> **Edgar Allan Poe**

In 1827 he enlisted in the army but was dismissed when he refused to carry out orders. He spent all his money in publishing his first volume, *Tamerlane and Other Poems*, which won scant notice. A second volume, *Al Aaraaf, Tamerlane and Minor Poems*, was printed in November 1829. The following year he entered the military academy at West Point but was still drinking, gambling, and quarrelsome and was again discharged in 1831. Soon after, he went to live with his aunt Maria Clemm in Baltimore. More poems appeared the following year and in 1833 the *Baltimore Weekly* awarded him first prize for his story *A MS Found in a Bottle*. He left Baltimore to join the staff of the *Southern Literay Messenger* in Richmond, but miserable at being separated from his thirteen-year-old tubercular cousin Virginia Clemm, with whom he had fallen in love, he returned to Baltimore, and the couple were married in 1836.

The marriage was a difficult one: Virginia was not well, and Poe continued to drink; he was also the subject of rumor and scandal over his alleged involvement with other women. He worked on various magazines, including the *Gentleman's Magazine*, and launched the short-lived *Penn Magazine*. He wrote his famous metaphysical poems, *Annabel Lee* and *The Bells*. Meanwhile he continued publishing his stories — perhaps his most famous, *The Fall of the House of Usher*, appeared in 1839 and in 1841 he published what has been called the world's first detective story, *The Murders in the Rue Morgue*. Contentment still eluded the writer, who was contin-

ually dogged by problems with money, health, drink, and opium. Living in great poverty, he moved his family to a poor cottage in Fordham, New York, where there was no heat and his wife slept on a straw mattress. Nevertheless, he continued to work, and in 1844 wrote one of his most striking poems, *The Raven*, which brought him much acclaim, and the famous *Balloon Hoax*, written as a news article announcing the crossing of the Atlantic by balloon. By now he had also achieved considerable recognition abroad, notably in France.

The death of his wife in 1847 proved a major setback leading Poe, not for the first time, into a kind of nervous breakdown, and he lived in dissipation and isolation. On his recovery, Poe courted a Mrs. Whitman, but she broke off their engagement and he became involved with his first love, the now widowed Elmira Royster. They were due to marry in Richmond in October 1849, but in September he went to visit a friend in Baltimore, disappeared for a few days, and was found unconscious in the street. He died a few days later.

Although he considered himself primarily a poet, it is for his short stories that Poe is perhaps best remembered. A writer in the romantic tradition and a contemporary of Herman Melville and Nathaniel Hawthorne, a major theme in Poe's work is the "terror... of the soul." His landscapes are largely interior: man is depicted as alone, accompanied only by his own fear. Images of madness, death, conspiracy, and revenge abound. Man struggles alone, while onlookers are passive, often uncomprehending, witnesses. Nature, eerie and foreboding in *A Ms Found in a Bottle*, oppressive and dark in *The Fall of the House of Usher*, reflects man's inner torment. Poe's houses, too, are prisons, characters inexorably drawn toward their sinister, beckoning center. Poe's insistence on the "single effect" increases the pervading atmosphere of claustrophobia and panic. Yet Poe was a versatile writer who was also capable of lightness and humor: the *Balloon Hoax* was only one of a number of elaborate jokes; while the mysteries, *The Murders in the Rue Morgue* and *The Mystery of Marie Roget* were unique in their day.

A controversial figure both in his life and in his work, Poe was often dismissed as absurd, even unreadable, yet he endures for his unique, tautly communicated vision of terror and its relentness.

B. L. Knapp, *Edgar Allan Poe,*, 1985.

J. Symons, *The Tell-Tale Heart: The Life and Works of Edgar Allan Poe*, 1978.

G. R. Thompson, *Poe's Fiction: Romantic Irony in the Gothic Tales*, 1973.

POLO, MARCO (1254–1324), Venetian traveler. Marco Polo, whose detailed account of his journeys through Asia fired the medieval imagination, was born in Venice. His father and uncle, Nicolo and Maffeo Polo, successful merchants in the trade in Asian goods that had made Venice one of the West's richest cities, were attracted to Constantinople, where they opened a branch of their business shortly before Marco was born. In 1260 they moved their business eastward to Central Asia. When warring Tartar tribes blocked their return, they continued moving eastward. Accepting an invitation to accompany an envoy en route to the Mongol chieftain *Kublai Khan, they eventually arrived at the Great Khan's court in Cathay, China, around 1265.

Distrusting the newly-conquered Chinese, Kublai preferred employing foreigners. He made the Polos his emissaries, sending them back to Europe with gifts and letters asking the pope for one hundred learned missionaries. They arrived back in Venice to find Nicolo's wife dead and the election of a new pope delayed. After waiting in vain for two years for a new pope to be elected, the Polo brothers, fearing the consequences of keeping Kublai waiting, decided to return to China and take fifteen-year old Marco with them. However, they were soon summoned back by the new pope, Gregory X, who supplied them with credentials and sent two friars to accompany them. The friars turned back at the first hint of danger, but the Polos pressed onwards, trusting that the gold tablet that they carried, which was inscribed by Kublai himself, would ensure their safe passage.

They took three years to reach the Mongol court, having remained a year in Afghanistan while Marco recovered from an illness. Soon after their arrival, Kublai utilized Marco's gift for languages, keenly accurate observation, and vivid description by sending him on fact-finding missions to various parts of the Mongol Empire. Marco discharged his responsibilities so well that he was rewarded by being granted the governorship of Yangchow for three years, while his family was honored and protected from jealous courtiers.

After seventeen years in China, the Polos, knowing that their position there would be precarious after Kublai's death, sought to overcome the eighty-year old khan's resistance to letting them return to Venice. He was loath to see them go but finally, when they offered to guide a princess to her Persian bridegroom through the southern seas with which Marco was familiar (he had just returned from a mission there), Kublai reluctantly consented, supplying them with fourteen ships and a golden tablet to ensuring their safe passage. Their voyage to Persia was extremely rough (only eighteen of their six hundred passengers survived) but they delivered the princess and continued on to Venice, arriving home after being twenty-five years.

The written account of Marco Polo's journeys came into existence by chance. He was captured while participating in a naval battle with Genoa soon after returning to Venice. Imprisoned in Genoa, his tales of the fabulous East fascinated prisoners, jailers, and visitors alike and were written down by a fellow prisoner, a writer of romances named Rustichello. The completed manuscript described lands Polo had visited (or heard about in the East), their produce and trade, people, customs, curiosities, religions, and interesting historical incidents. Peace was declared soon after Rustichello completed his task and Polo was released from prison. He returned to Vienna, became involved in the daily life of a prosperous merchant, married, and had several children; on his death, his Tartar slave was freed according to the provisions of his will.

His manuscript's fate was more exotic. Considered fiction since it seemed too fantastic to be real, it was an immediate success throughout Italy. Translated and retranslated, it spread throughout Europe. Widely considered no more than an inventive storyteller, Polo, when asked to confess the truth on his deathbed, responded: "I did not write half the things I saw." Some suspected that there might be some truth in his tales: Columbus set sail in search of the riches of the East whose location and extent Polo had so carefully chronicled. Later explorers and researchers discovered that Polo was indeed an accurate and serious geographer.

W. Forman, *The Travels of Marco Polo*, 1970.
M. Rugoff, ed., *The Travels of Marco Polo*, 1961.

POMPEY (Gnaeus Pompeius Magnus; 106–48 B.C.E.), Roman general and statesman, known as "Pompey the Great." Pompey was born in a time of both economic and social unrest for Rome, in which the empire was rich with the resources of the West and the treasures of the East. Booty and taxes from conquered provinces made the taxation of Roman citizens unnecessary and created new standards of Roman wealth. The republic had deteriorated into an oligarchy ruled by a rich, powerful, and corrupt nobility. Civil wars wracked the empire in which the supremacy of the nobility — the propatricians — was challenged by businessmen and the people — the proplebians. Cheap grain and slaves from conquered provinces had made the traditional small Roman farm unviable. Many farmers sold out to large land owners and became soldiers or moved to Rome. Rapacious economic exploitation had brought the conquered provinces to economic ruin, which endangered both cheap grain supplies and the new wealth.

Pompey's father was Pompeius Strabo, a general in the Social War (91–89 B.C.E.), fought between Rome and the Italian tribes over the granting of Roman citizenship to the rest of Italy. Though Strabo was a great general, he was hated and feared for his unprincipled greed for money and honors. At sixteen Pompey accompanied Strabo to war. Recklessly brave and popular with the soldiers, he is credited with facing down troops and saving his father from assassination. In 89 B.C.E. Strabo was elected consul, and when civil war broke out between proplebian and propatrician forces the following year, his intrigues for a second consulship prevented his taking sides. His refusal to commit himself turned both sides against him and led to his death.

The proplebians were victorious and started settling old scores. As Strabo's heir, Pompey received the animosity Strabo had aroused. He defended him-

Bust of Pompey the Great

- A dead man cannot bite.
- More worship the rising sun than the setting sun.
- In whatever part of Italy I stamp the earth with my foot, there will spring up forces, both footsoldiers and horsemen.

Pompey the Great

self eloquently in court, displaying poise and wit. Acquitted, he married the judge's daughter several days later and discreetly devoted the next few years to his estates and family.

The civil war resumed when the propatrician general Sulla returned from the East in 84 B.C.E. Pompey never bothered much about the issues behind the civil wars that brought him power, fame, and fortune, but fought for any side willing to give him what he wanted. When Pompey's offer to fight against Sulla revived old emnities and accusations against him, he withdrew again to his family estates and decided to offer his services to Sulla. To make himself more acceptable as an ally he raised, financed, trained, and equipped an army. Three armies were sent against him and he routed the nearest. His reputation spread and Sulla eagerly marched towards his only ally and showered the twenty-two year-old Pompey with honors. Pompey became Sulla's protégé, dependent on him for advancement. When Sulla ordered Pompey to divorce his wife and marry Sulla's pregnant, married stepdaughter, Pompey promptly did so.

The proplebian leaders had fled to Sicily, Spain, and Africa to continue fighting against Sulla. Pompey went to Sicily to fight them after his new wife miscarried and died. There he first showed the traits that were to characterize him as a leader of armies: ruthlessness toward opposition, moderation and kindness towards the vanquished, and efficient orga-

nization and administration of the subdued province. His strict control of his troops won over the population (swords were sealed in scabbards and each broken seal had to be accounted for). In Spain he swiftly defeated the rebel forces, tersely responding to a city's questioning the legality of his position with: "Stop reading laws at men who have swords strapped at their sides." Then he defeated the rebels in Africa in forty days. Upon returning to Rome he demanded an official "triumph" (parade for victorious Roman generals) and an appointment to the Senate, despite lacking the requisite years and rank. Sulla gave him his triumph, the title of "magnus," a new wife from an influential family, and an appointment as senator. As a senator he worked to promote Sulla's goals but was not particularly successful, due to lack of ability, statesmanship, and the carefully cultivated connections of the other senators.

He was elected consul for the year 70 B.C.E. Pompey now began to be proplebian rather than propatrician and restored the power of electing the tribune to the people. He contrived to be sent on military missions from which he would return victorious and laden with booty to parade through Rome in increasingly magnificent triumphs, enhancing his great popularity. In 67 B.C.E. he was empowered to tackle the pirate problem in the Mediterranean and cleared the sea within three months, settling the pirates on the land in the eastern provinces of the empire. In 66 B.C.E. he was appointed to take command against Mithradates VI of Pontus in the East and he defeated him as he did Tigranes of Armenia and Antiochus of Syria (which he annexed), and he then subdued the Jews of Judea, which henceforth was under Roman rule. His organization of the Eastern Empire was a great achievement and set patterns that were to last for five centuries. In 61 B.C.E. he was given his third triumph in Rome, but back in Rome, his power began to wane.

Pompey was not a policy maker and not adept in handling the Senate. Together with Julius *Caesar and the rich Crassus, he was a member of the powerful First Triumvirate (61 B.C.E.), and he married Caesar's daughter, Julia. More concerned with matters of personal importance (such as ratification of the treaties he had negotiated and gifts of land for his soldiers) than with larger issues, his power was weakened by Caesar's increasing strength and the opposition he aroused among the aristocracy. Nevertheless he and Caesar were elected consuls in 55 B.C.E.

In 52 B.C.E., when Caesar was away fighting in Gaul, civil disorder broke out in Rome; Pompey suppressed it with the aid of tropps brought in from elsewhere in Italy. The final break between Pompey and Caesar came at the end of 51 B.C.E. The Senate and nobles were divided and eventually civil war was declared between the two sides. At the beginning of 49 B.C.E. Caesar crossed the Rubicon, in defiance of the Senate and its armies, and won a decisive victory over Pompey at the Battle of Pharsalus the following year. Pompey fled for refuge to Egypt where he was murdered. His younger son, Sextus, raised a fleet and occupied Sicily, holding out until defeated in a sea battle and killed in 37 B.C.E.
R. Seager, *Pompey*, 1979.

POPE, ALEXANDER (1688–1744), English poet, satirist, and translator. Born in London, Pope was the son of a Roman Catholic linen merchant. In 1700 his family moved to Binfield and for a while Pope attended schools near Winchester and in London, but was principally self-educated at home. At the age of twelve he began to suffer from a malignant and disfiguring disease, which was assumed by his family to be the consequence of too much study. The illness seriously impaired his health and stunted his growth: his full-grown height was four feet, six inches.

Encouraged as a prodigy by retired dramatist William Wycherley, Pope soon became acquainted with other former members of John Dryden's circle in London. In May 1709 Pope's *Pastorals* were published by the leading publisher of poetry, Jacob Tonson, taking the place of honor in his *Poetical Miscellanies*. Pope's first major work, *An Essay on Criticism* (1711), was a statement of neoclassical critical principles in which he lectured his age on its ill breeding and narrow-mindedness. Its distinctive epigrams have become part of the proverbial heritage of the English language.

In 1712 Pope published the first version of his mock-epic *The Rape of the Lock*. This masterpiece was written to reconcile two families who had become embittered over an actual incident: a gentleman in one family had, as a joke, stolen a lock of hair from a lady in the other. Pope treated the ensuing controversy as though it were comparable to *Homer's turbulent dispute between Greeks and Trojans. His favorite meter was the ten-syllable, iambic pentameter, rhyming ("heroic") couplet, which he handled skillfully in his original compositions and also in his translations of the classics. Proposals for the first of these translations, the *Iliad*, were issued in 1713 and for a decade Pope worked on his verse translation of Homer. The *Iliad* was published in six volumes in 1720 and the five-volume translation of the *Odyssey* was completed, with assistance, in five volumes in 1726. The translations brought Pope critical acclaim and financial success and with the proceeds he acquired a villa on the Thames at Twickenham which was to be his home for the rest of his life. Twickenham became the

---

FROM POPE'S *ESSAY ON CRITICISM*

A little learning is a dang'rous thing.
To what base ends and by what abject ways,
Are mortals urg'd through sacred lust of praise!
Ah ne'er so dire a thirst of glory boast,
Nor in the Critic let the Man be lost.
Good-nature and good-sense must ever join;
To err is human, to forgive, divine.

For fools rush in where angels fear to tread.
Distrustful sense with modest caution speaks,
It still looks home, and short excursions makes;
But rattling nonsense in full volleys breaks,
And never shocked, and never turned aside,
Bursts out, resistless, with a thund'ring tide:

---

scene of Pope's frequent hospitality and it was there that he expended much effort in the cultivation of the garden with its famous grotto, to which he often refers in his writing, and spent time with his friends and his dogs.

The translation of Homer and Pope's edition of *Shakespeare, published in 1725, embroiled him in the literary infighting of the time. As a Roman Catholic his affiliations were Tory and his former relationship with the Whig essayists Richard Steele and Joseph Addison had become hostile by 1715 due to the political animosity at the end of Queen Anne's reign. Pope found new and lasting friends in Tory circles, men who encouraged Pope's translation of Homer in the face of Whiggish attacks. Together with four of his new acquaintances, namely Jonathan *Swift, John Arbuthnot, Thomas Parnell, and John Gay, Pope collaborated in a series of projected prose satires.

Wearied by the attacks of the past decade on his politics, religion, poetic ability and moral character, Pope attempted to end the opposition and defend his values. In *The Dunciad* (1728), Pope denounced his critic, Lewis Theobold, for representing the degenerate standards of society. The effect of the poem was sensational and signified the beginning of Pope's role as the principal satirist of his age. It was followed by the *Limitations of Horace* (1733–1738), a loose translation of Horace's *Epistles, Satires and Odes* which Pope adapted to the contemporary social and political scene. Between 1733 and 1734 Pope wrote *An Essay on Man*, a philosophical contemplation of the relations between man, God, and nature, which during his lifetime became his most popular work.

Pope supported his defense of his character by editing a selection of his letters. These were analyses of his own thoughts and feelings, revealing him as a man of modest living, honor, and integrity and a profound critic of society; he was one of the first English writers to publish his own letters.

His preeminence as a poet, letter writer, satirist, and critic was established in his lifetime both at home and abroad. He was the first English poet to be recognized in Europe, where he enjoyed contemporary fame throughout the continent. He remains the major English poet of the eighteenth century.
B. S. Hammond, *Pope,*1986.
M. Mack, *Alexander Pope*, 1985.

POUND, EZRA LOOMIS (1885–1972), poet, critic, fascist propagandist. Ezra Pound was born in Hailey, Idaho, the only son of middle-class parents (his father later was to work at the Philadelphia mint). Pound went to preparatory school, and then studied at Hamilton College, and the University of Pennsylvania. After completing his master's degree in 1906, he taught Romance literature in a college for one year in Indiana, but left his job under suspicion of a morals charge.

In 1907 he went to Europe, remaining there for most of the rest of his life. He published his first book of poetry, *A lume spento*, in Venice in 1908. The same year he went to London where he remained for twelve years.There he entered William Butler *Yeats's little circle of poets seeking new forms of expression. This antiromantic, avant-garde coterie was called the School of Images. Despite near poverty — he frequently sent appeals to his father asking for five dollars to help him get by — by 1914, when he edited *Des Imagistes*, he was considered the master of this new, modern school of poetry.

Imagism was "one of the most short-lived movements in English poetry," according to one critic, but with long-term and profound effects on the development of modernism. "An 'Image'," Pound himself explained, "is that which presents an intellectual and emotional complex in an instant of time." Brilliant and incisive, his images hit to the core — or vortex (the name of Wyndham Lewis's school of writing at the same time). In describing Lewis's influence, Pound wrote that the image "is a vortex or cluster of fused ideas and is endowed with energy." Pound's word plays were witty and colorful. He had translated some early Chinese poetry, (*Cathay*, 1915), and the Chinese ideograms appealed to his fancy and his crystallizing development of modernism. Pound, however, did of not always interpret the ideograms accurately — but rather saw in the Oriental symbols what he wanted to see. While in London, he began to write his *Cantos*.

In 1920 Pound moved to Paris, where he advised Ernest *Hemingway, James *Joyce, and T. S. *Eliot. In 1924 he settled in Rapallo, Italy, where he was the center of a group of young followers — ultimately calling themselves "students at Ezuversity." He expanded his ideas on economics. Eccentric at best, his theories derived from his poverty-stricken

---

**EZRA POUND:
POETRY AND PROSE**

- Literature is news that *stays* new.
- What thou lovest well remains,
  the rest is dross.
- What thou lov'st well shall not be reft from thee
  What thou lov'st well is thy true heritage.
- O, woe, woe
  People are born and die
  We also shall be dead pretty soon
  Therefore let us act as if we were dead already.
- Winter is icumen in,
  Lhude sing Goddamm,
  Raineth drop and staineth slop,
  And how the wind doth ramm!
  Sing: Goddamm.
- The concept of genius as akin to madness has been carefully fostered by the inferiority complex of the public.
- Music begins to atrophy when it departs too far from the dance...poetry begins to atrophy when its gets too far from music.

---

years as a young writer, critic, and editor. He had always been an elitist, holding that only the elite could produce culture, particularly poetry. His group had felt the need for a homogeneous society, where racially all would be the same. Pound believed that society owed a debt to its artists and should support them. As these strands of his economic and political philosophy became linked together, he grew increasingly bitter toward those he believed held the purse-strings of society — bankers, landlords, "usurers," Jews. He felt that *Mussolini's Fascist government offered answers to economic problems of the 1930s.

In 1930 he published *A Draft of XXX Cantos*, intended as an epic work on the history of mankind, in the manner of *Homer and with a nod to Walt *Whitman. Pound drew from multicultural and multilinguistic sources. Complex and often obscure, the *Cantos* met with mixed reviews, but has been recognized as a seminal work in modern poetry.

During World War II Pound made several hundred radio broadcasts from Italy that were an extreme expression of earlier attitudes he had expressed; they were pro-Fascist and pro-Nazi and virulently anti-Semitic propaganda. In 1945 he was arrested by American troops for treason; however, after serving only six months in a prison camp, he was considered "insane and mentally unfit for trial" in the United States. He was hospitalized for twelve years in an institution that gave him preferential treatment.

His followers, who idolized him, such as T. S. Eliot, either dismissed his political excesses, or excused it as an illness. Due to their championing his cause, he received the Bollingen Prize for poetry, amid much controversy, in 1949, for *The Pisan Cantos*. ("Can a bad man write a good poem?" was the critical question.) In 1958, after his devotees' pleading, he was released from the mental hospital and permitted to return to Italy; the charges against him were dropped by the administration of Dwight D. *Eisenhower.

Pound stayed for a time with his daughter, before returning to his wife, Dorothy Pound, at their Rapallo home. When he became increasingly ill, he went to live with his old friend Olga Rudge, who took care of him during his last years as Dorothy Pound was not well herself.

Pound profoundly influenced twentieth century literature and his impact can be detected in almost every significant literary movement. In particular, he was one of the central figures in modern poetry, admired for his subtlety and complexity and his contribution to liberating poetry from its previous conventionality.

C. Craig, *Yeats, Eliot, Pound and the Politics of Poetry*, 1982.

H. Kenner, *The Pound Era*, 1971.

J. Laughlin, *Pound as Wuz, Essays and Lectures on Ezra Pound*, 1987.

N. Stock, *The Life of Ezra Pound*, 1982.

PRIESTLEY, JOSEPH (1733–1804), English clergyman, political theorist, and physical scientist who made momentous discoveries. The eldest child of a cloth dresser from Leeds, Priestley showed an early aptitude and enthusiasm for learning; a sickly child, he read voraciously in an effort to educate himself. In 1752 his Calvinist parents sent him to the Dissenting Academy at Daventry, a school for children of families that did not conform to the practices of the Church of England. There, he trained as a theological student and served as assistant minister to an independent Presbyterian congregation in Suffolk from 1755; the development of his commitment to Unitarianism rendered him too unorthodox for the liking of his parishioners, so in 1758 he took up a new position in Nantwich, Cheshire.

Priestley opened a small school in Nantwich, and it was through his duties as a teacher that his interest in scientific experimentation first developed. In 1761 he became tutor in language and literature at the Warrington Academy and developed a vocational course for his Dissenting students, as well as producing the *Rudiments of English Grammar* as a teaching aid; revolutionary in relying on descriptions of actual language usage, this primer remained in widespread use for over fifty years. A number of distinguished educational texts followed, including the *Theory of Language and Universal Grammar* (1762), *Essay on a Course of Liberal Education* (1765), and *Lectures on History and General Policy* (1765). Under Priestley's influence Warrington came to be recognized as one of the finest schools of its type in England. The University of Edinburgh conferred on him a doctor of law degree in 1765.

Priestley's experiments on electricity led to his being elected to the Royal Society in 1766, and with the encouragement of Benjamin *Franklin, whom he met in London, he wrote *The History and Present State of Electricity*. Once he became minister of Mill Hill Chapel, Leeds, in 1767, he enjoyed more leisure time for writing and experimentation, and he discovered four new gases (then called "airs"): nitrous oxide, nitric oxide, nitrogen dioxide, and hydrogen chloride. His 1771 publication, *On Different Kinds of Air*, came to the attention of Antoine-Laurent *Lavoisier, who was to provide the theoretical interpretation of Priestley's experimental findings.

With his 1769 *Essay on the First Principles of Government, and on the Nature of Political, Civil and Religious Liberty*, Priestley produced a powerful statement of eighteenth century liberal individualist values (which Jeremy *Bentham acknowledged as having inspired his axiom concerning the "greatest happiness of the greatest number"), while as a result of his 1772 work on optics he was offered a place on Captain James *Cook's second voyage; this was subsequently withdrawn due to mounting opposition to his Unitarianism, although the technique he invented for carbonizing water — he was the inventor of soda water (seltzer) — was used on the expedition and won him the Royal Society's Copley Medal in 1773.

Priestley moved into the employ of the earl of Shelburne in 1773, acting as his literary companion and librarian, and tutor to his two sons. It was on the Shelburne estate that he first identified a gas that supported and caused vigorous combustion; he called it "dephlogisticated air," believing it to be air free of phlogiston, that substance which was then commonly believed to saturate ordinary air when it no longer supported combustion or life. It was left to Lavoisier to work out the implications of Priestley's new discovery, to name the new gas "oxygen," and to point out the revolutionary nature of the new theory of the process of combustion that its discovery necessitated. Priestley himself was never to subscribe to Lavoisier's conclusions and remained one of the last and staunchest proponents of the phlogiston hypothesis long after it was generally regarded as obsolete.

Priestley later discovered the gases ammonia, sulphur dioxide, silicon tetrafluoride, nitrogen, and carbon monoxide, and noted the importance of light for plant growth, and that plants give off oxygen. In 1779 he left Shelburne's employ to become minister of the New Meeting congregation, subsisting on an annuity from Shelburne and money raised by friends. He now devoted his energies to religious and political issues, rapidly becoming regarded as an antagonist of all political and religious establishments; his *History of the Corruptions of Christianity* rejected fundamental Christian beliefs, while his support for the French Revolution led to the destruction of his house by an antirevolutionary mob in 1791. Three years later, in 1794, Priestley moved to the United States to escape the hostility and opposition he was facing in England, making friends there with such like-minded individuals as John *Adams and Thomas *Jefferson. His *Memoirs* were published in 1805.

K. S. Davis, *The Cautionary Scientists*, 1966.

F. W. Gibbs, *Joseph Priestley: Adventurer in Science and Champion of the Truth*, 1965.

PROUST, MARCEL (1871–1922), French novelist, author of the semi-autobiographical *Remembrance of Things Past*, one of the most influential novels of the twentieth century. Proust's father was a Catholic, while his mother came from a distinguished Jewish family. He respected his father, who had a brilliant career as a physician, but his mother was the focus of his passions and emotions, and he liked to smother her with his kisses and be beside her at all times, even when studying and sleeping. A key theme in his novel is the memory of the goodnight kiss given to the hero by his mother when he was a child.

Proust was plagued by poor health from his earliest years; he suffered from indigestion and hay fever, and when nine he suffered his first attack of asthma, which was to affect him for the rest of his life. He always had to watch his diet and dose himself with bicarbonate of soda and iodine. Despite his efforts to avoid fatigue, his asthma often kept him awake and he suffered from spells of melancholy.

Proust attended the Lycée Condorcet, where he was a good student, although often at home ill and not particularly popular with the other boys because of his delicate temperament. Despite his bourgeois and half-Jewish background, however, he ingratiated himself with the wealthy and sometimes aristocratic families of his schoolmates. By the time he was seventeen he was visiting literary salons and finding his way in Parisian society. As he grew older he discovered that his intellectual talents brought him popularity, and found that he was happiest and at his best in the company of older women.

When he graduated from the lycée, he was set on a literary career, but his parents insisted on a profession. The impasse was temporarily solved by his decision to volunteer for a year in the army, but he was not cut out for military life. Upon completion of his service, he entered university to study law and political science as a concession to his parents, but his literary ambitions remained and his student status simply gave him the freedom to continue devoting himself to his real interests — literature and society. He appeased his parents by continuing with his legal studies and eventually qualified as a lawyer but convinced them to allow him to go on studying. He was now a rather eccentric figure, continuing to live at home on an allowance, arising in

---

THE OPENING OF *REMEMBRANCE OF THINGS PAST*

For a long time I used to go to bed early. Sometimes, when I had put out my candle, my eyes would close so quickly that I had not even time to say "I'm going to sleep." And half an hour later, the thought that it was time to go to sleep would awaken me; I would try to put the book away which, I imagined, was still in my hands and to blow out the light; I had been thinking all the time, while I was asleep, of what I had just been reading, but my thoughts had run into a channel of their own, until I myself seemed actually to have become the subject of my book: a church, a quartet, the rivalry between Francis I and Charles V. This impression would persist for some moments after I was awake; it did not disturb my mind but it lay like scales upon my eyes and prevented them from registering the fact that the candle was no longer burning.

---

the late afternoon and going to bed at dawn. In his mid twenties he came to terms with his homosexuality. The collected works of his youth were published in 1896 as *Le Plaisir et les Jours*, which enjoyed little success among either reviewers or readers.

Proust was profoundly affected by the Dreyfus Affair in 1897, and, unlike his father and most of the society hostesses whom he visited, was convinced of Alfred *Dreyfus's innocence. He persuaded Anatole France to sign the pro-Dreyfus Petition of the Intellectuals and attended every session of the trial of Émile *Zola.

In the fall of 1900 Proust moved to a new house, which was opulent even though his own room was comparatively bare. There his life became a struggle to breathe, sleep, and avoid dependency on drugs. During difficult periods he would sleep in the day, when his asthma was least troublesome, and work through the night. Eventually he had his room lined with cork to keep out the dust and noise. His daily pattern was to wake at three or four in the afternoon and ring for breakfast. Hot coffee helped him breathe and he burned Legras powder for his asthma. Then, dressed by his servants in prewarmed clothes, he would go out to visit friends. He would often arrive just as they were going to bed, apologize profusely, say he was just leaving and then stay on talking interminably in the same parenthetical style that he used for writing.

After the death of his parents in the early 1900s, Proust abandoned his career as a man of the world to concentrate on literature, although he never entirely ceased social activities. His extensive experience in society now formed the raw material of his literature. In 1910 he began his masterpiece, sealing himself in his bedroom and from time to time sending out progress bulletins to his friends. The first volume was rejected by four publishers and only appeared at the author's expense in 1913. By the time that the second volume appeared in 1919, Proust was an acclaimed celebrity and won the Goncourt Prize. He remained, however, reclusive and a semi-invalid. On one occasion he emerged for a midnight supper party for Diaghilev, Pablo *Picasso, and Igor Stravinsky. There, he met James *Joyce; since neither author had read the other's work, they discussed their main subject of mutual interest — their health.

For the last three years of his life, Proust was bedridden (partly through illness, partly to escape the demands of literary celebrity), surrounded by galley proofs, manuscripts, and medicines. Four volumes of *Remembrance of Things Past* appeared before his death, the other three, posthumously. His early novels, *Jean Santeuil* and *Sainte Beuve*, only appeared in the 1950s.

Remembrance of Things Past is an involved psychological novel of some three thousand pages. Its labyrinthine sentences, slow unfolding, and constant time shifts — which mean that many clues are only solved long after they appear in the work — make it a difficult literary experience. One concept central to Proust's writing is that of memory, and, basing his ideas on the philosophy of Henri *Bergson (whose wife was Proust's cousin), he set out to exalt the place of involuntary memory in the recreation of the past. The *Remembrance*'s originality of concept and style, its breadth, its great humor, and its language have brought it recognition as a key contribution to modern literature.

R. Hayman, *Proust*, 1990.

G. D. Painter, *Marcel Proust: A Biography*, 2 vols., 1965.

R. Shattuck, *Proust*, 1974.

PTOLEMY, CLAUDIUS (c.100–170), mathematician, astronomer, and geographer.

Little is known about Ptolemy's early life except that he was born in Alexandria, then one of the world's great centers of learning, of Greek and Egyptian parents. Demonstrating an encyclopedic breadth and depth of erudition he gathered all the theories that were prominent in his time and tested them against the knowledge of the physical world that had been accumulated. Although his knowledge was necessarily limited by ancient theories, Ptolemy's use of mathematics and derivation of precise observation makes him a precursor of later scientific method. Indeed, his synthesis was so powerful that it lasted for thirteen centuries, dominating European thinking and acting as the cornerstone of scientific knowledge until the Copernican Revolution.

Ptolemy inherited a wealth of Greek philosophical, astronomical, and geographical works: from the philosophy of *Plato he adopted the assumption that the earth was that most perfect of geometric forms, a sphere; following *Aristotle, he further saw the earth as the center of the universe, surrounded by fixed celestial spheres, including one which held the multiplicity of stars (another trend in Greek thought, that placed the sun at the center of the universe, was thereby ignored); from *Hipparchus, the preeminent astronomer of antiquity, Ptolemy inherited a star map with the locations of 850 stars, the first such compilation of its kind, which increased the number of charted stars to 1,022. He also adopted Hipparchus's tradition of dividing a circle or sphere into 360 degrees, and invented the map grid charting longitude and latitude, which is still utilized to the present day. With his sphere projected on a flat surface divided by latitude and longitude Ptolemy charted the locations of eight thousand places in the known world, including the entire Roman Empire, which spanned the known continents of his times — Africa, Asia, and Europe. His maps situated the northern lands at the top of the page with east at the right, a convention still observed in cartography.

Ptolemy erred in his estimate of the size of the earth: attributing fifty miles to one degree of latitude, he underestimated the circumference of the planet by some thirty percent. Moreover, on Ptolemy's maps the majority of the earth's surface is covered by land (which in fact only accounts for some one-quarter of the planet's surface area), incorrectly making the distance from Europe to its neighboring continent seem smaller than it really is. Ptolemy studied spherical geometry, inventing a sundial that was of great significance in an age before the advent of the mechanical clock. He also worked in harmonics, measuring the lengths of chords, and propounded theories in optics for phenomena that had previously escaped scientific explanation. In addition, he developed a calendar that indicated meteorological factors as well as charting the locations of stars at sunrise and sunset.

Ptolemy's major work in astronomy is the thirteen-volume *Almagest*. Ptolemy put the earth at the center of the universe, followed by the Moon, Mercury, Venus, the Sun, Mars, Jupiter, and Saturn. He correctly placed the planets closer to earth than the stars, which he believed were held in fixed positions by a crystalline sphere. Like Aristotle, he held that the outermost sphere was set into motion by the Prime Mover. The planets were conceived of as revolving around the earth on a circular course known as a deferent. The system was complicated by the need to account for the occasional dimming of a planet's light that could be observed. A more significant problem was the observation of retrograde motions, when planets seemed to move backward in their course. Ptolemy explained this phenomenon by proposing that while the planet revolved in its larger circles around the earth, they also turned in an epicycle, a smaller cycle that gave the planet a second revolving course.

The *Almagest* also offered proofs for a geocentric universe, based on the observable fact that an object when dropped falls toward the earth and not toward

> I know that I am born for a day, but when I follow the serried multitude of the stars in their circular course, my feet no longer touch the earth; I ascend to Zeus himself to feast me on ambrosia, the food of the gods.
>
> **Ptolemy**

some other center. It also argued that the earth was stationary for otherwise an object dropped from a height would land at a distant location.These beliefs, consistent with the teaching of the church, remained unchallenged until the fifteenth century when accumulated observation made the Ptolemaic system less tenable than a heliocentric model. C.L. Stevenson, *Geography*, 1932.

PUSHKIN, ALEKSANDR SERGEYEVICH

(1799–1837), Russian poet. Aleksandr Puskin was born in Moscow, where his parents were minor aristocrats; his maternal great-grandfather was reputedly an Ethiopian prince who married a Balto-German gentlewoman (Pushkin was to speak of "my brother blacks"). His family was not particularly interested in him but gave him the run of the large family library where he became acquainted with French literature from an early age. He was deeply impressed by the Russian folktales related to him by his old nurse. When he was twelve he was sent to school at Tsarkskoye Selo (now Detskoye Selo), where *Alexander I intended to train an elite generation of soldiers and public servants (his French teacher was a brother of Jean Paul *Marat). There his gift for writing first became evident and his first poem was published when he was fifteen. He was similarly precocious in his love affairs.

During his school years he was elected to the Arzamas club, a group of progressive students, and as a young man, he joined the Green Lamp, a more revolutionary group that had some associations (though Pushkin himself was unaware of them) with the initiators of the Decembrist plot of 1825. On graduation from school, he received an appointment in the ministry of foreign affairs, but spent most of his time carousing. In 1820, Czar Alexander had him exiled in order to rid him of the liberal tendencies in his poetry, which were occasionally directed against the czar himself. He carried a letter of recommendation from the foreign minister that stated "there is no excess in which this young man has not indulged, as there is no perfection which he cannot attain by the high excellence of his talents." Through the intervention of his literary friend V. A. Zhukovsky, he escaped confinement in a monastery on the White Sea, and was sent instead to south Russia to serve on the Board of the Protection of Foreign Colonists. There he spent more time writing poetry, gambling, and falling in love than actually working for the Russian civil service. In 1824 he was formally expelled from the civil service and ordered to live on his mother's estate in northwest Russia. During this period his literary output was considerable; it was not long before he became known as "the Russian *Byron."

When Alexander died and the Decembrist coup was staged against Nicholas I in 1825, many of Pushkin's friends were exiled to Siberia, and five leading Decembrists, among them one of his friends, were hanged. Pushkin himself, with the assistance once again of Zhukovsky, was summoned to Moscow for a meeting with the czar. He was given permission to come out of exile and write freely. At court the czar presented Pushkin to a group of courtiers with the words "Gentlemen, permit me to introduce a new Pushkin; please forget the old one." In effect, however, for the rest of his life he was under surveillance, listed by the police as a reckless gambler, and his work was censored.

In 1827 Pushkin went to Saint Petersburg where he married a young, beautiful, and extravagant woman who severely taxed his finances, enjoyed the Moscow social life tremendously, and cared little for her husband's poetry. Pushkin, on the other hand, was bored and longed to return to the country, but was compelled to remain in Saint Petersburg in order to retain the czar's permission to enter the state archives so that he could gather material for a study of the Pugachov rebellion under *Catherine the Great. He was appointed a Gentleman of the Bedchamber, probably so that his popular wife could attend court balls, and hated the role of courtier he was called upon to play.

When his wife's brother-in-law, a French royalist emigré, Baron Georges d'Anthès, began to pay court to her, Pushkin was incensed and challenged the young man to a duel. He was fatally wounded and died two days later. To avoid the anger of the public, who suspected the authorities of condoning the duel, his body was smuggled out of the capital in the middle of the night for burial in Mikhailovkoye, where he had requested to be buried beside his mother.

Pushkin wrote of himself, "Perhaps I am elegant and genteel in my writings; but my heart is completely vulgar." Yet he was one of the greatest

---

"I LOVED YOU ONCE"

I loved you once, nor can this heart be quiet:
For it would seem that love still lingers here;
But do not you be further troubled by it;
I would in no wise hurt you, oh, my dear.
I loved you without hope, a mute offender;
  What jealous pangs, what shy despairs I knew!
A love as deep as this, as true, as tender,
God grant another may yet offer you.

A. S. Pushkin

national poets in Russia, and virtually founded Russian literature. He had had only Western authors for inspiration, among them Lord *Byron and William *Shakespeare. He was a supreme lyricist, diverse, exuberant, and inexhaustibly imaginative yet concise and restrained in style. His works include *Eugene Onegin* (1833), a novel in verse marked by a rare humor into which it was said he put "all his life, all his soul, all his love, feelings, views and ideals," *Poltava* (1828), *Ruslan and Lyudmila* (1820), *Boris Godunov* (1831), *The Queen of Spades* (1833–1834), and *The Captain's Daughter* (1836).

J. Bayely, *Pushkin, A Comparative Commentary*, 1971.
S. Sandler, *Distant Pleasures*, 1989.
W. N. Vickery, *Alexander Pushkin*, 1970.
G. Ziegler, *Alexander S. Puschkin*, 1979.

PYTHAGORAS (c.580–c.500 B.C.E.), Greek philosopher. If, as Alfred North Whitehead claimed, European philosophy is simply, "a series of footnotes to Plato," Pythagoras can rightfully be considered the father of philosophy — a term he coined — and of mathematics, physics, and astronomy. Although his teachings were handed down secretly to a select body of disciples, contemporary scholars have been able to reconstruct much of what he said and present plausible interpretations of the numerous cryptic maxims attributed to him.

The events of Pythagoras's life have been obscured by countless legends promulgated by fervent devotees attempting to deify their master. Some considered him the incarnation of the Hyperborean Apollo; others claim that Apollo was his father. Actually, Pythagoras was probably the son of Mnesarchus, a merchant or jeweler from the island of Samos, then a major Mediterranean commercial center. To explain his preoccupation with numbers, some biographers claim that he trained to be a bookkeeper. More likely, he studied under the three foremost contemporary thinkers: Pherekydis of Syros and Thales and Anaximander of Miletus, to each of whom central elements of his doctrines can be traced. He seems to have rejected the Hellenic ideal of physical perfection, possibly because of a large golden birthmark on his thigh, which he later pointed to as evidence of his divine origins.

The reasons for Pythagoras's sudden departure for Egypt remain obscure. In one account, he fled the dictator Polycrates, but that same source claims that he brought with him a letter of introduction signed by Polycrates. Another possibility is that, having mastered astrology under Anaximander, he wanted to continue his studies under Thales, but the latter, being too old, encouraged him to study abroad. Whatever the reason, his twenty years there proved vital in formulating his philosophy. He was initiated into several esoteric sects and adopted many of their beliefs. Most notable was the belief in reincarnation — he later claimed to remember his previous lives — and in a living universe governed by mathematical principles.

PYTHAGOREAN MAXIMS

- Go not beyond the balance — Transgress not justice.
- Sit not down on the bushel — Do not loaf on the job.
- Wear not a narrow ring — Seek freedom; avoid slavery.
- Always put salt on the table — Settle problems with justice.
- Do not cut wood on the public road — Never use public utilities privately.
- Feed not yourself with your left hand — Support yourself through work, not theft.
- Write not in the snow — Do not trust precepts to inconstant figures.

Egypt was conquered by Cambyses in 525 and Pythagoras was exiled to Babylon. For ten years, he mastered Chaldean mysticism, including the use of opium to attain enlightenment and the complicated procedures of ritual purification, before returning to Samos to establish his ideas.

Back home, however, Pythagoras, who now sported long hair, an unshaven beard, and trousers, was regarded as an eccentric figure, more barbarian than Greek. Since no one would attend his school, he bribed a young boy to study mathematics with him. The boy then shared his knowledge with his peers who became increasingly fascinated by Pythagoras. Suddenly, Pythagoras refused to teach unless he was paid. Not only the boy, but many other young aristocrats flocked to him until, unwilling to fulfill disagreeable social obligations, Pythagoras fled to Croton.

There, Pythagoras quickly reestablished his brotherhood of disciples, called mathematikoi. Its beliefs were a well guarded secret, but probably included the belief that the entire universe was a living organism governed by mathematical principles. Man's soul was immortal, but subject to reincarnation, possibly as an animal or even a plant. Ritual purity was essential; his followers were strict vegetarians who also abstained from eating beans because of the similarity between their shape and that of the human embryo. The brotherhood was governed by a strict moral code that emphasized communal property and, above all, secrecy. Pythagoras encouraged the reputation that he was divine by refusing to eat or perform other physical needs in public. He was surrounded by legends — on one occasion, a heavenly voice called out his name. He once stopped a dog from being beaten because he recognized in its whining the voice of a dead friend, while on another occasion, he made a fisherman agree to release his catch if he told him exactly how many fish were in the net.

The Pythagoreans governed Croton for about fifteen years, until a native rebellion forced

Pythagoras to flee to Metapontum amidst rumors that he committed suicide. Conflicting accounts exist as to how Pythagoras died; one disciple later claimed that he rose bodily to heaven. His school, however, continued to function for four hundred years, influencing many prominent Greek philosophers, among them Plato. Today, it is difficult to determine what was originally taught by Pythagoras and what was discovered by his pupils — they generally attributed all their knowledge to him. In mathematics, he is attributed with the Pythagorean Theorem (the square of the hypotenuse of a right angle triangle is equal to the sum of the square of both sides). In physics, he taught the mathematical relationship between the length of a string and its tone when plucked. In astronomy, he was the first to propose that the earth was spherical and that the evening star and the morning star were the same planet, which he identified as Aphrodite (later known as Venus).

P. Gorman, *Pythagoras: A Life*, 1979

D. J. O'Meara, *Pythagoras Revived*, 1988.

K. S. Guthrie, *The Pythagorean Sourcebook and Library*, 1986.

Pythagoras, from a fresco by Raphael

Q

QUEZON Y MOLINA, MANUEL LUIS

(1878–1944), first president of the Philippines. Born in Baler, Tayabas province, Quezon quit school to participate in Emilio Aguinaldo's failed uprising against American colonial rule. Aguinaldo was defeated in 1901; after six months in jail for his role in the rebellion, Quezon returned to law school, convinced that the cause of independence was best served by negotiating with the American authorities.

After completing his degree in 1903, Quezon was appointed prosecuting attorney for the provinces of Mindaro and his native Tayabas. In 1905 he was elected governor of Tayabas, and in 1909 one of the two resident commissioners for the Philippines in Washington. There, the "Patrick Henry of the Philippines" became a vociferous champion of independence. As a nonvoting member of Congress, he questioned whether the Jones Act (1916), enabling the formation of a local legislature for the Philippines, went far enough in ensuring self-rule. The act depicted a continued American military presence on the islands even if independence were, at some future date, achieved. He, nonetheless, returned to the islands and was elected speaker of the newly formed Senate, the most prestigious post open to native Filipinos.

Similar reservations led Quezon to oppose deferred independence as proposed in the Heres-Hawes-Cutting bill of 1933. In 1934, however, he accepted the Tydings-McDuffie Act assuring complete independence by 4 July 1946. In view of Japanese expansionism in the Pacific, he recognized that only the American military was capable of defending the islands, while the proposed transitional Commonwealth of the Philippines would allow him to formulate an independent policy to tackle the pressing problems of the islands. The following year, Quezon was elected president of the new commonwealth.

The Americans were shocked to discover that Quezon's grand design for the islands exhibited totalitarian tendencies. He described the country as a "distributive state," in which the state allocated accumulated wealth so that "all citizens receive the means to live." Although essentially democratic, Quezon spoke of a "dictatorship of persuasion," and eventually of banning political parties. Essential to his doctrine of attaining total self-reliance was the establishment of a national defense force, for which he employed his old friend, American general Douglas *MacArthur, a former governor and outspoken proponent of independence. Other problems he confronted included the settlement of the large southern island of Mindanao to quell a local Muslim revolt and corruption at all levels of government. At one point, Quezon studied the option of closer cooperation with the Japanese, and even made a state visit there in 1938 but concluded that the Japanese were already intent on occupying the country.

In 1941, with a Japanese invasion well underway, Quezon was elected to a second term as president by a seven to one margin. A heavy air raid shook Manila during the inauguration ceremonies, forcing the president and his entourage to flee to the U.S. garrison of Corregidor. After seventy-seven days and an impassioned plea from President Franklin D. *Roosevelt, Quezon finally agreed to leave the Philippines. MacArthur received $500,000 to take Quezon and his immediate family to Australia, and in 1942, Quezon reached the United States to organize his government in exile.

Although Quezon had earlier decided to retire from politics in 1943, Roosevelt urged him to postpone his resignation until the Philippines were liberated in return for a promise of immediate independence. Quezon, however, died of tuberculosis in August 1944; the American invasion began in October of that year and only succeeded in liberating Manila in February 1945. Although Quezon never lived to see the Philippines liberated, he is considered the father and first president of his country. A new city built near Manila was named Quezon City in his honor.

E. Goettel, *Eagle of the Philippines: President Manuel Quezon*, 1970.

A. Gopinath, *Manuel Quezon*, 1987.

C. Quirino, *Quezon, Paladin of Philippine Freedom*, 1971.

R

RABELAIS, FRANÇOIS (c.1494–1553), French writer and humanist. His exuberant two-part work, *Gargantua and Pantagruel*, is both a literary classic and one of the world's satirical masterpieces. A provincial lawyer's son, François Rabelais was born and raised near Chinon in Touraine, which he later called the "garden of France." Educated by priests, he entered a Franciscan monastery (where he spent about fourteen years) and took holy orders in 1520. By then, he and some fellow monks were engaged in the clandestine study of law and the sciences, also building a small library of works in Greek. Their hyperorthodox superiors, who believed that Greek was an heretical language since it opened up the original New Testament and allowed for the study of the Greek Fathers of the Church, opposed their studies. Rabelais and his friends took refuge in the neighboring abbey of Maillezais, which had a more liberal outlook. There he was permitted to transfer his allegiance from the Franciscan to the Benedictine order, as well as to continue broadening his knowledge. In 1527, however, Rabelais left the abbey and eventually became a secular priest. At the end of 1530 he took his bachelor's degree in medicine at the University of Montpellier and then settled in Lyons, an important center of Renaissance culture and publishing, where he worked as a physician at the city hospital (1532–1534).

From then until the year of his death, Rabelais combined the practice of medicine with the development of his scholarly reputation as a humanist who corresponded with (and was influenced by) great contemporaries such as Desiderius *Erasmus. He learned Arabic and a smattering of Hebrew, gave lectures on medical subjects, took his medical degree in 1537 and published a variety of learned texts. At the same time, he managed to acquire several eminent protectors (notably Cardinal Jean du Bellay, his martial brother Guillaume, and Cardinal Jean de Lorraine), who took Rabelais into their service and, when necessary, interceded on his behalf at the French court and at the papal court in Rome.

Such protection was often a vital necessity once it became clear that the irreverent, boisterous satires entitled *Pantagruel* (1532) and *Gargantua* (1534), given out as the work of a mysterious Dr. Alcofrybas Nasier, had actually been written under that anagrammatical pen name by the erudite François Rabelais. His rambling, fantastic stories about two gigantic rulers, Gargantua and his son Pantagruel, scarcely disguised the author's true purpose, which was to pour scorn on the religious obscurantism and educational backwardness of his time. Thanks to their deliberately coarse humor and the widespread controversy they aroused, these two books had a phenomenal sale and placed Rabelais in the front rank of European writers. He later published two sequels (1546, 1552), resuming the adventures of Pantagruel and his companions but reducing the grotesque element to a minimum; a fifth volume (1564), printed long after his death, may well be a forgery. Rabelais attacked pious humbug, dogmatism, and superstition, even venturing to question papal authority, but he never abandoned Catholicism and mocked John *Calvin as the "Genevan impostor."

- It is in the nature of man to laugh.
- Appetite comes with eating, but thirst goes away with drinking.
- *Fay ce que vouldras* — Do what you will (the utopian Abbey of Theleme's only rule).
- Science without conscience is the ruin of the soul.
- A disease known as being short of cash.
- Speak the truth and shame the Devil.
- Performed to a T.
- As plain as the nose in a man's face.
- This is a great year for cuckolds.
- Everyone to his taste, as the woman said when she kissed the cow.
- Everything comes to those that wait.
- Half the world doesn't know how the other half lives.
- Ring down the curtain, the farce is over (supposed last words).

François Rabelais

Although a man of the Renaissance in his attitudes and ideas, Rabelais was a typical product of the Middle Ages in his undisciplined style and expression. To the arbiters of seventeenth-century French classicism, he seemed remote and uncouth; for the Victorian public, even bowdlerized translations of *Gargantua* and *Pantagruel* were scandalously "Rabelaisian." A more appreciative and realistic view has prevailed in the twentieth century. Far from being a lecherous buffoon, Rabelais is now consdiered to have championed enlightenment, tolerance, common sense, and a healthy regard for life, negating hypocrisy, prejudice, and all forms of tyranny. His innumerable coinages and telling phrases vastly enriched the language of France; his bawdy humor, characteristic of the *esprit gaulois*, hid many a profound thought; and his satirical genius would impress itself on many other great writers for centuries to come.

D. G. Coleman, *Rabelais: A Critical Study in Prose Fiction*, 1971.

L. Febvre, *The Problem of Unbelief in the 16th Century: The Religion of Rabelais*, 1985.

D. M. Frame, *Francois Rabelais*, 1977.

M. A. Screech, *Looking at Rabelais*, 1988.

RACINE, JEAN (1639–1699), French dramatist, whose eleven tragedies are considered the greatest in the French language. Born into a provincial family of modest means, Jean Racine was left motherless at one and fatherless two years later. Consigned to the care of his paternal grandparents, in 1655 he entered the important Jansenist school (see Cornelis *Jansen) at Port Royal des Champs, where he remained until 1658. It was at Port Royal that Racine was introduced to Latin, Greek, and, most important, to the world of classical literature. Here he began to write verse and also showed a taste for romance, which distressed his instructors. The year 1660 saw the beginnings of Racine's literary career with *Amasie*, which was never published, and his first published work, *The Nymph of the Seine*, on the marriage of *Louis XIV, as well as an ode dedicated to the queen.

In 1661 he was sent to the cathedral of Uzès in the south of France, where his uncle, Antonin Sconin, was a vicar general of the diocese. However, despite his uncle's influence, he was unable to obtain an ecclesiastical benefice and returned to Paris, where he, Jean-Baptiste *Molière, and Jean de La Fontaine formed a famous friendship. His first tragedies to be performed, *La Thébaïde* (The Story of Thebes, 1664) and *Alexandre le Grand* (1665), resembled the works of Pierre *Corneille. *Alexandre* had its premier at Molière's theater but Racine made a lifetime enemy of Molière by permitting a rival company, the Hotel de Bourgogne, to put it on while it was still being performed by Molière's theater. Racine also conducted a public quarrel with his former teachers and mentors at Port Royal by defending the morality of the theater against the Jansenists.

With the tragedy *Andromaque* (1667), Racine replaced Corneille as France's premier dramatist. In 1668 *Les Plaideurs* (The Litigants), Racine's only comedy, was produced, in which he satirized the law courts. He then returned to his favorite form with two tragedies set in imperial Rome, *Britannicus* and the moving *Bérénice*, which firmly established him as a master of French classical tragedy. A success, *Bérénice* overshadowed Corneille's version of the story of two lovers separated by history, *Tite and Bérénice* (Titus and Bernice). Always attempting to chart new courses, Racine's next subject involved contemporary scandal. *Bajazet* (1672) was set in a Turkish harem and was full of intrigue and excitement.

In 1673 Racine reaped his professional rewards. His tragedy, *Mithridate*, was a popular success and he was made a member of the French Academy, the official body that arbitrates French literature and language. His next play, *Iphigénie* (1674), signaled a return to Greek tragedy and was an adaptation of *Euripides's *Iphigenia at Aulis*. In the same year Racine, whose income had been supplemented by royal allowances, improved his financial situation by becoming treasurer for the region of Moulins. The year 1677 was significant in Racine's life; after a concerted attack on his latest play, *Phèdre*, he gave up the theater, was happily married to Catherine de Romanet who brought him wealth and seven children, and together with the writer Nicolas Bolieau-Despreaux, was appointed official historiographer to the king.

It was not until 1689, upon the request of Madame de Maintenon, Louis XIV's second wife, that Racine wrote again. *Esther* (1689) and *Athalie* (1691) were composed for the girls of the school under her patronage at Saint-Cyr. These plays differ from his other works in their religious content and by their use of a chorus.

Although he never wrote any more plays, Racine remained a man of letters, editing and revising new editions of his earlier works as well as composing a number of religious songs which were published posthumously. In the last years of his life he re-

---

- Great crimes never come singly; they are linked to sins that went before.
- Flight is lawful when one flees from tyrants.
- Without money, honor is a malady.
- Extreme justice is often unjust.
- The heart that can no longer love passionately, must with fury hate.
- I have loved him too much not to hate him.
- The face of tyranny is always mild at first.
- There may be guilt when there is too much virtue.

Jean Racine

newed his contact with Port Royal and led a life compatible to the demands of Jansenism.

J. P. Giradoux, *Jean-Baptiste Racine*, 1982.
G. Lucien, *Racine*, 1981.
D. Maskell, *Racine: A Theatrical Reading*, 1991.
J. Rohov, *Jean Racine*, 1992.

RALEIGH, SIR WALTER (1552–1618), English courtier, soldier, adventurer, poet, and prose writer. The son of a Devonshire squire, Raleigh studied at Cambridge but never completed his degree. Adventure called and he went to France to fight for the Protestant cause. Later he studied law in London but found more interest in the wild tavern life of the city, once going to prison for six days for his part in a fight.

Since law was not to be his livelihood, he invested in an expedition to America organized by his half-brother. A fight with Spanish warships aborted this venture and Raleigh exploited family influences at court to acquire an army commission. He took part in the ruthless suppression of an insurrection in southern Ireland, showing himself a brave officer but merciless with captured rebels. He hoped Ireland could be colonized with men from his native Devon.

In 1581 Raleigh was back in London, and ambitious as ever, secured a position for himself at court. He cut a dashing figure: handsome features adorned with the most expensive clothes and jewelery. His looks and his gallantries won the favor of Queen *Elizabeth I. Raleigh's placing his expensive cloak over a puddle so she would not have to dirty her shoes typified his chivalrous manner.

Raleigh was rewarded with a knighthood and in 1586 the captaincy of the royal guard. Elizabeth also granted him land in England and Ireland and trading monopolies including tin and playing-cards. Raleigh became a very wealthy man, arousing jealousy in other courtiers not only with his money but with pride openly displayed.

He spent money lavishly, on his own appearance, his properties, and especially on grand schemes, foremost of which was the founding of a new English settlement in North America, although he himself never visited the American continent. The colony was named Virginia in honor of Queen Elizabeth. For Raleigh it proved a financial disaster, native attacks destroying the settlement.

He did not live to see the development of Virginia, but he had a role in popularizing the substance that would enrich it — tobacco. A trend setter in fashion, Raleigh's enthusiasm for smoking spread through society. The novelty took some getting used to — one of his servants tried to empty a bucket of water over him to put out the fire! Raleigh's other famous American import, the potato, had equally outstanding success. Following introduction on his Irish estates, it became a staple foodstuff in Ireland.

Rivalry from the earl of Essex for the queen's favor displaced Raleigh in 1589 and he took up residence in Ireland. Here he befriended the poet

> ### RALEIGH WROTE
>
> - Eat slowly; only men in rags
>   And gluttons old in sin
>   Mistake themselves for carpet bags
>   And tumble victuals in.
> - The nightingale got no prize at the poultry show.
> - If she seems not chaste to me,
>   What care I how chaste she be?
> - Prevention is the daughter of intelligence.
> - Speaking much is a sign of vanity; for he that is lavish of words is a niggard in deed.

Edmund Spenser and encouraged him in his monumental work *The Faerie Queene*.

Raleigh's marriage to Elizabeth Throckmorton, one of Queen Elizabeth's maids, again aroused the queen's anger for she did not tolerate rivals for her favorites' affection. Raleigh and his wife spent their honeymoon imprisoned in separate cells in the Tower of London. His fortune only improved when an expedition to Panama he promoted, captured a richly laden Spanish treasure galleon. The queen took most of the booty, with Raleigh seeing scant financial return, but he was allowed to keep his royal honors and his banishment from court ended and this was considered sufficient reward.

His fertile imagination now found expression in pursuit of El Dorado, the fabulously wealthy king-

Sir Walter Raleigh

dom believed to exist in South America, but his expedition of 1595 was another failure.

In 1596 Raleigh had a command in the British naval squadron that successfully destroyed a Spanish fleet and sacked Cadiz. He showed his capabilities at the height of battle and sustained a wound to his leg leaving a permanent limp. His share of the spoils once more proved disappointing compared with that of other officers.

During Elizabeth's final years, Raleigh seemed to have reached a new peak of power and influence at court and domestic tranquillity with his family at his favorite estate, Sherborne in Devon. It was the quiet before the storm. He was widely envied and disliked, especially by Sir Robert Cecil, Elizabeth's leading minister. Cecil poisoned the mind of the heir to the English throne, King *James of Scotland, telling him of Raleigh's alleged atheism and anti-Scottish sentiments. At the same time Cecil feigned friendship, so Raleigh was unprepared for the changed attitude when King James came to the throne in 1603. Within a few months he was under house arrest for treason.

Raleigh knew of a conspiracy to overthrow King James, though he was not involved. One of the arrested conspirators, Lord Cobham, accused him of instigating the scheme and he was confined to the Tower of London. In a fit of depression he tried to take his own life but only inflicted a slight wound. Cobham's withdrawal of the charge helped give him strength to face his trial.

The case against Raleigh was presented in a vindictive, insulting manner by the Crown. Cobham also renewed his accusation and the verdict of death was a foregone conclusion. Raleigh's spirited defense combined with the unfairness of the prosecution won him many sympathizers, and even Queen Anne, wife of King James, intervened on his behalf. The king suspended execution of the sentence. Raleigh was returned to the tower but lived there in style, free to entertain family and friends, carry out scientific experiments, and devote time to writing, including his most famous work *History of the World* (1614).

Raleigh's continual efforts to secure his release bore fruit in 1616, when ministers again shared his strong anti-Spanish opinions and the king became interested in the gold Raleigh claimed he could find in Guiana; he was freed to lead an expedition. The voyage ended in disastrous conflict with Spanish forces in which Raleigh's son was killed. He returned to England dejected, and stoically laid his fate in the hands of an unsympathetic King James. This time he was not allowed to defend himself in public. Good relations with Spain were again a high priority and Raleigh was an embarrassment. In 1618 he was beheaded in the Tower of London. To the very last he behaved with dignity: refusing a blindfold, he said to the executioner, "Think you I fear the shadow of the axe when I don't fear the axe itself?"

S. J. Greenblatt, *Sir Walter Raleigh*, 1973.
R. Lacy, *Sir Walter Raleigh*, 1974.
A. S. Stein, *The House of Death*, 1987.

RAMSES II (the Great; died 1237 B.C.E.), Egyptian pharaoh. Third king of the nineteenth dynasty of Egypt, Ramses reigned from 1304 to 1237 B.C.E. His wide-ranging military exploits brought Egypt to the height of its imperial power, and his battles were made known throughout the empire, inscribed on the walls of the numerous temples he built. This military prowess, together with his massive building projects and the prosperity that accompanied his reign, made him a legendary figure and a model for Egyptian kings who followed. It is thought by scholars that Ramses was ruler of Egypt during the end of the enslavement of the Jews and their exodus.

Ramses II's grandfather, Ramses I, was the first of his family to rule Egypt, having ascended to the throne after being the previous king's general and vizier, while his father, Seti I, ruled from 1318 to 1304 B.C.E., struggling for dominance in the region against the Hittites, who had become the most powerful nation in Asia; he also fended off a threat from the Libyans and reasserted control over the rebellious territories of Palestine and Syria. When his son, the future Ramses II, was still very young, Seti I made him crown prince, and at the age of ten he became coregent with all the accouterments of royalty, including a palace and a harem. His military rank of captain was largely symbolic at this time, perhaps an attempt to ensure his accession to the throne over an older brother whose presence is blotted from the records.The young prince, nevertheless, did accompany his father during his military exploits, and by the time he assumed power he was an experienced soldier and commander.

Ramses's dwelling place, called Per-Ramesse and located in the eastern delta, was actually a new city which became famous for its magnificence. Ramses incorporated into the four quarters of his new domicile the recently arrived gods of Asia: the north was presided over by Buto, the royal cobra goddess, the south by Seth, Amon was located in the west, and Astarte, the Syrian goddess, ruled in the east. The incorporation into Egypt of such Asian gods was a common practice at this time, and Ramses's behavior attests to his participation in local beliefs.

The period of Ramses II's rule was marked by vast changes in the Mediterranean world: new peoples of the region, notably the Greeks and later the Romans, were slowly establishing themselves as powers. Thus Ramses, in the first years of his reign, had to battle to drive off invaders from the sea, a Mediterranean people known as the Sherden. In the fourth year of his reign, he began a series of ambitious military campaigns designed to reassert Egyptian hegemony over Asia. He drove his troops through Palestine and Lebanon, subduing Syria and establishing a base for an attack against the Hittite nation at their fortress city of Kadesh. One year later he mounted the attack, splitting his army and sending a small force to take the seaport of Simyra. Before they could attack Kadesh, Ramses's forces were ambushed by the Hittites and all but a small royal guard fled. If not for the timely appearance of the second force marching to rejoin the main army, Ramses's forces would probably have been wiped out. As it was, the narrow escape from the Hittite ambush was the extent of Ramses's success. Although Ramses's own temple inscriptions publicized the pharaoh's personal courage in a "heroic victory," Hittite accounts reveal that he was defeated in the battle and retreated to Damascus.

This failure to take Kadesh lessened fear of Egypt among its client states to the north, and as a result Ramses was forced, once again, to put down rebellions in Palestine and Syria. In the sixth or seventh year of his reign, he reconquered Palestine and three years later he won victories over the Hittites, capturing Katna and Tunip. He found he could not control these regions against Hittite aggression from a distance and after sixteen years of war, a treaty with Egypt's foremost competitor was made in 1283 B.C.E., recorded in hieroglyphic and cuneiform. The treaty called for each side to respect the other's holdings in Palestine and Syria, with Egypt claiming Phoenicia for itself. Both nations also entered a defensive agreement in the event that a third nation attack these regions. The two powers were further united when Ramses married the Hittite king's eldest daughter, and possibly a second daughter as well.

Ramses also warred against the smaller kingdoms of Edom, Moab, and Negeb as well as defending the Nile delta from the attacks of the Libyans. Although his military ability has sometimes been questioned, the prosperity of his kingdom and his popularity among his people despite the frequency with which he waged war suggests that he must have been a force to reckon with.

In addition to his military exploits, Ramses left his mark with a vast number of monuments and temples. His most famous legacies are the two temples carved in the sandstone cliffs at Abu Simbel. The enormous statues of the pharaoh overlooking the Nile were moved to higher ground when the Aswan dam was built during the 1960s. Another extant monument, the Great Hypostyle Hall at Karnak, was attributed to Ramses, but it is possible he only adorned it with his own inscriptions and reliefs.

Of Ramses's many wives, his most beloved appears to have been Nefretari, his first queen, to whom he dedicated one of the temples at Abu Simbel. In addition to his many wives, the pharaoh had a harem, and all told more than one hundred sons were born to him, who themselves constituted a special class within Egyptian society. Ramses lived his life in opulence and ease, king of the greatest power of the ancient world. When he died his twelve oldest sons were already dead and he was succeeded by

Mer-ne-Ptah, his thirteenth son. The well-preserved mummy of Ramses II, in a mausoleum in Cairo, confirms hat he died as an old man.

Sir A. H. Gardiner, *Egypt of the Pharaohs*, 1961.
J. D. Schmidt, *Ramses II*, 1973.

RAPHAEL (Raphael Sanzio; 1483–1520), Italian painter whose work exemplifies the Renaissance interpretation of the classical ideal of perfect beauty. He was an inspired borrower who absorbed the best of the art of his time and renewed and perfected the forms, compositional devices, and motifs of antiquity. His style is characterized by an idealized representation of nature and a sweet and graceful manner by which he sought to capture the high ideals of humanism combined with a representation of the Divine. The renowned historian Giorgio Vasari held him in great esteem and his interpretation of Raphael's work formed the basis of much later study.

Raphael was born in Urbino, son of a poet-painter, and trained in the style of Perugino. In 1504 he went to Florence, then the center of the Italian Renaissance. The fevered tone of the Florentine style exemplified by Botticelli and Pollaiuolo contrasted sharply with the calm, disciplined style Raphael had developed. He was, however, always eager to emulate other artists' work in order to enhance his own style. He mastered the Florentines' drawing style and adapted their robust sculptural forms so well that his paintings eventually became the yardstick for fine draftsmanship. He worked on commissions all over central Italy, developing techniques of naturalism, perspective, color, and composition. Fra Bartolomeo, whose sweet, simple style was closely influenced by Leonardo *da Vinci, was a formative influence on Raphael, as was Leonardo himself, whose Battle Cartoons prompted him to enliven his technique.

Donato Bramante, the leading architect of the Renaissance, was a townsman of Raphael's, and it is likely that it was he who suggested to him to leave for Rome, which had become the new center of Renaissance art. Raphael arrived there in 1508 and studied the numerous remains of antiquity and the works of masters such as *Michelangelo. He was criticized for emulating Michelangelo's style too closely: the latter even commented that "all he knows he learnt from me."

In Rome, Raphael's career and reputation soared. He received numerous commissions for portraits, easel pictures, religious and secular decorations, and tapestry cartoons. He was also commissioned to list and conserve the antique remains of Rome and was chosen by Pope Leo XI to succeed Bramante as architect of Saint Peter's.

A humane and charming person who exhibited the manners of a gentleman, Raphael was famous for his enthusiastic appreciation of women (Vasari ironically attributed his early death to this passion). His major commission (from Pope Julius II) and the culmination of his work came in 1509, when he decorated three rooms of the new papal apartments in the Vatican — the Stanze. The frescoes of the middle room, Stanza della Segnatura (1509–1511), explore the theme of divinely inspired intellect as represented by theology, philosophy, poetry, and law. In the second room, Stanza dell'Eliodoro (1511), Raphael's depiction of scenes from the New Testament was strongly influenced by Michelangelo's Sistine Chapel ceiling, the first part of which was completed in 1510.

After the Stanze, Raphael worked on architectural designs as well as painting. He received commissions for palaces in Rome and designed a villa for Cardinal Giulio de Medici. Throughout his career Raphael experimented with the theme of the Madonna and Child. While working on the Stanze he painted his most celebrated study of this theme, the *Sistine Madonna* (1513).

Raphael's last work, a study of the heads of apostles for the Transfiguration, was exhibited unfinished over the bier at his funeral; he was buried in the Pantheon. Despite the brevity of his career, his ability was universally admired and his work became the model for beauty and idyllic charm.

B. F. Davidson, *Raphael's Bible*, 1985.
L. Dussler, *Raphael*, 1971.
A. P. Oppe, *Raphael*,1970.
C. Pedretti, *Raphael: His Life and Work in the Splendors of the Italian Renaissance*, 1989.
J. Pope-Hennessy, *Raphael*, 1970.

Grigory Rasputin

RASPUTIN (1872–1916), Russian monk, mystic and charlatan. Grigory Yefimovich Novykh was born to a farmer in the Siberian town of Pokrovskoye. He received the name Rasputin, Russian for "debaucher," only later in life, as a result of his reputation among the Russian aristocracy. A coarse, uneducated peasant who earned a reputation for licentiousness, he was also suspected of being a horse thief. In 1895 he married and had four children.

While in his twenties, Rasputin underwent a religious conversion, following which he proclaimed himself a *starets*, or holy man. He became an ascetic and lived off charity. Rasputin joined the Khyltsy, or Flagellants, a Russian sectarian group that emphasized the importance of penitence. He often visited the Abalaksky Monastery, which housed many sectarian exiles, and was apparently attracted by many of their mystic teachings. It is supposed that there the seeds were planted for his own belief that one must sin in order to gain forgiveness. He had a strange building without windows, supposedly a bath-house, built on his property in which mysterious gatherings took place, often throughout the night. It is suspected that these consisted of strange religious rituals which included erotic dances and orgies.

After several years as a *starets* in his own province, Rasputin set out on a pilgrimage across Russia to the monastery of Mount Athos in Greece and then to the Holy Land. Although he was practically illiterate, Rasputin spent much time poring over obscure mystical tomes in the libraries he encountered. Without understanding the texts, he managed to memorize miscellaneous arcane passages which he later used as spells and incantations.

Rasputin arrived in Saint Petersburg in December 1904, where he rapidly gained a reputation as a mystic and healer. It was whispered that he had predicted a drought in a remote region of Russia and had successfully healed Grand Duke Nikolai's pet dog. He came to the attention of Bishop Hermogen and to the priest, Feofan, confessor to the Empress Alexandra. Feofan introduced Rasputin to the imperial family, to whom he became a close friend and confidant. Rasputin was taken to Czar *Nicholas's young son and heir Alexei, a sickly hemophiliac whom even the slightest bump would cause severe pain and swellings. Having won the boy's confidence by gently stroking him and telling him Siberian fairy tales, Rasputin proceded to hypnotize Alexei, bringing about a remission of the swellings. With tears in her eyes, the empress kissed the monk's hand and declared her eternal indebtedness to him.

Alexandra grew to love Rasputin, regarding him as a symbol of the mystic union between the peasants and the aristocracy. The czar also came to revere him, and even combed his hair with

Rasputin's comb before attending government meetings, claiming that it gave him the strength and courage he needed in face of the growing criticism of his regime.

In 1905, during the Russo-Japanese War, Rasputin was appointed lampkeeper in charge of the candles placed before the icons in the royal palace. This position gave him constant access to the royal family and his power increased accordingly.

Rasputin was unruly, filthy, and often drunk. He used foul language to offend and humiliate members of the nobility but because of the protection he received from the royal family, he was immune to any attacks on his character. Often, lower-ranking aristocrats would bribe Rasputin to wield his influence at court and obtain favors for them. To his benefit, it must be said that much of the money found its way to the poor and needy; Rasputin was far more interested in sex and both men and women found that granting him their sexual favors was to their benefit. His house was constantly filled with sexual supplicants who believed that physical contact with the monk would assure them of spiritual purification and he invited them to his bedroom, which he called "the holy of holies." Others complied with his enormous lust to better their positions at court. In one instance, the wife of a low-ranking provincial official came to Rasputin begging him to use his influence at court to obtain a promotion for her husband. The monk replied, "Come to me in a low-necked dress with no shoulders. And don't you dare come to me otherwise." Rasputin's wife shrugged off her husband's infidelities with the comment, "He has enough for all."

Rasputin's lecherous reputation cost him the respect of the church and senior government officials and every attempt was made to degrade Rasputin before the royal family. Feofan, who had brought the monk to the attention of the royal family, was removed from his post. Rasputin's former patron, Bishop Hermogen, attempted to have him anathematized, but suffered a similar fate. Prime Minister Stolypin was actually successful in forcing Rasputin to flee the capital but the monk rejoined the royal family in their palace in Kiev. Empress Alexandra was unwilling to forego the services of her loyal monk and confidant.

Because he was perceived as being a leading cause of the decline of the monarchy's popularity, an assassination attempt was made on Rasputin in 1913. A conspiracy of leading Russian nobles and clergymen was formed; they sent a deranged prostitute to ask Rasputin for charity. As he proceeded to give her alms, she plunged a knife in his chest, shouting, "I have killed the anti-Christ." Rasputin survived the attack but lay ill for many months. He later claimed his convalescence as the reason he was unable to dissuade Czar Nicholas from entering World War I. Rasputin had always promoted peace between Russia and her neighbors and had earlier convinced Nicholas not to enter the Balkan War.

> - Only through me can you be saved, and the manner of your salvation is this – you must be united with me in soul and body. The virtue that goes out from me is the source of light, the destruction of sin.
> - If I die, the Czar will soon lose his crown.
>
> **Rasputin**
>
> - If there had been no Rasputin, there would have been no Lenin.
>
> **Alexander Karensky**

In 1915, in the midst of World War I, Czar Nicholas appointed himself commander of the Imperial armies and left the capital to be with his troops in the field. Rasputin remained with Alexandra in the palace and became, in effect, ruler of Russia. He replaced many government officials with his own supporters and subverted the traditional authority of the country. Rasputin even went so far as to undermine the czar in military matters, using Alexandra to coax Nicholas into accepting Rasputin's positions. Certain letters, stolen from Rasputin's desk, even intimated a love affair between the monk and the empress.

By 1916 the whole of Russia was in an uproar over the power wielded by the uncouth monk. Three nobles, led by the czar's nephew, Grand Duke Dimitri Pavlovich, plotted to assassinate Rasputin; Prince Felix Yusupov invited Rasputin to a midnight party at his castle. Having been forewarned of an attempt on his life, the monk consumed large quantities of wine and cake laced with potassium cyanide to give himself total immunity. The conspirators, amazed at the monk's inhuman tolerance of the poison, shot and stabbed Rasputin and threw his still-breathing body into the Neva River. It was found under an ice floe two days later.

Some time after Rasputin's death his daughter Maria, in her biography of her father, denied the charges leveled against him. She made the unfounded claim that Rasputin, in fact a saintly man, was replaced by an imposter who created the roguish image of Rasputin as part of a foreign plot to destabilize Russia.

J. T. Fuhrmann, *Rasputin*, 1990.
M. Paleologue, *Rasputin*, 1990.

REMBRANDT (Rembrandt Harmensz Van Rijn; 1606–1669), Dutch painter and etcher. Rembrandt was born in Leiden to a wealthy miller, the family's name, Van Rijn, being derived from the proximity of their home to the Rijnmill malt mill. As a child he studied at the Leiden Latin School but as an adolescent was only briefly enrolled at the university as his parents soon realized that his painting skills

Rembrandt, a self-portrait

were worthy of greater attention. At the age of fifteen he was allowed to enter the workshop of the architectural painter, Jacob Issacz van Swanenburgh, with whom he served a three-year apprenticeship, which gave him only an elementary technical training, but the next six months spent with the painter Pieter Lastman were more beneficial and kindled in him an ambition to paint historical and biblical subjects. He also did numerous portraits of members of his family, and, somewhat unusually, often chose old people as models for his portraits.

In 1631 a desire for wider opportunities took him to Amsterdam, where he moved in with the dealer and painter, Hendrik van Uylenburgh, and began to establish a reputation as a portrait painter. His first large-scale group portrait, the famous *The Anatomy Lesson of Dr. Tulp*, which now hangs in the Mauritshuis in The Hague, was painted at the age of twenty-six, and proved his ability to surpass all his contemporaries in Amsterdam in the dramatic vividness of his work. His fame increased steadily, climaxing at the end of the decade. Marriage to Saskia van Uylenburgh also served to improve his standing as he came into a substantial sum of money that helped him extend his contacts in the city. He greatly enjoyed his wealth and prestige and was apt to indulge his extravagant taste, impulsively collecting objects of art and curiosities. His wife, whom he adored, and whom he represented, sometimes somewhat raucously, in his paintings, seems to have encouraged his tendency to ostentatiousness.

In 1639 Rembrandt purchased a large house (now a museum of his etchings) that strained his financial resources to the limit and contributed to his eventual financial collapse. His personal life also took a turn for the worse. He painted many inhabitants of

the Jewish ghetto, some of them incorporated into his biblical pictures. His mother died in 1640 and Saskia in 1642, just after the birth of their only surviving child, Titus. Rather than deterring his career, however, adversity seems to have purified and refined his outlook and infused his works with a heightened sensitivity to humanity, which was reflected in a move from baroque theatricality to more natural simplicity in his work. Titus, to whom he was devoted, appeared in many of the biblical paintings, while a frequent model for his perception of womanhood became Hendrickje Stoffles who entered his home as a servant but remained with him as his companion for the rest of his life.

His financial situation deteriorated and in 1656 he transferred his house to Titus and pleaded insolvency. The liquidation of his property and the sale of his paintings at prices below their value did not relieve the strain. Titus and Hendrickje came to the rescue with a business relationship whereby they made Rembrandt their employee and themselves sold his works of art, allowing him to avoid the creditors while earning something from his own work.

Hendrickje did much to create a positive atmosphere in their home, but his previous wife's will, which stipulated termination of the small income from her estate if he remarried, prevented them from legalizing their union. Her death in 1663 was a further blow to him, and although Titus continued to care for him and manage the business, he too died several months after his own marriage, leaving Rembrandt alone with the young daughter he had fathered with Hendrickje. He was buried in an unknown rented grave.

Rembrandt was a temperamental man and a nonconformist who preferred the society of the common people to mingling with aristocrats and intellectuals. Unlike other painters of his generation who yearned for Italy, he preferred to remain close to home and fully explore his immediate surroundings. Considered the outstanding painter of the Dutch school, and one of the greatest of all time, he is famous for his treatment of light and shade, his portraits, particularly of the aged, and a gift for rendering common objects, ordinarily seen as ugly, with beauty. He is also admired for his etchings. His earliest pictures, *Saint Paul in Orison* and *Saint Jerome* were painted in Leiden, but most of his work was done in Amsterdam after he settled there in 1631. His most famous works include *Presentation in the Temple, Anatomy Lesson, The Night Watch, Woman Taken in Adultery* and *The Good Samaritan* as well as self-portraits.

C. Brown et al, *Rembrandt: The Master and his Workshop*, 1991.

J. Rosenberg, *Rembrandt: Life and Work*, 1968.

G. Schwarz, *Rembrandt: His Life, His Paintings*, 1985.

RHODES, CECIL JOHN (1853–1902), South African statesman and financier. He was the fifth son of the vicar of Bishop's Stortford in England.

SAYINGS OF CECIL RHODES

- How could I dislike a sex to which your majesty belongs? (on being accused by Queen Victoria of hating women).
- They can't hang me! I am a Privy Councillor! There are only 200 of us in the British Empire (on the Jameson raid).
- These are the things that make life worthwhile (after putting down a Matabele rebellion).
- To be useful to my country (when asked his creed).

Unlike his brothers, he did not attend public school because he suffered from poor health. Instead, he went to the local grammar school. His health also prevented his going into the army or becoming a barrister or a clergyman, all careers that he had considered.

At the age of seventeen he followed his brother Herbert to Natal in South Africa and went to work on a cotton farm. In 1871 Rhodes moved to the diamond mines and harsh conditions of Kimberley. Still dogged by poor health, he soon returned to England. Between 1873 and 1881 he traveled between Kimberley and Oxford, from where he finally graduated in the classics. He then wrote the first of his seven wills, leaving the fortune he did not yet possess for the founding of a secret society aimed at extending British rule "throughout the world." He dreamed of "painting the map red" and of building a railroad from the Cape to Cairo.

After returning to Kimberley, he began to amalgamate first the operations of individuals, then of syndicates, continually extending his control, until by 1891 he had gained a virtual monopoly of production and marketing through his De Beers Consolidated Mines company, controlling 90 percent of the world's diamond production. In 1887 Rhodes also founded Consolidated Gold Fields, one of the most powerful goldmining corporations on the Witwatersrand.

He was more interested in power than in money. He envisioned a world led by Great Britain, Germany, and the United States. He now had the wherewithal to promote his dreams of the expansion of the British Empire from its base in the Cape Colony.

Rhodes entered Cape politics and became the prime minister of Cape Colony in 1881. In 1884, after being pushed aside by General Charles *Warren in Bechuanaland, he resolved that northward expansion beyond the Limpopo River would be carried out under the colonial, not the British, government, a policy of expansion and autonomy termed "colonialism." Further to this, he developed a friendship with Jan Hofmeyr, the head of the Afrikaaner Bond. They agreed on the necessity of keeping the British government out of South Africa's internal affairs and saw the future as dependent upon the cooperation of the Boers and the British, with the African tribesmen excluded from the political system. Their aim was to unite South Africa and have British imperial cooperation for trade and defense. However, they had not taken into account the determination of the Transvaal and the Orange Free State to remain independent. Led by President Paul *Kruger, who held that "Africa was for the Afrikaaners," the South African Republic was equally interested in territorial expansion and commercial autonomy. Rhodes found that Kruger was one man he could never buy off.

Rhodes failed in his bid to have the Cape Colony annex Bechuanaland, the route to the northern territories of Mashonaland and Ndebeleland (which became Rhodesia), but he cleverly managed to obtain an exclusive treaty of friendship with King Lobengula, ruler of the Ndebele. He had John Moffat, a missionary, one of the few people the king trusted, sent to do this work, and Charles Rudd also obtained an exclusive concession on Rhodes's behalf over metals and minerals. Rhodes then obtained a royal charter of incorporation for his British South Africa Company that gave it the authority to make treaties, mine resources, and maintain a police force. In 1890 the company's pioneers occupied Mashonaland, and as a gesture to Britain's prime minister, who did not trust Rhodes, the latter had a newly established fort, Salisbury, named after him. The "scramble for Africa" was in full swing as Rhodes tried unsuccessfully to claim Katanga in the Congo in 1890, but the Belgians preempted him. In 1893 he sent his medical adviser and longtime personal friend, Dr. Leander Starr Jameson, to put down a serious Ndebele uprising. This led to the crushing of the Ndebele and the death of Lobengula.

Although Rhodes met with Kruger in 1890, he could not persuade him to agree to a railway and customs union. The Transvaal steadily grew in political strength after the discovery of gold in Witwatersrand. In 1895 Rhodes decided to put a stop to the Transvaal's autonomous growth, which threatened his plans for a British South African dominion. An ingenious coup was plotted in which the Uitlanders (foreigners who had come to work in the gold mines and had no political rights) were to stage a revolt intended to cause the British government to intercede and force a settlement. Rhodes managed to get colonial secretary Joseph Chamberlain's backing and had his company, Consolidated Gold Fields, foot the bill. Although the Uitlanders decided not to go through with the plan as it had no real support, Jameson impetuously led an attack in the Transvaal from Bechuanaland in 1895, and his forces were routed. Rhodes accepted responsibility for the disastrous Jameson raid and resigned his post as prime minister of Cape Colony, although he was able to keep his parliamentary seat and hold on to the British South Africa Company by blackmailing Chamberlain with threats to publish letters showing his role in the raid. The raid also served to deepen the split between the Dutch and the British colonials, as Kruger consolidated his position.

Even in the last years of his life, Rhodes was not out of the news, as a rare liaison with an adventuress, Princess Radziwill, ended in a court case in which she was charged with forging letters and bills of exchange in his name. Rhodes died before the end of the trial and was buried in the Matopo Hills in Rhodesia (now Zambia/Zimbabwe). His will included the generous scheme of scholarships at Oxford (the Rhodes scholarships) for young men from the colonies, the United States, and Germany.

S. Cloete, *Against These Three*, 1979.

J. S. Galbraith, *Crown and Charter*, 1974.

J. G. Lockhart and C.M. Woodhouse, *Rhodes*, 1963.

R. I. Rotberg, *The Founder*, 1988.

RICARDO, DAVID (1772–1823), English economist. The most influential of the classical economists of the early nineteenth century and an important advocate of the principle of free trade, David Ricardo was born the son of a rich Dutch Jew who had settled in London. He entered his father's business in the stock exchange at an early age and showed immediate aptitude for the work. However, when he converted to Unitarianism and married a Quaker at the age of twenty-one, his father disinherited him and he was forced to make his own way. Remaining on the stock exchange, he quickly attracted the attention of a major banking house and within a few years had made his fortune.

Ricardo's interest in theoretical economics was prompted by Adam *Smith's *The Wealth of Nations*, which he read in 1799. Over the next ten years he was to pursue the study of economics with increasing seriousness, and in 1810 he published *The High Price of Bullion, a Proof of the Depreciation of Bank Notes* in response to the inflationary credit policies that the Bank of England adopted when, as a result of the bullion shortage, it was forbidden from paying its notes in gold. Ricardo's assertion that arbitrary increases in the money supply pushed up prices and influenced exchange rates, thus leading to a net outflow of gold, was confirmed by the Bullion Committee and led to the repeal of the Bank Restriction Act.

Four years later Ricardo was able to retire on the wealth he had accumulated through his business activities and moved to his substantial land holdings in Gloucestershire. Here he was able to pursue his varied interests in literature and science; he was a good mathematician and an accomplished chemist and geologist. He also maintained contact with a number of the other influential intellectual figures of his age, the pioneers of the ascendant radical movement in British philosophy and politics; James Mill (father of John Stuart *Mill) became his political and editorial counselor, while he had mutually fruitful contacts with both the eminent philosopher and jurist Jeremy *Bentham and the clergyman and economist, Thomas *Malthus (to whose controversial population theory he subscribed).

Ricardo's involvement in shaping the economic awareness of his age deepened with his 1815 *Essay on the Influence of a Low Price of Corn on the Profits of Stock*, which argued that increasing the tariff on imported wheat to compensate for a reduction in domestic wheat prices was counterproductive: it served only to increase the rent revenues of the landed gentry while squeezing manufacturers' profits. His antipathy to the landowning class, which he came to see as parasitic (despite his own ownership of land), is implicit both in this and his subsequent economic writings.

Ricardo's classic *Principles of Political Economy and Taxation*, published in 1817, has been credited with the invention of the labor theory of value adopted by Karl *Marx. Examining the distribution of social product between workers, owners, and landlords, Ricardo concluded that the exchange value of a commodity is entirely due to the labor expended in producing it; from here it was but a short step to the assertion that labor was therefore due all the reward and that the share obtained by landowner and capitalist must be simple extortion, the view subsequently supported by the socialist movement. He was also instrumental in expounding the principle of comparative advantage — which demonstrates that trade between nations can be beneficial to all parties, even if one of them is absolutely more efficient in producing all tradeable goods, as long as relative opportunity costs of production vary from country to country — which constituted an important theoretical statement of the necessity of international trade as an engine of growth. Such was his prestige as an economist that Ricardo's promulgation of free trade ideas was accepted with respect, despite the novelty of such notions at that time. He gained a new platform for these pronouncements when he entered the House of Commons in 1819. The first systematizer of economics, illness prevented him from further developing his theories; he died at the age of 51, his seminal writings having spanned little more than a decade.

G. A. Caravale, *Ricardo and the Theory of Value Distribution and Growth*, 1980.

M. Morishima, *Ricardo's Economics*, 1989.

J. C. Wood, ed., *Ricardo: A Critical Assessment*, 1985.

RICHARD I (known as Richard the Lion-Hearted; 1157–1199), king of England from 1189. The third son of Henry II and Eleanor of Aquitaine, he was born in Oxford. While still a child, he was granted the dukedom of Aquitaine, land Henry II had acquired on marriage. Richard ruled over his lands with a severity that brought him respect yet also aroused the resentment of the powerful barons he subjugated.

In 1173 Richard joined in a rebellion against his father instigated by his mother and elder brother, Henry. Richard supposedly said of his family origins: "We came from the Devil, and to the Devil we

- When one has a good reserve, one does not fear one's enemies.
- Friends have I many, but their gifts are slight;

- Shame to them if unransomed I, poor wight, Two winters languish here.

Poem written by Richard I in captivity

OPINIONS ABOUT RICHARD

- Richard's courage, shrewdness, energy and patience made him the most remarkable ruler of his times.

The Muslim historian Ibn al-Athir, on Richard's death

- If heroism be confined to brutal and ferocious valor, Richard will stand high among the heroes of the age.

Edward Gibbon

- A bad son, a bad husband, and a bad king, but a gallant and splendid soldier.

Steven Runciman

will return." Not long after peace was restored with his father, Richard was fighting his brother Henry. Denied any estate of his own, Henry was envious of his brothers and when the barons of Aquitaine rebelled against Richard's harsh rule, he supported them. Henry died suddenly and the rebellion ended, leaving Richard with the claim to his father's kingdom.

Henry II refused to concede the power Richard believed he had the right to demand and when they met in 1188, with King Philip Augustus of France, Henry II declined to recognize Richard as the rightful heir. Richard then switched allegiance to his father's enemy, the king of France, and during the war that followed, Henry died in 1189 and Richard became king of England and Normandy. His coronation was marred by a massacre of Jews who wished to attend the ceremony, and the violence spread to York. Richard took steps to stop the attacks, for the Jews were a valuable source of funds and regarded as the king's private property.

Richard was tall and well proportioned, with blond hair and blue eyes. He proved himself a fearless soldier and possessed a keen understanding of issues and a gift of conversation. At the same time he was arrogant, devoid of compassion, and sunk in a debauched lifestyle sharply in contrast with the heroic image of "Lion heart." He was as tyrannical to his own family as he was rapacious to his sub-

jects. His marriage to Berengaria of Navarre in 1191 was assuaged solely for its political expediency, for Richard was a homosexual.

Richard's interest in his new kingdom was largely financial, to obtain the funds he needed for an Anglo-French crusade to capture Jerusalem. Richard made victorious progress eastward, capturing Messina and Cyprus despite continual disputes with his French ally. The day after the capture of Acre in 1191, the two kings again quarreled as the French ruler, King Philip, accused Richard of trying to keep Cyprus for himself despite an agreement they had made to share their conquests. Richard replied: "The victory over the infidels in the Holy Land was indeed a joint endeavor but the conquest of Cyprus is no business of yours as I carried it off alone." After they captured Acre, Philip fell ill and returned to France, leaving Richard in charge. He was responsible for the massacre of twenty-seven hundred Muslim survivors of the garrison at Acre by having their throats cut. He moved his army down the coast and defeated *Saladin's armies at the Battle of Arsuf. Richard was then able to enter Jaffa, which he fortified to give himself a strong base on the coast. His reputation was now at its highest and, as a result of his behavior on the battlefield, he was seen as the incarnation of the demon of war. However, by delaying in Jaffa, he gave Saladin the opportunity to reorganize and when he moved on his real goal, Jerusalem, his attacks were beaten off. Richard was only able to see the city from a distance but never entered it.

In 1192 Richard concluded a peace treaty with Saladin whereby the coastal cities were left in the hands of the Christians and the interior of the country remained with the Muslims; pilgrims were permitted to visit the holy sites. Richard set off to return to England. Bad weather forced his boat to call at Corfu. Fearing that he might be taken prisoner by the hostile Byzantines, he disguised himself as a Templar knight and traveled on a pirate boat headed for the north Adriatic. The boat was wrecked and, maintaining his disguise, he journeyed through the territories of his bitter enemy, Leopold, duke of Austria. Resting at an inn near Vienna, he was recognized and led before the duke, who imprisoned him. Three months later he was handed over to another enemy, the emperor *Henry VI. He languished in prison for a year and was only released when his loyal subjects raised the huge ransom demanded after he gave the emperor an oath of vassaldom.

On his return, he found that his lands in England had been exposed to the intrigue of his brother, *John Lackland (the future King John). Richard's return to take over from John forms the background to the Robin Hood legend. Before long, Richard went to France where he spent the rest of his life at war with King Philip, defending his inheritance. A stray arrow shot by an archer during the siege of a castle in Limoges killed him.

J. A. Brundage, *Richard the Lion Heart*, 1974.
J. Gillingham, *Richard the Lion Heart*, 1978.

RICHELIEU, CARDINAL (Armand Jean Du Plessis; 1585–1642), French statesman, chief minister of Louis XIII, and cardinal of the Roman Catholic Church, later known as the "Red Eminence"; son of François de Plessis, seigneur de Richelieu. The family was of feudal origins but had risen in social stature by marriage and royal service. Left fatherless at the age of five with his family in strained economic circumstances, Richelieu was obliged to enter the church and become a bishop in order to keep the benefice of the bishopric of Luçon in the family. In 1607, at the age of twenty-two, he was ordained priest and became bishop of Lucon.

In 1614 he was elected a delegate of the clergy to the Estates General and in 1616 through his alliance with *Marie de Médicis, the queen mother, he was appointed secretary of state for foreign affairs. Richelieu's term of office was completed in 1617 when a palace revolution saw the young Louis XIII taking a more active role in government affairs. Richelieu went into exile until the king and queen mother were reconciled. In 1622 he was made a cardinal in a settlement deal between the king and the queen mother and in 1624 was admitted into the royal council, of which he became the leader.

Once in a position of power he sought to suppress all opposition from the Huguenots at home as well as the Habsburg threat from abroad. To Richelieu the Huguenots represented the greatest threat to internal stability and in 1628 he laid siege to their fortress-port of La Rochelle. Although he deprived them of any military power they had amassed, Richelieu allowed them to continue enjoying the free exercise of their religion. Abroad, France had problems with the Swiss valley of Valtelina and the duchy of Mantua on which Spain had designs. Once La Rochelle was secured, Richelieu led the army into the Swiss Alps in order to halt Spanish expansionism. However, his intervention against Spain angered the Catholics in France and, fueled by her growing jealousy, Marie de Médicis used this opportunity to stage a coup against Richelieu. The coup failed, as Louis XIII supported his chief minister and Marie de Médicis was exiled.

Richelieu's power was now firmly secured, and he concentrated on strengthening France's military position. Unwilling to enter into an open declaration of war on Habsburg power, Richelieu made alliances with the Netherlands and German Protestant states. He subsidized *Gustavus II Adolphus of Sweden against the Holy Roman Empire in the Thirty Years' War and continued to strengthen France's army and navy in preparation for war. In 1635 he signed an alliance with Sweden and shortly afterwards France entered the war. France's involvement resulted in heavy taxation, large loans, and internal rebellion. Although an amateur in economic affairs, Richelieu had great dreams for France and continued encouraging trade and industry, hoping to achieve economic self-sufficiency. He planned new canal systems and promoted companies to trade in the Indies and Canada. However, most of his schemes remained a dream as France struggled to finance its participation in the Thirty Years' War while maintaining domestic stability.

In his last years Richelieu was plagued by constant conspiracies against his life. In 1632 the king's brother Gaston d'Orléans, who had previously sided with Marie de Médicis against Richelieu, invaded with foreign troops and was aided in his mission by Duke Henri de Montmorency, governor of Languedoc. The plot failed and Montmorency was executed shortly afterwards. This did not deter others from attempting to assassinate Richelieu and in 1636 a plot by the king's confessor was discovered. A year later, Richelieu's spies found out about a plot planned by the king's favorite, Henri Cinq-Mars, who had joined with Gaston in a further attempt on Richelieu's life and in 1642, Cinq-Mars was executed.

Richelieu died after years of ill-health caused by abscesses, fits of nervous exhaustion, and a painful urinary tract disorder, and was buried in the chapel of the Sorbonne which he himself had financed.

J. Bergin, *The Rise of Richelieu*, 1991.
J. H. Elliot, *Richelieu and Olivares*, 1984.
R. J. Knecht, *Richelieu*, 1991.
V. L. Tapie, *France in the Age of Louis XIII and Richelieu*, 1984.

RILKE, RAINER MARIA (1875–1926), German poet. Born in Prague, Rainer Maria Rilke's early works included the *Lay of the Cornet*, the *Book of God*, and the *Book of Hours*; he became internationally known for his later works, the *Duino Elegies* and *Sonnets to Orpheus*. Rilke's early education and childhood he described in later years as a "nightmare" and a "distortion"; throughout his life he was possessed by the desire "to do over the unachieved childhood." His parents separated when he was nine. His father had ambitions that he become an officer in the military and sent him to a military academy; the experiences and hardships of those years were never forgotten by the poet. His university studies were both in Prague and in Munich. Before he finished his studies he had written his first book of poems (1894), which already bore the distinctly lyrical, mystical,and intuitive qualities that were to characterize his later verse. In 1896 he left Prague for Munich where at the age of twenty-one he met Lou Andreas-Salomé, who at thirty-six was one of the great emancipated women of her time. The meeting had a profound impact upon the young Rilke. They traveled together, twice to Russia where she became his teacher and guide in the Russian language and in Russian studies. This visit to Russia opened up the significance of pure feeling, the inwardness that transforms the external world, and had a powerful effect upon Rilke's life and upon his work. Their friendship lasted throughout his life. In 1901 Rilke married Clara Westhoff, a sculptor who studied with Auguste *Rodin and was part of an artists' colony in the village of Worpswede near

He who does not consent sometimes to what is terror in his life, with a final, nay jubilant determination, will never possess the infinite birthrights of our existence; he only passes along its edge; before the final judgement he will be found to have been neither alive nor dead. To prove the identity of the terrible and the beatific, these two faces of the same divine head, not this one sole face, which only appears this way or that according to the distance from which, or according to the condition in which we perceive it—this is the sense and essence of my two books.

R. M. Rilke's interpretation of the *Duino Elegies* and *Sonnets to Orpheus,* taken from his personal correspondence

Bremen, which Rilke had joined. In 1902 a daughter, Ruth, was born but shortly afterward the couple decided to separate.

In 1902 Rilke was commissioned to write a book on Rodin. In 1905 he became Rodin's secretary; he was dismissed by the sculptor in 1906. The relationship with Rodin also had a transforming influence in Rilke's life. Rodin's influence is especially seen in Rilke's work, *Neue Gedichte*, written between 1905–1908, where the poet explores through images, the sensuality of objects, of things, while revealing their inner spiritual qualities.

Rilke lived his life and wrote his works in various parts of Europe. He always returned to Paris, which became his main home. Each place he visited and every person he met added to his ideas and images. The last years of his life were spent mainly in Switzerland. World War I, in which he served briefly in the Austrian army, had a debilitating and almost paralyzing effect upon Rilke's life and work. In 1922, after not publishing any poetry for thirteen years, Rilke, while staying at a castle in the Rhone valley, at Muzot, was seized with inspiration. Within a few days he completed the *Duino Elegies* (the first two were begun in 1912 during his stay at Duino Castle near Trieste); and then in that same month produced the fifty-five poems that became the *Sonnets to Orpheus*. In a letter to Margot Countess Sizzo in 1923, he wrote the following: "I think I told you that these strange *Sonnets to Orpheus* were not an intended or expected occupation. They arrived quite unexpected, often many in a single day (the first part originated in about three days) of February last year, while I was really concentrating on the continuation of those other poems, the great *Duino Elegies*. I could not but accept simply and obediently the dictation of the inner urge. Except a few poems in the beginning of the second part, all the sonnets have kept the chronological order of their origin."

His verse was often about death, seen as "the other half of life" and to be considered as part of existence. A musical and thoughtful poet, he had a strong influence on subsequent poetry but he himself defined fame as "the sum total of all the misunderstandings that collect around a new name."
W. Leppmann, *Rilke: A Life*, 1984.
D. Prater, *A Ringing Class*, 1986.
Rainer Maria Rilke, *Selected Works*, translated by J. B. Leishman, 1960.

RIMBAUD, ARTHUR (1854–1891), French poet; a precursor of the Symbolist movement. He was born in Charleville in northern France and evinced literary talents as early as age seven. He left school before he was sixteen and ran away to Paris, where he had an experience (the nature of which is unclear) which caused him distress, psychological turmoil, and led to his experiencing a disgust with life. Returning to Charleville, he lived an unruly life, breaking away from all conventions and restrictions. At the same time, he was furiously writing poetry, which he no longer saw as an end in itself but as a means of exploring the beyond. He studied the occult, kabbalah, and alchemy, convinced that the poet must become a seer whose mind can penetrate infinity, beyond the veil of reality. His poetic doctrine, which he developed in a few weeks when he was sixteen, held that poetry is a state of mind and soul in which all will find their own language, and his use of trivial, scientific, and even obscene words was to prove influential in all twentieth century poetry. He was only seventeen when he wrote one of his greatest poems, *Le Bateau Ivre*.

Moving to Paris, he was welcomed by Paul Verlaine, then the outstanding French poet. The two men formed a fateful (and probably homosexual) relationship. Rimbaud lived a life of complete depravity, and was filthy (never changing his clothes), permanently intoxicated by absinthe, and thoroughly obnoxious — not least because of his arrogance and superiority complex. Meanwhile, Rimbaud continued to write verse; his best-known work, *Les Illuminations*, was written between 1872 and 1875, although published much later.

Rimbaud persuaded Verlaine to leave Paris with him and they went to London, where they lived a life of debauchery. By 1873 things were going badly between them and Verlaine went to Brussels, soon asking Rimbaud to join him. While intoxicated, Verlaine bought a revolver, and when Rimbaud announced that he was returning to Paris, shot at him from three yards: two bullets missed, the third lodged in Rimbaud's arm. After Rimbaud returned from hospital, Verlaine again threatened him, and, when Rimbaud called to a policeman for help, Verlaine was arrested and sentenced to two years' imprisonment.

Rimbaud now returned to his family in Charleville and finished another major work, *Une Saison en Enfer*. It was now that his life changed completely and he sought to break with his past. At the age of twenty-one he abandoned poetry and burned all his manuscripts. He spent five years journeying around Europe. When Verlaine was released, he visited Rimbaud in Stuttgart. The meeting ended with a violent quarrel in which Rimbaud hit Verlaine, who was found unconscious the next morning. The two then spent some days together before parting for the last time.

Rimbaud next enlisted in the Dutch army to get to Java. He was attached to an infantry battalion in Batavia but soon deserted. After a brief stint as a construction worker in Cyprus, he found work in Aden in a firm exporting coffee. Sent as the firm's agent to Harar (in Abyssinia, now Ethiopia), he published an article with the French Geographical Society, which brought him some fame as an explorer of the African interior.

When the Mahdi rebellion made the situation in North Africa uncertain, Rimbaud returned to Aden and took a menial position in a store. Having decided to make his fortune by gun-running, he took his savings and spent a year in a dreary village called Tajoura until his arms and camel transport were ready. In 1886 he set out for Ethiopia and after a nightmare journey arrived at the palace of the Emperor *Menelik II. The king needed arms and contracted to buy Rimbaud's stock but in the end, he cheated Rimbaud and robbed him of most of his capital.

Rimbaud returned to Harar, where he directed a trading station, selling chiefly arms and ammunition. He was now an industrious businessman, seeking to raise sufficient capital to give him independence. Scrupulously honest, he lived soberly and chastely, while his public spirit and generosity won him the respect of the African chiefs.

He spent twelve years in the Red Sea area, returning to France in 1891. Having contracted a painful illness of the leg, when he reached Marseilles his leg was amputated. He managed to pay a final visit to Charleville, where he was looked after by his mother and sister. On his death, he was buried there.

Rimbaud's poetic career lasted a mere four or five years in his late adolescence. He was an almost purely intuitive poet, who has deeply influenced twentieth century verse.

C. Chadwick, *Rimbaud*, 1973.
E. Starkie, *Arthur Rimbaud*, 1947.

ROBESPIERRE, MAXIMILIEN MARIE ISIDORE DE

ROBESPIERRE, MAXIMILIEN MARIE ISIDORE DE (1758–1794), French revolutionist and orator. Maximilien Robespierre's mother was the daughter of a brewer and his father, François, was an attorney. His mother bore five children and died when Robespierre was only six. His father abandoned the children soon afterward, and spent the rest of his life wandering around Europe. Robespierre and his siblings were left in Arras to be raised by their maternal grandparents, who educated them and who helped transform Robespierre from a rowdy, careless boy to the head of his family. He

went to a local school until age eleven, and then on a scholarship to the College Louis-le-Grand in Paris, where he presented a loyal address to *Louis XVI. In 1781 the school awarded him a law degree and six hundred livres, and he returned to Arras to practice law. A year later he was appointed one of the five judges on the court with jurisiction over the provinalship of the diocese. Although he resigned the position after a short while in order to avoid sentencing someone to death, he continued to practice law.

Becoming involved in literature and culture, Robespierre became one of the most popular writers of Arras, joined a literary and music society, and proposed reforms, although he wrote, "There is no need for us to change the whole system of our legislation; it is dangerous to look for the remedy for a specific ill in a general revolution." By 1788 his law practice was dwindling and he considered relocating to Paris, but with rumors that there would be the first meeting of the States-General (a national assembly that had not been called since 1614), he decided to seek election. Winning support by primarily dealing with local matters, he was elected, and left for Versailles in 1789.

The deputies encountered several disappointments at Versailles, chief among them the lack of the king's initiative in proposing reforms, which they had eagerly anticipated. Though he was unknown at first, Robespierre's passionate speaking — he made twenty-five speeches by the end of the year — gained him a following. He strongly believed in the philosophy espoused by Jean-Jacques *Rousseau, which maintained that nature had made man good and happy but society had corrupted him. He played no special role in the storming of the Bastille but wrote to a friend: "How pleasant a place the Bastille is now that it is in the hands of the people. I could scarcely tear myself away from this spot whose aspect gives feelings of pleasure and ideas of freedom to all citizens."

Robespierre continued to speak out in the National Assembly, and was soon recognized as one of the leaders of the Left. He had some admirers in the assembly, but most of his support came from the public. When he felt his ideas were not being received well in the Estates-General, he turned to the Society of the Friends of the Constitution, which later came to be known as the Jacobin Club. Jean-Paul *Marat, the popular journalist, called Robespierre "the only deputy who appears aware of the great principles, and perhaps the only true patriot sitting in the Assembly." In the following months, tensions between the different factions in the assembly mounted and the public turned more and more to violent crime while claiming revolutionary motives. After the monarchy was brought down in August 1792, Robespierre was elected to the National Convention, in the midst of massacres of monarchists and moderates. He was accused by the Girondins, a revolutionary group that favored political rather than social democracy, of dictatorship. During the king's trial in December, Robespierre spoke out several times calling for his execution. After the king's execution, however, Robespierre supported a decree indicting the Girondins, which passed in June 1793.

Because the stability of the country was being threatened by movements of federalism from within and by external forces on its borders, Robespierre decided that the best way to be victorious was to unite all the power into "one single will." As the head of the Jacobin Club and of the National Convention, he used his Committee of Public Safety to denounce those with whom he did not agree. and, in effect, instigated the Reign of Terror, executing thousands, including Jacques-René Herbert and Georges-Jacques *Danton and their followers.

Elected president of the National Convention by a vote of 216 to 4 in June 1794, Robespierre asserted to the convention that God exists and tried to rally them around the concept of a civil religion and a "Supreme Being." Once in office, he attempted to reshape the government, ridding it of "enemies of the regime." Opposition to Robespierre grew, and his ministers began to detest him. Frequent lectures and the pressure of his work plagued his health, and he appeared less frequently at the National Convention. He aired his views now only at the Jacobin Club meetings.

In July the opposition sought to have Robespierre, his brother Augustin, and three of his deputies arrested. The prison warden refused to jail them, however, and they were released for a short time, but the National Convention decreed him an outlaw, and though he had some support throughout Paris, he decided not to continue his struggle. He shot himself in the jaw, leaving his loyalists confused. The soldiers of the National Convention then stormed City Hall, where Robespierre and his followers sat, and captured them. On July 28, he was executed in front of a cheering mob at the Place de la Révolution (Concorde), and several of his followers were guillotined as well.

J. F. Bosher, *The French Revolution*, 1988.

N. Hampson, *The Life and Opinions of Maximilien Robespierre*, 1974.

S. Schama, *Citizens; A Chronicle of the French Revolution*, 1989.

ROCKEFELLER, JOHN DAVISON

(1839–1937), U.S. industrialist and philanthropist. He was born in Richford, Tioga County, New York, where his father traded in lumber and salt. At a very early age, Rockefeller showed an aptitude for numbers, displaying an attention to detail, especially where money was concerned. At the age of seven, he had his first successful business venture — selling turkeys. The family then moved to Ohio, and at age sixteen, Rockefeller went to work in Cleveland for a produce firm. In 1859 he formed a partnership with Colonel Maurice Clark to trade produce. When Clark discovered oil, they began trading Pennsylvania oil.

John Davison Rockefeller at sixty

The idea of accruing instant wealth from oil caught their fancy. In 1863, when a new railroad line put Cleveland in a position to compete, refineries sprang into existence. At first, Rockefeller thought refining would be merely a sideline. In 1865, after repeated arguments about expansion, he bought out his partner, Clark, for $12,500. With the purchase of the refinery, Rockefeller began to expand the business and poured his profits, plus borrowed money, into building a second refinery. He decided to open additional markets, and in 1866, put his brother William in charge of another firm in New York as the manager of the Atlantic coast trade and the export of kerosene. The growing popularity of the refining business led Rockefeller to comment: "All sorts of people went into it; the butcher, the baker, and the candlestick maker began to refine oil." His success was a result of his ability to cut costs as well as a ruthlessness in stifling competition.

In 1867 Rockefeller and his new partner Andrews brought Henry Flagler into the business as a third partner. Flagler became a valued colleague and a close friend. In 1870 Rockefeller and a few of his people incorporated the Standard Oil Company (Ohio) and the company prospered. Rockefeller bought out his competitors by using a new method of purchase — he gave stock in his company to acquire other companies. He never owned more than 27 percent of Standard Oil stock, but even so, he became the wealthiest man in the United States with a personal fortune exceeding one billion dollars.

By the early 1880s Standard Oil had bought out or driven out of business most of its competition in

Ohio. The company used its leverage to obtain reduced freight rates. It then bought pipelines, terminals, and began to buy competing refineries in other cities until Standard Oil almost had a monopoly. The company exploited every avenue to increase income and lower expenses. It not only received reduced freight rates but was also getting "drawbacks," collecting a percentage of the freight costs paid by the competition. This practice led to the enactment of anti-monopoly laws, first by the states and then by Congress. The Sherman Anti-Trust Act was passed by Congress in 1890, and the law was upheld in the Ohio Supreme Court in 1892.

Rockefeller was able to work around the law for a while by eliminating the Standard Oil "Trust" and renaming the company Standard Oil Company of New Jersey. The new company was the largest and most efficient producer of petroleum products. Standard Oil of New Jersey operated throughout the world, until 1911, when the Supreme Court ruled that the company was in violation of the Sherman Anti-Trust Act.

Rockefeller was a generous philanthropist. As a pious Baptist he began by making relatively small contributions to the Baptist church. In 1892 he was instrumental in founding the University of Chicago. It was suggested that Rockefeller gave his spare change to the university — amounting to thirty-five million dollars. From 1897 he devoted himself exclusively to philanthropy, joined by his son, John (1894–1960). They created the Rockefeller Institute for Medical Research, later renamed Rockefeller University. In his lifetime, John D. Rockefeller contributed over half a billion dollars to charity.

In his later years, Rockefeller was well known for his habit of carrying a pocketful of shiny new dimes that he would give to the small children he met in his travels. Despite his great wealth, he was frugal with regard to personal expenses. He would wear suits until they became shiny. When he died aged ninety-eight, he was worth twenty-six million dollars, including a single share in Standard Oil worth $43.94.

D. F. Hawks, *John D*, 1980.
D. Yergin, *The Prize*, 1991.

RODIN, AUGUSTE (1840–1917), French sculptor. His father, Jean Baptiste Rodin, was a poorly paid clerk and an upright family man. Auguste Rodin had two older sisters, Clotilde from his father's first marriage who transgressed in some unknown way and was never mentioned after a certain point, and Marie, two years his elder, to whom he was devoted.

Rodin was a poor student and at the age of nine was sent to a boarding school he described as akin to prison. There he spent most of his time drawing and was sent back home at thirteen, barely having learned to read and write. It was at this age that he discovered his passion. He wrote "I saw clay for the first time and I felt as if I were ascending into heaven." His father agreed to let him pursue sculpting as a profession and arranged an interview for

him with a master who recognized the boy's talent and recommended he try to gain admittance to the state art school. While his talents were apparent his style was too daringly naturalistic and not quite classical enough for the art establishment. He was rejected by the academy on three occasions.

Confident of his own abilities, Rodin continued sculpting and did whatever was necessary to support himself while at the same time attempting to continue his education on his own.

At the age of twenty Rodin faced a personal crisis. His sister Marie fell in love with a friend of his who paid her little attention and eventually announced his engagement to another woman. Marie teetered on the verge of insanity. She joined a nunnery for a short time and then underwent an unsuccessful operation and died. Rodin was heartbroken. He too attempted to escape by joining a monastery, but his basic unsuitability for such a life became apparent and he left before the end of two years.

Soon after he met Rose Beuret, who was to become his lifelong companion and who bore him an illegitimate son. A journey to Italy proved a turning point and his encounter with classical and baroque art brought a greater realism. He himself stated, "*Michelangelo freed me from academicism."

He worked for several years in Brussels with a partner and created the statue that brought him recognition. This statue, called *The Bronze Age*, depicted a Belgian soldier, so lifelike and human that the artist had to prove he had sculpted from a model rather than a mold. The sculpture is now in the Luxembourg Gardens in Paris.

Rodin's first big commission (1880) The Gates of Hell, was an all-consuming project that allowed him to unleash his imagination as never before. He worked quite prolifically at this period, turning out, among other works, his famed bust of poet Victor *Hugo, and the Burghers of Calais, whose creation took so long that by the time it was completed the mayor of Calais could no longer afford to pay him.

By the 1880s his work was in great demand and buyers were willing to pay him high prices. His personal life became more involved as well, as he began a stormy and finally tragic relationship with a talented young sculptress named Camille Claudel. Around this period he began work on what is arguably his greatest piece, the brooding portrait of the author Honoré *Balzac. This work was a particular challenge for the artist as he had to work for the first time without a model and with little in the way of photographs. He continued with other portrait sculptures of famous figures including George Bernard *Shaw, Georges *Clemenceau, and Vaslav Nijinsky.

In his later years Rodin retired to the countryside with Rose, whom he eventually married, twenty-five days before her death. While still producing, his judgment in personal matters began to slip. He gained a reputation as a womanizer, succumbing to one woman, an American-born marquise who took advantage of the aging artist.

As he got older he grew more and more tyrannical toward his apprentices and at the same time increasingly childlike in his personal dealings. After his death, his coffin was draped in the French national colors, a rare tribute reserved for artists of his stature. Thanks to limited-edition bronze casting, many copies of his works are to be found throughout the world. Before his death he presented his own collection of his works to the French nation and they are housed in the Rodin Museum in Paris.

B. Champigneulle, *Rodin*, 1967.

R. Descharnes and J. Chabrun, *Auguste Rodin*, 1967.

A. Elsen, *In Rodin's Studio*, 1980.

ROENTGEN, WILHELM CONRAD

(1845–1923), German experimental physicist who was the first recipient of the Nobel Prize in physics for his discovery of X-rays. Wilhelm Roentgen was born in Lennep in Rhenish Prussia. Roentgen had an unexceptional early academic career, but was appointed as an assistant to the noted physicist August Kundt at Würzburg. In 1876 he became a lecturer at Strasbourg; the position was unpaid, but it enabled him to offer his own courses for which he could charge fees, and he managed to make a comfortable living. He was made a full professor the following year at Hohenheim and after brief tenures at a number of other universities returned to Würzburg in 1888.

In 1895 an event occurred in his laboratory that was to become the starting point of modern physics and was the catalyst for the later work of Ernest *Rutherford, Max *Planck, and Niels *Bohr. On November 8 of that year Roentgen discovered X-rays.

Roentgen had been working with various cathode tubes for some time. These were glass tubes containing mercury vapor that had metal plates at either end connected to fine wires that passed through the walls of the tube. Through these wires a voltage could be applied to the metal plates which acted as poles, one the anode and the other the cathode (hence the term "cathode tube"). As the tubes are evacuated, a thick fuzzy spark forms across the poles, and with increasing vacuum the glass of the tubes begins to fluoresce a pale green.

For whatever reason, in the course of his experiments with these devices Roentgen had wrapped one such tube with black opaque paper. He noticed in his darkened laboratory that a screen of barium platinosulphide lying near his apparatus began to fluoresce brightly even though the tube was sealed to visible light. This phenomenon piqued his curiosity, and he achieved the same results with other types of cathode tubes. Thus it happened that this landmark discovery of the modern era was entirely accidental.

Intrigued, Roentgen conducted a series of experiments to determine the cause of the fluorescence. In 1895 he published an account of his discoveries in the proceedings of the local scientific society. In his first paper, he noted the discovery of a new kind of ray whose nature he had been unable to fathom, and hence he named it X-ray. However, he did describe the salient properties of these mysterious new rays as invisible, moving in straught lines unaffected by electromagnetic fields, able to pass through substances opaque to ordinary visible light, able to produce fluorescence in some materials, causing the ionization of gases and activating photographic plates. In this paper he dramatically presented a picture of the bones of a living hand.

Copies of the paper were in wide circulation by 1896 and it caused a sensation in both scientific circles and the popular press. The medical fraternity quickly adapted his discovery for diagnostic uses, and newspapers filled their pages with skeletal snapshots.

Despite the tumult surrounding him, Roentgen remained a rigorous researcher, guarding himself from hypothesizing before the facts were known. He was a dedicated practitioner of the experimental method and refused to be drawn into idle speculation and theorizing.

Not long after he had made his initial discovery, a noted British doctor visited Röntgen in his laboratory in Würtburg. Röntgen had described to him how he had fortuitously seen the screen shining in the darkened room when the cathode tube was charged. The doctor asked Roentgen what he thought on seeing the glow, to which Roentgen replied, "I did not think, I investigated!"

In 1900 Roentgen, whose name had become synonymous with the rays he had discovered, accepted a chair in physics in Munich. The following year he became the first recipient of the Nobel Prize in physics. He lived to see the X-ray enigma solved and its nature identified by other great men of science.

R. S. Bowen, *They Found the Unknown*, 1963.

O. Glasser, *Dr. W. C. Roentgen*, 1945.

ROMMEL, ERWIN JOHANNES EUGEN

(1891–1944), German general. Unlike most other German generals, who were descended from Prussian Junker (landed aristocracy) families, Rommel, born in Heidenheim, Wurttemburg, was the son of a schoolteacher. He enlisted as an officer cadet in 1910 and joined the 124th infantry regiment two years later with the rank of second lieutenant. Rommel received his first combat experience during World War I in the German advance on the Marne. He did not stay long in France, however; the remainder of his service was spent in Romania and Italy, where he performed with distinction. He was decorated several times during the war, receiving the Iron Cross Second Class for attacking three French soldiers at Varennes without any ammunition. He was also decorated for his infiltration of Gagesti, for his company's capture of Mount Cosna, and for his particularly daring exploits leading to the capture of Monte Matajur. This success turned the tide of the battle of Caparetto in Germany's favor and led to the capture of 250,000 Italian prisoners of war. Rommel, then just a lieutenant, was awarded Pour le Mérité, a

Major General Erwin Rommel

ian rule and Germany feared that Italian muddling would lead to the fall of their ally. His stated objective was to defend Italian interests in Libya but he later said, "I took risks against all orders and instructions because the opportunity seemed favorable." He led his armies from Tunisia through Cyrenaica and Tripoli, pushing the British as far back as El-Alamein. What was supposed to be a minor defensive action became a major German offensive. After reaching El-Alamein Rommel returned to Germany suffering from high blood pressure and a liver condition. On his way home he met with both *Mussolini and Hitler, cautioning them about the lack of adequate supplies reaching his beleaguered troops. Hitler did not take his advice but did promote him to field marshal, the youngest in the German army (Rommel wrote to his wife, "I would rather he had given me one more division.") Hitler's failure to heed Rommel's warnings only increased the field marshal's growing contempt for Hitler's incompetence.

Rommel was still recuperating when Hitler himself called to inform him of an impending British counteroffensive at El-Alamein. Despite his poor health Rommel agreed to return to Africa; Hitler ordered Rommel not to concede any territory. However, Rommel's troops were exhausted and, hearing of American landings in Algeria and French Morocco, Rommel chose to ignore Hitler's directives and began his 1,400-mile retreat to Tunisia.

decoration generally reserved for generals. With the decoration came promotion to captain.

After Germany's defeat in World War I Rommel served as a regimental commander. He was an instructor at the Dresden Infantry School (1929–1933) and at the Potsdam War Academy (1935–1938). In 1937 he published *Infantrie greift an*, a popular book on infantry tactics that brought him to *Hitler's attention. Hitler was fond of Rommel, finding in his simple origins someone to whom he could relate. Rommel, in turn, despite his general contempt for the Nazis – he never joined the party – admired Hitler for his stand on the Treaty of Versailles. Hitler's appreciation of the young soldier led to his rapid advance through the ranks. Rommel commanded the battalion charged with Hitler's safety during the occupation of Sudetenland and Prague. By the outbreak of World War II Rommel had reached the rank of major general and was in charge of Hitler's safety in Poland.

Rommel always said that he preferred serving with his troops on the battlefield than being behind the lines with the staff. During the war he asked to command an armored division and was given the 7th Panzer division, which took part in the invasion of France. Rommel's speed and agility earned his division the name "Ghost Division"; Rommel himself was nicknamed "the Knight of the Apocalypse."

In 1941 Rommel was put in charge of the Afrika Korps serving in Libya; Libya was then under Ital-

FROM ROMMEL'S PAPERS

- There are always moments when the commander's place is not back with his staff but up with his troops.
- War makes extremely heavy demands on the soldier's strength and nerves. For this reason, make heavy demands on your men in peacetime.
- The commander must establish personal and comradely contact with his men but without giving away an inch of his authority.
- If I am successful here, everyone else will claim all the glory. If I fail, everybody will be after my blood.

ON ROMMEL

- We have a very daring and skillful opponent against us, and may I say across the havoc of war, a great general.
    Winston Churchill

- He was a first-class commander, you couldn't go to sleep when he was about.

    Field Marshal Sir Claude Auchinleck

Once safe, Rommel made several counterattacks against the allies. The Italian General Giovanni Mosse was given command of the Axis forces in Africa and Rommel returned to Germany on sick leave. On his way home he pleaded with Hitler to abandon Africa and use the troops to protect the European mainland from an Allied invasion. Only after the Allies had successfully established themselves in southern Italy did Hitler comment, "I should have listened to you."

Rommel joined Hitler's staff in May 1943 and was soon sent to northern Italy where he was to assist field marshal Albert Kesserling in the defense against an allied invasion. Rommel found himself arguing with Kesserling about the ideal line of defense; he supported a line north of Rome while Kesserling advocated one to the south. Hitler moved Rommel to France where he was made commander in chief of the German armies from Holland to the Loire River. Rommel was aware that the Allies were planning an invasion somewhere along the coast and again found himself in conflict with the German high command. He believed that the German defenses should be strengthened on the beachfronts, that the Allies must never be allowed to have a bridgehead in continental Europe, and tripled the number of mines planted along the coast. Other commanders, notably Field Marshal Gerd von Runstedt, advocated a depth defense policy. The debate prevented Rommel from deflecting the Normandy invasion.

Rommel was driving near the French village of Livasot when he was injured in an air raid. Three days later an attempt was made on Hitler's life. Although Rommel apparently had nothing to do with the conspiracy – he advocated Hitler's arrest and imprisonment, not his murder – under torture one conspirator mentioned Rommel. On October 14, 1944, two generals visited Rommel at home and offered him the option of trial in a people's court or immediate suicide; Rommel chose the latter. Hitler declared national mourning for Rommel; his death was explained as the result of an embolism.

Rommel was one of the great generals of World War II, proving himself in both offensive and defensive actions. Even his greatest adversaries admired his military competence and adeptness, his great battles in North Africa earning him the epithet "Desert Fox."

C. Barnett, ed., *Hitler's Generals*, 1989.
M. Carver, ed., *The War Lords*, 1976.
C. Douglas-Home, *Rommel*, 1973.

ROOSEVELT, FRANKLIN DELANO (1882–1945), thirty-second president of the United States (1933–1945), and **Roosevelt, Eleanor** (1884–1962), social activist. Franklin D. Roosevelt — whose presidency saw America through the Great Depression and almost to the end of World War II — formed, with his wife Eleanor, an effective husband-wife team. Fifth cousins from the well-to-do, patrician Roosevelt family, they were both extremely energetic, educated in schools that stressed the idea of public service, and strongly influenced by the political career and exhortations of Eleanor's uncle, President Theodore *Roosevelt. However, Franklin Roosevelt's secure and indulged upbringing left him self-confident, frivolous, and convinced that his charm could overcome any opposition. Eleanor's grim childhood, separated from the weak, alcoholic father she adored and neglected by her guardian maternal grandmother, left her feeling shy, awkward, and unloved. At Harvard University, Roosevelt neglected his studies for socializing and work on the college newspaper.

Roosevelt went to Columbia Law School and afterwards worked for years in a New York law firm, but his real interest lay in politics. The Democratic party nominated him for state senator because it believed that the Roosevelt name would make him a creditable and prestigious candidate; however, they were so sure he would lose the 1910 election that they refused to help with his campaign expenses, a disadvantage he turned into an asset in his campaign speeches: "I accept nomination with absolute independence. I am pledged to no man. If elected, I will give my entire time to serving the people of this district." He was elected.

Roosevelt's successful rebellion against the notoriously corrupt New York State Democratic party machinery (Tammany Hall) made his name known throughout the United States. Tammany Hall opposition was not able to prevent his reelection in 1912, but it did succeed in blocking his nomination for the U.S. Senate in 1914. His efforts in Woodrow *Wilson's 1912 campaign for the presidency of the United States, however, were rewarded by an appointment as assistant secretary of the navy — a position he held throughout World War I.

In their personal life, Eleanor and Franklin moved apart, especially when she discovered his relationship with her social secretary. He rejected Eleanor's offer of a divorce and they rebuilt their marriage. Eleanor spent the next few years in a state of depression and deep unhappiness, about which she later wrote: "There are times in everyone's life when the wish to be done with the burdens and even the decisions of this life seem overwhelming." Roosevelt gained a reputation as one of the most promising young politicians in Washington. He was nominated for vice president in 1920 and regarded his defeat in the elections as just a temporary setback to his career. He accepted a position in a New York bank while awaiting the 1924 elections.

In 1921 Roosevelt contracted polio and spent the next seven years fighting spiritedly to regain his health ("I spent two years lying in bed trying to move my big toe"). His mother wanted to coddle him into invalidism, but his wife was sure that the only way he could overcome his illness was to live as normal and full a life as possible, and for Roosevelt this meant maintaining an interest in politics. He never regained the use of his legs and spent

Franklin D. Roosevelt signing the Lend-Lease bill

much of his life in a wheelchair. Convinced that his welfare depended on it, Eleanor finally threw off his mother's domination. She became her husband's political representative, bringing him information, attending meetings, and preventing him from sinking into political obscurity. Her involvement in promoting the role of women in politics had been growing steadily since 1918, but it was only after Roosevelt became ill that she really began to emerge as a political figure.

By the time he won the governorship of New York in 1928, his battle against polio had matured Roosevelt, broadening his vision and deepening his understanding and compassion. Roosevelt's efforts to alleviate the depression in New York — aiding the state economy and creating the first state relief agency — helped him win the Democratic presidential nomination in 1932. He accepted the nomination with words that named his plan for ending the depression: "I pledge you, I pledge myself, to a *new deal* for the American people." Roosevelt expressed his confidence that the depression could be beaten in his inaugural speech: "All we have to fear is fear itself."

Roosevelt started his New Deal reforms immediately. Both Democrats and Republicans were shaken by the country's condition and willing to follow his lead. A special session of Congress passed most of his bills into law as fast as they were presented, forging most of the legal basis for the New Deal reforms in the first hundred days of his presidency. The New Deal's goal was first to end the depression and then to reform the economic system so that another depression could not occur. Roosevelt first closed all banks, then allowed only sound banks to reopen, and finally reformed the banking system itself with the Federal Reserve Act. The New Deal's attempt to reform every aspect of the American economy had mixed results. It did, however, bring about an immediate rise in prices, increase in business, and lessening of unemployment.

The first part of Roosevelt's second term was spent countering opposition to the New Deal. After Japan's 1937 invasion of China, his attention was increasingly diverted to international affairs. He could not openly oppose the strong isolationist sentiment prevalent in America, but he tried to prepare the country for the war he considered inevitable

Re-elected for an unprecedented third term in 1940, Roosevelt convinced Congress to approve the Lend-Lease Act providing Great Britain with equipment on a "buy now, pay later" basis and issued the Atlantic Charter jointly with Winston *Churchill. The Japanese attack on Pearl Harbor in December 1941 ended opposition to American involvement in the war.

Roosevelt was involved in planning strategy, developing and maintaining relations with the Allies, and trying to shape the post war world. He appointed Dwight D. *Eisenhower as supreme commander of the Allied forces, favored the Allied policy of demanding unconditional surrender from the Axis, and participated in conferences with Churchill and *Stalin to plan the war and the post-war world.

Eleanor's contribution was considerable. Her image as a genuinely caring mother-figure involved in day-to-day matters, extending a helping hand to anyone in need was the perfect counterbalance to Rossevelt's amiable, fatherly, but more distant image. She provided an unofficial channel through

---

SAYINGS OF FRANKLIN ROOSEVELT

- A conservative is a man with two perfectly good legs who has, however, never learned to walk forwards. A reactionary is a somnambulist walking backwards. A radical is a man with both feet firmly planted — in the air.
- Never underestimate a man who overestimates himself.
- We look forward to a world founded on four essential human freedoms:

  The first is freedom of speech and expression — everywhere in the world.

  The second is the freedom of every person to worship God in his own way — everywhere in the world.

  The third is freedom from want — which translated into world terms means economic understanding which will secure to every nation a healthy peacetime life for its inhabitants — everywhere in the world.

  The fourth is the freedom from fear, which means a worldwide reduction of armaments to such a point that no nation will be in a position to commit an act of physical aggression against any neighbor — anywhere in the world.
- The core of our defense is the faith we have in the institutions we defend.

which his attention could be drawn to any subject (if she considered it necessary), preventing his staff from sealing him off from the world. She went on tours of inspection and good will missions and tried to keep New Deal reforms from being totally disregarded because of wartime exigencies. Although she trusted his political judgment and leadership, she did not hesitate to criticize him in private if she felt his actions were ethically wrong or that he was making concessions on important principles because of tiredness, impatience, or expediency. Despite their public partnership, however, they tended to lead separate lives.

Eleanor's sense of duty shaped her reaction to Roosevelt's running for president a fourth time in 1944. Once she was convinced that the Republican candidate could not cope with the demands of the presidency she supported her husband's decision to accept the nomination, well aware of what it might cost him; he was reelected. Hindsight blames exhaustion and ill-health for the many concessions he made to Stalin at their last conference, in Yalta, in 1945. However, at the time he was sure that Stalin's agreement to fight against Japan made it worthwhile. His health was failing, and he died two months after Yalta- and one month beforeGermany surrendered.

After Roosevelt's death Eleanor continued and even intensified her public career. She was a delegate to the United Nations and, as chairman of the UN Commission on Human Rights, tirelessly traveled the world. She wrote three autobiographical works, *This is My Story* (1937), *This I Remember* (1949), and *On My Own* (1958).

R. Aglion, *Roosevelt and De Gaulle*, 1988.

S. D. Cashman, *America, Roosevelt, and World War II*, 1989.

J. Lash, *Eleanor and Franklin*, 1971.

S. J. Savage, *Roosevelt*, 1991.

A. M. Schlesinger, Jr., *The Age of Roosevelt*, 1957.

ROOSEVELT, THEODORE (1858 – 1919), twenty-sixth president of the United States (1901 – 1909), popularly known as "Teddy," a name he disliked and forbade his intimates to use. He was the only president to have been born in New York City. As a youngster, Theodore Roosevelt suffered from asthma and had poor eyesight. Through sheer determination, he worked to improve his physical condition, exercising and teaching himself to box, ride, and shoot.

Born into an affluent family, Roosevelt was educated by private tutors and traveled extensively, broadening his experiences and expanding his knowledge. He entered Harvard and graduated in 1880. In his senior year he began work on a book entitled *The Naval War in 1812*, which was published in 1882 and enthusiastically received.

After graduation, he enrolled in Columbia University Law School but quickly discovered that he was more interested in history and politics than in law and dropped the idea of a legal career. He ran for and was elected to the New York state assembly where he served from 1882 to 1884. During those two years he demonstrated admirable leadership ability, which won him a place as delegate-at-large to the Republican national convention held in Chicago. In 1886 he ran for mayor of New York City but finished third.

In 1888 Roosevelt supported the winning presidential ticket and as a result was appointed in 1889 to the U.S. Civil Service Commission, which he headed for the next six years. During his tenure, he uncovered corruption, fraud, and discrimination against women, and instituted reforms. He also wrote several books on his philosophies of good government.

After the election of William McKinley in 1896, Roosevelt was appointed assistant secretary of the navy. With the outbreak of the Spanish-American War in 1898, he resigned from the cabinet and together with Leonard Wood, organized the first volunteer cavalry regiment, later known as the Rough Riders. Roosevelt led his cavalry up Kettle Hill in the battle of San Juan, winning promotion to the rank of colonel. He was popular with his troops and concerned for their welfare. The men, in turn, helped him in his political endeavors and when Roosevelt ran for governor of New York, his men escorted him up and down the state campaigning on his behalf; he won, albeit by a narrow margin.

Roosevelt and Thomas Collier Platt, the Republican party boss, did not see eye to eye on many political issues. Despite strong opposition from Platt, Roosevelt did well as governor. He was able to tax corporation franchises and put through much practical reform, including a bill to outlaw racial prejudice in public schools. After two years in office, Platt wanted Roosevelt out of state government and talked him into running for vice president under McKinley.

Roosevelt was a hard campaigner, and he and McKinley won handily. On 14 September1901, six months into his second term, McKinley was assassinated and Roosevelt became president. At the age of forty-two, he was the youngest man to serve in that position.

Upon assuming office, Roosevelt pledged to continue McKinley's policies. He soon discovered that there were newer philosophies being generated from abroad. Younger men like Robert M. La Follette were leading the crusade for reform in government. Even though Roosevelt kept the McKinley cabinet intact during his first term, he brought a new vitality to the office and changed many of the methods practiced in the White House.

Roosevelt turned over much of the official paper work to his subordinates while he concentrated on bringing dignity and formality to life in the White House. With his so-called tennis cabinet, he took part in games, rides, and hikes. Through these contacts, Roosevelt learned the inner workings of government and how to speed up the legislative process. He was the first president to use his office to fight the abuses of big business. He established

The term "teddy bear" derives from an incident in one of Roosevelt's hunting expeditions when he refused to shoot a bear that was cornered because it was too small.

- The only man who makes no mistakes is the one who does nothing.
- McKinley shows all the backbone of a chocolate eclair.
- The reactionary is always willing to take a progressive attitude on any issue that is dead.
- No President has ever enjoyed himself as much as I.
- The most successful politician is he who says what everybody is thinking most often and in the loudest voice.
- The great virtue of my radicalism lies in the fact that I am perfectly ready, if necessary, to be radical on the conservative side.

Theodore Roosevelt

ABOUT THEODORE ROOSEVELT

- One thinks of him as a glorified bouncer engaged eternally in clearing out bar-rooms — and not too proud to gouge when the inspiration came to him, or to bite in the clinches.

H. L. Mencken

the Bureau of Corporations, which had the power to inspect the books of businessmen engaged in interstate commerce. Using a revived Sherman Anti-Trust Act, he and his administration were able to sue forty-three major corporations in anti trust actions. He also intervened in the coal miners' strike, supporting the unions and infuriating their bosses. He referred to the above actions against industry and indirectly for labor as a "square deal."

Roosevelt reversed his hawkish approach to foreign affairs but maintained his support of a strong America and turned the country into a world naval power. In 1904, with Charles W. Fairbanks as his running mate, he was reelected by over two and a half million votes and by a margin of 336 to 140 in the Electoral College. His popularity with the people did not carry over to Congress, with whom he was constantly at odds. He said, "Congress does from one-third to a half of what I think is the minimum it ought to do."

Roosevelt's foreign-affairs philosophy as articulated in his statements, "Speak softly and carry a big stick," and "Don't hit at all if it is honorably possible to avoid hitting, but never hit softly," resulted in the acquisition of the Panama Canal Zone. His intervention in the Russo-Japanese War in 1905 won him

the Nobel Peace Prize. His internal affairs policy was carried out through a series of quick administrative changes. He was a pioneer conservationist, concerned with soil and water, the preservation of wildernesses, and the establishment of national parks. He was consistently opposed by Congress and criticized by the press. The scope and depth of his interests and involvement, however, were recognized and it was said that no president since Thomas *Jefferson had ranged his mind over so broad a field. Roosevelt coined such phrases as "lunatic fringe," "muckrakers," and "my hat is in the ring." Roosevelt supported William Howard Taft as his successor in 1908 and received a positive reaction from the public.

When Roosevelt left the presidency he was only fifty. He spent time big-game hunting and touring Europe. In 1912 he challenged Taft's presidential renomination but the party bosses supported Taft, and so Roosevelt founded the Progressive party, which split the Republican vote and ensured the election of the Democrat candidate, Woodrow *Wilson. Shortly before the election Roosevelt survived an assassination attempt — the bullet lodged in his chest — by an assailant who was declared insane. After the election he went exploring in the Brazilian jungle and won a libel suit against an article accusing him of excessive drinking. From the outbreak of World War I, he advocated the immediate entry of the United States into the war on the side of the Allies. His request to lead a volunteer division was refused and his son was killed on the battlefield.

J. M. Cooper, *Theodore Roosevelt*, 1983.
R. H. Callin, *Theodore Roosevelt: Culture, Diplomacy, and Expansion*, 1985.
L. L. Gould, *The Presidency of Theodore Roosevelt*, 1991.

ROTHSCHILD, family of financiers. The name was derived from the "red shield" sign over the family house in the Frankfurt-on-Main Jewish ghetto. Founder of the family was **Mayer Amschel Rothschild** (1744–1812). He was orphaned at the age of twelve and looked after by relatives. Intended for a rabbinical career, he left it to enter a Frankfurt banking firm, which within a few years he headed. He had a special interest in old coins and medals, producing an annual catalog that caught the attention of William IX, land owner of Hesse-Cassel, who had a great interest in numismatics. He was so impressed by Rothschild that in 1769 he appointed him supplier to the principality. When *Napoleon Bonaparte began to spread his influence across Europe, William provided funds to assist his fellow rulers in face of the challenge and employed Rothschild as his agent.

Rothschild became one of the richest men in Frankfurt and deployed his five surviving sons (he had nineteen children) in different key banking capitals in Europe — Paris, London, Naples, Vienna, and Frankfurt. When William had to flee from

Napoleon's armies, he entrusted his fortune to Rothschild, who first concealed it in underground hiding-places originally constructed by the Jews of Frankfurt as secret refuges in the event of danger. Rothschild was, however, able through his sons to invest the money in various countries (even in the form of loans to Napoleon) and as a result when William returned, he found his capital multiplied. He rewarded Rothschild with tax and trade concessions which allowed him to further increase his European operations.

Rothschild's sons, known as the "Frankfurt five," were all financial geniuses and through their cooperation the House of Rothschild became Europe's leading banking house. The youngest son, **James Jacob Rothschild** (1792–1868) established the Paris branch, Rothschild Frères. After the fall of Napoleon, he raised the money to help France pay its war indemnity. He continued as a leading government financier through successive regimes down to the time of *Napoleon III. He also played an important role in early French railroad construction. He was an obsessive collector of objets d'art and his home was one of the great salons of Paris, presided over by his talented wife, Betty, who was also his cousin (the Rothschilds married among themselves whenever possible). There, most European artistic luminaries could be encountered — Frederick *Chopin made his French debut there, and other frequent visitors included Franz Liszt, Gioacchino Rossini, Heinrich *Heine, and Honoré *Balzac (who dedicated books to both James and Betty). His son, **Mayer Alphonse Rothschild** (1827–1905), carried on his father's traditions in banking, art collecting, and philanthropy in both the general and Jewish communities. Like his father, he enabled the French government to pay off an indemnity after a military defeat — this time following the Franco-Prussian War (1870–1871).

The third of the brothers, **Nathan Mayer Rothschild** (1777–1836), was sent to England and after an initial stay in Manchester, moved to London. By 1815 he was the leading figure on the London stock exchange and raised money for the British campaign against Napoleon in the Peninsular War. The legend that carrier pigeon service brought him early news of the Battle of Waterloo on which he was able to profit is not authentic but both he and his brothers made early use of carrier pigeons and he was reputed better informed on developments in Europe than anyone in the British government. In 1825–1826, a period of a massive bank crash in England, he was instrumental in saving the Bank of England and bailing out the British government. Involved in many philanthropies, he set up a fund to assist victims of the Irish Potato Famine in the 1840s.

He was succeeded in the business by his son **Lionel Nathan Rothschild** (1808–1879). In 1847 he became the first practicing Jew elected to the British Parliament. However, because he refused to swear the Christian oath incumbent upon all members, he was not seated. He was reelected repeatedly but was still barred from Parliament. Finally the oath was changed, whereupon he took his place, sitting for another sixteen years in Parliament — but never once making a speech. Lionel Rothschild provided the funds for his friend Benjamin *Disraeli, the prime minister, to purchase shares in the Suez Canal and hence establish British control of the waterway.

F. Morton, *The Rothschilds*, 1962.

D. Gutwein, *The Divided Elite*, 1992.

D. Wilson, *Rothschild; A Story of Wealth and Power*, 1988.

ROUSSEAU, JEAN-JACQUES (1712–1778), philosopher, novelist, and political theorist. Born in Geneva, the son of a Calvinist republican, he left in 1728 and with the help of Mme de Warens, a convert to Catholicism whom he met in Savoy, journeyed to Turin, where he was received into the Roman Catholic Church. Over the next few years he found work as an engraver and a music teacher and maintained contact with Mme de Warens. In 1733 she became his mistress and the two lived together at Chambéry, where Rousseau first began to write.

During the years 1741–1745 Rousseau traveled to Paris on several occasions, hoping to break into the intellectual circles of the capital. His success was limited although a number of his works were published, among them the *Dissertation sur la musique moderne* (1743); an opera, *Les Muses galantes* (1745); and a comedy, *Les pisonniers de guerre*. In Paris, Rousseau was introduced to the philosopher Denis *Diderot and established a friendship with him which lasted for fifteen years. He wrote a number of articles on the subject of music and music theory for Diderot's *Encylopédie*, which he later published in his own *Dictionnaire de la musique* (1768).

In 1745 Rousseau met Thérèse Levasseur, an illiterate chambermaid at the hotel where he was staying. A long affair ensued and five children were born, all of whom were sent to an orphanage; Rousseau eventually married Levasseur in 1768. Encouraged by Diderot, Rousseau entered the Dijon academy's essay competition in 1750 and won first prize with his *Discours sur les sciences et les arts*, an attack on the sciences and arts as instruments of inequality fostering the corruption of society, exploitation of the poor, and the self-enrichment of the wealthy, particularly the clergy and monarchy.

Rousseau first revealed his political philosophy in his *Discours sur l'origine et les fondements de l'inégalité parmi les hommes* (1755), in which he put forward his account of the state of nature and the origin of societies. He proposed the idea that man in his natural state is solitary and brutish like other animals and only becomes a moral being in the process of adapting himself to life in society. According to Rousseau, it was only with the development of a predominantly agricultural economy and the discovery of iron that men became permanently dependent

A bust of Rousseau, by Houdon

on one another and the need for private property and the accumulation of wealth was created. This development enabled the rich to dominate the poor, who became filled with resentment, resulting in insecurity and violence. Rousseau suggested that at this point political society was established, as this dangerous state forced the wealthy landowners to impose a system of laws to protect their property.

After a visit to Geneva in 1754, Rousseau returned to Paris, where he began to dissociate himself from the *encyclopédistes*, claiming that their aims and interests were those of the bourgeoisie, and as such were not working to relieve the suffering of the masses. Finally, exasperated with life in Paris, Rousseau moved in 1756 to L'Ermitage, a country house near Montmorency, where he conceived his love story, *Julie, ou la Nouvelle Héloïse*. Published in 1761, this novel, dealing with philosophical, moral, and religious issues, was received with greater enthusiasm than any other published in the eighteenth century.

Scandal erupted in 1757 when the seventh volume of Diderot's *Encyclopédie* was published; it included an article, written by Jean d'Alembert and inspired by *Voltaire, which proposed the building of a theater in Geneva. Rousseau replied to the article in the *Lettre à d'Alembert* in which he attacked the rational philosophy of the *philosophes* in general and ques-

tioned the morality of theatrical performances. His stand against the *encyclopéistes* in this dispute marked the final break between him and Diderot.

In 1762 Rousseau produced his two major works, *Émile* and *Du contrat social*. In *Émile Traité, ou de l'éducation*, he propounded his views on education, emphasizing man's natural goodness. He explained how a child can be raised in a special environment until he has grown strong enough in his reasoning powers and character to resist the corrupting influences of society. At this stage the youth can be educated to make the best of a bad world and taught to be morally independent of it by rising above its vanities and prejudices. In *Du Contrat social* Rousseau described an ideal, free society in which sovereign decisions are made by the whole body of citizens; adherence to such laws is achieved through free and tacit consent by all members of society. He asserted that many nations are incapable of making good laws and that the only people in Europe still incorrupt and "capable of legislation" were the Corsicans, meaning that they alone could become a properly constituted state. In return for this compliment he was invited by the Corsicans, then struggling for independence, to prepare a constitution for them.

Following the condemnation of *Émile and Du Contrat social* by the Parlement of Paris as contrary to church and state, Rousseau left France for Switzerland. There too his works were banned, and he began to defend himself in articles written in reply to his most virulent critics. He was particularly shocked by the *Sentiment de citoyens*, an anonymous pamphlet actually written by Voltaire, revealing to the public that Rousseau had abandoned his children and supposedly expressing the opinion of the Genevese that Rousseau was an ingrate and a hypocrite. An order was issued for the burning of *Émile* and *Contrat social* and Rousseau responded with his *Lettres écrites de la montagne*, which only served to strengthen the opposition against him. After his house had been vandalized Rousseau decided to leave Switzerland and fled to England in 1766, where he was taken under the patronage of David Hume, the British philosopher. However, Rousseau's suspicion of Hume as a collaborator in a plot with the Paris *philosophes* to ruin his name resulted in an open altercation between the two and in 1767 Rousseau returned to France.

Over the next few years Rousseau wrote his autobiography, *Confessions* and in 1770 settled in Paris, determined once again to defend himself against his enemies. His final years were spent in seclusion with his wife Thérèse. Rousseau died in Ermenonville, where he was buried, but his remains were transferred to the Panthéon in Paris during the Revolution.

Rousseau's influence on social and political thought has been immense; his conception of freedom inspired the French Revolution and his eloquent writings had a broad influence on the development of eighteenth-century philosophy and served as a foundation for political theories of later generations.

P. France, *Rousseau: Confessions*, 1987.

R. M. Lemos, *Rousseau's Political Philosophy*, 1977.

A. Rapaczynski, *Nature and Politics*, 1987.

RUBENS, PETER PAUL (1577–1640), painter of the Flemish school and diplomat. Born in Siegen, Westphalia, he was taken as a child to Antwerp, where he received an education in the humanities and a knowledge of six languages. His mother was a widow and could not continue to provide for her children, forcing him to stop studying and enter the service of the countess of Lalaing. Very little detail is known about Rubens's personal life: he hid personal affairs from the public, and it is not known why he decided to become a painter, or when he

began to study. His first two masters were Adam van Noort and Octave van Veen.

In 1599 Rubens earned the title of master of the Brotherhood of Saint Luke in Antwerp, which entitled him to sell his own works. He dreamed, however, of going to Italy to study classical art and the work of the classical masters, and in 1600 he set out. He made his way to Venice to study the works of *Titian and Veronese and almost immediately had the good fortune to enter the service of Vincento Gonzaga, the duke of Mantua. His duties as court painter and gentleman of the court for the duke required painting portraits of the prince and his family, copying famous works for the duke's gallery, and decorating various rooms in the palace.

In 1603 he was put in charge of a shipment of presents to the Spanish king and in 1605 sent on a mission to *Philip II of Spain, thus establishing himself as a diplomat whose intellect, polish, and linguistic accomplishments suited him admirably to the task. His diplomatic assignments did not detract from his painting career and while in Madrid he painted many portraits of the Spanish nobility and several historical subjects. He settled in Antwerp and was appointed court painter in 1609 to Archduke Albert and his wife Isabella. His great triptych, the *Erection of the Cross*, in the cathedral of Antwerp, established him as the leader of the Flemish school of painting. It was followed by the equally impressive triptych *The Descent from the Cross*. In 1622 he was invited to France by *Marie de Médicis, the queen mother, who was decorating the palace of the Luxembourg in Paris, for which he completed twenty-one large works (now in the Louvre). In 1628 he was sent by Isabella on a diplomatic mission to Philip IV of Spain and in 1629 appointed envoy to *Charles I of England, his mission being a peace treaty. His negotiations were skillfully accomplished and while there he also completed the painting *Peace and War*, which hangs in the National Gallery in London, a portrait of the king and queen as Saint George and Cleolinde, which is on display in Windsor, and sketches for the apotheosis of *James I for the banquet hall in Whitehall. He was knighted by both Charles I and Philip IV.

Rubens continued to receive ambitious commissions from various parts of Europe although during the last decade of his life much of the actual painting was executed by his pupils. He is the outstanding representative of the Baroque school of painting, and his work is marked by its dramatic power and structure filled with movement. He introduced the Flemish naturalist tradition into classic Baroque, with its style, subject matter, and colors. His subjects were of the most varied, including portraits, biblical scenes, book illustrations, allegories, historial and mythological events, nudes, and everyday life of his times. His nude figures are particularly characteristic with their ample, voluptuous flesh. His landscapes paved the way for the nineteenth-century romantics. His influence on European art was great down to the end of the nineteenth century while in French art the dominant style at the end of the seventeenth century was known as "Rubensism."

R. Avermaete, *Rubens and His Time*, 1968.

J. S. Held, *Rubens and His Circle*, 1982.

C. V. Wedgwood, *The World of Rubens*, 1967.

RUSSELL, BERTRAND ARTHUR WILLIAM, THIRD EARL RUSSELL (1872–1970), English philosopher, author, educator, pacifist, political radical, and Nobel Prize winner. Precocious as a child, Bertrand Russell was greatly disappointed to learn from his elder brother that if he wanted to progress in his study of Euclidian geometry he would have to accept certain unprovable axioms as given. The reluctance to accept given norms, intellectual or social, uncritically, always stayed with Russell. In the public sphere, his many marriages and affairs, his condemnation of conventional sexual morality, his atheism, and his pacifism often shocked mainstream sensibilities. He lived in accordance with the dictates of his favourite biblical text, "Thou shalt not follow a multitude to do evil."

Heir to an earldom, Russell's childhood was an unhappy one; he was brought up by his puritanical grandmother after the death of his parents. A brilliant student, he took a first class degree in mathematics from Trinity College, Cambridge, in 1893. At Cambridge he was a member of the Apostles, an exclusive intellectuals' society, fell in and out of love with Hegelianism, and developed a close friendship with the philosopher G. E. Moore.

Russell went to the United States to lecture in 1894. He married his first wife, Alys Pearsall Smith, a Quaker from Philadelphia, in that year. It was to be the first of four marriages. Returning to England in 1896, he took up a lectureship at Trinity College.

The sheer volume of his publications and his subsequent fame as an eloquent popularizer of philosophical and scientific issues can obscure the fact that he was one of the most important twentieth-century philosophers in his own right. His original work in philosophy and mathematics is highly technical and analytical in character. *Principles of Mathematics* (1903) demonstrated a derivation of mathematics from a very small number of logical principles, while the three-volume *Principia Mathematica* (1910–1913), co-authored with A. N. *Whitehead, presented many further developments in the field of mathematical philosophy.

Russell reacted against the philosophical idealism represented by Hegelianism by denying ultimate reality to the relationships between things and by propounding the theory of logical atomism, which asserted that propositions can be unquestionably true in isolation. He also pursued the task of paring down to a minimum and to their simplest expression the pretensions of human knowledge. He was one of the first people to recognize the significance of the work of Ludwig *Wittgenstein, although he was less enthusiastic about the linguistic movement in philosophy that the latter's work heralded.

Despite being outspokenly antireligious, Russell said that it was a "mystic illumination" that transformed him into a pacifist. Because of his views he lost his Cambridge lectureship in 1916 and spent six months in prison in 1918. Although a leftist, Russell was very critical of what he saw in the Soviet Union on his visit there in 1920, stressing the regime's totalitarianism and predicting many of the aspects of what was later to be called Stalinism. His honesty earned him the enmity of his former political allies on the left. Allegations that Russell was an agnostic and an advocate of sexual immorality came to a head when he was appointed to a professorship at City College, in New York City in 1940. There followed an intense campaign against his appointment by ecclesiastical authorities and the Hearst press, and the appointment was annulled.

- I believe that nine out of ten who have had a conventional upbringing in their early years have become in some degree incapable of a decent and sane attitude towards marriage and sex generally.
- The important thing is not what you believe but how you believe it.
- I am myself a dissenter from all known religions, and I hope that every kind of religious belief will die out... I regard religion as belonging to the infancy of human reason and to a stage of development which we are now outgrowing.
- It seemed to me one vast prison in which the jailors were bigots (of Soviet Russia).
- I cannot believe that there can ever be any good excuse for refusing to face the evidence in favour of something unwelcome. It is not by delusion, however exalted, that mankind can prosper, but only by unswerving courage in the pursuit of truth.
- My sad conviction is that people can only agree about what they're not really interested in.
- The fundamental defect of fathers is that they want their children to be a credit to them.
- It's co-existence or no existence.
- Bad philosophers may have a certain influence, good philosophers never.
- There are two motives for reading a book: one, that you enjoy it; the other that you can boast about it.
- The point of philosophy is to start with something so simple as to seem not worth stating and to end with something so paradoxical that no one will believe it.

Bertrand Russell

N. Griffin, *Russell's Idealist Apprenticeship*, 1990.
C. Moorehead, *Bertrand Russell*, 1992.
R. M. Sainsbury, *Russell*, 1985.

Bertrand Russell

Russell's fame, nevertheless, continued to grow. With books such as the *ABC of Atoms, Sceptical Essays* and *A History of Western Philosophy*, along with dozens of others, he introduced many important but hitherto inaccessible theories to the public. He wrote with clarity, humour, and facility, usually at the rate of three thousand words per day. The advent of radio and television made him a household name and his slight build, precise speech, and refined features came to define many people's notion of the man of ideas. In 1950 he won the Nobel Prize for literature and received a hero's welcome at Columbia University when he returned to the United States in that year.

The awards and acclaim did not blunt his spirit and he espoused the antinuclear cause in the 1950s, coissued the Russell-Einstein (see Albert *Einstein) statement of protest by Nobel scientists, and founded the Campaign for Nuclear Disarmament in 1958. He further irked the establishment with his opposition to the war in Vietnam. Active until his death, Russell intervened with state heads during the Sino-Indian border conflict and the Cuban missle crisis in 1962. He chaired a "Who Killed Kennedy?"(see John F. *Kennedy) committee after the publication of the Warren Report (see Earl *Warren), and in 1963 established the Bertrand Russell Peace Foundation and the Atlantic Trust. Much of his time in his last years was devoted to writing his autobiography, in which he described the three passions that had dominated his life as "the longing for love, the search for happiness, and unbearable pity for the sufferings of mankind."

RUTHERFORD, LORD ERNEST (1871–1937),

British physicist whose research in atomic structure and radioactivity laid the foundation for the quantum theory. Born in a modest farmhouse near Nelson, New Zealand, Ernest Rutherford was a bright, active pupil apt to construct models and contraptions. He received a scholarship to Canterbury College, Christchurch, in 1890, receiving his master's degree in 1893 with honors in mathematics and physics. He then began some experimental research into Hertzian (radio) waves, but quickly realized that in New Zealand he was working in intellectual isolation. In 1895 he was awarded a scholarship to Cambridge and traveled to England.

In Cambridge, Rutherford continued his research into radio waves at Cavendish Laboratory under the direction of Joseph J. *Thomson. Within a year he had successfully detected electromagnetic waves with a device of his own creation at a distance of about two miles from their point of emission, a record at the time.

That year, 1895, was pivotal in another respect, for the German scientist Wilhelm *Roentgen had discovered X-rays. This discovery caused a sensation in scientific circles, and Thomson invited Rutherford to join him in investigating this new phenomenon, which brought him a great deal of prominence.

Rutherford then began experimenting with the rays emitted by uranium, which had been discovered by the Frenchman Antoine Henri *Becquerel. He set about measuring the penetration power of these rays, although before he published his results he had accepted a professorship at McGill University in Montreal. He was still only twenty-seven years of age. In a paper published in 1898 he noted that at least two distinct types of radiation, which he called alpha and beta radiation, with differential penetrative powers, emanated from uranium. It was some years, however, before he identified the nature of these rays.

At McGill, Rutherford began to attract a number of collaborators and devoted his laboratory to research into radioactivity. His first discovery, with Frederick Soddy, was of a new noble gas emitted from thorium, which they called thoron. This led to an account of the unique exponential decay of all radioactive substances, which spontaneously disintegrate into new elements. This fundamentally challenged the classical concept of matter. Rutherford also began investigating the alpha particles he had earlier discovered, and although the question was not settled until 1908, he was confident that they were in fact helium nuclei.

By 1903 Rutherford had observed and named gamma rays, although their nature remained elusive until 1914. In 1904 he published his seminal work

Radioactive Substances and Their Radiations. Thomson said of the work; "Rutherford has not only extended the boundaries of knowledge of this subject, but has announced a whole new province."

He returned to England in 1907, accepting a chair at Manchester University, where he remained until 1919. He amassed awards and honors and in 1908 received the Nobel Prize, not in physics but in chemistry. It seems that the Nobel committee felt that Rutherford was due a prize, and as the physics category had already been awarded that year, chemistry was a suitable alternative. In his acceptance speech Rutherford quipped that he had dealt with many quick transformations, but the quickest he had met with was his own in one moment from physicist to chemist.

While at Manchester, Rutherford began to develop a crude conception of the structure of an atom that proved to be his greatest contribution to science. However, it was not until Niels *Bohr came to work under him in 1911 that his model was built into quantum theory. The Rutherford-Bohr atom became the foundation for atomic physics.

Rutherford was knighted in 1914. World War I interrupted the frenzy of discovery in the scientific community. He found himself involved with problems connected with the war, specifically with the task of submarine detection. In 1918 he returned to his physics passionately. He was the first to transform artificially nitrogen into an oxygen isotope through bombardment with alpha particles. Then in 1919 he succeeded Thomson to the prestigious Cavendish chair at Cambridge. A few years later he was elected president of the Royal Society (1925), a special honor for someone of colonial origin. He was elevated to the peerage in 1931. When asked to nominate a place to be included in his title, he chose his home town of Nelson. Even in great honor, Lord Rutherford of Nelson maintained his simple manner and attitude. He was a genial man much admired for his cooperative nature.

Rutherford was outraged by the policies of the Nazi government that had risen to power in Germany. Not content to merely voice his disgust, in 1935 he established the Academic Assistance Council to help those non-Aryan scientists thrown out of German institutions.

His vigorous health allowed him to spend a great deal of time tending his garden. It was while cutting down a tree branch that he fell awkwardly and suffered fatal injuries.

E. N. da C. Andrade, *Rutherford and the Nature of the Atom*, 1964.

N. Feather, *Lord Rutherford*, 1973.

S

SALADIN (Salah ad-Din Yusuf Ibn Ayyub; c. 1137–1193), Muslim military hero who captured Jerusalem from the crusaders. Saladin was no less esteemed by his enemies than by his co-religionists and his chivalry was celebrated in countless legends. A century after Saladin's death, *Dante, in his *Divine Comedy*, placed him in limbo with the noble philosophers who died before the coming of Christ.

Saladin was the son of Ayyub, Kurdish governor of the city of Tikrit on the Tigris. Having lost favor with the caliph for helping a rebel Turk, Zangi, Ayyub fled to Aleppo in Zangi's new kingdom in Syria. Saladin was born on the day Ayyub left Tikrit. The family was well treated by Zangi and his heir, Nureddin. After two years in the local militia, Saladin, although only eighteen, was appointed deputy governor of Damascus. He resigned soon after over the dishonest practices of the court's accountant. Returning to Nureddin's capital, Aleppo, he served the sultan as a retainer.

When information reached Aleppo that crusader king Amalric of Jerusalem was planning to raid Egypt, Nureddin sent his own troops to that country. Not only was he defending Muslim territory from Christian "pagans" but the wealthy Nile basin itself was a desirable prize. With Amalric already in Cairo, Nureddin's troops, led by Saladin's uncle Shirkuh, moved south to Ashmunein, where they trapped the enemy by feigning a retreat between two hills. With the crusaders seemingly crushed, Shirkuh then led his troops marauding, leaving Saladin to guard his base at Alexandria. Amalric, however, had escaped the battlefield to mobilize a new army with which he surrounded Alexandria. Only bitter hunger, ravaging both Alexandria and the besieging forces, compelled the sides to agree to a truce.

The Fatimid caliph of Egypt then appointed Shirkuh his vizier, but Shirkuh died of consumption shortly after, leaving the post to his nephew (1169). Saladin, now vizier and commander of Nureddin's armies, soon received command of Egypt's own army, too, and the title *al-Malik al-Nasir* ("savior king"). This infuriated Nureddin, who wrongly suspected Saladin of planning a revolt.

Saladin, however, still regarded himself as Nureddin's vassal. He believed that only a united Muslim world could defeat the intruders. His fortunes changed in 1174, when both Nureddin and Amalric died within a space of two months. Amalric's heir was a thirteen-year-old leper, Baldwin; al-Salih, Nureddin's heir, was only eleven. As Nureddin's most capable military commander, Saladin proposed himself as guardian for al-Salih, and defeated all other claimants at the battle of Hamah. Al-Salih maintained nominal rule over Aleppo, but Saladin was Nureddin's true heir.

He proved a tolerant and understanding ruler whose sole interest was the welfare of his people, no matter what their religious affiliation. His court physician was the celebrated Jewish philosopher-doctor *Maimonides and he maintained cordial relations with local Christian communities. He tolerated even the harshest criticism and emphasized the Muslim practice of maintaining easy accessibility to his citizens. He was charitable to a fault; his treasurers often hid his money so that it would not be used as alms or for the army.

Control of a well-established empire surrounding the Frankish crusaders' enclave finally enabled Saladin to launch his ambitious recovery of the Holy Land. When his initial attempts failed, he negotiated a three-year truce to allow him to build up his troops and glean information from his extensive spy network. This network, unparalleled in its scope, even included notable Franks, such as the Countess of Antioch.

The truce was broken after Baldwin's death in 1187 and the succession of Guy of Lusignan to the throne of Jerusalem. Guy's succession brought the crusader kingdom to the brink of civil war. Saladin forged an alliance with the rival claimant, Raymond of Tripoli, permitting his troops to spend one day foraging in Galilee. News of this arrangement failed to reach the Frankish knights patrolling the region, and Saladin's party was attacked. Saladin retaliated with an assault on Tiberias. Only the fortress remained in crusader hands when news reached Saladin that a rescue party was on its way. The crusaders had mustered all their troops — only two

> • I do not want to lay down my arms until there is no longer a single infidel on earth.
> • My saddle is my council chamber.
> • Kings do not kill each other. It is not the custom.
> • I would rather be gifted with wealth, so long as it is accompanied by wisdom and moderation, than with boldness and immoderation.
>
> **Saladin**

knights were left in Jerusalem — while Saladin, by positioning his men on a steeply dropping plain overlooking the Sea of Galilee, hindered any possibility of their retreat. The site chosen by Saladin for battle was a small village between two rising hillocks, the Horns of Hattin. He had correctly deduced that the scarcity of water in the area would be to crusader disadvantage.

After forty days of siege, Jerusalem surrendered on October 2, 1187, which, according to the Islamic calendar, was the anniversary of the day on which *Muhammad rose from Jerusalem to Heaven to receive the Koran.

Confident of his success, Saladin pursued the crusaders along the coast. Only Tyre, commanded by Conrad of Montferrat, offered any resistance. Saladin even had Conrad's elderly father, taken prisoner at Hattin, brought before the walls and threatened with execution if his son would not surrender, but Conrad calmly called down that his father had lived long enough. Unwilling to risk a protracted siege, Saladin eventually abandoned Tyre and retreated to Acre for the winter. The mistake nearly cost him his empire.

News of the fall of Jerusalem was greeted in Europe with immediate plans for a Third Crusade, led by King Philip of France, *Richard the Lion-Hearted, and *Frederick I (Barbarossa). News of Frederick's sudden drowning in Cilicia did not deter the crusaders, assisted by reinforcements from Tyre, from establishing a mighty beachhead opposite Acre. Saladin's own men were weary and the Muslim world, led by the Caliph and al-Salih's supporters, were envious of the successes of the upstart Kurd. After a lengthy siege, Acre agreed to pay the heavy cost of surrender: 600 prisoners, 200,000 gold dinars, and a relic of the True Cross taken at Hattin. Yet despite the animosity and distrust between Richard and Saladin, the two, although they never met, cultivated a relationship based on respect and chivalrous behavior. Saladin provided Richard with fruits and even with snow upon learning he was suffering from the heat. In one battle, Richard's horse was killed; Saladin replaced it with two of his own chargers.

Harsh weather discouraged Richard from mounting an immediate attack on Jerusalem. Instead, he preferred to consolidate his position on the coast, while planning an eventual foray into Egypt. As spring approached, Richard prepared his assault on Jerusalem, but found himself suffering from the same lack of water that had led to defeat at Hattin. Finally, in 1192 troubles at home led Richard to abandon his crusade. He agreed to cease all aggression for four years in return for pilgrims' rights to visit Christian holy sites.

One year later Saladin died in Damascus. He was found to be penniless; all the bounty he had captured over the years had been distributed among his troops. At his funeral, a piece of his shroud was wrapped around a lance and paraded through the streets of Damascus. Accompanying it was a crier who called out, "This is all a man takes with him to the grave."

M. C. Lyons, *Saladin,* 1982.
P. H. Newby, *Saladin in his Time,* 1983.
G. Regan, *Saladin and the Fall of Jerusalem,* 1987.

SANDBURG, CARL (1878–1967), American poet and biographer. He was born in Galesburg, Illinois, to poor Swedish immigrants. His father was a railroad laborer who earned less than two dollars a day and could not afford to send his first son to high school. At age thirteen Sandburg went to work and for the next six years performed every kind of odd job from delivering milk to shifting scenery for traveling shows to farm labor. The hours he spent at some of his jobs, such as sweeping the floor and shining shoes at Humphrey's barbershop while eavesdropping on local conversation, gave him an intimate familiarity with the midwestern idiom, which was to imbue his poetry with colloquial color.

When he was sixteen his father secured him a railway pass and he was sent to Chicago, albeit almost penniless, to see the sights; these first impressions of the city were to form a base for his later Chicago poetry. By 1897 he was ready to see more of the United States and began traveling cross-country by rail, taking on odd jobs as he went and recording his impressions in an informal journal. When his wanderlust was satisfied he returned home and worked there briefly before enlisting in the army for the Spanish-American War. When he was transported to Puerto Rico, he took with him only the Infantry Drill Regulations and the New Webster Dictionary and Complete Vest-Pocket Library, in order not to lose contact with the language he loved so much.

On his release from the army Sandburg took advantage of the free year's tuition granted war veterans and enrolled at Lombard College (now Knox College). There he was befriended by his professor, Philip Green Wright, who recognized his talents and invited him to join the Poor Writers' Club that met regularly to discuss literature as well as their own writing.

Sandburg was a successful student but after four years at college his old wanderlust returned and he

BY CARL SANDBURG

Hog Butcher of the World,
Tool Maker, Stacker of Wheat,
Player with Railroads and Nation's Freight
Handler
Stormy, husky, brawling,
City of the Big Shoulders

From "Chicago"

- There are people who want to be everywhere at once and they get nowhere.
- The greatest cunning is to have none.
- To never see a fool, lock yourself in your room and smash the looking glass.
- Freedom is baffling:
  Man having it often
  Know not they have it
  Till it is gone and
  They no longer have it.
- Slang is a language that rolls up its sleeves, spits on its hands and goes to work.

was on the road again, taking on short-term jobs and absorbing local color as he went. When he returned home in 1904 he took a job as a fireman and continued to meet with Professor Wright, who had a hand press that he used to publish limited copies of some of Sandburg's early writing. It was not, however, until the publication of the poem "Chicago" in 1914, which won the Levinson Prize, that he began to truly earn recognition as a poet. In 1908 he married Lillian Steichen, sister of the great photographer Edward Steichen, about whom Sandburg wrote a biography.

His poetry is characterized by its use of non-rhyming free verse, imagist techniques, and emphasis on industrial themes; he was a master of colloquial idiom and impressionistic style. His *Chicago Poems,* published in 1915, were followed by other volumes of poetry, among them *Corn Huskers* (1918), *Smoke and Steel* (1920), *Slabs of the Sunburnt West* (1922), and *Good Morning, America* (1928). From 1913 to 1918 his poetry-writing career was also supplemented by a position as an editorial writer for the *Chicago Daily News.* At age seventy he published his first novel, *Remembrance Rock* (1948).

He was famous not only as a poet but as a biographer and author of six volumes on Abraham Lincoln. For *Abraham Lincoln: The War Years* (4 vols., 1939), which followed *Abraham Lincoln: The Prairie Years* (2 vols., 1928), he won the Pulitzer prize.

Sandburg was also widely known as a collector and singer of folk songs. He saw himself as one of the common people and could often be found, stud-

iedly casual in front of an audience, plucking a guitar and singing the songs of the American people. His other works include *The American Songbag* (1927), *The People, Yes* (1936), *Complete Poems* (1950 and winner of the Pulitzer Prize in 1951), and *Honey and Salt* (1963). He received the U.S. Presidential Medal of Freedom in 1963.

R. Crowder, *Carl Sandburg,* 1970.
J. Haas and G. Lovitz, *Carl Sandburg,* 1967.

SANGER, MARGARET (née Higgins; 1883–1966), birth control advocate, midwife, nurse. She was born the sixth of eleven children in the factory town of Corning, New York, and attributed her mother's death at age forty-eight to continuous childbearing. Her father was a stonecutter whose free thinking, advocacy of socialism and women's suffrage, and whose antagonism to the Catholic church, were reflected in Sanger's own beliefs.

Feeling that at least one of the children should have a good education and the chance to leave home, Sanger's two elder sisters paid her way to Claverack College, a prestigious co-educational preparatory school. She later studied nursing at White Plains Hospital and at Manhattan Eye and Ear Hospital. While a student nurse at Manhattan Eye and Ear in 1902, she met and married architect William Sanger.

Working as a visiting nurse and midwife in the tenements of Manhattan's Lower East Side, Sanger repeatedly treated women with unwanted pregnancies who were desperate to know how rich women avoided pregnancy. When one woman died in her arms after a self-induced abortion, Sanger sprang into action, beginning her long campaign for the promotion and legalization of contraception.

In 1913 Sanger went to Europe, where more advanced knowledge of contraception was available, and became the first person to systematically study the safety and effectiveness of various contraceptive methods.

While many arguments have been made (and later adapted by Sanger) for the use of contraception, her primary motivation was feminist. She believed that, freed from the fear of unwanted pregnancy and with control over their own bodies, women could escape repressive marriage and motherhood to develop themselves spiritually, sexually, and professionally. In addition, she succeeded in providing a public justification — the suffering of working-class women — for a practice which had been thought personal and selfish.

Upon her return to the United States in 1914 Sanger began her education campaign by publishing a periodical, *The Woman Rebel.* With subscribers recruited from labor union lists and under the banner "No Gods, no Masters" lifted from International Workers of the World leaflets, its goal was to convince working women to demand "birth control," a term Sanger had coined in the British Museum library reading room.

Sanger was soon arrested under the Comstock laws, which prohibited the circulation of obscene materials. Avoiding prosecution, she fled to Europe after writing *Family Limitation,* a pamphlet detailing contraceptive information, and instructing friends to circulate it only after her departure. While she was in Europe, William Sanger was arrested for obscenity, having unwittingly sold a pamphlet to a Comstock agent; he was imprisoned for thirty days.

Meanwhile, Sanger amassed more knowledge and skills for her cause in Europe. In Holland her visit to a contraception clinic convinced her that birth control was a matter requiring medical supervision, and that the vaginal diaphragm is the best method of contraception. In England Sanger developed a close friendship with Havelock Ellis, author of *Studies in the Psychology of Sex.* Sanger changed her tactics in England, lecturing to social leaders rather than going directly to the working-class masses. Additionally, Ellis helped her to develop more prudent propaganda, appealing more to the emotions while also cultivating a resemblance to social science.

By the time she returned to the U.S. in 1915, birth control had become the publicly debated topic she had hoped to make it; soon after the charges against her were dropped. Her rhetoric became more palatable to the general public; now she promoted birth control as a way to achieve both sex without fear and, through a lowered birthrate, to transform society without class conflict.

This more conservative line did not make Sanger's methods less confrontational. In 1916 she and her sister, Ethel Byrne, defying New York law, opened the first birth control clinic outside Holland, in the low income Brownsville neighborhood. Promoting the clinic in English, Yiddish, and Italian, the sisters treated 488 women in the nine days before police raided the clinic and arrested them. After one trial Sanger reopened the clinic, was rearrested, and served thirty days in prison. In Appeals Court a breakthrough came; the judge broadened the instances in which New York law allowed birth control to be used. The law, in agreement with Sanger's own beliefs, required medical prescription for contraception.

With a new, more permissive law on the books, Sanger pursued medical doctors to run birth control clinics. In keeping with the medical profession's policy of distance from this populist movement, no gynecologists wanted to work for the cause. Sanger found female doctors (whose sex made finding work difficult) whose private practices functioned as clinics, accepting referrals from the American Birth Control League (founded by Sanger in 1921) located across the hall.

In 1917 Sanger founded the National Birth Control League, which became the Planned Parenthood Federation of America, and launched *The Birth Control Review.* Between the wars Sanger went on tour throughout the United States, creating a network of birth control clinics nationwide, and

teaching physicians contraceptive technique, a subject not taught in medical schools.

In 1929, the year in which Sanger founded the National Committee on Federal Legislation for Birth Control, civil authorities forbade her to speak in Ford Hall, Boston. Sanger did not let her message go unheard: she simply stood with her mouth taped shut while Harvard historian Arthur M. Schlesinger, Sr. read her speech.

Sanger conducted battles against the Catholic church and in the courts, winning decisions which undercut the prohibitive Comstock laws. She organized research and recruited manufacturers for birth control devices. In 1922 and 1936 Sanger conducted world tours and in 1927 organized the first International Birth Control Congress in Geneva.

This was also a time of new alliances for Sanger. She divorced her first husband, whom she had left in 1912, and in 1922 married Noah Slee, a millionaire seventeen years her senior. Slee did not demand Sanger's fidelity (in keeping with her ideology of sexual exploration she had many lovers), providing her campaign with respectability and significant financial support. She campaigned for President Franklin D. *Roosevelt to incorporate birth control in the public health programs of the New Deal. By 1940 Eleanor Roosevelt publicly endorsed her campaign.

In her bid for wide-ranging support Sanger joined efforts with wealthy women and with eugenicists, who advocated a restriction of births among the more "unfit" elements of society. While it seems she was careful to define "unfit" as restricted to the physically handicapped and mentally retarded, this alliance cost her the support of the left wing circles in which her campaign had begun.

Sanger's alleged interest in maintaining exclusive control of the movement, her populist methods, and her combative nature may have hindered her movement's progress. However, at her death in 1966 she had succeeded in convincing much of the world to view birth control as a human right. She wrote *Woman and the New Race* (1920), *Happiness in Marriage* (1926), *My Fight for Birth Control* (1931), and an autobiography (1938).

E. Chesler, *Woman of Valor: Margaret Sanger and the Birth Control Movement in America,* 1992.

D. M. Kennedy, *Birth Control in America: The Career of Margaret Sanger,* 1970.

L. Lader, *The Margaret Sanger Story,* 1955.

SAN MARTIN, JOSÉ DE (1778–1850), Argentinian soldier and liberator. Born in Yapeyu in northern Argentina, where his father was a prominent official in the Spanish colonial administration, San Martin received a military education in Madrid, Spain, to where his family returned when he was six years old. In 1793 he was commissioned as a second lieutenant, rising to the rank of lieutenant colonel by 1808. During this period he saw action on the Portuguese frontier, against the British (by whom he was held captive for over a year from 1798), and in the Peninsular War, in which he served the British-backed Spanish guerilla forces opposing *Napoleon Bonaparte's rule in Spain.

In 1812 San Martin resigned his commission and, after getting permission to travel to the Peruvian city of Lima — which was the center of Spanish power in South America — went instead to Buenos Aires, where he offered his services to the revolutionary government in Argentina, then threatened by Spanish royalist forces. His sudden switch to opposition to Spain, which he had served loyally for nearly twenty years, may in part be attributed to the persistent prejudice he experienced from peninsular Spaniards, who looked down on anyone who had been born in the colonies. It has been suggested that he was recruited by British sympathizers to the cause of Latin American independence; his own explanation was that he could no longer be indifferent to the call of his native land.

San Martin decided that the only way to liberate Argentina from the Spanish threat was in the context of a continental liberation plan which involved attacking Spain in her Peruvian stronghold. To this end, he took his forces north, defeating the Spanish at San Lorenzo on the Parana River in 1813. The following year he was promoted to the rank of general and appointed commander of the army of Upper Peru, which had suffered a series of defeats at the hands of the Spanish on the Bolivian plateau.

In order to lay the foundations for his bid to conquer Peru, San Martin now feigned ill-health in order to justify ceasing the abortive campaign in which he was engaged, and had himself elected military governor of Cuyo, a district of northern Argentina. There, he spent three years developing his audacious and original plan to invade Chile and advance north towards Lima by sea, and drilled his soldiers into a force capable of such an ambitious venture. His task was made harder by the rout of the nationalist forces in Chile, with whom he had hoped to link up, and his army had to fight their way across the Andes. Their victory at the Maipo River in 1817 signaled the end of Spanish power in Chile.

Declining the Chilean presidency in favor of his lieutenant, Bernardo O'Higgins, San Martin set about creating the navy he needed to approach close enough to Lima for the final land-based attack. In 1820 his motley fleet of armed merchant ships set sail from Valparaiso with 4,500 soldiers on board. Disembarking at Parasian, his forces soon occupied the coast to within 150 miles south of Lima and roundly defeated the royalists at the Battle of Pisco, capturing the Spanish general and most of his artillery. San Martin rejected any terms that did not concede absolute independence and, when the royalists in Lima finally despaired of assistance from the Spanish king, was able to occupy the city virtually unopposed. Peruvian independence was declared on July 22, 1821, and San Martin was installed as "protector." In this capacity, he expelled the majority of Spaniards and introduced a number of liberal reforms, which included ending the exploitation of native Indian labor, abolishing slavery, and creating a system of annual redemptions of quotas of living slaves.

San Martin's political career ended abruptly after his secret meeting with Simon *Bolivar, the liberator of northern Latin America, in 1822. They met at Guayaquil, which Bolivar had annexed despite San Martin's hope that it would opt for incorporation into Peru. The substance of their discussion remains the subject of speculation, but shortly thereafter San Martin resigned his protectorship and military command and returned to Argentina. First and foremost a military man, he had been unprepared for handling such problems as his own officers' suspicions that he had dictatorial or even monarchical ambitions, or his uncertainty that the Peruvian people would remain loyal to the new order. In 1824 he sailed for Europe, thereby distancing himself from the chaos that followed Latin American independence; he remained in self-imposed exile until his death in Boulogne, France. In 1880 his remains were removed and reinterred in the cathedral in Buenos Aires.

Widely revered in the land of his birth, where he is hailed as the "Liberator of the South," San Martin evinced a dedication to continent-wide independence, and was in favor of a centralized constitutional monarchy for Latin America. As a military leader, he exhibited outstanding ability in training and motivating his forces, while his feat in leading his men across the Andes has led to comparisons with *Hannibal and *Napoleon.

J. C. Metford, *San Martin the Liberator*, 1971.
B. Mitre, *The Emancipation of South America*, 1969.

SAPPHO (c.610-c.580 B.C.E.), Greek lyric poet. She was born in Eresus on the Greek island of Lesbos to an aristocratic family. Probably due to civil strife, her family was forced to flee their homeland when Sappho was still quite young. They traveled first to Pyrrha and then to Syracuse in Sicily where they spent several years before returning to Mitylene in Lesbos. Little is known about Sappho's background although she had at least two brothers: Charaxos, a trader who may have squandered the family fortune to buy a mistress in Egypt, and Larichos, a cupbearer in Mitylene. Sappho married a merchant, Cercolas, from Andros to whom she bore a daughter, Cleis.

Like many noblewomen of her day, Sappho spent her time with a circle of young women organized to worship the Muses and Aphrodite. Her poetry describes her passionate feelings for this circle of friends and her jealousy toward rivals for the girls' affections; it is from these passionate expressions that the term "lesbian" originated. At the same time Sappho often wrote marriage hymns for her friends.

Little is known about Sappho's private life other than what is recorded in later legends. She is alternately described as beautiful and as being short,

"SEIZURE"

To me that man equals a god
As he sits before you and listens
Closely to your sweet voice
And lovely laughter – which troubles
The heart in my ribs. For now,
As I look at you my voice fails
My tongue is broken and thin fire
Runs like a thief through my body.
My eyes are dead to light, my ears
Pound and sweat pours over me.
I shudder, I am paler than grass
And am intimate with dying – but
I must suffer everything being poor.

From *Sappho* by W. Barnstone

dark, and ugly, "like a nightingale with misshapen wings." Legends about Sappho flourished and she is the subject of at least six Greek plays.

Sappho's lifestyle has caused her poetry to be the subject of much debate and scrutiny. Although some scholars have rejected the claim that Sappho was a lesbian, claiming that the erotic language of her poetry was common to the worship of Aphrodite (of which Sappho would then have been a priestess), others take for granted the sexual inclinations of the poet. One scholar has gone so far as to claim that there were two Sapphos, one a poet, the other a prostitute.

Alexandrine scholars edited her works and the little that is extant – only 700 lines – is known mainly from papyri. Only one complete poem has survived. Not only has her work been lost, it was often destroyed because of its sensuous nature. In about 380 C.E. Saint Gregory of Nazianzus ordered her books burned, calling her "a lewd nymphomaniac." As late as 1073 C.E. Pope Gregory VII ordered her surviving writings to be burned. Some of those that survived were discovered in Egypt, where they had been used to wrap mummies.

Sappho's known poetry is rich in natural imagery. She was one of the first in the western world to sing of romantic love, using images of flowers, the sun, the moon, and the stars in describing her emotions. Simplicity of expression is accompanied by the use of melodious words and varied meters. Her poetry, originally written in the dialect of Lesbos, was meant to be sung accompanied by a lyre.

Nothing is known about how or when Sappho died, though according to legend, she fell in love near the end of her life. When her love was unanswered she flung herself from a cliff on the island of Leucas.

M. Giebel, *Sappho*, 1980.

J. J. Winkler, *The Constraints of Desire*, 1990.

SARGON II (died 705 B.C.E.), Assyrian king, founder of the Sargonid dynasty. The name Sargon, known through the Bible, is the Hebrew rendering of Sharru-kin, "the righteous king." He succeeded his presumed father (actually more probably his brother), Tiglath-Pileser III, in 722 B.C.E.; his elder brother, who was next in line for the throne, may have died or been deposed.

Primary documentary sources of evidence about Sargon's reign are sparse, consisting of a few cuneiform inscriptions, but in conjunction with references in the Old Testament they provide some idea of his achievements. Confronted by a succession of rebellions that constantly broke out in various parts of his empire, he nonetheless managed to consolidate the conquests of his predecessor. The year after his accession was marked by the successful conclusion of the campaign which had been set into motion by Tiglath-Pileser, to destroy the northern kingdom of Israel. The Old Testament relates (2 Kings 17) how Sargon had the Israelites carried away to Assyria, an action which attests to his policy of transporting peoples from conquered regions to distant parts of the empire to prevent a subsequent reemergence of nationalist sentiment.

The defeat of Hamath and Damascus in 720 B.C.E. signaled the subduing of the major previously-unconquered states of Syria, while in 714 B.C.E. Sargon's forces succeeded in defeating those of Urartu (modern-day Armenia) and breaking the power of that rival kingdom. In 712 B.C.E. Sargon crushed Ashdod, thereby breaking up an Egyptian-Palestinian conspiracy against him; the latter part of his reign was marked by such insurrections, which were incited and masterminded by the Chaldean tribal chieftain Merodach-Baladan with the support of Hezekiah in Judah. Sargon eventually triumphed against his opponents, becoming king of Babylon in 710 B.C.E., but Merodach-Baladan managed to escape into exile and, after Sargon's death, returned to plague his son, *Sennacherib.

Sargon's rule was a time of great artistic and cultural accomplishments. He built a splendid new capital for his empire, the city of Dur Sharukin (modern Khorsabad, Iraq), which contained a magnificent palace adorned with remarkable stone reliefs, some of which are now on display in the Louvre Museum, Paris. One of the most outstanding relics of his rule is a poetically resonant record of his invasion of Urartu. Most probably commissioned and approved by Sargon, it consists of a dramatic reconstruction of the campaign and includes an arresting description of the might of his armies as they would have appeared to the anxious enemy soldiers viewing their approach from afar. The style and finesse of the composition testify to the levels of literary excellence which were achieved through the king's patronage, and suggest that the Assyrian court was a place of great sophistication.

Sargon died as he had lived, campaigning to preserve and strengthen his domain; he met his end during an expedition against the Cimmerian tribes of Asia Minor, to be succeeded by Sennacherib.

G. Godspeed, *A History of the Babylonians and the Assyrians*, 1978.

A. G. Lie, *The Inscriptions of Sargon II*, 1929.

SARTRE, JEAN-PAUL (1905–1980), French author and philosopher, one of the most influential of the immediate post-World War II thinkers. Born in Paris, he lost his father at the age of two and moved with his mother to her parents' home. Much of what is known about his childhood is drawn from his own autobiographical *Les Mots* (The Words, 1964).

Deprived of his father, Sartre was extremely close to his mother while his grandfather, Charles Schweitzer (uncle of Albert *Schweitzer), although never a replacement for his father, figured centrally in his early years. He spent hours in his grandfather's library, first painstakingly teaching himself to read and then devouring French and German classics and the Larousse Encyclopedia. For him the library was a sanctuary and a window on the world but his mother, worried that he was being pushed too hard, made sure that he was also provided with adventure stories and lighter literature. Immersed in words and awed by their power, he began to write, beginning with adventures in which he was the hero.

From 1924 to 1928 Sartre studied at the École Normale Supérieure, where he passed with top

> - The passion of man is the reverse of that of Christ, for man loses himself as man in order that God may be born. But the idea of God is contradictory and we lose ourselves in vain. Man is a useless passion.
> - The more absurd is life, the more insupportable is death.
> - I distrust the incommunicable; it is the source of all violence.
> - Man is nothing else but what he makes of himself. That is the first principle of existentialism.
> - Respectable society believed in God in order to avoid talking about him.
> - It is enough for one man to hate another for hate to gain, little by little, all mankind.
> - Hell is other people.
> - When we love animals and children too much, we love them at the expense of men.
> - The world could get along very well without literature; it could also get along even better without man.
> - The poor don't know that their function in life is to exercise our generosity.
>
> **Jean-Paul Sartre**

marks on the second attempt, and taught philosophy at various high schools in Paris. In 1939 he was drafted into the French army and in 1940 captured by the Germans and held prisoner for a year. Upon his release he returned to Paris, where he continued to teach philosophy as well as coming active in the resistance. The German authorities, unaware of his activities, permitted him to produce his antiauthoritarian play *Les Mouches* (1943; The Flies, 1946). By 1944, he had given up teaching to devote himself fully to writing. The novels and plays he wrote in the postwar years made him world-famous. From his student days he maintained a close relationship and partnership with Simone de Beauvoir. They lived in close proximity in an open liaison and collaborated on many projects including *Les Temps modernes*, a periodical devoted to political and literary issues of an existential nature in which the conflict between Marxism and existentialism was often central. He was awarded the Nobel prize for literature in 1964 but refused to accept it because he believed it would compromise his personal integrity as a writer.

After World War II he became highly involved politically and was a supporter of the USSR until the suppression of the Hungarian revolution in 1956; his admiration for Marxism became increasingly critical. He wrote a four-volume study of Gustave *Flaubert examined through the lens of Marxist or Freudian theories (see Karl *Marx; Sigmund *Freud).

Sartre's existential philosophy, an attempt to define the essence of human beings, places him in the tradition of Edmund Husserl, Martin Heidegger, Georg *Hegel and Marx, who all influenced his writing. Simone de Beauvoir writes in *The Prime of Life* that when he first learned of phenomenology he saw in it the thing he had been longing for years: "to describe objects just as he saw and touched them, and to extract philosophy from the process." In 1933 he traveled to Germany to study it firsthand. Phenomenology revealed human existence as being primarily a being-in-the-world, which meant that any ordinary object could be seen as a matter of philosophical concern, so that, as Sartre put it, one could philosophize about everything, "even the essence of a gas street lamp .

Sartre's work can be roughly divided into three stages, the first being his contributions to phenomenological psychology, the second centering on the ontology of human existence, and the third devoted to the integration of Marxism and existentialism. His first two works were *L'Imagination* (1936; Imagination, 1962) and *L'Imaginaire* (1940; The Psychology of the Imagination, 1950), in which he developed the seminal idea that consciousness allows the human being freedom because it has the capacity to negate, i.e., not to be what it is, and to be what it is not. The crux of *L'Etre et le néant* (1943; Being and Nothingness, 1956), his central work, was the existential dilemma of how a consciousness can relate positively to other people and things in the world when freedom is defined in opposition to what is other than the self. In this work Sartre develops the distinction between consciousness — what he called being-for-itself — and objects, being-in-itself.

Being —for itself — or human consciousness, constitutes itself as being other than its physical environment, past, body, etc., i.e., as other than the world, and is characterized by the capacity to negate and rebel. This construction was the basis for his definition of freedom, to which he was deeply committed, and by which he meant the option to choose between abandoning oneself to the status quo and attempting to transcend it. Denying our freedom in the name of some form of psychological determinism he called bad faith, whereas its antithesis was acceptance of freedom and a recognition that human beings are the origin of, and solely responsible for, their own acts. Man, he argued, first exists, and then defines himself — there is no such thing as a given human nature because every act and choice we make contributes to the constitution of our identity. Such freedom, however, is also a burden of responsibility that fills us with anguish — thus his assertion that we are *condemned* to be free.

Sartre's theory of existential psychoanalysis also asserted the responsibility of the individual for his decisions, while the necessity of moral action and political commitment were central in his plays and novels. The novels include *La Nausée* (1938; Nausea 1949), *L'Age de raison* (1945; The Age of Reason, 1947), *Le Sursis* (1945; The Reprieve, 1947), and *La Mort dans l'âme* (1949; Troubled Sleep, 1950). Among his plays were *Huis-clos* (1944; No Exit, 1947), *Les Séquestrés d'Altona* (1960; The Condemned of Altona, 1960), *La Putain respectueuse* (1947; The Respectful Prostitute), and *Le Diable et le Bon Dieu* (1951; Lucifer and the Lord, 1953). His postwar works reflected a growing interest in Marxism as he attempted to reconcile the conflicting claims of Marxism for collective revolution and of existentialism for individual freedom, a debate which figured centrally in *Critique de la raison dialectique* (The Critique of Dialectical Reason, vol. 1, 1960, vol. 2, 1985). In his later writings Sartre returned to the theme of the imagination and the study of creativity as it was experienced by writers such as Jean Genet, André Mallarmé and Gustave Flaubert, but until his death maintained his critical stance and outspokenness in the political arena.

S. de Beauvoir, *Adieux,* 1984.
A. Cohen-Solal, *Sartre: A Life,* 1987.
J. Gerassi, *Jean-Paul Sartre,* 1989.
I. Murdoch, *Sartre,* 1987.

SAVONAROLA, GIROLAMO (1452–1498),

Italian religious reformer. A monk who attempted to reform Renaissance morals, he has been regarded both as a throwback to medieval times and as a precursor of the Reformation. The grandson of the duke of Ferrara's court physician, Savonarola stud-

Savonarola, by Fra Bartolommeo

ied medicine at the university of Bologna, but was more interested in philosophy, particularly the works of *Thomas Aquinas. Appalled by the irreverent speech and behavior at the university, he returned home and spent long hours praying and fasting before running away at age twenty-three to a Dominican monastery. He sent a letter to his parents explaining that he had chosen the religious life because he could not bear the proliferation of vice in the world. He stayed in the monastery for six years before feeling himself ready to preach.

The man who became one of history's most famous preachers was unpopular at first. He was assigned to Florence, but his sermons there were too didactic, too concerned with fine theological points, too couched in rough colloquialisms to be acceptable in a city accustomed to elegant, polished sermons. Attendance dwindled and he was reassigned to missionary work in northern Italy. There he fasted and flogged himself, began to hear angels speaking to him, and preached his apocalyptic sermons about the corruption of the church, its punishment, and its redemption. His vivid denunciations of immorality and calls for repentance attracted thousands. In 1489 he was sent back to Florence.

Savonarola became prior of San Marco monastery in Florence (1491), where he preached against the exploitation of the poor by the rich: "The poor are oppressed by grievous burdens; and when they are called to pay sums beyond their means the rich cry unto them, 'Give me the rest.' There be some who, having an income of fifty, pay a tax on one hundred, while the rich pay little, since the taxes are regulated at their pleasure." He also objected to Renaissance knowledge and art which he felt was basically pagan, sensual, and anti-Christian, and was outspoken in his opposition to its patron, Florence's *Medici ruler, Lorenzo the Magnificent.

At first Lorenzo tried to mollify Savonarola with rich gifts, attending his sermons and sending influential citizens to beg him to tone down his remarks. Then Lorenzo tried to siphon off Savonarola's audience with another preacher, a Franciscan friar famous for his eloquence, but Savonarola's church could not hold the numbers who still flocked to hear him, and Savonarola had to preach in the cathedral. Attendance at his sermons grew when Savonarola prophecied the deaths of Lorenzo and the Pope and invasion by Charles VIII of France. When Lorenzo and the Pope died in 1492 many began to think that Savonarola was a prophet and he became the most powerful man in Florence.

Charles invaded Italy (1494) and forced Piero, Lorenzo's son, to agree to such unfavorable terms that Piero was deposed and had to flee with his family. For years Savonarola had warned Florence that Charles, God's chosen scourge, would soon be crossing the Alps to punish his unrepentant people for their evil ways. Awed by the fulfillment of this prophecy, the people of Florence called for Savonarola to lead them. He advised the Signory to accept Charles's terms, welcomed Charles in the name of God, urged him to treat Florence well, and persuaded him to continue onward before his men did too much harm. He suggested the type of constitution adopted by Florence's new republican government and proposed a program of political, economic, and moral reform. Most of all he called for Florence to repent so that "...then wilt thou be rich with spiritual and temporal wealth; thou wilt achieve the reformation of Rome, of Italy, of all countries, the wings of thy greatness shall spread over the world."

Savonarola attempted to bring about his reforms with laws. Interest rates were lowered; almost all taxes were abolished; horse races, obscene songs, profanity and gambling became illegal; lawbreakers were tortured. The pre-Lent carnival was changed from a semipagan frolic into a Christian celebration. Children were organized into bands that went about asking for charitable contributions, searching for gamblers, and stripping people of their ornaments. Florence was transformed; churches were filled, people sang hymns rather than secular lyrics, and servants and children were encouraged to inform against offending masters and parents. Women came to the public square to fling down their ornaments and Savonarola's followers made a "bonfire of vanities."

However, there was opposition to Savonarola's reforms in Florence. Medici supporters, skeptics, those who longed to indulge their vices, and Fran-

ciscans objecting to the preeminence of a rival order were called the *Arrabiati* (mad dogs) by Savonarola's supporters. In Rome Pope Alexander VI favored Savonarola's reforms but questioned his claim to divine inspiration and opposed his pro-French politic.

In 1495 Alexander asked Savonarola to come to Rome and explain his prophecies. When Savonarola refused to go, fearing that Alexander would not allow him to return to Florence, Alexander ordered him to submit to Church authority and stop preaching; Savonarola refused. Frequently carried away by his own rhetoric, he had come to believe himself infallible, often saying "Only if God errs, can I be said to err."

1496 was an eventful year for Florence. Charles withdrew from Italy, incessant rain spoiled most of the crops, subject cities demanded their freedom, trade suffered, the treasury was exhausted, and an *Arrabiati* became head of government. In 1497 people were dying of hunger in the streets, an *Arrabiati* riot disrupted Savonarola's Ascension Day sermon, and Savonarola was excommunicated.

There were outbreaks of plague in 1498 but Savonarola continued preaching, declaring the excommunication invalid and anyone upholding it heretic. When the Signory ordered him, at Alexander's request, to stop, Savonarola made a wild attempt to get rid of Alexander by writing to Europe's kings and asking them to call a general council to remove Alexander from the papacy. Alexander told the Signory that he would put Florence under interdict if Savonarola were not stopped. The Signory agreed, fearful that an interdict would harm Florentine trade.

A Franciscan friar declared that Savonarola was a false prophet and offered to prove it with an ordeal by fire. A Dominican monk accepted the challenge. The fires were prepared, processions of Franciscan and Dominican monks escorted their champions through crowds of people to the waiting piles of wood, but theological arguments prevented the ordeal from taking place. Most of Savonarola's supporters lost confidence in him, cheated of the promised spectacle and disillusioned at the lack of a miracle. Two weeks later an *Arrabiati* mob stormed San Marco, killing supporters and monks before the Signory sent troops to arrest Savonarola and lead him away through jeering crowds.

Savonarola and two monks were imprisoned and tortured for forty-three days. Savonarola broke, confessing anything while being tortured and retracting his confession between sessions. They were condemned by both church and state on a variety of charges, including schism and heresy, and were hanged and burnt at the stake. Alexander sent them absolution.

R. Erlanger, *The Unarmed Prophet, Savonarola*, 1988.

P. Van Paasen, *A Crown of Fire*, 1960.

D. Weinstein, *Savonarola and Florence*, 1970.

SCHILLER, JOHANN CHRISTOPH FRIEDRICH VON (1759–1805), German drama-
tist, poet, and critic; one of the most influential figures in European drama. Until the age of thirteen, Schiller attended the best schools; aspired to study theology and become a minister in the Protestant church, but Duke Karl Eugen of Württemburg, for whom Schiller's father was groundskeeper, exerted an inordinate influence over the Schiller family and insisted that young Schiller attend his newly opened military academy in Stuttgart. Schiller now began a period of his life that isolated him from the outside world, his family, and friends, and subjected him to the constant scrutiny of the duke.

The years he spent at the academy left Schiller resentful and boiling with rebellious creativity. The education he received under the duke was wide-ranging and introduced him to contemporary social and philosophical issues, but the constraints on his freedom were almost unbearable. After studying law for a time, he switched to medicine and on preparing for graduation wrote a paper that criticized the medical authorities, for which he was punished with an additional year of study. His final paper earned him release from the academy but, because he had not come from a university, he was limited to an army position where he had to dress in uniform — a further torment for him.

In 1781 Schiller published his first play, *Die Räuber* (The Robbers), an emotionally explosive work he had been developing during his final years at the academy. It tells the story of a father deceived by one brother into disowning the other. Karl, the brother cast out, organizes a band of robbers, but his idealistic intentions come to evil under the influence of the thugs who join him. To free himself from his oath to the group, he kills his beloved and penitently turns himself in to the authorities. This play culminated the *Sturm und Drang* (Storm and Stress) movement, a wild expression of native energy among Germany's writers, and catapulted Schiller to fame, the critics speaking of him as a German Shakespeare.

However, Duke Karl disapproved of Schiller's play and threatened that he would lose his position if he wrote anything other than medical treatises, so Schiller fled the security of his position and past in order to pursue his literary career. To escape the duke, he had to cross the frontier at night, heading for Mannheim with his friend, the musician, Andreas Steicher. In his possession was a new play, *Die Verschwörung des Fiesko zu Genua* (Fiesco; or, the Genoese Conspiracy), set in sixteenth-century Genoa and dramatizing the guile of an ambitious man who fails in his political rise. Schiller's play was rejected by the city's baron, who did not want to antagonize his neighbor, the duke from whom Schiller had fled. The author lived from hand to mouth until he was taken in by the family of one of his friends from the academy. Here he completed his third tragedy, *Kabale und Liebe* (the Minister) a powerful portrayal of the conflict between feeling and convention, and began work on a fourth play, *Don Carlos*, centering on the royal family of Spain, a political work of great length and complexity.

With the passage of time Schiller became an established figure in Mannheim, and in 1783 he became theater poet of the city. He fell in love with Charlotte von Kalb, the wife of a French army captain, the pain of his situation resulting in a series of poems of passion and resignation. In 1790 Schiller married Charlotte von Lengefeld, and despite the author's intensity and emotionality, the relationship remained stable and harmonious to the end of his life. From 1789, Schiller lived in Jena, where he was professor of history at the university; in 1799, he settled in Weimar.

In addition to his plays, Schiller is also known for his writings on the philosophy of aesthetics, published between 1793 and 1801. His essays, "On Grace and Dignity" and "On the Sublime," strive to reconcile morality and reason, which the German philosopher Immanuel *Kant had held in opposition. Schiller proposed their harmonization through aesthetics, beauty and grace joined through moral action, the soul in creativity combining the physical and moral in an unrestricted interchange.

In 1794 Schiller began a friendship with Johann Wolfgang *Goethe. The two collaborated on a number of literary works and Goethe was inspired to renewed creativity as a result of Schiller's influence. Schiller produced a series of historical dramas, beginning in 1800 with *Mary Stuart*, dramatizing the last three days of *Mary, Queen of Scots before her execution. In 1801, *Die Jungfrau von Orleans* (The Maid of Orleans) depicted, with heroic alterations, the life of *Joan of Arc. In 1803 he utilized Euripidean form in his tragedy *The Bride of Messina*. He also wrote *William Tell* and the trilogy, *Wallenstein*; he was also a noted poet and literary critic.

- Art is the right hand of nature. The latter only gave us being, but the former made us men.
- The greater part of humanity is too much harassed and fatigued by the struggle with want to rally itself for a new and sterner struggle with error.
- Happy is he who learns to bear what he cannot change.
- Subdue the bitterness of the heart. No good results when hatred is returned for hatred.
- A word may be recalled, a life never.
- With stupidity the gods themselves struggle in vain.
- Contempt is the real death.

Schiller

When Schiller was still at the height of his creative powers, brimming with plans for further plays, his health, never robust, was broken by a painful internal disorder. He slept during the day and wrote at night, but at the age of forty-five he succumbed to his disease.

H. B. Garland, *Schiller, the Dramatic Writer: A Study of Style in the Plays*, 1969.
I. Graham, *Schiller's Drama: Talent and Integrity*, 1974.
H. Koopman, *Schiller*, 1988.

SCHLIEMANN, HEINRICH (1822–1890), German archeologist who proved that the Heroic Age of Greece was not myth but reality. Schliemann was born at Neu Buckow in Mecklenburg-Schwerin to a poor pastor. Obsessed by the Homeric stories, he wanted to become a linguist and came to know eight languages apart from German, including ancient and modern Greek.

After being sent out to Saint Petersburg by a commercial house in 1846, he set up his own company and traded in indigo. He made a fortune during the Crimean War, partly as a military contractor. In 1868 he moved to Greece, where he spent his time visiting Homeric sites. He then published a book, *Ithaka, der Peloponnes und Troja*, (1869) in which he put forward two theories which he was later to test: that Hissarlik (some four miles from the mouth of the Dardanelles) rather than Bunarbashi was the site of Troy, and that the Atreid graves that Pausanias saw at Mycenae were within the citadel wall.

In 1870 he started working on Calvert's excavations at the former site and, believing that Troy was on the lowest level, cut downwards, disregarding the upper strata, where the remains of the Troy of *Homer that he was seeking in fact lay. In 1873, the day before he was due to cease his digging for the season, he made the sensational discovery of 8,700 pieces, which he called "Priam's Treasure." He had unearthed large fortifications and other remains of a very ancient city that had been burned. Although Schliemann announced that it was Troy, this city is now known to have belonged to the middle pre-Mycenaean period, a thousand years before Homer's Archaeans. At the time, he was widely supported in his claim; only later was it realized that he had in fact destroyed much of the remains of the real Troy.

In 1874 Schliemann was prohibited by the Ottoman government from continuing his work, as they were dissatisfied with their share of the treasure. Only two years later did he receive permission to resume his excavations. In the meantime he had published *Troja und Seine Ruinen* (Troy and its Remains, 1875) and gone to Mycenae. In 1877 he began investigating the dome-tombs and the area near the Lion Gate, and opened up a large pit just inside the citadel of Mycenae. Here he discovered the now-famous double ring of slabs and stone reliefs. In the rock shaft, six royal graves were discovered, containing the most valuable treasure trove known, including gold, silver, bronze, fine stone and ivory objects, proving the existence of a great pre-Hellenic civilization. The find was deposited in Athens, and Schliemann published *Mykenä* (Mycenae,1878), becoming famous for his discoveries. He had by then settled in Athens and married a Greek woman, building two magnificent houses that became notable centers for Athenian society.

Further excavations in Ithaca in 1878 were unsuccessful, and so he again took up his work at Hissarlik. Based on this, he published his *Ilios* (1881) and, in 1883, *Troja*. In 1880 he found the beautiful ceiling in the remains of the ruined dome-tomb of Orchomenus and in 1885, aided by Wilhelm Dorpfeld, cleared away earth on the rock of Tiryns, traditional birthplace of Hercules, to reveal a complete ground plan of a Mycenaean palace. This proved to be his last major discovery. He was unsuccessful in his searches for the Caesareum at Alexandria, the palace of Minos at Knossos in Crete, and the Aphrodite temple at Cythera (1888). He died while planning further digs at Hissarlik. His autobiography was published in 1892.

R. Payne, *The Gold of Troy*, 1958.
L. and G. Poole, *One Passion, Two Loves*, 1966.

SCHOENBERG, ARNOLD (Arnold Franz Walter Schönberg; 1874–1951), Austrian composer who pioneered atonality and profoundly influenced twentieth-century music. Schoenberg was born in Vienna to a Jewish family but was raised as a Catholic. At eighteen he became a Protestant and in 1933 he returned to Judaism as a reaction to nazism. He demonstrated musical talent early on, playing the violin and cello and composing chamber music. Nevertheless, he had to struggle for his livelihood, which he earned by orchestrating thousands of pages of other people's theater music and by conducting theater orchestras.

In 1899 he wrote his romantic and emotional string sextet *Verklärte Nachte* (Resplendent Night), and the large score for his choral-orchestral *Gurrelieder* (Songs of Gurra), which was influenced by Wagnerian idiom. Richard *Strauss awarded him the Liszt Fellowship on the strength of *Gurrelieder*, and arranged for him to have a place on the staff of the Stern Conservatory in Berlin.

In the following years Schoenberg developed his own style, which was mainly atonal, as shown in his *Three Piano Pieces* and *Five Orchestral Pieces*, the drama with music *Die glückliche Hand* (The Lucky Hand, 1913), and especially the cycle of twenty-one poems, *Pierrot lunaire* (1912), which was his best-known work. He maintained that "nothing must hinder the free expression of the subjective ego." For the next eight years from 1915, Schoenberg experimented with his "method of composing with the twelve notes of the chromatic scale," which he saw as the solution to the problem of organizing music without a tonal center. In 1923, after his years of public silence (which included a period in the Austrian army), he publicized his *Five Piano Pieces* and *Serenade*, among many other works. His innovativeness exposed him to widespread vilification from musical circles as well as in the press. However, although initially isolated, he became the leader of a school of musical revolutionaries.

In 1933 Schoenberg emigrated to the United States, becoming a naturalized citizen in 1940, and lived in Los Angeles, where he was a staff member at the University of Southern California and the Univeristy of California at Los Angeles. He produced his *Violin Concerto* in 1936, the *Ode to Napoleon* and the *Piano Concerto* in 1942, and arranged a string trio. He also demonstrated his identification with Judaism in his unfinished opera *Moses and Aaron, Kol Nidre,* and *Survivor from Warsaw.*

Schoenberg wrote a *Manual of Harmony* and one on *Counterpoint* in 1911; these were orthodox in their approach. In 1940 he produced the book The *Theory of Composition.* He also enjoyed painting, identifying himself with his friend Kandinsky an the Expressionist school.

M. F. Benson, *Arnold Schoenberg and the Crisis of Modernism,* 1991.

Q. M. Wham, *Schoenberg/Kandinsky,* 1991.

A. L. Ringer, *Arnold Schönberg: The Composer as Jew,* 1990.

SCHOPENHAUER, ARTHUR (1788–1860),
German philosopher. Bitter opponent of the absolute Idealist school of German philosophy represented by Georg *Hegel and Johann Fichte, Schopenhauer's influence on the thought and literature of today is considerable, although he only achieved recognition in the last few years of his life. "The philosopher of pessimism" had a great impact upon Friedrich *Nietzsche and hence on existentialism, inspired the "life philosophy" of Wilhelm Dilthey and Henri *Bergson, the cultural studies of the great Swiss historian Jacob Burckhardt, anthropology, and the psychoanalytic developments of Sigmund *Freud. In addition, his ideas affected the work of European artists as disparate as Richard *Wagner and Leo *Tolstoy, Joseph Conrad and Thomas *Mann.

The son of a wealthy Danzig merchant, Schopenhauer attended a private business school after having spent two years learning French in Le Havre between 1798 and 1800. It was at the school that he was first exposed to the spirit of the enlightenment and to the Pietistic sensitivity to the plight of humankind that was always evident in his own philosophy. His travels in Europe with his parents in 1803 only heightened his awareness of the poverty and misery that was the common lot of the poor.

With his father's death in 1805 Schopenhauer was able to forsake the business world and turn to study. At Berlin University he was influenced by *Plato and, crucially, Immanuel *Kant. He also became acquainted with, and came to reject, the doctrines of

Hegel's fellow Idealist, Fichte. Schopenhauer was awarded his doctorate in philosophy from the University of Jena in 1813. Meanwhile, his mother, Johanna, who was to achieve fame herself as the author of numerous novels, essays, and travelogues, had become a part of Johann *Goethe's circle in Weimar, and Schopenhauer himself went there in 1813–1814. He came into close and frequent contact with Goethe, and it was there that he first learned about the religion and philosophy of ancient India, and in particular the *Upanishads,* the Hindu holy texts that formed a base of his own philosophy. His misogynism can also be traced to his disapproval of his mother's supposed philanderings at this time.

It was during the four years he spent in Dresden between 1814 and 1818 that Schopenhauer composed the work for which he subsequently became famous, *The World as Will and Idea.* Rejecting the prevailing philosophical preoccupation with spirit and reason, he identified intuition, creativity, and the irrational as key features of human and social consciousness. Expressing his conviction that reality is inherently malignant and that the only way out for ordinary people lies in the world of selfless contemplation, he criticized Hegelianism for serving the material ends of its professors rather than the pursuit of truth; he also scorned its interpretation of human history as an inevitable march of progress.

Like Kant, Schopenhauer rejected the notion that reason can have knowledge of things-in-themselves; however, he further argued that we have another, nonintellectual access to reality which is provided by the will. Since Schopenhauer considered that our futile attempts to appease the appetites of the will constitute the main source of our suffering, he espoused art as the sole arena of human endeavor in which one may escape subjection to the will, through free esthetic contemplation. He even ordered the arts hierarchically, from architecture through poetry to music, in terms of their efficacy in facilitating such a suspension in the workings of the will.

A brash and egotistical young man, Schopenhauer marked his appointment to the post of lecturer at Berlin University in 1820 by scheduling his lectures at the same time those of Hegel; unsurprisingly, he attracted few listeners. He retired from his post in 1833, expressing his contempt for the academic philosophy of the age, and moved to Frankfurt, where he remained until his death. It was here that he adopted a punctilious and idiosyncratic lifestyle, living as a crotchety bachelor. Although he desired fame, he appears to have accepted its absence stoically, remarking with characteristic irony that "the truth can wait, for it lives a long time."

A second edition of *The World as Will and Idea* appeared, almost unnoticed, in 1844, but in 1853 Schopenhauer's fortunes changed and he achieved recognition as the tide turned against Idealism: "the Nile has reached Cairo," he remarked. Courses in his philosophical ideas followed, as did the approba-

- Men need some kind of external activity because they are inactive within.
- There is one respect in which brutes show real wisdom when compared to us – their quiet placid enjoyment of the present moment.
- Politeness is to human nature what warmth is to wax.
- With people of only moderate ability, modesty is a mere honesty; but with those who possess great talent it is hypocrisy.
- Every man takes the limits of his own field of vision for the limits of the world.
- Time is that in which all things pass away.
- To desire immortality is to desire the eternal perpetuation of a great mistake.
- We deceive and flatter no one by such delicate artifices as we do our own selves.

Arthur Schopenhauer

tion of wider intellectual public. His elegant and jargonless literary style, together with his astute individualism, was refreshing as well as important in an age dominated by often opinionated, portentous, and obscure prose.

D. W. Hamlyn, *Schopenhauer*, 1988.
C. Janaway, *Self and World in Schopenhauer's Philosophy*, 1989.
R. Safranski, *Schopenhauer and the Wild Years of Philosophy*, 1989.

SCHRÖDINGER, ERWIN (1887–1961), Austrian physicist who in 1933 was awarded the Nobel Prize for his discovery of wave mechanics. In 1906 he entered University of Vienna to study mathematics and physics, graduating at the top of his class in 1910.

After a year's compulsory military service as an officer he returned to civilian life and was immediately appointed assistant professor in experimental physics at Vienna University. By 1914 his reputation was widespread, yet two events nearly reshaped his life. First, he fell in love with a woman for whom he considered leaving the university to enter his family's textile business. The woman, however, was from a noble family and was dissuaded from marrying beneath her rank. Second, with the outbreak of World War I he was recalled to duty and he spent most of the war close to the Italian front, where he managed to write a few noteworthy papers.

In 1921 Schrödinger accepted a full professorship in Zurich, but arrived emotionally and physically exhausted. He was diagnosed as suffering from a mild case of tuberculosis and was forced to take a complete rest for several months in the Alps. Nevertheless, the next few tranquil years in Zurich enabled Schrödinger to advance his own thinking and begin correspondence with the other great physicists of the time. In 1924 a young French physicist, Louis de Broglie, expounded his theory on the wave/particle duality of light. Schrödinger quickly adopted the idea and in a few months began publishing a series of papers that presented a mathematical model for atomic structure that described electrons as "smeared" waves of energy. It was encapsulated in a mathematical relationship that became known as the Schrödinger Wave Equation, and formed the basis of wave mechanics.

The success of his model in accounting for observed phenomena was startling, even at a time of frenetic creativity among physicists. He had discovered the basic equations of quantum mechanics. All the same, his theory was competing with equally applicable alternative models, most notably those of Werner *Heisenberg and Paul Dirac. Schrödinger managed to demonstrate in later papers that the other models were in fact subsumed by his own. However, many questions remained, such as how could matter be smeared in a wavelike distribution. The answer was first proposed in 1926 by Max Born and J. Robert *Oppenheimer, who suggested that Schrödinger's wave equation did not describe an actual wave of matter, but rather the wave of probability that a particle would be found at a particular location in its orbit.

Schrödinger sent the last of his monumental papers for publication in 1926, and thus concluded his greatest achievement. Max *Planck, the German physicist, was so impressed by Schrödinger's work that he invited him to be his successor at Berlin University, which in 1927 had the preeminent institute for physics. Schrödinger was popular in Zurich and reluctant to leave, but in the end the lure of greater financial rewards, the prestige of the appointment, and the opportunity to work alongside Albert *Einstein, who also held a chair in Berlin and whom he admired above all other physicists, was too great. Schrödinger moved to Berlin, where he enjoyed his prominence and the lifestyle it afforded.

The year 1932 shattered his idyllic existence. Schrödinger, never political although perhaps mildly bigoted, was nonetheless outraged by the virulent anti-Semitism of the Nazi regime, even if he never publicly criticized the new government. In 1934 he left Berlin for Oxford without even resigning his chair. It was a slap in the face for the Nazis to see one of their most celebrated non-Jewish scientists turn his back on them. His arrival in Oxford was accompanied by the news that together with Dirac he had been awarded the 1933 Nobel Prize for physics.

In 1937 he returned to Graz in Austria. Despite his attempts to appease the Nazis after the *Anschluss* the following year, Schrödinger faced a withering and vengeful onslaught from them and was forced to flee to Rome. After spending some time in England and Holland, he accepted a chair at the newly established Institute of Advanced Science in Dublin, a scientific backwater but comfortably removed from the war. He remained there until 1956, when he was persuaded to return to Vienna and resume his own personal chair. In 1960 he had a relapse of tuberculosis and once again found himself recuperating in the Alps, but he died soon after. His best-known book is *What Is Life?*, which interprets the stability of genetic structure by quantum physics.

W. J. Moore, *Schrödinger*, 1989.
W. T. Scott, *Erwin Schrödinger*, 1967.

SCHUBERT, FRANZ PETER (1797–1828), Austrian composer. Born in Vienna, the youngest of twelve children, of whom only four survived infancy. His father taught him the violin and his eldest brother taught him the piano. At the age of nine, when it was obvious that young Schubert was a promising musician, his father sent him to study with an organist at a local church. His teacher once said; "If I wished to instruct him in anything fresh, he already knew it. Consequently I gave him no actual tuition but merely conversed with him and watched him with silent astonishment."

In 1808 Schubert, eleven years old at the time, was accepted as a choirboy in the imperial court chapel, which also meant admission to the Imperial and Royal City College. There he studied a variety of subjects and soon became the leader of the first violins of the students' orchestra. On occasion he also conducted the orchestra, an invaluable experience for a young musician who was also starting to compose at the time.

Schubert left the college at sixteen and entered a training school for elementary school teachers. A year later he was already teaching at his father's school and still made time to write some of his finest works. He was composing in a variety of mediums, from songs to symphonic work, from choral masterpieces to chamber music. In 1816 alone he wrote 110 songs, his fourth and fifth symphonies, a mass, nine sonatas, and an opera fragment, strongly believing that a successful opera could open many doors for him.

In July 1818 he accepted the position of music master to the daughters of Count Johann Esterhazy and resigned from his father's school never to return to teaching. After a few weeks in the court's court in Zseliz, Hungary, Schubert wrote to his friends, "Thank God, I live at last, and it is high time." In November he returned to Vienna and spent the summer of 1819 at Steyr, about one hundred and fifty kilometers west of Vienna, where he began composing his popular *Trout Quintet*. His name also became associated with stage music and he began to receive commissions to write music for stage plays.

By now Schubert was a famous composer whose songs and chamber music were performed regularly in Vienna. At the end of 1822, however, he contracted syphilis and half a year later was desperately ill, forced to move back to his father's home. Schubert's health was deteriorating but he continued to compose and even tried from time to time to succeed in the one genre he never was able to master, opera.

> I feel myself to be the most unhappy and wretched creature in the world. Imagine a man whose health will never be right again, and who, in sheer despair over this, ever makes things worse and worse, instead of better; imagine a man whose most brilliant hopes have perished, to whom the felicity of love and friendship have nothing to offer but pain...Thus joyless and friendless I pass my days.
>
> **Franz Schubert in a letter to a friend, 1824**

In 1825 Schubert recovered somewhat and resumed composing. Many of his works were published and performed not only in his native Vienna but also throughout Europe. In 1828, the year of his death, Schubert continued to write without rest, including some of his greatest masterpieces, such as the *Great Symphony in C major* (which was not performed until 1850). He also gave his only public concert, which was so successful that he was at last able to buy himself a piano. However, his health was declining and he could not afford the holiday he needed. Although there was a common belief that Schubert's death was caused by typhoid, it seems more likely that syphilis was the cause.

The works of Schubert are performed regularly all over the world. "Schubertiads," evenings featuring the music of Schubert, a tradition which began in his lifetime, are very popular in many places celebrations of the genius of a man who died too young.

Despite the poverty that plagued his life, music poured out of him and his legacy of melody is unparalleled. His symphonies are in the standard repertory with the *Unfinished Symphony* being one of the world's favorites; he also created the German *lied*. He wrote over 600 songs and set seventy poems by Johann *Goethe and forty-five by Johann *Schiller to music. Robert Schumann said of him: "He would set a placard to music." Opening by chance a volume of William *Shakespeare in a restaurant, he jotted down his setting of "Hark, hark the lark" on the back of the menu.

M. J. E. Brown, *Schubert Symphonies*, 1970.
G. R. Marek, *Schubert*, 1985.
B. Massin, *Franz Schubert*, 1978.

SCHWEITZER, ALBERT (1875–1965), German Nobel Prize-winning humanitarian, missionary, scholar, and musician. Schweitzer was born in Kaysensberg, Alsace, into the family of an Evangelical Lutheran pastor whose views and sense of mission were a strong and lasting influence. He was an able student, while his obvious musical talents were nurtured through his lessons with the master organist Eugene Munch. In 1893 he entered the University of Strasbourg, with which he was to remain associated until his departure for Africa.

While in Strasbourg studying theology and philosophy (on which he also lectured after being

Schweitzer at work in Lambaréné

awarded, in 1899, his doctorate for a thesis on Immanuel *Kant), Schweitzer was also a preacher at St. Nicholas's church; meanwhile his reputation grew as one of the foremost organists in Europe. As well as playing the instrument superbly, he also came to be a master of organ design and building. He was especially recognized as an unparalleled interpreter of J. S. *Bach's music; in 1905, he produced a biography of the composer, which became a standard work on its subject. Schweitzer portrayed Bach as a religious mystic, likening his music to the impersonal and cosmic forces of the natural world.

Schweitzer's next literary effort, his *Quest of the Historical Jesus*, published in 1906, had an epochal impact on biblical scholarship. He demonstrated the contradictory nature of much of the available evidence on the life and character of Christ, and pointed out that previous biblical scholars had been less rigorous than they should; rather than having the courage to follow the evidence wherever it led, they were content to stop their researches as soon as they had unearthed a picture of Jesus that could act as a focus for their own liberal projections. The Jesus whom Schweitzer revealed was an apocalyptic zealot who believed that the end of days was imminent and presented his teachings with appropriate prophetic and messianic vigor. Despite the tenor of these findings, the author himself remained firmly rooted in the Christian spiritual tradition and was greatly influenced by the nature of Christ's ministry among the poor and oppressed.

By the age of thirty Schweitzer was respected and renowned, with the promise of even more successes ahead. Then, to the shock and dismay of many of his colleagues and friends, he chose to make good an earlier resolve that at that age he would turn to devoting his energies to helping mankind. Moved to missionary work in the Congo as the vehicle for this service, he enrolled in the Strasbourg medical faculty to train as a doctor that he might be of more use to his African congregation.

Shouldering an enormous workload, Schweitzer financed his arduous medical studies by organ recitals and teaching, and with the aid of the royalties from his book on Bach. In 1912 he married Helen Bresslau, an accomplished scholar who trained as a nurse that she might be of more use in the Congo venture. On Schweitzer's qualification as a doctor in 1913, the couple journeyed to French Equatorial Africa (taking with them a zinclined organ), where they established a hospital on the Ogooue river "at the edge of the primeval forest ."

As the hospital mission grew, it became a place of pilgrimage. Nevertheless, some observers were disturbed by what they saw as Schweitzer's arbitrary, paternalistic, and dictatorial administrative techniques, but none could doubt his devotion to what he perceived as the well-being of his growing native Christian flock, even if they might object to his condescension towards them.

In 1915 a mystical experience he underwent while on a boat on the Ogooue converted Schweitzer to the philosophy of "reverence for life," which he outlined in the second volume of his magnum opus, *Philosophy of Civilization*. This boundless humanitarianism necessitated absolute nonviolence toward all sentient beings, and Schweitzer practiced what he preached with such vigor that he attempted to avoid harming the smallest insect; even such potential disease vectors as mosquitoes and flies were left unmolested.

With the exception of a period during World War I when he was interned by the French administration as an enemy alien, Schweitzer remained on the banks of the Ogooue until his death. In 1924 he relocated the hospital two miles upriver from its original site, where it grew until it accommodated 350 patients and their relatives, while the leper colony that was also established cared for some 150 people. Schweitzer's charisma and persuasive powers encouraged many people to come and work for him, so the project staff expanded until, at any given time, there were thirty-six white physicians and nurses and a varying number of native personnel in a complex of seventy buildings and 500 beds.

In order to maintain funding for the project Schweitzer occasionally returned to Europe, where he would give organ recitals and lectures on his work to raise money. He maintained a keen and intelligent interest in world affairs, and was quick to protest the terrible destructive capability of atomic power. In 1952 he was awarded the Nobel Peace Prize for his work. He wrote several works of autobiography, notably *Out of My Life and Thought*.

N. Cousins, *Dr. Schweitzer of Lambaréné*, 1960.
G. N. Marshall and D. Poling, *Schweitzer*, 1971.
G. Seaver, *Albert Schweitzer: The Man and His Mind*, 1969.

SCIPIO AEMILIANUS AFRICANUS NUMAN-
TINUS (the Younger; 185–129 B.C.E.), Roman soldier and statesman. Scipio was the son of Lucius Aemilius Paulus Macedonicus, a member of one of Rome's leading families who had led Rome to victory in the Third Macedonian War and divorced his wife soon after Scipio's birth. Scipio was later adopted by his cousin, Scipio Paulus, the sickly eldest son of *Scipio Africanus. Being heir to the traditions and expectations of two great Roman families overwhelmed the young man; he withdrew from the usual occupations of the Roman nobility — war and politics — and spent his time hunting.

The Greek historian Polybius became the slave-tutor of Scipio and his brother. A father-son relationship developed between Polybius and Scipio, which kindled both the latter's lifelong interest in Hellenistic culture and his military and political ambitions. Elected quaestor, he entered the Senate in 152 B.C.E., volunteering to go to Spain, where other Romans were reluctant to serve because it had been the site of a series of Roman military disasters; and there he distinguished himself for his bravery.

In 151 B.C.E. Carthage finished paying off its indemnity to Rome from the Second Punic War. Rome, outraged that Carthage had regained its prosperity, was determined to destroy it permanently and used Carthage's defending itself against Numidian attacks as an excuse to declare war (Carthage's treaty with Rome forbade making war without Rome's permission). Carthage tried to avoid war by meeting all of Rome's increasingly outrageous demands until, realizing that Rome's real goal was its destruction, it began to fight, resisting for three years until Scipio was made consul and commander of the forces besieging it. He completely destroyed Carthage by fire, enslaving its survivors, sowing its soil with salt, and cursing any attempt to rebuild it. With the defeat of Carthage, he was named "Africanus," Africa became a Roman province, and Rome ruled the Mediterranean.

Scipio then became the center of a group of Romans interested in Hellenistic literature and philosophy, particularly Stoicism. His reputation for generosity and stern temperance in a Rome where corruption and immorality were rapidly increasing, his conservatism, and his rhetoric led to his election as censor in 142 B.C.E.

Scipio's marriage to Scipio Africanus's grand-daughter Cornelia was not successful. At first he gave his support to his brother in law Tiberius Gracchus's agrarian reforms, which attempted to help the urban lower classes and solve the problem of rural depopulation by distributing state land to poor citizens. Elected consul in 134 B.C.E., he successfully concluded Rome's long war with Spain by starving the besieged rebels into surrender. Back in Rome, his support for Tiberius changed to opposition as the latter's proposed reforms became increasingly extensive and radical, until finally a group of senators charged the Forum and beat Tiberius to death with clubs.

When Scipio had the land redistribution laws suspended because of objections from large landowners, public opinion turned against him, he was denounced as a traitor to the sacred memory of Tiberius, and was found dead in his bed one morning. The exact cause of his death was never determined; the gossip of the day accused his wife and mother-in-law of murder.

A. E. Astin, *Scipio Aemilianus*, 1967.

SCIPIO AFRICANUS (the Elder; c.236–183
B.C.E.), Roman statesman and general. Scipio was a member of one of Rome's leading families at a time when the traditional stern Stoic virtues were both preached and practiced; Romans were, by law, on call for service in Rome's citizen's army from the age of sixteen to sixty. Scipio was seventeen when he saved his injured father during the Battle of Ticinus River, in which Rome was defeated by *Hannibal. At the age of nineteen he rallied Rome to form a new army and continue fighting after its defeat by Hannibal at Cannae. By the time he was twenty the Roman Senate, realizing that its traditional citizen's army could not defeat Hannibal, gave him command of Rome's forces in Spain until he defeated the power of Carthage there.

In Spain, Scipio's moderate rule converted many natives into allies. He won the devotion of his native troops, restored discipline, and revised their traditional military tactics. Spanish battlefields provided a training ground for Scipio's new tactics, and by 205 B.C.E. his military victories had made Spain into a Roman province, while his legions had turned into a professional army that was ready to meet Hannibal.

Appointed consul in 205 B.C.E., Scipio raised a new army and sailed for Africa to carry out his plan of defeating Hannibal by conquering Carthage. Carthage appealed to Hannibal for help and he left Italy, returned to Carthage, and formed a new army. Hannibal tried to reach an agreement with Scipio, but they were unable to come to terms and Carthage lost the subsequent Battle of Zama, despite Hannibal's wounding of Scipio in personal combat. The resultant peace treaty gave Rome control of the western Mediterranean, subordinated Carthage to Rome and cost it an enormous indemnity, but left its empire intact.

Scipio returned to Rome where he was very popular, to be rewarded with a triumph, the name "Africanus," and various positions of honor in the Senate, where he proved that he was a much better soldier than politician. Wary, the Senate refused to give him command of the army Rome sent to free Greek cities from Macedonian domination (the Second Macedonian War) because they were afraid that another victory would make him so popular and powerful that he might overthrow the Republic and make himself king. Reactionary senators were also hostile toward him because they felt that the Hellenistic culture and philosophy that his family, friends, and political allies (the Scipionic Circle) were known to favor would corrupt Rome's moral fiber.

Hannibal moved to fight corruption in Carthage in 196 B.C.E., but this was not approved by its oligarchy, who retaliated by sending word to Rome that he was plotting to renew the war. When the Roman Senate demanded his surrender — over Scipio's protests — Hannibal fled to Antiochus III of Syria and advised him to make war on Rome. Antiochus advanced into Western Asia, Rome was appealed to for help, and Scipio and his brother, Lucius Cornelius Scipio, set out from Rome. Scipio fell ill whereupon Antiochus released his captured son to him without demanding a ransom, so it was Lucius who led the first Roman army to set foot on Asian soil, defeating Antiochus at Magnesia, and beginning Rome's conquest of the East.

Scipio's victory in the Second Punic War converted Rome from an Italian to a Mediterranean power and also brought great wealth, increasing the demand for luxuries. The war itself decimated Italian farms and most of the peasants who survived left the land; they had either become too accustomed to the excitement of soldiering to settle back into farm life or could not face the effort required to restore war-devastated farmland. The vacant farmland was acquired by large landowners, who used them to grow fruit and livestock, and Rome became dependent on grain shipments from its conquered provinces.

B. H. Liddell Hart, *A Greater than Napoleon: Scipio Africanus,* 1971.

H. H. Scullard, S*cipio Africanus: Soldier and Politician,* 1970.

SCOTT, ROBERT FALCON (1868–1912), British explorer. Born in Devonport, one of six children of an established naval family. At age thirteen he entered the Britannia Naval College in Dartmouth as an officer cadet, after which he rose slowly in rank until by the early 1890s he had become a lieutenant.

When he learned that the Royal Geographical Society and the Royal Society were organizing an expedition to the Antarctic and wanted a naval officer to lead it, he recognized an opportunity to make his name. He managed to convince the president of the Society, Sir Clements Markham, that he was a suitable candidate.

The project was hampered from the start by Markham's romantic ideas of traveling only on foot, disdaining the use of skis and dogs. Before setting out Scott paid a courtesy call on the great Norwegian explorer Fridjtof *Nansen, who convinced him to take dogs and skis. However, Scott made no practical efforts to gain experience journeying over ice and was content to assume that he would be able to deal with each situation as it arose, 'muddling through' in the best amateur, gentlemanly tradition.

In August 1901 he set sail on a specially commissioned ship named *Discovery*, during the Cowes Week of yacht racing, one of the main events in the social calendar. The new king, Edward VII, and a glittering array of aristocrats were present to see Scott's expedition depart.

During the journey south, basic design faults in the ship became apparent; furthermore Scott failed to inspire the crew, who looked to junior officers for leadership. After repairs in New Zealand, Scott wrote to Nansen "I am distinctly conscious of a want of plan... face to face with the work I cannot but feel a lively sense of my own shortcomings."

Early in 1902 the *Discovery* entered uncharted waters and discovered the peninsula they named King Edward VII Land. It was a welcome taste of success but then they became trapped in a sea of icebergs and Scott panicked. The scene was not calculated to improve morale any more than the pointless daily washing of the decks on which he insisted; as soon as water was poured over them it turned to ice, which then had to be broken off.

The *Discovery* was trapped in the ice for two years. During this period Scott led several treks across land and reached the furthest point south yet seen. The achievement, however, was marred by his limited capabilities as a commander; lack of preparation brought needless suffering to both crew and animals, with overwork and illness taking a heavy toll. Scott's pettiness and isolation from his men and his recklessness with their lives almost ended in tragedy, as he insisted on trudging on although the scant provisions were almost exhausted. Skis and dogs were of limited use since the team had never learned how to use them properly. Despite gross mismanagement, there was enough of the heroic in the exploit to justify a letter of congratulations from Edward and promotion for Scott upon return to England in 1904.

Scott wrote *The Voyage of the Discovery*, glorifying this achievement of men pitted against the most adverse of environments. His concept of polar exploration was expressed in a passage where, though acknowledging the utility of dogs, he admitted his preference for travel on foot: "Surely in this case the conquest is more nobly and splendidly won."

Scott's book was popular but he felt dwarfed by the exploits of a former member of his team with whom he had often clashed, Ernest Shackleton. Shackleton returned to the Antarctic and reached within 300 miles of the South Pole. In 1908 Scott had married Kathleen Bruce, a woman with a far stronger personality than his. She spurred him on to return to the icy wastes and reach the Pole before any rival. There were several competitors also planning ventures, not least the seasoned Norwegian polar explorer Roald *Amundsen who had been preparing for the trek since 1907, although he kept the world believing that his target was the North Pole.

Scott did not absorb the lessons of his previous expedition. He remained convinced that dogs were of no help although now he decided to use motor-driven sledges and skis. His new vessel, the *Terra Nova*, was once more poorly stocked. In clothing, equipment and, most crucially of all, training, Scott's party was well behind that of Amundsen, who took a professional approach toward training and provisioning.

Scott's mismanagement and rashness again paved the way for disaster. Dogs and horses were purchased without proper supervision and arrived in poor condition. Expensive motor sledges were poorly constructed and in the end abandoned. The horses were unsuitable for the terrain and the group led by Scott to the Pole pulled the sledges on foot. Not only had he failed to procure the right equipment but he made a fateful miscalculation that left them with insufficient food supplies in store depots too far apart and badly indicated. Even the British flag was left behind by mistake in a hasty departure.

Scott and his colleagues reached the South Pole thirty-four days after Amundsen. Bitterly disappointed, brought low by illness and depression, they made a valiant struggle to return to base camp but never arrived. Captain Oates, knowing that his end was near, left the tent to die, saying, "I am just going outside and may be some time." Scott and his other two companions were found frozen to death in their tent, buried in a snow drift. Their diaries remained, literate and moving witness to Scott's tragic incapacity for leadership and its fatal consequences.

R. Huntford, *Scott and Amundsen*, 1979.
R. Pound, *Scott of the Antarctic*, 1966.
G. Seaver, *Scott of the Antarctic*, 1940.

SELIM I (1467–1520), Ottoman emperor. As the third son of Emperor *Bajazet II, there was little likelihood that Selim would ascend to the throne. After an abortive attempted coup, Selim fled to Crimea, where his son Süleyman was governor, to bide his time until a better opportunity presented itself. Meanwhile, his eldest brother Ahmed, began associating with the rebellious Shi'ite mystical sect, the Kizil Besh, for which he was barred from inheriting the throne. Selim forced his father to abdicate; on his way to retirement in Demotika, Bayazed suddenly died, apparently from poison administered at Selim's instigation. To assure his accession to the throne, he had his brothers Corcud and Ahmed strangled with bowstrings. Five young nephews were then murdered as Selim listened to their cries from an adjoining room. His cruelty earned him the epithet Selim Yavuz ("Selim the Grim").

When, in Persia, the Kizil Besh seized power under Shah Ismail, founder of the Persian Safavid dynasty, Selim massacred forty thousand of his own Shi'ite subjects to forestall any rebellion. Ismail sued for peace, but Selim, aroused by his self-proclaimed mission as a zealous defender of Sunni Islam, attacked him in Chaldiran, Armenia. Using European muskets and heavy artillery Selim easily defeated Ismail and occupied Eastern Anatolia and Tabriz in Azerbaijan. All prisoners were massacred except for some one thousand skilled craftsmen, who were taken to Istanbul to enhance Ottoman art.

With Ismail enfeebled, Selim now turned on the Mamelukes of Egypt, whom he believed to be in partnership with Ismail. He crushed their forces at Marj Dabiq, north of Aleppo, and swept through Syria to the Egyptian border. There, he offered the Mameluke ruler, Tuman Bey, the governorship of Cairo if he submitted, but the latter refused. Selim entered Cairo in 1517, cheered on by the masses, who despised the Mamelukes, and Tuman Bey was hanged from one of the city gates like a common criminal.

The Abbasid caliph then living in Cairo surrendered to Selim and was taken to Istanbul. He brought with him the standard and cloak of Muhammad, and the submission of the holy cities of Mecca and Medina. Although Selim never declared himself caliph, the Abbasid line was soon discontinued and the title was adopted by all Ottoman emperors. Selim, now the dominant figure in the Islamic world, declared that he had "no journey left to make except to the hereafter."

Despite his relative tolerance of Christian and Jewish minorities, Selim terrified his Muslim subjects, who were often executed at his whim. Among the victims were seven of his viziers, and the expression "May you be Selim's vizier" became a popular curse. Ever fearful of a sudden death sentence, the viziers began taking their wills with them whenever they were called to meet Selim. On one occasion, an audacious vizier asked when he would be killed. Selim answered, "I've actually been thinking about it for quite a while, but haven't yet found anyone to replace you." Despite this, Selim was a patron of literature and wrote poetry in Persian. He was succeeded by his son *Süleyman I the Magnificent.

M. A. Cook, *The History of the Ottoman Empire to 1730*, 1976.
Lord Kinross, *The Ottoman Centuries: The Rise and Fall of the Turkish Empire*, 1978.

SENNACHERIB (Hebrew form of Sin-ahhe-eriba; died 681 B.C.E.), Assyrian king. Ascending the throne in 705 B.C.E., Sennacherib inherited from his father, *Sargon II, an empire that extended from Babylonia to southern Palestine and into Asia Minor. However, an unavoidable concomitant of such a large and disparian kingdom, many of whose peoples resented Assyrian rule, was internal dissent and the predatory ambitions of jealous neighbors. He was able to counter these threats through the might of his well-trained and well-equipped armies, which drew on the increased resources made available as a result of the innovations of his reign.

In Babylonia, Sennacherib confronted the Chaldean and Aramean tribes which, as they grew in power, harried the old urban centers of the area, whose trade-minded inhabitants looked to their Assyrian overlords for protection. The uneasy peace in the region was broken in 703 B.C.E., when Sargon II's old enemy, the Chaldean chieftain Merodach-

Sennacherib seated on his throne

Baladan, reemerged to lead a tribal revolt which received the military backing of Sennacherib's rival, the southwest Iranian kingdom of Elam. Through skillful generalship, Sennacherib recovered northern Babylonia, drove out Merodach-Baladan, and appointed the native Babylonian Bel-ibni as sub-king. This marked the first of six campaigns he was forced to undertake in the region. He then went on to devastate the tribal areas of southern Babylonia.

In alliance with the Israelite king Hezekiah, Merodach-Baladan now instigated a further insurrection, this time in Palestine, with support from Egypt. Sennacherib's response was swift and effective, and his forces successfully captured all the rebel cities but Jerusalem, which only escaped conquest on payment of a substantial indemnity (although the Bible attributes its salvation to a miracle). Further intriguing by Merodach-Baladan necessitated another Assyrian campaign into the Chaldean area in 700 B.C.E. Defeated conclusively, Merodach-Baladan took refuge in Elam, where he soon died.

Sennacherib grew progressively more frustrated by having to face constant opposition in Babylonia, and by the suspicion and lack of support for him of its native population. As a result, he removed its native king and introduced direct Assyrian rule through his own son, Ashur-nadin-shum. This led to a brief period of stability, but soon he was faced with further conspiracies against him. In 691 B.C.E. the Assyrian army was defeated by a coalition of Babylonian and Elamite forces at Khaluli. Once he had recovered from this blow, an exasperated Sennacherib retaliated by laying siege to Babylon. The city held out for nine months before it was captured. It was then sacked, Sennacherib's ire outweighing his respect for the city in its capacity as the cultic center of the religion of the Assyrian empire.

Sennacherib's rule was notable for developments in architecture, agriculture, and industry, all of which contributed to the splendor of the new capital, Nineveh. Using prisoners-of-war as laborers, he built a new palace and extended and beautified the city, while the great inner and outer walls he built to surround it — which stretch for over eight miles — still stand. The building of Tarsus is also attributed to Sennacherib's initiative.

An expanding population meant increased demand for food and clothing: therefore, cotton plants were for the first time cultivated in the region (they were known as the "wool-bearing tree"), and an ingenious irrigation system, consisting of six miles of canals and a massive stone aqueduct, fed the Khost River with spring-water so that the extensive new plantations of fields and orchards could be adequately watered. Assyrian metalworkers developed a new system for bronze-casting, and better equipment was designed for raising water from wells.

Sennacherib eventually died by the hand of one of his sons.

B. S. Childs, *Isaiah and the Assyrian Crisis*, 1967.
L. Homer, *Sennacherib's Invasion of Palestine*, 1966.
H. W. Saggs, *The Greatness That Was Babylon*, 1962.

SETON, ELIZABETH ANN (Elizabeth Ann Bayley; 1774–1821), Roman Catholic saint and American religious figure. Seton was born in New York City to a wealthy and distinguished family. As a young woman, her concern for the sick and poor earned her the title of Protestant sister of charity. Her father was a well-known area physician who brought his children up in an Episcopal home.

In 1794 she married William M. Seton, a merchant, and in the ensuing years the couple had five children. In 1803 the family traveled to Italy to care for William's ailing health, but he failed to recuperate and died. Seton was left to mourn her husband in a foreign country, and was taken in by the Filicchi family, who were old acquaintances. The Filicchis were Roman Catholics, and it was their devotion that eventually led Seton to the Roman Catholic church. She returned to the United States and after an inner, spiritual struggle, she joined the Catholic church in 1805, becoming a member of Saint Peter's congregation in New York City. Her choice was not popular among her friends, most of whom were influenced by the anti-Catholic sentiment of that era.

In 1808 she moved to Baltimore, where she opened a grade school for girls. Several young women were placed under her care, and they soon took vows to be the Sisters of Charity of Saint Joseph. She moved the school to Emmitsburg, Maryland in 1810 and opened the first free parochial school in the United States for both boys and girls, laying the foundation for the American parochial school system. In her work for the Sisters of Charity, as the organization was now called, Seton brought many black children into the school. She was now called Mother Seton, although she was allowed to keep legal guardianship over her natural children. Through her work with the Sisters of Charity, Seton became known as the mother of American Catholic sister-school nuns, as well as the mother of the parochial school system in the United States.

She was not a mystical person in an unattainable niche. She battled against odds in the trial of life with American stamina and cheerfulness. She worked and succeeded with American efficiency.

Francis Cardinal Spellman at Seton's beatification ceremony in 1963

Her legacy outlived her. In 1852 the Sisters of Charity founded an orphanage, and in 1907 the case for her beatification was opened. In 1963 she was canonized by Cardinal Francis Spellman. In 1975, Pope Paul VI waived the usual requirement of four miracles for sainthood, and declared that in the case of Seton, three miracles were enough. Thus, she became the first native-born American saint of the Roman Catholic church. Her feast day is January 4.
A. Melville, *Elizabeth Bayley Seton, 1774–1821*, 1960.

SHAH JAHAN (Prince Khurram; 1592–1666), Indian emperor. The penultimate ruler among the six great Moghuls, Muslim leaders who ruled India between 1527 (*Babur's conquest) and 1707 (when the death of *Aurangzeb was followed by the empire's rapid disintegration), Shah Jahan is primarily remembered for the Taj Mahal, the exquisite mausoleum built as a final resting place for his beloved

wife, Mumtaz Mahal. However, this was only one of the many magnificent buildings constructed during his thirty-one-year reign, which saw the creation of some of the most vivid and permanent reminders of Moghul glory.

Third son of the emperor Jehangir and grandson of *Akbar, Khurram gained the title of Shah Jahan for his services to his father in the military campaign of 1617. The heir-apparent after his elder brother's assassination, he was in revolt against his father from 1624 but succeeded him in 1628 after ruthlessly having his male collateral relatives killed. His reign saw the culmination of Moghul rule in India, and the splendor of his court was a well known. However, although Shan Jahan was able to sustain the empire he inherited, even expanding it to the northwest, he did so at the price of delegating a degree of power to his sons, which subsequently cost him his throne.

The favorite of his three wives, Mumtaz Mahal, whom he married in 1612, was the niece of an equally remarkable woman: one of Jehangir's wives, Nur Jahan, who had been the real power behind the imperial throne. Despite the fact that raisons d'etat contributed to the expediency of the match, the couple were deeply in love; Shah Jahan was heartbroken when Mumataz died bearing their fourteenth child in 1631.

The building of the Taj, the white marble monument on the bank of the river Jumna in the Moghul capital of Agra, began in 1632 and was not completed until 1653. A total of twenty thousand workers from all over India and central Asia were involved in its construction, while experts were brought in from as far away as western Europe. The supervising architect was Ustad Isa, from Shiraz in Persia; Ismail Khan Rumi, from Constantinople, constructed the soaring marble dome. The ornamentation throughout the structure is of unsurpassed excellence, and here the Indian art of pietra dura — decorating marble with an inlay of semiprecious stones — reached its zenith.

A number of other superb architectural ventures were undertaken in Shah Jahan's time: the Red Fort and Jami Masjid (the largest mosque in India and religious center of the empire) in Delhi being, with the additions to Agra Fort and the great mosque in Agra, the most famous. The structures succeed admirably in evoking the sentiment recorded in the Red Fort's Hall of Public Audience: "If there be a Heaven on earth / It is this, it is this, it is this."

Shah Jahan's extravagant plans, which included the building of a replica of the Taj in black marble opposite the original, to house his own grave, were brought to an abrupt end when he was overthrown by his son Aurangzeb in 1658. He lived out his last years imprisoned in Agra Fort, within sight of his own breathtaking monument to his beloved Mumtaz, next to whom he was buried.
B. P. Saksena, *History of Shahjahan of Dihli*, 1962.

SHAKESPEARE, WILLIAM (1564 – 1616), English playwright and poet. One of eight children, he was born in Stratford-upon-Avon, and was educated locally, starting at age five with reading and the catechism and later entering the grammar school, where, he learned Latin. Play-acting was in fashion as a means of improving pupils' language skills and it is possible that Shakespeare first became interested in theatricals in his school days. In addition, the pastoral landscape surrounding Stratford was clearly an important source of lasting inspiration. Shakespeare's works demonstrate a knowledge of rural sports and pastimes such as hunting and fishing, indicating that he was a man who enjoyed an active physical life.

In the 1580s his father's fortunes declined, which could account for Shakespeare's not attending university. When he was eighteen he married Anne Hathaway, eight years his senior, a local girl who was pregnant by him. Six months later their daughter Susannah was born, followed by twins, Judith and Hamnet, in 1585. Shakespeare's occupation until the early 1590s is a matter of conjecture.

By 1592 Shakespeare had left Stratford and became an actor in London, probably joining one of the companies of traveling players; nothing is clear about his activities during this period. However, his theatrical talents soon came to the fore. In 1592 he wrote *The Comedy of Errors*, *Titus Andronicus*, *The Two Gentlemen of Verona*, and *Henry VI*. These plays were enthusiastically received, the eloquent flow of his imagination imparting a liveliness and humanity to the characters which delighted his audiences.

Shakespeare's arrival in London coincided with a period of national prosperity, but he had just made his debut on the London stage when plague broke out in the city, killing a sixth of the inhabitants. The city council forbade theatrical performances and Shakespeare's company had to be satisfied with the meager takings from provincial audiences.

Established actors in this period needed the patronage of the nobility. Shakespeare worked with Lord Strange's actors but also sought out the patronage of the Earl of Southampton, a handsome, extravagant young nobleman to whom he dedicated the poems "Venus and Adonis" and "The Rape of Lucrece." There is reason to believe that he gained Southampton's favor and received some financial assistance; Southampton is considered one of the most likely contenders for the mysterious fair youth of the *Sonnets*.

By 1594 London theater had revived and Shakespeare was a leading member of the Lord Chamberlain's company performing at the Cross Keys. The company was in effect under royal patronage and Shakespeare's connection was a mark of his success. The violent death of Christopher Marlowe removed the leading rival playwright, leaving Shakespeare preeminent in his field. He had been influenced by Marlowe's style of writing but not his lifestyle. He was described by his fellow thespians as having the bearing of a gentleman and also had the distinction of never having spent time in prison, in sharp contrast to violent, shadowy Marlowe.

The mid-1590s was a prolific period for Shakespeare. He produced a succession of plays, including *Romeo and Juliet* and *A Midsummer Night's Dream*, works that drew the applause of the audience and enthusiasm of fellow actors. He considered that he now enjoyed sufficient status to lay claim to that symbol of gentility, the family coat of arms. His prosperity was also reflected in the purchase in 1597 of New Place in Stratford, a large, fine house with orchards and gardens, the first of several properties he bought in the neighborhood.

In 1599 Shakespeare, along with fellow actor Richard Burbage, was one of the founders of the Globe Theater on the south bank of the river Thames. He had a 10 percent share in the enterprise and probably a contract as resident writer. With the accession to the throne of King James in 1603, Shakespeare's company received the seal of the new king's approval with letters patent granting them the privileges of royal entertainers and the title "the King's Men." Shakespeare's literary output showed no signs of diminishing, with works like *Hamlet* and *Measure for Measure* enhancing the reputation of England's foremost playwright. There was now another rival writer making a name for himself, Ben Jonson, yet their relationship appears to have been friendly.

Shakespeare wanted more visible demonstration in Stratford of his fame and status and set about acquiring the trappings of gentility he now thought himself entitled to. He purchased a share in the church tithes and along with it came the right to burial in the chancel of the church. His eleven-year-old son Hamnet had died in 1596, but he could still hope to marry his daughters into the gentry and in this way to become progenitor of a noble family.

In his later years Shakespeare spent more time in Stratford-upon-Avon. In 1607 his daughter Susannah married in 1607 the physician John Hall and Shakespeare's granddaughter Elizabeth was born. His other daughter, Judith, had a less satisfactory marriage to Thomas Quiney. Soon after their marriage it was discovered that another woman was pregnant by Thomas. Distressed by his son-in-law's behavior, Shakespeare altered his will to deprive him of the £150 he had wanted to settle on Judith.

If family upsets disturbed the genteel retirement he hoped for, there was still the consolation of his work, including *The Winter's Tale* and *The Tempest*. In all, sixteen plays were published in his lifetime but many of these were pirated, some obtained through smuggling out scripts from the theater. It was not until 1623 that the famous First Folio edition of Shakespeare's works was printed at the initiative of two actor friends who by this time were beneficiaries of his will.

In 1613 a major portion of his plays was almost destroyed. During a performance of *Henry VIII* guns were fired for dramatic effect but the result was

PHRASES FROM SHAKESPEARE

- Thereby hangs a tale.
  The Taming of the Shrew

- What's in a name?
  Romeo and Juliet

- What fools these mortals be.
  A Midsummer Night's Dream

- The quality of mercy is not strained.
  The Merchant of Venice

- As merry as the day is long.
  Much Ado About Nothing

- Lend me your ears.
  Julius Caesar

- The short and the long of it.
  The Merry Wives of Windsor

- All the world's a stage.
  As You Like It

- In my mind's eye.
- Something is rotten in the state of Denmark.
- Brevity is the soul of wit.
- To be, or not to be.
  Hamlet

- The green-eyed monster.
  Othello

- What's done cannot be undone.
  Macbeth

- More sinned against than sinning.
- Every inch a king.
  King Lear

- Age cannot wither her, nor custom stale / Her infinite variety.
  Antony and Cleopatra

more dramatic than anyone intended: the thatched roof of the Globe Theater caught fire and the building burned down. Shakespeare's playbooks were, however, rescued from the flames. The Globe was rebuilt the following year at the enormous cost of £1,400, to which Shakespeare contributed his share.

Like so much of his life, Shakespeare's death is also shrouded in mystery. According to one account it was a consequence of fever contracted after overindulgence at a convivial gathering with Ben Jonson and Michael Drayton. Much lamented in the acting fraternity, he was buried beneath a plain gravestone in Stratford church. The engraved epitaph suggested that he was far from confident that future generations would so honor him: "Blest be the man that spares these stones, And cursed be he that moves my bones." In his will he left his wife "my second-best bed."

While Shakespeare was admired in his own time, a century elapsed before he came to be was considered the supreme genius of the English language. His contemporary, Ben Jonson, who wrote tributes to him, also noted "It is mentioned as an honor that he never blotted out a line. My answer hath been, would that he had blotted a thousand." John Dryden in 1668 said that of all poets he had the most comprehensive soul, but noted "He is many times flat, insipid; his comic wit degenerating into clenches, his serious swelling into bombast." By the eighteenth century, Dr. Samuel *Johnson, wrote that above all other poets, Shakespeare "holds up to his readers a faithful mirror of manners and life."

He has long been accepted as a phenomenon — the world's greatest playwright, who emerged out of humdrum surroundings and without any broad education or travel experience, yet writing about an amazing variety of subjects and characters with broad erudition and an unparalleled gift of language and imagery. His works have never gone out of fashion and are the staple of the theater in all lands. His contribution to drama, poetry, and the English language remains unique.

M. C. Bradbrook, *Shakespeare: The Poet in His World*, 1978.
R. A. Fraser, *Shakespeare*, 2 vols., 1988–1992.
A. L. Rowse, *William Shakespeare*, 1963.
S. Schoenbaum, *William Shakespeare, A Compact Documentary Life*, 1977.

William Shakespeare

SHAMIL (c.1797–1871), religious, military and nationalist leader of the Caucasus Muslims in their fight against Russian expansionism. Shamil was the son of a Dagestan landowner from the town of Ghimri. As a child he proved an adept student in the Koran, Arabic, grammar, logic, and rhetoric. Much of his education was undertaken by the Mullah Djemal ud-Din, an advocate of Muridism, a fundamentalist Muslim doctrine that called for jihad ("holy war") against the Russians. Already recognized as a scholar, Shamil soon became an outspoken and acclaimed proponent of the doctrine.

The Muridist movement was under attack from without and within. The Russians perceived it as a threat to their territorial ambitions in the Caucasus, while local leaders often disapproved of the rigid implementaton of Islamic law it demanded. In 1832 the first Muridist Imam of Dagestan was killed by the Russians; the second was assassinated by his own supporters in 1834. Shamil's uncompromising attitude led to his election that year as the third Imam.

Shamil set several goals for himself including the unification of the warring Caucasus tribes, the establishment of the Shariah (Muslim religious law) as the law of his territory, and universal recognition of his role not only as leader but as prophet. In all he proved successful – the fierce Chechen tribesmen submitted to him and all opposition was annihilated. In his wars against the Russians Shamil proved an able tactician who preferred and mastered guerilla warfare. Initially the Russians were terrified of Shamil. The Crimean War limited the number of troops available to protect the Caucasus; the region, which had formerly been garrisoned by only fifty thousand soldiers, required two hundred thousand fresh troops to be sent each year to replace the dead and injured. Shamil's fighters believed fervently in their mission, fighting to their last gasp and sometimes, it seemed, beyond that. The Russian novelist Mikhail Y. *Lermontov commented in a novel about the war, "They don't seem to know when they ought to die!"

Shamil himself was a ruthless leader, willing to sacrifice even those most dear to him for his cause. He was intolerant of cowardice; any man suspected of shirking his duty in combat was instantly excommunicated until he proved himself. In one instance the Chechens were overcome by Russian troops; surrender seemed their only option, but no one had the courage to ask Shamil for permission to do so. Finally it was decided to send Shamil's mother to plead with her son to allow the Chechens to submit. Shamil sat with his mother determining what to do. After three days he came out of the mosque and addressed the crowd: "After much prayer and supplication, God has told me how to respond to the Chechens' foul request. One hundred lashes will be given to the first person to speak to me of surrender – my mother." Despite everyone's pleas his mother was taken out to be beaten. After five strokes, the old woman fainted. Shamil promptly demanded that he receive the remaining ninety-five lashes himself, vowing to kill his soldiers if they did not beat him vigorously. After the beating he sent the Chechens back to the front, ordering them to tell their companions all that they had seen.

Shamil led a precarious existence, often just barely eluding capture. The one time he was captured he managed to escape but lost his wife and infant son to Russian bullets. Another son was captured and brought to Saint Petersburg. The czar raised the child, hoping he would one day succeed his father and prove a capable ally.

Shamil was defeated in 1859. The Russian army sent two hundred thousand troops led by General A. I. Bariatinsky to surround the Murid rebels. Shamil was no match for the overwhelming number of troops, nor could his poorly armed men compete with the two hundred heavy guns the Russians had brought; after several fierce battles he was captured and taken to Saint Petersburg and then to Kaluga for imprisonment. The terms of his imprisonment were, however, somewhat lax since even the Russians respected the man who fought against them so bravely. Shamil died on a pilgrimage to Mecca.

It was said: "Muhammad is Allah's first prophet; Shamil is his second."
L. Blanch, *The Sabres of Paradise,* 1960.

SHAW, GEORGE BERNARD (1856–1950), Irish playwright, critic, essayist, and wit. He was born in Dublin to an alcoholic father whom he described as a "Protestant merchant-gentleman and feudal downstart" and to a mother with musical ambitions who left her husband to follow her music instructor to London. For the first thirty-five years of his life Shaw lived in poverty. At age sixteen he began to work in an estate agent's office and when he was twenty left Dublin to join his mother in London. He was largely self-educated, reading avidly, hearing music at home and visiting theaters and art galleries. His first job in London was ghostwriting music criti-

George Bernard Shaw

cism for his mother's music instructor. He remained financially dependent on his parents, writing, "I did not throw myself into the struggle for life; I threw my mother into it. I was not a staff to my father's old age; I hung on to his coattails. I steadily wrote my five pages a day and made a man of myself (at my mother's expense)."

With great enthusiasm, he joined the newly founded socialist Fabian Society and sat on its executive committee. He became its outstanding spokesman and began to show his genius as a pamphleteer. He was one of the intellectual founders of British socialism. His freelance writing opportunities expanded and he appeared regularly as book reviewer, art critic, and especially as music critic. His writings about music (he was a Richard *Wagner enthusiast) are treasured as classics, not only for their musical insight but for their witty style and literary quality.

He wrote five unsuccessful novels but discovered his metier as a dramatist, initially profoundly influenced by Henrik *Ibsen. His first drama, *Widowers' Houses* (1892), attacked slum landlordism and only ran for two performances but created a sensation, as did *Mrs. Warren's Profession* (1898), which became notorious when banned by the censor because it showed prostitution to be the consequence of capitalistic society.

Shaw now began to pour out plays and soon achieved an international reputation. By 1898 he had written *Arms and the Man, Candida,* and *The Devil's Disciple.* During that year, while recuperating from a serious illness he proposed to an Irish heiress, Charlotte Payne-Townshend, and they were married soon after. The marriage, which was happy but platonic, relieved Shaw of financial worries. He had a number of premarital liaisons and engaged in two passionate correspondences with the famous actresses Ellen Terry and Mrs. Patrick Campbell. Throughout his life he wrote thousands of letters and, more often, postcards, which were a further expression of his intellect, originality, wit, and iconoclasm. He also sent frequent letters to the newspapers, especially *The Times.*

In the first years of the twentieth century, he wrote some of his great masterpieces. *John Bull's Other Island* (1904) autobiographically contrasts twenty years of Shaw's life in Ireland and twenty years in England. In it Ireland and England are also metaphors for opposing philosophies of life, which Shaw attempted to reconcile. An exiled Englishman in *John Bull* says, "I wish I could find a country to live in where the facts are not brutal and the dreams not unreal."

Major Barbara (1905) also concerns young idealists seeking the fulfillment of their dreams who encounter a sometimes brutal reality. Yet Shaw believed in progress, in the possibility of political and economic reform. The strong influence on him of Henri *Bergson's concept of creative evolution is particularly marked in his *Man and Superman*

(1903). His most popular comedy, *Pygmalion,* was premiered in 1913.

When Shaw published his plays, he accompanied them with lengthy prefaces in which he expounded his motivations and the ideas he was attempting to project. In the preface to *Major Barbara* Shaw lamented the comparisons drawn between his scenes of the ironies of life and the critics' claims that he borrowed from Ibsen, Arthur *Schopenhauer, Friedrich *Nietzsche, and other continental Europeans. He claimed to be drawing from real life, as well as from English and Irish authors.

During World War I he spoke out for better treatment for both laborers and soldiers. His *Common Sense about the War* (1914), which included an appeal for fairness for conscientious objectors, created a storm of protest. Booksellers removed his books from their shelves.

After the war his popularity quickly revived, and three of his greatest plays appeared in the following years. *Back to Methuselah* (1921), a series of five connected plays, was again inspired by the idea of creative evolution; *Saint Joan* (1923) was a reassessment of *Joan of Arc, motivated by her recent canonization; the third was *Heartbreak House* (1920). He also wrote an exposition of socialism in *The Intelligent Woman's Guide to Socialism and Capitalism* (1928). In 1925 he was awarded the Nobel Prize for literature.

THE WIT OF BERNARD SHAW

- I often quote myself. It adds spice to the conversation.
- Assassination is the extreme form of censorship.
- When a stupid man is doing something he is ashamed of, he always declares it is his duty.
- If all economists were laid end to end, they would reach no conclusion.
- If you eliminate smoking and gambling, you will find that almost all an Englishman's pleasures can be, and mostly are, shared by his dog.
- We have not lost faith, but we have transferred it from God to the medical profession.
- Do not do unto others as you would they should do to you. Their tastes may not be the same.
- A fool's brain digests philosophy into folly, science into superstition, and art into pedantry. Hence university education.
- He who can, does. He who cannot, teaches.
- Marriage is popular because it combines the maximum of temptation with the maximum of opportunity.
- There are two tragedies in life. One is not to get your heart's desire. The other is to get it.

G.B.S., as he became known, was an institution. People everywhere hung on his words and he an international celebrity. In 1930 he visited the USSR and met Joseph *Stalin, who made a favorable impression on him. He also initially found some positive aspects in Adolf *Hitler's policy, especially on labor relations, but expressed his abhorrence of his treatment of the Jews. However, by 1937 he wrote *Geneva*, which satirized Hitler, Benito *Mussolini, and Francisco *Franco (as "Herr Battler," "Signor Bombardone," and "General Flanco de Fortinbras"). By this time he had become a popular broadcaster whose gentle Irish brogue and sly humor beguiled millions of listeners. Indeed, his paradoxical quips brought a new word to the English language: "Shavianism."

Shaw remained eloquent to the end, although his later plays did not achieve lasting success. Following a fall he died in his mid-nineties in his Hertfordshire home at Ayot Saint Lawrence, where he had lived since 1904. Shaw's plays were translated into many languages and reached a wide new public in film versions (especially *Pygmalion*, *Major Barbara*, and *Caesar and Cleopatra*), in Oscar Straus's musical comedy *The Chocolate Soldier* based on *Arms and the Man*, and especially — after his death — in *My Fair Lady*, the musical version of *Pygmalion*.

For his ninetieth birthday, in 1946, he was inundated by tributes from the world over. His wit was as sharp as ever. "I hope I shall interview you again on your 100th birthday," a young journalist said. "I don't see why not, you look healthy enough to me," Shaw replied.

J. Ditsky, *The Onstage Christ*, 1980.
M. Holroyd, *Bernard Shaw*, 3 vols., 1991.
H. Pearson, *Bernard Shaw*, 1961.

SHELLEY, PERCY BYSSHE (1792–1822), English Romantic poet and essayist. Shelley was born in Sussex into a wealthy family of landed gentry, received his early schooling at Syon House Academy, Brentford, and continued at Eton College, where his eccentricities earned him the sobriquet "Mad Shelley." In 1810 he went to University College, Oxford and in that year published his first novel, *Zastrozzi*, and a book of verse, *Original Poetry by Victor and Cazire*, written in part by his sister Elizabeth. After only five months, Shelley was expelled from Oxford, together with his friend Jefferson Hogg, for refusing to answer questions about a pamphlet, "The Necessity of Atheism," which the two had written. This untimely termination of his university career was the beginning of a breakdown in relations between Shelley and his father, further aggravated by Shelley's elopement and marriage to Harriet Westbrook, which resulted in a lifelong estrangement between father and son.

Shelley and Westbrook married in Edinburgh (1811) and settled in the Lake District, where Shelley became acquainted with the older poet Robert Southey. During the next three years that the Shelleys spent wandering throughout Britain, Shelley produced a number of political prose works and wrote little poetry except for *Queen Mab*, completed in 1813. He had been greatly influenced by the works of the writer and philosopher William Godwin; and in 1812 they became acquainted, but their relationship was to end in 1820 when Shelley withdrew financial assistance from the impecunious Godwin, who had been dependent on the young poet for a number of years. Throughout his life Shelley was fortunate to be relatively unburdened by financial concerns, particularly after his grandfather's death (1815), which left him with a steady income and the expectation of a large inheritance.

Shelley's marriage began to show signs of collapse as his intellectual life broadened through his

---

FROM SHELLEY'S POETRY

Hail to Thee, blithe spirit!
Bird thou never wert
We look before and after;
We pine for what is not;
Our sincerest laughter
With some pain is fraught:
Our sweetest songs are those that tell of saddest thought.

From "To a Skylark"

Scatter, as from an unextinguished hearth
Ashes and sparks, my works among mankind!
Be through my lips to unawakened earth
The trumpet of a prophecy! O, Wind,
If Winter comes, can Spring be far behind?

From "Ode to the West Wind"

Death is the veil which those who live call life:
They sleep, and it is lifted.
Familiar acts are beautiful through love.

From "Prometheus Unbound"

Can man be free if woman be a slave?

From "The Revolt of Islam"

EDWARD TRELAWNY ON SHELLEY

To know an author personally is too often but to destroy the illusion created by his works... Shelley was a grand exception to this rule. To form a just idea of his poetry, you should have witnessed his daily life... The truth was, Shelley loved everything better than himself.

association with Godwin and writers such as the classical poet Thomas Love Peacock, who became one of his closest friends, and the vegetarian John Frank Newton and his family. Shelley also began what was to become the first of many correspondences with various intelligent and beautiful women, signifying his tendency to idealize the intellectual female. In 1814 he and his wife separated. Shelley left England with Mary Godwin, the daughter of William Godwin and his first wife, Mary *Wollstonecraft, author of *Vindication of the Rights of Women.* The two traveled through France and Switzerland accompanied by Mary Goodwin's half-sister, Claire Claremont.

In 1816 Shelley published his beautiful poem, *Alastor,* and in the summer of that year, spent in Switzerland on the shores of Lake Geneva, Shelley and Lord *Byron developed a close friendship which was later complicated by the birth of Byron's child, Allegra, to Claire Claremont. Following his return to England, Shelley was shocked to learn of Harriet's suicide by drowning in the Serpentine.

Shelley married Mary Wollestonecraft three weeks later and the couple bought a house in Marlowe, Buckinghamshire. At this time James Henry Leigh Hunt became a close friend of Shelley, sharing his passion for reforming the world and encouraging him as a poet. Leigh Hunt and his family were frequent visitors to the house at Marlowe along with Peacock, Hogg, and Godwin. It was here that Shelley wrote his longest poem, *Laon and Cynthia* (renamed *The Revolt of Islam, 1818*).

The remaining years of Shelley's life were spent mostly in Italy. He and Mary journeyed from place to place in that "paradise of exiles" as Shelley called it. The years 1817–1818 were difficult, bringing the death of their two children; a third, Percy Florence born in 1819 was to be their only surviving child. In 1818 Mary Shelley published her famous novel *Frankenstein.* Shelley wrote his most mature poems in Italy including "Julian and Maddalo," "Lines written among the Euganean Hills", "Ode to the West Wind" and "The Cloud," and also produced his greatest lyrical dramas, *Prometheus Unbound* and *The Cenci. Prometheus* is Shelley's major claim to status and remains one of the greatest English romantic mythological poems.

The Shelleys settled in Pisa in 1820, where Shelley became the center of a literary-artistic circle and was visited by Byron and Trelawny. In 1821 Shelley wrote *Epipsychidion,* describing his search for ideal love. The poem was inspired by a young Italian girl introduced to the family, Emilia Viviani. Along with his poetry, Shelley wrote prose works, tackling a variety of issues in philosophy, religion, politics, and literature, the most famous being *A Defence of Poetry* (1821), described by W. B. *Yeats as "the profoundest essay on the foundation of poetry in English."

Shelley died sailing his yacht, the *Don Juan,* in the Gulf of Spezia on a return visit to Byron and Leigh Hunt in Pisa. Drowned when the boat was caught in a sudden storm. Shelley's body was found by Trelawny cast ashore at Viareggio where it was cremated and the ashes taken for burial in the Protestant cemetery in Rome, which Shelley had written "might make one in love with death."

G. Kim Blank, *The New Shelley,* 1990.
K. Everest, *Shelley Revalued: Essays,* 1983.
D. G. King-Hele, *Shelley: His Thought and Work,* 1984.
M. O'Neill, *Percy Bysshe Shelley,* 1989.

SHERMAN, WILLIAM TECUMSEH (1820–1891), American army commander. Born in Lancaster, Ohio, Sherman was the eldest of eight children. He had been named Tecumseh by his father as a token of respect to the elder Sherman's friend, an Indian chief. Orphaned at the age of nine, he was adopted by Thomas Ewing, who was active in national politics; Ewing's wife insisted on changing the child's name to William.

Through Ewing's influence, Sherman was given an appointment at the U.S. Military Academy at West Point, and in 1840 he graduated sixth out of a class of forty-two. He served as a second lieutenant in Florida and New Orleans, but was not very happy with army life, eventually leaving the army in 1853. He then joined a St. Louis banking firm as manager of its San Francisco branch. The bank failed and he then tried his hand at being a lawyer, quickly discovering that he did not possess the necessary temperament.

In 1859, Sherman was made superintendent of a new military college in Alexandria, Louisiana, a position he held until 1861. He proved an excellent teacher and developed the abilities and skills which were to endear him to his troops during the Civil War. For the first time in his life he found satisfaction in what he was doing, but was forced to resign his position when Louisiana seceded from the Union.

With the onset of the Civil War, Sherman rejoined the army and in May 1861 was appointed a colonel, leading his troops at the Battle of Bull Run. He was not satisfied with the results and questioned his own ability to command, but President Abraham *Lincoln disagreed and promoted him to the rank of brigadier general. At this point, General Henry W. Halleck discovered Sherman's ability as a military planner and requested that he prepare the battle plans for General Ulysses S. *Grant's campaign. Sherman served brilliantly as Grant's subordinate, and quickly became his devoted friend.

In 1862, under Grant's command, Sherman and several other generals were able to drive back the Confederates at the Battle of Shiloh. Shortly thereafter Sherman was promoted to major general and effectively engineered the Union victory at Vicksburg, strategically important to the Union forces because it was located on the eastern bank of the Mississippi.

- If we must be enemies, let us be men, and fight it out as we propose to do, and not deal in hypocritical appeals to God and Humanity.
- There is a soul to an army as well as to the individual man, and no general can accomplish the full work of his army unless he commands the souls of his men as well as their bodies and legs.
- There's many a boy here today who looks on war as all glory; but, boys, it is all hell.
- The true way to be popular with troops is not to be free and familiar with them, but to make them believe you know more than they do.
- What is grand strategy? Common-sense applied to the art of war.

William Tecumseh Sherman

Sherman succeeded Grant as the commanding general in Tennessee. During the following year he led his troops to victory on the Missionary Bridge and in Knoxville, Tennessee. With Grant's promotion to commander of all the Union armies, Sherman was put in charge of the armies in the south. With one hundred and ten thousand troops under his command, Sherman advanced toward Atlanta, Georgia, in May 1864. His army far outnumbered the Confederates, causing them to retreat again and again. By July 1864 Sherman's troops had reached the outskirts of Atlanta and on September 1, 1864, he sent a telegram to Lincoln saying, "Atlanta is ours and fairly won." After completing the destruction of the city, Sherman led his troops to the sea and they went on to capture Savannah, Georgia. Congress gave a vote of thanks to Sherman for his accomplishments. During this period, Sherman received orders that he and his troops were to live off the countryside. To this end, he destroyed the war supplies, public buildings, railroad lines, and factories of the enemy. He brought the war home to civilians by the destruction of goods rather than life. Sherman then marched his troops through the Carolinas to join Grant in Virginia.

Sherman received the surrender of J. E. Johnston at Durham, North Carolina, on April 26, 1865. From 1865 to 1869 Sherman commanded the military in Mississippi and when Grant became president of the United States, Sherman was promoted to general in command of the army, remaining in that position until his retirement in 1884.

In 1883 his name was put before the Republican Convention as a presidential candidate. In typical fashion he responded, "If nominated I will not accept; if elected, I will not serve." He remained a very popular figure, even after his retirement, and was often called upon as a speaker, especially at functions of war veterans.

R. Charles, *William T. Sherman: Military Leadership*, 1991.

J. T. Glatthaar, *The March to the Sea and Beyond*, 1985.

B. H. Liddell Hart, *Sherman: Soldier, Realist, American*, 1978.

J. F. Marzalek, *Sherman's Other War — The General and the Civil War Press*, 1981.

SHIH HUANG TI (Prince Cheng; c. 259–210 B.C.E.), emperor of China, founder of the Ch'in dynasty, first emperor to unite China. Cheng was prince of Ch'in in western China, one of several independent and warring states that made up China. Little is known about his early life, although he was probably educated in the Legalist rather than Confucianist tradition. It has been suggested that he was the son of Lu Pu-wei, a wealthy silk merchant who turned to politics, although it is more likely that Lu was his advisor.

Cheng assumed the throne of Ch'in in 246 B.C.E. Upon reaching maturity he set out on a series of campaigns intended to bring the other Chinese states under his jurisdiction. Although no one had before succeeded in uniting the kingdoms, Cheng was at an advantage in that he was the first to use iron weapons. Among the states conquered by Cheng were: Han (230), Chao (228), Wei (225), Ch'u (223), Yen (222), and Ch'i (221). Within just seven years, he had conquered all of China, earning the epithet, "Tiger of Ch'in." In 221 B.C.E. Cheng was named emperor of all China and assumed the name Shih Huang Ti, i.e., "First August Emperor."

Shih Huang Ti was not merely a conqueror. Under the guidance of his minister Li Ssu he instituted important reforms aimed at the political and social unification of his realm. He created a unified system of measurements, a much-simplified unified writing system, and a single currency similar to the one still used today. The former states were dissolved and the country was divided into thirty-six and then forty-two prefectures. Shih Huang Ti was also a great builder. Apart from a series of roads and canals intended to facilitate travel in the vast state, he completed the Great Wall in the north to protect the kingdom from nomadic herdsmen, the Hsiung-nu, who threatened invasion. Once the wall had been finished, Shi Huang Ti sent troops against the Hsiung-nu. In other expeditions he reached as far south as Vietnam and as far north as Korea.

Despite his military and political successes, Shih Huang Ti was an unpopular monarch who seemed intent upon depriving his citizens of their most basic rights. His vast building projects required great amounts of tax money and forced labor; people could not protect themselves – the bearing of arms was forbidden. Weapons were confiscated, melted down, and cast into twelve enormous statues in the capital, Hsien-yang. The nobility despised the emperor for depriving them of their ancestral estates. To assure their loyalty Shih Huang Ti ordered all noble families to relocate to the capital and its environs. One hundred and twenty thousand families took part in this transfer of populations.

Perhaps the most dramatic act of Shih Huang Ti's reign was the "burning of the books." Legalism was declared the sole acceptable school of thought in the kingdom; Confucianism, Taoism, and other schools were ruthlessly suppressed. To enforce this suppression all books, except those on medicine, agriculture, and divination, were burned in 213. This act of barbarism was followed by the execution of more than 400 aristocrats and scholars perceived as being a threat to the regime.

Shih Huang Ti died in 210 B.C.E. He was succeeded by his son, who took the name Shi-erh Huang Ti, or Second August Emperor. His son's reign was brief, however. Although the people were enraged by his father's decrees they dared not rebel for fear of him, but Shih-erh Huang Ti's weak rule led to open rebellion within a year of his ascension and the Ch'in dynasty collapsed in 206 B.C.E. Despite its brevity and unpopularity it paved the way for future dynasties to promote Chinese unification as a goal. Many believe that the name "China" is derived from Shih Huang Ti's Ch'in dynasty.

J. Gernet, *A History of Chinese Civilization,* 1982.
Y. Yap and A. Cotterell, *The Early Civilization of China,* 1975.

SITTING BULL (Tatanka Iyotake; c. 1831–1890), American Indian leader. Sitting Bull, the son of a Hunkpapa Sioux chieftain, was born near Grand River, South Dakota. At an early age he participated in pitched battles with rival Indian tribes (he fought the Crow Indians when only fourteen years old), and with American troops. During the 1860s and 1870s he participated in the Plains Wars against the American government. Despite occasional successes the Indians were no match for the better armed American forces.

A local gold rush and the expansion of the Northern Railroad in 1876 prompted the federal government to offer the Sioux a reservation. Sitting Bull considered the proposal an affront and refused the offer. Other chiefs followed Sitting Bull's example by refusing similar offers and the Indians and Americans prepared for war. Before the battle Sitting Bull had a recurring vision in which American troops fell into his encampment. This dream, interpreted as a good omen by the Indians, encouraged them to believe that they would soon defeat the white man. The U.S. 7th Cavalry (266 troops), led by General George A. Custer, faced 3,500 Sioux and Cheyenne warriors at Little Big Horn, Montana, on June 25, 1876. The Indian warriors were led by Crazy Horse; Sitting Bull remained in his camp to perform religious rites to assure victory. A three-hour battle ensued, in which the federal troops were massacred. Only one cavalry horse, suffering from seven bullet wounds, survived the battle.

Sioux chieftain Sitting Bull

Although Sitting Bull was not an active participant in the Battle of Little Big Horn he was blamed by the government for the massacre. American troops chased Sitting Bull and Crazy Horse through the Plains until finally defeating them on October 31 of that year. Sitting Bull escaped with his tribe and crossed the border into Canada but the Canadian government was unsympathetic to the Indian refugees and prevented them from settling in Canada, supposedly because they were not British subjects. Nevertheless, the Sioux ignored the Canadian government and remained in Canada until 1881, when Sitting Bull and his people were granted an amnesty and allowed to return to the United States.

His notoriety for the Battle of Little Big Horn earned Sitting Bull a certain degree of respect and recognition. He toured with Buffalo Bill's Wild West Show in 1885 and was often asked to speak at public functions, generally from prepared texts which would then be translated into English. On one occasion he ignored the prepared speech and said, "I hate all the white men. You are thieves and liars and have made us outcasts." The translator replaced Sitting Bull's statement with a text of his own and Sitting Bull received a standing ovation.

Further American expansion threatened to displace the Indians from what little land remained to them. Sitting Bull, when asked about the Indian response to the danger, declared, "Indians! There are no Indians left but me."

The distraught Indians of the Plains began participating in a mystical ritual, the Ghost Dance, upon the advice of a prophet who claimed that the ceremony would assure the impending disappearance of the white man from their land, the resurrection of Indian dead, and the restoration of their indigenous culture. Among the Indians encouraged by the Ghost Dance was Sitting Bull. The government regarded Sitting Bull's participation in the ceremony as a threat to the fragile peace they had enforced and in December 1890 forty-three Indian police came to arrest Sitting Bull. They were met by a large group of Ghost Dancers who attempted to interfere with them. One Indian, Catch a Bear, shot the arresting officer, and in the ensuing scuffle, Sitting Bull and his son Crow Foot were killed. No revenge was taken for the death of Sitting Bull. It was believed that the Ghost Dance would soon put an end to the white threat to the Indians.

D. Brown, *Bury My Heart at Wounded Knee,* 1970.
E. F. Connell, *Son of the Morning Star,* 1984.
F. V. Lefthand and J. Marshall III, *Soldiers Falling Into Camp,* 1993.

SKANDERBEG, GEORGE (originally George Kastrioti; 1405–1468), Albanian national and military hero. George Kastrioti was the youngest son of John Kastrioti, a leading Albanian noble, who had been defeated by the Ottoman Turks under Isak, governor of Skopje. As part of the terms of his surrender, Kastrioti was obliged to hand the fortress of Kruje to the Turks. To further insure his submission, his four sons were taken as hostages to the Ottoman court of Sultan Murad II. The sultan sent the boys to the military academy at Edirne, where George quickly showed his talents as an able soldier. Following his conversion to Islam, he became a favorite of the sultan, who attached him to his personal retinue. George was given the name Iskander, Turkish for Alexander; in addition, he received the title, bey. The name, Skanderbeg, is an Albanian corruption of his Turkish name, Iskander Bey.

Skanderbeg fought with the Turkish army against the Serbs and Venetians. In 1443, while fighting against the Hungarian nationalist Janos Hunyadi, news reached Skanderbeg that his homeland, Albania, had risen against the Turks. Skanderbeg led 300 Albanian troops back to Kruje, defeated the Turkish troops stationed at the fort, and hoisted the flag of his family, a red banner with a black eagle imposed on it. The flag still serves as the national flag of Albania. Skanderbeg realized that his own, limited troops would be unable to stave off impending Turkish onslaughts, and that he required the support of other Albanian chieftains and nobles. To obtain such support, he renounced Islam, declared himself a Christian, and later married the daughter of a local noble. The following year he organized a gathering of all Albanian nobles at Lezhe. The nobles responded enthusiastically to Skanderbeg's call for revolt. They agreed to cooperate in an alliance commanded by Skanderbeg. Each household was required to provide one soldier to Skanderbeg's army, thereby promoting unity among the troops.

The Venetians regarded Skanderbeg's revolt against the Turks as an ideal opportunity for them to occupy strategic Albanian territory. Skanderbeg found his army fighting the Venetians at Shkoder and Durres while defending his own base at Kruje. Alliances were made with the Serbian nationalists under Djuradj Brankovic and the Hungarians under Janos Hunyadi. Realizing that they were unable to defeat Skanderbeg, the Venetians finally reached a peace accord with him in 1448. Skanderbeg was now free to focus his energies against the Turks. Sultan Murad II himself led his troops against Kruje in 1450. Although support from his allies was meager, Skanderbeg was able to defeat the Turks after a five-month siege by using guerilla tactics. Victory was, however, costly — the countryside was ravaged and many leading Albanians had deserted. Nonetheless, Skanderbeg's victory against the Ottomans won him the admiration of the entire Christian world.

Skanderbeg set off to tour the capitals of Europe. Everywhere he received recognition for his successful campaign against the Turks. The Kingdom of Naples granted him a pension, troops, food and two hundred muskets. With his new-found support, Skanderbeg set out in 1455 to conquer the town of Berat; although he was unsuccessful, he did succeed in annihilating an entire Turkish army. He gained the reputation of a crusader against Islam, and was called by Pope Calixtus III, "captain general of the Holy See."

In 1455 Muhammad II, the new sultan of the Ottoman Empire, decided to crush the Albanian revolt. Leading an army of sixty thousand troops, he quickly conquered the Balkan lowlands. By 1457 he had breached the walls of Kruje, but was unable to conquer the fortress. Muhammad's army was routed the following year. Although he remained in Albania until 1462 he constantly suffered defeat by Skanderbeg.

In 1463 the Venetians, responding to Pope Pius II's call for a crusade against the Turks, sent troops to Albania. The crusade was short-lived. The pope died suddenly and the Venetians retreated. Skanderbeg was left to fight the Turks, now led by an Albanian deserter, Balaban Pasha, on his own. The sultan himself led his armies against Kruje in 1466, but his forces were crushed, and among the casualties was Balaban Pasha. Skanderbeg realized the Turks would not concede defeat. Dressed as a soldier, he traveled to Rome to receive support from the new pope, Paul II. The pope knighted Skanderbeg by giving him a sword and cap. He also gave him a sizeable grant. Skanderbeg returned to Albania and again defeated Muhammad II (1467). Skanderbeg died in Lezhe the following year. After his death the Albanian League was dissolved; within ten years, all of Albania fell to the Turks. Skanderbeg is regarded as the national hero of Albania, and his tomb, in the Cathedral of Saint Nicholas in Lezhe is a national shrine.

R. Marmallaku, *Albania and the Albanians*, 1975.
F. S. Noli, *George Castrioti Scanderberg*, 1947.

SMITH, ADAM (1723–1790), British economist. Smith was born in Kirkcaldy in Scotland, three months after the death of his father, Adam Smith, a customs officer. When he was three, he was carried away by a party of tinkers who found him playing on his own, but his uncle pursued the kidnappers, and with the aid of friends, rescued the child.

Smith's early education was in Kirkcaldy, where he was popular with the other children and was already distinguished by his love for books and excellent memory. More unusual was a childhood habit he never rid himself of — a fondness for talking to himself.

Between 1737 and 1740 Smith was at Glasgow University, and then for six years at Balliol College, Oxford University, studying moral and political science and languages. He returned to Kirkcaldy in 1746 and gave a series of lectures on English literature. In 1748 he took up residence in Edinburgh, where he was honored with election to the city's Philosophical Society.

In 1751 he accepted the professorship of logic at Glasgow University and a year later became professor of moral philosophy there. Now began the period he later looked back on as "by far the most useful, and therefore by far the happiest and most honorable period of my life." Smith made little use of notes in his lectures: he would begin in a hesitant manner but gather confidence in the course of the lecture and become highly animated. His views aroused much discussion while the idiosyncrasies of his presentation also provided a source of amusement.

Among the first of Smith's works to appear in print was a magazine article about Dr. Samuel *Johnson's *Dictionary*. Later, he met Johnson on his first visit to London, where he had journeyed to arrange for the publication of his first major work, *The Theory of Moral Sentiments* (1759), a book outlining his ethical views and observations on human nature, with sympathy accorded pride of place as a motive force in human behavior. It came to Johnson's attention that Smith had praised his fellow-Scotsman and philosopher, David *Hume. Johnson thought the praise undeserved since Hume was accused of atheism. There followed a clash of opinions between the two intellectual giants and for once the erudite Johnson was lost for words. His accusation to Smith that "you lie!" was met with equal bluntness, Smith's retort to Johnson that "you are the son of a bitch!" effectively ending the conversation. However, this disagreement did not prevent the development of their acquaintance.

Smith was given an honorary doctorate in law in Glasgow in 1762 but resigned his professorship to become tutor to the Duke of Buccleuch and his brother Hew Campbell Scott, embarking with them on their Grand Tour. In France he came into contact with leading intellectuals like the economist François Quesnay, whose views influenced his thinking. He probably began work on his most famous book, *An Inquiry into the Nature and Causes of the Wealth of Nations*, while in Toulouse. The murder of Hew Campbell Scott brought the tour to an end and Smith returned to Scotland. The next ten years he lived a quiet life at home in Kirkcaldy with his elderly mother, in a house kept for them by his cousin, Jane Douglas.

In *The Wealth of Nations* (1776) Smith eloquently made the case for free trade as opposed to government interference in commerce and industry. Left to operate naturally, economic forces would advance the common good, he argued. Countries should specialize in what they are best suited to produce and exchange their goods with others; the forces of supply and demand would determine a fair market price for each product. Every man should be allowed to pursue his own self-interest, since by so doing he advances the common good — if his concerns prosper, the wealth generated by them filters down through the economy. As Smith expressed the point: "It is not from the benevolence of the butcher, the brewer, or the baker, that we expect our dinner but from their regard to their own interest ."

The book became one of the most important works of political economy, gaining for its author an international reputation. It provided the philosophical foundation for the doctrine of free trade developed in the following century.

Between 1776 and 1778 Smith lived in London, a highly respected figure, mixing with Edmund *Burke, the historian Edward Gibbon, the journalist and biographer James Boswell, and other literary men in Dr. Johnson's exclusive circle. In 1778 the Duke of Buccleuch procured for him a sinecure position as commissioner of customs in Edinburgh. The income left him free to continue intellectual pursuits. In 1787 he was delighted to be appointed lord rector of Glasgow University.

Smith was devoted to his mother and was devastated by her death at age ninety. He never married, and when Jane Douglas died in 1788 he lost his only other close relative. Much of his money he contributed secretly to charities while at home he entertained his friends in a simple style and took pleasure in his library. During his fatal, painful illness he gave instructions for many of his manuscript writings to be burned.

C. Hsieh, *A Search For Synthesis*, 1983.
J. Rae, *Life of Adam Smith*, 1965.
D. R. Reisman, *Tawney, Galbraith, and Adam Smith*, 1982.
D. D. Raphael, *Adam Smith*, 1985.

SMITH, JOSEPH (1805–1844), American religious reformer; founder of the Church of Jesus Christ of Latter-day Saints (the Mormons). No biography of Joseph Smith can ignore the vast discrepancies in the accounts given by his adherents and those of his critics. The former portray him as a godly man, among the most recent in a long chain of prophets and seers who have championed God's word across the centuries and the continents; the lat-

Joseph Smith

ter depict a charlatan who fabricated a new religion for reasons of self-aggrandizement. The current state of the religion he founded owes much to his remarkable personality and to the confused yet impassioned time of religious revival during which he lived.

Joseph Smith Jr. was born in Vermont, the fourth of nine children of a poor farmer. When Joseph was ten years old the family moved to upstate New York to improve their fortunes. America was then in the throes of a religious revival as itinerant Methodist, Baptist, and Presbyterian preachers roamed the countryside seeking new devotees. Smith later wrote that, at fourteen, he too was caught up in the revivalist movement, but was confused by the variety of competing sects. Seeking solace in his Bible, he closed himself in his room to uncover the truth, when he encountered James's counsel, "If any of you lack wisdom, let him ask of God" (James 1:5). Smith went to pray in the forest, when suddenly a pillar of light far brighter than the sun descended on him. Looking up, he saw two figures, God the Father and *Jesus, hovering above him. When questioned, they told Smith that all religions were false, but that in time, they would reappear to teach him the truth.

In another revelation in 1823, the angel Moroni appeared to Smith to recount the events of Jesus's life after the resurrection. According to Moroni, Jesus traveled to North America to preach the gospel to the local inhabitants. These early American Christians were destroyed by rival tribes in the fifth century, but their own historical account, inscribed in hieroglyphics on gold plates, was hidden on a nearby hill. Smith retrieved the plates from the Hill of Cumorah in 1827. He also found the Urim and Thummim, magic spectacles with which he could interpret the writings.

No one apart from Smith ever saw these plates. Hiding behind a screen, he dictated their contents to three scribes. The finished product was the Book of Mormon, named for one of the last survivors of the righteous early Americans. Published in 1830, it created an immediate sensation by purporting to be equal in importance to the Bible. The book still remains at the crux of the controversy surrounding Smith. His supporters point out the improbability of any contemporary writing such an accurate historical account of the early peoples of America. His detractors point to numerous anachronisms and contradictions within the text.

Religion-starved rural America, however, was attracted to the book and its message. Unlike other Christian denominations, Smith's Church of Jesus Christ of Latter-day Saints was based on direct revelation rather than questionable interpretation of biblical passages. Three years later, Smith produced the *Book of Commandments*, followed in 1835 by the *Doctrines and Covenants*, expounding his new religion. Smith's growing popularity among the antagonized among the established American churches. His claim to have been baptized by John the Baptist and by the apostles Peter, James, and John was treated skeptically, while the apostasy of his original scribes caused considerable damage to the young church. Many people abandoned Smith; in one instance he was tarred, feathered, and driven out of town. There was, nonetheless, a core group of faithful who clung to his every word despite the controversy surrounding him. Unable to remain in hostile New York, Smith led his followers west.

After an unsuccessful attempt to settle in Kirtland, Ohio, the group migrated to Missouri. There, too, they were spurned by the non-Mormon population. The Mormons were abolitionists; Missouri supported slavery. Their secret Temple rituals were deemed satanic in the fertile imagination of their neighbors. Hard working and principled church members were a valuable asset to Missouri society, but the state governor, uneasy about the reported existence of a secret Mormon paramilitary organization, the Avenging Angels of Dan, with plans to exterminate all "Gentiles," issued his own extermination order against the sect. Rather than face the hostile mobs, Smith led his following across the Mississippi to Illinois.

The Mormons settled in Commerce, which they renamed Nauvoo. There too, despite numerous setbacks, the church prospered. Mormon converts streamed there from America and Europe, and the population, at fifteen thousand by 1840, was the largest in Illinois. Yet even in Nauvoo, Smith could not avoid the hostility of the local population. After half a year in jail for supposedly plotting to kill the Illinois governor, his acquittal increased his popularity even further. He now served as mayor of Nauvoo, commander of the local militia, and lieutenant governor, and even considered running for president of the United States.

New problems faced Smith, however, when he began instituting polygamy as official church doctrine. He himself married fifty wives, an act of lechery to some of his more staid following. Smith's most vociferous opponent was William Law, editor of the local newspaper. When Law learned that Smith was having an affair with his wife, he maliciously attacked the prophet on his front pages. In response, Smith, accompanied by the local sheriff, smashed Law's presses. Law was undeterred. He complained directly to the governor, who issued a warrant for Smith's arrest. Smith fled to the Rockies, pursued not only by the law but by his own followers who urged him not to abandon them at this crucial time. After careful consideration, Smith agreed to accompany them back to jail.

Three weeks later, an angry lynch mob broke into Smith's cell. He ran to the window and jumped to his death. According to some, he survived the fall, only to be propped up and executed by an impromptu firing squad. His martyrdom only strengthened his followers' resolve to carry on his legacy. Several schisms emerged, one led by Smith's own son, but the majority of Mormons, led by Brigham *Young, moved further west, to reestablish the church in the remote deserts of Utah.

L. J. Avrington, *The Mormon Experience: A History of the Latter-day Saints*, 1980.

R. L. Bushman, *Joseph Smith and the Beginning of Mormonism*, 1984.

D. Persuitte, *Joseph Smith and the Origins of the Book of Mormon*, 1985.

SMUTS, JAN CHRISTIAAN (1870–1950), South African statesman, soldier, and philosopher. Born into a family of French Huguenot and Dutch origin, Smuts enjoyed a carefree youth on his parents' farm in the British-controlled territory of Cape Colony, where he developed his deep love for and knowledge of the land. In 1891, after taking first-class honors in both science and the arts at Victoria College, Stellenbosch, he won a scholarship to study law at Christ's College, Cambridge University, England. He was regarded as a brilliant law student, was the first person ever to take both parts of the law tripos examinations in one year (and came first in both), and came first in the honors examination for the lawyers' Inns of Court in London.

Smuts also read widely in philosophy, poetry, and science, and was profoundly affected by reading Walt *Whitman, whose conception of the natural man in *Leaves of Grass* came as a revelation that freed him from the sense of guilt induced by his Calvinist upbringing. His book *Holism and Evolution*, published in 1926, grew out of a study of Whitman he wrote while at Cambridge, and constituted the fullest statement of the metaphysical background that informed his actions. Envisaged by Smuts as "an attempted ground-plan of the universe," it stresses the intrinsic unity of all creation and outlines his belief that "evolution is a rising series of wholes, of which man is the highest, most complex, but most intensely individualized." Evolution is characterized as a purposive process leading toward the realization of the virtues of truth, beauty, and goodness, which the author considered inherent in the world. The book holds out the hope that science will serve to support and justify a spiritual rather than purely mechanistic view of the universe. Smuts regarded the principle of cooperation as fundamental and absolute, and sought to actualize it through his life's work in the political and social arena.

Although a successful career in England was there for the taking, Smuts chose to return to his homeland, settling in Cape Town in 1895. Disgusted by Governor Cecil *Rhodes's connivance in the Jameson Raid on the Transvaal, he moved to Pretoria in 1898, where President Paul *Kruger appointed him Transvaal state attorney at the age of twenty-eight.

Smuts achieved international fame through his brilliant generalship during the Boer War (1899–1902), precipitated by British expansionism threatening the Boer republics of Transvaal and the Orange Free State. Although the British had many more troops, Smuts used hit-and-run guerrilla tactics to advance to within 120 miles of Cape Town in 1902. But his heroics came too late and he was forced to call off the siege of O'okiep and return to Vereeniging to help draft peace terms after the Boers finally had to give up the unequal struggle.

After the war, Smuts and Louis *Botha formed the organization Het Volk (The People) to lobby the British administration on Boer rights; they obtained self-government for Transvaal and the Orange Free State in 1906, and, in 1910, the creation of the Union of South Africa, which Smuts served as minister of defense from 1910 to 1920. After the outbreak of World War I, he was instrumental in orchestrating South African participation in the war against Germany, while suppressing rebellion in South Africa, conquering South West Africa, and launching a campaign in East Africa. Forced to tackle the civil rights campaign of Mohandas Karamchand *Gandhi, he recognized the latter's extraordinary human qualities, and the two men always respected each other, despite their political differences.

In 1917, Smuts visited England, where he so impressed British premier David *Lloyd George that he was made minister of air. He was responsible for organizing the Royal Air Force and was intimately involved in planning the war effort. At war's end, he attended the Versailles conference, where he was one of the principle progenitors of the League of Nations and advocated a modest peace settlement that would not wholly crush Germany, pleading for "a spirit of pity, mercy, and forgiveness... towards those who were yesterday our bitter enemies." His reputation as a statesman of international stature grew. His sensitive intervention was instrumental in paving the way for Anglo-Irish talks and the subsequent creation of the Irish Free State in 1921. A great lover of English life and manners, he was never so relaxed as when in the company of like-minded Englishmen of learning and culture, at which times his natural wit would flower.

On Botha's death in 1919, Smuts became prime minister of South Africa. However, he was never as popular at home as Botha had been, lacking the common touch and deep understanding of Afrikanerdom that the latter had shown. Smuts had a reputation for being cold and aloof, and was increasingly opposed by the Afrikaner population, who disliked his policy of maintaining close ties with Britain and the Commonwealth. He was called a lackey of empire, even a betrayer of his own people.

Defeated by a Labor-Nationalist coalition in 1923, Smuts returned to government in 1933 (in alliance with Herzog's Labor party, which he helped implement its racial segregation legislation) and was able to win support for his policy of declaring war against Germany in 1939. He again held the post of prime minister during World War II. After the war, he represented South Africa at the 1945 San Francisco Conference and played a significant role in drafting the charter of the United Nations, an organization that promised to fulfill his dreams of unifying the global community.

In 1948 Smuts lost to the Nationalists in the elections but held the position of chancellor of South Africa until his death two years later.

B. Friedman, *Smuts*, 1976.

W. K. Hancock, *Smuts*, 2 vols., 1968.

K. Ingham, *Jan Christiaan Smuts*, 1986.

SNORRI STURLUSON (1179–1241), Icelandic poet, historian, and political leader. Snorri Sturluson was born in Hvamm, Iceland, to an illustrious family. His father was a descendant of Snorri the Priest and Gudmund the Powerful; his mother was descended from Egil Skallagrimsson, all semi-legendary figures in Iceland's history. In keeping with Icelandic tradition, Snorri did not live at home but was raised by Jón Loptsson, chieftain of another influential family. He received a broad education at Loptsson's estate and remained there until Loptsson's death in 1197. In 1199 Snorri married the daughter of another influential clan leader and

---

FROM SNORRI STURLUSON'S
HEIMSKRINGLA

In this book, I have written old stories about the rulers who have had kingdoms in Scandinavia and who spoke the Danish tongue, according to how I have heard learned men tell them; also some of their family trees as I have been taught them. Some of this to be found in the genealogies in which kings and other men of distinguished birth have traced their descent; but some of it is written according to old poems or historical lays, which people have used to entertain themselves with. And although we do not know the truth of them, we do, however, know of examples when old and learned men have reckoned them to be true.

---

her dowry, added to Snorri's own ample inheritance, brought him significant wealth. He settled in Borgarfjord in western Iceland and embarked on an ambitious project to augment his wealth and power, becoming the most powerful clan leader in Iceland. He was not above deception to improve his status and plotted against any rivals who stood in his way, including family members, eventually succeeded in gaining the recognition he so coveted: in 1215, he was elected law speaker (president) of Iceland's indigenous parliament, the Althing.

Snorri held the position until 1218, when he embarked on his first journey to Norway. A talented poet, he endeared himself to the young King Haakon Haakonsson, whom he served as a retainer, and to his chief advisor.

Upon his return to Iceland, Snorri reverted to his old ways to augment his prestige. He was involved in several bloody intrigues and feuds, but was popular enough to be returned as law speaker from 1222 to 1231. He also found time to collect poetry and compose verses of his own, his favorite style of poetry being the traditional court-meter employed by the royal houses of Scandinavia. His vast literary knowledge resulted in the composition of the *Edda*, partly an account of the old gods of the north, partly a textbook for literary composition. He also composed the *Heimskringla*, an historical account of the kings of Norway until his own time, and several sagas, some of which, like the *Olaf Saga*, are universally recognized as Snorri's work. Others, such as the *Egil Saga*, have been attributed to Snorri because of his family ties to the eponymous heroes.

King Haakon of Norway sought to advance his own claims to Iceland by promoting the ever-present rivalries among the clans. Snorri and his nephew Sturla Stighvatsson were deeply embroiled in these feuds, which were eating away at Iceland; the period was later referred to as the Sturlung Age because of Snorri Sturluson's involvement in the ruthless disputes. Snorri was eventually forced to flee to Norway in 1237, and sought sanctuary with Haakon only to be refused, forcing him to seek the protection of Haakon's new adversary, Duke Skúli. Snorri remained with Skúli until 1239 when, hearing of his nephew's assassination, he believed it safer to return to Iceland than to remain in Norway.

King Haakon was enraged that Snorri had returned to Iceland despite his orders to the contrary. He sent word to Sturla's murderer, Gissur Thordvaldsson, an avowed enemy of Snorri (although his son-in-law) to return Snorri to him or to have him killed, should he refuse to return to Norway. Gissur broke into Snorri's estate while Snorri was asleep; Snorri escaped to the cellar, but was unarmed when Gissur's men finally found him. Rather than give him the option of returning to Norway, Gissur had Snorri hacked to death.

S. Bagge, *Society and Politics in Snorri Sturlson's Heimskringla*, 1991.
M. Ciklamini, *Snorri Sturlusson*, 1978.
S. Sturluson, *King Harald's Saga,* English trans., 1966.

SOCRATES (c.470–399 B.C.E.), Greek philosopher. One of the few things known with certainty about Socrates is that he met his end in 399 B.C.E. He left no writings and what is known of him is derived from the reports of those who claimed to know him, most particularly the works of his disciple *Plato and the military historian, *Xenophon. Although Plato made Socrates the central figure in many of his dialogues, it is extremely unlikely that he is merely recapitulating what he learned from him. However, even if none of the evidence can be regarded as historically certain, the fragmentary data nonetheless present information about Socrates's life and philosophy.

The picture left to posterity of the man whom Marcus *Cicero said "was the first to call philosophy down from the heavens" is an arresting one. He seems to have been remarkable for actually living the life he preached. All personal considerations, including his own survival, he considered secondary to "the supreme art of philosophy"; in later life his dedication to spreading his teachings made him neglect his personal affairs and he fell into poverty. Nonetheless, he remained content, in keeping with his belief that material goods are unimportant and that what matters is the pursuit and development of wisdom.

Socrates was no stranger to power and influence; his father was a friend of the family of Aristides the Just, who had founded the Delian League from which the Athenian empire sprang. Socrates himself was intimate with the Periclean circle then dominant in Athens. However, he was consistently notable since although he eschewed political power, he did serve as a member of the 500-man legislative council known as the Boule between 406 and 405 B.C.E.;

The Death of Socrates, by J. L. David

he would not, however, compromise his principles. His friendship with Critias, one of the leaders of the oligarchical terror of 404 B.C.E., was one of the reasons the resurgent democratic forces of subsequent years opposed his influence.

Socrates's personal wealth was sufficient for him to volunteer as a hoplite (a heavily-armed foot soldier) in the Peloponnesian War, where he is reputed to have distinguished himself by his courage. He also became famous among his admirers for his indifference to physical suffering; he went barefoot everywhere and withstood hunger and thirst uncom-

SOCRATES'S DEATH

All broke down in sobbing and grief, except only Socrates himself. What are you doing, my friends? he exclaimed. I sent away the women chiefly that they not offend in this way, for I have heard that a man should die in silence. So calm yourselves and bear up. He walked about until he said his legs were getting heavy and then he lay down on his back. The man who gave the poison began to examine his feet and legs from time to time; he pressed his foot hard and asked if there was any feeling in it and Socrates said No; and then his legs, and so higher and higher, and showed us that he was cold and stiff. And Socrates felt himself and said that when it came to his heart he would be done. He was already growing cold about the groin, when he uncovered his face which had been covered and spoke for the last time. Crito, he said, I owe a cock to Asclepius; do not forget to pay it. It shall be done, replied Crito. Is there anything else you wish? He made no answer to this question; but after a short interval there was a movement, and the man uncovered him and his eyes were fixed. Then Crito closed his mouth and eyes.

From Plato's *Phaedo*

plainingly. These qualities stood him in good stead in his peripatetic lifestyle; Socrates the philosopher took his message to the streets, to the forum, the market and the Gymnasium; debate and persuasion were the lifeblood of his teachings.

Socrates's focus on ethics was in part a reaction against the prevailing vogue for philosophizing about the nature of the universe, which he saw as specious and unverifiable. Saying "I have nothing to do with physical speculations," he concerned himself with showing how to "make one's soul as good as possible." Happiness, he argued, depended on the development in the individual of the capacity and wisdom to act rightly; the self-discipline of moral reason is what enables one to develop this capacity by freeing one from the distractions of irrational appetites.

No one willfully chooses bad over good, argued Socrates. What causes wrong choices is ignorance; therefore right conduct depends solely on knowledge. Socrates thus sought a practical science of morality which through its rational organization would be infallible, predictable, and teachable. Moreover, arguing that one cannot be good unless one first knows what goodness is, Socrates saw the prime practical concern of the philosopher as the examination of moral terms and the attempt to define them. This for him was a process of discovery.

Plato attributes to Socrates the doctrine of Forms: this says that every term which has an unequivocal denotation (such as good, beautiful, or just) refers to an object of a kind inaccessible to sense perceptions and apprehensible only through thought — the Form. The physical things to which these terms are applied have only a secondary or derivative reality: they become this or that by virtue of their participation in the Form. Thus Socrates envisaged an absolute morality which would be revealed to the diligent seeker.

Perhaps even more significant than the content of Socrates's philosophy was his manner of philosophizing. The Socratic dialogue involved question and answer investigations of ethical terms through inductive methods of analogy and concrete illustration; it usually elicited from Socrates's interlocutor the realization that his confidence in his own understanding of the term under consideration was unfounded and that a new and more accurate definition was required. It exemplified the Socratic belief that knowledge was not something that could be acquired secondhand but constituted a personal achievement which depended on continual self-criticism and a willingness to subject oneself to the force of reason. Socrates did not set himself up as an authority; he professed as great a perplexity as his dialogue partners, and often asserted that his wisdom simply consisted in having a clear understanding of the true extent of his own ignorance.

As an educator critical of received assumptions, Socrates was a revolutionary in a state where education and the state were closely identified, while his simple way of life constituted a critique of the Athenian emphasis on material values. Therefore, conservative authorities considered him a dangerous influence. What prompted charges being brought against him was in fact his opposition to democracy on the grounds that it put government into the hands of men who had not been trained to govern. Athenian democracy was in a fragile position at that time; it did not need the likes of Socrates undermining its validity.

In 399 B.C.E. he was indicted before an Athenian criminal tribunal on charges of not believing in the gods of Athens and for corrupting young men with his ideas. He refused to pacify his judges with prayer and flattery, as he could easily have done. He spoke eloquently at his trial, arguing that he best served the state by intelligently criticizing its shortcomings and expressed his sense of mission arising from his personal *daimonion* — the voice of god he would sometimes hear forbidding a contemplated action. By a vote of 281 to 220 he was sentenced to death by drinking hemlock, a poison. Execution of the sentence was delayed for a long time as it had to await the return of the annual Athenian mission sent to Apollo at Delos. Meanwhile he continued to meet with his disciples in prison. On the morning after the mission's return, he parted from this wife, Xanthippe, bathed in preparation for death, and drank the poison calmly, chiding his disciples for their display of grief.

Socrates's ideas were developed by Plato into the fundamental system of Western philosophy; all earlier Greek thought is termed "pre-Socratic."

J. Eckstein, *The Deathday of Socrates*, 1981.
I. F. Stone, *The Trial of Socrates*, 1989.
G. Vlastos, *Socrates*, 1990.

SOLOMON (tenth century B.C.E.), fourth son of King *David, third king of Israel, builder of the First Temple in Jerusalem, in Jewish tradition the wisest of all men. Most of the biographical material on Solomon is found in 2 Samuel, 1 Kings 1–11 and 2 Chronicles 1–9. His mother was Bathsheba; he acceded to the throne three years before his father's death and reigned for thirty-seven years after it.

Called Solomon by his father, he was named Jedidiah (literally, "friend of God") by Nathan the prophet (2 Samuel 12:24–25), who was instrumental in ensuring Solomon's nomination as his father's successor (1 King 1–2), even though he was among the younger of David's sons.

Solomon inherited from his father a substantial kingdom, stretching beyond the borders of Israelite settlement, "from the river [the Euphrates] to the land of the Philistines and to the border of Egypt." Except for Aram-Damascus in the north, he maintained his hold on all of it. Moreover, he added Hamath (modern Hama, Syria) and Tadmor (Palmyra, an oasis 150 miles northeast of Damascus).

Solomon's first acts upon taking the throne were zealous dealings with his opponents Adonijah, his brother who declared himself king; Joab, David's commander in chief and supporter of Adonijah; and

Shimi ben Gera, who had taunted and cursed David; all of whom Solomon had executed. He banished Abiathar the priest to Anathoth, relieving him of his priestly duties. The image of Solomon as his father's ruthless avenger is somewhat at odds with his depiction as pursuer of peace found in 1 Chronicles 22:5–9, where his name ("Shelomo" in Hebrew) is linked to the Hebrew word for peace, *shalom*.

On the whole his reign was quiet and his direction of his kingdom orderly. The names of his administrative staff and their job descriptions are given in 1 Kings 4:2–6, with the range of duties listed including that of priest, secretaries, household manager, and tax overseer. Solomon apportioned Israel into twelve administrative units, each headed by an appointee, to provide for the needs of the king's household and food one month a year. Two of the unit heads were married to Solomon's daughters.

Solomon's love for non-Israelite women is specifically noted (1 Kings 11:1). He had a total of seven hundred wives and three hundred concubines. A special wedding gift accompanying the daughter of the Egyptian pharaoh was the Canaanite city of Gezer. The Bible finds that rather than serving as cement for political or military alliances, these matches drew Solomon away from the ways of the Lord and attributes the subsequent split in his kingdom to this behavior.

To maintain his kingdom Solomon depended on military might — infantry, extensive cavalry, and chariots — aimed at control and protection of trade routes and established Israelite colonies where needed to accomplish this. The thrust of his empire was commercial and he worked along with rulers such as King Hiram of Tyre. The Queen of Sheba went to Jerusalem from her south Arabian kingdom, probably to expand trade relations (although later legend spoke of other relations, with the royal house of Ethiopia claiming descent from their union).

The most significant result of Solomon's construction efforts was the Temple in Jerusalem, which took seven years to build, and "there was neither hammer nor axe nor any tool of iron heard in the house while it was in building." Hiram of Tyre provided timber, and gold, receiving land and foodstuffs in return. Among other structures built by Solomon in Jerusalem were his palace, which took thirteen years to complete, and a city wall. He also established garrison cities and built fortresses throughout the empire.

Solomon's reputation for wisdom is based on biblical and extra-biblical material. In response to God's asking him in a dream "What shall I give thee?", Solomon requested a discerning heart. The biblical story of his judgment in the case of two women, each of whom claims to be the mother of the same child, gives perhaps the most famous illustration of this wisdom (1 Kings 3:16–28). Biblical books traditionally ascribed to him are Proverbs, the Song of Songs (also known as the Song of Solomon), and Ecclesiastes. Later works attributed to him are the *Odes of Solomon*, and the *Psalms of Solomon*.

Although Solomon's reign saw developments in the economy, agriculture, and administration of the empire, the cost to the nation in taxes and work levy outweighed the benefits as far as most people were concerned, and they were deeply dissatisfied. After his death, ten tribes rejected the rule of Rehoboam, his successor, and created their own kingdom of Israel. The remaining territory became Rehoboam's truncated kingdom of Judah.

F. Thieberger, *King Solomon*, 1947.

SOLON (c.630–c.560 B.C.E.), Athenian statesman. One of the fathers of Athenian democracy, Solon humanized the legal code, making it more egalitarian while protecting the wealth of the aristocracy. He was considered Athens's first poet and his political decrees were often given in poetic form; he was the first to apply the Greek religious tradition of moderation to matters of government.

Little is known about Solon's early life, but he was originally a poet and merchant, and witnessed the military defeat of Athens by neighboring Megara that resulted in cession of the island of Salamis. His patriotic poetry appealed to the Athenians to reverse this shameful defeat and his countrymen responded to the call. Their subsequent victory made Solon a national figure at a time when the Athenian aristocracy was grappling with popular discontent arising from harsh economic and social conditions.

After the age of thirty, when Athenian law permitted a man to assume political power, Solon became archon, leader of the council that ruled Athens, a position that rotated every year among the council members. He remained on the governing council for some twenty years before being called upon by the aristocracy to assume a position of supreme power in the hope of circumventing a national disaster.

The conflict between the aristocracy and the rest of the population was at its height, the discrepancies of wealth exacerbated by a harsh legal code. Under previous rulers, including Draco (from whose harsh decrees the term "draconian" derived), the laws of Athens had resulted in large numbers of poor farmers being dispossessed of their lands and then enslaved. Under Draco, even minor criminal offenses were punished by death. The time was ripe for revolution and a tyrannical takeover, a scenario that had been realized during this period in other Greek city-states. Fearing this danger, Solon instituted a series of reforms that weakened the aristocracy's monopoly but promised to stabilize society.

- In giving advice seek to help, not please, your friends.
- Look to the end, no matter what it is you are considering. Often enough, the gods give a man a glimpse of happiness, and then utterly ruin him.
- Laws are like spiders' webs which if anything small falls into them they ensnare it, but large things break through and escape.
- Nothing in excess.
- Put more trust in nobility of character than in an oath.
- Learn to obey before you command.
- If things are going well, religion and legislation are beneficial, if not, they are of no avail.

Solon

Solon released those freemen who had been enslaved and forbade the practice of mortgaging persons to secure debts that had cost so many their freedom. He repealed the legal code of Draco, eliminating the death penalty for all but the worst crimes and otherwise humanizing the system of criminal justice. He issued new weights and measures to standardize mercantile practices and minted an indigenous Athenian coinage. In addition to these measures, designed to increase national efficiency, he restructured the economy by providing more positions in the trades and professions. While Athens had already been one of the regional exporters of olive oil and pottery, Solon's innovations aimed for a more equitable distribution of wealth.

Popular sentiment favored making Solon sole ruler but the aristocracy was angered by his concessions to the poor and middle-sized landowners. Solon saw himself as a buffer maintaining a semblance of peace between these forces. He trusted that the gods, Zeus and Athene, would keep the peace of Athens so long as her citizens restrained themselves from extremes and kept to a path of moderation. While implementing his economic reform he also protected the wealthy aristocracy, whom he saw as endangered by the envy of the poorer classes. Nevertheless, his political reforms seriously eroded the foundations of aristocratic monopoly. He divided the population into four classes according to wealth, measured by their stores of grain, wine, and oil; from this time on, political power was vested in the wealthy classes regardless of aristocratic ancestry. This opened the general assembly to all Athenian citizens, investing them with the power to legislate, elect representatives, and decide court appeals.

Solon bound the Athenians to his reforms for a period of one hundred years, displaying his decrees on revolving wooden tablets. In order to avoid having constantly to defend and explain them further in the face of considerable public discontent he then stepped down from power and departed, spending the next ten years traveling throughout the known world. He visit Egypt and Cyprus, setting down his experiences in his poetry. When he returned to Athens, he found the country divided in a contest of regional powers, the strongest faction led by Peisistratus, who had been one of the generals in the war for Salamis. Solon warned — correctly — that his friend was trying to become tyrant of Athens but his message was ignored. Peisistratus ruled for a brief period before being overthrown.

Solon left Athenian society better off economically and socially, and with political institutions that carried the potential for democratic stability. His selection as one of the Seven Wise Men of Athens was later ratified by *Plato, and he remained one of Athens's founding heroes.

K. Freeman, *The Code and Life of Solon*, 1926.
I. M. Linforth, *Solon the Athenian*, 1919.
W. J. Woodhouse, *Solon the Liberator*, 1965.

SOPHOCLES (c.496–406 B.C.E.), Greek playwright. One of the three great ancient Greek tragedians (the others being *Aeschylus and *Euripides), Sophocles combined epic poetry and drama to create theater that brought the moral problems of humanity to the fore even as his characters were enmeshed in the inexorable grip of fate. He increased and changed the function of the chorus so that it came to resemble an audience, providing reactions to characters and events.

Sophocles was born at Colonus Hippios near Athens, into an important and wealthy family and lived during a period of Athenian ascendancy. His father, Sophilus, owned a metal factory producing swords and other weaponry — necessary commodities in a century racked by wars.

Statue of Sophocles, Roman copy

- It is a painful thing to look at your own trouble and know that you yourself and none else has made it.
- No enemy is worse than bad advice.
- Afterthought makes the first resolve a liar.
- In a just cause, the weak will beat the strong.
- You win the victory when you yield to friends.
- There are times when even justice brings harm with it.
- What you cannot enforce, do not command.
- Nobody likes the bringer of bad news.
- Stubbornness and stupidity are twins.
- Nobody loves life like an old man.
- It is terrible to speak well and be wrong.

Sophocles

Sophocles assumed many tasks as a public servant of Athens. He was twice chosen as general over Athenian troops in battle — under *Pericles in the suppression of the Samian revolt in 440 B.C.E., and later under Nikias. In 413 B.C.E. he was one of the commission of ten that took over the governing of Athens after the naval disaster at Syracuse. He was treasurer of the empire for a year in 443 B.C.E. and priest of the healing god Amynos, opening his own home as a temporary place of worship until the temple for Asclepius could be completed. He also worked toward the founding of a public hospital in Athens and set up a literary club.

Sophocles produced one hundred and twenty-three plays, achieving eighteen victories at the theater competition in the Dionysian festivals and another six successes at the Lenaia dramatic festivals. He also wrote literary criticism, odes, and paeans, now lost. Of his tragedies only seven survive: *Antigone, Philoctetes, Oedipus at Colonus, Ajax, Oedipus the King, Electra,* and *The Trachinia.* At twenty-eight he bested his elder, Aeschylus, at the Dionysia and thereafter won many victories over the elder playwright, as well as over the younger Euripides. In his earliest tragedies, Sophocles also participated as an actor, but his voice was not powerful enough for this rigorous medium.

Sophocles's earliest extant play appears to be *Ajax,* written in the 430s B.C.E. The play dramatizes the legend of Ajax, one of the great national heroes and native to the area of Salamis. His next play, *Antigone,* was perhaps his most popular, revolving around the issue of proper burial and more broadly the problem of private versus public duty. His most famous work is *Oedipus the King,* a play which shows the tragic and inevitable consequences of fate. The play begins with Oedipus and his wife Jocasta reigning as king and queen of Thebes, a city in the throes of a plague. When oracular advice is sought, the king is told that the city is polluted by the presence in Thebes of the murderer of the former king, Laïus, Jocasta's late husband. When Oedipus seeks to find the cause of the plague he eventually is led to himself. When he realizes that it was he himself who killed Laïus — not knowing him to have been his father — and married Jocasta, his own mother, Oedipus blinds himself and Jocasta commits suicide. Sophocles's last play, *Oedipus at Colonus,* returns to the story of Oedipus and tells of his last days.

Many times invited to reside in royal courts outside Athens, Sophocles always refused. *Aristophanes in the *Frogs* refers to Sophocles as well-liked and of genial temperament, in contrast to his rival Euripides, who was cantankerous and argumentative. Sophocles was a friend of the historian *Herodotus and shared an interest in similar subjects, which he developed in his plays. The playwright lived to an old age, perhaps ninety, outliving Euripides, whom he mourned with the chorus and actors of the theater. When Sophocles died shortly thereafter, he was given a hero's funeral.

S. M. Adams, *Sophocles the Playwright,* 1957.
R. G. Buxton, *Sophocles,* 1984.
B. M. Knox, *Word and Action,* 1979.

SPARTACUS (died 71 B.C.E.), Roman gladiator who led the Gladiatorial War against Rome in 73–71 B.C.E. Very little is known about his life before the war began except that he was originally from Thrace and had been captured in war and sold into slavery.

The economy of the Roman Empire then had become increasingly dependent on slavery. Slaves were numerous and cheap; the many wars and pirate raids yielded large numbers of captives whose fate was almost invariably to be sold into slavery. Roman administrators in the provinces could augment their already high incomes by organizing manhunts that enslaved anyone not under the protection of local officials. Cities and states unable to meet the taxes imposed by the Romans would sell their citizens into slavery. Many slaves were sold to the big farms where they were forced to work for minimal food and clothing. Little care was taken of them because they could easily be replaced. Slaves fared better inside Rome, where much of the work — handicrafts, trade, banking, manufacturing, building, domestic services — was done by them. Not only was skilled labor treated well, since replacements were hard to find and more expensive, but the personal ties created by frequent contact between master and slave in the city strengthened the bonds between them.

Slaves were also trained in schools as gladiators to fight each other or animals to the death in public arenas. At one such school in Capua, run by Lentulus Batiates, two hundred gladiators tried to escape; seventy-eight of them succeeded, armed themselves, and occupied a slope of Vesuvius, raiding the adjoining towns for food. They chose as their leader Spartacus who — according to Plutarch — was "a man not only of high spirit and bravery, but also in understanding and gentleness superior to his condition." He issued a call to all the slaves of Italy to rise up in revolt and soon had a following of seventy thousand men, hungering for liberty and revenge. He taught them to manufacture their own weapons and to fight with such order and discipline that for years they outmatched every force sent to subdue them.

Spartacus's victories filled the wealthy men of Italy with fear and its slaves with hope. So many slaves escaped to join him that when his army numbered one hundred and twenty thousand he was forced to refuse further recruits. He marched his men toward the Alps, intending to cross them and then let every man return to his own home. His followers did not share these refined and pacific sentiments and, revolting against his leadership, they began looting the towns of northern Italy.

The Roman Senate sent out both heavy enforcements against the rebels. One army met a detachment that had seceded from Spartacus and slaughtered it. The other attacked the main rebel body and was defeated. Moving again toward the Alps, Spartacus encountered a third army, led by Cassius, and decimated it, but finding his way blocked by yet more legions, he turned south and marched toward Rome.

Many of the slaves in Italy were on the verge of insurrection and in the capital no one could tell when the rebellion would break out in his own home. Italy's opulent society, which had enjoyed all the luxuries of slave ownership, trembled at the thought of losing everything — mastery, property, life. Senators and millionaires cried out for a better general, but few offered themselves, for they all feared Spartacus, their strange new foe. Eventually Crassus came forward and was given forty thousand men, including many of the nobility who had joined as volunteers to fight the slaves.

Knowing that he had the empire against him and that his men could never administer it or even its capital, Spartacus bypassed Rome and continued south to Thurii, marching the length of Italy in the hope of transporting his men to Sicily or Africa.

For a third year he fought off all attacks. Again his impatient soldiers rejected his authority and began pillaging the neighboring towns. They were met by Crassus and his army killed 12,300 of them, every man fighting to the last. Pompey's legions, returning from Spain, were sent to augment Crassus's forces. Despairing of victory over such a multitude, Spartacus flung himself on the army of Crassus and welcomed death by plunging in the midst of his foes. He killed two centurions but, struck down and unable to rise, he continued fighting on his knees. He was so badly wounded that his body could not later be identified.

The majority of his followers perished with Spartacus; some fled and became hunted men in the woods of Italy, and six thousand captives were crucified along the Appian Way to Rome (71 B.C.E.). Their rotting bodies were left to hang for months, for all masters to take comfort and all slaves to take heed. After Spartacus's death, three thousand Roman prisoners were discovered unharmed in his camp. His revolt led to less capricious treatment of slaves in the Roman Empire.

H. Fast, *Spartacus*, 1952.

SPINOZA, BARUCH (Benedict; 1632–1677), Dutch rationalist philosopher. Reviled in his own lifetime as an atheist (although his whole philosophy is dominated by the idea of God) and freethinker, Spinoza has often been misunderstood by subsequent generations. Derided throughout the eighteenth century (even the enlightened and tolerant Scottish philosopher David *Hume spoke of Spinoza's "hideous hypothesis"), his ideas gained respectability during the nineteenth, partly due to the attentions of romantic writers.

Spinoza was the first great philosophical advocate of toleration in the modern spirit. An enemy of all persecuting churches, he demanded a purely secular state that would be indifferent in matters of religious doctrine. These views, allied with his advocacy of the application of the historical method to the interpretation of biblical sources, earned him widespread antipathy. Nevertheless, Bertrand *Russell speaks of Spinoza as "the noblest and most lovable of the great philosophers. Intellectually, some others have surpassed him, but ethically he is supreme."

- Not only is liberty to philosophize compatible with devout piety and with the peace of the state...to take away such liberty is to destroy the public peace and even piety itself.
- Hatred is increased by being reciprocated, and can on the other hand be destroyed by love.
- The mind's highest good is the knowledge of God, and the mind's highest virtue is to know God.
- All things that are, are in God, and must be conceived through God... No substances can be granted outside God, i.e., nothing outside God can exist in itself. God is the immanent, but not the transcendent, cause of all things.
- God, insofar as he loves himself, loves men. The love of God towards men and the intellectual love of the mind towards God are one and the same thing.
- I have striven hard to laugh at human actions, not to weep at them, nor to hate them, but to understand them.
- A good thing which prevents us from enjoying a greater good is, in effect, an evil.
- A free man thinks of nothing less than of death; and his wisdom is a meditation not of death, but of life.

Baruch Spinoza

Born to a family of wealthy Jewish merchants who had escaped the Portuguese Inquisition and settled in Amsterdam, Spinoza studied traditional Hebrew subjects at the Jewish school he attended and was privately tutored to a high standard in Latin and all the major continental languages. As a young man he came to know a group of freethinkers interested in philosophy — the climate of revolt against tradition and authority was strong in seventeenth-century Holland, by far the most tolerant state in Europe at that time — and found it impossible to remain an Orthodox Jew. His heretical views led to excommunication and his formal expulsion from the Jewish community in July 1656, after threats and bribes had failed to silence him and after he had attempted to defend his views in the synagogue. The elders not only were alarmed at the voicing of such opinions within the community but believed that they could have repercussions affecting their newly-achieved tolerated status if the Christians of the Netherlands were to identify such views — which affected all religious thought — as authentically Jewish.

Thereafter Spinoza lived a quiet and ascetic life in The Hague, devoting himself to the development of his philosophy. The death of his father in 1654 had entitled him to a considerable inheritance; his stepsister contested the estate but was defeated in litigation. Nonetheless, Spinoza allowed her to keep nearly everything. When the Elector Palatinate of Heidelberg offered him a post teaching philosophy at Heidelberg University, under conditions of complete freedom, he politely refused, explaining that as a philosopher he preferred to remain free of public commitment Instead, he supported himself by grinding lenses for spectacles, telescopes, and microscopes. His occupation hastened his death; the consumption that killed him was exacerbated by the glass dust he inhaled when polishing lenses in his workshop.

Spinoza was greatly influenced by the new philosophy of René *Descartes, as well as by the Jewish intellectual tradition. The only work of his to appear under his own name in his lifetime was his version of Descartes's *Principia*, and he was never to abandon the Cartesian precepts of clarity and deductive rigor. However, unlike Descartes, he was above all a moralist; moreover, while accepting the materialistic and deterministic physics of the Cartesians, he rejected the notions of the transcendence of God, mind-body dualism, and free will.

In his masterwork, the *Ethics*, written between the early 1660s and 1675 and first published in 1677, Spinoza — taking *Euclid's geometry as a model — set out to derive a coherent and all-encompassing philosophy proceeding from self-evident axiomatic premises via rigorously demonstrated deductive argument to true conclusions about the nature of reality. The result is one of the most complete systems of metaphysics in the history of philosophy. It is also notorious as one of the most difficult to understand. Its central features are: the doctrine that the world as a whole is a single substance, the parts of which are merely aspects of the Divine Being and logically incapable of existing alone; the belief that everything is ruled by an absolute logical necessity so that free will and chance are illusory; the view that if one could perceive the whole one would understand that evil does not really exist. It was this latter feature that was most repugnant to orthodox believers in sin and damnation.

Spinoza's main concern was his moral philosophy, which he felt followed directly from his metaphysics. "Love for God must hold the chief place in the mind," he said. The virtuous man makes himself free by understanding the true order of nature, thus detaching himself from transitory interests. He does this by freeing himself from the passions that dominate him so long as he remains in a state of ignorance, desiring objects that are transient and changeable. However, Spinoza's ideal man is not the cold intellectual; he has emotions, but they are a function of the whole man and not (as the passions are) a mere part of him.

Spinoza also wrote *Tractatus Theologico-Politicus*, but for fear of persecution issued it anonymously and even gave the place of publication as Hamburg, although it was printed in Amsterdam. In it he maintained that the biblical laws were only valid when the Jews enjoyed a polity, that the Bible stories were not to be taken literally but were meant to point toward abstract thinking, and that the historical events related have no universal significance and are irrelevant to other peoples. In this book he pioneered modern Bible criticism, denying the traditional assignation of authors, and maintained that generations of copyists had introduced errors into the text, which is a human, not a divine, creation. However, the Bible does contain universal teachings concerning the existence and nature of God and morality.

Spinoza died in The Hague, unmarried and heirless, and his meager belongings were publicly auctioned; his real legacy, his manuscripts, were preserved and published by his admirers.

H. E. Allison, *Benedict de Spinoza*, 1987.

S. Hampshire, *Spinoza*, 1988.

C. Norris, *Spinoza and the Origins of Modern Critical Theory,* 1992.

R. Scruton, *Spinoza*, 1986.

STALIN, JOSEPH, (1879–1953), Russian dictator. Born Josif Vissarionovich Dzhugashvili in the small town of Gori in Georgia, he later adopted the name Stalin (from stal', Russian for "steel"). Stalin was a Georgianized Ossetian, a descendant of an Iranian tribe that had settled in Georgia. He was the son of a poor shoemaker; his childhood was poverty-stricken and wretched. Educated to the Orthodox priesthood in the Tiflis (Tbilisi) ecclesiastical seminary, which was a breeding ground for Georgian revolutionaries, he was expelled from the seminary in 1899 for reading forbidden literature (Fyodor *Dostoevsky and Karl *Marx, among others).

In 1901 Stalin was banished from Tiflis by a revolutionary court and went to Batum, where he engaged in political agitation, inciting a demonstration that was brutally suppressed by the police. He used the alias "Koba," the name of a folk hero who took revenge on the Russians for oppressing Georgians. In 1903 he was arrested and exiled for a short time to Siberia.

Stalin soon began to make his way in the revolutionary movement. He joined the Bolshevik ("Majority") faction of the Social Democrat party in 1902 or 1903 and embarked on a campaign to achieve power. He was inactive in the abortive revolution of 1905 but in that year he met Vladimir *Lenin for the first time at a meeting of revolutionaries in Finland.

In 1912, as the most prominent Bolshevik in the Caucasus, he was invited by Lenin to join the Central Party Committee. He also became an editor of *Pravda* ("Truth"), the Bolshevik party organ. His essay on *Marxism and the National Question,* commissioned and edited by Lenin, contains the essence of his fervent Russian nationalism — despite his being of Georgian origin — and the opposition to ethnic minorities that he was later to display when he took power. In 1913 he was arrested and exiled for life to Siberia.

Much has been written about Stalin's role in the pre-revolutionary movement. The lack of documentation and his penchant for rewriting Soviet history, especially that of the early years (after taking power he claimed to have met Lenin years before their real first meeting took place), lends scope for many claims to be made about his activities at this time.

The overthrowing of the czar in 1917 and the subsequent amnesty freed Stalin, with many others, from exile. In Saint Petersburg, he served for three weeks as acting head of the party until Lenin returned from Switzerland. Stalin served as people's commissar for nationalities in the cabinet set up by Lenin after the October Revolution and took an active part in the civil war as a political commissar in the Red Army. During this turbulent period his rivalry with Leon *Trotsky emerged.

In 1922 Stalin was named general secretary of the Communist party, a position that involved running the growing party bureaucracy. Lenin died in 1924, leaving his "Testament," a codicil of which advised that Stalin should be removed from his position (known to the party leaders, this was not made public until Nikita *Khrushchev's denunciation of Stalin at the Twentieth Party Congress in 1956). However, Lenin's request was disregarded; Stalin was one of the triumvirate (the others being Lev Kamenev and Grigori Zinoviev) who succeeded to the party leadership.

Stalin spent the next few years eliminating his opponents. In 1927 he succeeded in having his two chief rivals, Trotsky and Zinoviev, expelled from the party and became sole leader of the Politburo, in effect, dictator of the Soviet Union, without holding an official title. He set about changing all Lenin's policies and programs, while beginning the process of deification of the dead leader. In 1928 he substituted the first Five-Year Plan for Lenin's New Economic Policy. From 1929 to 1932 he forced industrialization and collectivization on the Soviet Union. It is estimated that five to ten million people were killed in these years, through direct purges or by "natural" causes such as starvation, during the implementation of Stalin's program.

In 1929 Stalin gained control of the secret police and thereafter ruled through total terror. During the Great Purges of the 1930s, a series of show trials ostensibly sparked by the assassination of his second in command, Sergei Kirov, Stalin further solidified his dictatorship by eliminating any possible opposition (Khrushchev was later to hint that Kirov's murder had been engineered by Stalin as a pretext for the purges). In this period, too, which culminated in the notorious "Show Trials" of former leaders in 1935–1938, millions of workers and intellectuals, engineers, scientists, writers were killed or sentenced to imprisonment in labor camps. Many others were exiled to the outposts of the Soviet Union. During these years the country was virtually cut off from Western influence in all areas, from music, art, and literature to medicine and science. Soviet artists were organized into unions to depict "Soviet socialist reality."

Lenin and Stalin (right) at Gorki in 1922

Stalin's goal of "monolithic unity" was achieved in 1938. He had shrewdly grasped that Bolshevik rule had no clear legal or popular justification except for the near-religious worship of Lenin by certain sequents of the population. For this reason he encouraged the deification of Lenin; from earliest years children were taught to sing hymns about "Ilyich," the "wise leader who loved little children." Statues and pictures of Lenin abounded, together with legends and stories. After World War II, the "Great Patriotic War," as it was called in Russia, the official near-adoration of Lenin was replaced by the cult of Stalin. At the same time Stalin discarded the programs and plans Lenin had formulated for the future of the Bolshevik party and the Soviet Union. His nationalist beliefs led him to stress the slogan of "socialism in one country" rather than the world revolution Trotsky had advocated. The Soviet Communist party never paid more than lip service to the Communist parties established in other countries.

In August 1939, shortly before the outbreak of World War II, Stalin concluded an alliance with Adolf *Hitler. Mass deportations were carried out of populations in the areas that now came under Soviet rule, including eastern Poland and the Baltic republics.

The Nazi-Soviet pact exploded when the Germans invaded Russia on June 22, 1941. Stalin was taken by surprise. His purges of the Red Army from 1937 to 1938 weakened the Soviet military structure, contributing to early German successes. He took over the premiership from Viatcheslav Molotov and assumed military leadership later in 1941, styling himself marshal in 1943 and generalissimo in 1945. He mobilized and armed the country and eventually the German invaders were driven back. Stalin proved himself an astute negotiator with Western leaders at the conferences during and following the war. Franklin *Roosevelt was not the only leader who believed that Stalin's natural simplicity and readiness to negotiate were foiled by his hardline Politburo "colleagues."

Stalin established Soviet domination over eastern Europe in the post war years and began to prepare Soviet resources for a war with the West. He also conducted campaigns of extreme terror in the USSR — utilizing the secret police ruthlessly — and his paranoid anti-Semitism led him to a persecution of his Jewish subjects. Only his death in 1953 saved them.

Stalin ruled the Soviet Union until his death. Millions of Soviet citizens worshiped him and felt bereft after his passing, as if they had lost their father figure. His portrait was to be found in both private homes and workplaces and stories were told of his kindness toward the common people. In private life he was a tyrant who ruled his family with the same paranoid cruelty with which he ran the country. The myth was eventually exposed by Khrushchev in a speech which, though delivered to a closed gathering in 1956 soon received wide circulation; Krushchev revealed the excesses of Stalin's dictatorship, his "intolerance, brutality, and abuse of power," and started a far-reaching process of "de-Stalinization."

M. Agursky, *The Third Rome*, 1987.
A. Bullock, *Hitler and Stalin; Parallel Lives*, 1991.
K. N. Cameron, *Stalin*, 1989.
R. Conquest, *The Great Terror*, 1991.
R. Medvedev, *On Stalin and Stalinism*, 1979.

STANLEY, SIR HENRY MORTON (1841–1904), Anglo-American journalist and explorer. Born in North Wales, his original name was John Rowlands, the illegitimate child of a plowman and a servant girl. His childhood was miserable; he lived for a time with his grandparents but was then sent to a workhouse, where the beatings he endured at the hands of the schoolmaster drove him to run away.

Stanley found a place as cabin boy on a ship bound for the United States, arrived in New Orleans in 1858, and began to work for a merchant named Henry Morton Stanley. He was adopted by his employer the following year and took his name. During the Civil War he enlisted in the Confederate army and was captured at the Battle of Shiloh in 1862. While imprisoned in Camp Douglas in Chicago, he decided to change allegiance and joined the Union navy.

In 1865 Stanley began working as a journalist, covering the Indian wars in the American West as well as areas of conflict in the Middle East. In 1868 he was hired as correspondent for the *New York Herald* by its ambitious proprietor, James Gordon Bennett, Jr. He was soon assigned to report on the British expedition against the Abyssinian empire and then sent to Spain for the latest news about the civil war.

In 1869 Bennett summoned Stanley to Paris and gave him his most famous mission — to go and find Dr. David *Livingstone, the British explorer who was missing deep in Africa. Although Stanley was told to go with supplies to relieve Livingstone, it was not primarily a humanitarian venture but a search for a news scoop. To make sure there would be no shortage of good items, Stanley was also asked to report on the opening of the Suez Canal and write a travellers' guide to Lower Egypt.

After many delays he set off into the interior of Africa in March 1871, with a well-equipped and efficiently organized team of 192 men. Stanley was a hard taskmaster and drove them on ceaselessly, not sparing the whip when he thought it necessary.

On November 10, 1873, the historic encounter occurred at Ujiji. When the two men met, Stanley uttered his famous greeting, "Dr. Livingstone, I presume." Muskets were fired, a crowd assembled, and there was much cheering and even weeping.

Livingstone was delighted with the tents, cooking pots, tin baths, and other accouterments of civilization that Stanley had brought. He was even more grateful for the human contact and the two adventurers struck up an immediate rapport. They journeyed together, exploring the northern edge of Lake Tanganyika and when, after four months, it was time for Stanley to depart, he wrote of how he wanted "to rebel against the fate that drives me from him."

Stanley's book, *How I Found Livingstone*, was written in a sensational journalistic style that motivated Florence *Nightingale to describe it as "the very worst book on the very best subject I ever saw in my life." Other readers were less discriminating and it proved popular.

After Livingstone's death in 1873, Stanley wanted to carry on his work of exploration and persuaded the London *Daily Telegraph* to sponsor the venture in partnership with the *New York Herald*. Between 1874 and 1877, with 356 porters at his service, he explored the Upper Congo and Lakes Victoria and Tanganyika. In his characteristic manner he forced his party to proceed at great speed and showed himself a brutal master to the Africans. The 280-meter Livingstone Falls (as Stanley named them) were just one of his dramatic discoveries. In *Through the Dark Continent* (published in 1878), he described the journey and coined the appellation often applied to Africa ever since.

Having failed to interest the British in the Congo basin, Stanley entered into an agreement with the Belgians. During the years 1879–1885 he established many steamer stations along the river, laying the foundations for the Belgian colony. On his last African adventure in 1889 he led a rescue mission for Emin Pasha, governor of equatorial Egypt, who had been isolated in 1885 by rebellion in the Sudan. The project was problematic from the start but there were also important discoveries, notably the Mountains of the Moon.

In 1890 Stanley returned once more to Britain and renewed his British citizenship. He married and launched himself on a new career as member of parliament for Lambeth, in London. He was knighted in 1899.

J. W. Buel, *Heroes of the Dark Continent*, 1971.
R. Jones, *The Rescue of Emin Pasha*, 1972.

STEINBECK, JOHN (1902–1968), American author. Born in Salinas, California, he grew up in the Central Valley and later roamed the countryside, working on the farms and ranches, sometimes in the stores and cafés of the small towns. He studied at Stanford University (1920–1925) but never graduated, and alternated periods of study with periods of working. His close experience of the land and the people who worked it forms the foundation upon which much of his work is built. Salinas Valley is the locus for some of his greatest works.

Steinbeck worked, without much success, as a reporter and freelance writer in New York and returned to California in 1927. He began to publish in 1929 and his first critical success came with *The Red Pony* (1934), followed by *Tortilla Flat*.

The first of his works to deal with the great social issues of the Depression years was *In Dubious Battle* (1936), which tells the story of the migrant workers' strike in California. Steinbeck had lived and worked with migrant workers; his passionate concern for their plight and his awareness of the social and political issues involved is clearly stated in what at the time was a controversial novel. The work is also notable for the emergence of another lifelong theme in Steinbeck's work, the relationship of the individual to the group. *Of Mice and Men* (1937) was both a popular and a critical success; adapted for the stage, it enjoyed a long run in New

---

- If a body's ever took charity, it makes a burn that don't come out.
- I'm learnin' one thing good. Learnin' it all a time, ever' day. If you're in trouble, or hurt or need — go to the poor people. They're the only ones that'll help — the only ones.
- The fields were fruitful, and starving men moved on the roads. The granaries were full and the children of the poor grew up rachitic and the pustules of pellagra swelled on their side. The great companies did not know that the line between hunger and anger is a thin line.
- You got to have patience. Us people will go on livin' when all them people is gone... Rich fellas come up an' they die, an' their kids ain't no good an' they die out. But we keep a-comin'.
- S'pose you got a job an' there's jus' one fella wants the job. You got to pay 'im what he asts. But s'pose they's a hundred men wants that job. S'pose them men got kids an' them kids is hungry. S'pose a nickel'll buy at leas' sompin for the kids. An' you got a hundred men. Jus' offer 'em a nickel — why, they'll kill each other fightin' for that nickel.

Steinbeck, from *The Grapes of Wrath*

York and was later made into a film. On the night of the opening Steinbeck was living in a migrants' camp in California, having traveled with them in an epic journey from Oklahoma. His great work *The Grapes of Wrath* (1939) synthesizes his concerns about the social issues of the Depression with his philosophical interests in "nonteleological" thinking and in the relationship of the individual to the group. For this book he was awarded a Pulitzer Prize in 1940.

The Log from the Sea of Cortez (1941), written in collaboration with marine biologist Ed Ricketts, recounts their voyage to the Sea of Cortez (now known as the Gulf of California) and their conversations and speculations on ecology and human relationships with other forms of life. Ed Ricketts was the model for the character Doc in the 1944 novel *Cannery Row*, a paradigm for "natural philosophers." *The Pearl* (1947) retells an ancient story as a parable. In the same year the novel *The Wayward Bus* was published, followed by *Burning Bright* (1950), *East of Eden* (1952), *Sweet Thursday* (1954), *The Short Reign of Pippin IV* (1957), and *The Winter of Our Discontent* (1961). For the last he was awarded the Nobel Prize for Literature in 1962.

H. Levant, *The Novels of John Steinbeck*, 1974.
P. Lisca, *John Steinbeck*, 1978.
I. Rosberger, *Alternative Worlds*, 1988.
E. Steinbeck, R. Wallsten, eds., *Steinbeck: A Life in Letters*, 1975.

STEPHENSON, GEORGE (1781–1848), pioneer English railroad engineer and promoter. Born in Wylam, Northumberland, the son of a colliery mechanic, Stephenson had no formal education but was sent out to work to contribute to the family income. When he was eight years old he worked on a farm and at the age of fourteen he began to assist his father at the colliery. By his late teens he was in charge of a Newcomen steam-powered pumping engine at Killingworth Colliery. His work provided the opportunity to further his interests in mechanics.

Stephenson enrolled in night school to make up for the schooling he missed in his childhood years; it was only then that he learned to read and write, motivated not only by his desire to improve his technical education but also by a keen interest in the momentous events on the other side of the English Channel during the Napoleonic wars.

Following his marriage he augmented his income by repairing clocks, mending shoes, and cutting cloth for miners' wives. In 1803 his son Robert was born and George wanted to ensure that he received a better start in life. Robert was sent to school in Newcastle and when he came home each evening, father and son would study his lessons in arithmetic together.

In 1812 he became the chief engineer at Killingworth Colliery. The following year, he witnessed the operation of an experimental colliery locomotive built by an engineer called John Blenkinsop. This engine moved with the assistance of a cogged wheel that traveled along a special rail. Stephenson received the support of the owner of Killingworth Colliery to build his own locomotive. He improved on Blenkinsop's engine by building one able to run along smooth rails. The Stephenson machine was able to move eight wagons loaded with thirty tons of coal at a speed of four miles per hour. Stephenson was a man of vision and foresaw a future for steam locomotives far beyond the confines of colliery transport.

In 1821 he heard of ambitious plans to lay a railway from Stockton to Darlington. The purpose of the line was the transportation of coal and the original intention was that the line would be worked by horse-drawn wagons, as were used on existing mine lines in the area. Stephenson impressed the promoter of the railway, Edwin Pease, with a radical plan for steam locomotives to draw the wagons. Consideration was also given to the use of stationary engines and a pulley system but in the end Stephenson's bold proposal was accepted and he was given the job of building the line. It opened in 1825, with his locomotive drawing a train of 450 passengers at fifteen miles per hour.

Although a landmark in Stephenson's career and Britain's railroad development, the Stockton-Darlington railroad can be considered as a continuation, albeit on a much grander scale, of the colliery railroad. The revolution in rail came five years later with the opening of the Manchester to Liverpool line; for the first time passenger traffic was the key factor in the railroad's success.

In 1829 at Rainhill, near Liverpool, a competition was held to decide who could build the best locomotives to work the line. A £500 prize was offered to the successful engineer. Stephenson's "Rocket" clearly outdid all its competitors, moving a load of seventeen tons at an average speed of fourteen miles per hour and at one point reaching thirty miles per hour. In his locomotives Stephenson incorporated a multi tubular boiler and a device called the steam blast, improvements which made his engines more efficient than those of his rivals.

It was not surprising that such a capable engineer was given the awesome task of constructing this forty-mile railway, a formidable engineering task involving taking the line across both a marsh and a gorge. If natural obstacles were not sufficient, there was vigorous opposition from local landowners, who feared sparks from the engines would set fire to their fields and that the line would ruin traditional country pursuits such as fox hunting. A parliamentary committee doubted Stephenson's ability to overcome the enormous difficulties facing the project; in his characteristic blunt northern manner, he responded, "I can't tell you how I'll do it, but I can tell you I will do it." He was true to his word. Helped by his son Robert, he surveyed the course of the line and solved its technical problems.

The Manchester-Liverpool Railway opened to lavish ceremony in 1830, with the Duke of

*Wellington and other key political figures in attendance. The opening was marred by the running over of Liverpool M.P. William Huskisson, a victim of his lack of familiarity with the speed with which the locomotive was traveling toward him; Stephenson drove him fifteen miles in twenty-five minutes to the hospital at Eccles. Huskisson did not survive but the railway was a success beyond expectations.

Stephenson became engineer to a number of other railway promotions, primarily in the English Midlands. The gauge to which he built all his lines (based on the width between the wheels of horse-drawn wagons) gained general acceptance in England and overseas. Robert Stephenson followed in his father's footsteps and became a prominent engineer in his own right. He is remembered as a skilled designer of railway structures, including the impressive suspension bridge carrying the line over the Menai Straits in Wales. Robert also entered public life, becoming a member of Parliament.

George Stephenson avoided public office and honors and retired to his country home near Chesterfield in Derbyshire. Here he spent his last years pursuing his interests in farming and gardening. For the Victorians he symbolized the ideal of the self-made man and his life was held up as an example to others of what an individual from a deprived background could achieve.

R. M. Robbins, *George and Robert Stephenson*, 1966.
L. T. Rolt, *The Railway Revolution: George and Robert Stephenson*, 1962.

STRABO (c. 63 B.C.E.–c. 23 C.E.), Greek geographer. Author of the only existing work describing all the peoples and lands of his time that were known to both the Greek and Roman civilizations, Strabo was born into a rich Greek/Asian family in the Hellenized city of Amasya in Asia Minor. He received a thoroughly Greek education, studying rhetoric, philosophy and the works of *Aristotle. Most of the other details about Strabo's life have been lost; any information about him has to be deduced from the contents of the *Geography*, which is his only surviving work.

It is known that Strabo traveled extensively, presumably on diplomatic missions. As he wrote in his *Geography*: "Westward I have journeyed to the parts of Etruria [country in central Italy] opposite Sardinia, towards the south from the Euxine [Black Sea] to the borders of Ethiopia; and perhaps not one of those who have written geographies has visited more places than I have between these limits." Strabo took advantage of his travels to gather information about legends, history, and geography. Since he described places far beyond the boundaries of the lands he personally visited and often referred to Greek manuscripts, it is assumed that he lived for some time in Alexandria, where such information could have been acquired from the city's famous library. Apparently he lived for a time in Rome, where he took advantage of being at the hub of the expanding Roman Empire to extend his knowledge of its newly acquired lands.

Strabo's first work was his forty-three volume *Historical Memoirs*, recounting the history of Rome from the destruction of Carthage in 146 B.C.E. to Octavian's capture of Alexandria in 30 B.C.E. This work has since been lost but it was an important source of material for*Plutarch's biographies and Josephus's histories. The *Geography*, which was published in 7 B.C.E., was designed as a sequel to his history.

The *Geography* was intended as a reference book for statesmen and contained "knowledge of things famous and ancient... in this work I must leave untouched what is small, and devote my attention to what is noble and great...useful or memorable or entertaining." It was the first attempt to collect all known geographical knowledge and analyze it systematically from the perspectives of mathematical, physical, political, and historical geography.

Strabo lacked scientific training for original work in mathematical geography — the analysis of the shape and size of the world and its relationship to the heavens — so he used the results of the geographer Eratosthenes (who calculated the circumference of the Earth), the astronomer *Hipparchus, and the stoic philosopher Poseidonius. He was far from being the only one to take advantage of the work of others; he was, however, unusual in his open acknowledgement of the sources he utilized.

The *Geography* does have several definite defects. Strabo's physical geography suffers from a lack of accurate information and sources, his political perception was influenced by his admiration for the Pax Romana, and his historical accuracy was effected by his love of legend (for example, he wrote about Hercules's voyages as if they had just taken place). However, for all these shortcomings, the information he provided about peoples, physical environments, mineral resources, production, trade, history, and politics is of invaluable help in understanding Strabo's world and its inhabitants. For example, Strabo describes the Gauls of his day as "simple, high-spirited, boastful—insufferable when victorious, scared out of their wits when defeated," and is scandalized by the intermingling between the sexes in some parts of Spain where "the women dance promiscuously with men, taking hold of their hands." Some of his descriptions also show how little things have changed in the thousands of years since he wrote them, such as his description of a Venice "provided with thoroughfares by means of bridges and ferries," and of the climate of London where "on clear days the sun is to be seen only for three or four hours."

Strabo believed that the earth was round and that India could be reached by sailing west from Spain. He also believed in the existence of additional, unknown continents, and suggested that they might be located in the Atlantic Ocean.

G. Aujac, *Strabon et la science de son temps*, 1968.

H. L. Jones, *The Geography of Strabo*, 8 vols., 1917-1932.

STRAUSS A Viennese musical dynasty that epitomized the Habsburg empire's golden age. Strauss waltzes and polkas "set Europe dancing" and their melodies have become world-famous classics.

Johann Strauss I (the Elder; 1804–1849), who established the family orchestra, studied music while completing his apprenticeship to a bookbinder and, after gaining experience in a dance band, played the viola in a quartet led by Josef Lanner, the "Father of the Waltz." Their partnership lasted for six years (1819–1825), during which time they expanded the quartet into a string orchestra and transformed German dances such as the *Laendler* into the enormously popular, artistic waltz. Strauss formed a new orchestra, which he conducted while playing the violin, and began to enjoy tremendous success, notably at the Sperl ballroom in Vienna. To augment the Strauss orchestra's repertoire, he also wrote compositions of his own.

From 1832 he served as bandmaster of the capital's First Militia Regiment and a year later he embarked on the first of many orchestra tours abroad. During a lengthy concert tour of the British Isles (April-December 1838), Strauss gave eight concerts at Buckingham Palace in honor of the young Queen Victoria's coronation. From 1846 he was imperial director of music for court balls in Vienna. His 251 numbered compositions include gallops, marches, quadrilles, and a host of waltzes, few of which are still performed. His *Radetzky March* (1848), celebrating an Austrian field marshal's victory over the Italians, was denounced by young radicals as an expression of support for Metternich and the old order, yet it remains Strauss the Elder's most popular and enduring work.

Johann Strauss II (the Younger, 1825–1899), eventually outshone his father and is known as "the Waltz King." Although his father left home in 1842 to live with his mistress, he had always wanted his legitimate sons to enter more secure and "respectable" professions, but all three defied his wishes. Johann, the eldest, was a talented child pianist and turned to the violin, learning composition in secret. By 1844 he was conducting his own orchestra, playing favorite overtures as well as Strauss waltzes at Dommayer's Casino. Father and son became rivals, choosing opposite sides in the revolutionary upheaval of 1848, and the contest ended only after Johann I's death when the two ensembles were merged into one Strauss family orchestra. Despite his brilliant professionalism, musical genius, and ever increasing popularity, Johann II remained a political suspect for fifteen years; to advance his career, he had to concentrate on playing for the nobility and making foreign tours. Thus,

while permitted to succeed Josef Lanner as bandmaster of the Second Militia Regiment (1845), he was denied his father's old post as imperial music director until 1863.

During the years 1856–1865, Strauss was engaged to conduct summer concerts at Pavlovsk, near Saint Petersburg. His *Coronation March* was written for Czar *Alexander II and other works dating from this period include several on Russian themes, as well as the *Tritsch-Tratsch Polka* (1958), named after an Austrin satirical weekly, and *Perpetuum Mobile* (1861), "a musical jest." So as to have more time for composing, Strauss entrusted the family's orchestra direction to his brothers in 1862.

While making innumerable concert tours of foreign cities, Stauss brought the charm and gaiety of "Old Vienna" to millions of admirers overseas. With his striking appearance and lively manner of conducting with a violin bow, he looked every inch the "Waltz King," even though he himself never danced. Nothing in Europe, however, compared with the experience awaiting him in the United States during Boston's "World Peace Jubilee and International Music Festival" (June-July 1872). There Strauss had to give six mammoth concerts — directing one hundred assistant conductors, a two- thousand member "orchestra," and twenty thousand singers in an auditorium holding upwards of fifty thousand people. After three more concerts in New York he rejected further offers and took the first available steamship home, vowing never to return.

Strauss wrote more than five hundred compositions. His greatest achievement was the Viennese waltz, in which he displayed unchallenged elegance and a mastery of rhythm, instrumentation, and melodic craftsmanship. Dozens of his celebrated waltzes were written or commissioned for special events. To dispel the gloom of defeat in the Austro-Prussian War (1866), Strauss agreed to write a new work for the Vienna Men's Choral Society. The original score, for unaccompanied voices, had no definite title but in its expanded orchestral form, *An der schönen, blauen Donau* (The Blue Danube, 1867), achieved immortality. The famous *Kaiser Waltzer* (1888), originally called *Hand in Hand*, marked a goodwill royal visit to Kaiser Wilhelm II of Germany.

Strauss wrote sixteen operettas, the two enduring favorites being *Die Fledermaus* (The Bat, 1874) and *Der Zigeunerbaron* (The Gypsy Baron, 1885).

Josef Strauss (1827–1870), the second child of Johann I, was a qualified architect, engineer, and inventor. He temporarily substituted for his elder brother as conductor and composer when Johann II suffered a nervous breakdown in 1853. After three years of intensive musical study, he became Johann's official deputy, accompanying him on several European tours. His compositions made him a serious rival to his brother; both signed their works "Strauss," provoking speculation as to which

- If it is true that I have some talents, then I owe its development to My beloved city of Vienna, in whose air lie the sounds which my ear catches, my heart takes in, and my hand writes down.
- For an operetta to become popular, everyone must find something that he likes in it. People in the gallery rarely have cash to spare for printed music, so one must insure that their ears retain something after they've left the performance.

Johann Strauss

Vienna without Strauss is like Austria without the Danube.

Hector Berlioz

I shall never forget the extraordinary playing of Johann Strauss, who often made the audience nearly frantic with delight. At the beginning of a new waltz, this demon of the Viennese musical spirit shook like a Pythian priestess on the tripod...Worship for the magic violinist attained bewildering heights of frenzy.

Richard Wagner

brother had composed them. Josef wrote over two hundred and eighty numbered works, including marches, several quadrilles after themes by Offenbach, and a host of polkas. Thwarted ambition, family quarrels, and the strain imposed by his concert tours undermined his health: while conducting in Warsaw he suddenly collapsed, dying two months later in Vienna.

Eduard Strauss (1835–1916), the youngest brother, joined the "Strauss" firm, making his debut as a harpist in 1855, and began conducting in 1861. Though at first overshadowed by his two brothers, "handsome Edi" proved to be an even more expert conductor; after Josef's death, he directed the Strauss family orchestra for nearly thirty years. He composed three works, including waltzes, quadrilles, and a series of fast polkas. Eduard's relations with Johann were often troubled, however, and he was excluded from Johann's will. After recouping his lost fortune, he disbanded the Strauss orchestra in New York (1901), retired, and published a volume of memoirs (1906), then burned cartloads of sheet music that had been the orchestra's stock-in trade, claiming that this was in fulfillment of a pledge to Josef.

E. Gartenberg, *Johann Strauss: The End of an Era*, 1974.

P. Kemp, *The Strauss Family*, 1989.

O. M. Stroud, *The Story of the Strauss Family*, 1974.

J. Wechsberg, *The Waltz Emperors*, 1973.

SUKARNO, AHMED (1901–1970), Indonesian nationalist; first president of Indonesia. Sukarno was born in east Java to a Javanese Muslim father and a Balinese Hindu mother. He graduated in 1925, from the Bandung Technical Institute, where he studied civil engineering, and found work as an architect. Racist jibes at the institute and at work aroused Sukarno's nationalist sentiments and in 1928 he helped found the Indonesian Nationalist party, dedicated to the liberation of the archipelago from Dutch colonial rule. Sukarno was a skilled orator who often found himself at odds with the colonial government. He was arrested in 1929 and sentenced to two years imprisonment. Upon his release in 1933 he was exiled to the remote eastern island of Endeh, where he remained until World War II.

The Japanese occupation of Indonesia (1942–1945) encouraged the nationalists to cooperate with the occupying army in return for self-government and Sukarno was allowed to leave his exile as the president of a nominally independent Indonesia. This period is one of the most controversial in Sukarno's life. Although he did manage to negotiate a degree of autonomy for the islands, in return he was responsible for supplying thousands of Indonesians for forced labor in Japanese factories. Yet Sukarno maintained his popularity among the masses and upon the collapse of Japan declared himself president of the independent United States of Indonesia. The Dutch were unwilling to forego their colonial empire and a bloody civil war ensued. For four years Sukarno and his vice president, Muhammad Hatta, fought the Dutch and their British allies. Negotiations over the formation of a Dutch and Indonesian union began in 1946, but it was only on November 2, 1949, that the Netherlands recognized the independence of Indonesia. Elections were called in which Sukarno received a unanimous acclamation as president by all representatives. He preserved the terms of the union treaty with the Netherlands until 1956, when he unilaterally abrogated it and repudiated Indonesia's debt to the Netherlands.

The early years of Indonesian independence were fraught with ethnic, religious, regional, and political strains. Western Java, Sumatra, and Celebes each sought various degrees of autonomy and the South Moluccas declared their independence. Muslims, composing 90 percent of the population, attempted to establish a theocratic state. Sukarno himself was not a democrat. He favored Marhaemism, his own brand of socialism that included the principle of "guided democracy" of economic and social reforms, costing him much of his popularity. Still, Sukarno was a committed socialist, which led to a breach between himself and Vice President Hatta. He also found himself at constant odds with the Dutch over possession of the western half of the island of New Guinea, not included in the Dutch offer for Indonesian independence (Irian Jaya, as the region is now called, was granted to Indonesia by the United Nations in 1963).

Sukarno, who maintained a traditional Muslim lifestyle and had four wives and several mistresses, regarded himself as a world leader. He sought to unite the newly independent states of the Third World into a bloc independent of the United States and USSR, aspiring to lead the non-aligned states himself. His own political position grew increasingly closer to the Indonesian Communist party, and efforts were made to forge close bonds with China. It was Sukarno's flirtation with communism that led to his downfall. An attempted coup in 1965 by communist-leaning officers was suspected of being orchestrated by Sukarno; many leading generals were killed in the bungled coup attempt, and the majority Muslim population felt threatened. Sukarno was unable to prevent a massacre of suspected communist sympathizers and the estimated death toll from the massacre ranges between three hundred thousand and one million casualties. In response to the failed coup attempt, Sukarno's supporters were pushed out of office. Sukarno himself was stripped of his titles and all powers in 1967; he died three years later in Jakarta.

B. Dahm, *Sukarno and the Struggle for Independence,* 1969.

J. D. Legge, *Sukarno,* 1972.

O. G. Roeder, *The Smiling General,* 1970.

SÜLEYMAN THE MAGNIFICENT

(c.1494–1566), one of the Ottoman Empire's most famous sultans, presiding over the era of the empire's greatest expansion. He was called Süleyman the Magnificent in Europe; within the empire he was referred to as Süleyman the Lawgiver, because in addition to leading troops in thirteen wars, Süleyman improved the empire's code of justice. He filled in loopholes in the existing code of law, and executed corrupt officials — including a son-in-law — a first in Turkish history. He also constructed numerous mosques, schools, and hospitals that rivaled the masterpieces of some of Europe's master builders. His wall still stands around the Old City of Jerusalem.

Süleyman came to power at the age of twenty-six in 1520, succeeding his father *Selim I. An only son, Suleyman was spared from fratricide (a ruler often killed his brothers and nephews). His father had sent him to study government in provincial capitals for ten years, so he had been well prepared to rule. He removed incompetent officials and instituted far-reaching internal reforms. During his youth, Süleyman had made a close friend of a Christian slave boy, Ibrahim, who held high office in his government.

The custom of his time provided for the sultan to have an enormous harem of slave girls. The first four to bear sons were elevated to the status of a sultana but, nevertheless, remained slaves. The highest ranking woman in the harem was the mother of the

Süleyman the Magnificent (right)

sultan. Süleyman's harem numbered three hundred women. He fell deeply in love with the second sultana, a Russian girl called Roxelana, and after the birth of their son, remained faithful to her. She convinced him to marry her, freeing her from slavery. A sultan had not taken a wife in six centuries, ever since the wife of a sultan had been captured and humiliated by her captors. The wedding was celebrated with a week of lavish feasting throughout Constantinople.

When Süleyman came to power, he had a standing army of fifty thousand troops, which he personally led into battle. Their first campaign was to take Belgrade. They then moved on to Rhodes and were successful, but the battle cost nearly one hundred thousand lives (1523). Süleyman retired from the battlefield for three years, during which time his relationship with Ibrahim grew much closer. They spent much time together and sometimes even slept in the same quarters. This aroused jealousy and anger among other officials, and in Roxelana, who had also began taking an active role in government, advising her husband and listening in on parliament meetings. Ibrahim, who developed a taste for luxury and led an ostentatious life, married the sultan's sister.

Süleyman's next campaign, in 1526, was against Hungary. At this time, the empire stretched across the Middle East, comprising parts of Europe, Asia, and Africa and included the cities of Carthage, Alexandria, Jerusalem, Damascus, Nice, Athens, and Belgrade. The navy ruled the Mediterranean, under the command of Barbarossa, a pirate whom Süleyman had bribed to serve the empire. After

Hungary was subdued, Süleyman turned to besiege Vienna (1529). Unseasonably heavy rains slowed the transport of Süleyman's heavy guns to the front and, although the Turks vastly outnumbered the defending Viennese, Süleyman's army was defeated, his first failure in seventeen years.

Returning to Constantinople, Süleyman slipped into a life of luxury and idleness while Ibrahim took over more and more power. When Ibrahim began boasting that it was really he who ruled the empire, Roxelana became incensed. She began a campaign against him, supported by his many enemies among the officers. Finally, she persuaded Süleyman that Ibrahim intended to usurp his power completely and the sultan arranged to have his long time friend strangled as he slept.

Ibrahim's first three successors came and went quickly, but the fourth became friendly with Roxelana and married her daughter. Together, they plotted against Mustafa, the sultan's eldest son and heir apparent. Roxelana wanted her son, Selim, to succeed Süleyman in power, but as the eldest son, Mustafa, stood next in line. Furthermore, Mustafa was an intelligent and well liked young man who was popular among the officers. As with Ibrahim, although this time with entirely fabricated "evidence," Roxelana managed to convince Süleyman that Mutafa was plotting against him. Süleyman arranged to have his beloved son strangled, and he is reported to have watched the murder from behind a curtain and emerged afterward showing no trace of emotion.

Five weeks after assuring her son's place in line for the throne, Roxelana died. Meanwhile, Süleyman's health had also begun to fail and he suffered stomach problems and occasional fainting spells. He stopped attending parliament meetings and began promoting favorites and relatives, the start of the corruption that was to plague the next several rulers, until it finally brought about the end of the empire.

Süleyman died in his tent on the battlefield during another campaign in Hungary. His death was kept secret for three weeks, until Selim could reach Constantinople, the sultan's physician having been murdered so he would not let the secret out.

E. Atil, *The Age of Sultan Süleyman the Magnificent*, 1987.

R. B. Merriam, *Suleiman the Magnificent*, 1966.

SUN YAT-SEN (originally Sun Wen; 1866–1925), Chinese statesman. He was born to a poor peasant family near Portuguese-held Macao, in the district of Hsiang-shan in Kwantung province.

At the age of twelve Sun was sent to Hawaii to join his brother Sun Mei, where he boarded at the Iolani Anglican school; much pressure was placed on the boarders to convert to Christianity. Sun became convinced that he wanted to be a Christian, and when Sun Mei returned to Hawaii in 1883, Sun was speedily dispatched to his home village, where it was hoped he would give up his new ideas.

Sun finished his secondary studies in Hong Kong and enrolled in medical school in 1886, concluding his studies in 1892. He combined Western and Chinese medicine, and practiced for a brief period in Macao and Canton. His medical training is apparent in his memoirs, where he devotes a detailed section to the intricacies of digestion.

During his training he met Dr. James Cantlie, with whom he developed a close friendship, translating for him in Chinese leper villages where Cantlie was carrying out research. This activity earned Sun a scholarship, which helped cover some of his expenses during this period. Dr. Cantlie considered him a skillful surgeon and assisted him in difficult operations.

In 1884, Sun's converted to Christianity, and his Chinese Christian pastor gave him the name Yat-sen, by which he was to become famous. During this year, he also conformed to traditional norms by returning to his village to marry the girl his family had chosen for him.

During his time in Hong Kong, Sun studied classical Chinese texts with a private teacher, specializing in dynastic histories. By 1893, when he left Hong Kong and returned to Honolulu, he had become convinced that reform in China was essential. He compared the tide of reform that was sweeping Victorian England with Chinese conservatism and corruption.

His studies of classical texts heightened his awareness of the leading role that secret societies had always played in the implementation of revolution in China. In Honolulu, Sun founded his first secret society, the Hsing Chung Hui (Society to Restore China's Prosperity). Although small, it was a successful pioneering attempt to enlist overseas Chinese in the funding of revolution.

In preparing for revolution, by 1895 Sun was coordinating groups as diverse as overseas Chinese, the criminal groups known as Triads, local bandits, Christian workers, and some Imperial Navy officers; he succeeded in raising millions of dollars. The revolution failed and he had to flee China for sixteen years, spending most of his time in America and England working for a republican revolution in China.

In Tokyo in 1905, Sun founded the Tung Meng Hui (Revolutionary Alliance), based on the three main principles of nationalism, democracy, and people's livelihood. This was the forerunner of the Kuomintang, formally established on August 25, 1912, within the new Chinese republic.

Sun's main philosophies resulted from a mingling of the many elements that had influenced his life. Although the influence of Western culture and religion was strong, Sun considered himself essentially Chinese, and his theories were colored by ethical Confucianism (see *Confucius). He was essentially a reformist rather than a social revolutionary, and believing that reform could be achieved without the social turmoil predicted in the works of Karl *Marx.

During a visit to London, the Manchu embassy attempted to kidnap Sun and managed to hold him in the embassy for several days, awaiting orders to ship him back to China for execution. Although contact with the outside world was denied him, Sun managed to smuggle a letter out to Sir James Cantlie. Sun was freed immediately and the Manchu government was greatly discredited in the resulting scandal.

Sun was in the United States during the 1911 revolution, which finally overthrew the Manchu dynasty. He hurried back and was immediately elected provisional president of the new republic, a position he resigned shortly thereafter to Yuan Shih-kiai, one of his rivals, who commanded the only effective military force in the country.

After his abdication Sun threw himself into local projects and established the Chinese General Railway Corporation, with himself as president. He began intensive negotiations toward establishing a joint venture with Japan to use Japanese capital for the development of Chinese raw materials. However, these activities were brought to an abrupt halt in 1914, when Yuan Shih-kiai dissolved the parliament, expelled the Kuomintang party established by Sun, and declared himself sole ruler of China.

Until his death, Sun fought a rearguard battle from Canton and Shanghai against the rulers in Peking, with the presidency of China as his ultimate goal. Although his official position was unclear during this period, he was spokesman for China on several occasions, including his opposition to Chang Hsun's restoration of the emperor, Pu-Yi, in 1917, and to China's declaration of war on Germany later that year. He also defended China's rights in the Versailles negotiations of 1919.

In 1917 Sun was elected Grand Marshal of Canton, but by 1918 the office was replaced by a seven-man directorate. Although Sun was one of them, he chose to retire to Shanghai. The last years of his life also saw the beginnings of the Sino-Soviet alliance and the inclusion of Communist leaders in the Kuomintang; Sun's own thinking became increasingly Marxist after 1917. He died of cancer of the liver in 1925, potentially on the verge of the presidency that had eluded him for so many years. His widow, Soong Ching-ling, eventually identified with the Communists and became a vice chairman of the Chinese People's Republic in 1950.

Sun Yat-sen has been described in many different ways by those who knew him. The Chinese people called him "Guo Fu" — Father of the Country.
T. Miyazaki, *My Thirty-Three Years' Dream*, 1982.
Z. Schiffrin, *Sun Yat-sen: Reluctant Revolutionary*, 1980.

SUVOROV, ALEXSANDR VASILYEVICH

(1729–1800), Russian military commander, tactician, and strategist. Suvorov was trained in the art of war by his father, General Vasilii Suvorov, a former comrade of Emperor *Peter I the Great. He was a frail child, and despite a vigorous regimen of physical exercise he never developed the staunch appearance of a fearsome fighter. He never attended school, yet became one of the most educated military men in Russia, fluent in eight languages, conversant with mathematics, philosophy, and theology, and an author of poetry.

When only thirteen Suvorov enlisted as a private in the Serryonovsky Guards regiment and by 1754 received his commission as lieutenant in the infantry, seeing his first battle during the Seven Years' War of 1756–1763. In 1762 he was promoted to colonel and received his first command. The following year he was posted to the Suzdai regiment, where he was to remain for the next six years.

Suvorov strongly believed in the value of realistic battlefield training maneuvers, whereas the traditional approach stressed parade-ground exercises. His first text, *Regimental Organization*, was published in 1765. He made heavy demands on his soldiers, but they appreciated him as "Father Suvorov." As the commander of his regiment, and then of a full brigade, he earned an enviable reputation as a battlefield tactician of considerable flair in the wars of 1768–1772 against the Polish Confederation of Bar.

Suvorov's talent drew widespread attention at the Russian court, and it seemed that he was destined for quick promotion. However, his unorthodox style and unattractive appearance did not endear him to the military hierarchy, and he was transferred throughout Russia on various duties, mostly of a support nature, Finally, in 1786 he was promoted to full general and recalled to the battlefield against the Turks. He was seriously wounded at the siege of Ochakov, and soon afterward rumors began to circulate that he was a drunk whose own ineptness had led to his injury. To his dismay, he drew an official reprimand. Nonetheless, in 1789 he was sent to Moldavia to fight alongside Russia's Austrian allies. The highlight of this campaign was his brilliantly executed storming of Izmail, which was accompanied by a massacre of the Turks. It came as a severe rebuff when in 1791 he was sent to Finland to supervise fortifications.

Though the imperial court did not feel compelled to honor Suvorov, it nevertheless appreciated his skills. Thus in 1794 he was recalled to crush a revolt in Poland, which he accomplished coldly and decisively, slaughtering those revolutionaries in the Warsaw suburb of Praga who stood against his forces. Yet he exhibited a humane attitude toward those rebels who surrendered, prohibiting looting and insulting behavior by his troops.

The following year Suvorov was promoted to field marshal in command of the Southern Army. His unorthodoxy continued to antagonize the new emperor, Paul I, who had reintroduced parade-ground exercises. In response, Suvorov wrote his famous work *The Science of Victory*, in which he none-too-subtly challenged imperial ideas on training and battle. This led to his dismissal from command in 1797, and to suspicions that he was guilty of treason.

However, when Russia joined the anti-French coalition in 1799, Paul turned to Suvorov to command the joint Russian Austrian army. Despite his age and deteriorating health, Suvorov eagerly returned to duty, and his troops routed the French forces in northern Italy; he was awarded the title of Prince of Italy. His wish to invade France was blocked by Austria which, with designs of its own, arranged to have him ordered to Switzerland to assist the Russian forces. After struggling through the Alps, Suvorov rescued most of his army from an utterly hopeless position.

Suvorov was recalled to Saint Petersburg and promoted to the unprecedented rank of generalissimo. By now his tremendous authority in the army was unquestioned, yet the imperial court still viewed him with suspicion. The emperor refused him an audience, finally reprimanding him for a number of trivial violations of command. Suvorov, already exhausted, fell ill and died soon after. Only after his death did he receive recognition as a national hero, while as a tactician he greatly influenced the Russian army in the nineteenth century.

P. Longworth, *The Art of Victory: The Life and Achievements of Generalissimo Suvorov*, 1965.

Emanuel Swedenborg

SWEDENBORG, EMANUEL (1688–1772), Swedish scientist, mystic, philosopher and theologian. A man of massive erudition, Swedenborg created a comprehensive, if bizarre, theology in his later years, and it is for this that he is best known; it has offended the prudish through its frank detailing of explicit sexual dreams while inspiring the spiritual seeker with its resonant and complex symbolism. However, it was not until he was nearly sixty that Swedenborg abandoned secular concerns; prior to this, he had already produced a significant body of work on the natural sciences. Much of this material received little attention until long after his death, by which time its findings had been largely superceded by subsequent developments; nonetheless, though unacknowledged, its originality testifies to his quality as a thinker.

Swedenborg's father was the bishop of Skara and a believer in guardian spirits and angels. However, young Swedenborg did not enter the clergy; rather, his interest was in mathematics and the natural sciences, which took him abroad for five years after his graduation from Uppsala University. He benefitted from the patronage of Charles XII on his return, and worked with the foremost mechanical minds in the country to produce Sweden's first scientific journal in 1715. Charles's death in 1718 led to a decline in Swedenborg's influence; he published nothing further for fifteen years,

After another European journey in 1733, his quiet labors were crowned by the publication, in 1734, of his *Principles of Natural Things*, parts of which an-

ticipated Immanuel *Kant and Laplace's nebular theory. A two year sojourn in Amsterdam produced *The Economy of the Animal Kingdom*, in which the "animal kingdom" is the human body — the kingdom of the animal, or soul. Swedenborg believed the soul to be located in the cellular cortex, and his researches to confirm this end led him to many useful and significant conclusions in the field of psycho-physics.

The period 1743–1744 was a critical one in Swedenborg's life, chronicled in his *Journal of Dreams*; he experienced prolonged, intense, and repeated spiritual visions and was moved to a painful reevaluation of himself and his faith. He details his travels among the realms of spirits and angels and his climactic vision of *Jesus. Swedenborg guiltily realised the extent of his own spiritual pride and desire to be recognized as a great man of science and, repentant, abandoned his secular writings forthwith, leaving a projected synthesis of his scientific writings unfinished. The remainder of his long life was devoted to the exegesis of his religious vision.

His doctrines, as summarized in his work *True Christian Religion*, clearly borrow many structural notions from his scientific theories. Thus his doctrine of correspondence suggests that everything outward and visible in nature has an inward spiritual cause; Swedenborg's earlier search for a universal language (a problem that had also interested René *Descartes) led him to believe that his doctrine enabled one to uncover the hidden, inner, spiritual meaning of sacred scriptures. Further, he envisaged the contents of the cosmos as forming an ordered hi-

- Life is one thing, nature another.
- All things in heaven conspire to the conservation on the minutest things in the body.
- Conscience is God's presence in man.
- Evil has an appetite for falsity and often seizes upon it as truth.
- We are because God is.
- Love in its essence is spiritual fire.
- Self-love and love of the world constitute hell.
- Thought from the eye closes the understanding but thought from the understanding opens the eye.

Emanuel Swedenborg

erarchical series culminating in man, while he attributed the rise of evil in the world to man's selfish desires, which divert his love from its appropriate object, God. Swedenborg's God has his essence in love and wisdom; furthermore he rejected the conventional notion of the Trinity and asserted that Christ was not the son of God.

The range of people influenced by Swedenborg is considerable and sometimes surprising. Kant was one of only four purchasers of the original published version of his mystical system and pronounced it "very sublime", while William *Blake's rich and complex symbolic universe is of an undeniably Swedenborgian character; he even annotated sections from Swedenborg for posterity. Although Swedenborg never preached his doctrines, the Church of the New Jerusalem was founded on the basis of his teachings after his death. His emphasis on a divine landscape mappable through observation of the workings of the microcosm that is man also attracted creative talents such as Honoré *Balzac, Baudelaire, Ralph Waldo Emerson, Strindberg, and W. B. *Yeats. He is fashionable again today among those who see parallels between his cosmology and esoteric Eastern religious doctrines, which also stress introspection as a means to revelation.

A. S. Sechrist, *A Dictionary of Bible Imagery*, 1973.
C. S. Sigstedt, *The Swedenborg Epic*, 1971.

SWIFT, JONATHAN (1667–1745), Anglo-Irish

writer and one of the great satirists of all time. His English father, a lawyer, died before Swift's birth and his mother returned from Dublin to her family in England when he was three years old. His upbringing was entrusted to an uncle, who sent him back to Ireland to be educated.

Swift's schooling continued when he was fourteen at Dublin's Trinity College but the civil unrest of 1688–1689 led him to leave for England. He began a decade-long association with Sir William Temple — twice interrupted by journeys to Ireland, during the second of which, in 1695, he took orders

in the Anglican church — a wealthy gentleman who engaged Swift to serve as his secretary, helping with the writing of Temples memoirs. At Sir William's house Swift made the acquaintance of an eight-year-old girl named Esther Johnston, for whom he developed an enduring affection that was expressed in letters and fine verse and, according to one account, an eventual marriage ceremony. The writings he dedicated to her using the pseudonym "Stella," (notably his *Journal to Stella*) were only a small part of a large literary output that made his name in London as a man of letters and brought him into the company of such famous writers as Alexander *Pope and Joseph Addison.

Swift's themes were religious and philosophical and later political. Using biting sarcasm and humor, he made his points with fluency and power. *Tale of a Tub* (1704) was among the wittiest and best known of his earlier writings satirizing religious and other hypocrisies. His articles in *The Tatler* newspaper increased his public profile. The Tory government that came to power in 1711 recognized his talents and availed themselves of the services of this skillful propagandist as editor of the progovernment paper *Examiner*.

The change of regime that came with the Hanoverian succession in 1714 deprived Swift of government favor. He retired to Ireland to attend to his clerical duties but did not give up his literary endeavors. In 1726 Swift published *Gulliver's Travels*, for which he is best known (it was also the only writing for which he received payment). It might have been meant as a political satire for his own time but the imaginative and witty plot won it a place among the world's literary classics. According to the author not everyone was convinced that it was solely a product of fantasy. Writing to Pope of how people had been fascinated by it, he described an Irish bishop who said that "the book was full of improbable lies, and for his part he hardly believed a word of it."

Swift was firmly committed to the Anglican church, a fierce opponent of concessions to the Dissenters. Serving the church in various capacities, including prebendary of Saint Patrick's Cathedral in Dublin (1701–1710), he discharged his clerical duties conscientiously and won popularity for his championing of Irish interests against British encroachments. In 1713, under Tory government patronage, he was appointed dean of Saint Patrick's.

While a clergyman of orthodox opinions, in behavior he displayed an irreverence that matched his writings. He conducted one of the strangest marriages on record. Traveling from London to Chester on foot, on his way back to Ireland, he sought refuge under a tree during a heavy storm. He was joined by a couple, the woman in an advanced state of pregnancy. They told Swift that they were on their way to get married and, being a clergyman, he kindly offered to save them the journey and marry them there and then. They were only too happy to

> - Satire is a sort of glass wherein beholders generally discover everybody's face but their own.
> - I never saw, heard or read that the clergy were beloved in any Christian nation. Nothing can render them popular but some degree of persecution.
> - The two maxims of any great man at court are: always to keep his countenance and never to keep his word.
> - So, naturalists observe, a flea
>   Hath smallers fleas that on him prey;
>   And these have smaller still to bite 'em,
>   And so proceed ad infinitum.
>   Thus every poet, in his kind,
>   Is bit by him that comes behind.
>
> **Jonathan Swift**

agree; after this impromptu wedding the sky brightened and they were about to go their separate ways when the bridegroom remembered that they lacked a certificate. This was no problem for the witty Dean Swift who wrote it out as follows: "Under an oak, in stormy weather, / I joined this rogue and whore together; / And none but he who rules the thunder / Can put this rogue and whore asunder."

A romantic episode in his life in London had been the passion he inspired in Esther Vanhomrigh, whom he called "Vanessa" and who followed him to Ireland. She died in 1723, five years before "Stella," to whom he was devoted to the end (he was buried beside her in Saint Patrick's Cathedral). His real relations with the two women remain unclear and have prompted much speculation.

Swift lived his last thirty years in Dublin and except for two short visits to London never left Ireland during this time. After Stella's death he was lonely and miserable, in dread of mental disease. On his birthdays he wore black and fasted. His last years were a period of torment after suffering a stroke, and guardians had to be appointed to manage his affairs.

I. Ehrenpreis, *Swift: The Man, His Works and the Age*, 2 vols., 1962–1967.

D. Nokes, *Jonathan Swift: A Hypocrite Reversed*, 1985.

M. Price, *Swift's Rhetorical Art*, 1973.

T

TACITUS, CORNELIUS (c.56–c.120), Roman historian and orator. Little is known about the personal history of the man who was one of the world's greatest historians. Even his name and the date and place of his birth are the subject of conjecture. He was probably of good family, which would account for the rapidity of his political advancement. The accepted dates of his birth and death mean that his lifetime saw the reign of nine emperors. He married the daughter of the consul Agricola (the most famous Roman governor of Britain) in 78, well aware that his father-in-law could have made a more advantageous match for his daughter (Tacitus later wrote a biography praising Agricola).

In 88 Tacitus served as praetor (magistrate), arguing his court cases with an eloquence that led some to view him as the greatest orator in Rome. The years he served in an increasingly powerless Senate during *Domitian's reign of terror gave him a bitter and undying hatred of tyrants. Domitian used the terrified Senate (including Tacitus, to his regret and shame) to try and condemn his victims. Tacitus advanced under Domitian's successors. Nerva appointed him consul in 97 and *Trajan made him proconsul of Asia. In his later years he turned to writing history. The third-century emperor Tacitus would claim descent from him.

Much is known about Tacitus's beliefs as they are revealed in his writings. He hated tyrants passionately but was cynical about democracy: the rabble is "fond of innovation and change, and ever ready to shift to the side of the strongest." He deplored the fact of Rome's political and social degeneration and doubted that it was reversible: "Most plans of reformation are at first embraced with ardor; but soon the novelty ceases, and the scheme ends in nothing." He was cautiously ambivalent on the subject of religion, feeling that events proved "the indifference of the gods to good and bad alike." He hated the alien races pouring into Rome: "The city of Rome, the common sink into which everything infamous and abominable flows like a torrent from all quarters of the world." He admired what he regarded as the superior morality of the barbarian tribes and deplored that contact with Rome would corrupt them: "By degrees the charms of vice gained admission to British

hearts... and the new manners, which in reality only served to sweeten slavery, were by the unsuspecting Britons called the arts of polished humanity."

Tacitus owed much of his powerful, persuasive writing style to Quintilian, who taught rhetoric at a time when every aspirant to fashion wrote poetry. His students learned more than the art of speaking well; they learned how to persuasively present the pros and cons of an argument. He also taught writing: "Erasure is as important as writing. Prune what is turgid, elevate what is commonplace, arrange what is disorderly, introduce rhythm where the language is harsh, modify where it is too absolute....."

Tacitus's brief biographical monographs dealt with the main characters in the long struggle for power between the Senate and the emperors. They were *The Dialogue on Orators,* about the deterioration in the way oratory was taught to children; *Life of Agricola,* about Agricola and his problems with Domitian; *Germans,* in which the German tribes were regarded as a permanent menace while admired for their higher morals contrasted with Rome's imperially based degeneracy; *Histories,* about the emperors from Galba (69) through Domitian (97), of which only four and one half of the original twelve books have survived; and *Annals,* dealing with the emperors from Tiberius through Nero, of which only nine books and some fragments remain.

As an historian Tacitus has serious limitations. His writings were never objective, but then his aim was to persuade, instruct, and moralize, not to present an impartial record of historical events. He felt that "The chief duty of the historian is to judge the actions of men, so that the good may meet with the reward due to virtue, and pernicious citizens may be deterred by the condemnation that awaits evil deeds at the tribunal of posterity." In so doing he refused to admit that the emperors had any virtues or accomplished any good.

He was an aristocrat, and in his biographies stoic nobles struggle heroically against vicious tyrants. This bias is natural, as most of his sources of information as well as his audience were aristocrats who naturally preferred works favoring if not glamorizing their own class. He also used histories, letters, governmental decrees, and gossip as sources — though they were sometimes of questionable veracity.

Tacitus is not remembered for his long years of political service to Rome, but for the historical biographies he wrote in his old age. The tone of his works is moralistic, moody, and sarcastic. As embodiments of his personal prejudices, their value as historical references has been compromised. Yet his vivid characterizations and pithily brilliant writing have earned him a lasting reputation as both writer and historian, and his general accuracy has meant that he is the best historical source for knowledge of a crucial period in western civilization.

L. S. Mazzolani, *Empire Without End*, 1976.
R. Syme, *Tacitus,* 2 vols., 1958.
R. Syme, *Ten Studies in Tacitus*, 1970.

TAGORE, SIR RABINDRANATH (1861–1941),
Bengali poet, author, philosopher, mystic, and Nobel Prize winner. Tagore's father, Debendranath, was descended from one of Calcutta's wealthiest families and was a renowned Hindu philosopher, religious iconoclast, and reformer, known as the "Great Sage" (Maharishi). Rabindranath was the fourteenth child of a family which produced some of India's leading writers and artists; his sister, Svarnakumari Devi, was Bengal's first woman novelist.

Tagore had a lonely and secluded childhood, living in a mansion in North Calcutta where he was brought up by servants. The family was cut off from the Orthodox Hindu community and regarded as degraded Brahmans because the grandfather traveled and ate meat, which was against Hindu custom.

Tagore loathed formal education and at thirteen stopped attending school. At seventeen he traveled to England to study law, but just as he was settling down to his new environment his father called him back to India, fearing he had fallen in love with an English girl. Tagore returned to India and went to live with his brother Jyotirindranath and his sister-in-law Kadambari-Devi. He was very attached to both of them, and when Kadambari committed suicide he was so shocked that he wrote a large number of poems, verses, and songs. In 1890 he published *Manasi,* a collection of his writings containing some of his most famous poems.

His father had in the meantime arranged a marriage for him with an eleven year-old girl, Mrinalini Devi, daughter of an employee on the family's East Bengal estate. In 1891 his father sent him to administer the family's remote properties. Tagore spent almost ten years on these estates, constantly reporting back to his father with the minutest details. His time there brought him close to the peasantry and many of his short stories deal with the lives of the villagers. His poems too show his love for the Ganges and its valley; Tagore idealized this rural life as the true foundation of Indian culture. He published a number of collections: *Sonar Tari* (The Golden Boat, 1893), *Chitra* (1896), and *Chaitali* (Late Harvest, 1896), *Kalpana* (Dreams, 1900),

- Life is given to us, we earn it by giving it.
- In the world's audience hall, the simple blade of grass sits on the same carpet with the sunbeam and the stars of midnight.
- Pleasure is frail like a dewdrop, while it laughs it dies.
- Profit smiles on goodness when the good is profitable.
- He who is too busy doing good finds no time to be good.
- Our names are the light that glows on the sea waves at night and then dies without leaving its signature.
- The soil in return for its service keeps the tree tied to her, the sky asks nothing and leaves it free.
- Praise shames me for I secretly beg for it.
- Asia must find her own voice.

Rabindranath Tagore

Naivedya (Offerings, 1901); two lyrical plays, *Chitrangada* (Chitra, 1892) and *Malini* (1895); and *Galpa Guccha* on "humble lives" (Bunches of Tales, 1912). He also wrote sonnets that contrasted East and West, and an important essay titled "Eastern and Western Civilization."

In 1901, Tagore moved to Santiniketan in West Bengal and started a famous boys' school modeled on ancient India's hermitages, where pupils were taught by sages.

His Indocentricity was much influenced by his father and the close contact he had with rural Bengal, as well as the rise of patriotic feelings in India. He came to play an important role in the *swadeshi* (patriotic self-help movement) in Bengal, but the killing of a British woman and her daughter by nationalist activists in 1908 was so repugnant to him that he withdrew from political life.

Tagore had already experienced a number of personal tragedies in the deaths of his wife (1902), his daughter, Renuka (1903), his father (1905), and the most gifted of his four children, his son, Samindranath (1907). Tagore wrote some of his finest religious poems in the *Gitanjali* (An Offering of Song, 1910), in which frequently-expressed themes were the longing of the lover for the beloved, of the soul for the divine. He also began writing *My Reminiscences*.

In 1912 Tagore visited England and brought along with him an English translation of *Gitanjali,* which he showed to his friend the artist William Rothenstein and to W. B. *Yeats. The poems were then translated by André Gide into French and reached a wide readership in Europe and the United States. In 1913 Tagore won the Nobel Prize for Literature, the first non-European so honored. He accepted a knighthood in 1915, which he gave up in 1919 as a protest against the Amritsar massacre (although he did not object to the use of the title when addressed).

Tagore became the leading exponent of the revival of Indo-Asian spirituality, and was a strong adherent of the ideal previously supported by nineteenth-century Bengali intellectuals, that of a cultural synthesis between eastern spiritualism and western practicality. Between 1916 and 1934 he went on many tours to the United States, Europe, and Asia expounding these ideals. Tagore continued to produce a vast body of writings, and was also a gifted painter and composer.

S. N. Hay, *Asian Ideas of East and West,* 1970.
K. Kripalani, *Rabindranath Tagore: A Biography,* 1962.
Sir W. Rothenstein, *Imperfect Encounter,* 1972.

TALLEYRAND-PÉRIGORD, CHARLES-MAURICE DE (Prince de Bénévent; 1754-1838), French statesman and diplomat whose name became synonymous with political survival. Born into a titled family, his clubfoot precluded military service and so he was educated for the church, attending the seminary of Saint-Sulpice in Paris. In 1775 *Louis XVI appointed him abbé of Saint-Denis in Reims and upon receiving his degree in theology from the Sorbonne, Talleyrand was ordained and appointed vicar general of Reims.

At the seminary, Talleyrand had also studied the works of contemporary liberal thinkers and it was this knowledge of and taste for political life that he developed at Reims. He knew that his road to real political power and influence lay with the church and so he maneuvered his way into being appointed agent-general of the clergy, thus becoming a representative of the French church before the crown; in 1788 his efforts were rewarded when he was appointed bishop of Autun.

When the Estates-General was summoned to meet on May 5,1789, Talleyrand represented the clergy of the diocese of Autun. After the transformation of the Estates General into the revolutionary body called the National Assembly, Talleyrand sided with the revolutionists and called for the transfer of church land to the state, thus abolishing privileges he had previously advocated, seen by many in the church as an act of treason. He caused another scandal by endorsing the Civil Constitution of the Clergy and in 1791 was excommunicated by the pope when he consecrated two constitutional bishops, thereby ending his clerical career.

In 1792 Talleyrand was sent on a diplomatic mission to England in the hope of persuading the British government to remain neutral. Although he was successful in securing England's neutrality, the storming of the Tuileries Palace on June 20 made it impossible for him to remain in England and in 1794 he left for the United States, where he remained until 1796.

On his return to Paris, Talleyrand accepted a seat in the Institut National. His paper on French foreign policy received considerable attention and in 1797 he became minister for foreign affairs. While foreign minister he was involved in the XYZ affair, an attempt to secure bribes from three U.S. envoys that caused a rift between France and the United States. His personal encouragement of *Napoleon's plan to seize Egypt was also seen as a diplomatic failure and after only two years as foreign minister, Talleyrand resigned from office. However, five months later he returned to his post following the establishment of the Consulate. He encouraged the signing of the Concordat between Napoleon and Pope Pius VII in July 1801 and helped secure Napoleon's position as emperor by organizing the kidnapping of the Duc d'Enghien, a Bourbon prince believed to be planning Napoleon's assassination. In 1804, when Napoleon was proclaimed emperor, he appointed Talleyrand grand chamberlain.

Although Napoleon made him prince and duke de Bénévent (1806), their relationship soured and after several violent arguments Talleyrand resigned his office in August 1807. Nevertheless, Napoleon continued to consult him on foreign policy and Talleyrand accompanied him to the Congress of Erfurt (1808), where Talleyrand conducted secret discussions with Czar *Alexander I in an attempt to persuade him to oppose Napoleon's policies against Austria. In a further attempt at preventing Napoleon from realizing his designs on Austria, Talleyrand helped arrange Napoleon's marriage to Marie-Louise of Austria. However, after the failure of Napoleon's attack on Russia in 1812 and the entry of the allies into Paris, it was Talleyrand who persuaded the latter that the only hope for peace in Europe was the restoration of the Bourbon monarchy.

The new provisional government immediately restored Louis XVIII to the throne and Talleyrand was appointed his foreign minister. In this capacity, he negotiated the first Treaty of Paris (1814), by which France retained its borders of 1792, and he represented France at the Congress of Vienna (1814–1815). Talleyrand remained in Vienna throughout the Hundred Days (the period during which Napoleon reigned in Paris after escaping from the Isle of Elba) but resigned in September 1815 after the Second Bourbon Restoration. Fifteen years later, at the age of seventy-six, he returned to political power under Louis Philippe whom he had helped become king in 1830. As ambassador to London, Talleyrand's last diplomatic feat resulted in the recognition of a neutral Belgium (1831) and the signing of the Quadruple Alliance between France, Great Britain, Spain, and Portugal in 1834.

Talleyrand survived seven regimes. Only a few hours before his death he signed a document reconciling him with the church he had abandoned so many years before. He was buried in his castle, the Chateau de Valencay.

J. F. Bernard, *Talleyrand: A Biography,* 1970.
A. Duff-Cooper, *Talleyrand,* 1964.
L. S. Greenbaum, *Talleyrand: Statesman-Priest,* 1972.
M. Poneatowski, *Tallyrand et l'ancienne France,* 1988.

TAMERLANE (Timur; 1336–1405), Mongol conqueror of the Islamic faith. Born in an oasis valley between Samarkand and the Hindu Kush mountains, he belonged to the Barlas clan, firmly rooted in the political, cultural, and economic heritage of Central Asia; he gloried in the nomadic tradition of his region and scorned the settled peasantry. Crippled from birth, he was mocked as "Timur Lenk" ("Timur the Lame") by his enemies, a cognomen that was corrupted to "Tamerlane" in the West, where the tales of his brutality inspired the historian Edward Gibbon to call him "the scourge rather than the benefactor of mankind."

Although not of imperial Mongol stock, so effective was Tamerlane as a leader, warrior, negotiator, and intriguer that by the 1360s he had established control over the whole of Transoxiana (modern-day Uzbekistan). Thereafter he dedicated himself to a further four decades of almost continuous campaigning during which his forces conquered an enormous swathe of territory from Mongolia to as far west as the Mediterranean.

In 1381, after subduing the ferocious inhabitants of the mountainous regions around Transoxiana, Timur moved southwest, invading Khurasan and overthrowing the ruler of Herát. Thereafter, annual westward campaigns into Iraq, Syria, and Anatolia (now Turkey) further extended his dominion. During the course of his "Five Years' Campaign," which began in 1392, his forces rampaged through Persia (Iran), where they ended the Muzaffand dynasty; Iraq, where they occupied Baghdad; and Caucasia. After passing along the Don valley, they entered the territory of the Golden Horde, the Mongol descendants of *Genghis Khan, where they destroyed Astrakhan and New Serai before returning to Tamerlane's capital of Samarkand in Transoxiana.

The desire for plunder, the predatory instincts of his warlords, the needs of his Central Asian kingdom, and Islam's call for *jihad* (holy war) constituted the motive forces for Tamerlane's conquests. Using mobility and surprise as their major weapons of attack, the mounted nomads seemed invincible; their victories were accompanied by acts of great cruelty, with cities ruthlessly sacked and entire civilian populations mercilessly put to the sword. Thus, at Isfahan in Persia, Tamerlane ordered the heads of seventy thousand of his victims to be piled into pyramids as a monument to his victory.

Although the loot and tribute consequent upon his successes made Samarkand one of the most splendid cities in Asia, he seldom sought to enjoy the comforts of court and palace, preferring to live the life of the nomad; on his return from a campaign, he would spend but a few days in the capital before returning to the tented encampment of his warriors outside the city walls, accompanied by his wives and concubines. Nevertheless, he was more than simply a brutish and unsophisticated butcher of men; although uneducated, he was not ignorant, enjoyed disputations on the finer points of Islamic theology, and was an able chess player. Learning was encouraged and flourished in many parts of his empire, which was also famed for the grandeur of its monuments. First and foremost, however, Tamerlane was a master of military techniques and an adept diplomat, skilled in using the arts of intrigue, negotiation, and alliance to serve his own ends when the need arose.

A long-term improvement in weather conditions in Central Asia meant that hitherto desert areas became fit pastureland for Tamerlane's nomads' herds, and this, allied to the weakening of the remnants of Genghis Khan's empire through factional strife, meant that the way was open for him to enjoy further conquests. The 1398 capture of Delhi was the occasion for the slaughter of some one hundred thousand captives, and the city took a century to recover from the effects of his devastation. The "Seven Years' Campaign" launched in 1399 saw incursions into Georgia and eastern Turkey, clashes with the Ottoman Sultan Bajazet I and the Mameluke sultan of Egypt, and the invasion of Mamluk-controlled Syria. There, Aleppo and Damascus were captured, while in Iraq, Baghdad was recaptured and its inhabitants massacred in their hundreds of thousands.

By 1402 Tamerlane had reached the Aegean and sacked the city of Smyrna. He then returned to Transoxiana to celebrate his victories and plan for what was to be his grandest campaign, the invasion of Ming-controlled China. However, before he could execute this most ambitious design, he died of a fever exacerbated by excessive drinking. His mausoleum, the Gúr-e Amír in Samarkand, is recognized as one of the masterpieces of Islamic architecture.

Tamerlane's death was followed by a war of succession among his kin that prompted the swift dissolution of the empire he had created; however, his line did not fail, and it was his descendant, *Babur, who conquered Delhi and founded the Mogul dynasty in the early sixteenth century.

R. Grousset, *The Empire of the Steppes,* 1970.
W. P. Hansen and J. Haney, eds., *Tamerlaine,* 1987.
H. Hookham, *Tamburlaine the Conqueror,* 1962.
B. F. Manz, *The Rise and Rule of Tamerlane,* 1989.

TASMAN, ABEL JANSZOON (c.1603–1659), Dutch explorer of the South Pacific. Tasman arrived in Batavia (modern-day Java) in 1634. This city was the headquarters of the Dutch East India Company, which exercised full administrative, judicial, and legislative authority over Dutch possessions in the East. In 1639 Tasman was appointed second-in-command of an expedition sent out by the company into the northeast Pacific to find "certain islands of gold and silver" that supposedly existed somewhere east of Japan. Little was known about the Pacific Ocean at that time and inaccurate navigational devices meant that islands were frequently discovered, inaccurately charted on maps, and then lost again. Some islands moved back and forth across the maps of the Pacific ocean for centuries, while others appeared in several different places on the same map, each time under a different name given them by their "discoverer."

Tasman worked for the company in the Indian Ocean as a merchant-captain. He was given command of the South Land expedition of 1642 planned by Governor Anthony Van Diemen to expand the Dutch colonial empire. Dutch navigators had already discovered parts of Australia and Tasman's assignment was to find out if Australia was part of the great Southern continent whose existence had been theorized. He was given a highly inaccurate chart and ordered to follow the route of a former explorer and the decisions of the expedition's council.

The expedition sailed southward, established that Australia was a separate continent, and discovered Tasmania (which Tasman named Van Diemen's Land). Tasman discovered New Zealand in November of 1642 and then headed northeast toward (according to his map) the Solomon Islands (which he had in fact long since passed). He soon discovered the Friendly Islands, where he was able to take on provisions.

The Fiji Islands were discovered in February of 1643, the middle of the hurricane season, but the expedition safely navigated the dangerous waters around them. According to the chart, they had almost reached South America (among its other defects, the chart greatly underestimated the size of the Pacific Ocean). Tasman's (correct) calculation of their location was completely different. The expedition's council voted to follow the chart and they turned back to Batavia.

Tasman's second expedition, in 1644, circumnavigated Australia and charted its coast. Tasman was not a favorite of the company, but after his successful second voyage it awarded him with the rank of commodore and made him a member of Batavia's Council of Justice and of a committee to negotiate a truce with the viceroy of Portuguese India. He commanded a trading fleet to Siam in 1647, and a war fleet against the Spanish Philippines in 1648. Tasman retired from the company in 1653, but continued to live in Batavia as one of its wealthiest inhabitants.

A. Sharp, *Tasman*, 1968.

TASSO, TORQUATO (1544–1595), Italian poet of the Italian Renaissance, best known for his romantic epic of the crusader conquest of the Holy Land, *Gerusalemme liberata* (Jerusalem Delivered), Temperamental of character, Tasso's stormy life as a court poet subjected him to the intrigues and competitiveness of his fellow poets and drove him to paranoia and insanity. The tragedy of his emotionalism made him a heroic figure during the Romantic period of literature.

Tasso's father, Bernardo Tasso, was himself a poet who sustained himself and his family on the patronage of the Prince of Salerno. In 1552, when the prince objected to imposing the Inquisition in Naples, the emperor opposed him, forcing him to abdicate and flee. Left without means of support, Bernardo left Naples for the north of Italy, taking with him his son. Separated from his mother at a tender age, the boy lived in poverty, moving with his father between Rome, Venice, Padua, and other cities. Nevertheless Tasso studied law and philosophy while assisting his father with his poetic pursuits. Beginning in his teens, Tasso was deeply engaged in composing his own verse, its style derivative of his father's classical poetry. In 1561, Tasso published his first known poems, and the following year the chivalric poetic narrative *Rinaldo* appeared, a poem of twelve cantos, highly disciplined but lacking the talent of his mature works.

Like many poets of his day, Tasso sought a patron who would grant him the security and means to enable him to develop his abilities. In 1565 he arrived at the court at Ferrara, to which he would remain attached for much of his life. It was a learned court that attracted many poets, but Tasso was soon recognized as outstanding. His poetry earned him the patronage and personal regard of two women, Lucrezia and Leonora, sisters of Duke Alfonso II d'Este at Ferrara, and some of his finest lyrics were inspired by these patrons.

In 1569 Tasso's father died, which profoundly affected him. In 1573 he published his pastoral *Aminta,* a lyric drama of simple brilliance reflecting the idyllic years at court in Ferrara.

From his earliest years as a poet Tasso had been working on an epic poem based on the history of the Crusades. In 1575 he completed the work, *Gerusalemme liberata,* reading a first version to the Duke at Ferrara. Its story was loosely based on the last phase of the First Crusade, which freed Jerusalem from Saracen control. The epic poem opens in the spring of 1099, as Godfrey of Bouillon, the new head of the Christian army, encircles Jerusalem to conquer it. As the battle nears its conclusion, the forces of Hell mount a series of desperate measures to fend off defeat, disguising themselves as temptresses who seduce the Crusader knights, haunting them in forests, subjecting them to drought and mutiny and strengthening their Saracen enemies. In spite of these efforts, the forces of Heaven are victorious and under the leadership of Godfrey the Crusaders retake the Sepulcher of Christ, rescuing Jerusalem from pagan control.

Because Tasso had no romantic model for his historical epic, he turned to *Virgil's Latin classic, The Aeneid,* achieving a synthesis of romantic and classic forms that was entirely original. It retained a classical unity of plot but Tasso, then thirty-one, infused his poem with sensuality and a heightened poetic diction that anticipate modern sensibilities.

The completion of Tasso's masterpiece foreshadowed a series of tragic events in his life. The forces of the Catholic church's Counter-Reformation had grown strong during the 1570s, and its doctrines against heresy were applied to literature as well as church writings. Once his poem became public, Tasso began to worry excessively that it had overstepped the bounds of propriety, and was hounded by the fear of being branded a heretic. His popularity with the duke and his sisters made him subject to the intrigues of other court poets jealous of his success, and some of his works were pirated for profit and prestige.

Tasso had began to suffer from paranoid delusion, at one point pulling a knife on one of the duke's servants. The duke had him locked in his room and then transferred to a nearby Franciscan convent, but Tasso managed to escape and made his way to his sister's house in Sorrento. He found succor with his family, but growing restless, eventually found his way back to Ferrara. When he arrived, the duke was preoccupied with contracting his third marriage and his attitude towards Tasso sent the poet raving. The duke had him taken to the madhouse of Saint Anna, where he remained for the next seven years, suffering the brutal conditions of this primitive institution until he was allowed his own quarters and access to his friends. Even during the time of his confinement, editions of *Gerusalemme liberata* continued to be published, but Tasso received none of the revenues.

In 1586 Tasso left Saint Anna at the invitation of the Prince of Mantua and began to write again. None of these later works had the beauty and ease of the earlier poems. In 1587, he began to wander again, going to Bologna, Loreto, and Rome. In Naples he started his poem *Monte Oliveto*. In 1589 he took ill in Rome and from this point on his health slowly declined. In 1593 he published a completely revised version of his masterwork, now called *Gerusalemme conquistata* (Jerusalem Conquered) which was considered vastly inferior to the work of his youth.

In 1594 Tasso was invited by Pope Clement VIII to Rome to assume the position of poet laureate once held by the poet *Petrarch, for which he was to receive a generous pension from the papacy. But Tasso's health had deteriorated and he died in 1595. His poetry influenced John *Milton and Edmund Spenser, the English writers of epic poetry, and in the Romantic era he became a heroic figure, the subject of Johann Wolfgang *Goethe's drama *Torquato Tasso* and Lord *Byron's *Lament of Tasso*.

C. P. Brand, *Torquato Tasso: A Study of the Poet and His Contribution to English Literature*, 1965.

A. Fichter, *Poets Historical*, 1982.

M. Murrin, *The Allegorical Epic*, 1980.

TCHAIKOVSKY, PYOTR ILICH (1840–1893),

Russian composer. Although Tchaikovsky studied music, he never showed any considerable talent as either a pianist or a composer, but at age twenty-one he was accepted at a newly inaugurated musical institution that would eventually become the Saint Petersburg Conservatory. There he studied composition with Anton Rubinstein and graduated in 1865, winning a silver medal for his cantata *Hymn to Joy*, set to Johann *Schiller's poetry.

In 1866 Tchaikovsky became a professor of harmony at the Moscow Conservatory, which was headed by Nicolai Rubinstein, and here he began composing seriously. Apart from composing and teaching, Tchaikovsky wrote music criticism for several Moscow newspapers. He also traveled extensively, including a visit to the first Wagner festival in Bayreuth in 1876, publishing his impressions in the Moscow daily *Russkyie Vedomosti*.

Tchaikovsky's closest friends were his brother Modest, who would eventually become his biographer, and his married sister, Alexandra Davidov. Tchaikovsky spent most of his summers at his sister's estate and the extensive correspondence between these three siblings sheds much light on the composer's true character.

He maintained a special friendship with Nadezhda von Meck, a wealthy widow with eleven children whom he never met but who played an extremely important part in his life. Von Meck learned of Tchaikovsky's financial difficulties and commissioned several compositions from him at very large fees. She then arranged to pay him a considerable annuity. For more than thirteen years Tchaikovsky corresponded with his patroness, even when they lived in the same city, and although she hinted more than once that she would like to meet the composer, Tchaikovsky always declined, saying time and again that he should not see his guardian angel in the flesh. The composer himself wrote to von Meck on art and philosophy and reported on his daily activities without mentioning his basic problems.

In 1877 Tchaikovsky married Antonina Milyukova, a conservatory student who declared her love to him. The composer hoped that his marriage would stop the ongoing (and true) rumors about his homosexuality. The result was disastrous and Tchaikovsky even attempted suicide by standing up to his neck at night in the icy river, hoping to catch pneumonia. After nine weeks of torment he fled to Saint Petersburg and never saw his wife again. His brother, arranged the separation. The two were never divorced, and Antonina died in an insane asylum in 1917.

Tchaikovsky told Nadezhda von Meck about the failure of his marriage but never revealed the real reason. She at once gave him more money and the composer traveled to Italy, Switzerland, Paris, and Vienna in 1877–1888. During these long journeys he completed his fourth symphony, which he dedicated to von Meck. In 1878 Tchaikovsky resigned from the Moscow Conservatory and devoted all his time to composition; financial matters were handled by von Meck.

In 1879 he premiered his most successful and best-known opera, *Evgeny Onegin*. Many of his works were not initially received enthusiastically but despite his continual depression, each new work brought some relief. Critics attacked his violin concerto, but the piece eventually became one of the most popular violin concertos in the repertoire. Other compositions, such as the fifth symphony and the ballets *Swan Lake* and *The Sleeping Beauty,* were successful from the start. In 1884 he was received by the czar and awarded a decoration and, in 1888, a pension for life.

At the height of his career von Meck informed Tchaikovsky that she was terminating her association with him. Although by this time the composer was financially secure, he was deeply hurt by her behavior; however, he did not let this personal blow distract him from composition. In 1891 he went to the United States and conducted in New York, Baltimore, and Philadelphia. He completed his acclaimed sixth symphony, the *Pathétique,* during this time and traveled to Saint Petersburg to conduct its premiere 1893. According to accepted history, there was a cholera epidemic in the city at the time and no one was supposed to drink unboiled water. Tchaikovsky did so and was infected at once, dying nine days after the concert. However, there is a growing belief that he committed suicide to avoid the disgrace attached to his homosexual attentions to the nephew of a duke at court.

Tchaikovsky left a substantial legacy comprising six symphonies, chamber music, songs, and works for the lyric stage. While it is his later symphonies and concertos that are performed, his uniqueness is revealed in his early symphonies, which have reemerged in recent years. His affinity for the stage brought forth masterpieces of opera and ballet; almost no other composer was able to create a fully developed symphonic ballet score as Tchaikovsky did with his three major ballets, *Swan Lake, The Nutcracker,* and *The Sleeping Beauty.* His many operas, like *The Queen of Spades, The Maid of Orleans, Mazepa, The Sorceress,* and *Iolanta* are as captivating as *Evgeny Onegin.*

D. Brown, *Tchaikovsky,* 4 vols., 1976–1991.
A. Poznansky, *Tchaikovsky: The Quest for the Inner Man,* 1991.
V. Volkoff, *Tchaikovsky,* 1974.
J. Warrack, *Tchaikovsky Ballet Music,* 1979.
H. Zajaczkowski, *Tchaikovsky's Musical Style,* 1987.

TEMPLE, HENRY JOHN SEE PALMERSTON, LORD

TENNYSON, ALFRED, LORD (1809–1892), English poet. He was the fourth of twelve children of George Clayton Tennyson, rector of Somersby in Lincolnshire. His two elder brothers also became poets of some renown. The prosperous Tennyson family had claims to gentility: Alfred's grandfather owned an impressive estate and his uncle was a member of Parliament. There were constant feuds in the family, intensified by inherited health problems. George Clayton Tennyson kept a home where literature and the arts were valued but he suffered from epileptic attacks and was a difficult father to live with. He turned to drugs and alcohol, threatening his family with violence.

Tennyson became shy and melancholy. After a hateful experience at school in Louth, he returned to the parsonage where his father intended to oversee his education, but his distressed state of health and mind aborted this scheme, so the boy continued his education by reading through his father's extensive library; medical books were a particular favorite and he soon was convinced that he was suffering from a multiplicity of diseases.

His medical interests were swamped by his poetic yearnings, manifest at the early age of five, when he could compose single lines of poetic merit. His grandfather gave him his first commission, to write an elegy on his grandmother for a fee of ten shillings. Unwilling to raise false hopes, the frosty old man commented sardonically: "This is the first money you have ever earned by your poetry, and, take my word for it, it will be the last."

When Tennyson went to study at Cambridge University, he found himself at last in a more congenial atmosphere, although his appearance was not in keeping with the image of a gentleman — clothes unwashed for days on end, hair unkempt, his eyesight so poor that he had to wear a monocle to see what he was eating, and to cap it all a strange country accent. Yet this untidy undergraduate could write sublimely and had a good sense of humor. Once a fellow student remarked on the state of Tennyson's shirt and Tennyson replied, "Yours would not be as clean as mine if you had worn it a fortnight."

He entered the circle of Arthur Hallam, a handsome and talented young gentleman who matched his ideal of all the finest human qualities. Hallam encour-

Tennyson reading 'Maud,' by D. G. Rossetti

> - Music that gentlier on the spirit lies
>   Than tir'd eyelids upon tir'd eyes.
>
> - The old order changeth, yielding place to new,
>   And God fulfills himself in many ways,
>   Lest one good custom should corrupt the world.
>
> - In the Spring, a young man's fancy
>   Lightly turns to thoughts of love.
>
> - Knowledge comes, but Wisdom lingers.
>
> - 'Tis better to have loved and lost
>   Than never to have loved at all.
>
> - Come into the garden, Maud
>   For the black bat, night, hath flown.
>
> - I chatter, chatter as I flow
>   To join the brimming river,
>   For men may come and men may go,
>   But I go on for ever.
>
> - Half a league, half a league,
>   Half a league onward
>   All in the valley of Death
>   Rode the six hundred.
>
>   Theirs not to make reply,
>   Theirs not to reason why,
>   Theirs but to do and die.
>
>   Cannon to right of them,
>   Cannon to left of them,
>   Cannon in front of them
>   Volley'd and thunder'd.
>
> **From Tennyson's Poems**

in a woodcarving machine, promoted by the owner of the asylum.

In spite of the mental anguish, or perhaps because of it, these middle years of his life were productive and saw him firmly established as the country's leading new poet. The widely acclaimed edition of his poems published in 1842 (which included "Locksley Hall," one of his best-known works) did much to enhance his reputation. He also made a generous arrangement with an American publisher to bring out a revised version of his 1833 book of poems in the United States.

In 1845 influential friends secured for Tennyson a government pension of £200 a year and in 1850 came the ultimate accolade when he was chosen to succeed William *Wordsworth as poet laureate. The two poets had met on several occasions and showed a grudging respect for each other.

By 1850 Tennyson felt his condition sufficiently improved and married Emily Sellwood, after which he settled down into a better regulated life. Though his wife was in poor health and from the late 1850s an invalid, she assumed a crucial role as business manager and provider of moral support and household order. Their first son died tragically at birth. Their second, Hallam, devoted himself to his father's service as secretary and later biographer, remaining on call even after his own marriage. Their youngest son, Lionel, was of a more independent disposition and his early death in 1886 embittered his parents' last years.

Tennyson held the post of poet laureate for over forty years and was elevated to the peerage. His poetic genius matured rather than weakened. In works like the "Ode on the Death of the Duke of *Wellington" and "The Charge of the Light Brigade," he captured the nation's mood. Many other poems of strong appeal well beyond his own generation were also written during these years, "Maud" and the "Idylls of the King," poems based on the Arthurian legend, being among the best known.

Fame also brought an excellent income, yet deep-seated insecurity still led Tennyson to confess his poverty to his friends and jealously defend his right to a pension from state funds.

Although he had attained a paramount position in English poetry he still felt a constant need to hear how his writing was appreciated. The slightest prompting provided an excuse to start a reading, and because these could last for hours — and Tennyson had no concept of an hour that was too late — even for those who enjoyed his poems these readings could be an ordeal. Although he enjoyed being the center of attention, there were limits; the hordes of tourists, especially Americans whom he found particularly brash and distasteful, caused annoyance by invading the privacy of the Tennyson home at Farringford, Isle of Wight.

Tennyson was one of the first among famous poets to leave recordings of his readings to posterity; these were made by the Edison company in

aged him to publish a selection of poems in 1833 but Tennyson was deeply hurt by the savage reviews. Hallam's tragic death at the age of twenty-three was one of the most poignant and tragic moments in the poet's life and inspired the work later entitled "In Memoriam," one of his finest poems.

In 1837 Tennyson became engaged to Emily Sellwood, whom he had known in Somersby. Haunting fears of epilepsy and blindness and an unjustified pessimism over the state of his finances decided him against the marriage and he took up a nomadic existence, lodging with a succession of friends and acquaintances, often overstaying his welcome. His terror of the onset of mental illness led him to admit himself as a voluntary patient at a London asylum in the mid 1840s. He also suffered great financial loss in an ill-considered investment

1890. He was buried in Westminster Abbey and a laurel from *Virgil's tomb was placed in his coffin.

P. Levi, *Tennyson,* 1993.
R. B. Martin, *Tennyson: The Unquiet Heart,* 1980.
C. Ricks, *Tennyson,* 1972.

TERESA OF ÁVILA, SAINT (Teresa de Cepeda y Ahumada; 1515–1582), Spanish religious. Author of three celebrated works of spiritual autobiography and two about stages of mystical prayer, Teresa also initiated the reform of the Carmelite order in the face of vast opposition and her own failing health.

Teresa was born in Ávila, Spain, daughter of an affluent merchant family. Her relationship with her mother was particularly close. At a very young age, Teresa's devoutness evidenced itself. At seven she left home with her brother to journey to the Moorish part of Spain in order to die a martyr's death by decapitation, hoping to thus come to see God. The two children were discovered on the way by their uncle, and thereafter Teresa's father kept a watchful eye on his daughter's enthusiasm.

On reaching her teen years, Teresa's interest in religion waned as her beauty increased. She read chivalric tales that were popular at the time and was involved romantically with her cousin. However, her mother's death when Teresa was fifteen turned her back to her religious foundations, as she sought comfort through a relationship with the Virgin Mary to fill the void.

What I want to explain is the soul's feeling when it is in this divine union. It is plain enough what union is; in union two separate things become one. O my Lord, how good You are! May You be blessed for ever O my God, and may all things praise You for so loving us that we can truly speak of Your communications with souls even here in our exile!

After this prayer of union, the soul is left with a very great tenderness, so much so that it would gladly dissolve, not in grief but in tears of joy. Quite unawares, it finds itself bathed in them, and does not know how or when it wept.

The soul is left, with so much courage that if it were torn asunder at that moment for God's sake, it would be greatly comforted. This is a time of vows, of heroic resolutions, and of strengthening desires, when the soul begins to loath the world and develops a clear realization of its own vanity. The benefits that it receives are more numerous and sublime than any from previous states of prayer and humility grows greater.

From *The Life of Saint Teresa*

In 1531 her father entrusted her education to Augustinian nuns and in 1535 she ran away from home and entered the Carmelite Monastery of the Incarnation at Ávila, finally donning the habit of a nun, an act to which her father ultimately became resigned. Teresa committed herself to a life of prayer and penitence but she soon became ill, her condition being perhaps of psychological origin; nevertheless, her health degenerated seriously over the next year. By 1539 she lapsed into a coma and when she regained consciousness she had lost the use of her legs, a paralysis that lasted for three years.

During her convalescence she developed her mental prayer but she remained split between her need for approval by friends, family, and religious fellows and her inner spiritual life. Finally, at age thirty-nine, she experienced a vision of Christ wounded that enabled her to decisively break with outer concerns. From this point on she frequently experienced ecstatic mystical states. Her inner turmoil and religious triumph are recorded in her autobiography, usually called *The Life of Teresa of Ávila,* composed in the years 1562–1565.

Three years after her spiritual awakening she initiated a reform movement within the Carmelite order, the thrust of which was to return the Carmelite movement to its original austere values, isolating the nuns from the world in chastity and poverty, completely dependent on the alms of the community so as to allow them to concentrate on God, penitence, and reparation for man's sins. Teresa's single-mindedness earned her the opposition of the Carmelite order and the community around her, which did not want an unsupported convent in their midst.

Nevertheless, in 1562 Pope Pius IV approved Teresa's reform and the same year she opened her first convent, Saint Joseph's of the Carmelite Reform. During the next five years of relative peace, she wrote her autobiography and another work, *Meditations of the Canticles.* In 1567 John Baptist Rossi arrived in Avila from Rome, giving the papal stamp to Teresa's work and directing her to establish more monasteries. It was at this time that she met Juan de Yepes (later to become Saint John of the Cross) and encouraged him to institute reforms in the Carmelite men's order parallel to her reforms for women. The men's reforms were instituted while Teresa another sixteen more convents throughout Spain, her reform order becoming known as the "discalced" or unshod (Primitive) Carmelites as opposed to the "calced" or shod Carmelites. The division within the order reached a crisis in 1575, when Teresa was commanded by her superiors in the Carmelite order to go to Castile and to cease founding new monasteries.

In 1579 a solution to the Carmelite impasse was worked out with the aid of King *Philip II of Spain, an admirer of Teresa's accomplishments. Teresa's Carmelites of the Primitive Rule were to have independent jurisdiction from this point on, a decision confirmed by Pope Gregory XIII in 1580. Once this was granted, Teresa, now in poor health, resumed her vocation, traveling throughout Spain to the sites of the Carmelite Reform convents, giving spiritual guidance and solving administrative problems. On her way home from Burgos to Ávila in 1582 Teresa collapsed and died. She was buried at Alba, a town sixty miles from her birthplace.

The prayer life written about in Teresa's autobiography is further developed in her work *The Interior Castle*. Here, the beginnings of prayer are compared to entering a palace composed of six concentric rings, each ring made up of separate mansions or apartments. The three outer rings describe the admirable life of a virtuous believer, consisting of humility, meditation, and exemplary conduct. The inner three represent the depths of contemplation as the soul begins to find union in God. The center or sixth circle is called the holy of holies where the soul is betrothed to God, overcome by divine light in direct communion with the Creator.

Teresa's writings, though banned by the Inquisition, enjoyed widespread subsequent influence. In 1622 Teresa was canonized by Pope Gregory XV, and in 1970 Pope Paul made her a doctor of the church. She is also the patron saint of Spain.

J. Blinkoff, *The Ávila of Saint Theresa,* 1989.
S. Clissold, *Saint Theresa of Avila,* 1982.
E. W. T. Dicken, *The Crucible of Love,* 1963.
Father Thomas and Father Gabriel, eds., *Saint Teresa of Avila,* 1963.

THEMISTOCLES

THEMISTOCLES (c.524–c.460 B.C.E.), Athenian general and statesman who made Athens into a sea power and defeated the Persians, thus bringing about the golden age of Greek civilization.

The new Persian king, *Xerxes, assembled a great invasion force to avenge his father's defeat at Marathon in 490 B.C.E. To counter Xerxes's threat, a Hellenic League with Sparta's military leadership was formed, with almost every Greek city-state contributed troops or supplies. Spartan forces at the pass of Thermopylae successfully held off the Persians until betrayal led to their defeat and the unopposed Persian army streamed south, capturing Athens. The Athenians fled to the island of Salamis.

Themistocles knew that he would be victorious if he could get the Persians to fight at Salamis, where their larger force would be hampered by having to fight in a small, confined space. He also took advantage of the long history of Greek aid to the Persians by "warning" Xerxes that the Greeks were planning to escape from Salamis and suggesting that if stopped they would divide into factions and start fighting among themselves. The Persians believed his message, blockaded Salamis, were drawn into battle, and defeated. Xerxes fled towards Asia.

After the war Themistocles persuaded Athens to rebuild its defensive walls, despite Spartan objections that this would strengthen the city. He directed Athens to finish building the walls as fast as possible and, feeling that Athens's future lay on the sea, also persuaded it to complete the work of fortifying Piraeus and converting it into the largest and finest harbor in Greece.

Themistocles tried to counter the increasing hostility of Athens's postwar rulers with frequent reminders of his accomplishments; when this did not have the desired effect, he asked: "Why do you grow weary of being benefited again and again by the same men?" He was finally ostracized in 471 B.C.E. Sparta then took its revenge against him, pursuing him unrelentingly from one fearful city-state to another. After several years he was forced to go to Asia and throw himself at the mercy of Xerxes's son, the new Persian king, Artaxerxes.

Artaxerxes provided for Themistocles with many gifts after accepting his claim that a debt was owed him for Xerxes's safe return after Salamis. Themistocles served Artaxerxes faithfully as governor until his death. Some sources suggest that he died by his own hand rather than help his new master in a war against Greece.

F. J. Frost, *Plutarch's Themistocles,* 1980.
R. J. Lenardon, *The Saga of Themistocles,* 1978.
A. J. Poldecki, *The Life of Themistocles,* 1975.

THEODOSIUS I

THEODOSIUS I (the Great; c.346–395), Roman emperor of the East (379–395) and of the West (394–395). Son of the Roman general Flavius Theodosius, Theodosius was raised in Spain. He fought beside his father against barbarian incursions in Britain, Gaul, and the Balkans, but retired to his property in Spain after conspiracies at Emperor Valens's court led to his father's execution. Meanwhile, the Visigoth remnant that had survived the Huns' attack had received permission from Valens to cross the Danube and settle in Thrace only to find themselves plundered and enslaved by the Romans there. Starving and desperate, the Visigoths laid waste to the region, killed Valens and defeated his army, and went on a rampage through the Balkans. Gratian, Valens's son and successor recalled Theodosius who, after defeating the barbarian Sarmatians, was appointed coemperor.

Theodosius ruled the eastern part of the empire, which had suffered the most from barbarian incursions. He rebuilt the depleted army by allowing large numbers of non-Romans (previously not considered for enlistment) to become soldiers and officers. Realizing that his army was not strong enough to expel the Visigoths, Theodosius made them into military allies in 382 with an agreement that allowed them to maintain their autonomy, live within the empire, and receive an annual sum for helping to defend it.

Baptized in 380 after a serious illness, Theodosius was increasingly anti-pagan: he was the first emperor to refuse the title "Supreme Guardian of the old Roman Cults," forbade temple sacrifices, and completely prohibited paganism in 392. The Second Ecumenical Council, which he summoned in 381, gave ecclesiastical sanction to the Nicene Creed to which he subscribed (believing that the Father, Son, and Holy Spirit are of the same essence) and it became a basic Christian tenet.

In 383 General Maximus, who was of Spanish origin, was proclaimed emperor by his troops, overthrew and killed Gratian, and in 387 invaded Italy in an attempt to overthrow Gratian's successor, Valentian II. Theodosius, who had married Valentian's sister, came to the latter's aid and restored him to his throne after defeating Maximus and having him put to death. Theodosius ensured that real authority over the empire was in his own hands by making his trusted general, Arbogast, Valentian's adviser and remaining in Italy until 391.

Most of Theodosius's time in Italy was spent in Milan, where he became both friend and antagonist of the Church Father, Bishop *Ambrose. Ambrose never hesitated to criticize Theodosius even though he supported his temporal leadership. When a mob in Thessalonica tore the imperial governor to pieces for imprisoning a popular charioteer, Theodosius ordered that the city be punished and seven thousand Thessalonicans were massacred by Roman soldiers. Ambrose refused to let Theodosius receive communion until he repented publicly for his deed, barring the way when Theodosius tried to enter the cathedral by force. Theodosius finally gave in and begged forgiveness for his sins; this was the first of many occasions in which mighty temporal rulers would bow to the spiritual authority of the church.

When Arbogast proclaimed a pagan, Eugenius, emperor of the West after Valentian's death in 393, Theodosius invaded Italy in an effort finally to rid the empire of paganism. He was victorious, Eugenius was killed, Arbogast committed suicide, and the Roman Empire was once again united under one ruler. However, Theodosius died the following year, the empire was divided between his two sons and, except during the reign of the Byzantine emperor, *Justinian, was never united again.

N. Q. King, *The Emperor Theodosius and the Establishment of Christianity,* 1961.

THEODORIC THE GREAT (c.454–526), Ostrogoth king. Theodoric was from the royal Ostrogoth family of Amoli, the fourteenth generation of the line. He was born near present-day Vienna two years after the death of *Attila the Hun and a subsequent victory by the Ostrogoths that restored them to independence from Hun enslavement.

Soon afterward, Theodoric's father Theodemir, in an attempt to improve the conditions of his people, entered into an alliance with Leo, emperor of the Eastern Roman Empire. To ensure Theodemir's compliance, Leo took the ruler's son, Theodoric, as ransom. Thus from the age of eight, Theodoric lived in Constantinople, held captive in amenable surroundings and given a traditional Roman education by the most capable teachers. When he was eighteen he returned to his people, whom Emperor Leo was treating as liberally and generously as possible so as to avoid trouble with any of the barbarian tribes.

THEODORIC TO EMPEROR ZENO

Although your servant is maintained in affluence by your liberality, graciously listen to the wishes of my heart! Italy, the inheritance of your predecessors, and Rome itself, the head and mistress of the world, now fluctuate under the violence and oppression of Odoacer the mercenary. Direct me, with my national troops, to march against the tyrant. If I fall, you will be relieved from an expensive and troublesome friend; if, with the Divine permission, I succeed, I shall govern in your name, and to your glory, the Roman senate, and the part of the republic delivered from slavery by my victorious arms.

During this time, Theodemir led the Ostrogoths in battle and they were able to establish themselves in Pannonia (present-day western Hungary). Nevertheless, the Ostrogoth people lacked food and clothing. Eager to get what they needed for survival, they approached Constantinople and the Byzantine court. Leo, fearing for the capital's safety, granted Theodemir control over the lower Danube in an effort to appease him. It was at this time that Theodoric replaced his father as tribal leader. Meanwhile, Zeno replaced Leo as emperor, and he and Theodoric came to work together cooperatively, although the latter was known for his occasional pillaging rampages.

The Ostrogoths' inability to make their fertile lands produce adequately meant that they remained a threatening presence; Theodoric himself was kept in opulence by the Roman emperor, but he refused to forget the miserable conditions of his people in a land they were ill-adapted to occupy. Realizing his power to threaten the stability of the empire, he proposed a plan of mutual benefit to his people and the emperor, offering to take his entire people, numbering over one hundred thousand, across to Italy to conquer the center of the former western Roman empire. Zeno agreed, calculating that this would finally remove the Ostrogoth threat.

In 488 the order was given and the Ostrogoths began their long march. They arrived in Italy in mid-489, engaging in battle the forces of the barbarian ruler Odoacer. Odoacer's forces were eventually vanquished, but the barbarian king retreated to the impregnable citadel of Ravenna, where he succeeded in fending off Theodoric's army for another three years; only treachery enabled the latter's forces to enter the fortress and kill Odoacer, his family and eventually his followers throughout Italy.

Having achieved total victory, Theodoric divided the spoils of war, parceling out one third of the territories to his soldiers. Although he had confiscated large tracts of Roman land, he now tried to ensure the peaceful coexistence of the two peoples by keeping his nation separate from the former inhabitants who had been already been Romanized. Theodoric maintained his people's distinct language, customs, and religion, while the Romans were permitted to live undisturbed under the remnant of the Empire's civil service and to worship according to their Catholic traditions; the Ostrogoths adhered to Aryan Christianity.

Theodoric shed the skins and furs of traditional Ostrogoth leadership and donned the purple robes of the empire. His thirty-three-year reign was remarkably peaceful, both because of his statesmanship and due to the fear of him. He was buried in a magnificent tomb in Ravenna that remains intact to this day. R. Macpherson, *Rome in Involution,* 1989.

THÉRÈSE DE LISIEUX, SAINT (1873–1897), French Carmelite nun, popularly known as the Little Flower. Originally named Marie Françoise Thérèse Martin, she was youngest of nine children of a devout watchmaker in Alençon, France. Her mother died when she was four years old and the family moved to Lisieux, where Thérèse attended the Benedictine convent as a day student. From an early age she was drawn to religious perfection, and when she was fifteen obtained permission to enter the convent of the Discalced Carmelites in Lisieux, where two of her older sisters had already been admitted.

It was in the convent that she spent the remaining nine years of her life before dying of tuberculosis. Her years at the convent were spent practicing and teaching her doctrine of the "Little Way" — a way of spiritual childhood, trust and absolute surrender, holy life that, in the words of Pope Pius XI, "did not go beyond the common order of things." It was this outlook that she taught to the novices whom she was appointed acting mistress of novices in 1893. She exemplified the Little Way, achieving goodness by performing the humblest of tasks. Six months before her death, her tubercular condition forced her to retire to the convent's infirmary.

The story of Thérèse's spiritual development, *L'Histoire d'une ame* (Story of a Soul), was written at the command of her superiors. Before her death she asked her sister, Mother Agnes of Jesus, to edit these memoirs which, published as her autobiography, have become one of the most widely read religious autobiographies. It is filled, as are her letters, with her message of seeking good with childlike simplicity, and greatly appealed to the ordinary people attracted by the message that sanctity could be attained not only through mortification but through ongoing renunciation in small matters, and her grave became a place of worship and pilgrimage, and a basilica in her name was built there. She was canonized in 1925 and throughout the Roman Catholic world many churches were dedicated to her. Meditations from her writings are also read by many of the devout. She is often represented in art carrying an armful of roses, because of her promise that "After my death I will let fall a shower of roses." She is the patron saint of aviators and foreign missionaries and was proclaimed by Pope Pius

XI, "the greatest saint of modern times." In 1947 she joined *Joan of Arc as patroness of France.

H. V. Balthasar, *Thérèse of Lisieux,* 1954.
I. F. Gorrës, *The Hidden Face,* 1959.
R. A. Knox, *Thérèse of Lisieux, Story of a Soul,* 1958.

THOMAS AQUINAS, SAINT (also called Angelic Doctor and Prince of Scholastics; 1225–1274), philosopher and political thinker. He was born to a noble family near Aquino, Italy, and educated at Monte Cassino, home of the Benedictine order. In 1243, however, while still a youth, he joined the Dominican order. To his family of feudal lords such a change of allegiance was a disgrace which would bring no honor to the family. In an attempt to dissuade him they confined him to the family castle for almost two years, but to no avail. His family released him in 1245 and he went to Paris to serve his novitiate. There he studied with the German philosopher *Albertus Magnus, whom he followed to Cologne in 1248. As Aquinas was heavyset and quiet, his fellow novices called him Dumb Ox but Magnus, who knew his student better,

---

Since we would not be thought ungrateful to the memory of so great a cleric, so mighty a father and doctor, we humbly beg, in the loving affection of our hearts, as a special boon that, as we could not have him restored to us when alive, now that he is dead, his remains may be given back to us.... For if justly the Church honors the bones and relics of saints, not unreasonably does it seem to us proper that the body of so great a doctor should be held in perpetual honor, and that the lasting memory of one whose fame lives among us by his writings, should also be forever fixed in the hearts of our posterity by his tomb.

Petition from the University of Paris that Aquinas's body be buried in Paris

I exhort you to be chary of speech, and to go into the conversation room sparingly. Take great heed of the purity of your conscience. Never cease the practice of prayer. Love to be diligent in your cell, if you would be led to the wine-cellar of wisdom. Ever be loving towards all. Do not bother yourself about the doings of others; nor be familiar with anyone, since too great familiarity breeds contempt.

From a letter by Thomas Aquinas to a novice who had asked for advice

Thomas Aquinas in "Allegory of the Catholic Religion"

is said to have predicted that "this ox would one day fill the world with his bellowing."

Aquinas was ordained c. 1250 and in 1252 returned to Paris, where he began to teach at the university. His first major work, *Commentaries on the Sentences of Peter Lombard,* appeared in about 1256. That year he received a doctorate in theology and was appointed professor of philosophy at the University of Paris. He gained fame rapidly and was highly regarded because of his method of using Aristotelian philosophy for theological purposes – later called the Thomist system of study. Thanks to him Aristotelianism rather than Platonism became the foundation of Christian thought. In 1259 he was summoned to Rome by Pope Alexander IV, and enjoyed great favor there. He was offered the archbishopric of Naples but turned down this and other preferred ecclesiastical positions. Upon his return he was plunged into controversy with the Averroists (see *Averroes), who based themselves on a different variation of Aristotelianism from Aquinas's own and threatened to destroy the positions he had built up so carefully with Magnus. In the contest between Aquinas and the Averroist representative, Siger de Brabant, Aquinas outlined his position in the treatise *On the Unity of the Intellect against the Averroists* (1270); he was victorious but the victory was hard-won and wearying. In 1272 he went to Italy to organize a new Dominican school and devoted himself to a life of prayer and contemplation. He died while traveling to the Second Council of Lyons, called by Pope Gregory X to attempt the union of the Greek and Latin churches.

Rulers, religious orders, and universities vied for Aquinas's body, which was eventually given by the pope to Toulouse. He was canonized by Pope John XXII in 1323 and proclaimed a Doctor of the Church by Pope Pius V in 1567.

Aquinas is regarded as an outstanding theologian and philosopher of the Catholic church. He was a prolific author and is credited with some eighty works. His *Summa theologica* (written 1266–1273), one of the earliest and longest essays dealing with the whole of Christian theology, was highly regarded by his contemporaries and successors. *Summa contra gentiles,* a treatise for Catholic missionaries, offered a brief presentation of Christian faith intended to persuade intellectual Muslims of the truth of Christianity. He also presented a new rationalist basis for many Christian doctrines, notably transubstantiation. In 1879 Pope Leo XIII decreed that Aquinas's system be the basis of all philosophy reading in Catholic institutions.

Aquinas's political ideas were expressed in *De regimine principum,* where he distinguished between laws of nature, divine law, and human law and concluded that the social establishment of his age was necessary in a Christian state. He also developed the concept that a monarchy should be bound by law and allowed full authority only within a legal framework. The latter idea led to his distinguishing between king and tyrant — a tyrant being a king who has lost the grace of God and who therefore could justifiably be condemned to death.

B. Davies, *The Thought of Thomas Aquinas*, 1992.
J. Haberman, *Maimonides and Aquinas*, 1979.
A. Kenny, *Aquinas*, 1980.
A. A. Maurer, *Saint Thomas and Historicity*, 1979.
R. M. Mcinerny, *Rhyme and Reason*, 1981.

THOMAS A KEMPIS (c.1380–1471), Dutch theologian. Born in Kempen near Cologne (hence his name), Thomas was sent to Deventer when he was thirteen to study at the school conducted by Florentius Radewijns and the Brethren of the Common Life; this community, founded by the Dutch mystic Gerard Groote, stressed and sought to emulate the simplicity and sincerity of the early Christians. Thomas wholeheartedly adopted the teachings of the Brethren, and was later to write biographies of both Radewijns and Groote.

In 1399 Thomas entered the Augustinian monastery of Mount Saint Agnes, near Zwolle in The Netherlands, where his elder brother John was prior; he remained there for the rest of his long life. Ordained in 1414, he held a succession of administrative posts within the monastic community, and was a prolific writer of sermons, hymns, popular spiritual treatises, contemporary chronicles and biographies.

Thomas à Kempis is credited with writing of *The Imitation of Christ,* one of the most famous and influential works of Christian literature. A complete Latin manuscript of the work became available in

- Man proposes but God disposes.
- O everlasting Light, surpassing all created luminaries, flash forth Thy lightning from above, piercing all the most inward parts of my heart.
- Let all teachers hold their peace; let all creatures be silent in thy sight; speak to me thou alone.
- A peaceable man doth more good than he who is well learned.
- When the Day of Judgement comes we will not be asked what we have read but what we have done.
- When man is out of sight, quickly is he out of mind.
- Would to God we had behaved ourselves in this world, even for one full day.

From *The Imitation*

1427; subsequently, some twenty persons were proposed as possible authors, but Thomas's right to be regarded as author of the definitive edition is now uniformly acknowledged, although many ascribe the basic composition to Gerard Groote himself. In the days before printing, it was relatively common for devotional works to pass through several hands, being modified along the way, while many authors were content to remain anonymous.

The *Imitation* marks a reaction against what many perceived as the excessive intellectualism of theological scholasticism and recommends simple piety, devotion, and renunciation as the foundations of a true Christian life. Consisting of aphoristic reflections and counsels written in a straightforward and familiar style, it comprises four books: the first looks at ways of liberating oneself from worldly concerns and preparing for the spiritual life; the second offers advice and admonitions concerning the life of devotion; the third discusses the consolation offered by Christ to those who earnestly follow him; and the fourth gives recommendations for receiving Holy Communion in a devout manner.

As the author of the *Imitation*, Thomas is probably the outstanding representative of "Devotia Moderna" (Modern Devotion). This late medieval religious movement sought to make religion intelligible in the context of the attitudes arising in the Netherlands at the end of the fourteenth century, and heralded the beginnings of an emphasis on personal Christian witness as a reaction against the spiritual shortcomings and materialistic pomp of the Catholic establishment. It laid great stress on education and achieved notable successes in capturing the imagination of young people who came to study at schools subscribed to the movement's views.

Both the movement generally and *Imitation of Christ* specifically had a profound impact upon the church; Martin *Luther and Deiderius *Erasmus, central figures in the massive religious upheavals of the sixteenth century, were influenced at an early age by Modern Devotion, while the *Imitation* was the favorite book of Ignatius of *Loyola, founder of the Jesuits, who spearheaded the Catholic Counter-Reformation. Subsequently, the *Imitation* affected individuals as diverse as the lexicographer and wit Samuel *Johnson and the religious reformer John *Wesley. Thus, its impact on the evolution of Protestantism in England and Germany during the eighteenth century was substantial.

A. Butler, *Thomas à Kempis*, 1908.

J. E. G. De Montmorency, *Thomas à Kempis: His Age and Book*, 1970.

THOMSON, SIR JOSEPH JOHN (1856–1940), English physicist, discoverer of electrons and 1906 Nobel prize winner for his research on the conduction of electricity through gases. Thomson was born at Cheetham Hill, Manchester, and began attending Owen College, Manchester, when he was fourteen. In 1876 he entered Trinity College, Cambridge, of which he was to remain a member for the rest of his life. In 1884 he was elected a fellow of the Royal Society and in the same year was appointed Cavendish professor of physics at Cambridge.

Showing an early interest in atomic structure, in 1883 Thomson published a study on vortex rings and in 1893 published *Notes on Recent Researches in Electricity and Magnetism.*

In 1896 Thomson gave a series of lectures at Princeton University that summarized his research on the discharge of electricity through gases. These were followed in 1904 by another series of lectures on electricity and matter, in which he made astute points regarding atomic structure. In the intervening years he produced the most important research of his life; his study of cathode rays. In it he measured the ratio m/e (where m is mass and e is the charge of the ion) and found out that its value was almost one thousand times less than in the electrolysis of liquids. He then measured the charge of electricity, e, carried by various negative ions, and discovered it to be the same in the gaseous discharge as in electrolysis. Hence, he established that the particles that make up cathode rays were of a much smaller mass than the smallest known atom. These particles are today called "electrons." Thomson announced his discovery at the Royal Institute in 1897.

In 1903 Thomson published one of his most important books, *Conduction of Electricity Through Gases*. He continued his research, discovering a new way to separate different kinds of atoms and molecules, which led to the discovery of a large number of isotopes. Under his direction, the Cavendish laboratories in Cambridge received international recognition; he was also a very popular teacher.

From 1915 to 1920 Thomson was president of the Royal Society and master of Trinity College from 1918 to 1940. In recognition of his work, his ashes were buried at Westminster Abbey. In 1936 his autobiographical *Recollections and Reflections* was published.

R. J. S. Rayleigh, *Life of Sir J. J. Thomson,* 1943.
G. P. Thomson, *J. J. Thomson and the Cavendish Laboratory in His Day,* 1964.

THUCYDIDES (c.460-c.400 B.C.E.), the world's first critical historian. An Athenian, he seems to have come from a well-connected and propertied family with rights to the gold mines in Thrace.

While noted as an historian of the Peloponnesian Wars — the intense military and naval rivalries between Athens and Sparta that convulsed ancient Greece from 431 to 404 B.C.E. — Thucydides was also an active participant in the events described. When he details the course of the plague that first struck Athens in the winter of 430–429 B.C.E., he writes from personal experience, as he himself was sick with the plague. When he graphically presents the heat, thirst, and crowding of those holed up in the dense quarters behind the city walls, where the citizens of outlaying areas had taken refuge from Spartan attacks, and cites this as contributing to the spread of the plague, he writes from personal experience.

His accounts of the military strategies and technical details of the battle scenes were also written as an eyewitness. He was more than thirty in 424 B.C.E. when he became one of ten *strategos* (generals) but was less successful as a *stratega* than as an historian. He commanded a fleet that had been sent to Amphipolis, in Thrace, but arrived too late to prevent its capture by Brasidas, the Spartan leader. Upon his recall to Athens he was tried and sentenced to twenty years in exile for this debacle, returning to Athens only four years before his death.

Thucydides had already begun an analysis of the events that led up to the declaration of war and kept precise notes on both the military battles and the accompanying political arguments. His exile afforded him the opportunity to better organize his material, to polish the narrative, and to accumulate additional data. He was able to travel and discover aspects of the Spartan version of events, which enhanced his wish to provide "an exact knowledge of the past as an aid to the interpretation of the future."

Thucydides wanted to conclude his history with the end of the war but the work ends in 411 B.C.E., some six and a half years before the war's end. By then Athens had lost a major portion of its fleet in the harbor of Syracuse on the Italian coast and the empire's doom was inevitable. The last few chapters are in a somewhat rougher form than the earlier parts of his work. Perhaps a sudden — and maybe violent — death prevented him from completing his work as planned.

Nevertheless, his is still considered the authoritative text on the Peloponnesian Wars. In fact, the war

Thucydides is one who, though he never digress to read a Lecture, Moral or Political, upon his own Text, nor enter into men's hearts, further than the Actions themselves evidently guide him, yet is accounted the most Politick Historiographer that ever writ. The reason whereof I take to be this: He filleth his Narrations with that choice of matter, and ordereth them with that Judgment, and with such perspicuity and efficacy expresseth himself that he makest his Auditor a Spectator. For he setteth his Reader in the Assemblies of the People, and in the Senates, at their debating; in the Streets, at their Seditions; and in the Field at their Battels [sic].

Thomas Hobbes on Thucydides

goes by that name because that is what Thucydides called it. An indication of Thucydides's standing in the ancient world is that the Greek historian *Xenophon, who followed Thucydides, began his account of Greek history exactly where Thucydides left off.

Thucydides developed and perfected the methodology of historical research and writing, insisting on verification of all events described (he required two witnesses for each event reported — even if he were one of them). His search for the principal causes of the war derives from the logical philosophers, the sophists, of his time.

Thucydides seemed to transcribe the exact words of the speeches of *Pericles, the Athenian proponent of democracy and moderation, whom he admired, and Cleon, the demagogue who followed Pericles and whom Thucydides disliked, along with the other major actors on the Greek political stage, but in so doing he demonstrates his own political acuity. He says in his introduction that the speeches could not, in fact, be the exact words of the politicians, but "what was in my opinion demanded of them by the various occasions..." In this Thucydides proves himself an astute political scientist, with a keen sensibility of the psychology of the polis.

J. H. Finley Jr., *Thucydides,* 1964.
A. Fuks, *Social Conflict in Ancient Greece,* 1984.
S. Hornblower, *Thucydides,* 1987.

THUTMOSE III (1504-1450 B.C.E., reigned c.1490-1436 B.C.E.), Egyptian pharaoh and military leader. He was the son of Thutmose II and a concubine and ascended the throne only because Thutmose's wife, Hatshepsut, failed to produce any male progeny. In order to confirm his rights to the throne he was wed to Hatshepsut's daughter, his half sister Meryte.

Thutmose inherited his father's throne at a young age, with Hatshepsut acting as regent. Hatshepsut was, however, an ambitious woman who declared herself pharaoh and ruled as such for twenty years; legends that she was of divine descent insured her grasp on power. Contemporary statues show her in full royal regalia, including an artificial beard she apparently wore to disguise her true sex.

Hatshepsut died when Thutmose was twenty-two years old; there is reason to believe that he was responsible for her sudden death. All documents and inscriptions pertaining to Hatshepsut's reign were destroyed and her advisor Senenmut was overthrown. His authority safeguarded, Thutmose chose to continue the Asian conquests begun by his father. He appointed two viziers, one in Thebes, the other in Memphis, to govern the kingdom in his absence, and set off for Asia.

At that time Palestine and Syria were divided into many small city-states governed by minor princes under nominal Egyptian suzerainty. Only southern Palestine remained loyal to Egypt; the Hyksos (invaders who had taken possession of Egypt) had formed a coalition of 330 northern princes to overthrow Egyptian rule. Thutmose led his armies to Megiddo, an important center of the coalition in northern Palestine, to subdue the city and break the coalition's resolve. When his officers suggested that Thutmose take a roundabout route to the city, leaving his armies less vulnerable to attack, he rejected their advice as cowardice. Thutmose reached Megiddo without encountering any resistance; the allied princes chose to make their stand outside the city's walls. The ensuing battle was an outstanding victory for Thutmose; he crushed the coalition forces, leaving the few remaining survivors to seek sanctuary within the city walls. Rather than attack the well-fortified town, however, Thutmose laid siege to it for seven months. With the fall of Megiddo, Thutmose was free to sweep through Syria toward the Euphrates.

Opposition crumbled before the advancing Egyptian forces and Thutmose overran Kadesh, Aleppo, Katna, and Carchemish. He crossed the Euphrates in cedarwood boats carried from Lebanon and set up a boundary stela on its far bank, next to the stela placed there by his father years before.

Having achieved his goal in the north, Thutmose began the journey home. Upon receiving news that the king of Kadesh had revolted, he encircled that city with his chariots; the king sent out a mare in heat, hoping to distract the Egyptian horses. Thutmose's general Amenemhab promptly cut off the mare's head and disembowelled the beast, calming the horses and allowing for an attack. Amenemhab further distinguished himself during an elephant hunt; when one of the animals charged Thutmose, Amenemhab rushed to the elephant and cut off its trunk.

Thutmose was a brilliant strategist who often preferred a ruse to brute strength. During the siege

> Come to me, rejoicing
> To see my beauty, O my son,
> My champion, Thutmose,
> I give unto thee valor
> And victory over every land;
> I place thy might
> And the fear of thee in all lands
> And the terror of thee as far as
> The four supports of the sky.
>
> **Hymn in praise of Thutmose III**

of Jaffa, the local king was invited to the Egyptian camp. The Egyptian general offered to show him Thutmose's famed war club, only to batter the king with it. Two hundred Egyptian soldiers were then hidden in baskets while five hundred others hid their arms under their cloaks. Soldiers were led to the city walls to report that the Egyptians had surrendered and were bringing two hundred baskets carried by five hundred Egyptian prisoners as booty. The queen opened the gates to receive the treasure when, to her surprise, the Egyptians removed their cloaks, jumped from the baskets, and captured the city.

Thutmose also made conquests in Nubia but it is assumed that he did not personally participate in these conflicts. He created an effective bureaucracy of commissioners and high commissioners to govern his realm, guaranteeing future payments of tribute. The bounty he brought Egypt led to Thutmose's reign being referred to as Egypt's golden age. In his final years Thutmose shared the throne briefly with his son Amenhotep.

Complete lists of the cities conquered by Thutmose can still be seen at the Temple of Karnak. Three lists contain the cities' names surrounded by an ellipse and an engraving of a captured prince with his arms bound, paying tribute to Thutmose.
G. Steindorf and K. C. Seele, *When Egypt Ruled the East,* 1957.

TIBERIUS (Tiberius Claudius Nero Caesar Augustus; 42 B.C.E.– 37 C.E.), Roman emperor. When Tiberius was four years old the Emperor *Augustus fell in love with Tiberius's pregnant mother, Livia, and married her after persuading her husband to release her. Livia became the power behind the throne, exerting great influence over Augustus.

Livia brought two sons to her marriage with Augustus: Drusus, whom Augustus loved and adopted, and Tiberius, serious even as a child, whom Augustus eventually respected but never loved. Tiberius was well educated, then sent off early to war, the custom for boys in Augustus's household. Following Augustus's policy of extending the empire on every frontier, Tiberius and Drusus commanded armies for the next ten years until 9 B.C.E., when Drusus sustained a deadly injury thrown from his horse while fighting German tribes. Tiberius loved his brother deeply; he rode from Gaul to be present at his death, then brought Drusus's body back to Rome for burial before returning to the battlefield.

That same year Augustus forced Tiberius to divorce his pregnant wife and marry Augustus's twice-widowed daughter, Julia, to end the gossip caused by Julia's numerous lovers. Tiberius tried to be a good husband, enduring Julia's many love affairs in the hope that Augustus would adopt him as his successor. When it became clear that Augustus preferred his own grandchildren, Tiberius resigned and went to live in Rhodes as a private citizen. Julia continued to go from lover to lover until Augustus banished her to a barren island, where she died sixteen years later, still imprisoned.

Augustus was left without a successor (his grandsons had died) and rebellion was brewing in several provinces. Seeing no other choice, in 2 C.E. he reluctantly summoned Tiberius, adopted him as his son and co-ruler, and sent him to the revolts. An extremely capable general who won by strategy, not by squandering his soldiers in bloodbaths, Tiberius ended the disturbances.

Tiberius returned to a Rome that accepted him as co-ruler even while it hated him for his austerity his and tightfisted monetary policies did not suit the society he ruled. Augustus's reign had yielded a long period of peace and prosperity; Egyptian treasure and prosperous Roman trade had created a luxurious society in which poetry, literature, art, and the pursuit of pleasure flourished while the populace was mollified with games and doles of corn. Tiberius the stoic, who idealized the old Roman virtues, had no place in this epicurean society.

Livia, his mother, felt that Tiberius owed his throne to her and that he therefore ruled only as her representative. She insisted on cosigning official documents during the first years of his reign, then wanted to rule alone, until Tiberius could no longer live with her and built a separate palace. He refused even to attend her funeral.

Tiberius was fifty-five when he became emperor in 14 C.E. A careful, conscientious ruler, his diligence ensured efficient government, but nothing he did pleased Rome. Without increasing taxes he repaired and built public buildings, distributed charity to stricken families and regions, and greatly increased the treasury; but the poor were upset because he gave them bread, not circuses. He kept the empire at peace and was slandered by those with imperialistic designs or an eye to plunder. He tried to restore the Republic and the power of a degenerate Senate that wanted honors and wealth, not responsibility. Believing in and protecting freedom of speech, he was the victim of gossip and lampoons.

His troubles made Tiberius gloomy and withdrawn. Sejanus, the prefect of the Praetorian Guards, took advantage of this by preventing anyone from seeing Tiberius without his approval and presence. Sejanus acquired more and more power, first by recommending people for office, then by selling the offices to the highest bidder, and finally by exiling his enemies.

Tiberius's son, named Drusus after his father's beloved brother, was an unintelligent youth much devoted to blood sports who died in 23 C.E. Overcome with disappointment and bitterness, Tiberius moved to Capri at age sixty-seven. He continued to carefully rule the Empire through Sejanus. Especially in his latter years he was cruel and depraved and the Roman historians recorded many of his monstrous acts. Increasing fear of Sejanus, his Praetorian Guard, and even Tiberius, made the Senate obey Tiberius's communications as royal commands, further diminishing the Senate's authority. Sejanus's "rule" only came to an end when his plot to kill Tiberius was discovered, whereupon he was executed. Old, lonely, and sick, Tiberius himself died seven years later.

B. M. Levick, *Tiberius the Politician*, 1976.
F. March, *The Reign of Tiberius*, 1931.
R. Seager, *Tiberius*, 1972.
G. Maranon, *Tiberius: A Study in Resentment*, 1956.

TIMUR SEE TAMERLANE

TIPU SULTAN (Fateh Ali Tipu; 1749 or 1753–1799), sultan of Mysore; Indian nationalist who opposed British expansion in the subcontinent. Tipu was the son of Hyder Ali, sultan of the southern Indian state of Mysore. His early years in his father's court were spent learning military tactics from French officers advising the sultan. Tipu showed remarkable skill; when only fourteen years old he commanded a cavalry corps in the invasion of the Carnatic (1769). He later distinguished himself in the Marathas War (1775–1779). His greatest victory, however, was in the Mysore War (1780–1784) against the British. Tipu, at the head of a large body of men, defeated Colonel John Brathwaite by the banks of the Coleroon River (1782). In later battles his troops actually succeeded in capturing the British commander, forcing the British to sue for peace. The Treaty of Mangalore was signed in 1784, providing for a mutual restitution of conquered territory.

The sultan, Hyder Ali, died in the midst of the Mysore War. Tipu was proclaimed sultan of Mysore in April 1783. He himself preferred the title of *padshah*, or king. Peace with the British, agreed to the following year, enabled Tipu to pursue the expansion of his own realm. A successul campaign in 1787–1788 led to the conquest of the Malabar coast and prompted him to attempt an attack on the rajah of Travancore, an ally of the British in southern India. Tipu's unprovoked attack on Travancore, however, led to British involvement in the dispute, sparking the Second Mysore War, which proved far less successful for Tipu. British troops, aided by the Marathas and Nizam, invaded Mysore in 1790; an attempted counterinvasion by Tipu led to his defeat by Lord Cornwallis near Seringapatam. He was forced to surrender half of his kingdom to the British and their allies, pay exorbitant compensation to his foes, and surrender two of his sons as hostages. Tipu sent emissaries to Arabia, Kabul, the Ottoman Empire, and even France begging for help in his fight against the British. He even carried on a correspondence with *Napoleon, then campaigning in Egypt, but all his entreaties failed; only the French territory of Mauritius was willing to help.

The British, under Lord Wellesley, offered to make an alliance with Tipu in 1798 but he rejected the offer outright; he was loath to compromise with the British occupiers of India. Offended by Tipu's attitude, the British attacked Mysore in 1799 and the country was invaded once again. Tipu and his remaining supporters fortified themselves in Seringapatam but the king was killed during the storming of the fortress. Wellesley was delighted at Tipu's death, correctly assessing it as the end of native resistance to British colonialism. Gathering a group of friends around Tipu's bullet-ridden body, he poured himself a glass of whiskey and said, "Ladies and gentlemen, I drink to the demise of India."

Tipu was something of a hero to the British; despite failed attempts to vilify him as a tyrant and religious fanatic, his courage and endurance were respected by all classes. Tippoo Sahib, as he came to be known, was the subject of several contemporary British poems and plays.

D. Forest, *Tiger of Mysore: The Life and Death of Tipu Sultan*, 1970.

K. Kaubor, *The Secret Correspondence of Tipu Sultan*, 1980.

TITIAN (Tiziano Vecelli; c.1488–1576), Italian painter of the Venetian school. Titian was born in Pieve di Cadore in the Italian Alps and apprenticed to a Venetian mosaicist when only nine years old. Although there is no surviving documentation of his activities before 1508, it is accepted that in the early 1500s he worked as an apprentice in the workshops of Giovanni Bellini and Giorgione. In 1508 he was a junior assistant to Giorgione, who had been commissioned to paint the frescoes for the facade of the Fondaco dei Tedeschi in Venice. In 1511 he received payment for his first commissioned work, frescoes of Saint Anthony for the Scuola di San Antonio in Padua. On the death of Bellini in 1516 Titian was appointed official painter of the Venetian Republic.

The death of Bellini marked a significant stage in Titian's artistic development. Prior to Bellini's death Titian's work was heavily influenced by the style and form of his master, but subsequently he began to develop his own style, which ultimately gained international recognition. In 1518 he began a series of altarpieces, starting with the *Assumption of the Virgin* for the Church of Santa Maria Gloriosa dei Frari in Venice. Although this attracted a storm of criticism from the religious community for its size, it was soon recognized as an original masterpiece. Titian continued this phase of his work with the *Madonna* of the Pesaro Family (1519–1526), also in the Frari, and the *Death of Saint Peter the Martyr* (1528–1530) for the Church of Santi Giovanni e Paolo, Venice.

During the following decade Titian concentrated on painting more natural forms and executed such masterpieces as the *Presentation of the Virgin* (1534–1538) and *Venus of Urbino* (1538). In 1533 he was appointed court painter to the Holy Roman Emperor *Charles V, who made him Count Palatine and conferred upon him the Order of the Golden Spur. Titian's fame spread and he was in great demand among the nobility for his portraits.

In 1545 Titian went to Rome as a celebrity and met with *Michelangelo. On his return to Venice he was invited to the imperial court at Augsburg, where he completed his most important portrait, that of Charles V on horseback at the Battle of Mühlberg (1548). During this period he also developed what was to become a longstanding relationship with the emperor's son, the future *Philip II of Spain. Between 1550 and 1560 he worked on a number of mythological paintings commissioned by Philip, which included the *Rape of Europa* (1559), *Venus and Adonis*, and the *Luteplayer* (1560). These mythological figures were based on classical texts from which Titian derived inspiration, while the models for his sensuous paintings were usually Venetian prostitutes.

Titian's final years were spent in Venice. Along with his friends the writer Pietro Aretino and the sculptor-architect Jacopo Sansovino, he formed the core of an elite that ruled Venice's cultural life. It was said that his home "was frequented by all the princes, learned men, and gallants of his time, for to genius he added also the most courtly manners.¢

In the later part of his life Titian would begin a painting by sketching directly onto the canvas, outlining the basic form of the figures, and then turn the canvas to the wall, often for weeks on end, periodically making critical adjustments until he was satisfied that he had eradicated all faults. Finally, he would then complete the painting, using his fingers as frequently as his brush. He continued to paint almost to his death, by which time he was probably in his mid-eighties (his birthdate is uncertain).

When Titian died, a public funeral march was planned to glorify the painter who was the most renowned master of the Venetian school. However, these plans were thwarted by the plague that then ravaged Venice. Acknowledged during his lifetime as a creative genius, Titian leaves a legacy that both influenced and reflected the development of Italian art in the sixteenth century.

U. Fasolo, *Titian*, 1980.

L. Freedman, *Titian's Independent Self-Portraits*, 1990.

D. Rosand, *Titian: His World and His Legacy*, 1982.

H. E. Wethey, *The Paintings of Titian*, 3 vols., 1969-1975.

TITO (Josip Broz; 1892-1980), Yugoslav leader. Broz was one of fifteen children of peasants living near Zagreb in Croatia. Living conditions were harsh and food was frequently in short supply, although the family was well off in relation to many other peasants, since they owned a garden and ten acres of land.

At fourteen Broz left home to work as a waiter but was then offered an apprenticeship by a locksmith and quickly learned the trade. He found employment in several German cities as well as within the Austro-Hungarian empire. From an early age he was a firm believer in socialism and was actively involved in promoting metal workers' trade unions and the Social Democratic Party.

In 1915 Broz overcame his ideological objections to World War I and served on the Russian front, winning a medal. Badly wounded, he was taken prisoner and held in Russia until 1920. Thus he was present during the heady days of the revolution and returned to Yugoslavia with a Russian wife and a strong Communist commitment.

During the 1920s and 1930s Broz lived in straitened circumstances; two of his children died as he struggled to make a livelihood. He reached a high position in the Yugoslav Communist party and became a constant irritant to the authorities. After one dramatic escape from the police, he was caught red-handed with bomb-making equipment in 1928.

Deprived of sleep and beaten under police interrogation, he nonetheless made a defiant stand in court, refusing to acknowledge any authority apart from the Communist party. His belligerence brought him to public attention but also earned him a six-year prison sentence.

Upon release, Broz resumed promoting the growth of Yugoslavian communism. He traveled abroad frequently and from 1935 to 1937 was in Moscow receiving training in Communist theory and leadership. The illegal nature of his activities within Yugoslavia led to him adopting a variety of disguises and false names — "Tito" was the name by which he became best known.

By the time of the German invasion in 1941, Tito had been chosen as Communist Party general secretary. He organized and led a ferocious partisan war against the German invaders and their Yugoslav collaborators. The struggle was bitter and merciless; several times Tito and his men were surrounded and fought their way out of German encirclement. By 1942 Tito's partisans were down to three bullets per man. As they waited for Russian supplies that never materialized, they were

Marshal Tito hears out an old peasant woman

forced to eat their horses for food and Tito fled to an island off the Yugoslav coast.

Winston *Churchill concluded that Tito was an effective ally against the Nazis and was willing to set aside political differences to help him. Supplies sent to Tito's men by Allied forces gave them the means to carry on fighting and they succeeded in liberating the country without the aid of foreign troops, founding a new Communist state in the process.

Tito had the distinction of being one of the few postwar European Communist leaders with a strong popular power base. This was confirmed by his victory in elections in 1946 and the deposing of King Peter II. The U.S. government grudgingly extended recognition to his regime "despite failure to implement the guarantees of personal freedom promised its people."

The shooting down of two U.S. planes and support for Communist subversion in Greece led to the withdrawal of American aid in 1947. Tito turned to his natural ally, the Soviet Union, for assistance, but here also there were strings attached. *Stalin wanted Tito to follow other East European leaders by making his country subservient to Russia's strategic needs, but Tito's independent nationalistic spirit led him to seek to develop Yugoslav industry and provide leadership in the Communist world himself. This was intolerable to Stalin and in 1948 Yugoslavia was expelled from Cominform (the international Communist organization) for "capitalist leanings." Despite a Russian trade boycott and threats of force, Tito remained resolute.

In 1955 the Soviet leader Nikita *Khruschev visited Yugoslavia and a reconciliation of sorts was affected, but it was short-lived; Tito's criticism of Soviet actions in Hungary in 1956 and Czechoslovakia in 1968 embittered relations once more. Now Yugoslav president, Tito oversaw increasing liberalization within the state-planned economy. His 1959 tour of African and Asian countries marked his emergence as a leader of the nonaligned nations.

With his reputation as a womanizer, his liking for fine food and drink, expensive clothes, and gaudy diamond rings, Tito remained until his death in 1980 the most nonconformist of Communist heads of state. His strong personality dominated Yugoslav politics to the exclusion of a viable alternative leadership and the Yugoslav state did not long survive his demise.

I. Banac, *With Stalin Against Tito*, 1988.
M. Djilas, *Tito*, 1980.
S. Stankovic, *The End of the Tito Era*, 1981.
Sir D. Wilson, *Tito's Yogoslavia*, 1979.

TOJO, HIDEKI (1884–1948), Japanese soldier and statesman; prime minister of Japan throughout most of World War II. His father was a Japanese career soldier and his mother the daughter of a Buddhist priest. Tojo's early life was directed toward military service. Despite an austere home life he was a spoiled child who was known as an opinionated and stubborn brawler. He was of average build, myopic, and suffered from severe acne.

In 1902 Tojo was enrolled in the military academy, where he was an unpopular student who maintained only average grades. His schoolmates nicknamed him Komisori ("razor"). The outbreak of the Russo-Japanese War in 1904 cut short his studies; at age twenty-one he left the academy with the rank of second lieutenant and was sent to serve in Manchuria. Although by that time Tojo's father was a general, Tojo's rise through the ranks was slow. He was made a full lieutenant at age twenty-three and captain at twenty-nine.

From 1919 to 1920 Tojo served as a military attaché, first in Switzerland and then in Germany. At the end of his tour of duty he returned to Japan by way of the United States. While he grew to admire the German spirit, he was disgusted by what he considered to be American decadence.

From 1928 on Tojo served as commander of the First Infantry Division. Japan invaded Manchuria on September 18, 1931, and Tojo's successful command of his division in a time of war led to further promotions. He was appointed commander of the gendarmerie at army headquarters in 1937 and served as chief of staff of the Kwangtung Army. Although sympathetic to the conspirators, Tojo did not participate in a 1936 military coup attempt. Prime Minister Fuminaro Konoye rewarded Tojo's loyalty to the regime by appointing him deputy minister of war in 1938 and minister of war in 1940.

> ### TOJO'S STATEMENT OF DEFENSE AT HIS TRIAL
>
> Never at any time did I conceive that the waging of war could be challenged by the victors as an international crime, or that regularly constituted officials of the vanquished nations would be charged individually as criminals under any recognized international agreements or under alleged violations of treaties between nations... I feel... that I did no wrong. I feel I did what was right and true.

Tojo was one of the few ministers who urged the government to reject an American ultimatum on China. Konoye, who urged talks with the Americans, was unable to withstand pressure from Tojo's faction in the government. He resigned his post and was succeeded by Tojo on October 16, 1941. Tojo pursued a pro-Axis policy which included the Greater East Asia Program promoting Japanese domination over the Pacific rim as a "liberating force." On December 7, 1941, Japan attacked Pearl Harbor, the leading American naval base in the Pacific; the following day the United States declared war on Japan. Japan also attacked Hong Kong, Malaya, Singapore, and the Philippines, extending the war throughout the Pacific. Tojo took advantage of the situation to declare himself chief of staff and minister of war and education. He had become virtual dictator of the country he now referred to as Dai Nippon, or Greater Japan.

The Japanese army, under Tojo's leadership, was no less cruel than the German army. Tojo, who hated English speakers and even attempted to purge Japanese of English loan words, was responsible for some of the most horrendous atrocities against prisoners of war during World War II. He ordered the Bataan death march, in which countless Allied troops lost their lives, and believed that prisoners should be "usefully employed," a euphemism for slave labor.

Despite early Japanese successes in battle, the Americans gradually achieved the ascendancy. Following the fall of Saipan in the Mariana Islands to American troops in 1944, Tojo was removed as chief of staff. He resigned his post as prime minister and lived in semiretirement until the American occupation in 1945. Following the occupation Tojo attempted harakiri, or ritual suicide, but was rescued by American troops who wanted him to stand trial for war crimes. Tojo, who accepted responsibility for Japanese atrocities during the war, was sentenced to death and hanged on December 23, 1948.

General Douglas *MacArthur was not content with merely executing Tojo; he felt that his remains would become a central shrine for Japanese ultranationalists. Tojo's ashes were therefore hidden and in 1955 were returned to his widow. In 1960 they were entombed with the remains of six other Japanese war criminals in a shrine known as The Tomb of the Seven Martyrs.

C. Browne, *Tojo: The Last Banzai*, 1967.
R. Storry, *A History of Modern Japan*, 1960.

TOKUGAWA IEYASU (1543–1616), military administrator and founder of a Japanese dynasty. Three strong rulers were said to have been responsible for the unification of Japan in the sixteenth century: Oda Nobunaga, *Toyotomi Hideyoshi, and Tokugawa Ieyasu. Two anecdotes illustrate the different roles they played and their personality differences. In the first, Nobunaga is said to have quarried the stones for an imaginary castle in a unified Japan, Hideyoshi to have shaped them, and Tokugawa to have laid them in place. In the second anecdote the three discuss how to make a caged canary sing. Nobunaga, said "I'll make it sing," Hideyoshi said, "I'll kill it if it doesn't sing," and Tokugawa answered, "I'll wait until it sings."

Tokugawa Ieyasu perfected the system of the shoguns, hereditary commanders of the Japanese army who, in effect, ruled the country, founded a dynasty of rulers, organized a powerful system of government that was continued by his descendants until 1868, and remained the deity of his successors for almost three hundred years. His mausoleum, huge and elaborate, is magnificently situated amid the greenery of the Nikko resort in Japan and annually attracts millions of Japanese and foreign visitors.

Ieyasu was born in a period of national strife to the noble family of Minamoto. He established a reputation as an excellent soldier and was taken on as an ally of Oda Nobunaga, a contender for the shogunate. He consistently worked to better his position and although Nobunaga was assassinated and Hideyoshi replaced him, Ieyasu continued gaining power. By the time Hideyoshi died, Ieyasu was the most powerful of the guardians of Hideyoshi's five-year old heir, Hideyori. Determined to consolidate his power through victory at the battle of Sekigahara, where he defeated rival feudal barons, he established full control

In 1603 Ieyasu made himself shogun of Japan. Two years later he abdicated in favor of his son Hidetada, thereby leaving himself free to strengthen and consolidate his family's position; he retained de facto control, treating the powerful nobles with respect, placing family members in key positions, and judiciously spending and investing his enormous wealth.

Ieyasu was primarily interested in a strong, unified, orderly Japan and identified this goal with the interests of his own family. To ensure, however, that there would be no challenge from the surviving members of Hideyoshi's family, he decided in the winter of 1614–1615 to eliminate any threat

and attacked Osaka Castle. Hideyori, his mother, and their remaining retainers committed suicide, while Ieyasu executed the last heir of Hideyoshi, his eight-year-old grandson Kunimatsu.

One year later the veteran of forty-five battles died in his sleep leaving twelve children from carefully chosen consorts, nine of them sons, to carry on his dynasty.

One of the more notable events of Ieyasu's reign was his relationship with Will Adams, the survivor of the shipwreck of a Dutch vessel, and apparently the first Englishman to reach Japan. Adams made a good impression on Ieyasu and the Englishman taught him about Europe, mathematics, navigation, and shipbuilding, and was persuaded to build him a European-style ship. Ieyasu used Adams as a diplomatic agent when Dutch and English traders began arriving in Japan, and in return gave him an estate as one of his vassals.

Adams warned Ieyasu against trade with Spain and Portugal, but the shogun wished to treat all possible trading partners impartially in the hope of benefiting from their rivalry. When Spain was slow to respond to his overtures, he became displeased and more amenable to Dutch and English trade.

Initially Ieyasu did not maintain Hideyoshi's anti-Christian policies. Toward the end of his reign, however, he grew suspicious of Japanese-Christian insurgence and began issuing anti-Christian edicts. The edicts of 1614 ordered all foreign priests out of Japan, all churches destroyed, and demanded the renunciation of faith by native Christians. The last fifteen years of his life were devoted to organizing his country, arranging for education in the system of Confucian ethics, and educating his son Hidetada to continue his work. He was interested in publishing, particularly books about Confucian studies, and had been involved in printing a political textbook.

A. C. Sadler, *The Maker of Modern Japan*, 1977.
C. D. Totman, *Tokugawa Ieyasu: Shogun*, 1983.

TOLSTOY, COUNT LEO (LEV) NIKO-LAYEVICH (1828–1910), Russian writer and philosopher. Born into an aristocratic family of landowners, Tolstoy was educated at home and in 1844 began to study law and Oriental languages at the University of Kazan. In 1847 he abandoned his studies without receiving a degree and then indulged, like other young men of his background, in a period of dissipation, broken by a naive attempt to improve the lot of his serfs by opening a school for them. Tiring of his aimless life, he joined the army in 1851 as a "junker" (a volunteer of noble birth). In 1852 he published an autobiographical work, *Childhood*, in the Russian Journal *Sovremennik (Contemporary)*. It was an immediate success and was later followed by *Boyhood* (1854) and *Youth* (1857). Tolstoy's moral and philosophical concerns are already discernible in these youthful works, which sought to reform all mankind. As a student his ideal was Jean-Jacques *Rousseau, whose portrait he wore in a medallion around his neck.

In 1854 he received his commission and requested a transfer to a regiment fighting the Turks in Wallachia. He joined the garrison of Sevastopol in November 1854, seeing active service in the Crimean War. His "Sevastopol Stories," which appeared in *Sovremennik* while the siege was still in force, caused quite a stir.

Tolstoy left the army in 1855 and went to Moscow and Saint Petersburg, where he was feted by the literary society of both cities, but bohemian life was not to his taste. He traveled abroad in 1857 and again in 1860–1861; in 1859 he once more started a school for peasant children on his estate, based on his own ideas of "free education." In 1862 he published a magazine, *Yasnaya Polyana* (Clear Fields), in which he claimed that rather than teaching the peasants, intellectuals had much to learn from them. In 1861 he became Arbiter of the Peace, a local office established to supervise the carrying out of the Emancipation Act.

Tolstoy's early diaries, from 1847, represent his first attempts at the relentless psychological analysis and quest for moral balance that were to mark his literary work as well as his private life. Most, if not all, of his writings set forth the questions he struggled with, both public and private, in his never-ending search to understand life's meaning and to come to terms with death. He did not deal with contemporary public issues beyond using them as settings. Writing for him was a way to capture reality, in the form of words. His literary style before 1880 was of the sort that has been referred to as "psychological eavesdropping," in which inner experience is dissected in such a way that the reader "recognizes" himself and which has caused *War and Peace* in particular to be hailed by many as the greatest novel ever written.

In 1862 he married Sonya Andreyeuna, an educated girl from a middle-class family. The couple lived on his family estate, Yasnaya Polyana, where over the years his wife bore him thirteen children. By all accounts the first fifteen years of marriage were happy; he devoted himself to his estate, continued his educational involvements, including the preparation of a popular reading book for schools, and wrote *The Cossacks* (1863), *War and Peace* (1865–1869), and *Anna Karenina* (1875–1877), among others. His first literary work after his marriage was the theatrical comedy *A Contaminated Family* in which a rational but meek man triumphs over his rebellious children. It was rejected by the Imperial Theater and published only after Tolstoy's death.

In the character of Lyovin in *Anna Karenina* Tolstoy has drawn an idealized self-portrait: the landowner who lives a life of good deeds and physical labor, working side by side with his serfs. Even Lyovin's unusual way of proposing marriage

Leo Tolstoy in pilgrim's garb

was based on Tolstoy's own proposal to his wife: he wrote his message down using only the first letter of each word. If she understood him, he felt, this would prove her the right partner for him.

It was while writing *Anna Karenina* that Tolstoy underwent a moral crisis sparked by a growing obsession with the idea of death (in 1876 he wrote to his

- What a strange illusion it is to suppose that beauty is goodness.
- Faith is the force of life.
- All happy families resemble one another; every unhappy family is unhappy in its own way.
- We do not love people so much for the good they have done us as for the good we have done them.
- Where is there any book of the law so clear to each man as that written on his heart?
- Boredom: the desire for desires.
- There are no conditions to which a man cannot become accustomed, especially if he sees that all those around him live in the same way.
- Write only when you leave a piece of flesh in the inkwell every time you dip your pen.

Tolstoy

friend, the poet Fet: "You are ill and think of death, and I am alive and do not cease thinking of and preparing for the same thing… "). Initially becoming more deeply attached to the Orthodox church, Tolstoy ultimately developed a humanistic belief that embraced Christian precepts of love and nonviolence and discarded theological or mystical aspects.

Tolstoy's spiritual crisis was publicly marked in his work *My Confession* (1879–1882); rejected by the Russian censor, it was circulated privately. In it he openly analyzed his own character and life and the conclusions he had drawn regarding the nature of life, religion, and death. This was followed by a series of pamphlets on rejection of state and church, private property, and the "demands of the flesh": *What Then Must We Do, What I Believe, An Examination of Dogmatic Theology, The Kingdom of God Is Within You, An Exposition of the Gospels,* and *The Christian Doctrine.* Many people were drawn to his theories of return to the simple, natural life, but there were also many others who were shocked by what they saw as blasphemy in his attacks on organized religion, and he was excommunicated in 1901. His socialist teachings attracted radicals and revolutionaries, who saw him as the "grand old man" of revolutionary theory, although they rejected his principles of nonresistance.

In *What Is Art?* (1897–1898) Tolstoy analyzed writers of all times and places. His own dislike of romanticism is clear. He criticizes *Shakespeare for being an immoral writer as well as a bad poet. *Homer, too, is classified as an immoral poet because he idealized violence. "Art," according to Tolstoy, "is that which transmits the simplest feelings of common life" and is "comprehensible to all men." Primitive folk art fits this description, while

*Pushkin, for example, does not. He criticizes his own earlier work no less harshly. One of Tolstoy's favorite stories, real "art" according to his definition, was the story of Joseph in Genesis.

The Death of Ivan Ilyich (1886) perhaps best expresses a conclusion Tolstoy's came to in *Confession,* that each man must seek and find the truth for himself when he is faced by the fundamental facts of life and death. The earlier, uncompleted, and tragic *Notes of a Madman* (1884) and the later *Master and Man* (1895) are also on the theme of an awakening to life in the face of inevitable death.

In *The Kreutzer Sonata* (1889) and *The Devil* (written in 1889 and published only after his death) Tolstoy dealt with sexual themes of obsession and jealousy. The former work, with its call for chastity within marriage as well as outside of it, was circulated privately before the censor's decision and caused a sensation. Tolstoy, unable to practice what he preached, noted in his diary; "What if another baby came? How ashamed I should be… " His wife, who also kept a diary, wrote; "If those who have read… ["The Kreutzer Sonata] could have one glimpse of [Tolstoy's] love life… they would hurl their idol down from the pedestal they have put him on." The book was not passed for publication but it had received such publicity that Tolstoy wrote an afterword attempting to explain and justify his conclusions.

Another work belonging to his period is *Resurrection* (1899), a long novel considered by many to be flawed by his insistence on preaching moral themes. To this period also belongs *Khadjhi-Murat,* a short novel about a brave caucasian warrior, which ranks among the great examples of Tolstoy's art. (1896, published posthumously 1911).

The last years of Tolstoy's life were not happy as he became increasingly estranged from his wife and family as a result of the marked changes he made in his lifestyle in an effort to live more simply and self-sufficiently. Tolstoy was hounded by a variety of self-proclaimed disciples, not all sincere or honest, who interfered in his family life. He attempted to give up his property, and money troubles became more pressing. Some of his work was only published posthumously to avoid the battles for their copyright waged by his wife. At last, ill and desperate, at the age of eighty-two, he decided to run away from home. He boarded a train, accompanied only by one of his daughters, but got no further than Astapovo, a local station, before becoming too ill to continue. He lay sick in the stationmaster's house for several days, still refusing to see his wife, until his death.

M. B. Green, *Tolstoy and Gandhi: Men of Peace,* 1983.

W. B. Korr, *The Shaburin Affair,* 1982.

T. Redpath, *Tolstoy,* 1969.

H. Troyat, *Tolstoy,* 1967.

TORQUEMADA, TOMÁS DE (1420–1498),

Spanish inquisitor general. Torquemada grew up in Valladolid, Spain, and at fourteen entered the Dominican Order. His reputation for learning and his austere piety led to his being elected prior of a monastery when he was just thirty-two. He also became one of the regular confessors of the pious Princess Isabella of Castile, later Queen *Isabella of Spain.

Torquemada's influence on Isabella was enormous. Fanatically opposed to any form of heresy, which he defined very broadly, he urged that the Pope be asked for a bull authorizing the establishment of the Inquisition in Spain. This was granted in 1480 but could only act against Christian heresies; convinced that Jews and Muslims were a heretical influence, Torquemada pushed for a holy war against Granada, the last remaining Muslim kingdom in Spain and, when it fell, sought the expulsion of both Jews and Muslims from the country.

Torquemada is best known for having shaped the Inquisition into an inescapable instrument of terror for rooting out heresy; in 1482 he became Spain's inquisitor general, first for Castile, later for Aragon and Barcelona. An extremely efficient administrator, he devoted himself to spreading the Inquisition's power throughout Spain and closing any possible loophole through which a heretic might escape: the rich and powerful were not immune, it did not matter how much time had elapsed since the heretical act was committed, and there were no extenuating circumstances.

Suspects were imprisoned and tortured into confessing. Punishments included confiscation of property, life imprisonment, or burning at the stake. Criticism or jokes about the church or church doctrine, such as commenting that the Inquisition seemed more interested in property than souls, meant the death penalty. Those who confessed and repented were "mercifully" granted a quick death before being burned. Even the dead were purged; bones of suspected heretics were dug up and burned and their property confiscated from their heirs. Voluntary confessions (including informing about suspected heresy in others) earned a pardon and a mild penance. However, if the confession was later found to contain an error or to have omitted even the smallest detail, the pardon was invalidated and the death penalty imposed.

Papal attempts to restrain the excesses were ignored by Torquemada, who said that nothing could interfere with the protection of the True Faith. In 1494 the Pope tried to limit his power by appointing four other inquisitors general, but Torquemada's reputation, Isabella's support, and King *Ferdinand's appreciation of the Inquisition's usefulness in subduing opposition meant that Torquemada remained the Inquisition's supreme authority. After his death the Inquisition softened its stance, holding mass burnings at the stake approximately once every seven years rather than once a month.

Two years after the Spanish Inquisition was abolished in 1834, Torquemada's tomb was broken open, his bones removed and burned, and his ashes scattered.

TOUSSAINT-L'OUVERTURE, FRANÇOIS-DOMINIQUE (c.1743–1803), leader of the slave revolt in Haiti. Born to an African slave in Haiti, as a boy he showed remarkable intellect, learning some French and Latin (although he preferred to speak the local patois, Creole), and mathematics. Unlike other slaves, who adhered to mystic voodoo rites, he was an ardent Catholic. His fellow slaves revered him for his abilities as a healer, but his true fascination was with military history, which he read as a child. His owners, the aristocratic de Noe family, recognized the young slave's potential and appointed him steward, and he was granted his freedom in 1777.

When the Slave Rebellion broke out in 1791, Toussaint expressed his gratitude to the de Noes by helping the family escape to America. He then joined the slaves in their struggle for emancipation, convincing them of his own conviction that he had been chosen by God to liberate the black and mulatto slaves of Haiti. An opportunity to prove himself came in 1794 when Spain, in possession of the eastern half of the island of Hispaniola (today Haiti and the Dominican Republic), invaded the French section. Toussaint led 9,000 of his followers in support of the Spanish and engaged in several successful encounters with the French. His remarkable victories earned him the epithet L'Ouverture ("The Opening") as he was always able to break through French positions. Toussaint was not, however, an advocate of Spanish hegemony; the condition of black slaves in Spanish Santo Domingo was no better than on the French half of the island. He supported Spain for military motives: the ill-trained Haitian forces had a better chance to defeat reduced French forces. Once the French were sufficiently disabled, Toussaint abandoned the Spanish and their invasion collapsed.

Following the French Revolution, slavery was abolished by the local French republicans (1793) of whom Toussaint was the acknowledged leader. The British, however, attempted to take advantage of the uncertain turn of events by invading the island. Toussaint, now promoted to the rank of brigadier general, attacked the British and forced their withdrawal in 1798. He was promoted to the rank of major general and appointed lieutenant governor of the island for his supposed victory; in fact, a yellow fever epidemic had forced the British evacuation.

With foreign threats suppressed, racial tensions on the island, flared. Léger Félicité Sonthonax, a Frenchman and radical republican stationed on the island urged Toussaint to massacre the white in-

> Toussaint, the most unhappy man of men!
> Whether the whistling Rustic tend his plough
> Within thy hearing, or thy head be now
> Pillowed in some deep dungeon's earless den;-
> O miserable Chieftain! where and when
> Wilt thou find patience? Yet die not; do thou
> Wear rather in thy bonds a cheerful brow:
> Though fallen thyself, never to rise again,
> Live, and take comfort. Thou hast left behind
> Powers that will work for thee; air, earth, and skies;
> There's not a breathing of the common wind
> That will forget thee; thou hast great allies;
> Thy friends are exultations, agonies,
> And love, and man's unconquerable mind.
>
> **William Wordsworth**
> **"To Toussaint L'Ouverture"**

habitants, but Toussaint recognized the value of the whites to the future development of the island and encouraged emigres to return. The true focus of hostilities was between blacks, led by Toussaint, and mulattoes, led by Andre Rigaud. Toussaint appealed successfully for American military and economic aid to fight the French-backed mulattoes and defeated them in 1800. Toussaint was now recognized as the most powerful individual in the colony. The "First of the Blacks," as he was now called, received a lifetime appointment as governor general.

In 1801 Toussaint invaded Spanish Santo Domingo to liberate the slaves and his successful campaign made him the de facto ruler of the entire island. He was a fair and competent leader who encouraged economic growth and hindered any attempts at dividing the inhabitants along racial lines. He abhorred atrocities, such as those committed during the island's lengthy wars, and had all perpetrators executed.

While Haiti flourished, France was coming under the influence of *Napoleon Bonaparte, who wanted to reintroduce slavery. Troops, commanded by Napoleon's brother-in-law General Charles Leclerc, were sent to restore French rule on the island. Even as competent a general as Leclerc, however, was unable to defeat the wily rebel leader, while a yellow fever epidemic threatened Leclerc's own men. Forgoing a military victory, Leclerc invited Toussaint to discuss the island's future, promising to renounce slavery if the rebels would lay down their arms. Toussaint agreed to attend the meeting, not suspecting that it was a trap, and was arrested imprisoned, and shipped to the French Alps. He died in captivity in 1803, but the revolutionary fervor he had ignited did not die. His legacy was carried on by his former partners-in-arms, Jean-Jacques Dessalines and Henri Christophe. Haiti achieved independence in 1804.

C. L. R. James, *The Black Jacobins: Toussaint-L'Ouverture and the Santo Domingo Revolution*, 1963.
R. Korngold, *Citizen Toussaint*, 1944.

TOYOTOMI HIDEYOSHI (1537–1598), Japanese statesman. Hideyoshi, born the son of peasants in Owari, Japan, achieved fame and became dictator of his country. No caste system existed in Japan at that time but even so, it was rare for a peasant to rise out of his class. At the age of fifteen, Hideyoshi left home to become servant to a vassal and later entered the service of the warlord Nobunaga as a sandal holder.

Hideyoshi won Nobunaga's recognition and rose in rank, eventually becoming a general. Nobunaga was involved in a campaign to unify Japan and bring its warlords and provinces under his rule. He had subdued thirty-two out of thirty-six provinces when, cornered in battle, he killed himself. Hideyoshi went to Kyoto, the capital, and killed in battle the generals, including Nobunaga's son, who challenged him for succession to the leadership. By 1590 he had subdued the remaining warring provinces and all warlords except one, *Tokugawa Ieyasu, capitulated completely to his rule, becoming his vassals.

Hideyoshi made a treaty with Ieyasu, solidifying the relationship by adopting Ieyasu's son, letting Ieyasu marry his sister, and giving him eight provinces as well as making Ieyasu his successor. Hideyoshi was given the title of *kampaku* (regent) in 1585 and *dajo daijin* (chancellor) in 1586. He also wanted the shogunate, but since that was traditionally given to members of a different clan, he gave up his quest for that title after becoming chancellor.

Hideyoshi was a cruel and vicious ruler, greatly feared by his vassals. A Jesuit missionary, Luis Frois, wrote of him that, "He is so feared and obeyed that with no less ease than a father of a family disposes of the persons of his household he rules the principal kings and lords of Japan." As an example of his cruelty the story is told of how, after vandals wrote abusive remarks on his gate, he had eight random townspeople arrested, had their noses cut off, then their ears and, finally, impaled them upside down on swords.

In 1587 Hideyoshi, who had previously been very tolerant of Christian missionaries, turned against them and issued a decree ordering them out of the country and forbidding converts to proselytize. He was critical of the Christian-run slave trade and of the eating of meat — a custom introduced by Christians — and issued decrees against both practices.

Wishing to establish a great East Asian empire, Hideyoshi launched an unsuccessful invasion of Korea, thinking he could subdue it as easily as he had subdued the Japanese provinces. He once told a Jesuit that "his sole ambition was to leave a great name behind him after his death, for which reason he had resolved to cross the sea at the head of a vast expeditionary force with the object of conquering Korea and China." After his troops were met by Chinese forces sent into Korea to stop him, he negotiated with the Chinese for two years, unable to reach a peace settlement. When he realized that the Chinese were not going to capitulate to his demands, he sent another force to invade, but died before the campaign was concluded.

Hideyoshi's domestic policies aimed at returning order to the war-ravaged country and at restoring the class-conscious social order. He issued proclamations ordering peasants, many of whom had left their farms during the warlord era, to turn in their weapons and return to the land. He reinstated sharp distinctions among the four classes: samurai, merchant, artisan, and peasant, and bound peasants to the land as serfs. He ordered a nationwide survey of population and wealth so that he could set tax rates, held firm control over gold and silver mines, and closely controlled the nation's merchants.

N. E. Berry, *Hideyoshi*, 1972.

TRAJAN (Marcus Ulpius Traianus; 53–117), Roman emperor. Trajan succeeded the Emperor Nerva, whose brief rule had aroused the resentment of the Praetorian Guard. Besieged and humiliated, Nerva looked for a successor able to control both the Guards and discontented frontier commanders in revolt. He chose Trajan, a respected and honored general in charge of Rome's armies in Cologne, adopted him as his son and died several months later in 98. Trajan continued his work on the frontier, summoning the rebellious frontier leaders to him one by one. They never returned.

Trajan, originally from Spain, was a soldier by profession and by nature. He was forty when he became emperor of a Rome weakened by moral decay. Sexual freedom had replaced political freedom. The poor lived off corn doled out to keep them quiet and passive, while the rich wallowed in decadent luxuries, unwilling to assume civic responsibilities. Senators wanted prestige without responsibility. Foreigners poured into Rome, making overcrowding a serious problem at the same time that family limitation practices combined with plague and malaria to seriously reduce the native population. Peasant families, dispossessed by the expansion large estates, migrated to the city to live off the dole.

Trajan arrived in Rome two years after being appointed emperor. In typically modest manner, he walked through the streets of Rome toward the Senate. His wife Plotina, by her very appearance an example of earlier strict Roman family virtues, walked by his side. He promised the Senate that he would not threaten but respect it and be its servant, not its master. He kept that promise and found that he could wield almost absolute power if he observed the forms of deferring to the Senate.

A conscientious administrator, he required an equal devotion from senators who wished to enjoy his favor. The rich began to work at the tasks of government. To encourage the birth of more children, Trajan expanded the corn dole so that both children and parents received their own doles, and extended the *alimentia* established by Nerva (a monthly state subsidy for each child of Italian peasant families). He helped the peasants keep their lands by establishing a state fund of low-interest loans; his careful financial management of the Empire, starting with the personal example of his household, placed its economy on a sound basis.

Rome had been paying Dacia (roughly equivalent to modern Romania) tribute in return for peace for fifteen years and Trajan refused to pay anymore; in 101 he set out to conquer Dacia. The two Dacian wars (101–102 and 105–107) resulted in the annexation of Dacia and eventually the creation in Rome of the still-standing Column of Trajan, carved with realistic reliefs commemorating incidents in the Dacian wars in a spiral style, each scene melting into the next. Roman culture was based upon that of Greece, but the realistic style of these carvings was far more expressive of the Roman character than was the classical Greek style.

War booty and Dacia's gold mines enabled Trajan to build extensively without raising taxes, countering demobilization unemployment. Trajan built or improved aqueducts, harbors, bridges, roads, canals, tunnels, and public buildings and aided disaster-stricken cities. His first priority was Rome, then Italy, and finally the provinces, which he saw as a source of wealth to be milked for Rome. Rome provided the provinces with order, economic security, and protection against their enemies in return for providing Rome with specific goods and taxes that were no more burdensome than those they had paid to their own preconquest rulers.

Essentially a man of war, Trajan experienced six years of peace and administrative duties as quite enough. In 113 he set out on a campaign of imperial conquest against Parthia, sweeping through Armenia, Assyria, and Mesopotamia to the Indian Ocean, creating new provinces as he went. Massive Jewish-led rebellions broke out and were put down with great force and bloodshed. Unable to consolidate his conquests because of ill health, he died at the age of sixty-four.

The new emperor, Hadrian, was Trajan's nephew, but incompatibility between Trajan's straightforward nature and Hadrian's complex personality prevented Trajan from adopting Hadrian as his heir; Hadrian's appointment as Trajan's successor was contrived by Plotina after Trajan's death.

B. W. Henderson, *Five Roman Emperors*, 1927.
T. Rossi, *Trajan's Column and the Dacian Wars*, 1972.

TROTSKY, LEON (Lev Davidovich Bronstein; 1879–1940), Russian revolutionary. Of Ukrainian Jewish origin, he was infected with the revolutionary fervor that broke out in Russia in 1896 and joined friends to set up the South Russian Workers' Union in Odessa, where he was a student. Arrested in 1898, he was imprisoned for two years (where he first encountered the writings of Vladimir *Lenin) before being sentenced to four years' exile in Siberia with his wife Aleksandra Sokolovshaya, who had also been active in the union.

There he met others who were to play a role in the Soviet system, and wrote for local papers, formulating his own theories and drawing closer to Marxism in the process. Trotsky was disturbed by the lack of cohesion in the rapidly growing revolutionary movement both in Russia and abroad. From material smuggled to him in Irkutsk, he heard of Lenin's Marxist journal, *Iskra* (*The Spark*) and his book, *What Is To Be Done*, which called for a central, professional body of revolutionaries. Trotsky's response was immediate: with two years still to serve, he escaped to Samara to join the new task. He had papers in the name of "Trotsky," which he later said he had selected at random although he had apparently had a jailer by that name in his first prison. His wife and two small daughters remained behind and the separation became permanent.

Joining the *Iskra* circle in Samara, he worked on its behalf until summoned to Zurich, and later to London, where he met Lenin and other members of his revolutionary circle. Sent abroad to lecture, he met and married his second wife, the revolutionist Natalia Sedova, in Paris in 1903.

In 1903 Lenin, urged by the board of *Iskra*, reluctantly transferred its editorial office to Geneva, along with Trotsky, whom he supported and encouraged in order to ensure himself a majority on the board. However, differences of opinion developed between Lenin and his associates, and the resulting split disturbed Trotsky greatly, ideologically attracted as he was to the side opposing Lenin.

The Russian Social Democrat Party now consisted of two factions, Menshevik (minority) and Bolshevik (majority). At first a Menshevik, Trotsky drifted away from them, but by the end of 1904 he concluded that the only solution was a workers' revolution and general strike; this stand took him still further from the Menshevik position.

"Bloody Sunday," the Saint Petersburg workers' march in 1905 led by a priest and brutally suppressed by *Nicholas II, brought Trotsky back to Russia. Sedova was arrested in May and Trotsky fled to Finland, where he put the final touches to his theory: the revolution, based as it was on the land question, could be carried out only by the workers and peasants under the leadership of the Social Democrats, and would result in the formation of a provisional government consisting mainly of the proletariat. He returned to Saint Petersburg in October 1905 on hearing that a general strike had started, helping to form the city's *soviet* (council of workers' deputies), most of whose decisions he shaped. He also started a newspaper, *Nachalo* (Beginning).

After the abortive 1905 revolution he was, in 1907, sentenced again to Siberian exile. However, on the way there he decided to escape; this sentence, unlike the first, was for an unspecified period. Making part of the return journey on deerback through blizzards, he doubled back to Saint Petersburg, where he, Sedova, and their two sons took the train for Finland. He then went to London for the party congress held there in 1907, and to Berlin. Supporting himself by journalism and by writing a book on German social democracy, he continued formulating his theories and attending socialist congresses throughout Europe. In 1908 he also began publishing a Russian language paper, *Pravda*.

In 1912, Trotsky was sent by a radical Kiev paper to cover the Balkan war, and he eventually traveled to the United States in January 1917. News of the Bolshevik revolution soon broke out and Trotsky sailed for Russia; the family was feted on arrival in Petrograd.

After a tumultuous few months, Trotsky was arrested by Aleksandr Kerensky, leader of the Russian Liberal government; released, he was made head of the Petrograd Soviet. Trotsky abandoned his theories to become one of Lenin's "lieutenants." As such, he played a key supporting role in the October revolution and its aftermath, the civil war.

Lenin offered him a central position in his new government but Trotsky's sensitivity to his Jewish origins led him to take the post of minister for foreign affairs. Lenin sent him to Brest-Litovsk to sign the treaty with Germany, with instructions to draw out the process in the hope that, given enough time, the revolution would spread to Germany and bring the war between Germany and Russia, which had begun in 1914, to an end without Russian territorial concessions. Using brilliant debating techniques, Trotsky kept negotiations dragging on from December 1917 to February 1918, until the Germans lost patience, invaded Russia, and forced Lenin to accept their harsh terms.

Its part in World War I now over, Russia faced civil war and counterrevolution. Appointed military commissar in 1918, he spent the two years of the civil war in a train traveling from base to base,

Leon Trotsky

organizing the Red Army and delivering stirring speeches to persuade thousands of reluctant conscripts that to avoid military service was tantamount to desertion.

While struggling to reorganize, reeducate the people, and run essential services, the new rulers of Russia adhered to their pattern of internal debate; meanwhile, Joseph *Stalin, a comparatively unknown outsider, was consolidating his power base. Until Lenin's death in 1924, Trotsky's relations with Stalin were strained at best, but as he gradually resumed his former internationalist tendencies in opposition to Stalin's views, matters grew worse. Within five years of Lenin's death, Trotksy had lost both party membership and citizenship.

Expelled from the USSR in 1929 after a year of exile in Turkestan, Trotsky began another period of wandering in Turkey, France, and Norway. In 1936 the Soviet government obtained his expulsion from Norway when he and his son Leon were "linked" with anti-Stalin plots in the 1930s Moscow show trials. Trotsky and his wife sailed to Mexico, which had offered him asylum. His son Sergei was arrested later in the Soviet Union and died in a concentration camp; in February 1938 Leon died mysteriously in Paris.

In Mexico City Trotsky resumed writing, including an unfinished work on Stalin and a treatise on revolutionary art with André Breton and Diego Rivera. He founded the Fourth International, a group devoted to pure communism, and continued to be a vociferous opponent of Stalin. Several Stalin-directed attacks were made on his life before a Spanish Communist armed with an ice pick succeeded in killing him in his home.

M. Agursky, *The Third Rome*, 1987.

P. Beilharz, *Trotsky, Totskyism and the Transition to Socialism*, 1987.

R. V. Daniels, *Trotsky, Stalin, and Socialism*, 1991.

A. M. Glotzar, *Trotsky*, 1989.

TRUMAN, HARRY S. (1884–1972), thirty-third president of the United States (1945–1953). Born in Lamar, Missouri, Truman's middle initial "S" resulted from his parents' indecision as to which grandfather to name him after, since both had names starting with S. In 1890 the Truman family moved to Independence, Missouri. Truman was unable to participate in sports because of poor eyesight and turned to playing the piano and reading books for relaxation. Family finances made it impossible for him to attend college, and he was rejected from West Point due to his eyesight. At twenty-two, after working for a railroad and later for two bands, he returned to his roots, taking over the management of his maternal grandfather's farm at Grandview. He remained with the farm for eleven years, during which time he began his political involvement by becoming active in the Democratic party and joining several organizations.

SAYINGS OF HARRY S. TRUMAN

- Men don't change. The only thing new in the world is the history you don't know.
- The best way to give advice to your children is to find out what they want and advise them to do it.
- The Un-American Activities Committee was the most Un-American thing in America.
- It's a recession when your neighbor loses his job; it's a depression when you lose yours.
- The atomic bomb is another powerful weapon in the arsenal of the righteousness.
- A politician is a man who understands government and it takes a politician to run a government. A statesman is a politician who's been dead ten or fifteen years.
- Whenever you have an efficient government, you have a dictatorship.
- If you can't convince them, confuse them.
- The White House is the finest jail in the world.
- The greatest epitaph in the country is in Tombstone, Arizona. It says "Here lies Jack Williams. He done his damndest." That's the greatest epitaph a man can have.
- My choice early in life was either to be a piano-player in a whorehouse or a politician. And to tell the truth, there's hardly any difference.

Harry Truman fishing

Truman's life changed drastically with World War I. He was commissioned as a captain in the National Guard and commanded a field artillery battery in France. He was involved in some major battles toward the end of the war and discovered that he had leadership talents; his men regarded him with affection and esteem and helped him in later years. When the war ended, Truman joined veterans' organizations and the army reserve and rose to the rank of colonel.

Returning home, Truman married his childhood sweetheart, Elizabeth (Bess) Wallace, and became a partner in a Kansas City haberdashery store, which failed. Shortly after, he entered politics with the help of Democratic leader Thomas Prendergast. In 1922 Truman was elected judge of the Jackson county court, but was not reelected in 1924. In 1926, however, he became presiding judge of the county court and was reelected in 1930. After eight years in county administration, he had achieved state-wide power and had a reputation for honesty and good management. Nevertheless, Prendergast refused to back him for governor in 1932 and did not allow him to participate as a delegate to the Democratic National Convention.

Truman thought his political career was finished, but in 1934 he accepted Prendergast's offer to run for the U.S. Senate, even though he was Prendergast's fourth choice. Truman won the election, entering the Senate in 1935. He worked under the cloud of being identified with and influenced by Prendergast, who was thought of as a crooked politician. However, Truman overcame the objections of his critics and in 1938, authored the Civil Aeronautics Act, as well as other legislation in 1940. Running as the underdog, he won re-election in a tough three-man race, by a small majority.

At the beginning of his second term Truman launched his major senatorial endeavor. His special committee investigating national defense exposed graft, waste, and inferior military products; this exposé brought him public acclaim. During this period, he was able to return previous political favors received from Robert E. Hannegan, who was appointed Democratic National Convention chairman in 1944. Hannegan and others convinced President F. D. *Roosevelt to drop vicePresident Henry A. Wallace for the fourth term and replace him with Harry S. Truman.

When Roosevelt died on April 12, 1945, Truman was thrust into the presidency after only eighty-two days experience as vice president. He only met with Roosevelt twice during that period and had little knowledge of the administration's programs and plans. When Truman took office, the universal feeling was that an era had ended and that a "courthouse politician" had succeeded a world figure. Very quickly, despite Truman's lack of knowledge and experience, he was forced into making many decisions including being involved in making final arrangements for the charter-writing meeting of the United Nations, and helping to arrange Germany's surrender on May 8, 1945. In July he attended the Potsdam Conference for the drafting of the peace settlement. It was Truman who made the decision to drop the two atomic bombs on Japan which led to Japanese surrender on September 2, 1945.

During his first five months in office Congress was very supportive. However, that changed in 1945 when he selected his own cabinet. Roosevelt's supporters were defeated in the 1946 congressional election and Republicans took the majority in Congress. Despite opposition, Truman was able to check Soviet imperialism and the developing Chinese problem. He was also able to rally the free world and see to it that Greece and Turkey received the necessary aid so that they did not succumb to communism. This program was known as the Truman Doctrine. The Marshall Aid Plan went into effect under his leadership, as did the North Atlantic Treaty Organization and the Point Four foreign technical aid program. His internal program, directed at full employment, increased social security, and opposition to racial discrimination, was dubbed the Fair Deal.

In 1948 everybody, including the Democratic leaders, felt that Truman could not be reelected. Truman was viewed as weak compared to Roosevelt. He, however, ran with Senator Alban W. Barkley as his running mate and beat Governor Thomas E. Dewey by a 114-electoral vote margin. He won with his "give 'em hell" campaign, whistle-stopping all over the country, and denouncing the Republican Congress as the "do nothing" Congress. One of the highlights of his second administration was his dismissal of General Douglas *MacArthur for insubordination for publicly advocating an attack on China.

While in office, Truman assumed full responsibility for his decisions, proudly displaying the sign "The Buck Stops Here" on his desk. Whereas he accepted and responded to criticism himself, he would not tolerate criticism of his daughter Margaret, an aspiring singer who was a favorite target of the press. When he left the presidency in 1953, Harry Truman became a very popular public figure. A warm and loving family man, he took great pride in his daughter and her four sons. In addition, he wrote *Year of Decision, 1946–1952: Years of Trial and Hope*, and *Mr. Citizen*.

E. A. Ayers, *Truman in the White House*, 1991.
R. D. Burns, *Harry S. Truman*, 1984.
R. Jenkins, *Truman*, 1986.
D. McCullough, *Truman*, 1992.

TU FU (712–770), Chinese poet of the T'ang period. Tu Fu was born in Shao-ling near the T'ang dynastys capital of Changan. Although not wealthy, his scholarly family was of noble blood. As a child, Tu Fu showed remarkable progress in his studies, and he approached the imperial examinations expecting to win high honors and a prominent position in the governing bureaucracy, but to everyone's surprise, he failed. This failure seemed inexplicable, although it is possible that he was too sanguine about his presumed success; it has also been said that Tu Fu's skills were far too advanced for the needs of a clerk. A second attempt by Tu Fu met with similar failure, although this time the fault was clearly not his. A corrupt minister failed all candidates to prove that all the best minds were already in government service. Despite his repeated rejection, Tu Fu was determined to succeed; he eventually entered the imperial service with a special dispensation offered to outstanding candidates.

Tu Fu regarded himself as a disciple of the contemporary poet *Li Po. The two met briefly and even carried on a correspondence of sorts. Li Po was obviously impressed with Tu Fu's compositions, although his early work hardly reached the zenith that Tu Fu was later to achieve. China then prospered under Emperor Hsuan Tsung. Poets, whose work in that period was more akin to present-day social commentators or journalists, found little to criticize in such an affluent period. Only after the death of Hsuan Tsung's consort did China enter the turbulent period that so influenced Tu Fu's poetry. Hsuan Tsung fell victim to the amorous pleasures of his son's concubine, neglecting affairs of state, and the country was plunged into turmoil. General An Lu-shan led a successful revolt against the emperor and Hsuan Tsung fled

---

> ### "LOOKING AT THE SPRINGTIME"
>
> In fallen States
> Hills and streams are found,
> Cities have Spring,
> Grass and leaves abound;
>
> Though at such times
> Flowers might drop tears,
> Parting from mates,
> Birds have hidden fears:
>
> The beacon fires,
> Have now linked three moons
> Making home news
> Worth ten thousand coins;
>
> An old grey head
> Scratched at each mishap
> Has Dwindling hair,
> Does not fit its cap!
>
> **Tu Fu**

---

the capital in 756. Tu Fu was captured by the rebel forces and enslaved for over a year. Although he had served in the Ministry of Works, his lowly status there did not merit his execution by the rebels. He eventually managed to escape his captivity, but the scars remained with him for the rest of his life and influenced his later poetry.

By the time of Tu Fu's escape, Hsuan Tsung had abdicated in favor of his son Su-tsung. Tu Fu joined Su-tsung at his temporary capital of Feng-hsiang and was appointed to a position in the emperor's entourage, but did not hold it for long as his frequent criticisms of the new emperor reduced his popularity. Tu Fu even risked losing his head at one point for his nagging defense of a companion in the emperor's disfavor. When Tu Fu wished to visit his family after several years absence, Su-tsung suggested that he ought not return to court. Tu Fu, who was in any case bored with government intrigues, gladly accepted the emperor's offer of retirement and spent his final years composing poetry as he wandered down the Yangtze River.

During his final years Tu Fu he had no regular income and remained unrecognized as a poet; his family was therefore plunged into poverty. One son died of starvation and Tu Fu was unable to find work to support his remaining children. He suffered from consumption, which eventually killed him. Only after his death was his poetry recognized for its greatness. Its somber moods reflect the essence of Tu Fu's own tormented life as he strove for recognition.

A. Cooper, *Li Po and Tu Fu*, 1973.
W. Hung, *Tu Fu: China's Greatest Poet*, 1952.

TUBMAN, HARRIET (c.1820–1913), escaped slave, abolitionist, and Union spy. Harriet Tubman was born a slave in Dorchester, Maryland; her given name was Araminta Ross. Separated from her mother when only ten years old, she received no education and remained illiterate throughout her life. She was to learn weaving but instead spent her time watching rat traps. A later attempt to teach her a trade was a similar failure, so Tubman was sent to work in the fields with the men. Once asked to help tie down a fellow slave for a thrashing, she refused; incensed by her impudence, her master threw a heavy iron weight at her head. The injury was permanent; even in her most active period she suffered from losses of consciousness, sometimes in midsentence.

In 1844 Harriet's master married her to John Tubman, whose name she assumed. Although it was stated in her master's will that his slaves would receive their freedom upon the deaths of himself and his immediate heirs, his death and that of his only son prompted the family to sell his slaves. Harriet Tubman refused to be put on auction. In 1849 she ran away, making her way to Auburn, New York, where she worked as a cook and a laundress. She also became active in the abolitionist movement. Her piercing eyes, deep voice, love of singing and oft-repeated motto, "Mah people mus' go free," endeared her to crowds in New York and Boston. Despite her illiteracy she contributed to the *National Anti-Slavery Standard*, and befriended such important abolitionists as John Brown, the essayist Ralph Waldo Emerson, and the novelist Louisa May Alcott.

Tubman's greatest role was as a conductor of the Underground Railroad, an abolitionist network helping slaves to escape to the North and Canada. After earning enough money for the fare, Tubman would travel south to guide slaves to their freedom. She took only the weakest who could no longer endure the hardships of their bondage. In nineteen trips she succeeded in helping over three hundred slaves — including her aged parents – to escape. Tubman became known as *Moses and her followers were "the black wool she had come to gather." The trips were carried out with considerable danger; there was a sizable reward, at one point reaching $40,000, for her arrest, yet neither she nor any of her followers was ever caught. Tubman was a large woman who was able to lift a heavy man and run with him. She always carried a pistol and frequently reminded her anxious followers that, "Dead Negroes tell no tales." Messages with obscure hints, such as "The good ship Zion will arrive shortly," were sent to elderly slaves prior to her appearance. She generally planned escapes for Saturday nights since no announcements of escaped slaves could be prepared until Monday. Routes were never planned in advance; Tubman would often knock on the doors of unsuspecting Quakers and other sympathizers late at night, asking them to harbor the fugitives.

Tubman was aware of the dangers she faced and was often saved by her own ingenuity. Traveling north on a train she heard her name mentioned. Turning around, she saw a placard advertising a 5,000 dollar reward for her capture. Tubman covered her face with her bonnet, remaining that way until the next station, where she got off and took a train back south to avoid suspicion by crossing state lines. Getting off near her hometown, she bought chickens and limped, pretending to be an elderly slave. She even passed her old master, who failed to recognize her.

During the Civil War Tubman served in the Union army as a nurse; her cure for dysentery, made from local roots, saved countless lives. Because of her intimate knowledge of the countryside she frequently served as a scout and spy, often infiltrating enemy lines to collect information on troop movements and numbers. Although her reputation in the Underground Railroad won her considerable fame, common soldiers often failed to recognize Tubman. On her final voyage north, accompanying a group of wounded Union soldiers, she was told by a conductor that she would not be allowed to travel with the soldiers in the first class coach. A scuffle ensued in which Tubman's arm was broken and she was thrown into a baggage compartment.

After the war Tubman returned to Auburn, where she founded a shelter for needy blacks. A biography, written by Sarah Bradford in 1869, made her something of a celebrity, yet, at the time of her death in 1913 Tubman was still struggling with the federal government to obtain a military pension.

S. Bradford, *Harriet Tubman: The Moses of Her People*, 1889, reprinted 1961.

H. Buckmaster, *Let My People Go: The Story of the Underground Railroad and the Growth of the Abolitionist Movement*, 1949.

TURGENEV, IVAN SERGEYEVICH (1818–1883), Russian writer. Born in Orel to a wealthy and aristocratic family, Turgenev witnessed the cruel injustice of the serf system by his despotic mother's treatment of the family serfs. He spent some time at the universities of Saint Petersburg and Moscow, completing his education at the University of Berlin from 1838 to 1841. These experiences outside Russia served to "europeanize" him and set the stage for his later move to France, where he spent much of his life.

He began his writing career in 1838 with verse, continuing until 1845. His first published poem ("Parasha," 1843) was greeted with acclaim and won him the friendship and patronage of Vissarion Belinsky, the critic, journalist, and radical thinker who was to discover Fyodor *Dostoyevsky. After 1845 he turned to writing short prose works that demonstrated a deep understanding of his generation.

In 1845 an event had occurred that was to have a deep effect on Turgenev. He quarreled with his mother, whom he had angered by failing to secure a post at the university of Saint Petersburg, by having left the civil service after two years to devote himself to literature, and by his love for the opera singer Pauline Garcia (Viardot). His mother stopped giving him money and until her death he lived on his earnings as a writer. In 1847 he followed Mme. Viardot abroad and lived with her and her husband and children (the relationship may have been platonic), only returning to Russia in 1850 upon his sadistic, eccentric mother's death, when he inherited her fortune.

From 1847 Turgenev published in *Sovremennik* (now edited by the poet Nikolai Nekrasov) a series of short stories dealing with the gentry, the peasants, and the serfs subtitled "From a Hunter's Sketches," which developed into *A Sportsman's Sketches* (1852). A triumph of psychological insight, the stories were an immediate success. When he wrote a piece lamenting the death of Gogol — which the government for political reasons was seeking to play down — he was arrested and sentenced to eighteen months of house arrest on his country estate, from 1852 to 1853. On his return to Saint Petersburg in 1853 he enjoyed several years as the uncrowned leader of literature in the city and spokesman of the reformist trend. This period, encompassing the early years of Alexander II's reign, was the summer of his literary popularity.

Turgenev also wrote plays during this period, only one of which was passed by the censor for performance, but the experience contributed to his artistic development, culminating in *A Month in the Country*, a forerunner of the work of Anton *Chekhov. Completed in 1855, the play was not staged until 1872; however, not until Konstantin Stanislavsky presented it in 1909 was it recognized as a masterpiece.

Turgenev's succeeding works appeared to great acclaim. His novels *Rudin* (1856), *A Nest of Gentlefolk* (1859), and *On the Eve* (1860) painted portraits of contemporary types and outlined problems of Russian society; influential thinkers and journalists made extensive use of his works in their own diatribes. *On the Eve* (i.e., of reform), in particular, aroused widespread interest and debate; people argued about the characters as if they were real. Critics noted that when Turgenev had depicted a man of action he had made him a Bulgarian, not a Russian; his reactions to the criticism came in his masterpiece *Fathers and Sons* (1862), with the powerful figure of Bazarov, his strong-willed "man of action." It was a brilliant picture of the young nihilists (a term coined by Turgenev) of the time, but was greeted with indignation by the younger radicals, as Turgenev believed in gradual reform rather than revolution. It was not well received and Turgenev, sensitive to the views of his friends, even contemplated destroying the manuscript. In the following years he wrote little and never returned to live in Russia for any length of time.

Fathers and Sons had also caused his breach with Leo *Tolstoy. Turgenev had given Tolstoy the still-unpublished novel to read before he left for Europe; Tolstoy began reading it immediately, but fell asleep, and Turgenev left Tolstoy's house without saying anything. However, the following day he picked a quarrel with Tolstoy, who wrote him a note challenging him to a duel, which Turgenev received only after he had arrived in Paris. While they never fought, the breach in their friendship lasted for seventeen years, and was only healed superficially at Tolstoy's initiative.

Although only forty-three, Turgenev felt he had passed the peak of his achievement; the rest of his life was comparatively uneventful. After the Franco-Prussian war, the Viardot ménage moved to Paris, where Turgenev concentrated on writing memoirs and stories based on his early experiences, with two exceptions, *Smoke* (1867), which satirized both the reactionary aristocrats and the radicals, and *Virgin Soil* (1887), on the revolutionary movement of his time.

In Paris Turgenev enjoyed the company of leading writers and attended regular dinners with Gustav Flaubert, Émile *Zola, Edmond Goncourt, and Alphonse Daudet, who called the occasions "the dinners of the authors who have been hissed." There, too, Turgenev enjoyed the popularity and renown he had lost in Russia and was elected vicepresident of an international literary congress (Paris, 1878); he received an honorary doctorate from Oxford in 1879. To crown these achievements, the return to "esthetics" in Russia in the late 1870s brought a revival of his former popularity, and his last visit there, in 1880, was a triumph, although he commented, "I realize they are not honoring me but using me as a stick with which to beat the government."

Turgenev's last work, *Poems in Prose* (1879–1882; originally called *Senilia*), is a set of short pieces, some almost like fables, expressing a pessimistic view of life, nature, and human frailty.

Despite his having been a spokesman of the enthusiasm for progress and reform that gripped Russian society, as well as the first Russian writer to become popular in the West, his writing was marked by a certain detachment and lack of passion. Although he wrote love stories, his personal life seems to have been restricted in passionate attachments. He never married, retaining his youthful infatuation for Mme Viardot, who brought up the daughter born to him by a peasant girl who lived on his estate at Spasskoye. Turgenev died in France, an old bachelor still cared for by Mme. Viardot, and was buried in Saint Petersburg.

H. Troyat, *Turgenyev*, 1988.
P. Waddington, *Turgenyev and England*, 1981.

TWAIN, MARK (pseudonym of Samuel Langhorne Clemens; 1835–1910), American writer. Born in Florida, Missouri, he received a basic education in Hannibal, Missouri, but after his father's death in 1847 became a printer's apprentice. He later began to write for his brother's paper, the *Hannibal*

- When angry, count four; when very angry, swear.
- Familiarity breeds contempt — and children.
- When in doubt, tell the truth.
- A one-horse town.
- To eat is human, to digest, divine.
- Reader, suppose you were an idiot. And suppose you were a member of Congress. But I repeat myself.
- I did not attend his funeral; but I sent a nice letter saying I approve of it.
- The reports of my death are greatly exaggerated (after his obituary appeared in his lifetime).
- Everyone talks about the weather but no one does anything about it.
- An ethical man is a Christian holding four aces.
- The coldest winter I ever spent was a summer in San Francisco.
- The holy passion of Friendship is so sweet and steady and loyal and enduring a nature that it will last a whole lifetime, if not asked to lend money.
- They spell it "Vinci" and pronounce it "Vinchy"; foreigners always spell better than they pronounce.
- Man is the only animal that blushes, or needs to.
- There is a sumptuous variety about New England's weather... In the spring I have counted 136 different kinds of weather within twenty-four hours.
- By trying we can easily learn to endure adversity. Another man's.
- It usually takes me three weeks to prepare a good impromptu speech.

Mark Twain

A Mark Twain poster announcing his performance

Journal, as well as working as a journeyman printer and then a steamboat pilot on the Mississippi, until the Civil War stopped all travel on the river.

He served briefly as a Confederate volunteer before moving on to the silver mines of Nevada in 1861. In 1862 he became a reporter on the Virginia City (Nevada) *Enterprise* and in 1863 began using the pen name Mark Twain, a phrase meaning "two fathoms deep" used by the leadsmen of Mississippi river boats when they took soundings.

In 1864 Clemens moved to San Francisco, where he began to take part in the activities of a group of well-known writers who contributed to the distinguished newspaper and literary journal, *Golden Era*. With the publication of his humorous sketch of frontier life, "The Celebrated Jumping Frog of Calaveras County" in 1865, he earned his first national recognition as a writer.

Clemens traveled in the United States and Europe in 1867 and his experiences in France, Italy, and the Holy Land were recounted in *Innocents Abroad* (1869), notable for the author's irreverence toward certain aspects of European and religious culture that awed the impressionable American tourist.

In 1879 Clemens married and settled in Hartford, Connecticut, where he was able to build an impressive mansion with the proceeds from his first book and support from his new wife's wealthy family. He lived there for twenty years, with his wife and their three daughters, until disastrous investments forced the family to give up the house and move to Europe.

The years in Hartford were a fruitful period for Twain, during which he published *Roughing It* (1872), an account of his early adventures as a miner and journalist; *The Gilded Age* (1873), a satire on post-Civil War days, written with Charles Dudley Warner; *The Adventures of Tom Sawyer* (1876); *A Tramp Abroad* (1880); *The Prince and the Pauper* (1882); *Life on the Mississippi* (1883), an autobiographical account of his experiences as a river pilot; *The Adventures of Huckleberry Finn* (1884); *A Connecticut Yankee at King Arthur's Court* (1889), and other works.

In 1884 Twain became a partner in the publishing firm of Charles W. Webster and Co., which was initially profitable when it published the *Memoirs of General Grant* and the *Life of Pope Leo XIII*, but subsequently went into bankruptcy (1894), requiring Twain to make a worldwide lecture tour to pay off his debts; *Following The Equator* was the literary result of these travels.

During the 1890s and 1900s his work became less creative and increasingly pessimistic and bitter, though he produced some better works such as *The Tragedy of Pudd'nhead Wilson* (1894) and *Personal Recollections of Joan of Arc* (1896). At his best his writing had been characterized by broad, irreverent humor, realism, love of democracy, and hatred of sham and oppression. He raised a voice of social protest in an era when American life was suffering the conventionalism and philistinism of the epoch of industrial expansion following the Civil War. In his essays he railed against imperialism, war, hypocrisy, and corruption and criticized his countrymen's avarice, racial oppression, and mindless violence. He had little respect for the common man, whom he consistently depicted as being stupid, mean spirited, intolerant, and racist; *Huckleberry Finn* is full of such characters.

He publicly opposed his country's policies in domestic and foreign affairs alike, generally exhibiting profound dislike and distrust for politicians as well as any form of religious establishment. Twain is venerated as one of the most significant American writers, a fame which derives particularly from his books about nineteenth-century life in the Mississippi valley; *Tom Sawyer* and *Huckleberry Finn* have become classics the world over.

H. H. Kruse, *Mark Twain and Life on the Mississippi*, 1981.
J. Steinbrink, *Getting To Be Mark Twain*, 1991.
E. C. Wagenknecht, *Mark Twain: The Man and his Work*, 1967.

TZ'U-HSI (Empress Dowager; 1835–1908), mother of the Chinese emperor, the power behind the Chinese throne. Beginning her career as a low-ranking concubine of the Hsien-feng emperor, Tz'u-hsi contrived, by dint of ruthless determination, to become the most powerful woman in the China of her day and de facto ruler of the empire for over forty years.

She initially rose in status and authority in her capacity as mother of the emperor's only son, whom she bore in 1856. Increased foreign demands for diplomatic and trading rights marked this as a particularly turbulent period domestically: when, in 1860, British and French armies moved on Peking in retaliation for the emperor's refusal to allow foreign diplomats into the Forbidden City, members of the court fled to Jehol, where the emperor died.

After an accommodation had been reached with the Britain and France, the court returned to Peking and Tz'u-hsi's son, aged only five, now became the T'ung-chih emperor. A regency council of eight older officials took charge of state affairs, but Tz'u-hsi, in alliance with Hsien-feng's former senior consort, Tz'u-an, swiftly usurped their authority; Hsien-feng's brother, Prince Kung, helped them in their intriguing and became prince counsellor. This triumvirate was responsible for quelling the Taipang and Nien rebellions, which had raged since the early 1850s.

China was forced to concede to many of the demands for modernization and socio-economic liberalization made upon it by trade-hungry Western powers: between 1864 and 1889 it was opened to Christian missionaries and its internal transport infrastructure was upgraded with the aid of Western know-how. From 1863 Sir Robert Hart built up a maritime customs service which came to generate a significant proportion of the Chinese government's revenues. Kung promoted the establishment of schools for the study of foreign languages, Western-style weapons' arsenals, and a Chinese foreign service. In 1876 the Chafoo convention opened up a further ten Chinese ports to foreign traders. Many Chinese were vehemently against Western interference in their affairs and the changes initiated at the foreigners' behest, and Tz'u-hsi came to align herself with these opponents of reform, who included many members of the traditional military and government hierarchies.

T'ung-chih attained his majority in 1873, but remained under the domination of Tz'u-hsi. She forcefully disrupted his personal life and may also have been responsible for encouraging the debauched excesses which contributed to his early death. With the backing of the army, she then overturned the traditional laws of succession and had her three-year old nephew, Kuang-hsu, named as the new heir to the throne, thus ensuring that she and Tz'u-an retained their positions as regents. Tz'u-an died in 1881 and three years later Tz'u-hsi successfully plotted to disempower Kung and sabotage his reform program; she was now without rival. Marrying Kuang-hsu to one of her nieces in an effort to maintain her hold on him, she nominally relinquished her control of government and retired to her palace in northwest Peking. Charming, intelligent, persuasive, and authoritative, she continued to manipulate court affairs, while diverting funds destined for the much-needed modernization of the Chinese navy into her own hands.

The shortcomings of the corrupt and anachronistic system that Tz'u-hsi had patronized were exposed by the defeat of China by Japan in the 1894–1895 war, which came as a devastating shock to a nation that had considered itself the unquestioned regional superpower. In 1898

Kuang-hsu, influenced by a coterie of foreign-educated student radicals led by Chang Chih-tung and K'ang Yu-wei, initiated a number of radical proposals designed to renovate and modernize government and eliminate corruption. During the period subsequently called the one hundred Days of Reforms, he struck hard at the vital interests of civil and military officials by abolishing sinecures and the Green Banner provincial armies and introducing a budget system. The offended interest groups turned to Tz'u-hsi, who used the military to institute a coup, reversed the reforms, imprisoned, executed, or banished the reformers, and had the emperor confined to the palace.

The following year Tz'u-hsi, a fierce traditionalist, lent her support to officials who were encouraging the Boxers (militia forces organized in Shantung and southern Chihli provinces) in their rebellion against foreign intervention in China. These rebellions took the form of persecution of visible representatives of the foreign powers, such as missionaries. Some 100 foreigners were killed during the hostilities, which culminated in 1900 with the murder of the German minister Baron Klemens von Ketteler and the siege of the foreign legations in Peking. The siege was lifted by a coalition of foreign troops who captured the capital and suppressed the uprising. Tz'u-hsi fled and was forced to accept the humiliatingly apologetic Boxer Protocol of 1901 before being allowed to return to Peking. Thereafter she implemented many of the reforms she had previously rejected, but still refused to allow Kuang-hsi to participate in government and, from her deathbed, issued the order that led to his death from poisoning a day before her own decease.

M. E. Cameron, *The Reform Movement in China 1898–1912*, 1974.
C. Haldane, *The Last Great Empress of China*, 1965.
H. Hussey, *Venerable Ancestor: The Life and Times of Tz'u Hsi*, 1949.
M. Warner, *The Dragon Empress*, 1972.

U

URBAN II (Odo of Lagery c.1032–1099), pope who launched the First Crusade. Odo, the son of a French knight, was educated for the church, joining the reformed Benedictine order at the monastery of Cluny. There, his reforming and theological abilities led to his being chosen prior superior. His firm loyalty to Pope *Gregory VII, who appointed him Cardinal-Bishop of Osten in 1078, earned him imprisonment by *Henry IV while serving as papal legate in Germany in 1084, nomination by Gregory as one of the four men worthy to succeed him as pope, and years of conflict with Gregory's old rival, the powerful antipope, Clement III.

Urban's papacy (1088–1099) extended many of Gregory's policies, with a series of synods upholding Gregory's condemnation of simony, lay investiture, and the marriage of clerics. Urban's excommunication of King Philip I of France for adultery echoed Gregory's Europe-shaking battles with Henry IV. Even the First Crusade, for which Urban is famous, was the fulfillment of Gregory's most cherished dream.

The ostensible reason for the First Crusade was the appeal of Byzantine Emperor Alexius at the 1095 Council of Piacenza for help in driving back the Seljuk Turks, who had conquered much of Asia Minor, including Palestine. However, reported mistreatment of pilgrims and the desecration of Christian holy places (mostly due to the upheavals of war) had prepared the way for Urban to convert Alexius's appeal for help to recover Byzantium's lost lands into a crusade to liberate the Holy Land.

Urban might have had visions of uniting all Christendom under a papal theocracy through a crusade, but he was shrewd enough to realize that victory was uncertain and defeat would be detrimental to Christian prestige. He therefore toured northern Italy and southern France for six months to ensure support before preaching the crusade to thousands at a council in Clermont. His speech aroused the support of the French by appealing to them as a "race beloved and chosen by God," by referring to Turkish anti-Christian atrocities, and by comparing their limited opportunities in a France stricken with famine and plague with what awaited crusaders in the rich, war-depopulated lands of the East.

Preachers traveled throughout France giving variations on Urban's speech, and Urban himself continued to preach the crusade from city to city for nine months. Rome greeted him enthusiastically upon his return in 1097, and crusaders passing through Italy on their way to Constantinople drove Clement out of Rome, firmly securing Urban's position as pope.

Urban devoted the rest of his life to promoting the crusade. He became, theoretically, the master of a Europe united in its enthusiasm and preparation for a holy war. He made crusaders the recipients of valuable privileges, including protection of their property while they were on crusade and exemption from taxes, and even freed prisoners if they would agree to go on crusade. It was he who granted the first of the church's plenary indulgences (full remittance of punishment for sinning) that were so abused by later prelates. Urban also forbade Christians making war on other Christians for the duration of the crusade — and almost succeeded in enforcing this.

Thousands from every class flocked to join the First Crusade. These multitudes formed five divisions that marched off across Europe toward Constantinople without adequate food, money, or notion of the distance involved. One division scattered after sating their desire for fighting non-Christians by devastating the German-Jewish communities along the Rhine. Two other divisions fought off starvation by pillaging the lands they marched through before being wiped out by outraged Hungarians. The remaining two divisions were welcomed and fed by Alexius, who quickly equipped them and sent them on their way toward Jerusalem after they began plundering Constantinople. Jerusalem was captured in 1099 and its Muslim and native population slaughtered. Urban died fourteen days after Jerusalem was captured — but before he heard the news.

H. Jedin and J. Dolan, eds., *Handbook of Church History*, vol. 3, 1969.
L. Paulet, *Un Pape François: Urbain II*, 1903.
S. Runciman, *History of the Crusades,* vol. 1, 1951.

V

VAN GOGH, VINCENT SEE GOGH, VINCENT VAN

VASCO DA GAMA SEE GAMA, VASCO DA

VEGA CARPIO, LOPE FELIX DE
(1562–1635), Spanish dramatist and writer. Born in
Madrid to peasant parents he inherited his father's
emotional approach to religion in an uneasy partnership with a lust for the pleasures of the flesh. The
father also passed on to his son the characteristic
that distinguished him from men of a similar background — a talent for poetry.

Vega Carpio wrote his first play at the age of
twelve and aged fifteen he attracted the attention of
the Bishop of Avila who thought him a suitable candidate for the priesthood. He attended the University
of Alcalá but did not proceed to take holy orders. He
left the university in pursuit of another man's wife.
In 1583 he was serving under admiral Álvaro de
Bazán in an expedition against the Azores.

In between the women and the war he had began
to make his mark in Madrid literary society. His famous compatriot Miguel de *Cervantes, noted him
as one of the city's leading wits in 1585. At this
time he was working as secretary to the Marques de
las Navas but he was becoming better known as a
promising young playwright.

Again he got involved in a liaison which had
repercussions for his career. The object of his affections was the daughter of a theater manager, Elena
Osorio, later portrayed as the heroine of his novel
Dorotea (1632). He decided to acquire such gentlemanly accomplishments as Latin and French to impress her and wrote enthusiastic odes in her praise
but eventually she left him for the nephew of a cardinal. Vega Carpio was livid with anger and wrote
vicious libels against her family. He was imprisoned
and then expelled from Madrid, living in Toledo
and various other Spanish cities till finally allowed
to return in 1605.

Punishment was insufficient to discourage further
adventures for he abducted the sixteen year old
daughter of the earl marshal of Spain and was
forced to marry her. The Spanish Armada expedition probably provided a welcome change of scene;

it also inspired an epic poem. His brother died in
this military disaster but he returned and resumed
his theatrical career in Valencia. He also found secretarial employment in the service of the Duke of
Alba and later with the Duke of Sessa in Madrid.
Presumably work did not place such heavy demands
on his time as to interrupt a prolific flow of writing
and a succession of mistresses; he had a predilec-
tion for actresses, though other men's wives also
still aroused his desires.

It was as a playwright that Vega Carpio attained
his greatest fame. Considered the Spanish William
*Shakespeare the amount of plays he produced was
astounding, his biographer, Montalvan, claimed he
wrote eighteen hundred. He described the operation
of this dramatic production line as follows: "more
than a hundred of my comedies have taken only
twenty-four hours to pass from my brains to the
boards of the theater." He established the three act
play as the definitive form of Spanish drama. For his
themes he found a fertile source of inspiration in
Spanish history and from his own experiences he had
plenty of material for the love intrigues and affairs of
honor that came to characterize his most famous
works like *The Dancing Master* and *The Widow of
Valencia*.

The death of a favorite son in 1612 and the death
of his second wife in 1614 prompted Vega Carpio to
religious reflections and he entered holy orders. He
might have changed his clothes and begun writing
on religious themes but he did not feel any need to
change his lifestyle. He therefore felt free to enter
an adulterous relationship with the wife of a merchant and she bore him a daughter. The affair
brought him severe censure but it was not sufficient
to disqualify him from attaining high clerical office.
He became a priest and familiar of the Inquisition
and the Pope later made him a doctor of divinity.

Vega Carpio's last years were embittered by the
blindness, insanity and finally death (in 1632) of
the merchant's wife he had seduced and to whom
he dedicated many poems under the name Amar-
ilis. A favorite son, Lope, died at sea in 1634 and
a beloved daughter Antonia Clara was abducted
by a gentleman of the court. Vega Carpio turned

for solace to his religion and imposed on himself a harsh penance of self-flagellation; the walls of his room he spattered with his own blood. These sessions of self-abuse contributed to, if not caused, his death in 1635.

H. A. Rennert, *The Life of Lope de Vega, 1562–1635*, 1904.

F. C. Hayes, *Lope de Vega*, 1967.

A. Flores, *Lope de Vega, Monster of Nature*, 1969.

VERDI, GIUSEPPE FORTUNINO FRANCESCO

(1813–1901), Italian composer. Born in Le Roncole, a village northwest of Parma, he was the son of an innkeeper and first learned music from the village organist. Encouraged by Antonio Barezzi, a local tradesman, who offered to pay his tuition fees at the Milan conservatory, Verdi went there in 1832, only to be refused admission on the grounds that he was over-age (nineteen) and "lacking in aptitude." Undeterred, he studied privately for the next three years with Vincenzo Lavigna, the composer conductor of La Scala, Milan, and then embarked on his career as director of music in the town of Busseto, where he married Barezzi's daughter, Margherita. In 1839 Verdi settled in Milan and the success of his opera *Oberto*, produced at La Scala, brought a commission to write more of them. This promising start nearly came to an end with a series of disasters: the death of his wife and two children, followed by the luckless premiere of his comic opera *Un giorno di regno* (King for a Day), in 1840.

La Scala's director, Bartolomeo Merelli, was astute enough to show Verdi the libretto he had received for a biblical work entitled *Nabucodonosor* by T. Solera. "Va pensiero sull'ali dorate" (Fly, Thought, on Golden Wings), the chorus of Hebrew slaves in Act III, roused the composer from his depression, kindling both his musical genius and his patriotism. When staged as *Nabucco* (Milan, 1842), this opera was a huge success and made Verdi a household name. Italians chafing under Austrian and Spanish Bourbon rule saw an allusion in the chorus to the fate of their own homeland and political exiles. In the course of the following decade, Verdi and his librettists drew their themes from literary works that could often be interpreted in the same nationalistic spirit.

Salvatore Cammarano was Verdi's librettist for *La battaglia di Legnano* and *Luisa Miller* (both 1849), the second of which derived from Friedrich *Schiller, while F. M. Piave wrote many more librettos for a host of successful operas, which often brought the composer and himself into collision with government censorship. Initially, these included *Ernani* (1844), after the French drama by Victor *Hugo, and *Macbeth* (1847), Verdi's first adaptation of a Shakespearean play.

Rigoletto (Venice, 1851), one of Verdi's best-loved operas, heralded a period of more subtle characterization and mature technique. The libretto by Piave, after Victor Hugo's *Le Roi s'amuse*, did not

> I was born poor, in a poor village, and had no money for an education. I was given a miserable spinet to play, and after some time I began to compose — one work after another. That's the whole story... And now, as an old man, I have grave doubts about the worth of these compositions!
>
> **Verdi**

beguile the Austrian censors, who considered it a "revolting" attack on the establishment and banned the opera's performance until various changes had been made. It was followed by two other famous operas, both premiered in Italy: *La traviata*, the text of which Piave based on the renowned play *La Dame aux camélias* by Alexandre *Dumas fils, and *Il trovatore*, after the Spanish Romantic drama by Antonio Garcia Gutierrez, for which Cammarano wrote the text.

By 1851, having achieved wealth and renown, Verdi was able to work at a more leisurely pace, to buy the Villa Sant'Agata and an adjoining estate near Busseto, and to enjoy life there with his mistress, the singer Giuseppina Strepponi, whom he eventually married in 1859. *Les Vepres siciliennes* (1855), produced during a three-year stay in Paris, was followed by *Simone Boccanegra* (1857) and *Un ballo in maschera* (A Masked Ball, 1859). New censorship difficulties faced both Verdi and his librettist, Antonio Somma, over *Un ballo in maschera*. Not long after the composer's arrival in Naples, the Kingdom of the Two Sicilies (1858), enthusiastic crowds had begun chanting "Viva Verdi!" whenever his operas were performed. This was actually a political slogan in acrostic form, "Viva Vittorio Emmanuele Re d'Italia!" — "Long Live Victor Emmanuel King of Italy!" (expressing the true allegiance of Neapolitan liberals). Understandably, therefore, Bourbon officialdom was not pleased. *Un ballo in maschera*, dealing with the murder of a Swedish king, roused particularly fierce objections. The censors only lifted their ban when some ludicrous changes were made: the locale was shifted to prerevolutionary Boston, Massachusetts, and an English colonial governor became the assassin's victim!

After the war of independence leading to Italy's unification, Verdi agreed to sit for a time in the national parliament (1860–1865) and, though a decided anticlericalist, he later composed a fine *Requiem* for the Italian national poet Alessandro Manzoni. However, Italian operatic conventions now irritated him and the freer hand that he enjoyed abroad led him to travel and conduct throughout Europe. Two major changes in his technique were the move away from individual "numbers" that audiences would traditionally applaud, and a new emphasis on "musical recall" through the use of a theme associated with a particular character or situation. *La forza del destino* (1862), in which Piave collaborated for the last time with Verdi, is nowadays best known for its overture, but *Don Carlos* (1867) demonstrated Verdi's musical and dramatic genius at its height. Based on another of Schiller's libertarian dramas, this opera romanticized its eponymous hero as a youthful democrat opposed to his despotic father, King *Philip II of Spain.

Verdi's improved relationship with La Scala, Milan, dates from 1869, and in that year he was commissioned by Ismail Pasha, the Egyptian khedive, to write a new opera with a Middle Eastern locale. It was meant for the inauguration of Cairo's opera house and not, as often claimed, for the opening of the Suez Canal. With a text by Antonio Ghislanzoni, and named after its heroine an Ethiopian princess, *Aïda* had its premiere two years later in Cairo, but the settings were Thebes and Memphis in the era of the pharaohs.

With the triumph of *Aida*, Verdi might well have retired, but in 1884 he read Arrigo Boito's draft text for *Otello*, a new work based on William *Shakespeare. It captured his imagination and, thanks to Boito's skillful adaptation, was acclaimed as Verdi's masterpiece after the premiere at La Scala (188/). At the age of seventy-six, Verdi joined forces with Boito once again to produce his last opera, based on another Shakespearean work, *Falstaff* (1893), which signaled his return to the field of comic opera after more than half a century.

Verdi died of a stroke at the beginning of 1901 and was buried at the home for retired musicians that he had established in Milan and to which he left most of his fortune.

J. Budden, *The Operas of Verdi*, 3 vols., 1984.

D. R. B. Kimball, *Verdi in the Age of Italian Romanticism*, 1981.

W. Weaver and M. Chusid, eds., *The Verdi Companion*, 1979.

VESALIUS, ANDREAS (1514–1564), Belgian

physician who revolutionized the study of modern medicine and anatomy. Born in Brussels to a family of physicians, Vesalius entered the University of Louvain at the age of fourteen, studying Latin, some Greek, and medieval writings on science; he also performed dissections on small animals.

His study of medicine began in earnest in 1533 at the University of Paris. One of his teachers, Johann Guinther, had translated *Galen's work on anatomy. Galenic anatomy derived from the dissection of animals, since Roman law had forbidden human autopsies, and extrapolated to what was presumed to be the human condition. Galen's theories were a marked advance on Hippocratic medicine, which had been more philosophical and less grounded in practical demonstration, but it still lacked real examples of human anatomy. Galen's work, imperfect as it was, had been forgotten during the Middle Ages, while lesser scientific attitudes prevailed; only with the beginning of the Renaissance was it

brought to light. During the rare dissections that were performed, the professor would read out from a text while a demonstrator, usually a barber or executioner, dissected the corpse, exhibiting its various parts. Even this limited exposure to real human anatomy was infrequent, Vesalius attended less than a handful of such demonstrations during his three years at the university.

Curious and frustrated, Vesalius stole from the charnel houses of Paris the bodies of those who had been executed or had been victims of the plague and buried in the Cemetery of Innocents. Using these dismembered parts, he performed his own dissections in order to see for himself the structures of the human body. In 1536, due to war conditions, he had to return to Louvain for a year. On the road into town he found a hung cadaver, which he stole; it was his first articulated skeleton. During that year he obtained permission from the burgomeister to obtain whatever body he sought. In 1537 he received his medical doctorate "with highest distinction." The next day he was appointed Professor of Surgery; the day after that he began teaching anatomy.

Vesalius, who performed his own dissections in front of his well-attended classes, also used sketches to illustrate the workings of the body. In 1538 he published *Tabulae Sex*, a series of six charts, of which three (drawn by him) mapped out the vascular system and three (drawn by Jan Stefan van Kalkar, a student of *Titian) illustrated the skeletal form. A year later he published his *Venesection Letter*, which presented actual observations of the body and greatly influenced William *Harvey in his studies of the circulatory system.

Meanwhile, Vesalius had already begun the great multivolume work that was to take him several years to complete: *De humani corporis fabrica libri septem* (The Seven Books on the Structure of the Human Body). This was significantly more accurate than any other medical work of its time, and more extensive than most published since. It is particularly famed for its cross referencing and its anatomical illustrations. *Fabrica* faced severe criticism for its modern approach, which exposed the weaknesses in Galen's works.

In 1543, the same year that *Fabrica* was published, Vesalius — still only twenty-eight — also produced *Epitome*, which was largely pictorial with little text, cheaper, and therefore more accessible to students. This popular work was dedicated to Philip (later *Philip II of Spain), son of the Holy Roman emperor, *Charles V. Vesalius presented his works to the emperor personally, received a court appointment, and gave up his academic career. During that winter his father died and he came into his inheritance, which included the family home in Brussels. As court physician during the war of 1544 he had the opportunity to perform autopsies on some of the victims of gunpowder. With the war's end, he returned home to settle on his estate.

During his years with the emperor, Vesalius gained experience in surgery and a reputation for giving accurate prognoses. In 1555 he published his augmented second edition of the *Fabrica*, with a corrected text based on his more recent findings. The following year Charles gave up his throne to Philip, granted Vesalius a lifetime pension, made him a count, and had him appointed to Philip's court. In 1559 Vesalius and his family moved to Madrid.

In Spain, Vesalius was not chief court physician but merely physician in ordinary. He found the atmosphere there contrary to his more rational and modern tendencies, and he was often involved in controversies with the other attending physicians, whom he considered little more than faith healers. In 1564 he was given permission to leave Spain and make a pilgrimage to Jerusalem. While traveling, he died; on the Greek island of Zante stands a grave with the inscription, "The tomb of Andreas Vesalius of Brussels, who died October 15 of the year 1564 at the age of fifty years, on his return from Jerusalem." C. D. O'Malley, *Andreas Vesalius of Brussels*, 1964. J. B. Saunders and C. D. O'Malley, *Illustrations from the Works of Andreas Vesalius of Brussels*, 1973.

VESPUCCI, AMERIGO (1454–1512), Italian navigator. Son of one of the most respected families in Florence, Vespucci was trained for a career as one of Florence's merchant bankers and became his family's main financial support after his father died in 1482, taking the position of business manager to the junior branch of the *Medici family. For the next sixteen years he managed their business affairs so profitably that he could afford to indulge his hobby of collecting maps and books on cosmography, astronomy, and geography. Then, in 1491, Lorenzo de Medici became suspicious of the honesty of his Spanish business partner and sent Vespucci to investigate.

The expulsion of Jewish merchants following the Inquisition had created tremendous business opportunities for foreigners in Spain and Vespucci became a prominent merchant in Seville, where he worked preparing ships for expeditions to the Indies. During this time, he met Christopher *Columbus, organizing provisions for one of his ships. His knowledge of geography and mapmaking was a great asset in analyzing the financial possibilities resulting from Spain's and Portugal's voyages of discovery. The rival claims of the two countries to the newly discovered lands made geography a political issue as well; disputes were partly resolved by the 1494 Treaty of Tordesillas, which established the line of demarcation between Spanish and Portuguese spheres of influence at 370 degrees west of the Cape Verde Islands.

Concluding that only discovery of a western passage would get Spain to the Indies before Portugal, Vespucci used his family and business connections to get royal permission for an expedition across the Atlantic in 1499. He headed south searching for the passage to the Indies and was the first to sail along the coast of South America to the equator, where he stayed awake night after night, studying the skies of the southern hemisphere. His priorities now changed from the pursuit of wealth to a passionate pursuit of knowledge.

Vespucci returned to Spain thirteen months later having explored and mapped over three thousand miles of hitherto undiscovered coastline. He had carefully observed the flora, fauna, and natives encountered, developed a method for determining longitude that would be used for the next three hundred years, brought back enough Indian slaves to pay for the voyage and show a profit, and contracted the malaria that would eventually kill him. King *Ferdinand II of Spain was so impressed with his achievements that he promised to provide him with three more ships for another voyage. Vespucci turned down Ferdinand's offer as he was convinced that the last part of his voyage south had been on the Portuguese side of the line of demarcation. This meant, according to the decision of the 1495 Official Convention of Spanish and Portuguese Pilots, Astrologers, and Mariners, that Portugal had the right to be informed of this discovery and to explore it.

King Manuel of Portugal commissioned him to conduct that exploration, sailed in 1501, crossing the southern Atlantic to the elbow of Brazil, then turned south, exploring the coastline and naming its landmarks until he calculated that he had reached the line of demarcation and the end of Portuguese territory. He then ceased detailed exploration but continued searching for the passage as far south as the Bay of Saint Julian (a total of 3,300 miles) before turning north again.

Vespucci's began to suspect the geography of *Ptolemy, which held that there were only three continents (Europe, Asia, and Africa) and that India was just on the other side of the Atlantic ocean traveling west from Europe. Now, while searching for the Strait of Catigara, which was supposed to bring one through to India from the easterly part of Asia, he had mapped and charted a land mass that extended too far south to be the Asian continent. In addition, the land was inhabited and the flora and fauna were other than traditional knowledge had indicated. All of these factors led Vespucci to conclude that this unmapped land mass could not be Asia. He then determined that the Atlantic Ocean reached only as far as this new continent and that another ocean lay between Europe and a westerly access to Asia. Vespucci had discovered not only a new continent but also a new hemisphere, of huge significance for the imperial interests he represented. Thus, while he failed to find the sought-after route to India, his discovery opened a new era of empire-building that enlarged the known world. The knowledge provided by his discovery of a new continent combined with his innovation of charting location based on movements of the moon enabled

Vespucci to calculate the circumference of the earth to within fifty miles of the true measurement.

Vespucci returned to Portugal in 1502 with all of his ships and men and then went back to Spain. Exact details and maps of the new discoveries were closely guarded state secrets in both Spain and Portugal, but Vespucci's reputation for honesty was such that both kings trusted him, correctly, not to reveal information about one's sphere of influence to the other.

In 1507 Amerigo Vespucci's name was immortalized by a German geographer and cartographer, Martin Waldseemüller, who issued a map that included the new world, to which he had given the name "America" (the feminine ending consistent with the continents Europa and Asia). Although the name was originally applied only to what is now called South America, it was later used for the northern continent as well. On Waldseemüller's map a picture of Ptolemy accompanied the old world while a portrait of Vespucci adorned the new.

In spite of Vespucci's desire to sail again to the new world, he was summoned to the royal court and appointed to a position with the Commercial House for the West Indies; he made no more voyages. In 1508 he was made chief navigator, with responsibility for licensing pilots for expeditionary voyages and for interpreting and mapping their findings upon return. He held the position until his death.

G. Arciniegas, *Amerigo and the New World*, 1955.
F. J. Pohl, *Amerigo Vespucci, Pilot Major*, 1944.

VICO, GIAMBATTISTA (1668–1744), Italian philosopher of history, who developed the modernist concept that man can be aware of the dynamics of culture-making and thereby become responsible for changing his society. Vico was born in Naples and his life was spent in southern Italy, where his ideas were largely ignored, his career as educator was unappreciated, and his life was marred by poverty and an unhappy marriage. Nevertheless Vico created a methodology of historical investigation and theory of culture that slowly spread through Europe, coming into prominence in the nineteenth century through thinkers like G. W. F. *Hegel and Karl *Marx in Germany, the Romantic historian Michelet in France, and the philosopher and critic, Samuel Taylor Coleridge in England, as well as influencing James *Joyce's *Finnegans Wake*.

Vico was educated by the Jesuits, whom he found uninspiring; he studied the masters of philosophy in private, his first idols being *Plato and *Machiavelli. When typhus broke out in Naples, Vico moved south to Vatolla, where he was employed as tutor to the daughter of the Duke della Rocca. He fell in love with his student, but class differences kept them separated and Vico poured out his passion in his poetry. When he returned to Naples he married a longtime friend, a kind but impractical and almost illiterate woman. Family life placed heavy burdens on Vico as the couple had eight children, three of whom died in infancy.

From 1699, the year of his marriage, until 1708 Vico held the chair in rhetoric at the University of Naples. Although his position provided some degree of prestige, he still lacked for money and sought a more honored and remunerative position — the chair in civil law, which he failed to obtain. As professor in rhetoric, he had to lecture at the beginning of each academic year. His last lecture of this series, "On the Method of Studies in Our Times," is a valuable treatise on education. It was followed by a watershed article attacking the narrow rationalism of Cartesian philosophy, (see René *Descartes) which limited the possible areas of philosophical investigation.

In 1721 an outline for *The New Science* appeared in Vico's voluminous work on jurisprudence, *Universal Law*. Without a wealthy patron, Vico had to publish the work himself; he was forced to sell some valuables and reduce the length of the book by two-thirds. Unfortunately the published work went unacknowledged in the intellectual circles of the eighteenth century with the exception of Johann Wolfgang von *Goethe, who praised the original conception of a spiralizing progression in history instead of the classic Greek cycles or Christian linearity.

In the nineteenth century Vico's works were influential in the thinking of many great philosophers. His notion of "Providence" in history, would be transformed in Hegel into the "cunning of Reason"; and while Marx would shy away from acknowledging his debt to the Italian thinker, Vico's spiral of history, in which each period creates within itself the basis for the next, was unmistakably prominent in Marx's system.

Vico's great work, *The New Science*, analyzes the development of civilization without the recourse to divine fiat of Christian doctrine or the explanations of Enlightenment thinkers based on their belief in "man's eternal reason." For Vico, the nature of man was not fixed but rather the product of his responses to his environment, varying from the immediacy and irrationality of myth in one era to the rational philosophy of another. These responses depended on man's needs and the natural demands of the environment together with the stage of human development already reached.

Thus, primitive man, who lived an animal-like existence, had first created community out of fear, making myths powerful gods and relying on a patriarch for protection. As these patriarchs banded together to protect themselves from rebellion within their own families and from "lawless vagrants," they formed an aristocratic authority. This produced the second stage of civilization, with its culture of heroes where poetry replaced religious rite and myth. This stage, with its authoritarian rule over the masses through harsh laws, gave rise to a third stage, in which the dispossessed struggled for equality not based solely on abstract principles as Enlightenment philosophers contended, but also out of

In the night of thick darkness enveloping the earliest antiquity, so remote from ourselves, there shines the eternal and never-failing light of a truth beyond all question: that the world of civil society has certainly been made by men, and that its principles are therefore to be found within the modifications of our own human mind. Whoever reflects on this cannot but marvel that the philosophers should have bent all their energies in the study of the world of nature, which since God made it, He alone knows; and that they should have neglected the study of the world of nations or civil world, which, since men had made it, men could hope to know.

Giambattista Vico

sheer class interest. There is then an inevitable decline into barbarism, the new barbarism co-opting the reason and philosophy of the previous cycle for its uncivilized goals of selfish individualism. With the return to barbarism, the cycle starts over again, followed by a new manifestation of the gods, albeit on a higher level than in the first cycle, and so on ad infinitum.

Vico saw his *New Science* as freeing man from the traditional belief that the changes in society were caused solely by fate or some other outside force. By understanding how man is instrumental in creating his culture he can affect the future by choosing the best path toward for development.

Sir I. Berlin, *Vico and Herder*, 1976.

L. Pompa, *Human Nature and Historical Knowledge*, 1990.

D. P. Jerene, *Vico's Science of Imagination*, 1981.

VICTOR EMMANUEL II (1820–1878), first king (1861–1878) of a united Italy. He was born in Turin to Charles Albert, king of Sardinia, from the Savoy family line, and Maria Teresa of Tuscany. He grew up primarily in Piedmont, where he acquired his love of the countryside and disdain for city life. A rude and boorish man, he was ill at ease with high society.

At the age of twenty-two he married Maria Adelaide, the daughter of Archduke Rainier of Hapsburg and she bore him five children. Despite his marriage, he was a notorious womanizer with many mistresses, including his favorite, Rosina, who bore him three children. A popular waggish saying in Turin claimed that "no sovereign has been more successful in becoming the father of his subjects." When duty forced him to attend state dinners, which he dreaded, he would not eat at all, but would leave as early as possible for dinner with Rosina or another mistress.

From 1848 to 1849, Victor Emmanuel fought in his father's losing cause against the Austrians and developed a liking for battle. He considered himself a great and courageous warrior, but most others thought him merely a braggart who loved to tell stories of the supposed dangers he had overcome. After the defeat at Novara, his father abdicated and Victor Emmanuel acceded to the throne of Sardinia as one of Europe's highest paid constitutional monarchs. However, his liberal regime brought him great popularity while he personally led the Piedmontese armies in the crucial battles of Magenta and Solferino.

A poorly educated and lazy man, he signed laws without reading them and generally left the business of government to his prime minister, especially Camillo *Cavour, who served in that post from 1852 until his death in 1861. Nonetheless, it was the king who was the symbol of the Risorgimento, the movement for Italian unification. Cavour, to the delight of the bloodthirsty Victor Emmanuel, sent troops to fight in the Crimean War with England and France and this set in motion the diplomatic processes which led to the 1859 war against Austria.

With the help of tremendous French forces, Austria was forced to cede the territory of Lombardy to Victor Emmanuel II and Modena, Parma, Romagna, and Tuscany soon followed. Meanwhile, in southern Italy, the great nationalist general, Giuseppe *Garibaldi, won stunning victories in Sicily and Naples. Garibaldi turned southern Italy over to Victor Emmanuel, whose reign was confirmed overwhelmingly by plebiscite, and, in 1861, was declared the first king of Italy, ruling the peninsula except for Rome, Venice, Trieste, and Trent.

In 1866, Victor Emmanuel was once again on the battlefield, taking personal command of the Italian troops fighting with Prussia against Austria. Though his campaigns were dismal failures, Prussia was victorious and the province of Venice was given to him as war spoils. When the French withdrew from Rome in 1870 this too was added to the Italian kingdom.

He spent his final years much as he had spent the previous ones, with his mistresses and his hunting. He hunted wild boar in Tuscany, ibex and chamois in the Alps, birds throughout Italy, and bears in the Abruzzi. Often he killed hundreds, even thousands of animals in a day, with hordes of gamekeepers hired to drive the game within his shooting range. One friend estimated that Victor Emmanuel II spent a third of his life hunting.

Despite the Pope's enmity for the captor of Rome, he allowed the body of Victor Emmanuel to be buried in the Pantheon.

D.M. Smith, *Victor Emmanuel, Cavour and the Risorgimento*, 1971; *Italy and Its Monarchy*, 1989.

VICTORIA (Alexandrina Victoria; 1819–1901), queen of the United Kingdom of Great Britain and Ireland and its longest-reigning monarch, whose reign became known as the "Victorian Age." The only child of the duke and duchess of Kent and fifth in line to the throne, deaths and the lack of other legitimate heirs led to her becoming next in line while still a child.

Her father died when she was eight months old and she had a lonely and insecure upbringing under the watchful eye of her mother and the comptroller of her household, the ambitious Sir John Conroy. The duchess was receptive to his scheme to isolate and protect Victoria from the rest of the royal family, whom the duchess strongly disliked, but Victoria resented this policy and the desolate childhood that resulted.

However, there were some happy times, with outings to the theater and opera and rare visits from her German cousins, the only boys with whom she was allowed to fraternize. Her negative childhood experiences embittered Victoria's relations with her mother but also contributed to her strong independent spirit. Nonetheless although she was capable of taking care of herself, the need for the comfort and counsel of men she could trust became a constant theme in her life.

Upon the death of her uncle William IV in 1837, Victoria was proclaimed queen. She was just eighteen, of plain appearance and only about 4 feet 10 inches tall. The position she inherited was daunting and it was fortunate she had capable politicians such as William Melbourne and Henry *Palmerston to guide her, becoming so dependent on Lord Melbourne that she could not bear the thought of his being out of office; her partiality evoked the anger of his Tory rivals.

The happiest years of Victoria's life began with her marriage to her first cousin, Prince Albert of Coburg, in 1840. This handsome and highly intellectual German prince gave the impression of being cold and austere but to the queen he was her "angel," a devoted husband and idol. At first many resented the alliance; Albert's German attitudes and mannerisms aroused traditional English bigotry. But his competence at palace administration and involvement in public charities and works, not least the fabulous 1851 Great Exhibition, gained him popularity.

Victoria and Albert had nine children (although she felt that women who were always pregnant were "disgusting — more like a rabbit or a guinea pig than anything else") and made every effort to be devoted parents. Both had been raised in one-parent families, which heightened their desire to provide their own children with a secure and happy childhood. In great measure they succeeded, but at a cost. The queen was determined that her sons would be formed in Albert's image, leading to continual conflict with her fun-loving son Edward, Prince of Wales. Edward's sheltered youth made him easy prey for his fellow recruits in army camp in 1861; they smuggled a notorious prostitute into his bed and the resulting scandal contributed, the queen believed, to Albert's death at the age of forty-two in 1861. It is more probable that he died from typhoid transmitted through the primitive plumbing system at Windsor Castle.

Albert's death left Victoria close to mental breakdown. His room was preserved as he left it, and twice each day his clothes were laid out and soap and towel changed. Victoria dressed mainly in black for the rest of her life and, always shy of public engagements, now had a good excuse to avoid them, much to the frustration of her ministers. She did not attend meetings of the privy council, but sat in the next room with the door open. Her retirement was accepted by the public at first but after several years satirical notices were fixed to Buckingham Palace railings, advertising its sale due to "the late occupants' declining business."

Victoria felt more at ease away from London in the Scottish Highlands; fondly-remembered excursions with Albert created nostalgic appeal and she was attracted by the plain-speaking, naturally dignified Highlanders. She developed a strong attachment to her footman John Brown, "The Queen's Highland Servant"; over the next eighteen years Brown became friend and comforter as much as footman. But his outspoken manner made enemies at court, contributing further to Victoria's unpopularity with the public at large.

During the 1870s the queen emerged from self-imposed isolation, with the prime minister, Benjamin *Disraeli, whom she called "Dizzy," playing a crucial role. He knew the right mixture of sympathy and flattery to win her heart, unlike his rival, the Liberal party leader William *Gladstone, who spoke

Queen Victoria, from an 1897 portrait

to her, she said, as if he were addressing a public meeting. Disraeli guessed Victoria's ambition to be an empress and in 1877 shepherded through Parliament the act making her empress of India. In turn, she supported Disraeli's policies. In 1878, when he favored moves to stop Russian expansionism, Victoria remarked to her daughter, "Oh if only the Queen were a man, she would like to go and give those Russians such a beating." When Disraeli lay dying in 1881 the queen continually telegraphed for news.

Victoria displayed amazing stamina until her last year, although by this time she had to be wheeled around in a chair and her eyesight was poor. She continued to stay up late working on government papers, took a keen interest in British and international politics, and was deeply saddened by casualties in the Boer War (1899–1902). She knitted scarves for her soldiers and had one hundred thousand tins of chocolate sent out to them. She was also kept busy by her constantly growing family. Her children and grandchildren linked her by marriage with most of the ruling dynasties of Europe. The Golden (1887) and Diamond (1897) Jubilees bore witness to the might of her empire and the affection of her subjects. When she died there was a feeling of national loss, as much for the passing of an era as for the loss of a formidable old lady.

G. St. Aubyn, *Queen Victoria: A Portrait*, 1991.

E. Longford, *Victoria RI*, 1964.

A. Cecil, *Queen Victoria and her Prime Ministers*, 1953.

VIRGIL (or Vergil; Publius Vergilius Maro, 70–19 B.C.E.), the greatest poet of Roman antiquity. Virgil is best known for his epic, *The Aeneid*, that tells the mythic history of the founding of Rome. Born on a farm near Mantua, northern Italy, away from the cosmopolitan center of Rome, Virgil spent his early youth among peasant farmers. His father, a potter and laborer for a wealthy landowner, married his overlord's daughter and was thus able to provide his son with the best education. Virgil studied at Cremona, Milan, and later Rome, learning the literatures of Greece and Rome, philosophy, and rhetoric.

After finishing his primary education he attempted a political career, speaking in the law courts, but when civil war broke out in 49 B.C.E., he resumed his studies in Naples. The civil war raged during Virgil's early manhood. After Julius *Caesar's assassination, his supporter *Mark Antony and his heir, Octavian (later the Emperor *Augustus), battled the usurpers, throwing Italy into chaos. Due to his poor health, Virgil did not take part in any military campaigns, and while war ravaged parts of Italy, he spent his time in study and scholarship. When the first period of civil war ended with the battle at Phillipi, in which the assassins of Caesar were killed, Antony and Octavian allotted civilian farm lands in Italy to the returning soldiers; Virgil's father's farm was confiscated and the family fled to Naples.

These events — the chaos and dread of war, the loss of the family home, and finally, the hopes for peace — provided the background for Virgil's first work, *The Eclogues*. These poems are songs of an idyllic countryside sung by the shepherds, telling of their love of the land and their sorrows at death and loss.

Meanwhile, as fighting began anew, pitting Octavian against Antony and *Cleopatra, the destruction of Italy continued. Agricultural activity was interrupted as both armies took farmers into their ranks. Virgil's *Georgics*, written from 36 B.C.E. to 29 B.C.E., during and after this period, are a passionate, if didactic, response to the loss of Italian country life that he always loved.

When the civil war ended in 31 B.C.E., Virgil began the composition of an epic work that would rededicate Romans to creating civilization and restore a sense of national destiny under a new emperor.

Virgil, who was thirty-eight when Augustus triumphed over Antony, spent the remaining twelve

VIRGIL

- Fortune favors the bold.
- I fear the Greeks, even when bringing gifts.
- The descent to Hell is easy.
- Labor conquers everything.
- He becomes more ill through remedies.
- Vice is nourished and kept alive by concealment.
- Arms and the man I sing (opening of *The Aeneid*).
- Why does trembling seize the limbs before the trumpets sound?
- Cease to hope that the gods' decrees are changed by prayer.

years of his life perfecting *The Aeneid*. His earlier poetry had given him access to the highest circles of Roman society, his family's wealth had been restored through his influential contacts, and he numbered among his friends other poets of note, including *Horace.

The Aeneid comprises twelve books that tell the story of Aeneas, son of the Trojan King Anchises, as he flees Troy after its sacking by the Greeks. As Aeneas and his army make their escape toward Italy, they are pursued by the god Juno and are diverted to north Africa. Aeneas falls in love with the Carthaginian queen Dido, but is told by the supreme god Jupiter to continue on his mission to found what would become the Roman Empire. When Aeneas leaves her, Dido kills herself. Aeneas stops in Sicily to celebrate funeral games for his father and is told that he must journey to the underworld.

There, the spirit of Anchises informs him that his journey of destiny is laying the foundations for the great achievements of Augustus. A series of battles for the conquest of Italy follow, and Aeneas eventually triumphs.

The basic pattern for Virgil's work comes from *The Iliad* and *Odyssey* of *Homer. Not only do the events follow on the heels of Homer's story, but the intertwining of Aeneas's voyage for home, the wars in Italy, and the romance with Dido run parallel to events in the Greek epic. The fact that Aeneas's success in his role as founder of Rome comes as the result of placing duty above all else is an expression of the Stoic values Virgil held in later life.

In order to finish revising sections of *The Aeneid*, Virgil journeyed to Greece, planning to remain there for three years. When he fell seriously ill at the beginning of the trip, he ordered that his unfinished manuscript be burned, but Augustus refused to carry out this wish. Instead, the poem was published and soon became the national epic, a celebration of renewal under Augustus. From that time until the dissolution of the empire the work also formed the basis of Roman education in literature. In the middle ages *The Aeneid* was subject to Christian allegorical interpretation and its style later formed the basis of the neoclassical period of English literature in the seventeenth century.

M. Murrin, *The Allegorical Epic*, 1980.

B. Otis, *Virgil: A Study in Civilised Poetry*, 1963.

K. Quinn, *Virgil's Aeneid*, 1968.

G. Williams, *Techniques and Ideas in the Aeneid*, 1983.

VLADIMIR I (Saint Vladimir of Kiev; c.956-1015), Russian ruler of pagan origin who brought Eastern Orthodox Christianity to Old Russia and who united Novgorod and Kiev into a single state, the forerunner of modern Russia. A descendant of the house of Rurik, which ruled the area from the tenth to the thirteenth century, Vladimir was declared ruler of Novgorod in 970.

In 972 his father, Svyatoslav, died, and he escaped to Scandinavia to seek the help of his uncles in overcoming Yaropolk, another of Svyatoslav's sons. His campaigns proved so successful that by 980 Vladimir ruled an area extending from the Ukraine to the Baltic.

A folk legend tells that Vladimir, in his search for a religion, rejected Islam because Muslims were forbidden to drink alcohol, and Judaism because the Jews were fated to wander throughout the world, finally turning to Byzantine Christianity, with its sumptuous church architecture and furnishings and awe-inspiring liturgy. In fact, Vladimir's conversion came about as a result of his pact with Byzantine Emperor Basil II, who sought military aid and offered Vladimir his sister as wife in exchange.

Their pact was sealed when Vladimir underwent baptism in 988. The ceremony was preceded by the solemn drowning of a wooden statue of Perun, the god of thunder, in the Dnieper river, where Vladimir's baptism took place. Boris and Gleb, two of his twelve sons, became the first Russian saints.

Also known as the "Bright Sun," Vladimir observed many of the precepts of Christianity literally; when he held feasts at court he had food distributed to the poor and, while he imported Byzantine laws, he interpreted them more mercifully until persuaded by the church that criminals should be put on trial and punished.

Vladimir also built churches in Byzantine style, but with typically Russian additions; within fifty years of his conversion, there were said to be over four hundred churches in Kiev, his capital. Vladimir's choice of Byzantine Christianity effectively blocked the spread of other forms of Christianity in his realm, notably Roman Catholicism.

After the death of his first wife, Vladimir married again, this time into the German Ottonian dynasty of the Holy Roman emperor. His daughter from this second marriage married Casimir I of Poland. In his later years, Vladimir was challenged by the sons of his earlier, pagan wives and he died while on an expedition against one of them.

Many epic songs of this period celebrate Vladimir's brave knights. The best-known epic of the time, the *Lay of Igor*, includes the story of Vladimir from his humble beginnings as the "son of a serving woman," the rejection of his marriage proposal by the daughter of the ruler of Povolsk, and his eventual conquering of the lands around Kiev.

Vladimir, now known as Saint Vladimir, was also eulogized in the *Oration of Law and Grace*, a very early Orthodox writing ascribed to Hilarion, the first Russian to serve as Metropolitan of Kiev (c.1037–1050).

H. Lamb, *The March of Muscovy*, 1948.

D. S. Mirsky, *A History of Russian Literature*, 1958.

VOLTAIRE (pseudonym of François-Marie Arouet; 1694–1778), French philosopher and writer. Born in Paris, he was educated at the Jesuit College of Louis-le-Grand, developing there a love of literature that led him to reject his father's wishes that he study law; upon leaving college he determined to pursue a literary career. Inspired by the enlightened thinkers of the time, Voltaire became associated with the French *philosophes*, maintaining a belief in the efficacy of reason. He frequented the Temple, the center of intellectual life in Paris, and earned a reputation as a poet and satirist; however, in 1717 he was exiled from Paris and then imprisoned in the Bastille on suspicion of having lampooned the regent. On his release, his tragedy *Oedipe* was performed in Paris with great success and soon after he published a national epic, *La Henriade*, based on the reign of the popular monarch *Henry IV. The poem was widely acclaimed by his contemporaries, who began to compare Voltaire with the classical writers *Virgil and *Homer. His work was also praised by members of the royal family, whose employ he entered as court poet. This position was short-lived, though, due to a quarrel with a courtier who had offended Voltaire. The result was a second term of imprisonment in the Bastille and three years' exile in England.

During his stay in England Voltaire was impressed by the Deists and espoused the philosophy that a rational man would believe in God but not in supernatural inspiration. He admired the intellectual activity he found among the English and their more tolerant form of government, and returned to France in 1729 determined to impart the liberalism he had experienced in England to his compatriots. He expressed this enthusiasm for the English and his condemnation for the French system of government in the *Lettres philosophiques* (1734). In this brilliant, concise work. Voltaire advocated religious toleration and illustrated man's potential fulfillment through science and art. The *Lettres* was a powerful indictment of the French political and religious establishment and following its publication, sale of the book was forbidden in France and a warrant was issued for Voltaire's arrest.

Voltaire took refuge at Cirey in the Haute-Marne, the country residence of the marquise du Châtelet, with whom he spent the next fifteen years of his life. His work during these years reflects the influence of this intelligent young woman and her interest in science and metaphysics; in 1738 he published *Eléments de la philosophie de Newton*, a collection of English scientific discoveries. At the same time Voltaire maintained his interest in historical literature and began work on *Le Siècle de Louis*

FROM THE WRITINGS OF VOLTAIRE

- If God made us in His image, we have certainly returned the compliment.
- Once the people begin to reason, all is lost.
- They squeeze the orange and throw away the peel (alluding to Frederick the Great, with whom he had quarrelled).
- Work banishes those three great evils – boredom, vice, and poverty.
- In this country (England) it pays to shoot an admiral from time to time, so as to encourage the others.
- That is true enough," replied Candide, "but we must cultivate our garden" (i.e., attend to our own affairs).
- This agglomeration which was called – and which still calls itself – the Holy Roman empire was neither holy, nor Roman, nor an empire.
- History is just the portrayal of crimes and misfortunes.
- Ecrasez l'infame! ("Crush the evil thing!"), referring to the Catholic church.
- If God did not exist, it would be necessary to invent Him.
- The secret of all art is to correct nature.
- The best is the enemy of the good.

Voltaire

XIV. He also wrote several popular tragedies during this period, most notably *Alzire* (1736) and his witty fictional work *Zadig* (1747). From 1739 Voltaire traveled with Mme. du Châtelet between Belgium, Cirey, and Paris, regained favor in the court of Versailles, and built up a vast fortune.

The death of Mme du Châtelet in 1749 had a profound effect on Voltaire, leaving him bereft of adviser and confidante. He further suffered the failure of some of his plays, a constant hostility from the religious party at court, and was disliked by *Louis XV. Disappointed and frustrated, Voltaire accepted an invitation to visit the court of *Frederick the Great of Prussia, with whom he had been in correspondence for several years. In Berlin and Potsdam, Voltaire completed his historical work *Essai sur les moeurs*, an overview of the universal history of customs and civilizations, and began work on his *Dictionnaire philosophique*. However, differences began to emerge between Voltaire and Frederick, and Voltaire left Prussia in 1753. Louis XV forbade his return to Paris and his diminished popularity in France compelled him to spend the next two years wandering from place to place. He finally settled near Geneva, where he was welcomed at first as a champion of tolerance. His scandalous "Pucelle d'Orléans" was a mock-heroic poem, suggesting that *Joan of Arc was perhaps not a "maid." However, he soon lost public approval and provoked the enmity of Swiss intellectuals. Voltaire retired to Ferney, the property he acquired in 1758, which remained his home for the rest of his life, and is now called Ferney-Voltaire.

In 1758 Voltaire wrote his most famous work, *Candide*, which deals with the problems of human suffering and the existence of evil. In this wittiest of novels, Voltaire rejects the philosophy that "all is for the best in the best of all possible worlds" (a criticism of the philosophy of G. W. *Leibniz) as personified by Candide's tutor, Dr. Pangloss, while acknowledging the resilience of human nature, illustrated by the survival of Candide in the face of misfortune.

The last twenty years of Voltaire's life have been described as his most brilliant and his most active.

At Ferney he developed a modern estate, participating in the contemporary movement of agricultural reform and establishing a colony of watchmakers. He won enormous popularity among the people of Ferney, embroiling himself in social disputes and espousing local political causes. He was famous throughout Europe, and wrote extensively, producing his *Dialogues* and the completed version of the *Dictionnaire philosophique*, which was published in small format in 1764. He sustained his energetic attacks against the tyranny and intolerance of church and state, vigorously opposing traditional beliefs in the divine right of kings and the infallibility of the church. He decried the privileges of the nobility as illegitimate and enunciated his hatred of the church in his severe criticism of the Bible.

As a moralist and intellectual, Voltaire became the leader of the *philosophes* and the guiding spirit of their movement. He repeatedly called for tolerance and respect among mankind, insisting on the importance of civil rights and the abolition of torture. He conducted numerous personal attacks against those whose beliefs he criticized and sustained a protracted opposition to the philosophy of Jean-Jacques *Rousseau, accusing him of sophistry and small-mindedness. This in turn led to a concentrated counterattack against Voltaire by Rousseau's followers.

After twenty-eight years of exile from the city, Voltaire returned to Paris in 1778 to participate in the direction of his play *Irène*. The performance was a resounding success and Voltaire was showered with praise by a wildly enthusiastic audience. He died at the age of eighty-four, shortly after this final triumphant visit to Paris, and was buried as a Christian in the Abbey of Scellières; his remains were transferred to the Pantheon during the French Revolution.

T. Besterman, *Voltaire*, 1969.

J. H. Brumfitt, *Voltaire, Historian*, 1958.

P. Gay, *Voltaire's Politics: The Poet as Realist*, 1959.

I. O. Wade, *The Intellectual Development of Voltaire*, 1969.

W

WAGNER, RICHARD (1813–1883), German composer. His father was a police registrar in Leipzig who died when Wagner was only six months old; eight months after the death of her husband, his mother married the actor Ludwig Geyer. It has been speculated that Geyer was actually Wagner's father. Wagner himself entertained the idea for a while but his origin became a real concern during the Nazi regime. Some believed that not only was Geyer Wagner's father, but that he was Jewish. That would have meant that Wagner himself, one of the favorite composers of the Nazi elite, had Jewish blood. However, to the Nazis' relief, a lengthy examination of documents revealed that Geyer was not a Jew.

In 1814 the Wagner family moved to Dresden where Geyer was an actor in the local court theater. Geyer died in 1821 and a year later Wagner entered the Dresden Kreuzschüle, where he studied for six years. In 1825, at the age of twelve, Wagner began to study piano and violin. Two years later he and his mother returned to Leipzig and in 1830 he entered the Thomasschüle, where he began to compose.

In 1832 Wagner began to write operas, the genre which was to make him famous all over the world. His first work for the stage, *Die Hochzeit* (The Wedding) was never completed. Next came *Die Feen* (The Fairies) which was rejected and not performed, and in 1834 Wagner began composing *Das Liebesverbot* (The Ban on Love), with a libretto after William *Shakespeare's *Measure for Measure*. At this time, Wagner became the music director at a theater company based in Magdeburg and made his debut conducting *Mozart's *Don Giovanni*. In 1836 he led the Magdenburg premiere of *Das Liebesverbot,* but the company soon ceased operation. Wagner married one of its actresses, Christine Wilhelmine (Minna) Planer who, however, soon left him for another man. Wagner traveled to Riga to become its music director; Minna soon came to Riga and was reconciled with her husband. In Riga Wagner worked on his next opera, *Rienzi*.

In 1839 Wagner left Riga with many debts and enemies and after a lengthy sea journey through Norway and England arrived with his wife in Paris. In October 1840 he was put in debtors' prison for almost three weeks. He therefore sold his newest libretto to the Paris Opera for 500 francs. The libretto, for the opera *Der fliegende Holländer* (The Flying Dutchman), was used by another composer for his own opera on the subject.

In the meantime, *Rienzi* was performed in Dresden and Wagner's *Der fliegende Holländer* was premiered there as well in 1834, with the composer on the podium. During the same year Wagner secured a job as an opera conductor in Dresden and in 1845 conducted the premiere of his next opera, *Tännhauser*, which he then revised. However, although his works were performed, Wagner was unable to publish his operas, and he remained in debt.

Wagner next worked on *Lohengrin* and followed that with initial sketches for his four-opera *Ring* cycle. He also joined the revolutionary *Vaterlandsverein* and participated in the May Day

Richard Wagner, a contemporary woodcut

- You only have time to clamber up a tree and hold on like grim death. Your hair is blown about, your face streaked with blood, but when the storm dies off and recedes a little, you get down from your shelter, you shake yourself and you enjoy the pleasure of having escaped a great danger. The hurricane, my dear child, is Wagner and Wagnerism. It is fearsome but it passes on. The important thing is not to let yourself be carried away.
- It has its great moments and boring half-hours.

Charles Gounod

- The supreme utterance of a soul at its highest paroxysm.

Charles Pierre Baudelaire

- A melodramatic rhetorician of the senses.

Friedrich W. Nietzsche

- Wagner's music is better than it sounds.

Edgar W. Nye

uprising of 1849. A warrant was issued for his arrest and he had to flee Dresden hidden in a goods wagon, arriving in Zürich in July 1849, where Minna joined him. There Wagner began writing articles about the nature of art and society. These included his *Judaism in Music,* a viciously anti-Semitic tract written to "prove" the destructive effect of Jewish participation in artistic endeavors, especially music. (His anti-Semitism — and his glorification of Nordic myths — made him the favorite composer of Adolf *Hitler and the Nazis, while public performance of his work is banned in Israel.)

In 1852 Wagner completed the libretto for the four operas that comprise *Der Ring des Nibelungen* (The Ring of the Nibelungs). The composer, who always wrote his own texts, would compose more than sixteen hours of music for this grand epic in which giants, dwarves, dragons, and gods fight for power. The *Ring* was produced in its entirety only in 1876. The first two operas, *Das Rheingold* (Rhinegold) and *Die Walküre* (The Valkyrie), were premiered in Munich in 1869 and 1870 respectively. The other two parts, *Siegfried* and *Götterdämmerung* (Twilight of the Gods) were first performed in Wagner's own theater in Bayreuth in 1876.

During the late 1850s Wagner left the *Ring* for quite a while to write other operas. He also continued to travel and fall in love with married women. His concert tour in London in 1855 was most successful and the composer was presented to Queen *Victoria. After traveling to Venice, where he composed parts of his next opera, *Tristan und Isolde,*

Wagner made his home in Lucerne, still keeping away from the Dresden authorities who wanted him to stand trial as a revolutionary. In Lucerne he completed Tristan.

In 1862 Wagner began composing *Die Meistersinger von Nürnberg* (The Mastersingers of Nürnberg), his only mature comedy, a humane drama about young love, the power of art, and human understanding. Two years later Wagner's fortunes changed dramatically as the newly crowned King Ludwig II of Bavaria, who had a passion for his music, invited him to Munich with a promise to help him.

During this time Wagner became intimately involved with Franz Liszt's daughter, Cosima, who was the wife of Hans von Bülow, a prominent conductors of Wagner's music. In 1865 she gave birth to Isolde, Wagner's daughter. In the summer of 1865 Wagner began dictating his autobiography to Cosima and in 1869 Wagner and Cosima celebrated the birth of their second child, Siegfried. They married a year later, after Minna's death and Cosima's divorce.

In 1871 Wagner announced that he was about to build his own theater in the city of Bayreuth, a place where only his works would be performed. Bayreuth soon became a mecca for music lovers from all over the world and remains so today, with its annual Wagner festival supervised by his descendants. His last opera, *Parsifal,* was premiered in Bayreuth in 1882. Wagner ordered that this work not be performed in any other theater but his own, and not until 1903 did New York's Metropolitan Opera stage *Parsifal,* despite the ban. Wagner died in Venice and his body was taken back to Bayreuth and buried in the garden of his villa.

M. V. Amerongen, *Wagner,* 1983.

J. Chancellor, *Wagner: A Classic Study of the Composer's Life and Works,* 1980.

B. Millington, *Wagner,* 1984.

P. L. Rose, *Wagner: Race and Revolution,* 1992.

WALLENSTEIN (VALDSTEIN), ALBRECHT EUSEBIUS WENZEL VON (1583–1634), general of the imperial forces of Emperor *Ferdinand II during the Thirty Years' War. Among history's greatest military minds, Wallenstein remains an enigma to modern historians. His own officers could only guess at his schemes and battle plans for the next day, much less his long-range ambitions. Was his first loyalty to the empire, to himself, or possibly to his own Czech nation?

As the son of a Czech nobleman from Bohemia, Wallenstein received a traditional Protestant education before enlisting in the imperial army in 1604. There, he rejected his Protestant upbringing under the influence of the Jesuits. Although he soon abandoned his professed commitment to the church in favor of astrology and the occult, the Jesuits arranged his marriage to a wealthy Moravian widow in 1609. Her sudden death in 1614 made him the wealthiest landowner in Bohemia. In 1624 Ferdinand reorganized the territory as the Duchy of Friedland; the following year Wallenstein was promoted to duke. His influence at court was fostered by his marriage to Isabella von Harach, the daughter of a close advisor to Ferdinand.

In 1625 Wallenstein recommended to the emperor that he be enabled to finance the establishment of an imperial army under his command. Ferdinand was eager to relax his military dependence on Spain, the autonomous princes-elector, and Maximilian of Bavaria, and therefore granted Wallenstein's petition. In turn, Wallenstein proved unexpectedly adept. Over twenty-four thousand mercenaries enlisted in the first weeks, lured by promises of rich bounty. His critics expected the heterogeneous multitude to quickly disintegrate, but Wallenstein further proved himself by instilling a sense of loyalty and, above all, discipline, in his troops. His private executioner was a constant companion, and the slightest infringements were immediately punished. Occasionally, Wallenstein's discipline seemed absurd to outsiders. No one was allowed to appear before him in boots or spurs, nor was any unnecessary noise tolerated. Cats and dogs were killed in any town that Wallenstein visited, while soldiers were punished for no more than talking loudly. Nonetheless, his soldiers adored Wallenstein and were willing to make any sacrifice for him. Opposition to Wallenstein came from the Catholic nobles in whose territories he camped. The army was financed under the axiom "War should finance war," applying not only to occupied Protestant lands but to supportive Catholic territories as well.

In 1626, Wallenstein conquered Mecklenburg, Holstein, and Pomerania, thereby extending Ferdinand's influence to the Baltic. In return, he was granted the territories of Schleswig, Sagan, and Mecklenburg. The Catholic princes, however, regarded him as no less a threat than the Protestants. He had relieved Ferdinand of his dependence on them, and allowed him to centralize power in his own hands. But Wallenstein was not invulnerable. He had failed in his campaign against Stralsund and in his attempt to monopolize Baltic trade. Using his enforced billeting of soldiers in Catholic lands as a pretext, they convinced the emperor to dismiss his general.

So grievously insulted was Wallenstein by Ferdinand's betrayal that he contemplated switching sides to France or even Sweden. His excessive demands hindered the negotiations, while his successor, Count Tilly, was unequal to him in military acumen. The Swedish king *Gustavus II Adolphus was advancing through the north while the Saxons were threatening Bohemia itself. In 1632 Ferdinand was forced to recall Wallenstein from retirement. Wallenstein's terms, accepted by Ferdinand, included not only virtual authority over the army, but extensive diplomatic powers as well. He proved himself by repulsing the Saxons and expelling Gustavus from Franconia and Bavaria.

After Gustavus's death, the Swedes challenged Wallenstein in Silesia in 1633. Rumors that Wallenstein had demanded that his soldiers swear fealty to him alone shook the imperial court and served to incite the emperor's advisors against the general. Forced to react, Ferdinand dismissed Wallenstein and declared him a traitor, but pardoned all but two of the other supposed conspirators. An imperial decree demanded that Wallenstein be brought to the emperor dead or alive. In what was a fatal error, Wallenstein assumed that his troops were still loyal to him, whereas in fact they preferred the emperor. Even Wallenstein's personal astrologer had deserted the general, leaving him with some 1,500 troops, many secretly detesting his overblown self-aggrandizement. While leading his dwindling forces to the Swedish frontier, he was assassinated by Irish and Scottish officers claiming to be acting for the emperor.

Wallenstein was later immortalized in Johann *Schiller's dramatic trilogy.

H. Hartmann, *Wallenstein*, 1987.
G. Mann, *Wallenstein, His Life Narrated*, 1976.
G. Parker, *The Thirty Years' War*, 1984.

WARREN, EARL (1891–1974), fourteenth chief justice of the U.S. Supreme Court. Born in Los Angeles but raised in Bakersfield, California, Warren attended the University of California at Berkeley, receiving a doctorate of jurisprudence in 1914. He spent a brief period in private law practice, followed by army service in World War I.

By 1919 he found himself in the public legal sector. He was deputy city attorney in Oakland, California (1919-1920) and deputy district attorney there from 1920 to 1925. From 1925 to 1939 he was district attorney of Alameda County, and in 1939 was elected attorney general of the state of California.

In 1943 Warren was elected Republican governor of California, a post he held for almost eleven years. He became a national figure and was induced to run for vice president on the Republican ticket with then-governor of New York, Thomas Dewey, running for president; they lost to the incumbent, Harry S. *Truman. Warren was nevertheless able to retain his office as governor of California, where he was reelected to serve a third term beginning in 1950. As governor Warren managed to reduce taxes while expanding state services.

In 1954 Warren's appointment as chief justice of the U.S. Supreme Court by President Dwight D. *Eisenhower was confirmed by voice vote of the Senate, just five months after he had been appointed. Two months after the Senate confirmation of his appointment, Warren wrote a landmark decision for a unanimous court in *Brown v. Board of Education*, finding racial segregation in public schools to be unconstitutional as it denied the legal right to equality of all citizens. In 1963 the "Warren Court" handed down the decision in *Gideon v. Wainwright* holding that anyone facing criminal charges who was too poor to hire a lawyer could not

SEPARATE EDUCATIONAL FACILITIES FOUND INHERENTLY UNEQUAL

To separate (Negro children) from others of similar age and qualifications solely because of their race generates a feeling of inferiority as to their status in the community that may affect their hearts and minds in a way unlikely to be undone... We conclude that in the field of public education the doctrine of "separate but equal" has no place. Separate educational facilities are inherently unequal.

Brown v. Board of Education **(1954)**

NEW GROUND RULES FOR ADMITTING CONFESSIONS

We hold that when an individual is taken into custody, or otherwise deprived of his freedom... and subjected to questioning, the privilege against self-incrimination is jeopardized... He must be warned prior to any questioning that he has a right to remain silent, that anything he says can be used against him in a court of law, that he has a right to the presence of an attorney, and if he cannot afford an attorney one will be appointed for him...

After such warnings have been given and such opportunity afforded him, the individual may knowingly and intelligently waive these rights... But unless and until such warnings and waiver are demonstrated by the prosecution at the trial, no evidence obtained as the result of interrogation can be used against him.

Miranda v. Arizona **(1966)**

has come to be used to describe a bold, liberal Supreme Court.

J. Downing, *Warren: The Man, the Court, the Era,* 1968.
L. Katcher, *Earl Warren, A Political Biography,* 1967.
E. and N. Warren, *The Memoirs of Earl Warren,* 1977.
J. D. Weaver, *Warren,* 1967.

WASHINGTON, GEORGE (1732–1799), commander-in-chief of the Army of Independence and first president of the United States (1789–1797). Of British ancestry, the eldest of five children of his father's second wife, Washington was born in a modest farmhouse (destroyed by fire in 1799) near Fredericksburg, Virginia. His education was limited — he was the only one of the first six presidents who did not go to college. The marriage of his beloved elder half-brother Lawrence into an aristocratic English family, the Fairfaxes, provided the young Washington with his first experience as a land surveyor.

In the early 1950s Britain and France both laid claim to the upper Ohio Valley. The Fairfax family recommended Washington to head a small expedition representing English interests, but tragedy resulted when Washington attacked a small French encampment, thinking they were spies. Ten men, including the diplomatic commander, were killed; the French claimed they were on a peace mission. The event exacerbated tensions that led to the French and Indian War. In 1755, although war had not been declared, Washinton served as an aide to British general Edward Braddock in his campaign to capture Fort Duquesne at the Forks of the Ohio. The campaign ended in catastrophic defeat for the British, although Washington drew praise from the British commanders for his "courage and resolution."

At twenty-two, Washington was elected commander of all Virginia forces, his main task that of protecting the Virginia border from Indian attacks. After the retreat of the French from Fort Duquesne the war ended, having engaged Washington from 1753 to 1759. Resigning from military life, he turned his energies to Mount Vernon, the plantation home he had rented from the widow of his half-brother, which would later become his permanent estate in Virginia. In 1759 he married Martha Dandridge Custis, a wealthy widow with two small children. The Washingtons were charitable landowners, believing that no needy person should be turned away from Mount Vernon "lest the deserving suffer." Though he employed slaves, Washington was greatly troubled by the institution of slavery all his life. In his will he granted all his slaves their freedom, the only Virginia founding father to do so.

In the mid–1760s Britain's policy of taxing its colonies precipitated the American Revolution. At

be assured of a fair trial unless he were provided with counsel. Indigents became entitled to counsel at public expense and public defender offices sprang up all over the United States.

Probably the most celebrated decision involving the rights of an accused in criminal proceedings was *Miranda v. Arizona* (1966), written by Warren himself. In effect, the law of confessions was rewritten: Warren ruled that the police must inform a crimminal suspect of his right to remain silent and to have counsel present before they question him, and that a confession obtained in defiance any of those requirements is inadmissable in court.

Following the assassination of President John F. *Kennedy, Warren reluctantly acceded to President Lyndon *Johnson's request to head the official investigatory commission. The Warren Commission, as it was to be known, found that Lee Harvey Oswald had acted on his own in killing Kennedy. Warren retired in 1969 and the term "Warren Court"

Washington with his cabinet

first Washington hoped that armed rebellion could be avoided. As a member of Virginia's House of Burgesses he protested the Stamp Act, which imposed taxes on the colonies to support the British army, and the Townshend Revenue Act, a tax on tea and other staples. In 1774 Washington was a delegate to the First Continental Congress in Philadelphia, which agreed to ban all British goods. Not until after the battles of Lexington and Concord and the convening of the Second Continental Congress in May 1775 did it become clear that the colonies would have to take up arms.

In the year preceding the signing of the Declaration of Independence (July 4, 1776), Washington created a navy of six ships that were ordered to capture British vessels; initiated a campaign to arrest and detain British Tories; and encouraged leaders of the colonies to adopt independence.

With the exception of Washington's stunning success at Trenton on December 25–26, 1776, when he recrossed the Delaware and surprised the Hessian mercenaries, his army had suffered several defeats in New York, culminating in the misery of the hard winter at Valley Forge. The battle of Monmouth (June 28, 1778), when Washington took the initiative boldly and drove the the British back to their strongholds in New York, was the critical breakthrough for the Continental Army. In September 1781 Washington's army, assisted by able French troops, defeated the British garrison at Yorktown, Virginia, thereby inducing Britain's war-weary withdrawal. Washington was lauded for his outstanding conduct of the war, personal courage, and his concern for the underfed and ill-equipped men of his army. His suffering with them in their harshest trials, and his leadership and organizational ability, were later recognized by Congress as indisputably qualifying him for the presidency. He was already being called "the father of his country."

A period of longed-for retirement from 1783 to 1787 ended when Washington was called on to attend the Philadelphia Convention in May 1787. Lack of foreign markets for American goods and Britain's prohibition of trade with the British West Indies had led to a shortage of money and mounting debts. Following a mass insurgency in Massachusetts in 1786 called Shays' Rebellion, in which farmers demanded liquidation of their debts, fears of anarchy led to the growing conviction that a strong federal government was necessary. Washington used his influence with all the delegates to draft the Constitution. Signed first by Washington, the proposed Constitution established a national government consisting of "a supreme legislative, executive, and judiciary." Washington wrote: "It is clear to my conception that no government before introduced among mankind ever contained so many checks and such efficacious restraints to prevent it from...oppression." By June 1788 ten of the thirteen states had ratified the Constitution and on April 30, 1789, after unanimous election by the Electoral College, Washington took the oath in New York City as first president of the United States.

The judicial system and executive departments (the latter later known as the cabinet) established by Washington during his presidency have remained American institutions to the present time. Describing Washington's selection of executive heads for the five departments established by Congress, John *Adams, the vicepresident, wrote, "He seeks information from all quarters and judges more independently than any man I ever knew." Perhaps no two appointments had more repercussions for Washington's administration than the appointment of Alexander *Hamilton as secretary of the treasury and Thomas *Jefferson as secretary of state. Beginning in Washington's first term, Jefferson's opposition to Hamilton's economic and political philosophy eventually gave rise to two distinct parties: the Republican party (later to become the Democratic party) represented by Jefferson of Virginia, advocating an agrarian-based economy, and the Federalists, represented by Hamilton, whose proposal for the Bank of the United States and for increased industrialization anticipated the business interests of modern America.

Washington's foreign policy emphasized avoiding involvement in a European war, seeking treaties with Britain and Spain to open up the Ohio Valley to American settlement, and promoting the nation's import trade. On April 22, 1793, two days after his re-election, again unanimous, to a second term, and ten days after hearing of war between Britain and France, Washington voted for the Proclamation of

THOUGHTS ON WASHINGTON

- On the whole his character was, in its mass, perfect, in nothing bad, in few points indifferent; and it may truly be said that never did nature combine more perfectly to make a man great.

Thomas Jefferson

- To add brightness to the sun or glory to the name of Washington is impossible. Let none attempt it.

Abraham Lincoln

- He is next only to divinity.

Lord Byron

- He is too illiterate, unread, unlearned for his station and reputation.

John Adams

- The prevailin' weakness of most public men is to Slop Over. G. Washington never slopt over.

Artemus Ward

- Washington is the last person you'd ever suspect of having been a young man.

Samuel Eliot Morison

- He had no nakedness, but was born with his clothes on, and his hair powdered, and made a stately bow on his first appearance in the world.

Nathaniel Hawthorne

- The crude commercialism of America, its materializing spirit, are entirely due to the country having adopted for its national hero a man who was incapable of telling a lie.

Oscar Wilde

Neutrality prohibiting Americans from sending war materials to either country.

Despite Washington's efforts to resolve the Indian problem on the western front peacefully, it proved necessary to send an army against the Northwestern Indians. General Wayne's victory at the battle of Fallen Timbers in 1794 led to the Treaty of Greenville in 1795. The Indians gave up nearly all their land in Ohio, enabling pioneers to establish a new state. The Treaty of San Lorenzo in 1795 with Spain granted Americans the right to trade on the Mississippi.

In his farewell address of September 17, 1796, Washington set forth his principles for the future well-being of the nation. He stressed the need for religion to guide public morality, warned against foreign entanglements and partisan politics, and enjoined Americans to respect the Constitution and cherish the Union. He retired to his Mount Vernon plantation and, three days before his death, drafted a long document planning the rotation of crops on his farm.

J. R. Alden, *George Washington*, 1984.

N. Emery, *Washington: A Biography*, 1976.

B. Schwarz, *George Washington*, 1987.

C. C. Wall, *George Washington, Citizen-Soldier*, 1980.

WASSERMANN, AUGUST VON (1866–1925), German bacteriologist who discovered a blood serum test for syphilis. Born in Bamberg, Germany, he took his medical degree at the University of Strasbourg in 1888 and was then appointed assistant to Robert Koch at the Koch Institute of Infectious Diseases in Berlin (1890-1906). In 1891, in collaboration with another scientist, Wassermann reported on the toxins of diptheria and became famous after publishing a paper on immunity and toxin fixation in 1892. His reputation was enhanced in 1898 by a further paper on tetanus toxin in which he showed its affinity to nervous tissue. This work led to the development of biological methods of differentiating animal albumins. The precipitin reaction he produced became important medico-legally. He also developed innoculations against cholera and typhoid.

He received the titular rank of professor in 1898 and was appointed professor at the University of Berlin in 1903. In 1906 Wassermann announced his development of a serodiagnostic test for syphilis (the Wassermann test) following Jules Bordet and Octave Gengou's discovery of complement fixation. Blood or spinal fluid producing a positive reaction indicates the existence of antibodies formed as a result of infection with syphilis. Wassermann also proved that tabes dorsalis and progressive paralysis were late results of syphilis. This achievement revolutionized the diagnosis, control, and treatment of syphilis.

In 1907 he became director of therapeutic and serum research at the University of Berlin. From 1913 he directed the department of experimental therapy at the Kaiser Wilhelm Institute of Experimental Therapy, at Dahlem, Germany. He was responsible for discovering diagnostic tests for tuberculosis.

Wassermann's main genius as a brilliant scientific worker was to adapt and develop the research of others into practical use. He wrote over sixty scientific papers on serology and immunology and published a book *Immune Sera, Haemolysins, Cytotoxins and Precipitins* in 1904 (translated into English). Together with the German bacteriologist

Wilhelm Kolle, he published the six-volume *Handbook of Pathological Microorganisms* (1903-1909). W. Bullock, *History of Bacteriology*, 1960.

WATT, JAMES (1736–1819), Scottish engineer and inventor of the modern condensing steam engine. Watt was born at Greenock and at the age of nineteen traveled to London to be apprenticed as an instrument maker but was forced to return home, unable to stand up to the hard work and poverty. In 1756, using knowledge he had acquired in London, he tried to set up as an instrument maker in Glasgow, but the city guilds refused to recognize him as a craftsman as he had not completed his apprenticeship. The University of Glasgow helped him, however, and in 1757 he was given the title of mathematical instrument maker to the university.

Watt became a close friend of Joseph Black, who had discovered latent heat, and his student John Robinson, who later became professor of natural philosophy at Edinburgh. By then Watt was already considering how to improve the best available steam engine, the Newcomen engine, which was mainly used for pumping water, notably in draining mines. In 1764 he was able to make some progress in his experiments when he was given a Newcomen engine to repair. Observing its huge consumption of steam, Watt began studying the properties of the latter, particularly the relationship between density and pressure in determining the temperature of steam. From his experiments he concluded that two factors were important for the economical use of steam in a condensing machine: the temperature of the condensed steam had to be as low as possible (1,000° F. or less) to insure a good vacuum and the cylinder had to be as hot as the steam that entered it.

In 1765 Watt successfully solved the problem by condensing the steam in a separate vessel, thereby keeping the temperature of the condensation low and that of the cylinder high. A vacuum was maintained by adding an air pump for the removal of condensed steam. In 1769 Watt took out a patent for his invention. As a repayment to John Roebuck, the founder of Carron ironworks, for his financial backing, Watt gave him two-thirds of the profits. An engine was built near Linlithgow, allowing Watt to make further improvements.

In 1768 Matthew Boulton of Soho engineering works in Birmingham took over Roebuck's share of the invention's proceeds, and in 1775 successfully applied to parliament to continue the patent for another twenty-five years. Watt moved to Birmingham, where steam engines were manufactured by the firm Boulton and Watt. He took out a second steam engine patent in 1781 that showed five methods of converting the reciprocating motion to the piston into a rotating motion, enabling the engine to be adapted for driving ordinary machinery. In 1782 Watt took out a third patent for his invention of the double-action engine, in which both ends of the cylinder came into contact with the boiler and con-

denser instead of just one. A fourth patent in 1784 covered the way he arranged the links so that the top of the piston rod was connected to the beam, giving it the ability to pull or push.

A later invention was the centrifugal governor, which ensured the control of the speed of the rotary engines and was an early application of feedback, an important aspect of automation. Watt also invented the indicator diagram which showed the relation between the steam's pressure to its volume as the strokes proceeded.

Watt's invention helped revive the mining industry, which had suffered greatly due to the difficulties of draining mines. By 1873 his engine had replaced all but one of the Newcomen pumping engines. Watt's first invention speeded up the work and increased the power of the steam engine, but it was essentially a steam pump; his later invention adapted the steam engine to drive all kinds of machinery.

In 1800, when the act extending the patent of 1769 expired, Watt handed over his share in the business to his sons, and spent the rest of his years at Heathfield Hall near Birmingham, where he continued his research in mechanics and inventing.
M. Boulton, *The Selected Papers of Boulton and Watt*, 1981.
E. Robinson, *James Watt and the Steam Revolution*, 1969.

WEBSTER, DANIEL (1782–1852), American statesman, lawyer, and orator. At great personal sacrifice, Webster's father sent him to Dartmouth College and Webster was admitted to the bar in 1805, pursuing his law practice until the outbreak of the War of 1812. It was not until August 1812, when he wrote a formal protest against the government's trade embargo and its declaration of war with Great Britain, that Webster entered politics. He was elected to Congress that year as a representative from New Hampshire, serving two terms.

In the Dartmouth College Case of 1818, Webster's extraordinary powers of reasoning and eloquence stunned the Supreme Court to awed silence. An eye witness account of the case described one judge sitting with pen in hand suspended during Webster's entire four-hour argument and Chief Justice John Marshall bent forward, his "eyes suffused with tears." Webster was arguing for the immunity of the Dartmouth College charter (and by implication all privately endowed charities) from federal or state interference.

The Dartmouth College Case established Webster as one of the foremost legal minds of his time. He argued more cases before the Supreme Court than any private lawyer before or since, and because many cases required close analysis of meaning and intent of the Constitution, he became known as "the Expounder of the Constitution."

Because of his great skill as an orator, Webster was asked to deliver keynote speeches on occasions of national significance. Among the most histori-

> - I shall know but one country. The ends I aim at shall be my country's, my God's, and Truth's. I was born an American; I live an American; and I shall die an American.
>
> - Whatever makes men good Christians, makes them good citizens.
>
> - When tillage begins, other arts follow. The farmers, therefore, are the founders of human civilization.
>
> - Liberty exists in proportion to wholesome restraint; the more restraint on others to keep off from us, the more liberty we have.
>
> - Inconsistencies of opinion, arising form changes of circumstances, are often justifiable.
>
> - Repression is the seed of revolution.
>
> **Daniel Webster**

cally memorable were the Plymouth Oration given in December 1820, marking the two hundredth anniversary of the landing of the Pilgrims; the Bunker Hill Oration given June 17, 1825, marking fifty years since the first battle of the American Revolution; and the oration on August 2, 1826, commemorating John *Adams and Thomas *Jefferson, the two principal framers of the Declaration of Independence, who had died within hours of each other a few weeks earlier. On this astoundingly singular conjunction of events, Webster delivered these words: "Both had been Presidents, both had lived to great age, both were early patriots, and both were distinguished and ever honored by their immediate agency in the act of independence. As their lives themselves were the gifts of Providence, who is not willing to recognize in their happy termination...proofs that our country and its benefactors are objects of His care?"

In January 1830 Webster delivered before the Senate the great rebuttal speech known as the Reply to Hayne. Robert Hayne, a senator from South Carolina, had agreed to indict New England for presumably undermining the sale of public lands in the West. This indictment was also an attack on Webster who, as a senator from Massachusetts, where he had taken up residence, was viewed by the hostile factions in the Senate as spokesman for New England. Hayne also declared South Carolina's right to abrogate the government's tariff laws and accused Webster of impugning the integrity of the South for maintaining slavery. With great strength of conviction, Webster defended the "honor" of New England and presented his deeply held ideal of the supremacy of the Union. Although he regarded slavery as an evil, he held that it was within the do-

main of the Southern states and therefore wrong for the government to interfere. Liberty was a noble goal, but not even the combating of slavery was worth disunion. His concluding words, "Liberty *and* Union, now and forever, one and inseparable!" can be said to have been the guiding principle of President *Lincoln in his conduct of the Civil War.

Webster gave his last great speech, known as the Seventh of March Speech, in 1850. In that year the Union was seriously threatened by radicals from the North and South. Webster defended the Compromise of 1850 which contained a fugitive slave law requiring state officials to abide by the Constitution and return fugitive slaves. In appealing to the moderates, Webster called down upon his head the bitter denunciation of the abolitionists and northern liberals.

Webster served as secretary of state in 1840 and again in 1850. In 1836 he ran for the presidency on behalf of the Whig party, but carried only the state of Massachusetts.

I. H. Bartlett, *Daniel Webster,* 1981.
P. D. Erickson, *The Poetry of Events; Daniel Webster's Rhetoric of the American Dream,* 1986.
S. Nathasa, *Daniel Webster and Jacksonian Democracy,* 1973.
M. D. Peterson, *The Great Triumvirate,* 1987.

WEIZMANN, CHAIM (1874–1952), Zionist leader, chemist, and first president of the state of Israel. Weizmann was born in Motol, a village near Pinsk in Russia, the son of a timber merchant. He studied chemistry in Berlin and at an early age was attracted to the newly-founded Zionist movement. In 1898 he went to Fribourg University in Switzerland to complete his doctorate in chemistry and in 1904 was appointed lecturer in chemistry at Manchester University.

Weizmann was a supporter of practical Zionism, which stressed the importance of Jewish settlement in Palestine. He was also one of the initiators of the idea of a Hebrew university to be established in Jerusalem. During World War I he moved to London and made an important contribution to the British war effort by his discovery of an original process to yield acetone, which was required for the production of munitions. This brought him into contact with leaders of the British government. By this time he had attained a prominent role in the Zionist movement and was the main force behind the Balfour Declaration of 1917, which promised the establishment of a Jewish national home in Palestine.

In 1920 Weizmann became president of the World Zionist Organization (WZO); a year previously he had represented Zionist interests at the Versailles Peace Conference. He received support from his well-developed contacts with British officials and from his close association with the Jewish Labor movement in Palestine. He also maintained good relations with Jewish financiers around the world. As president, he supported a policy of moderation and cooperation with the British and was greatly disappointed when the Arab riots of 1929 led to British restrictions on Jewish immigration and settlement. Though this policy was effectively restricted by the MacDonald Letter of 1931, Weizmann was not re-elected president of the WZO at the Zionist Congress that year. Following his resignation he established the Daniel Sieff Scientific Institute in Rehovot, Palestine, which was later to become the Weizmann Institute; he also built a home in Rehovot, dividing his time between there and London.

In 1935 Weizmann was once more elected president of the WZO. He supported the proposal of the Peel Commission appointed by the British government to solve the Arab-Jewish problem by partitioning Palestine, but this policy was not implemented at that time. Instead the British decided on a program ending Jewish immigration. While this was bitterly opposed by all Zionists, the outbreak of World War II and the fight against Adolf *Hitler presented other priorities. Weizmann firmly backed the British war effort and helped to establish the Jewish Brigade in the British army in 1944. His son, a Royal Air Force pilot, was killed during the war.

After the war, with the Jews living in Palestine launching an underground campaign against the British, who were preventing survivors of the Holocaust from entering the territory, Weizmann was seen as too pro-British. In 1946 he resigned the WZO presidency, but his reputation remained so great that he was nonetheless the principal Zionist negotiator in the United Nations' talks which led to the decision on the partition of Palestine and the establishment of the state of Israel.

When the state was proclaimed in May 1948, Weizmann was elected as its provisional president, and his position was officially confirmed by Israel's first Knesset (parliament) in February 1949. Thereafter, he made his home permanently in Rehovot, serving as president until his death, although chafing at being a mere figurehead. In his last years he published his autobiography, *Trial and Error*.

Y. Reinharz, *Chaim Weizmann: The Making of a Jewish Leader*, 1985.
N. Rose, *Chaim Weizmann*, 1987.

WELLINGTON, DUKE OF (1769–1852), Anglo-Irish military hero and statesman. He was born in Dublin into a prosperou̇ family of Anglo-Irish nobility. His father, Lord Mornington, was professor of music at Trinity College, Dublin.

Following three unhappy years at Eton public school, it was clear he was not destined for academic success; one of his chief consolations was playing the violin. As a younger son with limited inheritance prospects, he needed a career, so for lack of anything better he took a commission in the army. First he was dispatched to the Royal Academy of Equitation at Angers (France) to learn horsemanship and fencing, along with other subjects suitable for an officer and gentleman. In 1787 he was appointed ensign in the 73rd Highland Regiment but soon transferred to a regiment serving in Dublin.

In 1794, following a short time in the Irish Parliament, he burned his violin to demonstrate that from now on the army would be his sole occupation. After winning commendation in a disastrous campaign against the French in The Netherlands, he went to India to defend the possessions of the East India Company, achieving a major victory with the capture of Seringapatam in 1799. Colonel Wellesley (the spelling of the family name had been altered by this time) was installed as governor, and distinguished himself as a fair ruler of the conquered city, making efforts to stamp out corruption in the British administration.

After further successful campaigning against native rulers under French influence, Wellesley returned to England in 1805, where he was honored with a knighthood. Now Sir Arthur, Wellesley was appointed chief secretary to Ireland, a thankless task that he tried to perform fairly. His ambitions, however, lay elsewhere — in taking an active part in the war against *Napoleon in Europe. In 1807 he participated in the siege and capture of Copenhagen, taking the Danish fleet out of Napoleon's reaches. This was a quick war with relatively few casualties, and Sir Arthur won praise from the British government for his valor and from the defeated Danes for his "human and generous conduct."

During the years 1809–1814, Sir Arthur achieved national fame as commander of the joint British-Portuguese and Spanish force, fighting to free the Iberian Peninsula from Napoleon's armies, and was awarded a peerage in 1809. Wellington was plagued by delays of promised funding for his forces and was constantly fighting a losing battle against the riotous behavior of his troops after victories. Although he believed "we have in the service the scum of the earth as common soldiers" and the only way to run the army was "to have a hand of iron," he initiated measures to improve the lot of the ordinary soldiers, such as the use of tents for overnight camps instead of sleeping in the open, and the provision of prefabricated hospitals. He limited leave for his officers in Lisbon to forty-eight hours saying that is as long as any reasonable man can wish to stay in bed with one woman. He gained the confidence of his soldiers, transmitting his own, at times overbearing, self-confidence. He won widespread acclaim in England when at the Battle of Vitoria in 1813, French forces were decisively defeated and the war was taken over the border with Wellington entering Paris in triumph in 1814. He was created a duke, and awarded a country home and a gift of 500,000 lbs. of beef.

As British ambassador in Paris, Wellington enjoyed a cycle of balls, plays, and hunts with the attentions of fashionable society ladies. He was then sent to represent Britain at the Congress held in Vienna to redraw the map of Europe and restore its stability. While there news arrived of Napoleon's flight from exile in Elba and he traveled to Brussels to command the British, Dutch, and Belgian forces. Among his preparations for the coming battle was the purchase of a new pair of longer boots ordered from his bootmaker in London — the style has carried his name ever since.

The Battle of Waterloo of June 15, 1815, began with serious reverses for the allied forces. Inexperienced Dutch and Belgian soldiers broke ranks in the face of a French cavalry charge. Wellington had to make a dash for his life, taking his horse over a ditch filled with Gordon Highlanders, their bayonets fixed. The French were slow to exploit their advantage and Wellington had time to reorganize his army, employing British troops in square formations against which successive waves of enemy cavalry charges broke. The first day's fighting ended in a stalemate; British forces had gained ground but their Prussian allies had been heavily mauled. The duke decided on strategic withdrawal to the village of Waterloo. Here he assembled his battle lines and dressed in civilian clothes, rode up and down the ranks to inspire them. It was a close-fought battle but his skillful tactics and the timely arrival of Prussian reinforcements won the day and changed the history of Europe.

The victor of Waterloo (popularly known as the Iron Duke) did not return to England to retire but rather exchanged the battlefields of Europe for the lobby of Parliament, where he defended the old social and political order. Soon after he entered the Cabinet in 1818 there was serious unrest in the north of England, with calls for reform of the electoral system. Wellington supported local magistrates, who bloodily suppressed one such demonstration in Manchester's Saint Peter's Field and the massacre became known as Peterloo. He served as prime minister 1828–1829 and reluctantly introduced in 1829 a

Wellington receives captured French eagles

Catholic Emancipation Act in response to unrest in Ireland. Out of office in 1832, he led the opposition to the reform of Parliament and so strong was the popular feeling against him that his home, Apsley House, was attacked by London mobs several times. Later the duke was pelted with mud and an attempt was made to pull him off his horse. The duke, however, stayed firm in his belief that to give into demands for reform would be the first step to revolution. He told his confidante Mrs. Arbuthnot, "It may be relied upon that we shall have a Revolution. I have never doubted the Inclination and disposition of the lower Orders of the People. I told you years ago that the people are rotten to the core...They are not bloodthirsty, but they are desirous of plunder."

Despite the duke's vigorous opposition the Reform Bill finally passed. Wellington continued to be active in Parliament and as commander of the army. Although suffering from increasing deafness and rheumatism, he found plenty of time for a colossal amount of letter-writing and for lady friends. By the time he died he had become not just a great war hero but a national institution. He was given a lavish state funeral and buried in Saint Paul's Cathedral with ten thousand in the procession and public buildings draped in black; one and a half million people lined the route.

L. James, *The Iron Duke*, 1992.
E. Longford, *Wellington, The Years of the Sword*, 1969.
N. Thompson, *Wellington After Waterloo*, 1986.
D. Young, *Wellington's Masterpiece*, 1972.

WESLEY, JOHN BENJAMIN (1703–1791), English evangelical preacher and founder of the Methodist Society. He was born in Lincolnshire, the fifteenth of nineteen children, less than half of whom survived infancy.

BY AND ABOUT WELLINGTON

- I think it is indifferent how a soldier is clothed, provided it is in a uniform manner, and that he is forced to keep himself clean and smart.
- In Spain I shaved myself overnight and sometimes slept five or six hours; sometimes only two or three. I undressed very seldom, never in the first four years.
- None but the worst description of men enter the regular service.
- It was the most desperate business I ever was in; I never took so much trouble about any Battle; & never was so near being beat (on the Battle of Waterloo).

- Wellington was always at his coolest at the hottest of moments.

  Winston Churchill

His formal education, by his mother, began at the age of five. She was particularly fond of John, probably because of an event that occurred in 1708. He had been trapped in the nursery of the Epworth rectory as it was engulfed by fire but, exhibiting extraordinary presence of mind for a five-year-old, he pushed a chest to a window, stood on it, and attracted the attention of rescuers below. This was regarded by witnesses, and later by the Methodist church, as an indication of special divine interest in the boy.

At the age of ten Wesley went to the Charterhouse School in London and after six years there obtained a scholarship to Christchurch College, Oxford; in 1725 he was ordained as a deacon and, shortly after, a fellow of Lincoln College. At Oxford in 1728 his brother Charles had gathered together a group of young men with the intention of studying Bible and books of divinity. Wesley soon emerged as their leader and began to promote other activities, such as visiting the sick. The group became known derisively as "The Bible Moths," "The Holy Club," and, notably, "The Methodists," because of the curiously methodical religion they prescribed. Yet at this stage Wesley's "Methodism" was still concerned with personal holiness through inward searching rather than outward benevolence.

In 1735 the numbers in the club dwindled, and both John and Charles were searching for a new challenge. A chance meeting with General James Edward Oglethorpe, the founder of the American colony of Georgia, led to an invitation for John to become pastor at the new settlement of Savannah, and for Charles to be the general's personal secretary. John was captivated by the notion of preaching Christianity to the "noble American savages," and with their mother's encouragement they accepted the positions.

In December 1735 the Wesley brothers set sail for the colony. On board their ship was a party of twenty-six Moravian settlers. John was awed by the simple faith of these Christians when, during a violent Atlantic storm that shattered the ship's mast, they calmly and courageously sang hymns while he nervously contemplated his imminent demise. On their arrival in Georgia, the Moravians were met by their own minister, August Spangenberg, whom Wesley approached for counsel. Spangenberg, who later remarked of Wesley "that true grace dwelt and reigned in him," stressed in their brief conversation the two themes that were later to dominate Wesley's preachings — the inward witness of the Spirit and the knowledge of personal salvation.

Despite this inspirational beginning his time in Georgia proved a failure. His new parishioners were not pious Oxford students but a motley collection, mostly ex-convicts, who had no time for the strictures of Wesley's methods. The climactic event that ended his time in Georgia involved a young woman whom he considered marrying, but while he prevaricated, the woman married another suitor. Wesley, shocked by her behavior and perhaps harboring certain resentments, refused her communion, an action which resulted in his being sued for defamation of character. Not waiting for the issue to be resolved, Wesley left for England.

On his arrival in early 1738, the dejected Wesley sought out the small Moravian community that was on its way to America. He saw that he had been ineffectual because he had lacked a firm personal faith until, in his words, on May 24, 1738, while attending a Bible society meeting "the peace was granted." This marked a turning point in his religion and his life. His formidable personal energy and intellect, no longer focused on his own personal salvation, were directed outward.

In 1739 Wesley was invited to become pastor to a poor community of colliers in Kingswood Chase. At first he was reluctant to preach to people who in all likelihood would be uneducated and unwilling recipients, but he realized that this was a mission necessitated by his new convictions.

Wesley continued the pervious pastor's habit of preaching in fields and on street corners. Soon, with his sincere and penetrating message of personal salvation, he was drawing crowds; people yelled and convulsed in religious fervor as he spoke. His own reputation grew rapidly as he traveled to preach in prisons and other towns. Religious societies sprang up that drew their character from Wesley's teachings and were regarded as distinctly Methodist.

Many in England, however, believed that Wesley's teachings might stir up rebellious sentiments and others were apparently jealous of his remarkable success. The Church of England opposed his "enthusiastic" style and eventually banned him from their pulpits. He continued to travel throughout Britain, mostly on horseback, preaching in the open, usually four or five times a day. Occasionally he and his lay preachers encountered mobs organized to break up his meetings. His rule was always to stand up to a mob, despite sometimes barely escaping death.

Wesley was endowed with an extraordinary gift for organization. By 1745, through all the persecution, this small, intense man had established a nationwide network and held the first gathering of his clerical supporters. Recognizing that for the most part, his parishioners were from the lower classes, he determined a need to establish schools for the poor. In 1774 he was perhaps the first notable voice in England to speak out against slavery. He campaigned for improving the conditions in prisons and moved to establish clinics for the poor. His compassion for humanity and sense of social justice were in many ways generations ahead of their time. He preached his last sermon in 1791, at eighty-eight, and was buried in Westminster Abbey.

F. Baker, *John Wesley*, 1970.

M. Edwards, *John Wesley and the 18th Century*, 1955.

F. J. McConnell, *Evangelicals, Revolutionists and Idealists*, 1972.

M. Schmidt, *John Wesley*, 2 vols., 1971.

WHITEHEAD, ALFRED NORTH (1861–1947), English mathematician and philosopher. Born in Ramsgate, on the island of Thanet off the east coast of the county of Kent, Whitehead came from a religious family. His childhood in the island's quiet rural community left him with an abiding sense of man's connectedness with nature. His over-protective parents considered him too frail to go to school and he was educated at home until he was fourteen, mastering Latin at ten and Greek at twelve, and showing special interest in poetry and history; he then entered the ancient private school of Sherborne, where he was exceptionally successful and from which he won a scholarship to study mathematics at Trinity College, Cambridge University.

At Trinity, where he became a fellow in 1884, Whitehead joined the elite intellectuals' club, "The Apostles", and developed friendships with many of the most prominent men of philosophy and letters of his day. His most distinguished pupil was Bertrand *Russell, with whom he collaborated on the three-volume *Principia Mathematica*, published between 1910 and 1913 after ten years of work. This work, which seeks to derive mathematics from the principles of formal logic, has been described by the contemporary philosopher W. V. Quine as "one of the great intellectual monuments of all time."

In 1910, Whitehead left Cambridge for London University where, in 1914, he was elected Professor of Applied Mathematics at Imperial College of Science and Technology, where he remained until 1924. It was during this period that he did his most intensive work in the philosophy of science; his theories were firmly rooted in the empirical tradition of John *Locke, George Berkeley, and David *Hume: in *Principles of Natural Knowledge* (1919) and *The Concept of Nature* (1920) he developed a concept of nature as nothing more than that which is observed in perception through the senses. In so doing, he attacked the "bifurcation of nature" into apparent nature (that of immediate experience, with characteristics such as color and sound) and causal nature (the world as posited by science, consisting of particles in motion which do not themselves really possess color or sound but somehow give rise to our perceptions of them). He argued that natural science had to be an account of the content of perception rather than a speculation about the causes; he also developed an ingenious explanation of how certain concepts used in mathematics and physics which are not directly given in experience (such as those of "point" and "line") can be defined in terms of things that are.

Meanwhile, Whitehead had come to the attention of a wider public, both through his popular *An Introduction to Mathematics* (1911), and as an imaginative and original thinker in the field of education. He commented that "culture is the activity of thought, and receptiveness to beauty and humane feelings. Scraps of information have nothing to do with it," indicative of his view that education should encourage love of learning rather than force-feed facts. His theories and recommendations inspired many teachers and educationalists in Britain and the United States.

Whitehead was married in 1890, and had two sons and a daughter. However, tragedy struck the family in 1918, when one of the sons was killed in action during World War I. Nonetheless, although this made him even more alive to the horrors of war, Whitehead continued to resist the pacifism of Russell, although the two remained friends and Whitehead visited Russell when he was imprisoned for anti-war agitation. A warm and affectionate man, he was much beloved by those who knew him since, while often stubborn in his opinions, he seldom let them interfere with his friendships.

Whitehead left Britain for the United States and a chair in philosophy at Harvard University, which he held from 1924 to 1937. During this period he developed a system of metaphysics to compare in scope and complexity with those of G. W. *Leibniz or Baruch *Spinoza. In *Process and Reality* (1929) and *Adventures of Ideas*, he combined a critique of scientific materialism with a "philosophy of organism," an all-embracing view of reality in which each basic element (or "actual entity") is essentially a process of self-development, or self-creation, by selection and rearrangement of the material provided by its background: on completion of this process it in turn becomes material for the self-creations of the next generation of actual entities. While the obvious analogy is with the life cycle of plants and other organisms, Whitehead sought to apply this formulation to the interpretation of everything from physics to psychology.

This formidable attempt to characterize the concrete reality of the world reflects the influence of Whitehead's youthful sense of the unity of nature and his strong religious sentiment, tempered by his rigorous philosophical method. Although he founded no school of philosophy, his ideas continue to have an influence, especially in the United States. C. Hartshorne, *Whitehead's Philosophy: Selected Essays 1935-1970,* 1972.

WHITMAN, WALT (1819–1892), American poet. Whitman is the first poet of the new American experience: independent, progressive, and optimistic. Breaking from convention, he wrote free verse chants in the American vernacular, praising the varieties of individual and social expression in an expanding and confident America.

Whitman was born in rural West Hills on Long Island, New York, or Paumanok as the Indians called it and as Whitman referred to it in his poems. The natural scenes of early childhood became subjects of his poetry, as did the city of New York, where he would later live. He also grew up during the first manifestations of the American Renaissance, that period of American politics and literature that saw the rise of Jacksonian democracy, idealization of the commmon man, and the philosophy of Ralph Waldo

Emerson, leader of the Transcendentalists. With his doctrine of "self-reliance," Emerson proposed that every man is a center of the world both in spirit and worldly experience.

In 1835 Whitman began to work as a printer's assistant and then as a teacher. By 1841 he had begun a career as a journalist, editing a series of news papers in New York City. In 1848 Whitman left his editing job in New York and journeyed to New Orleans where he stayed a short time, picking up a smattering of French. Rejuvenated by this exotic American city, he returned by way of the Mississippi River to New York that same year and took charge of the *Brooklyn Weekly Freeman*, a Free-Soil Democratic party paper. As it modified its views to satisfy the more conservative elements in the Democratic party, Whitman found himself at odds with the traditional parties and his poems of this time expressing his disaffiliation and disaffection with politics foreshadowed the style of *Leaves of Grass*.

After 1849 Whitman worked as a carpenter. During this period he composed his works like other Transcendentalist writers, recording a few lines of inspiration and then, rather than perfecting their form along neoclassical lines, allowing new ideas to germinate freely until the poem was fully written.

He published the first edition of *Leaves* with his own money in 1855, his name appearing neither on the cover nor title page. Rather, he stamped his achievement of ninety-four pages with twelve poems of unconventional style and subject with an equally unconventional signature — a picture of himself casually posing in workingman's clothes with a beard and broad-brimmed hat.

This volume of poems, subjected to several revisions and additions over the years (eventually extending to nearly four hundred pages) contained a type of poetry unknown at the time — free verse chants, rhythmic and biblically oratorical. They described the multiplicity of American life: urban, rural, dockside, and communal. He wrote in this first volume poems celebrating the body and sexuality, comradeship, and the equality of all classes and races in society. He outraged many of his contemporaries when he wrote such lines as: I believe in the flesh and the appetites, / Seeing, hearing, feeling are miracles, / and each part and tag of me is a miracle. / Divine am I inside and out, / and I make holy whatever I touch / or am touch'd from, / The scent of these armpits' aroma finer than prayer, / This head more than churches, bibles, and all the creeds.

As the bard of democracy, Whitman wrote of the "en masse," the new social reality that formed in the urban centers, creating new energies that were to carry the young democratic nation into the future. Though a commercial failure, apparently because it was too radical a departure from conventional tastes, Whitman's first publication of a book of verse was lauded by critics including Emerson, the pre-eminent man of letters in New England at the time.

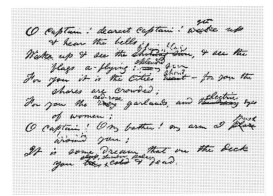

Whitman's manuscript of "O Captain! My Captain!"

The outbreak of the Civil War in 1861 marked a change in Whitman's vocation as he became the "Good Gray Poet," taking up the cause of the Union. In 1862, when Whitman's brother was wounded at the Battle of Fredericksburg, he traveled south to be with his brother and then stayed on in Washington, D.C., visiting soldiers both Union and Confederate, offering them solace. His poems published after the war show the effects of Whitman's exposure to its horrors, his works shifting toward greater realism.

In 1867 Whitman published the fourth edition of *Leaves,* including many new poems together with his old poems which had undergone significant revision. In 1871 he published his essay, *Democratic Vistas*, a pessimistic piece reflecting Whitman's disillusionment with the materialist tendencies of the nation after the Civil War and calling for a renewal of America's spiritual wellsprings. That year also saw the publication of *Passage to India*, a work showing a new international awareness on the poet's part.

From 1872 on Whitman's health began to deteriorate seriously and in 1873 he suffered his first stroke. His fortunes took a brief turn for the better in 1876 when, in commemoration of the American Revolution, Whitman's *Leaves of Grass* was published in England to much acclaim by that country's more radical elements. But once again Whitman, because of his views, fell into disfavor at home; the Boston edition of *Leaves* was withheld from the public by the Society for the Suppression of Vice. Nevertheless, Whitman was soon able to publish in Philadelphia and in 1884 earned enough royalties to purchase a house in Camden, New Jersey. This Philadelphia edition represents the final form in which the historic volume would appear.

Whitman continued to write in his last years, publishing *November Boughs*, a collection of sixty-two new poems. His poems established a new norm and inspired the great American poets who came after him; they placed the particular stamp of American culture and letters on the world with its mixture of mass culture and the glory of the individual, Ameri-

Thrive, cities — bring your freight, bring your shows, ample and sufficient rivers,

Expand, being than which none else is perhaps more spiritual,

Keep your places, objects than which none else is more lasting.

You have waited, you always wait, you dumb beautiful ministers,

We receive you with free sense at last, and are insatiate henceforward,

Not you any more shall be able to foil us, or withhold yourselves from us,

We use you, and do not cast you aside — we plant you permanently within us,

We fathom you not — we love you — there is perfection in you also,

You furnish your parts toward eternity,

Great or small, you furnish your parts towards the soul.

Taken from the final stanza of "Crossing Brooklyn Ferry," from *Leaves of Grass*

---

can myth and the penchant for vistas full of metaphorical meaning.

G. W. Allen, *Walt Whitman*, 1969.
P. Callow, *Walt Whitman*, 1992.
H. S. Canby, *Walt Whitman, an American: A Study in Biography*, 1943.
D. Zweig, *Walt Whitman*, 1984.

WILDE, OSCAR (1854–1900), Irish dramatist, writer, and wit. Born of wealthy parents, Wilde was raised in a highly literary family. His father was an author of archeological works and folklore, as well as being Ireland's leading ear and eye doctor, while his mother, from whom Wilde inherited his literary tastes, was a poet and scholar of Celtic myth and folklore. At nine years old, Wilde was sent to the Portora Royal School. Already noted for his wit, he was also a quick reader, and in his later years at the school he orally translated works by *Plato, *Virgil, and *Thucydides, winning prizes for his scholarship in Greek and classics.

At sixteen, Wilde entered Trinity College, Dublin, where he won additional prizes for scholarship; in 1874, he was awarded a scholarship to Oxford. There, he won the coveted Newdigate Prize for poetry and met two men who were to have a tremendous influence on his works, John Ruskin and Walter Pater. Ruskin, professor and author, believed that one can judge a civilization by its art and also encouraged privileged students to experience manual labor for themselves. Pater, on the other hand, taught "art for art's sake" and encouraged his students to live life as fully as possible by exploring new and strange experiences. The two promoted what was called the Aesthetic Movement, to which Wilde came to subscribe fully. He dressed sensationally, wearing silk stockings, knee britches, a braided velvet coat and a large green tie.

When Wilde moved to London in 1878, his personality, eccentric dress, and literary flair soon made him a celebrity, even though he had yet to publish any poetry outside of collegiate literary magazines and was an art critic simply by virtue of describing himself as such, which vindicated his belief that, "If one looks like a genius, and talks like a genius, then it is only a question of time — if one is invited to the right parties — before one comes to be perceived as a genius." He also became known for his cultivation of beautiful women, particularly the French actress Sarah Bernhardt, to whom he ingratiated himself by throwing an armful of lilies at her feet.

In 1881 Wilde published a collection of poetry that achieved moderate success. His real coup came when Gilbert and Sullivan's *Patience,* satirizing Wilde and the Aesthetic Movement, opened in London. Wilde was now a celebrity and went on a speaking tour of the United States (telling the bewildered customs man that, "I have nothing to declare but my genius") and was warmly received around the country.

Wilde then settled in Paris for three months, winning his way into the leading literary and artistic circles. While there, he wrote two plays, *Vera* and *The Duchess of Padua,* but neither achieved real success. Desperately needing money, he again went on a lecture tour, this time of Great Britain and Ireland, and in Dublin he met Constance Lloyd, whom he married in 1884.

The couple settled in London, where Wilde had his house completely redecorated with wallpaper

---

WILDE'S WIT

- To win back my youth...there is nothing I wouldn't do — except take exercise, get up early, or be a useful member of the community.
- Work is the curse of the drinking classes.
- Every woman is a rebel and usually in wild revolt against herself.
- He hasn't a single redeeming vice.
- To love oneself is the beginning of a lifelong romance.
- If one tells the truth, one is sure — sooner or later — to be found out.
- I can resist everything except temptation.
- One should never make one's debut with a scandal. One should reserve that to give an interest to one's old age.
- Prayer must never be answered; if it is, it ceases to be prayer and becomes correspondence.
- Philosophy teaches us to bear with equanimity the misfortune of others.

Wilde, by Henri de Toulouse Lautrec

imported from Japan, a minimum of furniture, and the ceiling in the drawing room adorned with peacock feathers. Constance gave birth to two sons. In 1887, Wilde secured a regular job, working as editor at *The Lady's World* magazine, which he soon renamed *The Woman's World* and transformed into a serious forum for women's opinions on literature, art, and modern life. He published *The Happy Prince,* a collection of fairy tales, in 1888, and a well-known essay, "The Decay of Lying," in 1889.

Upon leaving *The Woman's World* in 1889, Wilde entered his most productive period, finishing his novel *The Picture of Dorian Gray* within a year. In 1891 he published *Intentions, Lord Arthur Savile's Crime and Other Stories*, and *A House of Pomegranates*, and in the next year, he published his first great play, *Lady Windmere's Fan*; *Salome* and *A Woman of No Importance* followed in 1893.

Wilde's sexual identity had been ambivalent for some time, and he now began to experiment with homosexuality, having an affair with a Canadian named Robert Ross in 1886 and, later, with a number of male prostitutes. In 1891 he met the twenty-one year-old Lord Alfred Douglas, son of the eighth Marquis of Queensbury, codifier of boxing's Queensbury Rules. Douglas was talented, rich, attractive, and homosexual, and the two men became lovers. Wilde became obsessed with him, and when they were separated, wrote him love letters, one of which Douglas carelessly put in the pocket of a jacket he later gave away. The letter fell into to the hands of blackmailers, who brought the letter to Douglas's father.

By 1895 Wilde's career was at its peak, with production of the highly popular *An Ideal Husband* and *The Importance of Being Earnest* both running on the London stage. However in February of that year, he sued Queensbury for libel after the latter accused him of "posing as a sodomite"; in so doing, Wilde effectively put himself on trial for homosexuality. He lost the case, but the Marquis was not satisfied and convinced the public prosecutor to arrest and imprison Wilde on the then-criminal charge of homosexuality. His arrest was widely publicized, and public feeling against him ran high. After two trials he was found guilty and sentenced to two years of imprisonment with hard labor.

Wilde was now bankrupt, his goods sold at public auction, his home invaded by a mob rummaging through his papers. Meanwhile, he was kept in solitary confinement for twenty-three hours a day. After a near breakdown, his conditions were improved and old friends rallied to allow him more books and the privilege of using paper and ink; he began the composition of *De Profundis*.

Wilde was released from prison in 1897, whereupon he left for France, never to return to England. During the first few months after his release from jail, he wrote *The Ballad of Reading Gaol,* inspired by his prison experiences. In these few months, it seemed as though he might be reconciled with his wife, who had moved to Switzerland and later Italy as a result of the scandal. However, she asked to be assured that his relationship with Douglas was over, which he could not do, thus ending all hope for a reconciliation. She died seven months later, and after he and Douglas were reunited he ceased to work. Wilde began to drink absinthe heavily, and after he had moved to Italy, then Switzerland, and finally back to Paris, his health had deteriorated completely. He died at the age of forty-six from cerebral meningitis with the possible complication of syphilis.

R. Ellman, *Oscar Wilde,* 1987.
R. K. Miller, *Oscar Wilde*, 1982.
H. Montgomery-Hyde, *Oscar Wilde,* 1975.
H. Pearson, *The Life of Oscar Wilde,* 1946.

WILLIAM I, THE CONQUEROR (c.1027–1087), king of Normandy and England. William was born in Falaise, Lower Normandy, the illegitimate son of Robert, Duke of Normandy. With the death of his father in 1035 on a pilgrimage to Jerusalem, he succeeded to his father's title. Still a child, he was unable to exercise power and the country fell into a state of chaos and civil war. William was under the protection of guardians nominated from among his relatives, his life was thought to be in danger, and he often changed his residence.

In 1047 he defeated in battle his cousin Count Guy, a rival claimant for the dukedom. The odds were against William in this contest and he was rescued by the intervention of King Henry I of France. Later this same monarch feared Normandy becoming too powerful and, allied with William's enemies, attempted to invade the dukedom but was rebuffed.

As William entered early manhood, his skills as a warrior and the sheer strength of his will and personality became apparent. Stronger than many other soldiers, even on horseback he could draw a bow weaker men could not use and, being 5 feet 10 inches in height, was tall for the times. He defeated challenges to his authority from both neighboring magnates and his own family. By 1049 his reputation was such that the count of Flanders agreed to allow him to marry his daughter, Mathilda. This was more than a strategic alliance; there was genuine attraction involved — at least on William's part. He pursued Mathilda for seven years and eventually resorted to physical violence to get her to marry him. He was unusual among rulers of his time for remaining faithful to his wife. There is evidence she was just 4 feet 2 inches tall but still managed to bear twelve children.

William's firm rule in Normandy created stable conditions in which the economy flourished. He also brought surrounding territories into a Norman sphere of influence through skillful use of force of arms. He was a ruthless enemy, not hesitating to put to the torch the homes of those who stood in his way or mutilate those unlucky enough to fall into his hands. When he seized the neighboring territory of Maine, it is alleged that he had its ruler, Count Walter, and his wife murdered while they were his guests in Falaise.

However, he was careful to reward the nobles who supported him and he also cultivated good relations with the church. The building of abbeys and castles served as symbols of his power. By 1066 William was sufficiently secure to launch his most ambition venture: the invasion of England.

The English ruler, Edward the Confessor, had promised the crown to William in 1051 but this prospect was not welcomed in England. When Harold succeeded Edward to the throne in 1066, William was doubly aggrieved: Edward's promise was violated and Harold had also behaved falsely, since a few years earlier, when shipwrecked on the Normandy coast, he became a guest at William's court and joined him in a campaign in Brittany, after which he swore an oath of allegiance to William.

William invaded England with a force of some seven thousand men, landing in Pevensey on the south coast. Harold's army, after defeating an invading Norwegian army in Yorkshire, was forced to march rapidly south to confront William, hoping to catch the Normans by surprise with the speed of their advance; however, the Normans were forewarned. The English forces put up a brave struggle, driving back Norman cavalry and infantry charges, and it seemed that they might win the day, but William rallied his troops. A hail of arrows rained down on Harold and his men as the Norman knights charged once more, King Harold was fatally injured (according to tradition, with an arrow in his eye), the English ranks broke and William had won a kingdom.

After suppressing the last elements of serious resistance he returned to France with a rich harvest of plunder. For the rest of his life Normandy remained William's chief residence. He would visit England in order to put down rebellious outbreaks, such as the uprising in the north in 1069, which he quashed with customary ruthlessness, sacking the city of York. When Danish invaders linked up with English rebels, William again marched north. He trapped the Danes on the banks of the River Humber, enforced his peace terms on them, and destroyed the country between York and Durham so that it was left unplowed for nine years.

Although unabashed at resorting to force, William was keen to show that his rule over England was a legitimate continuation from the reign of Edward the Confessor. He held his coronation in Westminster Abbey in December 1066 and two years later had Mathilda crowned queen. In 1070 there was a further coronation by papal legates. He soon replaced the existing aristocracy and clergy with those of his own choosing. William's Norman supporters were rewarded with impressive estates. His half-brother Odo, already bishop of Bayeux, was made earl of Kent. Castles were built in strategic places to ensure the subjugation of hostile natives and the country was systematically exploited. Extensive areas were placed under draconian forest laws to preserve the game William loved to hunt. The Domesday survey of 1086 provided him with vital information for new tax assessments.

William I's last decade was troubled. The security of his dominions was undermined by family conflict. He had Bishop Odo arrested when his ambitions with regard to the papacy went a step too far. Then, his son Robert rebelled and joined his father's enemies bordering Normandy. He led raids across the frontier and in 1079 met William's forces in a battle in which Robert wounded his father in the hand. In 1080 a peace was concluded between them but this was not the end of William's problems. In reaction to raids from King Philip of France's territory, William led a punitive expedition across the border in 1087. While leading the sack of the town of Mantes he was thrown from his horse and died of internal injuries.

D. Bates, *William the Conqueror,* 1989.

R. A. Brown, *The Normans and the Norman Conquest,* 1969.

D. C. Douglas, *William the Conqueror,* 1964.

WILLIAM III (William of Orange; 1650–1702), Dutch prince and king of England from 1689. William was born in The Hague, Netherlands, to Princess Mary, widow of Prince William II of Orange and daughter of *Charles I of England; his father died shortly before his birth.

When France threatened to invade the Netherlands in 1672, William took command of Dutch forces. He was a fearless commander; under his direction Dutch forces were regrouped and succeeded in repelling the French and taking the war into Germany. War continued for most of that decade and William found fulfillment in leading his troops that made the routine of civil government pale in comparison.

In 1677 he married Mary, the fifteen-year-old daughter of James, Duke of York, his uncle and future king of England. It was not a love match, but their relationship blossomed. Won over by his military reputation and the genuine regard in which his men held him, Mary became a doting wife. William was a far from ideal husband, preferring the company of his mistress Elizabeth Villiers, but Mary's devotion remained steadfast.

William might have remained a relatively minor figure in European history but for the course of events in England. His uncle, Mary's father, came to the throne in 1685, becoming James II, and his favorable disposition toward Roman Catholicism alienated influential sections of his predominantly Protestant people. As Mary was next in line to the throne, it was felt that the future of Protestant England was secure in the long run, but in 1687 a son was born to James. Disaffected noblemen called on William to overthrow his uncle's regime and place Mary on the English throne. It was a priceless opportunity to free the Netherlands from the French threat by uniting the Dutch and English kingdoms.

William launched his invasion in November 1688. His Dutch force was joined by English supporters and proceeded slowly toward London, uncertain of the reception awaiting them. James had no stomach for a fight and his supporters were not enthusiastic enough to put their lives at stake for his cause; and he was swept away in the "bloodless" or "glorious" revolution. William chose to enter London in a closed carriage via a route that would not attract public attention. He jealously guarded his privacy and had little interest in the pomp and ceremony of royalty. Mary, however, was drawn to pageantry, and arrived in her new capital by colorful procession along the river Thames.

Mary was the real heir to the kingdom and could have ruled alone with William as consort, but he held such a lofty place in her estimation that she insisted on a joint monarchy. William threatened to return to Holland if he were not granted equal status to the queen. Although he was regarded as the savior of Protestant England, his cold and secretive manner did not gain him the same popularity as his beautiful, extroverted wife. In the words of a contemporary, "He spoke little...he hated business of all sorts. Yet he hated talking, and all house games, more." His preference for all things Dutch and his awarding English earldoms to Dutch friends also had a negative effect on public sympathies.

For much of their five-year joint monarchy, William was out of the country with his armies. On July 12, 1690, he decisively defeated James II's Catholic army at the Battle of the Boyne in Ireland, an event that has become a legend. Irish Protestants still celebrate the anniversary, with great enthusiasm for the memory of "King Billy." Having secured his British kingdom, William was able to turn his attention once more to fighting the French on the Continent.

Mary died in 1694 without having produced an heir and William was devastated by her death. He commanded a lavish funeral for her in recognition of the affection her subjects had for her. He then ruled alone for another eight years; his restraint in the exercise of royal power helped lay the foundation for the constitutional monarchy in Great Britain.

One of William's major ambitions had been the completion by Sir Christopher *Wren of one of the country's finest palaces, *Henry VIII's Hampton Court. The rebuilding was a triumph but the grounds were a setting for tragedy. In February 1702 his horse stumbled over a molehill and William was thrown, breaking his collarbone. The fracture did not heal and he died a few weeks later, little mourned by a people from whom he was distanced by character and nationality. Supporters of the house of James II, the Jacobites, drank toasts to "the little gentleman in black velvet" — the mole whose hill had caused the king's fatal fall.

S.B. Baxter, *William III*, 1966.
H. G. Horowitz, *Parliament, Policy and Politics in the Reign of William III*, 1927.
K. McLeod, *Drums and Trumpets — The House of Stuart*, 1977.
H. and B. Van Der Zee, *William and Mary*, 1973.

WILLIAM I (Wilhelm; 1797–1888), first modern German emperor. William, who united Germany and made it into the strongest European state of his time, was the second son of the Prussian king, Frederick William III. William's passionate lifelong interest in military matters began early: he became an officer at ten, fought against France in the Napoleonic Wars at seventeen, and received the Iron Cross for personal bravery at eighteen. After the war his military rank and responsibilities steadily increased as an enlarged Prussia became part of the new confederation of German states.

When William's father died in 1840, his childless older brother acceded to the throne and William became heir presumptive. Prussia was not spared the 1848 rebellions that swept Europe with demands for liberalized government, with violent street mobs calling for revolution. William was politically conservative but his wife, Augusta, was not, and William agreed that adopting a constitution seemed wise. However, he loved order, and wanted it restored before making political reforms. When government troops fired into a mob of Berlin demonstrators he became the most hated man in

Germany. A short vacation abroad seemed advisable and he took his family to England.

Britain's foreign policy focused on the adoption of British-type parliamentary governments by other countries and Queen *Victoria and the prince consort, Albert, approved of such liberal sentiments as William expressed. They betrothed their daughter to William's son (the future Frederick III) to help ensure that Prussia became a progressive ally for England. Upon William's return to Berlin he gave a speech in the national assembly in favor of adopting a constitution — and used force to swiftly crush a rebellion.

In 1858 William became regent of Prussia when his brother went mad, and was king from 1861. The opposition of Prussia's liberal parliament to his plan for reorganizing the army made William feel that he had to choose between abdication and bringing in someone strong enough to crush the liberals. He chose to make Otto von *Bismarck prime minister.

William's great ambition was to unite Germany under Prussian rule. His military reforms were responsible for Prussia's victory over Austria in 1866, which made Prussia the dominant German state, and over France in 1871, which made Germany the strongest country in Europe. He personally led Germany's army in several battles against France and was proclaimed emperor of the newly created, Prussian-controlled, German Empire in 1871.

As king, William had often disagreed with Bismarck although he usually ended up pursuing the latter's policies, either because he had come to agree with him or because Bismarck manipulated situations until William had no choice. As emperor, William was content to leave the running of the empire in Bismarck's hands, and for the rest of his life he was a figurehead whose upright and simple life made him respected and loved throughout Germany. Two socialist assassination attempts against him in 1878 were used by Bismarck as excuses to pass severe antisocialist laws.

T. Aronson, *The Kaisers,* 1971.
P. Wiegler, *William the First,* 1929.

WILLIAM II (Wilhelm II; 1859–1941), German ruler. The grandson of *William I of Prussia and Prince Albert and Queen *Victoria of England, William was the product of a marriage arranged to promote Anglo-Prussian friendship. Albert hoped that the marriage of his eldest daughter Victoria with Crown Prince Frederick of Prussia would help Prussia. Prussia had adopted a democratic constitution in 1850 and was on the road to industrial efficiency and commercial liberalism; Albert hoped to unite the German kingdoms and create a modern, liberal ally for England in the heart of Europe. William I favored the match because the connection with England greatly increased Prussia's prestige.

William II's birth was difficult and it crippled him. His emotionally high-strung and domineering mother hated him for being deformed, called him "cripple" even in public, and tried to cure him with painful and unsuccessful treatments: braces to force his tilted head upright, electric shocks to stimulate his stunted and paralyzed left arm, hot lotions poured into his left ear to restore his hearing and sense of balance, and lessons twelve hours a day, six days a week, to overcome what was possibly brain damage due to oxygen deprivation. William became determined to achieve at least the appearance of physical normality. He concentrated his energy and willpower on becoming proficient in swimming, tennis, shooting, riding, and the social obligations demanded by royal etiquette.

When Otto von *Bismarck reduced William's father, who disliked his son, to a political cipher, William responded by becoming closer to his adored grandfather, who groomed him, with Bismarck's help, to become king.

There were other influences on the future kaiser. His self importance was inflated with ideas of personal rule and of a strong king leading Germany toward its destiny. As a lieutenant in the First Regiment of the Guards, he became fascinated with the trappings of military life, acquired a military bearing and bark, but was never exposed to military realities. His many intellectual interests did not include the art and literature his mother favored and his politics were conservative: he was almost hysterically opposed to any suggestion of English interference in German affairs and he was extremely suspicious of his uncle, Edward VII of England.

William I and Frederick died in 1888, and William II became kaiser. Bismarck had been the real ruler of Germany and this might have continued under the new monarch had Bismarck not openly challenged him by defeating the political parties backed by William. The kaiser could not tolerate losing the appearance of power and authority and demanded Bismarck's resignation in 1890. William was both an absolute and constitutional monarch; he never exceeded his constitutional authority but opposition to his policies resulted in exclusion from the court and all chances of social or career advancement.

The conservative Prussian aristocracy exercised an inordinate influence over William. Three years of military service for all Germans became obligatory, spreading Prussian values of obedience to authority throughout Germany. A near-military discipline was extended to state schools, and the official state sponsored German culture was both patriotic and imperialistic. William stated that, "art which transgresses the laws and limits laid down by me can no longer be called art" and called any type of innovative artistic expression "gutter art."

William's conduct of Germany's foreign policy was also erratic. He tended to babble unwisely and his self-important and condescending attitude alienated many; he abandoned old alliances and impetuously entered into new ones. Many of his actions were actually conducive to peace, but his belligerent posturings and speeches demanding Germany's "place in the sun" were not. Fear of German

William II inspecting army and navy officers

aggression caused England, France, and Russia to band together in a defensive alliance.

With the outbreak of World War I — which William thought he could prevent with a word to his relatives, the other rulers of Europe — military rule was declared in Germany. The kaiser, discovering that he detested war, withdrew to his country estates and began suffering from psychosomatic illnesses. This did not stop anti-German propaganda from focusing on him — as Germany's Supreme War Lord — and caricaturing him in both picture and verse. "Little Willie," as he was called in England, played only a small, and typically inconsistent, role in the conduct of the war, first condemning, then condoning, unrestricted submarine warfare.

William abdicated the day before the Armistice was declared and spent the rest of his life living quietly in The Netherlands, passing his time chopping wood on a country estate at Drorn. He responded to the Nazis by behaving well to some of their victims, giving an archeology lecture in which he described the Nazi swastika as an ancient symbol of "night, misfortune, and death," and sending Hitler a congratulatory telegram when German armies entered Paris.
M. Balfour, *The Kaiser and His Times,* 1972.
J. von Kurenburg, *The Kaiser,* 1954.

WILLIAM I THE SILENT (1533–1584), leader of the Dutch rebellion against Spanish rule, king of the Netherlands. William was the eldest son of William, Count of Nassau-Dillenberg, whose religious tolerance enabled him to rule his domains throughout the religious wars of Emperor *Charles V and remain on good terms with both Catholic and Protestant neighbors. He adopted Lutheranism without becoming intolerant of Catholicism and accepted Charles's condition that William, his eleven-year-old son, had to convert to Catholicism before inheriting his cousin René of Orange's titles and lands, including the title of prince of the principality of Orange, in Provence, which included estates in the Low Countries.

Charles raised William as a Catholic prince, first making him his page, than a gentleman of his court. An astute statesman, Charles insisted that his fa-vorite, William, be present at councils of state. William became a competent soldier and a superb statesman and when he was eighteen, Charles arranged his marriage with the wealthy heiress, Anne of Egmont. The couple had two children and the match was a happy one, even though William's duties left them little time together.

Charles's son, *Philip II, became emperor and at first favored William with honors and position. This changed after the latter, now aged twenty-six, stayed with the King of France to ensure that France kept its peace treaty with Spain. The king, assuming that William knew about his secret agreement with Philip to use the Inquisition and the Spanish army to root out Protestantism in the Netherlands, began to talk about it. William did not reveal to the king his aversion to the plot but quickly organized the nobles of the Netherlands in opposition. His reticence on this occasion led to William — the most eloquent man of his day — being given the enduring nickname of "William the Silent."

Upon Anne's death, William insisted on marrying the Protestant heiress Anna of Saxony against both Catholic and Protestant opposition. He hoped to gain the powerful Lutheran nobles of central Germany as allies but they were not interested in helping the Dutch Calvinists. As a result, all William had to show for his ten years of marriage to an increasingly violent and abusive virago was two children; he eventually divorced Anna for adultery.

William wanted only to modify, not overthrow, Spanish rule of the Netherlands. He tried to accomplish this by urging the refusal of Philip's constant requests for funds unless Spanish troops were withdrawn. Philip, reluctant to drive his powerful nobles into armed rebellion, withdrew his army and appointed his half-sister, Margaret of Parma, as regent of the Netherlands. Philip and William then entered into prolonged negotiations to gain time: Philip to prepare a punitive army; William to prevent armed intervention by moderating violent opposition. Calvinist extremists went on a church-sacking rampage in 1566, Margaret suspended the Inquisition and granted freedom of worship, William restored order, and an enraged Philip appointed the duke of Alba head of his army.

Realizing that the Netherlands could not win against Spain on its own, William unsuccessfully sought support from abroad. He also tried to maintain order but revolts broke out and the other nobles, refusing to bear arms against Philip, suppressed the outbreaks violently. William resigned his offices, withdrew his daughter from Margaret's court, and left for Germany.

Alba entered the Netherlands with his highly trained army and instituted a reign of terror. He outlawed William, seized William's eldest son, massacred thousands, executed those loyal to William, and easily defeated the armies of mercenaries and untrained rabble sent against him. Deprived of his estates and home, denounced as a rebel by Lutherans and Catholics alike, William was totally ruined and the rumor spread that he was dead.

In fact, he was working constantly to raise funds and organize resistance to Alba. However it was the privateer Sea Beggars' (Orangist exiles who had taken to the sea to combat the king of Spain from foreign bases) successful harassment of the Spanish that turned the tide. Popular risings were triggered throughout Holland and Zeeland when Sea Beggars captured the port of Briel and declared for William in 1572. When the land attacks led by him and his brothers Louis and Henry failed, William committed himself completely to Holland and Zeeland, returning there personally to lead the resistance against Spain and becoming a Calvinist, despite his aversion to Calvinistic Puritanism and intolerance.

The desperate and tenacious resistance he met as he massacred his way through the Netherlands drained Alba. Between 1573 and 1578 William achieved the upper hand and conducted extensive negotiations with Spain; these proved fruitless as neither side was willing to compromise on the three issues William had considered essential from the beginning: freedom of religion, withdrawal of Spanish soldiers, and restoration of the Netherlands' ancient rights. William also made many attempts to unite the Netherlands' seventeen provinces, which failed because of irreconcilable differences of race, religion, and interests.

In 1575 William married Charlotte of Bourbon-Montpensier, a relative of the king of France and an former abbess, who became a Protestant. His insistence on marrying her over the objections of friends and relatives gained him a happy marriage, a good mother for his children, a peaceful family life even when surrounded by defeat and war, and six daughters. Charlotte died in 1582, when the shock of an assassination attempt that left William severely wounded was too much for her in her weakened, postnatal condition.

In 1578 Alexander of Parma arrived with a Spanish army that swept through the Netherlands, leaving death and defeat in its wake. William spent the rest of his life hopelessly trying to keep the provinces united and get the foreign support he saw as essential, while successfully countering rivals brought in by different factions striving for ascendancy (each of whom William courteously welcomed, foiled, used, and politely persuaded to leave). Meanwhile the Netherlands formally abjured Philip as their king in 1581, declared their independence, and made William count (Stadholder) of Holland soon afterwards.

William had been the target of assassination attempts for years, thanks to the rewards offered by Philip for his death. In 1583 William married Louise de Cologny, who gave birth to a son before the final assassination attempt was successful. William's sons continued to lead the rebellion against Spain for sixty-four more years before Spain recognized the Netherlands' independence with the Peace of Westphalia. His descendants rule the country to this day.
C. V. Wedgewood, *William the Silent,* 1967.

WILSON, THOMAS WOODROW (1856–1924), twenty-eighth president of the United States (1913–1921). He was born in Staunton, Virginia, but in 1870 the Wilson family moved to Columbia, South Carolina. Young Wilson was taught primarily by his father, Joseph Ruggles Wilson, who was a Presbyterian pastor.

At the age of seventeen Wilson had a powerful religious experience and joined the church. In 1874 he entered Davidson College in North Carolina and the following year, the College of New Jersey (which later became Princeton University), from which he graduated in 1879, going on to study law at the University of Virginia. He was admitted to the bar in 1881.

In 1882 Wilson opened a law office in Atlanta, Georgia, and enrolled in graduate school at Johns Hopkins University. He completed his doctoral thesis on congressional government in 1885. From 1885 to 1890 Wilson taught history at Bryn Mawr and Wesleyan Universities, and then became a professor of jurisprudence and political economics at Princeton, a position he held for twelve years. During this period he wrote nine books, including a biography of George *Washington and a five-volume *History of the American People*. He was the first nonclerical president of Princeton, serving from 1902 to 1910.

By 1906 Wilson was considered as a possible presidential candidate, especially by conservative Democrats. He entered politics upon completing his service as president of Princeton, and was elected governor of New Jersey in 1910. Although supported by a corrupt machine, he proved a reform governor, pushing through legislation for workmen's compensation and the regulation of public utilities. In 1912 he was nominated as the Democratic candidate for the US presidency, though not without a struggle — he was viewed by many as "professorial" and won only on the forty-sixth ballot. Even though he received only 42 percent of the popular vote, Wilson was elected president, along with a Democratic Congress, helped by the split in the Republican party between President William Howard Taft and Progressive leader Theodore *Roosevelt. He developed a domestic program called the New Freedom.

The Democratic party had been out of power for twenty years and Wilson had to build a completely new administration. However, during his first term he succeeded in legislating reforms such as the reduction of tariffs, the Federal Reserve Act, the establishment of the Federal Trade Commission to regulate unfair business competition, and the Clayton Anti–Trust Act. During Wilson's first two years in office, treaties were signed with thirty nations, despite the fact that he had serious problems with foreign relations.

BY AND ABOUT WOODROW WILSON

- The business of government is to organize the common interest against the special interests.
- Segregation is not humiliating but a benefit and ought to be so regarded by you gentlemen. The only harm that will come will be if you cause the colored people of the country to think it a humiliation (to a delegation of black leaders, 1913).
- If I said what I thought about those fellows in Congress, it would take a piece of asbestos two inches thick to hold it (in 1919 on Senate opposition to the Treaty of Versailles).
- We Americans have a great ardor for gain but we have a deep passion for the rights of man.
- The world must be made safe for democracy.

Mr. Wilson bores me with his Fourteen Points; why, God Almighty has only Ten.

Georges Clemenceau

Wilson stood for human decency. He stood weakly for human decency; but he stood where it is an honor to stand.

Sigmund Freud

In May 1914, Congress formalized Mother's Day as an annual celebration to be held on the second Sunday in May. Wilson asked that the flags be displayed to demonstrate "our love and reverence for the mothers of the country."

When World War I broke out in 1914 he sought to prevent the United States from taking part and he won reelection in 1916, although by only a narrow margin, under the slogan "He kept us out of the war."

However, despite Wilson's efforts, German submarine attacks led to war being declared on April 2, 1917, with Wilson declaring that "the world must be made safe for democracy." In January 1918 he set forth his Fourteen Points as a basis for peace, and in the fall of 1918, Germany, facing defeat, asked America for an armistice. The Armistice Agreement was signed on November 11, 1918. As head of the U.S. peace delegation to France, Wilson received a hero's welcome. However, due to disagreements with some of the Allies, he had to abandon most of his Fourteen Points.

At Wilson's insistence, the League of Nations was established to solve future conflicts by peaceful methods. Congress would not ratify the Treaty of Versailles unless certain changes were made, and this was unacceptable to Wilson. Remarking that "most members of Congress just had a knot on their shoulders to keep their bodies from unraveling," he declared, "I will carry to the people my case against the little group of willful men."

It was in the midst of an exhaustive campaign to raise public support for the treaty that he collapsed at Pueblo, Colorado, on September 26, 1919, suffering a stroke from which he never recovered. Partially paralyzed, he was an invalid for the rest of his life and was unable to prevent the Senate from rejecting the treaty. For the next seventeen months, the gravity of his condition was kept from the public while his wife, Edith, in effect ran the country. He wanted to run again in 1920, but the Democratic party chose James M. Cox, who lost the election on the issues of Wilson's leadership and the League of Nations.

Wilson received the Nobel Peace Prize in 1920 and retired to Washington, where he spent the rest of his life.

L. Aribrusius, *Woodrow Wilson and the American Diplomatic Tradition*, 1987.
K. A. Clements, *Woodrow Wilson*, 1987.
R. H. Ferrell, *Woodrow Wilson and World War I*, 1986.
A. Hechscher, *Woodrow Wilson*, 1991.

WITTGENSTEIN, LUDWIG JOSEF JOHAN
(1889-1951), Austrian-born British philosopher. Wittgenstein was the eighth child born to one of the wealthiest families in Vienna. Because his mother was Catholic, Wittgenstein was baptized, yet three of his grandparents were of Jewish descent. His father insisted upon his sons' working in the family business and consequently imposed upon his youngest the study of mechanical engineering and aeronautics. Not until Bertrand *Russell encouraged him and then only after three of his brothers had committed suicide, did Wittgenstein break away from this paternal stronghold. He began to pursue his true love, philosophy, at Cambridge University under Russell from 1912 to 1913, and on his own in Norway from 1913 to 1914. Russell was impressed by what he described as "perhaps the most perfect example I have ever known of genius as traditionally conceived — passionate, profound, intense, and dominating."

While an Austrian soldier in World War I, Wittgenstein completed the only work to be published during his lifetime, *Tractatus logico-philosophicus*, whose logical-structuralist approach had a formative effect upon the Vienna circle of logical positivists. The war left him questioning the "metaphysical explanations of the world" so that what followed were new meditations on esthetics, morality, and the soul. The great suffering he witnessed in the war convinced him that personal hardship and an absence of worldly distraction would lend meaning and focus to his life. Influenced by Leo *Tolstoy's understanding of Christian apostolic writings, Wittgenstein renounced his family wealth in favor of a life of asceticism and lived for a time as a schoolteacher in a southern Austrian village, and also worked as an architect in Vienna (1926-1928).

In 1938 he settled in Great Britain and was named professor of philosophy at Cambridge. He was a constant critic of academia, who denounced university life as devoid of purpose and meaning, believing that a professor could not be an authentic philosopher. Feeling that he was surrounded by people who did not understand him and that his best philosophical work was accomplished elsewhere, he retired from his chair in 1947.

Although he admitted to seeing the world in supernatural terms, Wittgenstein wrote little specifically on the subject of religion, claiming that it was far more important to speak to God than about God, and believing that instead of discussing the religious dimension or being able to prove it scientifically, it should be demonstrated in the way we live and die. Convinced that religious language no longer spoke to the current generation, he decided finally against dedicating one of his works (posthumously published as *Philosophical Remarks*), "To the glory of God".

Wittgenstein has been recognized as one of the major thinkers of the twentieth century. His primary philosophical concern was the nature of language as a means of understanding the world and ourselves (*Philosophical Investigations*, 1953). Accordingly, the role of philosophy is to clarify the usage and limits of language in order to resolve what Wittgenstein considered to be metaphysical anxieties inherent in the way we grammatically construct everyday sentences.

A seeker of solitude, Wittgenstein spent his last years in loneliness and melancholy, ill and impoverished, living as the guest of devoted students. His last words were: "I've had a wonderful life."

A. Kenny, *Wittgenstein*, 1973.
N. Malcolm, *Ludwig Wittgenstein: A Memoir*, 1958.
R. Monk, *Ludwig Wittgenstein: The Duty of Genius*, 1990.
R. Rhees (ed.), *Ludwig Wittgenstein: Personal Recollections*, 1981.

WOLLSTONECRAFT, MARY (Mary Godwin; 1759–1797), English author, advocate of education and social equality for women.

When a series of domestic misfortunes left London-born Wollstonecraft on her own, she resolved to support herself, first by running a school and then as a governess. She became involved in a circle of radical dissenters who used John *Locke's theory of natural rights to support demands for civil and political rights for all and the abolition of any aristocratic privileges.

Wollstonecraft's first work, *Thoughts on the Education of Daughters* (1787), foreshadowed her mature work on the place of women in society, but with the outbreak of the French Revolution she joined those attempting to refute the arguments of Edmund *Burke's *Reflections on the Revolution in France,* and published *A Vindication of the Rights of Man* in 1790. *A Vindication of the Rights of Women* followed in 1792.

The latter book, for which Wollstonecraft is now famous, can be considered the first major work of feminist literature. In it, Wollstonecraft contended that, as rational beings, women have a right to equality with and independence from men. She argued that women were commonly regarded as irrational and emotional only because society's existing conception of the appropriate education and way of life for them had conspired to prevent their developing their human capacities and virtues. Believing that women's real capacities could be determined only when they were given their freedom, and the opportunity and education to develop their talents, she stressed the importance of a proper education that would allow women to achieve independence, "the grand blessing of life, the basis of every virtue." She asserted that society as a whole, not just women, would be ennobled if the relations between men and women were marked by "a rational fellowship instead of slavish obedience."

In her own time, Wollstonecraft was better known for the then-scandalous elements of her life and conduct. While in France observing the French Revolution at first hand, she lived with an American, Captain Gilbert Imlay, by whom she had a child out of wedlock; when the relationship ended, Wollstonecraft attempted suicide. Back in England, she had a relationship with the anarchist philosopher William Godwin, who (along with Thomas *Paine, William *Blake, and William *Wordsworth) was part of the influential radical discussion group to which she belonged. When Wollstonecraft became pregnant, she and Godwin were married. She died eleven days after the birth of their daughter.

Her daughter by Godwin, **Mary Wollstonecraft Shelley** (1797-1851), eloped with and later married the poet Percy Bysshe *Shelley. She is most famous as author of *Frankenstein*, her tale of inventor Victor Frankenstein and the monster he creates, a powerful allegory of the creator's responsibility for mankind and the scientist's power to restructure nature.

E. Flexner, *Mary Wollstonecraft*, 1972.
M. George, *One Woman's "Situation"*, 1970.
C. Tomalin, *The Life and Death of Mary Wollstonecraft*, 1975.
J. M. Tood, *Feminist Literary History*, 1988.

WOLSEY, THOMAS (c.1475–1530), English cardinal and statesman.

Wolsey attended Magdalen College, Oxford, where he was ordained a priest and remained until 1500; in 1501 he became chaplain to Archbishop Dean, and in 1503, to Sir Richard Nanfan, deputy lieutenant of Calais, who was responsible for introducing Wolsey to *Henry VII. In 1506 the king took Wolsey as chaplain and also sent him on diplomatic missions to Scotland and the Netherlands; impressed by Wolsey, he eventually made him dean of Lincoln.

*Henry VIII, Henry VII's successor, continued supporting Wolsey and in 1509 appointed him his almoner. By 1511 Wolsey had become one of the king's most influential advisers and, against the wishes of Archbishop Warham and Bishop Foxe, urged the king to join the pope's "holy league" against France. During the war against France he displayed great organizational skill and after the French were defeated Wolsey arranged the "perpetual peace" and the marriage of Henry's sister, Mary, to Louis XII of France. For his services, Wolsey was awarded the bishoprics of Lincoln and Torunai and in 1514, the archbishopric of York. In 1515 the pope agreed that Wolsey become a cardinal, and Henry appointed him lord chancellor, greatly enhancing Wolsey's power and prestige.

Wolsey had a lasting influence on English history through his activities as chancellor. He presided over the Star Chamber public sessions, when the king's council exercised jurisdiction in semicriminal cases, exercising his power to the full. He upheld the authority of the central government in such cases as perjury, fraud, fixing of food prices, and the maintenance of law and order, and in insuring the supremacy of the sovereign's will. As he became increasingly drawn toward foreign affairs, he delegated much judicial work. He created a commission to hear piracy cases, which paved the way for the specialized admiralty courts; the development of the court of requests evolved from the four commissions for poor men's causes; and the delegation of northern and Welsh cases to the revived local councils at York and Ludlow helped in the evolution of separate courts within the official judicial system.

Wolsey also succeeded in gaining for himself a position in the church equal to that in the state, managing to obtain his own appointment from the papacy as legate *a latere*. In asserting his authority, the line between his role as a legate and chancellor became blurred, and the power of the chancery began impinging on the jurisdiction of the ecclesiastical courts. Although he wielded a great deal of power, he failed to reform the abuses in the church that had so angered the Commons. In dissolving certain monastic houses, he used their endowments to found his new college, Christ College, Oxford. He lived a worldly life, and enjoyed dressing extravagantly and entertaining lavishly. His arrogance and pomp alienated many people.

Wolsey was also instrumental in weakening the English clergy's affection for papal power, since he ignored local jurisdictions and privileges by right of the legatine authority Rome had granted him. He used his influence in unsuccessful attempts to gain the papacy on two occasions, in 1522 and 1523.

It was Wolsey's role in foreign policy that led to general hatred of him and the eventual distrust of the king, who took a lively interest in this field. Wolsey wanted England to balance the scale between the Holy Roman Emperor *Charles V and the king of France, *Francis I. In 1522 he extracted forced loans to finance campaigns in northern France, and tried to make the Commons

Cardinal Wolsey

grant £800,000 in 1523; he was also held mainly responsible for the 1525 "amicable grant" of £500,000 demanded of the laity by Henry to help destroy France, which almost caused a rebellion. After all this, England failed to regain its lost lands in France.

Wolsey's fate was sealed when he concluded an unpopular French alliance in 1527 and began an even more unpopular war to remove the pope from Charles V's grip. His fall came when the French were defeated in Italy in 1529, forcing the pope to make peace with Charles. Hated by the nobility and without the clergy's support, he could not turn to the public since they, too, hated him because of his taxation policy. The king had turned against him for his failure to persuade the pope to pronounce his marriage to Catherine of Aragon illegitimate. Indicted for a breach of *praemunire* (statutes designed to protect the crown against encroachments by the papacy) in the king's bench, he was permitted to keep the archbishopric of York and a yearly pension of £1,000 from the see of Winchester, but had to give up all his other offices and preferments.

Still wishing to regain royal favor, Wolsey entered into a secret and dangerous correspondence with the French and imperial ambassadors and with Rome. His plans to have a public enthronement at York in 1530 and his summoning of the northern convocation to meet him there alarmed the king, who had found out about his secret correspondence, and he was arrested on a charge of high treason. On the way to London to face the charges, he died at Leicester Abbey, where he was buried.

G. W. Bernard, *War, Taxation, and Rebellion in Early Tudor England*, 1986.
S. J. Gunn and P. G. Lindley, *Cardinal Wolsey,* 1991.
P. Gwynn, *The King's Cardinal*, 1990.

WORDSWORTH, WILLIAM (1770 – 1850),

English poet. He was born in Cockermouth in northwest England, to a family in comfortable circumstances, but parents died during his childhood and Wordsworth was sent away to grammar school in the village of Hawkshead. There, William boarded with an elderly lady named Mrs. Tyson, who became a substitute mother and gave Wordsworth freedom to explore the countryside at will; he would sometimes walk the hills late into the night.

From school he proceeded to Cambridge University but found formal studies irrelevant and hated examinations. Returning to the Lake District, he felt a heightened communion with his surroundings and realized his vocation was poetry. His first poem had been written at age fourteen at Hawkshead school, the subject, "what I did in my summer holiday."

Wordsworth visited France in 1789 and was caught up in the excitement of the Revolution, a period when "bliss was it in that dawn to be alive, But to be young was very Heaven!" On a second trip in 1791 he had a brief but intense affair with Annette Vallon in Orleans; war separated them and she gave birth to a girl. They maintained sporadic contact but this liaison was one of the great secrets of his life, hidden from all but closest friends.

Back in England Wordsworth lived with no fixed abode or income, committed to radical politics and speaking out against the domination of aristocracy and church. His first published poetry came in 1793, the subjects, the Lake District and revolution. Respectable relatives no longer tried to persuade him to take holy orders but instead distanced themselves. However, his sister Dorothy always stood by him and he enjoyed the closest of relationships; she was his confidante, housekeeper, secretary, and constant traveling companion.

Further stimulus was provided by his meeting with the poets Samuel T. Coleridge and Robert Southey in 1795. Initially Coleridge became Wordsworth's closest friend and literary collaborator and the Wordsworths took up residence near him in Somerset. Their frequent country hikes and broad northern accents aroused suspicion and the government sent a secret agent to investigate a possible French spy ring.

In 1800 the Wordsworths moved back to the Lake District, renting Dove Cottage in Grasmere. They were to live in this area for the rest of their lives. Coleridge soon joined them, taking a house in Keswick but often staying with the Wordsworths. Soon Southey also took up residence in the Lakes.

In 1798 Wordsworth and Coleridge had published a book of their poems entitled *Lyrical Ballads*. It received a hostile reception from the critics but after a year, sales picked up and a new edition was commissioned. Wordsworth's writing represented a revolutionary departure from the formalized conventions of eighteenth-century poetry — country scenes and the conversations of the peasantry were not considered noble themes for the poet. Literary critics annoyed him but could not impede increasing interest in the work of this new school of Romantic poetry — the Lake Poets.

In 1802 William married his childhood friend Mary Hutchinson and they had five children, three surviving infancy. His relationship with Dorothy continued at only slightly diminished intensity, as she moved in with them as companion and nurse. There was a falling-out with Coleridge following criticisms Wordsworth made of some of his friend's intemperate habits and Wordsworth became closer to Southey.

In 1813 Wordsworth was appointed collector of excise. He had sought a position because poetry yielded a poor income and he had a growing family. He was no longer hostile to the aristocracy and the church; the Reign of Terror in France had disillusioned him and he became an archconservative. He opposed parliamentary reform and the building of a railway into the Lake District, fearing it would bring an influx of the common masses to ruin the area.

Wordsworth's fame made him into a major tourist attraction in his own right and many came to try and catch a glimpse of him, and in 1843 he accepted the post of poet laureate.

F. W. Bateson, *Wordsworth, A Reinterpretation*, 1954.
H. Davies, *William Wordsworth*, 1980.

FROM WORDSWORTH'S POEMS

- A violet by a mossy stone
  Half hidden from the eye!
  Fair as a star, when only one
  Is shining in the sky.

- I traveled among unknown men
  In lands beyond the sea;
  Nor England! did I know till then
  What love I bore to thee.

- My heart leaps up when I behold
  A rainbow in the sky.

- Our birth is but a sleep and a forgetting;
  The Soul that rises with us, our life's Star,
  Hath had elsewhere its setting,
  And cometh from afar:
  Not in entire forgetfulness,
  And not in utter nakedness,
  But trailing clouds of glory do we come
  From God who is our home.

S. C. Gill, *William Wordsworth*, 1989.
M. Moorman, *William Wordsworth: A Biography*, 2 vols., 1957–1965.

WREN, SIR CHRISTOPHER (1632–1723), English architect and scientist. Although renowned as the architect who rebuilt Saint Paul's Cathedral after the Great Fire of London (1666), he began his career as a scientist. Turning to architecture late in life, he nonetheless achieved a prodigious output and popularized the Renaissance Palladian style.

Wren's family was prosperous and powerful; his father, the Dean of Windsor, was a devoted Tory and a staunch supporter of the Church of England. In 1641 Wren entered the Westminster School, which had a reputation for science, mathematics, and Latin, and performed brilliantly. In about 1646 he went to Oxford, graduating in 1653 with an M.A. He became an admired colleague among a brilliant circle who would be the leading scientists and scholars in England after the Restoration. He was a scientist, mathematician, and inventor and made significant scientific discoveries, especially in astronomy.

In 1657, upon his appointment as Gresham Professor of Astronomy in London, he pronounced in his inauguration speech that "Mathematical demonstrations being built upon the impregnable foundations of Geometry and Arithmetik are the only Truths that can sink into the mind of Man, void of all uncertainty." He was one of the founders of the Royal Society, and became Savillian Professor of Astronomy at Oxford in 1661, holding this position until 1673.

Wren ventured into architecture at a time when building was in a state of stagnation. The Italian Renaissance style had been introduced by Inigo Jones but was not widely accepted and the Civil War had discouraged building. Wren received his first architectural commission in 1662 to design the Sheldonian Theater at Oxford, which he modeled on the open air theaters of Roman antiquity. In 1665 he traveled to France to study art and architecture.

Wren returned from France inspired, loaded with books, engravings, and other materials on European architecture. These sources influenced his future work and his theories on beauty and taste, which he formulated in his essays on the development of architecture: "Architecture aims at eternity; and therefore the only Thing uncapable of Modes and Fashions in its Principals...Beauty, Firmness and Convenience are the Principles; the two first depend upon geometrical Reasons of opticks and staticks; the third only makes the Variety. There are natural Causes of Beauty. Beauty is a Harmony of Objects, begetting Pleasure by the Eye."

In London Wren became involved in planning the repair of Saint Paul's Cathedral but in 1666, days after his suggestions for an ambitious reconstruction were accepted, the Great Fire of London broke out. After most of London was destroyed in the fire Wren was appointed "Principal Architect" for the reconstruction of the city. His main project was the rebuilding of Saint Paul's and some fifty other city churches.

He was able to experiment with the designs for these churches, creating loose classical forms and devising ingenious solutions to the problems of cramped space and limited time. Most of the churches were based on plans of Roman basilicas. Saint Paul's Cathedral was conceived as a bold landmark for the newly-built London. The dome, influenced by the work of Donato *Bramante and *Michelangelo, dominates the skyline. A work group of master craftsmen was chosen and their exceptional workmanship established a precedent for masterly design in England.

Wren was also commissioned to design royal buildings such as the Kensington and Hampton Court palaces, and public buildings including the Royal Marine Hospital at Greeenwich, Chelsea Hospital, and the western towers and northern transept of Westminster Abbey. The royal palaces were built on a grand scale, influenced by glorious French Renaissance palaces such as Versailles. Wren was the first English architect to incorporate Baroque details into his buildings. The Doric order that encompasses the Chelsea Hospital foreshadows the Baroque style of the reign of Queen Anne and a number of his churches designed in the late 1600s embody a true Baroque vocabulary.

During his long and rich career Wren applied his genius so successfully to his work that he became a pivotal influence on the development of English architecture and a symbol of the flourishing of scholarship and the arts in seventeenth-century England. He was buried in Saint Paul's Cathedral.

M. S. Briggs, *Wren: The Incomparable*, 1953.
E. F. Sekler, *Wren and His Place in European Architecture*, 1954.
W. Whinney, *Christopher Wren*, 1971.

WRIGHT, WILBUR (1867–1912) and **ORVILLE** (1871–1948), American aviation pioneers. Their father was Milton Wright, bishop of the Church of the United Brethren in Christ. After finishing high school, the brothers set up the newspaper *West Side News*, which was printed on a homemade press. In 1893 they opened a bicycle repairing and manufacturing business.

Wilbur and Orville had already shown an interest in aerodynamics as boys, when they had access to a toy helicopter powered by rubber bands, and later closely followed the exploits of the German pioneer aviation engineer, Otto Lilienthal. His death in 1896 prompted them to undertake experiments in gliding based on his findings. They now read Lilienthal's *The Problems of Flying* and *Practical Experiments in Soaring;* and Octave Chanute's *Progress in Flying Machines*. Wilbur corresponded with Chanute and over the years the brothers kept him updated on their experiments.

Orville sought to improve flying machines through increased control. He also believed that sidewise balance could be attained by presenting the left and right wings at different angles to the wind; this was achieved by Wilbur twisting or warping the wings. When their initial experiments in increased control succeeded, they decided to build a man-carrying glider.

In 1900, after discovering from the U.S. Weather Bureau that Kitty Hawk, North Carolina, was the breeziest place in the country and that its sand hills made it suitable for gliding, they took their first man-carrying glider there. It spanned eighteen feet from tip to tip and was unique in having a horizontal front rudder or elevator which was approximately four feet in front of the lower main plane; the rear edge could be raised or lowered for fore-and-aft balance.

The brothers planned to fly the glider as a pilot-guided kite as a means of practicing, but they found that they could only do this when wind speed was over twenty-five miles an hour. Although the glider did not lift as it should have done according to Lilienthal's air pressure tables, Wilbur and Orville were encouraged by the success of their method of control. They then took their machine to Kill Devil Hill near Kitty Hawk and made a number of dives down the hillside. They were, however, dissatisfied with the glider's lifting ability and decided to return the following year with a larger machine with wings of deeper curvature.

Because of their problems with Lilienthal's tables and other air pressure figures which were used as standard references, the brothers began questioning the validity of the existing data and started to conduct their own experiments. The design of their glider of 1902 reflected their own calculations; it had a wing span of thirty-two feet and sported a tail with fixed twin vertical vanes: this was used for balancing, essential to add to the presentation of the wings at different angles to the wind. Using their new machine, the brothers made glides of over 600 feet and were able to glide at narrower angles of descent.

The following year the Wright brothers built a flying machine with a motor and on December 17, 1903, they took it to Kitty Hawk, where Orville made a flight of 120 feet, with Wilbur later flying 852 feet in 59 seconds. Between 1904 and 1905 they carried out further refinements which resulted in Wilbur flying as far as twenty-four miles. In 1908 they established their own company and received a contract with the U.S. War Department for the first army plane, development of which was completed the following year. Neither brother married; Wilbur died in 1912 of typhoid fever, while Orville survived him for another thirty-six years during which he made more important contributions to aviation.

R. Hallion, ed., *The Wright Brothers: Heirs of Prometheus*, 1978.

F. C. Kelly, ed., *Miracle at Kitty Hawk: The Letters of Wilbur and Orville Wright*, 1971.

J. E. Walsh, *One Day at Kitty Hawk*, 1975.

X

XAVIER, FRANCIS (1506–1552), Spanish Roman Catholic missionary. Born into a noble family in Navarre in northern Spain, in 1525 Xavier traveled to Paris, then the academic center of Europe, to continue his studies, earning his philosophy degree at the university there in 1530. He remained at the university as a lecturer in philosophy until 1534, when he transferred to theological studies.

It was in Paris that, in 1529, he met the man who was to conclusively shape his future life's course; Ignatius *Loyola, an ex-soldier fifteen years Xavier's senior, became his roommate and persuaded him to pledge his allegiance to the religious vision Loyola was developing. Xavier's original skepticism toward Loyola's plans abated, and he was one of the seven men who, on August 15, 1534, took a vow of poverty, celibacy, and devotion to the salvation of others. He had previously pursued the thirty days of "spiritual exercises" that Loyola had devised; the mystical insights they prompted were to remain an important influence on him for the rest of his life.

Saint Francis Xavier

Xavier and his colleagues were ordained in Venice in 1537 and then moved to Rome, where they founded the Society of Jesus under Loyola's command. Until 1540 Xavier was secretary of the new organization, later known as the Jesuits; then, Loyola chose him to lead the mission to those eastern regions that had become colonies of King John III's Portuguese empire. Xavier left for Goa on the Indian subcontinent, arriving there in 1542. He commenced a painstaking village to village ministry among the Paravas, poor pearl fishers of the southeast coast who had converted to Catholicism seven years earlier in the hope of winning Portuguese aid against their tribal enemies.

The villagers had received little pastoral care subsequent to their conversion, so Xavier concentrated on educating them in the tenets of their new faith. His missionary efforts bore fruit throughout the coastal area and into Ceylon; Xavier recorded baptizing over ten thousand villagers in one month alone. The converts he won during his mission to the islands of the Malayas and among the ferocious headhunters of the Mollucas were later forced to renounce their Christian faith as a result of persecution in the seventeenth century, but only after thousands had been martyred. On his return to India, Xavier took control of the diocese of Goa, stretching from the Cape of Good Hope on the southern tip of Africa, to China. The College of Holy Faith in Goa came under Jesuit control and trained native missionaries for continuing the proselytizing work.

Ever keen to spread the Christian gospel to new regions, Xavier was greatly excited by the possibility of converting the Japanese, whom he considered "the best people yet discovered." Reaching Japan in 1549, he was the first westerner to send reports of this mysterious new country and its culture back to Europe. Always able to communicate with people effectively, regardless of their age, race, or belief, he abandoned his poverty for a strategy of studied display, which was more impressive to the Japanese. Returning to India in 1551, he left behind him two thousand Japanese Christians in five communities.

Xavier's hopes of proselytizing China, which was then closed to foreigners, were never realized: he died aboard ship while attempting to enter the country. His body was taken back to Goa, where it was enshrined and remains an object of veneration to this day. Through his ministrations, thirty thousand people were baptized and Christianity was permanently installed in India.

Xavier's efforts were a key factor in promoting the importance of the Jesuits within the missionary and educational arm of the Roman Catholic church. He was also instrumental in determining the method, character, and approach of future Catholic missionary activity; he stressed the need for a missionary to learn the native customs and language of a country, and to promote the training of dedicated native evangelists to ensure continuing pastoral support for nascent Christian communities. Canonized in 1622, he was declared patron saint of all missions in 1927.

J. Brodrick, *Saint Francis Xavier, 1506–1552*, 1952. G. Schurhammer, *Francis Xavier: His Life, His Times*, 4 vols,, 1973–1982. M. Yeo, *Saint Francis Xavier: Apostle of the East*, 1932.

XENOPHON (c.431–c.352 B.C.E.), Greek historian and soldier. The Peloponnesian War (431–404 B.C.E.) continued throughout the first decades of his life and while he fought with an elite Athenian cavalry unit against Sparta, his sympathies were not with the democrats of Athens; he admired Spartan discipline and the aristocratic ideal. He identified with those who temporarily succeeded in conservative takeovers in 411 B.C.E. and 404 B.C.E. and was a *persona non grata* in the subsequent democratic restorations. His association with the controversial figure of *Socrates also caused him difficulty with the Athenian radicals and when democracy was restored in 401 B.C.E. he fled and was later officially banished from the city.

Xenophon then joined the campaign of Cyrus the Younger, pretender to the Persian throne, leading a Greek contingent of mercenaries in Cyrus's attempt to capture the throne of Persia from his older brother, Artaxerxes. When Cyrus died in Persia and his forces were routed, Xenophon was elected general of the remnant of twelve thousand troops and took them one thousand miles through the hostile mountainous terrain of Kurdistan and Armenia, back to the safety of Greece. In 400 B.C.E., with six thousand survivors, he arrived at Chrysopolis on the Sea of Marmara. His feat, accomplished by ingenious tactical maneuvers and leadership, brought him fame and wealth.

Xenophon, whose sympathies always lay with Sparta, was unable to return to Athens because of his banishment. He therefore served in Asia Minor under the Spartan king Agesilaus II. At Coronea he fought victoriously with Agesilaus against a coalition of Greek city-states, including Athens. For his loyalty to the Spartan cause he was awarded an estate near Olympia at Scillus, where he settled down,

married, and raised two children. There he led an aristocratic life, managing his farm, and writing the fourteen works for which he is known.

Xenophon's most famous work, and a key contribution to ancient historiography, is the seven-volume *Anabasis,* a lively account of Cyrus's bid to take the Persian throne and the subsequent retreat. The author appears as a youthful, romantic adventurer rising to the challenges of war. In his work *Hellika,* Xenophon takes a pro-Spartan stance on Greek history, covering the period from 411–362 B.C.E. *Cyropedia* gives an idealized picture of *Cyrus the Great, and in *Polity,* Xenophon renders a glowing account of Spartan education. *Agesilaus,* one of the earliest Greek biographies, sings the praises of the Spartan ruler under whom Xenophon served. His work *Cavalry Commander,* based on his experience in his elite unit, describes the duties and responsibilities of military command, while *On Horsemanship* details the art and is the most ancient treatise on the subject. *Fond of Hunting* proposes hunting as a means to learn the discipline necessary for military encounters. In *Ways and Means,* Xenophon details the management of an agricultural estate like his own and describes a proper wife as a woman of young enough age to adapt to the needs of her husband.

Xenophon's work *Hieron,* conducted as a dialogue, advises autocratic rulers how to treat their subjects. His *Symposium* is in the form of a discourse by Socrates on love and friendship, while *Socrates's Apology* sets out reasons for the philosopher's meager defense at his trial; *Memorabilia* is Xenophon's account of Socrates's life as a teacher of philosophy.

Xenophon's writings are practical and informative, though lacking the philosophical and historical sophistication of his contemporary, *Thucydides. His prose is straightforward and easy to read, and though repetitious and sometimes heavy-handed, contains brilliant insights into military tactics and interesting observations of humanity. The range of his writings earned him the cognomen "the Attic bee." L. V. Jacks, *Xenophon, Soldier of Fortune,* 1930.

XERXES I (the Great; c.519–465 B.C.E.), Persian king. He was the son of *Darius I, who had risen to power from the rank of spearbearer to *Cambyses II, and Attossa, the daughter of *Cyrus II (the Great). Xerxes was designated heir-apparent in preference to his brother, Artabazanes, and had already been governor of Babylonia for over a decade by the time he acceded to the throne on his father's death in 486 B.C.E. He inherited from Darius an efficient system for the exploitation of the resources of his empire, which was organized into satrapies (provinces), each with its own governor and responsible for providing a certain levy of taxes, produce, ships, horses, and soldiers to the emperor.

Soon after his accession Xerxes moved to pacify Egypt, where a usurper had been governing for two years: in 484 B.C.E. his forces overran the Nile Delta and ruthlessly restored imperial authority. He also violently suppressed a revolt in Babylonia: the rebels were tortured and slain, Babylon's city walls were destroyed, and the temple of Marduk, the largest and most prestigious in the oriental world, was razed to the ground.

Less tolerant of expressions of regional autonomy than his father, Xerxes was not prepared to brook any opposition to his status as absolute ruler. Zoroastrianism was the state religion and he regarded himself as the viceregent of its great god, Ahura Mazda. He was therefore keen to punish the Greek city-states for their participation in the Ionian revolt and the defeat of his father's armies at Marathon in 490 B.C.E. To this end, he embarked upon a diplomatic initiative which won him assurances of support from Carthage, Thessaly, Central Greece, Argos, and the Delphic Oracle. He then proceeded to muster a huge army; *Herodotus claimed that it numbered five million men, although a more likely figure is three hundred and sixty thousand soldiers and some eight hundred ships. Xerxes's engineers oversaw massive engineering works to support its passage, bridging the Hellespont and digging a canal through the Athos peninsula.

After overcoming heroic Spartan resistance at the pass of Thermopylae in 480 B.C.E., Xerxes's troops moved southwards, occupying Attica and pillaging Athens. Their Greek opponents were forced to retreat to their last line of defense, the Isthmus of Corinth. The wily Athenian leader, *Themistocles, overcoming the disunity among his allies who feared for the safety of their own cities and homes, then lured the Persian navy into combat off the is-land of Salamis. There, despite their superior numbers, they were defeated, losing some two hundred ships to ferocious ramming attacks from the Greek triremes. Xerxes was therefore forced to retreat for lack of a fleet large enough to supply his army. He left behind an occupying force in Thessaly under his brother-in-law Mardonius, but this too withdrew when the latter was killed.

The repulsion of Xerxes's attempt to subdue the rebel Greek states led to the defection of the Greeks of Asia Minor and signaled the onset of the decline of the Persian Empire. After the failure of this campaign, Xerxes became increasingly preoccupied with pomp rather than conquest, presiding over a vast and expensive construction program that developed his father's plans and transformed Persopolis into one of the most monumentally grand cities of the known world, although Susa remained the Persian Empire's administrative capital.

Xerxes distanced himself increasingly from affairs of state, becoming drawn into petty harem intrigues and leaving the administration of his realms to others, and information about his activities in the latter period of his reign is sparse. In the same year that the reconstruction of Persopolis was declared complete (an occasion marked by festivities, ceremonies, and the presence of tribute-bearing delegates from all parts of the empire, which stretched from the Caspian Sea to the Nile and from India to the Aegean), he and his eldest son were murdered by members of his court, among them his personal chief minister, Artabanus.

P. Green, *Xerxes at Salamis*, 1970.
C. Hignett, *Xerxes' Invasion of Greece*, 1963.

Y

YEATS, WILLIAM BUTLER (1865–1939), Irish poet and playwright, Nobel Prize winner and the outstanding figure in the twentieth-century Irish literary renaissance. He is noted for his role in bringing poetry back to the theater and for his fusion of realism with mystical vision.

Yeats was born in Sandymount, near Dublin. His father was a lawyer turned painter and money was often scarce. The family moved frequently between England and Ireland and the children spent a great deal of time with William's mother's parents in the west of Ireland. Yeats studied painting but also began to write poetry in his late teens and soon writing became his main occupation. This was the spring of the modern Irish nationalist movement and Yeats became a leading member in its cultural effervescence.

Yeats settled in London in 1887 and began to dabble in heterodox religious movements, exploring theosophy, Rosicrucianism, Platonism, Neo-Platonism, and even considering spiritualism and magic. He was particularly interested in the writings of William *Blake, whose works he coedited from 1891 to 1893. Under the influence of John O'Leary,

an old leader of the nationalist Fenian movement, Yeats became increasingly interested in nationalist politics. In 1896 he returned to Dublin, where he fell in love with the Irish beauty and patriot Maud Gonne. Through her he became more involved in the Irish nationalist movement; he dreamed of uniting the Irish parties, even briefly joining the secret extremist revolutionary Irish Republican Brotherhood.

In 1903 Maud Gonne's marriage to another man put an end to his own vain hopes and he began to produce love poetry much sparer, more personal, and more realistic than his previous lyrical and romantic poems to her had been. He also became disillusioned with Irish politics and learned to despise the revolutionaries he had formerly befriended so enthusiastically. He developed a distaste for the Irish middle class, whom he saw as philistines, and acquired an admiration for the aristocratic life. He returned to his old ambition of creating an Irish theater and in 1899, with the Irish writer Lady Isabella Augusta Gregory, helped found the Irish Literary Theater, which in 1904 became established as the Abbey Theatre, one of the world's great theatrical companies. Yeats became its guiding spirit, contributing plays in verse and prose and persuading other distinguished dramatists to write for it.

After the Easter rising of 1916 in Ireland, in which Maud Gonne's husband was executed, Yeats again proposed to her and then to her daughter, and was refused by both. In 1917 he married the Irish medium Georgie Lees. *A Vision* (1926), his account of the theories and myths reportedly communicated to his wife by supernatural beings, became a source of symbolism for his later work. This marriage at the age of fifty-two, to a woman half his age, brought order and happiness to his life. From 1922 to 1928 Yeats was senator of the Irish Free State and he received the Nobel Prize for literature in 1923.

Yeats's early poems and plays, drawn principally from ancient Irish folklore, include such romantic and lyrical works as *Poems* (1895) and *The Wind among the Reeds* (1899); prose works such as *The Celtic Twilight* (1893) and *The Secret Rose* (1897); and the verse drama *The Countess Kathleen* (1892).

> I have met them at close of day
> Coming with vivid faces
> From counter or desk among grey
> Eighteenth-century houses.
> I have passed with a nod of the head
> Or polite meaningless words,
> Or have lingered awhile and said
> Polite meaningless words
> And though before I had done
> Of a mocking tale or a gibe
> To please a companion
> Around the fire at the club,
> Being certain that they and I
> But lived where motley is worn:
> All changed, changed utterly:
> A terrible beauty is born.
>
> **From *Easter 1916***

With the turn of the century his style became more austere and restrained. Though still mystical he was less playful, as can be seen in verse plays such as *The Shadowy Waters* (1900), *Deirdre* (1907), and *The Green Helmet* (1910). *Responsibilities* (1914) demonstrated the replacement of his former mysticism and mystery with satire and criticism. In *The Wild Swans at Coole* (1919) and *Michael Robartes and the Dancer* (1921), however, he tempers his anger, fusing his appreciation of beauty with a sense of tragedy. The poetry of his last period, including *The Tower* (1928), *The Winding Stair* (1929), and *Last Poems* (posthumous, 1940), which is thought by many critics to have been his best, is richly symbolic. This last phase of poetry combines emotion and intellect in a celebration of man's contradictory nature.

Memories of Yeats's youth are recounted in *Reveries Over Childhood and Youth* (1915), *The Trembling of the Veil* (1922), and *Dramatis Personae* (1936).

A. N. Jeffares, *W. B. Yeats: Man and Poet*, 1988.
A. Martin, *W. B. Yeats*, 1983.

YOUNG, BRIGHAM (1801–1877), U.S. religious and pioneer leader, businessman, and second president of the Church of Jesus Christ of Latter-day Saints. He was born in Whitingham, Vermont, the ninth of eleven children of a Revolutionary War veteran. When he was three, his family moved to central New York state, then almost virgin land, settling at Sherburne when Young was ten. There, he had a vigorously physical upbringing, clearing land for agriculture, farming, and hunting. The family was a poor one and, especially after his mother's death in 1814, Young often knew hunger.

His father soon remarried and Young left home not long after. He worked successfully as a carpenter, painter, and glazier, married in 1824, and settled in Port Byron, New York, where he and his wife joined the Methodist church. It was through his brother Phineas, a traveling preacher, that he first received a copy of Joseph *Smith's *Book of Mormon* in 1830; he, his wife, and immediate family were baptized into the Mormon faith in 1832, and Young began his preaching mission soon after. Well-built, of greater than average height, sandy-haired, and with penetrating blue-gray eyes, Young was a charismatic individual and persuasive speaker responsible for the decision of many to embrace the Mormonism to which he devoted himself wholeheartedly.

In 1833, soon after his wife's death from tuberculosis, Young moved to Kirtland, Ohio, to join the nascent Mormon community under Joseph Smith's leadership. There he married a fellow-Mormon. His dedication and potential led to his election to the church's Quorum of the Twelve Apostles, a traveling high council charged with spreading the Mormon gospel. In this capacity he undertook missionary trips east each summer, returning to Kirtland in the winter to help build up the Mormon community.

Brigham Young

When disputes over Smith's leadership divided the Kirtland community, Young's support of the prophet prompted him to flee Kirtland. In 1838, he and others among the Kirtland faithful moved to Caldwell County, Missouri. The Mormons alienated veteran settlers there, who feared their bloc power, and they were dispossessed and violently driven from the state; with the senior Mormon leadership, including Smith, imprisoned, it was Young who organized the group's evacuation to Commerce (later renamed Nauvoo), Illinois.

Now quorum president, Young, despite illness exacerbated by the many hardships he had endured, directed the Mormon mission to Britain in 1840; this won eight thousand converts, nearly one thousand of whom emigrated to Nauvoo. Back in the United States, it was Young who took responsibility for the purchase of lands on which to settle the immigrant faithful.

Smith's teachings on plural marriage were only reluctantly accepted by Young, who feared the ammunition this practice might provide to the church's opponents. However, he went on to embrace the custom wholeheartedly, marrying twenty-six women by whom he had a total of fifty-seven children.

In Nauvoo, too, the Mormons' autonomy aroused the fear and suspicion of the non-Mormon citizenry. Shortly before his death while in custody, Smith advised the quorum to move to the Rocky Mountains. After Smith's death, Young led his followers on the great westward trek he deemed necessary to fulfill Smith's prophecies, escape persecution, and find a place suited for the creation of a new theocracy.

Under his inspirational leadership, nearly sixteen thousand Mormons set out in February 1846 on the pioneering journey by wagon train into unknown territory, with the more affluent helping those less fortunate than themselves so that none might be denied the opportunity to migrate. Upon first seeing the Salt Lake Valley, Utah, in July 1847, Young identified it as a place of appropriate harshness and isolation to "make Saints." Elected president of the church in December 1847 (a position he held until his death), he went on to supervise the organization and construction of Salt Lake City, directing cooperative efforts in building and clearing land for agricultural use. A perpetual emigrating fund was created to assist the emigration of Mormon converts from Britain and Europe. As the number of immigrants increased, so too did the number of colonies established to accommodate them; in all, Young was responsible for founding nearly four hundred colonies, making him one of America's great colonizers.

Poor relations between the Mormons and outside federal appointees led to rumors that they were flouting U.S. laws, and in 1857 U.S. president Millard Fillmore authorized the dispatch of federal troops to pacify what he had been led to believe was a self-declared Mormon state in rebellion. A violent confrontation was narrowly avoided, although the troops remained to occupy Camp Floyd, a post some forty miles from Salt Lake City.

A canny businessman who believed in adopting the newest technology to benefit his followers, Young contracted to build telegraphs and railroads in the Utah region and beyond, which served to connect Mormon communities to communication networks worldwide. In an effort to preserve Mormon identity in the face of the resultant increased exposure to outside influences, he also set up local manufacturing and merchandizing cooperatives and promoted the development of local resources. His commercial activities made him a rich man, to the benefit of both his family and community.

Bearded and prophet-like in his later years, Young remained active in his capacity as the social architect and guiding light of the community of Mormon faithful up until his death.

L. J. Arrington, *Brigham Young: American Moses*, 1985.

N. G. Bringhurst, *Brigham Young and the Expanding American Frontier*, 1986.

Z

ZAPATA, EMILIANO (1879–1919), Mexican revolutionary and advocate of agrarian reform. The son of a *mestizo* (mixed Indian and Spanish) peasant, he was born in the impoverished Mexican village of Anenecuilco. Orphaned at seventeen, he supported his younger brothers and sisters by working at menial jobs at the haciendas of local aristocrats. As a stable boy, he reflected on the contrast between the ceramic tiles on the stable floor and the dirt floor of his own home, and concluded that radical reform was needed to decrease the chasm separating the minority gentry and the peasant masses. Growing increasingly vocal in his support of *ejido*, the Indian practice of communal land ownership, he was arrested in 1897 for participating in a demonstration against the annexation of peasant lands by affluent hacienda owners. Upon receiving a pardon, he returned to his village to agitate for *ejido*, leading the local landowners to arrange to have Zapata drafted into the army. After serving for six months, he returned to his village and was elected president of the local defense board.

In 1911 the people of Mexico rose in revolt against the dictatorial policies of President Porfirio Diaz. Zapata was encouraged by the liberal promises of presidential contender Francisco Madero and sent men to occupy the strategic town of Cuautla on his behalf; with Zapata's backing, Madero was able to assume the presidency. While recognizing his deep personal debt to the rebel leader, the circumstances of his victory left Madero in a vulnerable position. He could not allow the continued existence of armed guerrillas such as those led by Zapata, nor could he forfeit the support of the aristocracy by encouraging *ejido*. Zapata begrudgingly accepted Madero's demand for disarmament, but was loath to relinquish the principle of land reform and rejected a generous offer of compensation. Pointing to Madero's gold watch, he asked, "Having a gun, I could easily rob you of your watch. Would it not be your right to steal it back later? This is how we feel about the haciendas."

The truce between Zapata and Madero collapsed when guerilla forces engaged in disarmament were attacked by government troops led by General Vic-

Emiliano Zapata

toriano Huerta. Madero disclaimed any knowledge of the attack but the damage had been done, and the revolution began anew. Zapata and his supporters drafted the Plan of Ayala, calling for the expropriation of one third of all hacienda lands; landowners who resisted would receive no restitution.

Huerta assassinated Madero in 1913. Upon assuming office he sent envoys to Zapata, calling for his support, but Zapata had never forgiven Huerta for attacking him while disarming, and the messengers were executed. Venustiano Carranza, a rebellious northern provincial governor, called a conference of rebel leaders in Aguascalientes to discuss a unified front to depose Huerta. Zapata's representatives were unimpressed by the aristocratic Carranza, but agreed to cooperate with the men of Pancho Villa, chief commander of the army of the north. The combined rebel armies of Zapata and Villa captured Mexico City on November 24, 1914. Its terrified inhabitants were surprised to find that the rebel troops, rather than sacking the city, went from door to door begging for provisions. Villa and Zapata agreed to share power until a civilian government could be elected. The Plan of Ayala was adopted as government policy and a bank was established to provide loans to peasant farmers for the purchase of land.

Zapata had won unrivaled support among the masses. He spoke to them in their native Nahuatl rather than in colonialist Spanish and told them, "Men of the South, it is better to die on your feet than live on your knees." Zapata and Villa's guerrillas continued their attacks against Carranza's Constitutionalist Army, earning Zapata the epithet, "Attila of the South." Zapata's supporters were executed; entire towns known to harbor rebels were burnt down. In response, Zapata engaged in acts of savage terrorism; in one attack he blew up a train, killing four hundred people.

Unable to defeat Zapata militarily, Colonel Jesús Guajardo plotted to assassinate him. Guajardo feigned interest in deserting the government to join the rebels, proving himself by executing all rebels who had deserted to the government army, and by capturing the town of Jonacatapec for Zapata. At a secret meeting between the two, Zapata was greeted by an honor guard. As he returned their salute, he was mortally shot. Guajarda strapped his body to a mule and escorted it to the city of Cuautla to prove Zapata had been killed.

Although Zapata's rebellion quickly crumbled, his legacy of peasant rights and agrarian reform were later adopted by the Mexican government, contributing to the first agrarian revolution in the twentieth century. He is commemorated throughout Mexico by numerous memorials and monuments.

A. Gilly, *The Mexican Revolution*, 1983.
R.P. Millon, *Zapata: The Story of a Peasant Revolutionary*, 1969.
J. Womack Jr., *Zapata and the Mexican Revolution*, 1972.

ZENO OF CITIUM (c.335-c.263 B.C.E.), Greek Stoic philosopher. Zeno, born in the Phoenician-Greek city of Citium in Cyprus, went to Athens when he was twenty-two, where he was comforted in his poverty by the teachings of the Cynic philosopher, Crates of Thebes, who taught the meaninglessness of possessions and the value of the pursuit of virtuous happiness. Zeno was also a student at *Plato's Academy and learned logic and dialectic from the Megarians. In 300 B.C.E., he started his own school of philosophy, whose adherents, originally called the Zenonians, later became known as the Stoics, referring to the *Stoa Poikile* or "Painted Porch" where Zeno delivered his lectures. Since mere fragments of Zeno's writings survive, the full extent of his teachings is known only through the later Stoics, particularly Diogenes Laertius, the third-century Roman historian of Greek philosophy.

Zeno rejected Plato's Ideal Forms, accessible only through pure intellectual activity, arguing that the real source of human knowledge is through physical perception of the natural laws that govern the world. His emphasis on natural law combined the ideas of earlier Greek thinkers with that of the pursuit of virtue. While the world man lives in is chaotic, even disruptive and violent, behind this lies a certain order providing man with meaningful obligations in his life. The goal of human life is not the acquisition of power or money, both of which are transient and unsatisfying; rather, man reaches perfection and

FROM DIOGENES LAERTIUS:
ZENO AND THE STOICS

The term Duty is applied to that for which, when done, a reasonable defense can be adduced, e.g. harmony in the tenor of life's process, which indeed pervades the growth of plants and animals. For even in plants and animals, they hold, you may discern fitness of behavior.

Befitting acts are all those which reason prevails with us to do, and this is the case with honoring one's parents, brothers and country, and intercourse with friends.

The good are genuinely in earnest and vigilant for their own improvement, using a manner of life which banishes evil out of sight and makes what good there is in things appear. At the same time they are free from pretence; for they have stripped off all pretence or 'make-up' whether in voice or in look. Free too are they from all business cares, declining to do anything which conflicts with duty.

They are also, it is declared, godlike; for they have something divine within them; whereas the bad man is godless.

finds happiness when his life conforms to the natural order of things, so the primary obligation of the individual is to understand his duties as a part of the natural scheme and to strive to fulfill them.

Zeno's philosophy reflected changes in the political realities of his time. After the deaths of *Aristotle in 322 B.C.E., and *Alexander the Great in 323 B.C.E., and the concomitant loss of Athens's ascendancy in culture and learning, educated Athenian citizens found themselves adrift in a political entity whose governing powers no longer made a moral claim to leadership. Zeno's philosophy, with its emphasis on the new concept of world citizenry that made each responsible for all, permitted an accommodation between these changed political realities and the continuing need for a meaningful structure in the daily life of Greece's citizenry. As opposed to *Epicurus's doctrine of withdrawal from worldly affairs in the pursuit of moderate pleasures, Zeno advocated playing an active part in the world community of which one is a member, whether the results are pleasant or not.

Zeno taught that the wise man ought not to have pity or mercy, but should follow right understanding without veering from his course for any reason. Two stories dramatically illustrate this point. The first recounts how the philosopher, having found a slave stealing, beat him. When the slave complained that he was destined to be a thief, Zeno replied, "Yes, and to be whipped too." On another occasion, having broken his toe while walking on the road, Zeno pounded the ground saying, "I come of my own accord, why then call me?" Because providence is knowable through nature, such an event was deemed to indicate Zeno's fate and he killed himself, according to some, by holding his breath where he had fallen.

Although Zeno's philosophy could be harsh, the Stoic notion of common humanity and brotherhood made it attractive and he had a large following, reflecting his positive effect on Athenian youth and the utter consistency between his life and his beliefs. Stoicism continued as an organized school down to the third century C.E., and has continued to influence philosophies stressing obligation to others and individual significance, such as humanism and existentialism.

C. C. Meinwald, *Plato's Parmenides*, 1991.

ZHUKOV, GEORGY KONSTANTINOVICH

(1896-1974), Soviet military commander and politician. After enlisting as a private in the Imperial Russian Army in 1915, he quickly made a name for himself as an able soldier and was twice awarded the prestigious Cross of Saint George. In 1917, with the rank of sergeant, he joined the Bolshevik revolutionary forces that became the Red Army the following year and continued his rapid rise through the ranks, commanding a cavalry corps by 1936.

Zhukov, an expert in employing armored troops in battle, used this proficiency to destroy the Japanese Sixth Army in Mongolia in 1939. His adeptness was noted by leading Soviet military figures, among them General (later Marshal) Semyon Timoshenko, with whom he developed a close relationship. To alleviate the increasing difficulties facing Soviet troops in the 1940 Russo-Finnish War, Zhukov was appointed chief of staff. Under his command, the war turned quickly in the Soviets' favor; he was rewarded with further promotions to several prestigious positions, including chief of staff for the Red Army and vice-commissar of defense.

In 1941, the year Zhukov joined the Politburo, he published an article praising the preparedness of the Soviet army and the rapid pace of development of new weapons technology; in reality, the Soviet army was among the most obsolete in Europe and weapons development was proceeding at a snail's pace. The blatant misinformation fabricated in the article was possibly an attempt to frighten Germany into avoiding confrontation, but might also have served as a means of pressuring the indomitable Soviet dictator Joseph *Stalin to proceed with much needed reforms. The campaign was a success; Germany's 1941 offensive into Russia was eventually halted. Zhukov, who had been charged with the defense of both Leningrad and the vital Ukrainian fronts, as well as with organizing reserve troops for the defense of Moscow, was now first deputy commissar for defense, second only to Stalin in conducting the war.

Zhukov's brilliant counteroffensive in defense of Stalingrad, in which he encircled the entire German Sixth Army on the Don river, earned him the rank of marshal. He continued to defeat the Germans in several important engagements such as the Battle of Kursic, the biggest tank battle of the war. He was enormously popular, both among the enlisted men for remaining at the front rather than seeking sanctuary in the Soviet capital, and with his officers, who prized the considerable independence he granted them. No one minded that his great victories, over which he loved to gloat, were often the result of his scant regard for human life and his willingness to sacrifice troops to obtain his objectives.

Zhukov was now charged with leading his Soviet troops in the race to Berlin. During the week-long battle for that city Zhukov never slept, preferring to tour the advanced Soviet positions despite heavy enemy bombardment, sipping cognac all the while to stay awake. After signing Germany's unconditional surrender on behalf of the Soviet Union, Zhukov remained in Berlin to oversee the Soviet occupation forces.

He returned to Moscow in 1946, to assume the position of deputy minister of defense and commander in chief of the Soviet ground forces. His popularity irked Stalin, as did his warm relationship with American commander Dwight D. *Eisenhower, and without warning, Zhukov was relieved of his posts and sent to command a remote outpost in the Crimea. Throughout his banishment, Zhukov never articulated his deepseated animosity toward Stalin, trusting that Stalin's unfounded suspicions would soon pass. Zhukov's estimation of Stalin was correct; in 1952, after an unexplained change of heart, Stalin reinstated Zhukov to all his former posts.

> - If we come to a minefield, our infantry attacks as if it were not there.
> - Bourgeois historians and former Nazi generals have tried to convince the public that the million picked German troops were beaten at Moscow not by the iron steadfastness, courage and heroism of the Soviet soldiers but by mud, cold, and deep snow. The authors of these apologetics seem to forget that the Soviet forces had to operate under the same conditions.
>
> **Marshal Zhukhov**

Stalin's death in 1953 finally enabled Zhukov to take his revenge on those responsible for his disgrace. He was instrumental in bringing Lavrenty Beria, Stalin's commander of the NKVD secret police force, to trial and execution. Zhukov supported the moderate Nikita *Khrushchev over his rival Georgy Malenkov. With Khrushchev firmly in power, Zhukov was appointed minister of defense. His loyalty to Khrushchev in suppressing the coup attempt of Malenkov and Vyacheslav Molotov in 1957 was rewarded with Zhukov's appointment to the Soviet presidium, the first soldier to earn this post.

Zhukov's time of glory lasted only six weeks. He was ousted for sponsoring an attempt to limit party control of the army, and lived in obscurity until 1964. With the fall of Khrushchev, Zhukov returned to public life. His book, *Toward Berlin*, an account of the final days of World War II, was serialized in the army press as proof of his rehabilitation.

O.P. Chaney Jr., *Zhukhov, 1972.*

H.E. Salisbury, ed., *Marshal Zhukov's Greatest Battles*, 1969.

G. Zhukov, *The Memoirs of Marshal Zhukov* (English trans.), 1971.

ZOLA, ÉMILE-ÉDOUARD-CHARLES-ANTOINE

(1840-1902), French social critic and naturalist novelist who depicted the seamier side of French society. Zola is also remembered for the courage he displayed in his pivotal role in the Alfred *Dreyfus Affair. Born in Paris, he spent most of his childhood living a quiet middle-class existence in Aix-en-Provence. This changed in 1856 with the unexpected death of his father, which left the family with no income.

With the aid of family friends, Zola was admitted to the Lycée Saint Louis in Paris in 1858. Until then, he had been a better than average scholar, but now, feeling confused and dejected, his grades began falling and he failed his final examinations. It was his literature professor who refused to pass him.

With no hope of continuing his education, he sought odd jobs on the Paris docks. He had a brief romance with a young prostitute, whom he hoped to redeem through the power of love. The frequent nights he spent destitute and hungry all helped provide him with a realist education, fueling his hatred of poverty and his ambivalence toward the society that tolerated it.

Zola emerged from this miserable period in 1862 ambitious and driven. A friend arranged for him to take a job as a clerk in Hachette's bookshop, where he worked for four years; the regularity of the work and income restored his health and self-respect. In 1864 his first book was published, a collection of largely romantic short stories of no great literary value. These were followed by his first novel, a crude, colorful, and semi-autobiographical work telling of life with a prostitute.

By now his writing was beginning to conflict with his clerical duties, and in 1866 he was asked to leave. Fortunately, Zola had just been offered a position as a journalist, with the promise of a greater salary and the power to influence an audience, which he accepted with relish. He compiled an enormous portfolio of articles as a political columnist, social reporter, literary chronicler, and art critic.

About this time Zola met Alexandrine Melley, whom he married in 1870. That same year there appeared in serialized form *Les Rougon-Macquart, the National and Social History of a Family During the Second Empire*, the first in a series of twenty novels that were to occupy him for most of his life. For many the series represents the supreme depiction of life in Second Empire France. Nevertheless, Zola was constantly striving for acceptance by the upper classes from which, by his lack of formal education and his poverty, he was excluded. It was probably this insecurity that made him attempt to shape his epic series as a scientific treatise, structured on theories concerning the heredity of character and intellect.

Zola achieved popular success in 1877 with the publication of *L'Assommoir*, a story concerning the miserable life around a lower-class tavern. This book made his fortune, whereupon he promptly surrounded himself with all the gaudy trappings of wealth. His most controversial novel, *Nana*, the scandalous story of a prostitute to the wealthy, appeared in 1880. Toward the end of that year he was struck by two tragedies: the deaths of Gustav Flaubert, whom he revered, and his mother. He pressed on with his writing but spent much of the following eight years in a deep depression, preoccupied with his own inevitable death. In 1888 he became involved with the young Jeanne Rozerot, his wife's former seamstress, who bore him a son and a daughter, his only children. Ironically, being a father, even illegitimately, gave him an added sense of respectability and newfound purpose. By the end of 1893 he completed the *Rougon-Macquart* series and eventually wrote six more novels.

The climax to his life came not in literature but through his vigorous and, initially, lone defense of Captain Alfred *Dreyfus, a Jewish French army officer who had been convicted of treason. Zola's involvement began in 1896 with his article in defense of French Jews, who were being portrayed as alien subversive elements. He then led a call for a review of Dreyfus's case as the facts began emerging, writing an open letter to the President of France. Published by Georges *Clemenceau under the title *J'Accuse* (which Clemenceau chose), this scathing letter accused the entire French military establishment of perpetrating a vile miscarriage of justice in defense of its own incompetence in the affair. Outraged rightist elements who supported the military arranged for a reluctant government

J'ACCUSE

It is my duty to speak. I do not wish to be an accessory. My dreams would be haunted by the spectre of the innocent man who is suffering the most frightful agonies for a crime he did not commit. Ah! The feebleness of the indictment. It is a monstrous iniquity that a man should be condemned on such a charge. I defy any honest man to read it without being filled with indignation and exclaiming in horror at the thought of the unbounded sufferings over there on Devil's Island. Dreyfus knows several languages, a crime; he sometimes pays a visit to the country of his birth, a crime; he is industrious, he wishes to know all about everything, a crime; he is not nervous, a crime; he is nervous, a crime...

It is a crime to have relied on the foul press...It is a crime, while hatching an impudent plot to deceive the whole world, to bring an accusation of disturbing France....It is a crime to mislead public opinion, perverting it to the point of delirium. It is a crime to poison the minds of the obscure and the humble while sheltering behind the vile anti-Semitism of which the great liberal France of the Rights of Man will die, if she is not cured. It is a crime to exploit patriotism in the cause of hatred, and it is a crime to make of the sword a modern divinity.

When truth is put underground it grows there, it assumes explosive strength, and when it bursts forth, it shatters everything.

to bring a libel suit against Zola. The trial was a mockery in which the jurors' names were published by the papers with veiled threats if Zola were acquitted, in addition to which a violent mob surrounded the courthouse. Unsurprisingly, he was found guilty. The verdict, however, was overturned on appeal.

The case was reopened amid great hostility, whereupon a reluctant Zola was persuaded to flee to England. In his absence, the tangle of official lies began unraveling, with one senior officer committing suicide and another escaping abroad, leaving behind a confession of sorts. A retrial for Dreyfus was ordered, and Zola returned home thinking this marked the rebirth of equity and honor in France. He was mistaken, as Dreyfus once again was condemned by the court, but this time with extenuating circumstances, and finally granted a pardon by the president. Zola was shocked, but the campaign to get an acquittal faded, not least because Dreyfus, an army man at heart, wished to return quietly to service without jeopardizing his career. Zola was also granted an amnesty, and the affair was effectively laid to rest.

Zola's death was sudden and, by some accounts, suspicious, although there was no evidence to suggest foul play. Returning to a chilly Paris in the fall of 1902 from their country home, the Zolas lit a fire in their bedroom and, as was their habit, closed the windows and went to bed. The chimney had become blocked during the previous summer, and by the morning Zola had died of asphyxiation.

C. Becker, *Zola*, 1990.
J. A. Bede, *Émile Zola*, 1974.
P. D. Walker, *Émile Zola*, 1968.

ZOROASTER (Zarathushtra or Zardust; c.628–c.551 B.C.E.), Persian religious leader; reputed founder of Zoroastrianism. Zoroaster was a priest, poet, prophetic seer, and original religious thinker. Virtually nothing is known about the historical figure of Zarathushtra (Zoroaster is the Greek rendition of his name); historical facts have been obscured by legend. Even the historical period in which he lived is the subject of considerable debate; according to some, he was born around 7000 B.C.E. Most scholars reject this date; much of what is known about his life would be anachronistic. The site of his birth also remains uncertain; a variety of locations, ranging from the Aral Sea to central India, have been suggested.

Zoroaster's name, meaning, "he who manages camels," perhaps indicates his birth to a wealthy family. Most accounts agree that he was the middle of five sons. According to legend, his birth was foretold in several ancient oracles. According to legend, Zoroaster was the only person in history to laugh rather than cry upon being born. The house filled with light, causing his father to think that the child was possessed by demons. On three occasions, a priest attempted to kill the frightening infant. At first, Zoroaster was placed in front of stampeding cattle. When these failed to kill him, he was cast in a fire, but escaped unscathed. Finally he was put in the den of a she-wolf, but was again miraculously preserved.

Brought up in polytheism, at fifteen Zoroaster studied for the priesthood. Unsatisfied, he left home at twenty to seek out the truth. For ten years he wandered through the countryside, often spending lengthy periods meditating in a cave. When he was thirty, he walked down to the river to draw water for ablutions. There, the Holy Immortal Vehu Manah appeared to him, clothed in light so bright that Zoroaster was unable to see his own shadow. Vehu Manah summoned him to the court of Ahura Mazda, Lord of Wisdom. In the ensuing conversation, Zoroaster asked and Ahura Mazda answered those questions that had plagued him for so many years. He asked about the three perfections and was told that they are: good thoughts, good words, and good deeds. Ahura Mazda also explained about the duality of the universe, and of his conflict with the evil spirit Ahriman. Only through man's actions would Ahura Mazda finally emerge victorious.

For ten years, Zoroaster wandered the countryside preaching his new belief in one eternal uncreated Being, Ahura Mazda, wholly wise, just, and good. Opposed to him is Angra Mainyu, the Evil Spirit, with a host of wicked forces. In this dualism, man must fight on the side of his creator. At that time, Zoroaster won only one convert, a cousin. Chased from his home, Zoroaster arrived at the court of Vishtaspa, king of Chorasmia. Queen Hutaosa was impressed by the prophet, but evil priests convinced the king to throw him in prison. At the time, the king's favorite horse suddenly became lame. Zoroaster agreed to cure the horse in return for a favor for each leg healed. For the first leg, he asked that Vishtaspa accept the new religion; for the second, that his son champion it; for the third he asked that the queen also accept the new faith, and for the fourth, that his enemies be put to death.

With Zoroastrianism as the official religion of Chorasmia, Zoroaster now prospered. Some accounts claim that he remained celibate. References to a daughter in one of the "Gathas," five hymns he allegedly composed, are understood to be an allegory. According to another account, he had one wife, Hvovi. Most Zoroastrians, however, believe that Hvovi was his third wife, who conceived three sons to be born by virgins at thousand-year intervals: Ukhshyatereta (he who makes righteousness grow), Ukhshyatnem (he who makes reverence grow), and Astvatereta (he who embodies righteousness).

Zoroaster, was killed at age seventy-seven, by a jealous priest. His religion, however, survives until today in Iran and India. It was adopted as the official state religion by the Persian Achaemenid (550–330 B.C.E.) and Sassanian (226–640 C.E.) dynasties, but was overthrown by Islam in the seventh century. The descendants of Persian religious refugees who fled to India are known as the Parsees. Through Gnosticism, Zoroastrian doctrines also influenced Judaism and Christianity.

M. Boyce, *A History of Zoroastrianism*, 2 vols., 1975–1982.

K. P. Mistree, *Zoroastrianism: An Ethnic Perspective*, 1982.

ZWINGLI, ULRICH (or Huldrych; 1484–1531), Swiss religious reformer. Born of pious Catholic parents in Wildhaus, he attended the universities of Vienna and Basel, graduating in 1504; he was ordained in 1506, by which time he was already a confirmed humanist. He studied Greek and Hebrew, and corresponded with the influential Dutch humanist scholar Desiderius *Erasmus, of whom he considered himself a follower.

Zwingli was pastor in the parish of Glarus from 1506, but left in 1516 when he became unpopular due to his opposition to Pope Leo X's recruitment of Swiss mercenaries. Moving to Einsiedeln, he began to criticize clerical abuses in his sermons; however, he remained doctrinally orthodox and, in 1518, was appointed to the position of People's Preacher at the Old Minster in Zurich, despite opposition from those who mistrusted his humanistic tendencies. In that capacity, and influenced by his exposure to the writings of Martin *Luther, he launched on a series of sermons on the New Testament liberally leavened with topical applications.

The plague that struck Zurich in 1519 marked an important turning point in Zwingli's life. While he contracted the disease but recovered, his brother died from it, and the experience led to the ripening of those dissident spiritual and theological elements in his thinking which had hitherto been overshadowed by humanistic concerns. The city council of Zurich supported him in his championing of the reform movement initiated by Luther: in 1520 they ordered that Holy Scripture should be taught "without human additions." Zwingli was now in open revolt against the established church, and his increasingly subversive sermons helped prompt revolts against fasting and clerical celibacy in 1522, making Zurich the second center of the Reformation after Wittenburg.

In 1523 Zwingli wrote the *Sixty-seven Articles;* they denied the authority of the pope, the doctrine of transubstantiation (the transformation of the bread and wine to the actual body and blood of *Jesus Christ during Mass), the veneration of saints, the state of purgatory, and fasting. Basing his arguments on them, he defeated papal representatives in two disputations that year; the outcome signaled the end of Catholicism in Zurich, and marked the beginning of liturgical reform there. Soon the local cathedral school was also functioning as a theological seminary training reform pastors.

Zwingli incisively elucidated the main tenets of the reformers. These rested on the fundamental belief in the supremacy of scripture over any worldly injunction, including that of the pope. Mass was rejected as an affront to the sacrifice and death of Christ, and images and pictures were banished from places of worship. Marriage was considered lawful for all and Zwingli himself married in Zurich Cathedral in 1524.

Zwingli continued to be the most influential figure in the Swiss reform movement. His *Commentaries on True and False Religion*, produced in 1525, helped spread the reforming doctrines from Zurich to other Swiss cantons, and soon a Christian civic alliance was formed among those cantons where the reform movement held sway.

In his *On Baptism* and *Tricks of the Catabaptists*, Zwingli was ruthless in his advocacy of the need to suppress the Anabaptists, who rejected his policy of accommodation between church and state, and advocated the creation of a pure church of true believers and an end to infant baptism: their leaders were later executed. Zwingli's own vision was of the preacher as the people's tribune before the civil rulers, reminding them of the views of those who legitimized their government while being prepared to accept some civil jurisdiction over church life.

Zwingli fell out with Luther over the latter's assertion that Christ was present in some form in the elements of the Mass. In *On the Lord's Supper*, Zwingli argued against any such real presence, choosing to interpret Christ's words "This is my body" and "This is my blood" figuratively rather than literally. The Marburg Colloquy of 1529 was convened to ameliorate disputes within the reform movement, but no agreement was achieved on this sensitive subject.

In 1529 the First War of Capel broke out, in which the Christian civic alliance of reform Swiss cantons launched a pre-emptive attack against the Catholic forest cantons (the five oldest Swiss cantons) who threatened them. This conflict ended inconclusively but hostilities soon broke out again. Accompanying the reform forces as chaplain carrying the banner, Zwingli fell in battle. His writings, often criticized as disjointed and over-intellectual, remained important.

U. Gabler, *Huldrych Zwingli*, 1986.

G. R. Potter, ed., *Huldrych Zwingli*, 1978.

W. P. Stevens, *The Theology of Huldrych Zwingli*, 1985.

ACKNOWLEDGMENTS

The Publishers wish to express their thanks to the following museums, libraries, and other institutions from whose collections works have been reproduced.

The Publishers have attempted to observe the legal requirements with respect to copyrights. However, in view of the large number of illustrations included in this volume, the Publishers wish to apologize in advance for any involuntary omissions or errors and invite persons or bodies concerned to write to the Publishers.

A. A. M. van der Heyden 54, 318; Fratelli Alinari, S.p.A. Florence 27, 50, 73, 102, 131, 223, 273, 332, 374, 413, 536; A.P. Photo 13, 339, 611; Archiv für Kunst und Geschichte 287; Bar David, Tel Aviv 301, 468; Beth Hatefutsoth Nahum Goldmann Museum of the Diaspora 334; Berhanena Salam Press, Addis Ababa 256; Bettman Archives, New York 213, 560; Bibliotek für Zeitgeschichte, Stuttgart 563; Bibliotèque Nationale, Paris 262, 358; Brandeis University Press 674; British Museum 9, 29, 108, 148, 420, 516, 592; Brooklyn Museum 22; Brown Bros. 533, 706; Bundesarchiv 241; Church of Jesus Christ of Latter-day Saints 604, 704; City Museum and Art Gallery, Birmingham 127, 633; Columbia University 166; Culver Service 164; Elsevier Publishing Projects, Amsterdam 58, 76, 81, 88, 90, 109, 112, 138, 144, 154, 188, 209, 270, 291, 297, 390, 399, 401, 423, 524, 595; Erica Anderson, Die Welt Albert Schweitzer, Frankfurt o.J. 588; Erich Lessing 504; Foto Italia 461; Foto Tanjug 645; Galleria dell'Accademia Carrara, Bergamo 84; Galleria del Prado, Madrid 118; George Allen and Unwin, Ltd. 465; G.G. The Jerusalem Publishing House, Ltd. 158, 456; Guillot de Saxe, H. Roger Viollet, Paris 688; Harrison Forman from Pix 409; Goldbeck Collection, Humanities Research Center, University of Texas at Austin 513; H. Gernsheim, London 168; Hodder and Stoughton 565; Imperial War Museum, London 366, 451, 692; India Office Library 21; Israel Museum, Jerusalem 305; Keter Enterprises, Ltd. 648; King Penguin Books 98, 129; Kedansha International Ltd. 284; Kunstammlunger der Veste, Coburg 198; Kupfertichtkabinet, Berlin 433; La Comedie Française 672; Mansell 615; Mary Evans Picture Library 170; Metropolitan Museum of Art 449, 607; Municipal Picture Gallery, Mannheim 427; Musée de Louvre 553, 569; Museo di Roma 230; National Archives 249, 310, 378, 508, 601; National Maritime Museum, Greenwich 326, 472; New York Historical Society 258, 495, 678; New York Public Library 659, 686; Pecci Blunt Collection, Rome 430 Penguin Viking Press 488; Phaidon Press, London 442; Picture Post Library, London 68, 85; Princeton University Library, Rare Book and Photo Collection 444; Spada Gallery 40; Radio Times Hulton Picture Library 44, 228, 478, 551, 669; Rijksmuseum 244; Royal Military Academy, Sandhurst 683; Scottish National Picture Gallery 93; Smithsonian Institution 182, 201; Syndics of the FitzWilliam Museum, Cambridge 80; Topkapi Museum, Istanbul 621; United Press International, 323; United States Air Force Photo 417; United States Army Photo 396; University of London 75; Weidenfeld and Nicolson 309; Wivenhoe 219.